The Routledge Handbook of
English Language Teaching

The Routledge Handbook of English Language Teaching is the definitive reference volume for post-graduate and advanced undergraduate students of Applied Linguistics, ELT/TESOL, and Language Teacher Education, and for ELT professionals engaged in in-service teacher development and/or undertaking academic study.

Progressing from 'broader' contextual issues to a 'narrower' focus on classrooms and classroom discourse, the volume's inter-related themes focus on:

- ELT in the world: contexts and goals
- planning and organising ELT: curriculum, resources and settings
- methods and methodology: perspectives and practices
- second language learning and learners
- teaching language: knowledge, skills and pedagogy
- understanding the language classroom.

The *Handbook's* 39 chapters are written by leading figures in ELT from around the world. Mindful of the diverse pedagogical, institutional and social contexts for ELT, they convincingly present the key issues, areas of debate and dispute, and future developments in ELT from an applied linguistics perspective.

Throughout the volume, readers are encouraged to develop their own thinking and practice in contextually appropriate ways, assisted by discussion questions and suggestions for further reading that accompany every chapter.

Graham Hall is Senior Lecturer in Applied Linguistics/TESOL at Northumbria University, UK. He is the author of *Exploring English Language Teaching: Language in Action* (Routledge, 2011), which was the winner of the 2012 British Association for Applied Linguistics (BAAL) book prize.

Routledge Handbooks in Applied Linguistics

Routledge Handbooks in Applied Linguistics provide comprehensive overviews of the key topics in applied linguistics. All entries for the handbooks are specially commissioned and written by leading scholars in the field. Clear, accessible and carefully edited *Routledge Handbooks in Applied Linguistics* are the ideal resource for both advanced undergraduates and postgraduate students.

The Routledge Handbook of Language Learning and Technology
Edited by Fiona Farr and Liam Murray

The Routledge Handbook of Language and Identity
Edited by Siân Preece

The Routledge Handbook of English for Academic Purposes
Edited by Ken Hyland and Philip Shaw

The Routledge Handbook of Language and Digital Communication
Edited by Alexandra Georgakopoulou and Tereza Spilioti

The Routledge Handbook of Literacy Studies
Edited by Jennifer Rowsell and Kate Pahl

The Routledge Handbook of Interpreting
Edited by Holly Mikkelson and Renée Jourdenais

The Routledge Handbook of Hispanic Applied Linguistics
Edited by Manel Lacorte

The Routledge Handbook of Educational Linguistics
Edited by Martha Bigelow and Johanna Ennser-Kananen

The Routledge Handbook of Forensic Linguistics
Edited by Malcolm Coulthard and Alison Johnson

The Routledge Handbook of Corpus Linguistics
Edited by Anne O'Keeffe and Mike McCarthy

The Routledge Handbook of World Englishes
Edited by Andy Kirkpatrick

The Routledge Handbook of Applied Linguistics
Edited by James Simpson

The Routledge Handbook of Discourse Analysis
Edited by James Paul Gee and Michael Handford

The Routledge Handbook of Second Language Acquisition
Edited by Susan Gass and Alison Mackey

The Routledge Handbook of Language and Intercultural Communication
Edited by Jane Jackson

The Routledge Handbook of Language Testing
Edited by Glenn Fulcher and Fred Davidson

The Routledge Handbook of Multilingualism
Edited by Marilyn Martin-Jones, Adrian Blackledge and Angela Creese

The Routledge Handbook of Translation Studies
Edited by Carmen Millán-Varela and Francesca Bartrina

The Routledge Handbook of Language and Health Communication
Edited by Heidi E. Hamilton and Wen-ying Sylvia Chou

The Routledge Handbook of Language and Professional Communication
Edited by Stephen Bremner and Vijay Bhatia

The Routledge Handbook of English Language Teaching

Edited by Graham Hall

Routledge
Taylor & Francis Group

LONDON AND NEW YORK

First published in paperback 2020
First published 2016
by Routledge
2 Park Square, Milton Park, Abingdon, Oxon OX14 4RN

and by Routledge
711 Third Avenue, New York, NY 10017

Routledge is an imprint of the Taylor & Francis Group, an informa business

British Library Cataloguing in Publication Data
A catalogue record for this book is available from the British Library

Library of Congress Cataloging-in-Publication Data
Names: Hall, Graham, 1969– author.
Title: The Routledge Handbook of English language teaching / by Graham Hall.
Description: Milton Park, Abingdon, Oxon ; New York, NY : Routledge, [2016] | Series: Routledge Handbooks in Applied Linguistics | Includes bibliographical references and index.
Identifiers: LCCN 2015046887 | ISBN 9780415747394 (hardback : alk. paper) | ISBN 9781315676203 (ebook : alk. paper)
Subjects: LCSH: English language—Study and teaching—Handbooks, manuals, etc.
Classification: LCC PE1065 .H23 2016 | DDC 428.0071—dc23
LC record available at http://lccn.loc.gov/2015046887

ISBN: 978-0-415-74739-4 (hbk)
ISBN: 978-0-367-47303-7 (pbk)
ISBN: 978-1-315-6762-0-3 (ebk)

Typeset in Bembo
by Apex CoVantage, LLC

Contents

Contents

Tables and figures

Acknowledgements

The writing and editing of this *Handbook* has been a cooperative and collaborative process to which many people have contributed, both directly and indirectly. First, many thanks to the contributors for their involvement and for enduring my editorial efforts with such good grace. I am also very grateful to the following for finding time to read and provide expert commentary and advice on chapters in the volume: Darío Banegas, Andrew Blair, George Braine, Martin Bygate, Mike Byram, Ron Carter, Mark Clarke, Alessia Cogo, Guy Cook, Ronayne Cowan, Yvette Coyle, Kata Csizér, Jim Cummins, Christiane Dalton-Puffer, Karen Dooley, Dacia Dressen-Hammouda, John Flowerdew, David Gardner, Christine Goh, Loretta Gray, Tony Green, Nigel Harwood, Suzanne Hilgendorf, Stephanie Houghton, Li-Shih Huang, Duncan Hunter, Chris Jenks, Hayriye Kayi-Aydar, Gerald Kelly, Charlotte Kemp, Philip Kerr, Richard Kiely, Judit Kormos, Kuchah Kuchah, Diane Larsen-Freeman, Alex Ho-Cheong Leung, Li Li, Chris Lima, Roy Lyster, Peter Mickan, Vera Menezes, Brian Morgan, Tom Morton, Carmen Muñoz, John M. Murphy, Rola Naeb, Lourdes Ortega, Amos Paran, Vai Ramanathan, Andrea Révész, Jack Richards, Damien Rivers, Peter Sayer, Philida Schellekens, Philip Seargeant, Olcay Sert, James Simpson, Richard Smith, Mike Solly, James Street, John Swales, Carolyn Turner, Ema Ushioda, Rémi A. van Compernolle, Aisha Walker, Steve Walsh, Robert Yates and Tony Young. My deepest thanks, too, to the *Handbook*'s advisory board – Guy Cook, Diane Larsen-Freeman, Amy Tsui and Steve Walsh – who have provided both insightful advice and generous encouragement throughout the development of the volume. I also wish to thank Ron Carter for his initial suggestion that I should edit the book and for giving me confidence to undertake it. Guy Mankowski provided a great deal of assistance in preparing the chapters for publication, whilst, at Routledge, Louisa Semlyen, Sophie Jaques and Laura Sandford have provided expert help and guidance in bringing the volume together.

Finally, thanks, yet again, to Helen. Editing the *Handbook* would not have been possible without her constant support and accommodation of my absences from family life. This book is dedicated to her and to our girls, Georgia and Rosa, who I learn from every day.

Every effort has been made to contact copyright-holders. Please advise the publisher of any errors or omissions, and these will be corrected in subsequent editions.

Contributors

Helen Basturkmen is Associate Professor at the University of Auckland, New Zealand. She has written two books on ESP/EAP – *Ideas and Options in English for Academic Purposes* (Lawrence Erlbaum, 2006) and *Developing Courses in English for Specific Purposes* (Palgrave Macmillan, 2010) – and has edited *English for Academic Purposes* in the *Critical Concepts in Linguistics* series (Routledge, 2015). She is an editorial review board member for the *Journal of English for Academic Purposes*.

Phil Benson is Professor of Applied Linguistics at Macquarie University, Australia. He has taught in Algeria, Kuwait, Seychelles, Malaysia, Japan and Hong Kong. His interests are in autonomy, out-of-class learning, and narrative research on language learning as life experience.

Mónica Stella Cárdenas-Claros is Adjunct Professor for the Institute of Literature and Language Sciences at Pontificia Universidad Católica de Valparaíso, Chile. Her research interests include computer-based L2 listening development, blended learning and technology integration in language classrooms.

Kevin S. Carroll is Associate Professor in the Department of English at the University of Puerto Rico Mayagüez, Puerto Rico. His research interests focus on bilingual education and language policy as well as language planning in the Middle East, Caribbean and the Americas.

Richard Clément is Professor of Psychology at the University of Ottawa in Ottawa, Ontario, Canada, where he serves as the Director for the Official Languages and Bilingualism Institute. He is the editor, along with Caroline Andrew, of *Cities and Languages: Governance and Policy* (Invenire Books, 2012).

Laura Collins is Associate Professor of Applied Linguistics at Concordia University, Montreal, Canada. Her research, both descriptive and experimental, is primarily focused on language learning in classroom contexts, exploring relationships between instructional practices and language learning outcomes.

Mary Carol Combs is Associate Professor in the Department of Teaching, Learning, and Sociocultural Studies, University of Arizona, USA. Her research interests include bilingual education, sociocultural theory, immigration and education, second language acquisition, sheltered instruction and English language learner teacher preparation.

Graham Crookes is Professor, Department of Second Language Studies, University of Hawai'i, USA. Originally from the UK, he has been resident in the Asia-Pacific area for most of his career. His major current research interest is critical pedagogy.

Janet Enever is Professor of Language Teaching and Learning at Umeå University, Sweden, specialising in early foreign language learning, language globalisation and language policy. She has advised on early language learning for ministries in Asia, Latin America and Europe.

Ana Frankenberg-Garcia holds a PhD in Applied Linguistics from the University of Edinburgh. She is Senior Lecturer in Translation Studies at the University of Surrey. Her research focuses on applied uses of corpora in language learning, lexicography and translation.

Glenn Fulcher is Professor of Education and Language Assessment at the University of Leicester, UK. His books from Routledge include *Practical Language Testing* (2010), the *Routledge Handbook of Language Testing* (2012; edited with Fred Davidson), and *Re-examining Language Testing* (2015). His website, http://languagetesting.info, is a major resource for testing.

Próspero N. García is Assistant Professor of Spanish Applied Linguistics at Rutgers University Camden, USA. His research interests lie in Spanish second language acquisition and pedagogy, Vygotsky's theory of mind, second language evaluation and assessment, and technology-enhanced language learning

Kathleen Graves is Associate Professor of Education Practice at the University of Michigan, USA, where she works in teacher education and curriculum development. Her books include *Teachers as Course Developers* (Cambridge University Press, 1996), *Designing Language Courses* (Heinle and Heinle, 2000) and, with Sue Garton, *International Perspectives on Materials in ELT* (Palgrave Macmillan, 2014).

John Gray is Reader in Languages in Education at the UCL Institute of Education, University College London, UK. He is the author of *The Construction of English* (Palgrave Macmillan, 2010), co-author with David Block and Marnie Holborow of *Neoliberalism and Applied Linguistics* (Routledge, 2012) and the editor of *Critical Perspectives on Language Teaching Materials* (Palgrave Macmillan, 2013).

Tammy Gregersen is Professor of TESOL and teacher trainer at the University of Northern Iowa in Cedar Falls, Iowa, USA. She is the author, with Peter MacIntyre, of *Capitalizing on Language Learner Individuality* (Multilingual Matters, 2014).

Paul Gruba is Senior Lecturer in the School of Languages and Linguistics, The University of Melbourne, Australia. His research interests include multimodal listening, blended programme evaluation and new media assessment.

Geoff Hall is Professor and Head of the School of English, University of Nottingham Ningbo, China (UNNC). He started working in ELT in 1978 and is author of *Literature in Language Education* (Palgrave Macmillan, 2015) and editor of the journal *Language and Literature*.

Graham Hall is Senior Lecturer in Applied Linguistics/TESOL at Northumbria University, UK. He is editor of *ELT Journal* and is the author of *Exploring English Language Teaching: language in action* (Routledge, 2011), which was the winner of the 2012 British Association for Applied Linguistics (BAAL) book prize.

Don Hinkelman is Professor of Foreign Language Education at Sapporo Gakuin University, Japan. His studies on blended language learning include video-recording for formative assessment, mass-collaborative authoring of multimedia teaching materials and developing interactive modules for open-source learning management systems.

Adrian Holliday is Professor of Applied Linguistics at Canterbury Christ Church University, UK, where he supervises doctoral research in the critical sociology of language education and intercultural communication. The first half of his career was spent in Iran, Syria and Egypt as a curriculum developer.

Karen E. Johnson is Kirby Professor of Language Learning and Applied Linguistics in the Department of Applied Linguistics at The Pennsylvania State University, USA. Her research interests include narrative inquiry as professional development, teacher learning in second language teacher education and sociocultural research and perspectives on language teacher professional development.

Richard Kern is Professor of French and Director of the Berkeley Language Center at the University of California, Berkeley, USA. He is an Associate Editor of *Language Learning & Technology*, and his most recent book is *Language, Literacy, and Technology* (Cambridge University Press, 2015).

Philip Kerr is a teacher trainer and materials writer. He is the author of *Translation and Own-Language Activities* (Cambridge University Press, 2014) and the co-author of the ELT coursebook series *Straightforward* and *Inside Out*, both published by Macmillan.

Claire Kramsch is Professor of German and Affiliate Professor of Education at the University of California at Berkeley, USA. Her research interests are foreign language learning and teaching, language and culture, and multilingualism. Her most recent book is *The Multilingual Subject* (Oxford, 2009).

Kuchah Kuchah is Lecturer in TESOL in the Department of Education, University of Bath, UK. His research interests are in teaching English to young learners, context-appropriate ELT methodology, teaching large and multi-grade classes, learner autonomy and teacher development.

Martin Lamb is Senior Lecturer in TESOL at the University of Leeds, UK, where he teaches courses in applied linguistics and ELT methodology. He previously taught English in Sweden, Bulgaria and Indonesia, from where arose his research interest in motivation.

Li Li is Senior Lecturer in Language Education and Director of the MEd in TESOL in the Graduate School of Education, University of Exeter, UK. Her research interests include teacher cognition, classroom discourse, developing thinking skills and integrating new technologies in language teaching.

Dilin Liu is Professor of Applied Linguistics/TESOL in the English Department at the University of Alabama, USA. His research focuses on corpus-based description/teaching of English lexis and grammar. He has published extensively on the topic, including books and numerous journal articles.

Enric Llurda is Senior Lecturer in Applied Linguistics at the Universitat de Lleida in Catalonia, Spain. His research interests are English as an international language or lingua franca, attitudes to languages, multilingualism in higher education and non-native language teachers.

Peter D. MacIntyre is Professor of Psychology at Cape Breton University in Sydney, Nova Scotia, Canada. He is co-editor, with Tammy Gregersen and Sarah Mercer, of *Positive Psychology in SLA* (Multilingual Matters, forthcoming).

Alison Mackey is Professor of Linguistics at Georgetown University in Washington, DC, USA. Her research interests include input and interaction, individual differences, research methodology and second language dialects. She is also the editor-in-chief of the *Annual Review of Applied Linguistics*, the official journal of the *American Association for Applied Linguistics (AAAL)*.

Emma Marsden is Senior Lecturer in Second Language Education at the University of York, UK. Her research focuses on instructed learning, particularly of grammar and vocabulary, and she has advised on policy and assessment. She is director of IRIS (www.iris-database.org), a large international repository of materials used for data collection.

Julia Menard-Warwick is Professor of Linguistics at University of California, Davis, USA. She has taught ESL to immigrants in the United States and worked within EFL teacher education in Chile. Her current research explores translingual identity development for individuals and communities.

Sarah Mercer is currently Professor of Foreign Language Teaching at the University of Graz, Austria. She has been teaching English as a foreign language since 1996. Her research interests focus on the psychology surrounding foreign language learning employing a complexity lens.

Daniel Moglen is a PhD candidate in the Department of Linguistics at the University of California, Davis, USA, with interests in language assessment and second language writing.

Miki Mori holds a PhD in Linguistics with an emphasis on Writing, Rhetoric and Composition Studies from the University of California, Davis, USA. She researches source use, paraphrasing and language appropriation. She currently teaches English as a Foreign Language in Mayotte, France.

Tom Morton is Honorary Research Fellow in the Department of Applied Linguistics and Communication, Birkbeck, University of London, UK, and Visiting Academic at the University of Southampton, UK, where he teaches on the University of Southampton/British Council online MA in ELT.

Eduardo Negueruela-Azarola is Associate Professor of Spanish Second Language Acquisition and Applied Linguistics at the Universidad de Navarra, Spain, and is director of the international research center: *Instituto de Lengua y Cultura Española* (ILCE). His research focuses on sociocultural psychology, second language learning and teaching, Spanish SLA and technology-enhanced language learning.

Robert Nelson is Assistant Professor of Applied Linguistics/TESOL in the English Department at the University of Alabama. His research interests include how probabilistically guided expectancies influence second language learning and the statistical description of learner language.

Jonathan Newton is Senior Lecturer and Director of the B.Ed. (TESOL) Programme in the School of Linguistics and Applied Language Studies, Victoria University of Wellington, New Zealand. He is the author, with Paul Nation, of *Teaching ESL/EFL listening and speaking* (Routledge, 2009).

Nathaniel Owen is a PhD candidate at the University of Leicester, UK. He also holds an MA in Applied Linguistics and TESOL from the University of Leicester. His PhD specialises in second language reading in high-stakes tests (IELTS and TOEFL).

Amos Paran is Reader in Second Language Education at the UCL Institute of Education, University College London, UK. His main interests are the teaching of reading and the use of literature in language classrooms. His most recent book (with Pauline Robinson) is *Literature* (Oxford University Press, 2016), a teacher resource book focusing on activities for using literature in EFL.

Hae In Park graduated in 2015 from the doctoral programme in Applied Linguistics at Georgetown University in Washington, DC, USA. Her research interests include bilingualism and cognition, language and thought and cross-linguistic influence. Her research has appeared in the journal *Bilingualism: Language and Cognition* and in edited collections.

Alastair Pennycook is the author of many books on the global spread of English, critical applied linguistics and language as a local practice. He is Professor of Language in Education at the University of Technology Sydney, Australia. His most recent book (with Emi Otsuji) is *Metrolingualism: Language in the city* (Routledge, 2015).

Annamaria Pinter is Associate Professor at the Centre for Applied Linguistics, University of Warwick, UK. She has published widely in the area of ELT. She is the author of *Teaching Young Language Learners* (Oxford University Press, 2nd Ed. 2016) and *Children Learning Second Languages* (Palgrave Macmillan, 2011).

Anna Reznik is a PhD candidate at University of California, Davis, USA. Her research interests include second language acquisition; heritage language transmission, especially in Russian immigrant communities; and the role of literacy in language learning.

Philip Seargeant is Senior Lecturer in Applied Linguistics at the Open University. He is author of *The idea of English in Japan* (Multilingual Matters, 2009) and *Exploring World Englishes* (Routledge, 2012), and editor of *English in Japan in the era of globalization* (Palgrave Macmillan, 2011) and, with Joan Swann, *English in the world today* (Routledge, 2012).

Fauzia Shamim is Professor and Coordinator, female section, in the English Language Centre at Taibah University, Saudi Arabia. Her research interests include teaching/learning in large classes, language teacher education and development and English as medium of instruction in EFL settings.

James Simpson is Senior Lecturer in Language Education at the University of Leeds, UK. His main research interests are the teaching and learning of English for multilingual students in migration contexts and language learning with new technology in the developing world.

Sue Starfield is Professor in the School of Education and Director of the Learning Centre at UNSW, Australia. She was co-editor of the journal *English for Specific Purposes* from 2009–2014. Her current research focus is on academic writing at an advanced level.

Agneta M-L. Svalberg teaches and supervises in Applied Linguistics and TESOL on master's and doctoral courses at the University of Leicester, UK. She is particularly interested in grammar. In her research on engagement with language, she uses a complex systems approach.

Kaitlyn Tagarelli holds a PhD in Applied Linguistics from Georgetown University, USA, and is currently a postdoctoral fellow in the Department of Psychology and Neuroscience at Dalhousie University in Halifax, Nova Scotia, Canada. Her research focuses on the neuro-cognition of second language learning.

Scott Thornbury is the author of a number of books on language and language teaching methodology. He currently teaches on an MA TESOL programme at The New School, New York, USA.

Kris Van den Branden is Professor of Linguistics and a teacher educator at the Faculty of Arts of the University of Leuven, Belgium. At the same university, he is the academic promoter of the Centre for Language and Education. He is the co-editor (with Martin Bygate and John Norris) of the book series *Task-based Language Teaching: Issues, Research and Practice,* published by John Benjamins.

Catherine Wallace is Professor of Language and Literacy Education at UCL/Institute of Education, London, UK. She is the author of numerous books on literacy, including *Learning to*

Read in a Multicultural Society (Pergamon Press, 1986); *Reading* (Oxford University Press, 1992); and *Critical Reading in Language Education* (Palgrave Macmillan, 2006). A recent publication, *Literacy and the Bilingual Learner* (Palgrave Macmillan, 2013), brings earlier work into focus by presenting case studies of bilingual learners, both adults and children, in London schools.

Steve Walsh is Professor and Head of Applied Linguistics and Communication in the School of Education, Communication and Language Sciences, Newcastle University, UK. He has been involved in English Language Teaching for more than 30 years in a range of overseas contexts. His research interests include classroom discourse, teacher development and second language teacher education.

Paige Ware is Professor and Chair of the Department of Teaching & Learning at Southern Methodist University in Dallas, TX, USA. She examines the use of technologies to foster language and literacy growth among adolescents and to promote intercultural awareness through online partnerships.

Mark Warschauer is Professor of Education at the University of California, Irvine, USA; director of the Digital Learning Lab; and editor of *AERA Open*. His recent books include *Learning in the Cloud: How (and Why) to Transform Schools with Digital Media* (Teachers' College Press, 2011).

Rosemary Wette is Senior Lecturer at the University of Auckland, New Zealand. She has designed and taught a range of EAP courses at undergraduate and postgraduate levels. She has published articles on topics in EAP writing in the *Journal of Second Language Writing, System* and *ELT Journal*.

Zhu Hua is Professor of Applied Linguistics and Communication and Head of Department at Birkbeck College, University of London, UK. Her research interests are intercultural communication, multilingualism and child development. Her most recent monograph is *Exploring Intercultural Communication: Language in Action* (Routledge, 2014).

Introduction

English language teaching in the contemporary world

Graham Hall

This *Handbook* surveys key topics in English Language Teaching (ELT), providing a clear and comprehensive overview of the field. The book is intended for a varied ELT audience: you, the reader, may be an ELT professional studying at graduate level after some time in the classroom; a language teacher engaged in in-service teacher development, either formally via a teacher training/education programme or informally as part of your own developing interest in the field; a student wishing to enter the ELT profession via an undergraduate or graduate qualification; or a teacher educator, academic or researcher seeking familiarity with elements of ELT that you know less well.

Mindful of the diverse pedagogical, institutional and social contexts for ELT, the *Handbook* aims to provide an understanding of both the principles and practice of ELT through insights gained from relevant academic disciplines such as applied linguistics, education, psychology and sociology. It is underpinned by the belief that professional practice can both inform and draw upon academic understanding. Consequently, the *Handbook* is not intended to be a guide to ELT practice in which 'experts' inform practitioners about 'best practice' (although chapter authors are indeed leaders in the field). Rather, it aims to stimulate professional and academic reflection on the key issues facing ELT practitioners working in a diverse range of contexts around the world. Chapters provide authoritative understandings and insights which enable readers to develop their own thinking and practice in contextually appropriate ways.

English language teaching (ELT)

Naming the field

English language teaching (ELT) is, of course, 'what English language teachers do'. Yet this statement of the obvious obscures the complexity of a field which incorporates teaching and learning English as second, additional or foreign language or as an international lingua franca; for specific, academic or more general purposes; in different countries and contexts; and at different levels (primary, secondary, tertiary or adult). Indeed, 'ELT' is not the only name given to the field as

1

a whole – we might also encounter 'EFL' (also incorporated into the *International Association of Teachers of English as a Foreign Language*, that is, *IATEFL*); 'ESL' (English as a Second Language); and 'TESOL' (both an umbrella term for Teaching English to Speakers of Other Languages and the name of the *TESOL International Association* for teachers).

As Howatt and Widdowson (2004: xv) note, establishing the origins of terminology and expressions is "a needle-in-a-haystack task with few clear-cut answers", yet the use of one term rather than another can reflect a particular perspective on the field and its development. Thus, as English in the twenty-first century is no longer a single entity and has multiple forms (i.e. we can talk of 'Englishes'; see Seargeant, this volume) and is increasingly a lingua franca in conversations between those who do not share a first language, 'English as a *Foreign* language' no longer seems to capture the scope of English and English language teaching in the contemporary world. Similarly, the now widespread recognition of the importance of bilingualism and multilingualism for individual and societal language use (see, for example, Martin-Jones et al., 2012) suggests that English will not be the *second* language of a substantial number of learners around the world.

Meanwhile, whilst 'ELT' was adopted in the UK in 1946 as the name of the British Council's new journal 'English Language Teaching' (now known as *ELT Journal*), the term 'TESOL' first clearly emerged with the foundation in 1966 of the professional association of that name in the US, as an inclusive take on the previously more widespread 'ESL' in that inward-migration context (Howatt with Widdowson, 2004). Thus, we might see a slight and perhaps somewhat stereotypical association between the term TESOL and the US, and ELT and the UK, although it is evident that the terms are interchangeable for most ELT practitioners and researchers (e.g. Pennington and Hoekje, 2014: 163).Yet, as a *Handbook* needs a title, this volume follows Howatt with Widdowson (2004), Smith (2005) and many others in adopting the journal's terminology, 'ELT', as the name for the field as a whole and as the focus of study and reflection in the chapters that follow.

Framing the field

The teaching of English has a long history that interconnects with the teaching of other languages (Kelly, 1969; Howatt with Widdowson, 2004; Pennington and Hoekje, 2014).Yet in the twentieth century, ELT emerged as a recognisable and distinctive entity, prompted in the first instance by increased migration, the internationalisation of education and the growth of multinational capitalism, particularly in the decades following World War II, and more recently by globalisation, the development of the Internet and online communication and the related continued spread of English around the world.

As a result of this range of forces, ELT can be characterised in a number of ways. As a *profession*, ELT is constituted by teachers, teacher trainers and educators, curriculum designers and materials writers, administrators and planners and so forth.Yet the profession is made up of many communities of practice (Lave and Wenger, 1991) within different countries or contexts and educational sectors (e.g. private or state) and levels (e.g. primary, secondary or tertiary), each with its own values, practices and understandings (Pennington and Hoekje, 2014). And these may conceive of their activity in differing ways, such as ELT as 'a business' or 'industry', as 'education' or as 'a service'.

However, ELT is also a *focus of study*, whether as an emerging discipline in its own right, or as a sub-field of, for example, applied linguistics or education. Here we might find research, debate and discussion which aims to inform the development of the field, focusing, for instance, on classroom methodology; curriculum and assessment design; how new technologies might be most effectively used for language teaching and learning; whether and how new knowledge about language, uncovered through corpus studies, might be introduced to learners; and whether and how the spread of English and subsequent changes in its uses and forms might be recognised in ELT classrooms and materials.

Of central concern, though, is the relationship between 'research/theory' on the one hand and 'practice' on the other, and it seems clear that, in a world of multiple perspectives and in which ELT professionals are subject to a range of competing demands and forces, academic perspectives offer prompts and possibilities for practice rather than neat, 'one-size-fits-all' solutions to the challenges and dilemmas of English language teaching today. Indeed, investigative approaches such as action research (e.g. Burns, 2009) and exploratory practice (e.g. Allwright and Hanks, 2009) offer teachers routes into researching matters of immediate interest, thus creating knowledge themselves.

'Navigating' the field

While offering a more realistic and potentially democratic and transformative view of the relationship between theory and practice, the suggestion that English language teachers need to find their own way through debates, options and possibilities in light of their own local professional experiences is challenging. As Canagarajah puts it, what do such debates and opportunities "suggest for teaching on a Monday morning" (2006: 29)? One response is for ELT professionals to develop personal strategies in line with their underlying assumptions about teaching and learning, as exemplified by Ellis (2006). A related approach is to recognise local contexts, needs and aims as the central lens through which all possibilities should be viewed, developing locally specific approaches which shape existing knowledge and practices in contextually appropriate ways.

Clearly, teachers' abilities to navigate and mediate professional and academic themes in ELT need to develop and, often, to be supported. This is a primary goal of language teacher education (Johnson, 2013) and of this *Handbook,* which aims to outline and explore key issues within ELT, providing space for readers to reflect upon the principles which inform their practice, to connect pedagogical theory and practice to wider social issues, and, where possible, to work together to share ideas (Giroux and McLaren, 1989: xxiii).

There is thus a clear challenge for this volume – to be informative but not directive, and to be authoritative whilst providing opportunities for readers to reflect on and react to the ideas discussed. I summarise below how the *Handbook* seeks to achieve this, outlining its subsections and chapters.

The scope of this volume

Each chapter in the *Handbook* focuses on a specific issue within ELT, and each follows broadly the same format. This comprises an introduction to the area (including the history of the topic as appropriate), a critical review of main current issues, discussion of key areas of debate and dispute, and an outline of possible future developments or contingencies. Chapters conclude with a number of subsections. First, authors provide a series of *Discussion questions* that prompt reader reflection on chapter content and seek to connect the issues discussed to readers' own ELT contexts and experiences. Second, in a field where issues, debates and themes intersect in complementary ways, chapters list *Related topics* in the volume. Each chapter then focuses on *Further readings*, providing a short annotated list of key works which readers might consult for a more detailed discussion of the area. Bibliographical *References* are listed at the end of each chapter, making each contribution to the volume self-contained.

In a volume of this size, surveying a field of such diversity, it is perhaps inevitable that chapters will at times examine topics, interpret debates and present dilemmas in ways that may not satisfy all readers on all occasions. Indeed, given the range of professional lives, narratives and experiences within the *Handbook*'s readership as a whole, it would be a surprise if this was not occasionally the case. Other readers may differ over the way the *Handbook* is organised or with the gaps in coverage which are inevitable in any volume of this breadth. Clearly, despite the intention to cover as much ground as possible, some areas have, for reasons of space, had to be omitted or dealt with only briefly. Nevertheless, the thirty-nine *Handbook* chapters are grouped into six main sections, progressing from 'broader' contextual issues which surround English language teaching in the world to a 'narrower' focus on the language classroom itself. I shall now outline each section in turn.

Part I
ELT in the world: contexts and goals

Pennycook describes English as a "worldly language" (1994: 36), a term which reflects "its spread around the world and its worldly character as a result of being used so widely in the world" – English, and the ways in which the language is used, both reflects and also shapes the world we live in. Equally, ELT is itself a "worldly" enterprise in which social, cultural and political developments and debates surrounding English underpin how, and indeed why, the language is taught in the early decades of the twenty-first century. Thus, this first section of the *Handbook* focuses on contexts for ELT as a contemporary global enterprise and activity.

In the volume's opening chapter, *World Englishes and English as a Lingua Franca: a changing context for ELT*, Philip Seargeant traces the way in which English today is a language which has an unprecedented global spread and is marked by diversity and variety. Drawing on two notable paradigms, 'World Englishes' and 'English as a Lingua Franca' of the chapter title, Seargeant explores the ways in which understanding the diversity and variety of English can inform ELT practices.

The two subsequent chapters take a more overtly critical position on English and ELT in the world. In Chapter 2, Alastair Pennycook makes explicit links between *Politics, power relationships and ELT*. Here, in an example of the debates surrounding ELT which the *Handbook* seeks to capture, Pennycook outlines what he sees as the shortcomings of the World Englishes, English as a Lingua Franca and Linguistic Imperialism paradigms, before suggesting that English language educators should question the wider implications of classroom language policies, textbook choices, language norms, work choices, knowledge of learners' own languages and, indeed, everything that is done in the classroom. Next, Claire Kramsch and Zhu Hua trace changes in the relationship between *Language and culture in ELT*. Questioning whether English has really become a 'culture-free skill', they observe that English carries discourses, identities, memories and social meanings that constitute global and local cultures. Consequently, they note that English language teaching requires a knowledge of history, awareness of discourse processes and enhanced reflexivity.

Drawing on these debates, Enric Llurda's chapter, focusing on *'Native speakers', English and ELT*, examines changing perspectives of the 'traditional' distinction between 'native' and 'non-native' speakers and the values that were once attached to each type of speaker. The chapter outlines how the classification of language users in these two apparently mutually exclusive groups makes no sense when actual speakers communicating in English in the 'real world' are considered and explores the implications for teachers and for teaching.

Finally in this section, Graham Crookes discusses *Educational perspectives on ELT*, considering the aims of English language teaching as they have manifested over time, as well as within indigenous, progressive and critical or transformative perspectives on education. Crookes draws on concepts drawn from the philosophy of education to explore the values teachers may have and the ways in which they are consistent (or not) with language teaching and educational traditions within which teachers might be working.

Part II
Planning and organising ELT: curriculum, resources and settings

Having examined the broad global trends and debates which frame ELT in Part I, the chapters in Part II examine the planning, preparation and resourcing of ELT in the more immediate context of the school, institution or educational system. As Richards (2001: 112) notes, "in deciding on [language teaching] goals, planners choose from among alternatives based on assumptions about the role of teaching and of a curriculum. Formulating goals is not, therefore, an objective scientific enterprise, but a judgement call". Thus, alongside conceptions of how languages are best learned, decisions concerning the planning and resourcing of ELT reflect wider value-based judgements about the purpose of and priorities for ELT in any given context, as the chapters in this section illustrate.

Opening this section, Kathleen Graves outlines key issues in *Language curriculum design*, which she addresses by describing three historical waves of curriculum content – each with different understandings of both language and how and why people learn a language. Graves highlights the important role of integrating planning processes to align the curriculum with its context. Published materials play a central role in the delivery of most language curricula and are the focus of John Gray's chapter, *ELT materials: claims, controversies and critiques*. Gray highlights the ways in which published materials represent both language for pedagogical purposes (and the simplifications and distortions this can entail) and the world and its inhabitants (and the denial of recognition to stigmatised social groups). Assessment is also a central consideration in language curriculum planning, and in *Dealing with the demands of language testing and assessment*, Glenn Fulcher and Nathaniel Owen outline ways in which teachers might understand and engage with the role of standardised language testing and of assessment in the language classroom.

Clearly, the enactment of any language curriculum depends on teachers' pedagogical knowledge and abilities. Thus, moving beyond components of the language curriculum *per se* to examine *Language teacher education*, Karen E. Johnson discusses the ways in which the development of knowledge for language teaching might take place through 'located teacher education', which links disciplinary knowledge to experiential knowledge.

Although many chapters in this *Handbook* identify new technologies as a key influence on current developments in ELT, Paul Gruba, Don Hinkelman and Mónica Stella Cárdenas-Claros' overview of *New technologies, blended learning, and the 'flipped classroom' in ELT* is the first of two in the volume in which technology is the central theme (for details of the other, by Kern, Ware and Warschauer, see Part VI). Examining two approaches to the language curriculum (i.e. 'blended' and 'flipped'), the chapter discusses how new technologies might spur curriculum innovation but may also disrupt established teacher and student routines, realigning our conceptions of language teaching and learning.

Subsequently, chapters outline key issues across a range of ELT fields and settings. Sue Starfield's overview of *English for specific purposes* (ESP) tracks the development of the field over time, noting the importance of students' needs and contexts and the development of genre-based instruction. She also points out the challenges raised by the global dominance of English; likewise, Helen Basturkmen and Rosemary Wette's chapter on *English for academic purposes* (EAP). Their discussion also examines the extent to which EAP students should balance the pragmatic accommodation of academic norms with the possibility of critically challenging them. The chapter on *English for speakers of other languages* (ESOL), by James Simpson, focuses in particular on language education and migration. Simpson presents an overview of the teaching and learning of English for adults who are migrants to English-dominant countries, focusing on how social, political and individual factors impinge on ESOL practice.

The final chapter in this section explores the phenomenon of *Bilingual education in a multilingual world*, focusing on language contexts where English is one of the bilingual target languages. Chapter authors Kevin S. Carroll and Mary Carol Combs outline the ways in which language ideologies underlie the design and implementation of differing forms of bilingual education, providing an overview of some of the current tensions in the field.

Part III
Methods and methodology: perspectives and practices

Historically, language teaching methods have been a key focus of ELT, with a search for the 'best method' through much of the twentieth century being an often cited characteristic of the field (e.g. Stern, 1983; Allwright and Hanks, 2009). However, from the 1990s onwards, new perspectives on and questions about Method (as an overarching concept), methods (as specific and pre-specified approaches to teaching) and methodology (what teachers actually do in class) have emerged. For many, the current plurality of methods in ELT is an accepted and welcome feature of the field. Others, however, view the concept of Method with suspicion: does Method create patterns of power and control within ELT? Are we entering a postmethod era? Is Method itself even a 'myth' – a pre-occupation of methodologists and researchers rather than a concern of teachers?

The current "profusion of methods" (Allwright and Hanks, 2009: 38) in contemporary ELT makes it impossible to deal with every current approach to language teaching within the *Handbook*; this section of the volume therefore balances accounts of debates about methods generally alongside overviews of specific approaches which are particularly influential within the field today. Additionally, many other chapters throughout the *Handbook* identify methodological trends and developments that are relevant to particular contexts and settings (e.g. *English for specific purposes, English for academic purposes* and *Teaching language skills*).

In the opening chapter of this section, therefore, Graham Hall provides an overview of the historical trends and current debates surrounding *Method, methods and methodology*. The chapter outlines a range of perspectives on the development of methods in ELT, narratives which, at times, diverge and offer conflicting accounts of the past and present, each having implications for the way we might make sense of contemporary debates and practice. Hall's chapter touches on a range of methods which are not examined in subsequent separate chapters and discusses the possibility of a postmethod era in ELT.

Following this, Scott Thornbury examines *Communicative language teaching in theory and practice*, exploring and disentangling the links between original conceptions of communicative language teaching (CLT) and learning and current practice around the world. Thornbury discusses whether CLT's influence as 'a brand' in ELT is matched by its impact on current classroom teaching. The next chapter, by Kris Van den Branden on *Task-based language teaching*, likewise reviews a communicative and interactive approach to teaching which has gained momentum in ELT but which can also be challenging to implement. Tom Morton then provides an overview of *Content and Language Integrated Learning* (CLIL) and assesses its relevance to ELT, focusing on the 'what', 'why', 'who' and 'how' of CLIL. Here, CLIL is identified as an umbrella term identifying a range of approaches to integrating content and language rather than as a label to identify specific programmes or a single pedagogical approach.

All chapters in this section note the challenges to teachers posed by methodological developments and the potential disparity between methods 'in theory' and 'in practice'; it is also clear that ELT practices are linked to wider social and intellectual trends. Adrian Holliday's chapter, focusing on *Appropriate methodology*, therefore closes this section by discussing how teaching methods need to be made meaningful to the existing, lived cultural and linguistic experiences of language learners and their teachers everywhere. Arguing for a critical cosmopolitan approach, Holliday suggests that teachers need to consider the cultural and linguistic value of what their students bring to their learning and to the classroom.

Part IV
Second language learning and learners

There are obvious reasons why an overview of ELT should focus on language learners and learning. "Only the learners can do their own learning", note Allwright and Hanks (2009: 2), and it is learners "that either will or will not effectively complement the efforts of teachers and other, more 'background' language professionals (like textbook writers and curriculum developers) to make language classrooms productive" (ibid.). Understanding what learners themselves bring to language learning can help guide ELT practice. In this regard, Second Language Acquisition (SLA) research provides insights into language learning processes. Although this research has, over time, been dominated by cognitivist perspectives which see learning as a mental process, alternative conceptions have recently emerged offering more socially-oriented explanations that situate learning in its social context. A focus on learners also leads us to consider students as individuals, with differing attributes and attitudes (for example, age, aptitude, motivation and anxiety).

The first two chapters of this section draw on contrasting accounts of how languages are learned. Laura Collins and Emma Marsden discuss *Cognitive perspectives on classroom language learning*, focusing on a range of complex mental processes that learners engage in to develop language knowledge. Meanwhile, Eduardo Negueruela-Azarola and Próspero N. García's account of *Sociocultural theory and the language classroom* reviews theoretical and pedagogical insights for ELT inspired by Vygotsky's research on the relationship between thinking and speaking. From this perspective, social context and cultural tools (such as language) mediate thinking and learning, and it is misleading to separate 'the cognitive' from 'the social'. Of course, ELT practitioners do not have to commit solely to one view of learning or the other and will find plausible insights in both accounts of language learning and their implications for classroom practice.

Subsequently, chapters in this section review a range of learner characteristics and their implications for language learning and teaching. In their overview of *Individual differences* (IDs), Peter D. MacIntyre, Tammy Gregersen and Richard Clément highlight a number of key ID factors such as anxiety, aptitude, language learning styles and strategies and willingness to communicate. The chapter then discusses how such factors may interact, grow together and operate in context. Also an ID, *Motivation* is explored in a separate chapter by Martin Lamb, reflecting its central role in language learning and the range of different approaches that theorists have taken to describe and research this phenomenon.

Although maintaining the focus on learning and learners, the final three chapters in this section pursue a more contextually and institutionally oriented approach to the issues and trends which they describe. Firstly, Phil Benson discusses how conceptions of *Learner autonomy* are changing in the context of the global spread of ELT, the emergence of research exploring relationships between learner autonomy and language learner identity and the roles that learner autonomy might play in postmethod ELT pedagogies. The subsequent two chapters then focus on the rapid recent growth of English language teaching to younger learners. Janet Enever traces the development of *Primary ELT*, highlighting the socio-political nature of decisions for, and reviewing pedagogic responses to, an early start to teaching and learning English. Subsequently, Annamaria Pinter's *Secondary ELT* chapter reviews core characteristics of teenage learners, and considers the current pedagogic opportunities and challenges of working with secondary level learners.

Part V
Teaching language: knowledge, skills and pedagogy

Part V of the volume examines a range of perspectives on *what* is taught in class, i.e. the language itself, and considers *how* the teaching of language knowledge and skills might be realised in practice. It is not the *Handbook*'s aim to provide a detailed examination of each aspect of linguistic knowledge (e.g. vocabulary, grammar, listening, reading, etc.) and specific instructional practices surrounding them. Rather, the six chapters deal with key themes and questions surrounding the language, and knowledge about language, that learners might need, and explore differing conceptualisations of how this might be developed in the classroom.

The first two chapters in this section deal with ways in which learners might engage explicitly with knowledge about language. Ana Frankenberg-Garcia provides an overview of the possibilities offered by *Corpora in ELT*, discussing both how corpus analysis has provided new insights into language and language use but also how corpora might be used for pedagogical purposes. Frankenberg-Garcia also discusses questions surrounding the use of 'authentic' or 'real' language in the ELT classroom. Subsequently, Agneta M-L. Svalberg's chapter discusses *Language Awareness* (LA), a term which incorporates knowledge about language, a movement with an ideological stance towards language-related issues and an approach to teaching and learning languages.

Whilst recognising that languages are not learned and not often taught in such a 'compartmentalised' way, the next two chapters examine first the teaching of language as a 'system' and then the teaching of 'language skills'. In *Teaching language as a system*, Dilin Liu and Robert Nelson draw on 'systemic functional linguistics' and 'cognitive linguistics' to present a 'comprehensive systems view' which might help ELT practitioners better understand language and language teaching, especially the teaching of grammar and vocabulary. Jonathan Newton's chapter on *Teaching language skills* then provides an overview of the critical issues surrounding the teaching of the 'four skills' of reading, writing, speaking and listening. Newton notes the complex interplay of these skills and discusses how integrating them within a 'fours strands' framework focused on learning opportunities may be a more effective pedagogical approach.

The final two chapters in this section explore aspects of English language teaching that are arguably somewhat overlooked in the mainstream literature of ELT. Amos Paran and Catherine Wallace's chapter on *Teaching literacy* clarifies the distinction between 'literacy' and 'reading and writing', with particular reference to learning literacy in a second language, and presents a view of literacy as a social practice embedded in the social and cultural lives of learners. Whilst noting the existence of many types of literacy (e.g. digital literacy, visual literacy), the chapter focuses on the development of reading and writing, but as a sociocultural practice and process. Finally, Geoff Hall reviews arguments for *Using Literature in ELT*. For Hall, using literature in ELT is a useful way of expanding learners' vocabulary, awareness of register, genre and general linguistic knowledge. However, a stronger claim within the chapter is that the ways in which language is used in literary texts are centrally relevant to the needs of students in a wide range of situations in everyday life.

Part VI
Focus on the language classroom

The final section of the *Handbook* brings us to the language classroom itself, described by Gaies (1980) as "the crucible" of language teaching and learning. Given the number of factors at play (from global trends in ELT to individual learner characteristics) and the varied contexts in which ELT takes place, what happens in a classroom is localised and situation-specific; experience tells us that no two classrooms are the same.

However, there are a number of key issues and questions that English language teachers and learners navigate in every classroom. These broadly relate to the ways in which teacher(s) and learners relate to each other and use language in class – whether that classroom is a physical or a virtual environment – and the opportunities this might create for learning. Yet while the questions teachers (and learners) face are similar – for example, how should errors be treated, what is the role of the learners' own-language in class – the ways in which these issues are addressed and resolved will vary; as Freeman (2002) notes, context is everything.

Sarah Mercer's chapter on *Complexity and language teaching* opens the section. Clarifying the difference between 'complex' and 'complicated', Mercer outlines how complexity theories, and seeing the classroom as a complex dynamic system, can help us understand ELT learning and teaching contexts and processes. The chapter also suggests that complexity theories can offer practitioners a framework for reflexive practice, systemic thinking or systemic action research.

Subsequently, Steve Walsh and Li Li look at the important relationship between *Classroom talk, interaction and collaboration*. Their chapter not only outlines how learners access and acquire new knowledge and skills through the talk, interaction and collaboration which take place but also suggests that teachers need to develop clear understandings of these processes in order to maximise opportunities for language learning in class. Alison Mackey, Hae In Park and Kaitlyn M. Tagarelli then examine a key aspect of classroom discourse, the ways in which teachers (and learners) might deal with *Errors, corrective feedback and repair*. Their discussion offers English language teachers an overview of the issues surrounding corrective feedback, informed by empirical findings from SLA research, and tackles decades-old questions about whether, when, how and by whom corrective feedback might or should be provided. Philip Kerr's chapter, *Questioning 'English-only' classrooms*, then examines own-language use (i.e. use of the 'mother tongue' or 'first language') in ELT classrooms. Kerr explores the tension between the widely held belief in English-only approaches (in the methodological literature of ELT, at least) and actual classroom practices, and argues the case for the principled use of the learners' own-language in class.

The final three chapters in this section examine issues which, whilst not about classroom discourse and language *per se*, examine contexts for interaction and language learning. Fauzia Shamim and Kuchah Kuchah discuss *Teaching large classes in difficult circumstances* and outline the need for practitioners to move away from a 'problem-solution' approach to pedagogy towards developing context-appropriate methodologies for large-class teaching. Richard Kern, Paige Ware and Mark Warschauer then describe a very different set of issues, examining the relationship between *Computer-mediated communication and language learning*. Their chapter focuses in particular on feedback on learners' writing and speaking and telecollaboration in language and intercultural learning, and addresses the key question of determining the 'effectiveness' of computer-mediated communication for learning. Finally, Julia Menard-Warwick, Miki Mori, Anna Reznik and Daniel Moglen explore *Values in the ELT classroom*, showing how the teaching of English always involves values, realised both in the decisions teachers make and how classes are organised, and in the values students and teachers express during lessons. Menard-Warwick et al.'s chapter thus reflects, at the level of the classroom, those broad issues of power, culture and educational philosophy raised in the opening section of the *Handbook*.

This Introduction has mapped out both the rationale for and the key areas discussed within the *Routledge Handbook of English Language Teaching*. Recognising the diverse nature of ELT, as a profession constituted by a range of communities of practice and professional interests but also as focus of study and professional reflection, the chapters that follow thus provide a comprehensive overview of the field whilst providing opportunities for you, the reader, to develop your own contextualised understandings of principles and practice in English language teaching.

References

Allwright, D. and Hanks, J. (2009) *The developing language learner: An introduction to exploratory practice*. Basingstoke, UK: Palgrave Macmillan.

Burns, A. (2009) *Doing action research in English language teaching*. London: Routledge.

Canagarajah, A.S. (2006) 'TESOL at forty: What are the issues?' *TESOL Quarterly*, 40/1. 9–34.

Ellis, R. (2006) 'Current issues in the teaching of grammar: An SLA perspective'. *TESOL Quarterly*, 40/1. 83–107.

Freeman, D. (2002) 'The hidden side of the work: Teacher knowledge and learning to teach. A perspective from North American educational research on teacher education in English language teaching'. *Language Teaching*, 35/1. 1–13.

Gaies, S. (1980) *Classroom-centred research: Some consumer guidelines*. Paper presented at the Second Annual TESOL Summer Meeting. Albuquerque, NM.

Giroux, H. and McLaren, P. (1989) *Critical pedagogy, the state and cultural struggle*. Albany, NY: SUNY Press.

Howatt, A. with Widdowson, H. (2004) *A history of English language teaching*. Oxford: Oxford University Press.

Johnson, K.E. (2013) 'Foreword', in S. Ben Said and L.J. Zhang (eds) *Language teachers and teaching: Global perspectives, local initiatives*. New York: Routledge. 23–26.

Kelly, L. (1969) *25 centuries of language teaching*. Rowley, MA: Newbury House.

Lave, J. and Wenger, E. (1991) *Situated learning: Legitimate peripheral participation*. New York: Cambridge University Press.

Martin-Jones, M., Blackledge, A. and Creese, A. (2012) *The Routledge handbook of multilingualism*. London: Routledge.

Pennington, M. and Hoekje, B. (2014) 'Framing English language teaching'. *System*, 46. 163–175.

Pennycook, A. (1994) *The cultural politics of English as an international language*. London: Longman.

Richards, J. (2001) *Curriculum development in language teaching*. Cambridge: Cambridge University Press.

Smith, R. (ed.) (2005) *Teaching English as a foreign language, 1936–1961: Foundations of ELT. Volume 1, selected papers*. London: Routledge.

Stern, H. (1983) *Fundamental concepts of language teaching*. Oxford: Oxford University Press.

Part I

ELT in the world

Contexts and goals

1

World Englishes and English as a Lingua Franca

A changing context for ELT

Philip Seargeant

Introduction: Englishes around the world

English in the world today is a language which has an unprecedented global spread, is marked by its diversity and variety, and plays a fundamental role in the lives of millions of people in countries all around the globe. This chapter gives an overview of the current state and status of the language, and considers the implications that its global standing has for ELT theory and practice. It looks at how two notable paradigms – World Englishes studies and English as a Lingua Franca – have been instrumental in theorising the nature of English in the modern world and in refocusing debates about how the language is perceived by those responsible for its regulation in terms of planning, policy and education. The chapter reviews the development and aims of these two paradigms and explores the implications that an understanding of the diversity and variety of the language has for ELT practices.

Let us begin looking at what it means for English to be a 'global' language by considering the question of how many people speak English in the world today. It is a challenging task to calculate with any degree of accuracy the number of English speakers globally, but the processes involved in making these calculations illuminate a number of key issues about the language as it exists today and thus offer a good starting point for our wider discussion. There are two main difficulties in estimating the total number of current English speakers globally. The first of these is a practical issue: no purposefully designed data-gathering procedures exist for recording the use of languages around the world. As such, figures need to be deduced and pieced together from various different sources, and this inevitably results in a wide margin of error for any total one puts together.

The second problem is a more theoretical one and involves issues which have direct relevance to ELT. The difficulty here concerns decisions about precisely whom one includes in the figures. If we wish to calculate the total number of English speakers in the world, we obviously need a stable idea of what counts as an 'English speaker'. And although at first glance the answer to this may seem self-evident, once we begin to take into account the great variety of ways in which people use and engage with English around the world, it soon becomes apparent that it is actually a rather complex issue. We need to decide, for example, what level of proficiency is necessary to qualify as a speaker of the language. Will everyday conversational ability (which is in itself difficult to define) do, or should the threshold for competence be set at a higher level? Then there is the question of what range of varieties should be included within the broad concept of 'English'. Should we include English-based pidgins, for example, or 'mixed' varieties such as Singlish? With English being spoken in communities stretching all around the globe, diversity of both form and function – how the language looks and sounds, and how it is used – is a fundamental element of its modern-day identity. But this diversity makes it increasingly difficult to define 'English' and 'English speakers' in a simple or straightforward way.

Despite these difficulties, there has been much work done on compiling statistics about the number of people who speak English in the world today, and, as we shall discuss below, the nature of these statistics – and the theoretical issues that are involved in the criteria upon which they are based – have important implications for the teaching of the language. In effect, they provide the broad context in which the teaching and learning of the language takes place, and as such they are a good place to begin when thinking about how English's global status might influence ELT.

David Crystal has estimated that, by the first decade of the twenty-first century, there were somewhere between 400 and 500 million first language speakers of English in the world (Crystal, 2012). This figure is arrived at by combining the numbers of first language users in all the English-dominant countries such as the UK, USA and Australia (while being mindful of the caveat that, in all these countries, large proportions of the population do not have English as their mother tongue, and that several of the countries are officially bi- or multilingual, such as South Africa) and adding to this estimates of people living elsewhere around the world who have English as a native language. (The concept of the 'native speaker' is a complicated and, at times, contentious one. I am using it here in its 'common-sense' frame of reference, while at the same time noting the complexities around its use. A full discussion of these can be found in Llurda, this volume.) The rough figures for the main English-dominant countries are as follows:

United States of America	approximately 250 million
United Kingdom	approx. 60m
Canada	approx. 24m
Australia and New Zealand	approx. 20m
The Caribbean	approx. 5m
Ireland	approx. 3.7m
South Africa	approx. 3.6m

This figure for native speakers is, however, only a part of the overall picture. In addition, there are approximately 60 countries (for example India, Nigeria and Singapore) where English is used as a second or additional language. In these societies, English has an official status alongside local languages and is often used as the primary means of communication in domains such as education, the law and bureaucracy. It has been estimated that only around 20 per cent to 30 per cent of the population in countries such as these are likely to speak the language, as use is predominantly clustered around urban areas and limited to white-collar workers (Mufwene, 2010). However, given the size of the population of some of these countries and the number of regions in which it is used, the total figure for speakers of English as a second or additional language around the world is in the vicinity of 600 million (Schneider, 2011).

A third and final category that can be included in the overall figures is those to whom English is taught/has been learnt as the primary foreign language: people who are or have engaged in formal education of the language for a number of years. This accounts for speakers in over another hundred countries (McArthur, 1998), further extending the reach of the language. By adding these three groups of speakers together, the total that Crystal arrives at is somewhere between one and a half and two billion people. In other words, somewhere between a quarter and a third of the world's current population currently speak English to some level of proficiency.

There are a number of interesting implications to note from these figures, even when we take into account the lack of precision in the overall total. The first point to make is that, although English is not the language with the most native speakers in the world – Chinese overshadows it in this respect with over 1.2 billion native speakers, while Spanish is also a close rival with around 414 million first language speakers (Ethnologue, 2014) – when one adds those who speak it as a second or additional language within their communities and those who use it as a foreign or international language, English emerges as very much the pre-eminent global language of the modern era. And, as the summary of figures above reveals, a significantly larger proportion of English users – a ratio of around four to one, in fact – are now non-native rather than native speakers. In other words, the majority of people around the world who speak English – and who use it as a fundamental resource in their daily lives – have learnt it as an additional or foreign language. ELT, therefore, has played a very significant part in the spread and current role of the language around the world.

A further important point of note, however, is that over two-thirds of the world's population do *not* speak English. Thus, although it can be described as the pre-eminent global language in today's world, when compared to other languages, it is not by any means a universal resource, and a majority of the global population do not speak it. Yet, given the range of functions and the nature of the domains in which it is used (e.g. its status as the language of global business, its role in the global knowledge economy, etc.), it nevertheless often still plays some role in the lives of those who do not have any practical knowledge of it and is a significant part of the environment in which they live. For example, such is the nature of contemporary global commerce that a farmer in rural Bangladesh may well need to find ways to decode the instructions on the pesticides he (and it usually is 'he') uses on his crops as these are printed in English, even if the language has little other existence in his life (Erling et al., 2012). In contexts such as this, therefore, access to English language education is often desirable or in some cases necessary, although such provision is often not provided or sufficiently resourced (for a critical perspective on the access or barriers to material benefits created by the spread of English, see Pennycook, this volume).

Theoretical paradigms: a multiplex of Englishes

World Englishes

The current status of English around the world, as well as the different ways it is used and exists in different societies, is a product of the language's global spread. The extent of this spread has meant that, since the 1980s, there has been a trend within scholarship to talk of it in the plural form. English in the world today is not a single entity; it is multiplex, with different forms, different identities and different histories. In the words of Braj Kachru, one of the pioneering scholars in this field, "The result of [its] spread is that, formally and functionally, English now has multicultural identities. The term 'English' does not capture this sociolinguistic reality; the term 'Englishes' does" (Kachru, 1992: 357).

The Three Circles of English

To highlight the multiplexity of the language, and the sociolinguistic profiles of these many 'world Englishes', Kachru (1992: 356–357) devised what has become a very influential descriptive model. Known as the *Three Circles of English*, this focuses upon a number of key issues responsible for the ways in which English is now used in particular countries. It views the language in terms of three concentric circles, each of which is composed of countries whose use of English is a product of the history of its spread, the patterns of acquisition in that country, and the ways it is used. In other words, he highlights the following three issues which he sees as fundamental for the identity the language has in different parts of the world:

- the historical process that has resulted in English occupying its current position in a particular country;
- how members of that country usually come to acquire the language (e.g. as a first language learnt from birth, as an additional language learnt via formal education later in life);
- the purposes or functions to which the language is put in that country.

Using these issues, he divides the world up into three broad groups which he terms the Inner, Outer and Expanding Circles.

The Inner Circle comprises those countries where English is the mother tongue for the great majority of the population and where it is used as the default language for most domains of society. Along with the UK, this includes countries such as the USA, Canada, Australia, New Zealand – i.e. those which were colonised by the British and where English displaced indigenous languages. Kachru (1992: 356–357) refers to these as "norm-providing" in that the type of English that is spoken by their populations has generally acted as the model for the English taught and learnt elsewhere in the world. That is to say, when people learn English in, for example, Japan, there has been a tradition of using standard American or standard British English as the model. American and British Englishes have been seen as the standards to which to aspire and viewed as 'authentic' forms of the language.

The second grouping is known as the Outer Circle, and this again comprises countries where English's current status is the product of a colonial history. The difference here, though, is that in these countries English did not displace indigenous languages but came to be used alongside them, often fulfilling specific functions in various institutional domains. English is therefore predominantly an additional language in this circle, used in contexts such as bureaucracy and education. In 1992, Kachru referred to these countries as "norm-developing" in that the varieties of English spoken here have their "own local histories, literary traditions, pragmatic contexts, and communicative norms" (1992: 359), and have thus become indigenised to a significant degree. They do not, however, have the same status as the Inner Circle varieties (they are occasionally known as 'new Englishes') and have thus not normally been used as teaching models in EFL contexts. Countries in this circle include places such as India, Kenya and Singapore.

The final grouping is what Kachru calls the Expanding Circle. This, in effect, comprises the rest of the world, i.e. countries in which English has been predominantly taught as a foreign language. The spread of English here is not tied specifically to a history of colonisation but is the result of other factors, predominant amongst which are processes of globalisation. Historically, these countries have been "norm-dependent"; these are the countries which have followed an Inner Circle standard English as their model. They can be categorised as English as a *Foreign* Language (EFL) countries in that the education system has, at least traditionally, assumed that English is taught for purposes such as foreign travel and engagement with foreign literature – although in recent years this has been added to by the notion of English for international communication in domains such as business. Countries in this circle include China, Japan and most of the countries of Europe.

Strengths and critiques of the Three Circles model

One of the major strengths of the Three Circles model – and one of its important legacies – has been the way it has focused scholarly attention on the diversity of English and particularly on the history and current cultural identity of non-native varieties. In promoting interest in these, the model – and scholarship which takes a World Englishes perspective – has done a great deal to legitimise these varieties as valid linguistic systems in their own right. By referring to these varieties as separate Englishes rather than simply non-native dialects, this approach makes a case for seeing what were often previously viewed as deficient versions of Inner Circle varieties (e.g. Quirk, 1990) as legitimate varieties in their own right, and research conducted in this field has provided empirical evidence of the ways in which these varieties are linguistically stable and have firm roots within the culture of the societies which use them.

Since the introduction and development of the Three Circles model, however, it has been subject to a number of critiques, focusing on certain limitations in its scope, detail or theoretical assumptions (e.g. Bruthiaux, 2003; Pennycook, 2007). In its attempt to generalise across the broad sweep of English speakers globally (a population which numbers, as we have noted above, up to two billion people), the model necessarily looks on a broad level at certain aspects of the phenomena it is explaining. Limitations to which people have drawn attention include the fact that it deals with language only at the level of the nation state, thus ignoring the immense amount of variety, e.g. the regional and social dialects, the domain-specific registers, which occur within countries. It has also been criticised for conceptualising varieties as separate and distinct entities (e.g. Indian English, Singapore English) rather than attempting to deal with the way that people often tend to mix English with other languages in an *ad hoc* manner, creating hybrid patterns of language use which draw on the various linguistic resources they have to hand (Pennycook, 2007). In other words, the critiques claim that the model is built on distinct national varieties that do not reflect the real-world fluidity of language use as experienced by speakers around the globe and thus gives a skewed picture of the sociolinguistic realities of much of the world's population.

Another problem concerns the way that several countries do not fit neatly within the categories used by the model. Kachru himself noted this weakness for the case of South Africa, which now has eleven official languages and where English exists as a mother tongue for large sections of the population but not for others. As noted above, several of the Inner Circle countries are officially bilingual, and thus even these complicate clear-cut distinctions between the three groupings.

A further problematic area (again intimated by Kachru in his early writings, e.g. Kachru, 1985) is countries such as those in Scandinavia, in which English is, on paper, a foreign language but where it now exists as such an integral part of everyday life that to all intents and purposes it operates more as an additional language. Despite these areas of critique, however, the model has been greatly influential, both in broadening the scope of research and debate about the nature of global English and in providing a conceptual vocabulary to talk about these phenomena.

Schneider's dynamic model

Other models for explaining the roots of the diversity of Englishes around the world have also been proposed, aiming to further refine our theoretical understanding of the current nature of the language. One such is that devised by Edgar Schneider (2011) who, like Kachru, focuses on the historical development of worldwide varieties and the way that patterns of contact between different speech communities that took place as a result of colonialism have shaped the current form and function of the language in post-colonial countries. Schneider identifies five broad stages that varieties in what are now post-colonial countries can pass through which influence the way the language is used and perceived. Not all territories go through all five stages – depending on the particular historical circumstances, different parts of the process will be more prominent than others for some territories – but as a model, this attempts to provide a more detailed explanation of the development of worldwide varieties than the Three Circles model.

The first stage – what Schneider calls "foundation" – sees English being brought to a territory where it was not previously spoken as part of the broader process of colonial expansion. In this first phase of contact, the two communities – the indigenous people and the newly arrived settlers – view themselves as distinct groups, and though some language contact takes place, communication is usually conducted via interpreters or high-status members of the communities.

In stage 2, "exonormative stabilisation", English starts to be spoken on a more regular basis in the territory, although it is confined mostly to domains such as education, administration and the legal system. The variety that is spoken is exonormative in that it is modelled on norms external to the territory itself – i.e. from the 'home' country (i.e. Britain) – and thus it has no distinct linguistic or cultural identity of its own. This is followed by Stage 3, "nativisation". At this point in the process, the cultural and political allegiances of the pre-colonisation period are beginning to wane, and the territory is instead developing a new cultural identity which includes a localised variety of English. The fourth stage of the process, "endonormative stabilisation", then sees this local variety become viewed as a legitimate entity in its own right, to the extent that it starts to be promoted as a significant element of the territory's culture. The population of the territory thus no longer looks to a British model of English but instead relies upon local norms, which often begin to be codified in national dictionary projects. This stage often occurs after political independence for the colony, and linguistic issues, along with other cultural issues (e.g. the promotion of a national literature), are part of the process of forging a distinct political identity.

Once the local variety is firmly established, the fifth stage of the process takes place, termed "differentiation" by Schneider. This refers to processes of internal linguistic variation that happen within a territory as different sectors of the community begin to establish their own specific usage patterns. For example, differentiation will occur between the way different geographical regions use the language, or between age groups, and the extent of this is such that these can be considered as separate dialects. The five-stage model thus maps a process which accounts for how diverse world varieties develop and the role that historical and cultural issues play in shaping this development. As we shall discuss later, when we look at implications for ELT, this historico-cultural background and the influence it has on the relationship between English and local identities is a key issue for teaching as it provides the background context for questions about language form and function.

English as a Lingua Franca

Research and debate in World Englishes has, then, done a great deal to highlight the full extent of the diversity of English around the world and the deep cultural roots it has in various world contexts, especially in so far as it is bound up with the cultural identity of different communities. There is another significant way in which English is presently used as a language across the globe, however, and this is as an international language: a *lingua franca* allowing communication between those who do not share a mother tongue. The phenomenon of English as a Lingua

Franca (ELF) is another important site for research for English language studies and one which also has implications for the teaching and learning of the language. The term 'lingua franca' originally referred to a trade language that was used in the Levant from the eleventh through to the nineteenth centuries. The name, the Latin for 'Frankish tongue', comes from the way that Muslims in the area would commonly refer to the Crusaders as Franks irrespective of their actual background. From the nineteenth century onwards, the term began to be used for any medium of communication between people who do not share a native language. As was noted above, the demographics of English use around the world today mean that non-native speakers outnumber native speakers significantly and thus, for a large proportion of interactions in which English is used, it has precisely this role, as a means for international dialogue in an increasingly globalised world.

Within scholarship focusing on English as a Lingua Franca, there is some debate about the scope of the term – whether it should include interaction which involves both native and non-native speakers (e.g. Firth, 1996) or whether it is best reserved for interactions where neither party have English as a native language. Given the complex patterns of mobility that now characterise the lives of great sections of the world population, an inclusive use of the concept seems most useful, focusing attention on how English is used in a variety of contexts and domains as the preferred medium for international communication. While early research on the topic looked to identify habitually used language features in ELF interactions (e.g. Dewey, 2007), recent research has moved to viewing ELF more as a function than a specific variety in its own right and to focusing on the range of strategies that people use in order to accommodate to each other's communicative practices (Jenkins et al., 2011; Seidlhofer, 2011). In essence, English as a Lingua Franca is an aspect of intercultural communication (see Kramsch and Zhu, this volume). Unlike varieties which are used by particular speech communities, it is better conceived of as something drawn upon by communities of practice who have shared interests, goals and emergent ways for engaging in these (Wenger, 1998). Research attention thus focuses on how people adapt their English usage to ensure that it is appropriate for the culturally and linguistically diverse contexts in which they are communicating. For example, those accustomed to using English in this way are likely to avoid the use of idioms, given that these are usually highly culturally specific; they will also adapt their pronunciation according to the audience they are addressing so as to ensure maximum clarity of expression.

In summary, both the above paradigms have had great influence in focusing research interest in, and raising general awareness of, the ways that English is actually used around the world today. Their findings have mapped out the diversity in form, function and beliefs about the language. In doing this they have played a role in countering attitudes which stigmatise usages that differ from standard British or American as being in some way 'broken' or imperfect. Thus, through the collection and analysis of empirical data, they have made the case for legitimising the diversity that is found in English around the world today. In the next section, we will go on to look at how our understanding of this diversity impacts on the teaching of the language.

Implications and challenges for ELT practice and practitioners

As we saw from both Kachru's and Schneider's models, the issue of norms – of how the systematised features of the language are spoken by a speech community – has been an important factor in how varieties are perceived and the status they are accorded. This is, of course, a crucial issue for ELT, as any language class needs to have a model of the language with which to work, and the insights from World Englishes and ELF both provide challenges for finding straightforward answers about what this model should be. In this section, we will examine the most prominent of these challenges, addressing the questions of what form(s) of English should be taught, as well as who should teach it and how should it be tested.

What model of English should be taught?

The issue of teaching models is relevant for almost all those who speak the language, both native speaker and non-native speaker alike. Those for whom English is a first language acquire its spoken form as a natural part of their development, but in doing so they learn the variety that is spoken around them, which, for the majority of the population, means a regional or social dialect which differs in various ways from standard English. When they then enter formal education, they are most likely to be taught using a model based on a standard form of the language, both for their writing and speech. The standard model used in institutional education thus has a strong influence on the sociolinguistic habits of all those who pass through the school system and frequently figures as the subject of political debate about what precisely constitutes standard English and the way it is positioned within the curriculum.

In non-mother-tongue countries, a similar and equally influential process occurs. As noted above, the majority of English speakers around the world acquire the language initially via some sort of formal schooling, and thus the ELT profession operates as a key mediator for the way the language is introduced to them. A fundamental question for ELT professionals, then, is which variety is best taught to students? The answer to this question involves issues relating to consequences for the learning process, to the practices and perspectives of students and teachers and to the politics of the language as it exists within society more generally. Three broad approaches can be taken. The first is to opt for a native speaker standard, i.e. one spoken in an English-dominant country such as the UK or USA. The second is to adopt a local variety as teaching model. In other words, the choice of model is between one which looks to external norms, i.e. those used in native speaker countries, and one which uses norms that have developed as the language has become indigenised by the local community (Kirkpatrick, 2007). The third option focuses less on specific models (i.e. choosing an Inner Circle or local variety as a teaching standard) and more on intercultural communication strategies, drawing on research on the ways English is used in lingua franca contexts.

In taking a decision about which of these alternatives is likely to be more appropriate, there are a number of factors to take into consideration. The exact nature of these factors will, however, vary considerably depending on the circumstances in which the language is being taught. There is thus no straightforward correct or incorrect answer which is applicable for all ELT contexts, and teachers working within particular contexts will be in the best position to judge what works for their students, taking into account the following factors: (1) how suitable the variety or ELF strategies are as a means of communication in the context for which the language is being learnt; (2) what implications the choice of variety has for the practice of teaching in that context; and (3) how the decision relates to the cultural politics of the variety as this is manifest in that context. For each of these factors, there are both practical and ideological concerns which relate to the purpose for which the language is being learnt, the status accorded to different varieties in particular contexts, the availability and suitability of resources, implications over the cost of accessing or generating materials and pedagogic concerns relating to motivation and attainability. The relative balance of these issues will differ depending on the contexts in which English is taught, and the challenge for educators is to make informed decisions which navigate these various factors while taking into account the insights about the use of language in a global context which research into World Englishes and ELF provides. For the remainder of this section, I will look at these factors in further detail, beginning with arguments in favour of native speaker teaching models.

A first argument in favour of using native speaker varieties as teaching models relates to their current status both around the globe and within the ELT profession itself. One of the motivations for many people learning English is that it has a global reach, and an argument in favour of using a standard British or American variety is thus based on the belief that their current status and history mean they are better placed than other varieties for offering wide-ranging intelligibility. As global sociolinguistic trends evolve and alter, the affordances that these varieties currently possess may also change, of course, and different varieties may, at some stage, emerge as candidates for a preeminent international standard. For the moment, however, not least because native speaker varieties are currently used globally as teaching standards, these varieties are the ones which come closest to acting as international standards. Yet the question of whether an international standard is necessarily any better for intelligibility purposes is a moot point, and thus this argument is one which, in many ways, relates more to perceptions rather than practicalities (Seargeant, 2012: 40).

On the other hand, an issue which does have specific practical implications is that standard British and American Englishes are already extensively codified; there are a range of available dictionaries and grammars for them which act as reference resources for the teaching of the language. In addition, the UK and USA both have large ELT industries which supply English language education expertise around the globe and provide for a wide range of teaching resources. The availability of these pre-existing materials is thus both convenient and cost-effective for those working in the profession, providing as it does a ready-made support structure (for further critical discussion of the claims and controversies surrounding ELT materials, see Gray, this volume).

Practicality issues alone will not determine the choice over variety, however. There are ideological issues to take into account as well. In the current 'marketplace' of world languages, native speaker varieties of English have prestige and legitimacy in many parts of the world in a way that local varieties do not, and this in turn makes them an attractive choice both for individual learners as well as policy makers and educationalists. Furthermore, the prestige of these varieties is often a motivational factor for learning them, as students will associate these varieties with aspirational lifestyles or with a range of instrumental benefits (Seargeant, 2009). However, the obverse of this is that a native speaker model is unlikely to be something a student will ever perfectly attain, and if acquisition of this model is the goal for the student, the learning journey may prove to be frustrating and, ultimately, disheartening (Kirkpatrick, 2007).

What then are the issues relating to the teaching of a local variety instead? As suggested above, one of the arguments given against local varieties is their lack of international intelligibility. As noted, though, evidence that this is actually the case is, at most, slight, and varietal difference need not be an impediment to international communication. Moreover, if the language is going to be predominantly used in local contexts – as is the case in Outer Circle countries where it is an official language – the local variety will probably be the more appropriate choice. Furthermore, from a motivational point of view, a local model is likely to be not only more familiar to the students but also more attainable.

Another issue to take into account with local varieties is that, whereas standard US or UK varieties are well codified, many local varieties are either only in the very early stages of this process or have not begun it at all. As such, teaching resources such as textbooks and assessment instruments do not exist for many local varieties, with possible financial and workload consequences for educators. However, adopting a local variety as a teaching model can lead to further codification projects, and thus, from a language policy perspective, the choice of a local variety can have long-term advantages in terms of enhancing its status and providing secure foundations for its identity as a distinct and legitimate variety. There are also other, more general, political arguments for the use of a local variety to act as a counter to the hegemony that US and UK varieties, and the cultures with which they are associated, continue to have in the world and which continue to have implications for issues related to global social inequality (see Pennycook, this volume).

The third approach to the issue reframes the question to concentrate less on the notion of alternative varieties and more on strategies for intercultural communication. Drawing on research into the way that people use English in Lingua Franca contexts, this approach aims to ensure that teaching is sensitive to the ways in which speakers co-create meaning using English as a resource (Jenkins et al., 2011).

Who should teach English?

Along with the question of which variety or strategy to use as a teaching model, there is also the issue of who should do the teaching. As different teachers speak differing varieties, they are often seen to represent differing cultural associations of English; thus, they can be viewed as an embodiment of the diversity in the language, and their own linguistic profiles can act as a key variable in the educational process. For example, a teacher's linguistic profile often plays a part in hiring practices in educational institutions and, in certain parts of the world, also becomes co-opted as part of the promotion of what counts as successful language teaching. Issues around this topic are again a mixture of the practical and ideological, while also having an ethical dimension.

As with the debate over teaching models, a basic distinction for categories of English language teacher is made between native-speaker teachers, i.e. those emanating from one of the English-dominant countries, and local teachers who have English as an additional language (see Llurda, this volume). Decisions over who teaches the language have effects both for learners and for teachers themselves. From the perspective of students, a native speaker teacher is often seen to be able to model what is viewed as an authentic form of the language as it is spoken in English-dominant countries and is also thought to have an intuitive knowledge about norms of usage. Additionally, if English is being learnt as part of the culture of one of the mother tongue countries, the native speaker's personal background provides an exemplar of that culture. This is, however, a rather simplistic view of the situation and does not correspond to the diversity of linguistic practices even within Inner Circle countries; nor does it reflect the patterns of mobility in modern societies.

An argument in favour of non-native speakers is that they are likely to be familiar with local educational and cultural practices in a way that teachers from outside the community are not and can also act as role models of successful later-life acquisition in that they have experience of learning English in circumstances similar to those of their students. They are also likely to be more attuned to the communicative strategies used in ELF encounters and thus have practical knowledge about how the language operates for these purposes.

There are also implications for teachers themselves from decisions around this issue. In many regions of the world where a standard British or American model is held in high esteem, there is often a tradition of ELT instructors being hired solely on their status as native speakers and of them having little or nothing in the way of professional teaching qualifications. This practice can obviously be to the detriment of the local teacher population – it can deprive them of work and also undermine their own status as professionals, not to mention the professional status of the teaching industry in general. The teaching of a local variety, on the other hand, can professionally favour local teachers and avoid a situation where promotion of a native speaker model has the effect of framing local teachers as imperfect speakers of the language. Additionally, local teachers will, by definition, be multilingual (knowing both the local language(s) and English) and will have been English learners themselves; this is likely to have positive benefits for their teaching (for further discussion, see Llurda, this volume).

How should English be tested?

The final element of the education process I wish to look at is testing, and here again, the pedagogy and politics of World Englishes and ELF are of relevance. Testing has an important role both within and beyond the classroom. As part of the education process, it acts as a means of evaluating learning as well as bringing into focus the aims of the curriculum. Beyond the classroom, it has an influential role in social organisation. These two roles relate to the effects of what are known as washback and impact. Washback is the effect the content of the test has on the teaching process. In other words, in so far as teachers shape their teaching to prepare students for passing tests, the content of the test will determine what is being taught. Impact, on the other hand, refers to the effects felt from the shape and role of the test in society more generally. For example, an immediate and practical purpose of learning English for many students is to pass what are known as high-stakes tests, i.e. those which regulate access to things such as employment and further education opportunities or act as determinants for people's right to citizenship in a country (McNamara and Roever, 2006). Tests such as these play an important role in the political regulation of society and have very real consequences for the lives of those who take them (Shohamy, 2006; see also Fulcher and Owen, this volume).

The salient issues around testing English are similar to those relating to its teaching. The majority of tests are based on the idea that English is composed of a set core of correct usages (usually understood as those of the idealised native speaker) and that design of the test is able to check for understanding of these usages. Within the context of World Englishes and ELF research, one major concern relating to mainstream English language tests therefore is that they are structured around linguistic norms which do not accurately represent the range of varieties and communicative strategies used around the globe (Davidson, 2006). A fundamental question for testing thus becomes: what norms should provide the standard for the test?

Here again, there are two traditions of answer, the first advocating the use of a standard native speaker variety, the second the ability to communicate fluently according to local communicative norms. The arguments for each are much the same as those outlined above for different teaching models. Recent research relating to ELF, however, has led to certain people, such as Suresh Canagarajah (2006), suggesting that this traditional dichotomy oversimplifies the way the language is actually used in the present day. Canagarajah's argument is that because English is a language of such diversity in today's world, proficiency in it necessitates being 'multidialectical', i.e. people need access to different types of English as they move from context to context. Tests, he therefore suggests, should examine communicative strategies which allow people to negotiate this diversity, and in this way their washback will influence teaching in such a way that it better prepares students for the actuality of modern-day globalised English use. Thus their impact will stop promoting the hegemony of native speaker varieties and help democratise the use of English around the world.

Conclusion

The challenges for ELT from the theoretical perspectives and empirical research provided by World Englishes studies and ELF are all to do with context. The overriding theme from this research is that English today is multiplex. It has different identities in different communities and operates on multiple levels, both local and translocal. In contexts where it is used as a lingua franca, it has an identity which is no longer tethered to any particular culture or nation and instead has become a functional means of communication which interlocutors can draw on for transactional purposes. In other contexts, localised varieties are embedded within the culture of the places in which they are used, and the language has come to reflect this local culture and become a part of its identity. This multiplex nature of English has implications for the way that it is taught, for decisions about who teaches it and for how it is tested. Given this multiplex nature, it is not possible to advocate straightforward approaches that will apply equally to all contexts. Instead, teachers and other ELT professionals need an awareness of the nature of the contemporary profile of the language and of the issues it raises – both in their context and globally, and for both learners, institutions and policy makers – and with this they can then tailor their professional practice to the particular circumstances of their students and to the contexts in which those students will be using the language.

Discussion questions

- What are the implications of the demographics of English speakers globally for the teaching of English?
- In what ways does the global spread of English complicate the notion of a single standard of the language?
- What practical implications can teachers draw from the theoretical insights of World Englishes and English as a Lingua Franca?
- In what sense will decisions about which variety should act as a teaching model be based on both practical and ideological concerns?
- In what ways is English used in your own local context? What functions does it fulfil, and what form does it take?

Related topics

Bilingual education in a multilingual world; ELT materials; Language and culture in ELT; 'Native speakers', English and ELT; Politics, power relationships and ELT

Further reading

Kirkpatrick, A. (2007) *World Englishes: Implications for international communication and English language teaching*. Cambridge: Cambridge University Press. (This introduces issues and debates around World Englishes, with a specific focus on the implications of the spread of the language for teaching and education.)

McKay, S. (2002) *Teaching English as an international language: Rethinking goals and approaches*. Oxford: Oxford University Press. (As with the Kirkpatrick book, this also focuses on the issues involved in teaching English in contexts where it operates as an international language.)

Seargeant, P. (2012) *Exploring World Englishes: Language in a global context*. Abingdon: Routledge. (This book examines issues around World Englishes from an applied linguistics perspective, focusing specifically on real-life challenges that are faced by language professionals in contexts such as language education and language planning.)

Seargeant, P. and Swann, J. (eds) (2012) *English in the world: History, diversity, change*. Abingdon: Routledge. (This is an introductory textbook about the global spread of English, tracing its historical development and examining its diversity today. It includes chapters by leading scholars such as David Crystal, Kay McCormick and Miriam Meyerhoff.)

Seidlhofer, B. (2011) *Understanding English as a Lingua Franca*. Oxford: Oxford University Press. (This provides an overview of the issues and debates relating to the use of English as an international lingua franca, including a chapter dedicated to implications of ELF for English language teaching.)

References

Bruthiaux, P. (2003) 'Squaring the circles: Issues in modeling English worldwide'. *International Journal of Applied Linguistics*, 13/2. 159–178.

Canagarajah, S. (2006) 'Changing communicative needs, revised assessment objectives: Testing English as an international language'. *Language Assessment Quarterly*, 3/3. 229–242.

Crystal, D. (2012) 'A global language', in P. Seargeant and J. Swann (eds) *English in the world: History, diversity, change*. Abingdon: Routledge. 151–177.

Davidson, F. (2006) 'World Englishes and test construction', in B. Kachru, Y. Kachru and C. Nelson (eds) *The handbook of World Englishes*. Malden, MA: Blackwell. 709–717.

Dewey, M. (2007) 'English as a Lingua Franca and globalization: An interconnected perspective'. *International Journal of Applied Linguistics*, 17/3. 332–354.

Erling, E. J., Seargeant, P., Solly, M., Hasan Chowdhury, Q. and Rahman, S. (2012) *Attitudes to English as a language for international development in rural Bangladesh*. London: British Council.

Ethnologue (2014) Retrieved from www.ethnologue.com.

Firth, A. (1996) 'The discursive accomplishment of normality: On 'lingua franca' English and conversation analysis'. *Journal of Pragmatics*, 26/2. 237–259.

Jenkins, J., Cogo, A. and Dewey, M. (2011) 'Review of developments in research into English as a lingua franca'. *Language Teaching*, 44/3. 281–315.

Kachru, B. B. (1985) 'Standards, codification and sociolinguistic realism: The English language in the Outer Circle', in R. Quirk and H. G. Widdowson (eds) *English in the world: Teaching and learning the language*. Cambridge: The British Council. 11–30.

Kachru, B. B. (1992) 'Teaching World Englishes', in B. B. Kachru (ed.) *The other tongue: English across cultures* (2nd ed.). Urbana and Chicago: University of Illinois Press. 355–365.

Kirkpatrick, A. (2007) *World Englishes: Implications for international communication and English language teaching*. Cambridge: Cambridge University Press.

McArthur, T. (1998) *The English languages*. Cambridge: Cambridge University Press.

McNamara, T. and Roever, C. (2006) *Language testing: The social dimension*. Oxford: Blackwell.

Mufwene, S. (2010) 'Globalization and the spread of English: What does it mean to be Anglophone?' *English Today*, 26/1. 57–59.

Pennycook, A. (2007) 'The myth of English as an international language', in S. Makoni and A. Pennycook (eds) *Disinventing and reconstituting languages*. Clevedon: Multilingual Matters. 90–115.

Quirk, R. (1990) 'Language varieties and standard language'. *English Today*, 6. 3–10.

Schneider, E. W. (2011) *English around the world: An introduction*. Cambridge: Cambridge University Press.

Seargeant, P. (2009) *The idea of English in Japan: Ideology and the evolution of a global language*. Bristol: Multilingual Matters.

Seargeant, P. (2012) *Exploring World Englishes: Language in a global context*. Abingdon: Routledge.

Seidlhofer, B. (2011) *Understanding English as a Lingua Franca*. Oxford: Oxford University Press.

Shohamy, E. (2006) *Language policy: Hidden agendas and new approaches*. New York: Routledge.

Wenger, E. (1998) *Communities of practice: Learning, meaning, and identity*. Cambridge: Cambridge University Press.

2

Politics, power relationships and ELT

Alastair Pennycook

Introduction: power and politics in ELT

That English language teaching (ELT) is inextricably bound up with multiple power relationships is indisputable. English did not spread globally as if it had a capacity to take over the world without human help. It was pushed by many forces that saw an interest in its promotion and pulled by many who also perceived value in acquiring it. A language only spreads because people learn it, and where learning happens, teaching is often (though not always) involved. So the global spread of English, with its connections to colonial exploitation and the contemporary inequalities fostered by globalisation and neoliberal ideologies (an emphasis away from equity, welfare and government spending towards privatisation, deregulation and the rule of the market; see Holborow, 2015; also Menard-Warwick et al., this volume), as well as its relations, for example, to travel, popular culture, technology and religion, cannot be understood outside such global forces. ELT, therefore, with its audience of 'Others' (a division between teaching English and speakers of other languages is embedded in acronyms such as TESOL) is inescapably caught up in questions of power.

As Joseph (2006) has observed, language is steeped from top to bottom in relations of power, or in other words it is profoundly political (the political here refers not so much to the tawdry battles fought out in our national parliaments but to the everyday struggles over whose version of the world will prevail). And because of its involvement in so much of what is going on in the world, English and ELT are even more so. Rather than the bland terms in which English is often understood – as a neutral medium of international communication, a language that holds out the promise of social and economic development to all those who learn it, a language of equal opportunity, a language that the world needs in order to be able to communicate – we need to understand that it is also an exclusionary class dialect, favouring particular people, countries, cultures, forms of knowledge and possibilities of development; it is a language which creates barriers as much as it presents possibilities.

Tollefson (2000: 8) warns that "at a time when English is widely seen as a key to the economic success of nations and the economic well-being of individuals, the spread of English also contributes to significant social, political, and economic inequalities." Bruthiaux (2002: 292–293) argues convincingly that English language education is "an outlandish irrelevance" for many of the world's poor, and "talk of a role for English language education in facilitating the process of poverty reduction and a major allocation of public resources to that end is likely to prove misguided and wasteful." As ELT practitioners, therefore, we cannot simply bury our heads in our classrooms and assume none of this has anything to do with us. Nor can we simply adopt individually oriented access arguments on the basis that any improvement in learners' English will likely bring them benefits. There is much more at stake here. For those "who do not have access to high-quality English language education, the spread of English presents a formidable obstacle to education, employment, and other activities requiring English proficiency" (Tollefson, 2000: 9), so ELT may have as much to do with the creation as the alleviation of inequality.

Ramanathan's (2005: 112) study of English and Vernacular medium education in India shows, how English is a deeply divisive language, tied on the one hand to the denigration of vernacular languages, cultures and ways of learning and teaching, and, on the other, dovetailing "with the values and aspirations of the elite Indian middle class". While English opens doors to some, it is simultaneously a barrier to learning, development and employment for others. Ferguson (2013: 35) explains that there is a "massive popular demand not just for English but for English-medium education" based on the reasonable assumption in the current global economy that "without English-language skills, one's labour mobility and employment prospects are restricted"; yet at the same time, English language education has many deleterious effects, including distorting already weak primary education sectors, advantaging urban elites over rural poor, constraining the use of other languages and diverting resources from other areas.

So for those of us involved in ELT, we need to consider how all that we do in the name of English teaching is inevitably connected to power and politics. What are the wider implications of promoting an English-only policy in a classroom, of choosing a textbook with glossy images of international travel, of deciding that 'furnitures' is acceptable or unacceptable, of choosing to work at a private language school, of knowing or not knowing the first language(s) of our students, of choosing to hire 'native speakers' at a school? In the next section, I will provide a brief overview of the prevailing paradigms for looking at the global spread of English – World Englishes, English as a Lingua Franca and Linguistic Imperialism – and point to their general shortcomings for understanding power and ELT. The following section will then look at local manifestations of ELT, ways in which ELT is bound up with local economies and education systems, racial and linguistic prejudice, styles of popular culture and economies of desire. The final section of the chapter will discuss the implications of all this for the practice of ELT.

Prevailing discourses: World Englishes, ELF and Linguistic Imperialism

Despite the evident connections, power has not always been sufficiently part of discussions of ELT. There are several reasons for this, including the lack of attention to power and politics in linguistics, applied linguistics and educational theory, and the role ELT plays as a form of service industry to globalisation. Discussion of the global spread of English has been dominated in recent times by the World Englishes (WE) (Kachru, 1992), and more recently English as a Lingua Franca (ELF) (Seidlhofer, 2011) frameworks (for further discussion, see Seargeant, this volume). Although Kachru's model of Three Circles of English – the Inner Circle where English is widely spoken as a first language, the Outer, postcolonial Circle where it is used internally as a second or additional language, and the Expanding Circle, where it is largely used for external, foreign language communication – has changed the ways in which we view varieties of English and norms of correctness (giving us multiple Englishes), and although the ELF programme has usefully drawn attention to the ways in which English is used in daily interactions among multilingual speakers, both approaches have been criticised for eschewing questions of power and presenting instead a utopian vision of linguistic diversity.

Kachru's (1992) Three Circle model of World Englishes posits a new list of standard varieties – based rather confusingly on a mixture of social, historical and geographical factors – but tends to overlook difference within regions. As Martin (2014: 53) observes in the context of the Philippines, there are at very least circles within circles, comprising an Inner Circle "of educated, elite Filipinos who have embraced the English language", an Outer Circle who may be aware of Philippine English as a variety but are "either powerless to support it and/or ambivalent about its promotion" and an Expanding Circle for whom the language is "largely inaccessible". Tupas (2006: 169) points out that "the power to (re)create English ascribed to the Outer Circle is mainly reserved only for those who have been invested with such power in the first place (the educated/the rich/the creative writers, etc.)." Thus, as Parakrama (1995: 25–26) argues, "the smoothing out of struggle within and without language is replicated in the homogenising of the varieties of English on the basis of 'upper-class' forms. Kachru is thus able to theorise on the nature of a monolithic Indian English." Whilst appearing, therefore, to work from an inclusionary political agenda in its attempt to have the new Englishes acknowledged as varieties of English, this approach to language is equally exclusionary. Ultimately, concludes Bruthiaux, "the Three Circles model is a 20th century construct that has outlived its usefulness" (2003: 161).

The more recent work on English as a Lingua Franca (ELF) (e.g. Jenkins, 2006; Seidlhofer, 2011) is perhaps a little more promising in that it does not work with either nation-based nor class-based linguistic models (though there is still insufficient attention to what we might call 'English from below' or the everyday interactions of non-elites). As O'Regan (2014: 540) notes, however, there is a "profound disconnect between the desire to identify and promote 'ELF' features and functions and the practical necessity of dealing with the structural iniquities of a global capitalism which will by default always distribute economic and linguistic resources in a way which benefits the few over the many and which confers especial prestige upon selective language forms". Thus while the ELF approach has been able to avoid some of the problems of the World Englishes focus on nation- and class-based varieties and can open up a more flexible and mobile version of English, it has likewise never engaged adequately with questions of power. While the WE approach has framed its position as a struggle between the former colonial Centre and its postcolonial offspring, the ELF approach has located its struggle between so-called native and non-native speakers (see Llurda, this volume). Yet neither of these sites of struggle engages with wider questions of power, inequality, class, ideology or access.

Phillipson's (1992, 2009) Linguistic Imperialism framework, by contrast, developed "to account for linguistic hierarchisation, to address issues of why some languages come to be used more and others less, what structures and ideologies facilitate such processes, and the role of language professionals" (1997: 238), places questions of power much more squarely in the picture. There are two discernible strands to Phillipson's argument. On the one hand, linguistic imperialism is concerned with the ways in which English is constantly promoted over other languages, the role played by organisations such as the British Council in the promotion and orchestration of the global spread of English (it was far from accidental), and the ways in which this inequitable position of English has become embedded in ELT dogmas, such as promoting native speaker teachers of English over their non-native speaker counterparts or suggesting that the learning of English is better started as early as possible (a trend that is continuing worldwide, with English language teaching occurring more and more at the primary and even pre-primary levels; see Enever, this volume).

On the other hand, linguistic imperialism "dovetails with communicative, cultural, educational, and scientific imperialism in a rapidly evolving world in which corporate-led globalisation is seeking to impose or induce a neo-imperial world order" (Phillipson, 2006: 357), thus drawing attention to the relation between English, neo-liberalism and globalisation. At stake, therefore, in this vision of English linguistic imperialism is not only the ascendency of English in relation to other languages but also the role English plays in much broader processes of the dominance of forms of global capital and the assumed homogenisation of world culture. For Phillipson (2008: 38), "acceptance of the status of English, and its assumed neutrality implies uncritical adherence to the dominant world disorder, unless policies to counteract neolinguistic imperialism and to resist linguistic capital dispossession are in force."

While Phillipson usefully locates English within inequitable relations of globalisation, there are several limitations to this view. Park and Wee (2012) explain that a "problem of linguistic imperialism's macrosocial emphasis is that it does not leave room for more specific and ethno-graphically sensitive accounts of actual language use" (p.16). As Holborow (2012: 27) puts it, in order to equate imperialism and linguistic imperialism, Phillipson has to "materialise language", a position that cannot adequately account for the ways in which English is resisted and appropri-ated, and how English users "may find ways to negotiate, alter and oppose political structures, and reconstruct their languages, cultures and identities to their advantage. The intention is not to *reject* English, but to *reconstitute* it in more inclusive, ethical, and democratic terms" (Canagarajah, 1999: 2). Phillipson's version of linguistic imperialism assumes processes of homogenisation without examining local complexities of cultural appropriation and language use (Pennycook, 2007; Bruthiaux, 2008). It is essential, as Blommaert (2010: 20) notes, to approach the sociolinguistics of globalisation in terms of a "chequered, layered complex of processes evolving simultaneously at a variety of scales and in reference to a variety of centres".

In order to place ELT – teaching practices, curricula, materials, tests – in the wider context of the global spread of English, it is essential to understand English in relation to globalisation, neoliberalism, exploitation and discrimination. But we need an understanding of language in relation to power that operates neither with a utopian vision of linguistic diversity nor with a dystopian assumption of linguistic imperialism. While we ignore Phillipson's warnings at our peril, it is important to develop a multifaceted understanding of the power and politics of ELT. Phillipson's critique of the global spread of English has compelled many to reflect on global inequities in which English plays a role, but his insistence that this should be seen in terms of imperialism has also narrowed the scope of the debate. The equation of a linguistic imperialism thesis with a critical standpoint, and the frequent dismissal of this totalising version of events on the grounds that it overstates the case, draws attention away from the necessity to evaluate the global spread of English, and the role of English language teachers as its agents, critically and carefully. What is required, then, is a more sensitive account of power, language and context and the implications for ELT.

Locality, desire and contingency: the embeddedness of English

A theory of imperialism is not a prerequisite to look critically at questions of power and politics in ELT, but if we reject linguistic imperialism for its monologically dystopian approach to lan-guage and culture in favour of the utopian visions of diversity in WE or ELF frameworks, we are equally poorly served. More important in relation to the power and politics of English are close and detailed understandings of the ways in which English is embedded in local economies of desire and the ways in which demand for English is part of a larger picture of images of change, modernisation, access and longing. It is tied to the languages, cultures, styles and aesthetics of popular culture, with its particular attractions for youth, rebellion and conformity; it is enmeshed within local economies and all the inclusions, exclusions and inequalities this may entail; it is bound up with changing modes of communication, from shifting Internet uses to its role in text-messaging; it is increasingly entrenched in educational systems, bringing to the fore many concerns about knowledge, pedagogy and the curriculum. We need to understand the diversity of what English is and what it means in all these contexts, and we need to do so not with prior assumptions about globalisation and its effects but with critical studies of the local embeddedness of English.

As Borjian (2013: 166) shows, English education in post-revolutionary Iran has been a "site of struggle, in which multiple forces compete". One major aspect of this was the state and religious (closely combined) opposition to Western forms of modernity, leading to an attempt to create "an indigenized model of English education, free from the influence of the English-speaking nations" (Borjian, 2013: 160). It is important to understand, then, that *indigenisation* of English education was not so much a local movement to make English their own but rather a state ideology to oppose Western influence. Meanwhile, the privatisation of ELT provision led to an opposing trend that tended more towards Anglo-American models of ELT. The point here, once again, is that ELT is always caught up in a range of political, religious, cultural and economic battles. In Algeria, by contrast, the growth of English education sits in a different set of complex historical and political relations, involving both French as the former colonial language as well as postcolonial processes of Arabisation. English, as a "new intruder in Algeria's sociolinguistic scenery", suggests Benrabah (2013: 124) may bring the benefits of helping Algerians to see both that there are other alternatives to French and that other languages, such as Berber, have much to offer alongside Arabic. Language conflicts around English, French, Berber and Arabic in Algeria, Benrabah shows, are always bound up with the complexity of other local political struggles.

There are several implications for ELT, since these perspectives force us to rethink what we mean by the idea of English. No longer can we consider it to be a pre-given object that we are employed to deliver; rather, it is a many-headed hydra (Rapatahana and Bunce, 2012) enmeshed in complex local contexts of power and struggle. From the relation between English and other languages in the Pacific (Barker, 2012) to its role in countries such as Sri Lanka (Parakrama, 2012), the position of English is complex and many sided. To understand the power and politics of ELT, then, we need detailed understandings of the role English plays in relation to local languages, politics and economies. This requires meticulous studies of English and its users, as well as theories of power that are well adapted to contextual understandings. As ELT professionals, we are never just teaching something called English but rather are involved in economic and social change, cultural renewal, people's dreams and desires.

There are therefore many Englishes, not so much in the terms of language varieties posited by the World Englishes framework but rather in terms of different Englishes in relation to different social and economic forces. In South Korea, for example, where 'English fever' has driven people to remarkable extremes (from prenatal classes to tongue surgery and sending young children overseas to study), English has become naturalised 'as the language of global competitiveness', so that English as a neoliberal language is regarded as a "natural and neutral medium of academic excellence" (Piller and Cho, 2013: 24). As a new destination for such English language learners, the Philippines markets itself as a place where 'authentic English' (an Outer Circle variety) is spoken, yet its real drawcard is that its English is "cheap and affordable" (Lorente and Tupas, 2014: 79). For the Philippines, like other countries such as Pakistan (Rahman, 2009) with low economic development but relatively strong access to English, the language becomes one of commercial opportunity, so that businesses such as call centres on the one hand open up jobs for local college-educated employees but on the other hand distort the local economy and education system and perpetuate forms of global inequality (Friginal, 2009).

As ELT practitioners, we need to understand not only these roles English plays in relation to the economy but also student motivations to learn English, which may concern more than just pragmatic goals of social and economic development (Kubota, 2011). Since English is often marketed in relation to a particular set of images of sexual desire, it is important to appreciate the gender and sexual politics involved in English language learning and the ways in which English, as advertised for language schools and presented in textbooks, "emerges as a powerful tool to construct a gendered identity and to gain access to the romanticized West" (Piller and Takahashi, 2006: 69). As Motha and Lin (2014: 332) contend, "at the center of every English language learning moment lies desire: desire for the language; for the identities represented by particular accents and varieties of English; for capital, power, and images that are associated with English; for what is believed to lie beyond the doors that English unlocks." The ELT practitioner, therefore, may become an object of desire, a gatekeeper, a constructor or destroyer of dreams.

Like Darvin and Norton's (2015) understanding of *investment* as the intersection between identity, ideology and capital, this notion of desire is best understood not as an internal psychological characteristic but rather, as Takahashi (2013: 144) explains in her exploration of Japanese women's 'desire' for English, as "constructed at the intersection between the macro-discourses of the West and foreign men and ideologies of Japanese women's life-courses in terms of education, occupation, and heterosexuality". Focusing on the ways in which these discourses of desire implicate white Western men, Appleby (2013: 144) shows how "an embodied hegemonic masculinity" is constructed in the Japanese ELT industry, producing as a commodity "an extroverted and eroticised White Western ideal for male teachers". Any understanding of the motivations to learn English, therefore, has to deal with relations of power not only in economic and educational terms but also as they are tied to questions of desire, gender, sexuality (Nelson, 2009), and the marketing of English and English language teachers as products (see also Gray, this volume).

An appreciation of the complicities of power – the ways in which ELT is tied up not only with neoliberal economic relations but also other forms of power and prejudice – sheds light on the ways in which assumptions of native speaker authority privilege not only a particular version of language ideology but are also often tied to particular racial formations (white faces, white voices) (Shuck, 2006; Ruecker, 2011). "Both race and nativeness are elements of 'the idealized native speaker'" (Romney, 2010: 19). People of colour may not be accepted as native speakers (who are assumed to be white): "The problem lies in the tendency to equate the native speaker with white and the non-native speaker with non-white. These equations certainly explain discrimination against non-native professionals, many of whom are people of colour" (Kubota and Lin, 2009: 8). Indeed, since teaching "second or foreign languages entails complex relations of power fuelled by differences created by racialization" (Kubota and Lin, 2009: 16), the field of ELT might be reconceptualised "with a disciplinary base that no longer revolves solely around teaching methodology and language studies but instead takes as a point of departure race and empire" (Motha, 2014: 129).

Before ELT practitioners consider the politics of their classroom, therefore, it is important to consider the local and contingent politics of English (Pennycook, 2010). It is often said that language and culture are closely tied together, that to learn a language is to learn a culture, yet such a proposition overlooks the contingent relations between linguistic and cultural forms or the local uses of language. Attention has been drawn to the connections, for example, between English language teaching and Christian missionary activity. As Varghese and Johnston (2007: 7) observe, the widespread use of English and the opportunities this provides for missionary work dressed up as English language teaching raises "profound moral questions about the professional activities and purposes of teachers and organizations in our occupation". In a post-9/11 world and with "American foreign and domestic policy driven increasingly by imperialist goals and guided by an evangelical Christian agenda" (ibid.: 6), English language education and missionary work present a contingent set of relations between language and culture.

The point here is not that to learn English is to be exposed to Christian values – as Mahboob (2009) argues, English can equally serve as an Islamic language – but that English may be called upon to do particular cultural and ideological work in particular pedagogical contexts. The promotion, use and teaching of English in contexts of economic development, military conflict, religious struggle, mobility, tertiary access and so on have to be understood in relation to the meanings English is expected to carry, as a language of progress, democratic reform, religious change, economic development, advanced knowledge, popular culture and much more. These connections are by no means coincidental – they are a product of the roles English comes to play in the world – but they are at the same time contingent. That is to say, they are a product of the many relations of power and politics with which English is embroiled.

Power, politics and pedagogy: responses to the politics of ELT

When we talk of English today we mean many things, many of them not necessarily having to do with some core notion of language. The question becomes not whether some monolithic thing called English is imperialistic or an escape from poverty, nor how many varieties there may be of this thing called English, but rather what kind of mobilisations underlie acts of English use or learning? Something called English is mobilised by English language industries, including ELT, with particular language effects. But something called English is also part of complex language chains, mobilised as part of multiple acts of identity and desire. It is not English – if by that we mean a certain grammar and lexicon – that is at stake here. It is the discourses around English that matter, the ways in which an idea of English is caught up in all that we do so badly in the name of education, all the exacerbations of inequality that go under the label of globalisation, all the linguistic calumnies that denigrate other ways of speaking, all the shamefully racist institutional interactions that occur in schools, hospitals, law courts, police stations, social security offices and unemployment centres.

Whether we see English as a monster, juggernaut, bully or governess (Rapatahana and Bunce, 2012), we clearly need to do something about this pedagogically. As Gray suggests, "ideologies associated with English which take it as self-evident that it is perforce the language of economic prosperity and individual wealth are also those of the ELT industry itself" (2012: 98). While we might, like ostriches (Pennycook, 2001), be tempted to bury our heads in the classroom and refuse to engage with these issues, we surely owe more to the educational needs of our students than to ignore the many dimensions of power and politics in ELT. One level of pedagogical response to the dominance of English is to see ELT not so much as centrally about the promotion of English but rather as a process of working out where English can usefully sit within an ecology of languages. When we observe the growth of Southeast Asian economies – their increased roles in the global economy and the resultant pressure to teach English earlier and younger in a region with wide linguistic diversity – there are real causes for concern that current language education policies favouring only the national language plus English will lead to Asian multilingualism being reduced to bilingualism only in the national language and English (Kirkpatrick, 2012).

As ELT professionals, therefore, we would do well to question the linguistic, educational and pedagogical ideologies behind "the one-classroom-one-language pedagogical straitjacket" (Lin, 2013: 540) that many current ELT approaches continue to endorse, and embrace instead a broader, multilingual approach to our classrooms. Approaches such as communicative language teaching are far from neutral pedagogical technologies (Pennycook, 1989) but are rather "intimately linked to the production of a certain kind of student and worker subjectivity suitable for participating in a certain kind of political economy" (Lin, 2013: 540). Rather than focusing so intently on English as the sole objective of our teaching, we can start to reimagine classes as part of a broader multilingual context, and, indeed, following Motha (2014), to engage in a project of *provincialising English*. Such multilingualism, furthermore, needs to be understood not so much in terms of separate monolingualisms (adding English to one or more other languages) but rather in much more fluid terms (see also Carroll and Combs, and Kerr, this volume).

Drawing on recent sociolinguistic approaches to *translanguaging* (García and Li, 2014) and *metrolingualism* (Pennycook and Otsuji, 2015), we can start to think of ELT classrooms in terms of *principled polycentrism* (Pennycook, 2014). This is not the polycentrism of a World Englishes focus, with its established norms of regional varieties of English, but a more fluid concept based on the idea that students are developing complex repertoires of multilingual and multimodal resources. This enables us to think in terms of ELT as developing resourceful speakers who are able to use available language resources and to shift between styles, discourses, registers and genres. This brings the recent sociolinguistic emphasis on repertoires and resources into conversation with a focus on the need to learn how to negotiate and accommodate, rather than to be proficient in one variety of English. So an emerging goal of ELT may be less towards proficient native-speaker-like speakers (which has always been a confused and misguided goal) and to think instead in polycentric terms of resourceful speakers (Pennycook, 2012) who can draw on multiple linguistic and semiotic resources.

Focusing on the politics of the classroom itself, it is important to understand on the one hand the permeability of the classroom walls – that is to say that what goes on inside the classroom is always tied to what goes on outside – and the local questions of power and politics within the classroom (Pennycook, 2000). Benson (1997: 32) outlines the ways in which "we are inclined to think of the politics of language teaching in terms of language planning and educational policy while neglecting the political content of everyday language and language learning practices". Shifting our thinking, he suggests, entails a political understanding of the social context of education, classroom roles and relations, the nature of tasks and the content and language of the lesson. According to Auerbach (1995: 12), "dynamics of power and inequality show up in every aspect of classroom life, from physical setting to needs assessment, participant structures, curriculum development, lesson content, materials, instructional processes, discourse patterns, language use, and evaluation."

Everything in the classroom – from how we teach (how we conduct ourselves as a teacher, as master, authority, facilitator, organiser), what we teach (whether we focus only on English, on grammar, on communication, on tests), how we respond to students (correcting, ignoring, cajoling, praising), how we understand language and learning (favouring noise over silence, emphasising expression over accuracy), how we think of our classroom (as a place to have fun or a site for serious learning), to the materials we use (off-the-shelf international textbooks, materials from the local community), the ways we organise our class (in rows, pairs, tables, circles) and the way we assess the students (against what norms, in terms of what language possibilities) – needs to be seen as social and cultural practices that have broader implications than just elements of classroom interaction. The point here is not that choosing what we might consider the preferable options listed above absolves us of questions of power, but that all these choices are embedded in larger social and ideological formations.

Critical pedagogical approaches to ELT (Morgan, 1998; Benesch, 2001; Crookes, 2013 and also this volume) have sought in various ways to address many of these concerns. Critical pedagogy itself embraces a range of different approaches. For Crookes (2013: 9), it is "teaching for social justice, in ways that support the development of active engaged citizens", that is to say a form of critical ELT that focuses on social change through learning English. Chun's (2015) overview of commonalities in critical literacy practices includes drawing on students' and teachers' historically lived experiences, viewing language as a social semiotic, focusing on power both within and outside the classroom, engaging with commonsense notions of the everyday, developing self-reflexive practice, renewing a sense of community and maintaining a common goal. There has been considerable resistance to such critical approaches to education. The classroom should, from some perspectives, be a neutral place for language learning, and to teach critically is to impose one's views on others. Such a view both misses the larger political context of the classroom and also underestimates the capacity of students to resist and evaluate what is before them (Benesch, 2001). Given the power and politics of ELT, a politically acquiescent position as an English language educator is an equally political position.

Other work has sought to develop critical responses to textbooks (Gray, 2012 and also this volume). Gray (2010: 3) shows how global coursebooks inscribe a set of values in English associated with "individualism, egalitarianism, cosmopolitanism, mobility and affluence", or the very cultural and ideological formations with which English is connected in international contexts. It is important from this point of view for teachers and students to work against the ways English-language classes interpellate students into particular ways of thinking, talking and being through these corporatised ELT materials. Testing is perhaps the hardest domain to struggle against, so powerful are the interests and operations of major language tests (Shohamy, 2001). The point for any of these critical approaches to pedagogy, literacy, materials or testing is not that they provide any easy solution to the complex relations among classrooms, language and power but that they address such questions with power always to the fore. Critical approaches to ELT view the politics of ELT as a given – not a given to be accepted but a given against which we must always struggle.

Conclusion

Discussions of ELT all too often assume that they know what the object of ELT is: this system of grammar and words called English. But clearly this is not adequate, since English is many things besides. The global spread of English and the materials and practices of ELT that support it cannot be removed from questions of power and politics. But to understand these political implications, we need an exhaustive understanding of relations of power. Rather than easy suppositions about domination, about some having power and others not, or assuming ELT inevitably to be a tool of neoliberalism, we need to explore the ways in which power operates in local contexts. Such an approach by no means turns its back on the broader context of globalisation but rather insists that this can never be understood outside its local realisations.

Such an understanding urges us on the one hand to acknowledge that what we mean by English is always contingent on local relations of power and desire, the ways that English means many different things and is caught up in many forms of hope, longing, discrimination and inequality. It also allows us on the other hand to avoid a hopelessness faced by immovable forces of global domination and instead to see that we can seek to change inequitable conditions of power through our small-scale actions that address local conditions of difference, desire and disparity, seeking out ELT responses through an understanding of translingual practices in the classroom, critical discussions of textbooks and ideological formations, questioning of the norms of ELT practices and their interests. Power and politics are ubiquitous in language and language education, but resistance and change are always possible.

Discussion questions

- Describe a classroom context with which you are familiar. Using a series of concentric circles (or arrows, or boxes or whatever works for you) show all the other factors involved in this interaction, from the gender and ethnicity of the participants and their hopes and desires, to the local and regional language policies and broader economic factors at play.
- What pedagogical responses do you consider would be appropriate and effective to deal with the issues outlined in the first question?
- It has been said that one is never 'just' an English teacher on two counts: English is never just English, and teaching is never just teaching. Describe to what extent you agree with this analysis, and explain what it implies for ELT generally.
- Using examples from your own experience, to what extent do English learning and use perpetuate inequality, open up opportunity, homogenise cultures and/or create diversity?

Related topics

Educational perspectives on ELT; Language and culture in ELT; 'Native speakers', English and ELT; Values in the ELT classroom; World Englishes and English as a Lingua Franca.

Further reading

Appleby, R. (2010) *ELT, gender and international development: Myths of progress in a neocolonial world*. Bristol: Multilingual Matters. (This volume provides good background for understanding the relations between English education and development.)

Chun, C. (2015) *Power and meaning making in an EAP classroom: Engaging with the everyday*. Bristol: Multilingual Matters. (A recent account of critical pedagogy in the context of English for academic purposes.)

Gray, J. (2010) *The construction of English: Culture, consumerism and promotion in the ELT global coursebook*. Basingstoke: Palgrave Macmillan. (A useful analysis of the global coursebook market.)

Motha, S. (2014) *Race, empire, and English language teaching: Creating responsible and ethical anti-racist practice*. New York, NY: Teachers College Press, Columbia University. (This book presents a strong case for understanding and resisting racism in ELT.)

Phillipson. R. (2009) *Linguistic imperialism continued*. London: Routledge. (This text reiterates Robert Phillipson's views on linguistic imperialism.)

References

Appleby R. (2013) 'Desire in translation: White masculinity and TESOL'. *TESOL Quarterly*, 47/1. 122–147.

Auerbach, E. (1995) 'The politics of the ESL classroom: Issues of power in pedagogical choices', in J. Tollefson (ed.) *Power and inequality in language education*. New York: Cambridge University Press. 9–33.

Barker, X. (2012) 'English language as a bully in the Republic of Nauru', in V. Rapatahana and P. Bunce (eds) *English language as hydra: Its impacts on non-English language cultures*. Bristol: Multilingual Matters. 18–36.

Benesch, S. (2001) *Critical English for academic purposes: Theory, politics and practice*. Mahwah, NJ: Lawrence Erlbaum Associates.

Benrabah, M. (2013) *Language conflict in Algeria: From colonialism to post-independence*. Bristol: Multilingual Matters.

Benson, P. (1997) 'The philosophy and politics of learner autonomy', in P. Benson and P. Voller (eds) *Autonomy and independence in language learning*. London: Longman. 18–34.

Blommaert, J. (2010) *The Sociolinguistics of globalization*. Cambridge: Cambridge University Press.

Borjian, M. (2013) *English in post-revolutionary Iran*. Bristol: Multilingual Matters.

Bruthiaux, P. (2002) 'Hold your courses: Language education, language choice, and economic development'. *TESOL Quarterly*, 36/3. 275–296.

Bruthiaux, P. (2003) 'Squaring the circles: Issues in modeling English worldwide'. *International Journal of Applied Linguistics*, 13/2. 159–177.

Bruthiaux, P. (2008) 'Dimensions of globalization and applied linguistics', in P. Tan and R. Rubdy (eds) *Language as commodity: Global structures, local marketplaces*. London: Continuum. 1–30.

Canagarajah, S. (1999) *Resisting linguistic imperialism in English teaching*. Oxford: Oxford University Press.

Chun, C. (2015) *Power and meaning making in an EAP classroom: Engaging with the everyday*. Bristol: Multilingual Matters.

Crookes, G. (2013) *Critical ELT in action: Foundations, promises, praxis*. New York: Routledge.

Darvin, R. and Norton, B. (2015) 'Identity and a model of investment in applied linguistics'. *Annual Review of Applied Linguistics*, 35. 36–56.

Ferguson, G. (2013) 'English, development and education: Charting the tensions', in E. Erling and P. Seargeant (eds) *English and development: Policy, pedagogy and globalization*. Bristol: Multilingual Matters. 21–44.

Friginal, E. (2009) 'Threats to the sustainability of the outsourced call center industry in the Philippines: Implications for language policy'. *Language Policy*, 8. 51–68.

García, O. and Li, W. (2014) *Translanguaging: Language, bilingualism and education*. Basingstoke: Palgrave Macmillan.

Gray, J. (2010) *The construction of English: Culture, consumerism and promotion in the ELT global coursebook*. Basingstoke: Palgrave Macmillan.

Gray, J. (2012) 'Neoliberalism, celebrity and 'aspirational content' in English language teaching textbooks for the global market', in D. Block, J. Gray and M. Holborow (eds) *Neoliberalism and applied linguistics*. London: Routledge. 86–113.

Holborow, M. (2012) 'What is neoliberalism? Discourse, ideology and the real world', in D. Block, J. Gray and M. Holborow (eds) *Neoliberalism and applied linguistics*. London: Routledge. 33–55.

Holborow, M. (2015) *Language and neoliberalism*. London: Routledge.

Jenkins, J (2006) 'Current perspectives on teaching World Englishes and English as a Lingua Franca'. *TESOL Quarterly*, 40/1. 157–181.

Joseph, J. (2006) *Language and politics*. Edinburgh: Edinburgh University Press.

Kachru, B (1992) *The other tongue: English across cultures*. Urbana: University of Illinois Press.

Kirkpatrick, A. (2012) 'English in ASEAN: Implications for regional multilingualism'. *Journal of Multilingual and Multicultural Development*, 33/4. 331–344.

Kubota, R. (2011) 'Questioning linguistic instrumentalism: English, neoliberalism, and language tests in Japan'. *Linguistics and Education*, 22. 248–260.

Kubota, R. and Lin, A. (2009) 'Race, culture, and identities in second language education', in R. Kubota and A. Lin (eds) *Race, culture and identities in second language education: Exploring critically engaged practice*. New York: Routledge. 1–23.

Lin, A. (2013) 'Toward paradigmatic change in TESOL methodologies: Building plurilingual pedagogies from the ground up'. *TESOL Quarterly, 47/3.* 521–545.

Lorente, B. and Tupas, R. (2014) '(Un)emancipatory hybridity: Selling English in an unequal world', in R. Rubdy and L. Alsagoff (eds) *The global-local interface and hybridity: Exploring language and identity*. Bristol, UK: Multilingual Matters. 66–82.

Mahboob, A. (2009) 'English as an Islamic language: A case study of Pakistani English'. *World Englishes*, 28/2. 175–189.

Martin, I. (2014) 'Philippine English revisited'. *World Englishes, 33/1.* 50–59.

Morgan, B. (1998) *The ESL classroom: Teaching, critical practice, and community development*. Toronto, ON: University of Toronto Press.

Motha, S. (2014) *Race, empire, and English language teaching: Creating responsible and ethical anti-racist practice*. New York: Teachers College Press, Columbia University.

Motha, S. and Lin, A. (2014) "Non-coercive rearrangements': Theorizing desire in TESOL'. *TESOL Quarterly*, 48/2. 331–359.

Nelson, C. (2009) *Sexual identities in English language education: Classroom conversations*. New York: Routledge.

O'Regan, J. (2014) 'English as a lingua franca: An immanent critique'. *Applied Linguistics*, 35/5. 533–552.

Parakrama, A. (1995) *De-hegemonizing language standards: Learning from (post)colonial Englishes about 'English'*. Basingstoke: MacMillan.

Parakrama, A. (2012) 'The *malchemy* of English in Sri Lanka: Reinforcing inequality though imposing extra-linguistic value', in V. Rapatahana and P. Bunce (eds) *English language as hydra: Its impacts on non-English language cultures*. Bristol: Multilingual Matters. 107–132.

Park, J. S-Y. and Wee, L. (2012) *Markets of English: Linguistic capital and language policy in a globalizing world*. New York: Routledge

Pennycook, A. (1989) 'The concept of method, interested knowledge, and the politics of language teaching'. *TESOL Quarterly*, 23/4. 589-618.

Pennycook, A (2000) 'The social politics and the cultural politics of language classrooms', in J. K. Hall and W. Eggington (eds) *The sociopolitics of English language teaching*. Clevedon: Multilingual Matters. 89–103.

Pennycook, A. (2001) *Critical applied linguistics: A critical introduction*. Mahwah, NJ: Lawrence Erlbaum.

Pennycook, A. (2007) *Global Englishes and transcultural flows*. London: Routledge.

Pennycook, A. (2010) *Language as a local practice*. London: Routledge.

Pennycook, A. (2012) *Language and mobility: Unexpected places*. Bristol: Multilingual Matters.

Pennycook, A. (2014) 'Principled polycentrism and resourceful speakers'. *Journal of Asia TEFL*, 11/4. 1–19.

Pennycook, A. and Otsuji, E. (2015) *Metrolingualism: Language in the city*. London: Routledge.

Phillipson, R. (1992) *Linguistic imperialism*. Oxford: Oxford University Press.

Phillipson, R. (1997) 'Realities and myths of linguistic imperialism'. *Journal of Multilingual and Multicultural Development*, 18/3. 238–248.

Phillipson, R. (2006) 'Language policy and linguistic imperialism', in T. Ricento (ed.) *An introduction to language policy: Theory and method*. Oxford: Blackwell. 346–361.

Phillipson, R. (2008) 'The linguistic imperialism of neoliberal empire'. *Critical Inquiry in Language Studies*, 5/1. 1–43.

Phillipson. R. (2009) *Linguistic imperialism continued*. London: Routledge.

Piller, I. and Cho, J. (2013) 'Neoliberalism as language policy'. *Language in Society*, 42. 23–44.

Piller, I. and Takahashi, K. (2006) 'A passion for English: Desire and the language market', in A Pavlenko (ed.) *Bilingual minds: Emotional experience, expression and representation*. Clevedon: Multilingual Matters. 59–83.

Rahman, T. (2009) 'Language ideology, identity and the commodification of language in the call centers of Pakistan'. *Language in Society*, 38/2. 233–258.

Ramanathan, V. (2005) *The English-Vernacular divide: Postcolonial language politics and practice*. Clevedon: Multilingual Matters.

Rapatahana, V. and Bunce, P. (eds) (2012) *English language as hydra: Its impacts on non-English language cultures*. Bristol: Multilingual Matters.

Romney, M. (2010) 'The colour of English', in A. Mahboob (ed.) *The NNEST lens: Non native English speakers in TESOL*. Newcastle: Cambridge Scholars Publishing. 18–34.

Ruecker, T. (2011) 'Challenging the native and nonnative English speaker hierarchy in ELT: New directions from race theory'. *Critical Inquiry in Language Studies*, 8/4. 400–422.

Seidlhofer, B. (2011) *Understanding English as a lingua franca*. Oxford: Oxford University Press.

Shohamy, E. (2001) *The power of tests: A critical perspective on the uses of language tests*. London: Longman.

Shuck, G. (2006) 'Racializing the non-native English speaker'. *Journal of Language, Identity, and Education*, 5/4. 259–276.

Takahashi, K. (2013) *Language learning, gender and desire: Japanese women on the move*. Bristol: Multilingual Matters.

Tollefson, J. (2000) 'Policy and ideology in the spread of English', in J.K. Hall and W. Eggington (eds) *The sociopolitics of English language teaching*. Clevedon: Multilingual Matters. 7–21.

Tupas, R. (2006) 'Standard Englishes, pedagogical paradigms and conditions of (im)possibility', in R. Rubdy and M. Saraceni (eds) *English in the world: Global rules, global roles*. London: Continuum. 169–185.

Varghese, M. and Johnston, B. (2007) 'Evangelical Christians and English language teaching'. *TESOL Quarterly*, 41/1. 5–31.

3

Language and culture in ELT

Claire Kramsch and Zhu Hua

Introduction

English language teaching (ELT), as it developed after World War II within the field of applied linguistics (Li 2014: 13), responded to the needs of an international market-based economy and the spread of an Anglo-Saxon form of democracy during the Cold War (Brutt-Griffler, 2002), and thus did not originally have much concern for culture (Corbett, 2003: 20). The link between language and culture in applied linguistics only became an issue in the 1990s with the identity politics of the time and the advances made in second language acquisition research. Until then, the research and methodological literature of ELT had, from the 1970s onwards, promoted the benefits of learning English through a functional, communicative approach based on democratic access to turns-at-talk and on individual autonomy in the expression, interpretation and negotiation of meaning (see Thornbury, this volume). This communicative approach had been deemed universal in its applicability because it was grounded in a view of language learners as rational actors, equal before the rules of grammar and the norms of the native speaker, and eager to benefit from the economic opportunities that a knowledge of English would bring. The negotiation of meaning that formed the core of the communicative approach applied to referential or to situational meaning, not necessarily, as was later argued (e.g. Kramsch, 1993), to cultural or to ideological meaning.

Since the end of the Cold War in 1990, and with the advent of globalisation, the increasingly multicultural nature of societies has made it necessary for English language teachers to factor 'culture' into ELT and to take into account the culture their students come from. Among the many definitions of culture, the one we retain here is the following: "Culture can be defined as membership in a discourse community that shares a common social space and history, and common imaginings. Even when they have left that community, its members may retain, wherever they are, a common system of standards for perceiving, believing, evaluating and acting. These standards are what is generally called their 'culture'" (Kramsch, 1998: 10). Risager (2007) has proposed the concept of *languaculture* to suggest that there is neither an "essentialist language-culture duality" (p. 162), nor a radical distinction between the two, but a "close connection, an interdependence, a complex relationship between language and culture" (p. 163).

In the case of ELT, therefore, which culture should be taught as part of the language's relationship with culture: for example, UK, US, Australian, Indian or Singaporean national culture? The global culture of commerce and industry? Or Internet culture? And, in increasingly multilingual classrooms, which learners' culture should be taken into account: their national, regional, ethnic, generational or professional culture?

In this chapter, we first examine the socio-cultural and socio-political changes of the last twenty years in terms of the relationship of language and culture in ELT. Next, we examine the rise of the field of intercultural communication and its relation to language teaching. We then discuss the main current issues and key areas of debate concerning the role of culture in ELT. We finally discuss future developments in the study of language and culture as they relate to the teaching and learning of English.

The changing goals of ELT from a socio-cultural and socio-political perspective

Unlike the teaching of languages other than English, and despite the fact that many English teachers still focus on US or UK culture in class, English language teaching (ELT) has not been primarily concerned with the teaching of culture *per se*, since it has seen itself as teaching a language of economic opportunity not tied to any particular national or regional space or history (for reviews, see Kramsch, 2009a, 2010; also Pennycook, and Gray, this volume). Some educators have felt that English is a (culture-free) skill that anyone can appropriate and make his/her own. Indeed, twenty years ago, Henry Widdowson eloquently argued that the ownership of English was not (or was no longer) the prerogative of the so-called native speaker. He wrote: "You are proficient in a language to the extent that you possess it, make it your own, bend it to your will, assert yourself through it rather than simply submit to the dictates of its form. . . . Real proficiency is when you are able to take possession of the language, turn it to your advantage, and make it real for you. This is what mastery means" (Widdowson, 1994: 384). Widdowson decried the discriminatory employment practices in ELT that privileged educated native speakers, i.e. speakers for whom the English language was tightly bound with a native Anglophone culture. (However, the delinking of ELT from the native speaker model for learners of English has not eliminated the privileging of native speakers as teachers of English around the world [i.e. native speakerism, Holliday, 2006; see also Llurda, and Holliday, this volume], nor, in many places, the privileging of native-speaker varieties of English in the ELT classroom, as we shall see.)

Since the 1990s, the link between language and culture has become more complex due to the global mobility of capital, goods and people and to the growing multilingualism of human communication, both in face-to-face and in online environments. English is not, in fact, a culture-free language which people can just appropriate for themselves and use as a tool to get things done. It bears traces of the cultural contexts in which it has been used and contributes to shaping the identity of speakers of English. Making the language your own is already a difficult enterprise linguistically, but the process is rendered more problematic by the pressure in the media, the film industry, social networks and popular culture to adopt consumerist lifestyles associated with the use of English as a global language. For many learners of English, these lifestyles might remain out of reach.

Thus, today, there are four ways of conceiving of the link between language and culture in ELT:

• As language of interest in or identification with Anglo-Saxon culture – a language taught in schools around the world, which, like other national languages, is attached to the national culture of English-speaking nation states, e.g. British English taught in French secondary schools.

- As language of aspiration with a multinational culture of modernity, progress and prosperity. This is the language of the 'American Dream', Hollywood and pop culture that is promoted by the multinational US and UK textbook industry, e.g. ESL taught to immigrants in the US and the UK or in secondary schools in Hungary, Iraq and the Ukraine.
- As language of communication with a global culture of entrepreneurial and cosmopolitan individuals, e.g. English-as-a-skill taught in China, English taught at business language schools in Europe.
- Spanglish, Singlish, Chinglish and other multilingual, hybrid forms of English as language of diaspora, travel, worldliness, resistance or entertainment (e.g. Lam, 2009; Pennycook, 2010).

Each of these forms of English is associated with learners from different classes, genders, race and ethnicities, with different aspirations and purposes. And there is, of course, some overlap in the Englishes learners need, learn and use depending on the conditions on the ground. For example, some learners might entertain aspirations of modernity and prosperity as well as an identification with Anglo-Saxon culture, and some learners might, in addition to standard British or American English, also use hybrid forms of English as bridges to other, less modern or equally modern, cultures. Additionally, given the transnational training of many English teachers in Anglophone countries like the UK, US, Australia or New Zealand, the distinction between English as a foreign, second or international language is sometimes difficult to uphold; for example, when Hungary's national school system hires British-trained or native English teachers, and uses British textbooks to teach English in Hungarian public schools, is British English being taught as a foreign language in Hungary or as an international second language or lingua franca?

Thus, English both facilitates global citizenship and prompts a return to local forms of community membership. It can serve to liberate learners from their own oppressive historical and cultural past (e.g. Germany) by standing for democracy, progress and modernity or by offering the prospect of a cosmopolitan future. It can also trigger renewed pride in local cultures perceived as countering the instrumental and profit-making culture of globalisation (Duchêne and Heller, 2012). Furthermore, the link between language and culture in ELT has moved from a view of (national or multinational) speech communities to communities of local practice and loose networks of language users (Kanno and Norton, 2003; Pennycook, this volume). These associations of learners and speakers of English, in many ways, resemble "imagined (national) communities" (Anderson, 1983) and offer transient, multiple, sometimes genuine and sometimes illusory friendships that replace the deep, horizontal comradeship offered and taken for granted by the nation-state. These associations are reflected upon within the field of intercultural communication.

A new emphasis on intercultural communication

Language learning and teaching is an interpersonal and intercultural process whereby learners come into contact with teachers and other learners of diverse personal histories, experiences and outlooks either face to face or virtually. Language learning and teaching thus has close connections with the field of intercultural communication (ICC), in particular where the notion of culture is concerned.

From culture-as-nation to interculturality

Whilst having its roots in anthropology, ICC as a field of inquiry was established out of concerns for national security in the post-Second World War period during the 1950s. The scholarly interest of that time was predominantly in understanding non-verbal and verbal aspects of communication of 'cultural' groups, which were used exchangeably with nationalities or indigenous people. In the 1970s and '80s, the scope of the field diversified to include interethnic and interracial communication (e.g. 'interethnic' in Scollon and Scollon, 1981; 'interracial' in Rich, 1974, and Blubaugh and Pennington, 1976). The change was the result of shifts of interests from building relationships with people from other cultures, including the cultures of enemy states, to addressing social tensions and understanding interactions among different races, ethnicities, gender, social classes or groups within a society. In the 1980s and '90s, however, ICC research became dominated by the comparative and positivist paradigms of cross-cultural psychology, in which culture is defined solely in terms of nationality and one culture is compared with another using some generalised constructs (e.g. Hofstede, 1991). Many broad, categorical terms used at the time in describing national cultures (e.g. individualism vs. collectivism, high- vs. low-power distance, masculinity vs. femininity, high vs. low uncertainty avoidance) have, in simplified and reductive form, taken root in public discourse and regularly appear in training manuals and workshops for people whose work may put them in direct contact with others of different nationalities. There were exceptions to this approach, however. Some publications (e.g. Meeuwis, 1994; Scollon and Scollon, 1995) began to question the notion of 'culture' and the nature of cultural differences and memberships. These studies challenge the practice of 'cultural account', which attributes misunderstanding in intercultural communication to cultural differences, and also raise the issues of stereotyping and overgeneralisation.

Since the 2000s, the field of ICC has shifted away from the comparative and culture-as-nation paradigm. Noticeable trends include a continued interest in deconstructing cultural differences and membership through interculturality studies, in which scholars seek to interpret how participants make aspects of their identities, in particular, socio-cultural identities, relevant or irrelevant to interactions through symbolic resources including, but not solely, language (e.g. Higgins, 2007; Sercombe and Young, 2010; Zhu, 2014). Scholars from a number of disciplines, such as sociolinguistics, critical discourse studies, education, ethnicity studies, communication studies and diaspora studies, have called for a critical examination of the way larger structures of power (e.g. situated power interests; historical contextualisation; global shifts and economic conditions; politicised identities in terms of race, ethnicity, gender, sexuality, region, socioeconomic class, generation and diasporic positions) impact on intercultural communication (e.g. Nakayama and Halualani, 2010; Piller, 2011).

From being to doing culture: a discourse perspective to ICC

One significant new emphasis within ICC, which is the most relevant to language learning/teaching and to ELT, is a discourse perspective to understanding how culture is produced or made (ir)relevant to interactions, by whom that is accomplished and why (e.g. Scollon and Scollon, 1995, 2001; Piller, 2012; Zhu, 2014). The discourse perspective, as Scollon and Scollon (2001: 543–544) explain, approaches intercultural communication as 'interdiscourse' communication, i.e. the interplay of various discourse systems – based on, for example, gender, age, profession, corporate membership, religion or ethnicity – and focuses on the co-constructed aspects of communication and social change. The insights offered through this perspective are, first of all, that culture is not given, static or something you belong to or live with, but something one does, or, as Street described it, "culture is a verb" (1993: 25). Treating culture as a verb means that one should not think of participants as representative of the group they are associated with and start with cultural labels they are assigned to (e.g. American vs. Japanese). Rather, the focus should be on the process of meaning making, that is, on what people do and how they do it through discourse (e.g. whether or how one orients to Japaneseness or Americanness in interactions) (Scollon et al., 2012).

The second insight from the discourse perspective is that discourse systems (including those of culture, gender, profession, religion, the workplace or the classroom) are multiple, intersect with each other and sometimes contradict each other as a reflection of the multiplicity and scope of identities that people bring along to or bring about through interactions. The identities that people 'bring along' are the knowledge, beliefs, memories, aspirations, worldviews they have acquired by living in a particular cultural community. The identities they 'bring about' in their interactions with native and non-native speakers emerge through the construction, perpetuation or subversion of established cultures through discourse (Baynham, 2015). They have been called *master, interactional, relational* and *personal* identities (Tracy, 2002), *imposed, assumed* and *negotiable* identities (Pavlenko and Blackledge, 2003), *audible, visible* and *readable* identities (Zhu, 2014), or self-oriented or prescribed-by-others identities (Zhu, 2014). Therefore, it is important to ask the question of how a particular kind of identity (e.g. cultural identity) is brought into interactions rather than, for example, how Americans and Japanese speak differently.

The third insight brought by the discourse perspective is that intercultural communication is *social* (inter-)action – a series of interrelated actions mediated by ideologies, societal structures, power (im)balances, self-ascribed and other-prescribed identities, memories, experiences, accumulated cultural knowledge, imagination, contingencies and the combined forces of globalisation and local adaptation and resistance. Seeing intercultural communication as social (inter)action means that we can no longer assume that the problems experienced in intercultural communication are merely cultural misunderstandings which can be made good or pre-empted if people can somehow see 'good intentions' in each other's actions or have sufficient cultural information or skills. These problems require intercultural competence, i.e. the ability to put yourself into others' shoes, see the world the way they see it, and give it the meaning they give it based on shared human experience. And we should remember that parties involved in intercultural communication are not necessarily in an equal power relationship, and they may not share similar access to resources and skills (e.g. linguistic skills, among others).

The discourse perspective to ICC raises questions about current practices in language learning and teaching. It decentres the notion of culture in the type of interactions that are usually described in textbooks and studied in the classroom and which are usually described as 'intercultural communication'; argues that not all the problems in intercultural communication are cultural; and moves away from *who* is involved in interactions and turns attention to the questions of *how* and *why* (i.e. how culture is done and made (ir)relevant, and for what purposes). It calls for an approach beyond the current integrated language-and-culture teaching practice which tries to integrate culture-as-discourse at all levels of language teaching. A case has been made: while it is important to know where the 'cultural faultlines' are (the term used by Kramsch, 2003; for example, the different reactions of the American and the German media to the 9/11 attacks in the USA), it is not good enough to explain everything a German or an American says by referring to their 'German' or 'American' culture. What is more important is the larger picture and a critical understanding of what is going on in social interactions *in situ* and how meaning is made, identities are negotiated, 'culture' is brought in and relationships are transformed discursively. What seems to be missing from communicative or task-based language teaching is a process- and context-oriented approach that is politically and ideologically sensitive, that goes beyond the here and now of problem solving and the negotiation of immediate tasks, and that raises historical and political consciousness.

Current issues and key areas of debate

This section reviews some issues raised by the view of culture as a context-oriented process that is at once politically and ideologically sensitive, and the debates that ensue. It reviews four current areas of debate.

Culture as historical context

It is a sign of the times that the head of a department of anthropology at an American university was overheard saying that anthropology these days is not about "studying culture, but studying historicity and subjectivity". As global technologies have made it possible to communicate with more and more people across space, the differences in the way people interpret historical events has become more visible and more intractable. For example, World War II is remembered differently by Americans and Russians, the Holocaust is interpreted differently by Israelis and Iranians, national security surveillance has a different meaning for Americans and Germans, and the Korean War is talked about differently in North and South Korea. To what extent, when and how is history relevant to interactions among individuals, even though they might all speak English?

The renewed attention to discourse "as the repository of cultural memory" (Freadman, 2014) has prompted some foreign language educators to suggest placing storytelling and story listening at the core of language instruction. Indeed, language teachers are now encouraged to use spoken and written narrative in their classes, not just in order to make learners talk and practice their grammar, but in order to make visible the invisible layers of history that constitute learners' experience and the subjective choices they make each time they narrate events (Kramsch, 2009c; Kramsch and Huffmaster, 2015).

Culture as both structure and agency

There are nowadays more non-native speakers of English around the world than there are native speakers (Graddol, 1997; see also Seargeant, this volume). Native speakers themselves live in multicultural societies or live abroad as expatriates with indeterminate cultural affinities. National cultures are being infiltrated by a global culture that speaks global English but might be making meaning differently from English native speakers, and whose cultural points of reference are multiple and changing. The large scale migrations ushered in by a globalised economy combined with the advent of global social networks have led to the interpenetration of national, regional and ethnic cultures and to their hybridisation. It is no longer sufficient to teach the pragmatics, sociolinguistics and semiotics of monolingual white middle-class speakers of British or American English. Applied linguists are now urging language teachers to teach stylistic variation (e.g. Pennycook, 2010) and to make their students aware of the different meanings that words have in the mouths of different people: for example, younger and older speakers, academics and businessmen or city dwellers and rural residents. They are also advocating teaching their students how to operate between languages in the form of 'translanguaging' (Garcia, 2009) or 'translingual practice' (Canagarajah, 2013) and other multilingual practices where English is combined with other languages to make meaning (see also Pennycook, this volume). These multilingual practices correspond to multicultural worldviews that are indexed by the linguistic codes used at any given time. Culture has to be seen as an agentive, discursive process that constructs new speaker or writer identities. For example, an immigrant learner of English might present a 'narratorial self' (Kramsch, 2009c: 73) when telling his/her story in English that might be different from the same story told to a relative in his/her native language (Norton, 2000). Teachers are now encouraged to let their students use their native languages in conjunction with English to express meanings they could not express in only one language (Canagarajah, 2013; see also Kerr, this volume).

But at the same time, culture has a material structure that cannot be ignored. There is, as David Block puts it, a tension between culture as *agency* and culture as *structure*. Culture is not only co-constructed by social actors with motivations and agency but also is made of institutions, practices and material interactions that constrain individual agency (Block, 2013). Block argues that structure and agency are mediated by the human capacity for reflexivity. For English language teachers, such reflexivity should be applied not only to grammatical or lexical structures but also to the historical 'conditions of possibility' of social and cultural events. For example, teaching students how to write a statement of purpose for admission to an American university requires teaching them not only how to write correct grammar and spelling but how to use culturally appropriate phrases such as *setting and achieving goals, overcoming adversity, showing leadership skills.* These phrases index a certain entrepreneurial culture made of individual tenacity and high achievement which the teacher should help the students recognise and understand. However, teaching culture is not giving them a recipe for success. It is not because English learners use these appropriate phrases that they will necessarily get admitted. They must also learn about their highly unequal chances of success at American universities depending on their race, ethnicity, gender and geographical origin.

Language and thought

The Sapir-Whorf hypothesis (Whorf, 1956), which argues that the language we speak shapes the way we perceive the world and that our culture influences the way we think (Kramsch, 2004), is still eminently relevant to the teaching of English. On the one hand, it makes sense that the language in which we were socialised should have an influence on the way we think of things and events. If native speakers of American English talk about 'challenges' and 'opportunities' rather than problems and fate, it is because the former evoke a can-do mentality that they may share with other American speakers. On the other hand, it is not certain that learners of English as a second or foreign language acquire a can-do mentality just by learning the lexical item 'challenge'. Indeed, should they be taught to adopt such a mentality? Or should they merely recognise and understand it when they hear native speakers use the word? Educators are divided on this issue, and they are rightly wary of stereotypes.

This language relativity hypothesis confronts the language teacher with the double task of teaching both linguistic form and living discourse meaning. If culture consists of common standards for perceiving, believing and evaluating events (see Kramsch, 1998; also above), then teachers are responsible for teaching not only the dictionary meanings of words but also the cognitive and affective values of these words and how they potentially channel a speaker's perceptions of social reality. Recent advances in cognitive linguistics shed light on precisely this aspect of language and culture. For example, cognitive linguists like George Lakoff (1996) remind us that the public can be manipulated into believing that 'torture' is merely an 'enhanced interrogation technique' and thus does not protest. Learners of English can be reminded by teachers that words do not change meaning on their own; they can be made to change meaning in order to arouse different emotions and thus serve different political interests. This is exactly what a culture-as-discourse approach encourages teachers to do (see previous discussion).

Language and online cultures

As learners of English around the world increasingly use computer-mediated communication (CMC) on the Internet and through social networks, English language educators generally welcome this opportunity to have their students use English for real-world purposes to connect with the rest of the world online (e.g. Danet, 1998; Grasmuck et al., 2009; Gardner and Davis, 2013). But they also have growing concerns regarding the transferability of communicative skills from online to face-to-face interactions, the nature of online vs. offline identities and the risks involved with the loss of privacy and the addictive nature of the medium.

Research on CMC in the last thirty years has shown that online communication can enhance both the quantity and the quality of the language produced by language learners; it makes them less timorous to voice their opinions and enables them to make friendships they would not normally make in the intimidating environment of a classroom (e.g. Lam, 2000, 2009, 2013; also, Kern, Ware and Warschauer, this volume). For example, the Chinese adolescent immigrants studied in the U.S. by Eva Lam, who connect online with a variety of interlocutors around Japanese anime comics or global hip-hop, find a way to improve their English and to create for themselves a 'third culture' (Kramsch, 2009b) in cyberspace. This third culture satisfies their emotional and aesthetic needs and enables them to eschew the discrimination they experience in real life.

However, many educators are concerned that online environments like Facebook or Instagram foster a culture of narcissism and personal display that is not conducive to the development of any deep communicative competence. Rather than connecting people, such environments risk isolating them in communities of like-minded peers, makes them vulnerable to electronic surveillance and makes them addicted to peer approbation and peer pressure. The challenge for ELT professionals is to balance these concerns with the evident opportunities for learning and personal development which online communication offers.

The four areas of debate surveyed in this chapter reflect the changing nature of culture in ELT as culture becomes denationalised, deterritorialised, decontextualised and associated with language use in real and virtual environments across social, ethnic, gender and generational boundaries rather than in terms of uniform or homogeneous national or state cultures.

Future developments and implications for ELT practitioners

How useful is the notion of culture for ELT practitioners? How shall language students, teachers and researchers engage with it?

There are many challenges in engaging with the notion of culture in language learning and teaching. The biggest hurdle, in our opinion, is how to translate the denationalised, deterritorialised and decontextualised forms of culture into classroom practice, when culture is still seen by many teachers "as a geographically, and quite often nationally, distinct entity, as relatively unchanging and homogenous, and as all-encompassing systems of rules or norms that substantially determine personal behavior" (Atkinson, 1999: 626). Additionally, for many researchers, national and linguistic groupings and memberships such as 'Chinese learners', 'Arabic speakers', 'Japanese students', continue to feature prominently either as a research context or as a contrasting variable. There is also reluctance or resistance towards teaching and learning culture in the classroom. When being asking their views on having 'Chinese culture' taught in the Chinese language class, one student reported that "I don't want to waste time in the class to be taught something that I can read on the internet" (Zhu and Li, 2014), and some language teachers feel their mandate is to teach language, not culture.

Despite such challenges, culture as a process of meaning-making itself has been and is still being used as a useful concept in language learning and teaching. Culture is getting both 'smaller' and 'bigger'. It is no longer the big 'C' culture of literature and the arts, or the culture of anthropologists or sociologists, but the way of life and everyday behaviours of speakers, readers and writers in daily communication (i.e. small culture). At the same time, paradoxically, culture is getting bigger and operates on a global scale (e.g. see the discussion on cultural globalisation in Kumaravadivelu, 2008). It manifests itself through different discourse levels, semiotic forms, verbal and nonverbal modalities and voices, and varies across time and contexts. Through the way we do things, new culture comes into being. Precisely due to its simultaneously open and bounded, reference-providing and reference-developing nature, we need to talk about culture more to understand how it works. A possible way forward, at the conceptual level, is to use culture "not as one thing or another, not as a thing at all, but rather as a heuristic . . . a tool for thinking" (Scollon et al., 2012: 3). At the analytical level, culture can be used as an interpretive, reflexive, historically grounded and politically sensitive lens to interpret differences or similarities experienced, perceived or constructed by social actors. At the operational level, culture is there to remind English language teachers that even though their students might use English words, these words might mean different things for them, evoke different memories and make sense of the world in different ways. It also invites them to distrust the ready-made meanings of the dictionary, to teach sociolinguistic variation and to help their students interpret the meaning of these variations.

How useful for language teachers is the notion of 'intercultural competence' as it is defined, used or sometimes idealised in the current literature?

Intercultural competence is a term defined, refined and debated across several disciplines including language and intercultural education, communication studies, interpersonal communication studies and international business and management studies (see, for example, Bennett, 1993; Byram, 1997; Risager, 2007; Byram and Hu, 2009). While the plethora of definitions and assessments of intercultural competence indicates its popularity among both ELT researchers and English teachers in many parts of the world, it also raises questions: why is it so difficult to pin down intercultural competence? Do such abstract notions as 'tolerance' and 'respect' mean the same to different people or in different contexts?

The biggest problem with the various interpretations of intercultural competence is that they are underpinned by 'static' and essentialised notions of culture and competence. Culture-specific knowledge is often mentioned as if it exists in the form of objective facts and can, therefore, be gleaned from books in the library or on the Internet as well as taught and relayed from one person to another. The question is: what is culture-specific knowledge? When people tell you: 'Chinese people do not open the gift in front of you and tend to decline gifts three times before accepting them', who are the Chinese people they have in mind? Are they reifying stereotypes and offering a reductionist profiling? How is the allegedly 'traditional' practice typical of the practice of the group it is associated with? In what way does it represent common practice, not a practice constructed or desired? And how current is the practice?

Similarly, the notion of competence is often treated as 'static', as something given. In fact, whether someone is competent or incompetent is very often a matter of ascription, either by speakers themselves or others in interactions. In Jiang and Zhu's work on children's interaction in an international summer camp (2010), a boy who is an L2 speaker of English found himself perceived to be less communicatively competent than another girl with a similar language background because he was 'quiet' in activities. Once the perception was formed, other participants in the activities kept asking the girl to translate for the boy. This example shows that the perception of belonging to a foreign culture is not the result of a linguistic deficiency but a social construction based on ideological values such as team spirit and participation.

These challenges raise the question of whether the notion of culture can be defined, modelled or benchmarked; indeed, whether it is possible to capture the essence of what is needed in intercultural interactions at all. As various researchers have shown (e.g. Kramsch and Whiteside, 2008; Kramsch, 2009c; Dervin, 2010; Clark and Dervin, 2014), what is needed for ELT practitioners is greater historical and political awareness, greater reflexivity in order to help learners understand the power dynamic behind intercultural exchanges, and the historical and symbolic components of what has been called 'symbolic competence' (Kramsch, 2009c) to supplement 'intercultural competence'.

How can we reclaim English as a language with a heart by attaching it neither to global economic interests nor to national hegemonies but to the deep aspirations of socially and historically situated social actors?

The current trend both towards more globalisation and towards renewed nationalist ideologies poses a challenge to English teachers who want to respond to the enormous demand for English as the language of technological modernity and economic prosperity but do not necessarily want to be associated with Anglo-American imperialism and the resurgent nationalist ideologies of English-speaking countries. The research reviewed in this chapter has broadened the concept of culture and intercultural communication to include many aspects that are not covered by a narrow definition of culture as the way of life, attitudes and opinions, foods, fairs and folklores of a nation's citizens. If culture is now seen as encompassing much larger historical processes – the memories and aspirations of people who identify themselves not necessarily by their nationality but by their language variety, their gender, race, ethnicity, age or occupation – then culture, thus understood, is likely to affect the way speakers of English use the English language. In this case, the Chinese learner of English who thought he could learn culture by consulting the Internet (see earlier in the chapter) might wonder why, when conversing with a native speaker, he still does not understand what the native speaker is saying even though he can comprehend every word, nor why he seems to have offended his interlocutor even though his grammar was perfect. Indeed, what he can get from the Internet is the WHAT of culture: the facts, information, explanations and expert advice on things to say or not to say. What he cannot get from the Internet is the WHY: why are people offended by what I have said? Why did they get so upset by what I have done? Why do they attach so much importance to particular things, people or events? It is not enough to understand people's words, opinions and feelings – one has to understand their intensity.

The task of English language teachers is to decide which aspect of culture, understood as a process, might be relevant to understanding this intensity. The growing complexity of global real-life encounters has increased the spatial and temporal scale of events English learners need to understand and put in relation with one another in order to achieve 'successful' communication. The training of English teachers thus increasingly requires training in semiotic awareness, discourse analysis and interpretation.

How can we manage the relationship between English and the other languages?

One of the things English learners now have to learn is when to use English and when to use other languages, with whom and on which topic. English, by its global nature, makes it possible to communicate with more people than ever, but it does not necessarily enable people to understand other people's motives, memories and aspirations. These are embedded in the language or language varieties in which their speakers were raised, socialised and schooled and in which they express their innermost aspirations. Like virtual technology, English creates a platform on which all other languages can be learned and used. But the very global spread of English makes it also possible to see how limiting English might be if it is used as the sole language, 'the only game in town'. English as a global language can be at its most useful as a supplement to, not as a replacement of, other local languages; in fact, it needs other languages to grow and change, like any other living language.

It is an ultimate irony that in order to promote understanding across cultures, English teachers must teach not English as it is spoken by monolingual nationals but English as a social semiotic system that mediates between global form and local thought, national and transnational interpretations of history, collective and individual apprehensions of reality. And they have to accept that their view of the value of English might not be the same as their students' views.

Discussion questions

- How far do you agree that learning another language implies learning another culture?
- Can you give an example of how you deal with culture in your teaching or language learning?
- What is your view of the relationship between English and culture in ELT? Is English a culture-free global lingua franca, or is it a language attached to a culture 'made in the West' but with global reach?
- To what extent do you think it is possible for teachers to focus on developing learners' 'intercultural communicative competence'? Do you think that ICC is a useful concept in your professional context?
- Think of a particular group of learners you have taught: to what extent will they engage multilingual practices in the future? How, where and when will they use English?
- Think of a time when you got really upset when someone from a different culture voiced opinions that were radically opposed to yours and that offended your moral system of values. How did you find out what the miscommunication was due to and how did you deal with it?

Related topics

Appropriate methodology; Communicative language teaching in theory and practice; Computer-mediated communication and language learning; ELT materials; 'Native speakers', English and ELT; Politics, power relationships and ELT; World Englishes and English as a Lingua Franca.

Further reading

Kramsch, C. (1998) *Language and culture*. Oxford: Oxford University Press. (Using insights from linguistics, sociology and anthropology, this book gives an overview of this field of research together with selected readings, study questions and annotated references.)

Kramsch, C. (2015) 'Language and culture'. *AILA Review*, 27. 30–55. (This essay gives an up-to-date overview of the methodology used to study language and culture in applied linguistics.)

Kumaravadivelu, B. (2008) *Cultural globalisation and language education*. New Haven: Yale University Press. (The book explores the impact of cultural globalisation on language education and critiques how Western notions of cultural assimilation, pluralism and hybridity impact the way culture is constructed in language classrooms.)

Scollon, R., Scollon, S. W. and Jones, R. H. (2012) *Intercultural communication: A discourse approach* (3rd ed.). Oxford: Wiley-Blackwell. (The recently updated edition provides an introduction to the discourse approach to intercultural communication.)

Zhu, H. (2014) *Exploring intercultural communication: Language in action*. London: Routledge. (The book examines how intercultural communication permeates our everyday life, what we can do to achieve effective and appropriate intercultural communication and why we study language, culture and identity together.)

References

Anderson, B. (1983) *Imagined communities*. New York: Verso.

Atkinson, D. (1999) 'TESOL and culture'. *TESOL Quarterly*, 33/4. 625–654.

Baynham, M. (2015) 'Identity brought about or along? Narrative as a privileged site for researching intercultural identities', in F. Dervin and K. Risager (eds) *Researching identity and interculturality*. London: Routledge. 67–88.

Bennett, M. J. (1993) 'Cultural marginality: Identity issues in intercultural training', in R. M. Paige (ed.) *Education for the intercultural experience* (2nd ed.). Yarmouth, ME: Intercultural Press. 109–135.

Block, D. (2013) 'The structure and agency: dilemma in identity and intercultural communication research'. *Language and Intercultural Communication*, 13/2. 126–147.

Blubaugh, J. A. and Pennington, D. L. (1976) *Crossing difference: Interracial communication*. Columbus, OH: Charles E. Merrill.

Brutt-Griffler, J. (2002) *World English. A study of its development*. Clevedon: Multilingual Matters.

Byram, M. (1997) *Teaching and assessing intercultural communicative competence*. Clevedon: Multilingual Matters.

Byram, M. and Hu, A. (eds) (2009) *Intercultural competence and foreign language learning: Models, empiricism, assessment*. Tübingen: Gunter Narr.

Canagarajah, S. (ed.) (2013) *Literacy as translingual practice: Between communities and classrooms*. New York: Routledge.

Clark, J. B. and Dervin, F. (eds) (2014) *Reflexivity in language and intercultural education: Rethinking multilingualism and interculturality*. London: Routledge.

Corbett, J. (2003) *An intercultural approach to English language teaching*. Clevedon: Multilingual Matters.

Danet, B. (1998) 'Text as mask: Gender, play, and performance on the net', in S. G. Jones (ed.) *Cyberspace 2.0: Revisiting computer-mediated communication and community*. Thousand Oaks, CA: Sage. 129–158.

Dervin, F. (2010) 'Assessing intercultural competence in language learning and teaching: A critical review of current efforts', in F. Dervin and E. Suomela-Salmi (eds) *New approaches to assessment in higher education*. Bern: Peter Lang. 157–173.

Duchêne, A. and Heller, M. (eds) (2012) *Language in late capitalism: Pride and profit*. London: Routledge.

Freadman, A. (2014) 'Fragmented memory in a global age: The place of storytelling in modern languages curricula'. *Modern Language Journal*, 98/1. 373–385

Garcia, O. (2009) *Bilingual education in the 21st century: Global perspectives*. Malden, MA: Blackwell.

Gardner, H. and Davis, K. (2013) *The App generation: How today's youth navigate identity, intimacy, and imagination in a digital world*. New Haven, CT: Yale University Press.

Graddol, D. (1997) *The future of English?* London: British Council.

Grasmuck, S., Martin, J. and Zhao, S. (2009) 'Ethno-racial identity displays on Facebook'. *Journal of Computer-Mediated Communication*, 15/1. 158–188.

Higgins, C. (ed.) (2007) 'A closer look at cultural difference: "Interculturality" in talk-in-interaction'. Special issue of *Pragmatics*, 17/1. 1–142.

Hofstede, H. (1991) *Cultures and organisations: Software of the mind*. London: McGraw-Hill.

Holliday, A. (2006) 'Native-speakerism'. *ELT Journal*, 60/4. 385–387.

Jiang, Y. and Zhu, H. (2010) 'Communicating in a lingua franca: Children's interaction in an international summer camp'. *Sociolinguistic Studies*, 4/3. 535–552.

Kanno, Y. and Norton, B. (2003) 'Imagined communities and educational possibilities: Introduction'. *Journal of Language, Identity and Education*, 2/4. 241–249.

Kramsch, C. (1993) *Context and culture in language teaching*. Oxford: Oxford University Press.

Kramsch, C. (1998) *Language and culture*. Oxford: Oxford University Press.

Kramsch, C. (2003) 'Teaching along the cultural faultline', in D. L. Lange and R. M. Paige (eds) *Culture as the core: Perspectives on culture in second language*. Greenwich, CT: Information Age Publishing. 19–36.

Kramsch, C. (2004) 'Language, thought, and culture', in A. Davies and C. Elder (eds) *The handbook of applied linguistics*. Oxford: Blackwell. 235–261.

Kramsch, C. (2009a) 'Cultural perspectives on language learning and teaching', in W. Knapp and B. Seidlhofer (eds) *Handbook of applied linguistics*. Berlin: Mouton de Gruyter. 219–246.

Kramsch, C. (2009b) 'Third culture and language education', in V. Cook and W. Li (eds) *Contemporary applied linguistics*. London: Continuum. 233–254.

Kramsch, C. (2009c) *The multilingual subject*. Oxford: Oxford University Press.

Kramsch, C. (2010) 'Language and culture', in J. Simpson (ed.) *Routledge handbook of applied linguistics*. New York: Routledge. 305–317.

Kramsch, C. and Huffmaster, M. (2015) 'Multilingual practices in foreign language study', in J. Cenoz and D. Gorter (eds) *Multilingual education*. Cambridge: Cambridge University Press. 114–136.

Kramsch, C. and Whiteside, A. (2008) 'Language ecology in multilingual settings: Towards a theory of symbolic competence'. *Applied Linguistics*, 29/4. 645–671.

Kumaravadivelu, B. (2008) *Cultural globalisation and language education*. New Haven: Yale University Press.

Lakoff, G. (1996) *Moral politics: How liberals and conservatives think* (2nd ed.). Chicago: University of Chicago Press.

Lam, W. S. E. (2000) 'L2 literacy and the design of the self: A case study of a teenager writing on the Internet'. *TESOL Quarterly*, 34/3. 457–482.

Lam, W. S. E. (2009) 'Multiliteracies on instant messaging in negotiating local, translocal, and transnational affiliations: A case of an adolescent immigrant'. *Reading Research Quarterly*, 4/4. 377–397.

Lam, W. S. E. (2013) Multilingual practices in transnational digital contexts. *TESOL Quarterly*, 47/4. 820–825.

Li, W. (ed.) (2014) *Applied linguistics*. Oxford: Wiley-Blackwell.

Meeuwis, M. (1994) 'Critical perspectives on intercultural communication: An introduction to the special issue'. *Pragmatics*, 4/3. 309–459.

Nakayama, T. K. and Halualani, R. T. (eds) (2010) *The handbook of critical intercultural communication*. Oxford: Wiley-Blackwell.

Norton, B. (2000) *Identity and language learning*. Harlow, England: Longman/Pearson Education.

Pavlenko, A. and Blackledge, A. (2003) 'Introduction: New theoretical approaches to the study of negotiation of identities in multilingual contexts', in A. Pavlenko and A. Blackledge (eds) *Negotiation of identities in multilingual contexts*. Clevedon: Multilingual Matters. 1–33.

Pennycook, A. (2010) *Language as a local practice*. New York: Routledge.

Piller, I. (2011) *Intercultural communication: A critical introduction*. Edinburgh: Edinburgh University Press.

Piller, I. (2012) 'Intercultural communication: An overview', in C. B. Paulston, S. F. Kiesling and E. S. Rangel (eds) *The handbook of intercultural discourse and communication*. Oxford: Wiley-Blackwell. 3–18.

Rich, A. (1974) *Interracial communication*. New York: Harper & Row.

Risager, K. (2007) *Language and culture pedagogy. From a national to a transnational paradigm*. Clevedon: Multilingual Matters.

Scollon, R. and Scollon, S. W. (1981) *Narrative, literacy and face in interethnic communication*. Norwood, NJ: Ablex.

Scollon, R. and Scollon, S. W. (1995) *Intercultural communication: A discourse approach*. Oxford: Blackwell.

Scollon, R. and Scollon, S. W. (2001) 'Discourse and intercultural communication', in D. Schiffrin, D. Tannen and H. E. Hamilton (eds) *The handbook of discourse analysis*. Oxford: Blackwell. 538–547.

Scollon, R., Scollon, S. W. and Jones, R. H. (2012) *Intercultural communication: A discourse approach* (3rd ed.). Oxford: Wiley-Blackwell.

Sercombe, P. and Young, T. (2010) 'Communication, discourses and interculturality: Introduction to the special issue'. *Special issue of Language and Intercultural Communication*, 11/3. 181–272.

Street, B. (1993) 'Culture is a verb: Anthropological aspects of language and cultural process', in D. Graddol, L. Thompson and M. Byram (eds) *Language and culture*. Clevedon: Multilingual Matters in association with BAAL. 23–43.

Tracy, K. (2002) *Everyday talk: Building and reflecting identities*. New York: The Guilford Press.

Whorf, B. L. (1956) *Language, thought, and reality*. Cambridge, MA: MIT Press.

Widdowson, H. G. (1994) 'The ownership of English'. *TESOL Quarterly*, 28/2. 377–389.

Zhu, H. (2014) *Exploring intercultural communication: Language in action*. London: Routledge.

Zhu, H. and Li, W. (2014) *Authenticity revisited: The teaching and learning of Chinese in the era of globalisation*. Keynote speech at language teaching and language learning seminar by British Association for Applied Linguistics Special Interest Group in Intercultural Communication, May 23–24, 2014, University of Edinburgh, UK.

4

'Native speakers', English and ELT

Changing perspectives

Enric Llurda

Introduction

Traditionally, ELT has tended to establish a dichotomy between native speakers (NSs) and non-native speakers (NNSs). In this chapter, I will show the problematic nature of the concept 'native speaker', I will provide arguments challenging this established division and I will discuss how such dichotomy has, until now, been responsible for the persistent disempowerment of NNSs within the profession.

Historically, many teachers of English have been L2 speakers, so-called NNSs, and they have been responsible for the teaching of English to millions of learners worldwide. Yet their identities, roles and contributions to the profession have, for the most part, been marginalised and remain invisible in mainstream accounts of ELT, whereas NSs have generally been regarded as ideal teachers of English. Additionally, teacher training and, more acutely, ELT materials writing have often been in the hands of NSs, who at the same time have also exerted control on professional practices such as the establishment of teaching goals, approaches and methodologies and models of language use across the profession (Phillipson, 1992).

We should also note from the outset that the term 'native' is rather strongly semantically loaded, even when it is used in areas that are totally unrelated to language and language teaching. Matsuda (2003), for example, argues that the term 'native' often carries positive connotations and there is a consequent negative meaning associated to 'non-native': "*Non-native* is marginal, and *native* is dominant. *Non*-native is negative, and *native* is positive" (Matsuda, 2003: 15). Even in the natural sciences, biologists and environmentalists refer to the negative impact of 'non-native species' invading the natural habitat of 'native' varieties. Non-natives in such a context are equated to 'aliens', as can be observed in the following text taken from a sign that I had the opportunity to read a few years ago at a state park in Minnesota, USA: "Many weeds have pretty flowers, but they are a growing pain. They crowd our native plants which provide wildlife with food and shelter. These invaders are called aliens or non-natives. They are biological pollutants." The term 'alien' is clearly associated with something dangerous that needs to be kept under control. Fortunately, 'non-native speakers' are normally not considered a dangerous species! However, the overall negative connotation of the term still covers NNSs, and they are often regarded as less efficient and less capable of conducting certain tasks involving language, particularly language teaching.

Current critical issues

Defining 'nativeness'

Noam Chomsky has often been blamed for imposing a vision of 'the native speaker' as the only valid speaker of a language. His often-cited words, "Linguistic theory is concerned primarily with an ideal speaker-listener, in a completely homogeneous speech-community . . ." (Chomsky, 1965: 3), have been taken as legitimising the native (ideal) speaker as the object of analysis in linguistics and applied linguistics. However, we must recognise that the relevance of Chomsky's words to ELT has been a misappropriation, as he never referred to *real* people teaching and learning any *real* language, nor did he claim that his work should inform language teaching.

In fact, the dominant status of the native speaker over non-native speakers is such a widespread phenomenon in society and in language teaching that it cannot be simply blamed on Chomsky's words. Rather, cause can be found in largely Western approaches to language that have established the unwritten norm that modern nations must have only one language in order to establish a unified national identity built around the use of that national language (see also Carroll and Combs, and Crookes, this volume). Such national and monolingual approaches have been the norm in most European countries since at least the 1500s, but this ideology can also be found in those non-European nations in which a strong fairly unitary national identity is promoted (e.g. Japan, China, Brazil, Colombia); exceptions include rather atypical cases such as Switzerland and, to some extent, Canada. Consequently, the motto 'one nation, one language' has led to the accompanying assumption of 'one person, one language' in those countries considered monolingual and where language diversity within their borders is hardly, if at all, recognised. Against this backdrop, language has been a determining factor in establishing who is entitled to 'belong' to a given nation or community of speakers, and the notion of 'nativeness' has for a long time been the ultimate measure of identity in such contexts.

Challenging 'nativeness': overlapping language skills and competencies

Recently, however, applied linguists have been concerned with the notion of 'nativeness' and have overtly questioned its usefulness. They have also shown the problems derived from artificially dividing speakers into 'natives' and 'non-natives' without actually attending to the complexities entailed in the act of speaking.

One of the pioneers in challenging nativeness was Paikeday (1985), who declared the native speaker 'dead'. Paikeday's early thesis revealed the need to problematise the native-speaker construct. However, the most influential challenge to the dominant notion of the native speaker comes through the work of Alan Davies, who very carefully attempted to deconstruct the native-speaker concept and ended by claiming that native-speaker competencies and characteristics are not in fact exclusive to speakers born into the language. According to Davies (2003: 210), there are six fundamental ways in which native speakers have been characterised in the research and methodological literature of ELT, of which only the first totally excludes second language speakers. They are:

1   The native speaker acquires the L1 of which s/he is a native speaker in childhood.
2   The native speaker has intuitions (in terms of acceptability and productiveness) about his/her Grammar 1 (idiolectal grammar).
3   The native speaker has intuitions about those features of the Grammar 2 (standard language grammar) which are distinct from his/her Grammar 1 (idiolectal grammar).

4   The native speaker has a unique capacity to produce fluent spontaneous discourse, which exhibits pauses mainly at clause boundaries (the 'one clause at a time' facility) and which is facilitated by a large memory stock of complete lexical items.

5   The native speaker has a unique capacity to write creatively (and this includes literature at all levels, for example, from jokes to epics, metaphor to novels).

6   The native speaker has a unique capacity to interpret and translate into the L1 of which s/he is a native speaker.

Apart from point one, which directly appeals to the order in which languages are acquired, none of these characteristics establish a firm division between first and second language users. Rather, they appeal to capacities and skills, and second language users can and do develop intuitions about their Grammars 1 and 2, produce fluent spontaneous discourse, write creatively, and interpret and translate. This leads Davies (2013: 5) to make the following claim:

> there are native speakers and there is 'the native speaker.' The first is all of us, the second an idealization. We are all native speakers of one or other code, language, idiolect. Some of us are educated, some not, some literate, some not, some creative orators, some not, and so on. The idea that all these native speakers are at C2, the highest level on the Council of Europe's framework for reference scale, makes no sense. Some perhaps are, but they are unusual.

'Nativeness' and ideology

Whilst Davies' discussion examines nativeness in terms of language users' capabilities, other authors have examined the ideological underpinnings of the concept. In 1992, Phillipson (1992) argued that a 'native speaker fallacy' had contributed to linguistic imperialism, whereby the belief that NSs were the ideal teachers of English facilitated the spread and influence of dominant UK and US language and culture around the world (see also Pennycook, this volume). And in the last fifteen years, several works have further examined the consequences of the simplistic dichotomy which divides all speakers of a language in the two categories of NSs and NNSs. Among such works, we may refer to Holliday's concept of 'native-speakerism' (2005, 2006; see also Holliday, this volume), which he defines as "a pervasive ideology within ELT, characterised by the belief that 'native-speaker' teachers represent a 'Western culture' from which springs the ideals both of the English language and of English language teaching methodology" (Holliday, 2006: 385). Leaving aside the fact that this definition might be interpreted as emphasising an 'East-West division', and accepting that native-speakerism can also affect language teaching and teachers within the Western world, it clearly accounts for the socially accepted superiority of the 'native speaker' over the rest of the world's speakers of English and assigns the former innumerable qualities and values that give them the aura of being the 'ideal language teacher'. The discourse of native-speakerism is evident in the bias against NNS teachers on the international job market (Clark and Paran, 2007; Selvi, 2010), for example, a point we return to later in the chapter.

Holliday (2005) further connects native-speakerism to the cultural narrative of Orientalism (Said, 1978) and to the much broader and perverse ideology supporting the basic division between 'in-groupers' (us) and 'out-groupers' (them): racism. Specific connections between native-speakerism and racism in ELT have been raised, for example, by Amin (1997), Chacón (2006), Kubota and Lin (2006, 2009) and Motha (2006, 2014). Holliday (2005, 2006) further argues that native-speakerism has imposed a preference for a certain type of classroom task and activity based around the idea of 'learner-centredness', and it identifies non-Western practices and cultures as, for example, 'hierarchical', 'passive', 'undemocratic' or 'traditional'. Consequently, he claims that "dominant professional discourses must be put aside if the meanings and realities of students and colleagues from outside the English-speaking West are to be understood" (Holliday, 2006: 386). More recently, Houghton and Rivers (2013: 14) have expanded the concept and define native-speakerism as "prejudice, stereotyping and/or discrimination, typically by or against foreign language teachers, on the basis of either being or not being perceived and categorised as a native speaker of a particular language, which can form part of a larger complex of interconnected prejudices including ethnocentrism, racism and sexism". In this, they are arguing that, in particular contexts (e.g. Japan), so-called native-speaker teachers can themselves be marginalised through stereotyping and discriminatory practices.

English as a global language

I hope to have made it clear by now that behind the apparently innocent term 'native speaker' lurks a stigmatisation of individuals who do not fit the socially established pattern of the 'ideal native speaker'. This pattern is often determined by a speaker's place of birth and his or her physical appearance rather than by linguistic and/or pedagogical competences; and this discourse can be applied to native and non-native speakers of all languages. However, focusing on the particular case of English, we observe that the language has spread all over the world in different waves of expansion, bringing it to places where the majority of speakers do not speak English as their first language. This phenomenon is reflected in the establishment of two paradigms in the applied linguistics literature that make these new contexts of English use their main focus – World Englishes (WEs, which, put simply, identifies and recognises the value of localised varieties of English, for example, Indian English or Nigerian English) and English as a Lingua Franca (ELF, which refers to English language communication between speakers who do not share first language) (see Seargeant, this volume). WEs and ELF showcase the need to deal with all users of English in the world today and to avoid restricting research to so-called native speakers.

The emergence of ELF, in particular, has challenged the theoretical division between NSs and NNSs. Communicative situations involve speakers who are capable of interacting successfully in English. The communicative success of such oral or written interactions does not depend at all on the place of birth of speakers or the order in which English was learnt (as a first, second or third language) but rather relies on the communicative skills of each of the participants. Thus, a distinction between NSs and NNSs is rendered irrelevant, as some 'native speakers' may fail to accomplish a successful interaction whereas some 'non-native speakers' will manage to reach their purported goal and satisfactorily conclude their interaction. Consequently, Modiano (1999) has proposed the "centripetal circles of International English", a classification of speakers of English as an international language inspired by, but significantly altering, Kachru's three concentric circles (Kachru, 1986, 1992; see Seargeant, this volume). In Modiano's view, an 'inner circle' of English is made up of speakers – both native and non-native – who are proficient in *English as an international language*; in other words, they can communicate in English, but do not necessarily have to follow 'native-speaker' models of English to be successful. Just outside this group, one could find speakers – again, both native and non-native – who are proficient in English but were not efficient communicators in *international* contexts. In other words, native speakers in this grouping can communicate well with other native speakers; non-native speakers communicate effectively in English with speakers who share the same L1 background as themselves. The last group is made of learners who are in the process of developing proficiency in English. The use of the word 'centripetal' to refer to these circles expresses the tendency of all speakers to gradually move towards the Inner Circle and reach the ultimate goal of being proficient international English speakers. In Modiano's model, therefore, English use and status is not based around 'nativeness' or notions of where speakers were born or the country they come from; rather, it focuses on speakers' proficiency in expressing themselves in English to other speakers of English as an international language.

From native/non-natives to language users

Languages develop and flourish in communities of practice (Lave and Wenger, 1991), and, until recently, such communities of practice were largely determined by geographical constraints, restricting languages to well-defined groups of speakers (with the occasional exceptions of foreign-born citizens who entered a new speech community). Globalisation, however, has lowered such geographical barriers, and now communities of practice exist among people living in distant places and sharing a particular interest or professional focus. Using online technologies or travelling regularly, such communities maintain a constant flux of communication that binds them together regardless of their place of birth and/or residence. These new global communities of practice are establishing a new use of English as a Lingua Franca, as we have seen, that is not necessarily connected to any group of native speakers (Seidlhofer, 2011). Rather, what characterises all these members of the global English-speaking community is that they are competent users of English. This leads us to the notion of English language *user* as opposed to *native* English speaker.

Several authors have suggested alternative terms that could successfully act as a substitute for *native speaker*. Noting that there is no reason to maintain the term *native speaker* as the "arbiter of grammaticality and acceptability of language", Paikeday (1985) embraced the alternative term *proficient user*, which more clearly captures contemporary concerns in the areas of linguistics, second language acquisition and language teaching. Rampton (1990), meanwhile, suggested *expert speaker* in order to include all successful users of a language, regardless of their mother tongue or place of birth. And Cook has extensively written about an alternative term – the *L2 user*. According to Cook (1999), this term suits the needs and reality of all speakers who have learned the language as an L2. Cook (2007) specifically claims that the goal of a language learner is to become a 'L2 user' rather than to become a 'native speaker', and therefore L2 teaching should be based on the L2 user as the target model for teaching (Cook, 2005). He further claims that using the native speaker as the goal of language teaching condemns all L2 learners never to reach this unachievable (i.e. NS) status and, therefore, to remain as perennial learners of the language regardless of the level of competence and achievement in English they attain. In Cook's view, once L2 learners can use the language and successfully function in the L2, they become L2 users, and this is, or should be, the goal of L2 language teaching.

When we look into the international dimensions of English and its role as the world's lingua franca, this idea of the L2 user becomes particularly relevant because it describes millions of speakers of the language who are running international organisations, participating at international conferences and meetings or doing business at a global scale for whom English is the main language of professional communication. Such a view is gradually challenging traditional notions of 'native speakers' being the goal, providing the language model and being the arbiter of success in second/English language teaching and learning. Although many language teachers and researchers (both native and non-native) still consider the native speaker the ultimate example of good language use, this perception is gradually changing. More and more of them are taking forward the arguments of those who question the authority of the native speaker, recognising that such authority is based on a fallacy or 'myth' which finds no match in 'real' and contemporary English language usage around the world.

Implications and challenges for ELT practice and practitioners

Within the field of ELT, these discussions have had a profound impact and have brought the issue of nativeness to the fore, making an increasing number of language teachers and teacher educators aware of the need to challenge pre-established assumptions and recognise the equivalent role that all kinds of English speakers can make to the ELT profession (Braine, 1999). Such pre-established assumptions were – and still are – visible in the higher prestige of NSs over NNSs within ELT and the many examples of discrimination suffered by non-natives across the profession, some of which have been reported in empirical studies, for example Mahboob et al. (2004), Clark and Paran (2007) and Selvi (2010). In all these studies, employers showed a preference for native speakers, and being a NS appeared to be an important feature in the selection of new teachers.

In addition to fighting discrimination by *employers* against non-native teachers, there is still a lot of work to be done to change the minds and preconceptions of many English *teachers* and *learners* in order for them to appreciate the values of different types of language teachers. Simultaneously, we need society at large to address and work towards changing stereotyped views. These are often presented in the media, as reported, for example, in a study showing how non-native speakers are often portrayed in Latin America as incompetent speakers and non-native instructors are considered responsible for the failure of English education policies, whereas native speakers are presented as the ideal solution to the problem of low proficiency in English (González Moncada and Llurda, 2016). Likewise, we need to be aware of problems and discrimination experienced by NSs teaching English in expanding circle countries, where their externally imposed 'native-speaker identity' causes them to suffer from discrimination by local citizens (Houghton, 2013; Rivers, 2013; Rivers and Ross, 2013; see also earlier in the chapter).

Implications and challenges for ELT practice

Once it is accepted that English no longer 'belongs' exclusively to its native speakers, as Widdowson (1994) convincingly argues and as posited by the World Englishes and English as a Lingua Franca paradigms, and if we accept Cook's argument (2005; see above) that learners should aspire to be successful L2 users rather than 'imitation' native speakers, then we need to question the common assumption in ELT that native speaker English should be the target for learners. What is the point in teaching specific aspects of a particular variety spoken by a restricted number of people if the goal is to communicate with a much wider and more global population? Consequently, what model of English (if any) should be given to learners? And what variety or varieties should be used in class? These questions are frequently asked by teachers who want to move beyond the dominant native speaker model of English and try to find an answer to their particular classroom needs.

Although the establishment of World Englishes and ELF research has provided powerful arguments for the need to reconceptualise models of English in ELT, the lack of descriptive work on ELF initially made it difficult for teaching professionals to incorporate an ELF approach into their teaching practice. Additionally, initial discussions as to whether ELF was a single variety or not (see Seargeant, this volume) led to questions about whether there would ever be a single standard of ELF to be implemented in language teaching. However, the abundance of current research on ELF has revealed the creativity of ELF users and the diversity of solutions found to solve communication problems. In effect, ELF is now seen as a function or range of practices rather than as a specific variety built around specific linguistic features of English, ending the debate on ELF unity versus diversity, and at the same time clearing the way for proposals that emphasise English language diversity over alignment with a single standard norm (Jenkins et al., 2011; Seidlhofer, 2011; Pitzl, 2012). Furthermore, a basic principle in language teaching should be the prioritisation of overall communication over the maintenance of particular native-speaker norms. The proof of successful learning is when a message reaches its target and is understood, rather than concerns about whether an L2 user's production matches the production of a selected group of native speakers. In other words, when we challenge the status of idealised native-speaker language as a target for learning, we automatically make intelligibility the ultimate goal in communication, as we no longer attempt to imitate an imagined native speaker but rather focus on conveying our message to a real audience. Negotiation of appropriate forms by all participants in a conversation – regardless of their L1 – is fundamental.

Thus, a realistic answer to the question of 'What model should be used in teaching?' must point to the need to expose learners to a diversity of *Englishes* in order for them to be well-prepared to understand English spoken by speakers from anywhere of the world. Obviously, each particular group of students will have specific needs and prospects for communicating with some groups of speakers of English more often than with others. Thus, teaching English in Singapore or Malaysia will have to take into account the fact that learners will be more likely to use English with Chinese and Australian speakers than with Irish or Germans; conversely, Italians will probably need to use English with other Europeans more often than with Japanese or Australians. Yet globalisation has made the world a fairly small place, and one should never discard the possibility of communicating in English with somebody living on the other side of the planet.

We also need to distinguish between the productive and receptive skills that English learners and users need. When it comes to receptive skills, given the wide range of possible English varieties that L2 users may encounter in their lives and the strong connection between intelligibility and familiarity with a particular variety (Gass and Varonis, 1984; Smith et al., 2014), the more varieties learners are exposed to, the more able to understand them the learners will be. However, if we are concerned about productive skills, then a different approach is obviously needed, as we cannot reasonably expect learners to speak several varieties of English. For learners to be able to convey their messages in an intelligible manner, they are likely to need to choose less marked forms of the language, avoiding local pronunciations or idiomatic expressions that may obscure the meaning to the nonmembers of their local community of English language practice. As Seidlhofer (2003: 22) indicates:

> Abandoning unrealistic notions of achieving 'perfect' communication through 'native-like' proficiency in English would free up resources for focusing on skills and procedures that are likely to be useful in EIL talk. (. . .) Needless to say, exposure to a wide range of varieties of English and a multilingual/comparative approach (. . .) are likely to facilitate the acquisition of these communicative abilities.

Two further fundamental aspects that need to be considered for ELT practice are language awareness and multilingualism. Throughout the twentieth century, much mainstream ELT pedagogy did not attend to language awareness, that is, explicit conscious knowledge about language (see Svalberg, this volume). This was in part due to the rise of audiolingualism in the 1940s/50s through to the 1960s/70s (see Hall, this volume, ch. 15), for example, and communicative language teaching from the 1970s onwards (see Thornbury, and also Hall, this volume, ch. 15). However, it was also partly due to the fact that language awareness was considered irrelevant for students aiming to achieve native-speaker competence. However, language awareness has been increasingly appreciated since the 1990s (James and Garrett, 1992; Schmidt, 1993; Andrews, 2007), and the challenge to native-speaker authority has emphasised more clearly the important role of language awareness in language education, as non-native teachers are often more aware of aspects of the language than native speakers, who may tend to rely on their intuitions rather than on their conscious knowledge of the language.

With regard to multilingualism, current approaches to language learning have increasingly questioned monolingual approaches to L2 teaching such as those proclaiming the need to use an 'English-only' approach in the ELT classroom, and the positive role of the L1 – and any previously known languages – in the process of L2 learning has been reappraised (see, for example, Kerr, this volume). Thus, there is an increasing literature claiming that using the learners' L1 in the second language classroom is more a help than a hindrance to language learning (Cook, 2001; Macaro, 2005), and, more recently, Creese and Blackledge (2010) and Garcia and Li (2014) have shown the positive effects of moving across languages (which they refer as *translanguaging*) in second language development.

Current developments in multilingual education clearly support the idea that we need to move away from traditional native (monolingual) approaches to ELT. In short, transcending the nativeness paradigm (Brutt-Griffler and Samimy, 2001) contributes new ideas and new foci of attention to ELT by detaching it from idealised visions of native-speaker models and goals and bringing "a more open view of language models and standards, calling into question the need to reproduce a restricted set of socially prestigious forms of language" (Llurda, 2015). This may appear as lacking in ambition to some professionals, who have worked hard to instil the native-speaker ideal in their students. But with the exception of those learners who are in the process of becoming citizens of an 'inner circle' country and who may wish to become as indistinguishable as possible from speakers from that country, the majority of ELT learners worldwide do not need to pass for native speakers. They simply need to be fully competent in using English as a Lingua Franca in any given context or situation they may encounter. Catering for these learners requires changing the way ELT is carried out.

Implications and challenges for ELT practitioners

This section is specifically devoted to issues surrounding NNS teachers. The changing perspectives on nativeness affect all actors in ELT, and teaching approaches need to be transformed and adapted to accommodate new realities. However, non-native teachers have suffered from a lack of self-confidence and a feeling of illegitimacy within the profession (Medgyes, 1994; Bernat, 2008), which has often led to their professional identity being based solely on their 'non-nativeness'. Here, I argue that the new perspectives on English and on nativeness discussed in this chapter will hopefully lead to changes to their identity. Establishing the L2 user (Cook, 2005) instead of the native speaker as the goal of ELT is a fundamental step in this direction, and an increase in opportunities for use of the L2 in class, plus awareness of the role and scope of English as a Lingua Franca, will lead to empowerment and increased self-confidence among NNS teachers of English (Llurda, 2009).

L2 speakers of a language cannot be permanently considered to be L2 learners. At some point, they are bound to be competent enough in using the L2 to be granted the term L2 users (Cook, 2005). When considering the distinction between L2 learners and L2 users, it may be useful to look at who might constitute each of these two groups. As can be seen below, teachers are difficult to classify, and they deserve to be included in a category of their own (Llurda, 2012):

i Learners: These are the people who initiate their language learning process. They generally hold a rather naïve perspective and may have an idealised vision of the learning process and its goal, which they may tend to think is to become similar (if not identical) to native speakers

(Xu et al., 2010). In the case of young learners, their parents are often willing to pay big sums of money for 'the correct model' and may complain if the teacher they are assigned is not a native speaker. This idealised vision constitutes a very lucrative business in some countries that receive vast numbers of young students who are sent there in order to learn 'proper' English.

ii   Users: This group of people is composed of those who have learned the language and have actually had the experience of using it with a diversity of speakers of different origins and accents. These speakers are aware of being speakers of English as a Lingua Franca and have appropriated the language, becoming *owners* of it, with the right to innovate and find new communicative solutions without feeling inadequate (Cook, 2002).

iii   Teachers: Paradoxically, not all non-native teachers regard themselves as users of the language, in spite of the fact that they have developed a high level of proficiency in English. Teachers' specific orientations towards mastering the formal aspects of the language, together with traditional training that used to place the native speaker centre stage, may have affected the way they perceive themselves. As a consequence, teachers can be divided into two further subgroups:

a   The *essentialists*, who promote the *essential* aspects of the English language and culture, projecting the idea of English as the exclusive property of native speakers. Here, we may encounter many university English departments, for example, anchored on traditional native-speaker values and on the supposed virtues of native varieties over any other variety or accent (Llurda, 2004). These teachers assume the role of ambassadors or even custodians of the *true* (i.e. native-speaker) language (Sifakis, 2009). These teachers often refuse to consider themselves as *users* and keep regarding themselves as *permanent learners* in pursuit of the elusive *native-speaker condition*.

b   ELF-aware teachers, who see themselves as L2 users and are aware that the goals of ELT are not to create pseudo-native speakers but to help learners become confident users who can communicate effectively in a diversity of situations and contexts. These teachers prefer to take on the role of *mediators* or *facilitators* rather than *custodians* or *ambassadors*. These teachers do not suffer from low professional self-esteem caused by their permanent quest for the native-speaker condition (Llurda, 2009) and project realistic goals onto themselves and their students.

Obviously, NNS teachers have a big challenge ahead of them, but NSs need to adapt to the new situation, as well. They all are competent users who have often been educated in the traditional paradigm of one standard language form that needs to be protected from *corrupted* forms of language. Many of them are not aware of being ELF users, which may lead to NSs imposing their own particular realisation of the language or may lead NNSs to fear not performing up to the expected (native) standard together with a fundamentalist fervour in defending the values of the native speaker. As pointed out by Sifakis (2007), a paradigm shift is taking place, and teachers need to gradually change their views along with it. A traditional orientation includes such aspects as standard language ideology, native speaker orientation, monolingual bias and negative attitude towards errors, whereas the new ELF-based orientation is based on such concepts as multilingualism, World Englishes, ownership and pre-eminence of intelligibility over native speaker imitation. Sifakis and Bayyurt (2015) report how a training programme in Turkey for non-native teachers with an ELF/WE perspective has engaged participants in a transformative journey. At the end of the process, they were more aware of their own condition as non-native teachers and of the issues involved in ELT, as well as broader issues related to their national educational system. Thus they became more reflective teachers, better prepared to critically take on the challenges of the profession.

Thus, the question that remains is: 'What kind of teachers are needed in ELT?' One may still wonder about the qualities of native and non-native teachers, but separating NSs and NNSs only distracts our attention from the key issue of teacher training and expertise. Thus, the answer to the above question can only be inclusive: all kinds of teachers are needed in ELT, as long as they develop professionally and show expertise in teaching the language as needed by their students. Medgyes (1994), for example, claims that cooperation between native and non-native is optimal, and similar conclusions have been reached by de Oliveira and Richardson (2004) and Matsuda and Matsuda (2004). Thus, all teachers add their specific talents to the profession, and it is funda-mental that they go through adequate and extensive training. Unfortunately, teachers and their employers often think that knowing the language makes good training unnecessary. However, in order to develop expertise, teachers must develop insights and skills, plus a critical stance, that can only be acquired through training. Teachers' biographies also play a role, and there are obvi-ously differences between teachers who have travelled around the world and those who have never left their hometown, as there are differences between those who have heard and spoken English since birth and use English as their main language of daily communication with their immediate relatives and those who have learned it as an additional language and mainly use it for professional purposes. But the relevant issue is that language teaching does not require teach-ers to be monolingual users of English but rather people with enough competence, awareness, and resources to help learners become confident users of the language. Different personalities, different biographies and different teaching styles are equally valid to reach such a goal. There still are teachers who lack self-confidence and who may feel inadequate for the job. Others may feel overconfident due to their 'native' condition. They all need to abandon the native-speaker paradigm, based on an ideal perception of language, and focus on their own condition as users, their teacher awareness and their teaching skills.

Conclusion

The main aim of this chapter has been to examine changing perspectives around the 'traditional' distinction between native and non-native speakers and the values that were attached to each type of speaker. Contemporary accounts suggest that the dichotomised classification of language users in these two apparently mutually-exclusive groups makes no sense when actual speakers commu-nicating in the real world are considered, particularly when the community of users of English worldwide is not restricted to members of a given localised community, but instead comes from each corner of the world. Changing perspectives on native speakers and on the nature of English as a global lingua franca have immediate implications for ELT practice and practitioners.

Thus, views on native and non-native speakers are changing, and these changes are bringing a paradigm shift in the way ELT is understood and practised. Such a transformation in perspective is not yet complete, as many teachers and learners are still guided by idealised, native-speaker oriented visions of English and English language learning. However, it is my contention that per-spectives are gradually changing in a process that will not stop until it has reached all members of the global ELT community.

Discussion questions

- Is it really possible to define a 'native speaker' of English? What difficulties can you think of regarding this concept?
- To what extent do 'native speaker' discourses prevail in your own professional context? Is there any element of discrimination based on the native/non-native distinction?

- What advantages for the learner may be derived from an approach that focuses on the 'L2 user' rather than the 'native speaker' as the goal of ELT?

Related topics

Appropriate methodology; Communicative language teaching in theory and practice; Language awareness; Language teacher education; Method, methods and methodology; Politics, power relationships and ELT; Questioning 'English-only' classrooms; World Englishes and English as a Lingua Franca.

Further reading

Braine, G. (2010) *Nonnative speaker English teachers: Research, pedagogy, and professional growth*. New York: Routledge. (This book is a readable compendium of where and how far research on non-native English speaker teachers has brought us.)

Davies, A. (2003) *The native speaker: Myth and reality*. Clevedon: Multilingual Matters. (This is an updated version of a book originally published in 1991 in which the author thoroughly dissects the meanings and implications of the native speaker concept.)

Llurda, E. (ed.) (2005) *Non-native language teachers: Perceptions, challenges and contributions to the profession*. New York: Springer. (A collection of papers showing how non-native teachers can contribute to the language teaching profession; it includes empirical studies expanding the scope of non-native teacher research, opening new directions and applying a diversity of methodologies.)

Medgyes, P. (1994) *The non-native teacher*. London: Macmillan. (The beginning of interest in non-native teachers, with innovative suggestions and implications for the language teaching profession.)

Moussu, L. and Llurda, E. (2008) 'Non-native English-speaking English language teachers: History and research'. *Language Teaching*, 41/3. 315–348. (A review article providing a comprehensive view of research, including an introductory discussion of the concept of nativeness and an overview of methods of research, with indications of possible future directions.)

References

Amin, N. (1997) 'Race and the identity of the non-native ESL teacher'. *TESOL Quarterly*, 31/3. 580–583.

Andrews, S. (2007) *Teacher language awareness*. Cambridge: Cambridge University Press.

Bernat, E. (2008) 'Towards a pedagogy of empowerment: The case of 'impostor syndrome' among pre-service non-native speaker teachers in TESOL'. *English Language Teacher Education and Development Journal*, 11. 1–8.

Braine, G. (ed.) (1999) *Nonnative educators in English language teaching*. Mahwah, NJ: Lawrence Erlbaum.

Brutt-Griffler, J. and Samimy, K. (2001) 'Transcending the nativeness paradigm'. *World Englishes*, 20/1. 99–106.

Chacón, C. (2006) 'My journey into racial awareness', in A. Curtis and M. Romney (eds) *Color, race, and English language teaching: Shades of meaning*. Mahwah, NJ: Lawrence Erlbaum Associates. 49–63.

Chomsky, N. (1965) *Aspects of the theory of syntax*. Cambridge, MA: MIT Press.

Clark, E. and Paran, A. (2007) 'The employability of non-native-speaker teachers of EFL: A UK survey'. *System*, 35/4. 407–430.

Cook, V. J. (1999) 'Going beyond the native speaker in language teaching'. *TESOL Quarterly*, 33/2. 185–209.

Cook, V. J. (2001) 'Using the first language in the classroom'. *Canadian Modern Language Review*, 57/3. 1–14.

Cook, V. J. (ed.) (2002) *Portraits of the L2 user*. Clevedon, UK: Multilingual Matters.

Cook, V. J. (2005) 'Basing teaching on the L2 user', in E. Llurda (ed.) *Non-native language teachers: Perceptions, challenges, and contributions to the profession*. New York: Springer. 47–62.

Cook, V. J. (2007) 'The goals of ELT: Reproducing native-speakers or promoting multicompetence among second language users?', in J. Cummins and C. Davison (eds) *International handbook of English language teaching*. New York: Springer. 237–248.

Creese, A. and Blackledge, A. (2010) 'Translanguaging in the bilingual classroom: A pedagogy for learning and teaching?'. *Modern Language Journal*, 94/1. 103–115.

Davies, A. (2003) *The native speaker: Myth and reality*. Clevedon: Multilingual Matters.

Davies, A. (2013) 'Native speaker', in C. A. Chapelle (ed.) *The encyclopedia of applied linguistics*. Blackwell Publishing Ltd. Retrieved from http://onlinelibrary.wiley.com/book/10.1002/9781405198431

De Oliveira, L. and Richardson, S. (2004) 'Collaboration between native and nonnative English-speaking educators', in L. Kamhi-Stein (ed.) *Learning and teaching from experience: Perspectives on nonnative English-speaking professionals*. Ann Arbor, MI: University of Michigan Press. 294–306.

García, O. and Li, W. (2014) *Translanguaging: Language, bilingualism and education*. New York: Palgrave Macmillan.

Gass, S. and Varonis, E. M. (1984) 'The effect of familiarity on the comprehensibility of nonnative speech'. *Language Learning*, 34/1. 65–87.

González Moncada, A. and Llurda, E. (2016) 'Bilingualism and globalisation in Latin America: Fertile ground for native-speakerism', in F. Copland, S. Garton and S. Mann (eds) *LETs and NESTs: Voices, Views and Vignettes*. London: British Council. 103–121.

Holliday, A. (2005) *The struggle to teach English as an international language*. Oxford: Oxford University Press.

Holliday, A. (2006) 'Native-speakerism'. *ELT Journal*, 60/4. 385–387.

Houghton, S. A. (2013) 'The overthrow of the foreign lecturer position, and its aftermath', in S. A. Houghton and D. J. Rivers (eds) *Native-speakerism in Japan: Intergroup dynamics in foreign language education*. Bristol: Multilingual Matters. 60–74.

Houghton, S. A. and Rivers, D. J. (2013) 'Introduction: Redefining native-speakerism', in S. A. Houghton and D. J. Rivers (eds) *Native-speakerism in Japan: Intergroup dynamics in foreign language education*. Bristol: Multilingual Matters. 1–14.

James, C. and Garrett, P. (eds) (1992) *Language awareness in the classroom*. London: Longman.

Jenkins, J., Cogo, A. and Dewey, M. (2011) 'Review of developments in research into English as a Lingua Franca'. *Language Teaching*, 44/3. 281–315.

Kachru, B. B. (1986) *The alchemy of English*. Oxford: Pergamon Press.

Kachru, B. B. (ed.) (1992) *The other tongue: English across cultures* (2nd ed.). Chicago: University of Illinois Press.

Kubota, R. and Lin, A. (2006) 'Race and TESOL: Concepts, research, and future directions'. *TESOL Quarterly*, 40/3. 471–493.

Kubota, R. and Lin, A. (eds) (2009) *Race, culture, and identity in second language education: Exploring critically engaged practice*. New York: Routledge.

Lave, J. and Wenger E. (1991) *Situated learning: Legitimate peripheral participation*. Cambridge: Cambridge University Press.

Llurda, E. (2004) '"Native/non-native speaker" discourses in foreign language university departments in Spain', in B. Dendrinos and B. Mitsikopoulu (eds) *Plurilingualism and language politics in the E.U.* Athens, Greece: University of Athens Press. 237–243.

Llurda, E. (2009) 'Attitudes towards English as an international language: The pervasiveness of native models among L2 users and teachers', in F. Sharifian (ed.) *English as an international language: Perspectives and pedagogical issues*. Clevedon: Multilingual Matters. 119–134.

Llurda, E. (2012) *Policies and attitudes to ELF: A Southern European perspective*. Plenary speech given at The Fifth International Conference of English as a Lingua Franca. Istanbul, Turkey. May 24–26, 2012.

Llurda, E. (2015) 'Non-native teachers and advocacy', in M. Bigelow and J. Ennser-Kananen (eds) *The Routledge handbook of educational linguistics*. New York and London: Routledge. 105–116.

Macaro, E. (2005) 'Codeswitching in the L2 classroom: A communication and learning strategy', in E. Llurda (ed.) *Non-native language teachers: Perceptions, challenges and contributions to the profession*. New York: Springer. 63–84.

Mahboob, A., Uhrig, K., Newman, K. and Hartford, B.S. (2004) 'Children of a lesser English: Status of nonnative English speakers as college-level English as a second language teachers in the United States', in L. Kamhi-Stein (ed.) *Learning and teaching from experience: Perspectives on nonnative English-speaking professionals*. Ann Arbor, MI: University of Michigan Press. 100–120.

Matsuda, P. K. (2003) 'Proud to be a non-native English speaker'. *TESOL Matters*, 13/4. 15.

Matsuda, A. and Matsuda, P. K. (2004) 'Autonomy and collaboration in teacher education: Journal sharing among native and nonnative English-speaking teachers', in L. Kamhi-Stein (ed.) *Learning and teaching from experience: Perspectives on nonnative English-speaking professionals*. Ann Arbor, MI: University of Michigan Press. 176–189.

Medgyes, P. (1994) *The non-native teacher*. London: Macmillan.

Modiano, M. (1999) 'International English in the global village'. *English Today*, 15/2. 22–28.

Motha, S. (2006) 'Racializing ESOL teacher identities in U.S. K–12 public schools'. *TESOL Quarterly*, 40/3. 495–518.

Motha, S. (2014) *Race, empire, and English language teaching*. New York: Teachers College Press.

Paikeday, T. M. (1985) *The native speaker is dead!* Toronto: Paikeday Publishing.

Phillipson, R. (1992) *Linguistic imperialism*. Oxford: Oxford University Press.

Pitzl, M-L. (2012) 'Creativity meets convention: Idiom variation and re-metaphorization in ELF'. *Journal of English as a Lingua Franca*, 1/1. 27–55.

Rampton, M. B. H. (1990) 'Displacing the 'native speaker': Expertise, affiliation, and inheritance'. *ELT Journal*, 44/2. 97–101.

Rivers, D. J. (2013) 'Implications for identity: Inhabiting the 'native-speaker' English teacher location in the Japanese sociocultural context', in D. J. Rivers and S. A. Houghton (eds) *Social identities and multiple selves in foreign language education*. London and New York: Bloomsbury. 33–55.

Rivers, D. J. and Ross, A. (2013) 'Idealized English teachers: The implicit influence of race in Japan'. *Journal of Language, Identity and Education*, 12/5. 321–339.

Said, E. (1978) *Orientalism*. New York: Pantheon Books.

Schmidt, R. (1993) 'Awareness and second language acquisition'. *Annual Review of Applied Linguistics*, 13. 206–226.

Seidlhofer, B. (2003) *A concept of international English and related issues: From 'real English' to 'realistic English'?* Council of Europe. Retrieved from http://www.coe.int/t/dg4/linguistic/Source/SeidlhoferEN.pdf

Seidlhofer, B. (2011) *Understanding English as a lingua franca*. Oxford: Oxford University Press.

Selvi, A. F. (2010) 'All teachers are equal, but some teachers are more equal than others: Trend analysis of job advertisements in English language teaching'. *WATESOLNNEST Caucus Annual Review*, 1. 156–181.

Sifakis, N. (2007) 'The education of teachers of English as a Lingua Franca: A transformative perspective'. *International Journal of Applied Linguistics*, 17/3. 355–375.

Sifakis, N. (2009) 'Challenges in teaching ELF in the periphery: The Greek context'. *ELT Journal*, 63/3. 230–237.

Sifakis, N. and Bayyurt, Y. (2015) Insights from ELF and WE in teacher training in Greece and Turkey. *World Englishes*, 34/3. 471–484.

Smith, R., Holmes-Elliott, S., Pettinato, M. and Knight, R. (2014) 'Cross-accent intelligibility of speech in noise: Long-term familiarity and short-term familiarization'. *The Quarterly Journal of Experimental Psychology*, 67/3. 590–608.

Widdowson, H. G. (1994) 'The ownership of English'. *TESOL Quarterly*, 28/2. 377–389.

Xu, W., Wang, Y. and Case, R. E. (2010) 'Chinese attitudes towards varieties of English: A pre-Olympic examination'. *Language Awareness*, 19/4. 249–260.

5

Educational perspectives on ELT

Society and the individual; traditional, progressive and transformative

Graham Crookes

Introduction

'Educational perspectives on ELT' means understanding ELT in light of larger movements within the domain of education that have influenced our field, movements which provide overarching educational aims for any particular perspective on formal instruction. In this chapter, I relate aims to curriculum concepts and philosophies of education associated with three major perspectives: first, 'traditional' forms of education and second, progressive education, with transformative perspectives presented as an optimistic third view more visible recently in ELT. The understanding of ELT in terms of its educational aims is important, as ELT is often thought of only in an instrumental way. An educational understanding relates, at an individual level, to what teachers themselves are aiming at, in terms of their personal values as articulated in their philosophies of teaching (though, clearly, educational perspectives are also of interest at broader levels, i.e. institutional/governmental, and also philosophical). Teachers who see ELT as a form of education would naturally want to determine what their educational values are and would therefore wish to be aware of trends or patterns in this area. In explaining this, I have drawn on a simple three-part category system that we inherit from specialists in the philosophy of education – they refer to these categories as 'philosophies of schooling'. On the face of it, such a simple system seems likely to oversimplify – surely an area as broad as this cannot be neatly fitted into just three boxes. Some simplification for purposes of initial exposition is defensible and necessary, though I note that this particular systematisation of educational ideas has its own history and reflects its own cultural and historical biases, having emerged in the US in the mid-twentieth century.

The concept of a philosophy of schooling is one alternative at hand when we are seeking general historically located understandings of ELT. The most common alternative account seeks an initial understanding of ELT by way of stereotypical classroom practices identified by analysts of ELT 'methods' (see Hall, this volume, ch. 15 for related discussion). There is some overlap in these two expository strategies. However, in this chapter, I present trends and positions in ELT through engaging with the general question of 'what is the overall educational aim for an individual student or for society or, more generally, of teaching English?' There can be more than one answer – and clearly, ELT teachers need to know these possibilities. A teacher's skill in the application of class-room practices and activities will not be sufficient for professional practice if s/he is unable to see to what basic end the learning and teaching is supposed to be put or might ideally be directed. A sense of purpose or meaning that a teacher can extract from his or her practice is highly valuable for personal growth and to enable one to bear up when things do not go as one would wish. With-out a vision of the overall goals of one's work, meaning may be absent, and thus the daily grind becomes just that – a chore or drudgery. Language teachers need to locate themselves in regard to broad educational aims; they need to think about how such aims are to be achieved through curricular choices and classroom practices (and in, or against, institutional and cultural contexts). They need to decide whether such aims are or are not consistent with their own philosophy of language teaching and how to position themselves accordingly. Some ELT professionals arrive as teachers via a pathway that does not include a first degree in education, maybe primarily through the disciplinary medium of applied linguistics or by way of unsupervised apprenticeships in the private language school sector; thus, some of us may not have been oriented explicitly to the val-ues dimension of our work. Similarly, some entrants to the field may identify only with a narrow conception of the role of language teacher, not fully appreciating its societal obligations, ethical constraints and values dimensions. Some may initially pick up only on the thinnest thread of this, which in the proprietary language school, for example, may be mainly related to the exchange of services for a fee. Nevertheless, ELT does play a major role in many societies and has philosophi-cal and values dimensions which deserve to be engaged with as an ELT practitioner develops. In general, this perspective is engaged with too rarely, as indicated by the existence of overview texts in our field whose titles include the phrase 'language education' yet make no connection to educa-tional systems or philosophies (e.g. McDonough, 2002; Nicholas and Starks, 2014).

Modern times and the emergence of mass education

The term 'traditional' can be useful when applied to the domain of education. It is at the same time a problematic catch-all term. I distinguish two senses of it here. First, there is 'traditional' in the sense of what educational institutions, curricula and teaching practices were in place before modern times. This will be close to meanings associated with the term 'indigenous'. And second, *within* modern times there is a sense of 'traditional' that is close to 'mainstream', 'dominant' and 'long-standing'. I will take up the second here and return to the first towards the end of the chapter.

The present period is often referred to as modern times, or 'modernity' (e.g. by Hall et al., 1996) – the period of time characterised both by the rise of the modern nation-state, notably in Western Europe (since the Treaty of Westphalia, 1648, which was instrumental in establish-ing concepts of the sovereign state), but also with characteristic linguistic, societal and person-related features. In developing one's values in language teaching, it is important to recognise that the nation-state developed hand in hand with the establishment of national languages. In this period and from this viewpoint, national languages are thought of as homogenous and important for communication and mutual comprehensibility among citizens of the state. Society is seen in terms of the nation-state, and the language is tied to, or circumscribed by, fixed borders; the people within a particular society are considered to be (or pressed to be) the same, culturally and linguistically. The nation-state also grew up along with *mass* education. Before there was mass education, most people simply did not have any education, although the elite had tutoring or went to a handful of special institutions often attached to other non-educational institutions, most obviously churches and temples. Mass education came along with the industrial revolution, as is indicated still by many older, factory-like school buildings. It is obvious that they were and are intended to deliver services to large groups of similar pupils, turning out a quality product – or at least a homogenous product – and one that fits the needs of the state and the taxpayers, the entities that foot the bill. Modernity also favoured science over religion and appeared in the West first, thus benefiting Western cultures over others.

Modern times: modern education as 'essentialist'

The nation-state of modern times is initially a European phenomenon. The advancement of Europe (and in due course, the USA) over other areas was attributed, at the time, to these countries' superior economic base in science and industry. This became a reason for providing a technical education for ordinary people. Educational reformers in favour of a national education system (as opposed to private schools) believed it would socialise citizens appropriately in accord with dominant political and moral values (Mitch, 1992; Crookes, 2009: 51). In the US, this was so that democracy would flourish (since democracy needs an educated electorate to function). But also in the US, it was so that the social classes would mix in a 'common school', and by the late nineteenth century, under pressure of immigration, it was so that the newcomers would be Americanised, becoming homogenous users of one language, graduating from one education system.

In the account so far in this section, I have not introduced ELT. But its forerunners were there, in a couple of guises. In the British colonies, specifically India, the initial administrators valued indigenous languages and cultures. What became established policy, however, was the promotion of English language and culture and, in support, English language teaching. This was articulated initially by Mill (1817) and more bluntly by Macaulay (1835, paragraph 34), who stated that the aim was to reproduce Indians as Englishmen: "We must at present do our best to form a class who may be interpreters between us and the millions whom we govern, – a class of persons Indian in blood and colour, but English in tastes, in opinions, in morals and in intellect."

Meanwhile, in the US, English instruction for immigrants was on the rise (though provision of education in immigrant first languages declined). Compulsory education laws, with English instruction specified, became common at state level. The 1906 Naturalization Act required US immigrants to show a command of English to become citizens. Elementary and high schools made no special provision for English instruction for immigrants, but night schools had special-ised classes (Ross, 1937).

In ELT, the Prussian method that became known as grammar-translation (Fick, 1800) man-ifested itself as highly routinised techniques, ways into the second language via its grammatical structures and a process of translation of isolated sentences. A "high priority [was] attached to meticulous standards of accuracy which, as well as having an intrinsic moral value, was a prereq-uisite for passing the increasing number of formal written examinations that grew up during the century" (Howatt, 1984: 132; see also Hall, this volume, ch. 15). For language teachers, this is the method most commonly thought of as 'traditional', and this is indeed how language teaching historian Kelly refers to it (1969: 53), while pointing out (following Rouse and Appleton, 1925) that it is "not older than the nineteenth century". Though beginning outside state schools (and driven by utilitarian needs), materials and curriculum for learning English (mostly as a foreign language) in state high schools in developed countries such as Germany, France and Japan during much of the twentieth century came to reflect this as the dominant perspective.

The aims of this kind of education and the conceptions of the individual and of society implied by it are summarised in the philosophy of education literature under the technical term 'essentialist', coined by US (Russian-expatriate) academic Demiashkevich (1935: 5–6). It conceived of

> the demands of social heritage, . . . standards of the good life that are cherished by the group (tribe, caste, religious organization, or nation) . . . [and] the standards of competence set by the occupational group (trade, vocation, profession). . . . [It expected] systematic . . . sequential curricula . . . [and] attention to fundamentals, such as the permanent moral values of humanity and the information, skills, aptitudes, and attitudes without which – in the judgment of educational authorities – neither the individual . . . nor the group can achieve the good life.

Key aspects were that curriculum should be determined by the needs of the "nation" and target "occupational group[s] . . . [or] profession[s]" (ibid.). An instrumental view of education is thus in place – something practical, useful and material is to be done with the education obtained; most likely, for the skill of ELT, it is to be used in the discharge of employment-related matters. More broadly, the essentialist aim of education is to prepare individuals to be good upstanding individuals who can fit into the existing order of society, with emphasis on character building, shared knowledge of a single culture that manifests in and unifies the nation-state and education preparing individuals for useful employment. Originating with the rise of the industrial nation-state in the West, this perspective rapidly expanded to developing countries during the twentieth century and now holds sway throughout the world.

This 'essentialist' perspective is still dominant today, but it has altered. The previously strong statist perspective – emphasising a unitary nation-state for which education makes citizens – has diminished in force and visibility. This change is signalled by the term 'neo-liberal', describing aspects of capitalist economies and countries in which the private limited-stock company is the dominant form of economic organisation, as opposed to publicly-owned or cooperatively-owned enterprises (see also Pennycook, and Menard-Warwick et al., this volume). This means that business corporations see their interests as less identified with the nation-state as before. The free movement of capital and labour across national boundaries is to the advantage of businesses, which themselves may be domiciled for tax purposes outside of their major market countries; consequently, the target of educational systems is now the creation of individuals who are flexible, mobile, not rooted in specific areas, not attached to an ancestral language and not identified with one set of job-related skills but willing to learn or relearn new ones, including, most especially, English as the international lingua franca (see Seargeant, this volume).

It is this perspective on the individual and learner which begins to be manifest in curricular statements and through the universal ELT coursebook (Chun, 2013; Gray, 2013). Despite many efforts at reform, it is still easy to find forms of English teaching which emphasise knowledge rather than use, teacher-fronted classrooms, memorisation, drill and practice and heavy use of standardised testing. In many cases, the English language is taught only for its use in sorting mechanisms, not actually as a means of communication. Where communication is used as the justification for teaching English, the language is advanced as the international language of business, or just as the main instrumentally dominant language, so considerations of efficiency and practicality are behind the aims of this so-called traditional form of language education.

This essentialist and instrumental line of thinking and practice, in modern times, has had one major counter-trend, to which I turn next.

Progressive education

At the same time as the central nation-states in Europe were beginning to industrialise, a counter-movement, opposed to rules, regimentation, rigid social structures and materialism, was beginning. The Romantic Movement of the late 1700s did support the idea of a nation (and was implicated in the initial modern version of France, and in the forces that eventually brought Germany into existence), but it also contained within it ideas of individual freedom and something of an opposition to rationality; certainly there was an emphasis on nature, natural growth and spirit. The visibility of these ideas in the realm of educational theory and then practice is attributed to Jean-Jacques Rousseau. He opposed dominant ideas about child-rearing and education – the idea that children were inherently bad, and that (according to Martin Luther, Calvin, Wesley and others in this tradition) it was essential to break the will of the child before education or even proper child-rearing could proceed. Thus when a teacher such as Pestalozzi (1801) took up Rousseau's ideas, put them into practice and reported results, he was able to describe a loving and supportive educational environment, much to the surprise of many conventional thinkers but to the delight of intellectuals and Romantics throughout Europe.

By the late nineteenth century in the English-speaking world, this tradition had become associated with the term 'progressive' and began to appear in private and public and mass and elite forms of education. The individual, more likely to be seen as a child than an adult in this tradition, is viewed as inherently good and capable of natural growth through experience. Other key themes in early progressive education were that it was child- or student-centred; activity and experience (rather than lecture and drill) formed the mainstay of the curriculum; a holistic perspective on individual development was called for; freedom or student choice rather than constraint and control was important; and education had the purpose of societal improvement, to foster democracy and equality. Not all of these matters would have been manifested in all progressive schools, and they would have been understood through nineteenth and early twentieth century eyes rather differently than how we might understand them today, in the multicultural, globalised twenty-first century; however, the themes are there, and we can also trace their continuation and modification, as an educational perspective, to the present day and through to some aspects of language education as well.

These ideas were taken on, and up, by many throughout Europe and elsewhere (the work of Tagore in India, Tolstoy in Russia, Tao in China, and the UK, for example, Skidelsky, 1969), though in a minority of schools. They were most successful in the US. John Dewey took over the already-progressive Parker School (Parker, 1891 [1937]), closely attached to his position as a professor of the University of Chicago, as an experimental school, while surveying and reporting on the alternative, progressive school scene as it was in the US (Dewey and Dewey, 1915). This led, through the work of the progressive education movement, to this perspective being instantiated substantially, for a while, in US state education. What this looked like in practice was a broadly democratic, project-oriented and yet practical curriculum, as reported in such works as *Were we guinea pigs?* (Ohio State University, University High School, 1938).

In that work, for example, the students of the high school attached to Ohio State University report the various curriculum projects they planned, initiated and carried out themselves, discuss how they researched and organised the physical aspects of their school and reflect on their overall ability to carry off complex organisational tasks and even fund-raise and arrange a field trip. The progressives' view of society was one in which local democracy, in the form of town meetings, was the target, and their view of the individual was a person prepared to take an active civic role. While educating for the 'growth' (Dewey's watchword) of the self-realised individual through a democratic curriculum and participatory classroom practices, students would be well-prepared to take on their civic duties (not merely economic roles) when they graduated from school.

However, beginning before World War II and intensifying afterwards, critics of progressivism (such as Bagley, 1934) worked to extinguish the more democratic elements of this educational perspective. Progressivism had always had two currents, an instrumental, scientistic one with a strong belief in the possibilities offered by science and a more social and political one. With the second current in retreat, the first altered into the life adjustment curriculum of the US high school in the immediate postwar period (Hartman, 2008). "Proponents of life adjustment education supported curriculum flexibility; student guidance; and attention to previously neglected areas of social living such as hygiene, family living, drivers' education, and social relations with peers. Emphasis was upon increasing the holding power of American high schools by presenting students with a more meaningful and relevant curriculum" (Fallace, 2011: 575). It was more likely to prepare the student to be a good worker and consumer than a good citizen and was driven by the first flush of the scientific, instrumentally oriented needs-assessment procedures (Tyler, 1949) that were to play a major role in language teaching developments to come. Certainly the individual and society were seen as having identifiable and real needs that should be addressed by education, and these were not merely the needs of business or industry, nor solely those of Deweyan civic duty.

Progressivism in ELT

Meanwhile, a self-aware ELT profession was developing, and progressive educational perspectives had an influence on it, if initially diluted and indirect. The major historian of ELT, Howatt (1984: 220–221, 275), explains that in the UK, this was partly a response to immigration. A materials and curriculum ELT project of the mid-1960s is identified by Howatt as a major turning point in the development of ELT approaches and the moment when progressive ideas become visible in ELT. Howatt initially describes this project in terms of a melding of the pre-existing "EFL tradition of the linguistically organized syllabus" with the recently developed UK "primary school tradition of activity methods". What the UK primary school 'tradition' looked like was certainly of international and especially US interest. Learning through doing and using, group and pair work, classrooms organised in terms of study centres, much use of teacher-produced materials, field trips, a relaxed approach to discipline and a generally student- or child-centred perspective characterised the best schools in this tradition.

In this period, the US Ford Foundation funded the Anglo-American Primary Education Project. It sent US teachers on study tours of UK schools and published descriptions of the British primary practices (e.g. Featherstone, 1971; see also Rogers, 1970) for the US audience, which were at the time signalled by the term 'informal education' (crystallised in the Plowden Report: Central Advisory Council for Education, 1967; Galton, 1987). These were seen as maintaining the progressive methods that had been pushed aside in the US during the same post-war period (e.g. Armytage, 1967), and it was from them that progressive practices entered ELT. A progressive orientation was also to be found in another early 1970s UK language teaching project that Howatt focuses on (Concept 7–9, 1972; authors, Wight, Norris and Worsley). Early UK ESL pushed back against a negative view of minority languages by focusing on practising in the academic high school classroom the specific kinds of language needed by immigrant L2 learners. Using the L2 to learn it (especially through group work and information-gap activities) has been a feature of communicative approaches ever since, but in Howatt's historical account, it is associated with language teachers who are acting on behalf of a minority group against mistaken mainstream conceptions of them which were not grounded in a real understanding of minority language use.

Thus, almost all aspects of what in ELT came to be called Communicative Language Teaching (CLT) can be found in the progressive tradition, and the primary means of this transmission seems to have been the maintenance of an activity-based, student-centred approach with strong roots in the pre-existing progressive perspective. In addition to activities as an area in which progressive education and ELT in its communicative conception came together, let me also point out the role of the teacher as a facilitator and the conception of the learner as one who explores through activities and active engagement with the subject matter, making mistakes and learning from them.

The aims of both progressive education as conceived in primary ELT and the emergent CLT of the 1970s and beyond, then, in simple terms, are focused on individual growth, reflecting individual (not state) needs and fostering the development of personal autonomy, with the communication that is to be achieved conceptualised in terms of functional communication about matters of personal concern and importance. The one 'progressive' aim that seems to have been lost along the way to CLT is the importance of preparing for citizenship. Progressive educational aims certainly included fostering and supporting democracy, which is not evident in CLT.

The 1970s saw the rapid international growth of a self-aware ELT profession and an associated academic discipline (applied linguistics). Progressive elements were to be found in some of the alternative 'humanistic' methods that flourished briefly in late twentieth century ELT (see, for example, Galyean, 1977, discussed in Crookes, 2009; also Hall, this volume, ch. 15) and more persistently in the efforts to promote learner autonomy in ELT (e.g. Benson and Voller, 1997; also Benson, this volume). Language schools that were entirely separate from the state sector and organised primarily for adults found themselves free to try out new ideas but were usually driven by profit considerations. Post-colonial English teaching in schools and universities maintained dominant or traditional perspectives, teaching structural and instrumentally driven English with the award of credentials as their main aim. On the other hand, the flows of migrants into the core English-speaking countries, many forced to displace from one country to another through wars of liberation or decolonisation, resulted in a growth within ELT of forms of adult ESL that had the potential to take the aims of progressive education on yet further. This perspective is summed up here under the heading of transformative education.

Transformative education

As the name suggests, transformative education is an educational perspective, a philosophy of schooling, in which the aim of education is to transform society (in a positive way, in directions signalled typically by a term such as 'social justice'). Historically, there are two (Western) versions of the story of transformative education. One is that in Europe, just as modern times were beginning and right from the beginnings of the Romantic movement around the 1790s, a radical version of progressive education had also come into existence (in, for example, the writings and actions of individuals such as William Godwin, Thomas Paine, and Mary Wollstonecraft [Simon, 1972]). Among its inheritors were anarchist educators like Ferrer who, in the 1910s, produced the Modern School, a small international network of schools that preserved radical political traditions (such as an activist role for the citizen, direct democracy and distrust of or opposition to the state) along with high levels of student autonomy in small private educational institutions that lasted until the 1950s. The other story, beginning a little later and independent of the first one, was that a more explicitly socialist wing of the US Progressive Movement developed, exemplified by Counts (1932) and Rugg (1931). This encouraged US and other progressive teachers to teach and to act politically inside and outside of school with the intention of radically reforming society – particularly during the Great Depression, when many felt that capitalism was truly destroying economies, that radical alternatives were needed and that teachers and education had a role to play in this transformation. Counts' development of the progressive tradition is called 'social reconstructionist'.

US opponents of the very idea of social justice and of the position that education should further it resisted these initiatives. The Progressive Movement was a much bigger target than its socialist left wing, the social reconstructionists, but both were attacked. The Cold War enabled opponents to label them 'unpatriotic', and most of the state manifestations of progressive and radical traditions in education in the US were, for a time, erased. Meanwhile, an avowedly socialist government took office in the UK immediately at the end of World War II (Lawton, 1977). I have already mentioned the somewhat atheoretical version of the progressive tradition which coalesced in the UK in the 1960s under the heading of 'informal education'. This eventually regrouped in the US as the 'open classroom' movement of the early 1970s (Cuban, 2004). These developments encompassed the increasingly radical and diverse currents in education, reflecting the social changes of the time. Adult education became a visible site for the manifestation of a transformative educational perspective. Recently exiled Brazilian literacy educator Paulo Freire spent time at Harvard University and had strong effects on second language and other adult educators through his best-seller, *Pedagogy of the Oppressed* (1970). Along with the massive, wrenching changes in society and the political upheavals around the Vietnam War and other wars of popular liberation, the anti-colonial struggle, movements for women and gay liberation and Black Power, transformative ways of doing school and L2 learning and teaching were sought out enthusiastically by many young people (students as well as teachers, not to mention radical academics).

The assumptions this educational perspective makes about learning, the learner, the teacher, materials and curriculum, and the wider socio-political context overlap and draw from the progressives but are more challenging. The conception of society is that it is a site of conflict. A critique of society is implied, and this suggests that a teacher implementing it views society as being seriously in need of improvement. The social goal of this kind of education is to improve society, but going beyond merely more and better democracy, a fairly radical transformation is called for. Materials and curriculum are not only to be activity-based, but the curriculum (or syllabus) is to be negotiated with learners and must reflect their needs as articulated by them in a process of dialogue with the teacher (this puts the student in an activist role and makes the classroom itself democratic). The teacher is not merely a facilitator but also someone willing to challenge students (without imposing on them) through articulating her or his perspective on materials, content and theories of language and society. The view of the individual learner is not merely as one active individual among others but as a person with class, race and gender whose identity both affects learning and also is changed in the process of learning (particularly of a second language). For ELT, these aims manifested, a few years after Freire's work became widely-published in English, in discussions such as Moriarty and Wallerstein (1979) and subsequently in published materials such as Auerbach and Wallerstein (1987).

What these published materials aim to do is enable adult immigrant ESL learners to raise in the classroom practical issues they face in daily life, and, using the classroom, fellow students and the teacher as resources, investigate the problem and the language needed to address it. Auerbach and Wallerstein's work, for example, includes units on 'the job search' (where the job search is not necessarily successful), 'talking with the boss' (not always understood), 'the deportation scare' and 'stress' (the result of overwork in garment-making), to mention just a few. I mention the most obviously challenging topics, but this should not suggest that only problems are focused on. However, the point is that problems are *posed*, and it is for the students collectively to consider how, using the L2, they will deal with them, bringing up their own topics as needed and negotiating the syllabus accordingly. (It is not the teacher's job, nor the role of the textbook materials, to solve the problems.) These materials and this philosophy of schooling do not indoctrinate the learner, nor even tell him/her what to do. But it hopes that by facilitating the ability to critically understand society and use language to improve the learner's own situation, this will carry forward to the learners themselves being able to use language to improve society. Much more recently, individual ELT specialists have explored the use of these ideas and associated classroom practices in a range of EFL countries and provided teacher-research reports of their efforts (some summarised in Crookes, 2011).

Back to the future? 'Traditional' education and ELT in the twenty-first century

As mentioned earlier, there is more than one form of 'traditional' education. Besides the traditions of mass education discussed earlier, there is also indigenous education. It is consistent with a transformative perspective on education that indigenous education should not be dismissed. Ideas and forces associated with the rise of the modern nation-state certainly did dismiss, indeed tried to expunge, traditional forms and indigenous values; but the transformative tradition sees that as an unethical exercise of power and identifies it as very much associated with colonialism, which it is opposed to.

As previously discussed, large-scale economic development, as well as mass education and its associated range of educational aims, came about first in the West. That makes 'non-Western' the other side of a relevant albeit simplistic dichotomy. So, a comprehensive discussion in this chapter should try to also engage with non-Western traditions in education. Non-Western education here includes both the traditions of very simple societies but also the traditions of non-Western civilisations. The latter were originally, in a sense, indigenous, but developed into urban and highly literate forms. Thus, they can be associated with the major non-Christian religions, philosophies, forms of science (Selin, 1992), civilisations and ways of life signalled by terms like Buddhist, Islamic, Hindu and so on (see Reagan, 1996). The individual, and the society, imagined or discussed thus far in the chapter has in fact been that of the Western, industrial, so-called developed and secular world. However, the perspectives implied by a phrase such as Buddhist civilisation should also be considered. ELT should have space for the Buddhist student, the Islamic teacher, the Confucian society and the associated philosophies of teaching and schooling, though published discussions of these interactions are rare.

Turning now to the more established understanding of 'indigenous' as a form of traditional education: while many indigenous cultures and peoples have indeed been exterminated by the 'modernising' forces of the twentieth century and continue to be under great pressure in the twenty-first century, they are themselves not static. They duck and feint and transform themselves, engaging with the modern world but endeavouring to remain true to their traditions even while those traditions may change.

There certainly are many academic treatises on indigenous education. However, the interface of indigenous education and ELT may be hard to perceive or imagine at first. That may be because where ELT has met indigenous cultures, this has usually been in the context of colonialism and Christian missionary work, and the result is usually a post-colonial education system rather than one which is still visibly indigenous. However, at the risk of oversimplifying, a few points can be made (following Gegeo and Watson-Gegeo, 2002; Jacobs, 2013).

The indigenous viewpoint is often presented as holistic. That is, the individual is located within the physical, social, familial and personal environment, and a spiritual dimension for that location is usually articulated as well (e.g. Wilson, 1999). There is no place for the individualist neoliberal worker here. And the individual's engagement with the environment is often presented as a spiritual, certainly an ethical one, with preservation and maintenance rather than transformation, let alone exploitation, as goals and responsibilities. This is a good form of conservatism; but being inward-looking, it perhaps does not lend itself to the learning of languages from outside, (but see Hornberger, 2008). On the other hand, it is clearly not necessarily a monolingual perspective. Some indigenous cultures engage with others at a linguistic level; other not entirely modern nations and cultures are explicitly multilingual or expect a degree of plurilingual competence from their members (Canagarajah and Wurr, 2011); many recognise the power of English but also its dangers. Gegeo and Watson-Gegeo (2002) report on the teaching of an indigenous language arts teacher in the Solomon Islands:

> We call Lindsay's teaching "counter-hegemonic" because his practices are grounded in indigenous epistemology, they model for students' indigenous critical praxis, and they prepare students for further schooling or returning to the village. In kindergarten, where the Ministry policy allows some use of children's first language, Lindsay alternates lessons in Kwara'ae and English (the official school medium of instruction); at higher grade levels, he uses English and SI [Solomon Islands] Pijin. In a discourse analytic study of Lindsay's kindergarten language arts lessons . . . we found that Lindsay uses village conversational discourse patterns and pieces of caregiver-child interactional routines known to his students, during literacy tasks. His interactive lessons contrast sharply with those of typical SI rural classroom teachers' recitation format inherited from colonial days. Most striking is Lindsay's use of a traditional Kwara'ae argument technique found in planning, debate, and oratory: 'ini te'ete'e suli ru'anga (literally, "inching with the fingers along it"). The metaphor (from gardening) refers to careful, step-by-step systematic reasoning well-supported with evidence, and involves a set of clearly marked discourse routines. Kwara'ae children are familiar with those routines not only from attending village events with their parents, but also from their use to teach children linguistic, social, and intellectual skills at home. We believe that Lindsay's use of this strategy is one factor in his students' success in learning English.

So, this exemplifies some important aspects of how traditional, in the sense of indigenous, remains a valuable educational perspective, even influencing some local delivery of ELT, while exemplifying positive values that are generally relevant even in a globalised world.

Implications for the individual teacher

What do these various perspectives mean for the individual developing English language teacher? I think that all teachers should make an effort to identify personally important aspects of what it is they want to be doing, as teachers, in the area of individual values and beliefs (Crookes, 2003). Language teaching should be more than a paycheck. We work with other humans; our efforts can help or harm them; we also are directly engaged in the multicultural aspects of the countries we work in and, as somewhat bicultural people ourselves, we almost certainly have a desire to make the spaces within which we work maximally accommodating to those with a foot in more than one culture. So we are almost inevitably engaged with the socio-cultural and thus political aspects of our countries of residence. Language teaching is a value-laden enterprise, and we would do well to recognise this reality. It should help, conceptually, for us to notice that the language teaching practices we deliver, engage with, and have been inculcated with themselves have values or philosophies underlying them. Even classroom practices that are not language-specific have morally right and morally wrong ways of being conducted. If we do not consider the educational underpinnings of language teaching practices (and consult relevant literature, and talk with our peers and our mentors), we will find ourselves obliged to implement practices we might not fully agree with. That in itself is not as problematic as implementing practices whose intellectual or moral bases we do not understand. Conscious compromise is not as bad as sleep-walking through what should be a moral, values-based practice.

However, the responsibility cannot be exclusively placed on the individual teacher. School administrators, teacher educators, directors of studies, section heads, all should be looking to foster professional development at levels beyond those of technique – at levels of personal consciousness and growth. A tall order, it might be said, but the materials for doing so are more easily available than before. What is less available than before, as work intensification and de-professionalisation proceed apace in neoliberal environments, is the time and space to support such development. It is nevertheless the right thing to do.

Future developments and conclusion

Discussions of future developments in the field of education are very much bound up with the massive implications of recent developments in educational technology in the Internet era (see, for example, Gruba, Hinkelman and Cárdenas-Claro, this volume). I think these do not necessarily favour any particular values or philosophical position, but they do enable the participatory aspects of transformative educational perspective to be implemented more easily; clearly, language students can talk to others using the target language in other places; they can also be actively involved in the creation of their own materials and the organisation of their own courses. Internet technology does also facilitate access to non-mainstream, nondominant strains of thought (government firewalls aside). But there are other real-world developments that may be more relevant to understanding the role of educational perspectives in ELT. I am thinking of the interpenetration of cultures within and across political borders, and the increasing non-homogeneity of institutions, from nation-state on down through school systems, to the classroom and to the village. These developments are not conducive to the statist, homogeneity-promoting position of essentialism. So under some working conditions, a language teacher who cares to, has greater ease than in previous decades in teaching with a values position opposed to essentialism. Of course, the power of English and its engagement with employment-related preparation will allow instrumentally oriented approaches in ELT to dominate. But the feasibility of alternative positions, which I personally see as the more desirable ones, is, I like to think, better as we look to the future – always provided that language teachers are willing to think, reflect and explore the alternatives that have been present almost as long as (English) language teaching has been in existence.

Discussion questions

- To what extent do you believe that it is the role of ELT professionals to engage in 'transformative' education?
- What are the needs of English language learners? How do different answers to this question indicate different perspectives in ELT education? Do you focus on learners' needs, and if so, why?
- What might Buddhist or Islamic approaches to ELT look like for the individual or for society? Why might these approaches not be best described as 'traditional'?
- Can indigenous education be transformative? If so, how? If not, why not?
- Do you have a philosophy of teaching that corresponds to any of the philosophies of schooling outlined in this chapter?

Related topics

Communicative language teaching in theory and practice; Method, methods and methodology; Politics, power relationships and ELT; Values in the ELT classroom

Further reading

Crookes, G. V. (2009) *Values, philosophies and beliefs in TESOL: Making a statement*. Cambridge: Cambridge University Press. (An extensive overview of the area briefly sketched out by this chapter.)

Crookes, G. V. (2013) *Critical ELT in action: Foundations, promises, praxis*. New York: Routledge. (Theory and practice for the transformative viewpoint outlined in this chapter.)

Pennycook, A. (2001) *Critical applied linguistics*. Mahwah, NJ: Lawrence Erlbaum. (A sophisticated and reflexive overview that encompasses the entire domain considered here within a transformative understanding of applied linguistics, including ELT.)

References

Armytage, W. H. G. (1967) *The American influence on English education*. London: Routledge & Kegan Paul.

Auerbach, E. R. and Wallerstein, N. (1987) *ESL for action: Problem-posing at work*. Reading, MA: Addison-Wesley.

Bagley, W. C. (1934) *Education and emergent man*. New York: T. Nelson and Sons.

Benson, P. and Voller, P. (eds) (1997) *Autonomy and independence in language learning*. New York: Longman.

Canagarajah, S. and Wurr, A. J. (2011) 'Multilingual communication and language acquisition: New research directions'. *The Reading Matrix*, 11/1. 1–15.

Central Advisory Council for Education (England) (1967) *Children and their primary schools*. [Plowden Report]. London: HMSO.

Chun, C. (2013) 'The 'neoliberal' citizen: Resemiotising globalized identities in EAP materials', in J. Gray (ed.) *Critical perspectives on language teaching materials*. New York: Routledge. 64–87.

Counts, G. S. (1932) *Dare the school build a new world order?* New York: John Day Co.

Crookes, G. V. (2003) *Values, philosophies, and beliefs in TESOL: Making a statement*. Cambridge: Cambridge University Press.

Crookes, G. V. (2009) *Values, philosophies and beliefs in TESOL: Making a statement*. Cambridge: Cambridge University Press.

Crookes, G. V. (2011) *Critical ELT in action: Foundations, promises, praxis*. New York: Routledge.

Cuban, L. (2004) 'The open classroom'. *Education Next*, 4/2. 68–71.

Demiashkevich, M. (1935) *An introduction to the philosophy of education*. New York: American Book Company.

Dewey, J. and Dewey, E. (1915) *Schools of to-morrow*. New York: E. P. Dutton & Co.

Fallace, T. D. (2011) 'The effects of life adjustment education on the U.S. history curriculum, 1948–1957'. *The History Teacher*, 44/4. 569–589.

Featherstone, J. (1971) *An introduction* (Informal Schools in Britain Today series). New York: Citation Press.

Fick, J. C. (1800) *Practische Englische Sprachlehre*. Erlangen, Germany: Walter.

Freire, P. (1970) *Pedagogy of the oppressed*. New York: Seabury Press.

Galton, M. (1987) 'Change and continuity in the primary school: The research evidence'. *Oxford Review of Education*, 13/1. 81–92.

Galyean, B. (1977) 'A confluent design for language teaching'. *TESOL Quarterly*, 11/2. 143–156.

Gegeo, D. W. and Watson-Gegeo, K. A. (2002) 'The critical villager: Transforming language and education in Solomon Islands', in J. W. Tollefson (ed.) *Language policies in education: Critical issues*. Mahwah, NJ: Lawrence Erlbaum Assocs. 233–252.

Gray, J. (ed.) (2013) *Critical perspectives on language teaching materials*. New York: Routledge.

Hall, S., Held, D., Hubert, D. and Thompson, K. (eds) (1996) *Modernity: An introduction to modern societies*. Cambridge, MA: Blackwell.

Hartman, A. (2008) *Education and the cold war*. New York: Palgrave Macmillan.

Hornberger, N. H. (2008) 'Multilingual education policy and practice: Ten certainties (grounded in indigenous experience)'. *Language Teaching*, 42/2. 197–211.

Howatt, A. P. R. (1984) *A history of English language teaching*. London: Oxford University Press.

Jacobs, D. T. (2013) *Teaching truly: A curriculum to indigenize mainstream education*. New York: Peter Lang.

Kelly, L. G. (1969) *25 centuries of language teaching*. Rowley, MA: Newbury House.

Lawton, D. (1977) *Education and social justice*. London: Sage.

Macaulay, T. G. (1835) 'Minute on Indian education', in H. Sharp (ed.) *Bureau of education: Selections from educational records, Part I* (1781–1839). Calcutta: Superintendent, Government Printing, 1920. Reprint. Delhi: National Archives of India, 1965. 107–117. Retrieved from http://www.columbia.edu/itc/mealac/pritchett/00generallinks/macaulay/txt_minute_education_1835.html

McDonough, S. (2002) *Applied linguistics in language education*. London: Edward Arnold.

Mill, J. (1817 [1858]) *History of British India*. London: Piper, Stephenson, & Spence.

Mitch, D. (1992) 'The rise of popular literacy in Europe', in B. Fuller and R. Robinson (eds) *The political construction of education*. New York: Praeger. 31–46.

Moriarty, P. and Wallerstein, N. (1979) 'Student/teacher/learner: A Freire approach to ABE/ESL'. *Adult Literacy and Basic Education, 3*. 193–200.

Nicholas, H. and Starks, D. (2014) *Language education and applied linguistics: Bridging the two fields*. New York: Routledge.

Ohio State University, University High School. (1938) *Were we guinea pigs?* New York: Henry Holt & Co.

Parker, F. W. (1891 [1937]) *Talks on pedagogics*. New York: John Day for the Progressive Education Association.

Pestalozzi, J. H. (1801 [1891]) *How Gertrude teaches her children*. Syracuse, NY: E. W. Bardeen.

Reagan, T. G. (1996) *Non-Western educational traditions: Alternative approaches to educational thought and practice*. Mahwah, NJ: Lawrence Erlbaum Assocs.

Rogers, V. R. (1970) *Teaching in the British primary school*. New York: Macmillan.

Ross, L. Q. (1937) *The education of H*Y*M*A*N K*A*P*L*A*N*. New York: Harcourt Brace.

Rouse, W. H. D. and Appleton, R. B. (1925) *Latin on the direct method*. London: University of London Press.

Rugg, H. (1931) *An introduction to problems of American culture*. Boston, MA: Ginn & Co.

Selin, H. (1992) *Science across cultures: A bibliography of books on non-Western science, technology, and medicine*. New York: Garland

Simon, R. (1972) *The radical tradition in education in Britain*. London: Lawrence & Wishart.

Skidelsky, R. (1969) *English progressive schools*. Harmsworth, UK: Penguin Books.

Tyler, R. (1949) *Basic principles of curriculum and instruction*. New York: Harcourt Brace.

Wight, J., Norris, R. A., and Worsley, F. J. (1972) *Concept 7–9*. Leeds, E. Schools Council.

Wilson, S. (1999) *Recognizing the importance of spirituality in Indigenous learning*. Retrieved from Australasian Corrections Education Association http://www.acea.org.au/Content/1999%20papers/Shaun%20Wilson%20-%20paper.pdf

Part II

Planning and organising ELT
Curriculum, resources and settings

Part II

Planning and organising ELT
Curriculum, resources and settings

6

Language curriculum design
Possibilities and realities

Kathleen Graves

Introduction

This chapter examines language curriculum design from two perspectives: the possible *content* of the curriculum, i.e. decisions about what students will learn, how they will learn and why, and the planning *processes* that guide these decisions. Curriculum content in language teaching is often described in terms of different kinds of syllabuses (e.g. notional/functional, task-based and so forth; see, for example, Thornbury, and Van den Branden, this volume). This chapter takes a different approach by describing three historical, overlapping waves of curriculum content that have their basis in different understandings of language and how and why people learn a language. Curriculum content must also be appropriate for the context in which it is enacted, hence the importance of having integrated planning processes. If the processes do not align, the curriculum may not be effective in its intended context.

Definitions: curriculum and syllabus

Curriculum and syllabus are both concerned with the same question: *what* students learn. The purpose of curriculum and syllabus design, therefore, is to determine what students will learn and to outline a plan for how they will learn it. Although there are regional differences in the way these terms are sometimes used (between, for example, the UK and the USA), for the purposes of this chapter, curriculum is the superordinate term and syllabus a subordinate term. Richards distinguishes the terms as follows:

> The term *curriculum* is used here to refer to the overall plan or design for a course and how the content for a course is transformed into a blueprint for teaching and learning which enables the desired learning outcomes to be achieved. . . . Once content has been selected it then needs to be organized into teachable and learnable units as well as arranged in a rational sequence. The result is a *syllabus*.
>
> *(2013: 6; italics added)*

As in Richards' definition, curriculum is commonly understood as a plan for learning as distinct from the actual learning experiences that occur in (or outside of) the classroom. Theorists in general education suggest that there are multiple dimensions of curriculum, which include, according to Ylimaki (2013), the *intended*, the *enacted*, the *assessed*, the *learned* and the *hidden* curriculum. The *intended* curriculum comprises the content learners are expected to learn, the *enacted* curriculum refers to what learners are actually taught, the *assessed* curriculum refers to the skills and knowledge learners acquire as documented through formative and summative assessments, and the *learned* curriculum is the effects, intended or unintended, of the educational experience. The *hidden* curriculum refers to what is implied to students by what (and who) is included or left out of the curriculum experience (Apple, 2004). For example, when immigrant students are taught about housekeeping and warehouse jobs rather than how to prepare for a career, the curriculum implies that they are only capable of the former, not the latter.

I suggest that a curriculum is the dynamic interplay of three interconnected processes: planning, enacting and evaluating. In this view, a curriculum is not just a design for learning, it is also the learning itself; it is both the plan and the enactment. The enacted curriculum is what happens in the classroom among learners and teacher – without enactment, the curriculum plan is just an artefact (Graves, 2008). Ideally, enactment is informed and guided by the design and made more effective as a result of both formative and summative evaluation, but this depends on how well curriculum planners have taken into account the realities of the classroom and educational context, and whether evaluation is actually carried out.

This chapter focuses on the planning process – how one makes decisions about what will be learned. In ELT, these decisions are complex for two reasons: language is not intrinsically a subject matter, and people learn languages for different purposes in different contexts.

Three waves of language curriculum

Despite how it is often perceived, language is not of itself an educational subject; it is a resource human beings use for meaning-making in all aspects of their lives. In order to be taught and learned in a classroom, language must be turned into curriculum content. Curriculum content in ELT has been influenced by research in linguistics and second language acquisition (SLA), and has been shaped by global trends in immigration and by the emergence and dominance of English as the language of business, science and technology. Below I outline three successive, overlapping waves of curriculum content: the *linguistic wave*, the *communicative wave* and the *third wave*. While they are in some ways chronological, there is considerable overlap among them, and they are each still very much in play today. Each wave carries some of what came before, and all draw from the same ocean.

First wave: the linguistic wave

A traditional view of curriculum content is that it is an external body of knowledge that is broken down into its components and built up, component by component, in order to reach some sort of mastery. In this view, all learners who are taught the curriculum are meant to master the same body of knowledge. The particular learners and their needs are irrelevant. In language teaching, this notion of curriculum as an external body of knowledge is based on a view of language as a set of grammatical, morphological and phonological rule-governed systems. Curriculum content is based on *grammatical patterns* and language features that are built up, pattern by pattern, to form sentences and dialogues. Typically, these patterns or features are coupled with *topic*-based or *situational vocabulary*. Language teaching materials for such a curriculum are usually organised around situational dialogues that include the target grammar and vocabulary, as well as grammar and pronunciation exercises. For example, a unit might focus on simple present tense, adverbs of frequency and the question *how often,* coupled with the topic of daily or weekly routines.

Second wave: the communicative wave

Developments in sociolinguistics in the 1970s and '80s brought about a major shift in understandings of language, ultimately leading to the development of a 'communicative approach' to language teaching (see Thornbury, this volume). Rather than a set of components to be combined and mastered, language was defined as socially situated communication in which appropriate use depended on the ability to speak, write, read and understand the language for different purposes in a range of settings. The linguistic curriculum was deemed inadequate, as it did not prepare students to actually *use* the language. Thus the purposes for which language is used, its *functions*, became a focus of curriculum content (Wilkins, 1976). Canale's model of communicative competence (1983), which included linguistic, sociolinguistic, strategic and discourse competence, became an influential framework. Analyzing learners' needs and contexts for using language entered curriculum thinking. This type of needs analysis was most highly developed in early work on English for specific purposes (Munby, 1978; see Starfield, this volume).

Thus, the notion of language proficiency in the four skills of *reading, writing, speaking* and *listening* for communication gained traction, and they became the building blocks of the communicative curriculum. Research into the skills, and their subskills and underlying processes, began to emerge (e.g. Omaggio, 1986). *Learning strategies*, which can be defined as behaviours or thinking processes that students use to enhance their learning, also became a component of curriculum content. Taxonomies of strategies were developed, for example by Oxford (1990) and O'Malley and Chamot (1990), that included, among other things, cognitive strategies such as making predictions based on the topic of a text and metacognitive strategies such as setting learning goals.

Research in the 1970s and '80s in the fledgling field of SLA focused on the processes of acquiring a language, particularly the importance of learning through interaction and negotiation of meaning. *Tasks,* which required communication between two or more learners in order to achieve an outcome, thus became an element of curriculum content (Long and Crookes, 1992). 'Task' has been defined and interpreted in different ways and has evolved in meaning from the early 1980s (Richards, 2013). In communicative language teaching, tasks are meant to mirror those that learners will be expected to perform outside the classroom, for example, ordering from a menu or completing a job application. In this second wave of curriculum content, therefore, tasks focus on communicative processes rather than mastery of specific linguistic content. Tasks are a-linguistic in the sense that how learners accomplish them depends on their using whatever linguistic resources are available rather than being constructed or defined by certain language choices. (See Van den Branden, this volume, for further discussion of task-based learning and teaching.)

The communicative wave thus introduced functions, strategies, the four individual macro skills of speaking, listening, reading and writing, and tasks as elements of curriculum content. These elements are aimed at developing skills in communication, or 'communicative competence'. Although communicative competence is based on an understanding of language as context-dependent, somewhat paradoxically descriptions of it tend to be a-contextual in the sense that they describe generic abilities in the four macro skills. For example, in the Council of Europe

Frame of Reference (CEFR), the self-assessment grid from the Common Reference Levels for a B1 ability in spoken interaction states:

> I can deal with most situations likely to arise whilst travelling in an area where the language is spoken. I can enter unprepared into conversation on topics that are familiar, of personal interest or pertinent to everyday life (e.g. family, hobbies, work, travel and current events).
>
> *(2001: 24)*

The descriptor is aimed at all learners and does not take into account actual contexts of use. Leung (2012: 165, cited in Richards, 2013: 27) points out:

> Quite clearly teachers will need to judge the appropriateness of the B1 descriptors (or any other within the CEFR scales) in relation to the students they are teaching. If one is teaching linguistic minority students in England who are learning to use English to do academic studies, then these descriptors would only be, at best, appropriate in a very vague and abstract sense.

A communicative view of language is not adequate for those who need English for specific professional or academic purposes, that is, for specific contexts of use, such as the linguistic minority students mentioned by Leung or adults who will use English in their professions.

Leung's comment also highlights an important feature of the complexity of language curriculum design — that the content can vary markedly depending on who the learners are, their purposes for learning and the contexts in which they are learning. One factor in that complexity is whether the students have immediate, identifiable needs for the language in or outside of the classroom. In other words, are they preparing to participate or do they already participate in a target discourse community? For these learners, it is possible to identify text types they will need to understand or produce, tasks they will need to perform and content they will need to learn. Work done in the classroom is thus actual language performance, as with immigrant children learning subject matter in and through English, or language performance that feeds into target performance, as with adults and young adults who are learning the genres and lexicon that will enable them to participate in their target discourse community.

In other environments, students' needs for the language are not linked with target discourse communities. These include school-age learners in most countries where English is a required subject, at an increasingly younger age. It also includes many adult learners who study English because it is supposed to give them economic and social opportunities. Depending on how the curriculum is designed, the classroom may focus on learning about language — the linguistic curriculum; or it may focus on learning English for communicative purposes, in which case the classroom becomes a rehearsal space for tasks that students may engage in at some later time. The curriculum may also create a context of use for the language through investigation of texts, through the learning of content or through project work.

Third wave

The third wave of curriculum content views language as a resource for meaning-making contingent on a context of use. The curriculum is organised around genre, texts, content and/or projects, each of which has the potential to engage learners in a context of use, either through apprenticeship into discourse communities as with genre and text or by creating a common focus for meaning-making through exploration of content or involvement in projects.

Genre and text-based learning

Genre and text-based approaches to syllabus are both concerned with context of use. They both view text as the unit of analysis of language. A text is language structured in a certain way "to achieve social purposes in particular contexts of use" (Hyland, 2007: 148). Genres, such as academic essays and research articles, are texts particular to a discourse community; as Paltridge points out, "Genres, in this view, both respond and contribute to the constitution of social contexts, as well as the socialisation of individuals" (2014: 303). In the language curriculum, genre is most closely associated with the teaching of writing for academic purposes. Learning genre is thus a matter of learning to construct the texts of a given discourse community in order to participate and gain membership in the community defined by the texts (see also Basturkmen and Wette, and Starfield, this volume).

Text as curriculum content is closely related to genre, and the two are often used interchangeably. According to Mickan, a curriculum that focuses on texts foregrounds their social purpose: "The priority is to determine what is going on in a context and how language is integral to what is taking place" (2013: 23). Texts are viewed as social practices that are chosen according to who the learners are and their target needs. Much of the work on texts has come out of Australia and is rooted in systemic functional linguistics (e.g. Halliday, 1975). In Australia, text-based syllabuses have served the needs of adult migrant populations and learners in schools (Feez and de Silva Joyce, 2012). For example, Mickan (2013: 64–65) describes a programme for migrant students in a secondary school science class who learn to participate in science practices through literacy events and lab work. Text practices include following textbook instructions, interpreting diagrams, conducting an experiment and interpreting and documenting results. Lexico-grammatical features of language such as 'let the solution cool' are learned while participating in the practices. In both genre and text-based approaches, the lexical and grammatical features of the language that construct the text go hand-in-hand with the expression of the text.

Content-based learning

A curriculum may also be built around subject matter content. In the secondary science example described by Mickan, the content is science. In a curriculum based on content (known as CBI or content-based instruction in US ELT and CLIL or content and language integrated learning in European ELT; see Morton, this volume), the subject matter determines the instructional texts and the kinds of tasks learners do. They investigate and demonstrate learning of the content, while also learning the language needed to understand it.

According to Ioannou-Georgiou, CLIL creates:

> an authentic setting of meaningful learning where the students can engage in exploring and finding out about the world while using a foreign language to do so. Moreover, CLIL creates a situation where the students use the language as they learn it rather than spending years 'rehearsing' in a language class for a possible opportunity to use the language some time in the future.
>
> *(2012: 496)*

The investigation of content has the potential to create a context of use in the sense that the content provides a common focus for meaning-making – exploring and finding out about the world – and for using the target language to do so; 'they use the language as they learn it.' It also makes use of the context of the classroom in ways that are congruent with its social practices. Classrooms are natural contexts for classroom texts, roles and activities that revolve around subject-matter. They are not natural contexts for other types of roles, texts and tasks, e.g. socialising, getting things done, etc. In the latter case, the classroom becomes a rehearsal space – to rehearse types of language use in the classroom that could later be 'performed' outside the classroom in target contexts or for target purposes, as in the second wave curriculum described earlier, in which learners might roleplay ordering food in a restaurant or complete simulated job applications.

Project-based learning

Project-based learning, like content-based learning, has the potential to create a context of use either in or beyond the classroom. Project-based language learning uses a project or projects as the focus of curriculum content. Learners work individually and cooperatively to complete a complex task through inquiry, research and problem solving in English. Projects involve ongoing exploration and activity and usually result in a product of some kind, such as a research report, a performance or a presentation (Beckett, 2006). For example, a teacher in Thailand (Knox, 2007) designed a course based on two student projects. The first involved planning and conducting group interviews with departing tourists at the airport about their experience in Thailand, followed by a presentation based on the interviews. The second involved organising a group tour of a temple. The projects combined work on language in preparation for and within actual contexts of use.

Technology as part of the third wave

Technology has played a role in both the linguistic and communicative curriculum waves, consonant with their underlying view of language (Dudeney and Hockly, 2012). For the third wave, especially for content and project-based learning, the Internet and Web 2.0 technologies have made it possible to design courses that are rich in content and provide means for authentic interactions and collaboration, as well as self-directed learning (Maggi et al., 2014). Since content is available for every possible theme or topic, curriculum designers, teachers and learners with Internet access have access to this wealth of content in multi-modal forms. The interactivity of Web 2.0 technology allows learners to use the language as a means for collaborating and communicating with others, thus breaking down the notion of the classroom as a closed context (see Gruba, Hinkelman and Cárdenas-Claras, this volume).

In summary, the third wave is concerned with how to organise the language curriculum so that language is used as a resource for meaning-making in contexts of use that engage learners in complex and cognitively challenging ways. Working with genre and texts prepares students to participate in contexts of use. Using content and projects takes advantage of the classroom and its technological extension as a natural context of use for investigation and research of subject matter. It should be noted that for school-age learners in countries like the US, Canada and Australia, the learning of content is a given, not a choice.

Table 6.1 summarises the three waves of curriculum according to curriculum content, the processes for learning content, and the role of student needs and context.

Making principled choices

Different ways of conceptualising language as curriculum content depicted in Table 6.1 represent understandings of language and how languages are learned based on research and theory in

Table 6.1 The three waves of language curriculum

First wave: linguistic
Language as a unified body of interrelated systems of linguistic knowledge, learned as sentence-level patterns which may be topic-based, by all learners irrespective of needs.
Second wave: communicative
Language as communication for various purposes and contexts, learned through interactions or tasks using the four macro-skills of reading, writing, listening and speaking.
Third wave
Language as contingent on particular content, social practices (genre/text) or projects, learned and used as a means to learn content, participate in practices or accomplish projects.

applied linguistics and related fields. In that sense, they are theoretical understandings of content. In practical terms, curriculum and course designers draw from different elements of these syllabuses when designing a course or programme. In this sense, there are a great many possibilities for curriculum content.

Mickan, however, cautions that the proliferation of elements has created a problem of cumulative overload in language curriculum design, noting that:

(1) There has been a continuing re-appraisal of what it is to teach a language, and in that process there has been a reluctance to give up previous conceptions of language. This is exhibited in the retention of grammar as a measure of language acquisition.

(2) In order to compensate for shortcomings in the description of language in structural terms, the models have added elements to the curriculum in a cumulative process. To syntax and lexis have been added . . . functions and notions, learners' roles and identities, communicative activities and tasks, composing strategies and learning strategies, and discourse features of text.

(Mickan, 2013: 24)

The proliferation of elements underscores a central challenge of language curriculum design: how to make principled choices among the elements. These choices depend on both a theoretical stance and a practical understanding of who the students are, the context in which they are learning and their purposes for learning. These choices are guided by the various processes of curriculum planning, the subject of the next section.

Curriculum planning processes

Curriculum planning involves a set of decisions that operate at the programme level or at the individual course level. The aim is to develop a plan for learning that is effective and realistic in enabling learners to meet the desired goals. Different curriculum specialists have labelled these processes in different ways (e.g. Richards, 2001; Nation and Macalister, 2010). For the purposes of this chapter, we will discuss the following:

- Stating guiding principles
- Analyzing contextual factors
- Assessing learner needs
- Determining aims, goals or objectives

- Deciding the scope and sequence
- Planning assessments and evaluation

While the processes appear as a sequence, in practice they overlap and mutually influence each other.

There are two major differences between planning at the programme versus planning at the course level. The first is *scale*. At the programme level, ranging from national curricula to institutional curricula, planning is aimed at designing a curriculum for different levels and, perhaps, different needs, over a span of time. At the course level, planning is aimed at designing a single course. The second, influenced by scale, is one of *alignment* among the various processes and communication among those who participate in them. In the discussion that follows, scale will be addressed with each process; alignment will be taken up in the discussion of issues in implementation.

Stating guiding principles or rationale

A statement of principles outlines the understanding of language, of learning and of learners on which the curriculum or course is based. These principles should derive from theories of language, and research on learning and on how languages are learned, and be clearly linked to learning in the classroom. Nation and Macalister caution that "There is a tendency for this connection not to be made, with the result that curriculum design and therefore learners do not benefit from developments in knowledge gained from research" (2010: 6). Stating principles helps to shape the overall aims and specific objectives of the curriculum and guide decisions about the content, process and assessment of learning.

Principles are context-dependent in the sense that they guide a particular curriculum or course for a particular group of learners in a particular context. For example, the principle below is from the US Commonwealth of Massachusetts Department of Education curriculum framework for adult learners:

> Principle 5: Language learning requires risk-taking. Adult learners will benefit from a classroom community that supports them in taking risks in authentic communication practice.
> *(Commonwealth of Massachusetts Department of Education, 2005)*

It is based on an understanding of the needs of adult learners and contributes to a common platform for administrators, materials developers and teachers as they support, design and enact curriculum.

Analyzing contextual factors

Context analysis, also called situational analysis and environment analysis, involves identifying factors in the environment, both the resources and constraints, that will have an impact on the curriculum. This process, along with learner needs assessment, is critical to creating a realistic plan and thus supporting successful enactment of the curriculum. Factors to consider include:

- Human resources, including teachers and administrative/support staff
- Physical resources, including materials, technology, space
- The educational environment: fit with other courses, examinations
- Social, cultural and political factors and related stakeholders
- Time

Once factors have been identified, decisions must be made about which factors will have the most impact and how they will be taken into account in the design of the curriculum.

Assessing learner needs

Needs assessment, also called needs analysis, involves gathering two kinds of information: about learners at the start of a programme or course and about possible or expected final outcomes. This information is then analysed to determine needs so that the curriculum can be designed to bridge the gap. An important consideration in needs assessment is whether and what type of target needs learners have. Target needs are related to where, with whom, why and how the learners are expected to use the language. Analysis of these needs enables the designer to choose tasks, texts and content the learners will read, listen to, produce or learn.

A course developer of a business English programme in Australia describes the process:

> To establish the aims and objectives, we engaged in a target situation analysis. We reviewed DEFS staff's course notes to give us an idea of the text types learners would need to master. We listed the types of texts that they would encounter and the types of assignments they would be expected to produce once they became university students. We then analyzed the assignments produced by previous international students to pinpoint the areas where they seemed to be having difficulties.
>
> *(Agosti, 2006: 103)*

As discussed earlier, one issue in the field of ELT is that learners do not always have identifiable target needs. Regardless of the context, information about the learners' background, language proficiency, interests and purposes for studying will help the designer to shape a curriculum that is at the appropriate language level, targets topics and materials that will interest them, employs approaches to learning that are appropriate to their cultural background and age, and so on.

At the course level, as most teachers do not meet their students until they start teaching them, they must rely on available information as well as previous experience they may have with such students. Needs assessment with the actual learners can be done in the initial stages of the course to gather or confirm information about learners' background, interests, learning preferences, target needs and other, similar concerns (Graves, 2000).

Determining goals, aims or objectives

Goals, aims and objectives are near-synonyms and thus are often used interchangeably. Aims and goals are generally broader and state what learners are expected to achieve by the end of the course or programme of study. Objectives are generally more specific descriptions of what students need to know or be able to do in order to achieve the goals; thus objectives 'unpack' the goals.

Table 6.2 describes the third year reading component of a three level integrated skills programme at a Turkish university. It shows a three-part structure: the overall expected outcomes related to types and lengths of text and use of strategies; how these are broken down into goals that will enable them to achieve the outcomes; and specific objectives that will enable them to achieve the goals.

Goals and objectives provide a basis for planning instruction as well as for planning both formative and summative assessments. They can be aligned with national or transnational outcomes frameworks such as the CEFR (Common European Framework of Reference) or the Canadian Language Benchmarks.

Table 6.2 Outcome, goals and objectives for Level 3 reading at a Turkish university

Overall reading outcome for Level 3

Students are expected to read and understand various factual and scientific articles and magazine and newspaper texts of 500–600 words and use various reading strategies effectively.

Goals for reading	Objectives for reading
The students will be able to:	The students will be able to:
read and summarise a text	understand grammatical items in context
be aware of the process of pre-,while and postreading	guess the meaning of vocabulary in texts
develop appropriate reading strategies	increase vocabulary knowledge
read and comprehend texts and	read for the gist
semi-technical texts	outline a reading text
read to support ideas	do decision-making tasks
read to learn technical terms	scan for specific information
read for pleasure	skim for the main idea
read up-to-date materials relevant to their field	paraphrase texts
read nonverbal information e.g. tables, graphs	

Source: Kirkgöz, 2007: 160. Reproduced with permission.

Deciding the scope and sequence of the programme or the course

Deciding the scope and sequence of the programme or course involves decisions about what should be taught and how it will be organised. At the course level, this also involves decisions about materials and methods. Decisions about programme or course content depend on the goals of the programme or course, which, in turn, depend on learners' needs, contextual factors and guiding principles. The goals are one way of defining content, as can be seen in Table 6.2, which outlines what students will do and learn with respect to reading. Deciding the actual scope of the content and its sequence shows how the content is learned in real time.

At the programme level, decisions are made about what should be taught over the entire span of the programme; how the content will be divided (e.g. into courses); what should be emphasised in each course; how the courses will complement or build on each other; and how they will be levelled and sequenced. In effect, the programme needs to be organised from a vertical perspective, i.e. how different courses for one level or group of students complement each other, and from a horizontal perspective, i.e. how courses are levelled and sequenced, and how they build on each other over time. Table 6.3 illustrates a US university ESL preparation programme for undergraduates.

The vertical curriculum shows the scope of the programme and what it includes: writing, reading, integrated skills, cross-cultural communication and content-based courses (Topics in ESL). Except for the latter, the horizontal curriculum outlines the progression of each of these components throughout the programme. For example, writing progresses to an increasingly academic focus.

The processes are similar at the course level, but on a different scale. Decisions are made about the following in a way that fits the time frame of the course:

- *what should be taught* over the span of the course, e.g. which macro skills, content, genres, grammar, vocabulary etc.

Table 6.3 IELI curriculum

	PROGRESSION			
	Level 1	Level 2	Level 3	Level 4
CONTENT	Writing I	Writing from sources	Writing from authentic texts	Writing from academic sources
	Reading I	Reading II	Reading authentic texts	Reading from academic sources
	Integrated skills	Integrated skills	Comprehending academic discourse	Comprehending lecture discourse
	Cross-culture talk	Cross-culture talk	Spoken discourse and cross-cultural communication	Academic discourse
	Topics in ESL I & II	Topics in ESL I & II	Topics in ESL III	Cross-cultural perspectives

Source: Adapted from Rawley and Roemer, 2007: 93. Reproduced with permission.

- *how the content will be divided* into modules or units of work and what they are organised around, e.g. specific themes or topics, projects, types of texts.
- *how the units of work will be sequenced* so that they build on each other (or are independent), and how the elements within the units will be interwoven.

For example, in 'Written communication for international business managers' (one of the Topics in ESL III shown in Table 6.3), students work in teams to form an imaginary company, choose a product and do market research for it. The course combines content (advertising, sales and marketing), discipline-specific vocabulary, writing business genres, as well as Internet and library research on their topic. The units of work are based on the steps of choosing the company, designing a logo, choosing a product and so forth (Rawley and Roemer, 2007).

Planning assessments and evaluation

Language assessments document student learning, for both formative and summative purposes, through tests and other instruments such as portfolios and performance assessments. Evaluation documents the effectiveness of a course or programme. Programmes engage in different types of language assessments for different purposes: for placement purposes, for diagnostic purposes, for achievement purposes, for exit from/entry to other levels. Planning for these assessments is a crucial feature of curriculum design. Planning programme evaluations is also an important part of curriculum design, as the information gathered in an evaluation about the effectiveness of the programme has an impact on its sustainability and relevance.

A key planning decision is the extent to which in-class assessments and course evaluations should be standardised across courses. This, in turn, has an effect on course assessment and evaluation. For example, an EAP programme in Canada found that separate exit tests used to progress to higher levels were too onerous for both students and teachers, and so integrated them into course final exams. Course objectives and assessment measures were standardised across levels and brought in line with Canadian Language Benchmarks (Royal et al., 2007).

At the course level, types of assessment reflect the type of content. A course that focuses on language as knowledge to be mastered will use more conventional assessment instruments such as so-called paper and pencil tests. A course that focuses on oral communication may use assessment instruments such as oral interviews. A course that focuses on mastering written genres may use assessment instruments such as rubrics.

In summary, an effective curriculum or course design is one in which the designers have:

- made explicit the educational principles that underlie the curriculum
- defined goals that are realistic for learners and account for their current abilities and future needs and are achievable with the resources and within the constraints of the context;
- chosen content and a sequence that enables learners to reach the goals;
- planned for assessments that will provide formative support toward the goals and summative information about how well the goals have been achieved;
- developed evaluations that will provide input into future iterations of the curriculum.

Why do curriculum plans often not work in practice?

As stated earlier, designing a programme and designing a course are different because of scale and the potential for misalignment between the processes. Scale has been addressed in the preceding sections by contrasting programme and course decisions. Misalignment will be addressed here. In his edited volume on curriculum in second language teaching, Johnson (1989) uses the term 'specialist' approach to describe cascading curriculum design processes in which each process is undertaken by a different group, with the results handed on to the next group until they finally reach the teacher and learners. He argues that this is, essentially, a recipe for curriculum incoherence. In order to have a coherent curriculum, these processes need to be aligned with overlapping actors at each stage. Misalignment occurs when there is a disconnect between two or more of the processes/products (e.g. policy, goals, materials, assessment) and those who carry them out. The greater the disconnect, the greater the potential for misalignment. Conversely, the closer the connection between the processes and those who carry them out, the greater the potential for alignment among the processes. We shall now look at some common examples of misalignment.

Misalignment between principles and goals on the one hand, and the context and learner needs on the other

Too often, those who develop guiding principles and programme goals design a curriculum that does not take into account or ignores contextual factors such as availability of materials, teacher experience or amount of time; or learner factors such as proficiency level and educational background. In effect, the designers state principles (or policy) and determine goals without undertaking a context analysis or needs analysis.

Misalignment between programme content and student needs

Programme content and materials are often at a proficiency level that is beyond the learners' capacity. The programme is 'aspirational' rather than realistic for the learners. The designers of a programme for Burmese adults describe such a gap, where teachers and educational decision-makers wanted the programme targeted at an upper intermediate or pre-university level, which was greatly at odds with the target students' proficiencies indicated on diagnostic testing (Julian and Foster, 2013).

The content may also be inappropriate for the learners' backgrounds and communicative needs. For example, an activity from a coursebook chosen to fulfil the government mandated communicative curriculum in Albanian secondary schools asked students to describe an accident while traveling abroad. However, as one teacher explained, "Most of them have neither been abroad nor witnessed an accident" (Seferaj, 2014: 98).

Misalignment between programme content and teacher preparation

At the programme level, accounting for or supporting teachers' understanding and acceptance of and preparation for the curriculum is one of the single most important factors in designing for successful enactment of the curriculum. For many of these teachers, the textbook is the *de facto* syllabus. Programmes based on communicative language teaching have been difficult for teachers in schools to teach because it presupposes a familiarity with sociocultural norms that the teachers, who have never participated in these contexts, do not have (Humphries, 2014). Moreover, the teachers' expected role may be at odds with their beliefs and expertise.

Misalignment between goals and intended outcomes and assessments

At both the programme level and at the course level, external assessments may be inappropriate for the content of the programme or course. In Japan, for example, government guidelines to teach language for communication in secondary schools are at odds with university entrance exams, which place a heavy emphasis on grammar and lexical knowledge (Sato and Takahashi, 2008). Thus the potential for negative washback from assessments needs to be taken into account in the curriculum planning process.

These misalignments describe disconnects between the design process and those for whom the design is intended: teachers and learners. While curriculum design should be underpinned by research and theory, it is aimed at practice – the curriculum enacted in the classroom by teacher and learners. This does not mean that curriculum should be designed for the status quo; it means that teachers need to be brought into the process in ways that respect their expertise and develop their potential.

Future directions

Future directions for the language curriculum revolve around third wave developments and the impact of technology. As English continues to grow as the global lingua franca for knowledge construction and dissemination, the third wave will continue to expand through curricula based on content, projects and social practices. In these curricula, learners use language as a *means* (e.g. to do research, to explore content, to solve problems), rather than as an *end* in itself (e.g. to learn vocabulary and dialogues). They draw on the learners' cognitive capacities in ways that allow them to learn challenging content, to work collaboratively and to direct their learning.

The expanded use of technology will continue to affect language curricula, both in terms of content and interactivity. It has become the source of materials for many third wave curricula, supplanting the traditional language textbook, which is an artefact of the first and second waves. By providing platforms for individual and collaborative learning both within and outside the classroom, it greatly expands opportunities for students to use language as a means to learn content and (co)construct knowledge.

Expansion of the third wave and the enrichment of curriculum content and learning processes through technology will not be possible, however, unless teachers are supported in learning to teach language through content, to guide, monitor and evaluate project work, to understand the relationship between text and context, and to incorporate technology in their work. This kind of support, in turn, can only happen when those who prepare teachers are themselves able to teach in ways that are consistent with these approaches, e.g. having teacher candidates unpack the relationship between text and context, engage in problem solving or connect through technology as they learn how to teach. Ideally, practicing teachers and teacher-educators would collaborate in the design of language curricula, research how they are enacted, evaluate their effectiveness and use the results of evaluation to both improve teacher education and language teaching and, ultimately, student learning.

Discussion questions

- Consider the language curriculum for a context you are familiar with. In what way does it draw upon first, second and third wave curriculum elements?
- Have you experienced incidents of curriculum misalignment and disconnect? What were the implications for subsequent teaching and learning? How were the misalignments addressed?
- What role do you think teachers should play in curriculum development?

Related topics

Communicative language teaching in theory and practice; Content and language integrated learning; English for academic purposes; English for specific purposes; New technologies, blended learning and the 'flipped classroom'; Task-based language teaching.

Further reading

Graves, K. (2000) *Designing language courses: A guide for teachers*. Boston: Heinle Cengage. (This book describes course design processes with teacher examples.)

Mickan, P. (2013) *Language curriculum design and socialisation*. Bristol, UK: Multilingual Matters. (An introduction to the theory underlying a text-based approach, with practical examples.)

Nation, I.S.P. and Macalister, J. (2010) *Language curriculum design*. London: Routledge. (This book uses a systematic approach to design, mainly at the course level.)

Richards, J. C. (2013) 'Curriculum approaches in language teaching: Forward, central and backward design' *RELC Journal,* 44/1/ 5–33. (An examination of input, process and output in three approaches to curriculum design.)

References

Agosti, C. (2006) 'Seizing the opportunity for change: The business preparation program, a new pathway to gain direct entry into Macquarie University', in M. A. Snow and L. Kamhi-Stein (eds) *Developing a new course for adult learners.* Alexandria, VA: Teachers of English to Speakers of Other Languages. 99–122.

Apple, M. (2004) *Ideology and curriculum* (3rd ed.). New York: Routledge Falmer.

Beckett, G. H. (2006) 'Project-based second and foreign language education: Theory, research and practice', in G. H. Beckett and P. C. Miller (eds) *Project-based second and foreign language education.* Greenwich, CT: Information Age Publishing. 3–16.

Canale, M. (1983) 'From communicative competence to communicative language pedagogy', in J. Richards and R. Schmidt (eds) *Language and communication*. London, UK: Longman. 2–27.

Commonwealth of Massachusetts Department of Education (2005) *Massachusetts adult basic education curriculum framework for English for speakers of other languages*. Retrieved from www.doe.mass.edu/acls/frameworks/esol.doc

Council of Europe. (2001) *Common European framework of reference for languages: Learning, teaching and assessment*. Cambridge, UK: Cambridge University Press.

Dudeney, G. and Hockly, N. (2012) 'ICT in ELT: How did we get here and where are we going?' *ELT Journal, 66/4*. 533–542.

Feez, S. and de Silva Joyce, H. (2012) *Text-based language and literacy education: Programming and methodology*. Sydney, N.S.W.: Phoenix Education.

Graves, K. (2000) *Designing language courses: A guide for teachers*. Boston: Heinle & Heinle.

Graves, K. (2008) 'The language curriculum: A social contextual perspective'. *Language Teaching, 41/2*. 149–183.

Halliday, M. (1975) *Learning how to mean: Explorations in the development of language*. London: Edward Arnold.

Humphries, S. (2014) 'Factors influencing Japanese teachers' adoption of communication oriented textbooks', in S. Garton and K. Graves (eds) *International perspectives on materials in ELT*. Basingstoke, England: Palgrave Macmillan. 253–269.

Hyland, K. (2007) 'Genre pedagogy: Language, literacy and L2 writing instruction'. *Journal of Second Language Writing*, 16. 148–164.

Ioannou-Georgiou, S. (2012) 'Reviewing the puzzle of CLIL'. *ELT Journal, 66/4*. 495–504.

Johnson, R.K. (1989) 'A decision-making framework for the coherent language curriculum', in R.K. Johnson (ed.) *The second language curriculum*. Cambridge: Cambridge University Press. 1–23.

Julian, K. and Foster, D. (2013) 'Design meeting context: A general English course for Burmese adults', in J. Macalister and I. S. P. Nation (eds) *Case studies in language curriculum design*. London: Taylor & Francis. 21–39.

Kirkgöz, Y. (2007) 'Innovation as a curriculum renewal process in a university in Turkey', in A. Rice (ed.) *Revitalizing an established program for adult learners*. Alexandria, VA: Teachers of English to Speakers of Other Languages. 135–160.

Knox, J. (2007) 'Foreign eyes on Thailand: An ESP project for EFL learners', in A. Burns and H. de Silva Joyce (eds) *Planning and teaching creatively within a required curriculum for adults*. Alexandria, VA: Teachers of English to Speakers of Other Languages. 119–142.

Leung, C. (2012) Outcomes-based language teaching. In A. Burns and J. C. Richards (eds) *The Cambridge guide to pedagogy and practice in language teaching*. New York: Cambridge University Press. 161–179

Long, M. and Crookes, G. (1992) 'Three approaches to task-based syllabus design'. *TESOL Quarterly, 26/1*. 27–56.

Maggi, F., Cherubin, M. and Pascual, E. G. (2014) 'Using Web 2.0 tools in CLIL', in S. Garton and K. Graves (eds) *International perspectives on materials in ELT*. Basingstoke, England: Palgrave Macmillan. 198–215.

Mickan, P. (2013) *Language curriculum design and socialisation*. Bristol, UK: Multilingual Matters.

Munby, J. (1978) *Communicative syllabus design*. Cambridge: Cambridge University Press.

Nation, I.S.P. and Macalister, J. (2010) *Language curriculum design*. London: Routledge.

Omaggio, A. C. (1986) *Teaching language in context*. Boston: Heinle and Heinle.

O'Malley, J. M. and Chamot, A. (1990) *Language learning strategies in second language acquisition*. Cambridge: Cambridge University Press.

Oxford, R. (1990) *Language learning strategies. What every teacher should know*. Boston: Heinle and Heinle.

Paltridge, B. (2014) 'Genre and second-language academic writing'. *Language Teaching*, 47. 303–318.

Rawley, L. A. and Roemer, A. (2007) 'Reading, writing, and web-page design: Content-based courses within a skills-based curriculum', in A. Rice (ed.) *Revitalizing an established program for adult learners*. Alexandria, VA: Teachers of English to Speakers of Other Languages. 79–99.

Richards, J. C. (2001) *Curriculum development in language teaching*. New York: Cambridge University Press.

Richards, J. C. (2013) 'Curriculum approaches in language teaching: Forward, central and backward design'. *RELC Journal, 44/1*. 5–33.

Royal, W., White, J. and McIntosh, H. (2007) 'Revitalizing a curriculum: The long and winding road', in A. Rice (ed.) *Revitalizing an established program for adult learners*. Alexandria, VA: Teachers of English to Speakers of Other Languages. 57–78.

Sato, K. and Takahashi, K. (2008) 'Curriculum revitalization in a Japanese high school: Teacher-teacher and teacher-university collaboration', in D. Hayes and J. Sharkey (eds) *Revitalizing a curriculum for school-age learners*. Alexandria, VA: Teachers of English to Speakers of Other Languages. 205–238.

Seferaj, K. (2014) 'Coping with new teaching approaches and materials: An east-European EFL teacher's interpretation of communicative teaching activities', in S. Garton and K. Graves (eds) *International perspectives on materials in ELT*. Basingstoke, England: Palgrave Macmillan. 89–103.

Wilkins, D.A. (1976) *Notional syllabuses*. Oxford: Oxford University Press.

Ylimaki, R. M. (2013) 'Create a comprehensive, rigorous and coherent curricular program', in R. M. Ylimaki (ed.) *The new instructional leadership: ISLLC standard two*. New York: Routledge. 27–44.

7

ELT materials
Claims, critiques and controversies

John Gray

Introduction

Although materials have been defined very broadly in the ELT literature as consisting of more or less "anything which presents or informs about the language being learned" (Tomlinson, 1998: xi; see also McGrath, 2002), three main types have been identified. The most significant and widely disseminated type consists of *published materials*, which includes an ever growing array of items such as textbooks, ancillary audio-visual accompaniments, workbooks, learner dictionaries, guided readers, online courses and online supplements to traditional textbook-based courses. Increasingly, online resources comprise interactive white board activities and programmes (apps) designed to run on mobile devices such as smartphones and tablets. A second type is made up of so-called *authentic materials,* consisting of newspapers, magazines, songs and all other content which was not designed for pedagogical use but which is brought into classrooms by teachers. Finally, there are *teacher-made materials,* which comprise the wide range of sources of input or practice material which teachers design themselves and use to supplement or to replace existing resources. Regardless of type, materials have consistently been accorded a key role in the literature of "pinning down the procedures of the classroom" and imposing structure on the complexities of second language teaching and learning (Hutchinson and Torres, 1994: 319). The focus of this chapter is on published materials, given their enduring centrality in classrooms around the world as purveyors of thematic content, syllabus and curriculum (particularly in the case of state school education, where specific values may have to be imparted) and as realisations of method and sources of examination preparation and practice.

To date, the most common type of published material has been the textbook, also known in the literature as the 'coursebook', a term which refers to the fact that specific courses taking students through a series of pre-determined levels tend to consist of several books. Despite a considerable amount of discussion about the move towards postmethod pedagogy (Kumaravadivelu, 2001; see also Hall, this volume, ch. 15), in which it might be expected that textbooks would play a less central role, scholars such as Akbari (2008: 647) have argued convincingly that "the concept of method has not been replaced by the concept of postmethod but rather by an era of textbook-defined practice". However, as the UK Publishers Association (2014: 53) points out, the concept of the textbook in ELT is undergoing significant change in the early twenty-first century, as "core sales are now derived not only from course books and reference books, but also more modular, flexible, blended and online solutions". Examples are the many online courses whose software profiles students in terms of level, tracks their progress and offers what is referred to as 'adaptive' or 'personalised' learning. Although these 'solutions' are currently being actively promoted by publishers globally, the textbook (for the time being) retains its centrality – although the form in which it is delivered is becoming increasingly diversified (see Gruba, Hinkelman and Cárdenas-Claros, this volume, for further discussion in the context of blended learning and the flipped classroom).

Before going any further, it should be noted that European and North American publishers exercise a powerful influence on ELT publishing globally. Although local publishers in many parts of the world *do* produce materials for their own markets, in some settings they are not always able to compete with global competitors – particularly when it comes to the introduction of specific methods such as communicative language teaching (CLT; see Thornbury, this volume) or task-based learning (see Van den Branden, this volume). Kumaravadivelu (2016) explains how educational reform aimed at accelerating the move towards CLT in China in 2001 did little for local publishing houses. Despite the decentralisation of textbook production and local publishers being authorised by the authorities to produce suitable materials for the change in policy, Kumaravadivelu (2016: 74–75) notes that, with few exceptions, ELT textbooks:

> continue to be produced by center-based publishing industries or their subsidiaries located in China. In other words, the official policy of decentralization of the textbook market has not resulted in the devolution of power and authority to the peripheral ELT community. The dominating agency of the center-based publishing industry is too powerful to overcome.

As will be suggested below, this appears to be a process which is likely to continue, if not intensify. This chapter proceeds by outlining briefly the case that has been made for the use of published materials in ELT and some of the arguments traditionally put forward against them. I then consider developments in materials research before focusing in greater detail on key areas of dispute and debate which surround materials. Finally, I consider the future directions of published materials and the implications and challenges these are likely to presuppose for English language teachers.

Published materials: for and against

The most common arguments proposed in favour of published materials are that they are a source of linguistic and thematic input for teachers, who are thus spared the time and effort of having to produce such content themselves; that they are increasingly designed to align with syllabuses such as the evermore globally disseminated Common European Framework of Reference for Languages (CEFR), which they structure for both teachers and students; that they prepare students to take the proliferation of high-stakes international tests, as well as tests which are country-specific; that they provide students with opportunities for independent learning (by providing, in some cases, grammar summaries, self-check exercises and learner training activities); and that, when accompanied by a teacher's manual, they provide novice teachers with on-the-job training (McGrath, 2002; Richards, 2014). In addition, it has been suggested that they frequently contain information about the target culture (Harmer, 2001) – selective and problematic though this has been shown to be (Gray, 2010a; see also Kramsch and Zhu, this volume, for further discussion of the potentially contentious notion of 'culture') – and that they are particularly useful for managing and effecting change in education sectors globally, where change (in the sense of curriculum renewal or implementation of new teaching methods or approaches to learning) has become endemic (Hutchinson and Torres, 1994).

Despite these claims, published materials – and textbooks in particular – have attracted a considerable amount of censure. Brumfit (1980: 30) famously argued that while textbooks (specifically those aimed at the global market) did have the potential to help teachers, "many of them don't . . . and masses of rubbish is skilfully marketed". He continued, drawing attention to what would become two of the most enduring charges levelled against them – their capacity to deskill teachers (Littlejohn, 1992) and their problematic status as educational tools which are also commodities whose "prime function [is] to earn their producers a living" (Apple, 1985: 149; see also Gray, 2013a). Deskilling refers to the way in which many such materials position teachers as mere deliverers of the content they contain rather than as decision makers who select, reject and modify content on the basis of specific local requirements. At the same time, it has been suggested that textbooks (when not produced locally) can be methodologically and culturally inappropriate – for example, failing to recognise that certain 'communicative' activities may be at odds with local educational culture or that the focus on consumerism often found in UK-produced textbooks for the global market may be alien to the students (Appleby, 2010; see also Holliday, this volume).

However, most criticism of published materials has been directed at the representational practices governing their production – on the one hand, the representation of language for pedagogical purposes and the inaccuracies and omissions this frequently entails (McCarthy and Carter, 1995; Wajnryb, 1996; Roberts and Cooke, 2009; Angouri, 2010); on the other hand, the representation of the world and the *mis*representation and/or erasure of specific categories of people and the consequences this may have for students (Gray, 2013b; Gray and Block, 2014; Chun, 2016). These issues are dealt with at some length in sections below.

Although many of these scholars are critical of the form published materials currently take, they are not necessarily against the idea of published materials *per se*. One critic who *is* against their centrality in teaching, however, is Thornbury (2000, 2001, 2013) who argues that languages are best learned through a materials-light pedagogy of scaffolded talk in which students experience language *use* (i.e. language deployed with communicative intent), as distinct from the study of language *usage* (i.e. language understood in terms of grammatical rules) of the kind found in published materials. From this perspective, textbooks and their inevitable attempts to pre-package learning represent an interference in a process which is understood as essentially experiential and "contingent on the concerns, interests, desires and needs of the user" (Thornbury, 2001: 11) – and he argues that language learning needs to remain so, if the conditions for learning are to be optimised.

However, persuasive as many have found his case to be, published materials look set to remain part of ELT for the foreseeable future. There are a number of reasons for this. On the one hand, instructed second language learning in most parts of the world is an activity of concern to ministries of education and testing bodies of various kinds, for whom pre-stated and measurable learning outcomes are considered essential. In such conditions, published materials continue to be seen as the most effective tools for guaranteeing that these outcomes are met – problematic though the implied cause-and-effect association between materials (if not teaching itself) and learning outcomes might be. On the other hand, as Akbari (2008: 646–647) has indicated, the material lives of many teachers are often difficult, and thus such artefacts, for all their shortcomings, are welcome, arguing that:

> Teachers in many contexts are not different from factory workers in terms of their working hours; in many countries, a typical language teacher works for 8 hours per day, 5 or even 6

days per week. . . . Textbooks now take care of all the details of classroom life, and most of them come with teacher guides that include achievement tests and even all the examples teachers need in their classes.

In such circumstances, published materials assume a centrality in teaching – even in settings where the teachers who use them may be critical of aspects of content. Indeed, it could be argued that one of the reasons published materials have proved so enduring is that most teachers are neither trained nor (crucially) paid to develop alternatives.

Developments in materials research

A focus on micro and macro issues

Surveying the development of research into ELT materials at the beginning of the second decade of the twenty-first century, Tomlinson (2012) noted that despite their centrality in instructed second language learning, it was surprising how little attention published materials had received traditionally in the applied linguistics literature – a situation he saw as having changed significantly in the mid-1990s. His own edited volume (Tomlinson, 1998) was significant in this change, and his subsequent work (e.g. Tomlinson, 2003, 2008, 2012), coupled with the appearance of a raft of books (mostly edited volumes) and academic papers (e.g. Chun, 2009, 2016; Gray, 2010a, 2010b, 2013c; Harwood, 2010, 2014; Mishan and Chambers, 2010; Littlejohn, 2012; Garton and Graves, 2014), are testament to the current vitality of research into ELT materials.

As this area of research has grown, two main interrelated tendencies have become noticeable in the literature – on the one hand, those involved in researching ELT materials are increasingly reflective about the nature of the field in which they work, and on the other, there is evidence of greater interdisciplinarity in the approach to research being carried out. With regard to the former tendency, one of the most commonly deployed terms in the growing literature is 'materials development', which is used by Tomlinson (2012: 143–144) as the superordinate term for *all* research in the area:

> 'Materials development' refers to all the processes made use of by practitioners who produce and/or use materials for language learning, including materials evaluation, their adaptation, design, production, exploitation and research.

Clearly this covers a wide range of very different activities, and, indeed, Tomlinson (2012), following Littlejohn (1992), points out that *materials evaluation* (a normative activity which considers how materials *should* be) and *materials analysis* (a descriptive and hermeneutical activity concerned with how materials *are* and why) are distinct activities. For this reason Gray (2013a: 13), whose work has focused mainly on materials analysis, suggests that:

> materials analysis, precisely because it is focused on content (including the ways in which content comes into being and the ways in which it is used in classrooms), is best understood as an activity which does not take place under the umbrella of materials development. While the aim of materials development is the (immediate) production of materials for use in specific classrooms, analysis tends to be more concerned with identifying and interpreting actually existing content (whether contemporary or historical). . . . From this perspective *materials research* might be a more appropriate superordinate, consisting of materials development on the one hand and materials analysis on the other.

This case for an enhanced role for ELT materials analysis is in line with the established tradition of (largely textbook) analysis in mainstream education, in which macro socio-historical issues are accorded the same attention as micro issues of design, evaluation and adaptation (e.g. Anyon, 1981; Apple, 1985; Apple and Christian-Smith, 1991; Provenzo et al., 2011). In a not dissimilar vein, Garton and Graves (2014: x) argue that research into ELT materials needs to be broadly based, pointing out that "[i]f we narrow our view of materials to embrace only issues of design, evaluation, and application, we obscure their indexical significance", by which they mean the political and ideological systems within which they are located. Similarly, Littlejohn (2012: 285) makes the case for consideration of the social and historical context of materials production:

> Materials production, in this view, can be seen as potentially resonating in tune with social forces far beyond language teaching itself, and far beyond the immediate discussions of language teaching professionals, even though, to borrow Marx's words, materials writers may imagine that such discussions form the real motives and starting point of their activity.

These concerns with indexicality and social structures also relate to the second tendency noticeable in the literature, namely the above-mentioned increase in interdisciplinary perspectives, particularly in the area of materials analysis. The move towards greater attention being paid to materials in applied linguistics from the mid-1990s onwards can be related to developments in the field more generally. During this period, Holliday (1996), Rampton (1997) and Edge and Richards (1998) made the case for much greater interdisciplinarity in the field. For all of them, this entailed a broadening of the scope of applied linguistics to encompass a much fuller intellectual engagement with the social sciences. Holliday (1996: 235) argued the need for those involved specifically in ELT research to develop a *sociological imagination* (a term borrowed from the sociologist C. Wright Mills), which he took to mean "the ability to locate oneself and one's actions critically within a wider community or world scenario". In fact, a number of scholars had already begun to draw attention to the need to consider ELT critically from a more macro social perspective than had hitherto been the case (Phillipson, 1992; Pennycook, 1994), and several had identified the centrality of materials analysis in this endeavour (Porreca, 1984; Auerbach and Burgess, 1985; Dendrinos, 1992; Littlejohn, 1992). In the long run, what this has meant is that the broader systems of relations within which published materials are imbricated – and specifically the political, commercial and ideological dimensions of these relations – have begun to assume greater significance in the literature.

Interdisciplinarity and academic rigour

This change of emphasis can be seen as a shift from a consideration of ELT materials exclusively as *curriculum artefacts* (in which the concern is with issues such as syllabus and methodology) to one in which they are also seen as *cultural artefacts* (in which the focus is on the meanings they seek to create for teachers and students, and the conditions of their production, circulation and consumption). Thus materials research currently reveals a variety of disciplinary influences which include cultural and media studies (Gray, 2010a; Harwood, 2014), sociology (Littlejohn, 2012) and theoretical perspectives derived from postmodernism (Kullman, 2003, 2013), Marxism (Gray and Block, 2014) and critical pedagogy (Thornbury, 2013; Chun, 2016).

At the same time, Harwood (2010, 2014) argues that while there has been a considerable amount of very useful qualitative analysis of textbook content, some research reveals the need for greater rigour, particularly with regard to coding procedures (such as rigorously determining categories for counting and analysis) and reliability checks (such as inter-rater reliability tests). He gives examples of two studies from the field of education which looked at mathematics textbooks and those for the teaching of L1 reading from which, it is suggested, ELT research could benefit (Valencia et al., 2006; Drake and Sherin, 2009). Both were conducted over several years, both were rigorously triangulated in terms of research design, and both consisted of sizeable data bases consisting of hours of classroom observation and multiple interviews with the teachers involved. In line with Tomlinson (2012), Harwood argues that it is to the detriment of research into ELT materials that no such longitudinal studies exist in our own field. Similarly, Gray (2013a) has drawn attention to the work of the Georg Eckert Institute (GEI) as an example of an orientation to materials research from which there is much to be learned. This materials research centre was established in Germany in 1975 and is described on the GEI website as being dedicated to 'research into school textbooks', in which "structures of knowledge and models of identities conveyed via state education", along with "[c]onstructions of the self and the other, processes of cultural translation, and practices of memory in the context of educational media" are key areas of investigation (www.gei.de). The GEI has been influential in carrying out extensive historical and contemporary textbook research in a range of international settings, as well as initiating in 2012 a major study of digital materials in the German state school system. The *UNESCO Guidebook on Textbook Research and Textbook Revision* (Pingel, 2009), which was written in conjunction with the GEI, argues the case for a socio-political perspective on materials analysis and provides clear methodological guidelines for approaches to textbook research. That such work – in addition to the work of a wide range of scholars from across the social sciences – is now being cited increasingly in the ELT materials literature could be seen as indicative of the emergence of a more sociological imagination on the part of materials researchers.

Key areas of dispute and debate

While the field of materials research may be said to be entering a period of maturity, a number of areas of dispute and debate surrounding materials themselves have proved enduring. As suggested earlier, these revolve around the representation of language for pedagogical purposes and the representation of the world and its inhabitants.

Representation of language

The issue of *authenticity* is central to ongoing discussions of ELT materials (McGrath, 2002; Waters, 2009; Harwood, 2010; Richards, 2014). Traditionally, *authentic language* referred to the kind of language found in what were called authentic texts – i.e. those which were not produced for pedagogical purposes but for audiences of so-called native speakers or highly proficient second language users. The rationale for the privileging of such language and such texts (particularly in CLT) was that exposure to language being used with communicative (as opposed to pedagogical) intent was held to give students "a taste of the real world" and served to prepare them "for that real world" (McGrath, 2002: 23) – in ways which exposure to contrived and simplified texts produced by materials writers did not.

From the late 1980s onwards, authenticity was also invoked in the case for a more corpus-based approach to the description of language in which attested examples of language-in-use were seen as providing more accurate models than those normally found in pedagogical grammar (Willis, 1990; see also Frankenberg-Garcia, this volume). The proliferation of various kinds of corpora (e.g. written English, spoken English, academic English, etc.) provided information about frequency and collocation, and also showed that much of what speakers and writers produced was pre-packaged and heavily reliant on fixed and semi-fixed chunks of language. In addition, corpora of spoken English (Carter and McCarthy, 1995; McCarthy and Carter, 1995) revealed that informal British speech was characterised by pervasive ellipsis (omissions as in 'Having a lovely time'), the use of vague language (expressions such as 'kind of', 'Where's that thing for propping the door open?'), reinforcement tags ('Nice drink, that'), varieties of syntactic 'dislocation' whereby elements within an utterance could be placed outside clause boundaries for greater emphasis ('They went to Greece, Mel and Debra, just to get away from it all') – to say nothing of false starts, overlaps, incomplete utterances and other disfluencies. Corpus studies also showed that many of the 'rules' of pedagogical grammar as described in published materials were not always confirmed, while additionally revealing that particular functions of certain grammatical forms were entirely absent (McCarthy and Carter, 1995).

Scholars such as Cook (1998), while recognising that corpus findings did have pedagogical implications, were quick to point out that new descriptions of language did not automatically translate into prescriptions for teaching. Given that ELT takes place in such diverse settings, not all students can be said to have the same needs or require access to the same kinds of English (see also Seargeant, this volume). For example, the idiomaticity of spoken British English may be relevant to migrants to the UK and those planning on studying there, but may be of less use to students whose needs are more focused on academic writing, those who may wish to learn North American English, or those living in countries where English is an established second language with its own local standard. And, indeed, Carter and McCarthy (1995) recognise that corpora need to chosen carefully if students, teachers and materials writers are to benefit from the descriptions they provide.

However, despite the impact of the corpus revolution in descriptive linguistics, corpora have made a limited impression on published materials such as textbooks (although they have impacted significantly on dictionaries and grammars). This is partly as a result of opinion being divided over the value of so-called authentic language in ELT generally (Waters, 2009; Tomlinson, 2012), with many scholars and teachers taking the view that such language may be of limited value and culturally too remote to be accessible to students and teachers, many of whom are L2 speakers, but also because contrived samples of language in which linguistic items can be artificially repeated for purposes of salience may be considered more useful from the perspective of learning. The limited impact of corpora can also be related to the lack of uptake of the first corpus-based course – the *Collins COBUILD English Course* (Willis and Willis, 1988). This course was based entirely on a lexical syllabus consisting of individual words selected on the basis of frequency, along with a high proportion of lexical chunks and an eschewal of what might be called traditional grammar. A product of the early days of the corpus revolution, the course simply proved too unfamiliar for many teachers.

Several years later, and keen to sound less corpus-driven, materials writers Gairns and Redman (2006) described an alternative approach. Their *Natural English* course is based on an initial analysis of a corpus of English language students' talk (which helped them determine what they felt students at various levels needed) and information derived from the British National Corpus. Their approach to the vexatious issue of the relevance of the kind of idiomaticity often found in corpora containing spoken data was clearly informed by the view that not all corpus descriptions were appropriate for pedagogy:

> We have, therefore, tried to focus on language which is used naturally by native speakers or proficient speakers of the language, but also sounds natural when used by L2 learners. So, at this elementary level for example, we want learners to use high-frequency and relatively

informal ways of thanking people such as *thanks* and *thanks a lot*; but we have not introduced the more colloquial phrases such as *cheers* or *ta*.

(Gairns and Redman, 2006: 6)

Although somewhat vague as to what sounding 'natural' actually means, their caution regarding 'more colloquial phrases' resonates with the views of teachers interviewed by Gray (2010a). These teachers took the view that when English was being learned as an international language, so-called native speaker idiomaticity was not a high priority. A similarly judicious approach to corpus data has been adopted in the *Touchstone* course (McCarthy et al., 2005). This is marketed as being corpus-*informed* – as opposed to corpus-*based* – and the course website states that it *draws on* (rather than *is driven by*) "extensive research into the corpus of North American English in the Cambridge English Corpus – a large database of everyday conversations and texts that show how people actually use English" (www.cambridge.org).

Such innovations aside, Waters (2009) points out that contrived texts and contrived samples of language continue to predominate in most published materials. While the case for such language has been convincingly made (Ellis, 1999), it has also been argued that greater use of corpora would provide students with the opportunity for exposure to naturally occurring language which many actually need (McCarthy and McCarten, 2010; see also Thornbury, 2005). A number of areas – all related to spoken discourse – have been identified as worthy of attention. Gray (2010a) has argued that despite the fact that English is being used increasingly as an international language, there are few instances in the listening components of published materials of students being exposed to authentic samples of English from Outer and Expanding Circle countries (Kachru, 1985; also Seargeant, this volume). He contends (in line with interview data he collected from teachers working in Spain, most of whom saw themselves as teaching English as an international language) that if students are to be empowered to decode the speech of those who do not speak with General American accents, Received Pronunciation (RP) or modified RP, the listening components of published materials might usefully include more diverse samples of naturally occurring speech than is currently the case. On the same theme of student empowerment, Wajnryb (1996) argued that the contrived dialogues found in textbooks being used in Australia were of little use in preparing students for the kind of interactions they were likely to have to engage in outside school. Her study revealed an absence of any consideration of the role of context in affecting linguistic choice. There was no attention to pragmatic meaning – for example, the way in which a statement such as 'It's hot in here' might actually be an indirect request to have a window opened. There was also a focus on interactions which were typified by symmetrical power relations which were devoid of all threats to face (Brown and Levinson, 1987). Threats to face, or face-threatening acts, most frequently refer to requests or commands which are generally worded in such a way so as to signal the speaker's awareness of the degree of imposition and the speaker's wish to show respect for the addressee's sense of self-worth – for example, 'I can see you're busy at the moment, but I just wanted to remind you I need those figures by 4 o'clock.' These charges can still be made of most published materials.

Other studies have compared the representation of particular speech events such as job interviews, doctor-patient consultations (Roberts and Cooke, 2009) and business meetings (Angouri, 2010) found in published materials with ethnographically gathered data. These have shown that the pedagogical representations are often seriously misleading – not only in terms of language used but also in terms of the way in which such events are structured. While recognising that ethnographic data, like corpus data, do not translate straightforwardly into recipes for teaching, Roberts and Cooke make a very plausible case for published materials being much more research-informed in this regard.

Representation of the world

A second area of concern in the materials literature is with the representation of the world and the people in it. This work has focused mainly on the cultural and ideological aspects of materials produced in Inner Circle countries (Kachru, 1985) aimed at the global market. Critics argue that, since the 1980s, celebratory discourses of individualism, entrepreneurialism and free-market capitalism have been, and continue to be, repeatedly deployed in these materials in ways which give cause for concern (e.g. Dendrinos, 1992; Pegrum, 2004; Chun, 2009; Gray, 2010a, 2010b, 2012). Referred to by publishers in interviews (Gray, 2010a) as 'aspirational content', the assumption appears to be that the repeated association of English with spectacular personal and professional success, effortless global mobility and the power to consume is what motivates students to learn (although there are no studies to support this). At the same time, such materials are shown to be typified by the progressive erasure of working-class characters, themes and concerns from the late 1980s onwards (Gray and Block, 2014) and a relentlessly heteronormative view of human relations in which lesbian, gay, bisexual and transgender (LGBT) characters are rendered invisible (Nelson, 2006; Gray, 2013b). Such practices, these writers suggest, have potentially negative consequences not only for those working-class and LGBT students who are denied recognition (see also Liddicoat, 2009) but for all students who are thereby presented with a skewed view of the world and who are simultaneously denied a vocabulary for talking about a reality in which social classes (and the inequalities they imply) and sexual minorities exist. Other scholars have identified the deployment of culturally and racially essentialised discourses in accounts of immigrant success stories in materials designed to teach English for academic purposes (Chun, 2016). Given the highly competitive nature of ELT publishing, it has been argued that such representational practices are in most cases commercially motivated – whether in terms of perceived market sensitivity regarding supposedly 'inappropriate' content or ascribed student aspiration (Gray, 2010a). And it is to the commercial aspect of published materials that the final section of this chapter now turns, given that this is likely to impact significantly on future developments.

Future developments

Across much of the world, education in the twenty-first century is increasingly being subjected to commercial forces under the aegis of neoliberal economic policies, which seek to extend the reach of the market. In such an environment, multinational companies (memorably described by Ball (2012) as 'edu-businesses') providing a range of 'educational services' and 'solutions' have come to occupy an important role, not only in the private sector but also in increasingly privatised public sectors. Ball cites Pearson, the world's largest education company, as emblematic of one such edu-business, which produces not only ELT materials and tests for the global market but also provides a raft of additional services. He reports that, in 2011, Pearson signed a new memorandum of understanding with the Chinese Ministry of Education and the General Administration of Press and Publishing (the agency responsible for regulating all print and digital media), which saw the company become involved in teacher training, translation and Chinese and English language teaching and assessment. Such involvement, Ball argues, means that edu-businesses (and Pearson is only one of many) are often powerfully positioned "*to agitate for policies which offer further opportunities for profit*" (Ball, 2012: 126) (emphasis added).

At the same time, as part of Pearson's declared aim to become "the world's pre-eminent provider of English language learning content, technology and services" (Pearson website, in Ball, 2012: 126), the company acquired the Wall Street Institute chain of language schools in 2009 and the Global Education and Technology Group (specialising in ELT testing) in 2011. The UK

Publishers Association (2014: 53) commented on the "striking case of Pearson" as indicative of the transformation of the ELT industry "into vertical integration, from curriculum design and other consultancy services through the traditional materials publishing to high-stakes assessment and continuing professional development for teachers". The Wall Street Institute has its own 'method' and, although students do have periodic access to a teacher in what are known as 'encounters' (rather than lessons), content is delivered digitally and learning takes place almost entirely online. As suggested earlier, 'solutions' to teaching and learning in which digital materials figure prominently are currently being promoted by most ELT publishers – partly because such materials are cheaper to produce and partly because of the opportunities they provide to further structure learning. In recent years, the UK Publishers Association (2010, 2014) has drawn attention to the commercial challenge posed by the increased costs of print production, increased storage and transportation costs, the fluctuating price of paper, the difficult economic situation in southern Europe and political turmoil in many parts of the world. For ELT publishers, it states, "this means continuing the push into digital" with the prospect of offering "complete solutions" (The Publishers Association, 2014: 54). Complete solutions refer not only to the learning management systems (LMS) which allow for the delivery of digital content but increasingly to *adaptive learning* – that is the ability of the LMS being used to profile the software user in ways which theoretically allow for more personalised learning. At the same time, adaptive learning is linked to assessment in ways that could be seen to be advantageous to those edu-businesses which are also test providers:

> It is more important than ever that publishers get close to their end users – the learners and teachers. This is the age of 'big data', which is nowhere more important than in education, where individualised learning can be possible only with better data about learning through continuous assessment. This data feeds back into more effective learning materials and better learning outcomes for students. In line with these trends and market demands, publishers are investing directly in and combining forces with assessment bodies, linking learning to assessment, providing formative and learning-orientated assessment for personalised learning, and tapping into the emergent technologies of adaptive learning.
>
> *(The Publishers Association, 2014: 54)*

Despite the case for the affordances of technologically mediated teaching and learning materials being addressed in the literature (e.g. Rahman and Cotter, 2014), a number of critical voices have been raised with regard to the ways in which this is happening and the interests which are ultimately being served (Selwyn, 2014). Significantly, a major systematic review of computer-assisted language learning concluded that an "exhaustive search of the literature on technology in primary and secondary teaching of English as an L2 has not yielded clear or sufficient evidence of its effectiveness", and added that this was "of some concern given the very large amounts of funding that are being made available worldwide for the purpose of encouraging its use for whatever reasons, political, economic or pedagogical" (Macaro et al., 2012: 24). Furthermore, as materials writer Kerr (2014) has pointed out, "[w]hat LMSs, adaptive software and most apps do best is the teaching of language knowledge (grammar and vocabulary), not the provision of opportunities for communicative practice." Ironically, as Kerr explains, such moves towards adaptive learning are being carried out (in conjunction with major publishing companies) in settings (he gives the example of Turkey) where the government's aim is precisely to make teaching more communicative. It could be argued that in such a scenario, the deskilling of teachers referred to by Littlejohn (1992) with regard to print materials is currently entering a new phase. The classroom event, traditionally seen as a co-production between teacher and students in interaction with materials (Allwright, 1981), is potentially being reconfigured as a co-production of students and personalised digital materials, to the near exclusion of teachers.

Conclusion

By way of summary, we can say that ELT materials research is enjoying a period of great vitality and, in common with developments in applied linguistics more generally, has assumed an increasingly interdisciplinary character. Meanwhile, in a globalised world where a plurality of varieties of English are used and are constantly evolving, the kind of English contained in published materials has become a matter of debate and looks set to remain so. At the same time, issues related to the representation of the world in published materials have been put firmly on the agenda, as indeed has the political economy of materials production, dissemination and consumption. More research is now needed in the area of materials-in-use and the ways in which inscribed meanings are recontextualised in classroom settings. Such work is necessary to complement the recent wave of textbook analyses, which has shed much needed light on the way materials currently are and the reasons for this. Against this backdrop of burgeoning research, published materials themselves are changing as new technologies are embraced by publishers. Such change tends to come with the promotional promise of enhanced learning – a claim which some have viewed with considerable scepticism. Certainly the implications of new technologies are likely to be central to debates about the role of published materials in ELT for decades to come.

Discussion questions

- What role, if any, should corpus descriptions of English play in materials design?
- What options do teachers have for dealing with ideological content and systematic omissions in published materials?
- Is it alarmist to suggest that adaptive learning 'solutions' have the potential to deskill teachers?
- Given the concerns and critiques of ELT materials outlined in this chapter, why do you think ELT textbooks continue to be so widely used in the profession?

Related topics

Appropriate methodology; Communicative language teaching in theory and practice; Corpora in ELT; Language and culture in ELT; Method, methods and methodology; Politics, power relationships and ELT; World Englishes and English as a Lingua Franca.

Further reading

Littlejohn, A. (2012) 'Language teaching materials and the (very) big picture'. *Electronic Journal of Foreign Language Teaching*, 9/1. 283–297. (This paper locates ELT materials production firmly within the macro social and historical context.)

Macaro, E., Handley, Z. and Walter C. (2012) 'A systematic review of CALL in English as a second language: Focus on primary and secondary education'. *Language Teaching*, 45/1. 1–43. (A comprehensive overview of the use of technology in second language learning which identifies the lack of evidence for its effectiveness.)

Tomlinson, B. (2012) 'Materials development for language learning and teaching'. *Language Teaching*, 45/2. 143–179. (A comprehensive overview of the state of research into materials development and the ways in which it is likely to develop.)

John Gray

References

Akbari, R. (2008) 'Postmethod discourse and practice'. *TESOL Quarterly*, 42/4. 641–652.

Allwright, R. (1981) 'What do we want teaching materials for?' *ELT Journal*, 36/1. 5–18.

Angouri, J. (2010) 'Using textbook and real-life data to teach turn-taking in business meetings', in N. Harwood (ed.) *English language teaching materials: Theory and practice*. Cambridge: Cambridge University Press. 373–394.

Anyon, J. (1981) 'Ideology and United States history books', in R. Dale, G. Esland, R. Fergusson and M. MacDonald (eds) *Education and the state: Politics, patriarchy and practice*. Basingstoke: The Falmer Press. 21–39.

Apple, M. W. (1985) 'The culture and commerce of the textbook'. *Journal of Curriculum Studies*, 17/2. 147–162.

Apple, M. W. and Christian-Smith, L. K (eds) (1991) *The politics of the textbook*. London: Routledge.

Appleby, R. (2010) *ELT, gender and international development myths of progress in a neocolonial world*. Clevedon: Multilingual Matters.

Auerbach, E. and Burgess, D. (1985) 'The hidden curriculum of survival ESL'. *TESOL Quarterly*, 19/3. 475–495.

Ball, S. J. (2012) *Global Education Inc.: New policy networks and the neo-liberal imaginary*. Abingdon: Routledge.

Brown, P. and Levinson, S. C. (1987) *Politeness: Some universals in language usage*. Cambridge: Cambridge University Press.

Brumfit, C. (1980) 'Seven last slogans'. *Modern English Teacher*, 7/1. 30–31.

Carter, R. and McCarthy, M. (1995) 'Grammar and the spoken language'. *Applied Linguistics*, 16/2. 141–158.

Chun, C. (2009) 'Contesting neoliberal discourses in EAP: Critical praxis in an IEP classroom'. *Journal of English for Academic Purposes,* 8. 111–120.

Chun, C. (2016) 'Addressing racialized multicultural discourses in an EAP textbook: Working toward a critical pedagogies approach'. *TESOL Quarterly.* 50/1. 109–131.

Cook, G. (1998) 'The uses of reality – a reply to Ronald Carter'. *ELT Journal*, 52/1. 57–63.

Dendrinos, B. (1992) *The EFL textbook and ideology*. Athens: N.C. Grivas.

Drake, C. and Sherin, M. G. (2009) 'Developing curriculum vision and trust: Changes in teachers' curriculum strategies', in J. T. Remilliard (ed.) *Mathematics teachers at work: Connecting curriculum materials and classroom instruction*. New York: Routledge. 321–337.

Edge, J. and Richards, K. (1998) 'May I see your warrant, please?: Justifying outcomes in qualitative research'. *Applied Linguistics*, 19/3. 334–356.

Ellis, R. (1999) 'Input-based approaches to teaching grammar: A review of classroom-oriented research'. *Annual Review of Applied Linguistics*, 19. 64–80.

Gairns, R. and Redman, S. (2006) *Natural English*. Oxford: Oxford University Press.

Garton, S. and Graves, K. (eds) (2014) *International perspectives on materials in ELT.* Basingstoke: Palgrave Macmillan.

Gray, J. (2010a) *The construction of English: Culture, consumerism and promotion in the ELT global coursebook*. Basingstoke: Palgrave Macmillan.

Gray, J. (2010b) 'The branding of English and the culture of the new capitalism: Representations of the world of work in English language textbooks'. *Applied Linguistics*, 31/5. 714–733.

Gray, J. (2012) 'Neoliberalism, celebrity and "aspirational content" in English language teaching textbooks for the global market', in D. Block, J. Gray and M. Holborow (eds) *Neoliberalism and applied linguistics*. London: Routledge. 86–113.

Gray, J. (2013a) 'Introduction', in Gray, J. (ed.) *Critical perspectives on language teaching materials*. Basingstoke: Palgrave Macmillan. 1–16.

Gray, J. (2013b) 'LGBT invisibility and heteronormativity in ELT materials', in J. Gray (ed.) *Critical perspectives on language teaching materials*. Basingstoke: Palgrave Macmillan. 40–63.

Gray, J. (ed.) (2013c) *Critical perspectives on language teaching materials*. Basingstoke: Palgrave Macmillan.

Gray, J. and Block, D. (2014) 'All middle class now? Evolving representations of the working class in the neoliberal era: The case of ELT textbooks', in N. Harwood (ed.) *English language teaching textbooks: Content, consumption, production*. Basingstoke: Palgrave Macmillan. 45–71.

Harmer, J. (2001) 'Coursebooks: A human, cultural and linguistic disaster?' *Modern English Teacher*, 10/3. 5–10.

Harwood, N. (ed.) (2010) *English language teaching materials: Theory and practice*. Cambridge: Cambridge University Press.

Harwood, N. (ed.) (2014) *English language teaching textbooks: Content, consumption, production.* Basingstoke: Palgrave Macmillan.

Holliday, A. (1996) 'Developing a sociological imagination: Expanding ethnography in international English language education'. *Applied Linguistics,* 17/2. 234–255.

Hutchinson, T. and Torres, E. (1994) 'The textbook as agent of change'. *ELT Journal,* 48/4. 315–328.

Kachru, B. (1985) 'Standards, codification and sociolinguistic realism: The English language in the outer circle', in R. Quirk and H. G. Widdowson (eds) *English in the world: Teaching the language and the literature.* Cambridge: Cambridge University Press/ British Council. 11–30.

Kerr, P. (2014) 'Adaptive learning markets: Talking Turkey'. [Adaptive Learning in ELT blog] Retrieved from https://adaptivelearninginelt.wordpress.com/2014/12/15/adaptive-learning-markets-talking-turkey/

Kullman, J. (2003) *The social construction of learner identity in the UK-published ELT coursebook.* Unpublished PhD thesis, University of Kent.

Kullman, J. (2013) 'Telling tales: Changing discourses of identity in the 'global' UK-published English language coursebook', in J. Gray (ed.) *Critical perspectives on language teaching materials.* Basingstoke: Palgrave Macmillan. 17–39.

Kumaravadivelu, B. (2001) 'Towards a postmethod pedagogy'. *TESOL Quarterly,* 35/4. 537–560.

Kumaravadivelu, B. (2016) 'The decolonial option in English teaching: Can the subaltern act?'. *TESOL Quarterly,* 50/1. 66–85.

Liddicoat, A. (2009) 'Sexual identity as linguistic failure: Trajectories of interaction in the heteronormative language classroom'. *Journal of Language, Identity, and Education,* 8. 191–202.

Littlejohn, A. (1992) *Why are ELT materials the way they are?* Unpublished PhD thesis. Lancaster University.

Littlejohn, A. (2012) 'Language teaching materials and the (very) big picture'. *Electronic Journal of Foreign Language Teaching,* 9/1. 283–297.

Macaro, E., Handley, Z. and Walter, C. (2012) 'A systematic review of CALL in English as a second language: Focus on primary and secondary education'. *Language Teaching,* 45/1. 1–43.

McCarthy, M. and Carter, R. (1995) 'Spoken grammar: What is it and how can we teach it?' *ELT Journal,* 49/3. 207–218.

McCarthy, M. and McCarten, J. (2010) 'Bridging the gap between corpus and course book: The case of conversation strategies', in F. Mishan and A. Chambers (eds) *Perspectives on language learning materials development.* Bern: Peter Lang. 11–32.

McCarthy, M., McCarten, J. and Sandiford, H. (2005) *Touchstone.* Cambridge: Cambridge University Press.

McGrath, I. (2002) *Materials evaluation and design for language teaching.* Edinburgh: Edinburgh University Press.

Mishan, F. and Chambers, A. (eds) (2010) *Perspectives on language learning materials development.* Bern: Peter Lang.

Nelson, C. (2006) 'Queer inquiry in language education'. *Journal of Language, Identity and Education,* 5/1. 1–9.

Pegrum, M. (2004) 'Selling English: Advertising and the discourses of ELT'. *English Today,* 20/1. 2–10.

Pennycook, A. (1994) *The cultural politics of English as an international language.* New York: Longman.

Phillipson, R. (1992) *Linguistic imperialism.* Oxford: Oxford University Press.

Pingel, F. (2009) *UNESCO guidebook on textbook research and textbook revision.* Paris/Braunschweig: UNESCO.

Porreca, K. (1984) 'Sexism in current ESL textbooks'. *TESOL Quarterly,* 18/4. 705–724.

Provenzo, E. F., Shaver, A. N. and Bello, M. (eds) (2011) *The textbook as discourse: Sociocultural dimensions of American schoolbooks.* London: Routledge.

Rahman, A. and Cotter, T. (2014) 'English language learning through mobile phones', in S. Garton and K. Graves (eds) *International perspectives on materials in ELT.* Basingstoke: Palgrave Macmillan. 159–177.

Rampton, B. (1997) 'Retuning in applied linguistics'. *International Journal of Applied Linguistics,* 7/1. 3–25.

Richards, J. (2014) 'The ELT textbook', in S. Garton and K. Graves (eds) *International perspectives on materials in ELT.* Basingstoke: Palgrave Macmillan. 19–36.

Roberts, C. and Cooke, M. (2009) 'Authenticity in the adult ESOL classroom and beyond'. *TESOL Quarterly,* 43/4. 620–642.

Selwyn, N. (2014) *Distrusting educational technology: Critical questions for changing times.* Abingdon: Routledge.

The Publishers Association (2010) *PA statistics yearbook 2009.* London: The Publishers Association.

The Publishers Association (2014) *PA statistics yearbook 2013.* London: The Publishers Association.

Thornbury, S. (2000) 'A dogma for EFL'. *IATEFL Issues,* 153. 2.

Thornbury, S. (2001) 'Coursebooks: The roaring in the chimney'. *Modern English Teacher,* 10 (3): 11–13.

Thornbury, S. (2005) *Beyond the sentence: Introducing discourse analysis.* Oxford: Macmillan.

Thornbury, S. (2013) 'Resisting coursebooks', in J. Gray (ed.) *Critical perspectives on language teaching materials*. Basingstoke: Palgrave Macmillan. 204–223.

Tomlinson, B. (1998) *Materials development in language teaching*. Cambridge: Cambridge University Press.

Tomlinson, B. (2003) *Developing materials for language teaching*. London: Continuum.

Tomlinson, B. (2008) *English language learning materials: A critical review*. London: Continuum.

Tomlinson, B. (2012) 'Materials development for language learning and teaching'. *Language Teaching*, 45/2. 143–179.

Valencia, S. W., Place, N. A., Martin, S. D. and Grossman, P. L. (2006) 'Curriculum materials for elementary reading: Shackles and scaffolds for four beginning teachers'. *The Elementary School Journal*, 107. 93–120.

Wajnryb, R. (1996) 'Death, taxes, and jeopardy: Systematic omissions in EFL texts, or life was never meant to be an adjacency pair'. ELICOS plenary delivered in Sydney, Australia.

Waters, A. (2009) 'Advances in materials design', in M. H. Long and C. J. Doughty (eds) *The handbook of language teaching*. Oxford: Blackwell. 311–326.

Willis, D. (1990) *The lexical syllabus*. London: Collins COBUILD.

Willis, J. and Willis, D. (1988) *Collins COBUILD English course*. London: Collins COBUILD.

8

Dealing with the demands of language testing and assessment

Glenn Fulcher and Nathaniel Owen

Introduction

A remarkable amount of teacher time is devoted to assessment and testing. Assessment is the broader term, encompassing any activity in which data is collected from learners from which we make judgments about their proficiency or progress. It includes, for example, informal classroom quizzes and peer- and self-assessment, and is free from the restrictions imposed by formal testing (Fulcher, 2010: 67–92). Testing is the more specific term that refers to formal or standardised testing for the purposes of certification or decision-making. Tests are usually constructed and provided by examination agencies with the authority to issue certificates that are recognised for purposes such as entry to higher education or employment.

The purpose of this chapter is to introduce teachers and students of applied linguistics to the key concepts and terminology needed to understand the role of standardised language testing and of assessment in the language classroom, and to utilise the testing and assessment literature. We discuss assessment for learning, i.e. how teachers can embed assessment into classroom activities to enhance learning opportunities. We consider the politics of externally mandated testing and the role of teachers in preparing learners to take examinations. This is a highly controversial area, and so we make recommendations for best practice based upon the concept of 'reverse engineering'. The chapter concludes with a discussion of assessment literacy for language teachers.

Critical issues and topics

Motivation and learning

Why do teachers spend so much time preparing learners to take tests and writing tests for their own use? Teachers often hold two related beliefs about the value of tests. The first is that a test acts as a motivational tool for study and learning, incentivising increased effort on the part of the learner (Eklöf, 2010). This is a long-held belief. Ruch (1924) referred to a test as "the day of reckoning", which encourages learning through establishing clear intermediate and long-term goals. It is also recognised that working towards a qualification is a source of motivation that may not otherwise be present. As Latham (1877: 146) recalls from the introduction of the very first school assessments, "The efficacy of examinations as a means of calling out the interest of a pupil and directing it into the desired channels was soon recognized by teachers."

The second belief is somewhat more contentious. In a nutshell, the view is that if tests are designed to carefully reflect the knowledge, skills and abilities (KSAs) that are the goals of an educational programme, the existence of the test will guide the efficient and effective learning of relevant content as well as motivate learning. This is usually termed *measurement driven instruction*. Popham (1987: 682) expresses the strongest form of this position: "It can be empirically demonstrated that a carrot-laden cart will provide a powerful incentive if placed in the path of an underfed pony." While this may be a classic case of putting the cart before the horse, the argument is clear: it is the test that creates a challenge.

Classroom-based assessment

Classroom-based assessment (CBA) is an overarching term for the use of assessment to promote learning and includes approaches such as assessment for learning (AFL) (Turner, 2012). Classroom assessments are designed to provide feedback that leads to learning. Swain (2000: 100) refers to this as the "notice the gap principle". Feedback is *descriptive* rather than *evaluative* (Rea-Dickins, 2006). The purpose is to help the learner to become aware of the current state of their L2 development and what needs to be learned to reach the desired target. Research suggests that appropriate classroom assessment practices lead to improved learner self-esteem and motivation, lower needs for extrinsic reward and raised levels of success (Black et al., 2003). It therefore relates directly to learner motivation (see Lamb, this volume). Classroom-based assessment activities are flexible and open, including the creation of portfolios, group discussions and presentations, process writing and multi-stage simulations. The guiding principle for the creation of activities is the engagement of learners in communication. For this reason, group work is highly valued. Similarly, the assessment of learning outcomes is not limited to the teacher. Self- and peer-assessment are highly valued, which requires learner training in the recognition of their current abilities in comparison with where they wish to reach. The role of the teacher is one of facilitation, and key teaching skills include effective questioning and providing quality feedback. The latter may include verbal or written information, but scores are not required. Much more important is ensuring classroom time for learners to respond to feedback. Managing effective classroom assessment requires exceptional classroom management and lesson-planning skills.

External tests

The reason for using external tests has been termed the *test mandate* (Davidson and Lynch, 2002). The mandate may be under the control of schools, as they select tests that best meet the certification needs of their learners. At other times, the test is imposed by an education authority in order to implement a national syllabus (measurement-driven education policy) or to introduce accountability practices for teachers and schools. The use of test data to construct school league tables or to rank order countries according to scores on language tests creates tools by which teachers and institutions are evaluated. Evaluations may be directly linked to interventions in the school, disciplinary measures or teacher pay (Mansell, 2007). Shohamy (2001) identifies this use of language tests as the primary reason for teachers' dislike and mistrust of testing. She argues that it enforces the values of the elite and punishes those who do not conform. While it is true that testing can have negative impacts such as social exclusion, history shows that in some cases it has also spurred curriculum development and been instrumental in achieving significant advances for the underprivileged and disenfranchised (Mill, 1859/1998: 118–119). For example, without the evolution of public examinations in the nineteenth century, the goals of opening the professions and civil service to the middle classes on meritocratic principles would not have been possible (Roach, 1971). The establishment of examination boards such as the Cambridge Syndicate was part of this reform movement (Watts, 2008: 40–41). The use of testing in social reform has arguably shaped the provision of unbiased access to educational and employment opportunities in societies across the world (Zeng, 1999). It is therefore possible to make a positive case for the role of testing as a tool for the maintenance of meritocratic processes in modern democracies (Fulcher, 2015).

Washback

The use of external tests has been shown to affect the work of teachers in schools and the expectations of learners. The study of testing effects is termed *washback* (Wall, 2012). Alderson and Wall (1993) developed a set of 'washback hypotheses'. These include: a test will influence teaching; a test will influence learning; a test will influence what teachers teach; a test will influence how teachers teach; a test will influence the rate and sequence of teaching; and so on. While it has been discovered that washback is endemic in education, it has been impossible to articulate a theory that predicts where or how washback will occur. Nor are we much closer to isolating contextual variables that are predictive of how teachers or learners will react to the use of tests. For example, under what conditions might a teacher revert to the use of 'past papers' as teaching materials, linked to a strategy of classroom test-taking followed by analysis of correct/incorrect answers? Concern over the impact of tests on education has also resulted in a new focus on test development. If new tests can be designed in such a way that they promote positive washback, we may be able to avoid the worst consequences of test-preparation (or cramming) that focuses only on test-taking strategies rather than language learning. As Fulcher and Davidson (2007: 144) argue, "The task for the ethical language tester is to look into the future, to picture the effect the test is intended to have, and to structure the test development to achieve that effect. This is what we refer to as '*effect-driven testing*.'"

Key concepts

Test purpose

Testing always has a purpose. Carroll (1961: 314) expressed this most eloquently: "The purpose of language testing is always to render information to aid in making intelligent decisions about possible courses of action." A test is constructed of one or more *prompts*, to which learners respond. The responses are treated as *evidence* for the existence of some knowledge, skill or ability (KSA) and the degree of its presence. In classroom-based tests, the evidence is treated *formatively*, which means that the evidence is used to enable learners to see where they are at present and how they may improve. In external proficiency tests, the evidence is treated *summatively*, which means that decisions are being made about an individual at the end of some programme of study. Other purposes for testing include placing learners in suitable classes so that learning materials are challenging but not too difficult, or assessing their achievement against a set of learning objectives over a specified time.

Stakes

The consequences of test outcomes may be fairly benign, as is always the case with classroom-based assessment. These are low-stakes assessments. However, in many cases the consequences are high-stakes. This is usually the case with external proficiency tests, the outcome of which may mean that the test taker cannot, for example, attend university, may not graduate or cannot apply for a job or move to another country. Teachers must understand whether an assessment or test is high stakes for their learners, as this is likely to impact upon their motivation and the kinds of activities or tasks that they wish to focus on in class.

Referencing

Tests are usually classified as either norm-referenced (NR) or criterion-referenced (CR). A NR test is so called because it is designed to create the maximum discrimination between test takers along a continuous scale. The main requirement for interpretation is the normal distribution of scores. The meaning of the score is its place in the continuum, because the test taker is being compared with all other test takers drawn from the same population. This may be useful when it is necessary to select a predetermined number of candidates, for example. A CR test focuses on a distinction between *mastery* and *non-mastery*, with reference to some absolute definition that resides in a real-world domain (Fulcher and Svalberg, 2013). CR test interpretation asks the question whether a learner has achieved mastery to perform as, for example, an air traffic controller or an international teaching assistant, irrespective of the scores of other test takers.

Validity

In high-stakes testing, validity is about whether and to what extent our inferences about the meaning of a test score are true. A validity argument sets out the evidence and theory to support the claim we make for score meaning. The kinds of evidence that we would typically expect to find in an argument may include a comparison of the test content with the kinds of communication we would find in the real world. We may find studies relating test scores to an external criterion, such as academic performance in the first year of university study. In some cases, the differential performance of known groups of *masters* and *non-masters* may show that the test is capable of discriminating between target groups. For example, we may find evidence from conversation analytic studies that show learner speech reflects a predicted range of functions or conversational features. Thus, the type of evidence required to support a validity argument depends upon the claims we make for the scores. The theory we expect to see in the validity argument provides the rationale for claiming that the evidence presented supports the proposed score interpretation. In low-stakes tests, particularly classroom-based assessments, validation evidence may be collected informally. Validity questions we might ask would include: has the feedback resulted in learner improvement? Are the tasks engaging and challenging for learners at this level? Is learner motivation improving?

Reliability and dependability

In high-stakes tests, it is essential to demonstrate that scores are *reliable*, which means that they are *consistent* across facets of the testing context. Such facets usually include time, place, interlocutor and rater/marker. If a test assesses proficiency to engage successfully in service encounters, the score should not change if the test is taken two or three times over one week, apart from normal random error due to chance factors; over longer periods of time, a score may of course change, either because of further study or attrition. Similarly, the score should not vary depending upon where the test is taken, who the interlocutor may be or who rates the performance, as these facets are irrelevant to what we wish to assess.

It should be noted that any claim regarding 'irrelevant facets' is directly related to the theory underlying the test. For example, if it is claimed that speaking is a socially co-constructed activity and that the demonstrated proficiency of an individual is variable depending upon the speaking partner, the interlocutor facet suddenly becomes relevant. In this case, it would be essential to collect a number of speaking samples holding all facets of the task stable but using a different interlocutor for each sample.

The concept of *dependability* is similar to that of reliability but applies to CR assessments. The question in this case is the extent to which individuals are classified in the same way across facets. It is not just a matter of obtaining reliable scores but of making dependable classifications of individuals to meaningful categories. Within educational institutions, for example, it would be highly desirable if any individual learner was classified as a master or non-master irrespective of the member of staff conducting the assessment or the particular task selected. If we are able to do this, our decision-making processes are strengthened and outcomes are more easily defended.

Reliability and dependability are important because they reflect concerns for *fairness* in all assessment practices. The overriding principle is that all learners should have an equal opportunity at the point of assessment. In practice, this implies that there should be no *bias* towards or against any subgroups of the population and that the scores should be *independent* of test method facets that are irrelevant to what we are assessing. In high-stakes contexts, it is also important to be aware that a failure to maintain either principle may lead to charges of discrimination against test takers (Fulcher, 2014).

Key areas of dispute and debate

Policy, politics and fairness

We have already intimated that external testing increasingly impinges upon language learners and teachers. There is a vocal critical applied linguistic voice arguing that "Test results have detrimental effects for test takers" (Shohamy, 2001: 15) because the very purpose is to *discriminate*. In testing, discrimination is usually considered to be a 'good thing' because it separates test-takers out for decision-making purposes. However, for critical applied linguists, *discrimination* retains its usual pejorative meaning.

Similarly, there is a view that all washback on teaching and teachers is negative. Smith (1991) has summarised the arguments that are now periodically rehearsed in the literature. When used for accountability purposes, test scores are published by school or region, and this can lead to negative morale among teachers whose students do not score highly. This potential shift in the use of test scores from the assessment of individual learning to reporting average group performance can be used to evaluate teachers and educational institutions. In turn, this puts pressure on teachers to spend more time attempting to raise average test scores rather than delivering a broad curriculum. This is precisely the opposite of Popham's claim (noted earlier in the chapter) that measurement-driven instruction improves learning. Many externally mandated tests also use large numbers of multiple-choice items. There is a very good reason for this. The multiple-choice item raises the reliability of any test because it allows the collection of more individual pieces of evidence about performance and it is possible to create items that discriminate exceptionally well for a known population. However, many teachers use multiple-choice items for teaching and examination preparation at the expense of creative language learning activities.

Standards

Accountability is facilitated by the growth in standards-based assessment, which is driven by the national or international use of *standards*, to which testing practices are obliged to conform (Hudson, 2012). Standards documents are usually made up of subject content with sets of arbitrary levels against which learners are matched (Cizek and Bunch, 2007: 18). In language testing, the most commonly used standards documents are those of the American Council on Teaching English as a Foreign Language (ACTFL), the Canadian Language Benchmarks (CLB) and the Common European Framework of Reference (CEFR) in Europe. Their use may be fairly benign, providing a framework for the development of assessments for particular purposes, or they may be used for the implementation of policy and the harmonisation of educational systems (Fulcher, 2004). In worse-case scenarios, teachers are required to align their tests to the standards, thus removing a great deal of professional discretion from classroom assessment. This could be interpreted as the 'invasion' of the classroom by standardised testing practices. Crease (2011) refers to such a super-system as a *metroscape*. It represents an attempt to ensure that the outcomes of all tests and assessments can be quantified in the same 'currency', which is given its value by the institution that prints the units and recognises them for use in education and employment. The effect has been the creation of an *alignment industry*, which has come to view mapping test scores to external standards as a validation process in its own right – for example, the mapping of institutional tests to the CEFR (e.g. Martyniuk, 2010). There are always (at least) two sides to every case. For some, the use of a common currency makes sense if qualifications and certificates are to be accepted across national borders (Jones, 2013). For others, it is a feature of unwanted political control that undermines the use of tests for defined purposes, subverts validity theory and threatens teacher independence (Fulcher, 2016).

Implications and challenges for ELT practice and practitioners

Living in the modern metroscape

The first challenge for ELT practitioners is to work out just where they stand on the contentious issues that we have outlined. Do you believe in measurement-driven teaching, or does the dominance of tests undermine your professionalism and the quality of the learning experience? Should you use tests to motivate learners or aim to develop intrinsic motivation for learning? Do you wish all your tests to be based on, and interpreted in terms of, an external set of standards? Or do you believe in an ecologically sensitive assessment where interpretation is context dependent? The answer to these questions does not come entirely from assessment theory, but from the values that you bring to the profession of language teaching.

In this section, we wish to illustrate the implications of value-driven choices in one particular area. We have already suggested that the use of external tests has a profound effect on teacher and learner behaviour. We know this from washback research. Learner motivation to pass external tests also brings pressure on teachers to engage in test-preparation practices. The metroscape also enlists parents or sponsors, principals and heads to create an environment in which the teacher is required to 'get students through the exam' and upon which their effectiveness is judged. This is a familiar scenario in language education the world over. We believe that teachers faced with these pressures can use classroom-based assessment practices to deal with the demands of external testing regimes.

Test preparation practices

Popham (1991: 13) suggests that classroom practice should be guided by two principles. The first is the educational correlate of the Hippocratic Oath, that "no test preparation practice should violate the standards of the education profession." This essentially rules out raising test scores by altering them during or after the test or assisting others to circumvent test security. It also prevents teachers from excluding learners expected to get low scores from taking the test in order to artificially inflate averages for the benefit of the institution's place in league tables. The second is the educational defensibility clause, which states that "No test preparation practice should increase students' test scores without simultaneously increasing student mastery of the content domain tested." This principle rules out focusing on test-taking strategies such as learning tricks for guessing the correct answer in a multiple-choice item or memorising canned responses to speaking or writing prompts (pre-prepared answers to lists of common questions). Haladyna et al. (1991) refer to the score-raising effect of these practices as 'score pollution'. In such cases, the inference from score to what a learner can do is weakened or destroyed completely. Validity is undermined. In very high-stakes contexts such as air traffic control, the results of unethical practice can also be extremely dangerous.

The question we therefore wish to address is how language professionals might ethically prepare learners for tests. This question is specifically considered with the impact of external tests upon teachers, and we choose this as a focus because we think it is one of the greatest challenges that teachers face in the metroscape that is set to dominate language education for the foreseeable future. What we wish to do is offer an approach to test preparation that maintains the principles set out by Popham.

Reverse engineering

One solution that we propose for language teachers is *reverse engineering* (RE). This is defined as "the creation of a test specification from representative sample items" (Davidson and Lynch, 2002: 41). A *test specification* is the blueprint, or design document, that states what the test is designed to assess and how it should do that. A test specification therefore contains a statement of the purpose of the test and the range of items or tasks that the test should contain. It may also include information about the topics that might be used, where texts should come from and how difficult they might be. It also contains sample items or tasks so that someone who is asked to write them could see what was intended by the test designer. Specifications are never put into the public domain. What teachers and learners see is a general description of the test, along with sample 'papers' that illustrate what might be expected to appear on any particular test form.

Reverse engineering is the process of analysing the content of the test in order to recreate the specification. The reverse-engineered specification does not have to be exact; it merely has to be accurate enough to identify the key skills, ability or knowledge that the test was designed to assess. The process may be aided by any documentation that the test providers do place into the public domain for test takers and teachers.

Fulcher and Davidson (2007: 57–58) identify test deconstruction reverse engineering as relevant to teachers who wish to prepare learners to take tests. The purpose of this type of RE, carried out by teachers, is to discover what the test is designed to assess, uncover the KSAs that the test writers value and relate these to the goals of learners in the institution. The intention is not to produce more items or tasks similar to those in the test but to design learning activities suitable for a classroom that target the skills valued by the assessment system. When teaching reading, for example, an analysis of the variety of genres used, topics, lexical range, difficulty and target audience may inform the search for learner reading material. The item types will reveal the reading skills valued, such as understanding explicit information, identifying main points, summarising detail, skimming, scanning, interpreting diagrammatic information, making inferences or comparing and contrasting different arguments across texts. Such an analysis provides a rich starting point for the design and production of creative learning activities that do not rely on testing practice or test-type items. It is hypothesised that the use of learning activities that are much closer to the kind of tasks found in classroom-based assessment are more likely to lead to learning than the use of the kinds of tasks found in tests. If this is the case, as the classroom-based assessment research claims, learners will acquire the target skills without engaging in test-taking strategies. Such learning, it is claimed, will translate into higher test scores if the tests are valid measures of those skills.

Examples of RE to support ethical test preparation are provided by Owen (2011). Analysing one item in relation to an IELTS reading text on population movement and genetics provides rich information to inform reading pedagogy; we reproduce two paragraphs from the text and the test item in Figure 8.1 and its RE deconstruction in Figure 8.2.

A: Text

An important project, led by the biological anthropologist Robert Williams, focused on the variants (called Gm allotypes) of one particular protein – immunoglobin G – found in the fluid portion of human blood. All proteins 'drift' or produce variants, over the generations, and members of an interbreeding human population will share a set of such variants. Thus, by comparing the Gm allotypes of two different populations (e.g. two Indian tribes), one can establish their genetic 'distance', which itself can be calibrated to give an indication of the length of time since these populations last interbred.

Williams and his colleagues sampled the blood of over 5,000 American Indians in western North America during a twenty-year period. They found that their Gm allotypes could be divided into two groups, one of which also corresponded to the genetic typing of Central and South American Indians. Other tests showed that the Inuit (or Eskimo) and Aleut* formed a third group. From this evidence it was deduced that there had been three major waves of migration across the Bering Strait. The first, Paleo-Indian, wave more than 15,000 years ago was ancestral to all Central and South American Indians. The second wave, about 14,000–12,000 years ago, brought Na-Dene hunters, ancestors of the Navajo and Apache (who only migrated south from Canada about 600 or 700 years ago). The third wave, perhaps 10,000 or 9,000 years ago, saw the migration from North-east Asia of groups ancestral to the modern Eskimo and Aleut.

Glossary for the Whole Text

1   New World: the American continent, as opposed to the so-called Old World of Europe, Asian and Africa
2   modern Native American: an American descended from the groups that were native to America
3   Inuit and Aleut: two of the ethnic groups native to the northern regions of North America (i.e. northern Canada and Greenland)
4   DNA: the substance in which genetic information is stored
5   crown/root: parts of the truth
6   incisor/premolar/molar: kinds of teeth

Figure 8.1   An example of an IELTS test reading item

Source: Cambridge University Press, 2009: 70–73.

B: Test item

The reading passage refers to the three-wave theory of early migration to the Americas. It also suggests in which of these three waves the ancestors of various groups of modern Native Americans first reached the continent.

Question 22.

Stem: Classify the groups named in the table below as originating from:
A – the first wave; B – the second wave; C – the third wave.

Inuit   22. . . . .   **[ANSWER: C]**

Figure 8.1 (Continued)

Textual reference: "The third wave, perhaps 10,000 or 9,000 years ago, saw the migration from North-east Asia of groups ancestral to the modern Eskimo and Aleut."

Response Attribute: test taker should recognise wording 'three-wave theory' from question stem and scan the text to identify the corresponding paragraph (D). Test taker should then recognise textual cohesion throughout the paragraph ("the first . . . the second . . . the third . . ."). Lexical linking of stem words 'originating from' and text word 'ancestral' is required to answer question confidently.

Figure 8.2 Reverse engineering deconstruction of example test item

The first important observation is that no background knowledge is required to answer this item correctly. This is provided by the glossary, which may be substituted in a classroom environment by pre-teaching lexical items. The selection of the correct response then involves a three-stage process. The first is the identification of the paragraph that contains the required information, and this can be done by scanning to match lexical items from the prompt to text. The selection of answer C requires an ability to understand and identify the common textual structuring device of enumeration. Once identified, the Inuit group must be matched to the correct wave by recognising synonymy between prompt and text.

Armed with this analysis, the teacher may design reading tasks drawing upon texts of varying and increasing complexity that assist learners in scanning, identifying discourse structure markers and recognising synonyms/antonyms. This is good practice in reading pedagogy, not mindless test preparation (Grabe and Stoller, 2013).

Future directions

The language classroom has become increasingly complex. As language teachers, we are required to reconcile innumerable conflicting priorities and demands. We believe that the modern metroscape is perhaps the most significant factor that impinges upon classroom practice. This is perhaps not surprising – test scores have become a commodity. They are the vehicle by which learners travel on to further educational opportunities or acquire positions that will secure their economic future. The desire to get higher test scores can even become an end in its own right, which is why some learners begin to believe that short cuts (such as cheating) are a viable option. We are not going to change the market value of test scores. The challenge facing us is therefore engaging with learners, their sponsors and the institutions for which we work to show that sound pedagogy and ethical practice are not in conflict with success in tests.

The example of reverse engineering that we have given is a strategy to identify what is valued by high-stakes tests and to create non-test tasks that target those skills and abilities. These tasks may be used in classroom-based assessment for learning. This begins to break down the division between the summative and the formative. It does assume, of course, that the external test has been designed to assess abilities that we wish to teach and which are relevant to the future success of our learners. For the most part, the examination boards and agencies that create high-stakes tests do have a theoretical basis that links test content to a defined purpose. But if we believe and can show that this is not the case, we have a responsibility to look for alternative tests that will support rather than frustrate our pedagogy.

The ambition is to keep the responsibility for teaching and learning firmly with the classroom teacher. To deal with the challenges we have outlined, it is essential that all language professionals are assessment literate. In the coming years, one of the key challenges will be to continue to refine our definition of what language professionals need to know about assessment to improve learning (Fulcher, 2012) and devise new strategies for delivering that literacy in both initial teacher education and continuing professional development. This may be in the form of seminars and conferences. It may be largely delivered online. But best practice will surely be for teachers to work together in local contexts to develop their own learning materials and share best practice in using assessment for learning. Solutions that are ecologically sensitive to specific contexts and learners are almost always preferable to the alternatives. They empower learners and teachers to improve learning and, ultimately, test scores as well.

Discussion questions

- To what extent do tests motivate learners? How might you define 'motivation' and the types of tests that may impact upon it? A related additional reading and a video is available at: http://languagetesting.info/features/motivation/mil.html.
- Examine the principles and methods of assessment for learning (AFL) available at: http://languagetesting.info/features/afl/formative.html. How might you create the time to implement particular AFL strategies in your own teaching context?
- The Programme for International Student Assessment (PISA) is run by the OECD (Organisation for Economic Cooperation and Development). Their literacy tests compare country performance, and inferences are drawn about likely future economic performance. Examine the PISA tests and data at their website: http://www.oecd.org/pisa/home/. Are the inferences drawn from scores sound? Are there any flaws in the tests or the steps in the OECD arguments? What are the likely impacts of such testing on education policy in the country where you work? Is there any likely washback on your teaching environment?
- The three most widely used testing standards documents are:
  - ACTFL: http://www.actfl.org/publications/guidelines-and-manuals/actfl-proficiency-guidelines-2012
  - CLB: http://www.language.ca/
  - CEFR: http://www.coe.int/t/dg4/linguistic/Source/Framework_EN.pdf

Which do you think may be helpful in designing your own assessments? How would you use the document(s) in your own context?

- The International Language Testing Association (ILTA) publishes:
  - a Code of Ethics http://www.iltaonline.com/index.php/en/resources/ilta-code-of-ethics
  - Guidelines for Practice http://www.iltaonline.com/index.php/en/resources/ilta-guidelines-for-practice

To what extent do you think these offer reasonable guidance for your own classroom practice in test preparation and assessment?

Related topics

Educational perspectives on ELT; Language curriculum design; Values in the ELT classroom.

Further reading

The three texts recommended for further reading represent graded reading in language testing and assessment, from an introductory text to an advanced resource book. The advanced book was written first, and the other two commissioned at a later date to provide a coherent progression of topics and difficulty.

Douglas, D. (2010) *Understanding language testing*. London: Hodder Education/ Routledge. (An introductory text that explains basic terminology and key concepts in language testing, outlines the skills required to design and use language tests, and introduces simple statistical tools for test analysis. No prior knowledge of language testing is assumed.)

Fulcher, G. (2010) *Practical language testing*. London: Hodder Education/Routledge. (An intermediate text that deals with the purpose of testing in context and an analysis of test use in society. The text then follows the 'test development cycle' to explain in detail the process of test design, implementation and interpretation.)

Fulcher, G. and Davidson, F. (2007) *Language testing and assessment: An advanced resource book*. London & New York: Routledge. (The ten sections in this volume each address a key issue in language testing, including: validity, test specifications, the nature of constructs, designing and piloting tests, scoring, ethics and fairness. Each section is accompanied by a key article from the field and related activities for groups and individuals.)

Website: http://languagetesting.info (An extensive language testing website providing links to articles and journals, videos explaining key concepts, podcasts and features on a range of topics, study scenarios, statistical resources, and daily language testing news from the world's media.)

References

Alderson, J. C. and Wall, D. (1993) 'Does washback exist?' *Applied Linguistics*, 14/2. 115–129.

Black, P. Harrison, C., Lee, C., Marshall, B. and Wiliam, D. (2003) *Assessment for learning: Putting it into practice*. Buckingham, UK: Open University Press.

Cambridge University Press (2009) *Cambridge IELTS 7 self-study pack: Examination papers from University of Cambridge ESOL examinations (IELTS practice tests)*. Cambridge: Cambridge University Press. 70–73.

Carroll, J. B. (1961) 'Fundamental considerations in testing for English language proficiency of foreign students', reprinted in H. B. Allen and R. N. Campbell (eds) (1965) *Teaching English as a second language: A book of readings*. New York: McGraw Hill. 313–330.

Cizek, G. J. and Bunch, M. B. (2007) *Standard setting: A guide to establishing and evaluating performance standards on tests*. London: Sage.

Crease, R. P. (2011) *World in the balance. The historic quest for an absolute system of measurement*. New York and London: W. W. Norton & Company.

Davidson, F. and Lynch, B. K. (2002) *Testcraft: A teacher's guide to writing and using language test specifications*. New Haven and London: Yale University Press.

Eklöf, H. (2010) 'Skill and will: Test-taking motivation and assessment quality'. *Assessment in Higher Education: Principles, Policy & Practice*, 17/4. 345–356.

Fulcher, G. (2004) 'Deluded by artifices? The common European framework and harmonization'. *Language Assessment Quarterly*, 1/4. 235–266.

Fulcher, G. (2010) *Practical language testing*. London: Hodder Education/Routledge.

Fulcher, G. (2012) 'Assessment literacy for the language classroom'. *Language Assessment Quarterly*, 9/2. 113–132.

Fulcher, G. (2014) 'Language testing in the dock', in A. J. Kunnan (ed.) *The companion to language testing*. London: Wiley-Blackwell. 1553–1570.

Fulcher, G. (2015) *Re-examining language testing: A philosophical and social inquiry*. London and New York: Routledge.

Fulcher, G. (2016) 'Standards and frameworks', in J. Banerjee and D. Tsangari (eds) *Handbook of second language assessment*. Berlin: DeGruyter Mouton.

Fulcher, G. and Davidson, F. (2007) *Language testing and assessment: An advanced resource book*. London and New York: Routledge.

Fulcher, G. and Svalberg, A. (2013) 'Limited aspects of reality: Frames of reference in language assessment'. *International Journal of English Studies*, 13/2. 1–19.

Grabe, W. and Stoller, F. (2013) *Teaching and researching reading* (2nd ed.). London and New York: Routledge.

Haladyna, M., Nolen, S. B. and Haas, N. (1991) 'Raising standardized achievement test scores and the origins of test score pollution'. *Educational Researcher*, 20/5. 2–7.

Hudson. T. (2012) 'Standards-based testing', in G. Fulcher and F. Davidson (eds) *The Routledge handbook of language testing*. London and New York: Routledge. 479–494.

Jones, N. (2013) 'Defining an inclusive framework for languages', in E. D. Galaczi and C. J. Weir (eds) *Exploring language frameworks*. Cambridge: Cambridge University Press. 105–117.

Latham, H. (1877) *On the action of examinations considered as a means of selection*. Cambridge: Dighton, Bell and Company.

Mansell, W. (2007) *Education by numbers: The tyranny of testing*. London: Politico's Publishing.

Martyniuk, W. (2010) *Aligning tests with the CEFR: Reflections on using the Council of Europe's draft manual*. Cambridge: Cambridge University Press.

Mill, J. S. (1859/1998) 'On liberty', in J. Gray (ed.) *John Stuart Mill's on liberty and other essays*. Oxford: Oxford University Press. 2–128.

Owen, N. (2011) *Reverse engineering: A model and case study*. University of Leicester: Unpublished MA Dissertation.

Popham, W. J. (1987) 'The merits of measurement-driven instruction'. *Phi Delta Kappan*. 68/9. 679–682.

Popham, W. J. (1991) 'Appropriateness of teachers' test-preparation practices'. *Educational Measurement: Issues and Practice*, 10/4. 12–15.

Rea-Dickins, P. (2006) 'Currents and eddies in the discourse of assessment: A learning-focused interpretation'. *International Journal of Applied Linguistics*, 16/2. 163–188.

Roach, J. (1971) *Public examinations in England 1850–1900*. Cambridge: Cambridge University Press.

Ruch, G. M. (1924) *The improvement of the written examination*. Chicago: Scott, Foresman and Company.

Shohamy, E. (2001) The *power of tests: A critical perspective on the uses of language tests*. London: Longman/Pearson Education.

Smith, M. L. (1991) 'The effects of external testing on teachers'. *Educational Researcher*, 20/5. 8–11.

Swain, M. (2000) 'The output hypothesis and beyond: Mediating acquisition through collaborative dialogue', in J. Lantolf (ed.) *Sociocultural theory and second language learning*. Oxford: Oxford University Press. 97–114.

Turner, C. E. (2012) 'Classroom assessment', in G. Fulcher and F. Davidson (eds) *The Routledge handbook of language testing*. London and New York: Routledge. 65–78.

Wall, D. (2012) 'Washback', in G. Fulcher and F. Davidson (eds) *The Routledge handbook of Language Testing*. London and New York: Routledge. 79–92.

Watts, A. (2008) 'Cambridge local examinations 1858–1945', in S. Raban (ed.) *Examining the world: A history of the University of Cambridge Local Examinations Syndicate*. Cambridge: Cambridge University Press. 36–70.

Zeng, K. (1999) *Dragon gate: Competitive examinations and their consequences*. London: Cassell.

9

Language teacher education

Karen E. Johnson

Introduction

There are three fundamental questions that constitute the core of language teacher education (LTE): what is it that language teachers need to know? What is it that language teachers need to be able to do? And how are these best learned? How the profession answers these questions speaks directly to what constitutes the professional knowledge base of LTE and informs the content of LTE programmes, the pedagogies that are taught in those programmes, and the institutional forms of delivery through which both the content and pedagogies are learned.

All those involved in the education of language teachers make choices about how these fundamental questions are answered. Such choices emerge from and are situated in the social, political, economic and cultural histories that are located in the contexts where language teachers live, learn and teach. Yet while "located L2 teacher education" entails constructing locally appropriate responses that support the preparation and professionalism of language teachers (Johnson, 2006: 245), there are several persistent challenges that have shaped and will continue to shape the programmatic choices that are made about LTE. This chapter begins with a brief history of language teacher education – focusing in particular on the sub-disciplinary area now known as *teacher cognition* – followed by a discussion of persistent challenges faced by LTE programmes, including emerging areas of debate and calls for future research that will continue to inform the programmatic choices that shape the field.

Brief history of language teacher education

Language teacher education has emerged only relatively recently, both as a professional activity and as a focus of research. Responsibility for preparing language teachers in the North American context moved from schools to and within universities in the mid-twentieth century (Labaree, 2004); EFL teacher training courses in the UK only started in the 1960s, leading to the eventual emergence of the Cambridge ESOL CELTA and the Trinity Cert. TESOL qualifications (Borg, 2011). Meanwhile, published volumes of empirical research on the practices of teacher education (rather than research into the activity of teaching itself) only began to emerge in the late-1980s (Houston, 1990).

Prior to this, the theories and research that informed general teacher education until the 1970s failed to consider the *mental lives of teachers* (Walburg, 1977). Instead, teachers were considered to be 'doers' rather than 'thinkers', and the doing of teaching was conceptualised as a set of instructional behaviours that, if carried out systematically and efficiently, would ultimately lead to greater gains in student learning regardless of institutional and/or social context. Since then, numerous handbooks (e.g. Cochran-Smith et al., 2008) and commissioned reports (e.g. the American Educational Research Association (AREA) Report, Cochran-Smith and Zeichner, 2005; National Academy of Education (NAE) Report, Darling-Hammond and Bransford, 2005) have helped to consolidate the most up-to-date research on teacher education. And, although at times overshadowed by research on *teaching* rather than *teacher education* (Grossman and McDonald, 2008), more than three decades of research on *teacher cognition* in general teacher education (e.g. Cochran-Smith and Zeichner, 2005) and in L2 teacher education (e.g. Freeman, 2002; Borg, 2003; Johnson, 2006) has come to characterise teacher learning as normative and lifelong; it is built through experiences in multiple social contexts and is based on the assumption that knowing, thinking and doing come from participating in the social practices of learning and teaching in specific classroom and school situations.

Within the context of L2 teacher education, therefore, the learning of L2 teaching is no longer viewed as a matter of simply translating theories of linguistics and/or second language acquisition (SLA) into effective instructional practices but as a dialogic process of co-constructing knowledge that is situated in and emerges out of participation in particular socio-cultural practices and contexts (Freeman and Johnson, 1998; Johnson, 2009). Instead, the typical ways of acting and interacting, and the values, assumptions and attitudes that are embedded in the classrooms where teachers were once students, in the teacher education programmes where they receive their professional credentialing and in the schools where they work, shape the complex ways in which they come to think about themselves, their students, the activities of L2 teaching and the processes of L2 teaching-learning (Johnson, 2009).

Additionally, over the past four decades, two parallel paradigm shifts have also helped reshape our understanding of learning in general and teacher learning in particular. Within the field of applied linguistics, shifts in disciplinary knowledge about the nature of language and SLA have been informed by shifts in how various intellectual traditions have come to conceptualise learning – from behaviourist, to cognitive, to situated, social and distributed views of human cognition (Firth and Wagner, 1997; Putman and Borko, 2000; 'Second language acquisition reconceptualized?', 2007). In LTE, these shifts have been reflected in shifting characterisations of teachers and teaching respectively as: *doing* or enacting effective teaching behaviours as determined by others (external); as *knowing*, or interactive decision-making about subject matter content and teaching processes as determined by teachers themselves (internal); and as *interpreting,* or knowing what to do within the social contexts and situated meanings that are embedded in and emerge from the cultural practices and institutions where teachers and students live, learn and work (Freeman, 2002; Johnson, 2009).

Overall, this shifting epistemological orientation toward the so-called sociocultural turn (Block, 2003; Johnson, 2006) in our understanding of human cognition and a more nuanced understanding of the complexities of teacher learning and the activities of language teaching have created an array of persistent challenges for all those involved in LTE. Moreover, in the twenty-first century, the work of teacher educators and LTE programmes has expanded exponentially as a result of new technologies (see Gruba, Hinkelman and Cárdenas-Claros, this volume), the globalisation of English (see Seargeant, this volume), and an increasingly globalised world (see Pennycook, this volume). In newly emerging centres of ELT in Asia, East Asia, South America and across the African continent, today's language teachers are more likely to be non-native speakers of English (see Llurda, this volume), be required to implement national curricula in large-scale public sector institutional settings and, despite the promulgation of communicative language teaching (CLT) methods (see Thornbury, this volume), continue to teach mandatory English through the national language rather than in English. The changing demographics of English language learners and the teachers who teach them has intensified the challenges facing the preparation and professionalisation of the English language teaching force around the world.

Persistent challenges: the nature and role of disciplinary knowledge

Given this history, if disciplinary knowledge about language and SLA cannot simply be applied to the pedagogies of the language classroom, then the question remains: what constitutes the knowledge base of language teacher education? Answering this question is complicated because few would deny that knowledge of the formal proprieties of language, a meta-language to describe those proprieties (i.e. grammar terminology) and an understanding of how languages are learned and used, as well as insight into users and contexts of use, is essential for the development of language teacher expertise. In fact, this sort of disciplinary knowledge is what distinguishes a professional language teacher from someone who, simply by birthright, speaks the language. And despite attempts to debunk the native-speaker fallacy (Phillipson, 1992), in many regions of the world it is assumed that if someone speaks the language, he/she can teach it, and/or that a second language is learned best when taught by a native-speaker (see Llurda, this volume). Such socially constructed, historically and culturally perpetuated notions about language teaching and language learning have served to minimise the value of language teacher education as the quintessential institutional context for the professional development of language teachers. And given the globalisation of English, traditional English language teacher training programmes (such as the CELTA, mentioned above, which in the past involved mostly native speakers of English and small class sizes) can no longer realistically prepare large-scale public sector teachers who teach mandated curricula to the increasing numbers of diverse English language learners around the world.

The theory/practice dichotomy

While disciplinary knowledge about language and how languages are learned (i.e. SLA) has and will continue to play an important role in the professionalisation of language teachers, two persistent challenges remain for LTE. First, the nature of disciplinary knowledge about language and SLA has long been plagued by questions surrounding the relationship between theory and practice. While many SLA researchers have cautioned against attempts to inform practice directly from theory on the grounds that the activities, interests and goals of SLA researchers are simply incompatible with those of teachers as they operate is different discursive worlds (Ellis, 1997; Gass and Mackey, 2007; Long, 2007), more recently, others have argued that theory and practice are simply two sides of the same coin, that is, that educational practice is a form of scientific research, and theory is not for mere observation but an instrument for educational innovation and change (Stetsenko and Arievitch, 2004; Lantolf and Poehner, 2014). Working from a Vygotskyian socio-cultural perspective (Vygotsky, 1978, 1986), the notion of *praxis*, or the dialectical unity of theory and practice, emerges out of a process of reconsidering and reorganising lived experiences of teachers and their students through theoretical constructs and discourses of the professional discourse community, while simultaneously reconsidering and reorganising theoretical constructs and discourses as they are enacted in language classrooms (Lantolf and Poehner, 2014; see also Negueruela-Azarola and García, this volume). For language teacher educators, if disciplinary knowledge about language, SLA and the learning of language teaching are to have relevance for language teachers, they must be interconnected with the experiential knowledge that teachers bring with them to LTE programmes, while simultaneously grounding them in the actual activities of being and becoming language teachers in the setting and circumstances in which they live, learn and work.

The cognitive/social dichotomy

Scholarly agreement over what constitutes language and SLA also remains contested between the so-called cognitive versus social perspectives in the field of SLA in particular, and in applied linguistics more generally (Zuengler and Miller, 2006; Atkinson, 2011). Cognitive-oriented SLA research typically defines language as a stable, neutral and naturally ordered hierarchical system consisting of predetermined syntactic, phonological, morphological and pragmatic characteristics that reside on some deeper psycho-cognitive level in the individual (see Zuengler and Miller, 2006). Additionally, cognitive-oriented SLA research separates language *learning* from language *use* (Kasper, 1997; Gass, 2008) based on the underlying assumption that while systematicity and generativity can be found in fully formed native speakers (Chomsky, 1965), the goal of cognitive-oriented SLA research is to empirically document the increasing complexity and developing fluency of language learners' mental grammars (i.e. their interlanguage).

Social-oriented SLA research, on the other hand, foregrounds language use in real-world situations as fundamental, not ancillary, to language learning (Zuengler and Miller, 2006). In fact, Lantolf and Johnson (2007: 878) state emphatically that "it is not that social activity influences cognition, but that social activity is the process through which human cognition is formed". Social-oriented SLA research is grounded in the notion that humans develop as "participants in cultural communities" and "their development can be understood only in light of the cultural practices and circumstances of their communities – which also change" (Rogoff, 2003: 3–4). Social-oriented SLA research defines language learning as building capacity to function in relevant socio-cultural contexts; as positioning speakers in relation to others; as invoking particular cultural schema; as being fluid, dynamic and ultimately unstable; and as accessing resources and making choices about *how to be* in the target language community. Therefore, from this perspective, attention to participation in various socio-cultural practices is critical to understanding SLA, since the processes of language learning are negotiated with people in what they do, in what such practices collectively mean and in the resources people draw on and the choices they make to achieve their communicative goals.

Linking disciplinary and experiential knowledge

Given this state of affairs, LTE programmes are left to grapple with the difficulties of the theory/practice relationship and the cognitive/social dichotomy that persist in linguistic/SLA theory and research. Yet, by rejecting an 'applied science model' (Wallace, 1998), in other words, the direct application of theories of SLA to methods of language teaching, LTE programmes have begun to recognise the complexities of teachers' mental lives, the socially situated processes of learning to teach, and the dynamic nature of the teaching/learning processes that occur in language classrooms. By doing so, what becomes central to the knowledge base of language teacher education is not which ontological SLA camp to draw from but the need to ground relevant disciplinary knowledge about language and SLA in teachers' understandings of and experiences in the day-to-day activities of learning to teach and being a language teacher.

Put more directly, an essential element of becoming a professional language teacher is gaining a deep understanding of the disciplinary knowledge that reflects the history and current debates that define what language is, how second languages are learned and how language can best be taught. However, this disciplinary knowledge is not the same kind of knowledge that teachers use to teach languages, nor is it the same kind of knowledge that learners use to learn languages (Freeman, 2004). Thus, while an important part of language teacher professionalism is knowledge of the most up-to-date disciplinary knowledge about language and SLA, an equally important dimension of that professionalism is the development of a specialised kind of knowledge that teachers use to actually teach language.

Discussed in greater depth in the next section, the knowledge that teachers use to teach language does have a great deal of disciplinary knowledge in it, but it is also shaped by experiential knowledge that emerges from teachers' own lived experiences as students, language learners and language teachers. In fact, it is this interconnectedness between lived experiences and disciplinary knowledge that is most influential in the development of teacher expertise (Kennedy, 1999).

A powerful example of this process can be found in a collection of 'dialogues' between *TESOL Quarterly* readers (classroom teachers) and *TESOL Quarterly* authors of previously published *TESOL Quarterly* articles (researchers, drawing on theoretical perspectives) that focused on issues of language, culture and power (see Sharkey and Johnson, 2003). For instance, as an experienced language teacher enrolled in a post-secondary teacher education programme, Jordan (2003) recalls the "discomfort and embarrassment" she felt after reading Auerbach's (1993) critique of the USA English-only ideology and its detrimental impact on the language and literacy development of English language learners. Because Jordan had long considered herself an "advocate for native language rights" and an "educational progressive", Auerbach's article led her to question her long-held assumption that "any departure from English in my ESL classroom was not good teaching practice" (p. 37). Jordan narrates how, over an eight-year period, her approach to teaching shifted toward seeing students' L1 as a resource that, when integrated into her daily instructional practices, fostered greater student engagement, more authentic communication and greater gains in students' L2 literacy. Projects such as the *TESOL Quarterly Dialogues* highlight the complex ways in which teachers actively link disciplinary knowledge to their own experiential knowledge as they reframe the way they describe and interpret their teaching/learning experiences as a result of engagement in LTE programmes.

Another productive means of building the interconnectedness between teachers' lived experiences and disciplinary knowledge is to develop what Andrews (2007) refers to as teacher *language awareness*. Such awareness entails not only developing a conscious understanding of and the meta-linguistic terminology to explain both structural and functional features of the language but also developing language teachers' competence as language users, language analysts and language teachers (Wright, 2002; Andrews, 2007; see also Svalberg, this volume). This process involves not only the ability to use the language appropriately in a variety of situations but also to develop explicit awareness of the social and pragmatic norms which underlie appropriate use. It encompasses a deeper understanding of the grammatical, semantic and pragmatic resources that are available to language users and how it is that users choose and manipulate these resources to accomplish their communicative goals. And it involves understanding how to create and exploit language learning opportunities within the activities of the language classroom that will help language learners develop the capacity to generate meaning from and function in the target language community.

Disciplinary knowledge of all stripes will most certainly continue to inform, in part, the knowledge base of LTE programmes. However, for disciplinary knowledge to be relevant to the work of language teachers, it must be grounded in the actual activities of being and becoming a language teacher, it must be made accessible in ways that enable teachers to reframe how they interpret their lived experiences and it must be reconstituted in such a way that it becomes a kind of specialised knowledge that language teachers are able to use to make the content of their lessons relevant, usable and accessible to their students.

The development of knowledge for language teaching

In the mid-1980s, Shulman (1987) and his colleagues at Stanford University embarked on a research project to define teacher knowledge not only in terms of the disciplinary foundations of what teachers need to know about the subject matter that they are expected to teach but also the knowledge that teachers rely on to make that subject matter accessible, relevant and useful to students. Coined *pedagogical content knowledge* because it combines knowledge of content, pedagogy, curriculum, learners and educational context, Shulman emphasised this knowledge as being "of special interest because it identifies the distinctive bodies of knowledge for teaching" (p. 8). Pedagogical content knowledge is neither fixed nor stable but instead emergent, dynamic and contingent on teachers' knowledge of particular students, in particular contexts who are learning particular content for particular purposes. As a result, its development emerges out of engagement in the activities of teaching since its very nature constitutes and is constitutive of the interconnectedness of content, context, students and pedagogical purpose.

Given its dynamic nature, pedagogical content knowledge develops as teachers engage in the actual activities of teaching. This creates a conundrum for pre-service teacher education programmes because it requires that learners of teaching perform as teachers before they have the necessary competence to do so. Yet it is precisely through engaging in the activities of teaching and the teacher educator/teacher interactions about those activities that teachers are enabled to develop deeper understandings of their actions. They will become consciously aware of the subject matter content and pedagogical resources that form the basis of their instructional decisions and activities.

While most pre-service LTE programmes do require supervised practicum and/or internship experiences, these often come near the end of the programme, remain disconnected from academic coursework and are apprenticeship-like, in that they invoke a 'discovery learning' conceptualisation of teacher learning. If, as the research on teacher cognition suggests, participation in particular socio-cultural practices and contexts shapes what and how teachers learn to teach, then LTE programmes must create multiple and varied opportunities for teachers to engage in theoretically and pedagogically sound instructional practices within the socio-cultural contexts in which they teach. More importantly, these opportunities, by design, must create spaces for teacher educators to offer expert mediation that supports language teachers as they are engaged in the processes of being and becoming a teacher.

Thus, while typical practicum activities include teaching a class, self-observation, observing other teachers, the use of teaching journals or discussions in seminars (Gebhard, 2009), new technologies that support computer-mediated communication (e.g. discussion boards, moodles, blogs) have helped to open up these activities by exposing teachers' thoughts, feelings and concerns as they are participating in the processes of learning to teach, while simultaneously fostering greater teacher educator/teacher dialogue around the activities of planning, teaching and reflecting on teaching (see Yoshida, 2011; Johnson and Golombek, 2013). For example, a study of the private, asynchronous online blog exchanges between novice ESL teachers and a teacher educator during a 15-week MA TESL teaching practicum (Johnson and Golombek, 2013) highlighted the case of Kyla, who struggled to construct a teaching persona that would enable her to function successfully while completing her practicum in a post-secondary ESL oral communication course. Through her weekly blog posts, she expressed this struggle through emotive language that shifted from overconfidence to deep disappointment. The dialogic blog exchanges between Kyla and her teacher educator provided Kyla with emotional support, offered concrete instructional strategies and modelled expert thinking, all of which appeared to work in consort to assist Kyla as she worked to overcome the dissonance she was experiencing between her imagined teaching persona and the instructional experiences she was attempting to create for the students in her practicum placement.

Additionally, various forms of inquiry-based professional development (i.e. teacher study groups, peer coaching, lesson study, see Johnson, 2009), particularly those that allow for self-directed, collaborative, inquiry-based learning that is directly relevant to teachers' classrooms, have helped to create structural arrangements where teachers and teacher educators can engage in sustained collaborative dialogue that make explicit the dynamic nature of the pedagogical content knowledge that teachers come to rely on as they make the content of their instruction accessible, relevant and useful to students.

A persistent challenge for language teacher education is to create learning/teaching opportunities that foster the development of language teacher pedagogical content knowledge. What makes this challenge so persistent is, as the original definition suggests, because it is emergent, dynamic and contingent on teachers' knowledge of particular students, in particular contexts and who are learning particular content for particular purposes, it cannot be acquired in one context and then simply applied to another. At best, LTE programmes must make teachers aware of the emergent, dynamic and contingent qualities of pedagogical content knowledge and create varied and multiple experiences where teachers must draw together their knowledge of content, context, students and pedagogical purpose in ways that enable them to develop a disposition for *reasoning teaching,* that is, "when teachers are able to assemble and apply their knowledge of their professional landscape flexibly so that it can be used in different situations and for different purposes ... the kind of reasoning that will enable them not only to recognise that it depends, but to articulate what it depends on" (Johnson, 1999: 2). Developing a *reasoning teaching* disposition for language teaching leads us to another persistent challenge in language teacher education: recognising the powerful role that context plays in learning-to-teach and teaching.

The challenge of context in learning-to-teach, teaching and educational innovation

In his 2002 review of three decades of research on LTE, Freeman (2002: 11) claimed that "[i]n teacher education, context is everything". As such, context is not just the physical classrooms where language teaching/learning occurs but also the socio-cultural processes that make up the norms of schooling and which reflect the cultural values and social practices that dictate what teachers and students accept as normal (Denscombe, 1982). Likewise, teacher socialisation that takes place in different contexts has a long reach, emerging from teachers' schooling histories, intertwining with their professional development experiences in teacher education programmes and extending to the schools and classrooms where they eventually teach (as noted earlier). Participation in these various contexts works in consort to socialise teachers into particular ways of conceptualising themselves as teachers, carrying out their teaching practices and supporting student learning.

Additionally, the power of context in language teacher education makes pedagogical innovation and/or educational reform a persistent challenge. Nowhere has this challenge been more acknowledged than in the 'importation' of 'Western methods' into instructional settings where policy makers and government officials seek to reform traditional grammar-based English language educational systems. As has been the case in South Korea, shifting English language instruction toward more communicative-oriented outcomes through curricular reform (i.e. the introduction of communicative language teaching) and mandated policies (i.e. teaching English through English) has failed to take into account the limited oral language proficiency of the local teaching force, the washback effect of the grammar-translation-oriented examination system and the normative ways of schooling that South Korean teachers and their students are socialised into. As a result, despite decades of educational reform efforts, English language teachers in Korea have been found to enact their supposedly communication-oriented curricula in very traditional, non-communicative ways (Ahn, 2011; Kim, 2011).

In emerging ELT contexts around the world, ministries of education have also begun to mandate English language instruction at the primary level to prepare their citizens for an increasingly globalised economy (Graddol, 2006; see also Enever, this volume). Such educational policies are placing increasing demands on LTE programmes to prepare teachers with the necessary English language proficiency to teach English in English and to enact nationally mandated curricula so that all students have access to high-quality English language instruction. Well-known frameworks of language proficiency such as the Common European Framework of Reference (CEFR) and the American Council on the Teaching of Foreign Language (ACTFL) Proficiency Guidelines are often not within the reach of the teachers who work in large-scale public sector institutional settings. LTE programmes are therefore left with the dual challenge of increasing teachers' overall language proficiency while simultaneously preparing them with theoretically and pedagogically sound instructional practices that meet the local language learning demands of the students in the contexts where they teach.

Moreover, the language learning context in which language teacher education takes place matters as well. In the field of English language teaching generally, much is made of the English as a foreign language (EFL) versus English as a second language (ESL) distinction. Obviously, the goals for language learning differ, the opportunities for language use differ, the motivation of language learners differ and the intended outcomes of language teaching differ. Similar claims can be made for ESL/EFL language teacher education. EFL teachers are typically more concerned with how to teach 'language as content', while ESL teachers are more concerned with how to teach 'content through language'. EFL teachers often have to contend with high-stakes testing and a mandated curriculum, while ESL teachers are charged with keeping ESL students on grade-level with their English-speaking peers. Slogans such as 'teacher-centred' versus 'student-centred' are sometimes invoked to distinguish between the instructional styles of EFL versus ESL teachers. Yet the research on language teacher cognition is quite clear: the lived, language learning and schooling experiences that teachers have been socialised into will no doubt influence how they make sense of the content and pedagogies of their teacher education programme. Thus, the same can be said whether language teacher education takes place in ESL or EFL instructional contexts. In language teacher education, context matters.

Thus, recognising that context shapes both the processes of learning to teach and the activity of teaching remains a persistent challenge for LTE programmes. It requires that language teachers learn to scrutinise and navigate the consequences that various contexts, and the values and norms embedded in those contexts, have had or will continue to have on their daily classroom practices. This can be accomplished through autobiographical introspection about the schooling contexts from which teachers have come, for example, through teacher-constructed learning-to-teach histories (Johnson, 1999). It can take place through narrative-inquiry practitioner research where teachers seek to expose the normative values that regulate their own instructional practices and/or how students respond to innovative instructional practices (Johnson and Golombek, 2002). It can become salient to teachers as they read case studies of local language teaching/learning practices that demonstrate the cultural complexities implicit in classroom language learning (Canagarajah, 2003). It can emerge as language teachers attempt to create alternative identities for their language learners (e.g. 'I don't need to sound like a native-speaker') or assist language learners as they fulfil aspirations to develop new identities in the target language community (Norton, 1995).

Ultimately, recognising the role of context in language teacher education means recognising the social, cultural, political and economic realities within which language teachers live and work, or for many, hope to live and work. Language learners' ethnicity, gender, heritage, educational level, socioeconomic status and even the perceived status of their L1, all work in consort to situate and construct learners, teachers and the activities of language teaching in particular ways. If, in teacher education, 'context is everything', then LTE programmes must recognise how changing socio-political and socio-economic contexts impact upon the ways in which language teachers come to conceptualise themselves as teachers, how they enact their teaching practices and, most importantly, the kinds of learning environments that they are willing and able to create for their students.

Emerging areas of debate

Which English should teachers teach?

With the globalisation of English and the increasing legitimacy of the varieties of English that are spoken throughout the world (see Seargeant, this volume), an emerging area of debate for language teacher education is 'which English should teachers teach?' While commercial textbooks, high-stakes tests and language policies tend to propagate native speaker standards, in many regions of the world, non-standard varieties of English are not only widely spoken but widely accepted (Jenkins, 2006). Here again, the mantra 'context is everything' can be invoked, because historical, cultural, social, economic and political issues embedded in different contexts will determine which English teachers can and/or should teach.

Scholars working to promote World Englishes and English as a Lingua Franca (ELF) continue to struggle against dominant native speaker standards despite claims that native speaker standards in and of themselves are difficult to define, that the number of non-standard speakers of English around the world far exceeds those deemed in the Inner Circle (Kachru, 1992) and that Outer Circle speakers can and should develop their own norms rather than conforming to those of the so-called native speaker (Seidlhofer, 2005). Yet despite the increasing legitimacy of World Englishes in scholarly circles, there has been very little pedagogical uptake within the field of English language teaching (Jenkins, 2006). At best, scholars agree that teachers and learners should be made aware of what World Englishes are, what they represent to those who speak them and why they serve a valuable function in different contexts around the world. For LTE programmes, this reiterates the point made above: it is precisely the power of context – in particular, contexts with high-stakes exams, language policies and/or public discourses that view varieties of English as linguistic deficiencies – that will in large part determine which English teachers will choose to teach and which English students will be willing to learn.

Where should English language teacher education take place?

Largely due to the globalisation of English, the demand for English language teachers around the world finds increasing numbers of EFL teachers seeking professional development in ESL instructional settings. Within LTE programmes, teachers who have been socialised into typical ways of acting and interacting in EFL instructional settings often find the ESL classrooms where they are expected to learn-to-teach to be qualitatively different in terms of the norms for interaction, teacher/student roles and language learning expectations. The same can be said for teachers who have been socialised into typical ways of acting and interacting in ESL instructional settings when they enter EFL instructional settings. LTE programmes are left to determine whether the content and pedagogies taught in LTE programmes in ESL settings are appropriate for the professional development of EFL teachers, and vice versa. Often the dilemma of making sense of professional development experiences in different instructional settings is left to the individual teacher once he/she enters the profession. Anecdotal evidence often indicates that much of what might be possible in ESL instructional contexts is not possible in EFL instructional contexts, and what is typical in EFL instructional contexts may not be appropriate in ESL instructional contexts. For LTE programmes, understanding the extent to which the language learning settings in which language teacher education takes place adequately prepares language teachers for any and all instructional contexts in an under-researched yet highly relevant emerging area of debate.

What is the relationship between teacher learning and student learning?

One might assume, as much of the public discourse on educational improvement does, that greater teacher professional development will lead to greater gains in student achievement. Yet direct causal links between what teachers learn as part of their teacher education programme and what students learn as a result of what and how teachers teach have yet to be adequately addressed in the educational literature (Ball et al., 2005; Freeman and Johnson, 2005). This remains an emerging issue of debate because defining learning depends, once again, on epistemological stance. Operating from a cognitive-oriented stance, language learning is believed to be located in the mind of the learner and separated from language use and reflects essentially the same outcome (e.g. so-called native speaker English) regardless of the context in which it is learned. Operating from a social-oriented stance, learning is believed to depend on the specific social activities in which students engage and the tools they use to engage in during those activities. As long as human agency and social context come into play, there will always be differences in how different people react to the same set of circumstances at different times (Lantolf and Johnson, 2007). Thus, the assumption that teacher professional development inevitably causes greater gains in student achievement implies an overly simplistic and inadequate understanding of the dynamic and complex nature of the activities of teacher learning, teaching and student learning.

While no one would argue against some sort of relationship between what teachers learn in their teacher education programmes and what students learn as a result of teachers' instruction, Freeman and Johnson (2005) argue for a *relationship of influence* rather than causality. In their study of a high school French teacher involved in a long-term teacher inquiry project, what became salient was not so much what the students learned about the French language but how their teacher's participation in the teacher inquiry project shaped how they experienced the learning of French. For them, learning French was an ongoing process of collaboratively co-constructing their understandings of the French lexicon and grammar while simultaneously expressing shared understandings of both the topic and the language used to talk about it. Likewise, a similar finding emerged in a narrative inquiry conducted by Herndon (2002) in a secondary ESL literature class for immigrant students in the New York public schools. Based on disciplinary knowledge that Herndon was exposed to in her LTE programme, she began to alter the modes of engagement in how her students interacted with literary texts from teacher-directed to student-directed. And as these new modes of engagement became the new norms for literacy activities in her classroom, her students began to engage with literary texts in much more communicative and personally meaningful ways. While much more research is certainly needed, these two studies provide hints into the challenges of uncovering the *relationship of influence* between teacher learning and student learning. Such research also points to the need to examine the practices of language teacher education that are instantiated in English LTE programmes around the world, the focus of future research, as discussed next.

Future research: reclaiming the relevance of L2 teacher education

While the research and scholarship in teacher cognition has transformed our understanding of how language teachers learn-to-teach and what is involved in the complexities of language teaching, traditional notions of teacher knowledge (i.e. a body of knowledge to be learned) and teacher learning continue to shape current models of second language teacher education practice (Tedick, 2009). In order to encourage greater uptake of teacher education practices that support the development of effective language educators who are skilled at enacting theoretically and pedagogically sound instructional practices in diverse settings, an area of future research is to determine empirically what language teachers actually learn by participating in the practices embedded their teacher education programmes. Such work can begin by examining what teacher educators are attempting to accomplish through these practices, the quality and character of their interactions as they engage in these practices, what teachers are learning as they participate in these practices and, most importantly, how their learning shapes the language learning environments teachers attempt to create for their students (Johnson, 2015). In essence, such empirical work seeks to establish the relevance of language teacher education by not only opening up the practices of LTE for closer scrutiny but also by holding teacher educators accountable to the language teachers with whom they work and, of course, the students their teachers teach. Until the profession establishes an empirical basis that justifies the practices of LTE, the relevance of language teacher education will remain in doubt and the false assumption that speaking a language is enough to teach it will prevail. Ultimately, empirical attention to the design, enactment and outcomes of the practices of language teacher education will establish the relevance of language teacher education *in* and *for* the professional development of language teachers.

Discussion questions

* How might language teacher education programmes (re)structure their content and pedagogies to deal with the debates surrounding the theory/practice and cognitive/social dichotomies that exist in SLA research?
* Hypothesise about what 'located language teacher education' might look like in the setting in which you teach?
* Reflect on the content and pedagogies of your own LTE programme or an LTE programme you have experienced. What choices were made about what language teachers should know and be able to do, and how is this best learned?
* Consider a teacher education practice that you experienced directly or that you routinely carry out in your teacher education programme. What are you attempting to accomplish through this practice? What did you or what did your teachers actually learned as they participated in this practice? What might be alternative ways of (re)structuring this practice to foster greater teacher learning?

Related topics

Cognitive perspectives on classroom language learning; Communicative language teaching in theory and practice; Language awareness; Method, methods and methodology; Politics, power relationships and ELT; Sociocultural theory and the language classroom; World Englishes and English as a Lingua Franca.

Further reading

Borg, S. (2006) *Teacher cognition and language education: Research and practice.* London: Continuum. (This book focuses specifically on the body of research that now exists on the study of teacher cognition – what teachers think, know and believe – and of its relationship to teachers' classroom practices.)

Burns, A. and Richards, J.C. (eds) (2009) *The Cambridge guide to second language teacher education.* New York: Cambridge University Press. (A collection of 30 original state-of-the-art articles on contemporary issues in second language teacher education.)

Johnson, K.E. (2009) *Second language teacher education: A sociocultural perspective.* New York: Routledge. (An overview of the theoretical underpinnings of a Vygotskian sociocultural theoretical perspective on human learning, and what it offers the field of second language teacher education.)

Kubanyiova, M. (2012) *Teacher development in action: Understanding language teachers' conceptual change.* London: Palgrave MacMillan. (A year-long investigation of how language teacher thinking and practices are transformed through formal teacher education programmes and how a teacher educator can facilitate the process.)

References

Ahn, K. (2011) 'Learning to teach under curricular reform: The practicum experience in South Korea', in K. E. Johnson and P. R. Golombek (eds) *Research on second language teacher education: A sociocultural perspective on professional development.* New York: Routledge. 239–253.

Andrews, S. (2007) *Teacher language awareness.* Cambridge: Cambridge University Press.

Atkinson, D. (2011) *Alternative approaches to second language acquisition.* New York: Routledge.

Auerbach, E. R. (1993) 'Re-examining English only in the ESL classroom'. *TESOL Quarterly, 27/1.* 9–32.

Ball, D., Hill, L. and Bass, H. C. (2005) 'Knowing mathematics for teaching: Who knows mathematics well enough to teach third grade and how can we decide?' *American Educator, 29/1.* 14–46.

Block, D. (2003) *The social turn in second language acquisition.* Edinburgh, UK. Edinburgh University Press.

Borg, S. (2003) 'Teacher cognition in language teaching: A review of research on what language teachers think, know, believe, and do'. *Language Teaching, 36/2.* 81–109.

Borg, S. (2011) 'Language teacher education', in J. Simpson (ed.) *The Routledge handbook of applied linguistics.* London: Routledge. 215–228.

Canagarajah, S. (2003) 'Subversive identities, pedagogical safe houses, and critical learning', in B. Norton and K. Toohey (eds) *Critical pedagogies and language learning.* New York: Cambridge University Press. 116–137.

Chomsky, N. (1965) *Aspects of the theory of syntax.* Cambridge, MA: MIT Press.

Cochran-Smith, M., Feiman-Nemser, S. and McIntyre, D. J. (eds) (2008) *Handbook of research on teacher education: Enduring questions in changing contexts* (3rd ed.). New York: Routledge.

Cochran-Smith, M. and Zeichner, K. (eds) (2005) *Studying teacher education: The report of the AERA panel on research and teacher education.* Washington, DC: The American Educational Research Association.

Darling-Hammond, L. and Bransford, J. (eds) (2005) *Preparing teachers for a changing world: What teachers should learn and be able to do.* San Francisco, CA: Jossey-Bass

Denscombe, M. (1982) 'The hidden pedagogy and its implications for teacher training: An ecological analysis'. *British Journal of Sociology of Education, 3/3.* 249–265.

Ellis, R. (1997) 'SLA and language pedagogy: An educational perspective'. *Studies in Second Language Acquisition, 19/1.* 69–92.

Firth, A. and Wagner, J. (1997) 'On discourse, communication and (some) fundamental concepts in SLA research'. *Modern Language Journal, 81/3.* 285–3000.

Freeman, D. (2002) 'The hidden side of the work: Teacher knowledge and learning to teach'. *Language Teaching, 35/1.* 1–13.

Freeman, D. (2004) 'Language, sociocultural theory, and L2 teacher education: Examining the technology of subject matter and the architecture of instruction', in M. R. Hawkins (ed.) *Language learning and teacher education.* Clevedon: Multilingual Matters. 167–197.

Freeman, D. and Johnson, K. E. (1998) 'Reconceptualizing the knowledge-base of language teacher education'. *TESOL Quarterly, 32/1.* 397–417.

Freeman, D. and Johnson, K. E. (2005) 'Towards linking teacher knowledge and student learning', in D. J. Tedick (ed.) *Language teacher education: International perspectives on research and practice.* Mahwah, NJ: Lawrence Erlbaum Associates. 73–95.

Gass, S. M. (2008) 'Apples and oranges: Or why apples are not oranges and don't need to be. A response to Firth and Wagner'. *Modern Language Journal*, 82/1. 83–90.

Gass, S. M. and Mackey, A. (2007) 'Input, interaction, and output in second language acquisition', in B. Van-Patton and J. Williams (eds) *Theories in second language acquisition: An introduction*. New York: Routledge. 175–200.

Gebhard, J. (2009) 'The practicum', in J. C. Richards and A. Burns (eds) *The Cambridge guide to language teacher education*. Cambridge: Cambridge University Press. 250–258.

Graddol, D. (2006) *English next*. Plymouth, UK: The British Council.

Grossman, P. and McDonald, M. (2008) Back to the future: Directions for research in teaching and teacher education. *American Educational Research Journal*, 45/1. 184–205.

Herndon, L. D. (2002) 'Putting theory into practice: Letting my students learn to read', in K. E. Johnson and P. R. Golombek (eds) *Research on second language teacher education: A sociocultural perspective on professional development*. New York: Routledge. 35–51.

Houston, R. W. (ed.) (1990) *Handbook of research on teacher education: A project of the Association of Teacher Educators*. New York: Macmillan.

Jenkins, J. (2006) 'Current perspectives on teaching World Englishes and English as a Lingua Franca'. *TESOL Quarterly*, 40/1. 157–181.

Johnson, K. E. (1999) *Understanding language teaching: Reasoning in action*. Boston, MA: Heinle & Heinle Publishing Company.

Johnson, K. E. (2006) 'The sociocultural turn and its challenges for L2 teacher education'. *TESOL Quarterly*, 40/1. 235–257.

Johnson, K. E. (2009) *Second language teacher education: A sociocultural perspective*. New York: Routledge.

Johnson, K. E. (2015) 'Reclaiming the relevance of L2 teacher education'. *Modern Language Journal*, 99/3. 515–528.

Johnson, K. E. and Golombek, P. R. (eds) (2002) *Teachers' narrative inquiry as professional development*. New York: Cambridge University Press.

Johnson, K. E. and Golombek, P. R. (2013) 'A tale of two mediations: Tracing the dialectics of cognition, emotion, and activity in teachers' practicum blogs', in G. Barkhuizen (ed.) *Narrative research in applied linguistics*. Cambridge: Cambridge University Press. 85–104.

Jordan, B. M. (2003) 'Dialogues around "re-examining English only in the ESL classroom"', in J. Sharkey and K. E. Johnson (eds) *TESOL Quarterly dialogues: Rethinking issues of language, culture, and power*. Alexandria, VA: Teachers of English to Speakers of Other Languages. 35–40.

Kachru, B. B. (1992) 'Teaching World Englishes', in B. B. Kachru (ed.) *The other tongue: English across cultures*. Urbana, IL: University of Illinois Press. 355–365.

Kasper, G. (1997) '"A" stands for acquisition: A response to Firth and Wagner'. *Modern Language Journal*, 81/2. 307–312.

Kennedy, M. (1999) 'Schools and the problem of knowledge', in J. Rath and A. McAninch (eds) *What counts as knowledge in teacher education?* Stanford, CT: Ablex Publishing Corporation. 29–45.

Kim, E. (2011), 'Ten years of CLT curricular reform efforts in South Korea: An activity theory analysis of a teachers' experience', in K. E. Johnson and P. R. Golombek (eds) *Research on second language teacher education: A sociocultural perspective on professional development*. New York: Routledge. 225–238.

Labaree, D. F. (2004) *The trouble with education schools*. New Haven, CT: Yale University Press.

Lantolf, J. P. and Johnson, K. E. (2007) 'Extending Firth and Wagner's ontological perspective to L2 classroom praxis and teacher education'. *Modern Language Journal*, 91/5. 875–890.

Lantolf, J. P. and Poehner, M. (2014) *Sociocultural theory and the pedagogical imperative in L2 education: Vygotskian praxis and the research/practice divide*. New York: Routledge.

Long, M. (2007) *Problems in SLA*. Mahwah, NJ: Lawrence Erlbaum.

Norton, B. (1995) 'Social identity, investment, and language learning'. *TESOL Quarterly*, 29/1. 9–31.

Phillipson, R. (1992) *Linguistic imperialism*. Oxford: Oxford University Press.

Putman, R. T. and Borko, H. (2000) 'What do new views of knowledge and thinking have to say about research on teacher learning?' *Educational Researcher*, 29/1. 4–15.

Rogoff, B. (2003) *The cultural nature of human development*. Oxford: Oxford University Press.

'Second language acquisition reconceptualized? The impact of Firth and Wagner' (1997). (2007) *Modern Language Journal*, 91, Focus Issue.

Seidlhofer, B. (2005) 'Standard future or half-baked quackery?', in C. Gnutzmann and F. Intemann (eds) *The globalization of English and the English language classroom*. Tubingen, Germany: Narr. 159–173.

Sharkey, J. and Johnson, K. E. (eds) (2003) *TESOL Quarterly dialogues: Rethinking issues of language, culture, and power*. Alexandria, VA: Teachers of English to Speakers of Other Languages.

Shulman, L. S. (1987) 'Knowledge and teaching: Foundations of the new reform'. *Harvard Educational Review,* 57/1. 1–22.

Stetsenko, A. and Arievitch, I. M. (2004) 'Vygotskian collaborative project of social transformation: History, politics, and practice in knowledge construction'. *International Journal of Critical Psychology,* 12/4. 58–80.

Tedick, D. J. (2009) 'K-12 language teacher preparation: Problems and possibilities'. *Modern Language Journal,* 93/2. 263–267.

Vygotsky, L. S. (1978) *Mind in society.* Cambridge, MA: Harvard University Press.

Vygotsky, L. S. (1986) *Thought and language.* Cambridge, MA: MIT Press.

Walburg, H. (1977) 'Decision and perception: New constructs for research on teaching effects'. *Cambridge Journal of Education,* 7/1. 12–20.

Wallace, M. (1998) *Action research for language teachers.* Cambridge: Cambridge University Press.

Wright, T. (2002) 'Doing language awareness: Issues of language study in language teacher education', in H. Trappes-Lomax and G. Ferguson (eds) *Language in language teacher education.* Amsterdam: John Benjamins Publishing Company. 113–130.

Yoshida, T. (2011) 'Model as a meditational space: Japanese EFL teachers' emerging conceptualizations of curriculum', in K. E. Johnson and P. R. Golombek (eds) *Research on second language teacher education: A sociocultural perspective on professional development.* New York: Routledge. 132–152.

Zuengler, J. and Miller, E. R. (2006) 'Cognitive and sociocultural perspectives: Two parallel SLA worlds?' *TESOL Quarterly,* 40/1. 35–58.

10

New technologies, blended learning and the 'flipped classroom' in ELT

Paul Gruba, Don Hinkelman and
Mónica Stella Cárdenas-Claros

Introduction

New technologies and media consist of blends of digital technologies, practices and social arrangements that people use to enable and extend their ability to share meaning, communicate through shared technical resources and build large networked communities (Lievrouw, 2011). Increasingly integrated into second language programmes, new technologies challenge ELT professionals to reconsider how they design, teach and assess their courses (Lotherington and Jenson, 2011).

Potentially, new technologies can enhance language teaching and learning when their use aligns with principles of second language acquisition (Chapelle, 2009), for example, by facilitating student interaction or through tasks explicitly designed to foster noticing. Technologies also contribute to language learning when they are used to encourage the development of 'new' or 'multi' literacies that are needed to meet the demands of twenty-first century living (Huber et al., 2015; see also Paran and Wallace, this volume). Once challenged to understand, produce and navigate through new media, students can learn to interact effectively in English across vast global digital networks (Lotherington and Jenson, 2011); accordingly, one key goal of modern ELT programmes is to foster the development of the language and digital skills that are needed to communicate in the modern world.

In this chapter, we discuss two ways in which ELT programmes are making use of new technologies. In a 'blended' approach, new media and technologies are integrated in face-to-face settings (Gruba and Hinkelman, 2012); in a 'flipped' approach, new media such as digital video are designed to prepare students in advance of a lesson so that class time itself is participatory (Lage et al., 2000). Both approaches to ELT programmes illustrate the ways that new media technologies spur innovation in the modern language curriculum (Cennamo et al., 2009; Kessler, 2009), and both may disrupt established teacher and student routines. We conclude the chapter with a discussion of the further possibilities of, and limits to, the use of new media and technologies in ELT programmes.

From CALL to blended language learning

Developments in CALL

Discussion of the role of technologies in language learning is often located in the field of 'computer-assisted language learning' (CALL). In general, work in CALL has mirrored pedagogical trends in ELT, adopting behaviourist, cognitive and socio-cultural views of language learning (Chapelle, 2001). Behaviourist perspectives, grounded in a belief that sequential study of grammar and vocabulary are key to successful language learning, can be found in techniques that saw early computers as 'patient tutors' that could endlessly deliver systematic content to students through tutorial CALL-based activities, such as flash cards, adaptive quizzes and level-based readers. Cognitive views, based on individualistic, psychological theories of learning, could be found in CALL applications that sought to teach learning strategies as a way to develop core language skills through, for example, guided Internet search activities. In tandem with socio-cultural theories that see participation as a way to acquire languages (Chau and Lee, 2014), CALL educators now increasingly foster student computer-mediated communication (CMC) exchanges in forums, blogs and wikis (see also Kern, Ware and Warschauer, this volume).

Defined as "the full integration of technology in language learning", CALL is now evolving to be "a dynamic complex in which technology, theory, and pedagogy are inseparably interwoven" (Garrett, 2009: 719–720). As predicted by Bax (2003), computers in language learning are set to 'disappear' into ELT programmes and become a normal, routine part of everyday language teaching (Chapelle, 2010). Nonetheless, normalisation continues to be a moving target as new media and technologies continue to redefine what it means to teach, learn and assess languages in the twenty-first century (Lotherington and Jenson, 2011). The concept of blended language learning, along with its ability to integrate pedagogy and technology, offers a comprehensive framework to understand the constant change that teachers, researchers and administrators must adapt to.

Reconceptualising teaching, learning and assessment

Reconceptualising teaching

One way that new media and technologies challenge established teaching practices lies in their potential to undermine the authority of ELT instructors (Corbel, 2007), alter the design and use of language tasks (Hampel, 2006), change concepts of spaces and timings (Gruba and Hinkelman, 2012) and upset traditional notions of a stepped curriculum (Waters, 2009). The authority of teachers is disrupted when freely available video and audio materials are available directly from the Internet. In addition, language task design is altered by a drive to incorporate a range of media. Spaces and timings are altered, as learners can interact with authentic input anytime and anywhere. Finally, teaching through a twenty-first century curriculum can no longer depend on educational structures originally modelled on nineteenth century industrial processes. That is, proponents argue, language acquisition cannot be based on a linear progression of skills neatly classified into beginning, intermediate and advanced levels of proficiency (Cameron and Larsen-Freeman, 2007); new technologies allow teachers and curriculum planners to respond to this in more flexible ways. Throughout, proponents argue that language learning can, and indeed must, integrate technologies to facilitate language proficiency in a world now full of new technologies and media.

Reconceptualising learning

Learning is altered by the use of new media and technologies as students acquire the 'new literacies' required for twenty-first century learning (e.g. Hafner, 2014). Briefly, 'new literacies' is an umbrella term for the skills needed to navigate, understand and produce digital texts (for an overview, see Coiro et al., 2008; Benson and Chik, 2010). Through participation in online communities of learning, for example, learners are guided as they develop proficiencies in microblogging, social network sites, digital video, discussion boards and mash-up news sites (Thomas, 2011). Without such exposure to technologies, students are seen to be handicapped by curricula that emphasise 'traditional' or 'flat' literacies which involve the less interactive learning of print material. This approach is often situated in environments where questioning, exploration and participation are discouraged in favour of the reproduction of information in formal assessments (Lotherington and Jenson, 2011).

For the learner, new technologies also pose a range of challenges brought on by a need to be more autonomous, more critical and more able to communicate across a variety of world Englishes. Autonomy is necessary for students working with new technologies because they themselves must direct their own efforts to learn within complex multi-literacy environments (e.g. Fuchs et al., 2012; see Benson, this volume, for further discussion of learner autonomy). Critical thinking comes to the fore, as students need to be able to sift through vast amounts of material to discern quality. The global use of English as a Lingua Franca, both in face-to-face and online settings, is now a central reason why learners must be able to adjust their communicative practices in ways that are appropriate to the local context (see Seargeant, this volume, for further discussion of World Englishes and English as a Lingua Franca).

Reconceptualising assessment

Potentially, if new media fundamentally redefine what it means to be proficient in a language (Lotherington and Jenson, 2011; Kress, 2013), there are several implications for language testing. Constructs, or the underlying principles of a skill area, have traditionally been demonstrated through competence with print in reading, audiotapes for listening, handwritten manuscripts for writing and face-to-face interactions for speaking. Such views are challenged when reading goes online, digital video is used for listening, collaborative writing is created through wikis and video conferencing links speakers across the globe (Gruba, 2014). In 2007, for example, Royce (2007: 374) called for "multimodal communicative competence" or "becoming competent in interpreting and constructing appropriate meanings multimodally" to be a key goal in language learning. Thus, as pedagogical goals move towards the acquisition of new literacies, it is clear that performance in new literacies must become the focus of assessment activities (Kress, 2013). Nowadays, for example, as contemporary students make frequent use of short message services (SMS) facilities and online social and visual media, handwritten responses in class may seem dated (Douglas, 2010). Despite reaching high levels of proficiency, language educators may be hesitant to 'recognise' these emerging means of personal and global communication (Kress, 2013). Indeed, language educators may still cling to tests of grammatical accuracy for reasons more aligned to embedded institutional practices than to a need to advance an ability to communicate in world Englishes (Brown, 2014), for example, or continue to test listening through audio-only files in an age dominated by on-demand video access sites.

Towards blended language learning in ELT

Having discussed the issues and challenges of CALL, how might these changes happen in practice – how might technologies 'disappear' through normalisation and 'proliferate' through multimodality? One way is through blended learning. Recent developments in blended learning, or the principled integration of new technologies and media in face-to-face classrooms, can be found in many mainstream education and ELT publications that include, for example, work by Garrison and Vaughan (2008), Picciano (2009) and Tomlinson and Whittaker (2013).

Approaches to blended learning in ELT can be based on ecological principles that emphasise the context in which learning occurs, where entities are seen to be less important than relationships (van Lier, 2004; Lafford, 2009). In an ecological framework, the teacher acts as an agent of intervention, configuring dimensions that are both embedded within a device and between devices, materials and spaces. Humans are not separated from the configuration (as in a device-centric view) but are part of all dimensions. Southgate and Murphy (2011) called this the 'nature' of the blend of teaching modes, tools and resources.

Extending this ecological approach to blended learning, Gruba and Hinkelman (2012) seek to refine and extend the work of CALL theorists such that technologies are used in ways that are appropriate, purposeful, sustainable and multimodal. To clarify their framework, they write that technology is appropriate when ELT educators are sensitive to the proficiency levels and socio-cultural contexts of their students. Gruba and Hinkelman suggest that, to be purposeful, technologies be used to add value to the language learning experience by providing real-world contexts through multi-media and by extending the time and places in which learning can take place. The sustainable use of technologies in ELT programmes, they argue, can be promoted by fostering an attitude of sharing and revision amongst learners and revision amongst educators. Finally, to recognise the consumption and production of new media by students, 'multimodal' texts and practices need to be integral to blended language learning.

In their work, Gruba and Hinkelman (2012) also identify five pedagogical dimensions of technologies that are useful in interpreting blended learning practices: actions, groupings, timings, texts and tools.

Actions

Based on seminal research in educational technology, Laurillard (2002) combined classroom and digital activities to propose five types of pedagogic technologies that occur in blended learning environments. Gruba and Hinkelman (2012) then mapped out these intentional actions as they take place in second language learning contexts. *Narrative* actions occur, for example, when materials are presented in a teacher-fronted lecture or digital video clip. *Interactive* actions are promoted when learners discuss and respond to narrative content through, for example, feedback, pair-work dialogues and online discussion boards. *Adaptive* actions, including role plays and games, may enable learners to modify their speaking and listening responses according to differing educational demands and learning styles. *Communicative* actions are best exemplified by small group work that involves problem solving. Finally, *productive* actions promote the creation and publication of student work for an audience through websites, conferences and online video clips.

Groupings

Gruba and Hinkelman (2012) place *groupings* as a dimension in their framework for blended learning to recognise how classroom activities may vary according to whether or not students are working individually, in pairs or in small or large groups. Recognition of grouping is important because it helps ELT instructors determine the amount and arrangement of physical resources that are required (e.g. a tablet for each student or moving chairs to allow groups of students to interact), as well as informing the design of blended tasks; for example, can some aspects of a task be completed individually in ways that lead to wider contributions to whole class activities? In blended approaches, what an 'individual' or 'collective' contribution consists of may be blurred when students work across face-to-face and online environments (Gruba, 2014); accordingly, groupings may need to be presented as flexible concepts to students, with task designs requiring multiple switches between individual, pair and group work.

Timings

The dimension of *timing* recognises that classroom activities can be based on technologies that are used in real-time (i.e. synchronous) activities or those that are grounded in recorded technologies (i.e. asynchronous). To take an example of a combined synchronous and asynchronous activity, a student can prepare for a live, face-to-face presentation in her classroom after reflecting on a series of recorded written conversations, or 'threads', that she participated in through an online discussion board. *Timings* also involves recognising the pacing or speed at which students are expected to work. Pacing can be periodic and/or intensive, that is, on the one hand, periodic pacing involves actions across an extended activity such as maintaining a blog on a weekly basis; on the other hand, intensive pacing may be required when students participate in fast-paced and competitive in-class language learning games (Neumeier, 2005).

Texts

Traditionally, *text* was understood to be writing on a piece of paper; contemporary views, however, are more likely to see text as a communicative artefact that has materiality and structure that is seen to generate meaning through multimodal semiotic resources (Graddol, 1994). For the ELT teacher, broader views of text may help when coming to terms with student-produced artefacts that may range from blogs to wikis to video clips across a number of social network sites (Levy and Stockwell, 2006). Even when simple slides are added to a presentation, the text expands to combine images and key words together with spoken words and physical gestures.

Tools

Tools, in Gruba and Hinkelman's framing, is a dimension which acknowledges the ways in which variations in the physical devices, classroom furniture, software applications and online networks (e.g. learning management systems [LMSs], social messaging services) may influence the production of tangible learning outcomes. Previously, in an early CALL perspective, tools were limited to the addition of desktop computers to language learning classrooms. However, the wide range of devices now installed in schools and carried by learners includes smartphones, interactive whiteboards, tablets, movable desks and flat screens. Tools are not only physical devices and furniture but also virtual, online systems and plug-ins. The concept of 'software' has also transformed from, for example, simple cloze or gap-fill programmes into complex online tools or apps that teach pronunciation, record presentations, play word games and correct written grammar.

Such dimensions of blended learning may be manifested in a task-based learning (TBLT) approach (Thomas and Reinders, 2010; González-Lloret and Ortega, 2014). In TBLT, the curriculum and lesson planning are built around a communicative goal and an assessable outcome. The wider curricula goals, outcomes, and assessments may be ignored in 'weak' versions of TBLT, which largely focus only on in-class tasks, but can be a focus in 'strong' versions of TBLT (see Van den Branden, this volume). In the past, tasks were often separated into classroom tasks and online tasks. However, blended language learning introduces the concept of the 'blended task', which includes both online/face-to-face or synchronous/asynchronous activity within the same task. Performing and recording a classroom role play or speech in live classroom activities and later doing self- and peer-assessment of the recording online is one example of this kind of blended task.

The 'flipped classroom'

Blended approaches to language learning may take the form of 'flipped' or 'inverted' classrooms. Rather than using an established pattern of instruction in which a language teacher presents the material, then follows with learners' practice and production (the PPP approach), a flipped approach moves the presentation of content online and asks students to interact with content before class and come prepared to participate in later discussions and activities within the classroom. Both teacher and student roles are affected. For their part, teachers must provide materials, for example in the form of video clips, discussion boards, quizzes and online resources, before leading classroom discussions; for students, the need to access materials and learn material before coming to class creates a much greater sense of responsibility to be self-directed and engaged throughout the learning process.

Many of the studies of flipped classrooms to date have been situated in discipline areas where there is a stronger emphasis to learn subject content (e.g. geography or science) rather than to encourage student participation, as in much of ELT (see, for example, Keengwe et al., 2014). However, although results are still tentative, researchers who have investigated flipped classrooms tend to agree that learners and instructors alike may benefit from using such approaches. Learners, for example, may benefit from being able to study at their own pace and revisit materials; instructors have found that they are able to give more attention to weaker learners needing review of the online content while other learners can move on to independent, interactive tasks (Bergmann and Sams, 2012).

ELT research in the use of flipped approaches is still preliminary. One study by Hung (2015) examined learning gains, perceived levels of students' participation in language tasks and students' learning attitudes regarding blended teaching. Seventy-five first-year English majors from Taiwan were assigned to flipped and non-flipped lessons. The students in the flipped lessons were required to view video material prior to and in preparation for in-class discussions and task development. For the non-flipped condition, the video viewing was done in class and materials were presented in printed format. To measure learning gains, vocabulary and listening comprehension tests were given to students after each lesson. Hung (2015) reported that students in the flipped lessons outperformed students in the non-flipped condition in terms of learning gains and student participation.

The important technological changes in the flipped approach are the inverted sequencing of individual work and group work and the addition of new media (e.g. interactive, online video tutorials). In this way, flipped techniques both re-order the sequence of learning activities and emphasise a greater use of multimodal materials. In Table 10.1, we outline two stages of three different types of learning sequences, ranging from a Type 1 'traditional' classroom learning environment (lecture/demonstration at first in class, followed by practice and homework), to a Type 2 environment with pre-class reading exercises (non-interactive class preparation using 'old' media), to Type 3 flipped, blended learning with pre-class interactive online video exercises ('new' media).

As a type of blended learning, flipped designs may emphasise narrative and interactive actions (lecture and quizzes) with texts that include video clips and complementary web or paper-based materials. Moreover, learners in flipped models can be required to complete short comprehension quizzes and/or bring questions to trigger in-class discussions (Fulton, 2012).

Ideally, flipped classes within a blended approach to ELT would promote a greater use of communicative activities. In these situations, the flipped approach would begin with out-of-class activities to reinforce vocabulary and structures with no communicative intention, followed by varied communicative activities in the face-to-face classroom sessions. Students would be expected

Table 10.1 Comparison of flipped learning with common models of classroom learning

	Stage 1: Lesson initiation	Stage 2: Lesson completion
Type 1: **Non-flipped, non-blended learning** (or, 'traditional classroom learning')	Space: <u>In the classroom</u> Actions: Teacher presentation, followed by teacher-initiated questions, immediate feedback Grouping: Large group, small group or pair-work Texts: Lecture notes on blackboard narrated with live voice, supported by printed handouts	Space: <u>Outside the classroom</u> Actions: Reading with no feedback or delayed feedback Grouping: Individual self-study Texts: Papers or textbooks
Type 2: **Flipped, non-blended learning** (pre-class study with 'old' media)	Space: <u>Outside the classroom</u> Actions: Reading textbook with no feedback or delayed feedback Grouping: Individual, self-study Texts: Paper prints or textbook	Space: <u>In the classroom</u> Actions: Open-ended questions with immediate face-to-face feedback Grouping: Large group, small group or pair-work Texts: Face-to-face activities with supporting handouts
Type 3: **Flipped, blended learning** (pre-class study with 'new' media)	Space: <u>Outside the classroom</u> Actions: Reading and watching video with closed-ended questions and immediate, automated feedback Grouping: Individual self-study Texts: Online, video lecture	Space: <u>In the classroom</u> Actions: Open-ended questions with immediate, face-to-face feedback Grouping: Large group, small group or pair-work Texts: Face-to-face activities with supporting handouts

to prepare for the lesson ahead of time through specific vocabulary, grammar and problem-posing material made available online. In this way, interactional and social views of language learning could be heightened by exploiting the capabilities of new technologies to present lower priority tasks and thus expand the opportunities to enact a much richer communicative and collaborative set of activities (Chapelle, 2001). Therefore, while some teachers may claim that flipping is 'nothing new', the blended way that flipping replaces printed text homework with online, interactive instruction leads to multi-modal variation and problem-posing models of foreign language education (Correa, 2015).

New technologies and ELT teacher education

The full impact of new technologies and media on language teaching and learning as yet remains unknown (Kern, 2014). Most research done in ELT settings has taken a primarily techno–centric approach, where the affordance for language learning offered by the hardware device or software application is more important than the underlying pedagogical principles for its use (Levy et al., 2015).

One area in need of urgent attention lies in the training of ELT teachers to work effectively with technologies (Motteram, 2014). Recently, Arnold and Ducate (2015) summarised three key issues facing language educators and technology: the impact of differing approaches to technology use in language programmes, as well as the extent and type of specific training that is needed; the ongoing development of learning to teach and the influence of prior experiences with technologies; and the continued encouragement of collaborative and self-evaluative activities amongst language teachers. One issue, for example, concerns how differing approaches to technology use may influence the extent and type of training needed. For instance, if a teacher promotes social media to foster out-of-class interaction, difficulties in establishing student online accounts and explaining the legal uses of such accounts will likely take more time than simply logging on to an established website. Another issue, the need for ongoing training as technologies evolve, raises difficulties related to funding and resourcing continual professional development. Finally, according to Arnold and Ducate (2015), any success in the use of new media and technologies eventually relies on the continued encouragement of collaborative and self-evaluative activities amongst language teachers. In addition, Godwin-Jones (2015) points to a need for language teachers to be trained in software coding, conduct action research with technologies and see themselves as responsible global citizens.

Another way to spur professional development in new technologies is to provide an overarching goal, or set of standards, for language teachers. For this reason, TESOL, the international teachers' association, released a 'Technology Standards Framework' that seeks to better establish "pedagogically solid ways of integrating and using technologies in all language classrooms" (Healey et al., 2009: 1). The framework is built on four main goals: acquiring and maintaining foundational technical skills; integrating pedagogies and technologies; applying technologies in assessment practices; and using technologies to communicate and collaborate efficiently. For his part, Kessler (2009) sees standards as a way to make the integration of new technologies into language classrooms more meaningful; others, however, may see the addition of yet another standard as implying that there is a shared responsibility across the profession for language teachers to be proficient in new technologies despite an already demanding workload (Tai, 2012). Teacher resistance in the use of new technologies may persist in settings where teachers fear losing control of their classrooms, especially those who come from teacher-centred training (Cárdenas-Claros and Oyanedel, 2015).

Gamification, gaming and mobile learning for ELT

Although not specific to ELT, the *Horizon Report*, released each year by the New Media Consortium, provides a way for ELT educators to see upcoming trends in the use of new technologies and media (Johnson et al., 2015). Based on the collected opinions of a range of global educational technology experts, the report sets out short-term, long-term and disruptive ('wicked') trends that lie ahead for higher education and secondary schools. To summarise the 2015 higher education report: short-term trends that will occur in one to two years include an increased uptake of blended learning and flipped classrooms and a need to redesign learning spaces for mobile devices; in the middle term, or three to four years from now, the report predicts a greater focus on measuring learning (learner analytics via LMS activity) and a proliferation of open educational resources (mass collaboration via Internet sites); changes that were seen to be particularly challenging in the long term, or five to seven years from the present, include a push for more innovation and increased cross-institutional collaborations. ELT professionals will need to keep pace with these mainstream educational trends. Wary of making predictions, and aware that technical fads come and go, we highlight gamification, gaming and mobile learning to illustrate how new technologies may continue to shape ELT practices in the classroom and across worldwide networks.

The first trend, gamification, is the process of integrating gaming techniques into learning environments, which is built on 'embedding motivational strategies' and deepening engagement in learning environments (Zourou and Lamy, 2013). Gamification strategies may include scoring systems, badges, challenges, rating systems and leaderboards added to already existing language learning tasks. Typically, gamification harnesses online tracking tools such as LMSs and SNSs to track participation and automatically give awards when achievement standards have been reached.

A second trend, digital gaming in ELT, can help L2 learners build problem-solving skills (Cornillie et al., 2012), offer contextualised communication (Reinders, 2012) and provide meaningful language input (Sykes and Reinhardt, 2013). In a recent study, Ryu (2013), for example, found that gaming promoted increased use of second language words, phrases and discourse through game interaction and repeated practice. Gaming may lead students to become absorbed in tasks that lead to a state of 'flow', that is, a sense of full immersion and engagement, during the language learning process (Egbert, 2003; see Csikszentmihályi, 1990, for discussion of 'flow'). Despite a critique that digital gaming is yet one more fad that will soon be abandoned (Peterson, 2013), such an approach may strengthen the growing integration of task-based language learning with new technologies (Thomas and Reinders, 2010; González-Lloret and Ortega, 2014).

A third major trend in new technologies for ELT is mobile learning, or the use of devices such as smartphones and tablets both in and out of the classroom. Use of these tools affects time, space and groupings of blended language learning environments (Gruba and Hinkelman, 2012). Online activities can be conducted individually or in groups at the learners' convenience, at home, while traveling or in public spaces. This reinforces the flipped learning approach because second language exercises can be assessed automatically with feedback and students are socialised to prepare for class ahead of the meeting time. Pegrum (2014) argues that mobile-assisted learning or 'm-learning' creates affordances and affordability across a wide spectrum of learners, opening access in developing countries and to low-income students, thereby crossing the potential 'digital divide' of 'haves' and 'have-nots'. He describes the 'ecosystem' of mobile devices and how learning artefacts such as blogs, slide shows and narrated videos facilitate or even force expanded forms of speaking, listening, reading and writing skills. Mobile devices applied in second language learning have also shown increases in EFL proficiency in extensive reading (Lin, 2014) and writing programmes (Hwang et al., 2014). In a comprehensive review of mobile assisted language learning (MALL), Duman et al. (2015) found the teaching of vocabulary to be the most prominent topic, although a significant number of the studies they examined lacked an explicit theoretical framework.

Future directions for ELT

As the chapter so far has indicated, the full integration of technologies in language teaching has a number of wide-ranging implications: ELT professionals will need to rethink how they teach, define core skills and meet the demands of new literacies, design language tasks, and create innovative language programmes (Lotherington and Jenson, 2011). Assessment practices, too, will change (Gruba, 2014). The demands of such an agenda will influence pre-service teacher training and professional development, put pressure on already heavy workloads and shift the boundaries of time, space and location for both formal and informal learning opportunities. As Kern (2014) states, such changes present both opportunities and challenges to language professionals and students; at the risk of simplification, we discuss the implications for ELT in terms of what new technologies integration may mean in the classroom, in programmes and across the field as a whole.

New technologies and the classroom

As the stable environment of a four-walled classroom breaks down into virtual and distributed 'spaces', learners and teachers are no longer confined to always attending a lesson at a specific time and location (either physical or virtual). Yet the concept of 'the classroom' is still useful as a way to discuss and locate pedagogical activities in bricks-and-mortar rooms and password-protected LMS class sites. For advocates of blended learning in ELT, the varied and intense use of technologies in face-to-face settings has a range of implications for practice for the teacher, the student and the use of resources.

For the classroom teacher, the effective blending of new technologies in the classroom presents a number of challenges. Not only do pedagogical actions require rethinking but so do fundamental considerations of power (Hinkelman and Gruba, 2012) as well as professional identities (Cárdenas-Claros and Oyanedel, 2015). Lesson preparation times, new media design and accountability may increase as teachers add materials development, outcomes reports and tool training to their workload. At the resource level, task and materials design are affected by the integration of technologies and, as such, their construction may require substantial effort (Thomas et al., 2013; González-Lloret and Ortega, 2014). Further, the widespread use of institutional LMS may become a platform for a greater scrutiny of student efforts made possible by learning analytics and other tracking technologies. Assessment for learning practices – for example, encouraging students to assess and reflect on their own work – will also require teachers to align their teaching to accord with new literacies proficiencies that include digital media production, social media usage and the navigation of virtual worlds (Kress, 2013).

Learner roles are also challenged by the integration of new technologies in their classrooms. Movements such as 'bring your own device' (Johnson et al., 2015) may heighten perceived inequalities, for example, and not all students are 'digital natives' capable of fluent uses of new technologies despite popular rhetoric surrounding the skills of a younger generation (Thomas, 2011). As with teachers, the use of learning analytics will come to foster greater accountability for students who may fundamentally come to shape how they go about the way they learn and how they direct their abilities.

New technologies and ELT programmes

For programmes located in academic institutions, technology integration is likely aimed to develop student proficiencies for further study. For example, an English for academic purposes (EAP; see Basturkmen and Wette, this volume) course would provide students with an ability to use an institutional learning management system (LMS) before they could pursue further studies in commerce and economics. In this case, meeting the students' EAP needs would place demands on the programme to provide sufficient training and technological resources.

ELT programmes situated in fully private or branded franchise schools are likely to have pressures to provide instruction for language test training or perhaps conversational interaction, for example, as well as to limit expenses such that the programme and institution can profit. In these programmes, there would be less of an incentive to fully integrate technologies in the short term, but long-term development would require a greater online presence to be able to sustain market share amidst an increasingly competitive range of educational options. Fee-paying students would need to be directed to make use of branded resources despite the global availability of low-cost and free materials that are available for learning English across social network sites (Lamy and Zourou, 2013). Professional development opportunities, as well as radical re-designing of teaching/learning approaches such as the flipped classroom, would likely be limited.

Some ELT programmes, often in low-resource countries, are built on the strength of individual or small group initiatives with an aim of serving local needs; in such cases, for example, a proficient English speaker may offer classes for a small fee to help students bolster test scores and gain practice in speaking. Technology integration in these programmes may rest on the use of agile resources that can be delivered across mobile devices.

The role of new technologies could be useful in accessing world Englishes to inspire students, for example, as well as to provide a means to practise language skills. Blending, of course, could occur when students are gathered in face-to-face settings but where the flipped classroom may well be considered a distant novelty.

New technologies and the ELT profession

As the publication of the TESOL Technology Standards (Healey et al., 2009; see above) implies, the ELT profession is well aware of the need to raise both language and new literacies proficiency in tandem, for students and teachers alike. Meeting such standards, however, requires a strong commitment to training in the effective use of new technologies in pre-service teacher training and professional development programmes as well as considerable revision of language learning goals, resources and assessment practices.

As recommended in the *Horizon Report* (Johnson et al., 2015; see earlier in the chapter), ELT professionals would need to follow the lead of mainstream educators to foster much greater cooperation across programmes to share resources and expertise, not only to contain costs but also to be able to maintain relevance. Contemporary students need to be assured that what they are learning in an ELT programme cannot simply be found through video sharing sites, for example, or in the playing of online games: what does a blended approach, run by dedicated ELT professionals, offer to learners that self-directed online learning does not? The answer may lie in the trends of gamification and flipped learning, where the social presence of mentors and peers is important and learning competitively and collaboratively in cohorts may spur greater motivation and achievement.

Additionally, ELT programmes may strive to meet a set of international standards established by one of its leading professional organisations. Progress may be slow and face barriers at times; nonetheless, the lack of sustained response would eventually undermine confidence in the ability of the profession to deliver instruction that is truly relevant to the complex demands of global communication for educational, social, economic and recreational purposes.

Future directions in ELT research

In their review of twelve years of research in 'mobile-assisted language learning' (MALL), Duman et al. (2015) found that a significant number of studies lacked theoretical framing. Their findings echo the conclusion of a meta-analysis of over 350 studies in the area of computer-assisted language learning: "most CALL studies seem limited to either describing the affordances offered by particular types of technology or measuring their effects on students' affective reactions" (Golonka et al., 2014: 92). To improve research, Golonka and her colleagues suggested that there be a greater emphasis on developing mature theories that are closely aligned with prevailing theories of learning. Importantly, they concluded, those working with technologies should not lose sight of the point that quality teaching depends on a 'blend' of technologies aligned to appropriate frameworks of instructional, cognitive and socio-cultural models of learning.

Confirming this belief, Levy et al. (2015) surveyed CALL professionals to find that the most prominent areas of their studies concerned 'pedagogy', 'design' and 'research'. Notably, areas such as 'psychology', 'linguistics' and 'technology' were ranked as much lower priorities for the field. In discussing the results, Levy and his colleagues agreed that the development of principled teaching practices, grounded in well-designed learning environments and backed by sound empirical studies, would continue to drive the field.

Summary

Years ago, Warschauer (2004: 24) wrote about the future of technologies with the astute observation that "the most important developments may not be those that occur in the technological realm, but rather those that take place in our own conceptions of teaching and learning". In this chapter, we have reviewed several ways that new technologies, blended learning and the flipped classroom will indeed continue to challenge us. In summary, they are set to realign our notions of literacies, professional development, assessment practices, mobile learning, and the role of games throughout our programmes as ELT develops in the twenty-first century.

Discussion questions

- Why is there a drive to integrate new technologies into ELT programmes?
- Describe an ideal blended language lesson that would be appropriate to your situation.
- How does the introduction of new technologies, blended approaches and flipped classrooms fundamentally alter the relationships between teachers and students and, indeed, amongst students themselves?
- New media and technologies often require significant resources. Are they viable for sustained use in developing countries or throughout low-technology contexts?
- Language programme evaluation is often grounded in a clear acknowledgement of national or state standards, and ELT programmes are measured on their success in attaining such standards. Do you think blended and flipped approaches should foster the development of a new set of standards to teaching?

Related topics

Computer-mediated communication and language learning; Task-based language teaching; Teaching language skills; Teaching literacy.

Further reading

Laurillard, D. (2012) *Teaching as a design science: Building pedagogical patterns for learning and technology*. New York: Routledge. (This major methodological work in pedagogic design provides a framework for iterative, cyclical change in building blended learning environments that incorporate both face-to-face and digital technologies.)

Pegrum, M. (2014) *Mobile learning: Languages, literacies and cultures*. Basingstoke, UK: Palgrave Macmillan. (Grounded in a solid understanding of mobile devices, this book provides insights into teaching with new media and includes a range of international case studies to illustrate mobile language learning in actual practice.)

Stanley, G. and Thornbury, S. (2013) *Language learning with technology: Ideas for integrating technology in the language classroom*. Cambridge, UK: Cambridge University Press. (A well-written and clear guide for classroom teachers who are seeking ideas and activities to integrate new technologies into their lessons, assessments and evaluation.)

Tagg, C. (2015) *Exploring digital communication: Language in action*. New York: Routledge. (Divided into sections that explore problems and practices, interventions and theory, this book examines contemporary issues of how language online is influencing a range of communication practices.)

References

Arnold, N. and Ducate, L. (2015) 'Contextualized views of practices and competencies in CALL teacher education research'. *Language Learning & Technology*, 19/1. 1–9.

Bax, S. (2003) 'CALL – Past, present and future'. *System*, 31/1. 13–28.

Benson, P. and Chik, A. (2010) 'New literacies and autonomy in foreign language learning', in M. J. Luzón, M. N Ruiz-Madrid and M. L. Villanueva (eds) *Digital genres, new literacies, and autonomy in language learning*. Newcastle upon Tyne: Cambridge Scholars. 63–80.

Bergmann, J. and Sams, A. (2012) *Flip your classroom: Reach every student in every class every day*. Alexandria, VA: International Society for Technology in Education.

Brown, J. D. (2014) 'The future of World Englishes in language testing'. *Language Assessment Quarterly*, 11/1. 5–26.

Cameron, L. and Larsen-Freeman, D. (2007) 'Complex systems and applied linguistics'. *International Journal of Applied Linguistics*, 17/2. 226–239.

Cárdenas-Claros, M. and Oyanedel, M. (2015) 'Teachers' implicit theories and use of ICTs in the language classroom'. *Technology, Pedagogy and Education*. January. 1–19.

Cennamo, K., Ross, J. and Ertmer, P. (2009) *Technology integration for meaningful classroom use: A standards-based approach*. Belmont, CA: Wadsworth.

Chapelle, C. A. (2001) *Computer applications in second language acquisition: Foundations for teaching, testing, and research*. Cambridge: Cambridge University Press.

Chapelle, C. A. (2009) 'The relationship between second language acquisition theory and computer-assisted language learning'. *Modern Language Journal*, 93. 741–753.

Chapelle, C. (2010) 'The spread of computer-assisted language learning'. *Language Teaching*, 43/1. 66–74.

Chau, J. and Lee, A. (2014) 'Technology-enhanced language learning (TeLL): An update and a principled framework for English for Academic Purposes (EAP) courses'. *Canadian Journal of Learning & Technology*, 40/1. 1–24.

Coiro, J., Knobel, M., Lankshear, C. and Leu, D. J. (2008) *Handbook of research on new literacies*. New York: Erlbaum.

Corbel, C. (2007) 'Teacher's roles in the global hypermedia environment', in J. Cummins and C. Davison (eds) *International handbook of English language teaching*. New York: Springer. 1113–1124.

Cornillie, F., Thorne, S. and Desmet, P. (2012) 'Digital games for language learning: Challenges and opportunities'. *ReCALL*, 24/3. 243–256.

Correa, M. (2015) 'Flipping the foreign language classroom and critical pedagogies'. *Higher Education for the Future*, 2/2. 114–125.

Csikszentmihályi, M. (1990) *Flow: The psychology of optimal experience*. New York: Harper and Row.

Douglas, D. (2010) *Understanding language testing*. London: Hodder.

Duman, G., Orhon, G. and Gedik, N. (2015) 'Research trends in mobile assisted language learning from 2000 to 2012'. *ReCALL*, 27/2. 197–216.

Egbert, J. (2003) 'A study of flow theory in the foreign language classroom'. *Modern Language Journal*, 87/4. 499–518.

Fuchs, C., Hauck, M. and Muller-Hartmann, A. (2012) 'Promoting learner autonomy through multiliteracy skills development in cross-institutional exchanges'. *Language Learning & Technology*, 16/3. 82–102.

Fulton, K. (2012) 'Upside down and inside out: Flip your classroom to improve student learning'. *Learning & Leading with Technology*, 39/8. 12–17.

Garrett, N. (2009) 'Computer-assisted language learning trends and issues revisited: Integrating innovation'. *Modern Language Journal*. 93/1. 719–740.

Garrison, D. R. and Vaughan, N. D. (2008) *Blended learning in higher education: Framework, principles, and guidelines*. San Francisco: Jossey-Bass.

Godwin-Jones, R. (2015) 'The evolving roles of language teachers: Trained coders, local researchers, global citizens'. *Language Learning & Technology*, 19/1. 10–22.

Golonka, E. M., Bowles, A. R., Frank, V. M., Richardson, D. L. and Freynik, S. (2014) 'Technologies for foreign language learning: A review of technology types and their effectiveness'. *Computer Assisted Language Learning*, 27/1. 70–105.

González-Lloret, M. and Ortega, L. (2014) *Tasks and technology: Exploring technology-mediated TBLT*. Amsterdam: John Benjamins.

Graddol, D. (1994) 'What is a text?', in D. Graddol and O. Boyd-Barret (eds) *Media texts: Authors and readers*. Clevendon: Multilingual matters. 40–50.

Gruba, P. (2014) 'New media in language assessments', in A. J. Kunnan (ed.) *The companion to language assessment*. London: John Wiley. 995–1012.

Gruba, P. and Hinkelman, D. (2012) *Blending technologies in second language classrooms*. Basingstoke, UK: Palgrave MacMillan.

Hafner, C. A. (2014) 'Embedding digital literacies in English language teaching: Students' digital video projects as multimodal ensembles'. *TESOL Quarterly*, 48/4. 655–685.

Hampel, R. (2006) 'Rethinking task design for the digital age: A framework for language teaching and learning in a synchronous online environment'. *ReCALL*, 18/1. 105–121.

Healey, D., Hegelheimer, V., Hubbard, P., Ioannou-Georgiou, S., Kessler, G. and Ware, P. (2009) *TESOL technology standards framework*. Alexandria, VA: TESOL.

Hinkelman, D. and Gruba, P. (2012) 'Power within blended language learning programs in Japan', *Language Learning & Technology*, 16/2. 46–64.

Huber, A., Dinham, J. and Chalk, B. (2015) 'Responding to the call: Arts methodologies informing 21st century literacies'. *Literacy*, 49/1. 5–54.

Hung, H. T. (2015) 'Flipping the classroom for English language learners to foster active learning'. *Computer Assisted Language Learning*, 28/1. 81–96.

Hwang, W., Chen, H. Shadiev, R. Huang, R. and Chen, C. (2014) 'Improving English as a foreign language writing in elementary schools using mobile devices in familiar situational contexts'. *Computer Assisted Language Learning*, 27/5. 359–378.

Johnson, L., Adams Becker, S., Estrada, V. and Freeman, A. (2015) *NMC horizon report: 2015 higher education edition*. Austin, TX: NMC.

Keengwe, J., Onchwari, G. and Oigara, J. N. (2014) *Promoting active learning through the flipped classroom model*. Hershey PA: Information Science Reference.

Kern, R. (2014) 'Technology as *pharmakon*: The promise and perils of the Internet for foreign language education'. *Modern Language Journal*, 98/1. 340–357.

Kessler, G. (2009) 'Technology standards in foreign language education', in K. Cennamo, J. Ross, P. Ertmer and K. Potter (eds) *Technology integration for meaningful classroom use: A standards-based approach*. Belmont, CA: Wadsworth. 1–26.

Kress, G. (2013) 'Recognizing learning: A perspective from a social semiotic theory of multimodality', in I. de Saint Georges and J. Weber (eds) *Multilingualism and multimodality: Current challenges for educational studies*. Rotterdam: Sens Publications. 119–140.

Lafford, B. (2009) 'Toward an ecological CALL: Update to Garrett (1991)'. *Modern Language Journal*, 93 (Supplement s1). 673–696.

Lage, M. J., Platt, G. J. and Treglia, M. (2000) Inverting the classroom: A gateway to creating an inclusive learning environment. *The Journal of Economic Education*, 31/1. 30–43.

Lamy, M-N. and Zourou, K. (2013) *Social networking for language education*. New York: Palgrave-MacMillan.

Laurillard, D. (2002) *Rethinking university teaching: A framework for the effective use of learning technologies* (2nd ed.). London: Routledge Farmer.

Levy, M., Hubbard, P., Stockwell, G. and Colpaert, J. (2015) 'Research challenges in CALL'. *Computer Assisted Language Learning*. 28/1. 1–6.

Levy, M. and Stockwell, G. (2006) *CALL dimensions: Options and issues in computer-assisted language learning*. Mahwah, NJ: Lawrence Erlbaum.

Lievrouw, L. A. (2011) *Alternative and activist new media*. Cambridge: Polity.

Lin, C. (2014) 'Learning English reading in a mobile-assisted extensive reading program'. *Computers & Education*, 78/September. 48–59.

Lotherington, H. and Jenson, J. (2011) 'Teaching multimodal and digital literacy in L2 settings: New literacies, new basics, new pedagogies'. *Annual Review of Applied Linguistics*, 31. 226–246.

Motteram, G. (2014) 'Re-aligning research into teacher education for CALL and bringing it into the mainstream'. *Language Teaching*, 47/3. 319–331.

Neumeier, P. (2005) A closer look at blended learning – parameters for designing a blended learning environment for language teaching and learning. *ReCALL*, 17/2. 163–178.

Pegrum, M. (2014) *Mobile learning: Languages, literacies and cultures*. Basingstoke: Palgrave Macmillan.

Peterson, M. (2013) *Computer games and language learning*. Basingstoke: Palgrave Macmillan.

Picciano, A. G. (2009) 'Blending with purpose: The multimodal model'. *Journal of the Research Center for Educational Technology (RCET)*, 5/1. 4–14.

Reinders, H. (ed.) (2012) *Digital games in language learning and teaching*. Basingstoke: Palgrave Macmillan.

Royce, T. D. (2007) 'Multimodal communicative competence in second language contexts', in T. D. Royce and W. Bowcher (eds) *New directions in the analysis of multimodal discourse*. New York: Lawrence Erlbaum. 361–390.

Ryu, D. (2013) 'Play to learn, learn to play: Language learning through gaming culture'. *ReCALL*, 25/2. 286–301.

Southgate, M. and Murphy, L. (2011) 'The nature of the "blend": Interaction of teaching modes, tools and resources', in M. Nicolson, L. Murphy and M. Southgate (eds) *Language teaching in blended contexts*. Edinburgh: Dunedin Press. 13–28.

Sykes, J. and Reinhardt, J. (2013) *Language at play: Digital games in second and foreign language teaching and learning*. New York: Pearson.

Tai, Y. (2012) 'Contextualizing a MALL: Practice, design and evaluation'. *Journal of Educational Technology & Society*, 15/2. 220–230.

Thomas, M. (2011) *Deconstructing digital natives: Young people, technology, and the new literacies*. London: Routledge.

Thomas, M. and Reinders, H. (eds) (2010) *Task-based language learning and teaching with technology*. London: Continuum.

Thomas, M., Reinders, H. and Warschauer, M. (eds) (2013) *Contemporary computer-assisted language learning*. New York: Bloomsbury.

Tomlinson, B. and Whittaker, C. (eds) (2013) *Blended learning in English language teaching: Course design and implementation*. London: British Council.

van Lier, L. (2004) *The ecology and semiotics of language learning: A sociocultural perspective*. Boston: Kluwer.

Warschauer, M. (2004) 'Technological change and the future of CALL', in S. Fotos and C. Browne (eds) *New perspectives on CALL for the second language classroom*. Mahwah, NJ: Lawrence Erlbaum. 15–26.

Waters, A. (2009) 'Managing innovation in English language education'. *Language Teaching*, 42/4. 421–458.

Zourou, K. and Lamy, M. (2013) 'Social networked game dynamics in web 2.0 language learning communities'. *Alsic*, vol. 16. Retrieved from http://alsic.revues.org/2642. doi: 10.4000/alsic.2642

11

English for specific purposes

Sue Starfield

Historical overview

The emergence of ESP

Learning and teaching English for specific rather than general purposes is an approach that began to develop during and after World War II and has shown continued growth since. Its origins are to be found in the enormous social changes and massive economic development that occurred with what has been called the third wave of globalisation (Robertson in Kumaravadivelu, 2006) as Europe struggled to rebuild itself post-1945 and newly independent Asian and African countries sought to modernise. The growth of multinational capitalism during this period and the emergence of the United States of America as a global superpower also encouraged the development of English for specific purposes (ESP) teaching. At the same time, ideologies of progress and the desire to facilitate international communication, understanding and student exchange in the hope of helping to prevent future wars were also influential in ESP's establishment. These somewhat contradictory aims and intentions are at the heart of ESP and are the focus of some recent critiques which will be discussed in this chapter (see also Starfield (2013b) for further discussion).

The ESP learner is not learning the language for general educative purposes or for the study of literature in which the language is the subject matter of the course, but rather as a means to the "acquisition of some quite different body of knowledge or set of skills" (Robinson, 1980: 6). Context and content thus became key issues in ESP pedagogy – in what context would the learner be using the language skills and what content would she or he need to access through the language (Starfield, 2013a). ESP was perceived by many ELT educators as a radical break with previous approaches; Strevens (1977: 146), for example, linked ESP to a "major, world-wide educational tide of change".

Growth of the field

From the 1960s onwards, ESP saw sustained growth and began to make a substantial contribution to the field of language learning and teaching. ESP was intended to meet the communication needs of rapidly industrialising nations, overcoming local barriers to communication, often by promoting 'global' languages such as English at the expense of local languages, and contributing to the growth of multinational corporations. In line with the modernisation agenda, ESP was also seen as more efficient, being targeted to the specific needs of the learners for their workplaces or academic settings. Benesch cites a presentation by Strevens at a 1971 conference on 'Adult English for National Development' held in Beirut: "The profession can now say . . . to the oil industry or to a shipping firm or even to a government . . . describe accurately the precise achievement in English that you require, we can 'engineer' a system that will reach this target" (Strevens, 1971, cited in Benesch, 2001: 30).

Organisations such as the British Council, the Ford Foundation, and the United States Information Agency were also actively involved in promoting ESP, contributing to the establishment of English as the dominant language of science, technology and commerce (Hutchinson and Waters, 1987; Benesch, 2001). Many of the early advocates of ESP cited in this chapter, such as Swales, Dudley-Evans and Robinson, developed their ESP approaches in newly independent states, often working on British Council-funded projects, while much of the early dissemination of their work and the work of others in the new field was through British Council publications in the *ELT Documents* series (see Robinson, 1980, for a comprehensive bibliography, and Swales, 1985a). The link to the postcolonial context is explicit in *The Linguistic Sciences and Language Teaching* (Halliday et al., 1964), an influential text that set out an agenda for ESP based on functional linguistics, in particular the study of register. The authors clearly articulate ESP's intention to provide an approach to language learning and teaching that distinguishes itself from traditional general purposes language teaching:

> only the merest fraction of investigation has yet been carried out into just what parts of a conventional course in English are needed by . . . power station engineers in India, or police inspectors in Nigeria; even less is known about precisely what extra specialised material is required.
>
> *(Halliday et al., 1964: 189)*

Register analysis

While Halliday et al. identify need and context as important categories, in their view, the task of the linguist was to carry out "detailed studies of restricted language and special registers" based on "large samples of the language used by the particular person concerned" (ibid.: 190). The importance of what came to be called 'authentic' texts – texts that learners were likely to encounter in their work or study situation – is also evident in their thinking. Halliday and colleagues' emphasis on specific sublanguages or registers was seminal to the development of the many ESP subfields that are still studied and taught today – for example, English for medical purposes; English for law; English for nursing; English for science and technology; English for academic purposes (EAP) (see Basturkmen and Wette, this volume); and occupational sublanguages such as English for business/occupational purposes and vocational/workplace English.

The initial focus of ESP on the language for science and technology was not surprising, as there was a "postwar boom in funding for sciences and technology by the United States and the United Kingdom [that] included subsidies for English language teaching" (Benesch, 2001: 5). English for science and technology (EST) research was influenced by register analysis and consisted of frequency studies of lexical items and grammatical features of science texts. Textbooks developed on the basis of register analysis include *A Course in Basic Scientific English,* from a study of three million words of modern scientific English (Ewer and Latorre, 1969). This approach has been criticised for confining its analysis to sentence level; the restricted range of grammar and lexis; the lack of authenticity of the reading passages; the focus on form at the expense of meaning and communication; and whether special registers could, in fact, be clearly identified (Robinson, 1980; Dudley-Evans and St John, 1998).

A rhetorical/functional approach

Partly as a response to the difficulties experienced with register analysis, and under the influence of communicative approaches to language teaching and theoretical frameworks such as speech act theory and functional linguistics, applied linguists began to examine texts beyond the level of the sentence in terms of their overall discourse structure and their rhetorical purpose or communicative function. *Industrial English* (Jupp and Hodlin, 1975) adopted a functional approach to analysing the language needed by factory workers in the UK, clearly moving away from the linguistic/structural syllabus to focus on what people do with language in the workplace. The nine volume *English in Focus* series (edited by Allen and Widdowson from 1974–1980) featured textbooks in areas such as physical science, mechanical engineering, medical science, education, social science and biology. The series followed a rhetorical/functional approach that saw scientific discourse as a set of rhetorical acts such as defining, classifying and exemplifying. This early interest in texts and the relationship between form and function laid the foundation for the development of studies of genre and the concept of discourse community, which have become central to ESP (see Swales, 1990, and further discussion here).

These early approaches to ESP were based on the belief that identifying the specific variety of language or discourse functions of the particular domain of future study would meet the learners' communicative needs and sustain student motivation. As most ESP learners were adults, they were also assumed to have more clearly identifiable needs than younger learners. Needs analysis was used to carry out target situation analysis in order to specify the communicative language functions required within the specific context and develop appropriate syllabus content (Hutchinson and Waters, 1987; Benesch, 2001). Munby's (1978) *Communicative Syllabus Design* attempted to provide a more theoretically informed and systematic approach to needs analysis through detailed lists of micro-functions which the ESP practitioner would need to identify prior to syllabus development. Although largely discounted today, the approach had the merit of placing needs analysis, situation, function and context at centre stage in ESP, alerting ESP practitioners to the multiple variables that needed to be considered when adopting a communicative approach. The more sophisticated needs analyses approaches in use today have evolved in part as a reaction to Munby's work.

Munby's needs analysis model used a pre-course analysis that the course developer carried out prior to implementation. In contrast, in Richterich and Chancerel's (1977) influential approach (developed for the Council of Europe to identify the needs of adults learning a foreign language), needs analysis is an ongoing process, not a one-off event carried out prior to the commencement of a course. Crucially, they not only focussed on the language needed in the target situation but also emphasised the role of 'present situation analysis', drawing attention to the gap between what students could currently do with the language and what they needed or wanted to be able to do at the end of the course. In this approach, the learners, the educational institution and the employer separately identify their needs, which may include available resources, objectives, curriculum and teaching methods. Methods used are largely quantitative and include surveys and questionnaires and content analyses but also non-directive interviews, language attitude scales and job analyses.

An established field

By 1981, with the founding of the first scholarly journal devoted entirely to English for specific purposes (known then as the *ESP Journal* and today as *English for Specific Purposes*), ESP could be said to have become an established field of study within English language teaching. Johns (2013:

6), however, points out that, "unlike many other research areas in theoretical and applied linguistics, ESP has been, at its core, a practitioners' movement" with a focus on "establishing, through careful research, the needs and relevant discourse features for a targeted group of students". While these concerns continue to drive much ESP research, as Hewings (2002) notes in his survey of articles published in *English for Specific Purposes* between 1981–2001, papers on course design, which proliferated in the earlier years, decreased over the period; meanwhile, empirical studies with a focus on written textual or discourse analysis became the norm. In all likelihood, this was due to the growing professionalisation and specialisation of the field and its need to meet established university definitions of research as, by the early 2000s, the journal was listed on the *Social Sciences Citation Index* (SSCI) (Hewings, 2002). Hewings also notes a decline in the proportion of papers that looked at ESP in general and a corresponding increase in papers on English for occupational purposes (EOP), particularly in business contexts. The biggest change, however, was the increase in papers dealing with EAP, to the extent that about 80 per cent of papers in later volumes focused on this area. This is more than likely due to most scholars being based in academia, where research and publication are an expectation (Flowerdew and Peacock, 2001). As EAP is the subject of a separate chapter in this *Handbook* (see Basturkmen and Wette, this volume), the focus in this chapter is on the sub-field known as EOP, which has a workplace and professional orientation. However, as Flowerdew and Peacock (2001) point out, there is no neat dividing line between EAP and EOP; categories may overlap, as when English classes for medical students could be considered to be preparing them for both their academic study but also their professional practice.

Current issues

In an overview of developments in ESP through the last decade of the twentieth century into the early years of the twenty-first century, Belcher (2006: 135) comments that there would probably be agreement that "needs assessment, content-based teaching methods, and content-area informed instructors have long been considered essential to the practice of specific-purposes language teaching". She goes on to point out that contemporary processes of globalisation are, at the same time, rendering these notions increasingly more complex. Learners are often mobile, diverse, multilingual populations with rapidly evolving needs, and our understandings of content and contexts are becoming more nuanced through the use of diverse methodologies and theories not only of language learning but of the relationships of individuals to society. Above all, the role of English has changed most dramatically from the early days of ESP sketched out above, as it has become the international lingua franca of business, industry and science (Kassim and Ali, 2010; Nickerson, 2013). Current issues in needs analysis and the roles of content and context are discussed in more detail below.

Needs analysis

While needs analysis can be seen as the "foundation on which all other decisions are, or should be, made" (Belcher, 2006: 135), that is, "the means of establishing the *how* and *what* of a course" (Hyland, 2006: 73 emphasis in original), understandings of needs analysis have evolved considerably from the early years described above. The 'objective' language needs of students in the target situation remain important, but interest in learners' more subjective needs, wants, larger life goals, motivations and investment in the communities they seek to join has widened the scope of needs analysis (Belcher, 2006; Norton, 2013). For example, the practising engineers surveyed by Kassim and Ali (2010: 179) identified English competency as essential to their desire to become "global engineers" and saw English as a "tool for self and professional development".

Hutchinson and Waters (1987: 54) had critiqued what they saw as a "language centred approach" to target situation analysis which used subject area texts to produce lists of linguistic features to be learnt, often leading to materials that were demotivating for students. They focussed instead on the learning needs of the learner: what the learner needs to do in order to learn. They argued that teachers needed to focus on the underlying competencies and learning skills that lecturers assume students will have and which should enable them to reach the target performance rather than concentrate simply on linguistic features of specialised texts. In arguing against the existence of specialised varieties of English, Hutchinson and Waters can be seen to favour what has become known as a 'common core' approach to ESP rather than a highly subject-specific one, which has obvious implications for the role of the ESP teacher (Dudley-Evans and St John, 1998 and later in this chapter).

Thus, needs analysis is now understood as an ongoing, iterative process that continues through course delivery as teachers learn more about their students' learning needs and which may actively engage learners themselves in the needs analysis process (Dudley-Evans and St. John, 1998; Hyland, 2006; Flowerdew, 2013). As our understandings of needs become more complex, so do our understandings of the contexts in which learners will be learning the language. As a consequence, the traditional methods of stakeholder surveys, interviews and text analysis are felt to be less than adequate. Moving beyond the language focus of the first wave of ESP studies, Swales (1985b: 219) stressed the need for ESP practitioners to both grasp the "conceptual structures of the disciplines and occupations" they are supporting as well as understand the "conventions of conduct that organise vocational and organisational life", urging them to engage in "thick description" and "ethnographic sleuthing". While Swales (1985b: 219) is often viewed as a major proponent of a text-focused approach to ESP, he has long been interested in ethnographic approaches to understanding needs, arguing that "it is not only texts that we need to understand, but the roles texts have in their environments; the values . . . placed on them by occupational, professional and disciplinary memberships; and the expectations those memberships have of . . . the genres they participate in".

Ethnographically oriented methods are therefore starting to be used in ESP needs analysis. These draw on insider understandings and triangulate multiple perspectives through observation, in-depth interviewing and other forms of data collection (see, for example, Bosher and Smalkoski, 2002), although, as Cowling (2007) points out, real-world constraints such as limited time often complicate the carrying out of more in-depth observation in EOP settings.

Critical needs analysis goes a step further, examining the unequal power relations in any institutionally based learning-teaching situation. Benesch's (2001: 108) call for "rights analysis" – a tool for "teachers and students to consider possible responses to unfavourable social, intuitional, and classroom conditions" – has highlighted that learners' needs and desires are frequently subordinated to institutions or corporations' dominant needs. Jasso-Aguilar (1999) adopted a critical ethnographic approach to needs analysis in the hotel industry, carrying out participant observation of the daily routines of maids in a Waikiki hotel in order to research their language needs. The multimethod approach adopted in this study drew on multiple sources and revealed a clear disjuncture between the hotel managers' views of the English needed by the maids and the maids' own understandings of their needs. Goldstein (1997) carried out a similar investigation on a factory assembly line in Toronto in order to establish the English needs of a group of immigrant workers. Her critical perspectives, intensive observation and the triangulation of multiple data sources helped explain why many of the workers were reluctant to embrace a programme designed to improve their English skills and their ability to participate in Canadian society.

While ESP initially relied on register analysis and functional notional analyses of language use to assist in the identification of learners' language-based needs, the 1980s saw the birth and continued growth of genre analysis. Genre analysis replaced the narrower understandings of language as register, adding to the complexity of needs analysis as students' socio-rhetorical needs in specific discourse communities needed to be addressed (Swales, 1990). Analysis of how specific genres are realised and function within these communities is now a key component of ESP needs analysis. A distinctive ESP school of genre analysis based primarily on the work of Swales and Bhatia emerged in the 1990s (Swales, 1990; Bhatia, 1993, 2004; Hyon, 1996). Genres are seen as staged communicative events which move through a series of prototypical stages called moves and steps in their realisation, and are the properties of specific discourse communities who use them to further their communicative purposes. Genres are also identifiable through their use of conventionalised language forms to realise specific communicative functions. Professional genres examined include corporate disclosure documents, letters of application, newspaper law reports, emails in multinational corporations, sales letters and popularised medical texts (Bargiela-Chiappini and Nickerson, 1999; Paltridge, 2013). Genre-based pedagogies are now a regular component of ESP teaching, as ESP practitioners carry out genre analysis of key genres learners will need to perform in the target situation, sometimes drawing on computerised corpus analysis tools (Henry and Roseberry, 2001; Upton and Connor, 2001).

More recently, rhetorical genre studies (Bawarshi and Reiff, 2010) have attracted the attention of ESP researchers. Such studies adopt more ethnographic approaches to genre analysis, focussing on the activities, attitudes, beliefs, values and patterns of behaviour of the discourse community using the genres being studied rather than on rhetorical structure or language patterns. In a study of how company audit reports are produced, Flowerdew and Wan (2010) fruitfully combined genre analysis with ethnographic observation and in-depth interviews with key informants at the Hong Kong branch of a large international accounting firm.

Contents and contexts

Closely linked to uncovering learners' needs is the development of learning materials and methods that enable "needs-responsive instruction" (Belcher, 2009: 3) that will assist students in the learning context and with the multiple purposes identified through the needs analysis. Ready-made, generic materials may thus not prove helpful in responding to the specific needs identified through the needs analysis (Belcher, 2009). While Dudley-Evans and St. John (1998) state that the content of ESP courses should not be language but that content should function as a carrier of language, the challenge for the ESP practitioner is to identify this carrier content and ensure that it is motivating for the students. Consequently, ESP courses have been described as having either a narrow-angle or a wide-angle approach to content selection (Dudley-Evans and St. John, 1998; Basturkmen, 2006; Belcher, 2006). Narrow-angled courses are aimed at learners with broadly similar needs and tend to be quite specialised in their subject matter, for example, pilots and nurses (Basturkmen, 2006), while wider-angled course are less specialised and aimed at learners who needs are less similar. Narrow-angled courses may put ESP teachers at a disadvantage, as their students may know more about the subject area than they do (Dudley-Evans and St. John, 1998; Belcher, 2009), so wide-angled, more general approaches are often preferred by ESP teachers for this very reason (Belcher, 2006). Narrow-angle approaches may work better with students in EOP settings (Belcher, 2009), the implication being that the teacher may need to become more familiar with domain knowledge (see Northcott, 2009).

Belcher (2009: 2) noted that the "fastest growing branches of EOP are those associated with professions that are themselves constantly expanding and generating offshoots": business communication, legal English and health care. Business English or English for business purposes or, more recently, business discourse (see Bargiela-Chiappini and Zhang, 2013) was historically under-researched as compared to science and technology, especially in discourse terms, but is now a rapidly expanding field of research. Key factors driving this expansion have been the dominance of Western business culture and the associated dominance of English under globalisation. English has become the lingua franca of global business, giving rise to extensive use of what is known as business English as a Lingua Franca (BELF) where English is used as a means of communication between speakers who are not native English speakers and do not share another native language (see Seargeant, this volume). While St. John (1996: 15) was able to refer to business English as "a materials-led movement rather than a research-led movement", there is now a considerable amount of research into both business English and business discourse (Nickerson and Planken, 2016). Key genres such as negotiations, meetings, business email and oral presentations have all been studied by ESP researchers (see for example Gimenez, 2000; Louhiala-Salminen et al., 2005; Nickerson, 2005; Planken, 2005). While initial work focussed on written texts, currently there is growing interest in spoken business genres (Rogerson-Revell, 2007; Planken and Nickerson, 2009; Evans, 2013).

The extent to which these findings are being taken into account in business English textbooks has been the focus of research which has identified a gap between the findings of applied linguistics studies and textbook depictions of communicative events such as, for example, meetings (Williams, 1988; Chan, 2009). Cheng and Warren (2005) found discrepancies between the treatment of certain speech acts in Hong Kong business English textbooks and the ways English was used in the Hong Kong Corpus of Spoken English business sub-corpus. Similarly, Gimenez (2000), comparing email and formal business letters produced in one company, found that the standard business letter format taught in a business English class would not prepare the students to produce appropriate email correspondence. Studies such as Bhatia and Candlin's (2001) multi-method needs analysis of business communication across several Hong Kong tertiary institutions have found similar mismatches between university courses and the skills needed in the workplace. Likewise, Crosling and Ward's (2002) comparison of typical university oral presentations with those in the workplace showed a mismatch with the 'real world', less formal styles common to the workplace.

Consulting domain experts has also proved helpful in course development. In order to develop an English programme at a large Japanese company, Cowling (2007) surveyed former trainees, now employed, about their English usage in the workplace. Somewhat unexpectedly, they reported the need for 'small talk' in important work situations such as interacting with foreign guests. They also reported that the language taught in previous business English classes at the company had not prepared them for the reality of language use in business meetings and that they would like more 'authentic' content.

In some domains, where English acts as a lingua franca, ESP training can have dramatic real world consequences. Wozniak's (2010) study of the English language skills needed by certified mountain guides in the French Alps highlights the importance of communication skills for guides in this potentially hazardous occupation. Similarly, aviation English – a highly specialised language used by pilots and flight engineers in the cockpit – is proving a domain of increasing interest in ESP research (Moder, 2013; Estival et al., 2016).

New needs emerge regularly in EOP as new contexts for English language use emerge in the rapidly globalising world of business; the growth in outsourcing to call centres in countries such as India and the Philippines is a case in point. A growing body of research is examining the language training needs of call centre operatives who are required to communicate telephonically in English, often with native speakers, under quite demanding and stressful conditions (Forey and Lockwood, 2007; Lockwood, 2012; Friginal, 2013).

Also of growing significance is the increasing use of technology in occupational and professional settings and the corresponding emergence of new genres or genre variants. In the multinational

Malaysian engineering workplace, Kassim and Ali (2010) found that teleconferencing was the oral communicative event in which English was most used, yet as their university did not possess this technology, they were unable to provide training for their students in this key area. In the modules developed on the basis of their needs analysis, they developed task-based scenarios for ESP training to simulate the workplace contexts in which engineering graduates would be likely to find themselves in, focussing on topics such as networking externally with clients, which requires highly developed oral communication skills. In fact, the communicative needs of engineers in contemporary professional workplace contexts have been found to include both engineering and business discourse, posing the considerable challenge to the ESP practitioner of developing courses that can meet the multiple needs of engineers using English in the global workplace (Spence and Liu, 2013).

Who should teach ESP?

Given the breadth of areas covered by ESP instruction, it is reasonable to ask who can teach ESP and how much content knowledge ESP professionals need. As mentioned above, Belcher (2006) refers to "content-area informed instructors", highlighting the many roles an ESP practitioner can be called upon to play – from needs assessor to curriculum and authentic materials developer, with the flexibility to cope with many different content areas. Many ESP teachers have humanities backgrounds which do not necessarily equip them well for the challenge of ESP teaching, and, although growing rapidly in number and extent, ESP components of graduate ELT programmes are still relatively limited. In Belcher's (2009) view, ESP instructors should show a willingness to "enter as a stranger into strange domains", as Sullivan and Girginer (2002) did in recording interactions in an airport control tower when asked to deliver an ESP programme in a civil aviation school in Turkey, where students were training to become pilots and air traffic controllers.

The degree of subject area knowledge required by language teachers and their relationship with content-area specialists and specialised texts are issues that continue to be posed in ESP. Flowerdew (2013: 339) comments that, in many EOP settings, courses are delivered by 'discipline-based practitioners' rather than ESP specialists. Master (2005), however, is of the view that ESP instructors are better prepared than content instructors in most settings, apart from highly specialised contexts like air traffic control. Team-teaching with a subject specialist, language and content integration, and linked courses (Kotecha et al., 1990; Dudley-Evans and St. John, 1998; Benesch, 2001) are some solutions that have been implemented in response to narrow-angle course needs. In the highly specialised contexts of legal English, for example, Northcott (2009) recommends the development of an equal partnership between ESP practitioner and legal specialist. Hyland (2002) argues for specificity as the cornerstone of ESP but does acknowledge that institutional constraints may hamper this.

New methodologies such as corpus studies (see Frankenberg-Garcia, this volume) are, however, making knowledge of professional discourse more widely available, and technologies such as video are making real world data and settings much more accessible and available for the production of teaching materials (Belcher, 2004). More qualitative approaches such as ethnography, used in combination with new technologies, can also help provide the ESP practitioner and researcher with access to authentic data for classroom use and research purposes, thereby mitigating the lack of insider knowledge.

ESP, ideology and neutrality

This chapter has highlighted the global desire for English, seen by many as the gateway to increased opportunity. At the same time, we should acknowledge that the spread of English can, as Belcher (2006: 143) reminds us, open the door to a "form of domination". Master (2005: 112) similarly evokes "the double-edged sword ESP practitioners wield in representing the most powerful nations on the planet while addressing the increasing demand for instruction in English as the lingua franca of the learning and working world". As Nickerson (2005) points out, the linguistic realities of the contemporary workplace are complex; English is used by first, second and foreign language speakers, often in co-existence with one or more other languages, and has effectively become the lingua franca of world business. Many have, however, questioned whether English can in fact play the role of a neutral lingua franca when it is associated with the negative experiences of colonialism, exploitation, dispossession and war (Pennycook, 1994; also, Pennycook, this volume). Indigenous business cultures, for example, may be disappearing as English and 'Western' business culture become dominant in the workplaces of Expanding Circle countries (Kachru, 1985). Nickerson (2013: 451) argues that the field needs to move beyond native speaker models and understand more about what constitutes "functional nativeness" in lingua franca contexts. Of course, as in ELT more generally, the majority of ESP practitioners across the globe are not native speakers, and those who research and write about ESP are increasingly located in Expanding Circle countries. Out of 19 articles published in the 2013 volume of *English for Specific Purposes,* over one third were authored by non-native speakers located in Expanding Circle countries underlining the extent to which ESP is no longer the exclusive 'property' of native speakers. (See also Llurda, this volume, for discussion of the contested and contentious term 'native speaker').

While in 1994, Swales could note that the field of ESP had been "strikingly unengaged by . . . issues of ideology . . . and learners' rights" (1994: 201), in the decades since, critical approaches to ESP have foregrounded these concerns, and many practitioners and researchers are sensitive to these perceptions about English and their role (Master, 2005; Belcher, 2006). Thus, the extent to which ESP practitioners and researchers should adopt a more critical stance towards the role of English and the role of ESP more broadly is an ongoing topic of debate. It has been argued, for example, that the dominant ideology of ESP seeks to help learners fit into rather than challenge existing power structures and economic realities (Starfield, 2013b).

Related to these issues are concerns about the potential restrictiveness of ESP in terms of access to limited discourses and lexis; the extent to which learner empowerment is a goal of ESP; and the extent to which ESP restricts learner access to the multiple identities and imagined communities that might enable them to thrive more than simply survive (Belcher, 2004). For example, a study of Cantonese-speaking bank personnel revealed that they felt inadequate and disempowered when speaking English, as they were not able to respond as quickly as those around them, either because they lacked appropriate discourse strategies or used a different set of strategies because of their cultural background (Chew, 2005). The move to discourse-based approaches that include socio-pragmatics may help to reduce this sense of disempowerment (Bargiela-Chiappini and Zhang, 2013). Nickerson (2005: 369) recommended "identifying those strategies that can be associated with effective communication in business, regardless of whether the speaker/writer is a native or non-native speaker", pointing to a shift in focus in English for specific business purposes from language skills to language strategy.

Future developments

The most significant developments in ESP since the early days outlined above have without doubt been the rise in English as a global language, and the concomitant realisation that native speaker models will become less relevant and that a degree of competence in English is now considered a basic constituent of a person's general education (Nickerson, 2013; Seargeant, this volume). Nickerson (2013) has predicted a shift towards the development of English lingua franca models rather than native speaker ones in business and workplace contexts. Corpora such as VOICE (the Vienna-Oxford International Corpus of English at https://www.univie.ac.at/voice/page/index.php) will provide instances of spoken interaction that may help drive these changes. In conjunction with this shift, the increasing use of multimodal and hybrid genres in these contexts will challenge ESP practitioners, researchers and learners. Clear distinctions between spoken and written discourse will blur, and research into these emerging genres is urgently needed.

As outlined above, needs analyses have become increasingly more sophisticated and multi-dimensional. Yet as the cornerstone of the ESP approach to curriculum development, needs analysis will need to continually broaden its scope to deal with the increasingly complex contexts in which learners are located. Belcher and Lukkarila (2011), for instance, called for needs analysis to broaden its focus on the learner to include multilingual learners' self-perception of their cultural identities and postitionings, both in terms of their current situation and the futures they imagine for themselves and the role English may play in this desired future. Conceptualising learners as multilingual subjects who are negotiating multiple identities in a globalised workplace has implications for ESP teachers and curricula, and certainly has the potential to move the field forward from the deficit views that tended to characterise the early years of ESP. Studies that adopt more critical perspectives such as those referred to above can only be welcomed as they challenge the perception of ESP as accommodationist (Starfield, 2013b).

As Belcher (2004) points out, there is much we still need to understand about the nature of expertise in the professions and in workplaces. Researchers should be encouraged to leave the academy and venture into the workplace so that innovative studies that draw on multiple methods become more frequent, such as, for example, Handford and Matous' (2011) study of spoken discourse at a Hong Kong construction site, which combines ethnographic observation with corpus examination of the discourse in use, and Gimenez's (2014) ethnographically-oriented study of the multi-communication practices in four contemporary multinational corporations. The affordances of technology have the potential to be of great pedagogic benefit, significantly increasing the ability of ESP researchers and practitioners to more fully account for workplace interaction, allowing us to "capture gesture, body movement and gaze in interaction" (Marra, 2013: 187). Marra and colleagues have pioneered methodologies that involve research subjects as active participants in the research process. In their studies of white collar workplaces in New Zealand, authentic data is often collected by the participants themselves who, after appropriate negotiation and trust building, take responsibility for "recording their own interactions based on negotiated research goals" (Marra, 2013: 177). As Swales (1985b: 221) noted, "ESP is required to operate within the multifarious universe of discourse denizened by other occupations, disciplines and professions". The challenge facing practitioners and researchers remains that of entering these worlds, understanding their meaning-making practices and assisting newcomers to successfully participate in these discursive worlds.

Many ESP researchers are also practitioners, and there are many ESP practitioners who do not themselves publish research but would be interested in learning more about courses and programme development in different contexts. Thus, it would be useful to have a range of fora for the dissemination of analyses of courses and programmes which, as indicated above, have largely disappeared from reputable academic journals as not being seen to be 'research-worthy'. The affordances of the digital world could be usefully harnessed for these purposes. The predominance of peer-reviewed SSCI-indexed journals that publish ESP research being mainly located in Centre countries is also an issue that requires addressing. The emergence in a diversity of locations of an increasing number of journals devoted to ESP testifies, however, to both the international nature of the field and its adaptive endurance, with ESP associations in countries such as Taiwan, Serbia and France, to list but a few, producing their own academic journals.

Summary

This chapter has reviewed key issues in the field of English for specific purposes. After providing a historical overview, it traced current key issues, including the centrality of needs analysis, the relationship between content and language in ESP, and debates surrounding the level of subject knowledge ESP practitioners require, and outlined some of the ideological questions surrounding ESP in the world. In the rapidly changing contemporary world, ESP faces a number of challenges, which necessitates both continued research and sharing of good practice in this dynamic field.

Discussion questions

- How would you go about developing an ESP course in an area for which you have very little content or contextual knowledge?
- How would you go about finding out about the specific needs of the learners on your course?
- To what extent do you think the ESP teacher should consider the learners' 'rights' as well as their needs?
- To what extent do you think an ESP teacher needs to be a specialist in the content area?

Related topics

Corpora in ELT; English for academic purposes; Politics, power relationships and ELT; World Englishes and English as a Lingua Franca.

Further reading

Belcher, D. (ed.) (2009) *English for specific purposes in theory and practice*. Ann Arbor: University of Michigan Press. (A good introductory collection focusing on the field of ESP.)

Belcher, D., Johns, A. and Paltridge, B. (eds) (2010) *New directions in English for specific purposes research*. Ann Arbor: University of Michigan Press. (A research-focussed collection that showcases ESP's ongoing vitality.)

Nickerson, C. and Planken. B. (2015) *Introducing business English*. London: Routledge. (An excellent introductory text for teachers of this expanding field.)

Paltridge, B. and Starfield, S. (eds) (2013) *The handbook of English for specific purposes*. Walden, MA: Wiley-Blackwell. (A collection of state-of-the-art chapters on ESP research by experts in the field.)

References

Allen, J. P. B. and Widdowson, H. G. (1974) *English in focus* (9 volumes). Oxford: Oxford University Press.

Bargiela-Chiappini, F. and Nickerson, C. (1999) *Writing business genres, media and discourses*. London: Longman.

Bargiela-Chiappini, F. and Zhang, Z. (2013) 'Business English', in B. Paltridge and S. Starfield (eds) *The handbook of English for specific purposes*. Walden, MA: Wiley-Blackwell. 193–212.

Basturkmen, H. (2006) *Ideas and options for English for specific purposes*. Mahwah: NJ: Laurence Erlbaum Associates.

Bawarshi, A. and Reiff, M. J. (2010) *Genre: An introduction to history, theory, research, and pedagogy*. West Lafayette, IN: Parlor Press.

Belcher, D. (2004) 'Trends in teaching English for specific purposes'. *Annual Review of Applied Linguistics*, 24. 165–186.

Belcher, D. (2006) 'English for specific purposes: Teaching to perceived needs and imagined futures in worlds of work, study, and everyday life'. *TESOL Quarterly*, 40. 133–156.

Belcher, D. (2009) 'What ESP is and can be: An introduction', in D. Belcher (ed.) *English for specific purposes in theory and practice*. Ann Arbor: University of Michigan Press. 1–20.

Belcher, D. and Lukkarila, L. (2011) 'Identity in the ESP context: Putting the learner front and center in needs analysis', in D. Belcher, A. M. Johns and B. Paltridge (eds) *New directions in English for specific purposes research*. Ann Arbor: University of Michigan Press. 73–93.

Benesch, S. (2001) *Critical English for academic purposes*. Mahwah, NJ: Lawrence Erlbaum.

Bhatia, V. (1993) *Analysing genre: Language use in professional settings*. New York: Longman.

Bhatia, V. (2004) *Worlds of written discourse: A genre-based view*. London: Continuum.

Bhatia, V. K. and Candlin, C. N. (2001) *Teaching English to meet the needs of business education in Hong Kong*. Hong Kong: Centre for English Language Education and Communication Research, City University of Hong Kong.

Bosher, S. and Smalkoski, K. (2002) 'From needs analysis to curriculum development: Designing a course in health-care communication for immigrant students in the USA'. *English for Specific Purposes*, 21. 59–79.

Chan, C. S. C. (2009) 'Forging a link between research and pedagogy: A holistic framework for evaluating business English materials'. *English for Specific Purposes*, 28. 125–136.

Cheng, W. and Warren, M. (2005) '// → well I have a DIFferent // _ THINking youknow //: A corpus-driven study of disagreement in Hong Kong business discourse', in M. Gotti and F. Bargiela (eds) *Asian business discourse(s)*. Frankfurt am main: Peter Lang. 241–270.

Chew, K. (2005) 'An investigation of the English language skills used by new entrants in banks in Hong Kong'. *English for Specific Purposes*, 24. 423–435.

Cowling, J. (2007) 'Needs analysis: Planning a syllabus for a series of intensive workplace courses at a leading Japanese company'. *English for Specific Purposes*, 26. 426–442.

Crosling, G. and Ward, I. (2002) 'Oral communication: The workplace needs and uses of business graduate employees'. *English for Specific Purposes*, 21. 41–57.

Dudley-Evans, T. and St. John, M. (1998) *Developments in English for specific purposes*. Cambridge: Cambridge University Press.

Estival, D., Farris, C. and Molesworth, B. (2016) *Aviation English: A lingua franca for pilots and air traffic controllers*. London: Routledge.

Evans, S. (2013) "'Just want to give you guys a bit of an update': Insider perspectives on business presentations in Hong Kong'. *English for Specific Purposes*, 35. 195–207.

Ewer, J. and Latorre, G. (1969) *A course in basic scientific English*. London: Longman.

Flowerdew, J. and Peacock, M. (2001) 'Issues in EAP: A preliminary perspective', in J. Flowerdew and M. Peacock (eds) *Research perspectives on English for academic purposes*. Cambridge: Cambridge University Press. 8–24.

Flowerdew, J. and Wan, A. (2010) 'The linguistic and the contextual in applied genre analysis: The case of the company audit report'. *English for Specific Purposes*, 29. 78–93.

Flowerdew, L. (2013) 'Needs analysis and curriculum development in ESP', in B. Paltridge and S. Starfield (eds) *The handbook of English for specific purposes*. Walden, MA: Wiley-Blackwell. 325–346.

Forey, G. and Lockwood, J. (2007) "'I'd love to put someone in jail for this": An initial investigation of English in the business processing outsourcing (BPO) industry'. *English for Specific Purposes*, 26. 308–326.

Friginal, E. (2013) 'Evaluation of oral performance in outsourced call centres: An exploratory case study'. *English for Specific Purposes*, 32. 25–35.

Gimenez, J. (2000) 'Business e-mail communication: Some emerging tendencies in register'. *English for Specific Purposes*, 19. 237–251.

Gimenez, J. (2014) 'Multi-communication and the business English class: Research meets pedagogy'. *English for Specific Purposes*, 35. 1–16.

Goldstein, T. (1997) *Two languages at work: Bilingual life on the production floor*. Berlin: Mouton de Gruyter.

Halliday, M.A.K., McIntosh, A. and Strevens, P. (1964) *The linguistics sciences and language teaching*. Longman.

Handford, M. and Matous, P (2011) 'Lexicogrammar in the international construction industry: A corpus-based case study of Japanese-Hong-Kongese on-site interactions in English'. *English for Specific Purposes*, 30. 87–90.

Henry, A. and Roseberry, R. (2001) 'A narrow-angled corpus analysis of moves and strategies of the genre: "Letter of Application"'. *English for Specific Purposes*, 20. 153–167.

Hewings, M. (2002) 'A history of ESP through *English for specific purposes'*. *ESP World*, 1. Retrieved July, 2014 from http://www.esp-world.info/Articles_3/Hewings_paper_Introduction.htm

Hutchinson, T. and Waters, A. (1987) *English for specific purposes.* Cambridge: Cambridge University Press.

Hyland, K. (2002) 'Specificity revisited: How far should we go now?' *English for Specific Purposes,* 21. 385–395.

Hyland, K. (2006) *English for academic purposes.* London: Routledge.

Hyon, S. (1996) 'Genre in three traditions: Implications for ESL'. *TESOL Quarterly*, 30. 693–722.

Jasso-Aguilar, R. (1999) 'Sources, methods and triangulation in needs analysis: A critical perspective in a case study of Waikiki hotel maids'. *English for Specific Purposes*, 18. 27–46.

Johns, A. M. (2013) 'The history of English for specific purposes research', in B. Paltridge and S. Starfield (eds) *The handbook of English for specific purposes*. Walden, MA: Wiley-Blackwell. 5–30.

Jupp, T. C. and Hodlin, S. (1975) *Industrial English.* London: Heineman.

Kachru, B. (1985) 'Standards, codification and sociolinguistic realism: The English language in the Outer Circle', in R. Quirk and H. G. Widdowson (eds) *English in the world.* Cambridge: Cambridge University Press. 11–30.

Kassim, H. and Ali, F. (2010) 'English communicative events and skills needed at the workplace: Feedback from the industry'. *English for Specific Purposes*, 29. 168–182.

Kotecha, P., Rutherford, M. and Starfield, S. (1990) Science, language or both? The development of a team-teaching approach to English for science and technology, *South African Journal of Education*, 10/3. 212–221.

Kumaravadivelu, B. (2006) 'Dangerous liaison: Globalization, empire and TESOL', in J. Edge (ed.) *(Re-) locating TESOL in an age of empire.* Hampshire: Palgrave Macmillan. 1–27.

Lockwood, J. (2012) 'Developing an English for specific purpose curriculum for Asian call centres: How theory can inform practice'. *English for Specific Purposes*, 31. 14–24.

Louhiala-Salminen, L., Charles, M. and Kankaanranta, A. (2005) 'English as a Lingua Franca in Nordic corporate mergers: Two case companies'. *English for Specific Purposes*, 24. 401–421.

Marra, M. (2013) 'English in the workplace', in B. Paltridge and S. Starfield (eds) *The handbook of English for specific purposes.* Walden, MA: Wiley-Blackwell. 175–192.

Master, P. (2005) 'Research in English for specific purposes', in E. Hinkel (ed.) *The handbook of research in second language teaching and learning.* Mahwah, NJ: Lawrence Erlbaum Associates. 99–115.

Moder, C. (2013) 'Aviation English', in B. Paltridge and S. Starfield (eds) *The handbook of English for specific purposes.* Walden, MA: Wiley-Blackwell. 227–242.

Munby, J. (1978) *Communicative syllabus design.* Cambridge: Cambridge University Press.

Nickerson, C. (2005) 'English as a Lingua Franca in international business contexts'. *English for Specific Purposes,* 24. 367–380.

Nickerson, C. (2013) 'English for specific purposes and English as a Lingua Franca', in B. Paltridge and S. Starfield (eds) *The handbook of English for specific purposes.* Walden, MA: Wiley-Blackwell. 445–460.

Nickerson, C. and Planken, B. (2016) *Introducing business English.* London: Routledge.

Northcott, J. (2009) 'Teaching legal English: Contexts and cases', in D. Belcher (ed.) *English for specific purposes in theory and practice.* Ann Arbor: University of Michigan Press. 165–185.

Norton, B. (2013) *Identity and language learning: Extending the conversation.* Bristol, UK: Multilingual Matters.

Paltridge, B. (2013) 'Genre and English for specific purposes', in B. Paltridge and S. Starfield (eds) *The handbook of English for specific purposes.* Malden, MA: Wiley-Blackwell. 347–366.

Pennycook, A. (1994) *The cultural politics of English as an international language.* London: Longman.

Planken, B. (2005) Managing rapport in lingua franca sales negotiations: A comparison of professional and aspiring negotiators. *English for Specific Purposes*, 24. 381–400.

Planken, B. and Nickerson, C. (2009) English for specific business purposes: Intercultural issues and the use of business English as a lingua franca, in D. Belcher (ed.) *English for specific purposes in theory and practice.* Ann Arbor: University of Michigan Press. 107–126,

Richterich, R. and Chancerel, J. L. (1977) *Identifying the needs of adults learning a foreign language.* Oxford, England: Pergamon Press.

Robinson, P. (1980) *ESP (English for specific purposes).* Oxford, England: Pergamon Press.

Rogerson-Revell, P. (2007) Using English for international business: A European case study. *English for Specific Purposes*, 26. 103–120.

Spence, P. and Liu, G-Z (2013) 'Engineering English and the high-tech industry: A case study of an English needs analysis of process integration engineers at a semiconductor manufacturing company in Taiwan'. *English for Specific Purposes,* 32. 97–109.

Starfield, S. (2013a) 'Historical development of language for specific purposes', in C. A. Chappelle (ed.) *The encyclopedia of applied linguistics*. Malden, MA: Wiley-Blackwell. 2485–2491.

Starfield, S. (2013b) 'Critical perspectives on ESP', in B. Paltridge and S. Starfield (eds) *The handbook of English for specific purposes*. Malden, MA: Wiley-Blackwell. 461–479.

St. John, M. (1996) 'Business is booming: Business English in the 1990s'. *English for Specific Purposes*, 15/1. 3–18.

Strevens, P. (1977) 'Special-purposed language learning: A perspective'. *Language Teaching*, 10/3. 145–163.

Sullivan, P. and Girginer, H. (2002) 'The use of discourse analysis to enhance ESP teacher knowledge: An example using aviation English'. *English for Specific Purposes*, 21. 397–404.

Swales, J. M. (1985a) *Episodes in ESP*. Oxford: Pergamon Press.

Swales, J. M. (1985b) 'ESP – the heart of the matter or the end of the affair?', in R. Quirk and H. G. Widdowson (eds) *English in the world*. Cambridge: Cambridge University Press. 212–223.

Swales, J. M. (1990) *Genre analysis*. Cambridge: Cambridge University Press.

Swales, J. M. (1994) 'From the editors'. *English for Specific Purposes*, 13. 199–203.

Upton, T. and Connor, U. (2001) 'Using computerized corpus analysis to investigate the textlinguistic discourse moves of a genre'. *English for Specific Purposes*, 20. 313–329.

Williams, M. (1988) 'Language taught for meetings and language used in meetings: Is there anything in common?' *Applied Linguistics*, 9. 45–58.

Wozniak, S. (2010) 'Language needs analysis from a perspective of international professional mobility: The case of French mountain guides'. *English for Specific Purposes*, 29. 243–252.

12

English for academic purposes

Helen Basturkmen and Rosemary Wette

Introduction

This chapter outlines developments in the increasingly influential field of English for academic purposes (EAP), a subfield of English for specific purposes (ESP; see Starfield, this volume). It begins with a definition and brief history of EAP, followed by a review of the key stages in EAP course planning and implementation, including discussion of teaching approaches and curriculum choices. It continues with an examination of debates in this field (such as differing views on the importance of disciplinary knowledge for teachers of English for specific academic purposes) and recent challenges to EAP's self-image as a socially and politically neutral enterprise. The chapter concludes by identifying a number of future directions, including continuation of the trend towards discipline-specific and ethnographic explorations of academic discourse communities.

The term EAP refers to the teaching of varieties of English to assist students of all ages to manage the linguistic, conceptual and social demands of academic study, as well as to support the dissemination and exchange of research and scholarship (Flowerdew, 2015). While this definition emphasises the specific, practical nature of EAP, any comprehensive description needs to also include research, both to build theory and to inform practice. EAP can involve students at primary, secondary or tertiary levels of education, although research interest to date has largely focused on the tertiary sector. It can refer to instruction taking place in English as a foreign language (EFL) teaching contexts where English is an academic subject or the medium of instruction, as well as courses offered in English-speaking countries. Students taking EAP courses in English-speaking countries can be short-stay international students, new migrants, refugees or students from English-speaking backgrounds who have been admitted to tertiary courses as 'second chance' learners under equity initiatives. In EFL contexts, students in EAP classes might be required to reach a certain level of proficiency to enter or exit tertiary study, or they might want to study at undergraduate or postgraduate level in an English-speaking country. Researchers and practitioners from non-English-speaking backgrounds who are obliged to publish or teach in English might also have an interest in EAP instruction, scholarship and research. The interests of EAP are therefore wide-ranging and predominantly real-world.

EAP has its origins in the 1960s. It was initially motivated by interest in possibilities for more applied, student-oriented, English language instruction in academic contexts, as well as by the growing importance of English globally (Strevens, 1977). Short courses in English for science and technology students were first developed for delivery in developing countries or for international tertiary students in English-speaking countries (Jordan, 1997). Distinct stages in the history of EAP have been identified (Flowerdew and Peacock, 2001), each one marked by expansion in the size, range, complexity and importance of the field. During its early years, the main area of interest was register analysis in order to identify word- and sentence-level characteristics of scientific English. Courses then began to include ways of selecting and organising information to create coherent texts (Halliday et al., 1964). By the mid-1970s, EAP scholars and teachers were also paying attention to study skills, which included note taking from readings and lectures, as well as referencing and learning skills (Candlin et al., 1978). Study skills soon came to be viewed as an essential component of EAP, particularly in courses for students coming to English-medium universities from home contexts with different educational practices. From the early 1980s, interest in needs analysis became a further stage in the development of EAP. Although less sophisticated or student-centred than the instruments and methods in use today, information from taxonomies (e.g. Munby, 1978) and questionnaire-based surveys of university staff and students (e.g. Ostler, 1980) about when, where, why and how students will need to use English in their academic studies provided teachers with context-based information about the level and types of proficiency required, and the relative importance of each of the four skills.

EAP today

Although EAP originated as one of two branches (with English for occupational purposes) of English for specific purposes, it has now outgrown its parent in size, range and importance to such an extent that its status as 'offspring' has been called into question (Hamp-Lyons, 2005). Such is the current dominance of English (often American English) as the primary language of instruction and research globally that the academic success of students, as well as the careers of their lecturers, is increasingly tied to competence in academic English (Hyland and Hamp-Lyons, 2002). In Hyland's words, English is now regarded by many as "less a language than a basic academic skill for many users around the world" (2013a: 54). In this section, issues and information relevant to the work of EAP teachers are reviewed.

Needs and context analysis

Awareness of the needs of students and the purposes for which students are learning English is a fundamental difference between EAP and English language courses with more general content, or content and language integrated courses (CLIL; see Morton, this volume), where the curriculum of a particular subject (e.g. geography or biology) is strongly influential. Needs analysis provides opportunities to investigate students' current, required and desired levels of proficiency, learning styles and intended post-study uses of the target language (Dudley-Evans and St John, 1998; Long, 2005a). Early approaches (e.g. Munby, 1978) were based almost exclusively on analysis of end-use and institutional needs (e.g. the texts that students will need to be able to interpret and produce and the degree of proficiency required) but were strongly critiqued for neglecting students' learning preferences and expectations (Hutchinson and Waters, 1987) and their rights with regard to matters such as discoursal identity and culturally inherited ways of writing (Benesch, 1999). Needs analysis is now more broadly defined and encompasses investigation of both learner (e.g. goals, backgrounds, language proficiencies, reasons for taking EAP courses, teaching and learning preferences) and disciplinary needs (Hyland, 2006). However, the identification and analysis of needs is not a simple, straightforward process. Scholars (e.g. West, 1994; Long, 2005b) have pointed out that information from students, especially if they are pre-experience, can be of uncertain quality and reliability, and they recommend that data be collected from multiple sources using a range of procedures. These may include interviews and questionnaires with students, language experts and subject experts (e.g. Deutch, 2003), lesson observations (e.g. Bosher and Smalkoski, 2002), student diaries, language audits and analysis of end-use genres and their discourse features (e.g. Swales, 1990; Hyland, 2000, 2008, 2009a; Thompson, 2003; Nesi and Gardner, 2012). (For further discussion of needs analysis in ESP, see Starfield, this volume.)

Another important consideration for EAP teachers is the institutional and socio-cultural context in which a course takes place. Examples of important contextual influences would be the availability of resources and materials, syllabus requirements, the relationship of the EAP course to other programme offerings, duration and frequency of classes, whether the course earns academic credit and a range of factors from the students' cultures of learning such as preferences with regard to a focus on text analysis or on production tasks, how assignment tasks are interpreted, cultural practices with regard to writing using sources and feedback expectations (Ballard and Clanchy, 1991). The qualifications, experience, motivation, degree of autonomy and working conditions of the EAP teacher (Crookes and Arakaki, 1999) might also play an influential role.

Choice of instructional approach

The progressive expansion and enrichment of EAP with regard to consideration of needs, context considerations and the analysis and production of a range of academic text types has already been outlined. A similar pattern is evident over the past fifty years with regard to instructional approaches, with each new development responding to and incorporating elements of its predecessors (Lea and Street, 2000). While study skills-type courses continue to be offered and textbooks are still published (e.g. Wallace, 2004), strong doubts have been expressed (e.g. Lea and Street, 2000; Wingate, 2006) about the restrictiveness of its view that the primary aim of EAP is to offer remedial instruction in technical, non-discipline-specific skills.

The introduction of genre-based instruction has therefore been a major development in EAP and one that indicates "an important new sphere of activity which is much broader than skills teaching: it locates EAP at the heart of university teaching and learning and of students' orientation to, and success in, their fields of study" (Hyland, 2006: 20). Genre approaches have their origins in register analysis. A primary goal is to socialise students into new academic discourses through instruction in how particular text characteristics and stages are used to construct knowledge (Swales, 1990; Johns, 2008) and also, through practice tasks of various kinds, to develop students' ability to construct texts independently. Genre-based instruction is now widely used to teach core text types such as academic essays, problem-solution and cause-effect texts and research reports (e.g. Swales and Feak, 2000, 2012). Genre approaches have incorporated influences from New Rhetoric (e.g. the use of analytic tasks such as case studies and simulations) and from systemic functional linguistics (e.g. the use of explicit, scaffolded instruction progressing through cycles of modelling, collaborative and independent text construction). It is also now generally acknowledged that genres are neither neutral nor unchanging and also that instruction in how to create an authorial identity and manage the writer-reader relationship is both necessary and important (Hyland, 2000).

However, genre-based pedagogies have been not been without critics. Advocates of the academic literacies approach (e.g. Lillis and Scott, 2007) claim that genre-based instruction can be overly prescriptive and that it pays scant attention to important issues such as bias, lack of transparency and power imbalances in the academy. They maintain that the basically assimilationist nature of genre pedagogies might well reduce the likelihood of students gaining the kind of knowledge and awareness that they will need in order to be able to challenge and possibly transform dominant disciplinary norms and practices.

Curriculum choices

EAP is an active field of research and scholarship, and teachers incorporate advances in knowledge into their teaching, also keeping in mind the needs of their student groups and contextual constraints. This section outlines current practices and recent scholarly developments as they relate to the teaching of listening, speaking, reading and writing in EAP courses.

In his review of recent research, Lynch (2011) notes that although listening is of vital importance to students as a main source of disciplinary information, it is a skill often neglected in EAP research and instruction. Although it is difficult to generalise across a broad range of interactive (e.g. seminars and discussions) and non-interactive (e.g. lectures) listening events, research suggests that if a spoken text employs clear discourse signalling cues (Jung, 2003), uses visual support displayed using PowerPoint slides (MacDonald et al., 2000) and provides opportunities for interaction and clarification, comprehension of spoken academic content will be assisted. Listening skill instruction in EAP draws on these findings to provide practice in managing multiple sources of input (e.g. PowerPoint, audio- or video-recorded texts, written texts displayed using a document camera), and in utilising top-down approaches such as predicting the content of lectures and seminars from prior knowledge and identifying the organisational structure of a spoken text (Salehzadeh, 2006), as well as intensive listening for main points of information. For less advanced students, teachers may need to make compromises between authenticity and accessibility when selecting texts. The importance of lexical knowledge gained from exposure to academic vocabulary in spoken as well as written texts has been noted (Vandergrift, 2006), and information now available from corpora of academic English has made possible investigations of the language features of spoken academic texts across disciplines (e.g. Hyland, 2000; Swales and Feak, 2012) that can be utilised for instructional purposes in EAP.

Speaking and oral interaction skills also tend to be less emphasised than written literacies in EAP instruction. However, Ferris and Tagg (1996) identified a number of areas of academic study where proficiency in speaking is highly desirable, including participating in tutorials and lectures, giving oral presentations and verbalising data in workshops or laboratories. Current EAP instruction aims to raise awareness of particular communicative functions such as asking for clarification, expressing an opinion, agreeing and disagreeing, and the language needed to negotiate meaning through spoken interactions (Basturkmen, 2002), as well as providing sufficient practice opportunities to build confidence and fluency. It has been pointed out that students need to attend to both language and delivery when giving oral presentations and describing data, with special attention to numerical information and graphic representations for the latter category (Jordan, 1997). They also need to become familiar with culture-specific non-verbal aspects of communication such as gestures and eye contact (Robinson et al., 2001).

The importance for successful academic study of being able to extract meaning from a variety of written texts is beyond question. It is now generally recognised that in order to become proficient readers, students need to be able to integrate an ability to use top-down (e.g. prior knowledge and contextual information) and bottom-up (e.g. word by word processing) processes, together with a range of strategies that includes predicting, skimming, scanning, differentiating between fact and opinion, making inferences and understanding how the text is organised (Jordan, 1997). Since vocabulary knowledge is strongly associated with reading comprehension ability, systematic learning of items from general and academic word lists based on frequency (e.g. Coxhead, 2000) has long been a component of EAP courses. However, in recent years, the availability of large corpora such as BAWE and MICASE has made possible explorations of variation in frequency and use across disciplines (Hyland, 2000) and registers (Biber, 2006), and, as a result, the importance of discipline-specific vocabulary is now increasingly emphasised (Hyland and

Tse, 2007). Other current developments include the use of concordancing programmes that can analyse frequently occurring lexical patterns in academic corpora (Hyland, 2008) which students can learn as appropriate collocations. In addition to instruction in appropriate reading strategies and the use of particular vocabulary items, the value of reading frequently and extensively, using top-down strategies and relinquishing word-by-word processing to the fullest extent possible is now widely acknowledged (e.g. Nuttall, 2005).

As the skill which produces a permanent, visible output and the one that is central to assessment in most academic disciplines, writing is for many students the most important of the four skills. Although no particular approach or technique has as yet been validated through empirical research as best practice (Hinkel, 2011), recently published guides for teachers (e.g. Hyland, 2002, 2005; Paltridge et al., 2009), recommend a curriculum that will develop awareness and understanding of the rhetorical and linguistic components of genres (e.g. essay, research report); of variability within genres; of individual thinking processes as they relate to the text construction; of the need to meet reader expectations, manage the information flow and develop an appropriate academic 'voice'; and of the shaping influence of social and contextual variables. In genre-based instruction, students are introduced to the main features of text exemplars before undertaking guided and independent practice to learn how to compose texts (Wette, 2014). Researchers advise that this process will be assisted if learners have knowledge of a metalanguage with which to discuss and analyse texts and if the teacher provides explicit, constructive feedback that is appropriate for the particular learner group (Bitchener, 2012). Developing students' ability to question and evaluate the subject content they encounter is now widely acknowledged to be an essential element of EAP instruction. It is best developed in relation to disciplinary content rather than as a generic skill (Swales and Feak, 2012) and after students have become familiar with and proficient in conventional academic practices. The aim of genre-based pedagogies is therefore to provide instruction that will ultimately build independent skill and the ability to challenge and transform conventional literacy practices if need be.

Key areas of dispute and debate

Narrow- and wide-angled course designs

A number of areas of debate are evident in EAP. One topic that has led to considerable discussion concerns decisions as to whether EAP courses can meaningfully be wide-angled and cater for students from a mix of disciplinary areas by focusing on English for general academic purposes (EGAP) or whether courses should whenever possible be narrow-angled and cater for students from a particular discipline or disciplinary area (English for specific academic purposes – i.e. ESAP), such as English for business studies or English for social studies. The debate is partly concerned with the needs of students. Students beginning university study need to be able to cope with university-wide demands of reading, listening, writing and interacting and using a general academic register, but they also need to be able to cope with the demands of studying in individual disciplines and the disciplinary-specific uses of language this involves (Hyland, 2013b). In reality, decisions about the focus of EAP programmes and courses are often made on a number of bases, including practical concerns such as the availability of teaching staff and universities' willingness to support and fund the development of programmes or courses for particular disciplines. However, at the centre of the discussion is a theoretical concern: to what extent is a generic version of EAP a meaningful construct? The idea of generic EAP may be problematic, as a considerable body of research has now documented the distinctive nature of language use in research writing in different disciplines (Hyland, 2000; Bruce, 2009).

A further body of research has investigated the kinds of writing students are expected to produce. This indicates that different disciplines can require different genres or text types (Nesi and Gardner, 2012). Research also suggests that although different disciplines or subjects within a discipline (Samraj, 2004, 2008) may use similar labels for genres of student writing (for example, the label 'essay'), there can be considerable differences in the practices of those genres, such as differences in the linguistic features commonly used or the ways they are organised (Gardner and Holmes, 2009) and the expectations and values held for the genres in different academic discourse communities (Hyland, 2009a). For example, one linguistic feature, personal pronouns, was found to be far more prevalent in student-written critiques and essays in certain arts and humanities disciplines, including philosophy and English, compared to student writing in these genres in engineering and biological sciences (Nesi and Gardner, 2012). Given such differences, questions can be raised about the nature of descriptions given in generic EAP (EGAP) instruction. There are some practices that are used across disciplines, such as the use of citations to support claims or the widespread use of the introduction-method-results-discussion structure in research reports. However, it can be argued that there is no generic English for academic purposes variety, but rather a set of disciplinary varieties of English (Bloor and Bloor, 1986). It is probably true to say that, at present, generic EAP courses are prevalent in many contexts, although the EAP teaching community has become increasingly aware of the debate that has arisen in the literature on this topic.

As mentioned above, there may be practical reasons why institutions may not be able to run ESAP programmes and courses. ESAP can appear more costly as courses for each of the different disciplines may need to be developed, and EAP teachers may feel unable to develop or teach courses for disciplines with which they are not familiar. In addition, in some situations, such as in pre-sessional EAP programmes which are taken before the students' main academic courses begin (Gillet and Wray, 2006) or EAP courses catering for students in their first year of university study, students' target disciplines may be unclear or changing.

Role of disciplinary content knowledge

Related to the above debate is the question of the role of disciplinary content knowledge in EAP teaching. In teaching English for a specific disciplinary area (ESAP), the question arises of how much knowledge of disciplinary forms of communication, language use and practices of genres is needed by the ESAP teacher. A number of perspectives have been evident in the literature (Ferguson, 1997; Basturkmen, 2014), and views range from those suggesting the need for relatively little subject knowledge to those suggesting the need for considerable expertise, and even that, in some situations, subject experts rather than language experts should teach communication skills. The extent of the disciplinary knowledge the ESAP teacher needs can be considered in relation to the level of disciplinary knowledge of the students. In during-experience or post-experience ESAP settings (that is, in settings in which the students are already studying or have previously studied their disciplinary areas), the teacher may need only some knowledge, since the students have knowledge that can be drawn on during teaching. However, in settings where the students are pre-experience (they have not yet studied their disciplinary area), the teacher might need more disciplinary content knowledge, since he or she might introduce concepts (for example, by introducing subject terminology) and would not be able to draw on the students' own knowledge. It is thus important to consider how the ESAP teacher can collaborate with subject experts to gain information, when needed, on subject content or on disciplinary uses of language. The question of the level of disciplinary knowledge needed by the ESAP teacher can thus be seen as one that is dependent on the context.

Pragmatic and critical aims

A further debate concerns the aims of EAP teaching. As EAP aims to help students meet the linguistic needs of studying in the academic community and to become aware of what is expected of student performance in this community, it may be construed as an essentially socially and politically neutral enterprise. However, in recent years, questions have been raised about whether EAP, through such instrumental endeavours, functions as a means of upholding the status quo and inadvertently as a force for accommodation in helping students fit into the norms and practices set by established members of the academic institution. But should EAP teaching only function in this way, or should it also aim to take on a critical function and at least in part show learners ways in which they might at times challenge existing norms and expectations? In teaching a paired ESL-psychology programme in a US college setting, Benesch (1999) reports how she observed interaction in the psychology lectures. She found that the ESL students resisted the power of the psychology lecturer with questions, complaints (for example, about the speed of the lecturers) and silence. Following this, some ESL class time was spent in discussion of ways the students might overcome some of the difficulties they faced as ESL learners on their psychology paper and how they might initiate change in a more constructive way. As a result, students in the ESL class wrote to the psychology professor to suggest ways to modify the situation. A series of articles on this topic, which became known as the pragmatic/critical debate, appeared in the journal *English for Specific Purposes,* in which Allison (1996) argued for the importance of EAP's pragmatic or instrumental role in helping students cope linguistically with the academic communicative practices and expectations they face. Although a pragmatic approach can be defined in various ways, in EAP it has been used to refer to teaching that is "sensitive to contexts of discourse and of action" (Allison, 1996: 87) and takes into account the needs of the learners in the local academic situation. Its objectives generally include helping learners develop their 'academic communicative competence' (Swales, 1990) and initiating learners into the discourses, communicative practices and forms of expression that are valued in their disciplines. These are seen as key objectives since students and academic alike tend to be evaluated by their "control of the discourses of their disciplines", mastery of which determines "educational life opportunities" (Hyland, 2006: 31).

Discussion in recent years has turned towards the means by which EAP teachers and course developers can include activities with a critical dimension into their instruction (such as class discussions questioning or suggesting changes to current practices) and how a focus on critical EAP can be incorporated into EAP teacher education (Morgan, 2009). The debate has been significant in leading writers and teachers to question the fundamental role of EAP teaching and to consider some of the socio-political implications of this branch of language teaching. Critical EAP (CEAP) widens the lens of academic purposes to take the socio-political context of teaching and learning into account, while continuing to serve the "on-the-ground requirements of academic genres and classroom interactions" (Benesch, 2009: 81).

The dominant role of English in academic publishing

The review of debates in EAP has thus far considered EAP from the viewpoint of the teachers and teaching. However, an emerging sub-field of EAP is English for research publication purposes, or ERPP (Charles, 2013), also termed English for professional academic purposes (EPAP) (Hyland, 2009b). One issue of concern for researchers around the world relates to the dominant role of English in academic publishing. English has become the "language of international scholarship and an important medium of research communication for non-native English speaking academics around the world" (Hyland, 2009b: 83). English can be seen as 'the' language of academic publication (Mur Dueñas, 2012: 141), and getting published in high impact journals as the key to institutional rewards. More than 95 per cent of all publications in the *Science Citation Index* are in English (Hyland, 2009b). Thus, EAP practitioners are increasingly called on to help novice researchers and postgraduate students develop their English for research publication skills, that is, to help them develop the writing skills and knowledge of academic writing conventions that may help them publish research articles in journals. The dominance of English in research publication, which privileges those with English as a first language or those who have had the opportunity to study through the medium of English, can be seen as a form of inequity, and it has led to the emergence of a thrust of research interest into the processes by which non-native English speakers come to acquire the ability to write for publication and enter the international research arena (see, for example, Buckingham, 2014).

Future directions

A major focus of interest in EAP to date has been the investigation of language use and forms of communication involved in academic genres. Conventionally, this interest has led to text or discourse analysis studies which have sought to describe the forms and features of study genres, such as academic lectures (Eslami and Eslami-Rasekh, 2007), and research genres, such as research article introductions (Loi, 2010); many such studies now are drawing on corpus analytical techniques (see, for example, Aktas and Cortes, 2008; Loi, 2010). However, there is growing recognition of the value of research that combines text or discourse analysis type research with ethnographic approaches, such as the use of interviews with disciplinary lecturers, to explicate the values and expectations of the academic community for academic writing in general or in a specific academic discipline (Dressen-Hammouda, 2013). A recent example of this can be seen in the work of Nesi and Gardner (2012), which sought to identify the types of assessed writing required of undergraduates in UK universities and provide corpus and genre-based analyses and description of these genres. In addition to text analysis, the methods included interviews with lecturers and students to provide contextual information and record their understandings of the values and norms of the genres of writing. This research trend is expected to continue. This focus on ethnographic approaches is also impacting on EAP teaching. There have been suggestions for EAP instruction to try to help learners develop the skills to investigate expectations for writing in the context of their disciplines/content classes, since "as literacy instructors we cannot predict what will be valued in students' disciplinary classrooms" (Johns, 2009: 51). Thus, genre-based teaching is widening to include not only a focus on the textual forms of academic genres (i.e. genre acquisition) but also a focus on the development of learners' genre knowledge, that is, the contextual knowledge needed for successful use of genres (Paltridge, 2009). It is expected that the aim of developing learners' genre knowledge (their understanding of contextual factors in successful genre use) will become more generally recognised as an aim of EAP writing instruction and that EAP practitioners will work on devising activities and materials to support learners in developing the ability to investigate genres and the values and expectations held for them in their disciplines.

The growth in EAP teaching worldwide described here has led to the need for EAP-oriented teacher education programmes. A limited number of EAP teacher education programmes appear to be available in certain contexts, although some TESOL programmes offer a module or unit on EAP (Basturkmen, 2014). Teaching EAP often requires teachers to have additional skills and knowledge. In only some cases can EAP teachers rely on published course books, which may appear to have limited relevance to their learners' specific needs, and they often develop in-house materials to match the precise needs of their learners. In addition, especially if developing a new ESAP course, teachers may need to know how to conduct some form of investigation of disciplinary communication (Basturkmen, 2010). EAP teachers thus often require skills in language and discourse analysis and, as described above, an understanding of ethnographic approaches to enquiry. A future direction for the field of EAP must surely be consideration of the needs of EAP teachers and delineating topics for EAP teacher education programmes. In some contexts, writing pedagogy could be an important topic for such programmes. For example, in the North American context, delivery of initial EAP tends to be through freshman or second-year composition courses (Johns, 2009). However, the situation may vary elsewhere.

EAP is taught globally and in many countries where English is used as a medium of instruction in tertiary education, although it is not the native language. Reports of EAP teacher education in particular contexts would be of potential interest to teacher educators elsewhere. EAP teachers' knowledge of general academic literacies may serve them well in certain situations, such as teaching first- or second-year tertiary students who have not as yet entered their major field of study (Belcher, 2009: 11). However, in teaching EAP at higher levels, and especially in teaching ESAP, teachers may need to collaborate with disciplinary specialists. Some reports of collaboration can be seen in Dudley-Evans (2001) and Basturkmen (2010). Further reports of the ways EAP teachers collaborate with content lecturers/disciplinary experts, especially in situations where the teachers could not rely on their understanding of general academic literacies, are needed.

Most EAP literature to date has largely concerned linguistic description (description of study and research genres and forms of communication) and teaching EAP (reports of teaching initiatives in developing and implementing EAP courses and materials). Although EAP learning has played a less central role in the literature, this is an emerging topic of research interest, and more studies of EAP learning are now being published. Recent studies, for example, have focused on the development of academic writing (Parkinson and Musgrave, 2014), the impact of EAP instruction on learning academic literacies (Storch and Tapper, 2009; Wette, 2010) and genre learning in an EAP instructional setting (Cheng, 2011). Future researchers might consider the learning of genres or academic literacies in non-instructed settings. This would be an important topic of interest, given that university students continue to meet new genres and forms of communication in the later years of university study, often when EAP classes or teaching support is no longer on offer. More information is needed on ways students approach learning *in situ* while studying in their disciplines.

Finally, the use of corpus analysis to investigate linguistic features of study and research genres is likely to continue in future years. Meanwhile, EAP practitioners will continue to consider how students can draw on corpus techniques in investigating language use in their disciplines and the kind of teaching materials that can be developed for the EAP classroom to introduce students to such techniques. (See also Frankenberg-Garcia, this volume.)

Summary

This chapter has outlined historical and current approaches to teaching EAP, identified issues and debates in the field and suggested directions that EAP is likely to move towards in coming years. Although EAP emerged as a sub-specialism of ESP and continues to this day to have common features with ESP (such as the important role of needs analysis in curriculum design), EAP has emerged as a field of teaching and research in its own right. As has been shown, EAP has grown significantly in size and importance in recent years. Concomitant with the increasing number of teachers and learners of EAP worldwide, there has been considerable development of instructional activities to support students and novice researchers and discussion of the aims and approaches of this branch of ELT.

Discussion questions

- What do you see as the main purpose of an EAP course? Is it to provide instruction in study skills, to show the way texts are written and used in students' disciplinary areas or to raise awareness of issues such as neutrality and equity in EAP? To what extent do you see the purpose as being a combination of all three?
- What information would you collect from learners at the beginning of an EAP course? What information would you also need to obtain from teachers or lecturers in students' disciplinary areas? Which source do you consider to be of most importance?
- What are your views on teaching a general or a specific variety of academic English writing? How do you deal with this issue in your teaching?
- Does teaching EAP require particular areas of knowledge or a particular set of skills? If so, what topics do you see as appropriate for an EAP teacher education programme?

Related topics

Corpora in ELT; English for specific purposes; Language curriculum design; Teaching language skills.

Further reading

Alexander, O., Argent, S. and Spencer, J. (2008) *EAP essentials: A teacher's guide to principles and practice*. Reading: Garnet. (This book supports teachers working with pre-university level students, outlining text analysis, context considerations, curriculum matters and teaching of the four skills.)

Bruce, I. (2011) *Theory and concepts of English for academic purposes*. Basingstoke: Palgrave Macmillan. (This volume outlines both practical and theoretical issues in the design and teaching of EAP courses.)

De Chazal, E. (2014) *English for academic purposes*. Oxford: Oxford University Press. (This introduces key terms and provides a comprehensive overview of typical and best practice in EAP teaching.)

Hyland, K. (2006) *English for academic purposes: An advanced resource book*. Abingdon: Routledge. (Focussing on approaches and debates in EAP, the volume includes extracts from previously published works to illustrate different perspectives.)

Nesi, H. and Gardner, S. (2012) *Genres across disciplines: Student writing in higher education*. Cambridge: Cambridge University Press. (Reporting on a corpus-based investigation into undergraduate student writing in UK, this book provides detailed descriptions of the range of written genres produced by students.)

References

Aktas, R. N. and Cortes, V. (2008) 'Shell nouns as cohesive devices in published and ESL student writing'. *Journal of English for Academic Purposes*, 7. 3–14.

Allison, D. (1996) 'Pragmatist discourse and English for academic purposes'. *English for Specific Purposes*, 15. 85–103.

Ballard, B. and Clanchy, J. (1991) 'Assessment by misconception: Cultural influences and intellectual traditions', in L. Hamp-Lyons (ed.) *Assessing second language writing in academic contexts*. Norwood, NJ: Ablex. 19–35.

Basturkmen, H. (2002) 'Negotiating meaning in seminar-type discussion and EAP'. *English for Specific Purposes*, 21. 233–242.

Basturkmen, H. (2010) *Developing courses in English for specific purposes*. Basingstoke: Palgrave Macmillan.

Basturkmen, H. (2014) 'LSP teacher education: Review of literature and suggestions for the research agenda'. *Ibérica*, 28. 17–33.

Belcher, D. (2009) 'What ESP is and can be: An introduction', in D. Belcher (ed.) *English for specific purposes in theory and practice*. Ann Arbor: University of Michigan Press. 1–20.

Benesch, S. (1999) 'Rights analysis: Studying power relations in an academic setting'. *English for Specific Purposes*, 18. 81–85.

Benesch, S. (2009) 'Theorizing and practicing critical English for academic purposes'. *Journal of English for Academic Purposes*, 8. 81–85.

Biber, D. (2006) *University language: A corpus-based study of spoken and written registers*. Amsterdam: John Benjamins.

Bitchener, J. (2012) 'A reflection on "the language learning potential" of written CF'. *Journal of Second Language Writing*, 21. 348–363.

Bloor, M. and Bloor, T. (1986) *Languages for specific purposes: Practice and theory. Occasional Paper No 19*. Dublin: Trinity College.

Bosher, S. and Smalkoski, K. (2002) 'From needs analysis to curriculum development: Designing a course in health-care communication for immigrant students in the USA'. *English for Specific Purposes*, 21. 59–79.

Bruce, I. (2009) 'Results sections in sociology and organic chemistry: A genre analysis'. *English for Specific Purposes*, 28. 105–124.

Buckingham, L. (2014) 'Building a career in English: Users of English as an additional language in academia in the Arabian Gulf'. *TESOL Quarterly*, 48. 6–33.

Candlin, C. N., Kirkwood, J. M. and Moore, H. M. (1978) 'Study skills in English: Theoretical issues and practical problems', in R. Mackay and A. J. Mountford (eds) *English for specific purposes: A case study approach*. London: Longman. 190–219.

Charles, M. (2013) 'English for academic purposes', in B. Paltridge and S. Starfield (eds) *The handbook of English for specific purposes*, Oxford: Wiley-Blackwell. 137–153.

Cheng, A. (2011) 'Language features as the pathways to genre: Students' attention to non-prototypical features and its implications'. *Journal of Second Language Writing*, 20. 69–82.

Coxhead, A. (2000) 'A new academic word list'. *TESOL Quarterly*, 34: 493–510.

Crookes, A. and Arakaki, L. (1999) 'Teaching idea sources and working conditions in an ESL program'. *TESOL Journal*, 8. 15–19.

Deutch, Y. (2003) 'Needs analysis for academic legal courses in Israel: A model of setting priorities'. *Journal of English for Academic Purposes*, 2. 125–146.

Dressen-Hammouda, D. (2013) 'Ethnographic approaches to ESP research', in B. Paltridge and S. Starfield (eds) *The handbook of English for specific purposes*. Oxford: Wiley-Blackwell. 501–517.

Dudley-Evans, T. (2001) 'Team-teaching in EAP: Changes and adaptations in the Birmingham approach', in J. Flowerdew and M. Peacock (eds) *Research perspectives on English for academic purposes*. Cambridge: Cambridge University Press. 225–238.

Dudley-Evans, T. and St. John, M-J. (1998) *Developments in English for specific purposes: A multi-disciplinary approach*. Cambridge: Cambridge University Press.

Eslami, Z. R. and Eslami-Rasekh, A. (2007) 'Discourse markers in academic lectures'. *Asian EFL Journal*, 9. 22–38.

Ferguson, G. (1997) 'Teacher education and LSP: The role of specialised knowledge', in R. Howard and G. Brown (eds) *Teacher education for LSP*. Clevedon: Multilingual Matters. 80–89.

Ferris, D. and Tagg, T. (1996) 'Academic listening/speaking tasks for students: Problems, suggestions, and implications'. *TESOL Quarterly*, 30. 31–58.

Flowerdew, J. (2015) 'Some thoughts on English for research publication purposes (ERPP) and related issues'. *Language Teaching*, 48. 250–262.

Flowerdew, J. and Peacock, M. (2001) 'Issues in EAP: A preliminary perspective', in J. Flowerdew and M. Peacock (eds) *Research perspectives on English for academic purposes*. Cambridge: Cambridge University Press. 8–24.

Gardner, S. and Holmes, J. (2009) 'Can I use headings in my essay? Section headings, macrostructures and genre families in the BAWE corpus of student writing', in M. Charles, D. Pecorari and S. Hunston (eds) *Academic writing: At the interface of corpus and discourse*. London: Continuum. 251–271.

Gillet, A. and Wray, L. (2006) 'EAP and success', in A. Gillet and L. Wray (eds) *Assessing the effectiveness of EAP programmes*. London: British Association of Lecturers in English for Academic Purposes. 1–11.

Halliday, M.A.K., McIntosh, A. and Strevens, P. (1964) *The linguistic sciences and language teaching*. London: Longman.

Hamp-Lyons, L. (2005) 'English for academic purposes', in E. Hinkel (ed.) *Handbook of research in second language teaching and learning*. Mahwah: Erlbaum. 89–105.

Hinkel, E. (2011) 'What research on second language writing tells us and what it doesn't', in E. Hinkel (ed.) *Handbook of research in second language teaching and learning.* New York: Routledge. 523–538.

Hutchinson, T. and Waters, A. (1987) *English for specific purposes: A learning-centred approach.* Cambridge: Cambridge University Press.

Hyland, K. (2000) *Disciplinary discourses: Social interactions in academic writing.* Harlow: Pearson.

Hyland, K. (2002) *Teaching and researching writing.* Harlow: Pearson.

Hyland, K. (2005) *Metadiscourse.* London: Continuum.

Hyland, K. (2006) *English for academic purposes: An advanced resource book.* London: Routledge.

Hyland, K. (2008) 'As can be seen: Lexical bundles and disciplinary variation'. *English for Specific Purposes,* 27. 4–21.

Hyland, K. (2009a) *Academic discourse.* London: Continuum.

Hyland, K. (2009b) 'English for professional academic purposes: Writing for scholarly publication', in D. Belcher (ed.) *English for specific purposes in theory and practice.* Ann Arbor: University of Michigan Press. 83–105.

Hyland, K. (2013a) 'Writing in the university: Education, knowledge and reputation'. *Language Teaching,* 46. 53–70.

Hyland, K. (2013b) 'Instructional discourses', in K. Hyland (ed.) *Discourse studies reader: Essential excerpts.* London: Bloomsbury Academic. 195–221.

Hyland, K. and Hamp-Lyons, J. (2002) 'EAP: Issues and directions'. *Journal of English for Academic Purposes,* 1. 1–12.

Hyland, K. and Tse, P. (2007) 'Is there an "academic vocabulary"?'. *TESOL Quarterly,* 41. 235–253.

Johns, A. M. (2008) 'Genre awareness for the novice academic student: An ongoing quest'. *Language Teaching,* 41. 237–252.

Johns, A. M. (2009) 'Tertiary undergraduate EAP: problems and possibilities', in D. Belcher (ed.) *English for specific purposes in theory and practice.* Ann Arbor: University of Michigan Press. 41–59.

Jordan, R. R. (1997) *English for academic purposes: A guide and resource book for teachers.* Cambridge: Cambridge University Press.

Jung, E. H. (2003) 'The role of discourse signalling cues in second language listening comprehension'. *Modern Language Journal,* 87. 562–577.

Lea, M. and Street, B. V. (2000) 'Student writing and staff feedback in higher education', in M. Lea and B. Stierer (eds) *Student writing in higher education: New contexts.* Buckingham: Society for Research in Higher Education and Open University Press. 32–46.

Lillis, T. and Scott, M. (2007) 'Defining academic literacies research: Issues of epistemology, ideology and strategy'. *Journal of Applied Linguistics,* 4. 5–32.

Loi, C. K. (2010) 'Research article introductions in Chinese and English: A comparative genre-based study'. *Journal of English for Academic Purposes,* 9. 267–279.

Long, M. H. (2005a) 'A rationale for needs analysis and needs analysis research', in M. H. Long (ed.) *Second language needs analysis.* Cambridge: Cambridge University Press. 1–16.

Long, M. H. (2005b) 'Methodological issues in needs analysis', in M. H. Long (ed.) *Second language needs analysis.* Cambridge: Cambridge University Press. 19–76.

Lynch, T. (2011) 'Academic listening in the 21st century: Reviewing a decade of research'. *Journal of English for Academic Purposes,* 10. 79–88.

MacDonald, M., Badger, R. and White, G. (2000) 'The real thing? Authenticity and academic listening'. *English for Specific Purposes,* 19. 251–267.

Morgan, B. (2009) 'Fostering transformative practitioners for critical EAP: Possibilities and challenges'. *Journal of English for Academic Purposes,* 8. 86–99.

Munby, J. (1978) *Communicative syllabus design.* Cambridge: Cambridge University Press.

Mur Dueñas, P. (2012) 'Getting research published in English: An ethnographic account of a team of finance Spanish scholars' struggles'. *Ibérica* 24. 139–155.

Nesi, H. and Gardner, S. (2012) *Genres across the disciplines: Student writing in higher education.* Cambridge: Cambridge University Press.

Nuttall, C. E. (2005) *Teaching reading skills in a foreign language.* Oxford: Macmillan.

Ostler, S. E. (1980) 'A survey of academic needs for advanced ESL'. *TESOL Quarterly,* 14. 489–502.

Paltridge, B. (2009) 'Afterword: Where have we come from and where are we now?', in D. Belcher (ed.) *English for specific purposes in theory and practice.* Ann Arbor: University of Michigan Press. 289–296.

Paltridge, B., Harbon, L., Hirsch, D., Shen, H., Stevenson, M., Phatiki, A. and Woodrow, L. (2009) *Teaching academic writing.* Ann Arbor: University of Michigan Press.

Parkinson, J. and Musgrave, J. (2014) 'Development of noun phrase complexity in the writing of English for academic purposes students'. *Journal of English for Academic Purposes,* 14. 48–59.

Robinson, P., Strong, G., Whittle, J. and Nobe, S. (2001) 'The development of EAP oral discussion ability', in J. Flowerdew and M. Peacock (eds) *Research perspectives on English for academic purposes.* Cambridge: Cambridge University Press. 347–359.

Salehzadeh, J. (2006) *Academic listening strategies: A guide to understanding lectures.* Ann Arbor: University of Michigan Press.

Samraj, B. (2004) 'Discourse features of student-produced academic papers: Variations across disciplinary courses'. *Journal of English for Academic Purposes,* 3. 5–22.

Samraj, B. (2008) 'A discourse analysis of master's theses across disciplines with a focus on introductions'. *Journal of English for Academic Purposes,* 7. 55–67.

Storch, N. and Tapper, J. (2009) 'The impact of an EAP course on postgraduate writing'. *Journal of English for Academic Purposes,* 8. 207–223.

Strevens, P. (1977) 'Special-purpose language learning: a perspective'. *Language Teaching,* 10. 145–163.

Swales, J. (1990) *Genre analysis: English in academic and research settings.* Cambridge: Cambridge University Press.

Swales, J. M. and Feak, C. B. (2000) *English in today's research world: A writing guide.* Ann Arbor: University of Michigan Press.

Swales, J. M. and Feak, C. B. (2012) *Academic writing for graduate students* (3rd ed.). Ann Arbor: University of Michigan Press.

Thompson, S. E. (2003) 'Text-structuring, metadiscourse, intonation and the signalling of organisation in academic lectures'. *Journal of English for Academic Purposes,* 2. 5–20.

Vandergrift, L. (2006) 'Second language listening: Listening ability or language proficiency?' *Modern Language Journal,* 90. 6–18.

Wallace, M. J. (2004) *Study skills in English: A course in reading skills for academic purposes* (2nd ed.). Cambridge: Cambridge University Press.

West, R. (1994) 'Needs analysis in language teaching'. *Language Teaching,* 27. 1–19.

Wette, R. (2010) 'Evaluating student learning in a university-level EAP unit on writing using sources'. *Journal of Second Language Writing,* 19. 158–177.

Wette, R. (2014) 'Teachers' practices in EAP writing instruction: Use of models and modelling'. *System,* 42. 60–69.

Wingate, U. (2006) 'Doing away with study skills'. *Teaching in Higher Education,* 11. 457–469.

13

English for speakers of other languages
Language education and migration

James Simpson

Introduction

The teaching and learning of English for adults who are migrants to English-dominant countries (e.g. the UK, Australia, Canada, the US) is most commonly known as English for speakers of other languages (ESOL, the term used in this chapter), and also as ESL (English as a *second* language). This chapter is about ESOL practice and, in particular, the need to understand the social, political and individual factors that impinge on such practice. The chapter is not principally concerned with English as a foreign language (EFL), taught to and learnt by people in parts of the world which are not English-dominant and, in those parts which are, by people who are not 'here to stay'.

Following this introduction, I locate the field of ESOL in the contemporary multilingual sociolinguistic setting. I then turn to how language education policies relating to adult migrants position ESOL students in certain ways. Subsequently, I sketch out a range of characteristics that relate closely to the ESOL student population and that typically affect their learning experience. The final section of the chapter focuses on practice in ESOL classrooms, as the sites where societal, political and individual concerns converge.

Migrants to English-dominant countries have two fundamental linguistic human rights, embedded in documents such as the Universal Declaration of Human Rights (UN General Assembly, 1948). First, they should be allowed to maintain the languages they grew up speaking, even as they and their families settle in a new country. Second, they are entitled to learn the main language of their new country, to learn to communicate in English. The central concern of ESOL is with the second of these: the right of newcomers to an English-dominant country to learn English and the provision of opportunities for them to do so. Certain sectors of the media and some politicians present this right as an obligation and even imply a reluctance on the part of some migrants to learn the language at all, as I discuss below. In fact, the majority of migrants to English-dominant countries do want to learn English (Rosenberg, 2007), but may face barriers of access to appropriate high-quality tuition (Simpson et al., 2011).

There is variation between countries which are English-dominant, at the scale of national policy, pedagogic practices and traditions, and the profile of the student body (Simpson and Whiteside, 2015). At root of this variety are many factors: whether the state is historically one of immigration (e.g. Canada, Australia, the US) or emigration (e.g. Ireland, Scotland); whether political and social structures are in place to enable and assist newcomers in settling in their new country; whether there is a history of coordinated language education for new non-English speaking arrivals; who the new arrivals actually are; and how those patterns change over time. Some countries have long experience of and commitment to publicly-funded ESOL, and others less so; this is reflected in the level of development of curriculum and statutory provision. Some countries adopt a curriculum nationally, specifying the theoretical principles upon which it should be based, while for others curriculum development happens locally, outside state policy structures. Questions of provision and funding are perennial for ESOL worldwide: which bodies are responsible for ESOL provision? How much state funding is available for language classes for adults? Who is eligible for them, and for how long? Some countries stipulate that statutory funding will be limited to certain groups of adult migrants, for example permanent residents or those actively seeking employment. Others, such as Australia, have a set number of hours for which migrants are eligible for free English classes. Some countries organise funding centrally on a national level (for example, England and Wales between 2001 and 2009), while in others it devolves to a provincial or local level (for example, the fragmented picture in the US).

There are commonalities too: ESOL, wherever it is practised, is closely related to national government policy on migration, integration and the social inclusion of new arrivals. A phenomenon in many countries in the West is a tightening of the relationship between language, immigration, citizenship and national security, seen most clearly in the rise of language and citizenship testing and teaching. How host countries plan and provide for newcomers is often a sign of prevailing attitudes towards immigration in general and towards broader issues such as race, ethnicity and social class, as I discuss below. Other points in common around the world of ESOL include its frequent alignment with adult basic skills and a growing focus on preparation for the workplace (Cooke and Simpson, 2008). Moreover, the way governments respond to the language learning needs of adult migrants tends not to take into account their experiences 'on the ground', typically in linguistically and socially diverse urban areas. Policies that promote the learning of English do not always recognise its position in individuals' multilingual daily lives.

The distinctiveness of ESOL as a branch of ELT is evident therefore through an interplay of life, learning and migration trajectories, of history and of government policies and the way these come together in practice. As this chapter will explore, there is a need to attend to how global processes relating to language and migration as well as language ideological debates are played out in students' life experiences and in the warp and the weft of actual practice, both outside class and within.

ESOL students in the sociolinguistic setting

A feature of twenty-first century globalisation is the growth of movement of people from one country to another. Around one in 35 people in the world are migrants, and the reasons for their migration vary. People move to a new country because of a shortage of labour in certain sectors, to be with their families, or as refugees to escape war, civil unrest, poverty or fear of persecution. While most refugees stay relatively near their home countries – the top four hosts for refugees in 2013 were Pakistan, Iran, Lebanon and Jordan (UNHCR, 2014) – migration to more peaceful and prosperous countries continues to grow, despite attempts by the governments of some of those countries to curtail it.

Countries around the world hosting ESOL students have experienced differing patterns of migration. Britain, for example, has since the nineteenth century experienced successive waves of migration (Rosenberg, 2007). The mid-twentieth century saw the arrival of migrants from the former colonies – particularly the Indian sub-continent and the Caribbean – who had a right to settle in Britain in response to the post-war demand for labour. Migration today differs in range and scale from these earlier waves, at least in part due to processes of globalisation associated with late modernity (Appadurai, 1996; Giddens, 1999). These include increased mobility and movement of people towards the developed West. Hence, Britain in recent years has seen inward migration from places such as Somalia, Congo, Iraq, Afghanistan and Syria, where the political and economic situation has driven people to uproot. While the picture is similar in other countries, also apparent are idiosyncratic patterns in the development of migration (and associated policies) related to divergent geographical, historical and ideological factors (see chapters in Simpson and Whiteside, 2015). In terms of geography, the long, sparsely populated US/Mexico border has facilitated the historical exploitation of Mexican guest workers (*braceros*) and undocumented labourers in the US. Canada, with its vast under-populated areas, has embraced immigration (though recently with financial strings attached), while Australia has a history of exclusionary migration policies targeting non-Europeans (McNamara, 2012). Post-colonial ties with 'sending' countries have characterised much policy, though not in countries with no such historical relationships. Countries with long histories of inward migration like the US and the UK, and with diverse populations, contrast with historically sending countries such as Ireland, which is legislating for language diversity for the first time (Sheridan, 2015).

Globalisation and migration help to shape the demographic make-up of English-dominant countries, which are experiencing *superdiversity* at a scale never before encountered (Vertovec, 2006, 2012; Blommaert and Rampton, 2011). Today's language use too, therefore, is affected by migration, as documented in a developing sociolinguistics of mobility (Pratt, 1997; Baynham, 2011; Canagarajah, forthcoming) and of globalisation (Blommaert, 2010). Notions such as *translanguaging* (Creese and Blackledge, 2010) and *metrolingualism* (Pennycook and Otsuji, 2015) are gaining currency in a communicative era where people with a range of multilingual resources are in contact (see also Carroll and Combs, and Pennycook, this volume). Garcia and Li define translanguaging thus:

> translanguaging is an approach to the use of language, bilingualism and the education of bilinguals that considers the language practices of bilinguals not as two autonomous language systems as has been traditionally the case, but as one linguistic repertoire with features that have been societally constructed as belonging to two separate languages.
>
> *(Garcia and Li, 2014: 2)*

Perhaps of all the branches of ELT, ESOL has the closest link to the consequences of migration and globalisation, processes which have brought large numbers and also huge variety to ESOL classes. Approaches to pedagogy which draw upon notions such as translanguaging for their theoretical bases would seem to be particularly fitting in educational settings in the global cities of today, where students may well be developing their competence in English as part of a multilingual repertoire (see also May, 2013).

How adult students engage with English outside class in the broader sociolinguistic setting is relevant for teachers. Approaches to language teaching generally should encompass a concern with students' needs. In the case of ESOL, this entails recognising the complexities inherent in students' daily lives. Newcomers to a country differ in terms of the degrees of integration they feel, for instance. Some suffer extremes of isolation and speak very little to anyone, even in their expert languages. Others move in large multilingual networks of migrants and refugees, while yet others have busy lives in large ethnic minority communities. Most people attending ESOL classes, however, express a certain sense of frustration at their progress and lack of opportunities to practise English with expert speakers of the language (Cooke and Simpson, 2008).

The advantages of speaking English in a new home in an English-dominant country (as well as in a globalised world), and speaking it well, are more than apparent to the majority of migrants, and many are highly motivated to learn. Bonny Norton (2000, 2011, 2013) proposes the construct of *investment* as appropriate to describe migrants' language learning, to complement more established understandings of language learner motivation (see Lamb, this volume). Investment signals "the socially and historically constructed relationship of learners to the target language and their often ambivalent desire to learn and practice it" (Norton, 2011: 322). For ESOL learners, this ambivalence relates to the way they, as migrants, settle into life in a new country. As Norton writes elsewhere (2006: 96), "while adult ESOL language learners may strive to make a productive contribution to their new societies, unless the host community is receptive to their arrival, they will struggle to fulfil their potential."

A question to ask of ESOL, therefore, is how do new arrivals invest in the language practices of the classroom and the local community? There are multiple reasons why those settling in a new country are motivated to learn English, ranging from the urgency of finding a job to the desire to socialise. Another motivational factor is the day-to-day difficulty of being a low-level speaker of English. Some ESOL learners experience fear, isolation and a feeling of disadvantage or incompleteness. Moreover, institutions such as government employment offices, welfare offices and banks loom large in the lives of linguistic minority people, and students' interactions in English can be coloured by miscommunication, hostility and sometimes racism. Encounters with service providers or bureaucrats are by their nature unequal and do not provide environments conducive to developing either spoken or listening competence. The power imbalances inherent in many such interactions have implications for the development of their understanding (Bremer et al., 1996; Carrier, 1999). At the same time, a feeling commonly reported by beginner learners of ESOL is discomfort at their dependence on interpreters, friends or even their own children to help with bureaucratic and medical encounters; many talk of their language learning achievements in terms of breaking this dependency (Baynham et al., 2007). This is why ESOL lessons remain important: instruction makes a difference generally (Norris and Ortega, 2000), and critical examination of daily encounters should be included in the context of such instruction in ESOL contexts, as we shall see later in the chapter.

ESOL and political discourse

Migration to English-dominant countries across the West outpaces the development of policies and infrastructure which address the presence of new migrants and the linguistic diversity that their arrival entails. National policies concerning language education for new arrivals tend to be inconsistent, contentious and contradictory (see later in this chapter), responding in uneven ways to the dynamic diversity associated with migration. That said, national governments generally accept that new arrivals should use the dominant language of their new country. Indeed, political and public rhetoric frequently makes reference to the obligation that migrants have to 'speak our language', often in the name of national unity. Such discourse is informed by deeply entrenched language ideologies, i.e. "beliefs, feelings, and conceptions about language structure and use which often index the political interests of individual speakers, ethnic and other interest groups, and nation states" (Kroskrity, 2001: 1). The ideology of a standard language that should be used in the public (and even private) sphere across a country is particularly well-established

(Wright, 2004). This 'one nation, one language' ideology is interlaced with other beliefs about national identity, for example, the ideal that the nation state should be as homogeneous – and as monolingual – as possible.

For many, understanding and using the dominant language of the new country is a *sine qua non* of integration and social cohesion. This stance assumes that acquiring competence in the standard variety of a language equips newcomers with the means to navigate a fresh social context. This extends to competence in reading and writing: an assumption is easily made that literacy in the standard variety is a pre-requisite for daily life and is the route to a successful future. From here, it is but a short step to another easy assumption – one that many learners also make – that once competence in the language has been achieved, all the problems one faces as a migrant will be solved, as if all social groups using the standard variety are natural allies. Yet the notion of a stable distribution of languages following national boundaries – and indeed the notion of languages themselves as stable and bounded – runs counter to lived language experience. As I have suggested, daily language use in migration contexts inevitably involves individuals drawing upon their multilingual repertoire as situations demand (Creese and Blackledge, 2010, 2011). But although multilingualism is the norm on the ground, monolingualism is hegemonic in many places: that is, it is accepted as an unquestioned common sense 'given' by the majority of people that one language stands above others as having particular status as the national language of the country. Monolingualist policies appeal to, and resonate with, everyday understandings of the importance of a standard language as a unifying 'glue' for a nation, and battles over monolingualist stances (e.g. the 'English only' movement in the US) abound. From such a perspective, the business of unifying (or homogenising) the nation is equated with positioning English as the only acceptable language of the public sphere (Ricento, 2003). The mobility of contemporary globalisation certainly presents something of a problem to the idea of the nation as a fixed entity. The imagined homogeneity of a nation (in linguistic terms) is maintained by national policy and political discourse but is challenged by mobility and diversity.

In the UK, policy and public rhetoric in recent years promotes the dominance of standard English to counter religious and political extremism (Simpson and Whiteside, 2012; Simpson, 2015). In Australia, where an understanding of cultural pluralism has only recently developed, the learning of English has historically been considered part and parcel of the process of assimilation into an Anglo-Australian culture (Nicholas, 2015). Adult migrant language education and immigration policy in the US, though confused, is underpinned by a largely unquestioning acceptance of English as the *de facto* national language (Wrigley, 2015). It should come as no surprise, then, that the understanding of language education for migrants at the scale of national policy rarely embraces multilingualism, that is, the development of competence in the dominant language as part of a multilingual repertoire. Even in places where multiculturalism and diversity are embraced, such concern tends not to extend to linguistic diversity.

In sum then, across the developed West, language education for adult migrants has in recent years become closely intertwined with policy on immigration and citizenship. Recent studies of language policy consider it not as a formation created at an abstract scale, however, but as multiple processes (Ricento and Hornberger, 1996) and as locally situated sociocultural practice (McCarty, 2011; Johnson, 2013). This raises questions of how 'needs' in ESOL are understood, whose stake in the identification of needs is most prominent and what are the consequences for ESOL students in classrooms and in their out-of-class lives. In ESOL pedagogy, there is a tradition of appropriating and subverting imposed policies, interpreting them in new ways in local contexts of practice. I give an example later in the chapter, where I describe an approach to ESOL pedagogy which adopts a far broader, student-defined notion of integration. Before that, however, I turn to ESOL students and the factors that distinguish them in practice.

ESOL students

As noted earlier, the world's urban centres now host multilingual and multicultural populations from potentially anywhere. Any particular group of adult migrants learning English will be equally diverse. This diversity is most notable, perhaps, in terms of language background and geographical origin but also in migrants' educational trajectory and schooled experience, command of literacy in their expert languages, immigration status and reasons for migrating, age and gender, and employment. Individuals who share a similar background differ as well, of course, in terms of personality, a sense of agency, investment in learning and aspirations for the future. In this section, I sketch out this range, identifying those salient issues which typically impinge on ESOL students' language learning and therefore on classroom practice.

Baynham et al. (2007) describe an intermediate-level class of English for speakers of other languages (ESOL) in North London with students from Spain, Brazil, Somalia, France, Turkey, Columbia, Albania, Chad, Congo, Cyprus and India. In 2013, an equivalent class at the same college again has students from Brazil, Somalia and Turkey but also from Yemen, Eritrea, Ethiopia, Angola and China. The profile of these classes reflects fast-moving patterns of migration. The picture also varies from country to country (depending on overall migration patterns), city to city, town to town and neighbourhood to neighbourhood. An intermediate ESOL class in Sydney or Toronto, or elsewhere in London, or in a large regional city, or in a rural area, would most likely exhibit a different but possibly equally varied profile.

Language background

An obvious difference between ESOL learners lies in the languages they speak. In England, a survey of ESOL classes (Baynham et al., 2007) found over 50 languages spoken by 500 ESOL students in London and the North of England; Simpson et al. (2011) found a similar number in a single area of one city alone. A 'census' view of languages, however, does not encapsulate the full complex picture of language use amongst ESOL students, nor show that many of the learners are multilingual and multi-literate. Multilingualism, as well as multi-literacy (including literacy in more than one script) is taken for granted by many ESOL learners, so much so that they often fail to mention it on official forms. As I have already stressed, ESOL learners are often surrounded by many languages, use several languages themselves and move between them (*translanguage*) as a matter of course, or use English as a Lingua Franca with speakers from diverse backgrounds. (See Makoni and Pennycook, 2007 for a trenchant critique of 'census ideology' regarding language use.)

Educational background and literacy

Moreover, diversity extends beyond countries of origin and first languages claimed. Also far from uniform amongst ESOL learners is their educational background and prior experience of literacy (see Paran and Wallace, this volume). It is not unusual to find in the same class people who have received a university education together with people with very little schooling and therefore with little literacy in their first languages. The teaching of literacy for new readers and writers is considered by many teachers to be the most challenging area of ESOL pedagogy (see for example Crevecoeur-Bryant, 2011; Young-Scholten, 2015). This is not surprising, considering that such students are learning to read and write for the first time as adults and in a new language. Language learning for adults without foundational literacy in a first or expert language also presents cognitive demands on other aspects of language processing, as described by Tarone and colleagues (2009). The reasons for ESOL students not acquiring literacy as children vary:

there are political, social, economic and cultural barriers to schooling. The upheaval caused by military conflict and war is a reason why some children do not attend school, even in societies where the literacy rate was previously relatively high. Others may come from societies which do not have a strong literate tradition, such as Somalia (Bigelow and King, 2015), or from a tradition which does not prioritise the education of girls (Kouritzin, 2000). Others still may have been deprived of an education because of poverty. For whatever reason, lack of access to literacy has huge implications in the literacy-saturated world of the adult migrant. Cooke and Simpson (2008) quote Kamal, an ESOL student from Sri Lanka living in London:

> Say if I get a letter from the immigration people today, I can't read that letter properly, I can't understand the meanings correctly and if I misread the words there'll be a lot of problems.
>
> *(Kamal, in Cooke and Simpson, 2008: 92)*

Adult migrants to the English-dominant West who had not previously regarded their literacy (or lack of it) as a problem are faced with a pressure to learn to read and write in English, their second or third language, sometimes at the very time that they are confronting the stresses of migration (Baynham and De Fina, 2005). Other students who arrived many years ago may have worked in jobs which required little from them by way of literacy; now unemployed, however, they are facing new demands from potential employers in the increasing textualisation of even the most unskilled manual work (Scheeres, 2004; see also Duchêne et al., 2013). That is, even menial jobs now entail employees having to negotiate written texts. And there are potentially serious problems for people unable to read English when they are faced with the bureaucratic demands made of migrants in English-dominant countries. This is particularly true for asylum seekers and refugees such as Kamal. Many people have access to community networks and resources to help them process important bureaucracy such as letters from the immigration authorities; they might also have recourse to official interpreters and translators. However, as mentioned earlier, one of the reasons people attend ESOL classes in the first place is to break their sense of dependency on formal or informal support.

Gender

ESOL is a gendered field: in the surveys cited above, two thirds of students were female. Migration and asylum affect women in different ways than men, and this extends to their experience of ESOL, impinging on their ability to access ESOL classes. For example, people-trafficking as part of forced prostitution affects women and girls almost exclusively (Eaves Poppy Project, n.d.; Mai, 2013). A less obvious but still important issue is the change in family patterns associated with migration. Traditional family patterns go through many shifts during and after migration. These are sometimes to the benefit of women but sometimes not; for example, many women migrants are single mothers who have been widowed due to war and conflict in their home countries and are therefore living in situations at odds with the traditional norms for their communities, as well as coping with increased poverty. A lack of access to childcare is a particularly acute problem for women wishing to raise young children and attend regular full-time ESOL classes. Consequently, their learning happens in a piecemeal way over a much longer period of time.

Employment

One of the most pressing reasons learners invest in English is for employment. ESOL students bring with them a wide array of qualities and attributes which would normally give them status in society – what Bourdieu (1986) termed *cultural capital*. This cultural capital includes previous education, language and literacy, a range of qualifications, skills, knowledge and prior experience. Skilled tradespeople and highly qualified professionals can certainly be found in ESOL classes. But ESOL learners who find work in their new country tend to be employed below their professional level and may remain in this position for years to come. Finding that their cultural capital has less value than it had at home can have an impact on their social identity (Simpson and Cooke, 2010). Moreover, people sometimes lack the linguistic and cultural knowledge to negotiate gatekeeping procedures such as job interviews. Roberts and Campbell (2006) have shown that job interviews present a major barrier to second language speakers and contribute to high levels of unemployment amongst linguistic minority people. As I detail later in the chapter, ESOL practice addresses the interactional demands of events such as job interviews only imperfectly.

In some parts of countries such as the UK, the US, Canada and Australia, the foreign-born population outnumbers the local-born population. Thus the points about difference and diversity made in this section will be familiar and even obvious to some readers, above all to ESOL teachers in the West's global cities. However, when it comes to teaching and learning, ESOL students are often treated as one 'group', so responding to their diverse needs, experiences and aspirations becomes an essential part of the work of the ESOL teacher and a major challenge to curriculum planners. With ever greater demand for ESOL classes and a high level of insistence from governments that migrants learn English for purposes of integration, the job of ESOL teachers goes way beyond teaching the forms and structure of the English language.

ESOL classes

Now we arrive at ESOL lessons and consider ways in which teachers might approach the challenges and maximise the opportunities offered by the remarkable mixture of people in their classrooms. Given the variation sketched out above, it is clear that no one method is appropriate for all ESOL students; no unified lesson content or single set of topics, activities or materials will cater to their diverse needs. Nonetheless, although some teachers of ESOL draw on other approaches, most have been influenced in some way by communicative language teaching (CLT; see Thornbury, this volume) to a greater or lesser degree, either directly through their professional training or indirectly through materials and textbooks written according to CLT principles. In communicative classrooms, there is an emphasis on effective communication in language that is appropriate to its contexts of use. Unlike for most EFL students, for ESOL students, those contexts usually relate to their immediate concerns of daily life as well as to future aspirations. An issue for ESOL students is that daily concerns present language challenges that are frequently beyond their ascribed 'level'. Here, I first consider appropriate materials for ESOL then turn to the matter of how the interactional challenges from outside class might be addressed in practice. Finally, I give examples of how ESOL teachers can productively enable aspects of their students' out-of-class lives to be brought into the classroom, where they can be critically examined.

Materials for ESOL

ESOL materials tend to reflect the political trends of the time. In Britain, for example, ESOL developed in response to the needs of large numbers of non-English speaking people who migrated from the 1950s onwards, especially from the Indian sub-continent. Students needed to be prepared for daily life; materials were home-produced and heavily functional, dealing with basic survival and adjustment to life in the new country and with activities such as shopping, going to the doctor's and filling in forms for welfare benefits. 'Survival English' was later criticised by writers such as Auerbach (1986) and Tollefson (1986) for its reliance on materials based on unreal situations in which problems are easily solved and people in positions of power are co-operative and helpful, and for its hidden curriculum "which prepares students for subservient social roles and reinforces hierarchical relations both in and outside the classroom" (Auerbach and Burgess, 1985:475). Perhaps inevitably, echoes of survival English can be seen in materials and methods used in the ESOL classrooms of today.

ESOL teachers also draw upon commercially produced materials such as the type of textbooks commonly used in the teaching of EFL around the world. EFL is a commercial endeavour, so coursebooks have to accommodate the globalising trends of English language learning and publishing. It is in publishers' interests to make coursebooks appeal to as wide a market as possible, hence the emergence of generic English language, or 'global' coursebooks that can be marketed and sold anywhere ELT is practised. However, the extent to which global textbooks are appropriate in ESOL classrooms is questionable. In particular, the sort of apolitical, carefree and overwhelmingly middle-class culture that such coursebooks present opens them up to criticism (Gray, 2002, 2013, and this volume).

Tackling real world challenges in the ESOL classroom

Moreover, global textbooks do not prepare students for the real world challenges faced by students as they adjust to life in a new, English-dominant country. The demands of the world outside the classroom range from everyday activities such as shopping to encounters with medical professionals, interactions with officials in settings such as welfare offices and employment bureaux, and interviews for employment. ESOL-specific materials writers do attempt to cater for the daily needs of ESOL students. For example, the authors of the materials developed to accompany the Adult ESOL Core Curriculum in England draw on the traditional ways in which English language pedagogy has attempted to prepare learners for real life interaction, for instance through the use of dialogues such as this, in which learners hear an exchange in a doctor's surgery:

> Receptionist: Hello. Ashlea Surgery
> Filiz: Hello, can I make an appointment for my daughter to see Dr Green please?
> Receptionist: Yes. What's the name?
> Filiz: Gulay Akpinar
> Receptionist: Can you spell her first name please?
> Filiz: Yes. It's G–U–L–A–Y. Gulay Akpinar.
> Receptionist: OK. Dr Green's next appointment is on Thursday morning.
> Filiz: Thursday. OK.
> Receptionist: Right. Is 9.30 OK?
> Filiz: Yes, that's fine. Thank you very much.
> *(DfES, 2003 Skills for Life ESOL learning materials Entry 1)*

In class, students might go on to use a dialogue such as this as a model, modify it with their own details, rehearse it, and perhaps learn it by heart to perform in front of the class. However, ESOL teachers often have a feeling that these dialogues do not exactly 'work' as learning activities and somehow fail to hit the mark in terms of what really goes on in encounters outside the classroom. Research in conversation analysis (Drew and Heritage, 1992) and interactional sociolinguistics (Sarangi and Roberts, 1999) has shown that language in institutional interactions is usually very different from that given as models to learners; there is a wide gap between real spoken interaction on the one hand, with its pauses, hesitations, false starts, repair and unequal power relations (as mentioned earlier), and orderly classroom dialogues on the other, in which interactive tasks are accomplished with the minimum of misunderstanding and with the maximum co-operation between participants (Roberts et al., 2007). Learners themselves sometimes echo the same frustration. In the lesson where the dialogue above was presented (discussed in Roberts and Cooke, 2009), they lamented that, in their own doctor's surgery, they would never be able to get an appointment so easily at a time to suit them or with the doctor of their choice.

The reality in the outside world, whether in institutional domains or in general daily life, often differs greatly from the imagined interaction of classroom dialogues. The question arises, then, of how ESOL teachers can best prepare their learners for the challenges they face outside classrooms. To teach about high-stakes encounters such as job interviews, for example, requires teachers and materials writers to have a deep knowledge of the language practices of modern interviews, which they often do not possess. Materials which are based on authentic interaction (e.g. Roberts et al., 2007) can at the very least raise awareness of real-life language issues. To do this comprehensively across interactional domains is dependent on more data being made available from different settings, which inevitably has implications for resources and funding and therefore depends on the political will to fund such research.

Participatory pedagogy in ESOL

Language pedagogy for adult migrants requires innovative responses to linguistic and cultural diversity and to the new mobilities of the twenty-first century. Descriptions of such responses can be found in chapters in two British Council publications focusing on practice in the UK (Mallows, 2012, 2014) and, with a global reach beyond ESOL, in Simpson and Whiteside (2015). A number of the chapters in these volumes promote an approach to ESOL teaching which can be described as broadly critical and participatory. Their authors recognise that many migrants are not only concerned with a wish to access English to enable them to operate effectively in daily life but are engaged in a struggle for recognition and equality. Inspired by the writings of the Brazilian Marxist educator Paulo Freire in books such as *Pedagogy of the Oppressed* (1970) and by others such as Elsa Auerbach (e.g. Auerbach, 1992), participatory pedagogy has been practised by some educators since the 1970s, particularly in the teaching of adult literacy. It was advocated for the teaching of ESOL in the 1980s (Baynham, 1988), but only recently has it been taken up seriously by ESOL practitioners. Participatory pedagogy advocates that participants set their own agenda, devise their own learning materials, take action on the issues which they identify as important and evaluate their progress and the effectiveness of their programmes as they go. The syllabus, therefore, is not brought along by the teacher but rather *emerges* from class to class; the direction of the instructional process is, as Auerbach (1992: 19) puts it, "from the students to the curriculum rather than from the curriculum to the students" (see also Menard-Warwick et al., this volume).

An example of a participatory ESOL initiative is the *Whose Integration?* project (Bryers et al., 2014a, b, c; Cooke et al., 2015), whereby teacher-researchers explored critical participatory ESOL pedagogy with their adult migrant students in London. This is part of a movement in ESOL practice which relates language and literacy learning to the critical concerns of students' lives on the students' own terms. This can equip students with critical skills which can be transferred beyond the classroom to effect social action. The project builds on work on speaking development in ESOL classrooms (Cooke and Roberts, 2007a, b). This work recognised first that development in oral competence required the production of turns of talk that were longer and more sophisticated than are typical in many ESOL classrooms (Swain, 2000). At the same time, the content of classroom discussions needed to suit students' out-of-class needs and interests. *Whose Integration?* addresses a contemporary concern – integration into a new society – of which "ESOL students are often the referents, but about which they are rarely asked their opinions" (Cooke et al., 2015). The authors hold that the "intensity of discussion in the classroom led some students to stimulate the same debates at home and with friends, and as teachers we found ourselves discussing the issues which arose in class long after the sessions were over."

Conclusion

I conclude by stressing the mutually informing interplay of the factors I have sketched out in this chapter. I maintain that ESOL teachers, teacher educators and students with an interest in language education in migration contexts need to develop a knowledge of individual concerns (investment, learning and migration trajectories), of the sociolinguistic setting and of the "wider social, political and philosophical issues in education" (Lawes, 2003: 24). In so doing, they will strengthen their ability to understand ESOL students and to critically evaluate the policies and structures to which the field of ESOL is subject, and which – to a greater or lesser extent – the field shapes.

Discussion questions

- *Student interaction outside class.* What do ESOL teachers typically need to know about their students' interactions outside class? How might knowing this information affect the way they plan their courses?
- *Contemporary superdiversity and ESOL students.* What are some of the challenges and opportunities that the diversity of students outlined in the chapter might present to ESOL teachers and curriculum planners?
- *Reflection on gender.* What issues (in class and outside) might affect women ESOL learners in a different way from men?
- *The multilingual milieu.* English might be just one of many languages which ESOL students encounter day-to-day, and they may well be 'developing their competence in English as part of a multilingual repertoire'. How might ESOL teachers and their students address this new reality in their classrooms?

Related topics

Bilingual education in a multilingual world; Educational perspectives on ELT; ELT materials; Politics, power relationships and ELT; Teaching literacy; Values in the ELT classroom.

Further reading

Blackledge, A. and Creese, A. (eds) (2014) *Heteroglossia as practice and pedagogy.* New York: Springer. (A collection offering theoretical interpretations and explanations of voice and heteroglossia, and its relevance to multilingual research and teaching.)

Cooke, M. and Simpson, J. (2008) *ESOL: A critical guide.* Oxford: Oxford University Press. (A research-informed overview of ESOL for teachers and teacher-educators.)

Norton, B. (2013) *Identity and language learning: Extending the conversation.* Bristol: Multilingual Matters. (The updated edition of a classic work on identity and language learning among adult English language learners in Canada.)

Simpson, J. and Whiteside, A. (eds) (2015) *Adult language education and migration: Challenging agendas in policy and practice.* London: Routledge. (An edited collection comprising a critical examination of policy and practice in language education for adult migrants in nine countries around the world.)

Tarone, E. M. Bigelow and Hansen, K. (2009) *Literacy and second language oracy.* Oxford: Oxford University Press. (A book documenting the impact of low literacy skills on second language oral processing, an issue which disproportionately affects ESOL students.)

References

Appadurai, A. (1996) *Modernity at large: Cultural dimensions of globalization.* Minneapolis: University of Minnesota Press.

Auerbach, E. R. (1986) 'Competency-based ESL: One step forward or two steps back?' *TESOL Quarterly*, 20/3. 411–427.

Auerbach, E. R. (1992) *Making meaning, making change: Participatory curriculum development for adult ESL literacy.* McHenry, IL: Center for Applied Linguistics and Delta Systems.

Auerbach, E. R. and Burgess, D. (1985) 'The hidden curriculum of survival ESL'. *TESOL Quarterly*, 19/3. 475–495.

Baynham, M. (1988) 'Action and reflection: The Freirean argument in ESL'. *Language Issues*, 2/1. 6–12.

Baynham, M. (2011) 'Language and migration', in J. Simpson' (ed.) *The Routledge handbook of applied linguistics.* London: Routledge. 413–427.

Baynham, M. and De Fina, A. (2005) *Dislocations/relocations: Narratives of displacement.* Manchester: St Jerome.

Baynham, M., Roberts, C., Cooke, M., Simpson, J., Ananiadou, K, Callaghan, J., McGoldrick, J. and Wallace, C. (2007) *Effective teaching and learning: ESOL.* London: NRDC.

Bigelow, M. and King, K. (2015) 'Somali immigrant youths and the power of print literacy'. *Writing Systems Research*, 7/1. 4–19.

Blommaert, J. (2010) *The Sociolinguistics of globalization.* Cambridge: Cambridge University Press.

Blommaert, J. and Rampton, B. (2011) 'Language and superdiversity'. *Diversities*, 13/2. 1–20.

Bourdieu, P. (1986) 'The forms of capital', reprinted in S. Ball (ed.) *The Routledge Falmer reader in sociology of education.* London: Routledge Falmer. 15–29.

Bremer, K., Roberts, C., Vasseur, M., Simonot, M. and Broeder, P. (1996) *Achieving understanding.* Harlow: Longman.

Bryers, D., Winstanley, B. and Cooke, M. (2014a) 'Participatory ESOL', in D. Mallows (ed.) *Language issues in migration and integration: Perspectives from teachers and learners.* London: British Council. 9–19.

Bryers, D., Winstanley, B. and Cooke, M. (2014b) 'Whose integration?', in D. Mallows (ed.) *Language issues in migration and integration: Perspectives from teachers and learners.* London: British Council. 19–35.

Bryers, D., Winstanley, B. and Cooke, M. (2014c) 'The power of discussion', in D. Mallows (ed.) *Language issues in migration and integration: Perspectives from teachers and learners.* London: British Council. 35–54.

Canagarajah, S. (forthcoming) *The Routledge handbook of language and migration.* London: Routledge.

Carrier, K. (1999) 'The social environment of second language listening: Does status play a role in comprehension?' *Modern Language Journal*, 83/1. 65–79.

Cooke, M. and Roberts, C. (2007a) *Developing adult teaching and learning: Practitioner guides – ESOL.* London: NRDC and Leicester: NIACE.

Cooke, M. and Roberts, C. (2007b) *Reflection and action in ESOL classrooms.* Retrieved from http://www.nrdc.org.uk/publications_details.asp?ID=112

Cooke, M. and Simpson, J. (2008) *ESOL: A critical guide.* Oxford: Oxford University Press.

Cooke, M., Winstanley, B. and Bryers, D. (2015) 'Whose integration? A participatory ESOL project in the UK', in J. Simpson and A. Whiteside (eds) *Adult language education and migration: Challenging agendas in policy and practice.* London: Routledge. 214–224.

Creese, A. and Blackledge, A. (2010) 'Translanguaging in the bilingual classroom: A pedagogy for learning and teaching?' *The Modern Language Journal*, 94/1. 103–115.

Creese, A. and Blackledge, A. (2011) 'Separate and flexible bilingualism in complementary schools: Multiple language practices in interrelationship'. *Journal of Pragmatics*, 43/5. 1196–1208.

Crevecoeur-Bryant, E. (2011) 'Identification of specific research-based instruction methods to teach pre-literate ESOL students,' in I. van de Craats, J. Kurvers and C. Schöneberger (eds) *Low-educated second language and literacy acquisition. Proceedings of the 6th Symposium, Cologne 2010.* Nijmegen: Centre for Language Studies. 21–32.

DfES (2003) *Skills for life ESOL learning materials entry 1*. London: Basic Skills Agency/ Department for Education and Skills. Published under Open Government Licence for Public Sector Information. Retrieved from http://www.nationalarchives.gov.uk/doc/open-government-licence/version/3/

Drew, P. and Heritage, J. (eds) (1992) *Talk at work: Interaction in institutional settings*. Cambridge: Cambridge University Press.

Duchêne, A., Moyer, M. and Roberts, C. (eds) (2013) *Language, migration and social inequalities: A critical sociolinguistic perspective on institutions and work*. Bristol: Multilingual Matters.

Eaves Poppy Project (n.d.) Website of the *Poppy Project*, support, advocacy and accommodation for trafficked women. Retrieved from http://www.eavesforwomen.org.uk/about-eaves/our-projects/the-poppy-project

Freire, P. (1970) *Pedagogy of the oppressed*. New York: Seabury Books.

Garcia, O. and Li, W. (2014) *Translanguaging: Language, bilingualism and education*. London: Palgrave Macmillan.

Giddens, A. (1999) *Runaway world: How globalization is reshaping our lives*. London: Profile.

Gray, J. (2002) 'The global coursebook in ELT', in D. Block and D. Cameron (eds) *Globalization and language teaching*. London: Routledge. 151–167.

Gray, J. (2013) *Critical perspectives on language teaching materials*. Houndmills: Palgrave Macmillan.

Johnson, D. C. (ed.) (2013) 'Ethnography of language policy: Theory, method and practice'. Special issue of *International Journal of the Sociology of Language*, 219. 1–140.

Kouritzin, S. (2000) 'Immigrant mothers redefine access to ESL classes: Contradiction and ambivalence'. *Journal of Multilingual and Multicultural Development*, 21/1. 14–32.

Kroskrity, P. (2001) 'Language ideologies', in J. Verschueren, J-O Österman, J. Blommaert and C. Bulcaen (eds) *Handbook of pragmatics*. Amsterdam: John Benjamins. 1–17.

Lawes, S. (2003) 'What, when, how and why? Theory and foreign language teaching'. *Language Learning Journal* 28. 22–28.

Mai, N. (2013) 'Embodied cosmopolitanisms: The subjective mobility of migrants working in the global sex industry'. *Gender, Place and Culture : A Journal of Feminist Geography*, 20/1. 107–124.

Makoni, S. and Pennycook, A. (2007) 'Disinventing and reconstituting languages', in S. Makoni and A. Pennycook (eds) *Disinventing and reconstituting languages*. Clevedon: Multilingual Matters. 1–43.

Mallows, D. (ed.) (2012) *Innovations in English language teaching for migrants and refugees*. London: British Council.

Mallows, D. (ed.) (2014) *Language issues in migration and integration: Perspectives from teachers and learners*. London: British Council.

May, S. (ed.) (2013) *The multilingual turn: Implications for SLA, TESOL, and bilingual education*. New York and London: Routledge.

McCarty, T. L. (ed.) (2011) *Ethnography and language policy*. New York and London: Routledge.

McNamara, T. (2012) 'Language assessments as shibboleths: A poststructuralist perspective'. *Applied Linguistics*, 33/5. 564–581.

Nicholas, H. (2015) 'Shaping Australian policy for Australian adult migrant English language learning', in J. Simpson and A. Whiteside (eds) *Adult language education and migration: Challenging agendas in policy and practice*. London: Routledge. 19–34.

Norris, J. M. and Ortega, L. (2000) 'Effectiveness of L2 instruction: A research synthesis and quantitative meta-analysis'. *Language Learning*, 50/3. 417–528.

Norton, B. (2000) *Identity and language learning: Gender, ethnicity and educational change*. London: Longman.

Norton, B. (2006) 'Not an afterthought: Authoring a text on adult ESOL'. *Linguistics and Education*, 17/1. 91–96.

Norton, B. (2011) 'Identity', in J. Simpson (ed.) *The Routledge handbook of applied linguistics*. London: Routledge. 318–330.

Norton, B. (2013) *Identity and language learning: Extending the conversation*. Bristol: Multilingual Matters.

Pennycook, A. and Otsuji, E. (2015) *Metrolingualism: Language in the city*. London: Routledge.

Pratt, M. L. (1997) 'The arts of the contact zone'. *Profession*, 91. 33–40.

Ricento, T. (2003) 'The discursive construction of Americanism'. *Discourse and Society*, 14. 611–637.

Ricento, T. and Hornberger, N. (1996) 'Unpeeling the onion: Language planning and policy in the ELT professional'. *TESOL Quarterly*, 30/3. 401–427.

Roberts, C. and Campbell, S. (2006) *Talk on trial: Job interviews, language and ethnicity*. London: Department for Work and Pensions.

Roberts, C., Campbell, S., Cooke, M. and Stenhouse, J. (2007) *FAQs: Frequently asked questions*. Leicester: JobCentre Plus and King's College London.

Roberts, C. and Cooke, M. (2009) 'Authenticity in the adult ESOL classroom and beyond'. *TESOL Quarterly*, 43/4. 620–642.

Rosenberg, S. (2007) *A critical history of ESOL in the UK, 1870–2006*. Leicester: NIACE.

Sarangi, S. and Roberts, C. (eds) (1999) *Talk, work and institutional order: Discourse in medical, mediation, and management settings*. Berlin: Mouton de Gruyter.

Scheeres, H. (2004) 'The textualised workplace'. *Reflect*, 1. 22.

Sheridan, V. (2015) 'English, everywhere and nowhere: ESOL policies in Ireland', in J. Simpson and A. Whiteside (eds) *Adult language education and migration: Challenging agendas in policy and practice*. London: Routledge. 149–161.

Simpson, J. (2015) 'English language learning for adult migrants in superdiverse Britain', in J. Simpson and A. Whiteside (eds) *Adult language education and migration: Challenging agendas in policy and practice*. London: Routledge. 200–213.

Simpson, J. and Cooke, M. (2010) 'Movement and loss: Progression in tertiary education for migrant students'. *Language and Education*, 24/1. 57–73.

Simpson, J., Cooke, M., Callaghan, J., Hepworth, M., Homer, M., Baynham, M., Allen, T., Grant, R. and Sisimayi, S. (2011) *ESOL neighbourhood audit pilot (Harehills): The HENNA project*. Leeds City Council/University of Leeds. Retrieved from http://www.education.leeds.ac.uk/research/projects/henna-project

Simpson, J. and Whiteside, A. (2012) 'Politics, policy and practice: ESOL in the UK and the USA'. *King's College London Working Papers in Urban Language & Literacies*. 87.

Simpson, J. and Whiteside, A. (eds) (2015) *Adult language education and migration: Challenging agendas in policy and practice*. London: Routledge.

Swain, M. (2000) 'The output hypothesis and beyond: Mediating acquisition through collaborative dialogue', in J. P. Lantolf (ed.) *Sociocultural theory and second language learning*. Oxford: Oxford University Press. 97–114.

Tarone, E., Bigelow, M. and Hansen, K. (2009) *Literacy and second language oracy*. Oxford: Oxford University Press.

Tollefson, J. W. (1986) 'Functional competencies in the US refugee program: Theoretical and practical problems'. *TESOL Quarterly*, 20/4. 649–664.

UN General Assembly (1948) Universal Declaration of Human Rights. Retrieved from http://www.un.org/en/documents/udhr/index.shtml

UNHCR (2014) *UNHCR global trends 2013*. Retrieved from http://unhcr.org/trends2013/

Vertovec, S. (2006) 'The emergence of super-diversity in Britain'. *Working paper no. 25*. Oxford: Centre on Migration, Policy and Society (COMPAS), University of Oxford.

Vertovec, S. (2012) '"Diversity" and the social imaginary'. *European Journal of Sociology*, 53. 287–312.

Wright, S. (2004) *Language policy and language planning: From nationalism to globalisation*. Basingstoke: Palgrave Macmillan.

Wrigley, H. S. (2015) 'Green Card English: New possibilities and enduring challenges in US immigration reform', in J. Simpson and A. Whiteside (eds) *Adult language education and migration: Challenging agendas in policy and practice*. London: Routledge. 225–243.

Young-Scholten, M. (ed.) (2015) *Adolescents and adults who develop literacy for the first time in L2*. Special issue of *Writing Systems Research*, 7/1.

14

Bilingual education in a multilingual world

Kevin S. Carroll and Mary Carol Combs

Introduction

In this chapter, we explore the phenomenon of bilingual education in an increasingly globalised, multilingual world. After defining key terms and explaining a variety of bilingual education programme formats, we focus our discussion on language contexts where English is one of the bilingual target languages. In doing so, we foreground two competing language ideologies that underlie the design and implementation of bilingual education – monolingualism and multilingualism – and analyse the way that these ideologies underpin both policy and practice. We conclude with a discussion highlighting key areas of dispute and debate, as well as a description of some of the implications and challenges for bilingual education practitioners. Because the issues involved in bilingual education both globally and locally are broad and complex, our discussion is not exhaustive. Instead, we hope to articulate some of the core findings within the field and provide an overview of some of the current tensions.

Essentially, when looking at the field of bilingual education from a global perspective, one can distinguish between contexts where acquiring English is a national priority and contexts with other linguistic and educational priorities. When the learning of English is a priority or is present at all, its power, prestige and status as a global lingua franca makes it a popular choice among parents as they work to provide a meaningful education for their children. Yet some of the most successful bilingual and multilingual programmes are established in areas around the world where English is not a language in play but where historically marginalised linguistic minorities are starting to receive what is often referred to as mother tongue-based multilingual education (MTB-MLE). While we discuss some of the successes that these MTB-MLE programmes have had around the world, we will focus primarily on language contexts where English is pursued as a local or national goal.

Key terms and types of bilingual education

Defining *bilingualism* depends largely on who defines it, in which contexts and for which populations. It is widely agreed that there is a continuum of bilingualism and biliteracy (Hornberger, 1989) and that bilinguals fall between two poles. For example, some bilinguals have barely the second language competencies to understand basic phrases and produce language on a rudimentary level in a limited number of contexts. Other bilinguals are much more fluent and versatile and possess language competencies that allow them to use their second language across a variety of domains of language use.

While bilingual competencies vary among users of two or more languages, 'balanced bilinguals' have well-developed language skills in both languages across many language domains and are able to command relatively equal levels of native-like fluency. And while balanced bilingualism is certainly something to aim for, such a goal is not always practical or even necessary, as many domains of language use in a person's life are relatively monolingual (Fishman, 1967). Thus, balanced bilinguals represent a small portion of the entire bilingual/multilingual population (Crawford, 2004), and most people who consider themselves bilingual fall somewhere between bilinguals with limited proficiency and balanced bilingualism. In some circumstances, they may have polished second language skills in their area of work or study but have fewer linguistic competencies in other domains, such as familial interactions or in religious life. Defining what it means to be bilingual becomes important in bilingual education because if the goal of a bilingual programme is balanced bilingualism, the programme may be judged to have failed because of the difficulty in attaining equal competence in two languages. However, if bilingualism is defined more loosely, bilingual education programmes might in fact develop a degree of bilingualism amongst students such that they remain dominant in their first language but also have more limited competencies in their second language.

Monolingual ideologies are pervasive in contexts where language diversity is seen as a problem or a threat to traditional or socio-historical ways of using language. Often associated with the 'one-nation-one-language' ideal (see also Crookes, this volume), these ideologies will invariably lead to only 'weak' forms of bilingual education, if any at all (Baker, 2001). When bilingual education is offered in contexts where monolingual ideologies prevail, the goal is to use students' first language to transition into the dominant target language, usually the national language. This model of bilingual education often leads to what is referred to as 'subtractive' bilingualism because the goal is not to maintain students' two languages but rather to assimilate them into the dominant language group. In a subtractive model, the students' first language is gradually removed – or subtracted – and replaced by the second language. Once students are able to function in classes taught in the dominant language, little to no support is offered to maintain their mother tongues.

Bi/multi-lingual ideologies describe contexts where languages are seen as a resource and efforts are undertaken to foster, create and/or maintain two or more languages. When bi/multilingual ideologies prevail, a 'strong' form of bilingual education is often implemented. In this case, 'additive' bilingual education, whereby a new language is added to the learners' linguistic repertoire, incorporates the languages of linguistic minorities and majorities alike in school curricula and pedagogy in order to develop or sustain a multilingual society. Such practices can provide a more equitable and meaningful education to children with non-dominant languages.

Bilingual education, therefore, "is a seemingly simple label for a complex phenomenon" (Cazden and Snow, 1990: 9). As there is no universally accepted definition of bilingualism, bilingual education thus depends entirely on the context in which it is implemented (Baker, 2001; García, 2009). What we argue here, therefore, is that just as it is difficult to define *bilingualism*, bilingual education similarly means different things to different people. While the label implies the use of two languages in a school setting, the type of programme selected and the pedagogies used within it depend on the language ideologies of the community, school district and geographical region and the particular social, political and educational goals of formalised schooling. Colin Baker (2001) has developed a useful typology to describe strong and weak forms of bilingual education. He distinguishes between language contexts that represent or promote monolingual or multilingual ideologies, as can be seen in Table 14.1.

As Table 14.1 shows, the primary societal goal of 'weak forms' of bilingual education is not bilingualism but assimilation into the dominant culture and monolingualism in the dominant language. Within these weak forms of bilingual education, students who become bilingual, in that they maintain their home language and learn the language of formal schooling, often do so because of positive influences from family and community outside school rather than due to the effects of their actual schooling.

The 'submersion' – or 'sink or swim' – model assumes that what students need to acquire the target language is sufficient exposure to it. Unfortunately, language minority students in submersion programmes often fall behind their native speaking peers in content areas. Historically, in the name of colonisation and nationalism, students in English-using contexts like the United States, Australia and New Zealand were exposed to such programmes (Crawford,

Table 14.1 Strong *vs* weak forms of bilingual education

Weak forms of bilingual education				
Type of programme	*Typical student*	*Language(s) used for instruction*	*Societal / educational goal*	*Individual / language outcome goal*
Submersion	Language minority	Majority language	Assimilation	Monolingualism
Submersion with pull-out language classes / sheltered instruction	Language minority	Majority language with 'pull-out' L2 lessons	Assimilation	Monolingualism
Segregationist	Language minority	Minority language (forced, no choice)	Apartheid	Monolingualism
Transitional	Language minority	Moves from minority to majority language	Assimilation	Relative monolingualism
Separatist	Language minority	Minority language (out of choice)	Detachment / autonomy	Limited bilingualism
Strong forms of bilingual education				
Type of programme	*Typical student*	*Language(s) used for instruction*	*Societal / educational goal*	*Individual / language outcome goal*
Immersion	Language majority	Bilingual with initial emphasis in L2	Pluralism and enrichment	Bilingualism and biliteracy
Maintenance / heritage language	Language minority	Bilingual with emphasis on L1	Maintenance, pluralism and enrichment	Bilingualism and biliteracy
Two-way/Dual language	Mixed language minority and majority	Minority and majority	Maintenance, pluralism and enrichment	Bilingualism and biliteracy
Mainstream bilingual	Language majority	Two majority languages	Maintenance, pluralism and enrichment	Bilingualism and biliteracy

Source: Adapted from Baker, 2001: 194.

1992; Skutnabb-Kangas and Phillipson, 1995; Orelus, 2014). Submersion models contribute to 'language shift' or the move, for language users, from Indigenous and minority languages into the dominant or majority languages (Fishman, 1991, 2001). While language rights legislation has mitigated the imposition of both English and non-English submersion programmes in some Western countries such as the USA and the UK and Denmark and Sweden, linguistic contexts in Africa, Asia and South America have often adopted submersion models with regard to both English and other dominant languages. While UNESCO and other international aid organisations are working to interrupt this trend, submersion education remains common, especially in parts of Africa (Bamgbose, 2000) and Southeast Asia (e.g. Cambodia and Laos, see Kosonen, 2005; Philippines, see Dekker and Young, 2005; Thailand, see Kosonen, 2008; Timor-Leste, see Taylor-Leech, 2013). Yet despite the historical prominence of submersion models of education, many grassroots organisations are working toward MTB-MLE, often with the help of local and governmental organisations (Clinton, 2013).

Another more contemporary form of weak bilingual education is the 'transitional' model, which uses students' first languages as a 'transition' into content instruction in the majority language. The rationale here is that students need from four to seven years to develop academic proficiency in the target language. Academic language proficiency was initially theorised by Cummins (1976) as a way to distinguish between what he called 'basic interpersonal communication skills' (BICS) and 'cognitive academic language proficiency' (CALP; see also Morton, this volume). More recent scholarship, however, has contested this theoretical distinction between social and academic language, arguing on the one hand that the lines between these dimensions are blurred, and critiquing the assumption that academic language can only be acquired in formal school settings on the other; an uncritical acceptance of this latter assumption implies that working class or language minority families do not practice academic discourses at home and can only acquire them at school (MacSwan and Rolstad, 2003; Faltis, 2013). Nonetheless, the BICS-CALP distinction underlies the reasoning behind many transitional programmes, which prepare students for monolingual content courses in their second language. Because the maintenance and development of students' first language is not a goal, transitional programmes are often shorter than stronger forms of bilingual education. Once students show sufficient academic language proficiency in L2, they are placed in classrooms with target language native speaking peers and L1 language support typically ceases (Wright, 2010; Ovando and Combs, 2011).

Alternatives to these weaker forms of bilingual education seek an additive approach where the goal is to foster or maintain students' L1 while they learn an L2. However, 'strong approaches' to bilingual education also vary and depend on the sociocultural and economic contexts in which such programmes are found. As goals and contexts change, so too do the ways in which programmes work to develop bilingual students. In the United States, for example, additive bilingual programmes have been inspired by 'immersion' programmes in Canada, which, in spite of their label, are actually strong bilingual programmes (Lambert, 1972; Genesse, 1995; Ricento and Burnaby, 1998). Historically, these Canadian programmes have served middle-class English-speaking children in the French-speaking province of Québec. These students attend classes taught in French for the better part of the day throughout their primary grades (Crawford, 2004). Participating students, who already have a wealth of social, economic and L1 linguistic capital, are merely adding French to their linguistic repertoires (Genesee, 1995). Similarly, students enrolled in many private schools on the largely Spanish L1 island of Puerto Rico attend bilingual schools where maths and science are taught in English, while social studies and certain electives are taught in Spanish (Schmidt, 2013).

'Heritage language' models, sometimes called 'maintenance' or 'developmental' programmes in the US, feature a family or community language which may – or may not – be the students' primary language but nevertheless carries a cultural and linguistic connection for them. Used as the medium of instruction, the heritage language reinforces its connection to ancestry while facilitating its contemporary use. Heritage language programmes have been implemented with some success with Indigenous languages students in different parts of the United States (Hinton and Hale, 2001; McCarty, 2002, 2013; McCarty and Zepeda, 2006). When used among caregivers in early childhood and preschool, these programmes are sometimes called 'language nests'. Language nests were popularised in New Zealand in the push for Maori language revitalisation and maintenance in a predominantly English-speaking environment (King, 2001). Similar language nest programmes have been adopted successfully in Hawai'i (Warner, 2001).

'Two-way' or 'dual immersion' models have also been successful strong forms of bilingual education. These programmes require relatively equal numbers of users of the two languages – dominant and non-dominant. Successful dual language programmes use a bilingual and bicultural curriculum where content is delivered in both the majority and minority languages. The language use in two-way programmes varies, but the two most common models use a 50/50 or 90/10 approach, meaning that half of the content areas are taught in the minority language and half in the majority language, or 90 per cent in the minority language and 10 per cent in the majority language, respectively. Additional language classes are also included in the curriculum in both the L1 and L2 of the students. Some schools organise instruction by time of day (e.g. L1 in the morning and L2 in the afternoon) or by alternate days or weeks (L1 the first week, L2 the second) (Wright, 2010).

Current critical issues and debates

Monolingual vs multilingual ideologies

As noted earlier, decisions about bilingual education are often determined by political, social and economic contexts (Blackledge and Creese, 2010). Although financial concerns about cost may affect the implementation of bilingual programmes, more important influences are the dominant language ideologies in particular contexts. Especially in the United States and the United Kingdom, groups and individuals often exercise their franchise to block bilingual programmes. Monolingual discourse has prevailed in these nations, reifying a 'language-as-a-problem' orientation toward the use of languages other than English (Ruiz, 1984). 'One nation-one flag' ideologies are expressed by elected officials, policy makers and voters, who may see the presence of speakers of other languages as a threat to their way of life on the one hand and to the dominant language on the other (Beardsmore, 2003). These 'language panics' (Hill, 2001) are rarely divorced from larger fears about racial, ethnic and cultural tensions that result from economic or demographic shifts, often accompanied by racialised backlashes against immigrants and speakers of other languages. Consequently, it is unsurprising that the primary goal of bilingual education in both the US and the UK has been to transition students, through weak forms of delivery, into the larger English-using environment of public schools.

Within the Western world, "debates about language are often debates about immigration, and about 'pluralist' or 'assimilationist' policy in relation to immigrant groups" (Blackledge and Creese, 2010: 26; see also Simpson, this volume). Some of the tension about bilingual education, especially in the United States, reflects broader ideological fears about the perceived encroachment of 'little' languages (Fishman, 1991) into majority language communities. These largely monolingual contexts regularly position speakers of other languages as a threat to the dominant language (Blackledge and Creese, 2010). For example, voters in California, Arizona and Massachusetts (USA) passed anti-bilingual education ballot initiatives in which media campaigns were waged through misleading, inflammatory and anti-immigrant sound bites (Johnson, 2005; Wright, 2005; Mora, 2009). The passage of such laws has resulted in a precipitous decline in the number of bilingual programmes in these states (Combs et al., 2005; Combs and Nicholas, 2012; Gándara and Hopkins, 2010; Arias and Faltis, 2012; Moore, 2014). And while the passage of these propositions worked to hurt large minority populations (such as L1 Spanish speakers), they have also affected Native American bilingual and language revitalisation programmes (Combs and Nicholas, 2012).

Unfortunately, language-as-problem-orientations toward linguistic minorities are not limited to the contexts where English is primarily used. Linguistic diversity in relatively new nations has prompted central governments to adopt a restrictionist orientation toward language pluralism, privileging dominant languages. In the Philippines, for example, restrictionist orientations have resulted in submersion models of bilingual education, though, as Dekker and Young (2005) document, relatively new MTB-MLE programmes allow an easier transition into future schooling in Tagalog and/or English. According to Kosonen (2005) and Kosonen and Young (2009), national unification movements in Southeast Asian countries have placed linguistic minority students at a decisive disadvantage. UNESCO, along with these and other applied linguists, argues that formal schooling should be a space where linguistic resources are viewed positively and that strong forms of bilingual education be adopted. This would entail the adoption of bilingual programmes that encourage literacy in students' first language because their first language is seen as a resource and is to be welcomed into the formal school environment (UNESCO, 2010).

In contrast, and differing from countries with well-established monolingual ideologies, countries and contexts where multilingual discourses are the norm often promote an additive form of bilingual education, where language is viewed from a rights or resource orientation (Ruiz, 1984). Bilingual education policy initiatives in Singapore (Silver, 2005), Luxemburg (De Korne, 2012), Catalonia, Spain (Urmeneta and Unamuno, 2008) and India (Mohanty, 2013) have taken a more additive view of bilingualism, mirroring the multilingual contexts of these countries. In all four contexts, regional languages are taught alongside national languages. In these contexts, English is also greatly emphasised, if not required (as in the case of Singapore and India). The adoption of multilingual ideologies has resulted in programme models that often entail the use of MTB-MLE in the primary grades in order to develop literacy. As students improve their first language literacy skills, they are gradually exposed to a second or even third language. This exposure often comes in the form of language courses but can also include content courses taught in these languages.

Determining the languages used for instruction

While the cognitive benefits of bilingualism have been documented (see Cummins, 1976; Lazaruk, 2007; Bialystok, 2009), the inclusiveness and equity that bilingual education can provide for a community are almost impossible to measure. Given the effect on linguistic minority communities of historical and continuing colonisation in parts of the world, minority language speakers almost everywhere are susceptible to the same restrictive ideologies manifested by dominant language speakers, for example, that there is little educational value inherent in school programmes designed to develop or maintain heritage languages (Smith, 1999). Even when stronger bilingual models replace submersion programmes, policy makers and teachers still face the uphill battle of convincing parents and community members of the merit of using mother tongue instruction in schools rather than English or another regional lingua franca (e.g. in South Africa, Webb, 2004; in Southeast Asia, Kosonen and Young, 2009).

After determining that bilingual education will be the programme of choice, school administrators, teachers and policy makers must create a programme that parallels the rigor and expectations of 'regular' classes and must find teachers qualified to teach these classes. Thus, hiring individuals who might not have state or national teaching credentials but do have advanced knowledge of the key languages in question must be considered. These issues are ever present in indigenous communities in the Americas, where few elders have advanced degrees and as such are typically precluded from teaching their native language in schools, despite the fact that they might be among the only remaining speakers with an intricate understanding of the minority language (Lomawaima and McCarty, 2006).

Once a bilingual programme is selected, policy makers, principals, teachers and parents must decide on the school's language policy. For instance, until recently it has been assumed that the two languages in a bilingual programme should be kept separate in order to minimise interference between them. However, this assumption has been challenged, and terms such as 'code-meshing' and 'translanguaging' have drawn attention to the legitimacy of connecting the languages in a productive way within bilingual instruction, both across the curriculum and in the classroom. Code-meshing is defined by Michael-Luna and Canagarajah (2007: 56) as "a communicative device used for specific rhetorical and ideological purposes in which a multilingual speaker intentionally integrates local and academic discourse as a form of resistance, reappropriation and/or transformation of the academic discourse". Translanguaging, on the other hand, "extends our traditional definitions of language and bilingualism. It refers to the ways in which bilinguals use their complex semiotic repertoire to act, to know, and to be" (García and Li, 2013: 137; see also chapters by Morton, Pennycook, and Simpson, this volume). The emergence of these conceptualisations has major implications for bilingual education. It will be interesting to see the extent to which these theoretical terms and concepts influence both pedagogy and practice in the development of bilingual education models around the world.

Implementation of bilingual education

As one would imagine, given the differences between bilingual programmes and the range in contexts that use bilingual models, no two bilingual programmes are identical. Bilingual education administrators must consider the teachers' language proficiency, students' proficiency in either L1 or L2, local and national linguistic contexts, and national accountability measures. While a bilingual programme might require some additional funding, the cost of running a bilingual programme might parallel the costs of a monolingual curriculum, if, for instance, bilingual teachers are not compensated for their linguistic abilities (a circumstance we do not necessarily advocate).

While describing every potential bilingual programme is beyond the scope of this chapter, we provide a snapshot of an average day (or week) in three different bilingual models in Table 14.2. It provides the reader with a visual representation of the ways that instructional time is allocated in various models. We encourage readers to compare the amount of time and the scheduling of the classes in each context to the goals of language programmes discussed earlier in the chapter in Table 14.1, and, for those working in bilingual education, to make connections to the models most familiar to you.

As Table 14.2 indicates, the Arizona model is strictly English-only for four hours daily, with the remaining two hours devoted to mathematics, lunch and recess/break. What makes Arizona's segregationist approach particularly problematic is the intentional withholding of content areas like science, social studies and language arts. Mathematics is taught because it is a subject assessed on the state's high-stakes assessment instrument, but teaching and assessment take place in English. The Japanese-English programme in Illinois is emblematic of a dual language programme;

Table 14.2 Three language programme schedules

Segregated (4 hours daily) 'Structured English Immersion' (Arizona, USA)			'Dual language' programme District Level (Schaumburg, IL, USA)	Mainstream Bilingual Abu Dhabi Education Council (Abu Dhabi, United Arab Emirates)
Programme goal English medium instruction after one year			**Programme goal** Maintenance and acquisition of students' L1 & L2 Japanese and English	**Programme goal** Bilingualism in Arabic and English
Grade K–5 daily time allocation 100% English			**Grade 1–6 daily time allocation** 75% English / 25% Japanese	**Grade 1–5 daily time allocation** Arabic 50% / English 50%
AZELLA* Pre-emergent and emergent	AZELLA* Basic level	AZELLA* Intermediate level	**English medium teaching** English literacy – 60min. • 15min. for shared reading • 45min. guided reading Maths – 60min. Science – 60min. **Japanese medium teaching** Japanese literacy – 60min. • 15min. shared reading • 45min. guided reading Social Studies – 30min.	**Arabic medium teaching** Arabic literacy – 96min. Islamic studies – 48min. Social studies- 24min. Music/art/health/ PE – 24min. ICT – 12min. **English medium teaching** Literacy – 144min. Maths – 60min. Science – 48min.
Oral English 45min.	Oral English 30min.	Oral English 15min.		
Grammar 60min.	Grammar 60min.	Grammar 60min.		
Reading 60min.	Reading 60min.	Reading 60min.		
Vocabulary 60min.	Vocabulary 60min.	Vocabulary 60min.		
Pre-Writing 15min.	Writing 30min.	Writing 45min.		
The remaining 120 minutes of the school day is divided into math, lunch and recess				

*AZELLA (Arizona English Language Learner Assessment) is the state's English language proficiency instrument.

though it still heavily favours English, it promotes literacy and the use of Japanese among the students. The Abu Dhabi curriculum, on the other hand, is a mainstream bilingual programme which weighs Arabic and English equally, representing the desire to maintain students' L1 but also gain valuable proficiency in English. The Arizona English-only programme is designed to do exactly what its name indicates – transition students into speaking only English. On the other hand, the English-Japanese curriculum at the primary school in Illinois provides basic literacy and vocabulary, which could potentially set a solid foundation for future Japanese acquisition if secondary curricula complement this bilingual approach. The Abu Dhabi curriculum provides students the best chance to develop bilingualism in both Arabic and English, as both languages share high prestige and status within the country and the curriculum provides a balanced approach where both languages are seen as a resource.

Who should 'become' bilingual through bilingual education?

The societal goals of bilingual education programmes have varied widely, as noted earlier. Is bilingual education merely a means to an end, with students' first language used only to acquire a basic foundation in the second? Is the development of bilingualism and biliteracy a viable goal? If yes, what is the best way to achieve it? How long should students remain in a bilingual programme? Should the languages be taught separately, or is some degree of translanguaging appropriate? Similarly, questions about which students will benefit the most from bilingual education surface from time to time. While proponents might justifiably declare that majority and minority language students alike can benefit from bilingual instruction, discussions about programme eligibility can be contentious. This is particularly the case when space in bilingual programmes is limited or when government-funded bilingual programmes are tied to students' lower socioeconomic status, as is the case in the United States. Ironically, in the United States today, there is a great deal of interest in dual language education, a model in which linguistic majority and linguistic minority students are grouped together and receive a portion of their instruction in the dominant language and the other portion in a second language. This model is the fastest growing type of bilingual programme, enjoying the support of language majority and minority parents alike (Howard and Sugarman, 2007; Howard et al., 2007; Thomas and Collier, 2012). According to the Center for Applied Linguistics (2014), there are nearly 450 dual language programmes in schools across the US, and the number is growing. The overwhelming majority of the programmes provide instruction in Spanish and English, although there are a few programmes featuring Japanese, Korean and Mandarin instruction, mostly in the state of California.

Some have questioned whether dual language education, popular among English-speaking Anglo families, actually helps students *acquiring* English as a second language. An early critique came from Guadalupe Valdés, a second language acquisition researcher at Stanford University. Valdés (1997) questioned whether instruction in Spanish, simplified for English-speaking Anglo children, would disadvantage the native Spanish speakers present in the same classroom. Valdés wondered whether instruction would prioritise the acquisition of basic Spanish for English-speaking children rather than focus on the acquisition of academic content in Spanish for Spanish-speakers. Beyond instructional and curricular issues, Valdés raises broader socio-political concerns about the potential appropriation of the minority language – and the symbolic power it represents in majority contexts – by middle class and affluent Anglo families. She quotes a long-time bilingual educator worried about the merits of implementing dual language: "Dual-language immersion education is not a good idea. . . . If they take advantage of us in English, they will take advantage of us in Spanish as well" (Valdés, 1997: 393). In a similar critique of dual language education, Crawford (2004) worried that its popularity might dilute scarce school district resources allocated for language minority students learning content and English through bilingual education. This circumstance thus raises issues about educational equity and spotlights the "asymmetrical power dimensions around whiteness, wealth, and English privilege" (p. 29) in the United States and elsewhere. On the other hand, at least in the United States, the most common alternative to dual language is transitional bilingual education, a model that has been criticised as ineffective and remedial.

Paradoxically, the development of bilingualism *per se* is not contested, but rather who becomes bilingual and for what purpose. Thus, if an individual decides to add another language to her linguistic repertoire, such a pursuit is worthwhile and praiseworthy. In contrast, if entire communities seek to preserve or enhance the community language, this effort may be viewed with suspicion. Kjolseth (1973) addressed this paradox in an early article on Spanish-English bilingual education in the American Southwest: "Spanish is only a prestige idiom in the United States where there are irrelevant numbers of Spanish-speakers. Where Spanish-speakers are a relatively large group, it is an idiom held in considerable contempt" (p. 7). Today, tensions between group and individual bilingualism remain virtually unchanged in this region of the US.

Implications and challenges for ELT practice and practitioners

Bilingual teacher preparation

Districts or ministries serving a large number of second language English learners who share the same native language may be able to establish a bilingual education programme more easily than if they served students speaking different languages. However, even when parents support the academic development of the first language and the district or ministry provides the financial resources to build the programme, schools must consider how to select and prepare teachers for bilingual classrooms. Proximity to university teacher education programmes might supply some of these teachers, assuming the teachers are fluent in both the second language and native language of their students. Other rural and urban districts may have to recruit teachers, and if financial incentives are offered as part of recruitment packages, additional resources will be required. Some school districts or ministries may initiate and support 'grow your own' programmes, in which individuals – often para-professionals or teacher aides – are encouraged to obtain a teaching certificate at a nearby university or community college. Typically, these districts or ministries will partner with the university in a grant project to fund the tuition costs. If obtaining grant funds is impossible, the district or ministries themselves may dedicate all or part of the financial resources necessary, though this kind of support may be difficult to provide when budgets are limited.

Once teachers are in the classrooms, their education and experience should continue through professional development opportunities provided by the school district or educational authority. Ideally, they should also attend local and regional education conferences or meetings to obtain information about theory and research in the field and innovative pedagogical applications. Bilingual educators also benefit from social and professional networks, not only to connect to the latest developments in the field but also to create a sense of solidarity with other bilingual teachers. These networks are particularly important in areas where bilingual education is contested or controversial. In the United States, bilingual education increasingly has been replaced with English-only approaches to the education of second language learners. Former bilingual teachers may find themselves in charge of English-dominant language classrooms and unable to use their bilingualism and bilingual training in their instruction of English learners. In other parts of the world, policy changes requiring teachers to take or retake language proficiency exams that reify or at least favour an idealised standard English variety of the language can also have real implications for bilingual professionals as they are passed over for jobs by monolingual, native speakers, as has occurred in many international contexts (Jenkins and Leung, 2013).

Opening the door for translanguaging in the bilingual classroom

Bilingual education has historically meant the strategic distribution of two languages within a school curriculum. However, the simultaneous use of both languages in a classroom is something that scholars are now beginning to examine (as noted above). Cummins (2005) reiterates the importance for those working within the field of bilingual education to "confront and critically re-examine our own monolingual instructional assumptions" (p. 590). The re-examination of such assumptions may work to further legitimise the use of language patterns that more closely mirror authentic language use in bilingual communities, where there typically is an unclear delineation between the languages used in natural discourse (see Kerr, this volume, for further questioning of the English-only classroom).

We predict that one of the future directions for bilingual education in the coming years will be the need to re-examine bilingual or multilingual contexts in order to understand the extent that translanguaging practices present themselves in formal teaching environments. Canagarajah (2011) and Li (2010) document how translanguaging is a common and ongoing strategy used by bilingual students to learn content subjects. Creese and Blackledge (2010) document the usefulness of such practices in 'complementary schools' or learning environments that take place outside of the traditional classroom context. The volume by Blackledge and Creese (2010) speaks to the variety of spaces where a combined use of formal language teaching and translanguaging practices can strengthen students' learning and comprehension. The increasing attention of recent research to these practices indicates that the research community has begun to question previously assumed 'best' teaching practices.

Concluding remarks

Bilingual education is not a new phenomenon, nor is it practised in the same way throughout the world. Historically, different approaches to instruction in two languages have resulted from political or social ideologies of local circumstances. Throughout this chapter we have discussed the complex issues involved in bilingual education, particularly its connection to macro level political movements and ideologies. Language ideologies in contemporary global contexts are often indexed by societies that promote a monolingual discourse versus those who actively seek multilingual approaches. Monolingual discourses often lead to transitional bilingual programmes or no bilingual instruction at all and thus work to maintain the status quo of a dominant majority language alongside a low-status minority language or languages. Countries and contexts where multilingual discourses dominate generally see foreign languages and their speakers as a resource and support the development of students' literacy skills and content knowledge in their first language as well as their second. Nevertheless, as globalisation continues to bring the world together, bilingual education will continue to change. These changes may result in more English being adopted as one of the languages used in bilingual programmes. Additionally, strict adherence to language separation may start to erode as translanguaging-like approaches gain in popularity.

We also discussed the complexity of language policy issues that must be addressed when developing any bilingual programme. These policy decisions are numerous and difficult, as they often result in the favouring of a particular language over another and, by extension, the speakers of that language over speakers of other languages. In highly multilingual contexts, such as parts of South Africa, even identifying students' mother tongue is just one of the many tensions that accompany bilingual education in the multilingual world. Determining a students' mother tongue can itself be difficult (Bamgbose, 2000).

Of the key questions regarding bilingual education, one of the most fundamental is: who should receive it? The majority population often covet additive forms of bilingual education for their own members. However, when minority languages and their speakers are perceived as a threat to local norms, bilingual programmes provided to minority communities may be seen as promoting a questionable interest. By this we mean that anti-bilingual sentiments work to justify and strengthen monolingual ideologies that stress the importance of assimilation and the use of the national or majority language in educational settings. This has historically been the case in English-dominant countries where monolingual ideologies have prevailed, resulting in little minority language maintenance and bilingualism.

Future directions for bilingual education will undoubtedly continue to document teachers' best practices in the classroom; however, we predict that more emphasis will be put on the socio-cultural variables that influence the implementation and success of bilingual education. Continued focus will examine how power relations and perceptions of threat dictate where programmes are thwarted and where they have been allowed to flourish (see Pennycook, this volume). Furthermore, if recent research is any indication, assumptions regarding the exclusive use of one language in the classroom will continue to be contested as research documents how instruction in bi/multilingual settings around the world use translanguaging practices that are more indicative of natural linguistic environments. This circumstance will undoubtedly influence the use of multiple languages in public education, especially in countries where multilingual discourses prevail. Unfortunately, more work needs to be done in curbing the monolingual ideologies typically associated with English dominant countries. So doing would put more value on the language and culture that linguistic minorities bring to their schools and communities.

Discussion questions

- What roles do ideology and power play in the creation of bilingual education programmes in your context?
- Given what you now understand about monolingual versus multilingual discourses, what discourse prevails in the country you currently live in? What are some examples?
- Do bilingual programmes exist in your region? If so, do they represent a weaker or stronger form of bilingual education? How and why?
- When working toward the creation of a bilingual programme, why is it important to consider the social and political context in which the programme will be implemented? What might be some of these considerations?

Related topics

Appropriate methodology; Content and language integrated learning; Dealing with the demands of language testing and assessment; Educational perspectives on ELT; English for speakers of other languages; Language teacher education; Politics, power relationships and ELT; Questioning 'English-only' classrooms.

Further reading

Baker, C. (2011) *Foundations of bilingual education and bilingualism*. Multilingual matters. (An excellent overview of the pillars of bilingual education, societal and individual bilingualism. Baker does excellent work in summarising the seminal works within this ever-expanding field.)

Crawford, J. (2004) *Educating English learners* (5th ed.). Los Angeles, CA: Bilingual Education Services. (A bilingual education advocate and historian, Crawford provides a rich history of bilingual education in the United States and highlights how politics has influenced the development of language policies and pedagogies throughout its history.)

García, O. and Sylvan, C. E. (2011) 'Pedagogies and practices in multilingual classrooms: Singularities in pluralities'. *The Modern Language Journal*, *95*/3. 385–400. (This text provides an excellent overview of the different pedagogies and practices that teachers use in multilingual classrooms. Highlighting best practices, the authors demonstrate how teachers can see their students' language practices as a resource and not as a deficit.)

Hornberger, N. H. (1989) 'Continua of biliteracy'. *Review of Education Research*, 59/3. 271–296. (A seminal piece; Hornberger describes the complexities of bilingualism and its intersection with literacy.)

References

Arias, M. B. and Faltis, C. (eds) (2012) *Implementing educational language policy in Arizona*. Bristol, England: Multilingual Matters.

Baker, C. (2001) *Foundations of bilingual education and bilingualism*. Clevedon, England: Multilingual Matters.

Bamgbose, A. (2000) *Language and exclusion: The consequences of language policies in Africa*. London: Lit Verlag.

Beardsmore, H. B. (2003) 'Who's afraid of bilingualism?', in J. M. Dewaele, H. B. Beardsmore, A. Housen and L. Wei (eds) *Bilingualism: Beyond basic principles: Festschrift in honour of Hugo Baetens Beardsmore*. Tonawanda: New York. Multilingual Matters. 10–27.

Bialystok, E. (2009) 'Bilingualism: The good, the bad, and the indifferent'. *Bilingualism: Language and Cognition*, 12/1. 3–11.

Blackledge, A. and Creese, A. (2010) *Multilingualism: A critical perspective*. London: Bloomsbury Academic.

Canagarajah, S. (2011) 'Codemeshing in academic writing: Identifying teachable strategies of translanguaging'. *Modern Language Journal*, 95/3. 401–417.

Cazden, C. B. and Snow, C. E. (1990) 'English plus: Issues in bilingual education'. *American Academy of Political and Social Science Annals*, 508. 9–11.

Center for Applied Linguistics. (2014) *Directory of two-way bilingual immersion programs in the U.S.* Retrieved June 5, 2014, from http://www.cal.org/jsp/TWI/SchoolListings.jsp.

Clinton, A. (2013) The long road to school in Cambodia [Text]. Retrieved May 6, 2015, from http://www.care.org/impact/stories/long-road-school-cambodia

Combs, M. C., Evans, C., Parra, E., Fletcher, T. and Jiménez, A. (2005) 'Bilingualism for the children: Implementing a dual language program in an English-only state'. *Educational Policy Journal*, 19/5. 701–728.

Combs, M. C. and Nicholas, S. E. (2012) 'The effect of Arizona language policies on Arizona indigenous students'. *Language Policy*, 11. 101–118.

Crawford, J. (1992) *Hold your tongue: Bilingualism and the politics of "English Only."* Reading, MA: Addison-Wesley Publishing.

Crawford, J. (2004) *Educating English learners* (5th ed.). Los Angeles, CA: Bilingual Education Services.

Creese, A. and Blackledge, A. (2010) 'Translanguaging in the bilingual classroom: A pedagogy for learning and teaching?' *Modern Language Journal*, 94/1. 103–115.

Cummins, J. (1976) 'The influence of bilingualism on cognitive growth: A synthesis of research findings and explanatory hypotheses'. *Working Papers on Bilingualism*, 9. 1–43.

Cummins, J. (2005) 'A proposal for action: Strategies for recognizing heritage language competence as a learning resource within the mainstream classroom'. *Modern Language Journal*, 89/4. 585–592.

Dekker, D. and Young, C. (2005) 'Bridging the gap: The development of appropriate educational strategies for minority language communities in the Philippines'. *Current Issues in Language Planning*, 6/2. 182–199.

De Korne, H. (2012) 'Towards new ideologies and pedagogies of multilingualism: Innovations in interdisciplinary language education in Luxembourg'. *Language and Education*, 26/6. 479–500.

Faltis, C. (2013) 'Demystifying and questioning the power of academic language', in M. B. Arias and C. J. Faltis (eds) *Academic language in second language learning*. Charlotte, NC: Information Age Publishing. 3–26.

Fishman, J. A. (1967) 'Bilingualism with and without diglossia; Diglossia with and without bilingualism'. *Journal of Social Issues,* 23/2. 29–38.

Fishman, J. A. (1991) 'How threatened is "Threatened"?: A typology of disadvantaged languages and ameliorative priorities', in J. A. Fishman (ed.) *Reversing language shift: Theoretical and empirical foundations of assistance to threatened languages*. Clevedon, England: Multilingual Matters. 81–121.

Fishman, J. A. (2001) *Can threatened languages be saved?* Clevedon: Multilingual Matters.

Gándara, P. and Hopkins, M (2010) *Forbidden language: English learners and restrictive language policies*. New York: Teachers College Press.

García, O. (2009) *Bilingual education in the 21st century: A global perspective*. Malden, MA: Wiley-Blackwell.

García, O. and Li, W. (2013) *Translanguaging: Language, bilingualism and education*. London: Palgrave Macmillan.

Genesee, F. (1995) 'The Canadian second language immersion program'. *Policy and Practice in Bilingual Education: Extending the Foundations*. 118–133.

Hill, J. (2001) 'The racializing function of language panics', in R. D. González and I. Melis (eds) *Language ideologies, Vol. 2*. Mahwah, NJ: Lawrence Erlbaum. 245–267.

Hinton, L. and Hale, K. (eds) (2001) *The green book of language revitalization in practice*. San Diego, CA: Academic Press.

Hornberger, N. H. (1989) 'Continua of biliteracy'. *Review of Educational Research*, 59/3. 271–296.

Howard, E. R. and Sugarman, J. (2007) *Realizing the vision of two-way immersion*. Washington, DC: Center for Applied Linguistics.

Howard, E. R., Sugarman, J., Christian, D., Lindholm-Leary, K. and Rogers, D. (2007) *Guiding principles for dual language education* (2nd ed.). Washington, DC: Center for Applied Linguistics.

Jenkins, J. and Leung, C. (2013) 'English as a Lingua Franca', in A. J. Kunnan (ed.) *The companion to language assessment* IV, 13/95. 1605–1616.

Johnson, E. (2005) 'Proposition 203: A critical metaphor analysis'. *Bilingual Research Journal*, 29/1. 69–84.

King, J. (2001) 'Te Kohanga Reo: Maori language revitalizaion', in L. Hinton and K. L. Hale (eds) *The green book of language revitalization in practice*. San Diego, CA: Academic Press. 147–176.

Kjolseth, R. (1973) 'Bilingual education programs in the United States: For assimilation or pluralism?', in P. R. Turner (ed.) *Bilingualism in the Southwest* (2nd ed.). Tucson, AZ: University of Arizona Press. 3–27.

Kosonen, K. (2005) 'Vernaculars in literacy and basic education in Cambodia, Laos and Thailand'. *Current Issues in Language Planning*, 6/2. 122–142.

Kosonen, K. (2008) 'Literacy in local languages in Thailand: Language maintenance in a globalised world'. *International Journal of Bilingual Education and Bilingualism*, 11/2. 170–188.

Kosonen, K. and Young, C. (2009) 'Mother tongue as bridge language of instruction: Policies and experiences in Southeast Asia'. *Bangkok: Southeast Asian Ministers of Education Organization (SEAMEO)*. Retrieved from http://www.sil.org/resources/archives/49906

Lambert, W. E. (1972) *Bilingual education of children: The St. Lambert experiment*. Rowley, MA: Newbury House Publishers.

Lazaruk, W. (2007) 'Linguistic, academic, and cognitive benefits of French immersion'. *Canadian Modern Language Review/La Revue canadienne des langues vivantes*, 63/5. 605–627.

Li, W. (2010) 'Moment analysis and translanguaging space: Discursive construction of identities by multilingual Chinese youth in Britain'. *Journal of Pragmatics* 43. 1222–1235.

Lomawaima, K. T. and McCarty, T. L. (2006) *"To Remain an Indian": Lessons in democracy from a century of native American education*. New York: Teachers College Press.

MacSwan, J. and Rolstad, K. (2003) 'Linguistic diversity, schooling, and social class: Rethinking our conception of language proficiency in language minority education', in C. Bratt Paulston and G. R. Tucker (eds) *Sociolinguistics: The essential readings*. Hoboken: NJ: Wiley-Blackwell. 329–340.

McCarty, T. L. (2002) *A place to be Navajo: Rough Rock and the struggle for self-determination in indigenous schooling*. Mahwah, NJ: Lawrence Erlbaum Associates.

McCarty, T. L. (2013) *Language planning and policy in Native America*. Bristol, England: Multilingual Matters.

McCarty, T. L. and Zepeda, O. (eds) (2006) *One voice, many voices: Recreating indigenous language communities*. Tempe, AZ: Center for Indian Education, Arizona State University.

Michael-Luna, S. and Canagarajah, S. (2007) 'Multilingual academic literacies: Pedagogical foundations for code meshing in primary and higher education'. *Journal of Applied Linguistics*, 41. 55–77.

Mohanty, A. K. (2013) 'Multilingual education in India: Overcoming the language barrier and the burden', in P. Siemund, I. Gogolin, M. E. Schulz and J. Davydova (eds) *Multilingualism and language diversity in urban areas: Acquisition, identities, space, education*. Amsterdam: John Benjamins. 305–326.

Moore, S. C. K. (ed.) (2014) *Language policy processes and consequences: Arizona case studies*. Bristol, England: Multilingual Matters.

Mora, J. K. (2009) 'From the ballot box to the classroom'. *Educational Leadership*, 66/7. 14–19.

Orelus, P. (2014) *Affirming language diversity in schools and society: Beyond linguistic apartheid*. New York: Routledge.

Ovando, C. J. and Combs, M. C. (2011) *Bilingual and ESL classrooms: Teaching in multicultural contexts* (5th ed.). New York: McGraw-Hill.

Ricento, T. and Burnaby, B. (1998) *Language and politics in the United and Canada*. Mahwah, NJ: Lawrence Erlbaum Associates.

Ruiz, R. (1984) 'Orientations in language planning'. *NABE: the Journal for the National Association for Bilingual Education*, 8/2. 15–34.

Schmidt, J. R. (2013) *The politics of English in Puerto Rico's public schools*. Boulder, CO: Lynne Rienner Pub.

Silver, R. E. (2005) 'The discourse of linguistic capital: Language and economic policy planning in Singapore'. *Language Policy*, 4. 47–66.

Skutnabb-Kangas, T. and Phillipson, R. (1995) *Linguistic human rights*. Berlin: Mouton de Gruyter.

Smith, L. T. (1999) *Decolonizing methodologies: Research and indigenous peoples*. New York: Zed Books Ltd.

Taylor-Leech, K. (2013) 'Finding space for non-dominant languages in education: Language policy and medium of instruction in Timor-Leste 2000–2012'. *Current Issues in Language Planning*, 14/1. 109–126.

Thomas, W. P. and Collier, V. P. (2012) *Dual language education for a transformed world*. Albuquerque, NM: Fuente Press.

UNESCO (2010) *Education for all. EFA global monitoring report 2010. Reaching the marginalized*. Retrieved from http://unesdoc.unesco.org/images/0018/001866/186606e.pdf

Urmeneta, E. C. and Unamuno, V. (2008) 'Languages and language learning in Catalan Schools: From the bilingual to the multilingual challenge', in C. Hélot and A. M. De Mejía (eds) *Forging multilingual spaces:*

Integrated perspectives on majority and minority bilingual education. Clevedon, England: Multilingual Matters. 228–255.

Valdés, G. (1997) 'Dual language immersion programs: A cautionary note concerning the education of language minority students'. *Harvard Education Review,* 67/3. 391–429.

Warner, S. L. N. (2001) 'The movement to revitalize Hawaiian language and culture', in L. Hinton and K. L. Hale (eds) *The green book of language revitalization in practice.* San Diego, CA: Academic Press. 133–146.

Webb, V. (2004) 'African languages as media of instruction in South Africa: Stating the case'. *Language Problems and Language Planning,* 28/2. 147–173.

Wright, W. E. (2005) 'The political spectacle of Arizona's proposition 203'. *Educational Policy,* 19/5. 662–700.

Wright, W. E. (2010) *Foundations for teaching English language learners.* Philadelphia, PA: Caslon Publishing.

Part III

Methods and methodology

Perspectives and practices

15

Method, methods and methodology

Historical trends and current debates

Graham Hall

Introduction

Whether conceptualised as a disciplinary field (Richards and Rodgers, 2014) or a profession (Pennington and Hoekje, 2014), ELT is often characterised as being in 'ferment' (Richards and Rodgers, 2001: 254) and subject to 'fashions and trends' (Adamson, 2004); debates surrounding language teaching methods and methodology have been central to this perceived flux. Yet we are also in an era when unifying narratives and overarching explanations of intellectual and social developments "are viewed with suspicion" (Canagarajah, 2006: 9); in attempting to explain and understand the past, histories are always partial because they are informed by particular viewpoints and biases (ibid.). Consequently, there are a number of differing accounts of the recent history of methods in ELT, each with its own emphases and each having implications for the way we might make sense of contemporary debates and practices within ELT. This chapter therefore aims to convey this range of perspectives on the development of methods in our field, narratives which, at times, diverge and offer conflicting accounts of the past and present.

All histories of methods involve an element of compromise – when to start, and what timescale to cover? With notable exceptions such as the longer histories of Howatt with Widdowson (2004) and Kelly (1969), most reviews have focused on the relatively brief period from the late nineteenth century to the present day, and this chapter too will review developments over this same period, the era when "language teaching came into its own" (Richards and Rodgers, 2014: 1). The chapter will review a number of perspectives, and will seek to address the 'short memory' of language teaching theory, which often leads us to "ignore the past or distort its lessons" (Stern, 1983: 76–77). First, however, the chapter explores key terminology.

'Method' and methods: an initial understanding

All professional communities of practice draw upon shared understandings of key concepts, as expressed through terminology. Yet 'method', and the associated terms 'methods' and 'methodology', are used in variety of ways within ELT. This section will therefore explore what might be characterised as a standard understanding of method in our field; later in the chapter, however, this conception will be questioned and critiqued.

Central to traditional explanations of method is the relationship between theory and practice, Hinkel (2005: 631) suggesting that teaching methods are "theories translated into classroom applications . . . ideally, the purpose of a method for second language (L2) teaching is to connect the theories or research findings on how second languages are learned with how they can be taught". Stern thus notes that a method is "more than a single strategy or a particular technique; it is a 'theory' of language teaching" (1983: 452).

Anthony (1963) characterises the relationship between theory and practice within a three-tier hierarchy, in which 'method' occupies a central level between 'approach' and 'technique'. Here, 'approach' is a set of assumptions about the nature of language and language teaching and learning (in effect, the subject matter to be taught); 'method' is the plan for how to present language in an orderly way, which is based on and does not contradict the higher-order approach; and 'techniques' are specific classroom activities consistent with the method, and thus with the approach (Anthony, 1963). Techniques might include, for example, dialogue-building, translation exercises and communicative tasks. Meanwhile, Richards and Rodgers (2014) draw upon Anthony's model to offer their own fuller account of method. They suggest that the overarching concept of 'method' comprises three elements, their 'approach' and 'procedure' broadly resembling Anthony's 'approach' and 'technique', now complemented by the additional notion of 'design', which includes: the objectives of a method; how the target language is selected and organised (i.e. its syllabus); types of teaching and learning activities; learner and teacher roles (including considerations such as learner-centredness and autonomy); and the role of any instructional materials in the method (pp. 29–35).

Bringing the various perspectives together, therefore, a method can be characterised by the perspectives it adopts on the following key concerns:

a)   the nature of language
b)   the nature of second language learning
c)   goals and objectives in teaching
d)   the type of syllabus to use
e)   the role of teachers, learners and instructional materials
f)   the activities, techniques and procedures to use.

(Richards and Schmidt, 2002: 330)

Consequently, how has the distinction between 'method' and 'methodology' been conceptualised? At the broadest level, methodology is "the *how* of teaching" (Thornbury, 2011: 185), a "general word to describe classroom practices . . . irrespective of the particular method that a teacher is using" (Thornbury, 2006: 131). For Waters, therefore, methods are "'prescribed' ways of teaching", whilst methodology is "ways of teaching in general" (2012: 440). Meanwhile, Kumaravadivelu (2006: 84) suggests that: "Method [refers to] established methods constructed by experts in the field . . . . Methodology [is] what practicing teachers actually do in the classroom to achieve their stated or unstated teaching objectives."

Yet in practice, the method/methodology distinction is not always clear (Thornbury, 2011: 186). In their classroom practices (i.e. in their methodology), teachers are likely to either draw upon a single method, adopt a variety of elements taken from different methods which seem 'plausible' to them (Prabhu, 1990) or follow instructional materials in class which adhere to a particular method. In other words, 'methodology' often recycles 'big ideas' found in method (Thornbury, 2011: 186). It is this likely difference between methods 'in theory' and methodology 'in practice' which forms the basis for a sustained critique of the whole notion of 'method', which we shall explore later in the chapter. Now, however, the chapter will continue by examining how a current 'profusion of methods' has emerged over time in ELT, outlining the differing ways in which this history of methods has been characterised.

Methods, paradigms and change

A profusion of methods

Many accounts of methods suggest that, for over a century, "language educators sought to solve the problems of language teaching by focusing almost exclusively on *Method*" (Stern, 1983: 452; also, Kumaravadivelu, 2006; Allwright and Hanks, 2009; Richards and Rodgers, 2014), as theorists and methodologists searched for the most effective method for English language teaching. (However, whether *teachers* followed or engaged in such debates is more open to question, as is the extent to which such discussions were recognised globally or were actually pre-occupations of a largely UK and USA-based methodological literature. We shall return to these points later in the chapter.)

Consequently, by the early twenty-first century, a "profusion of competing methods" had emerged in ELT (Allwright and Hanks, 2009: 38). Larsen-Freeman and Anderson (2011), for example, identify eleven language teaching methods. Presented in sequence, these are: grammar-translation; the direct method; the audio-lingual method; the 'silent way', desuggestopedia; community language learning; total physical response (TPR); communicative language teaching (CLT); content-based instruction (CBI, the North American term, also known as content and language integrated learning [CLIL] in Europe); task-based language teaching (TBLT); and a politically-oriented participatory approach. Larsen-Freeman and Anderson also discuss a number of further 'methodological innovations' (learner strategy training; cooperative learning and multiple intelligences; and the uses of technology in language teaching and learning). Meanwhile, Richards and Rodgers (2014) examine a total of sixteen approaches and methods, a discussion which differs from Larsen-Freeman and Anderson (2011) by exploring grammar-translation and the direct method in significantly less depth, but by additionally examining in detail the oral approach and situational language teaching; whole language; competency-based teaching; text-based instruction; the lexical approach; and the natural approach. Significantly, although adopting an "essentially methods-based perspective" (Hunter and Smith, 2012: 430), the latter two texts also reflect upon the possible role of methods within a putative postmethod era (we shall reflect further on 'postmethod' later in the chapter). It is also interesting to note that, despite the excellent accounts within these texts, there is no 'definitive list' of methods across the methodological literature of ELT as a whole. This absence could, according to one's perspective, be the result of a fast-moving and ever-changing field; a lack of agreement and theoretical consistency about method and methods (Pennycook, 1989, a point to which we shall return); or quite simply, the practical constraints of word and page limit facing any author! (A detailed review of each of these methods is beyond the scope of this chapter; CLT (Thornbury), CLIL (Morton) and TBLT (Van den Branden) are discussed in detail in this *Handbook*, whilst further explorations can be found, for example, in Larsen-Freeman and Anderson (2011), Richards and Rodgers (2014), and Allwright and Hanks (2009: 37–57)).

Paradigms and change over time

Most narratives exploring the development of methods tend to present them in a sequence reflecting their perceived emergence over time – the order of methods listed in the previous section is typical – and central to these accounts is the notion that methods have, over time, succeeded one another as 'paradigms' within the field. As "universally recognized achievements that for a time provide model problems and solutions to a community of practitioners" (Kuhn, 1970/1996: x), paradigms are the fundamental underpinnings of what constitutes 'normal' or 'proper' theory and practice in any particular era. Once a paradigm is established, it defines the key questions and rationales of that era so strongly that it is almost impossible for those working within it to conceive of alternatives. However, once discoveries, anomalies or inconsistencies emerge which a paradigm cannot adequately explain, a 'revolution' takes place to resolve the 'crisis', leading to the replacement of one paradigm by another as existing orthodoxies are replaced (Thornbury, 2011). Thus, whilst *change within* a paradigm is gradual and developmental, a *change of* paradigm leads to rapid, radical and "tradition-shattering" transformation (Jacobs and Farrell, 2003: 3). Thinking in terms of paradigms, therefore, captures the notion of 'academic fashions' and offers one way of conceptualising the development of ELT methods in the twentieth century.

A 'progressive' history of methods

Thus, a traditional view of the development of method over time is that "there has been a series of language teaching methods over the years, each being succeeded by a better one until we reach the present" (Pennycook, 1989: 597). This perspective suggests that developments in method have been progressive and cumulative, and language teaching has therefore become more effective as 'better' methods are developed. Rowlinson characterises this overview of methods as "continuous upwards progress through history" (1994: 7), with each method emerging as a result of the development and application of new paradigmatic ideas and the rejection of 'old' ideas.

From this perspective, language teaching in the late nineteenth and early twentieth centuries was dominated by *grammar-translation*, which had emerged as an identifiable approach in the late eighteenth century. Based around ideas from the teaching of classical languages such as Latin, grammar-translation required students to follow explicit grammatical rules in order to translate written sentences and was criticised for, amongst other things, leaving learners unable to communicate in the target language (Weihua, 2004). Consequently, the early twentieth century reform movement advocated a *direct method* in which speech was primary, with a more prominent role for teaching pronunciation in class; there was a move away from isolated sentences and word lists to 'connected texts' from which grammar might be learned inductively; and an oral classroom methodology was implemented which included, for example, question-and-answer exchanges between teachers and students and the use of pictures, objects and actions to introduce and 'explain' new language (Howatt with Widdowson, 2004).

The move from grammar-translation to the direct method is, within contemporary methodological accounts, often regarded as laying the foundations for subsequent developments in ELT and is thus viewed as inherently 'progressive'. Hall and Cook (2012) suggest that, until recently, most subsequent methodological developments were founded on a monolingual assumption, derived directly from the rejection of grammar-translation, which discouraged students from making use of their L1 (see also Kerr, this volume). (In fact, although translation of texts and sentences *was* rejected by strict proponents of the direct method, many reform movement teachers of the time actually continued to offer brief L1 'glosses' of occasional words and phrases (Howatt with Widdowson, 2004: 191–192)).

Yet the 'progress' offered by the direct method was accompanied by some methodological weaknesses which, in many accounts, are highlighted to explain its own subsequent decline in popularity. Its association with the practices of Berlitz schools (see, for example, Richards and Rodgers, 2014; but also, for a contested account of the direct method/Berlitz relationship,

Hunter and Smith, 2012) led to criticism that its success was due to small class sizes, individual attention and intensive study (Brown, 2001: 22). Similarly, the argument goes, by placing teachers at the centre of classroom activity, the success of the method relied too heavily on teacher skill (ibid.). Finally, for some, the direct method lacked a clear grounding in theory and was the product of "enlightened amateurism" (Richards and Rodgers, 2014: 13). Indeed, the work of reformers such as Henry Sweet, who looked to link the practical study of languages (1899/1964) with methodological recommendations, provided a precursor to the development of applied linguistics as a discipline, which subsequently informed the development of many language teaching methods.

This narrative continues, therefore, with the emergence, in the 1940s, of *audiolingualism* in the US, and the now arguably less well-known *situational approach* in the UK. In the development of audiolingualism, Charles Fries' application of structuralism to language teaching (1945) provided a systematic description of language which had been missing from the direct method. Conceiving of language as a system of structurally related elements such as phonemes, morphemes or words which combine to create meaning through phrases, clauses and sentences, instruction consequently relied on forms of learning such as memorisation and drilling of sentence patterns. In audiolingualism, therefore, learning took place via a process of stimulus–response–reinforcement and, incorporating principles from 'scientific' behavioural psychology (Skinner, 1957), was envisaged as 'good habit formation'. Within a 'progressive' narrative of methods, audiolingualism heralds the time when ELT enters the 'applied linguistic' age, and many histories begin their detailed accounts of developments in method from this point (e.g. Allwright and Hanks, 2009; Richards and Rodgers, 2014).

The oral method and, subsequently, situational language teaching are less often reviewed in contemporary methodological literature but emerged in the UK from the work of, for example, Harold Palmer and A. S. Hornby in the 1920s and 1930s (Howatt with Widdowson, 2004). The oral method emphasised the primacy of spoken language, with new language carefully selected (to ensure coverage of key vocabulary), graded (simple before complex forms) and presented; situational language teaching is a particular oral approach deployed in the 1950s and 1960s which, as its name suggests, presented and practised new language through 'situations'. Like audiolingualism, the situational approach derived from a structural view of language and an implicitly behaviourist conception of learning, classrooms therefore featuring sentence pattern practice and drilling; indeed, we can see in situational language teaching the antecedents of the still widely deployed PPP (presentation-practice-production) lesson (Richards and Rodgers, 2014). Emphasising our 'progressive' narrative, proponents of the oral method were very clear that it represented a break from and improvement on what had gone before, with Pattison (1964: 4) noting that:

> An oral approach should not be confused with the obsolete Direct Method, which meant only that the learner was bewildered by a flow of ungraded speech, suffering all the difficulties he [sic] would have encountered in picking up the language in its normal environment and losing most of the compensating benefits of better contextualization in those circumstances.
>
> *(cited in Richards and Rodgers, 2014: 46)*

Yet continuing the now-established pattern, these methods were in turn attacked. From a theoretical perspective, advocates of generative grammar (e.g. Chomsky, 1966) suggested that language is a property of the human mind and is not learned through behaviourist processes of habit formation. Additionally, pragmatic problems were identified, such as a 'failure to deliver';

the emphasis on imitation rather than linguistic creativity, with associated issues of learner boredom; and the realisation that only relatively few learner errors are a result of L1 interference rather than developmental realisations of a learner's interlanguage. This latter point was significant to proponents of CLT, which emerged subsequently (Thornbury, 2011).

Prior to addressing CLT, however, most progressive accounts of ELT methods devote considerable time to a range of "unique and highly specific packages" (Allwright and Hanks, 2009: 44) which emerged at the end of the audiolingual era in the late 1960s and early 1970s. Usually described as 'humanistic approaches', or, reflecting their failure to become truly paradigmatic within the field, 'fringe' (Allwright and Hanks, 2009), 'designer/guru' (Bell, 2007) or 'alternative' (V. Cook, 2008) methods, they are one of two parallel yet very different strands within ELT during this period (the other being CLT itself). Interestingly, although regularly discussed and critiqued within the methodological literature, they are often portrayed as being 'beyond' the overall progression of mainstream methods during the twentieth century.

Based around their shared reaction against the 'science' of audiolingualism, typical accounts of humanistic approaches group together a number of methods in a way which often overlooks differences between them; such narratives therefore offer a 'methodological tidiness' which arguably did not exist in practice. Hence, the *silent way* (Gattegno, 1972), *community language learning* (Curran, 1972) and *suggestopedia* (Lozanov, 1978) aimed to 're-humanise' the classroom, drawing upon humanistic approaches to psychology (e.g. Rogers, 1969) rather than applied linguistics. Such approaches emphasised learners' personal growth and self-realisation; respect for learners' own knowledge; recognition of the affective as well as cognitive nature of learning; and, consequently, the need to teach in a facilitative or enabling way which encourages learner self-discovery, independence and autonomy (Moskowitz, 1978; Stevick, 1980). Meanwhile, *total physical response* (Asher, 1977) and the slightly later *natural approach* (Krashen and Terrell, 1983) emphasised, in differing ways, that exposure to the target language and to comprehensible input would lead to acquisition; language development would thus follow a predetermined 'natural' route. These two *comprehension approaches* (Winitz, 1981) drew upon Chomsky's (1966) suggestion that language knowledge is an innate human faculty which develops through exposure to input rather than being learned through imitation, as posited by the behaviourist approach of audiolingualism.

The "unusual demands" these methods placed on teachers or learners (Richards and Rodgers, 2014: 313), such as the emphasis on the socio-emotional growth of individuals, are often cited as a reason why they did not become mainstream in ELT. Why, therefore, do they remain such a focus within the methodological literature? From a progressive perspective, their presence is less anomalous than it might first appear. Discussions of humanistic language teaching highlight perceived weaknesses in previous paradigmatic theory and practice, i.e. the difficulties surrounding audiolingualism. Furthermore, as most histories of methods note, it is clear that key notions such as learner-centredness, independence and autonomy, and a focus on affect in the classroom have subsequently become widespread within ELT. Discussions of humanistic methods therefore serve as a supporting step in the perceived cumulative development of current 'good practice'.

Arguably still portrayed as the most significant development within ELT over the last 50 years, the emergence of CLT in the 1960s and 1970s is generally regarded as a clear paradigmatic break with the past, indeed, as a 'communicative revolution' (Bolitho et al., 1983). As Thornbury documents (this volume), CLT emerged from a concern with language functions and notions and the idea of 'communicative competence' – the knowledge of "when to speak, when not, and … what to talk about with whom, when, where and in what manner" (Hymes, 1972: 277). Thus, it is usually argued, key reactions to previous theory and practice were the "marked shift away from a concern for what language is (and the way it is represented in the mind) to a concern for what language does (and the way it operates in the world)" (Thornbury, 2011: 188).

Following its emergence, CLT was portrayed as *the* dominant methodological paradigm within ELT in the late twentieth century. And yet, in the early twenty-first century, a unified vision of CLT has given way to an examination of 'strong' and 'weak' CLT, of whether CLT is appropriate for all contexts and cultures, and the development, or perhaps fragmentation, of CLT into related methods such as *task-based language teaching* (TBLT) and content-oriented approaches such as *content and language integrated learning* (CLIL), both merging content and language-teaching in ways arguably similar to 'strong' forms of CLT (see Thornbury, Van den Branden, and Morton, respectively, this volume, for fuller discussion). Such developments can be viewed in two very different ways. As a continuation of the progressive narrative outlined in this section, the emergence from CLT of something 'new' maintains a sense of cumulative development over time; problems within the dominant paradigm are identified, and subsequent emerging contemporary methods are a further step forward in the development of effective ELT. However, if, as argued in this chapter's introduction, unifying narratives of progress are now being questioned, then contemporary accounts of CLT methods which consider its strengths and weaknesses, examine the extent to which it is or is not appropriate in particular localised contexts and reflect the variety of practices which are said to be underpinned by a broadly communicative approach reflect this more nuanced and cautious approach to historical developments in ELT. Richards and Rodgers exemplify this change in perspective over time. Summarising the position of CLT in their 2001 edition of *Approaches and Methods in Language Teaching*, they wrote: "the general principles of Communicative Language Teaching are today widely accepted around the world" (2001: 151).

Yet by 2014, in a revised edition of the same text, they recognised both the difficulties of CLT and, at a more general level, the need to recognise alternative perspectives on methods more generally:

> By the twenty-first century, the assumptions and practices of CLT seem on the one hand to be commonplace and part of a generally accepted and relatively uncontroversial canon of teaching theory and practice.... On the other hand, language teaching today is a much more localized activity, subject to the constraints and needs of particular contexts and cultures of learning, and the use of global and generic solutions to local problems is increasingly seen as problematic. Research and documentation of local practices is needed.
>
> *(Richards and Rodgers, 2014: 107)*

It is to these alternative perspectives and histories that we now turn.

Critiquing 'progress': methods as products of their times

The progressive narrative surrounding language teaching methods has been widely critiqued. In contrast to notions of cumulative improvements over time, longer-term histories of language teaching suggest that methodological developments are essentially cyclical. In his history of 2,500 years of language teaching, Kelly (1969) demonstrates that apparently recent innovations have very often been practised in earlier eras – oral communication, for example, was emphasised in the Classical and Renaissance periods, whilst language teaching in the Middle Ages and Enlightenment focused more on written texts (see also Pennycook, 1989). For Kelly, therefore, "nobody really knows what is new or what is old in present day language teaching procedures. There has been a vague feeling that modern experts have spent their time in discovering what other men [sic] have forgotten" (1969: ix). Consequently, Pennycook (1989) suggests that histories which portray the linear advancement of methods over time are 'ahistorical', whilst Hunter and Smith (2012: 430) refer, somewhat acerbically, to notions of "self-proclaimed progress". From this perspective, developments in method are often likened to a pendulum which rejects then returns to key principles over time before once again swinging away to supposedly 'new' alternatives.

Cyclical accounts generally suggest that, as the goals of language teaching change over time, so do language teaching methods: "Different approaches to teaching English did not occur by chance, but in response to changing geopolitical circumstances and social attitudes and values, as well as to shifts in fashions in linguistics" (G. Cook, 2003: 30).

From this perspective, therefore, grammar-translation was appropriate to the era before mass travel and international communication, when languages were learned by relatively few people, often to develop the learners' intellectual abilities and enable literature to be read in the original language rather than to facilitate communication (Richards and Rodgers, 2014). Similarly, the emergence of the direct method in the early twentieth century can be linked not only to an academic focus on speech and phonology, but also to a wider societal interest in 'natural learning' which was a reaction against the 'authoritarian' and 'traditional' teacher role said to underpin grammar-translation (Crookes, 2009) and also to the advent of more widespread international travel and the associated need to communicate in foreign languages. Whilst the emergence of audiolingualism can be linked to academic trends such as the rise of behavioural psychology and structuralism in linguistics, the need to teach foreign languages to many US serviceman towards the end of the Second World War prompted a focus on oral drills and conversation practice (known as the 'Army Method') which informed subsequent audiolingual methodology (Richards and Rodgers, 2014). And it is perhaps not surprising that 'humanistic' language teaching emerged from the social ferment of the 1960s, whilst CLT coincided not only with an intellectual focus on language functions and communication but also during an era of mass travel where the ability to communicate in English is increasingly seen as an essential skill for workers in many key sectors of many societies around the world.

The recognition that contextual factors play a fundamental role in the development and subsequent implementation of methods leads Adamson (2004: 605) to suggest that "no method is inherently superior to another; instead some methods are more appropriate than others in a particular context". From this perspective, therefore, methods reflect contemporary (rather than 'best') ideas and practices (ibid.).

Consequently, it is rare to find, within most contemporary overviews of ELT methods, clear or straightforward recommendations of one method over another; most aim to take account of the "complex, but not necessarily progressive" nature of their development (Crookes, 2009: 46). Thus, Larsen-Freeman and Anderson's wide-ranging overview of *Techniques and Principles in Language Teaching* (i.e. methods) overtly states that the authors "do not seek to convince readers that one method is superior to another, or that there is or ever will be a perfect method" (2011: ix). Similarly, Richards and Rodgers (2014) discuss at some length, within their exploration of *Approaches and Methods in Language Teaching*, how teachers themselves will need to interpret and implement methods and methodological decisions in their own contexts.

Methods as 'control': a critical narrative

Critical discussion within ELT has focused on the relationship between method and issues of power and control within the field. Drawing on the notion that all knowledge is 'interested' (Pennycook, 1989), that is, knowledge reflects a political perspective of how society should be organised, the concept of method is said to create and uphold a particular set of interests that favours some groups to the detriment of others.

We have already noted how traditional explanations of method suggest that methods are theories translated into practice, constructed by experts to be implemented by teachers in classrooms. Thus, a critical narrative suggests that the idea of method and the development of methods over time have created and sustained power imbalances between (largely male) theorists and academics on the one hand and (largely female) teachers in classrooms on the other. Consequently, Pennycook (1989) argues, the concept of method frustrates teachers who, in the 'real world', are unable to implement and follow methods fully and consistently. Method also values 'scientific' (i.e. applied linguistic) knowledge over contextual and local knowledges; from this perspective, teachers are 'de-skilled', becoming 'technicians' who merely implement other people's ideas. We shall return to these ideas shortly when discussing the emergence of 'postmethod' thinking in ELT.

Additionally, critical accounts also question the spread of methods around the world over time. For example, Holliday (1994), focusing in particular on CLT, questioned the extent to which methods emerging from and reflecting assumptions and cultural norms in dominant **B**ritish, **A**ustralasia and **N**orth **A**merican (BANA) contexts were appropriate in non-BANA contexts (see also Holliday, this volume). From this perspective, the dominance of the concept of 'method' within ELT has favoured BANA over non-BANA teaching practices as methods have been 'exported' (or even imposed) around the world, driven by the political and/or commercial imperatives of 'the Centre' (i.e. the US, UK and other English-dominant countries), where most methods originated. Meanwhile, Phillipson (1992) critiques what he sees as ELT's role in 'linguistic imperialism', in which a Centre-to-Periphery 'methods trade' has roots in colonialism and imperialism (see Pennycook, this volume). Here, then, the history of methods is seen not as a series of progressive developments over time which has led to more effective teaching and learning, nor as the consequence of shifts in social and linguistic fashions; rather, methods have created and maintain specific patterns of power and control within ELT, favouring 'Western' 'one-size-fits-all' approaches to learning over non-Western and localised practices, as they are exported from 'the Centre' to 'the Periphery'. (Larsen-Freeman (2000), however, questions this perspective. Whilst agreeing that supposedly universal solutions which are culturally insensitive or politically naïve are damaging, she suggests that to consequently withhold methods from teachers outside BANA contexts or to assume they would be taken up unthinkingly and wholesale is to assume non-BANA teachers are "helpless victims" (p. 63) and disregard their agency in teaching/learning. Larsen-Freeman thus calls for judgements regarding the appropriacy of particular methods in particular contexts to be made by local educators.)

Challenging the narratives: the 'myth' of method?

Although apparently contrasting histories of ELT – 'progressive', 'cyclical/context-dependent' and critical – have been outlined in the discussion so far, all share a fundamental perspective – that a succession of methods can be identified and labelled across "bounded periods of history" (Hunter and Smith, 2012: 430). This view of methods and of ELT history has been critiqued in a number of ways.

Pennycook suggests, for example, that within ELT: "First, there is little agreement as to which methods existed when, and in what order; second, there is little agreement and conceptual coherence to the terms used; and third, there is little evidence that methods ever reflected classroom reality" (1989: 602).

Hunter and Smith (2012) develop these points, arguing that a "mythology" has developed around methods which has served to "package up", simplify and stereotype complex and contested past practices (pp. 430–431). For example, as we have seen, both progressive and context-oriented histories suggest that grammar-translation was replaced by the direct method in the first half of the twentieth century. Yet it is evident that grammar-translation is still used today in many parts of the world (furthermore, Hunter and Smith (2012) question whether a single label, grammar-translation, can really be applied to the range of practices oriented around translation and explicit grammar teaching). Similarly, most descriptions of the direct method suggest that translation was forbidden, yet this was not always the case in practice (or, indeed, in principle), as we have seen. Meanwhile, PPP-style teaching continues to flourish in many contexts, despite the supposed dominance of CLT and related content and task-based approaches. From this perspective, the conventional accounts of method and methods over the course of the twentieth century over-emphasise change and 'revolution', whilst overlooking methodological continuities and the locally-constituted nature of ELT practices (Smith, 2003).

Consequently, Hunter and Smith (2012) argue that such accounts prioritise the understandings and experiences of Anglo-American methodologists and overlook the varied teaching traditions and experiences of English language teachers working in a near countless range of contexts around the world. From this perspective, the complexity of ELT classrooms, now and in the past, is overlooked by the "methods-based perspective on history which tends to dominate our profession" (p. 432). Indeed, Smith (2015) has subsequently suggested that 'bottom-up' accounts of 'good practice' may be more fruitful than top-down definitions imposed from external academic sources. Braine (2005) similarly argues that the voices of teachers, outlining English language teaching in their own particular contexts, can provide important perspectives on ELT from outside the UK, US and other English-dominant countries. Braine's edited collection of accounts from 15 countries (ibid.) including, for example, Brazil, Germany, Hungary, India, Lebanon, Singapore and Turkey provides clear evidence of the complex relationship between social, political and other contextual factors and classroom teaching; the central place of textbooks in many contexts, with the continuing prevalence of drilling, translation and a focus on canonical English literature texts; and the challenges of implementing large-scale methodological change and development in ELT. Whilst methods and CLT are a point of reference in several chapters, it is clear that the experience of many teachers is far more complex than 'just' implementing a particular method in the classroom.

Thus, Pennycook (2004: 278) argues that the concept of method is intrinsically 'reductive', as it fails to describe adequately what really happens in language teaching and language classrooms.

Current debates: 'Beyond method'?

The critiques outlined above have had a major impact within ELT since the early 1990s, and most writers in the field now explicitly recognise, to varying degrees, that "teachers are not mere conveyor belts delivering language through inflexible prescribed and proscribed behaviours" (Larsen-Freeman and Anderson, 2011: xii–xiii) and that universal, standardised solutions which ignore local conditions, learner diversity and teacher agency cannot be found (Larsen-Freeman and Freeman, 2008). There is thus a strong current within the contemporary methodological literature of ELT of a "shift to localization" (Howatt with Widdowson, 2004: 369), in which pedagogical practices develop in response to local contexts and needs (Bax, 2003; Ur, 2013; Holliday, this volume).

But how might this recognition of the importance of local conditions and needs affect current perspectives on the continuing role or value of methods within ELT?

Methods as empowering options for teachers

Recognising the importance of local decision-making in developing context appropriate teaching, many writers now suggest that methods offer a range of possibilities which "empower teachers to respond meaningfully to particular classroom contexts" (Bell, 2007: 141–142). From this perspective, teachers need to be "well-versed in the pedagogical options available to meet the needs of the various ages, purposes, proficiency levels, skills, and contexts of language learners around the globe" (Brown, 2001: xi), with Bell (2007) arguing that teachers are open to any method which helps them meet the challenges of their particular teaching context. (We can note here a change from the initial understanding of method outlined earlier in this chapter; teacher agency is now significantly foregrounded.)

Larsen-Freeman and Anderson (2011: xi–xii) thus suggest a number of ways in which knowledge of methods might be useful to teachers. Firstly, they argue, knowing about methods provides a "foil for reflection" which can help teachers become consciously aware of the thinking which underpins their current classroom practices. Secondly, as teachers become aware of what they do in the classroom and why they do it, they can choose to teach differently, making informed choices based on the range of possibilities available. Clearly, teachers may choose not to teach differently or may face contextual constraints on what might be possible. However, knowledge of methods will facilitate a deeper understanding of possibilities in particular contexts. Additionally, a knowledge of methods can help expand a teacher's range of classroom techniques and practices (Larsen-Freeman and Anderson, 2011), leading to further professional development. For Larsen-Freeman and Anderson, knowledge of methods does not de-skill teachers but can help teachers articulate and transform their practice, empowering them to make decisions about their own classroom and possibly even challenging the implementation of top-down educational policies. From this perspective, therefore, "methods can be studied not as prescriptions for how to teach but as a source of well-used practices, which teachers can adapt or implement based on their own needs" (Richards and Rodgers, 2014: 16), and knowledge of methods acts as a potential source of teacher empowerment, acting via a process of 'principled eclecticism'.

Beyond methods? Towards postmethod pedagogy

A more radical response to the criticisms of 'method' has been a more complete rejection of the concept as a basis for classroom teaching, with many scholars now arguing that we have witnessed, or are witnessing, "the death of the method" (Allwright, 1991), or are moving "beyond methods" (Kumaravadivelu, 2003, 2006, 2012) into a postmethod era characterised by "Postmethod Discourse" (Akbari, 2008).

Arguing for a shift in the way we understand teaching, its proponents argue that postmethod pedagogy attends not only to issues which we might readily identify with 'method' (for example, teaching, materials, curriculum and evaluation), but also to the range of historical, political and sociocultural experiences that influence language education. Kumaravadivelu (2003: 33) thus argues that postmethod is not an alternative method, but an alternative *to* method, which is thereby the product of bottom-up rather than top-down processes, signifies teacher autonomy and draws on 'principled pragmatism' rather than 'principled eclecticism' (thus pedagogy is not constrained by teacher selections from conventional methods but is shaped and reshaped by teacher self-observation, self-analysis and self-evaluation). Postmethod clearly draws on teachers' 'sense of plausibility' (Prabhu, 1990, and identified earlier in the chapter), and their subjective understandings of their own teaching and context arising from their own experience, professional education and peer consultation (Kumaravadivelu, 2003). Consequently, according to Kumaravadivelu, postmethod pedagogy builds on three key principles:

- *Particularity*, which requires pedagogy to be sensitive to the local individual, institutional, social and cultural contexts of teaching and learning and of teachers and learners

- *Practicality*, which breaks the hierarchical relationship between theorist and teacher as producers and consumers of knowledge; thus teachers are encouraged to theorize from their own practices, and put into practice their own theories
- *Possibility*, which fosters the socio-political consciousness of teachers and learners so they can "form and transform their personal and social identity".

(Kumaravadivelu, 2012: 12–16)

Kumaravadivelu suggests that these principles should be operationalised through a series of macrostrategies which include, for example, maximising learning opportunities; facilitating negotiated learner-learner and learner-teacher interaction; promoting learner autonomy; and fostering language awareness (see Kumaravadivelu, 2003, for fuller discussion; also note Larsen-Freeman's view (2005) that the principles and macrostrategies of Kumarivadivelu's postmethod pedagogy in fact qualify it as another method).

Challenges and concerns

Both the principled, eclectic implementation of existing methods and postmethod's 'principled pragmatism' envisage an enhanced role for teachers in which they have both freedom and power to make decisions by drawing upon their own local and contextual expertise. Crookes (2009), however, suggests that we must recognise the constraints that most English teachers around the world are under. In general, teachers are not completely free to decide how they teach – they are constrained by school and ministry policies about what and how to teach; by learner, parent and peer expectations; and, more generally, by social convention. Akbari (2008) therefore warns against overlooking the complex realities of teachers' social, political and cultural lives, which may work against teacher autonomy and enhanced decision-making – teachers may not have the time, resources or inclination to take responsibility for methodological decisions in the ways outlined above. One further consequence of these debates, Akbari (ibid.) also suggests, is the possible replacement of methods by textbook-defined practice, which, like 'method', is seen to have the potential for deskilling teachers whilst also raising concerns over the representation of language and, indeed, society and groups within society (for further discussion of these issues, see Gray, this volume).

Summary: a variety of perspectives

Whilst different approaches to teaching English can be identified over time (more within the methodological literature than in practice, perhaps), it is also clear that our ways of interpreting past and present developments in method are also changing. Thus, this chapter has briefly reviewed a range of perspectives on the recent history of methods in ELT, noting a range of accounts which are all in some way 'partial'.

Recognising the complexity, constraints and opportunities presented by local contexts and needs, many scholars have put aside notions of 'progress' and the search for a 'best method', whilst retaining a belief that methods still have an important role to play in teachers' decision-making, development and classroom practice. Others have rejected the notion of method more forcefully, arguing that teachers can be empowered through postmethod pedagogy. And others still have suggested that the construct of method is itself a reductive 'myth' which has distorted our view of both the history of ELT and of local teaching practices and traditions. From this perspective, the 'methods narrative' (or methods narratives) does not reflect the methodological and classroom realities of teachers and learners, both in the past and in contemporary ELT.

It is impossible to reconcile these differing perspectives on the historical trends and current debates which surround method and methods into a single narrative. Instead, "what we have now is not answers or solutions but a rich array of realizations and perspectives" (Canagarajah, 2006: 29) to help us understand and learn from the past in order to inform and explain contemporary methodological practices in ELT.

Discussion questions

- Which of the accounts of methods presented in this chapter seems most plausible to you? Do you think methods have progressively become 'better' over time, or do you think that they are simply 'products' of their time and context? Do you think that we, ELT professionals and researchers, focus too much on language teaching methods?
- A number of criticisms of the concept of method have been raised in this chapter. Which, if any, do you agree with, and why? If method is such a problematic concept, why does it continue to be such a powerful concept in ELT?
- Are you an 'eclectic' or 'pragmatic' teacher; do you 'mix and match' aspects from different methods in your teaching? If so, what principles or beliefs inform your decisions about what to do?

Related topics

Appropriate methodology; Communicative language teaching in theory and practice; Content and language integrated learning; Educational perspectives on ELT; ELT materials; Politics, power relationships and ELT; Questioning 'English-only' classrooms; Task-based language teaching.

Further reading

Howatt, A. with Widdowson, H. (2004) *A history of English language teaching.* Oxford: OUP. (A thorough history of English language teaching from CE 1400 onwards.)

Kumaravadivelu, B. (2003) *Beyond methods: Macrostrategies for language teaching.* New Haven: Yale University Press. (A detailed framework for the design and implementation of postmethod teaching.)

Kumaravadivelu, B. (2006) *Understanding language teaching: From method to postmethod.* New Jersey: Lawrence Erlbaum. (An examination of methods and postmethod in ELT, from a postmethod perspective, which traces the putative move towards a postmethod era.)

Larsen-Freeman, D. and Anderson, M. (2011) *Techniques and principles in language teaching* (3rd ed.). Oxford: OUP. (An overview of a range of methods, giving clear insights into classroom practices and techniques.)

Richards, J. and Rodgers, T. (2014) *Approaches and methods in language teaching* (3rd ed.). Oxford: OUP. (A systematic survey of a wide range of language teaching methods and approaches, looking at underlying principles and classroom practices.)

References

Adamson, B. (2004) 'Fashions in language teaching methodology', in A. Davies and C. Elder (eds) *The handbook of applied linguistics.* London: Blackwell. 604–622.

Akbari, R. (2008) 'Postmethod discourse and practice'. *TESOL Quarterly, 42/4.* 641–652.

Allwright, D. (1991) 'The death of the method', *CRILE Working Paper*, No. 10. Lancaster, Lancaster University.

Allwright, D. and Hanks, J. (2009) *The developing language learner: An introduction to exploratory practice.* Basingstoke: Palgrave Macmillan.

Anthony, E. (1963) 'Approach, method and technique'. *English Language Teaching*, 17. 63–67.

Asher, J. (1977) *Learning another language through actions: The complete teacher's guidebook.* California: Sky Oaks Productions.

Bax, S. (2003) 'The end of CLT: A context approach to language teaching'. *ELT Journal*, 57/3. 278–287.

Bell, D. (2007) 'Do teachers think that methods are dead?' *ELT Journal*, 61/2. 135–143.

Bolitho, R., Gower, R., Johnson, K., Murison-Bowie, S., White, R. (1983) 'Talking shop: The communicative teaching of English in non-English-speaking countries'. *ELT Journal*, 37/3. 235–242.

Braine, G. (ed.) (2005) *Teaching English to the world: History, curriculum and practice*. Mahwah, NJ: Lawrence Erlbaum Associates.

Brown, H. D. (2001) *Teaching by principles: An interactive approach to language pedagogy* (2nd ed.). New York: Longman.

Canagarajah, A. S. (2006) 'TESOL at forty: What are the issues?' *TESOL Quarterly*, 40/1. 9–34.

Chomsky, N. (1966) 'Linguistic theory'. Reprinted in J. Allen and P. Van Buren (eds) *Chomsky: Selected Readings*. Oxford: Oxford University Press. 152–159.

Cook, G. (2003) *Applied linguistics*. Oxford: Oxford University Press.

Cook, V. (2008) *Second language learning and language teaching* (4th ed.). London: Hodder Stoughton.

Crookes, G. (2009) *Values, philosophies, and beliefs in TESOL: Making a statement*. Cambridge: Cambridge University Press.

Curran, C. (1972) *Counseling-learning: A whole person model for education*. New York: Grune and Stratton.

Fries, C. (1945) *Teaching and learning English as a foreign language*. Ann Arbor: University of Michigan Press.

Gattegno, C. (1972) *Teaching foreign languages in schools: The silent way* (2nd ed.). New York: Educational Solutions.

Hall, G. and Cook, G. (2012) 'Own-language use in language teaching and learning'. *Language Teaching*, 45/3. 271–308.

Hinkel, E. (2005) 'Introduction', in E. Hinkel (ed.) *Handbook of research in second language teaching and learning*. Mahwah, NJ: Lawrence Erlbaum. 631–634.

Holliday, A. (1994) *Appropriate methodology and social context*. Cambridge: Cambridge University Press.

Howatt, A. with Widdowson, H. (2004) *A history of English language teaching*. Oxford: Oxford University Press.

Hunter, D. and Smith, R. (2012) 'Unpackaging the past: "CLT" through *ELTJ* keywords'. *ELT Journal*, 66/4. 430–439.

Hymes, D. (1972) 'On communicative competence', in J. Gumperz and D. Hymes (eds). *Directions in sociolinguistics*. New York: Holt and Reinhardt. 35–71.

Jacobs, G. and Farrell, T. (2003) 'Understanding and implementing the CLT (communicative language teaching) paradigm'. *RELC Journal*, 34/1. 5–30.

Kelly, L. (1969) *25 centuries of language teaching*. Rowley, MA: Newbury House.

Krashen, S. and Terrell, T. (1983) *The natural approach: Language acquisition in the classroom*. Oxford: Pergamon.

Kuhn, T. (1970/1996) *The structure of scientific revolutions* (3rd ed.). Chicago: University of Chicago Press.

Kumaravadivelu, B. (2003) *Beyond methods: Macrostrategies for language teaching*. New Haven, CT: Yale University Press.

Kumaravadivelu, B. (2006) *Understanding language teaching: From method to postmethod*. Mahwah, NJ: Lawrence Erlbaum.

Kumaravadivelu, B. (2012) *Language teacher education for a global society*. London: Routledge.

Larsen-Freeman, D. (2000) 'On the appropriateness of language teaching methods in language and development', in J. Shaw, D. Lubelske and M. Noullet (eds) *Partnership and interaction: Proceedings of the Fourth International Conference on Language and Development, Hanoi, Vietnam*. Bangkok: Asian Institute of Technology. 62–71.

Larsen-Freeman, D. (2005) 'A critical analysis of postmethod: An interview with Diane Larsen-Freeman by Zia Tajeddin'. *ILI Language Teaching Journal*, 1. 21–25.

Larsen-Freeman, D. and Anderson, M. (2011) *Techniques and principles in language teaching* (3rd ed.). Oxford: Oxford University Press.

Larsen-Freeman, D. and Freeman, D. (2008) 'Language moves: The place of 'foreign' languages in classroom teaching and learning'. *Review of Research in Education*, 32. 147–186.

Lozanov, G. (1978) *Suggestology and outlines of suggestopedy*. New York: Gordon and Breach.

Moskowitz, G. (1978) *Caring and sharing in the foreign language class*. Rowley, MA: Newbury House.

Pattison, B. (1964) 'Modern methods of language teaching'. *English Language Teaching*, 19/1. 2–6.

Pennycook, A. (1989) 'The concept of method, interested knowledge, and the politics of language teaching'. *TESOL Quarterly*, 23/4. 589–618.

Pennycook, A. (2004) 'History: After 1945', in M. Byram (ed.) *Routledge encyclopedia of language teaching and learning*. London: Routledge. 275–282.

Pennington, M. and Hoekje, B. (2014) 'Framing English language teaching'. *System*, 46. 163–175.

Phillipson, R. (1992) *Linguistic imperialism*. Oxford: Oxford University Press.

Prabhu, N. S. (1990) 'There is no best method – why?' *TESOL Quarterly*, 24/2. 161–176.

Richards, J. and Rodgers, T. (2001) *Approaches and methods in language teaching* (2nd ed.). Oxford: Oxford University Press.

Richards, J. and Rodgers, T. (2014) *Approaches and methods in language teaching* (3rd ed.). Oxford: Oxford University Press.

Richards, J. and Schmidt, R. (eds) (2002) *Dictionary of language teaching and applied linguistics* (3rd ed.). Harlow: Longman.

Rogers, C. (1969) *Freedom to learn: A view of what education might become*. Columbus, OH: Charles E. Merrill.

Rowlinson, W. (1994) 'The historical ball and chain', in Swarbrick, A. (ed.) *Teaching modern languages*. London: Open University. 7–17.

Skinner, B. (1957) *Verbal behaviour*. New York: Appleton-Century-Crofts.

Smith, R. (ed.) (2003) *Teaching English as a foreign language 1912–36: Volume 1 Wren and Wyatt*. London: Routledge.

Smith, R. (2015) 'Review of *teacher research in language teaching: A critical analysis* by S. Borg'. *ELT Journal*, 69/2. 205–208.

Stern, H. (1983) *Fundamental concepts of language teaching*. Oxford: Oxford University Press.

Stevick, E. (1980) *Teaching languages. A way and ways*. Rowley, MA: Newbury House.

Sweet, H. (1899/1964) *The practical study of languages. A guide for teachers and learners*. London, Dent. Republished by Oxford University Press in 1964, edited by R. Mackin.

Thornbury, S. (2006) *An A-Z of ELT*. Oxford: Macmillan.

Thornbury, S. (2011) 'Language teaching methodology', in J. Simpson (ed.) *The Routledge handbook of applied linguistics*. Oxon: Routledge. 185–199.

Ur, P. (2013) 'Language-teaching method revisited'. *ELT Journal*, 67/4. 468–474.

Waters, A. (2012) 'Trends and issues in ELT methods and methodology'. *ELT Journal*, 66/4. 440–449.

Weihua, Y. (2004) 'Grammar-translation method', in M. Byram (ed.) *Routledge encyclopaedia of language teaching and learning*. London: Routledge. 176–178.

Winitz, H. (ed.) (1981) *The comprehension approach to foreign language instruction*. Rowley, MA: Newbury House.

16

Communicative language teaching in theory and practice

Scott Thornbury

Introduction

> All courses based on functional/notional models must take as their starting point that communication must be taught and is therefore the primary objective, not merely the bi-product of other objectives.
>
> (Alexander, 1975/1980: 246)

> From the work of David Wilkins we took as our starting point this quotation: *What people want to do through language is more important than the mastery of language as an unapplied system.*
>
> (Abbs et al., 1975: 4)

The above two quotes highlight a significant paradigm shift in language teaching methodology that took place in the early 1970s and whose effects were still reverberating at the end of the decade – and beyond. The significance of the first owes as much to the fact that its author was Louis Alexander, perhaps the most widely published ELT materials writer of the time, and who, only a few years previously, had written (in the introductory notes to his hugely successful *New Concept English* series): "The basic aim in any language is to train the student to use new patterns" (Alexander, 1967: xiii).

The significance of the second is that it prefaces one of the first textbooks to break ranks with the prevailing structural organisation, adopting instead a syllabus organised round communicative *functions* and semantic *notions,* and, in so doing, helped popularise what would become known as communicative language teaching (CLT). Both quotes, in turn, reflect a seismic shift in the field of linguistics: "a reaction against the view of language as a set of structures; [and] a reaction towards a view of language as communication" (Brumfit and Johnson, 1979: 3). However, as Howatt (2004: 339) observes, what was attractive about this new approach "was not so much the novel syllabuses as the refreshing sense of freedom that followed the end of the over-rigid structural syllabus and the welcome variety of classroom activities that accompanied the new approach". But what precipitated such a radical turn of events?

A theory of language

The immediate impetus to define curriculum objectives not as structural 'patterns' but in terms of 'functional/notional models' emerged out of a Council of Europe project in the early 1970s that aimed to reform and standardise the teaching of modern languages to adults across Europe, and, specifically, to devise "a framework for adult language learning, based upon the language needs of the learner and the linguistic operations required of him [sic] in order to function effectively as a member of the language community for the purposes, and in the situations, revealed by those needs" (Trim, 1973, quoted in Brumfit and Johnson, 1979: 102). In order to specify the components of such a needs-and-purposes-driven curriculum, the advice of various linguists was sought, including David Wilkins. To Wilkins and his colleagues, it was self-evident that a curriculum designed to enable the learner "to function effectively" should be "organized in terms of the purposes for which people are learning language and the kinds of language performance that are necessary to meet these purposes" (Wilkins, 1976: 13). It quickly became an article of faith that a purely formal organisation, as in a structural syllabus, inadequately reflects and poorly predicts the way language is used in order to communicate. If language teaching was to be concerned with effective communication, this would mean "beginning with the context and purpose of utterances and asking how these might be expressed, rather than taking a linguistic form and asking what might be communicated through it" (Wilkins, 1972: 148).

This alternative organisation, as elaborated for the Council of Europe both by Van Ek (1975/1980) and Wilkins (1976), prioritised semantic categories, specifically language *notions* and communicative *functions,* over structural ones (hence, such syllabi – and the teaching approach that entailed their use – were initially labelled *functional-notional*). The emphasis on what the learner will be able *to do,* i.e. concrete behaviours as opposed to abstract linguistic knowledge, is consistent with Wilkins' injunction (1976: 42; cited by Abbs et al., above) that "*What people want to do through language is more important than the mastery of language as an unapplied system*".

Of course, a concern for what people want to *do* through language was not new. Wilkins and his contemporaries were themselves the heirs to a long tradition in British linguistics whose emphasis on context, meaning and 'language as part of the social process' was in sharp distinction to the Bloomfieldian structuralism that reigned on the other side of the Atlantic. Probably the most influential figure in this tradition was Michael Halliday (e.g. Halliday, 1978), whose foregrounding of the social and functional aspects of language and the way that these aspects are instantiated as text (or 'social exchange of meanings') undergirds the whole communicative enterprise.

"*What people want to do through language*" also recalls the work of the philosophers J. L. Austin and J. R. Searle, and especially the former's *How to Do Things with Words* (Austin, 1962). Speech act theory argues that "speaking a language is performing speech acts, acts such as making statements, giving commands, asking questions, making promises, and so on" (Searle, 1969: 16). The analysis of real-life interactions (i.e. discourse analysis) in terms of speech acts was developed in Birmingham in the early 1970s (e.g. Sinclair and Coulthard, 1975). The same tools were enlisted to meet the growing need for instructional materials that targeted specific registers: discourse analysis underpinned the design of the first ESP (English for specific purposes) courses (see Starfield, this volume). Before long, general English courses were incorporating an explicit reference to discourse in their objectives. The Teacher's Book for *Building Strategies* (Abbs and Freebairn, 1979: iv), for example, identifies as one of its aims: "[to] build up the language skills needed for extended discourse e.g. for reporting, narrating, describing, explaining", and "[to] practise connected speaking and writing".

So far, the impression might have been given that CLT was a purely European or even British-inspired phenomenon. However, US-based scholars, particularly those working in the field of sociolinguistics, also contributed in a major way to its development. Not the least of these was Dell Hymes, and, in fact, it is to Hymes that Howatt (2004) attributes the single 'big idea' that underpins CLT and from which the approach derived its name: *communicative competence*. In contradistinction to Chomsky's limited conception of competence as being a purely linguistic construct, Hymes argued that "there are rules of use without which the rules of grammar would be useless" (1972: 278) and that a socially-sensitive notion of competence entails knowing "when to speak, when not, [. . .] what to talk about with whom, when, where, in what manner" (1972: 277). This notion of *communicative competence* – subsequently reconfigured to include *sociolinguistic, discourse* and *strategic competences* (Canale and Swain, 1980) – significantly extended the goals of teaching. The idea, for example, that strategic competence could be developed through pedagogic tasks was adopted by Savignon (1972) in a ground-breaking classroom-based study, and one which first introduced the term communicative competence into the discourse of teaching, thereby marking a bridgehead into the new paradigm.

A theory of learning

An elaborated *theory of language* was now in place, but what was singularly lacking was a *theory of learning* to complement it and a methodology to actualise it. To bridge the gap, procedures inherited from audiolingualism were retained and adapted. Hence, Rivers (1981) proposed *skill-getting* (including the use of pattern-practice drills) as a prerequisite for *skill-using,* while Littlewood's (1981: 85) framework distinguished between *pre-communicative* and *communicative* activities, the former being the stage when "specific elements of knowledge or skill which compose communicative ability" are practised in isolation before eventual integration into communicative tasks.

Subsequently, cognitivist accounts of language acquisition (e.g. McLaughlin, 1987; Johnson, 1996; Skehan, 1998), which in turn drew on information-processing models in cognitive psychology (principally Anderson, 1983), lent credence to the skill-getting/skill-using framework, where practice in 'real operating conditions' helps automatise declarative knowledge (Johnson, 1996). At the same time, interlanguage studies (e.g. Selinker, 1972; Corder, 1981) that posited a 'natural order' of acquisition and the inevitability of error seemed to lend force to the argument that an overemphasis on accuracy at the expense of (communicative) fluency was misguided and that, as Littlewood (1981: 32) puts it, errors should be recognised "as a natural and acceptable phenomenon in any situation where learners have an urgent need to communicate".

More radically, and perhaps partly influenced by innatist theories of first language acquisition, some scholars put the case for purely experiential models of learning, or "learning by doing". Allwright (1979: 170), for example, argued persuasively for a "minimal teaching strategy" whereby learners simply performed communicative tasks in the belief that "language learning will take care of itself". The 'minimal teaching strategy' received endorsement through the popularisation of Krashen's distinction between *acquisition* and *learning* (Krashen, 1981) and his argument that language acquisition occurs only when unconscious processes are activated by exposure to comprehensible input. Krashen's rejection of a role for 'formal instruction' offered support for the kind of experiential 'deep-end' approach advocated by Allwright.

Building on Krashen's 'input hypothesis', Long's 'interaction hypothesis' (e.g. 1983) claimed that input can be rendered comprehensible, and thus available for acquisition, through such interactional processes as conversational repair and 'negotiation for meaning', that is to say, the kind of modifications that had been observed when learners are performing an *information-gap task.* Continuing this line of thinking, Swain's 'output hypothesis' (Swain, 1985) suggested that when learners experience communicative failure, they are 'pushed' both into making their output more comprehensible and into reappraising their existing interlanguage system, which provides further justification for the classroom use of communicative tasks.

Thus, more than a decade after its inception, the communicative approach was beginning to gather the ingredients of a learning theory to complement its theory of language. Even so, the tension between the linguistic and psychological underpinnings persisted, suggesting to Stern (1981) that there were two distinct approaches to CLT: the L (or linguistic) approach, as embodied in functional-notional syllabuses, and the P (or psychological and pedagogic approach), in which naturalistic learning processes are activated through communication. Stern argued that the two approaches could, and should, be synthesised, with an experiential element complementing the more academic elements. Howatt (1984: 279) made a similar distinction: between the 'weak' version of CLT, involving the systematic and incremental teaching of the sub-components of communicative competence, and the 'strong' version, which "advances the claim that language is acquired through communication". (The 'strong' version evolved into what is now known as *task-based instruction*: see Van den Branden, this volume.)

Nevertheless, and in spite of these tensions, by the mid-1980s there was a palpable sense the CLT had come of age and "assumed the status of orthodoxy" (Richards and Rodgers, 1986: 83), at least in British teaching circles. In the United States, its adoption was a little slower, but by 1994, H.D. Brown was confident enough to answer the question "Is there a currently recognised approach that is a generally accepted norm in the field?" by saying, "the answer is a qualified yes. That qualified yes can be captured in the term **communicative language teaching** (CLT)" (Brown, 1994: 77; emphasis in original).

So far, the impression may have been given that the advent of CLT was an unanticipated watershed event and that it happened independently of other concurrent social, political, economic and philosophical developments. But, as Hunter and Smith (2012; see also, Hall, this volume, ch. 15) make clear, few if any developments in language teaching methodology represent a complete break with the past. For many educationalists, CLT was simply 'new wine in old bottles'. "CLT is not a new idea," Savignon (2001: 18) reminds us. "Throughout the long history of language teaching, there always have been advocates of a focus on meaning, as opposed to form, and of developing learner ability to *use* the language for communication." Even scholars working within an audiolingual framework had, for some time, been advocating communicative tasks as a complement to more mechanical activities. Rivers (1972: 74), for example, reported "an increasing interest in communication and on what are being called communication drills," while, even earlier, Prator (1969) proposed that the teacher's repertory should include not only manipulative drills but also a gamut of 'communicative activities', sequenced in terms of the teacher's decreasing control. As Hunter and Smith (2012: 437) discovered: "Some of the ideas now associated with CLT were rooted in earlier discourse."

Moreover, as Howatt (2004) suggests, the notion of 'communication' was very much a feature of the educational and ideological climate at the end of the 1960s – a climate that was both progressive in spirit and pragmatic in terms of its educational goals. Savignon (1991: 264) notes how the philosophy of Jürgen Habermas, with its emphasis on individual empowerment, impelled methodologists working in Germany in the 1970s (such as Christopher Candlin, Christoph Edelhoff and Hans-Eberhard Piepho) in the direction of greater learner autonomy and 'communicatively oriented English teaching'. Likewise, Crookes (2009) associates the emergence of CLT in Europe with post-war 'reconstructionism', i.e. the impulse towards social and political integration and international mobility. Courses in 'communication sciences' and 'communication studies' burgeoned in university social science departments from the 1950s on, while leading educationalists (e.g. Barnes, 1976) were invoking the notion of communication as being at the heart of the learning process. Indeed, the idea that learning is experiential and that communication is the means by which experiences are shared and made meaningful dates at least as far back as the educational philosophy of John Dewey in the early twentieth century. As Crookes (2009: 70) notes, "the activity-centred curriculum of the British primary school [in the 1960s and 1970s] was an inheritance (mainly) from Dewey."

CLT, then, was not only a product of its *Zeitgeist* but, as Savignon (1991: 265) notes, derived "from a multidisciplinary perspective that includes, at least, linguistics, psychology, philosophy, sociology, and educational research." Nevertheless, as Brumfit (1978: 34) observed at the time, "to some teachers the arrival of 'communication' has come with the force of a revelation." How was this 'revelation' realised in practical terms? What was (and is) communicative teaching *like?*

CLT in practice

By redefining the goals of language learning in terms of *communicative,* rather than of *linguistic,* competence, advocates of CLT compelled teachers to re-think their classroom practices both at the level of overall course and lesson design and in terms of specific activity types and materials, changes that, in turn, prompted a re-evaluation of the teacher's role. This section reviews the ways that CLT was realised (or was supposed to have been realised) in practice.

At the level of course design, the most salient change was the (admittedly short-lived) shift in focus from a structural syllabus to one whose aims were defined in communicative terms, and specifically as *functions* and *notions* (Wilkins, 1972; Van Ek, 1975/1980; Munby, 1978). Thus, in what was effectively the first coursebook by a mainstream publisher to enshrine communicative principles, Abbs et al. (1975) mixed functional, notional and thematic categories in their syllabus. For example:

> **UNIT 13**
> Set 1: Imaginary situations
> Set 2: Obligation and necessity (present and future)
>
> **UNIT 14**
> Set 1: Obligation and necessity (past)
> Set 2: Reasons and consequences
>
> **UNIT 15**
> Set 1: Facts
> Set 2: Speculating about the past
>
> *(Abbs et al., 1975: 5)*

However, the wholesale abandonment of a structural component met some resistance, partly because of the residual conviction that "mastery of the structural system is still the basic requirement for using language to communicate one's own meanings" (Littlewood, 1981: 77), and a variety of compromise approaches soon emerged. In their *Cambridge English Course,* Swan and Walter (1984), for example, advocated a multi-strand syllabus, interweaving grammatical, thematic and functional-notional categories, but without necessarily prioritising any, on the grounds that, according to Swan (1990: 89) "it is . . . essential to consider both semantic and formal accounts of the language when deciding what to teach". By 1986, the tension between 'semantic and formal accounts' had been decided categorically in favour of the latter, as evidenced by the publication of the first of the *Headway* series (Soars and Soars, 1986a and b) and its unapologetically grammar-based syllabus.

More enduring than the functional-notional syllabus was the communicative methodology itself, as implemented through specific classroom activities, particularly those that replicated features of real-life communication. Widdowson (1990: 159) summarises the methodological implications of CLT thus: "The communicative approach reverses the emphasis of the structural. It concentrates on getting learners to do things with language, to express concepts and to carry out communicative acts of various kinds." "Reversing the emphasis of the structural" suggested, at least to some scholars, that the traditional trajectory, in which the learner progressed from accuracy to fluency, should itself be reversed, or at least conflated, and that classroom instruction should start with "getting learners to do things with language." After all, as Allwright (1979: 167) had argued, "if communication is THE aim, then it should be THE major element in the process" (emphasis in the original). Brumfit (1979: 188) proposed, therefore, that "a communicative methodology ... would start from communication, with exercises which constituted communication challenges for students". This reversed the prevailing instructional model, where communication was seen as an *outcome* of instruction, and substituted for it a model that *began* with production, i.e. with learners performing communicative tasks using all their available linguistic and pragmatic resources.

By contrast, in the 'weak' version of CLT, as promoted by Littlewood (1981), *pre-communicative activities* (typically with a structural focus) preceded *communicative activities*. While allowing that it might be possible, especially at higher levels, to reverse this sequence, Littlewood's 'default model' is one in which mastery of the linguistic systems is viewed as being a precondition for communication. The reversion to the grammar syllabus in the mid-1980s (see below) helped cement this accuracy-to-fluency approach, and most published materials ever since have perpetuated it.

Given the reinstatement of a structural syllabus and a presentation-practice methodology, a sceptic might be forgiven for wondering what, in the end, was new? The answer seems to be that CLT was defined less in terms of curriculum design and more in terms of actual classroom practices. In fact, as Harmer (1982) reasoned, it was erroneous to label a syllabus or even a methodology as being 'communicative' *per se*: only activities can be so. Or, as Larsen-Freeman (2000: 129) notes, "the most obvious characteristic of CLT is that almost everything that is done is done with a communicative intent. Students *use* the language a great deal through communicative activities such as games, role plays, and problem-solving tasks." This approach had been spelled out by Abbs and Freebairn (1979: v) in the teachers' guide to their *Strategies* series:

> If emphasis is placed on learning a language for communicative purposes, the methods used to promote learning should reflect this. . . . A communicative methodology will therefore encourage students to practise language in pairs and groups, where they have equal opportunity to ask, answer, initiate and respond. The teacher assumes a counselling role, initiating activity, listening, helping and advising. Students are encouraged to *communicate effectively* rather than merely to produce grammatically correct forms of English.

Contrasting the attributes of 'non-communicative' and communicative activities, Harmer (1982) argued that the latter involve a *desire* to communicate, have a communicative *purpose*, are focused on *content*, not form, require a *variety of linguistic resources* (rather than being restricted to some targeted feature) and involve little or no *teacher intervention* or *materials control*.

Archetypal activities meeting these criteria included information-gap activities of various types, from the relatively controlled, such as *describe-and-draw* (learners describe a picture to their partners, who recreate it, sight unseen), to freer 'milling' activities, such as *find-someone-who*, whereby learners circulate in order to complete some kind of survey by asking and answering questions. And, in order to practise functional language, *role plays* and *simulations* became standard practice. For similar reasons, the use of *authentic* reading and listening materials was promoted, and classroom procedures for minimising the difficulties of these – such as the use of skimming and scanning strategies – became commonplace.

Finally, and in order to meet the challenge of managing a 'communicative' classroom in which learner interaction is maximised, the teacher's role was re-envisaged as "a facilitator of learning" (Littlewood, 1981: 92). This less-interventionist teacher role was, of course, perfectly in tune with concurrent tendencies in general education, particularly those influenced by a more learner-centred, humanist learning philosophy (e.g. Stevick, 1976).

In short, Dörnyei (2009: 33) summarises the attributes of CLT in the following terms:

- Activities promote real communication, that is, engage learners in the *authentic, functional use of language*.
- Classroom communicative situations should resemble *real-life communication* as much as possible.
- *Fluency* is more important than *accuracy*.
- Typical communicative activities are *role-plays, discussions, problem-solving tasks, simulations, projects* and *games*.

CLT and its discontents

Almost since its inception, CLT has been challenged on a number of grounds, not only in terms of the principles underpinning it but also with regard to its actual practices, including not only their (global) appropriateness and applicability but the way that they might have been (locally) misappropriated and misapplied. This section reviews some of the major criticisms.

From the outset, it became clear that, in the absence of clear specifications as to the learners' needs, the selection and sequencing of items for a notional-functional syllabus was fairly arbitrary. Unlike grammatical structures, notions and functions could not be easily plotted along a scale from simple to complex, while estimates of their relative frequency or utility were largely hit-and-miss. As we have seen, alternative organising principles for communicative syllabuses, often involving a covert grammatical syllabus, quickly emerged.

A more fundamental criticism, however, targeted the way that communicative competence was being too narrowly interpreted. Brumfit (1978: 41) was one of the first to warn against construing communicative competence as simply a checklist of notions and functions: "No inventory of language items can itself capture the essence of communication."

Brumfit (1984: 123) went on to argue that any attempt to base a methodology on linguistic description would be counterproductive, on the grounds that "language is impossible to acquire if the product is predefined; what will then be acquired is merely language-like behaviour." Instead, "the *processes* of classroom activity, which cannot by definition be described in detail, must be given much greater prominence" (1984: 122 – emphasis in the original). More recently, Leung (2005) has criticised CLT on similar grounds, arguing that construing communicative competence as an inert and stable 'body of knowledge' ignores the contingency, fluidity and 'participatory involvement' that is the nature of actual communication.

While the foregoing criticisms targeted the 'reification' of communicative competence at the expense of the actual processes of communication, a counter-argument soon emerged to the effect that the pressure to be 'communicative' may prejudice learners' ultimate achievement. Studies undertaken in immersion contexts (e.g. Harley and Swain, 1984) suggested that, despite plentiful exposure to comprehensible input, learners failed to acquire a target-like grammar, while studies of learner-learner interaction (e.g. Porter, 1986) challenged the view that pair- and group-work provide a fertile base for acquisition. Based on a study of 'plateau' effects in foreign language classrooms, Higgs and Clifford (1982: 74) hypothesised that "the premature immersion of a student into an unstructured or 'free' conversational setting before certain fundamental linguistic structures are more or less in place is not done without cost" – that cost being an overreliance on communicative strategies at the expense of target-like competence.

Studies such as these cast doubt on the foundational communicative belief that 'one can learn a language simply by using it' and compelled a number of scholars to militate for the rehabilitation of more traditional classroom practices, especially those that had been discredited for being too 'form-focused'. In a famous exchange with Widdowson in the pages of *ELT Journal*, Swan (1985, reprinted in 1990) argued for (amongst other things) the restoration of the grammar syllabus, while challenging the communicative predilection for authentic materials and information gap activities. As he later argued in 1996, "it does not follow that because students are communicating they are learning English; and some activities (such as learning by heart or mechanical structure-practice) unfashionable because they are totally uncommunicative, may none the less be very valuable" (Swan, 2012: 67).

The rejection of traditional classroom practices is one reason that, in many contexts, there was a reluctance, even refusal, to embrace communicative principles unconditionally. Over the years there has been a steady stream of articles (e.g. Sano et al., 1984; Medgyes, 1986; Burnaby and Sun, 1989; Ellis, 1996; Kramsch and Sullivan, 1996; Li, 1998; Hu, 2002; Bax, 2003) challenging CLT's exportability to contexts beyond those in which it was originally developed. This alleged 'lack of fit' has often been attributed to different educational and/or cultural traditions. Thus, Li (1998: 696) argues that "the predominance of text-centred and grammar-centred practices in Korea does not provide a basis for the student-centred, fluency-focused, and problem-solving activities required by CLT". In a similar vein, Burnaby and Sun (1989) label CLT a 'Western method', characterised by its learner-centred approach, the use of authentic materials and an emphasis on spoken communication in accordance with native-speaker models of linguistic and sociolinguistic competence. This contrasts with the Chinese educational model, with its emphasis on academic skills, the use of literary texts and a more teacher-fronted pedagogy, where the teachers are almost always non-native speakers of English. Given the Chinese mindset, Xiaoju (1990: 70) concluded that "it is really not surprising that a communicative approach to EFL should meet with stubborn and protracted resistance". Furthermore, as Medgyes (1986) had earlier argued, the linguistic demands placed on teachers by the more reactive, interactive and learner-centred approach that CLT presupposes necessarily limits its practicability in *any* context where the majority of teachers are non-native speakers – that is to say, virtually everywhere where English is taught as a foreign language.

Such criticisms have nurtured the belief that CLT represents a form of cultural imperialism whereby, in Holliday's (2005: 2) formulation, "a well-resourced, politically and economically aggressive, colonising, Western 'Centre' imposes its values, standards and beliefs on 'an undersourced, colonised 'Periphery'". Thus, the emphasis on student-centred learning that is so often associated with CLT is, according to Pennycook (1994: 173) "not only inappropriate to many contexts in which student and teacher roles are defined differently, but it also supports a very particular view of the individual, development and authority". Arguably, this 'particular view' is one that asserts the primacy of the individual over the group and of self-expression and originality over cultural reproduction and tradition.

Defenders of the universality of CLT have argued, on the other hand, that its critics are construing CLT too narrowly. Holliday (1994a: 165) counters his own critique of inappropriate methodologies by arguing that "much of the bad press which the communicative approach has attracted is due to myths which have been built around it . . . such as 'communicative equals oral work', 'communicative equals group work' or 'communicative equals getting rid of the teacher as a major focus in the classroom'". In a similar vein, Thompson (1996) identifies four misconceptions about CLT: (a) CLT means not teaching grammar, (b) CLT means teaching only speaking, (c) CLT means pair work, which means role play, and (d) CLT means expecting too much from the teacher (in terms of management and linguistic skills, for example). Thompson not only refutes these misconceptions but argues that the benefits of CLT are too important to risk being jeopardised by ignorance.

More recently, Holliday (2005: 143) has argued that a distinction needs to be made between communicative *principles*, on the one hand, and communicative teaching *methodologies*, on the other. While the former may be universally applicable (e.g. 'Treat language as *communication*'), the latter may be tailored to specific local contexts, "whereby the curriculum would be sensitive to the broader sociological nature of its 'ecosystem'" (2005: 147). Thus Hiep (2007: 200) found that, despite the difficulties of implementing CLT in a Vietnamese context, the teachers he surveyed willingly embraced its basic principles. Liao (2004: 270) goes further by arguing that, in the Chinese context, not only the principles but the practices of CLT offer a timely antidote to 'traditional' ways of teaching. (For further discussion of the issues surrounding 'appropriate methodology', see Holliday, this volume.)

With regard to China and other countries in that region, Beaumont and Chang (2011) argue that the much-cited contradiction between communicative principles and the Confucian educational tradition is a false dichotomy and one that is contradicted by research into the attitudes of both teachers and students in these contexts, who report being favourably disposed to group-work, learner autonomy and interaction (see, for example, Littlewood, 2000). Moreover, as Kubota (1999) argues, stereotyping 'Asian' learners as having attitudes and beliefs that are inimical to communicative principles is yet another 'colonial legacy', and she cites studies that "challenge cultural representations such as homogeneity, groupism, and lack of self-expression, creativity, and critical thinking found in the current dominant applied linguistics literature" (1999: 25).

Whether or not attributable to cultural, social or linguistic factors, the failure to fully implement CLT in many contexts has defused its initial promise. Nunan (1987: 144), for example, complained that "there is growing evidence that, in communicative classes, interactions may, in fact, not be very communicative after all". The growing evidence Nunan adduces includes studies that characterise teacher-learner interaction as being almost entirely teacher-led and dominated. In similar vein, Kumaravadivelu (1993: 13) observes: "Even teachers who are committed to CLT can fail to create opportunities for genuine interaction in their classrooms."

A number of studies have confirmed this discrepancy between teachers' beliefs about CLT and what they actually do in the classroom. Karavas-Doukas (1996: 193), for example, found that 40 secondary school language teachers in Greece generally held favourable attitudes towards CLT, but, "when the teachers were observed, classroom practices (with very few exceptions) deviated considerably from the principles of the communicative approach. . . . Most lessons were teacher-fronted and exhibited an explicit focus on form." Other teachers are less favourably disposed: in a study of 10 teachers of Japanese who notionally subscribed to a communicative methodology, Sato and Kleinsasser (1999: 509) found that "the observation data showed reluctance on the part of teachers to promote CLT and indicated that many teachers avoided (or at least challenged or mutated) the few conceptions of CLT that they held."

Teacher resistance may be partly motivated by resistance on the part of their students. Nunan (1988: 89), for example, reports that, while teachers often voice support for communicative practices, learners tend to favour traditional classroom activities such as grammar exercises. Gatbonton and Segalowitz (2005: 327) would seem to concur, arguing that "CLT provides little that is concrete or tangible for students". This is because (they claim) "there are no provisions in current CLT methodologies to promote language use to a high level of mastery through repetitive practice. In fact, focused practice continues to be seen as inimical to the inherently open and unpredictable nature of communicative activities". Accordingly, they suggest ways in which activities that target 'creative automaticity' through 'inherent repetition' can be integrated into a communicative approach.

Other attempts to redress some of the perceived weaknesses of CLT include Celce-Murcia et al. (1997: 141), who welcome a return to a more 'direct' approach to the teaching of communicative competence, "whereby new linguistic information is passed on and practised explicitly". More recently, Lightbown and Spada (2006) cite research that suggests that an explicit instructional focus combined with overt error correction compensates for the risks of an approach that focuses on communication alone.

Nowhere has this erosion of 'strong' communicative principles been more apparent than in general English textbooks. Indeed, it is arguable that the ELT publishing industry has not so much reflected as driven this trend. Certainly, since the publication – and phenomenal global success – of *Headway Intermediate* (Soars and Soars, 1986b), no publisher has attempted to revive the notional-functional syllabi that were so popular in the preceding decade. Rather, we have witnessed what Waters (2011: 321) describes as "the grafting of a communicative 'veneer' on to what has remained basically language-focused stock". And yet, when it was first published, *Headway* was not ashamed of its communicative pedigree: as the authors wrote in the *Teacher's Book* to the first edition (Soars and Soars, 1986b: iv): "*Headway* incorporates and encourages what is generally considered to be a *communicative methodology.*" However, by the time the elementary level book in the series was published (Soars and Soars, 1993), the authors' commitment to a communicative approach had become somewhat qualified: "There is almost an assumption that nobody learned a language successfully before the arrival of the communicative approach" (Soars and Soars, 1993: 4). Accordingly, they were now advocating an approach in which new language "needs to be practised not only in communicative, meaningful ways but in drills and exercises where the language is used for display purposes only" (ibid.). This concession to 'non-communicative' practices reflects Harmer's earlier call for a judicious balance between "the drill and the discussion" (1982: 164).

The increasingly prominent grammar focus of the *Headway* series has persisted into subsequent editions, as Waters (2012) observes, and it is a trend that continues unabated in all mainstream ELT publishing, despite a plea on the part of some 'revivalists' (e.g. Meddings and Thornbury, 2009) to resuscitate CLT's prelapsarian values.

Conclusion

Is it true, then, that, as Thornbury (1998: 113) puts it, "CLT – both in its weak and in its strong version – has had little impact on current classroom practice" and that, in Swan's (1990: 98) words, "it is likely to be seen as little more than an interesting ripple on the surface of twentieth-century language teaching"? Or is it the case that, as Harmer (2007: 71) claims, "the Communicative approach has left an indelible mark on teaching and learning"?

In fact, it may be the case that the concept of 'method' itself has been, if not interred, at least problematised (see Hall, this volume, ch. 15) and that the notion of a monolithic, universally applicable approach, as embodied in CLT, is incompatible with the diversity of contexts, interests, purposes and technologies that characterise the teaching of second languages nowadays.

Moreover, the socio-economic landscape is very different now than it was in the 1970s. The 'marketisation' of education (Gray and Block, 2012: 121) and its associated concepts of 'the knowledge economy', 'learning outcomes' and 'accountability' have shifted the focus from 'communication' to 'commodification'; "in such an educational climate, students are increasingly seen as customers seeking a service and schools and teachers are, as a consequence, seen as service providers" (ibid.). Language learning, like other subjects, has become commodified, and the measure of its success is less communicative competence than the results of high-stakes testing. In such an educational climate, concepts so fundamental to CLT as authenticity, fluency, discovery and collaboration seem outmoded or, at best, 'add-ons' for those who can afford the luxury of small classes of communicatively motivated learners. More likely, however, and given the appeal that still attaches to the word 'communicative', CLT will continue to prosper as a brand, even though its original ingredients may have long since been reconstituted. In the end, as Holliday (1994b: 10) argues, CLT was itself a development from previous methodologies, "and further improvement can only be achieved by further development, not by going back".

Discussion questions

- "Everything is 'communicative' these days" (Harmer, 1982: 164). Is this still the case? Is CLT still the current orthodoxy? If not, what is?
- How far do you think that 'a language can be taught simply by using it'? In what ways are your views reflected in your classroom practice (as a teacher) or your preferences (as a learner)?
- If CLT is defined less by its theoretical foundations and more by its actual classroom practices, what CLT practices do you think are definitive?
- To what extent do you agree that the principles that underpin CLT have had little impact on current classroom practice?
- Is CLT a 'Western-centred' method, in your view? How far is it appropriate in your professional context?
- If further improvement of CLT can be achieved only by further development, what developments should we be looking forward to? For example, how can CLT accommodate developments in educational technology?

Related topics

Appropriate methodology; ELT materials; Language curriculum design; Method, methods and methodology; Task-based language teaching.

Further reading

Brumfit, C. J. and Johnson, K. (eds) (1979) *The communicative approach to language teaching*. Oxford: Oxford University Press. (A foundational text with papers by the leading architects of CLT in its prime, including Allwright, Widdowson, Wilkins and its two editors.)

Harmer, J. (2015) *The practice of English language teaching* (5th ed.). Harlow: Pearson. (This is a comprehensive manual of classroom practice that is firmly anchored in communicative principles.)

Richards, J. and Rodgers, T. (2014) *Approaches and methods in language teaching* (3rd ed.). Cambridge: Cambridge University Press. (This is an updated version of a core text describing methods, including CLT, in terms of their underlying principles as well as their surface practices.)

References

Abbs, B. and Freebairn, I. (1979) *Building strategies: Teacher's book*. London: Longman.

Abbs, B., Ayton, A. and Freebairn, I. (1975) *Strategies: Students' book*. London: Longman.

Alexander, L. G. (1967) *New concept English: First things first (teacher's book)*. Harlow: Longman.

Alexander, L. G. (1975/1980) 'Appendix 4. Some methodological implications of Waystage and Threshold level', in J. van Ek (ed.) *Threshold level English*. Oxford: Pergamon. 235–251.

Allwright, R. (1979) 'Language learning through communication practice', in C. J. Brumfit and K. Johnson (eds) *The communicative approach to language teaching*. Oxford: Oxford University Press. 167–182.

Anderson, J. (1983) *The architecture of cognition*. Cambridge, MA: Harvard University Press.

Austin, J. L. (1962) *How to do things with words*. Oxford: Clarenden Press.

Barnes, D. (1976) *From communication to curriculum*. Harmondsworth: Penguin.

Bax, S. (2003) 'The end of CLT: A context approach to language teaching'. *ELT Journal*, 57/3. 278–287.

Beaumont, M. and Chang, K-S. (2011) 'Challenging the traditional/communicative dichotomy'. *ELT Journal*, 65/3. 291–299.

Brown, H. D. (1994) *Teaching by principles: An interactive approach to language pedagogy*. Upper Saddle River, NJ: Prentice Hall Regents.

Brumfit, C. J. (1978) '"Communicative" language teaching: An assessment', in P. Strevens (ed.) *In honour of A.S. Hornby*. Oxford: Oxford University Press. 33–44.

Brumfit, C. J. (1979) '"Communicative" language teaching: An educational perspective', in C. J. Brumfit and K. Johnson (eds) *The communicative approach to language teaching*. Oxford: Oxford University Press. 183–191.

Brumfit, C. J. (1984) *Communicative methodology in language teaching: The roles of fluency and accuracy*. Cambridge: Cambridge University Press.

Brumfit, C. J. and Johnson, K. (eds) (1979) *The communicative approach to language teaching*. Oxford: Oxford University Press.

Burnaby, B. and Sun, Y. (1989) 'Chinese teachers' views of Western language teaching: Context informs paradigms'. *TESOL Quarterly*, 23/2. 219–238.

Canale, M. and Swain, M. (1980) 'Theoretical bases of communicative approaches to second language teaching and testing'. *Applied Linguistics*, 1/1. 1–47.

Celce-Murcia, M., Dörnyei, Z. and Thurrell, S. (1997) 'Direct approaches in L2 instruction: A turning point in communicative language teaching?' *TESOL Quarterly*, 31. 141–152.

Corder, S. P. (1981) *Error analysis and interlanguage*. Oxford: Oxford University Press.

Crookes, G. (2009) *Values, philosophies and beliefs in TESOL: Making a statement*. Cambridge: Cambridge University Press.

Dörnyei, Z. (2009) 'The 2010s. Communicative language teaching in the 21st century: The "principled communicative approach"'. *Perspectives*, 36/2. 33–43.

Ellis, G. (1996) 'How culturally appropriate is the communicative approach?' *ELT Journal*, 50/3. 213–218.

Gatbonton, E. and Segalowitz, N. (2005) 'Rethinking communicative language teaching: A focus on access to fluency'. *The Canadian Modern Language Review*, 61/3. 325–353.

Gray, J. and Block, D. (2012) 'The marketization of language teacher education and neoliberalism: Characteristics, consequence and future prospects', in D. Block, J. Gray and M. Holborow (eds) *Neoliberalism and applied linguistics*. London: Routledge. 114–143.

Halliday, M.A.K. (1978) *Language as social semiotic*. London: Edward Arnold.

Harley, B. and Swain, M. (1984) 'The interlanguage of immersion students and its implication for second language teaching', in A. Davies, C. Criper and A. Howatt (eds) *Interlanguage*. Edinburgh: Edinburgh University Press. 291–311.

Harmer, J. (1982) 'What is communicative?' *ELT Journal*, 36/3. 164–168.

Harmer, J. (2007) *The practice of English language teaching* (4th ed.). Harlow: Pearson.

Hiep, P.H. (2007) 'Communicative language teaching: unity within diversity'. *ELT Journal*, 61/3. 193–201.

Higgs, T. and Clifford R. (1982) 'The push towards communication', in T. Higgs (ed.) *Curriculum, competence, and the foreign language teacher*. Skokie, IL: National Textbook Co. 33–41.

Holliday, A. (1994a) *Appropriate methodology and social context*. Cambridge: Cambridge University Press.

Holliday, A. (1994b) 'The house of TESEP and the communicative approach: The special needs of state English language education'. *ELT Journal*, 48/1. 3–11.

Holliday, A. (2005) *The struggle to teach English as an international language*. Oxford: Oxford University Press.

Howatt, A. (1984) *A history of English language teaching*. Oxford: Oxford University Press.

Howatt, A. (2004) *A history of English language teaching* (2nd ed.). Oxford: Oxford University Press.

Hu, G. (2002) 'Potential cultural resistance to pedagogical imports: The case for communicative language teaching in China'. *Language, Culture and Curriculum*, 15/2. 93–105.

Hunter, D. and Smith, R. (2012) 'Unpacking the past: "CLT" through ELTJ keywords'. *ELT Journal*, 66/4. 430–439.

Hymes, D. (1972) 'On communicative competence', in J. B Pride and J. Holmes (eds) *Sociolinguistics: Selected readings*. Harmondsworth: Penguin Education. 269–293.

Johnson, K. (1996) *Language teaching and skill learning.* Oxford: Blackwell.

Karavas-Doukas, E. (1996) 'Using attitude scales to investigate teachers' attitudes to the communicative approach'. *ELT Journal,* 50/3. 187–198.

Kramsch, C. and Sullivan, P. (1996) 'Appropriate pedagogy'. *ELT Journal,* 50/3. 199–212.

Krashen, S. (1981) *Second language acquisition and second language learning.* Oxford: Pergamon.

Kubota, R. (1999) 'Japanese culture constructed by discourses: Implications for applied linguistics research and ELT'. *TESOL Quarterly,* 33/1. 9–36.

Kumaravadivelu, B. (1993) 'Maximizing learning potential in the communicative classroom'. *ELT Journal,* 47/1. 12–21.

Larsen-Freeman, D. (2000) *Techniques and principles in language teaching* (2nd ed.). Oxford: Oxford University Press.

Leung, C. (2005) 'Convivial communication: Recontextualizing communicative competence'. *International Journal of Applied Linguistics,* 15/2. 119–144.

Li, D. (1998) '"It's always more difficult than you plan or imagine": Teachers' perceived difficulties in introducing the communicative approach in South Korea'. *TESOL Quarterly,* 32/4. 677–704.

Liao, X. (2004) 'The need for communicative language teaching in China'. *ELT Journal,* 58/3. 270–273.

Lightbown, P. and Spada, N. (2006) *How languages are learned* (3rd ed.). Oxford: Oxford University Press.

Littlewood, W. (1981) *Communicative language teaching: An introduction.* Cambridge: Cambridge University Press.

Littlewood, W. (2000) 'Do Asian students really want to listen and obey?' *ELT Journal,* 54/1. 31–35.

Long, M. (1983) 'Native speaker/non-native speaker conversation and the negotiation of comprehensible input'. *Applied Linguistics,* 4. 126–141.

McLaughlin, B. (1987) *Theories of second-language learning.* London: Edward Arnold.

Meddings, L. and Thornbury, S. (2009) *Teaching unplugged: Dogme in English language teaching.* Peaslake: Delta.

Medgyes, P. (1986) 'Queries from a communicative teacher'. *ELT Journal,* 40/2. 107–112.

Munby, J. (1978) *Communicative syllabus design.* Cambridge: Cambridge University Press.

Nunan, D. (1987) 'Communicative language teaching: Making it work'. *ELT Journal,* 41/2. 136–145.

Nunan, D. (1988) *The learner-centred curriculum.* Cambridge: Cambridge University Press.

Pennycook, A. (1994) *The cultural politics of English as an international language.* Harlow: Longman.

Porter, P. (1986) 'How learners talk to each other: input and interaction in task-centred discussions', in R. Day (ed.) *Talking to learn: Conversation in second language acquisition.* Rowley, MA: Newbury House. 200–222.

Prator, C. H. (1969) 'Adding a second language'. *TESOL Quarterly,* 3/2. 95–104.

Richards, J. and Rodgers, T. (1986) *Approaches and methods in language teaching.* Cambridge: Cambridge University Press.

Rivers, W. M. (1972) 'Talking off the tops of their heads'. *TESOL Quarterly,* 6/1. 71–81.

Rivers, W. (1981) *Teaching foreign-language skills* (2nd ed.). Chicago: University of Chicago Press.

Sano, M., Takahashi, M. and Yoneyama, A. (1984) 'Communicative language teaching and local needs'. *ELT Journal,* 38. 170–177.

Sato, K. and Kleinsasser, R. C. (1999) 'Communicative language teaching (CLT): Practical understandings'. *Modern Language Journal,* 83/iv. 494–517.

Savignon, S. J. (1972) *Communicative competence: An experiment in foreign language teaching.* Philadelphia: Center for Curriculum Development.

Savignon, S. J. (1991) 'Communicative language teaching: State of the art'. *TESOL Quarterly,* 25/2. 261–277.

Savignon, S. J. (2001) 'Communicative language teaching for the twenty-first century', in M. Celce-Murcia (ed.) *Teaching English as a second or foreign language* (3rd ed.). Boston: Heinle Cengage Learning. 13–28.

Searle, J. R. (1969) *Speech acts: An essay in the philosophy of language.* Cambridge: Cambridge University Press.

Selinker, L. (1972) 'Interlanguage'. *International Review of Applied Linguistics,* 10. 209–231.

Sinclair, J. M. and Coulthard, R. M. (1975) *Towards an analysis of discourse.* Oxford: Oxford University Press.

Skehan, P. (1998) *A cognitive approach to language learning.* Oxford: Oxford University Press.

Soars, L. and Soars, J. (1986a) *Headway intermediate (students' book).* Oxford: Oxford University Press.

Soars, L. and Soars, J. (1986b) *Headway intermediate (teacher's book).* Oxford: Oxford University Press.

Soars, L. and Soars, J. (1993) *Headway elementary (teacher's book).* Oxford: Oxford University Press.

Stern, H. H. (1981) 'Communicative language teaching and learning: Toward a synthesis', in J. E. Alatis, H. B. Altman and P. M. Alatis (eds) *The second language classroom: Directions for the 1980's.* New York: Oxford University Press. 131–148.

Stevick, E. W. (1976) *Memory, meaning & method.* Rowley, MA: Newbury House.

Swain, M. (1985) 'Communicative competence: some roles of comprehensible input and comprehensible output in its development', in S. Gass and C. Madden (eds) *Input in second language acquisition*. Rowley, MA: Newbury House.

Swan, M. (1990) 'A critical look at the communicative approach', in R. Rossner and R. Bolitho (eds) *Currents of change in English language teaching*. Oxford: Oxford University Press. 73–98.

Swan, M. (2012) *Thinking about language teaching: Selected articles 1982–2011*. Oxford: Oxford University Press.

Swan, M. and Walter, C. (1984) *Cambridge English course, 1*. Cambridge: Cambridge University Press.

Thompson, G. (1996) 'Some misconceptions about communicative language teaching'. *ELT Journal,* 50/1. 9–15.

Thornbury, S. (1998) 'Comments on Marianne Celce-Murcia, Zoltán Dörnyei, and Sarah Thurrell's "Direct approaches in L2 Instruction: A turning point in communicative language teaching?" A reader reacts....'. *TESOL Quarterly,* 32/1. 109–116.

Trim, J. (1973) *Systems development in adult language learning*. Strasbourg: Council of Europe.

Van Ek, J. (1975/1980) *Threshold level English*. Oxford: Pergamon.

Waters, A. (2011) 'Advances in materials design', in M. H. Long and C. J. Doughty (eds) *The handbook of language teaching*. Oxford: Wiley-Blackwell. 311–326.

Waters (2012) 'Trends and issues in ELT methods and methodology'. *ELT Journal,* 6/4. 440–449.

Widdowson, H. (1990) *Aspects of language teaching*. Oxford: Oxford University Press.

Wilkins, D. (1972) *Linguistics in language teaching*. London: Edward Arnold.

Wilkins, D. (1976) *Notional syllabuses*. Oxford: Oxford University Press.

Xiaoju, L. (1990) 'In defence on the communicative approach', in R. Rossner and R. Bolitho (eds) *Currents of change in English language teaching*. Oxford: Oxford University Press. 59–72.

17

Task-based language teaching

Kris Van den Branden

Introduction

Task-based language teaching (TBLT) has gained considerable momentum over the past thirty years; in some countries, like New Zealand and Vietnam, TBLT has even been propagated by the national government as the most favoured approach to second and foreign language teaching. International conferences are devoted to this particular approach, task-based syllabuses are being developed in a growing number of educational settings and tasks are used by researchers in studies exploring the processes that drive second and foreign language acquisition (SLA). In this chapter, I will first describe the basic principles of TBLT and provide a brief historic overview of its development. Next, I will discuss what a task-based curriculum looks like and discuss a number of critical issues and key areas of debate. I will then move on to discuss the implementation of TBLT by teachers around the world, exploring the potential and opportunities that working with tasks in the classroom can give rise to on the one hand and the difficulties and tensions teachers are facing when trying to implement TBLT on the other hand. At the end of the chapter, I will point out a number of future challenges related to task-based language teaching.

What is TBLT? and what is a task?

Historically, TBLT grew out of applied linguists' and pedagogues' discontent with the prevailing approach to second/foreign language teaching during the second half of the twentieth century. Long (1985) argued that in many second language classes, language was approached as a system of elements and rules which were explicitly taught in a piecemeal and decontextualised fashion. Learners were supposed to first digest the explicit information about a particular linguistic item (e.g. a word or a grammar rule), then practise the item in isolated sentences until its application had been automatised; only then were learners encouraged to try and use the linguistic item in the exchange of meaningful messages for communicative purposes. Long argued that this approach to language *teaching* is largely inconsistent with the way people *learn* a language. Firstly, the language input that learners are exposed to is bound to be artificial, merely serving to illustrate 'the structure of the day' and failing to show learners how target language users really talk outside the classroom. Secondly, learners are typically asked to produce errorless output at a very early stage of acquisition (to show that they have absorbed the explicit information about the rule flawlessly), while normal processes of second language acquisition are gradual and naturally involve errors that can even be informative and useful to learners. Thirdly, according to Long, there is a huge difference between practising a rule in isolated sentences (and being allowed to just focus on that single rule) and integrating the context-appropriate use of the rule with the application of a wide range of other sub-processes (such as mobilising the right words, pronouncing an utterance appropriately, monitoring the interlocutor's reactions and so forth), which together constitute the complex challenge that second language learners face when making spontaneous conversation in the target language.

In natural, non-classroom-based processes of language acquisition (which typically can be observed with very young children acquiring their mother tongue or immigrants acquiring a language outside school, for instance when watching television, playing games, working or socialising in a second language context), people do not first acquire metalinguistic information about the elements of a language; rather, from the early developmental stages onwards, they intend, and therefore try, to comprehend and produce meaningful messages in the target language to achieve particular goals, many of which will be non-linguistic. Tourists at beginner levels who are travelling abroad, for instance, may be particularly eager to quickly pick up words and expressions they need to find a toilet, order drinks and food and find their way around; young adolescents who get absorbed in a fascinating digital game in a foreign language are equally eager to quickly acquire the language they need to play the game and talk about it; immigrants who have just found a new job in their new environment may be particularly motivated to try to comprehend/produce crucial messages related to doing their job well.

In India, Prabhu (1987) was one of the first to seriously explore this idea and organise a language-learning curriculum around a series of task-based projects (the 'Bangalore Project'), which hinged on the basic hypothesis that people learn real and useful language more quickly if they try to use it for non-linguistic ends. Around the same time, Long (1985) and Pica (1987), amongst others, also coined the term 'task-based' in the United States. These, in fact, were not the first attempts to challenge the grammar-based, teacher-dominated, explicit approach to language teaching noted earlier. Drawing on pragmatic and sociolinguistic approaches to the study of linguistics, communicative language teaching (CLT) had been introduced in the 1970s, raising awareness among language teachers of the need to base language learning in communication (Widdowson, 1978; Brumfit and Johnson, 1979; see Thornbury, this volume). However, as Long (1985) argued, both in curriculum and syllabus design on the one hand and in classroom practice on the other, CLT (especially the 'weaker' forms of CLT) rapidly became incorporated into the mainstream explicit approach to language teaching; although many teachers and textbooks were inspired by CLT to extend the third phase of the present-practice-produce paradigm, neither the basic structure of classroom activity nor the linear, incremental, structure-based view on language acquisition underpinning it turned out to have been significantly challenged by CLT.

What the early proponents of TBLT aimed for was the reversal of the basic pedagogic model; language learners needed to be exposed to meaningful input from the very early stages onwards, try to communicate by using whatever limited linguistic resources they had already built up, focus on meaning rather than on linguistic accuracy and try to reach intrinsically interesting, personally relevant goals while doing so. From their attempts to understand and produce meaningful messages for functional purposes and the exemplar-based linguistic repertoire they were building up, learners were presumed to gradually induce explicit language knowledge. From this perspective, explicit, conscious knowledge about language is based on and stems from the implicit knowledge that learners build up while trying to make conversation, rather than the other way round. This resonates strongly with the original CLT baseline of using language to learn it, or as Hatch (1978: 63) put it, "language learning evolves out of learning how to carry on conversations, out of learning how to communicate."

This brings us to the definition of 'task', the central concept in the TBLT-approach. As Table 17.1 illustrates, various definitions of 'task' have been proposed by different scholars over the past three decades, but all of them share a common core: a task is a goal-oriented activity that people undertake and that involves the meaningful use of language.

One fundamental question that proponents of task-based language teaching need to answer is how learners' attempts to *use* the language can be integrated with learners' (conscious or unconscious) attempts to *learn* a language. Don't people need to learn language first before they can use it? How can you use something that you have not learnt yet? How can you comprehend and/or produce previously unlearnt linguistic items? As studies of first language acquisition and language acquisition outside school indicate (cf. Ellis, 2008; Bavin, 2009), to pick up new words and expressions and unravel their meaning, language learners can be greatly aided by the extra-linguistic context in which the communicative activity is integrated, by the linguistic context in which linguistic items the learner is unfamiliar with are embedded, and by the interaction with their teacher and fellow-students. The latter may be supportive in many different ways (Mackey and Goo, 2007). For example, learners can negotiate the meaning of difficult words and expressions with their interlocutors; in a similar vein, interlocutors may negotiate the meaning that the second language learner is trying to convey, hence 'pushing' the output of the learner. Thus, teachers and peers may react to the learner's attempts at meaning-making in all kinds of supportive ways, for instance by recasting a non-target-like utterance in richer, more accurate, appropriate or adequate terms and in this way illustrating how the language works without interrupting the flow of the conversation. Or teachers may explicitly correct an error, scaffold learners' problem-solving

Table 17.1 Examples of definitions of 'task'

Long (1985: 89)	by 'task' is meant the hundred and one things people *do* in everyday life, at work, at play, and in between. 'Tasks' are the things people will tell you they do if you ask them and they are not applied linguists.
Prabhu (1987: 24)	an activity which required learners to arrive at an outcome from given information through some process of thought and which allowed teachers to control and regulate that process was regarded as a task.
Nunan (1989: 10)	a piece of classroom work which involves learners in comprehending, manipulating, producing or interacting in the target language while their attention is primarily focused on meaning rather than form.
Willis (1996: 23)	activities where the target language is used by the learner for a communicative purpose (goal) in order to achieve an outcome.
Bygate et al. (2001: 11)	an activity, influenced by learner choice, and susceptible to learner reinterpretation, which requires learners to use language, with emphasis on meaning, to attain an objective.
Ellis (2003: 16)	a workplan that requires learners to process language pragmatically in order to achieve an outcome that can be evaluated in terms of whether the correct or appropriate propositional content has been conveyed. To this end, it requires them to give primary attention to meaning and to make use of their own linguistic resources, although the design of the task may predispose them to choose particular forms. A task is intended to result in language use that bears a resemblance, direct or indirect, to the way language is used in the real world. Like other language activities, a task can engage productive or receptive, and oral or written skills, and also various cognitive processes.
Van den Branden (2006: 4)	A task is an activity in which a person engages in order to attain an objective, and which necessitates the use of language.

by prompting, or briefly provide metalinguistic information on how a particular grammar rule works while the learner is having trouble understanding or producing an utterance in which the rule is activated (see Mackey, Park and Tagarelli, this volume, for further discussion of error, feedback and repair).

From the above, it can be inferred that an explicit *focus on form* is an integral part of a task-based approach. TBLT is sometimes misunderstood as an approach that begins and ends with mere 'meaning-making', in which all instances of explicit, metalinguistic teaching are principally banned. However, this view is inconsistent with the basic principle that TBLT aims to be a research-based pedagogy (Van den Branden et al., 2009): it aims to dynamically respond to whatever research has to offer in terms of what works in the language classroom. The position of focus on form in the TBLT approach is a clear example of this: a considerable body of empirical evidence has built up over the past twenty years that indicates that explicit teaching aids language learning, particularly when it is skillfully integrated with the performance of holistic, situated, purposeful and meaningful activity (cf. Norris and Ortega, 2000; Ellis, 2008; Long, 2009; Collins and Marsden, this volume).

What does a task-based curriculum look like?

The discussion above thus suggests that the learners' language learning needs constitute the starting point for the development of a task-based curriculum. Most language learners aim or need to acquire the target language for functional purposes; consequently, their motivation to engage in classroom activity may be enhanced by linking classroom activity directly to the things they want to do with the target language in the outside world. Teachers may realise this link in different ways, such as incorporating authentic language material in the classroom, involving the students in negotiating the curriculum, working with semi-authentic tasks and using modern technology to give students real-life opportunities to use the language with native or expert speakers. Ideally, a fully developed TBLT programme would be structured via a full-blown needs analysis of the language tasks that learners need to be able to perform (Long, 2006; Norris, 2009).

Needs analyses are used to yield a list of essential *target tasks* which constitute the ultimate goals of the instructed language learning process in which the students are to engage. From the target tasks, a sequence of pedagogic tasks can be derived. Pedagogic tasks are more or less detailed scenarios ('workplans') for classroom activity which gradually present increasingly complex approximations of target tasks (Long, 1985; Long and Crookes, 1992). For example, second language learners enrolled in a L2 vocational course for immigrants aiming to find a job in administration who, amongst other things, need to develop the proficiency to place and handle all kinds of orders (e.g. through e-mail or telephone) may start out with a very simple version of the target ordering task. For instance, for a first stage, they might be asked to read a short written order from a customer for comprehension, and then to match the ordered items with pictures in a catalogue. In this early stage, students could be asked to do this task in pairs so that they can negotiate and support each other while performing it. Building on this basic task, all sorts of variations may follow in sequence, adding some degree of complexity pertaining to aspects such as the number and kinds of items that need to be ordered, the length and complexity of the message, the modality (written versus oral orders), the complexity of the situation (e. g. a wrong delivery that needs to be followed up), the interlocutors involved, the time pressure and so on. Meaning would be paramount throughout.

In the example above, learners work their way up from one task to the next. So, from the very beginning, classroom activity is task-*based;* however simple the vocabulary and grammatical structures involved in the first pedagogic tasks may be, students are still invited to exchange meaningful messages (i.e. comprehend and produce them themselves) in an attempt to reach a communicative solution and a (simulated or real) non-linguistic goal. In this approach to language learning, students not only acquire language *in order to* use language to reach functional goals, they also do so *while* trying to achieve those goals. In contrast to task-based approaches, a task-*supported* approach does not take 'task' as the central organising unit of classroom activity from beginning to end. In the latter case, tasks are integrated within classroom activity to complement language-focused classroom activity. For instance, learners may be presented with the rules for forming comparatives and superlatives in English, practise these rules in isolated sentences first, and then spend the final quarter of an hour performing a task in which they are asked to compare authentic advertisements to decide upon the best buy (Ellis, 2003).

Even though task-based classroom activity can take different shapes and guises, a number of influential pedagogical guides in the field have introduced a three-stage model which consists of pre-task activities, the actual task performance and post-task activities (e.g. Willis and Willis, 2007). During the *pre-task phase*, teachers and learners typically prepare the task performance cognitively, socio-emotionally and from an organisational point of view. From a cognitive perspective, the topic or non-linguistic goal is introduced, and the learners' prior knowledge (both content knowledge and useful linguistic knowledge) gets mobilised. In this stage, some teachers may ask students to rely on their own linguistic resources, while other teachers may present some vocabulary that will be useful or even crucial to perform the task at hand. From a socio-emotional point of view, the teacher will address students' interest and task motivation and may also want to encourage students to speak out, take risks while producing output, and signal their non-understanding when trying to comprehend input. From an organisational point of view, the teacher will need to give clear task instructions and, where appropriate, put the students in groups. During the stage of actual task performance, students will be working on the task individually, in pairs or in groups (or a combination of both) and will discuss task outcomes and task performance strategies and deal with any obstacles they may meet; this may happen via interim whole-class discussions or personalised teacher-learner interactions or within their pairs or groups. It is during this stage that interactional support serves the crucial functions of dealing with students' personal or shared misconceptions; responding to learners' form-focused and meaning-focused questions; providing learners with feedback on the quality of their ongoing work and monitoring their progress; encouraging students to keep up the good work or persevere when tasks are challenging; and maintain students' motivation, self-confidence, and task engagement. Finally, during the post-task phase, task outcomes will be reported and reviewed and task performance discussed as appropriate. Focus on form may be embedded in this stage, for instance when the teacher invites the students to practise specific rules or linguistic items that prominently featured in the tasks the learners performed.

In Table 17.2, two examples are given of task-based classroom activities that follow this three-stage structure. As both examples in the table show, task-based classroom work typically involves the integration of different skills. Students are invited to read articles, report back on them (orally or in written form) and discuss what they have read in groups, which entails listening and speaking, all during the same classroom activity. Task-based language teaching, then, is not necessarily compartmentalised the way more structure-based approaches to second/foreign language teaching tend to be, as, in real life, people also need to deploy different skills and knowledge in order to perform authentic tasks. In a similar vein, focus on form or strategies is integrated in the meaning-focused work. In a task-based syllabus, form follows function; explicit attention to form is primarily devoted to linguistic items that are deemed task-essential by the learner, by the teacher or both. While in a task-supported approach, tasks can still be used to practise the 'structure of the day', in a

Table 17.2 Examples of task-based classroom activity following a triadic component structure

Task 1: Safe passwords	Task 2: A new mobile phone?
Pre-task	*Pre-task*
• Students debate the features of safe Internet passwords with the teacher and share thoughts on why safe passwords are important. • The teacher puts preliminary answers on the board and invites students to sit in groups of four. • The groups are each given a text that describes one feature of a safe password.	• Students are shown a picture of a mobile phone with a broken glass screen and are told that this is how a phone they ordered online came out of the box upon delivery. They are told they will need to write a letter of complaint (by email) to the phone company. • In small groups, they debate the contents of this letter (what crucial information should be included?). • The groups are then given four samples of letters of complaint (relating to a similar, but different problem) and are asked to rank them according to their overall quality and effectiveness. The groups are asked to spell out the criteria they used.
Task performance: Information gap task	*Task performance: Writing a letter of complaint*
• Students read their texts in groups of four (a different text for each group). • Group members discuss the contents of their text because they will be invited to exchange this information with other groups (without being allowed to take their text with them). • Students regroup and are asked to exchange their information orally. They are shown five passwords, which they rank according to degree of safety. • Students create a new password for themselves and check it against the password safety criteria the group has used.	• Students now write the first draft of their letter (making use of the criteria they discussed in the previous stage). • Peers then provide feedback on drafts, and student revise letters accordingly. • At the end of the first session, the students hand second drafts to the teacher, after which the teacher discusses the criteria for good letters of complaints with the whole class. • After consensus has been reached, the teacher takes the drafts home and adds his/her own written feedback. During a second session, students revise their letters again and incorporate student and teacher feedback.
Post-task phase	*Post-task phase*
• Students summarise what they have learnt on the features of safe passwords, and reflect on the group work they have done and the contribution of individual group members. • Teacher provides follow-up activities that give students the opportunity to practise further specific vocabulary that featured in the articles they read.	• Students receive another set of letters of complaints (pertaining to another problem), and are asked to provide feedback and rank them according to their overall quality. During this stage, a focus on relevant language forms may be added.

task–based approach, primarily those structures are practised that play a vital role in the 'task of the day'.

In line with this, the assessment component of a task-based curriculum is built around the performance of tasks. What needs to be assessed in the first place is the extent to which learners are increasingly able to do functional things with language and to use language to reach all kinds of goals (Norris, 2009). Tasks, then, constitute the central unit of analysis not only for determining the goals of a curriculum (target tasks) and organising classroom activity (pedagogic tasks) but also for following, monitoring and evaluating learners' ongoing language development (assessment tasks). From this, it naturally follows that discrete-item tests (e.g. vocabulary tests measuring the knowledge of isolated words or tests measuring the explicit knowledge of particular grammar rules) are less informative than more holistic assessments in which learners are observed when performing communicative tasks. Besides formal test-taking situations, a wide range of instruments and procedures may be utilised for task-based assessment purposes, including observations of tasks-in-action (both inside and outside the classroom), peer- and self-assessment and portfolio assessment. Student rating will primarily focus on evaluating the extent to which the learner can perform the task to criterion and reach the intended goal rather than the students' ability to produce particular words or phrases. By comparing learners' performance of specific tasks with these same learners' performance of similar tasks or easier versions of the same task type, teachers can keep track of learners' language development. In other words, comparing learners with themselves may be more crucial than comparing learners with other learners (as is typically done in many classrooms around the world).

From a task-based perspective, formative assessment is as important as summative assessment. While summative assessment primarily serves to determine the students' current level of language proficiency, formative assessment aims to inform and support the learners' development, for instance by providing them with feedback on the basis of the assessment. In line with recent empirical research into the crucial value of feedback on learning processes (Hattie and Timperley, 2007; Hattie and Yates, 2014), feedback based on task-based assessment may provide learners with detailed insights into their current level of development and where they can move next; it may alert learners to misconceptions they have (e.g. about the meaning of particular words), systematic errors they make, particular strategies they fail to use and specific points of attention (for instance, with regard to the pragmatic use of particular expressions). In all of these cases, the feedback may also contain information about possible solutions to such problems or invite the students to try to come up with a solution themselves. Assessment, then, can (and should) do more for learners than merely inform them about the level they have reached and the class they will be allowed to enter next; assessment becomes more powerful as it feeds students' language learning process in a personalised, learner-tailored way. As such, it can add to learners' motivation by making their progress visible and by showing them how they can move from their current stage of development to the next.

Critical issues and points of debate

Sequencing tasks

One critical issue that designers of a task-based syllabus and teachers working with tasks need to address is the sequencing of tasks in the curriculum. As mentioned above, pedagogical tasks are increasingly complex approximations of target tasks; this, however, implies that the parameters that determine the relative complexity of pedagogical tasks can be identified and manipulated as required, and that theories of second language learning are sufficiently clear on the ways in which these parameters need to be manipulated to produce teaching sequences that are more or less in line with, or at least do not conflict with, developmental sequences (i.e. the order in which certain features of the language are acquired). However, determining the complexity of tasks constitutes a very complex puzzle in itself. To date, it is still largely unclear which particular task features are crucial in this respect, even if much of the recent research in the fields of applied linguistics, SLA research and language pedagogy which explicitly refers to task-based learning and/or teaching has been devoted to determining the relative impact of specific features of the task itself, the conditions under which tasks are performed on task complexity and the difficulty specific tasks pose to learners.

Based on the available empirical research, different theoretical frameworks have been proposed and put to the test, two of which have been particularly prominent over the past two decades: Robinson's 'cognition hypothesis' (Robinson, 2011) and Skehan's 'tradeoff hypothesis' (Skehan, 2014). Although these frameworks have been presented as diametrically opposed to each other, including by the authors themselves, they have a great deal in common: both mainly focus on the cognitive dimensions of tasks and primarily measure the impact of specific task features and task performance conditions on the fluency, accuracy and complexity of the output language learners produce. Robinson's and Skehan's models mainly differ in their view of the interplay between cognitive task features and the capacity of the learner's brain to handle task complexity (and the impact this has on learning trajectories). While Skehan emphasises that the learner's working memory capacity is limited, as a result of which a rise in task complexity will lead to loss of either accuracy, complexity or fluency, Robinson maintains that a trade-off need not be the case: manipulating the complexity of tasks may be expected to push learners' output and promote heightened attention to formal aspects of the target language. To date, however, the available research results are mixed. While the lists of factors that are included in Robinson's and Skehan's frameworks are long and the parameters are of a very diverse nature, the relative contribution of the different parameters remains unclear. Equally, the extent to which the relation between parameters (in determining task complexity) is stable across task types, for different types of learners and in different types of communicative contexts is still a matter of debate. In addition, it remains to be seen to what extent this research can be instructive for measuring the relative complexity of reception-based tasks (and sequencing them), the extent to which task complexity has a systematic impact on the way different types of learners perceive and approach different tasks, and how far the dimensions explored in this research can be systematically implemented in the design and use of tasks.

In this respect, it should also be noted that research has yet to take adequate account of the full range of dimensions involved in characterising language development. In particular, the focus on the impact of task features on the complexity, accuracy and fluency of students' output (commonly abbreviated as the CAF-measures) may reveal only a fragmented picture of what it takes to become better at using a language for functional purposes. In 'real life' outside the classroom, the output of second language learners will be evaluated along a wider range of dimensions than the CAF-measures used to date; moreover, these dimensions may differ depending on the context in which communicative activity takes place. For example, in real life, the sociolinguistic and pragmatic appropriateness of learners' output and the degree to which they can be understood by their interlocutor may have a far greater impact on the successful and smooth flow of communication, and hence on successful task performance, than the accuracy or complexity of the output that is produced. In a similar vein, learners' vocabulary reach (both in terms of understanding the words used by the interlocutor and producing context-appropriate vocabulary themselves) may have a strong impact on the degree to which tasks in real life are performed to criterion. In this respect, it should also be noted that second language learners' accuracy, fluency and complexity gains may be highly context- and genre-specific: while some learners may become able to perform tasks relating to a particular domain/genre increasingly better as they get ample opportunity to learn to do so, their performance in terms of accuracy, complexity and fluency may stabilise or fail to grow in other domains or genres that do not feature in the same learners' needs profiles.

Individual learner differences

This brings us to another critical issue in the task-based domain: the impact of individual learner differences on task-based learning. As can be inferred from the previous paragraph, in TBLT, the learner is prototypically addressed and identified as an active participant to task-based communication, as someone who deliberately sets out to reach a particular goal he or she finds intrinsically interesting and therefore launches into action. Even if the teacher is still a crucial participant in task performance in terms of organising classroom activity, interactionally supporting task-based work and assessing learners' development, the learners' agency is pivotal in TBLT. As a result, as in any approach, task-based language teaching will only have an effect on task-based learning to the extent that learners actively engage in task performance, participate in the task-based interaction and deploy the mental activity that results in the processing of information and, ultimately, in language development. Teachers cannot do the language learning *for* learners; similarly, tasks do not *cause* learning. Tasks may be powerful vehicles for the kind of mental processing that can lead to learning, but much will depend on the learner's willingness to engage in task performance and on learners' ability to deal with task exigencies. The implications of this insight are considerable: a wide range of learner-related variables, which researchers have barely begun to explore, enter into play and may shake up the basic view that particular types of tasks have systematic and relatively predictable effects on different learners' second language development (see Dörnyei, 2009, for an overview; also, MacIntyre, Gregersen and Clément's review of Individual Differences, this volume). Cognitive variables include (amongst others) the learner's memory and brain capacity, general knowledge, prior language knowledge (including the knowledge of other languages than the target language), IQ and preferred learning approach; socio-emotional variables include (amongst others) the learner's overall motivation to learn languages and the target language in particular, task motivation, self-confidence, well-being, relationship with the teacher and peers and language anxiety; other learner-related variables that should be taken into consideration include the learner's age, gender, prior educational background and socio-economic status. As recent research into learning processes amply show (Hattie and Yates, 2014), all of these have a potential impact on an individual's approach to learning tasks and, hence, on the learning that comes out of it. To date, however, there is very little research that illustrates how task-based work in second language classrooms is affected by these variables.

The implementation of TBLT in 'real' classrooms

Over the past three decades, a great number of teachers around the world have become acquainted with the basic principles of TBLT and have started to work with tasks in their classrooms; in many countries, tasks are now included in mainstream syllabuses, textbooks and handbooks. However, the available research on the implementation of TBLT in actual classrooms, which is still relatively limited (Van den Branden et al., 2009), clearly indicates that 'pure' forms of task-based language teaching are rare. In most cases, tasks have been integrated in eclectic, hybrid approaches which appear to present teachers with an acceptable mix of the traditional approaches they are familiar with and the innovations they are able, and willing, to digest (e.g. Van den Branden et al., 2007; East, 2012; Shehadeh and Coombe, 2012). In some regions, such as in parts of Southeast Asia, the actual implementation of TBLT proceeds with great difficulty, even though governments are trying to push the approach; the fact that the basic tenets of TBLT have been shown to clash with teachers' and learners' deeply ingrained beliefs about hierarchic teacher-learner relations in the classroom and the importance of explicit teaching and accuracy, and with the sheer size of most classes as well as the form-focus of the official exams that students need to prepare for, makes the implementation of a full-blown task-based approach to second and foreign language teaching extremely challenging (e.g. Carless, 2003; Shehadeh and Coombe, 2012). In fact, many of these factors also turn the implementation of TBLT in Western classrooms into a real challenge for many teachers.

All this boils down to the fact that the nature of an approach such as TBLT (like any other approach) is bound to be shaped by the people who choose to work with it. Tasks on paper are merely workplans. Once they enter into the hands of actual teachers, they become reinterpreted and reshaped to fit the latters' predispositions, capabilities, educational beliefs and established classroom practices. A growing body of empirical evidence (e.g. Van den Branden et al., 2007; East, 2012; Shehadeh and Coombe, 2012) vividly illustrates the myriad ways in which teachers and learners alike produce highly different versions of tasks-on-paper (as designed by syllabus designers), sometimes resulting in classroom activities that should be regarded more as manifestations of a grammar-based, explicit, teacher-dominated approach rather than a task-supported, let alone a task-based, form of language teaching. As argued by Van den Branden (2006), language teaching itself does not become task-based overnight simply by importing tasks into the classroom; neither do teachers become eager and/or proficient at using tasks to create powerful language learning environments just by being handed a task-based syllabus. As much as learners need interactional support to bridge the gaps between task demands and their current proficiency, teachers need to be supported while integrating tasks into their current approach. This support may take different shapes, but to support implementation in the classroom, it should preferably be as practice-based and teacher-oriented as possible, for, in the end, it is the teachers who are in the centre of this progressive dynamic. In their own schools, teachers can profit, for example, from team-teaching and discussing tasks (and task-based lessons) among each other, from videotaping themselves or being observed by/observing colleagues working with tasks, from asking students about their experiences with TBLT and from deliberating with colleagues about target tasks and task-based approaches to assessment. At regional and nation-wide levels, the availability of task-based syllabi, materials and assessment tools could make a crucial difference for teachers. In addition, more classroom-based research into the practice of TBLT is sorely needed. This could generate rich descriptions of task-based work and video clips that could inspire many teachers or even provide models they can learn from. Likewise, this kind of research could generate practice-based recommendations on how to work with tasks in specific kinds of classrooms.

In this respect, much of the available research into the classroom-based use of tasks shows the strong potential impact of working with tasks on second language acquisition. Not all of this research is subsumed under the explicit heading 'task-based', which may actually be considered an advantage in view of the fact that researchers who set out to prove the merits of the educational approach they favour in their pedagogically oriented writings tend to be distrusted by practitioners. In fact, much can be learnt nowadays from the 'evidence-based' approach to classroom-based research, as summarised by Hattie (2011) and Marzano et al. (2001), amongst others. The meta-analyses produced by these researchers, which are based on thousands of empirical studies, provide strong indications that a classroom approach that is centred around the performance of functional, motivating and challenging reading and writing tasks in which the explicit focus on reading and writing strategies and on particular linguistic forms is tightly embedded within a meaningful task has strong effects on the development of reading and writing skills. For the productive skills, feedback (in the shape of a varied repertoire of interactional moves and devices), embedded within the performance of complex tasks calling for higher reasoning and functional interaction, has been shown to be of crucial value to language learning; Hattie's empirical research provides ever-clearer indications of which types of feedback are most productive, and these are clearly in line with the results of available meta-analyses on the impact of interaction on second language learning (e.g. Mackey and Goo, 2007). In a similar vein, the importance of task repetition, as well as the fact that learning is cumulative and builds upon repeated, prolonged deliberate practice rather than being the result of one particular instance of task performance, is strongly supported by the empirical evidence summarised in the publications on evidence-based teaching mentioned above. On the whole, the evidence-based approach to classroom-based research strongly indicates that if higher-order, functional, holistic skills constitute the major goals of the curriculum, then learners should get ample opportunity to try and perform motivating, challenging (yet doable) and meaningful tasks that demand the application of the target skills. But, as mentioned above, to turn this into the kind of material that teachers can profit from, these research-based insights need to be translated into worked-out examples of tasks (preferably with annotations describing how certain research-based principles are at work), video recordings of teachers working with tasks and practice-based recommendations. It is high time we moved from meta-analyses of research to mega-banks of classroom data focusing on teachers working with tasks.

Future challenges

The conceptualisation, theoretical underpinning, research-based revision and refining, and the practical implementation of task-based language teaching can all be referred to as 'work-in-progress'. Though a large number of publications are now available which describe the basic principles of task-based language teaching (see this chapter's suggestions for further reading), TBLT, aiming to be a research-based approach to language teaching, is dynamic and, by definition, open to constant reinterpretation.

Clearly, current theory on second language learning and on the impact of formal education on learning, which underpins the pedagogical outlook of TBLT, is in need of further refinement. Though referring back to learning theories proposed by distinguished educationalists like Dewey and Vygotsky – which emphasise holistic learning, learner activity and meaningful interaction – theory regarding the exact relationship between tasks, learning and teaching still remains relatively vague. In essence, task-based language teaching is derived from a view of language learning that is largely based on the notions of *contingency* and *agency*. The first refers to the hypothesis that what learners learn (and can learn) is strongly contingent on the kind of exposure to language and language use they get (hence, explicit grammar knowledge does not automatically result in learners' competence to use the known grammar rule for communicative purposes, much as listening skills do not automatically transfer to speaking skills). Future research will need to inform our understanding of contingency in task-based work and, amongst other factors, the relative contribution of implicit and explicit learning processes. The second notion, agency, refers to the hypothesis that tasks do not cause learning but are useful vehicles for launching the agency of second language learners in the deliberate practice of communicative language use and verbal interaction and, in this process, engaging those conscious and unconscious attentional processes that lead to learning. Directly related to the notion of agency, the theory-building underpinning TBLT increasingly acknowledges the crucial importance of socio-emotional, cognitive, physical, affective and motivational learner characteristics (Verhelst, 2006; Long, 2015). The learner is the agent of his or her own learning, but it will take a considerable degree of further theorising (and research which empirically supports the theory) to get a firm grip on the relative impact of the many variables that are here at play.

In a similar vein, the development of task-based curricula, courses and materials present many challenges, some of which have been so poorly addressed (on a conceptual level) that just about anything that people do in a language classroom has been labelled 'a task'. Besides the issue of sequencing (noted earlier), many other questions besiege the task-based syllabus and course developer: how might teachers differentiate between learners during a task-based lesson? In which stage of the three-stage model is form-focus most effective? How might technology be integrated into the task-based classroom? To what extent should accuracy and the use of specific linguistic items be included in the grading rubrics of a task-based test?

Another huge challenge related to TBLT is the training of teachers. As inspiring and refreshing as task-based language teaching may seem to second language learners and many of their teachers, the actual implementation of TBLT will succeed only to the extent that it takes heed of practitioners' current educational beliefs and the context in which they are operating. The implementation of task-based language teaching should be duly acknowledged as a task for teachers, one many teachers may find intrinsically motivating and challenging but one that they should also consider as doable, rewarding (both for themselves and their students) and effective.

A major challenge underlying these challenges at the theoretical, conceptual and practical level is the accumulation of practice-based and practice-oriented research that documents what teachers and learners actually do with tasks in their classrooms, what the learners ultimately learn from them and which variables have the greatest effect on the impact of the classroom work on the learning. As much as form follows function in TBLT theory, theory-building follows practice and research, at least if we have the latter at our disposal.

Conclusion

Task-based language learning is an exciting, motivating, communicative and interactive approach to language learning. Because of their holistic nature, tasks can be used as educational tools to create learning opportunities in which the full complexity of language use may be experienced in real operating conditions and in which interactional work built up around shared, goal-directed projects offers rich affordances for exploring how language forms can be used to create meaningful messages that serve the pursuit of social/functional goals. Future research may, it is hoped, further document the strengths and weaknesses of the approach. Ultimately, however, the effectiveness of task-based language education relies upon the extent to which it allows and supports learners to learn to do the things with language that matter in their personal lives outside the classroom.

Discussion questions

- Do you believe task-based language teaching is possible from the very beginner stages of language acquisition?
- Do you think task-based language teaching is an effective approach for all language learners?
- Do you think task-based language teaching is a feasible approach for all teachers?

Related topics

Cognitive perspectives on classroom language learning; Communicative language teaching in theory and practice; Errors, corrective feedback and repair.

Further reading

Ellis, R. (2003) *Task-based language learning and teaching.* Oxford: Oxford University Press. (This volume provides a good overview of the principles underpinning TBLT and the empirical research supporting them.)

Samuda, V. and Bygate, M. (2008) *Tasks in second language learning.* London: Palgrave. (This volume contains reports of studies exploring both the theory and the practice of TBLT.)

Van den Branden, K. (ed.) (2006) *Task-based language education: From theory to practice.* Cambridge: Cambridge University Press. (This volume describes the implementation of TBLT in Flanders and vividly illustrates how TBLT takes shape in authentic syllabi and classrooms.)

Van den Branden, K., Bygate, M. and Norris, J. M. (eds) (2009) *Task-based language teaching: A reader.* Amsterdam: John Benjamins. (This volume compiles all major influential articles on TBLT published between 1985 and 2008.)

Willis, J. and Willis, D. (2007) *Doing task-based teaching: A practical guide to task-based teaching for ELT training courses and practising teachers.* Oxford: Oxford University Press. (This volume offers teachers a lot of practice-based advice on how to work with tasks in the classroom.)

References

Bavin, E. (2009) *Cambridge handbook of child language.* Cambridge: Cambridge University Press.

Brumfit, C. J. and Johnson, K. (ed.) (1979) *The communicative approach to language teaching.* Oxford: Oxford University Press.

Bygate, M., Skehan, P. and Swain, M. (2001) *Researching pedagogic tasks: Second language learning, teaching and testing.* Harlow: Longman.

Carless, D. (2003) Factors in the implementation of task-based teaching in primary schools. *System, 31.* 485–500.

Dörnyei, Z. (2009) *The psychology of second language acquisition.* Oxford: Oxford University Press.

East, M. (2012) *Task-based language teaching from the teachers' perspective.* Amsterdam: Benjamins.

Ellis, R. (2003) *Task-based language learning and teaching.* Oxford: Oxford University Press.

Ellis, R. (2008) *The study of second language acquisition.* Oxford: Oxford University Press.

Hatch, E. (1978) 'Discourse analysis and second language acquisition', in E. Hatch (ed.) *Second language acquisition: A book of reading.* Rowley, MA: Newbury House.

Hattie, J. (2011) *Visible learning for teachers: Maximizing impact on learning.* London: Routledge.

Hattie, J. and Timperley, H. (2007) The power of feedback. *Review of Educational Research, 77/1.* 81–112.

Hattie, J. and Yates, G. (2014) *Visible learning and the science of how we learn.* London: Routledge.

Long, M. (1985) 'A role for instruction in second language acquisition: Task-based language teaching', in K. Hylstenstam and M. Pienemann (eds) *Modelling and assessing second language acquisition.* Clevedon: Multilingual Matters. 77–99.

Long, M. (2006) *Second language needs analysis.* Cambridge: Cambridge University Press.

Long, M. (2009) Methodological principles for language teaching. In M. H. Long and C. J. Doughty (eds) *Handbook of language teaching.* Oxford: Blackwell. 373–394.

Long, M. (2015) *Second language acquisition and task-based language teaching.* Chicester: Wiley.

Long, M. and Crookes, G. (1992) 'Three approaches to task-based syllabus design'. *TESOL Quarterly, 26.* 27–56.

Mackey, A. and Goo, J. (2007) 'Interaction research in SLA: A meta-analysis and research synthesis', in A. Mackey (ed.) *Conversational interaction in second language acquisition.* Oxford: OUP. 407–452.

Marzano, R., Pickering, D. and Pollock, J. (2001) *Classroom instruction that works.* Alexandria, USA: ASCD.

Norris, J. M. (2009) 'Task-based teaching and testing', in M. Long and C. Doughty (eds) *Handbook of language teaching.* Cambridge: Blackwell. 578–594.

Norris, J. and Ortega, L. (2000) 'Effectiveness of L2 instruction: A research synthesis and quantitative meta-analysis'. *Language Learning, 50.* 417–528.

Nunan, D. (1989) *Designing tasks for the communicative classroom.* Cambridge: Cambridge University Press.

Pica, T. (1987) Second language acquisition, social interaction, and the classroom. *Applied Linguistics, 8.* 1–25.

Prabhu, N. (1987) *Second language pedagogy.* Oxford: Oxford University Press.

Robinson, P. (ed.) (2011) *Second language task complexity: Researching the cognition hypothesis of language learning and performance.* Amsterdam: John Benjamins.

Shehadeh, A. and Coombe, C. (2012) *Task-based language teaching in foreign language contexts.* Amsterdam: Benjamins.

Skehan, P. (ed.) (2014) *Processing perspectives on task performance.* Amsterdam: John Benjamins.

Van den Branden, K. (ed.) (2006) *Task-based language education: From theory to practice.* Cambridge: Cambridge University Press.

Van den Branden, K., Bygate, M. and Norris, J. M. (eds) (2009) *Task-based language teaching: A reader.* Amsterdam: John Benjamins.

Van den Branden, K., Van Gorp, K. and Verhelst, M. (eds) (2007) *Tasks in action: Task-based language education from a classroom-based perspective*. Cambridge: Cambridge Scholars Publishing.

Verhelst, M. (2006) 'Task-based language education: From theory to practice', in K. Van den Branden (ed.) *Task-based language education: From theory to practice*. Cambridge: Cambridge University Press. 197–216.

Widdowson, H. G. (1978) *Teaching language as communication*. Oxford: Oxford University Press.

Willis, J. (1996) *A framework for task-based learning*. Essex: Longman.

Willis, J. and Willis, D. (2007) *Doing task-based teaching: A practical guide to task-based teaching for ELT training courses and practising teachers*. Oxford: Oxford University Press.

18

Content and language integrated learning

Tom Morton

Introduction

This chapter provides an overview of content and language integrated learning (CLIL) which aims to enable readers to assess for themselves its relevance to the field of ELT. The chapter is organised into four main sections, focusing respectively on the 'what', 'why', 'who' and 'how' of this approach to language education. The 'what' of CLIL takes in its origins and history and defines its key characteristics in relation to similar approaches, such as immersion, content-based instruction (CBI) and English-medium instruction (EMI); CLIL is used as an umbrella term to identify a variety of pedagogical approaches to integrating content and language rather than a label for identifying particular programmes or a single approach. The 'why' of CLIL covers a range of current theoretical issues and debates: the focus on 'pluriliteracies'; arguments for CLIL based on second language acquisition (SLA) research and communicative language teaching (CLT); the balance between language and content outcomes in CLIL research; methodological issues in CLIL research and the dangers of elitism; and multilingual approaches to CLIL. The 'who' focuses on CLIL teachers. Then, moving on to the 'how' of CLIL, practical issues of classroom teaching, assessment, resources and materials are addressed. The chapter concludes with implications and challenges for ELT raised by the issues and debates surrounding CLIL.

What is CLIL? Historical overview and defining terms

Historical developments

CLIL, in its origins, was a specifically European phenomenon. Although related to, and drawing inspiration from, other approaches to bilingual education such as immersion in Canada, the development of CLIL can be seen against the backdrop of European language policies which promoted multilingualism as a way of both celebrating diversity and building a common European identity. According to Dalton-Puffer et al. (2014), when the acronym was coined by participants in transnational European projects in the mid-1990s, the fact that it was seen as new, a-historical and value-free was seen as advantageous in encouraging policy makers to expand multilingual education. It was hoped that bringing together content and language learning would introduce fresh approaches to 'traditional' foreign language teaching (i.e. foreign languages as a 'subject', often with a focus on grammar) and stimulate pedagogical innovation in other subject areas (ibid.: 214). Around this time, there was also an increase in grass-roots classroom activity, with enthusiasts at the local level starting to teach curricular content through foreign languages on a small scale. For example, in the UK, a geography teacher with good French skills might volunteer to teach the whole subject, or a few topics, in French.

By the early 2000s, CLIL was attracting policy makers' attention, with EU policy documents mentioning it as a way of promoting language learning and language diversity. However, CLIL provision in Europe remains very uneven and variable, with some countries taking it up as a matter of national education policy and others leaving it more to local initiative. For example, Sylvén (2013), points out that Spain and Finland have more structured CLIL provision, more developed teacher education programmes and more research activity than Germany and Sweden. In Spain, many regional governments have well-developed bilingual education programmes, in which the subjects taught, the curriculum time devoted to content taught in foreign and regional languages, and the language requirements of teachers are stipulated by official policy. In Sweden, as Sylvén (2013) points out, CLIL is not mentioned in any official policy documents at national level, and no specific level of language proficiency for teachers is required.

Interest in CLIL has recently been gathering pace outside Europe, and it is thus becoming a global phenomenon. In Asia, CLIL initiatives have been reported from primary to tertiary level in such countries as Japan (Yamano, 2013), Taiwan (Yang and Gosling, 2014) and Turkey (Bozdoğan and Karlidağ, 2013). In Latin America, CLIL sections are being included in ELT textbooks for use in secondary schools in Argentina (Banegas, 2014). However, some researchers, such as Turner (2013) in Australia, point out the need to subject CLIL to similar levels of scrutiny as in Europe before introducing it to non-European contexts. Yang and Gosling (2014) suggest that, in Asian contexts, there should be cross-cultural comparison studies to investigate students' expectations and attitudes towards CLIL and whether educational authorities have to deal with universal or local difficulties in implementing CLIL in their respective settings.

Defining CLIL

Coyle et al. (2010: 1) define CLIL as "a dual-focused educational approach in which an additional language is used for the learning and teaching of both content *and* language" (italics in original). Georgiou (2012) claims that it is the "dual focus" that distinguishes CLIL from other approaches, which either use content to support language learning or simply use a foreign language as a medium of instruction, with no focus on language. However, debates about CLIL have been bedeviled by confusion about its essential characteristics and the extent to which it is the same as or different from other approaches to content and language integration, and even to language teaching in general. For example, Mehisto et al. (2008: 12) claim that CLIL can include 'language showers' (i.e. short bursts of exposure to L2 for children, often through songs, games etc.), student exchanges, camps, local projects, work-study abroad and a range of types of immersion. As Cenoz et al. (2014: 4) point out, such a broad definition is problematic, as "... the possible forms that CLIL can take are so inclusive that it is difficult to think of any teaching or learning activity in which an L2/foreign language would be used that could not be considered CLIL".

Thus, Lasagabaster and Sierra (2010), for example, argue that there are clear differences between CLIL and immersion programmes, whether in the Canadian context or for the teaching of minority languages in Europe. These differences relate to the role of the language of instruction (which is a foreign language in CLIL, but a second language in immersion); teachers ('native' in immersion, 'non-native' in CLIL – see Llurda, this volume, for discussion of these complicated terms); learners (CLIL learners start later); materials (the same as those for native speakers in immersion, but adapted in CLIL); language outcomes (native speaker competence as the target in immersion, whilst this is not an expectation in CLIL); immigrant students (who may be excluded from CLIL programmes); and research (more research has been undertaken in immersion contexts than in CLIL) (Lasagabaster and Sierra, 2010: 4–7).

However, Cenoz et al. (2014) and Somers and Surmont (2012) argue that there may in fact be more similarities than differences between what are labelled 'CLIL' and 'immersion' programmes. For example, Somers and Surmont point out that immersion students, like CLIL students, may not have much contact with the language of instruction (for example, in Canada, English speakers may not interact much with speakers of French). Additionally, in terms of language outcomes, Cenoz et al. show that some European CLIL programmes (for example, in Sweden and the Netherlands) set very high standards for achievement, while some immersion programmes for majority language students in Canada (French), the USA (Spanish) and Japan (English) do not aim for native-like proficiency but expect students to attain advanced levels of functional proficiency (Cenoz et al., 2014: 7). Llinares and Lyster (2014), in a comparative study of corrective feedback in two immersion contexts (French and Japanese immersion) and one European CLIL context, found that the Japanese immersion classrooms had more in common with the CLIL classrooms than with the French immersion contexts.

Similar arguments can also be made regarding another commonly-used label for programmes which integrate content and language, content-based instruction (CBI). CBI has a long tradition in the United States and can be applied to a wide range of programme types, such as sheltered ESL classes (in which content is delivered to English language learners in ways that is more accessible to them), various types of bilingual programmes in which learners receive instruction in their primary language (see Carroll and Combs, this volume), immersion programmes and theme-based foreign language teaching (Tedick and Wesely, 2015). Cenoz (2015a) proposes that CBI and CLIL programmes are essentially the same as each other in terms of the use of an L2 as a medium of instruction, their linguistic, social and educational aims, and the types of learners. She argues that preferring one term over another is a question of contextual or accidental considerations.

Another commonly used term is English-medium instruction (EMI), which is often associated with the use of English as the language of schooling in Outer Circle countries such as Malaysia, Hong Kong and Singapore, where English is a second language (see Seargeant, this volume, for further discussion of the Inner, Outer and Expanding Circle terminology). It is also frequently used to refer to the use of English as a medium of instruction in tertiary education worldwide (Smit and Dafouz, 2012). In primary and secondary education in Expanding Circle countries (i.e. where English is a foreign language), the preferred term is CLIL, as in the studies cited above in Japan, Taiwan and Turkey. CLIL can be distinguished from EMI in that EMI refers solely to the teaching of content through the medium of English, without implying that there is any 'dual focus' on content and language. However, EMI is relevant to CLIL in that English is by far the language most used in CLIL programmes globally, with Dalton-Puffer et al. (2010) suggesting that CEIL (content and English integrated learning) might be a more appropriate acronym. Graddol (2006) identified CLIL (along with teaching English to young learners and English as an international language) as one of the key future trends for the teaching and learning of English throughout the world.

It can be seen, then, that there are many overlapping features of approaches which are labelled in different ways. Thus, as Dalton-Puffer (2011) points out, whether a specific programme is labelled 'immersion' or 'CLIL' is often more dependent on cultural and political issues than on any of its actual features. Cenoz et al. (2014) highlight the dangers of erecting boundaries between CLIL and other approaches such as immersion and CBI, as this may lead

CLIL to cut itself off from the possibility of learning from and exchanging ideas with other approaches. They propose that, rather than attempting to isolate CLIL, it may be better to see it as an umbrella term which covers a wide range of approaches in which language and content teaching are combined. This would suggest avoiding the use of the acronym CLIL to refer to programme types, or, as Paran (2013) argues, to refrain from seeing CLIL as a policy and to see it as a pedagogy. In this view, CLIL would be seen as a set of pedagogical approaches and options for combining content and second/foreign language instruction which could inform, and be descriptive of, the range of specific programme types discussed in this section and throughout the chapter. This is the approach taken in this chapter, with the discussion focusing on theoretical and pedagogical issues relating to the integration of content and language, with examples being drawn from a range of contexts, irrespective of whether they label themselves as CLIL, immersion, CBI or EMI.

Why (not) CLIL? Current critical issues and debates

This section examines current critical issues and topics in CLIL theory and research. These are: subject-specific literacies and SLA-informed approaches to CLIL; CLIL research on language and content learning outcomes; methodological shortcomings in some CLIL research and the danger of elitism; and the 'multilingual turn' in CLIL.

Subject-specific literacies and SLA-informed approaches

Recent work in CLIL has focused on the need to take into account the specificities of developing literacy across languages in different academic subjects and schooling in general. Meyer et al. (2015) argue that CLIL needs to develop a sound theory for integrating content and language. They propose a 'pluriliteracies' approach, which refers to learners' ability to use language in combination with other modes of communication (e.g. visual, graphic) to think, write and talk about subject-specific concepts and knowledge in ways that conform to the expected purposes and organisation of communication in these subjects. In this view, 'language' cannot be seen as separate from literacy skills across languages (hence *pluri*literacies) through which learners consume and produce the written and spoken texts through which subject knowledge and skills are construed. A pluriliteracies approach builds on and refines earlier distinctions between 'everyday' types of communication and more specialised types required for academic study, particularly Cummins' (1979) distinction between BICS (basic interpersonal communicative skills) and CALP (cognitive academic language proficiency; see also Carroll and Combs, this volume). Rather than seeing these as separate and sequential, this approach highlights the need to support learners in making connections between everyday and academic oral and written language (and other modes) in both their primary language(s) and the CLIL language of instruction.

Researchers taking this subject-literacies perspective often draw on systemic functional linguistics (SFL – Halliday and Matthiessen, 2013), which, rather than seeing language as an abstract formal system, links grammar, vocabulary and text type to the content activities learners and teachers are involved in. A key concept in SFL is that of genre – broadly, the text-types through which academic knowledge is expressed and accessed. Llinares et al. (2012) provide descriptions of key genres used in commonly taught subjects in CLIL, such as science and history, with guidance on how CLIL teachers and learners can be made more aware of their characteristics. Also within this 'integrative' perspective, Dalton-Puffer (2013) identifies 'cognitive discourse functions' (CDFs), which refer to verbalisations of cognitive processes such as defining, classifying and explaining as recurring linguistic patterns during classroom interaction. Identifying and teaching these patterns enables the integration of linguistic objectives in CLIL with the cognitive processes at the heart of knowledge construction across academic subjects.

Turning to approaches based on SLA research, two main issues can be discerned: the extent to which interaction in CLIL classrooms provides an environment for the development of communicative competence and the need to include focus on form in meaning-focused interaction. Dalton-Puffer (2007: 3) points out that CLIL is considered by enthusiastic advocates as the 'ultimate dream' of communicative language teaching (see Thornbury, this volume) and task-based learning (see Van den Branden, this volume) 'rolled into one', as the tasks are provided by the content activities and texts and content learning provides the context for meaning-focused language use. However, Dalton-Puffer's own research on Austrian CLIL classrooms does not paint such a rosy picture. In these classrooms, there was dominance of the IRF pattern (Initiation-Response-Feedback, in which teachers ask known-answer questions, students respond, teacher gives feedback on the answer), which led to a rather impoverished environment for the students to produce language. Dalton-Puffer (2009) suggests the need for a 'reality check' regarding the benefits of CLIL classrooms for developing communicative competence, arguing that, in most respects, CLIL classrooms are just like EFL or any other type of classroom, with relatively limited affordances for the expression and development of a broad range of communicative functions.

Turning to 'focus on form', there is a broad consensus that meaning-focused communication around academic content alone is not sufficient to move learners towards target-like performance. Furthermore, much research on CLIL contexts suggests that a language focus, where it exists, tends to be brief and incidental to the main business of working with content-related meanings. For example, Pérez-Vidal (2007), in a study of primary and secondary CLIL classrooms in Catalonia, found virtually no focus on language forms in the teachers' input to the learners. When form-focused instruction does appear, it is often limited to lexis or pronunciation, with little or no focus on grammar. For example, in a higher education context, Costa (2012) found that the focus was almost always on lexis, and even this was dealt with superficially. In order to redress this imbalance, Lyster (2007) proposes a 'counterbalanced' approach in which learners have their attention directed to linguistic features that they might not otherwise notice while they are engaged in content-learning activities.

Language and content outcomes in CLIL research

Despite the reservations outlined above, in terms of L2 learning outcomes, CLIL research has generally reported positive findings. Lorenzo et al.'s (2010) evaluation of a large CLIL programme in Andalusia found that primary and secondary pupils outperformed their non-CLIL peers in speaking, listening, reading and writing, as well as showing gains in the structural variety of language use and discourse features typical of academic language. Ruiz de Zarobe's (2011) review of research on CLIL learners' L2 proficiency outcomes suggests that CLIL benefits reading, listening, receptive vocabulary, oral fluency, fluency and complexity in writing, some areas of morphology and affective outcomes. However, the findings are less positive on syntactical development, productive vocabulary, informal (non-technical) language, accuracy and discourse skills in writing and pronunciation (degree of foreign accent).

However, CLIL research's emphasis on L2 as opposed to content learning outcomes has been criticised by Cenoz et al. (2014), who argue that the focus on ESL/EFL results leads to a neglect of outcomes in subject domains such as maths and science. In one of the relatively few studies on content learning outcomes in CLIL, Jäppinen (2005) found that Finnish science and mathematics students taught through English, French or Swedish achieved levels of thinking and content learning similar to those taught in L1 Finnish, with the 10–14 age group showing, at times, even faster development than those taught in L1. However, in a Spanish context, Anghel et al. (2012) provide evidence that primary pupils studying content in English, and whose parents were not educated to upper secondary level, performed worse in content learning than peers with similar characteristics who studied in Spanish. The picture regarding content learning through CLIL thus remains unclear.

Methodological issues in CLIL research and the danger of elitism

Research into CLIL, however, has been criticised by Bruton (2011), who identifies methodological and design problems which, he argues, compromise the positive results claimed. He reinterprets the results of studies which reported positive outcomes for CLIL students, highlighting four problematic areas: (1) researcher interest may bias the interpretation of results; (2) some studies are very limited, with results questionable in terms of pretesting, sampling and (lack of) observation data on actual instruction; (3) in most of the studies, the non-CLIL groups start out as less proficient, and possibly less motivated, with the CLIL groups attracting the 'best' students; (4) thus, the rather narrow advantages reported for CLIL students are not very promising, given that the CLIL students typically start off with higher levels of attainment and motivation. In relation to point (3), Bruton raises the important issue of the possibility of elitism in CLIL, particularly in the selection of pupils for bilingual streams. In a later paper (Bruton, 2013), he points out that, in spite of claims about egalitarianism in CLIL, there is evidence that there is selection of pupils into CLIL programmes who are more motivated and from families with a higher socio-economic status than students who remain in 'mainstream' ELT classes.

The 'multilingual turn' and CLIL

According to May (2014), the field of ELT has been marked by a 'monolingual bias', which treats the acquisition of an additional language as "an ideally hermetic process uncontaminated by knowledge and use of one's other languages" (p. 2). This has also been the case in some CLIL programmes in English, in which there has been a separation of languages at both curriculum and classroom levels through an 'English-only' policy. However, there are clear signs that CLIL, at least at the research level, is becoming more and more a part of what May calls 'the multilingual turn'. In a discussion of content-based education in Hong Kong, Cenoz (2015b) argues that there has been a paradigm shift away from a monolingual perspective which isolates the target language, sees the aim of language learning as emulating the native speaker and pays very little attention to language learners' existing linguistic repertoires.

A key concept in the new multilingual paradigm is that of 'translanguaging', which "refers both to pedagogical strategies that use two or more languages and to spontaneous discursive practices with shifting boundaries between languages" (Cenoz, 2015b: 348; see also Carroll and Combs, Pennycook, and Simpson, this volume). CLIL teachers can use translanguaging deliberately as a pedagogic strategy, such as having students read a text in one language and write/talk about it in another, and/or they can encourage/allow students to express multilingual identities through spontaneous use of the resources they have available to them. An example of the former approach is that of Lin (2015), who advocates an approach to CLIL which "allows for the planning of systematic and functional use of L1 and L2 in different stages and phases of the learning process" (p. 83). She proposes a "Multimodalities/Entextualization Cycle" consisting of three stages, each involving use of L1 and L2, and communication in a range of non-language modes. In the first stage, learners are provided with a rich experience in various modes (video, demonstrations, discovery activities) and encouraged to think, talk, inquire and read about the topic using everyday (non-academic) language in L1 and L2. In the second stage, the students read an L2 academic text on the topic and are encouraged to 'unpack' it by using everyday language in their L1 and L2, combined with other modes, for example by producing mind maps, visuals, description, story-boards or comics. In the third stage, learners are asked to 'entextualise' the experience by producing L1 or L2 academic genres relating to the topic (e.g. explanation, experimental design, description of procedure) and scaffolded with language support such as writing frames, prompts etc.

The 'who' of CLIL: characteristics and needs of teachers

While a focus on CLIL learners and learning may be implicit in the preceding discussions, it is only relatively recently that there has been an explicit focus on CLIL teachers, with an increase in studies investigating the identities, beliefs, knowledge and training needs of teachers who teach academic content in L2. In a secondary CLIL vocational education programme in Austria, Hüttner et al. (2013) found that the content teachers saw themselves as experts in their subjects but as co-learners with their students of the language used for teaching the subject, English. Tan (2011) found that Malaysian maths and science teachers who taught their subjects in English held beliefs about the roles of language in their subject teaching which often prevented them from focusing productively on language in their classes. And Cammarata and Tedick (2012), in a North American immersion context, describe how content teachers struggle to balance content and language, arguing that achieving such a balance entails a transformation from seeing oneself as purely a content teacher to embracing an identity as a teacher responsible for students' content and language learning.

Cammarata and Tedick point out that content teachers struggle to balance content and language because they lack sufficient knowledge about language and its roles in content teaching and learning, and they claim that current teacher training provision fails to equip them with this knowledge. One study in a US content-based teacher training context (Baecher et al., 2014) found that trainee teachers were able to write clear content objectives in their lesson plans but were less successful in identifying appropriate language objectives, which were often too broad and general and not focused at the level of individual lessons. This resonates with a survey of CLIL teachers' training needs in Europe, in which Pérez-Cañado (2014) found that the most pressing needs were not for the development of their linguistic or intercultural competence but for improved understanding of theoretical underpinnings of CLIL and ongoing professional development and, to a lesser extent, training in methodology and access to materials and resources.

The 'how' of CLIL: teaching, assessment and materials

Having dealt with aspects of the 'what', 'why' and 'who' of CLIL, this section now turns to the 'how' and examines a range of practical issues and options. These are: methodological guidelines for teaching in CLIL, approaches to assessment, and materials and resources.

Methodological options in CLIL

As Coyle et al. (2010: 86) point out, there is "no single CLIL pedagogy", and it is the "effective-practice pedagogies associated with individual subjects" that should guide CLIL teachers. This means that the main task for CLIL subject teachers is to adapt their subject teaching pedagogies to the reality of using a second/foreign language as a medium of instruction. Coyle and her colleagues have developed the '4Cs framework', in which the Cs stand for content (subject matter), communication (language learning and using), cognition (learning and thinking processes) and culture (developing intercultural understanding and global citizenship) (Coyle et al., 2010: 41). They point out that, while content should drive the overall planning of a teaching unit, there should be an integration of all 4Cs.

Within 'communication' in the 4Cs approach, there is a 'language triptych', consisting of the 'language *of* learning', 'language *for* learning' and 'language *through* learning' (Coyle et al., 2010: 36). The 'language of learning' is the language needed for the expression of content-related concepts and knowledge, including subject-specific terminology. 'Language for learning' is used by learners to participate in classroom activity, for example by asking questions, giving opinions, explaining or defining. 'Language through learning' emerges during the learning process as learners engage in cognitively demanding activities and explore new areas of meaning and is thus by definition unlikely to be predictable in advance. This framework enables content teachers to think about the language involved in teaching content topics.

An important construct underpinning CLIL pedagogy is that of 'scaffolding', that is, the actions taken by more expert others (often teachers) to provide temporary support for learners in carrying out tasks which may be just beyond them so that they can later do them on their own. A scaffolding approach to CLIL, then, entails not watering down the academic content but providing support for learners to access this content through the target language. An example of this approach is that of Dale and Tanner (2012), who provide a structure for implementing CLIL which supports teachers with activities divided into six different areas: activating, guiding understanding, focus on language, focus on speaking, focus on writing, and assessment, review and feedback. While respecting the pedagogic aims and cultures of different subjects (their book includes specific sections on subjects such as art, design and technology, business studies, geography, history and ICT), the activities have in common an emphasis on an imaginative, engaging and hands-on approach.

A scaffolding approach to CLIL pedagogy emphasises providing graphic and visual support for learners in dealing with new concepts in an unfamiliar language. Guerrini (2009) suggests that such scaffolding can be provided by the use of illustrations with labels and captions; explicit teaching about content area text types (genres), vocabulary and language; the use of graphic organisers such as charts, tables and diagrams; and the use of ICT. Bentley (2010), in a course for CLIL teachers, also emphasises the use of multi-media and visual organisers in supporting learners with the language demands of CLIL activities. Another aspect of scaffolding is providing learners with explicit support for the language demands of specific activities, particularly with texts that they may have to read and/or produce. Chadwick (2012) offers tools to help teachers develop language awareness to enable them to support their learners in meeting the language demands of content learning in subjects such as history, geography and science. For example, one activity helps teachers to distinguish between vocabulary items which require explicit teaching and those which learners can cope with by themselves, or can be safely ignored.

Assessment in CLIL

As in any educational context, three main questions arise in considering assessment in CLIL: the 'what' (i.e. content and/or language), the 'how' (i.e. which assessment methods are most suitable for CLIL contexts) and the 'when' (i.e. during and/or at the end of a teaching unit). In terms of the 'what', CLIL teachers are often uncertain about whether they should assess language as well as content, what aspects of language should be assessed and whether learners can be assessed in their L1 on content learned through an L2. Bentley (2010) suggests that CLIL teachers and curriculum planners need to decide which learning outcomes they want to focus on, and these can include not only content and language but communicative and cognitive skills (three of the 4Cs in Coyle et al.'s framework) and attitudes to learning. One way to ensure clarity of focus in assessment is to design rubrics, which are grids or matrices which include the criteria for content and language assessment (or any other areas that are the focus of assessment). These can be produced at the beginning of the teaching/learning process and used as guides to monitor progress and as tools for assessing learning outcomes at the end. Dale and Tanner (2012: 236) propose that CLIL learners themselves can be involved in brainstorming criteria to include in a rubric. They give an example of a rubric for assessing an oral presentation on a history topic divided into three columns: subject-specific criteria (e.g. correct information on dates and events), language criteria for speaking (e.g. intonation, word stress, correct grammar and fluency) and task-specific (presentation) criteria (visual support, eye contact, audience involvement).

Turning to the 'how' of assessment in CLIL, Coyle et al. (2010: 130) argue that "content knowledge should be assessed using the simplest form of language which is appropriate for that purpose". Generally, the key principle is that a wide range of assessment tools should be used to prevent language issues from becoming a barrier to the expression of content skills and understanding. Assessment in CLIL should align with the teaching, in that the types of scaffolding used to support CLIL learners in accessing content learning (e.g. visual organisers, a wide range of hands-on activities) should be reflected in the assessment tools used. Dale and Tanner (2012) suggest that, in addition to written assignments, other forms of assessment such as oral presentations or drawings can be used to show understanding.

As for the 'when' of assessment in CLIL, there is increasing interest in assessment *for* learning (assessment which is intended to boost performance during learning), as opposed to assessment *of* learning (the measurement of what learners know and can do at the end of a learning experience) (Black and Wiliam, 1998). Dale and Tanner (2012) point out that assessment for learning is particularly important in CLIL, in that teachers can develop both formal and informal assessments that develop both content and language, for example by asking learners to make authentic products such as brochures and posters. Such activities provide opportunities to both introduce the content and language objectives identified at the beginning of the unit and to assess the extent to which learners are able to cope with both.

Materials in CLIL

Moore and Lorenzo (2007) observed that there was a 'dearth' of commercially produced CLIL textbooks, and Coyle et al. (2010) report CLIL teachers mentioning the lack of readily available resources and therefore the need to find and create their own materials. However, the situation may be changing, at least for CLIL in English, as more and more CLIL materials for specific subjects are appearing. However, in spite of the growing availability of CLIL-specific textbooks and resources in some contexts, CLIL teachers do express a number of concerns about finding, using and creating materials. Morton (2013), in a study of European CLIL teachers' perceptions about materials, found that the most frequently mentioned concern was their appropriateness for learners, in terms of both cognitive and linguistic content. The second concern was the design of the materials, with many teachers expressing a desire for more graphic and visual support. Other concerns were the increased workload involved in finding, selecting and designing materials, and the suitability and match of the materials with the local educational context and its curricular aims.

Another related trend is the inclusion of 'CLIL' sections in commercially produced ELT coursebooks. Banegas (2014) looks at how CLIL is included in ELT coursebooks for school students in Argentina. Worryingly, he found that the content was over-simplified and had no relationship with the topics in the school curricula, and the activities, rather than engaging students with the content, mainly focused on reading and lower-order thinking skills. He concludes that the CLIL sections in the ELT coursebooks he analysed are little more than superficial add-ons that do not promote a genuinely bilingual form of education. Studies like this are a warning for ELT in how it conceives of its relationship with CLIL. It would be a disservice to both types of language education if CLIL were to appear in ELT materials as watered-down 'content' which merely acts as a disguise for language structures and skills exercises.

Conclusion and implications for ELT

This concluding section brings together some of the key topics and issues discussed in the chapter and looks at how they may be relevant to the broader field of ELT. The issues are treated tentatively and formulated more as prompts for reflection than as concrete suggestions and recommendations.

Turning again to the 'what' of CLIL, we can problematise the links and overlaps between CLIL and ELT. Dalton-Puffer et al. (2014) point out that CLIL is timetabled in schools as subject lessons, not as language lessons, so it seems clear that CLIL is not primarily considered a form of L2 pedagogy. However, a 'soft' version of CLIL may be incorporated into language classes, with content topics included as part of the language syllabus. Whether or not everyone would want to call this 'CLIL' is another question, however. As CLIL provision continues to grow, questions may be raised about the role of ELT in schools – is English necessary as a specific and separate subject? Will it have a 'supporting role' helping learners with the (academic) language they need to study other subjects? Graddol (2006) predicted that English will become a 'basic skill' facilitating access to other parts of the curriculum. This could have implications for the integrity of English language as a subject in itself in many institutions.

Revisiting the 'whys' of CLIL, we can ask to what extent ELT is or should be concerned with the development of academic literacy. There may be an overlap with English for academic purposes (EAP; see Basturkmen and Wette, this volume), and some EAP specialists have experimented with CLIL-like approaches (e.g. Garner and Borg, 2005). In some CLIL contexts, for example in bilingual programmes in Spain, English language lessons have shifted from an EFL approach to a focus on the kinds of literacy issues dealt with in language arts classes in students' L1 contexts. The focus on academic skills also raises questions about the appropriateness of assessment frameworks such as the Common European Framework of Reference (CEFR), which, some researchers (e.g. Little, 2007) have pointed out, is inadequate for CLIL. A further reflection is that the emphasis on CLIL as a context for meaningful communicative interaction could possibly release ELT lessons from the burden of providing massive amounts of input and practice and would free up space for more explicit approaches to language teaching, of the types described in Leow (2015).

As for the 'who' of CLIL, i.e. the teachers, we can ask if CLIL and ELT can be taught by the same people. At primary level, in fact, this is often the case – individual teachers often teach both CLIL and ELT; however, it is less common at higher levels of education, except in contexts where teachers have a double subject teaching qualification. Clearly, however, a key role for ELT teachers in CLIL contexts will be as collaborators with colleagues who teach other subjects through English. This raises issues of professional status and could either enhance the status of ELT teachers as they become across-the-curriculum language and literacy experts or could devalue them if seen as having a more subservient role.

Finally, turning to the 'how' of CLIL, we can reflect upon the methodological options in bringing content into English language lessons. There already is a long tradition of including content in ELT classes, whether this be topics and themes, project work, literature or work on intercultural awareness. Does bringing in to these English language lessons content from other subjects add anything to the students' experience? If such content is being dealt with by subject experts in CLIL classes, is there even any point in bringing it in to students' English classes, especially if it is done in the trivial manner that Banegas (2014) criticises? Looking at the pedagogical recommendations for CLIL practice, we can see that many (if not most) of them are very recognisable to ELT practitioners. And both CLIL and ELT share an increasing interest in multilingual and multimodal approaches to teaching. Perhaps what makes CLIL distinctive, and where it raises most challenges for ELT, is in its explicit attention to links between language and cognitive development in the context of developing pluriliteracies.

Discussion questions

- To what extent do you see CLIL as a threat or an opportunity for ELT professionals?
- What, if anything, do you think ELT practitioners can learn from CLIL methodology?
- Which theoretical justifications for CLIL do you find most/least convincing?
- Do you think the resources invested in CLIL in English would be better used in support of non-content integrated English language teaching? Why/why not?

Related topics

Bilingual education in a multilingual world; Communicative language teaching in theory and practice; ELT materials; Task-based language teaching; World Englishes and English as a Lingua Franca.

Further reading

Coyle, D., Hood, P. and Marsh, D. (2010) *CLIL: Content and language integrated learning*. Cambridge: Cambridge University Press. (Still the best introduction to and overview of CLIL.)

Dale, L. and Tanner, R. (2012) *CLIL activities*. Cambridge: Cambridge University Press. (Not only a very useful compendium of practical activities, but a good overall introduction to CLIL.)

Llinares, A., Morton, T. and Whittaker, R. (2012) *The roles of language in CLIL*. Cambridge: Cambridge University Press. (A thorough introduction to an SFL-based, subject-literacies approach to CLIL.)

Lyster, R. (2007) *Learning and teaching languages through content: A counterbalanced approach*. Amsterdam: John Benjamins. (A clear argument for, and methodological guidance on, incorporating a focus on form in all forms of content-based language teaching.)

References

Anghel, B., Cabrales, A., Carro, J. M. and Centre for Economic Policy Research (Great Britain) (2012) *Evaluating a bilingual education program in Spain: The impact beyond foreign language learning*. London: Centre for Economic Policy Research.

Baecher, L., Farnsworth, T. and Ediger, A. (2014) 'The challenges of planning language objectives in content-based ESL instruction'. *Language Teaching Research*, 18/1. 118–136.

Banegas, D. L. (2014) 'An investigation into CLIL-related sections of EFL coursebooks: Issues of CLIL inclusion in the publishing market'. *International Journal of Bilingual Education and Bilingualism*, 17/3. 345–359.

Bentley, K. (2010) *The TKT course CLIL module*. Cambridge: Cambridge University Press.

Black, P. and Wiliam, D. (1998) *Inside the black box: Raising standards through classroom assessment*. London: School of Education, King's College London.

Bozdoğan, D. and Karlidağ, B. (2013) 'A case of CLIL practice in the Turkish context: Lending an ear to students'. *Asian EFL Journal*, 15/4. 90–111.

Bruton, A. (2011) 'Is CLIL so beneficial, or just selective? Re-evaluating some of the research'. *System*, 39/4. 523–532.

Bruton, A. (2013) 'CLIL: Some of the reasons why . . . and why not'. *System, 41/3*. 587–597.

Cammarata, L. and Tedick, D. J. (2012) 'Balancing content and language in instruction: The experience of immersion teachers'. *Modern Language Journal*, 96/2. 251–269.

Cenoz, J. (2015a) 'Content-based instruction and content and language integrated learning: The same or different?' *Language, Culture and Curriculum, 28/1*. 8–24.

Cenoz, J. (2015b) 'Discussion: Some reflections on content-based education in Hong Kong as part of the paradigm shift'. *International Journal of Bilingual Education and Bilingualism*, 18/3. 345–351.

Cenoz, J., Genesee, F. and Gorter, D. (2014) 'Critical analysis of CLIL: Taking stock and looking forward'. *Applied Linguistics, 35/3*. 243–262.

Chadwick, T. (2012) *Language awareness in teaching: A toolkit for content and language teachers.* Cambridge: Cambridge University Press.

Costa, F. (2012) 'Focus on form in ICLHE lectures in Italy: Evidence from English-medium science lectures by native speakers of Italian'. *AILA Review*, 25. 30–47.

Coyle, D., Hood, P. and Marsh, D. (2010) *CLIL: Content and language integrated learning.* Cambridge: Cambridge University Press.

Cummins, J. (1979) 'Cognitive/academic language proficiency, linguistic interdependence, the optimum age question and some other matters'. *Working Papers on Bilingualism*, 19. 121–129.

Dale, L. and Tanner, R. (2012) *CLIL activities.* Cambridge: Cambridge University Press.

Dalton-Puffer, C. (2007) *Discourse in content and language integrated learning (CLIL) classrooms.* Amsterdam: John Benjamins.

Dalton-Puffer, C. (2009) 'Communicative competence and the CLIL lesson', in R. de Ruiz de Zarobe and R. M. Jiménez Catalán (eds) *Content and language integrated learning: Evidence from research in Europe.* Bristol: Multilingual Matters. 197–214.

Dalton-Puffer, C. (2011) 'Content and language integrated learning – from practice to principles?' *Annual Review of Applied Linguistics*, 31. 182–204.

Dalton-Puffer, C. (2013) 'A construct of cognitive discourse functions for conceptualising content-language integration in CLIL and multilingual education'. *European Journal of Applied Linguistics*, 1/2. 1–38.

Dalton-Puffer, C., Llinares, A., Lorenzo, F. and Nikula, T. (2014) 'You can stand under my umbrella: Immersion, CLIL and bilingual education. A response to Cenoz, Genesee and Gorter'. *Applied Linguistics, 35/2*. 213–218.

Dalton-Puffer, C., Nikula, T. and Smit, U. (2010) 'Language use and language learning in CLIL: Current findings and contentious issues', in C. Dalton-Puffer, T. Nikula and U. Smit (eds) *Language use in content and language integrated learning (CLIL).* Amsterdam: John Benjamins. 279–291.

Garner, M. and Borg, E. (2005) 'An ecological perspective on content-based instruction'. *Journal of English for Academic Purposes*, 4/2. 119–134.

Georgiou, S. I. (2012) 'Reviewing the puzzle of CLIL'. *ELT Journal, 66/4*. 495–504.

Graddol, D. (2006) *English next: Why global English may mean the end of 'English as a foreign language'.* London: The British Council.

Guerrini, M. (2009) 'CLIL materials as scaffolds to learning', in D. Marsh, P. Mehisto, D. Wolff, R. Aliaga, T. Asikainen, M. Frigols-Martin, S. Hughes and G. Langé (eds) *CLIL practice: Perspectives from the field.* Jyväskylä, Finland: University of Jyväskylä. 74–84.

Halliday, M.A.K. and Matthiessen, C.M.I.M. (2013) *Halliday's introduction to functional grammar* (4th ed.). London: Routledge.

Hüttner, J., Dalton-Puffer, C. and Smit, U. (2013) 'The power of beliefs: Lay theories and their influence on the implementation of CLIL programmes'. *International Journal of Bilingual Education and Bilingualism*, 16/3. 267–284.

Jäppinen, A-K. (2005) 'Thinking and content learning of mathematics and science as cognitional development in Content and Language Integrated Learning (CLIL): Teaching through a foreign language in Finland'. *Language and Education*, 19/2. 147–168.

Lasagabaster, D. and Sierra, J. M. (2010) 'Immersion and CLIL in English: More differences than similarities'. *ELT Journal*, 64/4. 367–375.

Leow, R. P. (2015) *Explicit learning in the L2 classroom: A student-centered approach.* New York: Routledge.

Lin, A.M.Y. (2015) 'Conceptualizing the potential role of L1 in CLIL'. *Language, Culture and Curriculum*, 28/1. 74–89.

Little, D. (2007) 'The common European framework of reference for languages: Perspectives on the making of supranational language education policy'. *Modern Language Journal*, 91/4. 645–655.

Llinares, A. and Lyster, R. (2014) 'The influence of context on patterns of corrective feedback and learner uptake: A comparison of CLIL and immersion classrooms'. *Language Learning Journal*, 42/2. 181–194.

Llinares, A., Morton, T. and Whittaker, R. (2012) *The roles of language in CLIL*. Cambridge: Cambridge University Press.

Lorenzo, F., Casal, S. and Moore, P. (2010) 'The effects of content and language integrated learning in European education: Key findings from the Andalusian bilingual sections evaluation project'. *Applied Linguistics*, 31/3. 418–442.

Lyster, R. (2007) *Learning and teaching languages through content: A counterbalanced approach*. Amsterdam: John Benjamins.

May, S. (2014) *The multilingual turn: Implications for SLA, TESOL and bilingual education*. New York: Routledge.

Mehisto, P., Marsh, D. and Frigols, M. J. (2008) *Uncovering CLIL: Content and language integrated learning in bilingual and multilingual education*. Oxford: Macmillan Education.

Meyer, O., Coyle, D., Halbach, A., Schuck, K. and Ting, T. (2015) 'A pluriliteracies approach to content and language integrated learning – mapping learner progressions in knowledge construction and meaning-making'. *Language, Culture and Curriculum*, 28/1. 41–57.

Moore, P. and Lorenzo, F. (2007) 'Adapting authentic materials for CLIL classrooms: An empirical study'. *VIEWZ: Vienna English Working Papers*, 16/3. 28–35.

Morton, T. (2013) 'Critically evaluating materials for CLIL: Practitioners' perspectives and practices', in J. Gray (ed.) *Critical perspectives on language teaching materials*. Basingstoke: Palgrave. 137–160.

Paran, A. (2013) 'Content and language integrated learning: Panacea or policy borrowing myth?' *Applied Linguistics Review*, 4/2. 317–342.

Pérez Cañado, M-L. (2014) 'Teacher training needs for bilingual education: In-service teacher perceptions'. *International Journal of Bilingual Education and Bilingualism*. doi: 10.1080/13670050.2014.980778

Pérez-Vidal, C. (2007) 'The need for focus on form in content and language integrated approaches: An exploratory study', in F. Lorenzo, S. Casal, V. de Alba and P. Moore (eds) *Models and practices in CLIL. Revista Española de Lingüística Aplicada (RESLA) Volumen monográfico*. Logroño: Asociación Española de Lingüística Aplicada. 39–53.

Ruiz de Zarobe, Y. (2011) 'Which language competencies benefit from CLIL? An insight into applied linguistics research', in Y. Ruiz de Zarobe, J. M Sierra and F. Gallardo del Puerto (eds) *Content and foreign language integrated learning: Contributions to multilingualism in European contexts*. Bern: Peter Lang. 129–154.

Smit, U. and Dafouz, E. (2012) 'Integrating content and language in higher education: An introduction to English-medium policies, conceptual issues and research practices across Europe'. *AILA Review*, 25/1. 1–12.

Somers, T. and Surmont, J. (2012) 'CLIL and immersion: How clear-cut are they?' *ELT Journal*, 66/1. 113–116.

Sylvén, L. K. (2013) 'CLIL in Sweden – why does it not work? A metaperspective on CLIL across contexts in Europe'. *International Journal of Bilingual Education and Bilingualism*, 16/3. 301–320.

Tan, M. (2011) 'Mathematics and science teachers' beliefs and practices regarding the teaching of language in content learning'. *Language Teaching Research*, 15/3. 325–342.

Tedick, D. J. and Wesely, P. M. (2015) 'A review of research on content-based foreign/second language education in US K-12 contexts'. *Language, Culture and Curriculum*, 28/1. 25–40.

Turner, M. (2013) 'CLIL in Australia: The importance of context'. *International Journal of Bilingual Education and Bilingualism*, 16/4. 395–410.

Yamano, Y. (2013) 'Using the CLIL approach in a Japanese primary school: A comparative study of CLIL and EFL lessons'. *Asian EFL Journal*, 15/4. 160–183.

Yang, W. and Gosling, M. (2014) 'What makes a Taiwan CLIL programme highly recommended or not recommended?' *International Journal of Bilingual Education and Bilingualism*, 17/4. 394–409.

19

Appropriate methodology

Towards a cosmopolitan approach

Adrian Holliday

Introduction

An early rationale for appropriate methodology, as expressed in the (1994) publication of *Appropriate Methodology and Social Context*, was a suggested conflict between two educational domains. On the one side was the largely private ELT sector originating in Britain, Australasia and North American (BANA). This was perceived to be an aggressive promoter of a particular and narrow interpretation of communicative teaching methodology through teacher training and education, international professional qualifications, curriculum projects and the prolific international publishing of textbooks (see Gray, and Pennycook, this volume). BANA also directly or indirectly promoted the so-called 'native speaker' teacher to be the best model both for teaching methodology and language (see also Llurda, this volume). On the other side was the mainstream tertiary, secondary, primary state education across the world (TESEP), where the majority of ELT takes place. This is perhaps the largest market for BANA methodology, and the majority of teachers are so-called 'non-native speakers'. The appropriate methodology quest was therefore to make BANA methodology appropriate to TESEP. A political dimension to this quest was the potential linguistic imperialism implicit in the domination of the BANA domain, which Phillipson (1992) describes as the West maintaining power over the rest of the world through the power of English and a false idea that the 'native speaker' is superior. (I use inverted commas here and throughout to remind us that the native-non-native speaker division is highly contested; again, see also Llurda, this volume.)

In assessing the concept of appropriate methodology, this chapter will evaluate the validity of this original BANA-TESEP model in the light of developing understandings of the cultural politics of ELT. It will suggest that, rather than focusing on distinct social or cultural TESEP contexts, there needs to be a more cosmopolitan model in which learning and teaching methodology is appropriate to the lived experience of *all* language learners and teachers *regardless* of whether they come from so-called BANA or TESEP backgrounds. It will suggest that, rather than being driven by what appears to be a 'centred' BANA perception of the ELT world, appropriate methodology needs to be 'de-centred' in the often-unrecognised worlds of language learners and teachers. I will begin by looking at the issues with the BANA-TESEP model and then move to the arguments for a more cosmopolitan model.

Problems with the BANA-TESEP model

The problem with the original BANA-TESEP model of appropriate methodology was signalled in Canagarajah's review of *Appropriate Methodology and Social Context*. He argued that it was designed to help BANA ELT professionals to solve the 'problem' of TESEP, as though they were a 'Centre', Western power speaking down to 'Periphery' communities (1996: 81–82). The reference here to 'the West' is not to a particular geographical place but to an idea inferring 'developed' and 'desirable' (Hall, 1996: 186). A useful definition of Centre is a location of power that always defines, whereas the Periphery is subjugated to this power by always being defined (Hannerz, 1991). This therefore means that, while the intention might be an innocent application of BANA methods to make ELT more effective in TESEP settings (e.g. Waters, 2007), there is a hidden politics in which TESEP is defined by BANA as a series of simplistic descriptions of national 'contexts' which only focus on problems. In effect, a culturally idealised BANA Others (i.e. reduces) TESEP 'contexts' to descriptions of cultural deficiency.

An association with an essentialised notion of non-Western national cultures has fed this image of TESEP deficiency. Essentialism here refers to view of culture that completely encases and defines the individual within it. There is continued recognition within critical applied linguistics of how this essentialism has been built around an exaggerated and simplistic association between collectivism, 'non-native speakers' and a lack of the self-directed autonomy that is thought to characterise successful ELT (Nayar, 2002; Holliday, 2005; Kubota and Lin, 2006; Kumaravadivelu, 2012). It is thus easily imagined that all the students and teachers who inhabit so-called TESEP 'contexts', most often framed as national cultures, have the same values, attitudes, practices, cultural preferences and behaviours, often ignoring the normal, expected differences in sector, institution, classroom makeup, teacher and student personality, individual classroom politics and so on. A consequence of this, in my personal experience, is that TESEP teachers often describe their contexts through national cultural generalities at conferences and in postgraduate assignments and are just assumed to 'know' everything about their national culture (a problematic concept in itself) because they are insiders. Acceptance of the unitary simplicity of these contexts means that there is no apparent need to challenge generalisations about them. It is an inconvenient truth that often-cited issues with class size, examinations, timetabling, teacher status, ministries, motivation and so on are often common to particular educational *sectors* in many parts of the world rather than to particular *places*. The implacability of this cultural politics is demonstrated when TESEP contexts anywhere in the world become 'non-Western' by virtue of being describable in simplistic terms. It is therefore how ELT professionals talk and think of or construct themselves and others, rather than who they might really be, that is the problem here.

BANA's strong association with individualism is presented as the ideal for the person-interactive classroom. It also claims the exclusive, superior and arrogant 'freedom' for people to be different to each other and have different views about things (Holliday, 2013: 70). This characterisation and positioning of BANA will always take on a Centre, Western identity. It is therefore not possible for British, American or Australian teachers to describe *their* own 'contexts' in simplistic generalised terms; the BANA default is individuality. Yet, at the same time, TESEP 'contexts' are only ever thought to be collectivist and must always therefore fail to attain this BANA ideal. This Othering of TESEP represents a long-standing, dominant Western marginalisation of world cultures that serves globalised markets (e.g. Hall, 1996). This divisive cultural politics, hidden beneath a rhetoric of celebrating diversity, resembles a broader 'West as steward' discourse (Holliday, 2013: 110–114) in which a deep sense of welcoming well-wishing is nevertheless patronising to the extent of thinking that only by being in the West or learning from the West can non-Western outsiders do well.

It would, however, be a mistake to think that this polarised politics is represented by two distinct groups of actual people – those who are 'Western' versus those who are 'non-Western'. BANA is no longer a specific group of British, Australasian and North American professionals and their practices. It is rather a dominant, Centre, global professional discourse, a way of representing ideas (Hall, 1996: 187) which constructs particular ELT practices as a superior force and is subscribed to in varying degrees by professionals everywhere. It is driven by the ideology of native-speakerism (i.e. the belief in the superiority of Western English and teaching methodology) that is also not particularly associated with its original BANA location (Holliday, 2005; Houghton and Rivers, 2013: 6). It is certainly not the case that all teachers who are labelled as 'native speakers' are native-speakerists. Native-speakerism is to greater or lesser extent subscribed to across the world both in professional and popular belief – from Asian American teachers being labelled 'non-native speakers' by employers in the UAE because they are not 'white' (Ali, 2009: 39) to the proliferation of newspaper advertisements in Mexico which sell language schools by how many 'native speaker' teachers they have (Lengeling and Mora Pablo, 2012; see also Kramsch and Zhu, this volume).

A critical cosmopolitan appropriate methodology

The rest of this chapter will consider how this divisive cultural politics can only be undone by somehow removing the BANA-TESEP tension and seeking to make methodology everywhere potentially appropriate to language learners and their teachers everywhere. This means moving away from the narrow communicative method originally associated with BANA, which has advocated a particular and culture-specific type of oral interaction, and looking at deeper communicative principles – capitalising on the immense 'communicative knowledge' and intelligence which all students bring to the classroom (Breen and Candlin, 1980: 93). Hence, important 'macrostrategies' for communicative teaching include utilising "learning opportunities *created by* learners" and activating their *existing* 'intuitive heuristics', or models of making sense of the world (Kumaravadivelu, 1993: 13–14, my emphasis). Also, this communicative curriculum should apply not only to students but to all the people concerned, which includes teachers, because they are a part of the learning process as they carry out the informal research to enable them to 'communicate' with what their students bring to the classroom (Hutchinson and Waters, 1984).

An appropriate methodology that follows this principle is by no means specific to BANA or distant from TESEP. It is an educational approach that can relate to any classroom, class size, institutional setting, cultural background and subject of study. As well as relating to the existing communicative knowledge and intelligence of students, it must relate to their existing cultural experience and also to that of their teachers and the other parties concerned and their communities. It is this relationship that gives authentic meaning to the educational process rather than any imagined BANA criterion.

This revised appropriate methodology that seeks to build on the intelligence and existing communicative and cultural experience of all students everywhere can be related to a critical cosmopolitan sociology which recognises the potential for the positive, creative and innovative contribution across cultural boundaries (Delanty, 2006). It is *critical* of the traditional essentialism which imagines solid and objectified national cultures such as those represented in TESEP 'contexts'. It is *cosmopolitan* in that it could relate to any sort of ELT setting anywhere in the world, from inner-city state education in London to private language institutes in China. It also resonates with a social action model of culture that emphasises a creative dialogue between individuals and the structures of their societies that makes their existing cultural experience sufficiently dynamic to engage across boundaries (Weber, 1964; Holliday, 2013).

A major task within this critical cosmopolitan approach is to bring about a shift:

- *From cultural disbelief* that TESEP contexts have the cultural richness to contribute positively to English language learning without change and the development of critical thinking and autonomy
- *Towards a cultural belief* – that the cultural backgrounds of all language learners and teachers have the richness to provide them with the linguistic and cultural experience to contribute positively to English language learning.

To recap, the emphasis here is to move away from an appropriate methodology that seeks to solve the problem of introducing BANA methods to TESEP contexts. It instead seeks to serve the intelligence and communicative and cultural experience of all students, and their teachers, in all settings. I shall first look at the case of students and then at the case of their teachers.

The worlds of students – 'I am not what you think I am'

Belief in the contribution of the existing communicative and cultural experience of our students, whatever their backgrounds, requires finding out what this contribution is. This might not be an easy task because their cultural backgrounds may be unrecognised and hidden by the dominant Western, and indeed BANA, view of who they are – that if they are non-Western they are likely to have restrictive collectivist cultures and therefore have little to offer. A cosmopolitan-appropriate methodology therefore needs to be underpinned by a research methodology that is equipped to fathom the marginal nature of hidden sites of learning. It needs to be de-centred, without the agenda of whether or not a Centre, Western BANA method is appropriate. It has to see around dominant preoccupations and prejudices that have Othered TESEP and needs to incorporate localised perspectives and to ask questions that seek out the unexpected. Ethnographic approaches are common here because they apply the disciplines of making the familiar strange and putting aside established prejudices, and are set up to appreciate unrecognised cultural realities in the lived experiences of students and teachers (Holliday, 2014). Much of the research into the worlds of students follows this approach.

"I am not what you think I am" is a statement from one of the participants in Yamchi's (2015) qualitative study of Emirati women college students' experience of academic writing. The statement indicates that the student is aware that her teachers do not recognise what she brings to the classroom. Yamchi, who was both teacher and researcher during this study, finds that only when her students talk to her outside the classroom about how they deal with the formal tasks of the writing curriculum do they demonstrate high degrees of criticality that have remained invisible inside the classroom. While, in the classroom, they appear uncritical while going through the motions of writing tasks that they do not feel ownership for, outside the classroom, they speak critically about the politics of the writing tasks. The student's statement therefore epitomises how what we need to learn from our students is often hidden and very different from what we as teachers imagine about them.

An appropriate methodology that searches out and recognises the cultural contribution of students in this way can be labelled as cosmopolitan because these contributions cross the cultural boundaries that have been dominant in the BANA-TESEP model. Becoming aware of hitherto hidden cultural contribution will also undoubtedly change teachers' classroom and other practice as their students, rather than BANA ideals, become their main resource.

That the most important aspects of what we need to know about our students have remained at the margins of the formal aspects of learning and teaching resonates with Canagarajah's (1996) reference to the Periphery being ignored by the original BANA-TESEP model. It is the margins that are the key to a cosmopolitan appropriate methodology because, as Hall maintains, the margins are in the process of contesting world orders as they struggle to occupy centre ground (1991: 53). It is at the margins that we can find out what makes English meaningful to the lives of language learners and what they therefore bring to the learning event. The 'we' here no longer refers to BANA teachers learning about TESEP students but to all of us appreciating the unexpected qualities of our students.

These hidden, marginalised qualities can be found in activities that are out of sight of the formal aspects of lessons and institutional assessment but that are essentially cosmopolitan in the way in which they relate to the wider world. They are the things that students get on with "relatively free from surveillance" (Canagarajah, 2004: 121). They include such things as "asides between students, passing of notes, small group interactions, peer activities, marginalia in textbooks and notebooks, transition from one teacher to another, before classes begin, after classes are officially over". They take place in "the canteen, library, dorms, playgroups, and computer labs". They are also very evident "in cyberspace" with "email, online discussion/chat". He notes that "students can make almost any site in the educational environment free from surveillance by colluding in constructing a culture of underlife behaviour" (ibid.). Language learners bring expectations, meanings and relationships which are formed in the corridors, in their friendship groups, their families, the media and so on (Allwright and Bailey, 1991; Prabhu, 1992). They have perceptions of what teachers and classrooms are like even before having to deal with them directly. That these invisible sites have immense impact on the classroom reinforces the view that we cannot think of the classroom and language learning only in terms of the instrumentality of second language acquisition or visible task-based talk. We must instead think of them as 'coral gardens' of behaviour in which much of what is going on always remains out of sight of the teacher (Breen, 2001).

Revealing a hidden and unrecognised student life that is rich with creativity, criticality and self-direction, which goes against the established stereotypes that are rooted in cultural disbelief, has been the task of ethnographic studies. The focus of these studies is what goes on between students, often out of sight of their teachers, outside the classroom and in moments within classrooms out of the teacher's line of sight. An example of this is where Taiwanese students in a British university study skills course are perceived by their teachers to lack autonomy because they do not perform the tasks they are given. The key to a very different interpretation can be found, however, outside the classroom, where the students, who do not understand what their teachers want, practice autonomy in their own terms to get the information they need through their own devices, consulting Taiwanese undergraduate students, using the library and forming their own self-help groups (Holliday, 2005: 94, citing Chang). Another example is where secondary school teachers in Hong Kong think their students cannot carry out communicative activities because of their 'Confucian culture'. In sharp contrast to this, observation from the back of the class reveals extensive evidence of the students' communicative engagement with English, often in resistance to their teachers, for example working in groups in the classroom when the teacher asked them to perform tasks individually and self- and group-study in the library (Holliday, 2005: 97–98, citing Tong).

Much has been written about how the processes of teaching and learning designed by teachers and educational institutions can hide and perhaps be in conflict with the social interaction between students and the expectations and identities they bring from the broader society. This conflict is expressed variously as the aim of education to reproduce established social norms versus students' individual identities (Canagarajah, 2004: 119–120; see also Crookes, this volume); the lesson as designed by the teachers versus the lesson as imagined by each student (Holliday, 1994: 142–159); the transaction of teaching and learning versus the social interaction that goes on between students (Widdowson, 1987); and pedagogical images of classroom seating arrangement versus those determined by how students wish to seat themselves according to friendship groups (Shamim, 1996).

The worlds of teachers

It would, however, be a gross mistake always to demonise teachers as representatives of the institutional domain that fails to understand the cultural contribution of their students. They are also participants in the educational process who need to be understood within the cosmopolitan model of appropriate methodology. They too have their freedoms limited by institutional and other structures. They can also be the victims of social, political and economic forces acting on the classroom from the wider society that they cannot control, as well as from the micro-politics, the favourability of their position in the timetable and so on from within the institution. They also bring into the classroom important identities from their own professional, reference and peer groups (van Lier, 1988: 8; Holliday, 1994: 17). Teachers also need to deal with the conflict between formal and informal orders, the impossibility of quality assurance régimes, the pressures to meet customer policy or institutional statements of quality versus the realities of scarce resources and the real challenges of everyday professional life (Swales, 1980; Coleman, 1988). Teachers, therefore, like students, can also have secret and unrecognised lives in institutions. Rather than teachers, it is institutions and resources within environments of state and local politics, managerialism, neoliberalism and hidden curricula related to other agendas that limit understanding (Holly, 1990).

There are many cases where teachers themselves struggle to find deeper educational meanings in the spaces between the pressures of examinations and prescribed syllabuses (e.g. Lin and Cheung, 2014) and where teachers in the most difficult circumstances collaborate out of school time to create highly innovative appropriate methodologies. Naidu et al. (1992) research how to interpret the diversity of their students in very large classes in India as a resource rather than a problem (see also Shamim and Kuchah, this volume). In Zhejiang Teacher's University in China, local teachers refuse to lecture and instead find ways to develop a bilingual and project-based communicative curriculum where teachers only teach what they are interested in and allow the students to develop their own syllabus as they move from teacher to teacher (Wu, 2005). In both these cases, the teachers go off-campus, where they can develop ideas away from institutional pressures.

While the cosmopolitan appropriate methodology model applies to teachers everywhere, it provides particular encouragement for teachers who have felt marginalised within a so-called TESEP context and whose attention may have been diverted away from the major resource of the cultural contribution of their students by the image of a better-resourced and unattainable BANA ideal.

Cosmopolitan cultural engagement

The possibility of a cosmopolitan appropriate methodology is underpinned by a social action approach to culture. Following the sociology of Max Weber (1964), this recognises that while different societies and communities do have particular features that make us, our cultural practices and our languages different, they do not necessarily prevent individuals from moving creatively beyond their boundaries. This can be seen in further ethnographic studies of student life.

The classic example is Canagarajah's description of how Sri Lankan secondary school students write their own agendas into the margins of their textbooks. They show a complex range of what might be considered local and foreign cultural influences that express a cosmopolitan attitude towards English that travels across boundaries:

> Romance, sex, and cinema all show influences from international 'pop culture', and the lifestyle of Western entertainment media and youth groups; traditional cultural values and practices are based on Hindu religious roots; the modern Marxist-influenced political discourse is slanted towards nationalistic tendencies.
>
> *(Canagarajah, 1999: 90)*

The Web 2.0 phenomenon, the generation of Internet-based material that students can interact with and write into, can help bring this cosmopolitan activity in hidden sites of learning into formal learning events. Lin and Cheung (2014: 141) report how students in a low-resourced secondary school in Hong Kong build on the multiple literacies they bring with them. They engage with "print, visual and multimodal" texts from "pop-music culture (e.g. songs, magazines, concerts, festivals, comics, interviews with pop stars, and so on)". They suggest that this is "especially important for young people as they go through the often-difficult adolescent stage", "searching for their identities", "constructing their self-image, and finding their self-worth" (Lin and Cheung, 2014: 140). They go on to comment that the cosmopolitan perspective which these students possess comes "with the globalisation of English popular cultural texts", "English-language pop cultural texts and genres" and "the lingua franca to interact with each other and with their cross-national and cross-cultural fans".

This crossing of cultural boundaries amongst language learners may be considered as a claiming of the world by the margins within a process of bottom-up globalisation. There has been much talk of a top-down globalisation as a fairly new phenomenon that has spread English across the world, with the threat of destroying cultures; and there is certainly an element of this in the West defining cultural profiles across the world described earlier. It is also, however, argued that a cosmopolitan world existed across a broad network of local communities long before European colonialism divided the world with artificial boundaries, before European nineteenth century nationalism brought us the now traditional one-culture-one-language model (Rajagopalan, 2012: 207). There is therefore nothing necessarily new about a bottom-up globalisation emerging from the Periphery that enriches rather than threatens its cultural communities in opposition to a Western hegemony. An example of this is the changes to English brought about by young people across the world using it on the Internet and through text messaging and the appropriation of rap and hip hop (Pennycook, 2003: 513; Graddol, 2006: 42). There have always been resilient local communities from which students can bring rich cultural and linguistic resources to the learning of new languages – and more recently to the learning of English. This is very evident in deeply multilingual societies like India. Here, people manage to communicate effectively across multiple language boundaries on a daily basis. They deal with different languages as though they are multiple genres (Amritavalli, 2012: 54; Rajagopalan, 2012: 209).

Cosmopolitan appropriate methodologists need therefore to consider the potential for students to engage creatively across cultural boundaries and their probable hunger for such engagement. Web 2.0 is an interesting phenomenon in this respect. While many students do not have the opportunity to engage with Web 2.0 because of economic circumstances, access and institutional policy, those students who do have access demonstrate potential that relates to all students. Web 2.0 therefore lays bare the creative learning potentials that students bring with them and shows teachers what they need to engage with and the role they need to fulfil. Norton (2014) shows us a similar process with language learners with digital cameras becoming journalists. While their students have the multiple literacies for accessing and engaging with complex cosmopolitan material, they need their teachers to guide them in what to do with it (Warschauer, 2012).

Choice of what is authentic

Researching what takes place in hidden sites makes it clear that students will make their own choices about what they feel is authentic. This is very evident in interviews with secondary and primary school students across China about their attitudes to textbooks (Gong and Holliday, 2013). In rural areas, many of them complained about content about urban life, such as asking the way and planning a trip to Europe, which they do not find meaningful to their lives. Some of them felt that this content devalued their 'home culture'. This did not, however, mean that they were not interested in the world. The issue was not with strangeness but with interest. Indeed, many students showed interest in world affairs, music, international media and "topics on friendship, love and life skills". There was a deeply cosmopolitan desire to communicate with the world about identity (2013: 46–48). The texts that they complained about were chosen by the Chinese textbook writers because they were presumed authentic examples of 'native speaker' English and 'Western culture' (2013: 45). Cosmopolitan appropriate methodologists are trying to address what the students said by rewriting the national curriculum for teacher training in issues of language and culture. Thus, as Widdowson suggests, "it is probably better to consider authenticity not as a quality residing in instances of language but as a quality which is bestowed upon them, created by the response of the receiver" (1979: 165). In this sense, it is to do with being meaningful to language learners.

However, language learners cannot be told what sort of English they should learn or what to use it for. University students in Kuwait, despite showing little motivation in the classroom, engage in sophisticated play with English among their friends and perceive it as a means to be themselves in a globalised world (Kamal, 2015). Mexican university students talk about how they stamp their identity on English by using it to discuss post-colonial politics (Clemente and Higgins, 2008), British secondary school students in multilingual London engaged in sophisticated play with each other's languages which looks as though they are misbehaving in the classroom (Rampton, 2011). At the same time, teachers and other ELT professionals do need to be able to make their own decisions, as language specialists, about what sort of English is to be taught, while taking heed of the cry for authenticity that students bring with them (Kuo, 2006).

Small culture engagement: case study 1

A further understanding of the nature of culture helps us understand better what students bring to the learning event and how we can respond to their expectations within a cosmopolitan appropriate methodology. There is a broad and significant domain of underlying universal cultural processes that enable all of us to read and engage creatively with culture and language wherever we find it. At the centre of this is our ability to engage with small cultures such as family, school, classroom and sports groups on a daily basis as we move through life. This is something we all share across nations and communities, and it enables cultural travel. Just as young people find ways to make sense of and be themselves when they visit their friends' families, they can also make huge sense of others' cultural realities without losing their identities. They can also expand their identities by finding ways to innovate within them (Holliday, 2013: 19–20).

An example of this small culture engagement can be seen in the study of Iranian students doing a six-month technical English course at Lancaster University in 1980 (Holliday, 1994: 144–146; 2005: 102). Halfway through the course, they began to refuse to do the communicative tasks set by the teacher and appeared to be talking about other things and just misbehaving.

However, when the researcher looked into what the students were saying, it was discovered that they were complaining that the tasks were not meaningful and were not communicative enough. They wanted to work with the material in their own way, and when the teacher agreed, the students had more opportunity to communicate meaningfully with texts and the teacher; moreover, their test results soared. To work out this strategy for change, they had engaged with the small culture of the classroom. They had worked out how it operated, how to apply their intelligence to it and how to preserve their identities within its structures. However, when we engage with small cultures, we do not always get what we want. We have to negotiate, and it does not always work because there will be conservative forces acting against us. We all have the potential for cultural travel and innovation, but sometimes existing power structures work against us. The Iranian students had got ahead of their teachers by working out from watching them what 'communicative' was and then demanding even more. When their demands were initially unrecognised by their teacher, they went into the hidden site of apparent misbehaviour, rather like many of the students referred to earlier in this chapter.

Statements about culture

What acted against finding an appropriate methodology for the Iranian students were the stereotypes the teachers possessed about where they came from. When they first arrived, the students complained that all they wanted to do was learn grammar in formal lectures because of their 'national culture'. This 'our context' statement was taken literally at the time by the teachers, and this influenced how the students were perceived for the remaining three months until the incident above took place. If the teachers had simply accepted at face value the Iranian students' statement that their culture only allowed the lecturing of grammar, and a researcher had not looked more deeply into what was going on, their immense linguistic and cultural abilities would never have been recognised.

The social action approach tries to work with such statements about culture in a different way. They are understood as conscious or unconscious strategic projections of how one wants to be seen by others, very often in response to how one is being treated. Grimshaw's (2010) study of how Chinese students in British universities self-stereotype to gain personal space and social capital in the face of cultural disbelief on the part of British students and teachers is useful here and links to considerable social research on how marginalised, Periphery communities often appear to buy into the imagery imposed upon them to maintain their own security. Statements about culture therefore need to be taken as cultural products rather than as descriptions of culture. They are produced by the culture but do not define it.

It would be naïve to imagine that a cosmopolitan appropriate methodology will simply do away with essentialist descriptions of TESEP cultures. These descriptions must be taken seriously as being meaningful to the people who make them, and cosmopolitan appropriate methodologists need to get to the bottom of why these statements are made and what therefore is meaningful to the people involved. There are many iconic statements in the ELT profession that are let go as easy answers. An example is the superior-inferior framing of the native-non-native speaker issue. Whether or not teachers are constructed as 'native' or 'non-native', it is the politics behind this construction that become key data in devising an educational methodology to resolve it – as it would be if there was discrimination against any other parties in the setting.

Making connections across settings: case study 2

Moving away from a narrowly context-driven BANA-TESEP approach recognises the need to look more widely in determining a cosmopolitan appropriate methodology. When student teachers from a university in Hong Kong came to Britain for a language immersion programme, they immediately seemed to conform to the common East-Asian stereotype by not speaking in the classroom. It would have been easy to take this as indicative of the context they came from. Instead, ethnographic research was carried out to get to the bottom of what was really going on (Holliday, 2005: 88–107). This research primarily involved observing their behaviour during all aspects of the course – in class, during drama classes, on campus, in staff-student evaluation sessions, in their home room where they worked on projects, when visiting schools to which they were attached as assistant teachers and group presentations. This research produced the initial finding that they were only quiet in the classroom when the tutor was present. Everywhere else, they were keen to interact with everyone they met and were, moreover, sharply observant to the extent that the review they presented at a primary school at the end of their programme was a highly sophisticated satire of British society.

Understanding that the stereotype was not valid was not, however, sufficient to unlock the reason for the silence in the classroom and where a more appropriate methodology may lie. A number of critical incidents within the research project helped, sometimes beyond the immediate environment of the course. These included: seeing the same students in a phonology lecture in their university in Hong Kong; comparing this with a sociology lecture in a British university; being surprised that the students bought postcards about expressionist art while visiting a gallery in London; the students taking over the classroom to get on with project work when their teacher left to get something; them not noticing him when he visited them in their home room because they were getting on with their projects; seeing evidence of describing the students as though they were children in the researcher's ethnographic descriptions; and a student telling the researcher that he was not prepared to talk in class because he felt too much under scrutiny. Two other research projects also contributed to these findings. Video sequences of Japanese secondary school students showed them supporting each other with bilingual 'private talk' with other students, under the surface of the formal part of lesson, while the teacher was talking but not acknowledged by him (Holliday, 2005: 90–91). Japanese students in a British language class were talkative outside the classroom and when the teacher was out of the class but 'froze' and went silent when the teacher was there (Holliday, 2005: 90, citing Hayagoshi).

Putting all this together, it was possible to say that the students were *uncharacteristically* silent in the classroom because there was insufficient personal space in the high-scrutiny U-shape seminar room for them to feel comfortable enough to speak. It was intimidating that every single word they said was being scrutinised. This was in contrast to the space that was available in all the other activities they were engaged in during the programme and to the space available in their university lectures in Hong Kong. This anxiety might have been exacerbated by their adult identity as university students having been overshadowed by being forced into the more childlike image of language learners and by their knowledge of science, art, social science and so on not having been appreciated. The outcomes of the research enabled a significant change in the methodology for teaching them. 'Meetings', with chairs placed close together at one end of the room, replaced 'lessons' in the traditional U-shape. The students were never silent again.

Conclusion: elusive meanings

To conclude, cosmopolitan appropriate methodologists need to look widely and deeply at whatever it takes to unlock how to engage with the existing communicative and cultural experience of their students. This search must not, however, be stylised within prescribed notions of 'context', especially where they correspond with national cultural profiling and any notion of cultural deficiency. Cosmopolitan appropriate methodology research needs to be sufficiently open-ended, creative and interpretive to connect wide-ranging factors in such a way that unexpected meanings can emerge. Always starting from the assumption that students are intelligent and capable, it is necessary to address and interrogate attitudes, prejudices, power structures, histories, preoccupations, destructive stereotypes and theories about culture and values. The social action approach tells us that there is nothing in the cultural domain which is not negotiable and that boundaries can more often be crossed than not, as long as opportunities are there. Much of the original focus of appropriate methodology is still relevant here. This involves appreciating how the classroom is part of a wider social world, through which there is the development of a sociological imagination (Mills, 1970) – the ability to locate oneself and one's actions critically within a wider community or world scenario.

Discussion questions

- Remember examples of when you made strong statements about your ELT context. What did you exaggerate and why?
- Take the two sections in the chapter about the Iranian and the Hong Kong students. Either (a) read the original references or (b) use your own experience to imagine the detail. Draw a diagram that represents the process of arriving at an appropriate methodology for these scenarios.
- Consider anything you have recently read about cultural context. In what sense was any part of this essentialist? On what basis do you make this judgement?
- Is it really the case that differentiating TESEP and BANA leads to the objectification of TESEP?

Related topics

Communicative language teaching in theory and practice; ELT materials; Language and culture in ELT; 'Native speakers', English and ELT; Politics, power relationships and ELT; Teaching large classes in difficult circumstances.

Further reading

Breen, M. P. (2001) 'The social context of language learning – a neglected situation?', in C. N. Candlin and N. Mercer (eds) *English language teaching in its social context*. London: Routledge: 122–144. [Originally published in *Studies in Second Language Acquisition* 7/02: 135–58, 1985.] (This seminal paper explores how most of the culture of the classroom, as well as how students apply their existing cultural competence to language learning, remains hidden beneath the surface.)

Breen, M. P. and Candlin, C. N. (1980) 'The essentials of a communicative curriculum in language teaching'. *Applied Linguistics*, I/2: 89–112. (This early presentation of a communicative approach sets out the principles for using the communicative experience that students bring to the classroom as a major resource. It presents a broad educational approach that can be applied to any cultural setting.)

Holliday, A. R. (2005) *The struggle to teach English as an international language*. Oxford: Oxford University Press. (This book revisits appropriate methodology within the context of the hidden politics of native-speakerism. It deals with the roots of the essentialist cultural profiling that is common in ELT professionalism and suggests non-essentialist solutions.)

Widdowson, H. G. (1987) 'The roles of teacher and learner'. *ELT Journal*, 41/2. 83–88. (This early seminal paper sets out the two key elements of the language classroom – the *transaction* of teaching and learning and the *interaction* between the students – to show us that teachers can only ever have minute influence on what is going on between their students in the classroom.)

References

Ali, S. (2009) 'Teaching English as an international language (EIL) in the Gulf Corporation Council (GCC) countries: the brown man's burden', in F. Sharifian (ed.) *English as an international language: Perspectives and pedagogical issues*. Bristol: Multilingual matters. 34–57.

Allwright, R. L. and Bailey, C. (1991) *Focus on the language classroom*. Cambridge: Cambridge University Press.

Amritavalli, R. (2012) 'Visible and invisible aspects of language ability', in R. K. Agnihotri and R. Singh (eds) *Indian English: Towards a new paradigm*. New Delhi: Orient Black Swan. 49–62.

Breen, M. P. (2001) 'The social context of language learning – a neglected situation?', in C. N. Candlin and N. Mercer (eds) *English language teaching in its social context*. London: Routledge. 122–144. (Originally published in *Studies in Second Language Acquisition* 7/02: 135–58, 1985.)

Breen, M. P. and Candlin, C. N. (1980) 'The essentials of a communicative curriculum in language teaching'. *Applied Linguistics*, I/2. 89–112.

Canagarajah, A. S. (1996) 'Appropriate methodology and social context'. *ELT Journal*, 50/1. 80–82.

Canagarajah, A. S. (1999) *Resisting linguistic imperialism*. Oxford: Oxford University Press.

Canagarajah, A. S. (2004) 'Subversive identities, pedagogical safe houses, and critical learning', in B. Norton and K. Toohey (eds) *Critical pedagogies and language learning*. Cambridge: Cambridge University Press. 96–116.

Clemente, A. and Higgins, M. (2008) *Performing English as a postcolonial accent: Ethnographic narratives from México*. London: Tufnell Press.

Coleman, H. (1988) 'Analysing language needs in large organisations'. *English for Specific Purposes*, 7. 155–169.

Delanty, G. (2006) 'The cosmopolitan imagination: Critical cosmopolitanism and social theory'. *British Journal of Sociology*, 57/1. 25–47.

Gong, Y. and Holliday, A. R. (2013) 'Cultures of change', in K. Hyland and L. Wong (eds) *Innovation and change in English language education*. London: Routledge. 44–57.

Graddol, D. (2006) *English next*. London: The British Council.

Grimshaw, T. (2010) *Stereotypes as cultural capital: International students negotiating identities in British HE*. Paper presented at the British Association of Applied Linguistics Annual Conference: Applied Linguistics: Global and Local, University of Aberdeen.

Hall, S. (1991) 'Old and new identities, old and new ethnicities', in A. D. King (ed.) *Culture, globalisation and the world-system*. New York: Palgrave. 40–68.

Hall, S. (1996) 'The West and the rest: Discourse and power', in S. Hall, D. Held, D. Hubert and K. Thompson (eds) *Modernity: An introduction to modern societies*. Oxford: Blackwell. 184–228.

Hannerz, U. (1991) 'Scenarios of peripheral cultures', in A. D. King (ed.) *Culture, globalisation and the world-system*. New York: Palgrave. 107–128.

Holliday, A. R. (1994) *Appropriate methodology and social context*. Cambridge: Cambridge University Press.

Holliday, A. R. (2005) *The struggle to teach English as an international language*. Oxford: Oxford University Press.

Holliday, A. R. (2013) *Understanding intercultural communication: Negotiating a grammar of culture*. London: Routledge.

Holliday, A. R. (2014) 'Researching English and culture and similar topics in ELT'. *The EFL Journal*, 5/1. 1–15.

Holly, D. (1990) 'The unspoken curriculum – or how language teaching carries cultural and ideological messages', in B. Harrison (ed.) *ELT Documents 132: Culture and the language classroom*. London: Modern English Publications & The British Council. 11–19.

Houghton, S. and Rivers, D. (2013) 'Introduction: Redefining native-speakerism', in S. Houghton and D. Rivers (eds) *Native-speakerism in foreign language education: Intergroup dynamics in Japan*. Clevedon: Multilingual Matters. 1–14.

Hutchinson, T. and Waters, A. (1984) 'How communicative is ESP?' *ELT Journal*, 38/2. 108–113.

Kamal, A. (2015) 'Interrogating assumptions of native-speakerism from the perspective of Kuwait university English language students', in A. Swan, P. J Aboshiha and A. R. Holliday (eds) *(En)countering native-speakerism: global perspectives*. London: Palgrave. 124–140.

Kubota, R. and Lin, A. M. Y. (eds) (2006) *TESOL Quarterly, special issue on race* (Vol. 40).

Kumaravadivelu, B. (1993) 'Maximising learning potential in the communicative classroom'. *ELT Journal*, 47/1. 12–21.

Kumaravadivelu, B. (2012) 'Individual identity, cultural globalisation, and teaching English as an international language: The case for an epistemic break', in L. Alsagoff, W. Renandya, G. Hu and S. McKay (eds) *Principles and practices for teaching English as an international language*. New York: Routledge. 9–27.

Kuo, I. C. (2006) 'Addressing the issue of teaching English as a Lingua Franca'. *ELT Journal*, 60/3. 213–221.

Lengeling, M. and Mora Pablo, I. (2012) 'A critical discourse analysis of advertisments: Contradictions of our EFL profession', in R. Roux, I. Mora Pablo and N. Trejo (eds) *Research in English language teaching: Mexican perspectives*. Bloomington, IN: Palibro. 89–103.

Lin, A. M. Y. and Cheung, T. (2014) 'Designing an engaging English language arts curriculum for English as a foreign language students: Capitalising on popular cultural resources', in P. Benson and A. Chik (eds) *Popular culture, pedagogy and teacher education: International perspectives*. London: Routledge. 138–150.

Mills, C. W. (1970) *The sociological imagination*. Harmondsworth: Pelican.

Naidu, B., Neeraja, K., Ramani, E., Shivakumar, J. and Viswanatha, V. (1992) 'Researching heterogeneity: An account of teacher-initiated research into large classes'. *ELT Journal*, 46/3. 252–263.

Nayar, B. (2002) 'Ideological binarism in the identities of native and non-native English speakers', in A. Duszac (ed.) *Us and others: Social identities across languages, discourse and cultures*. Amsterdam: John Benjamin. 463–480.

Norton, B. (2014) '*Intercultural identity, digital storytelling, and the African Storybook Project*'. Paper presented at the TESOL 2014 International Convention: ELT for The Next Generation, Portland, USA.

Pennycook, A. (2003) 'Global Englishes, Rip Slyme, and performativity'. *Journal of Sociolinguistics*, 7/4. 513–533.

Phillipson, R. (1992) *Linguistic imperialism*. Oxford: Oxford University Press.

Prabhu, N. S. (1992) 'The dynamics of the language lesson'. *TESOL Quarterly*, 26/2. 225–241.

Rajagopalan, K. (2012) 'Colonial hangover and the new 'hybrid' Englishes', in R. K. Agnihotri and R. Singh (eds) *Indian English: Towards a new paradigm*. New Delhi: Orient Black Swan. 206–215.

Rampton, B. (2011) From 'multi-ethnic adolescent heteroglossia' to 'contemporary urban vernaculars'. *Language and Communication*, 31/4. 276–294.

Shamim, F. (1996) 'In or out of the action zone: Location as a feature of interaction in large classes', in K. M Bailey and D. Nunan (eds) *Voices and viewpoints: Qualitative research in second language education*. Cambridge: Cambridge University Press. 123–144.

Swales, J. (1980) 'The educational environment and its relevance to ESP programme design'. *Projects in materials design, ELT documents special*. London: The British Council. 61–70.

van Lier, L. (1988) *The classroom and the language learner*. London: Longman.

Warschauer, M. (2012) 'The digital divide and social inclusion'. *Americas Quarterly*, Spring. 130–135.

Waters, A. (2007) 'ELT and "the spirit of the times"'. *ELT Journal*, 61/40. 353–359.

Weber, M. (1964) *The theory of social and economic organisation*. New York: The Free Press. (Originally published as *Wirtschaft und gesellschaft*, 1922.)

Widdowson, H. G. (1979) *Explorations in applied linguistics*. Oxford: Oxford University Press.

Widdowson, H. G. (1987) The roles of teacher and learner. *ELT Journal*, 41/2. 83–88.

Wu, Z. (2005) *Teachers' knowing in curriculum change: A critical discourse study of language teaching*. Beijing: Foreign Language Teaching and Research Press.

Yamchi, N. (2015) '"I am not what you think I am": EFL undergraduates' experience of academic writing, facing discourses of formulaic writing', in A. Swan, P. J. Aboshiha and A. R. Holliday (eds) *(En)countering native-speakerism: Global perspectives*. London: Palgrave. 177–192.

Part IV

Second language learning and learners

20

Cognitive perspectives on classroom language learning

Laura Collins and Emma Marsden

Introduction

Although there is a long history of second and foreign language *teaching* methods – Kelly's (1969) historical overview goes back to 500 BC – the focus on the cognitive *learning* processes involved in language acquisition is much more recent. This is because the field of cognitive psychology only emerged in the mid-twentieth century, with a shift away from the view of learning as conditioned behaviour to one focused on the complex mental operations involved in learning, such as memory and attention (Smith, 2001). The field of linguistics contributed to the development of this cognitive perspective: Chomsky's ideas on mental representations of language (1957) and his critique of behaviourist accounts of language (1959) are key moments in the 'cognitive revolution' (Gardner, 1986/1998; Miller, 2003).

The new discipline of second language acquisition (SLA) emerged at about the same time. It broadened the scope of inquiry from the language itself and how to teach it to include the learner's knowledge and use of the second language (L2). This new perspective viewed errors not simply as bad habits but rather as revealing how the L2 was represented and accessed (Corder, 1967; Selinker, 1972). The contributions from cognitive psychology have increasingly influenced our understanding of how language is perceived, processed, stored and retrieved for use. Within SLA, this has meant moving beyond borrowing concepts from cognitive psychology to the elaboration of sophisticated research methodologies and theoretical constructs. And as more of the research is now conducted in classrooms, in addition to the more controlled laboratory environments, there are clear implications for teaching.

We adopt the broad definition of cognition proposed by DeKeyser and Juffs (2005: 437): knowledge, how it is acquired and how it is accessed in performance. This clearly encompasses many phenomena; however, we will focus on those with particular relevance for classroom L2 learning (we use the terms 'acquisition' and 'learning' interchangeably in this chapter).

Current critical issues

We begin by describing five issues relevant to teaching and learning that have been well-researched and about which some level of consensus has been reached.

Implicit and explicit learning and explicit and implicit knowledge

One central issue is the extent to which language can be *learned* implicitly (i.e. without intention to learn or awareness of learning) and the extent to which language *knowledge* itself may be implicit (i.e. not easily accessible for conscious reflection). If learners can 'pick up' language without being aware of doing so, then pedagogy can focus on other, perhaps more interesting and motivating aspects, such as meaningful interaction using the L2. Implicit knowledge (which is likely to result from implicit learning) is also thought to be more readily available under communicative pressure and more durable than explicit knowledge (more likely to result from explicit learning).[1]

Pioneering research into implicit learning by cognitive psychologists demonstrated that humans are sensitive to patterns in meaningless strings of letters (Reber, 1996) and that language regularities can be induced by a computer network that is not given any predetermined rules or meaning (summarised in Mitchell et al., 2012). Most directly relevant for language teaching is recent research that looks at the extent to which humans can learn language phenomena implicitly. Studies increasingly use more sophisticated methods, including evidence about brain activation (Morgan-Short et al., 2015), to help document that participants are not aware of learning the targeted feature of language during training or following it; the resulting knowledge that they demonstrate is found to be implicit (e.g. Rebuschat and Williams, 2012).

Classroom-based research comparing the effectiveness of teaching approaches that draw learners' attention to aspects of the language (promoting intentional and explicit learning) with those that do not (promoting incidental learning, which could be explicit or implicit) (Norris and Ortega, 2000; Spada and Tomita, 2010[2]) has most convincingly demonstrated that intentionally and explicitly orienting students' attention to features of the language tends to lead to larger learning gains than instruction that hopes to do so incidentally and/or implicitly. However, capturing the learning of implicit knowledge has proven challenging: the measures of learning used (judgments of linguistic acceptability, for example) often favour the use of explicit knowledge (Doughty, 2004). A better understanding of the characteristics of linguistic forms that may be learned with minimum teacher guidance would allow for more efficient use of class time. We currently know more about features that are good candidates for instruction (see discussion below on redundancy and L1-influence, for example), but the increased availability of longitudinal L2 student production corpora holds great promise for highlighting problematic and less problematic aspects of language across a variety of classroom contexts (e.g. Hasko, 2013; Thewissen, 2013).

Practice and automatisation of explicit knowledge

A group of theories, broadly known as information processing theories, purports that some learning begins with explicit knowledge; that is, some awareness of the phenomenon to be learnt. One could be aware that *yes/no* questions in English contain 'do + subject + lexical verb'; that *his* and *her* refer to the possessor, not only to the possessed entity; or the position the tongue needs to adopt to pronounce *th*. With practice, this *declarative* knowledge (i.e. learners can talk about it) can be drawn upon to produce and comprehend language with increasing speed and accuracy (DeKeyser, 2007a). During this *proceduralisation* stage, some researchers argue that processes such as 'chunking' combine separate representations of knowledge in the brain to generate new, more holistic, representations. The learning can then move into a stage of *automatisation*, characterised by fast access and stable performance (whether target-like or not). At this point, knowledge may become context-dependent and skill specific, and thus not easily transferable, for example from comprehension to production or from oral to written modalities (Morgan-Short, 2012a and 2012b).

Which aspects of language learning and teaching have been researched from this point of view? It is claimed that grammar-based approaches are underpinned by this learning theory: the provision of grammatical rules is followed by opportunities to practise those rules in comprehension and production with feedback, in increasingly less controlled settings (DeKeyser, 1997; Sanz and Morgan-Short, 2004). Some research has found correlations between learners' ability to articulate knowledge about language with their ability to use that knowledge in specific tests or with their general proficiency (Roehr, 2007), although clear, linear relations between declarative knowledge and more automatised use of that knowledge are not consistent (Marsden and Chen, 2011). Several studies have focused on how practice improves fluency (e.g. de Jong and Perfetti, 2011). Others have provided learners with input that repeatedly makes particular features of the language essential for understanding the intended message, thus giving learners practice in connecting forms to a particular meaning or function (e.g. verb inflections to convey tense and number, Marsden, 2006, or morphosyntax to convey subject/object assignment; see VanPatten, 2004, for an overview). Another operationalisation of practice encourages learners to articulate declarative knowledge whilst working with other learners or with the teacher ('languaging', Swain, 2005). Here the idea is to help learners establish reliable knowledge and begin to proceduralise it. A great deal of research has examined the provision of different types of corrective feedback in response to learners' inaccuracies during production (Lyster et al., 2013; see also Mackey, Park and Tagarelli, this volume). The assumption is that learners establish some conscious representation (declarative knowledge) of 'what went wrong' and/or 'the language that should be used to communicate better'. The nature of learners' declarative knowledge, how it changes over time and the usefulness of different types of practice can be influenced by factors such as the language phenomena (e.g. morphosyntax, vocabulary/figurative language, phonology, pragmatics) and learner characteristics (e.g. age, proficiency, learning style) (R. Ellis, 2002; N. Ellis, 2005). We explore some of the teaching implications in later sections of this chapter.

Roles of working memory and attention

Working memory (WM) is the notion that we have a memory system that both holds information for a short time and simultaneously allows processes to be done with that information. Measurements of learners' WM capacity are increasingly considered as a proxy for language learning aptitude; that is, a stable, possibly innate, set of characteristics (such as the ability to analyse patterns in an unknown language or recall streams of sound) which may facilitate language learning (see also MacIntyre, Gergersen and Clément, this volume). Cognitive psychologists have proposed various components of WM, each fulfilling different functions (see Wen et al., 2015, for research into WM and SLA).

How does WM serve language learning during the processing of new language? It is thought that it helps learners to retain information about the sounds or visual forms of language whilst it is being assimilated into comprehension. A processing ('executive control') component allows learners to connect temporarily stored information with previously stored information. Language examples include linking to stored concepts such as 'pastness' or 'plurality' or co-indexing one part of the input with another (e.g. -s verb inflection with a third person singular subject). WM is also believed to control where learners direct their perceptual attention, influencing what is temporarily stored or rehearsed. Learners with higher WM capacity may be more likely to notice features in the input, as they have more attentional resources to simultaneously extract meaning and attend to form (Sagarra, 2008; Révész, 2012). Some cognitive models of WM include both a conscious dimension where learners are aware of controlling their attention and an automatic dimension where learners are unaware of how their attentional resources are being controlled (Cowan, 2011). WM capacity may be most beneficial when some level of awareness about the language is required, but it may have less of a role where learning or processing is largely implicit (Roehr, 2008; Roberts, 2012; Williams, 2012).

The notion of WM could be considered in pedagogy in several ways. Instruction can be designed to place lower demands on the functions of WM (Gathercole and Alloway, 2008). For example, because WM effects may be mediated by factors such as topic familiarity (Leeser, 2007), providing thematically linked content or task-based sequences may enhance students' opportunities to make connections between form and meaning. Activities can manipulate where and when attention is directed, so that low proficiency learners, for example, are not expected to both comprehend an utterance and notice key new grammar features simultaneously (VanPatten, 2004; Sagarra, 2008; Marsden, Altmann, and St. Claire, 2013). Measures of WM may predict which learners may be more likely to learn languages faster or to a higher level under different conditions. Finally, although WM has largely been considered as a relatively fixed trait that increases with maturity and reaches a stable capacity in early adolescence, there is increasing interest in whether some components can be improved with training (Holmes et al., 2009; Klingberg, 2010). If this proves to be so, teachers may consider practice tasks to help students become more effective learners.

Characteristics of the input influencing learning

A central question in SLA is why some features of language are more difficult to learn than others. To explain this, cognitive perspectives assign a large role to the characteristics of the input itself, i.e. the frequency, saliency, distribution and redundancy of language features. How frequently a feature is encountered is thought to determine fairly reliably how easily something is learnt, particularly the lexicon, though findings vary on the optimum number of exposures for learning a particular vocabulary item (Edwards and Collins, 2013). Critically, however, the relationship between frequency and learning morphosyntax is not linear. For example, highly frequent items such as *a/the* and third person *-s* (Bybee and Hopper, 2001) can be learnt relatively late, and native-like mastery of usage is not reliable even amongst proficient L2 speakers. Saliency is how prominent the feature is, whether it is at the start of a sentence, stressed, multi-syllabic or bounded to a word (e.g. *-s*), and may influence how likely particular learners' attention will be drawn to it. Similarly, however, saliency cannot fully account for why some aspects of language are more quickly learnt than others. For example, a word final *-s* has several functions – indicating plurality, third person present singular, possessive, contracted *be* auxiliary. All these functions are not learned simultaneously despite the form being physically the same. Other characteristics of the input must be at play.

One such characteristic is how the form is distributed in the input and the effect this has on how communicatively useful (or, conversely, how redundant) it is. Features of language tend to co-occur and convey the same or similar functions. For example, lexical items such as temporal adverbs are often associated with conveying tense (e.g. *last year, next year*) or aspect (e.g. *whilst, every day*), and so are frequently distributed with morphosyntax such a *-ed, am + ing, was + ing*. If one of the co-occurring features is more salient (i.e. *last year* versus *– ed*) and/or has an equivalent in the L1, then this may reduce the likelihood that the learner attends to the other feature. Assuming attention is helpful for learning, the less attended features may not be learnt easily or quickly (Sagarra and Ellis, 2013). Forms may also occur in constrained contexts that do not provide key cues for learning. For example, *his/her* in classroom speech occurs mainly with inanimate objects (e.g. *her sweater*) rather than with gendered objects that demonstrate a key characteristic of the forms in English: possessives agree with the possessor, not the object (e.g. *She called her* father) (Collins et al., 2009).

Making form-meaning connections

Directing attention to the function and distribution of features in the input in age- and learner-appropriate ways offers a promising way of helping classroom learners establish connections between morphosyntax and its meanings and functions. Making features of the input essential to task completion (Loschky and Bley-Vroman, 1993) addresses the problems of low salience and redundancy discussed above. A simple example is providing the *-ed* inflection in a sentence without a temporal adverb and asking learners to decide whether the event occurred in the past or is ongoing, and juxtaposing this with sentences in which the *-ed* is absent (Marsden and Chen, 2011). Giving visual response options (a picture of a completed action versus an ongoing action) connects features to a 'meaning' or 'concept'; providing aural exemplars further promotes the perception of the relevant phonemes. Note the difference between this and the more typical textbook practice activities, such as gap fills, which ask learners *first* to attend to the very cue that they over-rely on (e.g. *yesterday*) and then to match a form (e.g. *Yesterday, I ___ the TV (watch)*).

Key areas of dispute and debate

The debates over different cognitive accounts of L2 learning have often involved dichotomies (e.g. deductive versus inductive[3] or intentional versus incidental learning). However, as the field has matured, there is less emphasis on showing the superior explanatory power of one side of a dichotomy and more on determining the *relative* contribution of key factors. In this section, we highlight three areas of debate: one related to language knowledge and two to language use.[4]

Influence of previously learned languages

Although the phenomenon of L1 knowledge influencing L2 learning is in itself relatively uncontroversial, there is debate concerning the *magnitude* and *nature* of the effect, including its possibly diminished role among multilingual speakers. Current research is focused on understanding how prior language learning experiences may block or facilitate learners' attention to particular features of the L2 (Sagarra and Ellis, 2013) or influence how learners use relevant cues (such as word order or verb inflections) for interpreting subjects and objects (MacWhinney, 2012).

A fundamental question is how much of L2 learning can be explained by developmental processes common to learners from different L1 backgrounds and how much can be attributed to the particular L1. Some researchers argue that regardless of the L1, SLA relies heavily on using lexical items and/or semantic-pragmatic 'guessing' skills to get meaning (Clashen and Felser, 2006; Bley-Vroman, 2009; VanPatten, 2012). In addition, processes such as simplification and overgeneralisation can result in developmental trajectories that are similar across learners and across L2s (and can also resemble L1 development). An oft-cited example is learners' use of pre-verbal negation (*I no like*). This would not be surprising among Spanish learners, who have such a structure in their L1, but it has also been observed among learners whose L1 does not, including Swedish (Hyltenstam, 1977) and German (summarised in R. Ellis, 2008). Similar patterns within L2s and across different L1s have been observed for other features, including tense-aspect and word order (Ortega, 2009). L1 knowledge can, however, affect the *rate* at which learners progress to more advanced use of a complex feature. Spanish speakers may take longer to go beyond the pre-verbal negation stage in English than speakers whose L1s have post-verbal negation (Schumann, 1979). French speakers' acquisition of the inversion stages of questions in English may be slowed down by their reluctance to apply subject–auxiliary inversion to questions involving noun subjects (*Is the dog hungry?*), which is disallowed in French (Spada and Lightbown, 1999). They have also been shown to take longer to master the simple past than Japanese learners, needing to sort out the differences between the English present perfect and the French *passé composé* (similar in form but only partially similar in meaning) (Collins, 2004). L1 influence does not appear to result in substantial alterations to the *route* of development, but there is increased interest in documenting deviations from observed patterns across different L1 groups (e.g. Luk and Shirai, 2009).

An additional issue for teachers to bear in mind is that many students in L2 classrooms arrive already knowing two or more languages. There is considerable discussion of the factors that determine how the languages of multilingual speakers may influence the learning of a new language (either positively or negatively), including recency of use/learning, proficiency and degree of similarity between the target language and a known language (typology) (Jarvis and Pavlenko, 2008; Falk and Bardel, 2010). Indeed, the L1 may be less influential than other known L2s, as learners operate in a 'foreign language' mode, activating other L2s while suppressing knowledge of their L1 (De Angelis, 2007).

Benefits of comprehension and production practice

While all accounts of L2 learning recognise the importance of *exposure* to language (input) for acquisition, there is much less consensus on the role of *using* the language (output). A number of teaching approaches during the 1970s and '80s prioritised comprehension over production, on the assumption that input is a key factor driving acquisition. There is classroom research supporting this view, especially for early stages of learning (e.g. Lightbown et al., 2002). There are also techniques, such as the structured input described earlier, that provide practice at interpreting language features. VanPatten (2012) has argued that input processing practice is necessary for establishing new knowledge of particular features and should therefore precede production practice.

This secondary and delayed role for output in acquisition has also been challenged. One argument is that production helps learners test hypotheses about the target language and to notice and repair gaps in their knowledge (Izumi, 2002; Toth, 2006), especially when teachers can set up conditions that successfully encourage learners to attend to the most appropriate language forms for conveying intended meanings (Swain's (1995) 'pushed output'). A related argument, deriving from skill acquisition theory, is the importance of matching practice type (e.g. speaking practice) to targeted skill (e.g. oral production): according to this view, comprehension practice alone does not enhance production, especially beyond the initial stages of learning (de Jong, 2005; DeKeyser, 2007b).

What does the research contribute to the debate? In a meta-analysis of 35 studies, Shintani et al. (2013) found that both comprehension and output-based practice were effective at developing both receptive and productive knowledge, underscoring an observation DeKeyser (2007b: 294) made that speaks directly to teachers: "The question is not so much whether comprehension and production skills both have to be practiced but what constitutes good comprehension practice and good production practice, and how there can be cross-fertilization between the two."

Contributions of formulaic language and exemplars to learning

Instruction usually includes a number of phrases which are practised and used as fixed, routinised formulae. These can be defined as "multimorphemic sequences which go well beyond learners' grammatical competence" (Myles, 2004: 139), ranging from *How are you?* and *Put it down* to the idiomatic *by and large*. There is general consensus that such formulae aid fluency by allowing fast access to language which does not require effortful online computation and that they enable L2 speakers to participate in conversational exchanges, thereby creating opportunities for interaction, input and practice. However, beyond these benefits, there is debate over the role that formulae play in actual learning.

One idea is that interlanguage development depends on first memorising and then unpacking and analyzing formulae. Myles et al. (1999) found that learners who had a good store of formulae in L2 French (e.g. *comment tu t'appelles? what's your name?*) tended to go on to use related syntax (e.g. interrogatives) creatively in target-like ways. Myles (2004) proposes that learners move from an initial lexical-functional representation of whole formulae to establish syntactic representations of the component parts of these multi-word units and, critically, of the verb. Other researchers ascribe a more limited role, emphasising the preponderance of such formulae which remain unanalysed, unless the communicative need arises (Wray, 2002). An example could be using *What's your name?* when in fact *What's HIS name?* is required. Wray argues that memorised chunks can reduce processing load but they can in turn reduce expressive flexibility and accuracy. The challenge for the classroom emerging from both these lines of work is determining how to help learners store and break down some of these chunks at appropriate moments in their development.

Another perspective is that highly frequent constructions (e.g. *She put the X on the Y*) serve as prototypes – representative of a verb argument structure (e.g. S V O PREP O) that learners use as a frame, or template, into which other lexical items can slot (N. Ellis et al., 2014; see also Robinson and Ellis, 2008). This view has focused on documenting how prototypicality operates both in input and learners' output with particular lexical items in specific constructions. Research exploring the role of type frequency (a reliable characteristic of prototypicality) on classroom learning suggests that, in the initial stages, it may facilitate the detection of some patterns such as word order in questions (McDonough and Kim, 2009) but be less helpful with complex constructions such as English ditransitives (e.g. *Sarah gave Simon her old computer*) (Year and Gordon, 2009). For the latter, more explicit guidance may be required. Identifying appropriate prototypical structures is complex, requiring corpus-based and computer simulations, but this research could provide guidance for materials writers in creating practice opportunities that include modifications to authentic input that are biased towards such structures. This would complement the unmodified language samples that teachers often provide for students, which inevitably contain a wider range of lexical and functional distributions of particular constructions.

Implications and challenges for ELT practice and practitioners

In addition to the implications for language teaching already identified, we elaborate here upon two broader aspects of pedagogy as informed by cognitive perspectives.

Time on task

Parodying advertisements for language learning success in 10 days, Leveen (2014) titled a blog "Learn French in 10 years", referring to the oft-cited amount of time needed to acquire expertise (Chase and Simon, 1973), sometimes referred to as the 10,000-hour rule (Ericsson et al., 1993). People's expectations for L2 learning are frequently unrealistic, fuelled by academic and employment goals. Learning mechanisms such as memory, attention, the automatisation of knowledge and the use and breakdown of formulae take much more time than the few hundred hours of classroom instruction typically experienced. One crucial challenge is helping students learn *how* to learn, so that they can engage in effective practice on their own; another is setting attainable goals for the time available. For example, recognising the *emergence* and not just the *mastery* of new knowledge as an indicator of progress (Pienneman, 1998; Håkansson, 2013) (e.g. initial use of present perfect in some contexts versus accurate use in all contexts) has implications for language assessment. It entails tolerance of typical interlanguage behaviour such as backsliding to earlier, less accurate language, and indeed of errors in general (Ågren et al., 2012).

Reflecting on language and how it works

One way to promote autonomous learning is to train students to pay attention to language and its patterns through inductive learning activities. Students may be given samples of language containing a target feature and then guided to articulate a pattern or explanation for how it is used. Inductive approaches have been shown to be effective for learning some aspects of language (e.g. Rosa and O'Neill, 1999; Haight et al., 2007), including practice in comprehending structured input in which learners induce a rule from the feedback given (Sanz and Morgan-Short, 2004; Marsden and Chen, 2011). Some textbooks do include an inductive component embedded into meaning-based activities, but the provision of a rule/pattern followed by practice (deductive approach) tends to be more common.

Raising language awareness through reflection on previously learned languages can also enhance learning (Horst et al., 2010; Hall and Cook, 2012; see also Kerr, this volume), helping students identify useful similarities and confront problems that derive from the influence of known languages. The use of cross-linguistic comparisons as a learning tool is not common in published teaching materials; however, recent initiatives include the Downes' Discovering Language project (Barton et al., 2009; Downes, 2014) and Oxford University Press' *Clockwise* coursebook series, in which students periodically consider how a feature of English is rendered in their L1.

Future directions

A number of under-researched cognitive aspects of language learning have been mentioned above. We propose three additional directions that would further inform decisions on what to teach, when, and how.

Linking learning conditions to subsequent language use

The relationship between the conditions under which something is learned and the subsequent use of that knowledge in actual performance is highly relevant to teaching. The concept of *transfer appropriate processing* (TAP), for example, asserts that it is easier to remember something that has been learned if the new situation for use resembles the learning situation (Franks et al., 2000). This suggests benefits for matching instructional learning conditions to students' goals for language use (Segalowitz and Lightbown, 1999). Thus, if a student aims to use the L2 to interact outside the classroom, TAP predicts advantages for drawing students' attention to language forms during actual communicative practice rather than in separate grammar lessons (Spada and Lightbown, 2008). A related proposal is that the retrieval and transfer of knowledge to new situations may be more effective if the initial learning phase has some built-in challenges that require additional effort. Bjork (1994) has called these 'desirable difficulties'. They include varying the way the learning material is presented and practiced (iteration); creating 'contextual interference' such as unpredictability during the learning phase; and using testing phases as *learning* events for consolidating knowledge and identifying future needs. Lightbown (2008) and Larsen-Freeman (2013) propose applications of these ideas to L2 learning that merit pedagogical and research consideration.

The role of repetitive practice

Performing the same task more than once can enhance L2 learning, resulting, for example, in the use of more complex forms (Van den Branden, 2007). Fluent, automatic use of language is the result of considerable practice, and repetition clearly plays a role in the process. However, there is surprisingly little classroom research on the types of repetitive practice that may be beneficial to students for learning different aspects of language. There is little theoretical support for the mindless repetition of forms provided by mechanical, structural drills, but some scholars have made the case for 'mindful repetition' (N. Ellis, 2002: 177), which can reinforce the link between form and meaning (DeKeyser, 1998). Examples include communicative drills requiring genuine rather than rote responses and the contextualised pattern practice provided by some songs and poems. However, as DeKeyser noted, there are aspects of phonological and morphosyntactic form that are not tied to meaning, the learning of which may be enhanced by mechanical practice. Consider, for example, stress patterns in multi-syllabic words, reductions in complex conditional forms (e.g. *If I'd known, I wouldn't 've gone*) and possibly also form-related challenges stemming from L1 influence (e.g. the erroneous use of resumptive pronouns in relative clauses by Arabic learners of English; the under-use of inversion with noun subjects in English questions for French learners).

Manipulating the input

Studies of classroom input to students have demonstrated that some key features of language (such as the simple past) are infrequent and occur in contexts in which it is difficult to notice their form and function (Collins et al., 2009). Skewing the input may help learners to establish useful templates for learning particular morphosyntactic constructions, but this has yet to be established in rigorous classroom studies. The effectiveness of priming learners' use or perception of particular forms through careful activity design (e.g. giving an interlocutor a script enriched with prepositional datives or advanced question structures) is also promising (Trofimovich and McDonough, 2011), but this research has largely been carried out in laboratory conditions. The role of priming for learning *novel* morphosyntax and, critically, the *kind of knowledge* that results, also remain open questions (Marsden, Williams, and Liu, 2013); priming mechanisms may be more effective at consolidating existing knowledge (N. Ellis, 2002).

Concluding comments

In this chapter, we have highlighted insights from research on the cognitive dimensions of language learning that can inform teachers' practices and expectations. Not all phenomena of interest have been examined in the real world complexity of classrooms, and even those that have are obviously constrained in generalisability by the particular contexts in which they were investigated. One promising avenue for enhancing the generalisability of research and increasing its accessibility for teachers, however, is the digital repository IRIS (Instruments for Research into Second Languages; www.iris-database.org; Marsden et al., 2015). IRIS makes the materials used to collect data for published research, including areas covered by this chapter, freely available. We have also identified aspects of learning that are currently not well understood, as this information is equally important when assessing teaching materials, evaluating student progress and interpreting one's own experiences.

Discussion questions

- Of the different concepts and perspectives on language learning that have been reviewed in this chapter, are there any that are particularly relevant for explaining your own classroom learning or teaching experiences? Provide concrete examples to illustrate the links between theory and experience that you have in mind.
- Consult an ELT course book/series. Categorise the presentation and practice of an aspect of language (grammar, pronunciation, vocabulary, pragmatics *etc.*) using a set of relevant descriptors from this chapter (e.g. comprehension/production; proceduralisation/automatisation; inductive/deductive *etc.*). How does this categorisation inform the way you would use, adapt or supplement the material?
- Imagine you must identify priority research areas for improving teaching and learning in an ELT context that you are familiar with. Identify some under-researched and/or disputed issues highlighted in this chapter that merit investigation in your chosen context, explaining how these new studies could potentially inform pedagogy and enhance learning.

Related topics

Classroom talk, interaction and collaboration; Dealing with the demands of language testing and assessment; Error, corrective feedback, and repair; Individual differences; Language awareness; Teaching language skills.

Further reading

DeKeyser, R. (ed.) (2007) *Practice in a second language: Perspectives from applied linguistics and cognitive psychology*. New York: Cambridge. (This volume provides chapter overviews of cognitive dimensions of learning and relates these factors to pedagogy across different classroom settings.)

Ellis, R. and Shintani, N. (2014) *Exploring language pedagogy through second language acquisition research*. Abingdon: Routledge. (Newcomers to the field may find the practice to theory organisation of this introductory textbook refreshing.)

Gass, S. and Mackey, A. (eds) (2012) *The Routledge handbook of second language acquisition*. London: Routledge. (Part III of the handbook contains seven chapters on different language learning principles.)

Rich, K. R. (2009) *Dreaming in Hindi: Coming awake in another language*. Boston: Houghton Mifflin Harcourt. (An autobiographical account of an adult learning Hindi as an L2 in India provides an informal introduction to a variety of SLA concepts and processes from a student perspective.)

Notes

1 Defining these terms and measuring these constructs continues to attract debate (Rebuschat, 2013).
2 These are sometimes also referred to as 'explicit' and 'implicit' *instruction* but should not be confused with the *learning* itself. Instructional intentions, learning processes, and outcomes could each have different (and independent) degrees of explicitness.
3 Inductive learning involves the extraction of patterns or rules from examples (similar to discovery learning); deductive learning involves the application of a given rule to examples, thereby engaging learners in practice to consolidate knowledge of the rule.
4 Whether L2 learning is driven by general cognitive mechanisms or the result of language-dedicated functions of the brain is also debated. The latter 'universal grammar' (UG) approach is more focused on language knowledge than on the processes that result in the knowledge, so is not treated further here. (For examples of how UG insights may inform L2 teaching, see Whong et al., 2013).

References

Ågren, M., Granfeldt, J. and Schlyter, S. (2012) 'The growth of complexity and accuracy in L2 French: Past observations and recent applications of developmental stages', in A. Housen, F. Kuiken and I. Vedder (eds) *Dimensions of L2 performance and proficiency investigating complexity, accuracy and fluency in SLA.* Amsterdam/ Philadelphia: John Benjamins. 95–120.

Barton, A., Bragg, J. and Serratrice, L. (2009) '"Discovering Language" in primary school: An evaluation of a language awareness programme'. *Language Learning Journal*, 37/2. 145–164.

Bjork, R. A. (1994) 'Memory and metamemory considerations in the training of human beings', in J. Metcalfe and A. Shimamura (eds) *Metacognition: Knowing about knowing.* Cambridge, MA: MIT Press. 185–205.

Bley-Vroman, R. (2009) 'The evolving context of the fundamental difference hypothesis'. *Studies in Second Language Acquisition*, 31/2. 175–198.

Bybee, J. and Hopper, P. (eds) (2001) *Frequency and the emergence of linguistic structure.* Amsterdam: John Benjamins.

Chase, W. G. and Simon, H. A. (1973) 'The mind's eye in chess', in W. G. Chase (ed.) *Visual information processing.* New York: Academic Press. 215–281.

Chomsky, N. (1957) *Syntactic structures.* The Hague: Mouton.

Chomsky, N. (1959) 'A review of B. F. Skinner's "Verbal Behaviour"'. *Language*, 35/1. 26–58.

Clashen, H. and Felser, C. (2006) 'How native-like is non-native language processing?' *Trends in Cognitive Sciences*, 10/12. 564–570.

Collins, L. (2004) 'The particulars on universals: A comparison of the acquisition of tense-aspect morphology among Japanese- and French-speaking learners of English'. *Canadian Modern Language Review*, 61/2. 251–274.

Collins, L., Trofimovich, P., White, J., Cardoso, W. and Horst, M. (2009) 'Some input on the easy/difficult grammar question: An empirical study'. *Modern Language Journal*, 93/3. 336–353.

Corder, S. P. (1967) 'The significance of learners' errors'. *International Review of Applied Linguistics*, 5/1–4. 161–169.

Cowan, N. (2011) 'Working memory and attention in language use', in J. Guandouzi, F. Loncke and M. J. Williams (eds) *The handbook of psycholinguistics and cognitive processes.* London: Psychology Press. 75–97.

De Angelis, G. (2007) *Third or additional language acquisition.* Clevedon, UK: Multilingual Matters.

De Jong, N. (2005) 'Can second-language grammar be learned through listening? An experimental study'. *Studies in Second Language Acquisition*, 27/2. 205–234.

De Jong, N. and Perfetti, C. A. (2011) 'Fluency training in the ESL classroom: An experimental study of fluency development and proceduralization'. *Language Learning*, 61. 533–568.

DeKeyser, R. (1997) 'Beyond explicit rule learning: Automatising second language morphosyntax'. *Studies in Second Language Acquisition*, 19/2. 195–221.

DeKeyser, R. (1998) 'Beyond focus on form: Cognitive perspectives on learning and practicing second language grammar', in C. Doughty and J. Williams (eds) *Focus on form in classroom language acquisition.* New York: Cambridge University Press. 42–63.

DeKeyser, R. (2007a) 'Skill acquisition theory', in J. Williams and B. VanPatten (eds) *Theories in second language acquisition: An introduction.* Mahwah, NJ: Lawrence Erlbaum. 97–113.

DeKeyser, R. (ed.) (2007b) *Practice in a second language: Perspectives from applied linguistics and cognitive psychology.* Cambridge: Cambridge University Press.

DeKeyser, R. M. and Juffs, A. (2005) 'Cognitive considerations in L2 learning', in E. Hinkel (ed.) *Handbook of research in second language teaching and learning.* Mahwah, NJ: Lawrence Erlbaum Associates. 437–454.

Doughty, C. (2004) 'Effects of instruction on learning a second language: A critique of instructed SLA research', in B. VanPatten, J. Williams, S. Rott and M. Overstreet (eds) *Form-meaning connections in second language acquisition.* Mahwah, NJ: Lawrence Erlbaum Associates. 181–202.

Downes, P. (2014) *Discovering language.* Retrieved from http://sha.org.uk/Home/About_us/Projects/ Discovering_language/Project_rationale/

Edwards, R. and Collins, L. (2013) 'Modelling second language vocabulary learning', in S. Jarvis and M. Daller (eds) *Vocabulary knowledge: Human ratings and automated measures.* Amsterdam: John Benjamins. 157–184.

Ellis, N. C. (2002) 'Frequency effects in language processing: A review with implications for theories of implicit and explicit language acquisition'. *Studies in Second Language Acquisition*, 24/2. 143–188.

Ellis, N. C. (2005) 'At the interface: Dynamic interactions of explicit and implicit language knowledge'. *Studies in Second Language Acquisition*, 27/2. 305–352.

Ellis, N. C., O'Donnell, M. B. and Römer, U. (2014) 'The processing of verb-argument constructions is sensitive to form, function, frequency, contingency, and prototypicality'. *Cognitive Linguistics*, 25/1. 55–98.

Ellis, R. (2002) 'Does form-focused instruction affect the acquisition of implicit knowledge?' *Studies in Second Language Acquisition*, 24/2. 223–236.

Ellis, R. (2008) *The study of second language acquisition*. Oxford: Oxford University Press.

Ericsson, K. A., Krampe, R. T. and Tesche-Römer, C. (1993) 'The role of deliberate practice in the acquisition of expert performance'. *Psychological Review*, 100/3. 363–406.

Falk, Y. and Bardel, C. (2010) 'The study of the role of the background languages in third language acquisition: The state of the art'. *International Review of Applied Linguistics*, 48/2–3. 185–219.

Franks, J. J., Bilbrey, C. W., Lien, K. G. and McNamara, T. P. (2000) 'Transfer-appropriate processing (TAP) and repetition priming'. *Memory and cognition*, 28/7. 1140–1151.

Gardner, H. (1998) *The mind's new science: A history of the cognitive revolution*. New York, NY: Basic Books. (Original work published 1986.)

Gathercole, S. E. and Alloway, T. P. (2008) *Working memory and learning: A practical guide*. London: Sage.

Haight, C. E., Herron, C. and Cole, S. P. (2007) 'The effects of deductive and guided inductive instructional approaches on the learning of grammar in the elementary foreign language college classroom'. *Foreign Language Annals*, 40/2. 288–310.

Håkansson, G. (2013) 'Processability theory: Explaining developmental sequences', in M. P. Garcia-Mayo, M. J. Gutierrez-Mangado and M. Martínez Adrián (eds) *Contemporary approaches to second language acquisition*. Amsterdam: John Benjamins. 111–128.

Hall, G. and Cook, G. (2012) 'Own-language use in language teaching and learning'. *Language Teaching*, 45/3. 271–308.

Hasko, V. (2013) 'Capturing the dynamics of second language development via learner corpus research: A very long engagement'. *The Modern Language Journal*, 97/S1. 1–10.

Holmes, J., Gathercole, S. E. and Dunning, D. L. (2009) 'Adaptive training leads to sustained enhancement of poor working memory in children'. *Developmental Science*, 12. F9–F15.

Horst, M., White, J. and Bell, P. (2010) 'Interaction of first and second language knowledge'. *International Journal of Bilingualism*, 14/3. 331–349.

Hyltenstam, K. (1977) 'Implicational patterns in interlanguage syntax variation'. *Language Learning*, 27/2. 383–411.

Izumi, S. (2002) 'Output, input enhancement, and the noticing hypothesis: An experimental study on ESL relativization'. *Studies in Second Language Acquisition*, 24/4. 541–577.

Jarvis, S. and Pavlenko, A. (2008) *Crosslinguistic influence in language and cognition*. New York: Routledge.

Kelly, L. G. (1969) *25 centuries of language teaching*. Rowley, MA: Newbury House.

Klingberg, T. (2010) 'Training and plasticity of working memory'. *Trends in Cognitive Sciences*, 14/7. 317–324.

Larsen-Freeman, D. (2013) 'Transfer of learning transformed'. *Language Learning*, 63: Suppl. 1. 107–129.

Leeser, M. (2007) 'Learner-based factors in L2 reading comprehension and processing grammatical form: Topic familiarity and working memory'. *Language Learning*, 57/2. 229–270.

Leveen, S. (2014) *Learn French in 10 years*. Retrieved from http://www.huffingtonpost.com/steve-leveen/learn-french-in-10-years_1_b_5579270.html

Lightbown, P. M. (2008) 'Transfer appropriate processing as a model for class second language acquisition', in Z. Han (ed.) *Understanding second language process*. Clevedon: Multilingual Matters. 27–44.

Lightbown, P. M., Halter, R., White, J. and Horst, M. (2002) 'Comprehension-based learning: The limits of "Do it yourself"'. *Canadian Modern Language Review*, 58/3. 427–464.

Loschky, L. and Bley-Vroman, R. (1993) 'Grammar and task-based methodology', in G. Crookes and S. Gass (eds) *Tasks and language learning: Integrating theory and practice*. Clevedon, England: Multilingual Matters Ltd. 123–167.

Luk, Z. P. and Shirai, Y. (2009) 'Review article: Is the acquisition order of grammatical morphemes impervious to L1 knowledge? Evidence from the acquisition of plural -s, articles, and possessive 's'. *Language Learning*, 59/4. 721–754.

Lyster, R., Saito, K. and Sato, M. (2013) 'Oral corrective feedback in second language classrooms'. *Language Teaching*, 46/1. 1–40.

MacWhinney, B. (2012) 'The logic of the unified model', in S. Gass and A. Mackey (eds) *The Routledge handbook of second language acquisition*. Abingdon: Routledge. 211–227.

Marsden, E. (2006) 'Exploring input processing in the classroom: An experimental comparison of processing instruction and enriched input'. *Language Learning*, 56/3. 507–566.

Marsden, E., Altmann, G. and St. Claire. M. (2013) 'Priming of verb inflections in L2 French amongst beginner learners, and the effects of orientation of attention during different instructional activities'. *International Review of Applied Linguistics for Language Education*, 51/3. 271–298.

Marsden, E. and Chen, H.-Y. (2011) The roles of structured input activities in processing instruction and the kinds of knowledge they promote'. *Language Learning*, 61/4. 1058–1098.

Marsden, E., Mackey A. and Plonsky, L. (2015) 'Breadth and depth: The IRIS repository', in A. Mackey and E. Marsden (eds) *Instruments for research into second languages: Empirical studies advancing methodology.* Abingdon: Routledge. 1–21.

Marsden, E. J., Williams, J. and Liu, X. (2013) 'Learning novel morphology: The role of meaning and orientation of attention at initial exposure'. *Studies in Second Language Acquisition,* 35/4. 1–36.

McDonough, K. and Kim, Y. (2009) 'Syntactic priming, type frequency, and EFL learners' production of wh-questions'. *Modern Language Journal,* 93/3. 386–398.

Miller, G. (2003) 'The cognitive revolution: A historical perspective'. *Trends in Cognitive Sciences,* 7/3. 141–144.

Mitchell, R., Myles, F. and Marsden, E. (2012) *Second language learning theories* (3rd ed.). Abingdon, UK: Routledge.

Morgan-Short, K. (2012a) 'Declarative memory and knowledge', in P. Robinson (ed.) *The Routledge encyclopaedia of second language acquisition.* New York/London: Routledge. 157–160.

Morgan-Short, K. (2012b) 'Procedural memory and knowledge', in P. Robinson (ed.) *The Routledge encyclopaedia of second language acquisition.* New York/London: Routledge. 509–512.

Morgan-Short, K., Faretta-Stutenberg, M. and Bartlett, L. (2015) 'Contributions of event-related potential research to issues in explicit and implicit second language acquisition', in P. Rebuschat (ed.) *Implicit and explicit learning of languages.* Amsterdam: John Benjamins. 349–384.

Myles, F. (2004) 'From data to theory: The overrepresentation of linguistic knowledge in SLA'. *Transactions of the Philological Society,* 102/2. 139–168.

Myles, F., Mitchell, R. and Hooper, J. (1999) 'Interrogative chunks in French L2: A basis for creative construction?' *Studies in Second Language Acquisition,* 21/1. 49–80.

Norris, J. M. and Ortega, L. (2000) 'Effectiveness of L2 instruction: A research synthesis and quantitative meta-analysis'. *Language Learning,* 50/3. 417–528.

Ortega, L. (2009) *Understanding second language acquisition.* New York: Routledge.

Pienneman, M. (1998) *Language processing and second language development: Processability theory.* Amsterdam: John Benjamins.

Reber, A. S. (1996) *Implicit learning and tacit knowledge: An essay on the cognitive unconscious.* Oxford: Oxford University Press.

Rebuschat, P. (2013) 'Measuring implicit and explicit knowledge in second language research'. *Language Learning,* 63/3. 595–626.

Rebuschat, P. and Williams, J. N. (2012) 'Implicit and explicit knowledge in second language acquisition'. *Applied Psycholinguistics,* 33/4. 829–856.

Révész, A. (2012) 'Working memory and the observed effectiveness of recasts on different L2 outcome measures'. *Language Learning,* 62/1. 93–132.

Roberts, L. (2012) 'Individual differences in second language processing'. *Language Learning,* 62/s-2. 172–188.

Robinson, P. and Ellis, N. C. (eds) (2008) *Handbook of cognitive linguistics and second language acquisition.* London: Routledge.

Roehr, K. (2007) 'Metalinguistic knowledge and language ability in university-level L2 learners'. *Applied Linguistics,* 29/2. 173–199.

Roehr, K. (2008) 'Linguistic and metalinguistic categories in second language learning'. *Cognitive Linguistics,* 19/1. 67–106.

Rosa, E. and O'Neill, M. D. (1999) 'Explicitness, intake, and the issue of awareness'. *Studies in Second Language Acquisition,* 21/4. 511–556.

Sagarra, N. (2008) 'Working memory and L2 processing of redundant grammatical forms', in Z. Han (ed.) *Understanding second language process.* Clevedon, UK: Multilingual Matters. 133–147.

Sagarra, N. and Ellis, N. (2013) 'From seeing adverbs to seeing morphology: Language experience and adult acquisition of L2 tense'. *Studies in Second Language Acquisition,* 35/2. 261–290.

Sanz, C. and Morgan-Short, K. (2004) 'Positive evidence vs. explicit rule presentation and explicit negative feedback: A computer-assisted study'. *Language Learning,* 54/1. 35–78.

Schumann, J. (1979) 'The acquisition of English negation by speakers of Spanish: A review of the literature', in R. Andersen (ed.) *The acquisition and use of Spanish and English as first and second languages*. Washington, DC: TESOL. 3–32.

Segalowitz, N. and Lightbown, P. M. (1999) 'Psycholinguistic approaches to SLA'. *Annual Review of Applied Linguistics*, 19. 23–43.

Selinker, L. (1972) 'Interlanguage'. *International Review of Applied Linguistics in Language Teaching*, 10/1–4. 209–241.

Shintani, N., Li, S. and Ellis, R. (2013) 'Comprehension-based versus production-based grammar instruction: A meta-analysis of comparative studies'. *Language Learning*, 63/2. 296–329.

Smith, E. E. (2001) 'Cognitive psychology: history'. *International Encyclopaedia of the Social and Behavioural Sciences*. Amsterdam: Elsevier. 2140–2147.

Spada, N. and Lightbown, P. (1999) 'Instruction, first language influence, and developmental readiness in second language acquisition'. *Modern Language Journal*, 83. 1–22.

Spada, N. and Lightbown, P. M. (2008) 'Form-focused instruction: Isolated or integrated?' *TESOL Quarterly*, 42/2. 181–207.

Spada, N. and Tomita, Y. (2010) 'Interactions between type of instruction and type of language feature: A meta-analysis'. *Language Learning*, 60. 263–308.

Swain, M. (1995) 'Three functions of output in second language learning', in G. Cook and B. Seildlhofer (eds) *Principles and practice in applied linguistics: Studies in honour of H. G. Widdowson*. Oxford: Oxford University Press. 125–144.

Swain, M. (2005) 'The output hypothesis: theory and research', in E. Hinkel (ed.) *Handbook of research in second language teaching and learning*. Mahwah, NJ: Lawrence Erlbaum. 471–484.

Thewissen, J. (2013) 'Capturing L2 accuracy developmental patterns: Insights from an error-tagged EFL learner corpus'. *Modern Language Journal*, 97/S1. 77–101.

Toth, P. D. (2006) 'Processing instruction and a role for output in second language acquisition'. *Language Learning*, 56/2. 319–385.

Trofimovich, P. and McDonough, K. (2011) *Using priming methods to study L2 learning and teaching*. Amsterdam: John Benjamins.

Van den Branden, K. (2007) 'Second language education: Practice in perfect learning conditions?', in R. DeKeyser (ed.) *Practice in a second language: Perspectives from applied linguistics and cognitive psychology*. New York: Cambridge University Press. 161–179.

VanPatten, B. (ed.) (2004) *Processing instruction: Theory, research, and commentary*. Mahwah, NJ: Lawrence Erlbaum Associates.

VanPatten, B. (2012) 'Input processing', in S. M. Gass and A. Mackey (eds) *The Routledge handbook of second language acquisition*. Abingdon: Routledge. 268–281.

Wen, Z., Mota, M. and McNeill, A. (eds) (2015) *Working memory in second language acquisition and processing*. Bristol: Multilingual Matters.

Whong, M., Gil, K. and Marsden, H. (2013) *Universal grammar and the second language classroom*. Dordrecht: Springer.

Williams, J. N. (2012) 'Working memory and SLA', in S. M. Gass and A. Mackey (eds) *The Routledge handbook of second language acquisition*. Abingdon: Routledge. 427–441.

Wray, A. (2002) *Formulaic language and the lexicon*. Cambridge: Cambridge University Press.

Year, J. and Gordon, P. (2009) 'Korean speakers' acquisition of the English ditransitive construction: The role of verb prototype, input distribution, and frequency'. *Modern Language Journal*, 93/3. 399–417.

21

Sociocultural theory and the language classroom

Eduardo Negueruela-Azarola and Próspero N. García

Introduction

The present chapter reviews theoretical and pedagogical insights in the field of ELT inspired by Vygotsky's (1986) research on the relationship between thinking and speaking and by consequent research into second language acquisition (SLA) from a *sociocultural theory* (SCT) perspective (Negueruela-Azarola, 2003; Lantolf and Thorne, 2006). From this, we examine the teaching of conceptual thinking in the ELT classroom, grounded in the idea that language learning is a transformative activity.

The chapter begins by situating the historical origins of SCT in the work of Vygotsky and his colleagues. Next, we briefly explain the SCT constructs relevant to language teaching: *monism, dialectics, cultural mediation, verbal thinking internalisation*. Then, we focus on a key area of debate for ELT: teaching language as a transformative activity grounded in the notion of pedagogical praxis. From this perspective, teaching communities are prompted to consider communication not only as a source of meaning exchange and learning but also as a source of personal transformation and development. This requires us to understand a relatively complex theoretical issue: the dialectical (contradictory) unity formed by language learning and conceptual development. We conclude the chapter by focusing on two applications inspired by SCT principles: concept-based teaching (CBT) and dynamic assessment (DA).

Historical origins and central constructs of SCT

During the 1920s and 1930s, Vygotsky's research group began working on a socio-historical approach to human thinking, also known as sociocultural theory. Their objective was to understand the unique cultural nature of human activity when compared to other species. The underlying principle was recognising that human beings act upon and interact with the world using cultural artefacts and means, chief among them language.

Monism: unity of cognitive and social activity

Vygotsky's research group proposed that focusing *only* on private cognition through introspection or *only* on social activity through description was a reductionist way of understanding our unique relationship with the world (Van de Veer and Valsiner, 1991). In other words, the human mind and social activity can be seen as a unified whole (perceiving reality as a single entity is termed *monism*). Vygotsky's research programme was based on (1) constructing a comprehensive psychological theory that recognised the centrality of cultural activity in human psychological and social functioning and (2) offering a theoretical framework applicable and relevant to real and pressing world challenges in fields such as education and clinical psychology, in which a theory of human consciousness, learning and development was unavoidable. Consequently, a sociocultural approach based on a Vygotskian framework to the study of human thinking, learning and development highlights how the social and the cognitive are culturally interrelated and form a 'dialectic'.

Dialectics

Dialectics is the logic used within a SCT perspective to describe how apparently opposed processes or phenomena can function together, forming a more complex unity (Novack, 1971: 17). In dialectical logic, defining complex phenomena implies studying contradictory relationships without separating objects of study. Of course, separating the cognitive, the cultural and the social in human beings is a convenient epistemological move: it is easier to study the social, the cultural and the psychological in three separate disciplines (e.g. sociology, anthropology and psychology). This, however, is an ontological mistake, as human beings are social and private at the same time. In other words, it is misleading to see people as only social since we are also private beings in social settings who think through cultural artefacts such as language; conversely, we are social and public even in private settings. For instance, reading a book alone is a social activity where a text 'talks' to us in a private context. Our identities are social, psychological, historical and cultural at the same time.

Cultural mediation

The key to finding the connection between the social and the private is *cultural mediation*, as humans do not interact directly with their environment but through the mediation of physical and psychological tools. 'Mediation' implies that conscious human activity is guided, shaped and transformed by material (e.g. a screwdriver, a computer, a pencil) and psychological tools and artefacts (e.g. speech, literacy, logic, geometry). These psychological tools in turn change our environment through human activity, as well as affect how we think and orient our lives. In other words, the origin and essence of human thinking is participation in culturally mediated human activity. Mediation in human activity becomes the key principle to understand the cultural origins of human thinking.

As a consequence, SCT proposes that social context and cultural tools mediate thinking. They not only influence or guide it, but also – and mainly – transform and shape human activity. SCT approaches the study of human thinking by focusing on the emergence of higher forms of human consciousness (e.g. intentional memory, voluntary attention, categorisation and organised planning). These social forms of thinking are social activity mediated by symbolic cultural artefacts, which become tools for thinking, learning and communicating (Kozulin, 1998). Languages such as English or Spanish, as well as any other symbolic system (such as mathematics and music), are symbolic cultural artefacts; they are both content and tools for thinking processes in human beings.

Intermental functioning, transformation, verbal thinking and internalisation

For SCT, any psychological function begins *intermentally* in communicative activity (for instance between caregiver and infant or between expert and novice) and is transformed *intramentally*

(Vygotsky, 1978). This transformation implies changing social communicative activity into personal inner dialogue. In formal educational settings, communicative development could originate, for example, from meaningful dialogical interaction between instructor and learners or among the learners themselves (Swain et al., 2015), who then make these communicative interactions their own (intramental), thereby transforming them (i.e. understanding them in their own way, that is, from interaction and explanation to internal conceptual understanding). The centrality of languages as key meditational means in sociocultural functioning in the world (as well as in the classroom) and their dual quality (both social/communicative and private/cognitive) explain the transformation of social activity and experiences into verbal thinking (Vygotsky, 1986).

Verbal thinking originates in cultural social activity through shared intentionality and social collaboration (Tomasello, 2014). This is the theoretical basis for understanding *internalisation* as the process of transforming ideas from others into ideas for the self. The learner is also transformed when developing new ideas about language. In the field of instructed SLA, and applicable to ELT, internalisation is directly connected with the notion of mindful conceptual engagement, which is the transformative process taking place when learners focus and engage on 'conceptual categories' as tools for understanding and reflection (Negueruela-Azarola, 2013b), for instance, when learners develop a conceptual understanding of the language necessary to construct their grammatical choices. Conceptual categories that learners might focus on in an ELT classroom include grammatical concepts such as verbal tense, verbal aspect, motion and directionality; textual concepts such as coherence in texts; or pragmatic notions such as intentionality, normativity, solidarity or refusal.

Key insights for language teaching from a SCT perspective

Objectivist, interactionist and transformative language teaching

From a SCT perspective, language teaching may generally be interpreted through three basic approaches: objectivist, interactionist and transformative. An *objectivist* approach is based on the implicit or explicit idea that teaching a language such as English is the teaching and learning of a static systematic object, an empty structure that has morphology, syntax and a lexicon. This systematic object needs to be presented, described, explained and mastered by learners through understanding and practising. In other words, in this approach, explaining forms is explaining language.

This objectivist study and teaching frames language as an object to be placed in the 'container-mind' of learners. Indeed, the very phrase 'second language acquisition' leads to thinking about language as if it were an object that can be acquired, placed and stored somewhere in our minds as if they were containers (van Lier, 2000). We are also drawing here on Lakoff and Johnson's (1980) suggestion that metaphor is not just a linguistic phenomenon – it reveals the fundamentals ways in which people understand the world around them. The 'mind-as-container' is a metaphor which conveys a particular view of the mind, and also of language.

The objectivist approach constructs language as a system and foregrounds its formal properties. Logically, linguistic subfields based on form (morphology and syntax) are concrete and easier to systematise for teaching when compared to profiling other areas based on meaning, such as semantics (meaning and interpretation) and pragmatics (intentionality and context). Objectivist understandings may be linked to form-focused and structure-based approaches to language teaching.

Alternatively, an *interactionist* approach to language teaching highlights interaction in communication. Language as interaction may be taught through promoting communicative transactions where meaning is central. This is the approach followed in conventional communicative classrooms where a fluency approach to teaching (Omaggio, 2001) is foregrounded (i.e. teachers devising pedagogical tasks, which are conducive to interaction). Considerable advances in L2 pedagogy began to be made when scholars and language teachers realised that teaching a language was not about teaching a code or a systematic object but about teaching communication (Widdowson, 1978; see also Thornbury, this volume). In other words, language learners need to engage in meaning-making communicative activity to develop communicative abilities. A strong view of communicative language teaching (CLT) (Howatt, 1984; Howatt with Widdowson 2004), based on the idea that 'communication leads to learning' rather than 'learning leads to communication', precisely addresses the issue of language as meaning-making activity. Thus, although CLT did not originate from SCT, SCT thinking overlaps and develops communicative language teaching. For SCT, communicative approaches are needed in the classroom – participation in communicative events is critical to develop proficiency in a second language (Hall, 2002).

Finally, a *transformative* approach is inspired by SCT principles. Teaching does not just imply acquiring an object that is systematic or even promoting communicative transactions in the classroom: SCT-inspired transformative teaching is the activity of promoting conceptual reflection (i.e. the internalisation and thus transformation of new ideas through thinking on and about these new ideas) through communicative activity. ELT as transformative participation is about mediation, as mediation by language in social communicative activity promotes understanding. Consequently, learners themselves are also transformed as they internalise new ideas and knowledge.

The key in the classroom, therefore, is to promote strategic social interaction (DiPietro, 1987) and meaningful significant intra-action in which learners make new knowledge 'their own' (Negueruela-Azarola, 2003). ELT teachers should promote systematic conceptual communication, that is, reflection using concepts (ideas with functional relevance in concrete tasks). This also promotes the internalisation of new ideas. As will be illustrated below, transformative pedagogies for the ELT classroom are about engaging and contributing with others in social interaction. This is the origin of conceptual intra-action in L2 learning and development (Negueruela-Azarola et al., 2015). From this perspective, language teaching is essentially about personal transformation (defined as change based on conceptual development) both for learners and teachers.

Educational praxis and transformative pedagogies

An SCT-inspired pedagogical approach to language learning and conceptual development as a transformative practice does not 'understand' theoretical research as a separate process from pedagogical practices. There is nothing as practical as a good theory of L2 learning and development, and there is nothing as theoretical as the effective practice of L2 teaching and testing. This is the basis for educational praxis. In Vygotsky's SCT, theory and practice are interconnected in a dialectical relationship, in which theory guides practice and practice feeds theory, fostering change in both when needed in a bi-directional fashion (Lantolf and Poehner, 2014).

SCT, therefore, views research and practice as interdependent, paying special attention to actual classroom activity and its impact on learning and development (Lantolf, 2011). On the one hand, ELT researchers in classrooms need also to be practitioners whose role is not only observing development but additionally trying to foster it through direct instruction. On the other, ELT teachers need to become researchers in a transformative sense. From this perspective, the goal of a transformative approach to teaching as culturally mediated activity is to apply sociocultural theory to facilitate learning *and* to promote critical conceptual development, rather than just observing language learning processes. A transformative approach also aims to document and explain not only learners' behaviour (i.e. their performance) but also, and more importantly, to capture the dynamics of their conceptual development as mediated through language in reflective activity. For instance, L2 learners as sense-making beings should engage in reflective conceptual tasks where they are pushed to discover and find contradictions between their communicative choices and how they make sense of them. Reflecting on the conceptual reasons for our communicative choices, for instance, implies thinking about why we use a certain preposition in a specific utterance by constructing a model of motion events (Aguiló-Mora and Negueruela-Azarola, 2015), or reflecting on why we begin a paragraph with a specific thematic sentence by applying the notion of genre (Ferreira and Lantolf, 2008). Further examples of conceptual models follow later in the chapter.

In sum, a conceptual approach to ELT based on mindful-conceptual engagement has implications not only for communicative development but also for the internalisation of new thinking frames through which learners think about communication in new ways. This transformative perspective requires creating a classroom dynamic and tasks that promote both communication and conceptual reflection. Meanwhile, from a research perspective, data collection is a teaching process. In the ELT classroom, teachers must become investigators in the most applied sense of the word. A first step for transformative pedagogies, therefore, is to frame ELT classes both as a conceptual and a communicative environment. In this sense, we need to develop appropriate pedagogical explanations and materials for complex conceptual notions such as tense, aspect, mood, sarcasm, social distance, genre and text, which are directly relevant to communication in the ELT classroom.

The zone of potential development (ZPOD)

A transformative approach to teaching as a culturally-mediated activity is based on potential development. This is grounded in the Vygotskian distinction between learning and development. 'Learning' is about knowledge and skills, for example knowing verbal morphology or recognising a lexical item and using them appropriately in a text. 'Development' is defined here as the internalisation of functional conceptual meanings through which we orient concrete oral and written communicative activity. For example, development implies that a learner is morphologically accurate when speaking or writing not because they 'just' know the forms or they have the skill to deploy endings, but because they understand and are able to apply the notion of tense and aspect to orient their communicative choices. The key is to promote conceptual development and not only language learning as a skill or knowledge.

Such a stance is the basis for transformative pedagogies: to focus on 'the future in the making' or on the zone of potential development (ZPOD). The ZPOD is inspired by Vygtosky's original proposal on the zone of proximal development (ZPD). The ZPD as defined by Vygotsky (1978) was an alternative to IQ testing (i.e. 'intelligence quotient' – a standardised test to assess human intelligence). The ZPD is the difference between solo and assisted performance, i.e. it is the 'place' where, working with peers and 'better others', learners can work at a level that would otherwise be beyond their reach. In Vygotskian psychology, it is understood as a key element for assessing development in children. (For further elaborations which discuss how the ZPD fits with the teaching of second languages, see, for example, Mahn, 2015; Thorne and Hellermann, 2015.)

In the same way, the ZPOD is used specifically for second language development and emerges when learners consciously apply concepts (pragmatic, textual, grammatical) that they do not possess – and by using these meditational tools, they begin to master and internalise them (Negueruela-Azarola, 2008). By using the ZPOD concept, we understand language development to be the result of a process of appropriation and internalisation of concepts mediated by social and interpersonal activities (García, 2012). More importantly, by shifting from proximal (ZPD) to potential (ZPOD) development, we imply that "there is a potential for the internalization of a given concept" (ibid.:16), but that this does not necessarily lead to language development in all cases. In this sense, the ZPOD is the activity created by teachers/learners to explore potential areas of conceptual development by engaging in mediated thinking through conceptual engagement. The key to the ZPOD in ELT is in understanding that conceptual meanings are also the critical components to be presented and manipulated by learners in a coherent, organised and complete manner. However, not all reflections create new systematic and functional ideas or concepts as tools for thinking. There is a potentiality for development, but not a guarantee.

Ways ahead in ELT classroom practice

Classrooms are social contexts in which the aim is to organise learning in the most productive and significant way, and they are the ideal setting for promoting personal transformations (Kozulin, 1998). SCT scholars are beginning to explore a transformative stance in language learning for the ELT classroom. In what follows, we focus on two areas of interest: *concept-based teaching* (CBT) and *dynamic assessment* (DA).

Concept-based teaching in the ELT classroom

Using concepts as tools for understanding (Vygotsky, 1986) is the critical process for promoting conceptual development and language learning (Negueruela-Azarola, 2003). In CBT, teaching conceptual thinking in the ELT classroom is thus about promoting the emergence of categories of meaning to orient and facilitate communicative performance. In CBT, language is not only a tool used for communicative purposes (a 'tool for results'), but rather is a 'tool and result' in concept formation, as it is both the content and the tool that mediates thinking (Negueruela-Azarola, 2008; García, 2012). Thus, the key to promoting conceptual development becomes pedagogical tasks that facilitate and promote learner engagement by exploring concepts. Such pedagogical tasks include, for example, asking learners to reflect on a specific grammatical issue using a concept (we shall shortly see how this might take place).

From an SCT perspective, in many L2 classrooms, the learning of a new language is not constructed as the internalisation of conceptual tools (i.e. as a transformative approach, see earlier in the chapter) but as the acquisition of forms and basic interactional abilities (i.e. an objective or interactionist approach, see earlier in the chapter). Teaching and learning based on *incomplete* presentations or explanations of language, unsystematic representations of grammatical, textual and communicative knowledge, or a lack of effectively organised and guided conceptual reflection by learners does not lead to the growth of coherent and complete communicative development in learners (Negueruela-Azarola, 2003). This is a problem for classroom learners because they are not able to develop a coherent understanding of complex conceptual meanings, especially grammatical meanings, which may be typologically different between English and the learners' first language. For instance, in the case of learners of English whose first language is Spanish, this would include grammatical meanings such as tense, aspect and modality.

Internalising complex ideas with functional significance in communicative activity is challenging, but it is a developmental and transformative activity that is part of learning. As such, CBT focuses on learners' mindful engagement with grammatical, textual and pragmatic concepts as tools for thinking in meaningful reflective activities (Negueruela-Azarola, 2013a). To pursue a CBT approach in the L2 classroom, teachers need to apply three basic principles: (1) develop a complete and pedagogically adequate explanation of the point to be taught based on a conceptual category of meaning; (2) present a concise visual representation of the targeted concept; (3) and finally – and most importantly – the learner needs to engage in social interaction with the self that leads to intra-action, i.e. conceptualisation: a dynamic process where learners represent ideas to the self and others through creating representations (written and oral verbalisations). We shall now expand on these three points.

The first step to implement CBT is therefore to develop better pedagogical explanations and materials for complex conceptual notions such as tense, aspect, mood, sarcasm, social distance, genre and text. These explanations need to be coherent, complete and pedagogically feasible so learners can assign the notions a functional value that should allow them to understand and create meaningful utterances through them. Negueruela-Azarola (2013a) observes that many of the explanations found in textbooks are lists of simple uses in very concrete contexts for basic intermediate language courses, or are too long and cumbersome in advanced courses.

For instance, teaching a grammatical point such as tense and aspect in the ELT classroom based on a list of rules generally oversimplifies the grammatical issues and provides the learners with structures that can only be used in specific and constrained contexts. Similarly, describing all possible contexts of use is too cumbersome and prevents learners from assigning functional value to the concept as a whole. In the case of teaching grammar conceptually, the argument is that explanations for grammatical use should be based on categories of meaning. For instance, tense might be explained looking at the relative distance between the speaker and the event (Fauconnier, 1998), and aspect may be explained based on the notion of 'boundness' vs. 'unboundness' (Gánem-Gutiérrez and Harun, 2011: 102–103). Developing conceptual explanations of communicative issues is a research task for teaching communities, as not only learners but also teachers need to transform their understandings of language and communication.

Second, appropriate explanations of challenging communicative issues need to be introduced to language learners through concrete graphic representations, to aid learners in constructing functional understandings. These graphic representations as pedagogical aids for learners may be given to or developed by students in the form of diagrams, outlines, schemas or flow charts. The key to developing these material graphic representations is to capture, at a glance, basic meanings in a grammatical, textual or pragmatic way. Examples of these types of pedagogical and graphic tools for learners in an ELT context can be found in Gánem-Gutiérrez and Harun (2011), Lee (2012), White (2012) and Kim (2013). For example, Figure 21.1 (adapted from Gánem-Gutiérrez and Harun, 2011: 111) represents a pedagogical representation of the notions of tense and aspect. Understanding of how to mark tense appropriately is based on relative distance from the event, and each tense is represented by a 'mental space' (Fauconnier, 1998) encapsulated within the temporal line. Aspect, on the other hand, is based on the notions of boundness and unboundness and whether an action can be encapsulated (i.e. Event 1: Yesterday, David _studied_ for two hours) or not (i.e. Event 2: Yesterday David _was studying_ when Mary called).

Notwithstanding, these learning aids need to become thinking devices for learners, and, in this respect, the third step becomes critical in a CBT approach to ELT: learners need to start using language as a tool for internalising complex L2 categories of meaning. These categories of meaning, i.e. concepts, include grammatical (tense, aspect and modality), rhetorical (text, metaphor) and pragmatic (intentionality, voice) categories. Learners need to engage in conceptual tasks where they are pushed to reflect on communicative issues in conceptual ways, that is, using the concept to consciously guide their linguistic choices. For example, Figure 21.2 shows how this would be operationalised as a basic activity for an intermediate ELT classroom, developing the focus on tense and aspect outlined in Figure 21.1. In this basic task, learners are expected to consciously manipulate the concept of aspect in oral and written communication

Pedagogical tool for understanding the concepts of tense and aspect in English

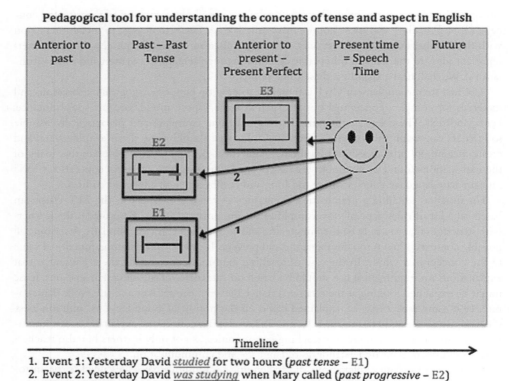

1. Event 1: Yesterday David _studied_ for two hours (*past tense* – E1)
2. Event 2: Yesterday David _was studying_ when Mary called (*past progressive* – E2)
3. Event 3: David _has studied_ a lot this academic year (*present perfect* – E3)

Figure 21.1 A pedagogical tool for understanding the concepts of tense and aspect in English

Source: Adapted from Gánem-Gutiérrez and Harun, 2011: 111. Reproduced by permission of Taylor & Francis Ltd, www.tandfonline.com.

to justify their aspectual choices, as a tool for internalisation. And other pedagogical tasks are of course possible.

When learners are not pushed to conceptualise communicative issues through concepts, they tend to provide simplistic explanations of linguistic and conceptual challenges based on rules of thumb or quick and superficial reasoning (Negueruela-Azarola, 2003; García-Frazier, 2013; Polizzi, 2013; García, 2014). Avoiding simplistic explanations through mindful conceptual engagement (the pedagogical process of constructing, explaining and using conceptual representations to think through communicative choices, i.e. explicitly explaining their own language choices to others) is the key to internalisation in CBT. Although different types of reflective practices abound in language classrooms, explicit conceptual reflection of the type advocated in this chapter is, for the most part, absent in ELT classrooms (see White, 2012 on the teaching of English prepositions from a conceptual perspective). The place where a more reflective conceptual approach seems to emerge in language classroom is in writing instruction in intermediate and advanced courses. In these ELT writing courses, sentence-level grammar generally fails learners and teachers when they want to address the meaning and intentionality that learners want to capture in their texts (see Ferreira and Lantolf, 2008, on the teaching of writing through the notion of genre).

I. ORAL AND WRITTEN COMMUNICATION

Tell a personal and interesting anecdote about something that happened to you this last year.
   Use *past tenses* for your narrative.

Steps:
(A) First, record yourself telling your story to your teacher. Improvise from your memories. Do
    not write your story.
(B) Listen to your own recording.
(C) Write down your story for analysis.

II. CONCEPTUALISATION TASK

Reflect on the meaning that you construct by using different tenses in English using the notion
   of verbal tense and aspect. Use the diagram to help you.
(A) Analyse five of your utterances. Explain each utterance and your use of tense/aspect using
    an abstract conceptual category. Use the ABSTRACT reasons studied so far. These reasons
    need to be based on abstract grammatical meaning (e.g. I present the action as completed
    because . . .). Do not use simple grammatical rules to justify your linguistic choices, such as
    an expression like '*Suddenly*' requires *simple past*.
(B) Explain why for you a particular form is appropriate and meaningful in each context. Are
    other options coherent or appropriate for the meaning you want to convey?
(C) Point out how you use each verb to either set the background of the story or the foreground.

Figure 21.2   A conceptualisation task for an intermediate ELT classroom

Dynamic assessment in the ELT classroom

Dynamic assessment (DA) is the direct application of Vygotsky's ZPD to the language classroom. DA uses assessment procedures that take into account the learner's ZPD as a dynamic and collaborative 'place' for learning.[1]

Thus, assessment in a SCT-inspired ELT classroom should not be understood only in terms of 'testing' but also as a process through which dynamic, fluid and collaborative intervention by peers and teachers opens, ascertains and promotes learners' development. While static and individualist (i.e. non-dynamic) assessment is found in classrooms when learners are asked to complete tasks that focus both on the 'here and now' and on what students have already learned (for example, via a grammar cloze test), DA, by contrast, explores learners' potential and fosters future L2 development as a collaborative process. It allows for interaction and offers mediation aimed at the learner's ZPD.

DA places assessment at the centre of teaching/learning activity, whilst teaching/learning activity becomes a critical part of assessment procedures. Active and dynamic intervention, mediation and help, which are all elements of everyday teaching and learning activity (and are thus not just 'testing'), are integrated during the DA process, both to diagnose learning success and to promote transformative language development in learners. DA is thus an evaluative procedure that considers learning and assessment as two sides of the same coin.

Collaborative dynamic mediation provided during DA allows the teacher to: (1) examine the reasons why students are – or are not – able to successfully complete a language task independently; and (2) establish how much and what type of help (i.e. external mediation) is needed to complete a task successfully, hence establishing learners' potential development. DA provides the instructor with a better idea of the type and amount of instruction and mediation that learners need in order to function independently.

In the context of ELT and L2 instruction, DA focuses on promoting significant interactions that lead to transformative intra-action (i.e. noticing of complex language features in collaborative interactions so as to develop linguistic abilities). The implementation of DA in the language classroom allows the instructor to offer mediation tuned to the learners' needs, creating a space where independent problem solving becomes the goal rather than the means of the evaluative process. Even though co-construction of knowledge among its participants plays a fundamental role in DA, mediation tuned to the ZPD "necessarily entails a level of challenge to learners, as they strive to push beyond what they are capable of achieving comfortably" (Lantolf and Poehner, 2014: 159). Learners are not provided with the 'right answer' to a particular task, but they are not expected to achieve it on their own, either. Rather, when engaged in DA, the learner and teacher work together towards a common objective in an activity where their "forms of participation and contribution may shift as new capabilities are formed" (Lantolf and Poehner, 2014: 158). This is precisely because the ultimate goal in DA is promoting learners' agentive development and self-regulation (García, 2014). Mediation in DA is a tool that aims at fostering self-regulation and learners' language development through and during pedagogical activity.

Research on DA in L2 and ELT learning and teaching has focused on issues such as establishing a prognosis of L2 development or exploring how mediation is internalised by the learner; that is, whether the mediation provided during DA has been effectively appropriated by the learner. Aljaafreh and Lantolf (1994), Antón (2009) and García (2011), among others, have focused on reporting the implementation of DA as a tool to establish a prognosis of language learning and potential development.

In their pioneering study, Aljaafreh and Lantolf (1994) illustrated how the development and use of English tense, articles, prepositions and modal verbs by three adult ESL learners could be documented through shifts in the type of mediation (in this case corrective feedback) offered by the practitioner while co-constructing knowledge with the learners. As illustrated in Figure 21.3, this mediation was organised from the most implicit (point 0) to the most explicit (point 12), and the more we move down the scale, the more teacher mediation is needed (hence mediation

0. Tutor asks the learner to read, find the errors and correct them independently, prior to the tutorial.
1. Construction of a 'collaborative frame' prompted by the presence of the tutor as a potential dialogic partner.
2. Prompted or focused reading of the sentence that contains the error by the learner or the tutor.
3. Tutor indicates explicitly that something may be wrong in a segment.
4. Tutor rejects unsuccessful attempts at recognising the error.
5. Tutor narrows down the location of the error.
6. Tutor indicates the nature of the error, but does not identify the error.
7. Tutor identifies the error.
8. Tutor rejects learner's unsuccessful attempts at correcting error.
9. Tutor provides clues to help the learner arrive at the correct form.
10. Tutor provides the correct form.
11. Tutor provides some explanation for use of the correct form.
12. Tutor provides examples of the correct pattern when other forms of help fail to produce an appropriate responsive action.

Figure 21.3 Regulatory scale of implicit (strategic) to explicit mediation

Source: Adapted from Aljaafreh and Lantolf (1994: 471). Reproduced by permission of John Wiley & Sons.

becomes more explicit). Teacher mediation is aimed towards the learners' ZPD, with the instructor adjusting this mediation according to the learners' responses and uptake over a period, in this particular example, of two months.

With respect to the regulatory scale in Figure 21.3, Aljaafreh and Lantolf (1994) observed that learner development could be traced by analyzing shifts from explicit to more implicit mediation. Although similar types of feedback may happen in many classrooms, the point of DA is to expand this type of feedback not only to teaching but also to testing and assessment. In Excerpt 1 below, we find an interaction with a learner (F) struggling with the notion of tense in English. He is working with his instructor (T) on the modal sentence 'I called other friends who can't went to the party.'

Excerpt 1

1   T: Okay what else? What about the verb and the tense? the verb and the tense . . .
2   F: Could
3   T: Okay, here.
4   F: Past tense.
5   T: Alright, okay, 'who [alright] could not.' Alright? And? . . .
6   F: To.
6   T: Here [points to the verb phrase], what is the right form?
7   F: I . . . go.
8   T: Go. Okay, 'could not go to [that's right] to the party . . .'
         (Aljaafreh and Lantolf, 1994: 479; reproduced with permission of John Wiley & Sons)

In the second excerpt, we can observe a similar situation arising a week later with the same learner. However, the type of mediation needed appears to have changed:

Excerpt 2

9   T: Is there anything wrong here in this sentence? 'I took only Ani because I
10   couldn't took both' . . . Do you see anything wrong? . . . Particularly here
11   'because I couldn't took both'
12   F: Or Maki?
13   T: What the verb, verb . . . something wrong with the verb . . .
14   F: Ah, yes . . .
15   T: That you used. Okay, where? Do you see it?
16   F: (points to the verb)
17   T: Took? okay.
18   F: Take.
19   T: Alright, take.
         (Aljaafreh and Lantolf, 1994: 479; reproduced with permission of John Wiley & Sons)

The learner's response to mediation in Excerpt 2 in relation to Excerpt 1 shows a different degree of control over the corrective feedback: the learner needs less mediation (both in terms of quantity and quality). The locus of control in the second session seems to be moving gradually from the teacher to the learner, who points to the incorrect verb and provides an appropriate verb form with less mediation (lines 15–19).

In addition to establishing a prognosis of conceptual language development, Kozulin and Garb (2001) implemented DA for a group of adult learners in an EFL context, exploring ways to foster their abilities to learn and use reading comprehension techniques. Their investigation showed critical differences between students who had not experienced a DA type of assessment and those who had been exposed to DA. Kozulin and Garb's (2001) study indicated that learners' with a similar performance level demonstrate different, and in some cases dramatically different, reactions to mediation when co-constructing new knowledge related to new EFL text comprehension strategies.

Researchers have also pursued DA as a tool for diagnosing and promoting learning in the classroom and creating a collective ZPD. Davin (2013) proposes combining a model of standardised DA (i.e. the mediation provided comes from a set of limited scripted forms planned before the DA session is conducted) with instructional conversation (IC). IC, according to Goldenberg (1991: 1), is discussion-based lessons in which the instructor promotes students' participation and encourages them to use their own ideas so they can build new notions with the teacher's guidance and arrive at deeper and more sophisticated levels of understanding. Although framed within the construct of the ZPD as a way to foster conceptual and linguistic development, instructional conversations focus on teaching rather than assessment. Notwithstanding, both IC and DA are characterised by the use of mediation – offered by the instructor or a more skilled peer – to achieve higher levels of performance that will lead to learners' development.

Davin (2013) suggests that his DA-IC model should be staged in a predetermined order whereby the instructor would receive a learner request for clarification on a given topic and identify whether or not the scripted forms would provide the necessary support; if they did not, the instructor would then engage students in conversation, address the whole class and co-construct the new knowledge together. Davin (2013: 318–319) thus implies that instructors should use the IC framework to introduce novel concepts and DA to review notions that have already been covered. The unique contribution of DA as a transformative approach to the ELT classroom is to highlight that interaction is a critical part of not only teaching but of testing and assessment. This is critical to provide a more realistic picture of language learners' development. DA in the ELT classroom has the potential to break the instruction-evaluation dichotomy and provide learners with the mediation needed to realise their true potential.

Conclusion

Sociocultural theory is a psychological approach that studies human thinking, learning and development in social activity through cultural mediation. When thinking about ELT, SCT-inspired transformative pedagogies focus on conceptual development. Language learning in the ELT classroom has the potential to promote development of the socially mediated mind. In this sense, L2 development is about internalising conceptual meanings with functional relevance in communicative contexts.

The development of teaching practices in concept-based teaching and dynamic assessment for the ELT classroom is still a work in progress. In this chapter, we have proposed teaching/testing conceptual thinking in the ELT classroom through mindful conceptual engagement activity, a dynamic and conscious process by which learners reflect on their communicative choices by using concepts with the intent of constructing new understandings. We have provided three principles to implement a mindful conceptual approach in the ELT classroom. We have also included examples of dynamic assessment procedures based on collaboration and interaction, which need to be a source of learning and development, rather than a technique for testing. ELT practitioners interested in developing transformative pedagogies and assessment procedures might start from the principles outlined in this chapter and find feasible applications in their own teaching contexts.

To conclude, therefore, ELT teachers/researchers working from a sociocultural theory perspective aim to create, develop and adapt pedagogical tools that allow learners to engage in sense-making activity with grammatical, rhetorical and pragmatic categories of meaning. Ultimately, a mindful conceptual engagement approach to language teaching and testing challenges teaching communities to start thinking about communication not only as a source of meaning exchange but also as a source of personal transformation.

Discussion questions

- Can you give examples of specific teaching and testing practices in the ELT classroom that illustrate objectivist, interactionist and transformative approaches to language teaching? Which of those most closely corresponds to your own teaching approach?
- What is unique about SCT perspective and transformative pedagogies when applied to the ELT classroom? What does it offer you that may be new? How does it challenge you to change or adapt your current teaching and testing practices? How do you understand the notion of transformation or transformative practices for ELT in your own teaching context?
- Some of the concepts explored in the ELT and second language teaching/learning literature have included tense, mood, aspect, voice, social distance and sarcasm. How would you approach the design and instruction of one of these concepts from a CBT perspective? How would you apply the idea of mindful conceptual engagement in your own teaching of concepts?
- In your opinion, are assessment instruments static or dynamic in the ELT classroom? Do they appropriately capture the distinction between actual and potential development? What are some of the consequences of applying DA to testing and assessment of communicative development in your own teaching context?

Related topics

Cognitive perspectives on classroom language learning; Communicative language teaching in theory and practice.

Further reading

Lantolf, J. P. and Poehner, M. E. (eds) (2008) *Sociocultural theory and the teaching of second languages.* London: Equinox. (Aimed at both researchers and practitioners, this volume offers fourteen original studies reporting the implementation of pedagogical and assessment approaches rooted in Vygotsky's sociocultural theory in the second language classroom.)

Lantolf, J. P. and Poehner, M. E. (2014) *Sociocultural theory and the pedagogical imperative in L2 education. Vygotskian Praxis and the Research/ Practice Divide.* London: Routledge. (This volume explores the notion of praxis in the field of second language education, explaining the inherent connection between language teaching and research from a sociocultural perspective.)

Negueruela-Azarola, E., García, P. N. and Buescher, K. (2015) 'From inter-action to intra-action: The internalisation of talk, gesture, and concepts in the second language classroom', in N. Markee (ed.) *The handbook of classroom interaction.* Malden: Wiley-Blackwell. 233–249. (Inspired by Vygotsky's views on collaboration and mediated activity, this chapter proposes that conceptual interaction is the source of internalisation or intra-action.)

Swain, M., Kinnear, P. and Steinman, L. (2015) *Sociocultural theory in second language education: An introduction through narratives* (2nd ed.). Toronto: Multilingual Matters. (This updated version covers some of the fundamental notions of sociocultural theory through the use of English language learners' and teachers' narratives.)

Note

1 In this chapter, we have already argued that the ZPD is also a potentiality: a zone of potential development or ZPOD. The ZPD becomes the ZPOD – and it is transformative in nature – when the learning process focuses on conceptual categories that become significant for the learner. In the case of DA and second language instruction, there has been a primary focus on collaborative activity for promoting learning through interaction, hence creating a ZPD.

References

Aguiló-Mora, F. and Negueruela-Azarola, E. (2015) 'Motion-for-the-other through motion-for-the-self: The complexities of giving directions for advanced second language learners of Spanish and English', in K. Masuda, C. Arnett and A. Labarca (eds) *Cognitive grammar and sociocultural theory in foreign and second language teaching.* Boston: De Gruyter Mouton. 73–100.

Aljaafreh, A. and Lantolf, J. P. (1994) 'Negative feedback as regulation and second language learning in the zone of proximal development'. *Modern Language Journal*, 78/4. 465–483.

Antón, M. (2009) Dynamic assessment of advanced second language learners. *Foreign Language Annals*, 42/3. 576–598.

Davin, K. J. (2013) 'Integration of dynamic assessment and instructional conversations to promote development and improve assessment in the language classroom'. *Language Teaching Research*, 17/3. 303–322.

DiPietro, R. J. (1987) *Strategic interaction: Learning languages through scenarios.* Cambridge: Cambridge University Press.

Fauconnier, G. (1998) 'Mental spaces, language modalities, and conceptual integration', in M. Tomasello (ed.) *The new psychology of language: Cognitive and functional approaches to language structure.* Mahwah, NJ: Lawrence Erlbaum. 251–280.

Ferreira, M. M. and Lantolf, J.P. (2008) 'A concept-based approach to teaching writing through genre analysis', in J. P. Lantolf and M. E. Poehner (eds) *Sociocultural theory and the teaching of second languages.* London, UK: Equinox. 189–227.

Gánem-Gutiérrez, G. A. and Harun, H. (2011) 'Verbalization as a mediational tool for understanding tense/aspect marking in English: An application of concept-based instruction'. *Language Awareness*, 20/2. 99–119.

García, P. N. (2011) 'Dynamic assessment and the Spanish classroom: Implications for teaching'. Proceedings from the *IX Congreso Internacional de Lingüística General.* Valladolid, Spain. June 21st–23rd, 2010.

García, P. N. (2012) *Verbalizing in the second language classroom: The development of the grammatical concept of aspect.* Unpublished PhD thesis. University of Massachusetts, Amherst, USA.

García, P. N. (2014) 'Verbalizing in the second language classroom: Exploring the role of agency in the internalization of grammatical categories', in P. Deters, X. Gao, E.R. Miller and G. Vitanova (eds) *Theorizing and analyzing agency in second language learning: Interdisciplinary approaches.* Bristol, England: Multilingual Matters. 213–231.

García-Frazier, E. (2013) *Concept-based teaching and Spanish modality in heritage language learners: A Vygotskyan approach.* Unpublished PhD thesis, University of Massachusetts, Amherst, USA.

Goldenberg, C. (1991) Instructional conversations and their classroom applications. Educational Practice Report 2. Paper EPR02. Santa Cruz, CA: National Center for Research on Cultural Diversity and Second Language Learning. Retrieved from http://www.escholarship.org/uc/ item/6q72k3k9.

Hall, J. K. (2002) *Methods for teaching foreign languages: Creating communities of learners in the classroom.* Englewood Cliffs, NJ: Prentice-Hall.

Howatt, A.P.R. (1984) *A history of English language teaching.* Oxford: Oxford University Press.

Howatt, A.P.R. with Widdowson, H.G. (2004) A History of Teaching English (2nd ed.). Oxford: Oxford University Press,

Kim, J. (2013) *Developing a conceptual understanding of sarcasm in a second language through concept-based instruction.* Unpublished PhD thesis. The Pennsylvania State University, University Park, PA, USA.

Kozulin, A. (1998) *Psychological tools: A sociocultural approach to education.* Cambridge, MA: Harvard University Press.

Kozulin, A. and Garb, E. (2001) *Dynamic assessment of EFL text comprehension.* Paper presented at the 9th Conference of the European Association for Research on Learning and Instruction. Fribourg, Switzerland.

Lakoff, G. and Johnson, M. (1980) *Metaphors we live by.* Chicago: University of Chicago Press.

Lantolf, J. P. (2011) 'The sociocultural approach to second language acquisition: Sociocultural theory, second language acquisition, and artificial L2 development', in D. Atkinson (ed.) *Alternative approaches to second language acquisition*. New York: Routledge. 24–47.

Lantolf, J. P. and Poehner, M. E. (2014) *Sociocultural theory and the pedagogical imperative in L2 education. Vygotskian Praxis and the Research/ Practice Divide*. London: Routledge.

Lantolf, J. P. and Thorne, S. L. (2006) *Sociocultural theory and the genesis of second language development*. Oxford: Oxford University Press.

Lee, H. (2012) *Concept-based approach to second language teaching and learning: Cognitive linguistics-inspired instruction of English phrasal verbs*. Unpublished PhD thesis. The Pennsylvania State University, University Park, PA.

Mahn, H. (2015) 'Classroom discourse and interaction in the zone of proximal development', in N. Markee (ed.) *The handbook of classroom interaction*. Malden: Wiley-Blackwell. 250–264.

Negueruela-Azarola, E. (2003) *Systemic-theoretical instruction and L2 development: A sociocultural approach to teaching-learning and researching L2 learning*. Unpublished PhD thesis, Pennsylvania State University, USA.

Negueruela-Azarola, E. (2008) 'Revolutionary pedagogies: Learning that leads (to) second language development', in J. P. Lantolf and M. E. Poehner (eds) *Sociocultural theory and the teaching of second languages*. London, UK: Equinox. 189–227.

Negueruela-Azarola, E. (2013a) 'Metalinguistic knowledge becoming intrapsychological tools: Concepts as tools for second language development', in K. Roehr and G. A. Gánem-Gutiérrez (eds) *The metalinguistic dimension in instructed second language learning*. London: Bloomsbury. 221–242.

Negueruela-Azarola, E. (2013b) 'Internalization in second language acquisition: Social perspectives', in C. A. Chapelle (ed.) *The encyclopedia of applied linguistics*. Hoboken, NJ: Wiley-Blackwell. 1–8.

Negueruela-Azarola, E., García, P. N. and Buescher, K. (2015) 'From inter-action to intra-action: The internalization of talk, gesture, and concepts in the second language classroom', in N. Markee (ed.) *The handbook of classroom interaction*. Malden: Wiley-Blackwell. 233–249.

Novack, G. (1971) *An introduction to the logic of Marxism*. Atlanta, GA: Pathfinder Press.

Omaggio, A. (2001) *Teaching language in context*. Boston: Heinle & Heinle.

Polizzi, M. (2013) *The development of Spanish aspect in the second language classroom: Concept-based pedagogy and dynamic assessment*. Unpublished PhD thesis, The University of Massachusetts, Amherst, USA.

Swain, M., Kinnear, P. and Steinman, L. (2015) *Sociocultural theory in second language education: An introduction through narratives* (2nd ed.). Toronto: Multilingual Matters.

Thorne, S. and Hellermann, J. (2015) 'Sociocultural approaches to expert-novice relationships in second language interaction', in N. Markee (ed.) *The handbook of classroom interaction*. Malden: Wiley-Blackwell. 281–297.

Tomasello, M. (2014) *A natural history of human thinking*. Harvard: Harvard University Press.

Van der Veer, R. and Valsiner, J. (1991) *Understanding Vygotsky: A quest for synthesis*. Oxford: Basil Blackwell.

van Lier, L. (2000) 'From input to affordance: Social-interactive learning from an ecological perspective', in J. P. Lantolf (ed.) *Sociocultural theory and second language learning*. Oxford: Oxford University Press. 254–269.

Vygotsky, L. V. (1978) *Mind in society*. Harvard: Harvard University Press.

Vygotsky, L. S. (1986) *Thought and language*. Cambridge, MA: MIT Press.

White, B. (2012) 'A conceptual approach to instruction of phrasal verbs'. *Modern Language Journal*, 96/3. 419–438.

Widdowson, H. G. (1978) *Teaching language as communication*. Oxford: Oxford University Press.

22

Individual differences

Peter D. MacIntyre, Tammy Gregersen and Richard Clément

Introduction

Every person is unique; it is not possible to find two identical language learners. For teachers, differences among individuals can be difficult to deal with because they make it virtually impossible to predict exactly what will happen during the language learning process or to specify in advance exactly what its outcomes will be. Teaching techniques, cultural exchange programmes and contact with other speakers of the target language (TL) can produce both successes and failures in the same cohort of students. Additionally, the actions and reactions of any specific individual will also change over time and are potentially influenced by a wide range of factors.

One of the reasons for the difficulty in predicting the outcomes of learning is the range of factors that influence the process, but, more importantly, the ways in which those many factors interact with each other (DeKeyser, 2013). Perhaps an analogy will help to illustrate the issue. Televisions sets and LCD projectors produce millions of colours on a screen using only three lights – red, green and blue. Subtle changes in combinations of the light provide the many different colours we see. Therefore, it is possible to begin with a few basic elements that interact to produce enormous diversity of outcomes. In some cases, the presence or absence of a specific factor can play a mediating role in the relationship between two other factors. For example, the link between anxiety and enjoyment appears to be somewhat different for men and women (Dewaele and MacIntyre, 2014). When we consider the many possible interactions among learner factors, we can see how the infinite number of different individuals and their learning outcomes can be possible.

In this chapter, we will discuss some of the reasons why individual differences arise and what the research suggests about them. Throughout the chapter, we identify trends in the research literature that have influenced ways in which individual difference (hereafter, ID) factors are conceptualised and studied.

The chapter is organised into four sections. The first reviews several prominent ID factors. We have decided not to classify the IDs into categories. Potential frameworks such as 'affective' versus 'cognitive' IDs can be problematic because there are both affective and cognitive dimensions to all of the concepts discussed below. Similarly, the concepts could be considered through a time-perspective, contrasting some IDs which can fluctuate rapidly, such as anxiety, with those that are quite stable, such as learner personality traits. However, all IDs show both stability and the capacity to change. Thus, classifying or grouping IDs would invariably clarify some dimensions of these variables while it clouds other dimensions. We have therefore chosen to review them individually, in alphabetical order, to emphasise that each of these concepts is complex and multifaceted.

The second section of the chapter deals with how the ID factors fit together; we use two different approaches, one that has been used extensively in the research literature (statistical modelling) and one that is rather new to the field (complex dynamic systems theory). The third section isolates key areas of dispute and debate in the area of ID factors. Finally, we discuss how language practitioners might capitalise on their learners' individuality.

ID factors

Anxiety

Anxiety is the most widely studied emotion in the SLA field, whilst teachers are concerned about language anxiety because of its potential negative effect on both classroom interactions and assessment. MacIntyre and Gardner (1991b) defined language anxiety as the worry and neg-ative emotion reaction aroused when learning or using a second language. Early research focused on two key questions: (1) how to define and measure the concept and (2) is anxiety a cause (or merely an effect) of poor performance?

In defining and attempting to measure anxiety related to language learning, Horwitz et al. (1986) argued that there is something about second/foreign language situations that produces a unique form of anxiety that functions like a personality trait. MacIntyre and Gardner (1991a: 297) theorised that language anxiety begins as an undifferentiated, negative response to some aspect of language learning, but repeated occurrences solidify the association between anxiety and the L2. This process helps to differentiate language learning and use from other anxiety-arousing situations that a learner might encounter, such as public speaking.

Horwitz et al. (1986) discuss three interrelated ingredients to anxiety reactions in the lan-guage classroom: communication, fear of negative evaluation and testing. Communication that is incomplete or incomprehensible can generate anxious feelings, as can worry about what others think of us because of misunderstanding or misspeaking the TL. Testing done as part of a course and for other purposes (e.g. university entrance, job applications) has the potential to generate anxiety that will interfere with the testing process, as when students 'freeze up' and cannot demonstrate what they have learned. The research literature has identified many other potential sources and consequences of language anxiety (Gregersen and MacIntyre, 2014).

As teachers think about anxiety, it might be best to consider it as *both* a cause and a con-sequence of difficulties with language and communication. Taken as a cause of difficulties in language, the emotional arousal and distractions that accompany anxiety can affect all stages of the learning process. For example, an experiment by MacIntyre and Gardner (1994) divided TL vocabulary learning into input, processing and output stages. At the input stage, where new words were originally encountered, anxiety arousal (i.e. increased anxiety) was shown to reduce attention and act as a distraction; thus, anxious learners' focus was divided between dealing with the emotional arousal and the linguistic task at hand. At the processing stage, where the meaning of new words is learned, higher levels of anxiety generated both increased effort to memorise the words and reduced accuracy of correctly identifying them – an unfortunate combination from a learner's perspective. Finally, anxiety arousal at the output stage, where learners use the new words in sentences, reduced the amount and quality of communication (see also Steinberg and Horwitz, 1986).

Anxiety is a consequence of, and can be triggered by, a long list of items, including competi-tiveness among learners, a mismatch between learner and teacher beliefs, harsh error correction and perfectionism (Gregersen and MacIntyre, 2014). Research has shown that difficulties in linguistic coding (such as not being able to recognise the sounds of a TL) contribute to anxiety reactions (Ganschow et al., 1994). Although speaking might be considered the most anxiety-arousing of the skill areas (Kim, 2009), language anxiety can also occur when listening, reading and writing. Gregersen (2006) further notes that anxiety may be heightened when a student has significantly stronger skills in one area (e.g. listening) than another (e.g. speaking). Many learners have described the feelings of fear, embarrassment and even panic associated with anxiety arousal (see MacIntyre, 1999).

Aptitude and multiple intelligences

The meaning and implications of concepts such as *ability, aptitude* or *intelligence* have been debated extensively over the years. From the controversy has emerged a set of concepts that have evolved from seemingly monolithic, fixed entities to a more nuanced account of modifiable abilities that work together. Early studies treated language aptitude as a stable ability determined early in life, one that is not based on training or prior experience (Carroll, 1973). Prior to the advent of language motivation research in the 1960s, aptitude was considered *the* major individual difference factor affecting learning. Thirty-five years later, Ehrman and Oxford (1995) reported that aptitude was the ID variable with the strongest prediction of L2 proficiency.

In spite of such empirical support, many language practitioners have been sceptical about aptitude; Skehan (2002) proposes three reasons for the concern. First, the original aptitude research was conducted during the period when the audiolingual approach was dominant in language pedagogy, and the teaching methodology of the field has changed substantially over the past 20 to 30 years. Second, there is now a greater appreciation for the whole learner, including affect and motivation. Third, the aptitude concept itself might be seen as anti-egalitarian, especially when used to stream learners into groups (Skehan, 2002).

Current research on language aptitude emphasises that it is a dynamic and potentially trainable ID factor (Robinson, 2007) that interacts with learner motivation and opportunity (Ranta, 2008). Robinson's work on aptitude emphasises cognitive abilities as they combine with other ID factors into aptitude complexes that can be matched with teaching techniques for maximum effect. Meanwhile, Skehan (2002) has argued that aptitude is multi-faceted, linked to stages of the learning process.

Like aptitude, the concept of intelligence also has undergone a significant change over the years, developing into a multi-dimensional and increasingly dynamic concept. Early research into intelligence involved a search for 'g', or general intelligence applicable to all situations. As intelligence research progressed, however, the concept became more diversified, and specific facets of intelligence were defined more specifically. Howard Gardner's (1993) theory of multiple intelligences defined at least seven different areas: linguistic, logical-mathematical, spatial, bodily-kinesthetic, musical intelligence, interpersonal intelligence and intrapersonal intelligence. The core idea is that various intelligences represent different ways of knowing and understanding the world, both around us and within us. Despite its intuitive appeal, the notion of multiple intelligences has drawn its share of criticism, and there is a paucity of empirical research to support specific application to language classrooms (Richards and Rodgers, 2001; Ghamrawi, 2014).

Beliefs

Beliefs carry assumptions about the learning process such as how long it should take, how an accent should sound and how teachers and learners should act. Beliefs influence students' receptivity to teaching practices and the choice of language learning strategies (Gregersen and MacIntyre, 2014). Beliefs can be explicitly taught or be implicit, acquired by listening and observing but often without critical evaluation (Wenden, 1999). Implicit beliefs, because they are unexamined, can be troublesome for teachers and learners at times. A learner's unique belief system develops from her or his own experience, combined with culture and personality, to form a coherent framework for interpreting the world that is both stable over time and somewhat open to change (Mori, 1999; Wenden, 1999).

Horwitz (1988) noted that learners are likely to be exposed to widespread and sometimes conflicting beliefs about language learning. Whether or not they are justified, helpful or ill-advised, learners act on their beliefs as if they are true (Stevick, 1980). For example, the belief that language aptitude or intelligence is a fixed, unchanging characteristic of a learner can exert a powerful effect on the learning process. Mori (1999) argues that a student who believes that intelligence can be increased through practice has the potential to be more successful than her counterparts who believe in innate, unchanging aptitude. Beliefs are connected to the larger emotion and motivation systems of learners; therefore, explicitly asking about beliefs can provide a window into how teachers and learners think IDs function in practice.

Identity

Language learning and usage involve how one defines oneself, particularly in interactions (see Edwards, 2009), because language fulfils multiple functions including communication, thinking, cultural transmission and symbolic representation, to name but a few. Early on, Lambert (1981) proposed that learning and using another language could have one of two consequences. It could result in the accumulation of two identities, a phenomenon he labelled additive bilingualism, or in the loss of the first identity, what he dubbed subtractive bilingualism. These ideas have strong intuitive appeal and have influenced both teachers' and researchers' thinking about identity.

Concern over the potential for subtractive bilingualism has generated a number of research studies that show generally positive effects of being bilingual. Gilette (2013) summarises the numerous advantages of bilingualism gleaned from scientific research, including improved attention to details, improved memory, early onset of conflict management skills, improved executive control, lessening of symptoms associated with cognitive decline, improved social skills and reduced stress and risk of depression. Other research has documented positive consequences of bilingualism for stronger family cohesion (Portes and Hao, 2004) and the valuation of bilingual children by their own community (Portes and Rumbaut, 2006). Bilingual children also show higher academic achievement (e.g. Golash-Boza, 2005) and higher self-esteem (Portes and Hao, 2004). Han (2010), however, warns that the advantages of bilingualism present among first generation immigrants tend to dissipate with subsequent generations.

Recent research has conceptualised the possibility of a hybrid identity, that is, a form of simultaneous identification to the two groups which may involve identity switching or fusion. Through sharing the same community activities, close ties are developed through peer groups and exogamic marriages, and support for one language becomes associated with support for the other (Gaudet and Clément, 2009), with a new form of identity emerging (e.g. Benet-Martinez and Haritatos, 2005). There is ample evidence from classroom research for the emergence of a fused identity (see, for example, Amicucci, 2012). Thus, social context plays a significant role in matters of identity. Landry et al. (2013) identified a phenomenon called 'resistance bilingualism', wherein a state of over protectiveness towards one's own language and identity is prompted by a perception that the group is under threat. Consistent with this idea, Freynet and Clément (2015) found that bilingual individuals whose language had the lowest distinctiveness and prominence in the community showed *better* attitudes and engagement towards their own language than groups whose language had higher vitality.

Work in the area of identity emphasises ways in which identities are complex and continuously being negotiated. Norton (2013) describes the investments learners make and how they imagine the TL communities to be (see also Lamb, this volume). The negotiation of identity is tied to how learners understand their imagined identities, which reflect "the way a person understands his or her relationship to the world, how that relationship is constructed across time and space, and how the person understands possibilities for the future" (p. 4). Teachers also work with complex issues of identity development and transformation (Duff and Uchida, 1997). Therefore, it appears that the relationship between language acquisition and identity is quite complex, involving the effects of social-structural factors moderated by cognitive integration mechanisms and ideological considerations.

Language learning strategies and styles

Strategies are what learners do mentally or physically to facilitate their language learning and communication (Rubin, 1975; Griffiths, 2008). Strategies can be taught and become easier to use over time, making them appealing to teachers and learners alike (see Griffiths, 2008; Cohen, 2007, 2012; Oxford, 2012). The function of strategies is to allow learners to "regulate or control their own learning, thus making it easier and more effective" (Oxford, 2012: 12). The idea that strategies provide a means of self-regulation helps to tie them to the learners' motivation system, as learners are viewed as being autonomous and active in the learning process (Dörnyei and Skehan, 2003; Cohen, 2007). However, ties to other ID factors have led to controversy over the definition of language learning strategies; specifically, how does one differentiate strategies from non-strategies? What should be counted and what should not be counted as a language learning strategy?

Broadly speaking, the most prominent taxonomies of language learning strategies converge on similar concepts (O'Malley and Chamot, 1990: Oxford, 1990, 2012; Cohen and Macaro, 2007). For example, Oxford (2012) identified: (a) cognitive strategies that allow learners to manipulate or transform the TL through identification, retention, storage and/or retrieval; (b) social strategies that enhance communication and practice in the TL; (c) affective strategies that help to regulate emotional experiences; and (d) metacognitive strategies that are used to manage the deployment of other types of strategies. Cohen (2012) advocates adding additional categories to the typology, including (a) communication strategies that allow for meaningful expression of ideas; (b) retrieval and rehearsal strategies that activate previously learned material in memory; and (c) cover strategies that project a positive image of oneself.

Language learning styles also have been difficult to define with precision (see Ehrman et al., 2003; Dörnyei, 2005). Yet the notion that people have preferences for thinking and learning in different ways has strong intuitive appeal – we all have ways of doing things that we find comfortable (Gregersen and MacIntyre, 2014). Reid (1987) reviewed a number of taxonomies of styles and chose six for comparison internationally: visual (seeing language), auditory (listening to language), kinesthetic (physical movement), tactile (hands-on experience), preference for individual-learning and preference for learning in groups. It seems quite natural to suggest that language teachers try to match their instructional style to learners' preferences, such as assigning readings to a learner with a visual style or movement for a learner with a kinesthetic style. Yet even the idea of style-matching has been controversial, as authors argue whether it is better to design instruction consistent with strengths of a learner or challenge learners to overcome their particular areas of weakness. It is important to emphasise that a preference for one or another style modality does not imply the inability to learn from non-preferred methods. Indeed, it is important for teachers and learners alike to keep in mind that styles are assessed on a continuum; labelling of persons as either 'this or that' style simply is not recommended.

Motivation

No discussion of ID factors should ignore motivation. The topic has been well established in the literature as perhaps the key ID factor (alongside aptitude), from early research (Gardner and Lambert, 1959) to the present day. This *Handbook* features a separate chapter on motivation (see Lamb, this volume).

Personality

In psychology, the topic of personality is virtually synonymous with the term 'individual differences'. Yet personality has not been studied as widely in the SLA field as other topics in this chapter. Indeed, there has been something of a conflicted relationship between SLA and personality-related topics such as tolerance for ambiguity, risk taking, perfectionism and the like (for a review, see Ellis, 2004). Identification of relevant personality traits was hampered for a long time by the plethora of personality theories and measures that were available in the psychology literature. Some consistency in the study of personality was achieved by the description of "the Five Factor Model" (Costa and McCrae, 1992) and its conceptual cousin "the Big Five" personality traits (Goldberg and Rosolack, 1994). Using Goldberg's Big Five terminology, the five major dimensions or personality traits are: extraversion/introversion, conscientiousness, agreeableness, emotional stability/neuroticism and openness to experience/sophistication/intellect. It is generally agreed that these five factors form a reasonable taxonomy for investigating personality traits, though there has been criticism of this perspective (McAdams, 1992; Block, 1995).

Of the Big Five, the extraversion-introversion dimension is the most widely studied in language learning. Yet the research results have been somewhat equivocal, leading researchers to call extraversion the 'unloved variable' in applied linguistics research (Dewaele and Furnham, 1999). The mixed bag of results in the literature on personality and various aspects of language learning stems in part from the issue of breadth versus depth in the definition of personality traits. For example, extraversion might work in favour of learners who wish to talk in order to learn (Skehan, 1998) but introversion might work in favour of detail-oriented cognitive learning tasks that are prevalent in formal language instruction (MacIntyre et al., 2004). By definition, personality traits apply across situations, yet the more broadly a concept is defined, the less capable it is of predicting specific behaviour or outcomes (Doll and Ajzen, 1992). The expectation seems reasonable that traits *should* predict language acquisition, but it might be too simple to define a broad trait, such as extraversion, and expect that it will relate consistently to the wide variety of specific indices of language achievement that are available. Thus, rather than personality traits, ID research in SLA has tended to examine specific concepts such as language anxiety, identity and motivation for language learning.

Willingness to communicate

One of the most important decisions that a learner faces is whether or not to speak the TL when the opportunity arises. The concept of willingness to communicate (WTC) is based on the idea that there are both long-lasting tendencies and immediate situational influences on the decision to speak or to remain quiet; even in the native language, there is a wide range of

WTC. MacIntyre et al. (1998) took the concept of WTC, as originally defined in the literature on native language communication, to emphasise stable tendencies in approaching or avoiding communication (McCroskey and Richmond, 1991) and re-conceptualised it as a rapidly changing, situational ID variable. Their 'pyramid' model captured a wide range of enduring and transient influences on WTC, many of which are included in this chapter. Research supports the model's prediction that higher levels of WTC are strongly correlated with both the perception of competence and lower levels of language anxiety (Clément et al., 2003; MacIntyre et al., 2003).

More recently, the dynamics underlying changes in WTC from moment to moment have come into focus (MacIntyre and Legatto, 2011). Qualitative research shows that a highly nuanced psychological process underlies fluctuations in WTC; the situations in which learners are most willing to communicate are not radically different from those in which they are least willing (MacIntyre et al., 2011). From this perspective, language competencies serve communication goals in the classroom (Kang, 2005). Yashima (2012) emphasises that communication is inherently social, meaning that the psychology of more than one individual comes into play during communication as people interact with each other. If communication is the ultimate goal of language teaching, then a language programme that does not create WTC among its learners has failed to achieve its prime objective (MacIntyre et al., 1998).

How do ID factors fit together?

Readers might have noticed that the discussion above does not feature a consideration of the links among ID factors. There is a large number of studies that have established correlations among subsets of the factors above, too many studies to review here. Here, we will call this research tradition the 'variable-analytic approach' because its goal is to understand the relationships among ID variables using statistical analysis. In this tradition, an ID factor refers to the relative positioning of individuals within a group with respect to a specific characteristic (for example, one learner's scores for anxiety, extraversion or WTC relative to other learners'). For example, a correlational study might ask whether the students in a sample who are relatively low in aptitude tend to show relatively higher levels of anxiety and, if so, whether theory can offer an explanation for the relationship. In some cases, studies have used multiple regression analysis to predict the scores for one ID factor based on a statistical combination of several other factors or to use a chosen set of ID factors to predict selected measures of language achievement.

An influential set of studies in this tradition integrate a large number of ID factors into conceptual models that can be tested statistically, providing evidence on how ID factors fit together. For example, Gardner's (1985, 2010) socio-educational model showed that support for languages in the social milieu, combined with positive attitudes toward the teacher and course, support what he called an integrative motivation for language learning (see also Lamb, this volume). Individual differences in integrative motivation predicted various language learning outcomes in both formal (e.g. school) and informal (e.g. in the community) learning contexts. A related model, Clément's (1986) social context model, emphasised that the language learning process is psychologically different for members of a minority group compared with members of a majority group. Clément suggested that minority group members can experience a tension between pressures to integrate with a larger group and at the same time fear assimilation and loss of their native language/culture. MacIntyre et al. (1998) developed the 'pyramid' model of WTC to show how factors as diverse as personality, intergroup climate, various motivational processes, anxiety and the desire to speak to a specific person combine to foster a willingness to enter into communication in the TL at a specific time. The approach to empirically testing all of these models has been to measure the various ID factors using questionnaires and then apply complex statistics (path analysis and structural equation modelling) to assess whether or not the pattern of correlations emerges as the theory would predict.

In recent years, an alternative approach to ID factors has been developed. Complex dynamic systems theory (CDST, Larsen-Freeman and Cameron, 2008; see also Mercer, this volume) exists alongside the variable-analytic tradition but has a long list of differing assumptions. CDST emphasises relationships among factors that are nonlinear, sometimes chaotic and sometimes stable and tied closely to the context in which the system is operating. Dynamic models emphasise that the parts of a system are continuously interacting in complex ways. In this research approach, IDs can refer to changes within a person over time, as language develops along unique, personal trajectories. For example, a case study might examine how a highly anxious student deals with language aptitude difficulties over the semester, focusing on various ways in which strategy instruction and his/her competitive personality facilitate language development.

Although the assumptions underlying the variable-analytic and CDST traditions are quite different, each approach has the potential to inform teaching and learning. For example, variable analytic studies have identified ID factors that appear to be most relevant to success in language learning. The strength of the CDST approach lies in a focus on describing the messy process that comes from a number of factors interacting with each other in a specific context. Teachers might find one or the other approach more appealing in conceptualising the IDs that they observe among learners and how language learning in their specific context changes over time.

Key areas of disagreement

Contrasting the variable analytic tradition with the CDST tradition can help to put three perennial controversies into perspective. In the literature, there has been a consistent issue with respect to correlation versus causation, definitions and how to use ID information in teaching. We will address briefly each of these issues.

1 *Correlation versus causation:* A perpetual controversy within the ID research tradition is the question of correlation versus causation. Introductory texts on research methods will emphasise that observing a correlation does not mean one factor causes the other. For example, it has been observed that students with higher anxiety also show deficits in aptitude and lower levels of achievement. Thus, Sparks and Ganschow (1991) took the position that aptitude differences, specifically having difficulties in the area of linguistic coding, cause both higher levels of anxiety and lower levels of achievement. However, MacIntyre and Gardner (1994) used an experimental method to show that increasing anxiety arousal can cause reductions in language input and output. Therefore, anxiety can be seen as both a cause and a consequence of poor performance.

2 *Definitional issues:* Controversies about definitions continue to affect ID research. Most, if not all, of the ID factors reviewed above have generated controversy over their definitions that continues to affect the ways in which those concepts are understood. For the most part, a core idea can be identified, but there is difficulty in finding its boundaries. For example, if an individual is high in a personality trait such as extraversion that generates a lot of socialising, then is it proper to think of conversations with strangers as this person's language learning strategy or is it simply a consequence of personality? Ehrman (1996) frames personality constructs such as extraversion-introversion as 'personality-based learning styles', but Griffiths (2012) argues strongly that extraversion and similar variables should not be classified as learning styles. A teacher might encounter an individual learner who talks a lot in the classroom – does this reflect a personality trait, a learning style, a strategy, a belief or

something else? When a teacher interprets such behaviour, the definitions of all of these concepts can be considered, but with the implicit understanding that choosing a focal concept does not imply that nothing else is relevant. Alternatively, the learner herself might understand that s/he talks a lot because of a convergence among personality traits, styles, strategies and beliefs, along with concurrent attitudes, emotions and aptitudes.

3   *Using ID research:* 'Am I a teacher or a psychologist?' This question was posed to two of the authors during a webinar for TESOL International (MacIntyre and Gregersen, 2014). The question raises an interesting point that teachers might wish to consider. The review earlier in this chapter of individual difference factors shows that much has been learned about making the learning process more efficient and effective, allowing teachers to take into account both stability and change in the learner and how she or he learns. Yet what is the responsibility of the teacher – are teachers to act as psychotherapists for students? Of course it is inappropriate to ask teachers to take on such responsibility. But it is fair to note that every teaching style, lesson strategy and choice of activity reveals something about a teacher's approach to ID factors. To the extent that a teacher can be informed by a nuanced understanding of ID factors and how they work together dynamically, teachers can make better-informed decisions and be in a position to evaluate the consequences of those choices. If the study of IDs has taught us anything, it is that one-size-fits-all solutions are very rare and that diversity is the rule rather than the exception. Activities that work well in some classes and not others are those that fit the ID profile of the students to a greater or lesser extent respectively.

Implications for teachers and practitioners

From a teacher's perspective, the sheer number of ID factors that impinge on learning and the complexity they bring can seem overwhelming. One approach to dealing with learner IDs that teachers might find useful would be to choose a single ID factor for detailed consideration, exploring how it relates to other relevant factors and processes, much as the variable-analytic approach to research has done (but without the statistics). For example, there are many causes and consequences of anxiety in a given classroom; teachers who understand how anxiety operates can develop ways to deal with it. A close inspection of any one of the IDs (e.g. anxiety, beliefs or WTC) will implicate a number of connections among many of the other IDs noted above, plus other factors, much as the CDST perspective has emphasised. When IDs interact, the relative influence of one factor on another also fluctuates in language classrooms. For example, a classroom roleplay activity might be embraced enthusiastically by some extraverted students, arouse anxiety among almost all students and conflict with the widely held learner beliefs about what counts as proper teaching. A subtle change in the activity, such as adding an element of choice to the role play, might alleviate some anxiety and increase WTC but leave beliefs unchanged.

ID factors work together because they grow together – they become mutually dependent and intertwined. Teachers and learners can experience difficulty in the ID field when they think of these factors as if they were parts of a machine to be assembled or ingredients in a recipe (see the epilogue in Gregersen and MacIntyre, 2014). Instead of a predictable recipe that works the same way every time, it is important to acknowledge that individual differences combine in ways that make sense but often remain somewhat unpredictable. Thinking about individual differences, we therefore recommend *not* using a recipe as a guiding metaphor. Instead, consider the metaphors emerging from the development of weather systems, fluctuations in the stock market or even the outcome of professional sports contests. Each of these three areas have rules that govern the activities within them and have outcomes that are often predictable in the long run but also carry an element of unpredictability that makes them interesting to contemplate. Within the complexity of IDs in language learning lie numerous opportunities for engaged teachers to capitalise on learner differences.

We believe that an explicit awareness of the processes and emotions that unfold during language learning can lead students to notice both their own uniqueness and what they share with other learners. Greater awareness can be achieved through self-analysis, autonomy and effective management of affective, psychological and cognitive issues. In their role as facilitators, it is important that teachers consider the relevance of IDs within and among learners, openly discuss them and provide learners with guidance on how to manage them. Teachers who exercise sensitivity to learner IDs can adapt to some of the unpredictable events that occur in teaching. Learners themselves can also become more sensitive to their own pattern of IDs and use self-regulation strategies that increase their constructive emotions and actions, reducing the impact of those factors that are unproductive and detrimental (Young, 1991). Through classroom (and other) community building activities, creating social networks and personal relationships, language learners can tap into those ID components that support their language learning.

Finally, the breadth of the collection of ID variables might leave teachers feeling a bit overwhelmed if they try to accommodate all learners at all times. It might seem a daunting task to try to accommodate all of the ID factors present in the classroom. Indeed, there can be a positive effect of growth when learners are exposed to something new, as when trying out new learning styles and strategies. It is said that 'variety is the spice of life', and for this reason, teachers might consider a 'mixed and many' approach to managing IDs in a classroom, at times matching and at other times conflicting with learner preferences, but always within a supportive context. Learner IDs do not necessarily imply one correct formula or recipe for success. Instead, teachers might consider instructional methods that allow them to capitalise on both variety and choice and also help learners find ways to do this for themselves inside and outside the classroom (Gregersen and MacIntyre, 2014).

Conclusion

A concern for ID factors is a concern for individuality, its regular patterns and change. The powerful interactions among ID factors will help to determine how a person proceeds with learning, how quickly learning takes place and some of the long-term effects of language learning, such as intercultural friendships, international travel and opportunities for personal growth and well-being. Even as research demands that certain factors be isolated for study, it is important to consider how IDs grow together and operate in context. Language learners arrive in classrooms as integrated, whole persons; informed teachers find ways of accessing the pressure points that drive positive change among their learners. In the ecology of the classroom, diversity is a source of strength.

Discussion questions

- What ID factors do you, or teachers/learners in general, view as most relevant and how might they affect learning in your context?
- To what extent do you think teachers need to be 'psychologists' in the classroom?
- We have suggested that ID factors do not fit together like baking a cake from a recipe or building a machine from its parts but that we prefer metaphors drawn from weather systems and sports. In thinking about how ID factors work together, finish the following phrase in ways which make sense to you: 'Individual differences among learners operate like a(n) _____.'

Related topics

Cognitive perspectives on classroom language learning; Complexity and language teaching; Motivation.

Further reading

Dörnyei, Z. and Ryan, S. (2015) *The psychology of the language learner – Revisited*. New York: Routledge. (This text is an update of Dörnyei's 2005 text covering research into key ID factors.)

Gregersen, T. and MacIntyre, P. D. (2014) *Capitalizing on language learner individuality*. Bristol: Multilingual Matters. (Directed primarily at teachers, the text reviews relevant ID research and presents numerous classroom activities along with suggestions for adapting those activities to different teaching situations.)

Pawlek, M. (2012) *New directions on individual differences in second language learning*. Berlin Heidelberg: Springer. (This edited volume combines theoretical and practical contributions, primarily from European authors.)

References

Amicucci, A. N. (2012) 'Becoming "American-Italian": An immigrant's narrative of acquiring English as an L2'. *Critical Inquiry in Language Studies*, 9. 312–345.

Benet-Martinez, V. and Haritatos, J. (2005) 'Bicultural identity integration (BII): Components and psychological antecedents'. *Journal of Personality*, 73. 1015–1050.

Block, M. E. (1995) 'Development and validation of the children's attitudes toward integrated physical education- revised (CAIPE-R) inventory'. *Adapted Physical Activity Quarterly*, 12. 60–77.

Carroll, J. B. (1973) 'Implications of aptitude test research and psycholinguistic theory for foreign language teaching'. *International Journal of Psycholinguistics*, 2. 5–14.

Clément, R. (1986) 'Second language proficiency and acculturation: An investigation of the effects of language status and individual characteristics'. *Journal of Language and Social Psychology*, 5/4. 271–290.

Clément, R., Baker, S. and MacIntyre, P. D. (2003) 'Willingness to communicate in second languages: The effects of context, norms, and vitality'. *Journal of Language and Social Psychology*, 22. 190–209.

Cohen, A. D. (2007) 'Coming to terms with language learner strategies: Surveying the experts', in A. Cohen and E. Macaro (eds) *Language learner strategies*. Oxford: Oxford University Press. 29–46.

Cohen, A. D. (2012) 'Strategies: The interface of styles, strategies, and motivation on tasks', in S. Mercer, S. Ryan and M. Williams (eds) *Language learning psychology: Research, theory and pedagogy*. Basingstoke, Hampshire: Palgrave. 136–150.

Cohen, A. D. and Macaro, E. (2007) *Language learner strategies: 30 years of research and practice*. New York: Oxford University Press.

Costa, P. T. and McCrae, R. R. (1992) *NEO PI-R: Revised NEO personality inventory and NEO five-factor inventory (NEO-FFI)*. Odessa, FL: PAR.

DeKeyser, R. M. (2013) 'Age effects in second language learning: Stepping stones toward better understanding'. *Language Learning*, 63/1. 52–67.

Dewaele, J. and Furnham, A. (1999) 'Extraversion: The unloved variable in applied linguistic research'. *Language Learning*, 49/3. 509–544.

Dewaele, J. M. and MacIntyre, P. D. (2014) 'The two faces of Janus? Anxiety and enjoyment in the foreign language classroom'. *Studies in Second Language Learning and Teaching*, 4/2. 237–274.

Doll, J. and Ajzen, I. (1992) 'Accessibility and stability of predictors in the theory of planned behavior'. *Journal of Personality and Social Psychology*, 63/5. 754.

Dörnyei, Z. (2005) *The psychology of the language learner: Individual differences in second language acquisition*. Mahwah, NJ: Lawrence Erlbaum Associates, Inc.

Dörnyei, Z. and Skehan, P. (2003)' Individual differences in second language learning', in C. J. Doughty and M. H. Long (eds) *The handbook of second language acquisition*. Oxford: Blackwell. 589–630.

Duff, P. A. and Uchida, Y. (1997) 'The negotiation of teachers' sociocultural identities and practices in post-secondary EFL classrooms'. *TESOL Quarterly*, 31. 451–486.

Edwards, J. (2009) *Language and identity*. Cambridge: Cambridge University Press.

Ehrman, M. E. (1996) *Understanding second language difficulties*. Thousand Oaks, CA: Sage Publication.

Ehrman, M. E., Leaver, B. S. and Oxford, R. L. (2003) 'A brief overview of individual differences in second language learning'. *System,* 31. 313–330.

Ehrman, M. E. and Oxford, R. L. (1995) 'Cognition plus: Correlates of language learning success'. *Modern Language Journal,* 79/1. 67–89.

Ellis, R. (2004) 'Individual differences in second language learning', in A. Davies and C. Elder (eds) *The handbook of applied linguistics.* Oxford: Blackwell. 525–551.

Freynet, N. and Clément, R. (2015) 'Bilingualism in minority settings in Canada: Fusion or assimilation'. *International Journal of Intercultural Research,* 46. 55–72.

Ganschow, L., Sparks, R. L., Anderson, R., Javorsky, J., Skinner, S. and Patton, J. (1994) 'Differences in language performance among high-, average-, and low-anxious college foreign language learners'. *Modern Language Journal,* 78/1. 41–55.

Gardner, R. C. (1985) *Social psychology and second language learning: The role of attitudes and motivation.* London: Edward Arnold.

Gardner, H. (1993) *Frames of the mind: The theory of multiple intelligences 10th anniversary edition.* New York: Basic Books.

Gardner, R. C. (2010) *Motivation and second language acquisition: The socio-educational model.* New York: Peter Lang.

Gardner, R. C. and Lambert, W. E. (1959) 'Motivational variables in second-language acquisition'. *Canadian Journal of Psychology,* 13. 266–272.

Gaudet, S. and Clément, R. (2009) 'Forging an identity as a linguistic minority: Intra- and inter-group aspects of language, communication and identity'. *International Journal of Intercultural Research,* 33. 213–227.

Ghamrawi, N. (2014) 'Multiple intelligences and ESL teaching and learning: An investigation in KG II classrooms in one private school in Beirut, Lebanon'. *Journal of Advanced Academics,* 25/1. 25–46.

Gilette, H. (May 11, 2013) 'Bilingual children and adults experience significant health benefits' *Voxxi.* Retrieved from http://www.huffingtonpost.com/2013/04/10/bilingual-children-healthier_n_3054 493.html

Golash-Boza, T. (2005) 'Assessing the advantages of bilingualism for the children of immigrants'. *International Migration Review,* 39. 721–753.

Goldberg, L. R. and Rosolack, T. K. (1994) 'The Big Five factor structure as an integrative framework: An empirical comparison with Eysenck's PEN model', in C. F. Halverston, Jr., G. A. Kohnstamm and R. P. Martin (eds) *The developing structure of temperament and personality from infancy to adulthood.* 7–35.

Gregersen, T. S. (2006) 'The despair of disparity: The connection between foreign language anxiety and the recognition of proficiency differences in L2 skills'. *Lenguas Modernas,* 31. 7–20.

Gregersen, T. and MacIntyre, P. D. (2014) *Capitalizing on language learner individuality.* Bristol: Multilingual Matters.

Griffiths, C. (2008) 'Strategies and good language learners', in Griffiths, C. (ed.) *Lessons from good language learners.* Cambridge: Cambridge University Press. 83–98.

Griffiths, C. (2012) 'Learning styles: Traversing the quagmire', in S. Mercer, S. Ryan and M. Williams (eds) *Psychology for language learning.* New York: Palgrave MacMillan. 151–168.

Han, W-J. (2010) 'Bilingualism and socioemotional well-being'. *Children and Youth Services Review,* 32. 720–731.

Horwitz, E., Horwitz, M. and Cope, J. (1986) 'Foreign language classroom anxiety'. *Modern Language Journal,* 70. 125–132.

Horwitz, E. K. (1988) 'The beliefs about language learning of beginning university foreign language students'. *Modern Language Journal,* 72. 283–294.

Kang, S. (2005) 'Dynamic emergence of situational willingness to communicate in a second language'. *System,* 33. 277–292.

Kim, S. (2009) 'Questioning the stability of foreign language classroom anxiety and motivation across different classroom contexts'. *Foreign Language Annals,* 42. 138–157.

Lambert, W. E. (1981) 'Bilingualism and language acquisition'. *Annals of the New York Academy of Sciences,* 379. 9–22.

Landry, R., Allard, R. and Deveau, K. (2013) 'Bilinguismesme et métissage identitaire : Vers un modèle conceptuel [Bilingualism and identity mixing : Towards a conceptual model]'. *Linguistic Minorities and Society,* 3. 56–79.

Larsen-Freeman, D. and Cameron, L. (2008) 'Research methodology on language development from a complex systems perspective'. *Modern Language Journal,* 92/2. 200–213.

MacIntyre, P. D. (1999) 'Language anxiety: A review of literature for language teachers', in D. J. Young (ed.) *Affect in foreign language and second language learning.* New York: McGraw Hill Companies. 24–23.

MacIntyre, P. D., Baker, S. C., Clément, R. and Donovan, L. A. (2003) 'Talking in order to learn: Willingness to communicate and intensive language programs'. *Canadian Modern Language Review/La Revue Canadienne des Langues Vivantes,* 59/4. 589–608.

MacIntyre, P. D., Burns, C. and Jessome, A. (2011) 'A dynamic system for approach to willingness to communicate: Developing an idiodynamic method to capture rapidly changing affect'. *Applied Linguistics,* 32. 149–171.

MacIntyre, P. D., Clément, R., Dörnyei, Z. and Noels, K. A. (1998) 'Conceptualizing willingness to communicate in a L2: A situational model of L2 confidence and affiliation'. *Modern Language Journal,* 82. 545–562.

MacIntyre, P. D., Donovan, L. A. and Standing, L. (2004) 'Extraversion and willingness to communicate in second language learning'. Paper presented at the annual conference of the Canadian Psychological Association, Saint John's NL, June 2004.

MacIntyre, P. D. and Gardner, R. (1991a) 'Investigating language class anxiety using the focused essay technique'. *Modern Language Journal,* 75. 296–304.

MacIntyre, P. D. and Gardner, R. (1991b) 'Language anxiety: Its relationship to other anxieties and to processing in native and second languages'. *Language Learning,* 41. 513–534.

MacIntyre, P. D. and Gardner, R. (1994) 'The subtle effects of language anxiety on cognitive processing in the second language'. *Language Learning,* 44. 283–305.

MacIntyre, P. D. and Gregersen, T. (2014) 'Talking in order to learn: Insights and practical strategies on learner anxiety and motivation'. TESOL International Webinar. Retrieved from http://www.tesol.org/connect/tesol-resource-center/page/5/#sthash.nWORambO.dpuf

MacIntyre, P. D. and Legatto, J. (2011) 'A dynamic system approach to willingness to communicate: Developing an idiodynamic method to capture rapidly changing affect'. *Applied Linguistics,* 32. 149–171.

McAdams, D. P. (1992) 'The five-factor model in personality: A critical appraisal'. *Journal of Personality,* 60. 329–361.

McCroskey, J. C. and Richmond, V. P. (1991) 'Willingness to communicate: A cognitive view', in M. Booth-Butterfield (ed.) *Communication, cognition, and anxiety.* Newbury Park, CA: Sage. 19–37.

Mori, Y. (1999) 'Epistemological beliefs and language learning beliefs: What do language learners believe about their learning?' *Language Learning,* 49. 377–415.

Norton, B. (2013) *Identity and language learning: Extending the conversation* (2nd ed.). Bristol: Multilingual Matters.

O'Malley, J. M. and Chamot, A. U. (1990) *Learning strategies in second language learning.* New York: Cambridge University Press.

Oxford, R. (1990) 'Styles, strategies, and aptitude: Connections for language learning', in T. S. Parry and C. W. Stansfield (eds) *Language aptitude reconsidered.* Englewood Cliffs, NJ: Prentice Hall. 76–125.

Oxford, R. (2012) *Teaching and researching language learning strategies.* Harlow, UK: Longman.

Portes, A. and Hao, L. (2004) 'The schooling of children of immigrants: Contextual effects on the educational attainment of the second generation'. *Proceedings of the National Academy of Sciences of the United States of America,* 101. 11920–11927.

Portes, A. and Rumbaut, R. G. (2006) *Immigrant America: A portrait.* Berkeley: University of California Press.

Ranta, L. (2008) 'Aptitude and good language learners', in C. Griffiths (ed.) *Lessons from good language learners.* Cambridge: Cambridge University Press. 142–155.

Reid, J. (1987) 'The learning style preferences of ESL students'. *TESOL Quarterly,* 21. 87–111.

Richards, J. C. and Rodgers, T. S. (2001) *Approaches and methods in language teaching* (2nd ed.). Cambridge: Cambridge University Press.

Robinson, P. (2007) 'Aptitudes, abilities, contexts, and practice', in R. M. DeKeyser (ed.) *Practice in a second language: Perspectives from applied linguistics and cognitive psychology.* Cambridge, UK: Cambridge University Press. 256–286.

Rubin, J. (1975) 'What the "good language learner" can teach us'. *TESOL Quarterly,* 9. 41–51.

Skehan, P. (1998) *A cognitive approach to language learning.* Oxford: Oxford University Press.

Skehan, P. (2002) 'Theorising and updating aptitude', in P. Robingson (ed.) *Individual differences and instructed language learning.* Amsterdam: John Benjamins. 69–93.

Sparks, R. L. and Ganschow, L. (1991) 'Foreign language learning differences: Affective or native language aptitude differences?' *Modern Language Journal,* 75. 3–16.

Steinberg, F. S. and Horwitz, E. K. (1986) 'The effect of induced anxiety on the denotative and interpretive content of second language speech'. *TESOL Quarterly,* 20. 131–136.

Stevick, E. W. (1980) *Teaching languages: A way and ways.* Rowley, MA: Newbury House.

Wenden, A. (1999) 'An introduction to metacognitive knowledge and beliefs in language learning: Beyond the basics'. *System,* 27. 435–441.

Yashima, T. (2012) 'Willingness to communicate: Momentary volition that results in L2 behavior', in S. Mercer, S. Ryan and M. Williams (eds) *Language learning psychology: Research, theory and pedagogy.* Basingstoke, Hampshire: Palgrave. 119–135.

Young, D. J. (1991) 'Creating a low-anxiety classroom environment: What does language anxiety research suggest?' *Modern Language Journal,* 75. 426–439.

23
Motivation

Martin Lamb

Introduction

Motivation is widely acknowledged, among both teachers and researchers, as one of the key issues in language education. Dörnyei (2001: 2), for example, suggests that "99 per cent of language learners who really want to learn a foreign language (i.e. who are really motivated) will be able to master a reasonable working knowledge of it as a minimum, regardless of their language aptitude." Yet everyone involved in language education also knows that the proportion of school pupils who do achieve "a reasonable working knowledge" of a foreign language falls far short of 99 per cent – in fact, it is probably a small minority. This state of affairs would suggest, then, that motivation is frequently a problem in ELT and the teaching of other foreign languages.

Before considering why this might be so, it is necessary to establish what the term 'motivation' refers to. A succinct definition in educational psychology is: "the process whereby goal-directed activity is instigated and sustained" (Pintrich and Schunk, 2007: 5). As a process internal to the person, it cannot be directly observed but only inferred from what they do or say. A number of different human attributes are implicated in this process, and when describing or measuring the motivation of English language learners, researchers have sought to identify some of the following:

- The person's *motives* or *reasons* for learning English (traditionally called 'orientations' in L2 motivation research)
- Their personal or academic *goals*, in the short or long term
- The strength of their *desire* to achieve those goals
- Their *attitudes* towards English, English-speaking peoples and Anglophone cultures
- Their *interest* in the subject and *enjoyment* of the learning process
- The *effort* they put into learning, in both formal and informal settings
- How they *self-regulate* their learning effort over time, in the face of distractions and competing goals

In the last two attributes, motivation overlaps with, and is sometimes considered a prerequisite of, learner autonomy (see Benson, this volume).

Motivation is most commonly thought of as an individual attribute, something that differentiates one learner from another and their likelihood of success (see MacIntyre, Gregersen and Clément, this volume). However, it is important to recognise that it is also a social construction;

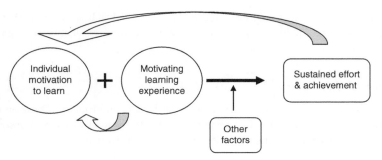

Figure 23.1   A simple representation of motivational processes

that is, we come to strive for certain things in life as a result of our socialisation in a particular community or society, and the extent to which we can act on our desires is also constrained by our social environment. Some researchers therefore prefer to use terms like *investment* (Norton, 2000) or *agency* (Deters et al., 2015) to emphasise how people depend upon certain resources (psychological and material) being available to them and need to feel empowered to act on their desires.

When thinking about motivation and English language learning, a broad distinction can be made between the motivation that learners bring to the task of learning and the motivational effects of the learning itself, both in or outside class. Clearly, these two elements interact with each other, and where both are strong, we may expect an optimal level of motivation that will produce sustained effort. Success along the way may feed back into motivation, producing a positive cycle of reinforcement that leads ultimately to mastery of the language, as portrayed in Figure 23.1.

In fact, statistical studies typically find that the correlation between learners' degree of motivation and their actual achievement is relatively modest (e.g. Masgoret and Gardner, 2003; Vandergrift, 2005; Lasagabaster, 2011), the reason being that many other factors will mediate this relationship, such as the learners' aptitude for languages, the efficiency of their learning strategies, the quality of instruction and the inherent difficulty of the language for a particular L1 speaker. Indeed, recognition of the complexity of motivational processes has encouraged researchers to look beyond linear 'cause and effect' models (e.g. the expectation that having a goal will result in the learner actively and persistently pursuing that goal) towards a dynamic systems perspective which focuses on the ongoing interactions between different contextual and temporal factors (see later in this chapter; also Mercer, this volume, for further discussion of complexity and language teaching).

Acknowledging these caveats, I will use the two circles in Figure 23.1 as an organizing principle for this chapter, as they represent two distinct areas of research, as well as perhaps reflecting how many teachers conceive of language learning motivation. In the final part of the chapter, I will highlight promising avenues of contemporary motivation research which should bring important new insights in the coming decade.

Competing perspectives on individual learner motivation

As in other areas of the social sciences, scholars interested in understanding L2 motivation have generally taken one of two approaches: either they have studied large groups of learners and sought to characterise their motivation in the terms of one or more psychological theories in order to identify the factors which seem most important for that population (e.g. Chen et al., 2005), or they have taken a few individual cases and tried to gain a more detailed and holistic understanding of their motivation in the belief that this can give us essential insights into how people think, feel and act in contexts of interest (e.g. Lamb, 2013). It is fair to say that the former approach has dominated the field, but that in the last decade more qualitative and mixed-method approaches have gained traction (Dörnyei and Ushioda, 2011).

Psychological theories

A wide range of psychological theories and concepts have been brought to bear on the issue of what motivates people to learn English. I will first deal with those that have been most influential and then more briefly review other theories that have potential relevance.

Social-psychological perspectives on L2 motivation

Systematic research into the motivation to learn a foreign language was initiated by Gardner and associates in Canada in the 1960s as part of a broader impetus in the post-war years to understand and promote better intercultural communication and relations between communities and nations. Gardner and Lambert (1972) argued that a person's attitudes towards the people who spoke a foreign language were likely to influence their desire to learn that language; this distinguishes language from other subjects on the academic curriculum, since "the learning of a second language involves taking on features of another cultural community" (Gardner, 2010: 2). Gardner (1985) elaborated this notion in his "socio-educational model of second language acquisition", which posited two main orientations (or motives) for learning an L2, the *integrative* – having positive attitudes towards the L2 group and desiring to interact with them – and the *instrumental* – seeing pragmatic benefits in the L2, such as passing exams and enhancing one's career potential. In interaction with other important factors, such as the individuals' attitude to the learning situation and their aptitude for language study, these orientations were predicted to affect learners' ultimate success in gaining proficiency in the language. Other researchers suggested further possible orientations to learning an L2, such as 'knowledge', 'travel' and 'friendship' (Clément and Kruidenier, 1983). Reviewing the many research studies based on the socio-educational model, Masgoret and Gardner (2003) concluded that there was strong evidence that 'integrativeness' was an important element in the motivation of learners of many different foreign languages, and Gardner (2010) continues to assert that motivation is "supported by a willingness and ability to take on the features of another cultural community" (p. 175).

While these ideas may well have relevance for the learning of certain languages by certain groups of learners – not least, perhaps, the learning of other languages by Anglophones – there is a growing consensus among ELT motivation researchers that intense globalisation over the past 30 years has lessened their usefulness for understanding why people would want to learn English. As it has gained a status as the world's lingua franca, English is gradually losing its association with Anglophone countries and cultures (see Seargeant, and Kramsch and Zhu, this volume), so it is difficult to see how individuals' attitudes towards Anglophone people or culture could be relevant to their desire to learn or use English. Moreover, in school curricula worldwide, English is not so much a foreign language as a basic skill like numeracy and L1 literacy (Graddol, 2006), a foundation on which higher level knowledge of other academic subjects is built, and thus a pre-requisite for many jobs and professions. Listening to the voices of diverse English language learners, whether Indonesian villagers (Lamb, 2013), South African multilinguals (Coetzee-Van Rooy, 2006) or the middle-class clients of British Council language centres (Borg, 2009), it is difficult to distinguish integrative from instrumental motives; their reasons for wanting to achieve mastery of English relate more to their perception of its general significance in their present lives and to the wider horizons it may open up for them in the future.

The implications of intense globalisation for ELT motivation theory are profound, for, as Ushioda has asked,

> [s]ince we are referring to a global community of English language users, does it make sense to conceptualise it as an 'external' reference group, or should we think of it more as part of one's internal representation of oneself as a *de facto* [or potential] member of this global community?
>
> *(2013: 3)*

The key to understanding people's motivation to learn English, therefore, seems to lie within their own self-conceptions.

The L2 motivational self-system

Dörnyei's L2 motivational self-system (2009) reconceptualises L2 motivation to take these new conditions into account, while building on what was already known to be important. It has three components:

- *The ideal L2 self* – this is our vision of ourselves as future L2 users, e.g. as an international traveller, a student abroad or a jet-setting businessperson. The clearer and more powerfully 'felt' the vision, the more likely it is to engender effort to learn, as we constantly compare our actual self with this future self and work to overcome the discrepancy we notice between the two. Dörnyei (2009) claims that this captures the motives formerly labelled 'integrative', with the 'integration' being more with a future version of the self rather than with any external body of L2 speakers. It can also capture the more internalised instrumental motives, i.e. those aspirations which one truly desires for oneself in the future.
- *The ought-to L2 self* – this is our sense of what significant others would like us to become; it engenders a feeling of duty and obligation, which may translate into effortful learning but may also lead learners to *avoid* negative outcomes rather than strive towards the positive. It may capture too those instrumental motives which are felt to be more externally imposed (e.g. getting good results in the end-of-term exam because our parents and the teacher demand it).
- *The L2 learning experience* – this relates to the motives engendered by the process of actually learning the language, recognised as important in almost all previous studies of L2 motivation and, indeed, general academic motivation. Relevant factors might include the teaching methods and available materials, the attitudes of peers and the experience of success or failure in the course of learning.

In recent years a number of researchers have found this framework valuable in portraying the pattern of learners' motivation for English (other languages have been far less studied) (see, for example, chapters in Dörnyei and Ushioda, 2009; Apple et al., 2013). Typically the ideal L2 self and the L2 learning experience are found to be the most powerful influences on people's intended learning effort. There is some evidence that the ideal L2 self has the most influence in later secondary and in tertiary levels of education (Kormos and Csizér, 2008) and is less influential on the motivation of older learners or those in early adolescence, whose future visions may still be vague or fantastical (Lamb, 2013). There is also likely to be interaction between the ideal L2 self and the L2 learning experience; learners with a vivid ideal L2 self, for instance, may draw satisfaction from their English classes even if they are not intrinsically enjoyable; equally, inspiring lessons may help the learners develop ideal L2 selves.

The role of the ought-to L2 self is more doubtful; most studies suggest it has less motivational power than the other two components of the self-system, as Dörnyei's framework would predict. However, there is also evidence that it has a larger role to play in the supposedly collectivist cultures of the 'East' than the individualist cultures of the 'West', that is, where individuals' personal motives may be more easily influenced by parents and other prominent figures in the milieu or even subordinated to relational motives, like those of the family or nation (Chen et al., 2005; Islam et al., 2013). On the other hand, proponents of self-determination theory have long argued that it is a universal human characteristic to act on motives that are internalised, whether these originate in one's own aspirations or those of significant others, and therefore the key to understanding learner motivation is to measure the degree of internalisation (Ryan and Deci, 2000). It is to this influential theory of motivation that I now turn.

Self-determination theory

Self-determination theory (SDT) has so far had more influence on general academic motivation research than on L2 motivation research, perhaps due to the perception that languages are different from other curriculum subjects. However, its main precepts are well-known to language teaching methodologists, who have long emphasised the distinction between intrinsic and extrinsic motivation (e.g. Harmer, 2007). Intrinsically motivated learners are said to study a language because they like it; that is, they are stimulated by new knowledge, enjoy the challenge of learning tasks or gain satisfaction from their increasing mastery of the subject. Extrinsically motivated learners do it in order to gain some other kind of benefit distinct from the process of learning. The key insight of SDT, however, is that this is a continuum – our goals may be externally imposed by circumstances or other people and we feel compelled to pursue them, or they may be more aligned with our personal goals, in other words, 'self-determined' and internalised, and "with increasing internalization (and its associated sense of personal commitment) come greater persistence, more positive self-perceptions, and better quality of engagement" (Ryan and Deci, 2000: 60–61).

Importantly for educators (and parents), the theory also proposes how learner motives can *become* internalised – by having their basic human need for autonomy, competence and relatedness satisfied in their learning activity. Learners who are given choices about what and how to learn, for example, may come to feel that they are learning English autonomously, for their own purposes (see Benson, this volume, for further discussion of learner autonomy). Those who are set appropriate challenges in their courses and given helpful feedback on their performance are likely to gain a sense of competence and thus feel confident to persist in learning. Those who are made to feel they 'belong' in a learning community and have warm relationships with teachers and peers are likely to stretch themselves further and take more risks (Noels, 2013). Conversely, as Ushioda (e.g. 2012) has consistently argued, teachers who attempt to motivate learners through traditional 'carrot and stick' approaches will likely produce a form of controlled extrinsic motivation that might have short-term benefits (e.g. learners will make an extra effort to do their homework tasks, in order to please the teacher) but will not produce the autonomous motivation necessary to sustain learners' efforts over the long term.

Other psychological concepts

While the theories outlined above have tended to dominate L2 motivation research, other psychological concepts have also been shown to influence individual learners' motivation. Here is a brief selection:

- How learners interpret their past success or failures, in particular whether they attribute them to factors under their control (see Williams et al., 2001)
- Learners' linguistic self-confidence, usually derived from their past success in L2 communication, and self-efficacy, their feeling of mastery over particular learning tasks (see Iwaniec, 2014)
- Learners' 'mindsets', i.e. their beliefs about the malleability of intelligence and talent, which may be particularly important for L2 motivation given the common perception that some people are born with a 'gift' for languages (see Mercer and Ryan, 2010)
- The distinction between one's private and public self, especially for adolescents learning English in school, who may be wary of evincing a strong motivation to study for fear of ridicule from peers (see Taylor, 2013).

Holistic perspectives on learner motivation

The danger in all such theoretical approaches is that they oversimplify human motivation, giving precedence to whatever cognitive or affective factors the theory presupposes are most important. Based usually on questionnaire data, published results are almost always averages and so may disguise the extent of individual variation. Conducted at one point in time, they cannot measure changes in motivation over a long period or its fluctuations over the short term. Such studies also often hypothesise a cause-effect relationship between the selected variables, which may give a false impression of their predictability in actual contexts of learning, where a complex array of internal and situational factors will interact with each other, potentially affecting the willingness and ability of learners to study or use the L2.

In response to these shortcomings, Ushioda (2009) has called for a complementary approach to be taken, wherein a language learner is viewed not as a theoretical abstraction with a set of identified characteristics but as a "thinking, feeling human being" living "in a fluid and complex system of social relations, activities, experiences and multiple micro- and macro-contexts" (p. 220). Such an approach is in tune with a wider social turn in SLA (Block, 2003) which has foregrounded the sociocultural and socio-historical nature of language learning rather than cognitive and psycholinguistic processes and adopted a range of "socially and contextually grounded theoretical frameworks" (Ushioda, 2009) and qualitative research methods such as interviews, classroom observations and discourse analysis. In fact, there are already several studies in this emerging paradigm which have provided real insights into the nature of EFL motivation, even though motivation may not have been a central focus of the research.

Perhaps the best known of these is Norton's (2000) longitudinal study of immigrant women in Canada learning English as an additional language. Although in conventional terms all the women were highly motivated, she shows how they did not always take up opportunities to use and learn the language; and although they were all striving to gain a 'voice' in English so they could participate in their new communities (both real and imagined), their actual investment in L2 learning and use was mediated by ongoing identity issues and, for some, the day-to-day struggle to survive. Like those researchers working with the 'self' psychology outlined earlier in the chapter, then, Norton sees individuals' 'visions of the future' as central to their motivation to learn English, but her case study approach enabled her to show that the "real world is messy and contradictory" (Kramsch, 2013: 198), that individuals' desires were often ambivalent and changeable, their agency in constant tension with the structuring forces of powerful institutions, discourses and people. As Kramsch puts it, in many twenty-first century contexts, "the dream of renewed identities is clouded by the ruthless realities of economic and cultural globalization" (ibid; see also Kramsch and Zhu, this volume).

One line of enquiry of particular interest to language educators is exploring the way that learners' identities – both how they see themselves and how they are positioned by others – may affect their motivation to participate in language classrooms. Language is our primary means of self-expression. Thus, learning a new language potentially expands our repertoire of symbolic resources for communication, but, in the process of learning, we may also feel as if we are being deprived of these resources or that our existing resources are no longer valued. To take two examples, Canagarajah (1999) and Skilton-Sylvester (2002) describe Sri Lankan school pupils and Cambodian women immigrants respectively resisting participation in English classes, despite being ostensibly motivated to learn, because they felt important aspects of their identities were not being recognised in classroom processes. In contrast, Lamb and Budiyanto (2013) describe young teenagers in Indonesian state schools reacting with excitement to the cultural challenges of English, tentatively performing new cosmopolitan identities in the language while struggling to reconcile them with more traditional, local identities. Focussing on the discourse of the communicative language classroom, Luk (2005) and Richards (2006) demonstrate how subtle differences in the way teachers position learners in class may encourage or discourage their engagement; broadly speaking, treating learners as more than just pupils, for example by recognising their aspirant identities beyond the classroom, is likely to promote engagement, if done with sympathy and humour.

The motivational effects of English teaching

We have already moved here into the second circle in Figure 23.1, above, the 'motivating learning experience'. The question of what should happen in language classrooms cannot and should not be separated entirely from what the learner brings to the classroom (see MacIntyre, Gregersen and Clément, this volume, for discussion of learners' individual differences), but this section will focus explicitly on what is known about the motivational dimension of language teaching, starting with what, arguably, is the most common learner experience – demotivation – and then looking at the burgeoning collection of research studies on motivational teaching strategies.

Demotivation

As Pintrich (2003: 680) notes, "Over the course of the school years student motivation on the average declines or becomes less adaptive, with a large drop as students enter the junior high school or middle school years." A certain loss of motivation may be inevitable in almost any long-term course of learning, as Dörnyei and Ushioda (2011) point out; novelty wears off, other interests develop. Nevertheless, it seems "there is something about the very organization of teaching and learning that, for many learners, systematically *kills* their motivation to learn" (Littlejohn, 2008: 216, original italics). Recent research has highlighted these 'external' demotivators as prominent in certain educational contexts:

- Boring teaching methods, such as the monotonous provision of grammar exercises, rote memorisation of vocabulary and translation (e.g. Falout and Maruyama, 2004). However, it is important to note that a 'grammar-translation' approach is not *always* demotivating – Lamb and Wedell (2015) found Chinese school classrooms where this approach, practised effectively and with enthusiasm, appeared to inspire learners.

- Lack of opportunities to practise the language, both inside and outside the classroom, which may also prevent learners feeling any sense of progress (especially a problem in rural areas; see, for example, Hu, 2003, on China).

- Relentless exam pressure during secondary school, which may promote anxiety and have more subtle effects on learners' motivation, displacing intrinsic motives with short-term extrinsic goals (see, for example, the studies of test washback in Cheng et al., 2004).

- Poor teacher-student relations, especially where teachers are 'distant', perhaps because they lack motivation or self-confidence themselves (e.g. in Korean primary schools, Kim and Seo, 2011).

- A dissonance between the frequent creative use of English in leisure pursuits outside the classroom, such as digital gaming, and the grammatical/lexical knowledge orientation of the classroom – particularly felt by relatively advanced-level European secondary school students (Henry, 2013).

It is too early to say whether the general trend of starting to learn English earlier, in primary school, will have the beneficial motivational effect that some proponents assert, or whether inappropriate teaching methods may even exacerbate the problem (see Enever, this volume, for further discussion of primary-level ELT).

Motivational strategies

The good news is that many of these demotivating factors can be overcome by skilful teaching. Not surprisingly, teachers who are identified as highly competent tend to have motivated learners (Brosh, 1996), and the ability to develop positive attitudes in learners is accepted as an essential skill that teachers need to develop. A primary rationale for the introduction of a new teaching methodology is its capacity to motivate, or re-motivate, learners; most recently, for instance, advocates of content and language integrated learning (CLIL) argue precisely this – that it can avoid the common pattern of demotivation that afflicts regular language-focussed instruction (see Lasagabaster, 2011; also Morton, this volume, for further discussion of CLIL).

There is an emerging body of research which aims at identifying teaching practices which boost the motivation of language learners. Some of the theoretical approaches to learner motivation described above offer their own implications for pedagogy. Hadfield and Dörnyei (2013), for example, offer teachers a variety of techniques and materials based on the notion that learners need to develop rich and vivid ideal L2 selves as well as detailed plans for realising them, and Magid and Chan (2012) provide some empirical support for the value of this approach when used with Chinese university students. Self-determination theory has also inspired researchers to design interventions to boost language learner motivation. For example, Wu (2003) found that Chinese primary school teachers who deliberately tried to boost their pupils' perception of competence (e.g. by presenting tasks with the right level of challenge) and perceived autonomy (e.g. by offering choices of activity) did help improve their learners' intrinsic motivation.

Other research studies are not so theory-based but instead attempt to find empirical support for the effectiveness of particular motivational strategies. The stimulus for this research was Dörnyei's (2001) taxonomy of 35 'macrostrategies' based on the stated preferences of Hungarian teachers of English and organised into four groups to reflect the different stages of the language learning process:

1   To provide fertile ground for motivation to grow, teachers and institutions need to establish a pleasant learning environment and create positive group dynamics (see Dörnyei, 2007, for especially valuable advice on this).
2   To help generate initial motivation, teachers should help learners form ideal L2 selves, set realistic personal goals and become confident about their ultimate success.
3   Once a learner has gained motivation, it needs to be carefully nurtured, for example through the provision of stimulating tasks, the encouragement of autonomous learning and the setting of achievable targets that lend a sense of progress.
4   The teacher needs to anticipate learners' motivational needs once a course is over, for instance by providing constructive feedback and promoting healthy motivational attributions (see earlier in the chapter).

Recognising that such a full and detailed list could be intimidating to teachers, Dörnyei and Ushioda (2011) emphasise that a reasonable professional aim is to be a "good enough motivator" using "a few well-chosen strategies that suit both the teacher and the learners" (p. 134).

Since Dörnyei produced his taxonomy, a number of research studies have been carried out to discover whether the strategies do actually motivate learners. Guilloteaux and Dörnyei (2008), for example, found that Korean school pupils with teachers who used motivational strategies, such as connecting lesson content to pupils' lives and using pair or groupwork, tended to have more positive attitudes and to engage more fully in class activities. Papi and Abdollahzadeh (2012) obtained similar results in Iranian classrooms. Moskovsky et al. (2012) went further by directly comparing the classroom motivation and attitudes of Saudi learners studying with teachers who did and did not use a set of selected motivational strategies. Over an eight-week period, they were able to demonstrate a causal link between strategy use and learners' motivation.

While it is encouraging to know that teachers can positively influence learner motivation, it is unlikely that the same set of techniques will motivate all learners in all contexts. Cheng and Dörnyei (2007) found that while Taiwanese and Hungarian teachers agreed on the value of some strategies, such as boosting learner self-confidence and creating a pleasant classroom climate, they gave different priority to other methods: the Europeans, for example, emphasised the importance of promoting learner autonomy, the Asians the need to recognise and praise students' efforts. Meanwhile, Guilloteaux (2013) found that Korean secondary school teachers attached much less importance to creating a pleasant classroom climate or fostering positive group dynamics, instead prioritising the development of learners' self-discipline and moral values.

In short, at the moment, the research evidence is too partial to validate any particular motivational strategy as universally applicable; and while a set of macro-strategies (as in Dörnyei, 2001) can be useful for beginning teachers, experienced teachers will know that they must always be adapted to the needs and preferences of each unique set of learners.

One further caveat regarding the 'motivational strategies' approach concerns the possible assumption that stimulating classroom experiences have *long-term* effects on pupils' motivation. Dörnyei and Ushioda (2011: 136) note that there is a critical difference between "motivating" students and "developing their motivation", defining the latter as "socializing and generating healthy forms of internally driven motivation"; students who are motivated by a teacher in a relatively short-term course may lose that motivation once they part company. Lamb and Wedell (2015) investigated whether there might be particular teacher behaviours that generate longer-term motivation by asking Chinese and Indonesian learners to recall inspiring teachers of English they had had in the past. Though their results suggested that inspiring teachers do deploy a range of motivational strategies in class, the common feature among them was that they themselves were highly committed to the profession and cared deeply about their learners, and it was possibly this that led them to be remembered so fondly by their former pupils.

Future directions for ELT motivation theory and research

The academic study of ELT motivation is thriving, and here I outline some of the key areas which will command the attention of researchers and practitioners in the coming decade.

Understanding the dynamism and complexity of learner motivation

As noted earlier, researchers are becoming increasingly aware of the complexity of internal and contextual factors that affect an individual's motivation to learn a language and how these factors interact and change in often unpredictable ways. Dörnyei and Ushioda (2011: 69) argue that L2 motivation research is entering a 'socio-dynamic' phase, and one of the most exciting developments has been the application of dynamic systems theory (or complexity theory; see Mercer, this volume) to the investigation of motivational issues. For example, Waninge et al. (2014) use experience sampling methods to chart the rise and fall of individual learners' motivation over a sequence of lessons, showing how these fluctuations may be responses to events within the lesson interacting with aspects of the learner's own personality and predilections. MacIntyre and Serroul (2015) employ an even more microscopic lens, finding quite dramatic fluctuations in individuals' motivation while engaged on various communicative tasks, with basic factors like 'topic' being hugely influential. Another promising theoretical concept is directed motivational current (DMC) (Muir and Dörnyei, 2013; Dörnyei et al., 2016), which is hypothesised to be a period of intense motivation during which individuals have a strong vision of how they want to be (e.g. getting fit, or achieving top grades in an exam), plan a sequence of action and sub-goals, and channel their energies towards these goals in such a way that their life changes significantly for that limited duration (typically a few weeks or months). Understanding the nature of DMCs in education may mean that, in the future, we can plan teaching interventions to initiate their operation simultaneously within a group of learners, for instance through a carefully-designed class project.

More focused contextual studies of L2 motivation

As the complexity of motivation becomes clearer and the number of English learners continues to grow, we may find more systematic variations among regions and nations and between ages, genders and other social groupings. Two recent edited volumes have purposefully examined learner motivation in particular global contexts. Ushioda (2013) looks at motivational challenges facing teachers and policy makers in 11 different countries, in both the developed 'North' and the developing 'South', whilst Apple et al. (2013) focuses on motivational issues in Japanese ELT; and we can expect to see more such contextually focused publications, as they are of value not only to readers from the same settings but to theorists and practitioners from elsewhere who are inevitably prompted to compare their own learning conditions and motivational practices. Learners of different ages have distinct characteristics (see chapters by Enever, and Pinter, this volume, for discussion of primary and secondary ELT), and as ministries grapple with the dilemmas of introducing English into earlier stages of the national curriculum, we need more longitudinal studies like those of Heinzmann (2013) in Switzerland, which charted changes in young learners' attitudes over several school years, and Carreira (2011) in Japan, which focused on children's language learning preferences in years 3–6.

Similarly, it is well-known that girls tend to do better in foreign language than boys. Some research has already implicated motivation in this gender achievement gap; for instance, Williams et al. (2002) showed how teenage boys perceived French as a 'feminine' language and preferred the more 'manly' sounding German, while Jones (2009) found that language teachers have strong expectations about the superior motivation and aptitude of girls and suggested that this itself may be a factor in perpetuating the gender gap. This issue is of more than academic interest, as the shortage of male students studying English at advanced levels is a matter of national concern in some countries. Another problem in many developing countries is the urban-rural divide, which some recent research (Islam et al., 2013; Lamb, 2013) suggests is not just due to inequitable educational opportunities but also to a possible motivational deficit: village children may lack the role models of competent English-speaking compatriots from which to form ideal L2 selves and also miss the support of parents and other family members who could help sustain motivation over the school years. Given that rural (and marginal urban) learners in developing countries make up the majority of English language learners worldwide, and that access to the global lingua franca may dramatically enhance their life prospects, their plight is worthy of much more research attention than they currently receive.

Recognising the importance of English teacher motivation

As noted above, inspiring teachers are very often those who, as Csikszentmihalyi (1997: 79) puts it, "showed by their dedication and their passion that there was nothing else on earth they would rather be doing". But it is also apparent that there is a teacher motivation crisis in many parts of the developing world (Bennell and Akyeampong, 2007). How can we expect children to be motivated to learn English if their teachers have to work in hot and crowded classrooms with minimal resources, managerial support and material reward? Of course, teacher stress and burnout is not limited to the developing world, and the problem is beginning to receive attention in general education research, but it is largely unexplored in ELT. Extrinsic factors like salary and accountability cannot be ignored, but it is probably the more intrinsic components which directly affect learners' motivation – that is, teachers' enthusiasm for their job and for their subject, their sense of competence (self-efficacy) and their sense of autonomy, all of which may be undermined by continual curriculum reform or overbearing assessment pressures (Wedell and Malderez, 2013). The rapid development of educational technologies impinges on teachers' motivation too – as an opportunity, where embraced to make their teaching more appealing, or as a threat, when teachers feel that their position as the 'language authority' is undermined by pupils' easy access to online resources that they themselves are not familiar with.

Conclusion

In this chapter, L2 motivation has been presented as the product of two distinct but interconnected elements: the individual's attitudes, goals and self-concepts, and the experience of learning. Mediating the connection is, among other important people, the teacher. It therefore seems appropriate to conclude the chapter with an endorsement of Ushioda's (forthcoming) proposal that teachers and learners research motivation together, carrying out small-scale localised research that focuses on the issues and challenges that they feel warrant attention: such projects may produce results of immediate relevance and boost the motivation of both parties in the process.

Discussion questions

- How far do you think the preeminence of English as a global language is affecting young people's motivation to learn other languages, in Anglophone countries and elsewhere?
- Reflecting on your life so far, do you think a strong 'ideal self' or 'ought-to self' was a major factor in motivating you to strive towards your main achievements? How have your ideal selves changed during your lifetime? As a teacher, do you think your learners have ideal English-speaking selves? If not, how might they be promoted?
- Is it true, as most theorists argue, that the most powerful motivators 'come from within'? Or are they underestimating the motivational power of external factors like class tests and national exams, for example?
- Can you think of teachers who inspired you to learn a subject at school? Did they use certain motivational strategies in class? If so, which ones? Or did their influence on you derive from some other aspect of their behaviour or presence?
- If you are a teacher of English, have you noticed any systematic fluctuations in your pupils' motivation to learn? Or in your own motivation to teach?

Related topics

Appropriate methodology; Complexity and language teaching; Individual differences; Learner autonomy.

Further reading

Dörnyei, Z., MacIntyre, P. and Henry, A. (eds) (2015) *Motivational dynamics in language learning.* Bristol: Multilingual Matters. (A collection of challenging but cutting-edge papers taking a complex dynamic systems perspective on L2 learning.)

Dörnyei, Z. and Ushioda, E. (2011) *Teaching and researching motivation.* Harlow: Pearson Education. (A comprehensive, balanced and clear text – the essential handbook for anyone interested in L2 motivation.)

Pink, D. H. (2009) *Drive: The surprising truth about what motivates us.* Edinburgh: Canongate. (A popular psychology paperback that applies the tenets of self-determination theory to everyday life; perhaps not 'paradigm-shattering' as its blurb claims, but entertaining and persuasive.)

Ushioda, E. (2012) 'Motivation', in A. Burns and J. Richards (eds) *Pedagogy and practice in second language teaching.* New York NY: Cambridge University Press. 77–85. (A brief, lucid argument for why motivation has to come from within and how teachers can help it germinate.)

References

Apple, M. T., Da Silva, D. and Fellner, T. (eds) (2013) *Language learning motivation in Japan.* Bristol: Multilingual Matters.

Bennell, P. and Akyeampong, K. (2007) *Teacher motivation in Sub-Saharan Africa and South Asia.* London: Department for International Development (DfID).

Block, D. (2003) *The social turn in second language acquisition.* Washington, DC: Georgetown University Press.

Borg, S. (2009) *The impact on students of British Council teacher centre EFL courses.* London: British Council. Retrieved August 21, 2014, from http://www.education.leeds.ac.uk/assets/files/staff/borg/The-Impact-on-students-of-British-Council-EFL-classes.pdf

Brosh, H. (1996) 'Perceived characteristics of the effective language teacher'. *Foreign Language Annals,* 29. 125–136.

Canagarajah, A. S. (1999) *Resisting linguistic imperialism in English teaching.* Oxford: Oxford University Press.

Carreira, J. M. (2011) 'Relationship between motivation for learning EFL and intrinsic motivation for learning in general among Japanese elementary school students'. *System,* 39. 90–102.

Chen, J. F., Warden, C. A. and Chang, H.-T. (2005) 'Motivators that do not motivate: The case of Chinese EFL learners and the influence of culture on motivation'. *TESOL Quarterly*, 39. 609–633.

Cheng, H-F. and Dörnyei, Z. (2007) 'The use of motivational strategies in language instruction: The case of EFL teaching in Taiwan' *Innovation in Language Teaching and Learning*, 1/1. 153–174.

Cheng, L., Watanabe, Y. and Curtis, A. (eds) (2004) *Washback in language testing: Research context and methods.* Mahwah, NJ: Lawrence Erlbaum Associates.

Clément, R. and Kruidenier, B. G. (1983) 'Orientations in second language acquisition: The effects of ethnicity, milieu and target language on their emergence'. *Language Learning*, 41. 469–512.

Coetzee-Van Rooy, S. (2006) 'Integrativeness: Untenable for World Englishes learners?' *World Englishes*, 25. 437–450.

Csikszentmihalyi, M. (1997) 'Intrinsic motivation and effective teaching: a flow analysis', in J. L. Bess (ed.) *Teaching well and liking it: Motivating faculty to teach effectively.* Baltimore, John Hopkins University Press. 72–89.

Deters, P., Xuesong, A. G., Miller, E. R. and Vitanova, G. (eds) (2015) *Theorizing and analyzing agency in second language learning.* Bristol: Multilingual Matters.

Dörnyei, Z. (2001) *Motivational strategies in the language classroom.* Cambridge: Cambridge University Press.

Dörnyei, Z. (2007) 'Creating a motivating classroom environment', in J. Cummins and C. Davison (eds) *International handbook of English language teaching.* New York: Springer. 719–731.

Dörnyei, Z. (2009) 'The L2 motivational self system', in Z. Dornyei and E. Ushioda (eds) *Motivation, language identity and the L2 self.* Bristol: Multilingual Matters. 9–42.

Dörnyei, Z., Henry, A. and Muir, C. (2016) *Directed motivational currents: Frameworks for focused interventions.* New York: Routledge.

Dörnyei, Z. and Ushioda, E. (eds) (2009) *Motivation, language identity and the L2 self.* Bristol: Multilingual Matters.

Dörnyei, Z. and Ushioda, E. (2011) *Teaching and researching motivation.* Harlow: Pearson Education.

Falout, J. and Maruyama, M. (2004) 'A comparative study of proficiency and learner demotivation'. *The Language Teacher*, 28. 3–9.

Gardner, R. (1985) *Social psychology and second language learning: The role of attitude and motivation.* London: Edward Arnold.

Gardner, R. C. (2010) *Motivation and second language acquisition.* New York: Peter Lang Publishing Inc.

Gardner, R. and Lambert, W. E. (1972) *Attitudes and motivation in second language learning.* Rowley, MA: Newbury House.

Graddol, D. (2006) *English next.* London: British Council.

Guilloteaux, M.-J. (2013) 'Motivational strategies for the language classroom: Perceptions of Korean secondary school English teachers'. *System*, 41. 3–14.

Guilloteaux, M. J. and Dörnyei, Z. (2008) 'Motivating language learners: A classroom-oriented investigation of the effects of motivational strategies on student motivation'. *TESOL Quarterly*, 42. 55–77.

Hadfield, J. and Dörnyei, Z. (2013) *Motivating learning.* Harlow: Longman.

Hall, D. and Hewings, A. (eds) (2001) *Innovation in English language teaching: A reader.* London: Routledge.

Harmer, J. (2007) *The practice of English language teaching.* Harlow: Pearson.

Heinzmann, S. (2013) *Young language learners' motivation and attitudes.* London: Bloomsbury.

Henry, A. (2013) 'Digital games and ELT: Bridging the authenticity gap', in E. Ushioda (ed.) *International perspectives on motivation.* Basingstoke: Palgrave Macmillan. 133–155.

Hu, G. (2003) 'English language teaching in China: Regional differences and contributing factors'. *Journal of Multilingual and Multicultural Development*, 24. 290–318.

Islam, M., Lamb, M. and Chambers, G. (2013) 'The L2 motivational self system and national interest: A Pakistani perspective'. *System*, 41. 231–244.

Iwaniec, J. (2014) 'Self-constructs in language learning: What is their role in self-regulation?' in K. Csizer and M. Magid (eds) *The impact of self-concept on language learning.* Bristol: Multilingual Matters. 189–205.

Jones, C. (2009) 'Parental support and the attitudes of boys and girls to modern foreign languages'. *Language Learning Journal*, 37. 85–97.

Kim, T. Y. and Seo, H. S. (2011) 'Elementary school students' foreign language learning demotivation: A mixed methods study of Korean EFL context'. *Asia-Pacific Education Researcher*, 21. 160–171.

Kormos, J. and Csizér, K. (2008) 'Age-related differences in the motivation of learning English as a foreign language: Attitudes, selves, and motivated learning behaviour'. *Language Learning*, 58. 327–355.

Kramsch, C. (2013) 'Afterword', in B. Norton (ed.) *Identity and language learning: Extending the conversation.* Bristol: Multilingual Matters. 192–201.

Lamb, M. (2013) "Your mum and dad can't teach you!': Constraints on agency among rural learners of English in Indonesia'. *Journal of Multilingual and Multicultural Development*, 34. 14–29.

Lamb, M. and Budiyanto (2013) 'Cultural challenges, identity and motivation in state school EFL', in E. Ushioda (ed.) *International perspectives on motivation: Language learning and professional challenges*. Basingstoke: Palgrave Macmillan. 18–34.

Lamb, M. and Wedell, M. (2015) 'Cultural contrasts and commonalities in inspiring language teaching'. *Language Teaching Research*, 9. 207–224.

Lasagabaster, D. (2011) 'English achievement and student motivation in CLIL and EFL settings'. *Innovation in Language Learning and Teaching*, 5. 3–18.

Littlejohn, A. (2008) 'The tip of the iceberg: Factors affecting learner motivation'. *RELC Journal*, 39. 214–225.

Luk, J. (2005) 'Voicing the self through the 'other' language: Exploring communicative language teaching for global communication', in A. S. Canagarajah (ed.) *Reclaiming the local in language policy and practice*. Mahwah, NJ: Lawrence Erlbaum Associates. 247–268.

MacIntyre, P. and Serroul, A. (2015) 'Motivation on a per-second timescale: Examining approach-avoidance motivation during L2 task performance', in Z. Dörnyei, P. MacIntyre and A. Henry (eds) *Motivational dynamics in language learning*. Bristol: Multilingual Matters. 109–138.

Magid, M. and Chan, L. (2012) 'Motivating English learners by helping them visualise their ideal L2 self: Lessons from two motivational programmes'. *Innovation in Language Learning and Teaching*, 6. 113–125.

Masgoret, A. M. and Gardner, R. (2003) 'Attitudes, motivation and second language learning: A meta-analysis of studies conducted by Gardner and associates'. *Language Learning*, 53. 123–163.

Mercer, S. and Ryan, S. (2010) 'A mindset for EFL: Learners' beliefs about the role of natural talent'. *ELT Journal*, 64. 436–444.

Moskovsky, C., Alrabai, F., Paolini, S. and Ratcheva, S. (2012) 'The effects of teachers' motivational strategies on learners' motivation: A controlled investigation of second language acquisition'. *Language Learning*, 63. 34–62.

Muir, C. and Dörnyei, Z. (2013) 'Directed motivational currents: Using vision to create effective motivational pathways'. *Studies in Second Language Learning and Teaching*, 3. 357–375.

Noels, K. (2013) 'Learning Japanese, learning English: Promoting motivation through autonomy, competence and relatedness', in M. T. Apple, D. Da Silva and T. Fellner (eds) *Language learning motivation in Japan*. Bristol: Multilingual Matters. 1-34.

Norton, B. (2000) *Identity and language learning: Social processes and educational practice*. London: Longman.

Papi, M. and Abdollahzadeh, E. (2012) 'Teacher motivational practice, student motivation, and possible L2 selves: An examination in the Iranian EFL context'. *Language Learning*, 62. 571–594.

Pintrich, P. R. (2003) 'A motivational science perspective on the role of student motivation in learning and teaching contexts'. *Journal of Educational Psychology*, 95. 667–686.

Pintrich, P. R. and Schunk, D. H. (2007) *Motivation in education: Theory, research and applications* (3rd ed.). Upper Saddle River, NJ: Merrill Prentice Hall.

Richards, K. (2006) "Being the teacher': Identity and classroom discourse'. *Applied Linguistics*, 27. 51–77.

Ryan, R. M. and Deci, E. L. (2000) 'Intrinsic and extrinsic motivations: Classic definitions and new directions'. *Contemporary Educational Psychology*, 25. 54–67.

Skilton-Sylvester, E. (2002) 'Should I stay or should I go? Investigating Cambodian women's participation and investment in adult ESL programs'. *Adult Education Quarterly*, 53. 9–26.

Taylor, F. (2013) *Self and identity in adolescent foreign language learning*. Bristol: Multilingual Matters.

Ushioda, E. (2009) 'A person-in-context relational view of emergent motivation, self and identity', in Z. Dörnyei and E. Ushioda (eds) *Motivation, language identity and the L2 self*. Bristol: Multilingual Matters. 215–228.

Ushioda, E. (2012) 'Motivation', in A. Burns and J. Richards (eds) *Pedagogy and practice in second language teaching*. New York, NY: Cambridge University Press. 77–85.

Ushioda, E. (ed.) (2013) *International perspectives on motivation: Language learning and professional challenges*. Basingstoke: Palgrave Macmillan.

Ushioda, E. (forthcoming) 'Thinking allowed'. *Language teaching*.

Vandergrift, L. (2005) 'Relationships among motivation orientations, metacognitive awareness and proficiency in L2 listening'. *Applied Linguistics*, 26. 70–89.

Waninge, F., Dörnyei, Z. and De Bot, K. (2014) 'Motivational dynamics in language learning: Change, stability, and context'. *The Modern Language Journal*, 98. 704–723.

Wedell, M. and Malderez, A. (2013) *Understanding language classroom contexts*. London: Bloomsbury.

Williams, M., Burden, R. and Lanvers, U. (2002) '"French is the Language of Love and Stuff": Student perceptions of issues related to motivation in learning a foreign language'. *British Educational Research Journal,* 28. 504–528.

Williams, M., Burden, R. L. and Al-Baharna, S. (2001) 'Making sense of success and failure: The role of the individual in motivation theory', in Z. Dörnyei and R. W. Schmidt (eds) *Motivation and second language acquisition.* Honolulu: University of Hawai'i at Manoa. 171–184.

Wu, X. (2003) 'Intrinsic motivation and young language learners: The impact of the classroom environment'. *System,* 31. 501–517.

24

Learner autonomy

Phil Benson

Introduction

Since its introduction into the field of language teaching in the 1970s, interest in learner autonomy has grown rapidly. This chapter outlines the evolution of definitions of autonomy and
its history in language teaching research and practice. Issues of particular interest to ELT are
highlighted – conceptions of autonomy in the context of the global spread of ELT, relationships
between autonomy and the development of identity in language learning, and the status of
autonomy in 'postmethod pedagogies'. The terms of persistent debates on the roles of teaching,
assessment and individuality are also discussed.

Definitions of autonomy in language learning

Among the many definitions of learner autonomy in the literature, Holec's (1981: 3) "the ability
to take charge of one's own learning" remains the most widely cited. Describing this ability in
terms of planning, monitoring and evaluation, Holec essentially explained what autonomous
language learners are able to do. Later, Little (1991: 4) shifted the emphasis from learning behaviour to the psychology of learning by describing autonomy as a capacity for "detachment, critical reflection, decision-making and independent action". Later still, Benson (2001: 47) defined
autonomy as "the capacity to take control of one's own learning" and identified a variety of
dimensions of control over language learning under three headings: the day-to-day management
of learning, the cognitive processes involved in language acquisition, and decisions about learning content. These definitions all acknowledge that autonomy is multidimensional, not "a single,
easily described behaviour" or a "steady state" (Little, 1990: 7), and that it takes different forms
according to the learner and the object and context of learning. In ELT, autonomy is likely to
take very different forms among, for example, young learners in a primary classroom in Asia,
EAP students in a university classroom in the United Kingdom or adult learners studying English outside the classroom in South America. In each case, individual differences (see MacIntyre,
Gregersen and Clément, this volume) related to learners' goals and purposes, prior experiences
and predispositions toward language learning will also come into play.

Other definitions of learner autonomy have additionally emphasised its social dimensions.
Jiménez Raya et al. (2007: 1) describe the autonomous learner as "self-determined, socially
responsible and critically aware", while Murray (2014: 4) makes the point that "individuals can

only be autonomous in relation to some social context". In ELT, social context could mean a number of things. We might think, for example, of ELT itself as a broad social context for learner autonomy, of the narrower contexts of regions or educational settings, of the social contexts of specific classrooms or of the social ecologies in which particular individuals learn languages and live their lives (van Lier, 2004; Palfreyman, 2014).

There is also an important situational aspect to learner autonomy. From the teacher's point of view, autonomy is not so much a matter of teaching autonomous learning skills but of creating an environment in which learner autonomy can be exercised and enhanced. Teachers who orient their teaching towards autonomy create conditions in which students make meaningful choices about their learning and produce diverse and personally relevant learning outcomes. Viewed in this way, autonomy might be understood as a conceptual toolkit for teachers to use in decision making at a variety of levels, ranging from curriculum design to minute-by-minute practice in the classroom. At each level, we might ask who makes the decisions about student learning and whether our choices as teachers help or hinder the development of learner autonomy.

Autonomy is viewed as an attribute that is worth developing for several reasons. Although learner autonomy is not exactly a theory, it does have a theoretical basis in the idea that language learning is more effective when students are more involved in decision-making about their own learning. Little (1994: 431) argues that "all genuinely successful learning is in the end autonomous", although we should bear in mind that "successful", in this context, implies not only a certain level of proficiency but also personal relevance and a capacity to use a foreign language for purposes that are recognisably the learner's own. According to Macaro (2008: 59–60), autonomy implies "taking control not only of the language being learnt, but also of the goal and purpose of that learning", and it resides in "being able to say what you want to say rather than producing the language of others". Autonomy has also been shown to be at the root of language learning motivation, which is enhanced when students are enabled to make choices and decisions about their learning (Ushioda, 2011; see also Lamb, this volume).

A brief history of learner autonomy

Starting points for the history of autonomy in ELT can be found in the 1970s in the experimental work of Henri Holec and his colleagues at the Centre de Recherches et d'Applications on Langues (CRAPEL) in France and Leni Dam and her colleagues in Danish secondary schools (Dam, 1995; Smith, 2008). Subsequent work has followed parallel paths inside and outside the classroom. At the CRAPEL, innovative work focused on opportunities for self-directed adult language learning using authentic materials in the 'Sound and Video Library'. Learners used the library with the guidance of 'counsellors' who engaged learners in self-directed processes of 'learner training' (Holec, 1980). From these beginnings evolved a range of practices involving self-access (Gardner and Miller, 1999), language advising (Ludwig and Mynard, 2013) and learning strategies (Cohen and Macaro, 2008; see also MacIntyre, Gregersen and Clément, this volume). Learner autonomy is often seen as the goal of these practices, without which they lack direction. Autonomy has also played a similar role in relation to distance language learning (White, 2003), tandem learning (Lewis and Walker, 2003), self-instruction (Fernández-Toro, 1999) and computer-mediated language learning (Lamy and Hampel, 2007; see Gruba, Hinkelman, and Cárdenas-Claros, this volume).

During the 1970s and 1980s, the emphasis in work on learner autonomy fell outside the classroom, for example, on how learners exercised autonomy in self-study. Although autonomy was also the focus of classroom work, it was not until Little (1991) and Dam (1995) that classroom autonomy became an important theme. Dam (1995) provided a detailed account of how learners were given a considerable share of the responsibility for planning and carrying out activities in Danish ELT classrooms. Classroom-based experiments elsewhere introduced the process and negotiated syllabus (Breen and Littlejohn, 2000), in which the content and methods of learning were either determined by the students or negotiated between students and teachers, and collaborative learning (Nunan, 1992; Ribé and Vidal, 1993), in which teaching and learning focused on independent project work carried out in groups. In these classroom contexts, the concept of autonomy lent meaning to a variety of practices that emphasised learner choice and decision-making.

The paths of out-of-class and classroom autonomy have seldom been far apart and frequently cross. Research on autonomy in language learning tends to be practice-driven (Little, 2007; Smith, 2008). In addition to journal papers and postgraduate theses, collections of papers from conferences, symposia and workshops that bring together practitioners from a variety of teaching and learning contexts are prominent in the dissemination of research (e.g. Morrison, 2011; Murray et al., 2011; Irie and Stewart, 2011; Barfield and Alvaro, 2013; Murray, 2014). In these collections, autonomy often plays the role of the theoretical 'glue' that holds together the diverse areas of practice mentioned above within a shared matrix of assumptions on the benefits of learners taking more active roles in decision making inside and beyond the classroom. While interest in autonomy stretches across languages, the majority of studies are now ELT based. The impact of this is difficult to assess, but it is clear that the ELT industry has facilitated both the internationalisation and what is sometimes perceived as the 'mainstreaming' of interest in autonomy (Pennycook, 1997). Whether autonomy has truly become a mainstream ELT concept is open to question, however. Little (2007), for example, suggests that interest in autonomy among researchers is not widely reflected in the practice of mainstream language education. Borg and Al-Busaidi's (2012) study of teachers' beliefs about autonomy, on the other hand, suggests that the concept is now deeply embedded in the professional consciousness of the ELT community.

Main current issues in the theory and practice of learner autonomy in ELT

Thinking about the nature of language learner autonomy has developed considerably over the past three decades or so. Three main current issues stand out that are largely inspired by thinking on autonomy from the perspective of ELT: conceptions of autonomy in the context of the globalisation of ELT, relationships between autonomy and the development of learners' identities, and the status of the concept of autonomy in postmethod pedagogies.

Autonomy and the globalisation of ELT

The rapid growth of ELT from the 1960s up to the present day has been both a consequence of and a factor in globalisation. The expansion of foreign travel for business, education and pleasure and the growth of global information technology and media networks has created both a demand for English and conditions that facilitate its acquisition, but the ELT industry has also helped speed these developments (Edge, 2006; Graddol, 2006; Phillipson, 2012; see Pennycook, this volume). The same is true of national education policies, which are increasingly subject to forces of convergence, leading to shared policies focusing on the individual as a resource in the struggle to maintain a competitive edge in the global 'knowledge economy'. In educational policy around the world, English language competence is now part of a 'generic skill' set tied up with communication, information technology and lifelong learning skills, which leads to English language education policies that often favour approaches focused on communication, information technology and autonomous learning skills.

Miliander and Trebbi (2008) have gathered data on language education policies favouring autonomy in seven European countries from Norway to Bulgaria. Studies have also documented policies involving autonomy in China (Shao and Wu, 2007), Thailand (Akaranithi and Punlay, 2007) and Japan (Head, 2006). These policies have kept alive the debate, initiated by Riley (1988), around the extent to which the idea of learner autonomy is essentially 'European' in character, which has largely focused on the 'appropriateness' of practices associated with autonomy in non-European education systems (Smith, 2001; Sonaiya, 2002; Holliday, 2005). Further critiques from Chinese researchers have tended to target communicative language teaching (see Thornbury, this volume). These critiques draw on similar arguments to those that were earlier directed at learner autonomy (e.g. Hu, 2002; Yu, 2012), the essential point being that ELT methods that are constructed as being 'progressive' in comparison to 'traditional' Chinese approaches may be culturally and ideologically inappropriate to local settings.

Thus, in a broader critique, Holliday (2005) sees autonomy as a central construct in dominant ELT discourses that oppose the 'active' Western student to the 'passive' non-Western 'Other'. Schmenk (2005) also critiques the alignment of the idea of autonomy with globalisation. According to this critique, wider interest in learner autonomy in language learning can be explained by its presence in global education policies and its promotion by the ELT industry. It is important, however, to untangle the internationalisation of autonomy in language teaching and learning 'on the ground' from these higher-level global processes. The rise of autonomy could be seen as a product of (problematic) 'top-down' processes of globalisation, yet as Smith (2008) points out, international interest in the practice of autonomy has evolved largely through 'bottom-up' processes involving networks of practitioners who often pursue autonomy as a minority interest in the systems in which they work.

It is also important to separate critique of the principles of learner autonomy from the forms in which it often appears through top-down, policy-driven approaches. For example, Sonaiya (2002) interprets the introduction of CALL (computer-assisted language learning) in place of classroom teaching in Nigeria as an initiative intended to facilitate learner autonomy, yet this top-down development appears to have done little to encourage learner decision making or control over learning. Valuable theoretical work that is attempting to develop culturally appropriate accounts of autonomy is being carried out by, for example, Wu (2011) who has explored roots for the broad idea of autonomy in learning in Confucian scholarship, and Huang (2013), who has carried out ethnographic work in a Chinese provincial university that teases out the relationship between ELT students' aspirations for autonomy and their expectations of community and care within the institution. Kuchah and Smith (2011) have explored the potential for autonomy in what they call the 'difficult circumstances' of large and low-resourced ELT classrooms in Africa. Kuchah devised pragmatic solutions to teaching in crowded classes of 200 or more which included teaching outdoors, negotiated rules and work plans, and creative writing as a response to the lack of textbooks (see also Shamim and Kuchah, this volume).

Autonomy and identity in ELT

The global spread of English is also leading some researchers to rethink the meaning of learner autonomy in the context of ELT. In an important contribution to the literature, Illés (2012) notes two developments affecting English language learners around the world – the growing role of English as a Lingua Franca (see Seargeant, this volume) and the role of English in computer-mediated communication (CMC; see Kern, Ware and Warschauer, this volume) – that are leading to a shift in emphasis from language learning to language use. The task of ELT, Illés argues, is to "help learners develop self-reliance and autonomy, which will help them to communicate successfully in international settings" (p. 506). In the new contexts of English language use, "learners can be considered autonomous only if they can meet the increased problem-solving demands the use of English in international and CMC settings presents" (p. 512). For Illés, this also implies a shift of emphasis in the definition of learner autonomy away from control of teaching and learning processes (which is best left to the pedagogical expertise of teachers) to control over language use. This is a challenging view from the perspective of ELT, which accords, for example, with new ways of looking at motivation that are similarly inspired by considerations of motivations to learn English as an international language (Ushioda, 2006; see also Lamb, this volume). It also accords with Littlewood's (1996: 81) model of autonomy, which identified "autonomy as a communicator" as an intermediate stage between "autonomy as a learner" and "autonomy as a person". From this perspective, the significance of autonomy in language learning lies in its impact on the learners' capacity to exercise personal autonomy in their lives through communication in a second language.

Much of the most interesting research on learner autonomy at present is taking place around the intersections of autonomy, identity and motivation and is largely inspired by thinking about the potential of ELT to enhance international mobility and change individual lives (Murray et al., 2011; Ushioda, 2011; Benson and Cooker, 2013). Recent research that links autonomy to issues of identity calls attention to ways in which learning a new language involves acquiring and experiencing new identities that may, in turn, contribute to the learner's personal autonomy. This research also links to motivation, especially where motivation is understood in terms of the 'ideal L2 self', or learners' imaginings of who they might become as users of a foreign language (Dörnyei and Ushioda, 2009; see also Lamb, this volume). From a practical perspective, ELT practitioners are encouraged to pay attention to the impact of learning English on the lives and identities of learners and the ways in which autonomy in their language learning is connected to autonomy in their lives (Benson, 2012).

Autonomy and postmethod pedagogy

Kumaravadivelu (2003) argues that the days in which researchers searched for the best 'methods' of teaching languages are long gone and that we now live in a 'postmethod' era in which language pedagogy is informed by 'macrostrategies', among which autonomy is one (see also Hall, this volume, ch. 15). It has long been emphasised that autonomy is not a 'method' of teaching or learning but a matter of encouraging learners to play a role in deciding what the most appropriate methods will be both in and out of the classroom. In its earlier incarnations, autonomy most often appeared as the goal of experimental approaches, where it was often as important as the goal of actually learning the language, if not more so. In more recent work, autonomy tends to be subordinated to language learning goals in approaches in which it is one, but not necessarily the most important, consideration in the planning of language courses or lessons. As a consequence, autonomy is no longer seen as a 'specialist' concern, and there are now sections on autonomy in language teaching overviews by, for example, Harmer (2001), Hedge (2000), Cameron (2001), Nation (2001), and Thornbury (2005). From this perspective, autonomy might be seen not as an overarching goal for ELT but as one of a number of elements around which postmethod language pedagogies might be built.

At the same time, the term 'pedagogy for autonomy' has emerged to refer to the various ways in which the idea of autonomy might be built into the practice of language education (Smith, 2003). This term implies teaching for the purpose of developing autonomy, but it is also understood that pedagogies for autonomy can be "weak" or "strong" (Smith, 2003), "narrow" or "broad" (Kumaravadivelu, 2003), or "gradualist" or "radical" (Allford and Pachler, 2007). For

Allford and Pachler (2007), gradualist approaches treat autonomy as a long-term goal to be achieved through the acquisition of autonomous learning skills, while radical versions emphasise learners' right to autonomy. For Smith (2003), weak pedagogies for autonomy assume that learners lack autonomy and need training towards it, while strong pedagogies begin from the assumption that learners are already autonomous to some degree. Ribé (2003) also makes a distinction between 'convergence' models of autonomy directed at shared, 'other-directed' curriculum goals and 'divergence' models which involve choices "affecting almost all levels of control, management and strategic decisions".

Although these are theoretical distinctions, they highlight a number of practical pedagogical questions. Is learner autonomy to be a course goal, or does it inform teaching within a course that has other objectives? Is the aim to develop learner autonomy or to build on the autonomy the students already have? Are the learners working towards a shared, externally defined goal such as an examination or towards individual targets and outcomes? The answers to these kinds of questions will determine whether a 'strong' or 'weak' approach is most appropriate and whether it is to be adopted at the level of course planning or day-to-day teaching.

Key debates about autonomy

Throughout the history of research and practice on learner autonomy, three persistent and unresolved issues have provoked discussion and debate: the roles of teachers and of assessment and the 'individualistic' character of autonomy.

Do autonomous learners need teachers?

A persistent question for debate is whether or not learner autonomy means, or at least implies, learning without a teacher or instructional materials, as it has sometimes been defined (e.g. Dickinson, 1987). Although this is now seen as a poor definition, it is also understood that autonomous language learners should, in principle, be capable of directing their own learning. One problem with this view is the suggestion that a second language can be learned, implicitly or naturalistically, in much the same way as a first language, whereas it is now clear that first language acquisition sets up barriers to naturalistic second language learning later in life that can only be overcome through explicit learning (Ellis, 2008). In light of this, it may be more accurate to say that autonomous language learners should be capable of self-directing whatever instructional, self-instructional or conscious learning processes prove necessary to their learning. This view does not preclude a role for teachers and teaching. At the same time, research and practice on learner autonomy has often explored modes of learning that involve alternatives to classroom instruction.

On the other hand, there is a school of research and practice on learner autonomy that values teachers and teaching and sees autonomy operating and developing mainly in language classrooms. This perspective has tended to focus on alternatives to direct instruction that give students more control over teaching and learning processes in the classroom. It has also focused on the qualities of teachers and, in particular, the notions of teacher autonomy and teacher education for learner autonomy (Benson and Huang, 2008; Smith and Vieira, 2009). The premise of much of this work is that in order to help students develop learner autonomy, teachers must be autonomous in respect to their own learning, professional practice and development and the exercise of discretion in the classroom.

In evaluating the role of teaching in the development of learner autonomy, it is perhaps important to bear in mind that teachers are apt to think of learner autonomy as something that depends on their actions rather than those of the students (Benson, 2008). At the same time, the trend for institutions to reduce the costs of ELT mean that any initiative that promises both learner autonomy and reduced expenditure on classroom teaching is likely to be welcomed. Thus, ELT practitioners need to be wary of simply providing an educational rationale for cost-cutting measures in the form of arguments for learner autonomy. The best way to approach this issue may be from the perspective of what learners need to do in order to learn a foreign language. The current state of research suggests that both explicit instruction *and* self-directed learning outside the classroom are needed for learners who achieve high levels of proficiency (Benson, 2011). This suggests the value of an approach to learner autonomy that attends both to classroom and out-of-class learning, which is reflected in recent work that has explored language learning beyond the classroom and how teachers can attend to it (Benson and Reinders, 2011; Nunan and Richards, 2015).

Does assessment have a role to play in autonomous learning?

From one perspective, there is considerable antipathy between the concepts of autonomy and language assessment, especially where the stakes in testing are high. While autonomy is associated with diverse learning outcomes and heterogeneity, assessment systems often aim at convergent outcomes and homogeneity (see Fulcher and Owen, this volume, for further discussion of language testing and assessment). In mass education systems, washback effects of external assessments are often the main constraint on teacher and learner autonomy as teachers are forced to 'teach to the test'. Arguably, the potential for autonomy is greatest where external assessment regimes are weak and assessment is internally managed, although several studies have argued that students are capable of exercising autonomy in preparing for public assessments such as IELTS (Barrett-Lennard, 1997; Morrison, 2011). Among international assessment tools, the Common European Framework of Reference for Languages (CEFR) and European Language Portfolio (ELP) have been seen as particularly conducive to autonomy because of their open-endedness and use of self-assessment procedures (Little, 2005; Kühn and Pérez Cavana, 2012). In this context, Little has argued, from a Vygotskian perspective, for the value of external assessment as a stage leading to the internalisation of capacities for self-assessment. Nevertheless, there has been a preference in the field of autonomy for localised formative assessment, and self- and peer-assessment especially (Everhard, 2015). Localised assessment is seen as a means by which autonomous leaners reflect on their plans and adjust them according to internal and external feedback (Dam and Legenhausen, 2010).

Another side to this problem concerns the place of assessment of autonomy in language teaching and learning. Arguably, learner autonomy is a means to the end of better language learning and does not need to be assessed independently of language proficiency, although the fact that we often talk of students 'developing' autonomy or becoming 'more autonomous' begs the question of the measurable criteria that might lie behind such statements. Benson (2010) argued that autonomy is potentially measurable in terms of degrees of control over a variety of dimensions of learning but that such measurements can only be approximate, due to the large number and contextual variability of the dimensions involved. Everhard and Murphy's (2015) recent collection on assessment and autonomy includes three proposals for the measurement of autonomy. Here, Murase (2015) describes a questionnaire instrument designed for self-assessment of autonomy along 'technical', 'psychological', 'socio-cultural', and 'political-philosophical' dimensions. Tassinari (2015) proposes a qualitative assessment model based on dynamic relationships among competencies and skills identified in the learner autonomy literature. And Cooker (2015) proposes a self-assessment process, conceived as "assessment *as* learning", that enables learners to align themselves with one of six modes of autonomy. While the practical purposes of assessing autonomy may be questioned, the authors claim that their models have value as diagnostic and self-development tools.

Is autonomy individualistic?

One of the more persistent charges levelled against the concept of autonomy is its focus on the individual, which has recently been discussed from a variety of theoretical perspectives in Benson and Cooker's (2013) and Murray's (2014) edited collections on the individual and social dimensions of autonomy in language learning. This question was first tackled in the 1980s, as advocates of autonomy sought to extricate the term from its associations with 'individualisation' (Brookes and Grundy, 1988) and 'self-instruction' (Dickinson, 1987). Thus, once the preferred term in ELT, 'learner independence' has also now largely been replaced by 'learner autonomy' as the view that autonomy implies 'interdependence', rather than 'independence', has come to the fore (for example, the International Association of Teachers of English as a Foreign Language [IATEFL] Learner Independence Special Interest Group [SIG] changed its name to the IATEFL Learner Autonomy SIG in the mid-2000s). Little (1994) argued this view from a Vygotskian sociocultural perspective (see Negueruela-Azarola and García, this volume) and later researchers have drawn on, for example, theories of "community" (Murray, 2011), "sociality" (Lewis, 2013) or "social ecology" (Palfreyman, 2014).

In spite of an insistence that autonomy is a social construct, the tension between the individual and social sides of autonomy remains and has been the object of recent critiques from the direction of social theory. Critics tend to associate autonomy with Cartesian conceptions of the self-determining mind and often prefer to use the term 'agency' to denote a culturally conditioned, socially mediated and constrained capacity for individual action (Lantolf, 2013). For many advocates of learner autonomy, this view of agency is consistent with their own views of autonomy as a social construct, yet the concept of learner autonomy ultimately rests on the assumption of an individual 'self' that is capable of making its own decisions about learning, albeit in interaction or conjunction with others. The strongest challenge to this assumption comes from research on 'social cognition' (Hamilton, 2005), which goes beyond the idea of self-determining individuals acting in concert to the idea that individual cognition itself, including our sense of self and individual agency, emerges from and is dependent on the social interactions that we are engaged in over the course of our lives (Shook, 2013). This view is increasingly supported by neuroscience research that fails to find evidence of physical structures in the brain that correspond to everyday conceptions of the autonomous self and calls into question whether individual minds are, in fact, separate from the minds of others (Iacoboni, 2008; Lakoff, 2013).

In practical terms, a social conception of learner autonomy entails a recognition that language learning depends on interaction, which might lead to a preference for group work, collaboration, and out-of-class activities that bring learners together in communication with other learners. At the same time, it seems important that a social view of autonomy retains a focus on individual differences, the diversity of experiences and purposes that individuals bring to language learning, the value of divergent learning outcomes, and the contribution of experiences of second language learning to the unique identities of individual learners. Benson (2013) argues that if the focus on the individual were removed from learner autonomy, its distinctive contribution to language pedagogy would be diminished. At the same time, we need to evolve a view of individual language learners, both in theory and practice, that attends to the social contexts of their learning as more than background information and foregrounds their individuality within frameworks of social conditioning, interaction and mediation.

Future developments

The debates around the nature of learner autonomy and its roles in the practice of language teaching and learning are likely to continue into the future. This chapter concludes with comments on two emerging issues that are likely to feed into these debates: the roles of language learning beyond the classroom and some implications of neuroscience research for the concept of autonomy in learning.

After a period in the 1990s and 2000s in which it was somewhat marginalised, there has recently been something of a resurgence of interest in language learning beyond the classroom (Benson and Reinders, 2011; Nunan and Richards, 2015). This interest is prompted in part by new digital contexts for language learning and awareness that learners who previously lacked access to out-of-class opportunities to learn English now find abundant opportunities through online media and social networking services (Lamy and Zorou, 2013). Renewed interest in language learning beyond the classroom is also prompted by increased mobility and, in particular, the opportunities for a closer integration of language learning and everyday life afforded by mobile, hand-held devices. In research on language learning beyond the classroom, there also appears to a significant shift from the provision of opportunities and resources to an understanding of how learners make use of the opportunities and resources available in their everyday environments. In a discussion of language learning skills for a 'mobile world', Kukulska-Hulme (2013: 5) argues for a shift from the design of language learning programmes based on transmission pedagogies to a learner-centred view of mobile devices as "personal tools that can also support self-directed forms of language learning and greater learner autonomy". These developments are likely to have a significant effect on research and practice on learner autonomy. Interest in autonomy in classrooms developed because teachers sought to make autonomy relevant to learners who mainly learned languages in classrooms. The imperative in the future, however, may well be for ELT practitioners to adapt classroom teaching to their learners' autonomous learning outside the classroom.

On a somewhat different note, we may also expect research on autonomy in language learning to be challenged by neuroscience research, which is already having an impact on research in fields such as 'neurosociology' (Franks and Turner, 2013), 'neuroeconomics' (Camerer et al., 2005) and 'neurolinguistics' (McGroarty, 2008). The idea of learner autonomy rests, fundamentally, on the assumption that human beings possess cognitive capacities that allow them to control learning behaviour through planning and reflection. Research on neural systems in the brain, however, is increasingly calling this assumption into question (Camerer et al., 2005). It suggests, for example, that the mental processes that account for much of our behaviour, and language processing in particular, are automatised and inaccessible to introspection. Moreover, we are apt to exaggerate the importance of controlled, conscious behaviour because introspective access to such cognitively controlled processes is much stronger than access to automated processes, which take place below the level of conscious awareness. Neuroscience research also points to the interaction of emotion and cognition in decision-making, showing that cognition is insufficient in itself to cause action without the support of emotion processes, which often overwhelm it. Lastly, there is some evidence that, because it draws resources from the regions of the brain that are responsible for cognition, conscious reflection on decision making may actually diminish control over behaviour. In other words, people who reflect upon and give reasons for their decisions do not necessarily make better decisions. While neuroscience at present stands at some remove from research on autonomy in learning, it deserves attention for what it might tell us about the limits of control, and hence autonomy, over language learning.

Conclusion

Given the many different ways in which learners can go about learning a second language and the many different outcomes they may achieve, research and practice on learner autonomy offers a set of ideas about language learning and approaches to language learning that promise satisfactory outcomes for individual learners. Autonomy is associated with better learning and, more importantly, with personally relevant outcomes. In indicating some of the key issues in its development in the field of language teaching and learning, this chapter has attempted to show both the flexibility and adaptability of the concept, related debates and concerns, and the openness of its advocates to new ideas and new practices.

Discussion questions

- What is the role of teaching in the development of learner autonomy? How should teachers incorporate out-of-class learning into teaching for learner autonomy?
- Does language proficiency assessment help or hinder the development of autonomy? Is there a purpose to the assessment of learner autonomy itself?
- Does learner autonomy imply an excessive concern with individuality in language learning? What do you understand by a 'social' approach to autonomy?
- To what extent do you agree or disagree with the view that autonomy is an essentially 'European' or 'Western' concept?

Related topics

Appropriate methodology; Cognitive perspectives on classroom language learning; Communicative language teaching in theory and practice; Educational perspectives on ELT; Individual differences; Method, methods and methodology; New technologies, blended learning and the 'flipped classroom'; Politics, power relationships and ELT; Sociocultural theory and the language classroom; World Englishes and English as a Lingua Franca.

Further reading

Benson, P. (2011) *Teaching and researching autonomy* (2nd ed.). London: Pearson. (A comprehensive account of research and practice on autonomy in language teaching and learning.)

Everhard, C. J. and Murphy, L. (eds) (2015) *Assessment and autonomy in language learning.* Basingstoke: Palgrave Macmillan. (This collection of papers is the first in the field to thoroughly discuss the question of how to assess autonomy.)

Morrison, B. and Navarro, D. (2014) *The autonomy approach: Language learning in the classroom and beyond.* Peaslake: Delta Publishing. (A teacher development book designed for teachers, advisors, trainers and materials developers, with activities to foster autonomy.)

Murray, G. (ed.) (2014) *Social dimensions of autonomy in language learning.* Basingstoke: Palgrave Macmillan. (This collection of papers by experts in the field discusses the social aspects of autonomy from a variety of theoretical points of view.)

Nunan, D. C. and Richards, J. (eds) (2015) *Language learning beyond the classroom.* London: Routledge. (This collection of short chapters describes a variety of techniques for integrating out-of-class language learning into language teaching.)

References

Akaranithi, A. and Punlay, S. (2007) 'Tensions in policy and practice in self-directed learning', in A. Barfield and S. Brown (eds) *Reconstructing autonomy in language education: Inquiry and innovation.* Basingstoke: Palgrave Macmillan. 43–55.

Allford, D. and Pachler, N. (2007) *Language, autonomy and the new learning environments.* Oxford: Peter Lang.

Barfield, A. and Alvaro, N. G. (eds) (2013) *Autonomy in language learning: Stories of practice.* Canterbury: IATEFL.

Barrett-Lennard, S. (1997) 'Encouraging autonomy and preparing for IELTS: Mutually exclusive goals?' *Prospect,* 12/3. 29–40.

Benson, P. (2001) *Teaching and researching autonomy in language learning.* London: Longman.

Benson, P. (2008) 'Teachers' and learners' perspectives on autonomy', in T. E. Lamb and H. Reinders (eds) *Learner and teacher autonomy: Concepts, realities and responses.* Amsterdam: John Benjamins. 15–32.

Benson, P. (2010) 'Measuring autonomy: Should we put our ability to the test?', in P. Amos and L. Sercu (eds) *Testing the untestable in language education.* Bristol: Multilingual Matters. 77–97.

Benson, P. (2011) 'Language learning and teaching beyond the classroom: An introduction to the field', in P. Benson and H. Reinders (eds) *Beyond the language classroom.* Basingstoke: Palgrave Macmillan. 7–16.

Benson, P. (2012) 'Autonomy in language learning, learning and life'. *Synergies France,* 9. 29–39.

Benson, P. (2013) 'Drifting in and out of view: Autonomy and the social individual', in P. Benson and L. Cooker (eds) *The applied linguistic individual: Sociocultural approaches to identity, agency and autonomy.* London: Equinox. 75–89.

Benson, P. and Cooker, L. (eds) (2013) *The applied linguistic individual: Sociocultural approaches to identity, agency and autonomy.* London: Equinox.

Benson, P. and Huang, J. (2008) 'Autonomy in the transition from foreign language learning to foreign language teaching'. *DELTA: Documentação de Estudos em Linguística Teórica e Aplicada,* 24. Especial. 421–439.

Benson, P. and Reinders, H. (eds) (2011) *Beyond the language classroom.* Basingstoke: Palgrave Macmillan.

Borg, S. and Al-Busaidi, S. (2012) 'Teachers' beliefs and practices regarding learner autonomy'. *ELT Journal,* 66/3. 283–292.

Breen, M. P. and Littlejohn, A. (eds) (2000) *Classroom decision-making: Negotiation in the language classroom.* Cambridge: Cambridge University Press.

Brookes, A. and Grundy, P. (eds) (1988) *Individualization and autonomy in language learning.* ELT Documents 131. Modern English Publications in association with the British Council/Macmillan.

Camerer, C., Loewenstein, G. and Prelec, D. (2005) 'Neuroeconomics: How neuroscience can inform economics'. *Journal of Economic Literature,* 43. 9–64.

Cameron, L. (2001) *Teaching languages to young learners.* Cambridge: Cambridge University Press.

Cohen, A. and Macaro, E. (eds) (2008) *Language learner strategies: 30 years of research and practice.* Oxford: Oxford University Press.

Cooker, L. (2015) 'Assessment as autonomous learning', in C. J. Everhard and L. Murphy (eds) *Assessment and autonomy in language learning.* Basingstoke: Palgrave Macmillan. 89–113.

Dam, L. (1995) *Learner autonomy 3: From theory to classroom practice.* Dublin: Authentik.

Dam, L. and Legenhausen, L. (2010) 'Learners reflecting on learning: Evaluating versus testing in autonomous language learning', in P. Amos and L. Sercu (eds) *Testing the untestable in language education.* Bristol: Multilingual Matters. 120–139.

Dickinson, L. (1987) *Self-instruction in language learning.* Cambridge: Cambridge University Press.

Dörnyei, Z. and Ushioda, E. (eds) (2009) *Motivation, language identity and the L2 self.* Bristol: Multilingual Matters.

Edge, J. (ed.) (2006) *(Re-)locating TESOL in an age of empire.* Basingstoke: Palgrave Macmillan.

Ellis, N. (2008) 'Implicit and explicit knowledge about language', in J. Cenoz and N. H. Hornberger (eds) *Encyclopedia of language and education* (2nd ed.), Volume 6. New York, NY: Springer. 1–13.

Everhard, C. J. (2015) 'Investigating peer-assessment and self-assessment of oral skills as stepping-stones to autonomy in EFL Higher Education', in C. J. Everhard and L. Murphy (eds) *Assessment and autonomy in language learning.* Basingstoke: Palgrave Macmillan. 114–142.

Everhard, C. J. and Murphy, L. (eds) (2015) *Assessment and autonomy in language learning.* Basingstoke: Palgrave Macmillan.

Fernández-Toro, M. (1999) *Training learners for self-instruction.* London: CILT.

Franks, D. D. and Turner, J. H. (eds) (2013) *Handbook of neurosociology.* Dordrecht: Springer.

Gardner, D. and Miller, L. (1999) *Establishing self-access: From theory to practice.* Cambridge: Cambridge University Press.

Graddol, D. (2006) *English next. Why global English may mean the end of 'English as a foreign language'.* London: British Council.

Hamilton, D. (ed.) (2005) *Social cognition: Key readings in social psychology.* New York, NY: Psychology Press.

Harmer, J. (2001) *The practice of English language teaching* (3rd ed.). London: Pearson Education.

Head, E. (2006) 'Learner autonomy and education reform in Japan: Asking the students', in E. Skier and M. Kohyama (eds) *More autonomy you ask!* Tokyo: JALT Learner Development SIG. 9–31.

Hedge, T. (2000) *Teaching and learning in the language classroom.* Oxford: Oxford University Press.

Holec, H. (1980) 'Learner training: Meeting needs in self-directed learning', in H. B. Altman and C. Vaughan James (eds) *Foreign language learning: Meeting individual needs.* Oxford: Pergamon. 30–45.

Holec, H. (1981) *Autonomy in foreign language learning.* Oxford: Pergamon. (First published 1979, Strasbourg: Council of Europe.)

Holliday, A. (2005) *The struggle to teach English as an international language.* Oxford: Oxford University Press.

Hu, G. (2002) 'Potential cultural resistance to pedagogical imports: The case of communicative language teaching in China'. *Language, Culture, and Curriculum*, 15. 93–105.

Huang, J. (2013) *Autonomy, agency and identity in foreign language learning and teaching.* New York: Peter Lang.

Iacoboni, M. (2008) *Mirroring people.* New York, NY: Farrar, Strauss and Giroux.

Illés, E. (2012) 'Learner autonomy revisited'. *ELT Journal*, 66/4. 505–513.

Irie, K. and Stewart, A. (eds) (2011) *Realizing autonomy: Practice and reflection in language education contexts.* Basingstoke: Palgrave Macmillan.

Jiménez Raya, M., Lamb, T. and Vieira, F. (2007) *Pedagogy for autonomy in language education in Europe: Towards a framework for learner and teacher development.* Dublin: Authentik.

Kuchah, K. and Smith, R. C. (2011) 'Pedagogy of autonomy for difficult circumstances: From practice to principles'. *International Journal of Innovation in Language Learning and Teaching*, 5/2. 119–140.

Kühn, B. and Pérez Cavana, M. L. (eds) (2012) *Perspectives from the European language portfolio: Learner autonomy and self-assessment.* New York, NY: Routledge.

Kukulska-Hulme, A. (2013) *Re-skilling language learners for a mobile world.* Monterey, CA: The International Research Foundation for English Language Education.

Kumaravadivelu, B. (2003) *Beyond methods: Macrostrategies for language teaching.* New Haven, CT: Yale University Press.

Lakoff, G. (2013) 'Neural social science', in D. D. Franks and J. H. Turner (eds) *Handbook of neurosociology.* Dordrecht: Springer. 9–26.

Lamy, M-N. and Hampel, R. (2007) *Online communication in language learning and teaching.* Basingstoke: Palgrave Macmillan.

Lamy, M-N. and Zorou, K. (eds) (2013) *Social networking for language education.* Basingstoke: Palgrave Macmillan.

Lantolf, J. P. (2013) 'Sociocultural theory and the dialectics of L2 learner autonomy/agency', in P. Benson and L. Cooker (eds) *The applied linguistic individual: Sociocultural approaches to identity, agency and autonomy.* London: Equinox. 17–31.

Lewis, T. (2013) 'Between the social and the selfish: Learner autonomy in online environments'. *Innovation in Language Learning and Teaching*, 7/3. 198–212.

Lewis, T. and Walker, L. (eds) (2003) *Autonomous language learning in tandem.* Sheffield: Academic and Electronic Press.

Little, D. (1990) 'Autonomy in language learning'. In I. Gathercole (ed.) *Autonomy in language learning.* London: CILT. 7–15.

Little, D. (1991) *Learner autonomy. 1: Definitions, issues and problems.* Dublin: Authentik.

Little, D. (1994) 'Learner autonomy: A theoretical construct and its practical application'. *Die Neuere Sprache*, 93/5. 430–442.

Little, D. (2005) 'The Common European Framework and the European Language Portfolio: Involving learners and their judgments in the assessment process'. *Language Testing*, 22/3. 321–336.

Little, D. (2007) 'Introduction: Re-constructing learner and teacher autonomy in language education', in A. Barfield and S. Brown (eds) *Reconstructing autonomy in language education: Inquiry and innovation.* Basingstoke: Palgrave Macmillan. 1–12.

Littlewood, W. (1996) 'Autonomy: An anatomy and a framework'. *System*, 24/4. 427–435.

Ludwig, C. and Mynard, J. (eds) (2013) *Autonomy in language learning: Advising in action.* Canterbury: IATEFL.

Macaro, E. (2008) 'The shifting dimensions of language learner autonomy', in T. E. Lamb and H. Reinders (eds) *Learner and teacher autonomy: Concepts, realities and responses.* Amsterdam: John Benjamins. 43–62.

McGroarty, M. (2008) *Neurolinguistics and cognitive aspects of language processing.* Cambridge: Cambridge University Press.

Miliander, J. and Trebbi, T. (eds) (2008) *Educational policies and language learner autonomy in schools: A new direction in language education.* Dublin: Authentik.

Morrison, B. (ed.) (2011) *Independent language learning: Building on experience, seeking new perspectives.* Hong Kong: Hong Kong University Press.

Morrison, B. R. (2011) 'Self-directed learning modules for independent learning: IELTS exam preparation'. *Studies in Self-access Learning,* 2/2. 51–67.

Murase, F. (2015) 'Measuring language learner autonomy: Problems and possibilities', in C. J. Everhard and L. Murphy (eds) *Assessment and autonomy in language learning.* Basingstoke: Palgrave Macmillan. 35–63.

Murray, G. (2011) 'Older language learners, social learning spaces and community', in P. Benson and H. Reinders (eds) *Beyond the language classroom.* Basingstoke: Palgrave Macmillan. 132–145.

Murray, G. (ed.) (2014) *Social dimensions of autonomy in language learning.* Basingstoke: Palgrave Macmillan.

Murray, G., Gao, A. and Lamb, T. (2011) *Identity, motivation and autonomy in language learning.* Bristol: Multilingual Matters.

Nation, I.S.P. (2001) *Teaching and learning vocabulary in another language.* Cambridge: Cambridge University Press.

Nunan, D. C. (ed.) (1992) *Collaborative language learning and teaching.* Cambridge: Cambridge University Press.

Nunan, D. C. and Richards, J. (eds) (2015) *Language learning beyond the classroom.* London: Routledge.

Palfreyman, D. and Smith, R. C. (eds) (2003) *Learner autonomy across cultures: Language education perspectives.* Basingstoke: Palgrave Macmillan.

Pennycook, A. (1997) 'Cultural alternatives and autonomy', in P. Benson and P. Voller (eds) *Autonomy and independence in language learning.* London: Longman. 35–53.

Phillipson, R. (2012) Linguistic imperialism alive and kicking. *The Guardian,* 14.03.2012. Retrieved from http://www.theguardian.com/education/2012/mar/13/linguistic-imperialism-english-language-teaching

Ribé, R. (2003) '*Tramas* in the foreign language classroom: Autopoietic networks for learner growth', in D. Little, J. Ridley and E. Ushioda (eds) *Learner autonomy in foreign language classrooms: Teacher, learner, curriculum and assessment.* Dublin: Authentik. 11–28.

Ribé, R. and Vidal, N. (1993) *Project work.* London: Heinemann.

Riley, P. (1988) 'The ethnography of autonomy', in A. Brookes and P. Grundy (eds) *Individualization and autonomy in language learning.* ELT Documents 131. London: Modern English Publications in association with the British Council. 12–34.

Schmenk, B. (2005) 'Globalizing learner autonomy'. *TESOL Quarterly,* 39/1. 107–118.

Shao, H. and Wu, Z. (2007) 'Nurturing language learner autonomy through caring pedagogic practice', in A. Barfield and S. Brown (eds) *Reconstructing autonomy in language education: Inquiry and innovation.* Basingstoke: Palgrave Macmillan. 95–107.

Shook, J. R. (2013) 'Social cognition and the problem of other minds', in D. D. Franks and J. H. Turner (eds) *Handbook of neurosociology.* Dordrecht: Springer. 33–46.

Smith, R. C. (2001) 'Group work for autonomy in Asia'. *The AILA Review,* 15. 70–81.

Smith, R. C. (2003) 'Pedagogy for autonomy as (becoming-) appropriate methodology', in D. Palfreyman and R. C. Smith (eds) *Learner autonomy across cultures: Language education perspectives.* Basingstoke: Palgrave Macmillan. 129–146.

Smith, R. C. (2008) 'The history of learner autonomy', in L. Dam (ed.) *Papers from the 9th Nordic Conference on Developing Autonomy in Language Learning.* Copenhagen: CVU. Retrieved from http://www2.warwick.ac.uk/fac/soc/al/research/groups/llta/circal/dahla/histories/the_history_of_learner_autonomy.pdf

Smith, R. C. and Vieira, F. (eds) (2009) '*Teacher education for learner autonomy: Building a knowledge base.* Special issue of *Innovation in Language Learning and Teaching,* 3/3.

Sonaiya, R. (2002) 'Autonomous language learning in Africa: A mismatch of cultural assumptions'. *Language, culture and curriculum,* 15/2. 106–116.

Tassinari, M-G. (2015) 'Self-assessing and evaluating learner autonomy: A dynamic approach', in C. J. Everhard and L. Murphy (eds) *Assessment and autonomy in language learning.* Basingstoke: Palgrave Macmillan. 64–88.

Thornbury, S. (2005) *How to teach speaking.* London: Longman.

Ushioda, E. (2006) 'Language motivation in a reconfigured Europe: Access, identity, autonomy'. *Journal of Multilingual and Multicultural Development,* 27/2. 148–161.

Ushioda, E. (2011) 'Language learning motivation, self and identity: Current theoretical perspectives'. *Computer Assisted Language Learning,* 24/3. 199–210.

van Lier, L. (2004) *The ecology and semiotics of language learning: A sociocultural perspective*. Boston, MA: Kluwer Academic Publishers.

White, C. (2003) *Language learning in distance education*. Cambridge: Cambridge University Press.

Wu, Z. (2011) 'Interpretation, autonomy, and transformation: Chinese pedagogic discourse in a cross-cultural perspective'. *Journal of Curriculum Studies*, 43/5. 569–590.

Yu, L. (2012) 'Communicative language teaching in China: Progress and resistance'. *TESOL Quarterly*, 5/1. 94–98.

25

Primary ELT

Issues and trends

Janet Enever

Introduction

This chapter sets out to identify current issues and major trends in primary ELT today. The scope is global, reflecting the large-scale reform that has occurred in primary school curricula world-wide over the past fifty years regarding the teaching of English as a second or foreign language (Cha and Ham, 2008: 317). In this chapter, I focus principally on contexts where English has recently been introduced as a new curriculum subject regionally or nationally in primary schools, examining learning in instructed or formal contexts rather than language development in the more naturalistic environment of the home or family. Given the limited space and the huge scale of reform, I will only touch briefly on contexts where English has been the medium of instruction (EMI) during former periods of colonial influence (e.g. parts of Africa, India, Hong Kong).

The trend towards an early start for primary-level English now appears to be fairly settled at something between the ages of 6 and 9 years old (Rixon, 2013), although there are discussions about a still earlier start of 3 to 4 years old in some pre-primary contexts (Lee, 2009; Rokita-Jaskow, 2013). Here, I use the term primary to indicate the age range 5/6 – 11/12 years old, although terminology for this first phase of schooling can vary across countries and may be known elsewhere as elementary, basic, lower primary or other similar terminology (Ellis, 2014). The chapter following this focuses on the older secondary or teenage phase of schooling, from 12 years old upwards (see Pinter, this volume). Possibly this older age group should no longer be described as 'young learners' – at least, with regard to ELT.

Policy developments over time

From the early part of the twentieth century, foreign languages have been taught in primary schools. Initially, this tended to occur only in a small number of elite or private schools world-wide. While EMI is beyond the scope of this chapter, it is important to note that English as the language of schooling was present in the majority of schools established in the former colonies of the United Kingdom, ranging from India to parts of Africa, Singapore, Hong Kong and the West Indies, amongst others. On gaining independence, some countries made the decision to establish schooling in a regional or national language, while others have retained a stronger presence of English; for further reading see, for example, Makoni and Makoni (2009); Meganathan (2011).

From 1960–1970, some interest in an early start to foreign language teaching/learning was evident in Europe, with a number of small-scale pilot studies conducted in various European languages, often initiated by university-based applied linguists (Vilke, 2007). These projects lost direction, however, as a result of a pilot study publication in England which reported that there was no advantage to be gained by an early start at primary level (Burstall et al., 1974). Despite subsequent weaknesses identified in the interpretation of the research findings (see Gamble and Smalley, 1975 for a critique of the findings), the publication of the Burstall Report precipitated the closure of many similar projects across Europe.

During the late 1980s, a new wave of initiatives for introducing primary ELT began to emerge as a result of major political and policy reforms across the world. The first wave of initiatives was precipitated by the political changes in Eastern Europe following the collapse of the Berlin Wall in 1989, resulting in the almost universal introduction of English, firstly at secondary school level, then subsequently at primary level, across the former Soviet bloc countries of Eastern Europe and countries of the former Yugoslavia. The unprecedented scale of reform in the rush towards English has been consolidated over the first two decades of the twenty-first century, as huge populations of primary-aged children across Asia (including former colonies where English has been retained or has been newly introduced at early primary level), together with other Eastern European and Latin American countries, have begun to learn English, increasingly from the first phase of compulsory schooling or earlier (see Butler, 2015 for an overview of East Asian developments in particular). Cautiously, it can now be proposed that this trend is becoming established as an accepted strand of early primary education. However, future-gazing in matters concerning language policy is a notoriously precarious and very political business (Grin, 2003: 5) with nothing remaining 'fixed' for very long.

Contexts for primary ELT

The introductory section of this chapter briefly clarified the approximate age group in focus for ELT at primary levels of schooling worldwide. Given the wide range of contexts where English is now a feature of the primary curriculum, it is also important to understand how each of these contexts differs, if we are to distinguish between the likely outcomes that might be anticipated. Firstly, at a global level, contexts range from extracurricular private language schools to public (state) school classrooms. Without doubt, across such a range of contexts, funding and resource issues vary considerably; hence, outcomes will similarly vary.

Pedagogical approaches to learning English at primary level also vary widely today. These may include contexts where English is the medium of instruction (EMI), whereby all (or most) subjects may be taught in English from either the very beginning of schooling or perhaps introduced from the age of 9 or 10 years. In essence, this pedagogical approach has quite similar aims to the immersion approaches of the former colonial contexts outlined above, albeit with very different histories of implementation. Immersion schooling in English can be found today in a number of private international school contexts worldwide, many of which tend to cater for a relatively global mobile elite. Moving along the continuum somewhat, bilingual or partially bilingual contexts at primary level have become more popular in recent years. This pedagogical approach introduces English fairly intensively within the broad primary curriculum, generally at a ratio close to 50:50 between English and the national language. In some contexts (particularly Europe), this is increasingly described as content and language integrated learning (CLIL, which I shall return to later in the chapter), although the intensity of provision at primary level may be quite limited, expanding towards the upper primary and secondary levels. On a global scale however, the most commonly found model of English provision is where English is regarded as a subject, with anything from one to four lessons per week included in the primary curriculum. The varied pedagogical approaches summarised here have been established based on a mix of theory, empirical evidence and sociopolitical grounds. The emergence of these influences over the past fifty years are outlined in the following section.

An emergent rationale for an early start to foreign languages

Many of the initial arguments put forward for the advantages of an early start to foreign language (FL) learning were based on Lenneberg's (1967) hypothesis that an optimal period for language acquisition existed somewhere between childhood and early adolescence, known as the critical period hypothesis (CPH). This claim, relating to children's biological abilities in their native language (sometimes known as mother tongue or first language) was soon adopted as a rationale for introducing children to learning an additional language from a young age. Evidence in support of this hypothesis came mainly from two sources: first, from the naturalistic setting of bilingual homes; second, from immersion education in some parts of Canada, where children from English-speaking homes attended primary schools with French as the medium of instruction. Evidence of their success operated as a powerful signal for the potential gains of an early FL start (Lambert and Tucker, 1972). Much contradictory evidence about this hypothesis has since been recorded, however, both from naturalistic settings and from classrooms. Given the limitations of space, I will refer the reader to Muñoz and Singleton's (2011) review for a helpful overview of the evidence related to the CPH. Importantly, their critical review questions the assumption that attainment should be based on native-like performance and suggests that the focus on age as the crucial variable has resulted in a lack of attention paid to the many other linguistic and contextual variables at play (p. 2). In particular, they report that an increasing number of studies provide empirical evidence for the impact of variables reflecting both individual and contextual factors. They also refer to evidence from recent brain research indicating that the young child's brain may function differently from older peoples', and thus process language differently (p. 21). However, as they note, there is still quite limited knowledge of how the brain functions in relation to language learning in general and the question of the CPH in particular (p. 25).

This clearly indicates that insufficient evidence currently exists for claiming that in an ordinary school classroom, with anything from 20–70 pupils or more, an early start to ELT will make a significant difference to final achievement levels. Nonetheless, the CPH, together with classroom evidence and a number of empirical studies (for example, Mihaljević Djigunović and Vilke, 2000; Wang, 2002; Edelenbos et al., 2006; Enever, 2011), have proved sufficient for policy makers and parents to be convinced that ELT should be introduced from the very earliest phase of schooling. This socio-political rationale has been driven mainly by a concern for future economic security – both at individual levels for the next generation and at the national level of engagement in what can be loosely termed as the 'global marketplace'. Parents have often been highly influential here, keen that their children will have the best advantage possible for future employment. An example from southern India illustrates this point well. In the state of Tamil Nadu, education authorities have recently supported the introduction of primary English in government schools in an effort to limit the trend for parents to send their children to fee-paying private schools which promote themselves as offering EMI (Enever, 2015). For politicians, there is often a perception that a policy for introducing English early will be perceived as 'modernisation of the curriculum', ensuring their popularity and success in the next round of elections. In the following sections, I will review some of the current trends and raise many questions regarding the complexities of satisfactory provision.

Recent trends in primary ELT

Pedagogical trends

Experiential learning and activity-based approaches

Arguably, the most important trend in primary ELT has been the gradual change in classroom approaches to teaching and learning. Medgyes and Nikolov (2010: 268) note how the paradigm of communicative language teaching (CLT; see Thornbury, this volume) "has permeated the language teaching scene since the 1970s". This paradigm shift was reflected in the development of primary foreign languages (FL) pedagogy in Europe from the 1980s onwards, supported by a range of Council of Europe initiatives to establish an earlier start to teaching FLs in the primary school (Doyé and Hurrell, 1997). During this period, a trend towards activity-focused classroom approaches also emerged in Europe for teaching primary ELT (note, however, that given the different history of EMI, traditions in former colonies tended not to follow this same trajectory). Such activities are exemplified by the 'Washing Line' game in Figure 25.1.

Underlying this approach were understandings related to the characteristics of young children that may help them in learning languages. Komorowska (1997: 58) summarises points referred to in many publications, including: curiosity and sense of enquiry; a sense of imitation; love of repetition for its own sake; a sense of fun; a lack of inhibition about speaking; willingness to make errors; a predisposition for kinaesthetic learning modes; and a sense of competitiveness. At the time, little systematic research underpinned claims that these characteristics were advantageous in learning foreign languages early; nonetheless, publications for teachers suggested that they enabled children to benefit from an early start to FL learning, providing an activity-based approach was used. This approach differed substantially from analytically-based approaches to FL learning commonly used with secondary school learners at the time.

In essence, activity-focused pedagogy is rooted in a usage-based theory of language learning (Tomasello, 2003), perceiving language learning as a sociocognitive phenomenon whereby learners build competence in the FL through frequent usage in authentic or simulated authentic activities. This theory is itself constructed on a Vygotskian understanding of language learning as taking place within a specific social context (Vygotsky, 1978). It is argued that in creating an appropriate social context within the school environment, children will engage in effective learning. In primary ELT, this approach has brought the introduction of classroom activities such as songs and rhymes; drama and role play; listening to stories and sharing storybooks; language

---

Washing Line game

1 Prepare two boxes containing identical clothing items.
2 Set up rope 'washing line' at front of class with two children holding the ends.
3 Organise class into two teams.
4 Call out one clothing item for first team member to find and hang on line, e.g. 'Hang a red sock on the washing line.'
5 First team to select and hang correct item wins a point.
6 Team with most points wins when box is empty.

Figure 25.1   The Washing Line game (vocabulary consolidation)

Source: Adapted from Halliwell, 1992: 48.

games; drawing and painting activities; simple cookery tasks; and science experiments (for an extensive list of activities, see Garton et al., 2011:12). Frequently, activities are integrated within a framework that focuses on the four language skills (speaking, listening, reading, writing), together with the inclusion of a strong emphasis on learning key lexis (Mihaljević Djigunović and Lopriore, 2011: 46).

Recognising variability

A more nuanced understanding of the relationship between the characteristics of young children and the processes of early language learning is now developing, although the area is substantially under-researched in many contexts. For example, Mihaljević Djigunović and Medved Krajnović (2015) have contributed a valuable analysis of longitudinal data from two substantial studies conducted in Croatia. The collective analyses from their research team provide important understandings of the significant variability between individual learners in the "cognitive, linguistic and affective" areas of development over time (p. 217). With an emphasis on the 'learner as an individual', they demonstrate the "complex, dynamic and idiosyncratic linguistic process" of language learning, shedding new light on the many factors that may define individual progress (ibid.: 217).

Given the extensive growth of early ELT in many contexts worldwide today, much further research of this kind is needed. A critical examination of the principles discussed above also suggests that, from a global perspective, many modifications may be necessary to adapt key principles to contexts where schooling is viewed as a substantially more formal endeavour, whereby enjoyment and motivation have not traditionally been prioritised as essential pre-requisites to effective learning. Indeed, Hu and McKay (2012: 356) claim that the introduction of a focus on oral communication has "raised significant issues concerning contextual and cultural influences/ constraints on pedagogical practices".

Models of increased intensity: bilingualism/CLIL

Recent studies of primary English provision have indicated a typical pattern of one to four lessons per week in many primary schools (Enever, 2011; Hu and McKay, 2012; OECD, 2011). In some contexts, schools, municipalities or central governments have chosen to provide a more intensive model, thus increasing the weekly proportion of English lessons at primary level. This has mainly occurred in contexts where it may be compulsory or optional to study some or all curriculum subjects through the medium of English (EMI) during the secondary school phase.

One trend reflecting interest in the provision of a more intensive start for primary ELT has been the expansion of a model where some parts of a subject are taught in the FL (in this case, English). At primary level, this cross-curricular approach has been evident for many years. For example, the teacher might begin by sharing a picture storybook such as *The Very Hungry Caterpillar* (Carle, 1969), then build on this storyline to create a cross-curricular topic about life cycles. Such a topic is likely to draw strongly on the discipline of biology and may also include other aspects of science, maths and art, with the thread of English language running throughout. While this age-appropriate way of combining subject areas and including a strong language focus is ideally suited for integrating within a model of primary ELT comprising 1–4 lessons per week, a more intensive model of provision might allow for delivering substantial areas of the curriculum in English, assuming the availability of highly skilled teachers. In some parts of Europe this approach has spread, particularly at secondary school level, with provision in primary schools now increasing (for example, in parts of Spain and Italy). In some contexts, this model (together with the model previously known as cross-curricular) has become known as content and language integrated learning (CLIL), intended to convey the meaning that the language curriculum area is combined with another curriculum area, so both are learnt at the same time. However, the most recent data reporting on the primary school context available in Europe (Eurydice Network, 2012: 39) records that "CLIL exists in some form in a number of countries but is not widespread across education systems" (for a more detailed overview of CLIL, see Morton, this volume).

The delivery model of CLIL shares much in common with models of bilingual or dual-language schooling, initially developed in North America and parts of Europe (Murphy, 2014; see Carroll and Combs, this volume). Drawing on evidence of the effectiveness of immersion schooling (Lambert and Tucker, 1972), interest in bilingual primary schools offering a combination of the national language plus English has grown substantially since the 1990s. This trend is further influenced by parental perceptions of the added advantage of English for their children's future economic prosperity (as noted earlier).

Bilingual provision continues to increase, with a variety of models now in Latin America, where private schooling catering for the wealthier middle class has promoted it (Banfi and Day, 2004). This Latin American trend is also spreading to state schools in some urban areas. Similarly, across urban regions of the world (e.g. Vienna, London, Shanghai), bilingual primary schools have been established within the state school system, albeit on a small scale. Most notably perhaps, the development of two large-scale government-supported initiatives in Spain are of interest here. In one instance, the Spanish government, working in partnership with the British Council, has supported the development of 43 bilingual state primary schools across Spain since their inception in 1996 (Dobson et al., 2010). Following a similar pattern, the regional government of Madrid has established 303 bilingual state primary schools (Rico, 2013). In both contexts, the approach has been to introduce English incrementally across some subject areas, with other subjects maintaining delivery in Spanish. This modified form of additive bilingualism – where the FL is viewed as an *addition* to the first language – aims to equip learners to function effectively in both languages by the end of compulsory schooling. The overall achievements of both programmes are significant, although sustaining the quality of bilingual teacher expertise is proving problematic in some instances (Dobson et al., 2010; 143).

Digital technologies

While digital technologies are widely claimed to offer much potential in ELT (for further discussion, see Gruba, Hinkelman and Cárdenas-Claros, this volume), their availability in many low economy contexts is currently very limited, particularly in primary schools. Only one or two large-scale studies have so far been conducted in primary schools that offer initial evidence of some possible contributions towards enhanced learning opportunities for this age group. In this section, four examples are briefly discussed.

Interactive whiteboards

At the level of national policy, ministries in some contexts have equipped classrooms with projection facilities and/or interactive whiteboards (IWBs). Such facilities offer the possibility of screening teaching materials, accessing Internet information/materials for the class and setting up links to school classrooms in other parts of the world (Phillips, 2010). The screen-based trend has been particularly widespread in China. For example, Wu (2012: 10) reports that in a survey of 1,099 teachers across six Chinese provinces conducted between 2007–2009, 82 per cent of schools were equipped with multimedia facilities, with 57 per cent of primary teachers using them during English lessons. Hockly (2013: 357) questions the rationale for the investment in IWBs, arguing that there is little evidence to indicate that they actually contribute to enhanced learning opportunities. She proposes that greater attention should instead be paid to other forms of mobile and hand-held devices.

Remote teaching

Banegas (2013) reported on an innovative national initiative in Uruguay, which equipped all primary school teachers and children with cheap laptops in an effort to overcome the digital divide that learners from low-income communities may experience (Warschauer, 2003). The introduction of a blended learning environment for primary ELT, using remote learning in which the teacher is in a different location to the learners but teaches via screen technology, is still at an experimental stage; however, the large-scale nature of this project offers an opportunity to explore new ways of employing digital technologies to meet the needs of primary ELT classrooms when insufficient local teacher expertise is currently available. If successful, it could provide a useful model for adaptation to other contexts.

Gaming practices

Butler et al. (2014) reported on the use of online games in English with children aged 4–12 years in Japan. Data from 3,945 children examined the young learners' game-playing behaviours and their relationship to learning outcomes. The focus on the use of educational games online is of particular interest, given the enormous growth of the gaming market in recent years. However, their research findings indicated that not all of the more popular games actually contributed to children's learning, "at least as measured by the test scores" (p. 271).

Learning online in and out of school

Butler et al. (2014) comment further on the increasing overlap of learning between home and school precipitated by the digital age. Internet use (via various mobile technologies) has become a daily activity in middle-income homes globally. Internet usage websites report that over 40 per cent of the world's population now has Internet access (an increase from less than 1 per cent in 1995) (Internet Live Stats, 2015). In a further study, Lindgren and Muñoz (2013) report on the extent to which children are now accessing the Internet in English for a variety of purposes, including chatting with children in other countries for fun, visiting web pages to find information and watching programmes online with no subtitles. Their analysis (n=1,400) indicated a wide degree of difference both within countries and across the seven countries studied (Croatia, England, Italy, Netherlands, Poland, Spain and Sweden). Significantly, most evidence of interactions in English was reported by boys aged 10–11 years old engaging in the online game of 'World of Warcraft'. Further research on the significance of the age factor in the use of gaming for social purposes might be a valuable line of future enquiry.

Although a wealth of small-scale classroom studies are now beginning to emerge in the field of primary ELT (e.g. Pim, 2013), substantially more research is now needed throughout the primary sector if we are to fully understand how to effectively integrate digital technologies within the language learning environment to achieve enhanced learning, both in English and in children's competency in learning through technology.

Pre-school / kindergarten ELT

Whilst the focus of this chapter relates to ELT trends in compulsory education, the growth of provision within pre-school and kindergarten contexts deserves a brief mention here, acknowledging its now substantial presence in some country contexts. Collecting reliable data globally on the scale of this development is simply an impossible task, given the range of contexts, the lack of national statistics and the difficulty in ascertaining the validity of any evidence provided. Two recent publications are reported here, together with one national survey, which provide indicative evidence of the growth pattern that has occurred since approximately the start of the twenty-first century.

Within Europe, a policy handbook has been compiled by European ministry officials and high-ranked academics in the field of early language learning, offering guidelines and recommendations on quality, effectiveness and sustainability in pre-primary provision (European Commission, 2011). The handbook records evidence of provision, much of which is driven at the local level by parents "who realise that with increasing globalisation the acquisition of languages other than their first language/mother tongue opens their children's minds and is an asset for their future social and working life" (European Commission, 2011: 9). Significantly, the European Commission (EC) has strongly promoted diversity in language learning for many years. Despite the many guidelines, projects and reports to this effect, however, increasingly, the first choice of schools and pre-schools is to include English in the curriculum. While the report includes no data on which languages are available at pre-school level in Europe, it does refer to a quite limited choice, as a result of parental preferences and challenges linked to locally available teachers and to what it describes as "utilitarian considerations" (European Commission, 2011: 10). This may imply a preference for English in many contexts (reflecting evidence at primary levels in Europe), but the relevant wording of the report is unclear.

Further evidence of the spread of English at pre-school level is recorded in a survey conducted by Rixon (2013). The survey reported a range of evidence on primary and pre-primary English in 64 countries and regions worldwide. To date, this is the largest scale study conducted under conditions of systematic sample selection. With reference to pre-primary, Rixon reports that "in a substantial number of contexts English teaching is widespread in state Early Years education" (Rixon, 2013: 12). She notes that over half the respondents from state funded pre-schools report that "English is not a compulsory part of the state Early Years curriculum but is frequently taught at this stage" (Rixon, 2013: 12). Survey respondents from private pre-schools also recorded English provision in 34 per cent of contexts. Parental demand was often cited as influential, with evidence of parents paying for lessons in a number of contexts.

Findings from these two studies are also reflected in evidence from smaller scale studies of individual countries (Lee, 2009: 99; Mourão, 2012). In the following section, I will consider the nature of challenges to be overcome as a result of this trend towards an earlier start to ELT, both at the primary and pre-primary stages of education.

Challenges for primary ELT

It can no longer be claimed that there is little research in the field of primary ELT. However, while the wealth of linguistic, socio-cultural and education-focused research worldwide is now strongly developing in the field of primary ELT, there remain a number of areas still hardly explored by empirical research. One significant area where greater understanding is needed concerns the different classroom models of provision (e.g. frequency and intensity). Linked to this, a deeper understanding of how specific contextual factors may be modified to ensure maximum benefit from the early start would be valuable. In this section, I will take some cautious steps towards highlighting those areas most urgently needing attention.

Teacher expertise

With the rapid expansion of primary ELT, the demand for well-qualified primary teachers with English competency has proved challenging to meet in many contexts globally. A further contributory factor has been the limited availability of appropriate teacher preparation courses, either at pre- or in-service levels. As a result, many teachers are expected to introduce those important first steps in English despite themselves having fluency levels which are not much above beginner levels (Hoque, 2009; Nikolov, 2009; Hu and McKay, 2012; Matthew, 2012; Wu, 2012; Rixon, 2013).

Debate on the most appropriate teacher model for the provision of primary ELT has continued to affect provision, with no clear evidence on whether a specialist English language teacher or generalist primary teacher with expertise in English is more likely to be effective. For example, whilst there is a broad recommended preference for a generalist model in Europe, many contexts continue to employ a specialist English teacher who may or may not have the skills to implement an age-appropriate methodological approach to the introduction of primary English (Enever, 2011: 26). Butler (2015) reports on heated discussion of this issue in both Korea and Japan. In her survey, Rixon identifies the predominance of specialist English teachers in primary classrooms, finding a generalist (class) teacher as the sole or main teacher of English in only 10 per cent of the contexts surveyed (Rixon, 2013: 20). Much of this lack of provision may relate to inadequate or inappropriate initial teacher preparation and to the very limited provision of in-service training available in many contexts. For example, Wu (2012) reports on situations in China where primary English teachers may only have a qualification in a different subject area, suggesting that this is particularly acute in rural areas (p. 17). Much further development is needed in many contexts before supply is able to meet demand. As an approximate illustration of the size of the shortfall, Rixon (2013: 18) reports that, in 64 per cent of the contexts covered by her survey, "there was a problem either over the whole territory or in parts of it concerning primary English teacher supply."

Linked to the question of teacher expertise, patterns of provision continue to present challenges in many contexts. Understandings about what may be achieved with quite limited intensity of provision (2–3 lessons per week) are often confused, and much work is still needed in developing curricula that meet with the frequency and intensity model that is to be implemented. The following section reviews the challenges of achieving this.

Curriculum design and intensity of provision

The rapid introduction of primary English has necessitated an equally rapid response from curriculum and materials developers in terms of new materials and curriculum guidelines designed to support teachers of younger children, together with revised materials to provide appropriate continuity for teachers of older children. In a number of contexts, this challenge has not yet been fully met. In some cases, the course materials previously used with beginners aged 10, for example, are simply being re-used with beginners aged 8, with little or no adjustment made for the differing cognitive abilities and interests of this younger age group. In other cases, countries have attempted to phase in an increasingly earlier start over time, with a staged lowering of the start age every two or three years. For example, in South Korea, such developments resulted in revision of teaching materials for each age group every two years in order to keep up with each new stage of the phasing-in process (Chang, 2007; Hu and McKay, 2012). This has proved to be an extremely demanding task, both for curriculum developers and for teachers adjusting to each new set of materials.

Altogether, the challenge of introducing an earlier start to FL learning appears to be quite unique in terms of curriculum design. Whilst most school subjects have a curriculum planning mechanism that starts with an introductory phase from the first school year right through to the end of schooling (for example, in the case of mathematics and literacy development), the recent lowering of the start age for the subject area of English has necessitated a complete revision of curricula from start to finish. Indeed, Johnstone (2009: 36) describes the introduction of early FL learning as "possibly the world's biggest policy development in education". Given the scale of this policy change, it is unsurprising perhaps that *full* curricular change has not yet been implemented in a number of contexts, resulting in a situation where little or no continuity or cohesion of the learning programme currently exists between phases of schooling (see Yoshida, 2012 for a discussion of this phenomenon in Japan). This challenge is discussed further in the next section.

A further challenge highlighted by Johnstone (2009) is the connection between the model of delivery (including frequency and duration of weekly lessons) and anticipated outcomes at each stage of schooling. Very little research has been attempted to compare models, and much clearer information on this is needed if we are to fully understand what can realistically be achieved under a particular set of circumstances.

Continuity of provision in transition

Somewhat surprisingly, the decision to introduce primary ELT often fails to include planning for the careful management of continuity between classes and from phase to phase in the schooling system. As indicated above, where there are no clear curriculum guidelines and no required course materials, there may be a tendency for teachers to include a range of learning activities which simply repeat what has already been covered, resulting in boredom and eventual lack of motivation for the learner. In those contexts where each phase of schooling is provided in a separate building or institution, curriculum cohesion across phases may be challenging to achieve. For example, teachers and school principals in the large-scale ELLiE study (Enever, 2011) reported limited or no contact with the next phase of schooling in situations where schools were placed some distance apart. Evidence from China (Wu, 2012: 18) similarly indicates a lack of communication across school phases regarding achievement levels, or even whether or not English classes have been provided at primary level. On a slightly different note, Yoshida (2012: 30) reports that the decision to introduce English in Japan from the final year of primary school in 2011 has revealed a disconnect between the methodology of primary and junior high schools.

Whilst finding a workable solution in specific learning contexts may prove to be an incremental process, evidence from an Australian project (Chesterton et al., 2004) suggests a possible way forward. The project comprised a cross-over programme of study in which teachers from upper primary met with lower secondary school teachers to develop a continuous cross-phase programme of work for learners moving from primary to secondary schooling. In this, they identified an outstanding model for establishing a coherent programme of FL learning. However, they acknowledged that achieving "initial and continuing cooperation, communication and support among partner schools" is crucial to the effectiveness and sustainability of the initiative (Chesterton et al., 2004: 56). This may prove a challenging remit in some circumstances, given its reliance on the expertise and commitment of teachers, together with the full support of the wider school community.

Conclusions

The scale of reform necessary for the introduction of primary ELT appears to have been underestimated in some contexts. A lengthy period of consolidation is now needed for equity of provision to be achieved in each national context. The quality of provision will finally depend on the political will to invest in a programme of teacher preparation to provide an adequate supply of well-trained primary English teachers equipped to refine and extend provision.

Parallel to the expansion and consolidation of primary English, we can now anticipate that pre-primary provision seems likely to expand considerably further. Over time, this may have the undesirable effect of increasing inequality, given the tendency for pre-primary provision to be funded privately by parents in many contexts worldwide. As a consequence, it is possible that the difficulties of varied competency levels currently experienced at the point of secondary school entry may simply move down a level to the primary school entry point over time. For ministries of education, this remains a complex problem to address.

Given the limitations of space, it has not been possible in this chapter to discuss the possible impact of trends in migration. Nonetheless, a brief note on this is appropriate here. As a general point, it appears that on current indications, migratory patterns are likely to increase due to a number of political and economic factors. Under such conditions, English may become increasingly important in primary schools, acting as a lingua franca, at least during the introductory period whilst the newly arrived children find their feet in the national/regional language. Within this scenario, English might adopt the role of *transitional language,* facilitating communication in and out of the classroom as children move between their home language and increasing competency in their new language context.

As a final note of caution in this conclusion, it is important to acknowledge the extreme changeability of language fashions. History has shown how quickly languages can fall out of favour, for any number of reasons. Despite the growth of primary ELT for over fifty years now, changed circumstances will bring new demands on languages and their speakers, taking them in unpredictable new directions. This degree of uncertainty adds to the challenge of planning for sustainability.

Discussion questions

- Do you consider that there are benefits of an early start to learning foreign languages generally, and English in particular? If so which are the most significant?
- Which model of early English learning would be most appropriate in your national schooling context? Identify the conditions that would need to be put in place to ensure sustainability.
- Grin (2003) claims that "The economic advantages may not outweigh the pedagogical advantages in all circumstances." Discuss this viewpoint with reference to the introduction of primary ELT in a national context you are familiar with.

Related topics

Bilingual education in a multilingual world; Communicative language teaching in theory and practice; Content and language integrated learning; Secondary ELT; Sociocultural theory and the language classroom.

Janet Enever

Further reading

Bland, J. (2015) *Teaching English to young learners: Critical issues in language teaching with 3–12 year olds.* London: Bloomsbury Academic. (An edited collection of research papers and pedagogical themes related to early language learning.)

Butler, Y. G. (2015) English language education among young learners in East Asia: A review of current research (2004–2013). *Language Teaching,* 48/3. 303–342. (This paper provides a comprehensive overview of recent research in Japan, China, Taiwan and Korea.)

Cameron, L. (2010) *Teaching languages to young learners.* Cambridge: Cambridge University Press. (This book offers teachers an understanding of what happens in classrooms where children are being taught a foreign language.)

McKay, P. (2006) *Assessing young language learners.* Cambridge: Cambridge University Press. (This volume provides a comprehensive overview of why and how to assess young language learners, drawing on examples from around the world.)

Murphy, V. (2014) *Second language learning in the early school years: Trends and contexts.* Oxford: Oxford University Press. (This book examines L2 research evidence in bilingualism, second and foreign language learning in the early years.)

References

Banegas, D. L. (2013) 'ELT through videoconferencing in primary schools in Uruguay: First steps'. *Innovation in Language Learning and Teaching,* 7/2. 179–188.

Banfi, C. and Day, J. (2004) 'The evolution of bilingual schools in Argentina'. *Bilingual education and bilingualism,* 7/5. 394–411.

Burstall, C., Jamieson, M., Cohen, S. and Hargreaves, M. (1974) *Primary French in the balance.* UK, Slough: NFER.

Butler, Y. G. (2015) 'English language education among young learners in East Asia: A review of current research (2004–2013)'. *Language Teaching,* 48/3. 303–342.

Butler, Y.G., Someya, Y. and Fukuhara, E. (2014) 'Online games for young learners' foreign language learning'. *ELT Journal,* 68/3. 265–275.

Carle, E. (1969) *The very hungry caterpillar.* London: Hamish Hamilton.

Cha, Y.K. and Ham, S.H. (2008) 'The impact of English on the school curriculum', in B. Spolsky and F. Hult (eds) *The handbook of educational linguistics.* London: Blackwell. 313–238.

Chang, K.S. (2007) *Korea: Innovation in PELT and management of change.* Primary Innovations Conference Presentation, Hanoi, March 7, 2007.

Chesterton, P., Steigler-Peters, S., Moran, W. and Piccioli, M. (2004) 'Developing sustainable language learning pathway: An Australian initiative'. *Language, Culture and Curriculum,* 17/1. 48–57.

Dobson, A., Perez Murillo, D. and Johnstone, R. (2010) *Bilingual Education Project Spain. Evaluation report.* Spain: Ministerio de Educación / British Council.

Doyé, P. and Hurrell, A. (1997) (eds) *Foreign language education in primary schools.* Strasbourg: Council of Europe.

Edelenbos, P., Johnstone, R. and Kubanek, A. (2006) *Languages for the children of Europe: Published research, good practice and main principles.* Retrieved May 2, 2015, from http://ec.europa.eu/languages/policy/language-policy/documents/young_en.pdf.

Ellis, G. (2014) '"Young learners": Clarifying our terms'. *ELT Journal,* 68/1. 75–78.

Enever, J. (2011) *ELLiE. Early language learning in Europe.* London: British Council. Retrieved September 9, 2014, from http://www.teachingenglish.org.uk/article/early-language-learning-europe

Enever, J. (2015) *Accounting for contemporary challenges in primary languages in India: Questions of history and development?* Conference paper: Teaching English to young learners as a second and foreign language. Poland: University of Warsaw.

European Commission (2011) *Language learning at pre-primary school level: Making it efficient and sustainable: A policy handbook.* Brussels: European Commission. Retrieved May 2, 2015, from http://ec.europa.eu/languages/policy/language-policy/documents/early-language-learning-handbook_en.pdf.

Eurydice Network (2012) *Eurydice: Key data on teaching languages at schools in Europe.* Brussels: Commission of the European Communities. Retrieved May 1, 2015, from https://webgate.ec.europa.eu/fpfis/mwikis/eurydice/index.php/Publications:Key_Data_on_Teaching_Languages_at_School_in_Europe_2012

Gamble, C. and Smalley, A. (1975) 'Primary French in the balance – "Were the scales accurate?"' *Journal of Modern Languages*, 94/7. 4–97.

Garton, S., Copland, F. and Burns, A. (2011) *Investigating global practices in teaching English to young learners*. London: British Council. Retrieved May 2, 2015, from https://www.teachingenglish.org.uk/article/global-practices-teaching-english-young-learners

Grin, F. (2003) 'Language planning and economics'. *Current Issues in Language Planning*, 4/1. 1–66.

Halliwell, S. (1992) *Teaching English in the primary classroom*. Harlow: Longman.

Hockly, N. (2013) 'Interactive whiteboards'. *ELT Journal*, 67/3. 354–358.

Hoque, S. (2009) 'Teaching English in primary schools in Bangladesh: Competencies and achievements', in J. Enever, J. Moon and U. Raman (eds) *Young learner English language policy and implementation: International perspectives*. Reading, UK: Garnet Education. 61–70.

Hu, G. and McKay, S. L. (2012) 'English language education in East Asia: Some recent developments'. *Journal of Multilingual and Multicultural Development*, 33/4. 345–362.

Internet Live Stats (2015) *Trends and more (statistics)*. Retrieved May 20, 2015, from http://www.internetlivestats.com/internet-users/#trend.

Johnstone, R. (2009) 'An early start: What are the key conditions for generalized success?', in J. Enever, J. Moon, and U. Raman (eds) *Young learner English language policy and implementation: International perspectives*. Reading, UK: Garnet Education. 31–42.

Komorowska, H. (1997) 'Organisation, integration and continuity', in P. Doyé and A. Hurrell (eds) *Foreign language education in primary schools*. Strasbourg: Council of Europe. 51–62.

Lambert, W. E. and Tucker, G. R. (1972) *The bilingual education of children: The St. Lambert Experiment*. Rowley, MA: Newbury House.

Lee, W. K. (2009) 'Primary English language teaching in Korea: Bold risks on the national foundation', in J. Enever, J. Moon and U. Raman (eds) *Young learner English language policy and implementation: International perspectives*. Reading, UK: Garnet Education. 95–102.

Lenneberg, E. (1967) *Biological foundations of language*. New York: Wiley & Son.

Lindgren, E. and Muñoz, C. (2013) 'The influence of exposure, parents and linguistic distance on young European learners' foreign language comprehension'. *International Journal of Multilingualism*, 10/1. 105–129.

Makoni, S. and Makoni, B. (2009) 'English and education in Anglophone Africa: Historical and current realities', in M. Wong and S. Canagarajah (eds) *Christian and critical English language educators in dialogue: Pedagogical and ethical dilemmas*. New York: Routledge, Taylor, & Francis. 106–119.

Matthew, R. (2012) 'Young learner English language policy and implementation: A view from India', in B. Spolsky and Y. Moon (eds) *Primary school English language education in Asia*. London: Routledge. 83–105.

Medgyes, P. and Nikolov, M. (2010) 'Curriculum development in foreign langauge education: The interface between political and professional decisions', in R. B. Kaplan (ed.) *The Oxford handbook of applied linguistics* (2nd ed.). Oxford: Oxford University Press. 263–274.

Meganathan, R. (2011), 'Language policy in education and the role of English in India: From library language to language of empowerment', in H. Coleman (ed.) *Dreams and realities: Developing countries and the English language*. London: British Council. 57–86.

Mihaljević Djigunović, J. and Lopriore, L. (2011) 'The learner: Do individual differences matter?', in J. Enever (ed.) *ELLiE. Early Language Learning in Europe*. UK: British Council. 43–60.

Mihaljević Djigunović, J. and Medved Krajnović, M. (2015) (eds) *Early learning and teaching of English*. Bristol, UK: Multilingual Matters.

Mihaljević Djigunović, J. and Vilke, M. (2000) 'Eight years after wishful thinking vs. facts of life', in J. Moon and M. Nikolov (eds) *Research into teaching English to young learners*. Pécs, Hungary: Pécs University Press. 66–86.

Mourão, S. (2012) 'Repeated read-alouds and picture book illustrations: A discussion around language development in a foreign language context', in H. Emery and F. Gardiner-Hyland (eds) *Contextualising EFL for young learners: International perspectives on policy, practice and procedure*. Dubai: TESOL Arabia Publications. 361–379.

Muñoz and Singleton (2011) 'A critical view of age-related research on L2 ultimate attainment'. *Language Teaching*, 44/1. 1–35.

Murphy, V. (2014) *Second language learning in the early school years: Trends and contexts*. Oxford: Oxford University Press.

Nikolov, M. (2009) 'The dream and the reality of early programmes in Hungary', in J. Enever, J. Moon and U. Raman (eds) *Young learner English language policy and implementation: International perspectives*. Reading, UK: Garnet Education. 121–130.

OECD (2011) *Education at a glance 2011: OECD indicators*, OECD Publishing. Retrieved May 2, 2015, from www.oecd.org/dataoecd/61/2/48631582.pdf

Phillips, M. (2010) 'The perceived value of video-conferencing with primary pupils learning to speak a modern language'. *Language Learning Journal*, 32/2. 221–238.

Pim, C. (2013) 'Emerging technologies, emerging minds: Digital innovations within the primary sector', in G. Motteram (ed.) *Innovations in learning technologies for English langauge teaching*. London: British Council. 15–42.

Rico, P. (2013) *Information about Bilingualism. Madrid, España*. Comunidad de Madrid. Retrieved September 6, 2014, from http://www.slideshare.net/auldreikie/bilingualism-madrid-spain-prico.

Rixon, S. (2013) *British Council survey of policy and practice in primary English language teaching worldwide*. London: British Council.

Rokita-Jaskow, J. (2013) *Foreign language learning at pre-primary level*. Krakow: Wydawnictwo Naukowe Uniwersytetu Pedagogicznego.

Tomasello, M. (2003) *Constructing a language. A usage-based theory of language acquisition*. Cambridge, MA: Harvard University Press.

Vilke, M. (2007) 'English in Croatia. A glimpse into past, present and future'. *Metodika*, 8/14. 17–24.

Vygotsky, L. (1978) *Mind in Society: The development of higher psychological processes*. Cambridge, MA: Harvard University Press.

Wang, Q. (2002) 'Primary school English teaching in China – New developments'. *English Language Teacher Education and Development*, 7. 99–108.

Warschauer, M. (2003) *Technology and social inclusion: Rethinking the digital divide*. Cambridge, MA: MIT Press.

Wu, Xin (2012) 'Primary English education in China', in B. Spolsky and Y-I. Moon (eds) *Primary school English language education in Asia*. London: Routledge. 1–22.

Yoshida, K. (2012) 'Issues of transition of English education from elementary schools to secondary schools', in B. Spolsky and Y.-I. Moon (eds) *Primary school English langauge education in Asia*. London: Routledge. 23–37.

26

Secondary ELT

Issues and trends

Annamaria Pinter

Introduction

Adolescents are considered by many a difficult group to teach. Stereotypically, teenagers are excitable, moody, exuberant and impulsive; they are obsessed with whether their appearance looks 'cool' to others; they question everything; and they are in a continuous search for their 'true self', which often involves getting into conflicts with parents, teachers and other figures of authority. Teenage identity-seeking translates into experimenting with a wide range of expressive styles in music, clothing and other modes of self-expression (Legutke, 2012), recognised widely as 'youth culture' (Diller et al., 2000; Blossfeld et al., 2006). Teenagers can bring a great deal of their creativity, energy and enthusiasm into the classroom, but, at the same time, their turbulent lives and their constant questioning of the status quo can also be a source of challenge and even frustration for those working with them.

Adolescence or the teenage years fall between childhood and adulthood, and their boundaries are marked by the biological changes occurring in puberty on the one side and the transition to adult status on the other side. The Society for Research on Adolescence (SRA), according to Goossens (2006), divides adolescence into three distinct stages: early adolescence (between the ages of 10–15), mid-adolescence (between the ages of 15–18) and finally late adolescence (between the ages of 18–22 years old). In most parts of the developed world, the period of adolescence is lengthening because of the earlier onset of puberty as well as the need to stay dependent longer on parents, sometime up to ages well beyond 22 years old. Most teenagers between the ages of 10–16/18 are in secondary education; thus, although there is a great deal of variation across different contexts with regard to the exact age secondary education begins and ends, in most countries, this period covers early and mid-adolescence.

Secondary-level learners make up by far the largest group of all English learners worldwide, and they learn in a variety of contexts, ranging from classrooms where the latest technology such as fast Internet connections and other learning resources are readily available to difficult, rural contexts where a school may have a single computer with only intermittent Internet access, no books and scarce learning resources (see Shamim and Kuchah's discussion of teaching large classes in 'difficult circumstances', this volume). Overall, L2 English learning has had a much longer tradition in the secondary sector, in contrast to primary English learning, which has only recently spread to state elementary school curricula across the world (see Enever, this volume).

In this chapter, my aim is to identify some core characteristics of teenage learners as thinkers and language learners related to general theories of physical and cognitive development, as well as SLA research and specific studies in different L2 contexts. The chapter will also consider the opportunities and challenges in the current global context due to English being the dominant lingua franca worldwide and due to the technological advances available to current generations of teenage learners worldwide.

Background: characteristics of teenagers

Physical and cognitive development

According to Lightfoot et al. (2013), following babyhood, physical growth is fastest in the teenage years. Boys may grow as much as 23 centimetres in height and girls 15–18 centimetres. Adolescents experience emotional highs and lows and a general emotional intensity due to hormone development. They are prone to sensation seeking and have a desire to participate in highly arousing activities (Martin et al., 2002). Neuroscientists suggest that this behavioural transition toward novelty-seeking and adventurousness is associated with the physical changes in the body, such as the development of the limbic system. Adolescence is a turbulent time overall, although, over the course of adolescence, emotions become gradually less intense, with ups and downs becoming less frequent, and, by the end of the teenage years, most teenagers become more effective and better at controlling their emotions (Steinberg, 2005). Larson et al. (2002) report that the average level of happiness declines in adolescence for both genders compared to younger children, although girls seem to have slightly more positive emotions than boys. It is only in late adolescence or early adulthood that the cortex and executive functions of the brain mature, increasing the individual's ability to control the way s/he thinks, feels and acts in particular situations (e.g. Steinberg, 2010).

Major changes occur in brain development during the adolescent years, which means that teenagers are able to learn faster and more efficiently than younger children. For example, the speed of retrieving information from long-term memory improves steadily in adolescence (Slater and Bremner, 2011). In addition to increasing memory capacity, teenagers also develop ever more effective learning strategies to help both memory and meta-memory, i.e. their awareness of memory functions. Adolescent strategy use is more flexible and broader in scope, and it is in aid of a wider range of tasks, as compared with that of younger children.

Teenagers fall within the Piagetian 'formal operation' period (beyond the age of 12). Piaget's developmental model is one of the most well-known models of child development, and it suggests that human development unfolds in stages which are universally predictable. These stages include the *sensory-motor stage* from 0–2 years of age, the *pre-operational stage* from 2–7 years of age, *the concrete operational stage* from 7–12 years of age and finally the *formal operational stage* beyond the age of 12. All children progress steadily through these stages, and they become more logical and more able to de-centre and to think in a systematic fashion. The qualitative change that separates teenagers from the previous stage is their ability to think logically even when they are presented with abstract problems. The concrete operational child is already able to understand analogies when these are limited to very familiar content, while teenagers, who are formal operational thinkers, have a much more flexible, abstract understanding (Slater and Bremner, 2011).

Piaget described the core formal operational ability as 'hypothetical-deductive reasoning', which means being able to judge a problem or argument on the basis of its logical properties alone. When teenagers are presented with the well-known 'balance scale problem' and they are asked about what factors influence the movement of the scales, learners at this stage of development are able to ascertain that both variables are important (i.e. the weight on each arm or the distance of each arm from the fulcrum) by thinking systematically about multiple dimensions of the problem and by considering the interaction between both weight and distance. In contrast, younger, concrete operational children tend to try different combinations of weights and distances randomly, in an unsystematic manner. It seems that only learners above the age of 12 are able to offer multiple hypotheses, isolate factors one by one, test the impact of each factor systematically while keeping other factors constant and then proceed to test the effect of two factor combinations.

These cognitive achievements, combined with a questioning attitude and a general openness to the world, make teenagers potentially very powerful thinkers. In terms of language teaching, this means that teachers can certainly experiment with abstract problems and tasks, complicated games or puzzles, or debates about controversial issues. Due to their advanced thinking skills, vast memory capacity and an ability to look at problems from various angles, learners will enjoy working with more challenging and unusual tasks.

Critics maintain, however, that overall, Piaget's claims about adolescence were too ambitious. Cultural differences and schooling play important roles as to whether individuals reach the formal operational stage at all. In addition, studies have also identified development that takes place post-adolescence, e.g. in terms of reasoning and decision-making (e.g. Halpern-Felsher and Cauffman, 2001), so that the formal operational period is not the end of the road when it comes to development.

Thus, in contrast to Piaget's developmental theory based on universal stages, Vygotsky's (1978) socio-cultural approach to development puts the emphasis on the continuous process of development which unfolds through careful scaffolding and focuses on the mediating role of adults, experts and more knowledgeable peers. From this perspective, any learning is social in origin, and therefore the use of talk as a mediating tool between experts and novices is central in helping learners' understanding and growth (for further discussion of sociocultural theory and the language classroom, see Negueruela-Azarola and García, this volume).

Younger children, especially those under the age of 9–10, are less efficient communicators, i.e. they might find talking to people they do not know difficult, might not appreciate the needs of listeners in conversations, or might not be able to verbalise their thoughts and ideas very succinctly. They may not be able to acknowledge lack of understanding or take a few steps back and reflect on one's learning or ideas. However, by the age of 12, these skills grow exponentially. Since teenage learners have the ability to use language powerfully to question ideas, to clarify their own and others' thoughts and reflect on ideas and problems, they become skilled at managing peer collaboration and participation in collaborative dialogue.

In terms of classroom learning, therefore, peer interaction between teenage learners has been the focus of many studies. In Swain and Lapkin's study (2002), for example, two 12-year-old girls were working on writing a story together, and when they were invited to reflect on the reformulations a tutor made to their writing, they were able to talk through the text, get a deeper understanding of the grammatical structures and learn new language as a result of co-constructing their joint understanding. In collaborative dialogue, learners verbalise their own thoughts, question and reflect on these verbalisations, and pull their knowledge and ideas together. In another study by Tsui and Ng (2000) in a Hong Kong secondary school with grade 12 students, it was found that teenage learners were able to benefit from peer feedback specifically focussed on grammar, even though they considered teacher feedback more authoritative. In particular, researchers have been interested in the quality of their peer interaction when they were focussing on grammatical difficulties. This type of 'languaging', according to Swain (2006), refers to a form of verbalisation which mediates cognitively demanding activities. In a further study by Suzuki and Itagaki (2009), it was found that even low-intermediate level Japanese secondary school students were able to learn from their peers while engaged in different types of languaging, depending on the task. The authors suggest that teachers should encourage such languaging in their classes and that, in particular, translation tasks in monolingual classes might be useful for this kind of collaborative language work.

For English language teachers, there are clear implications with regard to encouraging collaborative learning. For example, learners might be asked to write stories together or work on projects where different members of the group will take on different roles. With regard to the role of language, activities that require reflection, for example, through self-assessment and peer-assessment or through using the metacognitive cycle of planning, monitoring and evaluating learning, will also be suitable. Due to their ability to stand back and reflect on their learning, teenage learners also enjoy strategy training, whereas younger children tend not to be able to carry over any strategy training gains to new tasks.

Social development and identity growth

While younger children think about themselves mainly in terms of observable characteristics, adolescents are able to reflect on their own thoughts, desires and motives more readily (Slater and Bremner, 2011). One challenge is to identify how one is unique as an individual and how one still is similar to others; maintaining individuality while still fitting into a group is an important task all teenagers need to tackle. This requires a great deal of experimenting with different possible identities. For example, it may be that a teenage boy is interested in music or dancing, but he decides to keep these interests to himself because of the suspicion that his peer group might consider these unusual and/or feminine. How much of yourself you decide to reveal to others is a careful process of experimentation that takes time and confidence to manage.

By the time teenagers are in secondary schools, they spend twice as much time with their peers and friends as they do with their parents and other adults (Lightfoot et al., 2013). There are two kinds of peer relationships in the teenage years: those with close friends and those with a wider network of acquaintances. Adolescent friendships are sophisticated, based on reciprocity, emotional sharing, interests, commitment, loyalty and equality. However, there are important differences between the qualities of friendships of girls and boys. Boys are generally less intimate and less trusting and tend to avoid talking about emotionally charged experiences. They are also often more competitive than girls and engage in competitive play activities more readily when together. Hendry and Kloep (2006: 252) suggest that young people typically spend a great deal of their leisure time either with their best friend or a group of friends or both, often 'not doing anything' but chatting, giggling and just hanging around. Fooling around and laughter may seem rather aimless and pointless to an outsider, yet these are perceived as among the most fulfilling of activities by adolescents themselves (Csikszentmihalyi and Larson, 1984). When friends cannot meet face-to-face, in many contexts, mobile phones and computers become important devices to enable the chatting to continue.

Recently, scholars have been emphasising the importance of identity development and its links with autonomy and motivation in adolescence (e.g. Ushioda, 2013). Teenagers' natural inclination to explore their identities can be meaningful through using a second language. English as a 'lingua franca', a language that is universally understood, can be motivating for teenagers to learn, especially if they are encouraged to develop and reflect on their 'ideal self' (Dörnyei, 2009; see also Lamb, this volume) as competent English speakers participating successfully in the global online community. Arnett (2002: 777) argues that some youths develop a bicultural identity, with one part of their identity rooted in their own local culture and another part "stemming from an awareness of their relation to the global world" though English.

Lamb and Budiyanto (2013) point out that for many L2 English-speaking teenagers, identity development as a process coincides with a phase in their lives when their childhood identities are broken down and their new developing sense of self is in a flux. In their study in provincial Indonesia, they interviewed 12–14 year olds about their English learning experiences. The data suggests that successful interactions with native speakers are motivating for Indonesian teenagers because these interactions allow space for identity work. In these authentic interactions with native speakers, the learners can see themselves and their own local cultures through a different lens, i.e. the eyes of the outsider.

Many teenagers lead busy and rich social lives with hobbies, getting together with their friends regularly to play computer games, or sports and other activities. In general, compared to younger children, a wider range of out of school experiences are available to most teenagers. Henry (2013), writing about Swedish teenage learners of English, argues that digital game playing, in particular, in English is an important pastime activity for this age group (we shall return to online gaming towards the end of this chapter). He also comments that there is a serious discrepancy between 'out of school English' and 'school English' in that the intensity of interaction that takes place during games cannot be replicated in the classroom. This paper suggests that it is important for teachers to 'make connections' between classroom English and outside classroom English. Such connections can be made, for example, by inviting students to do short presentations about the rules of some games, and also by encouraging them to reflect on what language it is they need in these games and where their current language gaps might be.

Teenage language learners and SLA

Having considered the physical, cognitive and social development of the teenage years and some of their implications for teachers, this next section gives a brief overview of teenage learners from a psycholinguistic angle.

Within SLA research, studies that have focussed on the 'age factor' in second language acquisition have contrasted young children (those who started a second/foreign language after puberty, generally meaning after 12 years of age) and older learners to try to tease out the exact effects of age based on the critical period hypothesis originally suggested by Lenneberg (1967) (see also Enever, this volume). While there is no space here to discuss this literature in full, it is important to acknowledge that, overall, this body of literature suggests that teenage learners are in fact faster and more efficient language learners than younger children. This comes as something of a surprise when contrasted with anecdotal observations based on stories of immigrant families, where adults typically do not progress beyond a particular level of L2, while children tend to become native-like – younger children do have some limited advantages in naturalistic contexts such as acquiring implicit grammatical rules or native-like pronunciation in the early years (DeKeyser, 2012). However, in most English as a foreign language (EFL) contexts, i.e. in formal classrooms where children are learning English as a school subject, the notion of the critical period does not carry much meaning, because the learning environment is far from naturalistic and it often lacks high quality input, opportunities to interact with a variety of competent speakers and a strong need/motivation to fit in a new context. Muñoz (2008) summarises the characteristics of classroom learning contexts as offering limited instructional time, limited exposure to L2 in terms of both quantity and quality, and most importantly, perhaps, the target language is not used by peers or outside the classroom.

In such formal classroom contexts, when comparisons are made between young and older learners, studies indicate that younger learners cannot capitalise on their 'critical period', whilst older learners (such as teenagers) can rely on more efficient learning strategies and larger memory stores and can focus on the learning task with sustained intensity. All these qualities make them faster and more efficient language learners. Based on a very large data source, Muñoz (2006), for example, reports that teenage learners in Spanish schools progress faster than younger learners in learning English (L2), and even after longer periods of time, younger learners do not outperform those who only started in their teenage years, except perhaps in pronunciation (Muñoz, 2008).

The implications for teachers and classroom practice from this research are in line with what has been suggested earlier. Even if learners start a second/foreign language at the age of 12 or later, they will be able to progress quickly, tackle complex tasks and work collaboratively, and they are unlikely to come short in terms of their progress/proficiency when compared to those who started the L2 in formal classroom contexts earlier/at a younger age in childhood.

Learning English in the connected, globalised world

The spread of English and secondary ELT

Because of the unprecedented spread of English as a global lingua franca, the number of English learners is growing steadily all over the world (see Seargeant, this volume, for further discussion). In Europe, for example, almost all countries have introduced English into the primary curriculum, so, in theory, learners enter secondary education with some 'basic' English skills to build on, and in some contexts they add another foreign language to the curriculum at the age of 14–15.

Despite the fact that in most contexts English is now taught at primary level, in very few contexts has the difficulty of transition from primary to secondary been solved. In many contexts, children who progress from primary to secondary school with some English knowledge will still have to start all over again because of lack of communication and planning between primary and secondary institutions (see also Enever, this volume). There is also a competing private sector which offers additional classes to those who can afford it on top of their standard school English education. As a result, teenage classes are often heterogeneous, with learners of various proficiency levels. Due to global travel and mobility, teenage classes are also more multilingual and multicultural than ever before, and the challenges for teachers of all subjects in these classes are therefore formidable. Large heterogeneous classes naturally call for differentiation, group work, project work and other approaches to teaching and learning that take into account learner differences and build on learners' individual strengths and needs and interests. Reflecting these realities, teenage EFL materials tend to promote learner training, autonomous ways of working and systematic reflection on one's progress (for further discussion of learner autonomy, see Benson, this volume).

Content and language integrated learning (CLIL) has also recently become very popular both in Europe and beyond (e.g. Llinares et al., 2012; Morton, this volume). CLIL presents great challenges in terms of developing suitable materials in local contexts, but the success of these programmes is undeniable, with learners achieving much higher levels of proficiency and good quality content knowledge as compared to their mainstream EFL counterparts. Banegas (2013) argues that when selecting materials for content, learners should be consulted. They then become more motivated because they have the opportunity to work with authentic materials that are naturally engaging and responsive to their local context and needs. They can engage in meaningful language use and learn/explore something new about the world through English as a second language.

With the spread of English, standardised testing has also spread across most contexts. In some contexts, learners need to pass English exams to gain entrance to good universities, and many are encouraged to pass national and/or international tests such as the PELT (Practical English level tests for elementary English), or Cambridge Proficiency exams, or the International English Language Test (IELTS) to prepare them for study in an English-speaking country. International tests are popular, and parents pay large sums of money for certificates. In many countries, large-scale testing starts at an early age (elementary level), and one unfortunate effect of this is that it leads to students being driven solely by narrowly instrumental motives. Parents are committed to sending their children to attend private classes to enhance their chances in the job market, but this is usually the privilege of the well-to-do. As a consequence, the gap is widening in most contexts between those who become competent speakers due to their favourable socio-economic background and those who cannot afford extra provision, or fees for tests, trips to study abroad.

Intercultural encounters and the Internet

Due to technological advances, many teenagers have real and authentic opportunities to communicate with their peers across the globe via Skype, Facebook or Twitter. For example, teenage friends often stay in touch by Facebook after moving to a new country, and families staying temporarily abroad can maintain wider family relationships or friendships by using Skype or Facetime. Within the European Union, through programmes such as Comenius or E-twinning, teachers and learners have opportunities to link up with classrooms in other parts of the world. These are exciting developments that the current generation of teachers are the first to take advantage of.

Stanley (2013), for example, describes how an Egyptian teacher working with a lower secondary class collaborated with another teacher in Argentina. The students in Egypt, who were learning about rainforests, interviewed some learners and their teacher about the topic in Argentina by Skype. Afterwards, the Egyptian teenagers completed a writing task based on the information they had learnt. Student feedback was overwhelmingly positive, and following the Skype sessions, a Facebook group was set up to continue the interaction between the Egyptian and the Argentinian teenagers.

> The learners joined the group voluntarily asking each other questions about a range of topics, and sharing information about their own lifestyle, culture, traditions, festivals, and some linguistic points, idioms and expressions.
>
> *(Stanley, 2013: 50)*

This genuine communication was motivating for all, and, in this example, the Egyptian teacher carried on using Skype 'to invite guests' into her classroom. She also made recordings of these interviews which she could re-use with other learners and thus provide motivating, authentic tasks for them. (For further discussion of computer-mediated communication and language learning, see Kern, Ware and Warschauer, this volume.)

The Internet plays a major role in many teenagers' lives beyond the classroom. According to Palfrey and Grasser (2008), adolescents are 'digital natives'. At least in many parts of the world, Internet content creation by teenagers continues to grow. Over 70 per cent of teenage Internet users create and post material regularly on social networking websites (Lenhart et al., 2011). A great deal of Internet use is devoted to keeping in touch with friends or just hanging out (Boyd, 2007). Online sites such as Facebook offer opportunities for self-expression by constructing a 'self-image' while exploring one's relationships with others. As Lightfoot et al. (2013: 577) comment: "Indeed even the size and shifting content of one's online friends can be both used and interpreted as signs of social status and general coolness." Teenagers are also actively shaping the Internet as well as being shaped by it. One example to illustrate this dual process is the phenomenon of young YouTubers (e.g. Deyes, 2014). Without the mass viewing by mainly teenage audiences, these upcoming YouTube teenage celebrities would not be able to gain and maintain popularity. Their YouTube content is continuously shaped by viewers' feedback, but at the same time they are shaping the lives and the habits of millions of teenagers. This digital culture is relatively new, and for many, it is beginning to replace books and face-to-face interactions outside school. How this new way of functioning and spending time will affect the "process of coming of age for adolescents" struggling for autonomy and identity is not yet clear (Slater and Bremner, 2011: 561). Future research will be important in this respect.

L2 learning and the Internet

Teenage Internet and computer-mediated technology use has been explored in relation to L2 language learning. Macaro et al. (2012) reviewed research investigating the linguistic benefits of using CALL (computer-assisted language learning) in secondary classrooms and concluded that there is certainly plenty of evidence for linguistic development. CALL can help secondary learners with listening and writing, and even speaking can be improved. Non-linguistic benefits also occur, such as positive attitudes and heightened motivation. CALL is also attractive because it helps teenage learners connect with their genuine interests. Since learning content needs to be relevant and motivating, materials for teenagers place a great deal of emphasis on pop culture, cultural issues in general and study skills and focus on authenticity and the living language through the use of slang (Varanoglulari et al., 2008). Legutke (2012) also argues that in materials for teenagers, we need frequent opportunities for creative expression, experimentation and personalisation, and teenagers should be exposed to poetic texts, music, teenage fiction and young adult literature (Bushman and Parks, 2006).

Since technology and computer-mediated learning opportunities are readily available in a growing number of contexts, teachers can experiment with using Wikis, as described, for example, in a paper by Lund and Rasmussen (2008). In this paper, Norwegian high school students worked with an open-ended, collectively oriented task (a Wiki) which asked them collectively to build a typical British town. Small groups of learners appropriated the task and reported benefiting from the collaborative process; however, challenges such as not using all the intended features of the Wiki were also mentioned. Another example of exploiting computer-based technologies for language learning is reported by Comas-Quinn et al. (2009). In this study, learners were encouraged to try blogging for the purpose of language learning and appreciating culture. While on a study abroad trip, the students were invited to use their own mobile phones, digital cameras and MP3 recorders to select samples of authentic language to upload to a shared website. These recordings may have taken place in restaurants, on buses, inside tourist sites or shops. As a next step, students were encouraged to comment on and discuss aspects of the language or culture represented in these recordings. This approach hands over control to the learners, in that they can decide what to upload and share. This makes students alert to both linguistic and cultural content while they are immersed in it, and they can constantly evaluate their linguistic experiences in ways that would not be possible within the teacher's tight control. Mobile technologies, when used for language learning purposes, support the principles of Vygotskian social constructivism as learners create the learning materials collaboratively, using language as a mediating tool while commenting on or asking about each other's postings. Mobile learning technologies also promote the principles of learner-centredness, and informal learning. Despite all these attractive features, though, the authors admit that assessing such highly individualised and organic learning is challenging, and learning outcomes will differ from student to student.

Meanwhile, in ESL contexts, immigrant youths have exploited the Internet to develop hybrid identities through interacting with a range of different interlocutors online. Their positive experiences online are often in sharp contrast with their experiences as less successful language learners in their ESL classrooms and thus serve to boost their confidence in using the second language. For example, Lam's study (2000) of a Chinese immigrant teenager in America illustrates how a marginalised youth who is struggling with English in his institutionalised classes can have a transformative experience by engaging in L2 English writing on the Internet. Almon (the Chinese student in Lam's study) designed a home page in GeoCities about a young Japanese pop idol. His homepage attracted attention from a variety of online chat-mates from Canada, Hong Kong, Japan, Malaysia and the United States. This website afforded him regular contact and opportunities for asynchronous chats with a variety of interlocutors. He enjoyed interacting with his online friends and was aware of the fact that, in writing, he could express himself in English more easily compared to the difficulties he was having trying to talk in his English classes. The frequent practice led to a gradual increase in his fluency levels. "Almon was learning not only more English but also more relevant and appropriate English for the World Wide Web community he sought to become part of" (Lam, 2000: 476).

Another example is related to L2 learners' 'fan communities' (Black, 2006, 2008). Black describes some students who used their L2 English to compose and publicly post fictional narratives on fanfiction.net. Fan fiction writers typically rework an original text by integrating new materials and extending it in different directions, such as adding new chapters and volumes to the Harry Potter books. These sites promote informal participatory types of learning because writers get regular feedback through reader reviews. Black (2008) describes a student, Nanako, who successfully improved her English through participating in a fan fiction site. Over the time she was engaging with the fan fiction site, she improved her writing as she responded to the audience's feedback and revised and then reposted her writing, which incorporated some of her readers' suggestions and ideas. Teachers might encourage learners to share experiences about sites where such authentic English language use and learning occurs.

Online games and incidental learning

Thorne et al. (2009: 808) suggest that "social virtualities and massively multiplayer online games (MMOs) arguably comprise the most socially and cognitively complex forms of interactive media currently available", and there are many teenagers who play these games through English because the players are international and English is the accepted lingua franca of this context. In MMO games, thousands of people can simultaneously interact. The goal-oriented activities that become increasingly difficult as gamers gain experience offer opportunities for continual intellectual challenge. Some students' motives for foreign language learning may be related to their desire to participate in digitally mediated communities. For example, Chik's (2011) study with Chinese-speaking gamers in Hong Kong shows that learners use electronic dictionaries to make sense of the game in English and also enjoy frequent authentic opportunities to chat with international gamers and thus pick up new English phrases. Gamers participating in the study said that the repetition of language items that reoccur during play helps with their practice and language learning. They also suggested that learning English through gaming can be, for some, a deliberate endeavour. In fact, most of them played a mixture of educational and authentic games and made use of online discussion forums and online gaming platforms to extend their practice. What seems to make this learning so successful is that winning and getting further in the game is the priority, and language learning is only a secondary aim. This is related to purposeful learning, as, for example, in task-based learning (see Van den Branden, this volume), where learners always have a motivating non-linguistic outcome to drive them forward. If played regularly, the game context guarantees exposure to English as well as frequent opportunities for output (Swain, 2000).

The implications for language teachers are many. For example, in classes of teenagers where such games are played regularly by most of the students, teachers may organise debates or quizzes around games or get the students to evaluate a range of games advertised on the market. They may want to write a piece of persuasive text to get others interested in new games. Some teenagers might also like to design their own games and describe them/sell them to others. Teachers can invite learners to put themselves in the shoes of different characters in games and write/talk about contentious issues presented from their point of view. For young people, whose personalities, views and ideas are in flux, tasks where they play another character may be a safe way to experiment expressing uncertain views.

Teenage research participants in ELT research

Overall, research reported in mainstream applied linguistics journals does not necessarily differentiate between studies with teenage or adult participants. This is because, as research participants, adolescents are supposed to be very similar to adults, unlike young children, where all kinds of accommodations may be appropriate when conducting research, because children cannot write or cannot reflect on their learning very well, at least not when tools designed for research with adults are used.

Teenagers' status is ambiguous when it comes to consenting to participate in research. On the one hand, teenagers are still protected (in the UK) by The Children's Act (1989), which covers all young people under the age of 18. In this sense, they are treated the same way as younger children, even though they are clearly more able to take decisions for themselves and act autonomously about a range of issues in their lives. On the other hand, good ethical practice dictates, as France (2004: 184) argues, that young people's views and opinions are fully taken into account, so it is necessary to go beyond parent/guardian consent.

> Good practice should include a continual review of consent to ensure that young people remain happy with their involvement. The right to withdrawal has to be emphasised regardless of how uneasy we might feel about losing our cohort.

Each group of learners in any context will present some ethical and methodological dilemmas for researchers, and some of the dilemmas we face with younger learners may apply to teenagers as well (e.g. Pinter, 2014). For example, in secondary schools, the normal power gap between teachers and students naturally contributes to the real or perceived pressure to participate and do or say the 'right thing' in research studies. In teenage classrooms, just like with younger children, it may be difficult for an individual to withdraw consent when the rest of the class are all participating in a study. In fact, the effect of peer pressure may be greater than in the case of younger children.

An exciting type of research with teenagers that is lacking in ESL/ELT at present is where teenagers are enabled to participate actively to contribute to the actual research process in various ways, such as by identifying priorities for research or by helping with data collection, analysis and dissemination. Because of their general openness to new ideas and their interest in materials and approaches that bring authenticity into the classrooms, it may be feasible for them to work alongside adults as co-researchers (Fraser et al., 2003).

Conclusion

Overall, teaching English to teenage learners is a challenging task. The work reviewed in this paper suggests that it is important for teachers to foster a positive classroom culture and build good connections between the teaching materials and the students' lives, use peer interaction and peer collaboration, and teach explicit learning strategies to help teenagers to gain control over their own learning. Getting students to work in groups where they can collaborate with each other, engage in joint problem-solving and prepare short presentations, quizzes or other materials for the rest of the class generally accommodates their physical, cognitive and social stage of development. In this way, gradually, teachers are able to pass control over to their students and let them take charge of their own learning through more flexible, learner-centred tasks. Teachers also need to invest time into getting to know the students, establishing communities of peers working together. Since teenagers have a growing ability to take decisions for themselves, teachers might want to involve students in selecting materials and developing rules and expectations in the classroom and for learning, rather than just impose those on them.

Discussion questions

- What motivates teenagers to learn English in your context, both generally and in class?
- What 'in class' and 'out of class' English do your students have access to, and how do they engage with it?
- What online activities are most typical for teenagers in your context? How can the use of technology be incorporated into your own teaching?
- What are the challenges of teaching adolescents in your particular context?

Related topics

Computer-mediated communication and language learning; Content and language integrated learning; Motivation; Learner autonomy; Primary ELT; Sociocultural theory and the language classroom.

Further reading

Legutke, M. L. (2012) 'Teaching teenagers', in A. Burns and J. C. Richards (eds) *The Cambridge guide to pedagogy and practice in second language teaching*. Cambridge: Cambridge University Press. 112–119. (A concise overview of the topic, from a language teacher's point of view. It draws on current theory, research and practice in order to address key questions teachers in teenage classrooms may face, including teenagers' needs and how to accommodate these with appropriate topics, tasks and texts.)

Motteram, G. (ed.) (2013) *Innovations in learning technologies for English language teaching*. London: British Council. (Freely available online from the British Council, this volume contains seven chapters covering a range of issues related to English language teaching and CALL, including primary, secondary, adult contexts and assessment. The second chapter by Stanley is devoted to successful practices described in case studies by teachers working in the secondary sector. Each chapter offers valuable practical ideas to practising English teachers.)

Palfrey, J. and Grasser, U. (2008) *Born digital: Understanding the first generation of digital natives*. New York: Basic Books. (This interesting text focuses on Internet users born after the 1980s, termed 'digital natives'. The authors discuss the opportunities and challenges associated with the Internet as a social space, discussing issues surrounding young people's privacy and vulnerability as Internet users, and Internet regulation both in Europe and the USA.)

Slater, A. and Bremner, J. G. (2011) *An introduction to developmental psychology.* London: Wiley. (This is a state-of-the-art, comprehensive and authoritative overview of child development from birth to adolescence. It is thematically organised and discusses theories, empirical research and key debates in an international context. It has an excellent overview of the teenage years.)

References

Arnett, J. J. (2002) 'The psychology of globalisation'. *American Psychologist,* 57/10. 774–83.

Banegas, D. L. (2013) 'The integration of content and language as a driving force in the EFL lesson', in E. Ushioda (ed.) *International perspectives on motivation.* Palgrave Macmillan. 82–97.

Black, R. W. (2006) 'Language, culture, and identity in online fanfiction'. *E-learning,* 3/2. 170–184.

Black, R. W. (2008) *Adolescents and online fan fiction.* New York: Peter Lang.

Blossfeld, H. P., Klijzing, E., Mills, M. and Kurz, K. (eds) (2006) *Globalisation, uncertainly and youth in society.* London: Routledge.

Boyd, D. (2007) 'Why youth love social network sites: The role of networked publics in teenage social life', in D. Buckingham (ed.) *Youth, identity and digital media MacArthur foundation series on digital learning.* Cambridge MA: MIT Press. 119–142.

Bushman, L. and Parks, K. (2006) *Using young adult literature in the English classroom.* Upper Saddle River, NJ: Pearson Education.

Chik, A. (2011) 'Learner autonomy development through digital gameplay'. *Digital Culture and Education,* 3/1. 30–45.

Comas-Quinn, A., Mardomingo, R. and Valentine, C. (2009) 'Mobile blogs in language learning: Making the most of informal and situated learning opportunities'. *ReCALL,* 21/1. 96–112.

Csikszentmihalyi, M. and Larson, R. (1984) *Being adolescent: Conflict and growth in the teenage years.* New York: Basic Books.

DeKeyser, R. (2012) 'Age effects and second language learning', in S. Gass and A. Mackey (eds) *The Routledge handbook of second language acquisition.* London: Routledge. 442–460.

Deyes, A. (2014) *The pointless book.* Dorking: Blink Publishing.

Diller, H. J., Erwin, O. and Sratmann, G. (eds) (2000) *Teens and tweens in British culture.* Heidelberg: Winter.

Dörnyei, Z. (2009) 'The L2 motivational self-system', in Z. Dörnyei and E. Ushioda (eds) *Motivation, language identity and the L2 self.* Bristol: Multilingual Matters. 9–42.

France, A. (2004) 'Young people', in S. Fraser, V. Lewis, S. Ding, M. Kellett and C. Robinson (eds) *Doing research with children and young people.* London: Sage publications in association with The Open University. 175–190.

Fraser, S., Lewis, V., Ding, S., Kellett, M. and Robinson, C. (eds) (2003) *Doing research with children and young people.* London: Paul Chapman Publishing.

Goossens, L. (2006) 'Adolescent development: Putting Europe on the map', in S. Jackson and L. Goossens (eds) *Handbook of Adolescent Development.* Hove and New York: Psychology Press. 1–9.

Halpern-Felsher, B. L. and Cauffman, E. (2001) 'Costs and benefits of a decision – decision-making competence in adolescents and adults'. *Journal of Applied Developmental Psychology,* 22. 257–273.

Hendry, L. B. and Kloep, M. (2006) 'Youth and leisure: A European perspective', in S. Jackson and L. Goossens (eds) *Handbook of adolescent development.* Hove and New York: Psychology Press. 246–263.

Henry, A. (2013) 'Digital games and ELT: Bridging the authenticity gap', in E. Ushioda (ed.) *International Perspectives on Motivation.* Basingstoke: Palgrave Macmillan. 133–155.

Lam, W. S. E. (2000) 'L2 literacy and the design of the self: A case study of a teenager writing on the Internet'. *TESOL Quarterly,* 34/3. 457–482.

Lamb, M. and Budiyanto (2013) 'Cultural challenges, identity and motivation in state school EFL', in E. Ushioda (ed.) *International perspectives on motivation.* Basingstoke: Palgrave Macmillan. 18–34.

Larson, R., Moneta, G., Richards, M. and Wilson, S. (2002) 'Continuity, stability and change in daily emotional experience across adolescence'. *Child Development,* 73. 1151–1165.

Legutke, M. L. (2012) 'Teaching teenagers', in A. Burns and J. C. Richards (eds) *The Cambridge guide to pedagogy and practice in second language teaching.* Cambridge: Cambridge University Press. 112–119.

Lenhart, A., Purcell, K., Smith, A. and Zickuhr, K. (2011) *Social media and young adults: Pew Internet and American life project.* Washington, DC: Pew Research Center. Retrieved from http://pewinternet.org/reports/2010

Lenneberg, E. H. (1967) *Biological foundations of language.* New York: John Wiley and Sons.

Lightfoot, C., Cole, M. and Cole, S. R. (2013) *The development of children.* New York: Worth Publishers.

Llinares, A., Morton, T. and Whittaker, R. (2012) *The role of language in CLIL.* Cambridge: Cambridge University Press.

Lund, A. and Rasmussen, I. (2008) 'The right tool for the wrong task? Match and mismatch between first and second stimulus in double stimulation'. *Computer-Supported Collaborative Learning,* 3. 378–412.

Macaro E, Handley, Z. and Walter, C. (2012) 'A systematic review of CALL in English as a second language: Focus on primary and secondary education'. *Language Teaching,* 45/1. 1–43.

Martin, C. A., Kelly, T. H., Rayens, M. K., Brogli, B. R., Brenzel, A. and Smith, W. J. (2002) 'Sensation seeking, puberty, and nicotine, alcohol and marijuana use in adolescence'. *Journal of the American Academy of Child and Adolescent Psychiatry,* 41. 1495–1502.

Muñoz, C. (2006) 'The effects of age on foreign language learning; The BAF project', in C. Muñoz (ed.) *Age and the rate of foreign language learning.* Bristol: Multilingual Matters. 1–40.

Muñoz, C. (2008) 'Symmetries and asymmetries of age effects in naturalistic and instructed L2 learning'. *Applied Linguistics,* 24/4. 578–596.

Palfrey, J. and Grasser, U. (2008) *Born digital: Understanding the first generation of digital natives.* New York: Basic Books.

Pinter, A. (2014) 'Child participant roles in applied linguistics'. *Applied Linguistics,* 35/2. 168–183.

Slater, A. and Bremner, J. G. (2011) *An introduction to developmental psychology.* London: Wiley.

Stanley, G. (2013) 'Integrating technology into secondary English language teaching', in G. Motteram (ed.) *Innovations in learning technologies for English language teaching.* London: British Council. 43–66.

Steinberg, L. (2005) 'Cognitive and affective development in adolescence'. *Trends in Cognitive Sciences,* 9/2. 69–74.

Steinberg, L (2010) 'A dual system model of adolescent risk-taking', *Developmental Psychobiology,* 52. 216–224.

Suzuki, W. and Itagaki, N. (2009) 'Languaging in grammar exercises by Japanese EFL learners of differing proficiency'. *System,* 37. 217–225.

Swain, M. (2000) 'The output hypothesis and beyond: Mediating acquisition through collaborative dialogue', in J. P. Lantolf (ed.) *Sociocultural theory and second language learning.* Oxford: Oxford University Press. 97–114.

Swain, M. (2006) 'Languaging, agency and collaboration in advanced language proficiency', in H. Byrnes (ed.) *Advanced language learning: The contribution of Halliday and Vygotsky.* Continuum: London. 95–108.

Swain, M. and Lapkin, S. (2002) 'Talking it through: Two French immersion learners response to reformulation'. *International Journal of Educational Research,* 37. 285–304.

Thorne, S. L., Black, R. W. and Sykes, J. M. (2009) 'Second language use, socialisation, and learning in the Internet communities and online gaming'. *Modern Language Journal,* 93. 802–823.

Tsui, A.B.M. and Ng, M. (2000) 'Do secondary L2 writers benefit from peer comments?' *Journal of Second Language Writing,* 9/2. 147–170.

Ushioda, E. (ed.) (2013) *International perspectives on motivation: Language learning and professional challenges.* Basingstoke: Palgrave Macmillan.

Varanoglulari, F., Lopez, C., Gansrigler, E., Pessanha, L. and Williams, M. (2008) 'Secondary EFL course survey review'. *ELT Journal,* 62/4. 401–19.

Vygotsky, L. (1978) *Mind and society.* Cambridge, MA: Harvard University Press.

Part V

Teaching language

Knowledge, skills and pedagogy

27

Corpora in ELT

Ana Frankenberg-Garcia

Introduction

This chapter begins with an explanatory definition of corpora and covers different types of corpora available for ELT. It then proceeds to explain what corpus software does and how corpora can be used in ELT. It concludes with a discussion of key areas of debate surrounding the use of corpora for language teaching and future directions in this domain. The chapter does not assume any prior knowledge of corpora.

What is a corpus?

In very simple terms, a corpus is a collection of texts in electronic format. Although many people use the word 'corpora' simply to refer to a body of texts, in the present chapter, the word is being used in the corpus linguistics sense, where those texts must be in a machine-readable format. Thus, texts that are only available in print will need to be digitised before inclusion in a corpus. Likewise, in order to include spoken language in a corpus, speech needs to be recorded and then digitally transcribed into text. It is important to bear in mind that, unlike electronic libraries, which store texts for their intrinsic value, the texts compiled into a corpus are normally selected so as to be fit for a particular purpose. A corpus that is to be used to teach English academic writing, for example, may include academic essays, journal articles and dissertations in English, but not genres such as fiction and news.

Many scholars also believe that the texts in corpora need to have been produced for authentic communicative goals (e.g. Sinclair, 1991; Tognini-Bonelli, 2001). A corpus for teaching business English, for example, should include business letters and transcripts of business meetings that actually took place rather than letters invented for the purpose of teaching business English or transcripts of staged meetings recorded solely for the purpose of language teaching. This is because it is believed that only "genuine communications of people going about their normal business" (Tognini-Bonelli, 2001: 55) can give us a true picture of the language that is actually used in those circumstances. Studying such texts reveals facts about language that would otherwise remain unnoticed.

Two other key aspects of corpora are their size and representativeness. Common sense dictates that corpora should be large enough to allow one to make useful generalisations about the language represented in a particular corpus. For example, one cannot draw any conclusions about how to write abstracts by analysing only one or two abstracts. However, a small corpus of, say, forty medical journal abstracts can help one detect patterns about the language and organisational structure of this highly specific genre. On the other hand, corpora used for the analysis of general language often need to be quite large, for they must contain a sufficient number of texts which are representative of a wide range of situations. The ideal size of a corpus will ultimately depend on what the corpus is for. This can range from small, specialised language corpora for teaching ESP, with just a few thousand words (see Gavioli, 2005), to very large reference corpora with millions or even billions of words used in corpus-based lexicography.

The four essential characteristics of corpora described above are neatly summarised by McEnery et al. (2006: 5), for whom a corpus is "a collection of (1) *machine-readable* (2) *authentic texts* which is (3) *sampled* to be (4) *representative* of a particular language or language variety".

Different types of corpora

In the same way as there are different types of texts in the world, there are also different types of corpora. Table 27.1 lists a selection of open-access online corpora that can be used directly by EFL teachers and learners.

The British National Corpus (BNC; see Table 27.1), for example, was compiled in the early 1990s with the purpose of providing of snapshot of British English; thus it can be said to be a general language corpus. It contains a wide variety of texts, from formal academic writing to transcripts of spoken teenage language. Although it is still widely used in research and teaching, the BNC does not contain words or meanings that are relatively new in English; it reflects British English at a particular point in time. Thus a word like *wireless* will appear in the BNC in its rather old-fashioned sense meaning *radio*, but not in its current widely used form as a modifier in phrases like *wireless phone* and *wireless network*. With 100 million words, the BNC is also relatively small by today's standards. The dramatic increase of digital texts in the world since the 1990s has made corpora much easier to compile. The corpus underlying SkELL (Sketch Engine for English Language Learning; see Table 27.1), for example, contains over one billion words gathered from British and American websites (Baisa and Suchomel, 2014), providing a good coverage of everyday, standard, formal and professional English.

As explained above, however, corpora do not have to be huge to be useful. The academic language corpora in Table 27.1, for example the British Academic Written English corpus (BAWE), are much smaller. Likewise, the Business Letter Corpus (BLC; see Table 27.1), with just one million words, is a good example of a small, specialised corpus of American and British business letters that can be used in teaching business English.

Corpora consisting of speech also tend to be small, because it takes time to transcribe speech and not all forms of conversation are easy to capture. While parliamentary debates and radio and television talk shows are recorded anyway, in order to collect transcripts of other forms of speech, it is first necessary to ask volunteers to go around recording their own everyday conversations. For this same reason, the spoken component of general language corpora like the BNC or the Corpus of Contemporary American English (COCA; see Table 27.1) tend to be much smaller than the written one.

Table 27.1 A selection of open-access corpora with integrated online concordancers that can be used directly by teachers and learners of English

Corpus	Size in words (millions)	Brief description	URL	Relevance to ELT
British Academic Spoken English Corpus (BASE)	1 M	British university lectures and seminars	https://ca.sketchengine.co.uk/bonito/run.cgi/first_form?corpname=preloaded/base	Spoken academic English
Michigan Corpus of Academic Spoken English (MICASE)	1.8 M	Academic speech at the University of Michigan	http://quod.lib.umich.edu/m/micase/	
British Academic Written English Corpus (BAWE)	6.5 M	British university student essays	https://ca.sketchengine.co.uk/bonito/run.cgi/first_form?corpname=preloaded/bawe2	Written academic English
Michigan Corpus of Upper-Level Student Papers (MICUSP)	2.6 M	American grade A student papers	http://micusp.elicorpora.info/	
Business Letter Corpus (BLC)	1 M	British and American business letters	http://www.someya-net.com/concordancer/	Business English
British National Corpus (BNC)	100 M	British English from the early nineties	http://corpus.byu.edu/bnc/ (also available from other online concordancers)	General English
The Corpus Of Contemporary American English (COCA)	450 M	American English from 1990 to 2012	http://corpus.byu.edu/coca/	
Corpus Of Global Web-Based English (GloWbE)	1.9 B	Web pages from different English-speaking countries	http://corpus2.byu.edu/glowbe/	
SkELL	1 B	An interface-cum-corpus conceived for ELT based on recent texts gathered from the web.	https://skell.sketchengine.co.uk/run.cgi/skell	
Vienna-Oxford International Corpus of English (VOICE)	1 M	Speakers from different first language backgrounds using ELF	http://www.univie.ac.at/voice/page/corpus_availability_online	ELF
OPUS, the Open Parallel Corpus	open-ended	A collection of source texts and translations in English and various other languages, with several specialised language subcorpora for ESP	http://opus.lingfil.uu.se/	Use of L1 to teach English

In addition to corpora of speech and writing, there have been recent efforts to compile multi-modal corpora, such as the Padova Multimedia English Corpus (Coccetta, 2011). These corpora contain written transcripts of speech aligned with video recordings so that it is possible to study how language and non-linguistic elements such as gesture, facial expressions and gaze are used in conjunction to create meaning.

When referring to a corpus of English, the default is to assume the texts in the corpus were produced by native speakers (this chapter will not deal with the debates surrounding the term 'native speaker'; however, see Llurda, this volume, for further discussion). However, there are certain types of corpora that focus precisely on the language of non-native speakers. Learner corpora, made with texts produced by learners of English, are compiled to research learner error and second language development. The International Corpus of Learner English (Granger, 2003) is a notable example of this kind of corpus. Likewise, there are also corpora that have been assembled to study English as a Lingua Franca (ELF; see Seargeant, this volume), like the Vienna-Oxford Corpus of English (VOICE; see Table 27.1), which comprises transcripts of conversations by users of English as an international language.

In addition to monolingual corpora, there are also parallel corpora consisting of source texts aligned with their translations into another language. These corpora tend to be smaller, specialised language corpora – of parliamentary debates, of fiction, of film subtitles, for example – because they can only include texts belonging to genres that are available in translation. As shall be seen later in this chapter, parallel corpora can be particularly useful in ELT when one wishes to highlight L1 and L2 contrasts.

Finally, while all corpora consist of plain text, some corpora contain extra information attached to the text that is not normally visible to the corpus user. The two most common add-ons are 'lemmatisation' and 'part-of-speech tagging'. Lemmatisation involves labelling each word in a corpus with its base form, i.e. its lemma. Thus in a lemmatised corpus, 'hidden' behind the sentence *I was fifteen minutes late* is the information shown below in brackets:

*I*_[lemma=I] *was*_[lemma=BE] *fifteen*_ [lemma=FIFTEEN] *minutes*_ [lemma=MINUTE] *late*_[lemma=late]

Lemmatisation allows one to carry out queries which, in a single action, retrieve all the inflections of a given word. For example, a corpus search for [*lemma=BE*] followed by *late* will retrieve *am late, 'm late, is late, 's late, are late, was late, were late, been late* and *being late,* which is more practical than looking up each of these separately. This is also a good way of retrieving sentences for gapping exercises for learners to practice the verb *to be.*

Part-of-speech (POS) tagging, in turn, involves labelling each word in a corpus with its POS category. The example above would be tagged as follows:

*I*_[pos=PRONOUN] *was*_[pos=VERB] *fifteen*_ [pos=NUMBER] *minutes*_ [pos=NOUN] *late*_[pos=ADJECTIVE]

This kind of tagging allows one to carry out sophisticated queries involving POS categories. For example, a search for *I* [*pos=VERB*] *late* will retrieve *I am late, I slept late, I arrived late, I work late,* and so on. This is a practical way of retrieving sentences that can be transformed into a vocabulary exercise for learners.

Apart from lemmatisation and POS tagging, it is possible to add all sorts of extra information to a corpus that will help one search the corpus more efficiently. Learner corpora, for example, are tagged for errors so as to facilitate their retrieval and analysis.

Corpus software

Containing many thousands or even billions of words, corpora are used in conjunction with special text-retrieval software known as concordancers. Concordancers enable one to manipulate and interrogate a corpus in a way that is very different from reading texts from start to finish, often providing insights into the language represented by the corpus which are not visible to the naked eye. Concordancers perform three basic types of operations, generating concordances, word lists and collocation statistics. These will be now be explained.

Concordances

Concordance queries work in a way similar to the *find* function of a normal electronic text editor. However, instead of skipping from one occurrence of whatever we look up to another, the concordance option lists all such occurrences together, displaying them vertically along with the context in which they appear, as exemplified by the sample concordances for *married* in Figure 27.1. This simple key-word-in-context (KWIC) display allows one to scroll down the computer screen and notice various patterns of how *married* is used. The concordances in Figure 27.1 have been sorted alphabetically one word to the right of *married*, enabling learners to focus on the patterns used after *married with*. This could be useful for those who make errors like ★'*She is married with a Frenchman.*'

1839, but after his father died, his mother	**married**	William Viscount Beresford the Marshal
offices and awards of merit. In 1910 he	**married**	Winifred, daughter of Algernon Lyon of
fighter David Morris from Hereford. He was 35,	**married**	with 2 children and had been in the brigade
Leominster, a part-timer for 13 years, also	**married**	with 2 children. They died when part
occur. HISTORY Peter West, aged 35, is	**married**	with 2 young children. He is self employed
he had received hospital treatment. He is	**married**	with a 5 year old child. He receives invalidity
extra-mural Diploma and my war service. But I was	**married**	with a baby then, and, in 1949, this was

Figure 27.1 Sample KWIC concordances for *married* from the BNC

In addition to the standard KWIC display in Figure 27.1, which focuses the user's attention on the right- and left-hand co-text of a word or string of words, many concordancers allow users to switch to a full sentence view instead. This can be particularly important when teaching discourse, as can be seen from the sample concordances in Figure 27.2, all of which highlight the sentence-final position of the adverb *tomorrow*. Some concordancers also allow users to expand the co-text of each concordance line so as to retrieve more context preceding and following a given concordance.

My son is turning 30 years old **tomorrow**.
The trial was adjourned until 10am **tomorrow**.
The tours are supposedly being indefinitely suspended effective **tomorrow**.
My summer young artist applications are due **tomorrow**.
The city board holds its regular monthly meeting **tomorrow** night.
A small shift today becomes a disaster **tomorrow**.
I promise you something less serious **tomorrow**.

Figure 27.2   Sample full-sentence concordances for *tomorrow* from SkELL

Concordance queries in parallel corpora will in turn retrieve parallel concordances consisting of aligned source text and translation segments. Figure 27.3 contains a selection of parallel concordances from the COMPARA corpus (open access at www.linguateca.pt/COMPARA; Frankenberg-Garcia and Santos, 2003) which draw attention to the fact that the Portuguese adverb *atualmente* does not translate into its English cognate *actually*. This could clearly be useful for learners when considering lexical 'false friends', for example.

O original pertenceu mais tarde a Luís XIV e **atualmente** está no museu do Louvre.	The original was later a possession of Louis XIV and hangs now in the Louvre.
— Que meios de subsistência tem ele **atualmente**?	'What are his **present** means of subsistence?'
Como está ela **atualmente**?	How's she **these days**?
Atualmente finjo que não ouço.	I tend to ignore it **nowadays**.
Atualmente existe uma espécie de epidemia de falta de amor-próprio em Inglaterra.	There's something like an epidemic of lack of self-esteem in Britain **at the moment**.

Figure 27.3   Sample parallel PT > EN concordances for *atualmente* from COMPARA

Note finally that concordance queries need not focus on single words. Users can also search for conventional strings of words like *if I were you* (Figure 27.4), and, as explained above, depending on the corpus, it is possible to carry out more sophisticated queries involving lemmas, POS categories and other types of corpus annotation. Figure 27.5 exemplifies concordances for *a [pos=ADJECTIVE] escape*.

I should stay lying down **if I were you**.
I would leave **if I were you**.
I'd move on **if I were you**.
I should try to forget it **if I were you**.
I'd go home **if I were you**.
I would watch my step **if I were you**.

Figure 27.4   Sample concordances for *if I were you* from SkELL

> I never saw such **a fast escape**.
> They might have had **a miraculous escape**.
> He had **a lucky escape** from execution.
> They shot him during **an alleged escape**.
> It had been **a narrow escape** and I was impressed.
> Write a short story about **a daring escape** attempt.

Figure 27.5 Sample concordances for *a [pos=ADJECTIVE] escape* from SkELL

Word lists

Word lists are simply lists of all the words in a corpus along with information about their frequency and rank in the corpus. From the perspective of ELT, they can be very useful to help one determine what vocabulary to teach first. According to Zipf's law (Zipf, 1949), the top most frequent words in a language cover a very large proportion of the language as a whole, so if learners are able to understand and use, say, the 3,000 most frequent words, they should in theory be able to get by in most situations. As Cook (1998: 58) stated, however, corpora can only supply us with "information about production but not about reception". Corpus frequencies alone should therefore not be the sole criterion used when selecting what language to teach.

Apart from plain word lists, some concordancers also allow one to extract 'keyword' lists. This is typically done by comparing word frequencies in a specialised language corpus with word frequencies in a general language corpus. The words that are particularly salient in the former will be ranked first, highlighting the peculiarities of the specialised language in question. For example, by comparing verb frequency in the BLC with verb frequency in a corpus of general English, Someya (1999) was able to generate a list of verbs like *thank, enclose, appreciate, request, order, receive, schedule, attach, purchase, discuss* and so on that are particularly significant in business letters. Of course, it was only possible to isolate verbs in this way because the BLC is tagged for POS.

Using the same methodology, it is also possible to extract frequency lists of strings of words in order to identify key phrases in a corpus. Examples of core five-word strings in the Business Letter Corpus are: *thank you very much for, look forward to hearing from, do not hesitate to contact, please let me know if* and so on. Careful scrutiny of such a list can be very useful when it comes to identifying and selecting phrases that are typical of business letters.

Collocations

Proficient language users know instinctively which words go together in a language and which words sound awkward when combined. Some collocations are dictated by logic, like the verb *drink* followed by liquids like *water, beer* and so on, while others are purely arbitrary and often differ from language to language. For example, it is conventional to say *auburn hair*, but people do not say *auburn scarf*, even when the two are exactly the same colour. The concept of collocation (Firth, 1957) pre-dates corpus linguistics and collocation statistics. However, with the emergence of electronic corpora, it is now possible to list collocations in seconds by running automatic statistical calculations that compare the overall frequency of particular words in a corpus with their frequency in the immediate context of another word. This will show how likely it is for the words in question to combine. Imagine a learner trying to think of a verb to follow the noun *situation*. A collocation query would automatically list verbs like *arise, worsen, escalate, deteriorate, exist, warrant, change, improve, affect* and so on, which is more efficient than running a concordance query for *situation* and scrolling down the results until a suitable verb was found. It would be equally simple to run a collocation query in order to list adjectives that collocate with *situation,* like *dire, hopeless, desperate, untenable, tense, emergency, current, financial, stressful, win-win* and so on. This can be extremely useful to help learners expand their vocabulary and write more idiomatically.

Types of concordancers

As explained in the beginning of this section, most concordancers will allow users to run concordance, word list and collocation queries. However, their interfaces vary, and so does the query language associated with them. Some concordancers are more sophisticated than others, allowing users to run queries that are not possible in simpler software. Users can install proprietary stand-alone concordancers like WordSmith tools (Scott, 2012) or freeware like AntConc (Anthony, 2014) and use them to interrogate corpus files stored on their personal computers. Alternatively, as previously exemplified in Table 27.1, there are numerous open-access corpora that can be interrogated remotely via an online interface without any software installation. SkeLL was purposefully conceived for ELT (Baisa and Suchomel, 2014) and is arguably the most user-friendly English corpus-cum-concordancer available today.

Uses of corpora in ELT

Corpora are used to develop various general language tools that have become commonplace in people's lives, including spell checkers, autocorrect options in text editors and web browsers, and even sophisticated machine-translation programmes.

In state-of-the-art pedagogical lexicography, corpora are employed to research word use, and this information is collated to select which headwords (i.e. words listed in a dictionary) are important to include in learners' dictionaries, which senses of polysemous words to present first, which words to use in the definitions, and which grammatical properties and collocations of words to draw attention to. Modern learners' dictionaries also provide corpus-based examples that can help learners see how words are used in context and utilise data from learner corpora to draw attention to recurrent errors. For example, the word *information* in the *Macmillan English Dictionary* online is marked with three stars, meaning it is a very frequent word in English. The entry for *information* also shows common collocates and phrases, such as *get/obtain/collect information, information about/on/regarding, a piece of information, relevant/useful information, further information,* contextualised examples a such as *We were able to get the information we needed from the Internet,* and a 'get it right' rubric explaining that *information* 'is never used in the plural or comes after *an* or a number'. This explanation is then exemplified with learner corpus data of what is wrong − *★TV helps people to get an important information* − and how to correct it: *TV helps people to get important information.*

Apart from dictionaries, at least in the ELT market, there is a growing body of grammars, coursebooks and even language tests that draw on corpus data to develop their content in a number of different ways. Corpus frequencies may be used to inform what words and phrases to include in a syllabus and to distinguish between language that is typically spoken, written, formal and informal (see Biber et al., 1999, for example). Concordance lines may be incorporated into dialogues and exercises, learner corpus data may be used to identify problematic areas that

Cambridge Dictionary of American English
Cambridge International Dictionary of English
Cambridge Grammar of English
Collins COBUILD English Dictionary for
    Advanced Learners
Collins COBUILD English Usage
Collins COBUILD Intermediate English Grammar
Longman Dictionary of Common Errors
Longman Dictionary of Contemporary English
Longman Grammar of Spoken and Written
    English

Macmillan English Dictionary
Macmillan Collocations Dictionary
Natural Grammar (Oxford)
Oxford Advanced Learner's Dictionary
Oxford Collocations Dictionary for Students
    of English
Practical English Usage (Oxford)
Touchstone series (Cambridge)
Vocabulary in Use series (Cambridge)

Figure 27.6 Examples of corpus-based ELT publications

Source: Frankenberg-Garcia, 2014.

require special attention, and so on. In the Touchtone Series (McCarthy et al., 2005), for example, learners are informed that 'People say *Sometimes I* seven times more often than *I sometimes*' (p. 46). Figure 27.6 lists a few well-known corpus-based ELT publications.

The publications in Figure 27.6 contain language that has been selected from raw corpus data and edited by lexicographers, corpus linguists and materials designers. Of course, the amount of language that can be presented in this polished format is limited, simply because language is infinitely bigger and more complex than what can be summarised in a book or any other language learning aid. Language learners (and their teachers) often have questions for which there are no answers or which are not treated in sufficient detail in dictionaries, coursebooks, grammars and other educational publications.

Thus, another option is for teachers and learners to use corpora directly. Corpora can provide more language and can disclose solutions to language queries that have not been dealt with in edited language resources, propelling language users to completely new levels of learner autonomy (see Benson, this volume, for further discussion of learner autonomy). The direct use of corpora has come to be known as discovery or data-driven learning (DDL). For Johns (1991: 3), the founding father of DDL, "What distinguishes the data-driven learning approach is the attempt to cut out the middleman . . . and give direct access to the data so that the learner can take part in building up his or her own profiles of meanings and uses."

Language teachers do not normally have time to compile corpora and conduct corpus-based ELT research, but they can resort to ready-made corpora to complement their teaching in two basic ways. They can prepare corpus-based handouts and exercises for their students, and they can teach learners to use corpora on their own. Gabrielatos (2005) has referred to this distinction as the 'soft' and the 'hard' approach to using corpora in the classroom, while Boulton (2010) prefers to call this the 'hands-off' and the 'hands-on' approach. An example of the former is given in Frankenberg-Garcia (2012a). A group of Portuguese learners of English did not understand the meaning of *aisle* when they were exposed to the word via a dialogue in their coursebooks. The word appeared in the context of air travel, and its meaning in that sense was briefly explained. For the following lesson, the teacher prepared the exercise in Figure 27.7 in order to expand and consolidate the learners' previous one-off contact with the word. As can be seen, the *aisle* exercise enhances the learners' exposure to the new input by presenting them with concentrated doses of the word in context. The learners were able to figure out that aisles exist not just on aeroplanes (which was the original context in which they had seen the word) but also in places

---

A. Read the sentences below and make a list of the sort of place where aisles are found.
B. Does aisle translate into Portuguese always in the same way?

1. The air hostesses inquired what I was making and a man passing in the **aisle** quite genuinely complimented me on my work.
2. I arrived at Salisbury Cathedral, just as the bride was about to go up the **aisle**.
3. As she looked around she felt a twinge of sadness that in a carriage where 70 per cent of the commuters were men there were five women forced to stand in the **aisle**.
4. They looked at the passports and then started to walk down the **aisle**, pointing their guns at the passengers.
5. He hurried up the **aisle** of the church.
6. She picked up her suitcase and made her way along the **aisle**.
7. The layout of the store, with wide **aisles**, gives customers room to move around.
8. I spend much of my time at the shops; wandering through the **aisles**, faltering, never knowing what to buy.

Figure 27.7 Handout with selected BNC concordances for *aisle*

Source: Frankenberg-Garcia, 2012a: 40.

like trains, shops, churches and supermarkets. Additionally, the concordances served to help the learners notice that there is a distinction between aisles and corridors, which does not apply to their native language.

Frankenberg-Garcia (2012a) also gives an example of hands-on corpus consultation during a session in which learners were looking at different ways of ending business letters. One of the students was not happy about *I look forward to hearing from you*. She said her former tutor (a native speaker of English) had told her that the right way of saying this was using the present continuous: *I am looking forward to hearing from you*. The teacher (a non-native speaker) felt both forms were correct, but for reassurance she and the student looked up the strings *look/looking forward to hearing/seeing* in the BLC. The results summarised in Table 27.2 showed the student, and confirmed to the teacher, that not only it was perfectly acceptable to end a letter with *look forward to hearing/seeing*, but also that it seemed in fact to be more conventional than *looking forward to hearing/seeing*.

At a more advanced level, Charles (2012) has taught non-native PhD students to build their own corpora in their specialised domains to help them research the specialised terminology and phraseology of their fields of study.

To summarise, therefore, corpora have been used by linguists and lexicographers to write dictionaries, grammars and coursebooks and by teachers to prepare materials for their students or to help themselves and their students learn more about a language by consulting corpora directly.

Table 27.2 Distribution of *looking/look forward to seeing/hearing* in the BLC

Search string	Corpus Frequency
look forward to hearing	212
looking forward to hearing	19
look forward to seeing	156
looking forward to seeing	15

Key areas of debate

Authenticity

One of the most widely debated issues surrounding the use of corpora in ELT is the actual language represented in corpora. As explained earlier, corpora are made of texts taken from real-life communications between people. Corpus-based ELT materials therefore draw on attested language use rather than on language invented for the purpose of teaching. Attested language is often described as 'authentic', 'genuine' or 'real' language, and corpus-based publications have capitalised on this to market their products. For instance, Cambridge's Touchstone series (McCarthy et al., 2005) claims to teach "English as it's really used [and] presents natural language in authentic contexts". Similarly, the motto of Collins COBUILD (n.d.) Dictionary online is "supporting learners with authentic English since 1987", and the *Longman Dictionary of Contemporary English* online advertises that "155,000 natural examples bring English to life".

Widdowson (2000), however, points out that corpus data cannot be regarded as authentic once it has been uprooted from its original context. In other words, a text can only be regarded as authentic by those who use it for natural communicative purposes; when reused in a classroom for the purpose of teaching and learning a language, strictly speaking, it can no longer be said to be authentic.

Possibly more important than discussing the term authenticity, however, is the fact that because corpora are made of genuine communications, they may include errors, taboo words, sensitive topics that are not appropriate for classroom use and, in particular, language that is simply too difficult for learners. The argument here runs that unreal or scripted language is more accessible for learners and therefore more pedagogically appropriate. For Widdowson (1998: 714–715),

> the whole point of language learning tasks is that they are specifically contrived for learning. They do not have to replicate or even simulate what goes on in normal uses of language. Indeed, the more they seem to do so, the less effective they are likely to be.

Yet the point of using corpora in ELT is not to impinge raw corpus data on learners, but, as seen in the examples given in the previous section, to process this data so as to extract from it facts about language that are often unavailable elsewhere, promoting learner autonomy. If preparing hands-off corpus based hand-outs and exercises beforehand, teachers need to use their common sense so as to edit out corpus data that is unsuitable for teaching purposes. This cannot of course be done when learners use corpora hands-on, in which case teachers must be prepared to deal with exposing learners to raw corpus data. While this is very far from the idealised language that we normally see in ELT materials, it must be recognised this is also language people in the streets actually use. It could therefore be argued that corpora provide a golden opportunity for language learners to be able to get in touch with the language people use outside the classroom in the sheltering presence of a teacher.

Apart from the fact that attested uses of language can better prepare learners to communicate effectively and competently in real life outside the classroom, concordance data is often more interesting and thought-provoking than the sometimes insipid and contrived language used in scripted textbook dialogues and exercises. Römer (2004: 153) stresses this point by comparing particularly unrealistic sentences from a traditional German textbook dialogue like '*Where are the girls? Are they packing? Yes, they are.*' with spoken data from the BNC like '*What's happening, does anybody know? Are you listening to me?*'

There are however many very good course materials that are not corpus-based. Moreover, simplifying and adapting a language so as to make it more accessible to language learners is not necessarily a bad idea. Parents do this instinctively when speaking to babies and toddlers, and native speakers tend to do this when communicating with non-native speakers; whatever their pitfalls, coursebooks with invented sentences and scripted dialogues have been useful in helping people to learn foreign languages for many generations.

Although there are a number of studies on how teachers and learners react to corpora (see Boulton and Pérez-Paredes, 2014, for example), the fact is that further research is needed in order for us to come to a better understanding of how presenting learners with attested instances of language use from corpora compares with the idealised language that we often see in more traditional ELT textbooks.

Corpora for ELT

Another important issue is choosing a suitable corpus for classroom use. Traditional ELT materials tend to have been written, or at least edited, by native speakers of English, and corpus-based ELT publications on the market follow suit by using large native-speaker corpora (albeit often with insights from non-native, learner corpus data).

Since the language of these corpora may be too difficult or unsuitable for learners, some scholars believe in creating corpora purposefully designed for language teaching rather than using general language corpora like the BNC or COCA (see Table 27.1). The SACODEYL project (Widmann et al., 2011), for example, provides online access to very small pedagogic corpora in seven European languages consisting of video-recorded interviews with 13- to 17-year-old teenagers. This is an example of a corpus that was purposefully compiled for teaching young learners.

With the emergence of ELF, it is also important to consider how relevant corpora like the VOICE corpus in Table 27.1 might be for ELT (Seidlhofer, 2004). The question of whether ELF corpora are purely for linguistic research or whether they can or even should be used to inform ELT teaching is part of the ongoing debate on recognising L2 English users as speakers in their own right rather than as 'failed' native speakers.

Another issue related to the type of corpora used for language teaching is in what situations it is legitimate to use parallel corpora, since parallel concordances will inevitably put learners in contact with (a) L1 and L2 contrasts and (b) translated language. Frankenberg-Garcia (2005, 2007) argues that parallel corpora can be especially useful in teaching monolingual classrooms in a number of situations where comparing L1 and L2 is beneficial (see Svalberg for discussion of similar ideas in relation to language awareness, and Kerr for discussion of use of learners' own-language in the ELT classroom, both this volume).

Direct uses of corpora by teachers and learners

A further key area of debate surrounding the use of corpora in ELT is teachers' and learners' reactions to direct uses of corpora in the classroom. Even though the number of corpora that can be used by anyone with access to computers and the Internet has taken a giant leap over the past few years, there are still very few teachers, let alone learners, who feel comfortable using corpora directly. One of the problems is that most corpora were compiled for research rather than for teaching purposes, and the use of most concordancers is not very intuitive. There are a number of studies (for example, Kennedy and Miceli, 2001; Frankenberg-Garcia, 2012b) that show that corpus skills do not come naturally and need to be taught.

However, mastering the basics of corpora (i.e. how to select an appropriate corpus, how to work with concordances, word lists and collocations, and, most importantly, how to interpret corpus data) is not the only difficulty. The next major problem is how and when to transpose this expertise to the classroom. The fact that a ready-made ELT publication or a custom-made exercise or activity prepared by a teacher is corpus-based does necessarily mean that it is good. As with any other ELT material, corpus-based teaching aids must be relevant, useful and accessible to the particular group of learners they were designed for. Likewise, there are hundreds of ways in which learners can explore corpora on their own, but first they must develop a sense for what queries might be useful to them and understand what to do with the data retrieved. Unfortunately, there seem to be quite a number of corpus-based activities exemplified in the literature which have more to do with linguists' interest in language research than with language learners' actual needs. Language learners (and their teachers) cannot be expected to compile corpora and be captivated by analysing corpus data just because this is fascinating to linguists.

A final problem presented by data-driven learning is how to fit it in with the rest of the teaching curriculum. The few teachers who are using corpora today seem to be teachers who do research in corpus linguistics and work in an environment – mostly universities – where they have a great deal of autonomy regarding what and how they teach. However, this is not the case in the majority of ELT scenarios. As discussed in Frankenberg-Garcia (2012b), most teachers are not researchers. They normally have a syllabus to follow and do not have much time for devising corpus-based activities, let alone compiling corpora. Moreover, language lessons do not normally take place in computer labs that enable hands-on access to corpora.

Future directions

While the tendency is for there to be more and more corpus-informed ELT publications on the market, the direct use of corpora by teachers and learners is something that has yet to be addressed. The need for training pre-service and in-service teachers to use corpora is acknowledged by several scholars (for example, Mukherjee, 2004; Römer, 2009; Frankenberg-Garcia, 2012b; Lenko, 2014). It is only when language teachers have learnt how to use corpora that their expertise can trickle down to benefit language learners as well. Even teachers who do not have the time or are not willing to use corpora with their students can use corpora for their own benefit to look up information about language that is not available elsewhere. With the click of a mouse, corpus users can be empowered via the combined intuitions of hundreds of other language users. Although there are already a number of Master's programmes in TESOL, TEFL or ELT that offer students optional modules in corpus linguistics, there do not seem to be many programmes where, instead of receiving training in general corpus linguistics, teachers are being specifically trained in applied uses of corpora for language teaching. This would be an important development if corpora are to become more relevant and present in everyday teaching.

Another need for the future is further development of corpora and concordancers for ELT. Some advances in this direction have already been made, as seen earlier in Coccetta (2011) and Widmann et al. (2011), although the corpora described in those studies are very small and have very limited uses. Another example is the *Compleat Lexical Tutor*, developed by Tom Cobb (Cobb, n.d.), which contains specific tools for creating data-driven learning exercises. *For Better English* (http://forbetterenglish.com/) developed by Kilgarriff et al. (2008), though originally conceived for lexicography, is a tool which automatically filters out concordances from a very large general English corpus so as to prioritise full sentences that are not too long or too short and also sentences exhibiting typical patterns of usage, while at the same time leaving out concordances which contain infrequent, more difficult words. SkELL (see Table 27.1), in turn, is a further development of the corpus-filtering technology developed in *For Better English*, presenting novice corpus users with an extremely simple and intuitive interface of the highly sophisticated Sketch Engine tool (Kilgarriff et al., 2004). In order for these and a number of other corpus tools and resources conceived for language teaching to be further developed, however, it is important that they should be tried out and tested by actual teachers and learners.

Beyond this, in the future it should also be possible to integrate corpora and concordancing software with other applications, such as CALL software and simple text editors. Indeed, some progress in this direction has already been made, such as the Concord Writer tool in the previously mentioned *Compleat Lexical Tutor*, where learners can input their own text and link the words they write dynamically to concordances.

Conclusion

This chapter began by explaining corpora and corpus analysis tools. Examples of how different corpora can and have been used in ELT were given, and key points of debate were raised. The chapter concluded with some ideas for the future of corpora in ELT. While the growing influence of corpora seems to be undeniable, it remains to be seen whether one day they will become as essential to language teachers and learners as other, more conventional ELT materials and resources.

Discussion questions

- To what extent should language data from corpora be edited or simplified for pedagogic purposes?
- In what situations would it be appropriate to use parallel corpora in ELT?
- Discuss scenarios where the direct use of corpora by language learners can be useful in ELT writing.
- In your own professional context, to what extent is it realistic to expect teachers to develop corpus skills and use corpora with learners?

Related topics

ELT materials; Language curriculum design; Language teacher education; Learner autonomy; Language awareness; 'Native speakers', English and ELT; Questioning 'English-only' classrooms; World Englishes and English as a Llingua Franca.

Further reading

Flowerdew, L. (2011) *Corpora and language education*. London: Palgrave Macmillan. (A comprehensive overview of corpora in language education.)

Frankenberg-Garcia, A. (2012) 'Integrating corpora with everyday language teaching', in J. Thomas and A. Boulton (eds) *Input, process and product: Developments in teaching and language corpora*. Brno: Masaryk University Press. 36–53. (A discussion and examples of how the direct use of corpora can be integrated with everyday teaching.)

Gavioli, L. (2005) *Exploring corpora for ESP learning*. Amsterdam: John Benjamins. (A good introduction to corpora for those involved in teaching ESP.)

O'Keeffe, A., McCarthy, M. and Carter, R. (2007) *From corpus to classroom: Language use and language teaching*. Cambridge: Cambridge University Press. (An account of using corpus data to produce ELT coursebooks.)

Online tutorials on the use of corpora in language teaching are available at

- http://calper.la.psu.edu/corpus_portal/tutorial_overview.php
- http://www.ict4lt.org/en/en_mod3-4.htm
- https://eltadvantage.ed2go.com/

References

Anthony, L. (2014) *AntConc 3.4.3.* Tokyo: Waseda University. Retrieved from http://www.laurenceanthony.net/software/antconc/

Baisa, V. and Suchomel, V. (2014) 'SkELL: Web interface for English language learning', in A. Horák and P. Rychlý (eds) *Proceedings of recent advances in Slavonic natural language processing.* Brno: Tribun EU. 63–70.

Biber, D., Johansson, S., Leech, G., Conrad, S. and Finegan, E. (1999) *Longman grammar of spoken and written English.* Harlow: Longman.

Boulton, A. (2010) 'Data-driven learning: Taking the computer out of the equation'. *Language Learning,* 60/3. 534–572.

Boulton, A. and Pérez-Paredes, P. (eds) (2014) *ReCALL special issue: Researching uses of corpora for language teaching and learning.* Cambridge: Cambridge University Press.

Charles, M. (2012) 'Proper vocabulary and juicy collocations: EAP students evaluate do-it-yourself corpus-building'. *English for Specific Purposes,* 31/2. 93–102.

Cobb, T. (n.d.) *Compleat Lexical Tutor.* Retrieved from http://www.lextutor.ca/

Coccetta, F. (2011) 'Multimodal functional-notional concordancing', in A. Frankenberg-Garcia, L. Flowerdew and G. Aston (eds) *New trends in corpora and language learning.* New York: Continuum. 121–138.

Collins COBUILD. (n.d.) *English for Learners.* Retrieved from http://www.collinsdictionary.com/dictionary/english-cobuild-learners

Cook, G. (1998) 'The uses of reality: A reply to Ronald Carter'. *ELT Journal,* 51/1. 57–63.

Firth, J. R. (1957) 'Modes of meaning', in *Papers in linguistics 1934–1951.* Oxford: Oxford University Press. 190–215.

Frankenberg-Garcia, A. (2005) 'Pedagogical uses of monolingual and parallel concordances'. *ELT Journal,* 59/3. 189–198.

Frankenberg-Garcia, A. (2007) 'Lost in parallel concordances', in W. Teubert (ed.) *Corpus Linguistics: Critical concepts in linguistics.* London: Routledge, IV. 176–190.

Frankenberg-Garcia, A. (2012a) 'Integrating corpora with everyday language teaching', in J. Thomas and A. Boulton (eds) *Input, process and product: Developments in teaching and language corpora.* Brno: Masaryk University Press. 36–53.

Frankenberg-Garcia, A. (2012b) 'Raising teacher's awareness of corpora'. *Language Teaching,* 45/4. 475–489.

Frankenberg-Garcia, A. (2014) 'How language learners can benefit from corpora, or not' *Recherches en didactique des langues et des cultures: Les Cahiers de l'Acedle,* 1/1. 93–110.

Frankenberg-Garcia, A. and Santos, D. (2003) 'Introducing COMPARA: the Portuguese-English Parallel Corpus', in F. Zanettin, S. Bernardini and D. Stewart (eds.) *Corpora in Translator Education.* Manchester: St. Jerome. 71–87.

Gabrielatos, C. (2005) 'Corpora and language teaching: Just a fling or wedding bells?' *Teaching English as a Second Language Electronic Journal (TESL-EJ),* 8/4. 1–35.

Gavioli, L. (2005) *Exploring corpora for ESP learning.* Amsterdam: John Benjamins.

Granger, S. (2003) 'The international corpus of learner English: A new resource for foreign language learning and teaching and second language acquisition research'. *TESOL Quarterly,* 37/3. 538–546.

Johns, T. (1991) 'Should you be persuaded: Two samples of data-driven learning materials'. *English Language Research Journal,* 4. 1–16.

Kennedy, C. and Miceli, C. (2001) 'An evaluation of intermediate students' approaches to corpus investigation'. *Language Learning & Technology,* 5/3. 77–90.

Kilgarriff, A., Husák, M., Mcadam, K., Rundell, M. and Rychlý, P. (2008) 'GDEX: automatically finding good dictionary examples in a corpus', in E. Bernal and J. Decesaris (eds) *Proceedings of the XIII EURALEX International Congress.* Barcelona: Universitat Pompeu Fabra. 425–433.

Kilgarriff, A., Rychly, P., Smrz, P. and Tugwell, D. (2004) 'The sketch engine', in *Proceedings of Euralex.* Lorient, France. 105–116.

Lenko, A. (2014) 'Is this enough? A qualitative evaluation of the effectiveness of a teacher-training course on the use of corpora in language education'. *ReCALL,* 26/2. 260–278.

Longman Dictionary of Contemporary English. Retrieved from http://www.ldoceonline.com/about.html

Macmillan English Dictionary. Retrieved from http://www.macmillandictionary.com/

McCarthy, M., McCarten, J. and Sandiford, H. (2005) *Touchstone. Student book 1*. Cambridge: Cambridge University Press. Retrieved from http://www.cambridge.org/gb/cambridgeenglish/catalog/adult-courses/touchstone

McEnery, T., Xiao, R. and Tono, Y. (2006) *Corpus-based language studies*. London: Routledge.

Mukherjee, J. (2004) 'Bridging the gap between applied corpus linguistics and the reality of English language teaching in Germany'. *Language and Computers,* 52/1. 239–250.

Römer, U. (2004) 'Comparing real and ideal language learner input', in G. Aston, S. Bernardini and D. Stewart (eds) *Corpora and language learners*. Amsterdam: John Benjamins. 151–168.

Römer, U. (2009) 'Corpus research and practice: What help do teachers need and what can we offer?' in K. Aijmer (ed.) *Corpora and language teaching*. Amsterdam: John Benjamins. 83–98.

Scott, M. (2012) *WordSmith Tools 6.0*. Lexical Analysis Software and Oxford University Press. Retrieved from http://www.lexically.net/wordsmith/

Seidlhofer, B. (2004) 'Research perspectives on teaching English as a lingua franca'. *Annual Review of Applied Linguistics,* 24. 209–239.

Sinclair, J. (1991) *Corpus, concordance and collocation*. Oxford: Oxford University Press.

Someya, Y. (1999) *A corpus-based study of lexical and grammatical features of written business English*. MA dissertation. University of Tokyo.

Tognini-Bonelli, E. (2001) *Corpus linguistics at work*. Amsterdam: John Benjamins.

Widdowson, H. G. (1998) 'Context, community and authentic language'. *TESOL Quarterly*, 32/4. 705–716.

Widdowson, H. G. (2000) 'On the limitations of linguistics applied'. *Applied Linguistics,* 21/1. 3–25.

Widmann, J., Kohn, K. and Ziai, R. (2011) 'The SACODEYL search tool. Exploiting corpora for language learning purposes', in A. Frankenberg-Garcia, L. Flowerdew and G. Aston (eds) *New trends in corpora and language learning*. London: Bloomsbury. 167–178. Retrieved from www.um.es/sacodeyl/

Zipf, G. (1949) *Human behavior and the principle of least effort: An introduction to human ecology*. New York: Hafner.

28

Language Awareness

Agneta M-L. Svalberg

Introduction

In this chapter, I will first define Language Awareness (LA) and provide a brief history of it as a movement in a social context. The next section looks at the theoretical foundations of LA, including cognitive and sociocultural aspects of LA and how individual learners/language users construct their LA. I then address issues of research and teaching; LA is discussed from a complexity perspective before the focus shifts to an LA approach in the language classroom. There are links and references to how LA has been implemented and some examples of common tasks and techniques. Throughout the chapter, I will show that despite their very wide range and diverse manifestations, LA approaches have common theoretical and ideological foundations in first language classrooms (e.g. James and Garrett, 2013) and in second and foreign language classrooms (e.g. Wallace (2013) on critical LA; Eslami-Rasekh (2005) on pragmatic LA; Svalberg (2005) and Zangoei et al. (2014) on consciousness raising).

What is 'Language Awareness'?

Although Language Awareness is usually seen simply as a state of knowledge, it is also an ideological stance towards language and language related matters, and an approach to language teaching. As shown by the definition provided by the Association for Language Awareness (ALA; http://www.languageawareness.org/web.ala/web/about/tout.php), it covers a very wide and disparate field:

> [LA is] explicit knowledge about language, and conscious perception and sensitivity in language learning, language teaching and language use.

A key word in the definition is *about*. LA is knowledge *about* language, not the ability to use it (proficiency). LA covers not only language structure and vocabulary but also, for example, how language works socially and culturally, people's perceptions of and beliefs about language, and how languages are taught and learnt.

The meaning of 'sensitivity' in the definition is not entirely clear, but it seems a useful term to cover the kind of LA which is partly conscious and partly intuitive: for example, a poet's understanding of the effects of linguistic choices on readers or a language-aware speaker's understanding of what is appropriate language in a given context.

LA thus has a cognitive component (explicit knowledge, conscious perception and sensitivity), and an equally important socio-cultural element (learning, teaching and use). The latter is more evident in van Lier's (1995: xi) much quoted definition:

> Language awareness can be defined as an understanding of the human faculty of language and its role in thinking, learning and social life. It includes awareness of power and control through language, and the intricate relationships between language and culture.

Fairclough (2013, first published 1992) considers LA essential, but with the proviso that "a critical orientation is called for by the social circumstances we are living in" (p. 6). Critical Language Awareness (CLA), building on and incorporating critical discourse analysis, thus focuses on the relationship between language and power. A number of researchers, for example contributors to Fairclough (2013), have researched the implementation of CLA in language teaching (see also Janks, 1999; Wallace, 1999).

Hudson (2010) and Mulder (2010) distinguish between LA and *knowledge about language* (KAL). Both authors use the latter term, KAL, to refer to the explicit study, teaching and learning of language structure and LA to encompass all other aspects of language, such as the social, cultural and power dimensions referred to above in van Lier's definition. More frequently, however, LA and KAL have been used as synonyms (e.g. Carter, 1990; van Lier and Corson, 1997), and this practice will be adopted in this chapter.

'The Language Awareness movement': ideological foundations and social context

In the 1970s, demographic and social changes in the UK and resulting social tensions added to concerns about low literacy and lack of interest in modern foreign languages (MFL) among UK school children, providing the impetus for 'the LA movement'.

There had been a wave of West Indian immigration to the UK in the post-war period, and, in 1972, Asian East Africans were expelled from Uganda, with many settling in the UK. An example is the city of Leicester in central England, where a large number of ethnically Indian migrants arrived within a short time span of ten years: Gujarati is now the city's second language, spoken by over 11 per cent of the city's population (UK Census, 2011). As well as its positive effects (such as shaping the UK into the multicultural and multilingual society it is now), for a couple of decades, migration also led to increased racism in some parts of the population and a strong anti-racist reaction in others. In this climate, Eric Hawkins, the founder of the Language Awareness movement, suggested that LA could help foster tolerance and inclusiveness.

These social concerns added to the main impetus for the LA movement, the low English language literacy levels and low uptake of MFLs in UK schools already noted. Hudson (2010) describes it as a teacher-led grassroots movement. Hawkins first proposed LA as a school subject which would bridge the gap between mother tongue English and MFL study in the 1970s (Hawkins 1974, 1999; James, 2005). It would include both learning to investigate language and learning to learn. As a bridging subject, it would create a 'language apprenticeship', requiring MFL and English teachers in schools to collaborate. However, by 1999, Hawkins felt that despite a healthy debate about LA issues, progress on LA in UK schools had been patchy.

Nevertheless, the LA movement has undeniably had an impact. In the UK, work by linguists such as Michael Halliday (from the 1960s), David Crystal, Ron Carter, Dick Hudson and others has brought about a change in thinking, and LA ideas have now become part of the UK school curriculum (Hudson, 2010). Hudson points to the influence of linguistic research and to the active engagement of linguists in language education issues as a source of improvements in MFL teaching and also in the teaching of English (to UK English L1 speakers), which is now less prescriptive and more descriptive, referring to a range of written and spoken varieties alongside standard and literary English. It aims to develop the students' LA by having them investigate, observe and compare languages and acquire the metalanguage to talk about them (ibid.: pp. 35–36). At the same time, Hudson (2010) concedes that provision of these excellent features is by no means guaranteed: "every child *should have* experienced at least *some of these elements* during their school life, subject to obvious reservations about *teacher competence*" (p. 36, my italics). In a study by Pomphrey and Moger (1999), English mother tongue teachers' lack of grammar knowledge impeded their collaboration with MFL teachers, indicating that work still remains to be done to turn LA into more widespread and systematic actual practice.

The UK experience is not entirely unique. Mulder (2010) describes how grammar teaching in Australian schools, when it was re-introduced, having been absent from the syllabus for years, was hampered by gaps in the teachers' subject knowledge. In response to this situation, linguists and teachers collaborated to create a new 'English Language' subject for the last two years of secondary school. Mulder (2010) provides examples of the types of LA tasks used in the course. They involve the explicit study of language, focusing on grammar in context and using real-world texts.

The need for LA in schools has increased rather than diminished due to social developments, and not only in the UK. In Europe, multilingual and multicultural school populations have become the norm rather than the exception. Breidbach et al. (2011: 11), referring to a European Union context, consider that LA as a bridging subject has the potential to link "home and school languages, inside and outside the classroom experiences and the inner personal self with the social context in which the learner lives". LA here clearly encompasses a much wider sphere than just language structure. In addition to what they call the linguistic-systematic dimension, they distinguish cultural-political and social-educational dimensions of LA (p. 13). Breidbach et al. (2011) emphasise the critical and reflective nature of LA and the fact that when it promotes the noticing of differences between languages and varieties, it does so descriptively, without value judgement.

The Association for Language Awareness (ALA) was founded in 1994 to support and promote LA in research and practice "across the whole breadth of Language Awareness". Although it originated in the UK, the organisation now has an international membership, runs a biennial international conference and edits a peer-reviewed research journal (*Language Awareness*). In Francophone and German-speaking Europe, the EDiLiC association (*Education et Diversité Linguistic et Culturelle*) has a similar mission but focuses more specifically on teaching in schools. It also organises biennial international conferences. As is evident in the EDiLiC name, it shares the LA ideology of tolerance and inclusiveness.

Language Awareness and second/foreign language learning: theoretical foundations and social attitudes

In the 1970s and 1980s, the LA proposition that conscious linguistic knowledge would facilitate language learning contrasted both with earlier behaviourist views and with Stephen Krashen's very influential theories (Krashen, 1985), which posited that second/foreign languages (L2s) were acquired in a manner very similar to children's learning of the mother tongue (L1), primarily through exposure to new language. Early communicative language teaching (CLT; see Thornbury, this volume), which relied on unconscious acquisition through meaningful input and practice and excluded explicit instruction of form, seemed validated by Krashen's theories, which helped make explicit teaching/learning about language unfashionable in the UK and the US and countries most influenced by them. In this context, an LA approach, such as that proposed by Eric Hawkins at this time, was downright 'heretical' (James, 2005).

In its early, exclusively meaning-focused version, CLT did not live up to its promise. Observing this, EFL teachers in particular started reintroducing the explicit teaching of form alongside more communicative, meaning-focused elements. In this, they were supported by Long's (Long, 1991; Long and Robinson, 1998) 'focus on form' construct, which referred to the teaching of specific grammar features as and when student difficulties first became evident in a communicative context. Focus on form contrasted with a traditional approach to grammar teaching, where grammar was pre-sequenced in the language syllabus, and which Long called focus on forms. An indication of how far grammar teaching had fallen out of favour is the title of Doughty's (1991) paper, which started by stating what may now seem obvious: "Second language instruction does make a difference." It showed that learners produced more accurate relative clauses if they had been explicitly taught about them than if they had simply been exposed to them as input.

Whatever the fashion in ELT, LA proponents in the UK in the 1980s and 1990s continued their efforts to influence teaching and learning. Sporadically, the UK government supported their efforts, most notably by funding the Language in the National Curriculum (LINC) project, led by Ron Carter (1989–1992), which produced language teaching materials for schools and organised related teacher training (Carter, 1990, 1994; see chapter references for *LINC* sample material). The project incorporated principles of critical LA and critical discourse analysis. Historical, social and dialectal variation was discussed. The descriptive, inclusive approach to language was, however, seen as subversive and a poor model for school children and so, having spent over £20 million on the project, the UK government stopped the already completed materials from being printed.

Governments and social attitudes, however, change. A recent sign of progress was a project which produced materials, now freely available, on English speaking and listening skills for 14- to 19-year-olds (Shortis et al., 2011, *All Talk*, funded by British Telecom; see chapter references for link). Its interactive, awareness-raising tasks deal with English as used in the UK, often examining non-standard language, and give young people the opportunity to reflect on their own language, including identity issues and the effect of linguistic choices. It signals a substantial shift in social attitudes to language in which the LA movement has played an important part.

Below I will discuss some cognitive and sociocultural factors which support the argument for conscious learning about language, especially in foreign language learning.

Cognitive factors in developing LA

Although the relationship between instruction and learning is complex, research has shown that, for other than very young children, the explicit study of and conscious reflection on language facilitate learning (see extensive reviews in Ellis, 1994; Spada, 1997; see also Collins and Marsden, this volume). The case for LA has been particularly bolstered by research findings regarding the role of 'noticing' and attention in language learning. Based initially on observations during his own learning of Portuguese, Schmidt (1990, 1995) suggested that noticing was a necessary first step in the learning process. A large body of research has since helped us understand the role of noticing and attention in more depth. It generally confirms that noticing facilitates learning, but also that it may not be sufficient. In an effort to unravel why, Schmidt (1995) differentiates between levels of awareness, for example whether something has merely been noticed or noticed and understood (see also Truscott, 1998). Izumi (2002) takes this further, arguing that the effect of noticing on learning depends on how the noticed information is processed. In-depth process-ing might include learners making links to prior knowledge, making sense of what they have noticed and retaining it in long-term memory. Some of the research on noticing is concerned with teachers' corrective feedback (Mackey, 2006; see also Mackey, Park and Tagarelli, this vol-ume), or more generally with if and when learners 'notice the gap' (Swain, 1995) between their own output and an output model provided, for example, by the textbook or a more proficient speaker.

A challenge for teaching and learning is that any kind of noticing requires attention, which is a limited resource. Hence, learners will only notice some, but not all, of the information about the language potentially available in the input, and not necessarily what the teacher wishes them to notice. What they notice is partly idiosyncratic and partly due to natural inclinations. For example, we all normally attend to meaning before form (Van Patten, 1990), so learners may not notice the word order or the form of verbs in a text.

To promote and direct learners' noticing, teachers and researchers sometimes use a technique called visual input enhancement, or textual enhancement of input (TE). In written text, TE con-sists of formatting, size or colour to make specific linguistic features more salient, for example underlining words indicating future time in a text or using highlighter on expressions of degree, thereby drawing the learners' attention to them. Research suggests that TE increases the likeli-hood of learners' noticing the enhanced features (what the teacher wants them to notice), but studies are difficult to compare because of variation in, for example, the type of TE applied and the features targeted (Han et al., 2008).

Furthermore, LA is naturally enhanced by bi/multilingualism. Knowing another/other lan-guages affords a range of general cognitive advantages (Adesope et al., 2010) such as heightened noticing ability, improved problem-solving skills and increased creativity (Furlong, 2009). Jessner (1999, 2008) and Herdina and Jessner (2000) argue that third (and subsequent) language acquisi-tion is different from L2 acquisition due to the LA the multilingual learner has already developed.

Engagement with language (EWL)

The predominant view of learning among LA proponents is sociocultural (Vygotsky, 1978; Lantolf and Becket, 2009; see Negueruela-Azarola and García, this volume) and constructivist (Kaufman, 2004); that is to say, learning is said to emerge from a process of interaction in which the learner is actively involved. Knowledge about the language is not primarily transmitted either from the teacher, peers or materials, but is constructed by the learner. The environment in which this takes place can be teacher–student interaction or pair/group work in a classroom, or it might be social interaction outside the classroom. Individual learners/language users may also notice features of the language and reflect on them on their own, but it is assumed that interac-tion for the purpose of learning (inside or outside the classroom) at some point will facilitate this conscious construction of knowledge.

Svalberg (2009) has called the process through which LA is created *engagement with language* (EWL). As Figure 28.1 shows, during EWL, the learner draws on the LA they already have (prior knowledge) to create new or enhanced LA, which they can then draw on in further EWL, and so on.

EWL is different from learning processes in other subjects, for example, maths or history, in a number of ways. One is that language is both the object and the medium of learning, i.e. we teach and learn language through language. Another important difference is the essentially social nature of language, which means that EWL can take place as much outside the classroom as inside it. Language-aware individuals might, for example, notice and reflect on features of

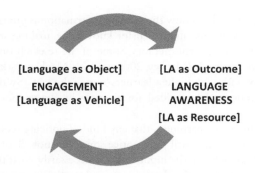

Figure 28.1   The Engagement with Language – Language Awareness cycle

Source: Svalberg, 2009: 248. Reproduced with permission.

language in the newspaper they read or in the interaction with traders in the fruit and vegetable market. Whether the language used is their first, second or a foreign language, such EWL is likely to enhance their LA. The social aspects of language also mean that identity and cultural issues are likely to play an important part in the learning process. EWL thus has cognitive, affective and social characteristics which interact mutually and with external factors. Ideally, the engaged individual is focused on the language task, willing and interactive. The LA practitioner strives to create a learning environment which facilitates high quality EWL.

Chik (2011) suggests that LA is developmental. In a narrative enquiry of the LA of 8- to 18-year-old English language learners in Hong Kong over 2.5 years, interviews revealed that the students developed awareness of English as an academic subject first, followed by English as a language system, followed by English use in context. She concluded that their awareness of themselves as language learners in a particular socio-cultural and education context was, and needed to be, the first stage in their English language development.

The affective dimension of EWL can have a decisive influence on its quality, and hence on the knowledge that emerges from it. Bolitho et al. (2003: 256) suggest that affect, our emotions, can stimulate "a fuller use of the resources of the brain. Positive attitudes, self-esteem, and emotive involvement help to fire neural paths between many areas of the brain and to achieve the multidimensional representation needed for deep processing of language". This applies at any age but plays an especially important role with very young learners (Kearney and Ahn, 2014), whose cognitive EWL may not be very deep for developmental reasons.

Language Awareness and complexity

Both language itself and the language learning process are complex dynamic phenomena (Ellis and Larsen-Freeman, 2010), and many LA researchers adopt a complexity approach to research (Jessner, 1999, 2008; Herdina and Jessner, 2000; van Lier, 2004; see also Mercer, this volume, for further discussion of complexity and language teaching). EWL is complex and dynamic, and learning emerges from it through the interaction of multiple internal factors (cognitive, affective and social) and external influences.

Feryok (2010) argues for the use of a complex systems theory framework in teacher cognition research. Considering student teachers' EWL as complex and dynamic helped Svalberg (2015a) and Svalberg and Askham (2014) understand how learning emerged from collaborative grammar awareness group-work. It showed individuals enacting engagement in very different but potentially equally effective ways. The case study in Svalberg and Askham (2014), drawing on diary, interview and interaction data, shows how a particular learner, 'Emily', despite usually saying very little, is deeply engaged and benefitting from listening to more talkative peers. She learns not only when they are right but also from their errors and doubts. At the same time, her occasional contributions are valuable to the group's knowledge construction. Her approach contrasts with that of 'Isabelle', who, being aware of often being wrong, still prefers to develop knowledge by verbalising her understanding and receiving peer feedback. In the group of five to six students (depending on the session), Emily and Isabelle complement each other, contributing positively to each other's learning and to the EWL of the whole group.

The implications for research of taking a complex systems perspective are discussed with great clarity by Larsen-Freeman and Cameron (2008). One is a greater emphasis on understanding the dynamic learning *process* than on measuring learning at specific points (although the latter may complement the former); absence of a measurable learning gain does not necessarily mean that no learning has taken place. Zheng (2014: 369), for example, describes the development of learners' awareness of L1–L2 semantic differences as "slow, unpredictable, and characterized by phases of incremental growth, stabilization, and attrition". Svalberg (2015b) observes student teachers developing an understanding of different aspects of the term 'phrase' (e.g. noun phrase, adjective phrase) and has paraphrased the stages of understanding as: "'phrase' is a label attached to some strings of words", "one phrase can be inside another phrase" (i.e. the idea of embedding), "each phrase has a head" and "a phrase can consist of just one word". Although all are correct and necessary insights for the acquisition of the construct, none on its own would necessarily result in measurable success in identifying phrases in a text. The gradual process we call learning involves assembling and connecting a number of such insights over a period of time.

Complexity-oriented research tends to take a holistic approach, drawing on, for example, case studies, ethnographic research and certain types of action research. There is thus great scope for language teachers to carry out LA research in their own classrooms (Svalberg, 2012). The challenge for the researcher and the teacher-researcher is to decide how to delimit the complex system they are investigating to a manageable set of factors.

Teachers' Language Awareness

As explained above, LA is about much more than grammar, but grammar is what studies on teachers' LA tend to focus on. They tend to find that LA about grammar is less than expected or less than most researchers consider necessary for teaching (e.g. in Hong Kong, Andrews, 1999; in the UK, Alderson et al., 1997, and Alderson and Horák, 2010), but in Brazil, for example, the opposite has also been found (Bailer et al., 2014). Teachers who themselves have not been taught grammar explicitly may develop their LA by teaching, for example, from pedagogic grammars – though knowledge acquired in this way is not necessarily accurate (Berry, 2014), and some teachers instead use strategies to avoid teaching grammar or answering students' grammar questions (Borg, 2001, 2005; Sanchez and Borg, 2014). Hence, it is important that student teachers develop explicit grammar awareness during language teacher education (LTE; see Johnson, this volume).

Well-developed LA has the potential to make teachers autonomous (Kumaravadivelu, 2012), i.e. not dependent on textbooks but able to adopt, adapt, supplement or replace material according to their learners' needs. Andrews (2003) points out that in addition to proficiency and knowledge about the language, teachers need pedagogical content knowledge, that is, knowing how to apply their LA in the classroom. Language teachers need to be able to explain and answer student questions; evaluate the appropriateness of text books and materials for their own students and teaching context; and design their own tasks when necessary.

On many LTE programmes, grammar is taught separately from pedagogy. Wright (2002) is critical of this practice, emphasising the need to make the connection between theoretical knowledge and classroom practice explicit. Wright emphasises that LA development in LTE requires working with data, for example corpus data, classroom talk samples and learner language, which the student teachers respond to affectively and analyse linguistically. He emphasises the need for time to talk about the material and suggests that a development session about a specific grammatical feature be immediately followed by a task where the student teachers write materials and/or plan a lesson to teach the feature to a specific group of learners.

Student teachers are likely to model their own teaching on teaching they have experienced themselves, including sessions experienced during LTE programmes. Hence, using an LA approach with student teachers may not only be effective in achieving the immediate curriculum goals (e.g. enhanced grammar awareness) but can also provide the students with a model they can reflect on and draw on in their own practice if and when it is appropriate. Next, I will discuss what characterises an LA approach in the classroom.

A Language Awareness approach to language learning and language teacher education (LTE)

LA approaches to language learning and teaching are used all over the world for a range of purposes, and hence adapted to local contexts. They are related by their adherence to the LA principles discussed earlier and expanded on here.

In the USA, for example, some states provide school children with experiences of languages other than English which are not taught as subjects in themselves but for the bridging, 'language apprenticeship' purpose envisioned by Hawkins and discussed earlier. The languages may be ones present in the local community or spoken by an available member of staff. Parents who speak other L1s may be asked to contribute to sessions where they share their own language and their culture with the students. This is called *world language learning* (WLL; see chapter references). The emphasis is very much on language and culture, and fostering positive attitudes in the children to languages other than English and to the communities that speak them. Kearney and Ahn (2014) describe the engagement with language (EWL) of preschool children in a WLL class. The children are not meant to fully master the Korean and Spanish to which they are exposed in this class, but they are excited to try to understand and perhaps use the new and different sounds and script. Their eagerness to engage makes it likely that some learning will emerge, whether in the form of memorised language or changes in beliefs and attitudes.

In Europe, and sometimes elsewhere, the term *awakening to languages* (AtL) is widely used to refer to similar LA practices for bridging purposes in schools, often with young learners. Lourenço and Andrade (2014) describe AtL classes in a pre-primary school in Portugal, where the students are exposed to a range of languages. Activities include listening to songs, comparing words in different languages, writing in a different script and so on. The study focused on one particular aspect of the lessons and found that an AtL group of students increased their phonological awareness, while a control group did not. Examples and accounts of AtL practice in a number of countries can be found on the EDiLiC website (see chapter references).

Borg (1994), Wright and Bolitho (1993) and Wright (2002) outline some common characteristics of an LA approach in some detail (see also Kumaravadivelu, 1994). Although they refer to language teacher education, the same principles apply to LA in second/foreign language teaching and also to LA to teach L1 or world languages (see earlier). The different contexts and purposes of learning in these settings clearly have an important bearing on how LA is implemented, but the principles remain the same.

LA practitioners do not try to transmit knowledge to their learners. Instead, they involve the learners both cognitively and affectively in exploration and investigation of language (i.e. EWL). Samples of language in use are treated as data, which the learners analyse, for example, to discover a rule, correct and explain errors, or to interpret and discuss a writer's reasons for choosing a particular word, phrase or grammatical form over another. In Kearney and Ahn's (2014) study with young learners, the affective aspect of EWL arguably played a relatively greater role than it might with adults, who are able to draw on more developed cognitive resources, but the principle of active engagement applies equally to both.

An LA approach to language teaching/learning thus involves the learners in the analysis and discussion of language (also called 'languaging', Swain et al., 2002; or 'grammaring', Larsen-Freeman, 2003). Some of the discussion may be with the teacher, but typically there is a great deal of peer interaction. The learners' active involvement and hence their interest in the task is crucial, as the aim is high quality EWL. LA tasks do not on their own develop learners' communicative competence. In a language course (in contrast to a language teacher education programme), they may be combined with communicative practice tasks to give the students opportunity to apply their enhanced LA in meaningful practice. LA thus does not replace but complements more communicative, meaning-focused activity.

An LA approach to language teaching will often involve so called *consciousness raising* (CR) tasks. CR is synonymous with 'awareness raising', but CR is the more frequent term. Such tasks can refer to any aspect of the language or language learning and teaching, for example attitudes to language varieties, pragmatic conventions, phonological features, genre characteristics, learning styles – the list is potentially endless. Tomlinson (1994) provides examples of pragmatic awareness tasks, and Svalberg (2005) shows a set of grammar awareness tasks, both intended for EFL contexts. In relation to L1 teaching, Alim (2005) discusses the use of critical LA (Fairclough, 2013) in US schools as a means of helping children understand sociolinguistic issues that affect them, often negatively, and empowering them in the process. The previously noted 'All Talk' material for UK schools (Shortis et al., 2011) is similar in that it raises the students' awareness of varieties of English in their social context and issues surrounding their use.

In the teaching of grammar, CR tasks contrast with practice activities. As pointed out by Ellis (2002) with respect to EFL, the two differ primarily in their purpose and in what they require learners to do. A practice activity helps learners move knowledge from short-term memory to long-term memory, usually by repeated production opportunities. The purpose of a CR task is instead to help learners develop explicit understanding of the target feature. It will involve noticing, but it may or may not involve production. Typically, the learners will be asked to identify a specific feature in a text and to discuss or draw some conclusions from what they have noticed. Ellis (2002: 173) concludes that a CR approach "accords with progressive views of education as a process of discovery through problem-solving tasks".

Some textbooks include so called 'discovery' tasks. The teacher needs to evaluate them critically. Are they sufficiently challenging to make learners engage with the language in some depth? Are they likely to seem relevant and interesting to the learners? A good CR/discovery task should result in cognitive, affective and social EWL. To make the task more meaningful and less mechanical, it needs to generate 'cognitive conflict' (Svalberg, 2015a, 2015b; Tocalli-Beller and Swain, 2005); the level of challenge should stimulate peer negotiation and require the students to justify their solutions.

Teachers using an LA approach tend to focus on how language is actually used, what speakers' and writers' choices mean, and what alternatives were available to them. A frequently used technique in LA is TE (textual enhancement; see above). The TE may be done by the teacher or text book writer, but it can also be learner-produced (Svalberg, 2012: 383), as when learners are asked to underline or highlight particular features in text. They may then be asked to draw some conclusion about the language on the basis of their observations. Another popular awareness raising task type is dictogloss, of which there are many variations and which can be used at any level (see for example Shak, 2006, for its use in a primary school).

Learners can also carry out corpus-based enquiries in class, for example on language varieties, collocations or word grammar (Sinclair, 2004). Corpus data provide examples of authentic use of both written and spoken language of different kinds. Links are provided at the end of this chapter to the freely available British National Corpus Sampler (2,000,000 words of spoken and written English) and the related 'simple search' facility provided by the British Library. Corpus data may take the form of simple lists of examples or sets of 'concordance lines' with a certain number of words to the left and right of the target feature. Gabrielatos (2005) and Frankenberg-Garcia (this volume) provide examples of the use of corpus data and point out some of the pitfalls. One limitation is that teachers may require some training in how to use corpora and, depending on the task, so might students. In L2 teaching, the fact that each line represents a different context, which is not even a complete sentence, can make text less meaningful and potentially harder to process. But, especially at higher levels of proficiency and in teacher education, corpus-based tasks can be a useful awareness raising tool (Farr, 2008).

The recognition that explicit reflection and discussion about language is facilitative has also renewed interest in using the learners' L1 knowledge as a resource in developing LA. Comparisons of L1 and L2 can be carried out on all aspects of the language, for example sentence structure, or how politeness is expressed. In a bilingual context, White and Horst (2012) found that raising Canadian school children's awareness of cognates in English and French was successful and useful to the learners. In foreign language classes where students and teachers share an L1, it allows them to draw on prior knowledge and has the potential to foster noticing of features in both languages (see Kerr, this volume, for further discussion of own-language use in ELT).

Conclusion

This chapter has provided an overview of LA as a state of knowledge, as a language-related ideology and as an approach to language learning and teaching. The sociocultural and political context from which it emerged, and in which it still exists, is one of population movements and consequent increases in multilingualism and multiculturalism (e.g. 700 Syrian refugees per week arriving in Sweden in 2014). LA has an important role to play in this context. Learning each others' languages takes time and is often not practicable, but learning *about* them and what they express (e.g. culture, identity) can happen more quickly and could reduce a sense of 'otherness'.

The LA inquiry approach is also a way of teaching regular language classes, whether modern foreign languages, English as a foreign or second language, or learners' L1. By training learners and teachers in noticing and analytical skills, it encourages learner autonomy and criticality. Asking the simple question 'What is it language users/language learners need to become aware of?' forces us to formulate not only how language works as a system but also how it works socially and for whom. The ideological dimension of LA then becomes as important as its teaching approaches and techniques.

Discussion questions

- What is your perspective on the place of grammar terminology (metalanguage) in language teaching and learning? What are the implications in your classroom?
- To what extent do you think learners in your particular context might (or might not)

benefit from an LA approach in a specific area (e.g. language attitudes, language and power, language and culture, academic writing, grammar, pronunciation etc.)?

• How well do you understand your learners' EWL (engagement with language)? Obtain your students' permission to record them solving a consciousness-raising task. Listen to/view it repeatedly (or transcribe it) and note down how cognitively, affectively and socially engaged they are and how they go about being engaged. Try to understand what might have helped or hindered each student's EWL, and how the task – or the surrounding setting – might be improved.

Related topics

Bilingual education in a multilingual world; Cognitive perspectives on classroom language learning; Communicative language teaching in theory and practice; Complexity and language teaching; Corpora in the classroom; English for speakers of other languages; Errors, corrective feedback and repair; Language teacher education; Method, methods and methodology; Sociocultural theory and the language classroom.

Further reading

Language Awareness is the official journal of the *Association for Language Awareness*. It publishes papers across the whole range of LA fields and concern and can be found at: http://www.tandfonline.com/loi/rmla20#.VcsGe3FVhHw

Berry, R. (2012) *English grammar: A resource book for students*. London: Routledge. (This resource is likely to enhance the grammar awareness of both teachers and students by drawing attention to the atypical as well as the typical. Examples and tasks, often using authentic language, are interesting puzzles, and the explanations are very clear.)

Bolitho, R. and Tomlinson, B. (2005) *Discover English: A language analysis for teachers*. London: MacMillan. (This book focuses on grammar and vocabulary and contains exercises with solutions. It is designed to train teachers' language analytical skills and enhance their LA in these areas.)

Fairclough, N. (ed.) (2013) *Critical language awareness*. London: Routledge. (An excellent introduction to language and power issues.)

van Lier, L. (1995) *Introducing language awareness*. London: Penguin. (A very accessible introductory text. van Lier's definition of LA, quoted at the beginning of this chapter, gives a good indication of the author's sociocultural approach to LA.)

References

Adesope, O. O., Lavin, T., Thompson, T. and Ungerleider, C. (2010) 'A systematic review and meta-analysis of the cognitive correlates of bilingualism'. *Review of Educational Research*, 80/2. 207–245.

Alderson, J. C. and Horák, T. (2010) *Metalinguistic knowledge of undergraduate students of English language and linguistics*. Final report on a project funded by the Subject Centre for Languages, Linguistics and Area Studies in Higher Education, Lancaster University. Retried August 27, 2014, from https://www.llas.ac.uk//resourcedownloads/3324/final_report_on_hea_project.pdf

Alderson, J. C., Steel, D. and Clapham, C. (1997) 'Metalinguistic knowledge, language aptitude and language proficiency'. *Language Teaching Research*, 1/2. 93–121.

Alim, S. H. (2005) 'Critical Language Awareness in the United States: Revisiting issues and revising pedagogies in a resegregated society'. *Educational Researcher*, 34/24. 24–31.

Andrews, S. J. (1999) 'All these like little name things' – A comparative study of language teachers' explicit knowledge of grammar and grammatical terminology'. *Language Awareness*, 8/3–4. 143–59.

Andrews, S. J. (2003) 'Teacher Language Awareness and the professional knowledge base of the L2 teacher'. *Language Awareness*, 12/2. 81–95.

Bailer, C., Nogueira, V. C., D'Ely, R. C. and Souza, F. (2014) 'An investigation on explicit knowledge with Brazilian EFL teachers'. *Revista Intercâmbio*, 28. 111–131.

Berry, R. (2014) 'Grammar myths'. *Language Awareness,* 24/1. 15–37.

Bolitho, R., Carter, R., Hughes, R., Ivanic, R., Masuhara, H. and Tomlinson, B. (2003) 'Ten questions about Language Awareness'. *ELT Journal,* 57/3. 251–259.

Borg, S. (1994) 'Language awareness as a methodology: Implications for teachers and teacher training'. *Language Awareness,* 3/2. 61–71.

Borg, S. (2001) 'Self-perception and practice in teaching grammar'. *ELT Journal,* 55/1. 21–29.

Borg, S. (2005) 'Experience, knowledge about language and classroom practice in teaching grammar', in N. Bartels (ed.) *Applied linguistics and language teacher education.* New York: Springer. 325–340.

Breidbach, S., Elsner, D. and Young, A. (eds) (2011) *Mehrsprachigkeit in Schule und Unterricht, Vol. 13: Language awareness in teacher education: Cultural-political and social-educational perspectives.* Frankfurt am Main, DEU: Peter Lang.

Carter, R. (1989–1992) *LINC* material sample. Retrieved from ftp://ftp.phon.ucl.ac.uk/pub/Word-Grammar/ec/linc1–12.pdf

Carter, R. (1990) *Knowledge about language and the curriculum: The LINC reader.* London: Hodder & Stoughton.

Carter, R. (1994) 'Knowledge about language in the curriculum', in S. Brindley (ed.) *Teaching English.* London: Open University Press. 223–234.

Chik, A. (2011) 'Learner Language Awareness development among Asian learners and implications for teacher education', in S. Breidbach, D. Elsner and A. Young (eds) *Mehrsprachigkeit in Schule und Unterricht, Vol. 13: Language awareness in teacher education: Cultural-political and social-educational perspectives.* Frankfurt am Main, DEU: Peter Lang. 23–39.

Doughty, C. (1991) 'Second language instruction does make a difference. Evidence from an empirical study of SL relativization'. *Studies in Second Language Acquisition,* 13/4. 431–469.

Ellis, N. C. and Larsen-Freeman, D. (eds) (2010) *Language as a complex adaptive system.* Oxford: Wiley-Blackwell.

Ellis, R. (1994) *The study of second language acquisition.* Oxford: Oxford University Press.

Ellis, R. (2002) 'Grammar teaching; practice or consciousness raising?', in J. C. Richards and W. A. Renandya (eds) *Methodology: An anthology of current practice.* Cambridge: Cambridge University Press. 167–174.

Eslami-Rasekh, Z. (2005) Raising the pragmatic awareness of language learners. *ELT Journal,* 59/3. 199–208.

Fairclough, N. (ed.) (2013) *Critical Language Awareness.* London: Routledge.

Farr, F. (2008) 'Evaluating the use of corpus-based instruction in a language teacher education context: Perspectives from the users'. *Language Awareness,* 17/1. 25–43.

Feryok, A. (2010) 'Language teacher cognitions: Complex dynamic systems?' *System,* 38/2. 272–279.

Furlong, A. (2009) 'The relation of plurilingualism/culturalism to creativity: A matter of perception'. *International Journal of Multilingualism,* 6/4. 343–368.

Gabrielatos, C. (2005) 'Corpora and language teaching: Just a fling or wedding bells?' *TESL-EJ,* 8/4. 1–34. Retrieved from http://tesl-ej.org/ej32/a1.html

Han, Z., Park, E. S. and Combs, C. (2008) 'Textual enhancement of input: Issues and possibilities'. *Applied Linguistics,* 29/4. 597–618.

Hawkins, E. (1974) 'Modern languages in the curriculum', in G. Perren (ed.) *The space between: English and foreign languages at school.* London: CILT.

Hawkins, E. (1999) 'Foreign language study and Language Awareness'. *Language Awareness,* 8. 124–142.

Herdina, P. and Jessner, U. (2000) 'The dynamics of third language acquisition', in J. Cenoz and U. Jessner (eds) *English in Europe: The acquisition of a third language.* Clevedon, UK: Multilingual Matters. 84–97.

Hudson, R. (2010) 'How linguistics has influenced schools in England', in K. Denham and A. Lobeck (eds) *Linguistics at school. Language awareness in primary and secondary education.* Cambridge: Cambridge University Press. 35–47.

Izumi, S. (2002) 'Output, input enhancement and the noticing hypothesis (an experimental study on English second language relativization)'. *Studies in Second Language Acquisition,* 24/4. 541–577.

James, C. (2005) 'Eric Hawkins: A tribute on your ninetieth birthday'. *Language Awareness,* 14/2–3. 80–81.

James, C. and Garrett, P. (2013) *Language awareness in the classroom.* Abingdon, UK: Routledge.

Janks, H. (1999) 'Critical language awareness journals and student identities'. *Language Awareness,* 8/2. 111–122.

Jessner, U. (1999) 'Metalinguistic awareness in multilinguals: Cognitive aspects of third language learning'. *Language Awareness,* 8/3–4. 201–209.

Jessner, U. (2008) 'A DST model of multilingualism and the role of metalinguistic awareness'. *Modern Language Journal,* 92/2. 270–283.

Kaufman, D. (2004) 'Constructivist issues in language learning and teaching'. *Annual Review of Applied Linguistics,* 24. 303–319.

Kearney, E. and Ahn, S.-Y. (2014) 'Preschool world language learners' engagement with language: What are the possibilities?' *Language Awareness*, 23/4. 319–333.

Krashen, S. (1985) *The input hypothesis: Issues and implications*. London: Longman.

Kumaravadivelu, B. (1994) 'The postmethod condition: (E)merging strategies for second/foreign language teaching'. *TESOL Quarterly*, 28/1. 27–48.

Kumaravadivelu, B. (2012) *Language teacher education for a global society*. London: Routledge.

Lantolf, J. P. and Beckett, T. G. (2009) 'Research timeline: Sociocultural theory and second language acquisition'. *Language Teaching*, 42/4. 459–475.

Larsen-Freeman, D. (2003) *Teaching language: From grammar to grammaring*. Boston, MA: Thomson/Heinle.

Larsen-Freeman, D. and Cameron, L. (2008) 'Research methodology on language development from a complex systems perspective'. *Modern Language Journal*, 92/2. 200–213.

Long, M. (1991) 'Focus on form: A design feature in language teaching methodology', in K. de Bot, R. Ginsberg and C. Kramsch (eds) *Foreign language research in cross-cultural perspective*. Amsterdam: John Benjamins. 39–52.

Long, M. and Robinson, P. (1998) 'Focus on form: Theory, research, and practice', in C. Doughty and J. Williams (eds) *Focus on form in classroom second language acquisition*. Cambridge: Cambridge University Press. 15–63.

Lourenço, M. and Andrade, A. I. (2014) 'Promoting phonological awareness in pre-primary education: Possibilities of the 'awakening to languages' approach'. *Language Awareness*, 23/4. 304–318.

Mackey, A. (2006) 'Feedback, noticing and instructed second language learning'. *Applied Linguistics*, 27/3. 405–430.

Mulder, J. (2010) 'Envisioning linguistics in secondary education: An Australian exemplar', in K. Denham and A. Lobeck (eds) *Linguistics at school. Language awareness in primary and secondary education*. Cambridge: Cambridge University Press. 62–75.

Pomphrey, C. and Moger, R. (1999) 'Cross-subject dialogue about language: Attitudes and perceptions of PGCE students of English and modern languages'. *Language Awareness*, 8/3–4. 223–236.

Sanchez, H. S. and Borg, S. (2014) 'Insights into L2 teachers' pedagogical content knowledge: A cognitive perspective on their grammar explanations'. *System*, 44. 45–53.

Schmidt, R. (1990) 'The role of consciousness in second language learning'. *Applied Linguistics*, 11/2. 129–158.

Schmidt, R. (1995) 'Consciousness and foreign language learning: A tutorial on attention and awareness in learning', in R. Schmidt (ed.) *Attention and awareness in second language learning*. Honolulu, Hawai'i: Second Language Teaching and Curriculum Center, University of Hawai'i. 1–63.

Shak, J. (2006) 'Children using dictogloss to focus on form'. *Reflections on English Language Teaching*, 5/2. 47–62.

Shortis, T., Blake, J. and Powell, A. (2011) *All talk. English 14–19*. BT Learning and Skills. Retrieved from http://www.btplc.com/BetterFuture/ConnectedSociety/LearningAndSkillsFreeResources/AllTalk/

Sinclair, J. (ed.) (2004) *How to use corpora in language teaching*. Amsterdam: John Benjamins.

Spada, N. (1997) 'Form-focussed instruction and second language acquisition: A review of classroom and laboratory research'. *Language Teaching*, 30/2. 73–87.

Svalberg, A. M.-L. (2005) 'Consciousness raising activities in some Lebanese English language classrooms: Teacher perceptions and learner engagement'. *Language Awareness*, 14/2–3. 70–190.

Svalberg, A. M.-L. (2009) 'Engagement with language: Developing a construct'. *Language Awareness*, 18/3–4. 242–258.

Svalberg, A. M.-L. (2012) 'Language Awareness in language learning and teaching: A research agenda'. *Language Teaching*, 45/3. 376–388.

Svalberg, A. M.-L. (2015a) 'Peer interaction, cognitive conflict and anxiety on a grammar awareness course for language teachers', in C. Finkbeiner and A. M.-L. Svalberg (eds) *Awareness matters – language, culture, literacy*. 137–156.

Svalberg, A. M-L. (2015b) 'Reclaiming the relevance of language teacher cognition: Understanding the complex processes in developing student teachers' knowledge about grammar', in M. Kubanyiova and A. Feryok (eds) *Modern Language Journal, Special Issue: Language Teacher Cognition in Applied Linguistics Research: Revisiting the Territory, Redrawing the Boundaries, Reclaiming the Relevance*. 99/3. 529–545.

Svalberg, A. M.-L. and Askham, J. (2014) 'Student teachers' collaborative construction of grammar awareness: The case of a highly competent learner'. *Language Awareness*, 23/1–2. 122–136.

Swain, M. (1995) 'Three functions of output in second language learning', in G. Cook and B. Seidlhofer (eds) *Principles and practice in applied linguistics: Studies in honour of H. G. Widdowson*. Oxford: Oxford University Press. 125–144.

Swain, M., Brooks, L. and Tocalli-Beller, A. (2002) 'Peer-peer dialogue as a means of second language learning'. *Annual Review of Applied Linguistics*, 22. 171–185. doi:10.1017/S0267190502000090.

Tocalli-Beller, A. and Swain, M. (2005) 'Reformulation: The cognitive conflict and L2 learning it generates'. *International Journal of Applied Linguistics*, 15/1. 5–28.

Tomlinson, B. (1994) 'Pragmatic awareness activities'. *Language Awareness*, 3/3. 119–129.

Truscott, J. (1998) 'Noticing in second language acquisition: A critical review', *Second Language Research*, 14/2. 103–135.

van Lier, L. (2004) *The ecology and semiotics of language learning: A sociocultural perspective.* Dordrecht, the Netherlands: Kluwer.

van Lier, L. (1995) *Introducing Language Awareness.* London: Penguin.

van Lier, L. and Corson, D. (eds) (1997) *Encyclopedia of language and education, vol. 6: Knowledge about language.* Amsterdam: Kluwer.

Van Patten, B. (1990) 'Attending to form and content in the input: An experiment in consciousness'. *Studies in Second Language Acquisition*, 12. 287–301.

Vygotsky, L. (1978) *Mind in society.* Cambridge, MA: Harvard University Press.

Wallace, C. (1999) 'Critical Language Awareness: Key principles for a course in critical reading'. *Language Awareness*, 8/2. 98–110.

Wallace, C. (2013) Critical literacy awareness in the EFL classroom. In N. Fairclough (ed.) *Critical Language Awareness.* Abingdon, UK: Routledge. 50–81.

White, J. L. and Horst, M. (2012) 'Cognate awareness–raising in late childhood: Teachable and useful'. *Language Awareness*, 21/1–2. 181–196.

WLL (World Languages; Early Language Experiences.) State of Washington, Office of Superintendent of Public Instruction. Retrieved from http://www.k12.wa.us/WorldLanguages/WorldLanguageExperiences.aspx

Wright, T. (2002) 'Doing LA. Issues for language study in language teacher education', in H. R. Trappes-Lomax and G. Ferguson (eds) *Language in language teacher education. Part 2.* Amsterdam: John Benjamins. 113–130.

Wright, T. and Bolitho, R. (1993) 'Language awareness: A missing link in language teacher education?' *ELT Journal*, 47/4. 292–304.

Zangoei, A., Nourmohammadi, E. and Derakhshan, A. (2014) The effect of consciousness–raising listening prompts on the development of the speech act of apology in an Iranian EFL context. *SAGE Open,* 4/2. 1–10.

Zheng, Y. (2014) 'The fluctuating development of cross–linguistic semantic awareness: A longitudinal multiple case-study'. *Language Awareness,* 23/4. 369–388.

Online sources

Association for Language Awareness. Retrieved from http://www.languageawareness.org/web.ala/web/about/tout.php

British National Corpus Sampler (written and spoken English). Retrieved from http://www.ota.ox.ac.uk/desc/2551

British National Corpus Simple Search (written and spoken English). Retrieved from http://www.natcorp.ox.ac.uk/using/index.xml?ID=simple

EDiLiC (Education et Diversité Linguistic et Culturelle) – Awakening to languages around the world. Retrieved from http://www.edilic.org/gb/gb_monde.php?monde=site

UK Census (2011) Concentration of languages across local authorities. Retrieved from http://www.ons.gov.uk/ons/rel/census/2011-census-analysis/language-in-england-and-wales-2011/rpt – language-in-england-and-wales—2011.html

29

Teaching language as a system

Dilin Liu and Robert Nelson

Introduction

While language has been accepted as a system composed of subsystems (e.g. morphological and syntactic systems), ideas about what it encompasses and how it works constantly evolve. Earlier linguistic theories, such as *structural linguistics* (Saussure, 1916; Bloomfield, 1933) and *generative linguistics* (Chomsky, 1957), consider language a largely autonomous system of structural rules, paying inadequate attention to meaning and use (i.e. to pragmatics – how language users convey and interpret meanings in a given context). Contemporary linguistic theories, such as *systemic functional linguistics* (SFL) and *cognitive linguistics* (CL, referring specifically to the linguistic theory developed by, among others, Langacker, 1987, 1991), develop a more comprehensive view that considers meaning and use as central. SFL treats language as a paradigmatic system for social interaction – a system of choices created and made by language users for communicating meaning in various social contexts. In this view, form, meaning and function interact to create a unified meaning-making "system network" (Halliday, 1994: xxvi); meaning is primary in this system network. Similarly, CL (Langacker, 1987, 1991) also considers meaning central in language, but it differs in that it considers human cognition key in the understanding and use of language. This theory treats language as a usage-based and conceptualisation-driven symbolic system for communication. Most importantly, in addition to form, meaning, context and use, language users and their *construals* (i.e. how speakers may frame an event differently or choose to select/focus on different aspects of it) play an extremely important role in meaning-making. This is because in each communication event, ultimately it is the language user who assesses the choices of form in context and decides which choices to make in order to best convey the meaning at hand. Furthermore, the choices made by language users will in turn affect the language system itself, making language a dynamic rather than a static system (Larsen-Freeman and Cameron, 2008; for further discussion of dynamic systems, see Mercer, this volume).

These more inclusive perspectives regarding language advocated by SFL and CL help form what we would like to call a 'comprehensive systems view'. This view has three important assumptions, drawn from the previous discussion. First, every language is simultaneously embedded in social systems and conceptual systems. Second, the function and meaning of a system are latent in its form, as mediated by speaker/writer construal. Third, language, being embedded in and interacting with social and conceptual systems mediated by the human mind, is a complex, dynamic system. This chapter will examine how such a comprehensive systems view might help us better understand language and, consequently, language teaching, especially the teaching of grammar and vocabulary, or *lexicogrammar*.

Understanding this view is important for language teaching because which language system view is adopted has a significant impact on how language is taught. For example, embodying the autonomous system view inherent in structural linguistics, traditional approaches to language teaching, such as the grammar-translation and audiolingual methods, focused mostly on form, as evidenced by the heavy grammar explanation in the grammar-translation method and the extensive use of sentence pattern drills in the audiolingual method and by the little attention that was paid to the meaningful use of the target language (see Hall, this volume, ch. 15 for further discussion of these methods). In contrast, embracing the comprehensive systems view that language is a usage-based system of choices embedded in social and conceptual systems requires language teaching to focus on function, meaning, use and context (including discourse, cultural and situational contexts) so as to help students develop the ability to use language for effective communication in the social contexts in which they find themselves.

Below, we first describe the critical theoretical issues related to language and language learning from the comprehensive systems view. Then we explore, with specific lexicogrammatical examples, the pedagogical implications of these principles. Finally, we briefly discuss the challenges and debates involved in language teaching informed by this comprehensive systems view.

Critical theoretical issues

Meaning and function are central

The first issue to understand is that, while form is important, meaning and function are central in language use and learning. The centrality of meaning/function directly affects how we analyse and organise language. For example, in SFL, language or its form serves three main functions: *ideational* (expressing experience/understanding about our world, e.g. *Mexico is in North America*), *interpersonal* (enacting our complex interpersonal relations, e.g. *Excuse me, Johnny*), and *textual* (organising communication in a cohesive manner, e.g. *Let's switch gears/topics*) (Halliday, 1994). Therefore, SFL language analysis considers not only syntactic but also semantic and pragmatic functions, as illustrated in Figure 29.1.

Such semantic/functional analysis enables us to better understand language as a system of choices for meaning-making. For example, it helps us understand that the subject in the Figure 29.1 utterance is the *agent* of the action (i.e. the person/thing directly affected by the verb), rather than the recipient or patient, and that the agent is chosen as the subject because it is the *theme* (which is often known information), as we typically begin a sentence with known information and proceed to the *rheme* (which is usually new information, presented typically in the predicate). We also know that '*surprisingly*' expresses the speaker's mood/modality about the event to the listener (hence performing an interpersonal function). Such an analysis enables us to see that language choices are not made in isolation but in meaningful discourse and situation

	Surprisingly,	*John*	*cooked*	*Jennifer*	*a dinner.*
Syntactic:	adverbial	subject	verb	indirect object	direct object
Semantic:	interpersonal theme	actor/agent	process	recipient	patient
Pragmatic:	mood adjunct	theme	rheme →		

Figure 29.1 An example of the syntactic, semantic and pragmatic functions within SFL analysis

contexts. As a very simple example, the choice of which greeting form to use (e.g. *How are you? What's up?* or *Howdy?*) will be determined by, among other things, the kind of relationship you have with the greeted person and the physical and social contexts of the greeting. Understanding the important role of discourse/situation context is imperative in language learning, as it tells learners how to use such information to make appropriate, meaningful language choices (Celce-Murcia and Olshtain, 2000).

Meanwhile, CL posits that meaning is inherent in all language forms, including grammatical structures; this meaning is rooted in our embodied experience (the experience gained through our body, i.e. its five senses) and our powerful capacities for conceptualisation. The claim that meaning is embodied is the claim that meaning "is structured by our constant encounter and interaction with the world via our bodies and brains" (Gallese and Lakoff, 2005: 456). Even the most pedestrian functions of language, like the use of repetition for emphasis (e.g. *He is very, very good*), are based on an embodied conceptualisation, in this case, the embodied schema that repetition increases intensity, or that more form signifies more meaning (Kövecses, 2006). Also, our everyday language usages are largely based on embodied conceptual metaphors. For example, based on our embodied experience that being balanced enables us to stand firmly while being unbalanced often causes us to fall, we use expressions where *balanced* means positive while *unbalanced* means negative, such as *balanced vs unbalanced approach/budget*. Similarly, because of the fact that when we are healthy, we are usually 'up' and active, but when we are very ill, we tend to lie 'down', expressions with *up* are generally positive while those with *down* are often negative, as can be seen in *brighten/cheer/go/thumbs up* vs. *break/go/let/thumbs down*.

It is also important to note that in CL, the atomic elements of language as a system are *symbolic units*, or *constructions*, which are pairings of form and meaning. Each of these pairings is understood to contain a *phonological pole* (form) and a *semantic pole* (meaning). As such, constructions may vary in size, ranging from something as small as a morpheme (e.g. the plural-*s*) to something as large as a sentence (e.g. *What's up?*). Hence, there is no rigid separation between lexis and grammar in this approach to language structures, an issue we will return to later. Constructions fall into three subcategories: filled (prefabricated) constructions (e.g. *What's up?/kick the bucket*), partially-filled (semi-prefabricated) constructions (e.g. *cut [someone] short* and *what's this [dog] doing [on my sofa]?* also known as the WXDY construction), and unfilled, schematic constructions (i.e. the productively abstract patterns such as the V+N+N 'cause to receive' construction, as instantiated by *gave someone a book/knitted someone a sweater*) (Holme, 2009: 184–204). While the first two kinds of constructions are clearly associations of form and meaning, the real advance of CL was showing that even the most schematic sentence frame, the unfilled construction, was also a form/meaning pairing (Goldberg, 1995, 2006). As such, the latter type is also the most productive, as its meanings are likewise maximally schematic. For example, while verbs like *cook* or *knit* do not inherently contain the meaning of 'cause to receive', when used in constructions like *She knitted him a sweater/He cooked her dinner*, they inherit the cause-receive meaning from the schematic construction they are embedded in. According to CL, language learning is essentially the learning of these three types of meaningful constructions.

Language as a usage-based system

The second critical theoretical issue to understand is that, rather than being an autonomous innate system, language is a usage-based system built on embodied experience and conceptualisation. This understanding has important implications for how we teach language. First, being usage based, language learning requires adequate input and output in meaningful communication. In the case of learning schematic constructions, students need both high *token* frequency and high *type* frequency in exposure. Tokens are individual instances of a construction, while types are different categories of the construction. For example, while *gave someone a book/gave someone money* are different tokens (although the same type) of the schematic 'cause to receive' construction, *give someone something, cook someone something* and *knit someone something* are each different types of this schematic construction.

Also, because this system is rooted in our embodied experience/conceptualisation, we see patterns of use that are motivated by embodied conceptualisations. Beyond employing repetition for emphasis and the embodied conceptualisation of 'being *balanced/up* meaning being positive', we see this motivated nature of language in the conflation of time and space. For instance, while it is widely and intuitively understood that we speak of time in terms of space (e.g. *I've got a big day in front of me*), what is less well described is the way we exploit this relationship to achieve pragmatic, social goals. For example, the use of the past tense for a present event to show politeness (e.g. *Could you help me?/Here is little something I thought you might like*) is based on our conceptualisation of time in spatial terms: because the use of the past tense creates distance from the present, the present request/suggestion becomes less imposing, hence more polite.

Importantly for language teachers, the experience that shapes language usage and construal is often culture-specific (Kövecses, 2006). This can help explain many of the differences in usages between different languages. For example, English speaking cultures are *low-context cultures*, where things often need to be specifically stated. In contrast, many Asian cultures (e.g. Chinese and Japanese) are *high-context cultures*, where many things are often unsaid but understood from contextual information. This may explain the lack of number/tense inflections in these Asian languages. Contextual information makes such inflections redundant, e.g. the adjective *three* in *three book* clearly indicates the plural nature of the noun and the time adverbial *yesterday* in *Yesterday I see a movie* makes clear the past time of the event in some Asian languages. Similarly, a difference in preference over how to express the manner and path (direction) of motion has resulted in two different types of languages: *verb-framed* languages (e.g. Romance languages) and *satellite-framed* languages (e.g. Germanic languages) (Talmy, 2000). In the former, the path of motion is encoded in the verb (e.g. *enter/exit* verbs of Latin origin), whereas in the latter the manner of motion is encoded with the path expressed by a prepositional/adverbial phrase (e.g. *walk into/walked out of the room*). This fact about language differences speaks strongly about the need to address culture and experience in language teaching. In short, exploring and understanding the conceptual motivations in language usages may help make language learning more interesting and effective (see Langacker, 2008).

The important role of construal

The third theoretical issue to understand is that speaker/writer construal plays a key role in language use and in helping make language a dynamic, rather than a static, system. This understanding calls for special attention to construal and the dynamic nature of language in language teaching. Construal operations are automatic in language use, and they affect our lexicogrammatical choice in a given context. For example, although both sentences, *He went over the report* and *He went through the report*, refer to the same event, they have each resulted from a different construal, with the former (*went over*) focusing on the completion of the activity and the latter (*went through*) highlighting the care or effort put into reading the report. Understanding how construal operates is especially important in learning lexicogrammatical usages related to prepositions, tenses/aspects and articles. Also, given the embodied nature of human conceptualisation as, explained earlier, embodied learning-based activities (i.e. gestures/movement/visuals) are especially effective in language learning (Holme, 2009).

One more important point related to this theory of language as a dynamic system shaped by language users is that teachers must value learners' creative use of language, including their errors, because errors are often signs of learning taking place and may help us better understand students' learning processes. In the section on construction learning later in the chapter, we discuss ways that learner error tells us exactly which constraints they have not acquired. Furthermore, because language is a dynamic adaptive system, the errors of today may become the standard usage of tomorrow; consider the present use of *less* for modifying count nouns (as in *ten items or less*) and *their* used as a singular possessive pronoun (as in *Everyone should do their best*). The point here is that often learner errors are not aberrations but a part of the natural ecology of language, according to the systems view.

Lexicogrammar

The fourth important theoretical issue is that grammar and vocabulary are the two ends of a single continuum, rather than two rigidly separate domains. This approach to grammar and vocabulary is based on the fact that syntactic structures are often lexically confined, while the use of a lexeme almost always has grammatical implications (Hunston and Francis, 2000). For example, *enjoy* and *love* are near-synonymous verbs, but while *love* can take as its object either an infinitive or a gerund (*love to read books* and *love reading books*), *enjoy* may take only a gerund object, *enjoy reading books*. Numerous corpus studies have demonstrated the close interconnection between lexis and grammar (e.g. Biber et al., 1999; Hunstan and Francis, 2000). Such findings from corpus research provide strong empirical support for SFL's view of language as a system of co-constraining choices (choices of, among other things, grammar and lexis simultaneously) and CL's view of language as a symbolic system made up of symbolic constructions. Corpus research has also shown that prefabricated constructions comprise a large part of natural language and perform important functions (Sinclair, 1991; Biber et al., 1999). Thus, language teaching should integrate lexis and grammar and pay close attention to collocations and constructions (Howarth, 1998; Lewis, 2000), including prefabricated multi-word constructions (which have been variously labelled as formulae, lexical bundles, etc.) and the structural patterns within which a lexical item typically occurs (what Hunstan and Francis (2000) call *pattern grammar*). It is necessary to note that while some cognitive linguists define a 'construction' as "any linguistic structure that is analysable into component parts" (Taylor, 2002: 561), others do not consider a construction to be entirely analysable because "aspects of its form or function is not strictly predictable from its component parts . . ." (Goldberg, 2006: 5). We are using the term 'construction' in the former sense.

Pedagogical implications

In this section, we show useful teaching practices guided or supported by the comprehensive systems view, using examples that are related to some basic but universally challenging lexicogrammatical issues (i.e. articles, tense/aspect and prepositions). It is important to note that many of the examples of teaching practices provided here are not new; they are given because they exemplify the teaching principles advocated by the systems view. Before we proceed, a word about sequencing in language teaching is also in order. Given the high importance of meaning/function in the systems view, the key criteria for determining instructional sequence are seen as meaningfulness and usefulness, as determined by students' needs and proficiency level. In general, we should begin with lexicogrammatical usages that are not only the most meaningful/useful but also the easiest for students to grasp based on what they already know. Hence, a beginning survival English class will start with the most basic useful survival expressions, accompanied by accessible lexicogrammatical and pragmatic usage information related to the expressions, and then move on to more complex but less essential ones. In contrast, an introductory intensive English programme (IEP) class might begin with the most basic expressions for academic interactions before moving on to more complex ones. Admittedly, it is not always easy to determine what language is most meaningful and useful for a given group of students – great effort is often needed to provide students a systematic, gap-free coverage of the lexicogrammar they need.

Teaching English articles, tense/aspect and word order: focusing on meaning/context

As is language in general, the English article system is dynamically integrated into our cognitive systems. Therefore, it is inadequate in language teaching simply to invoke the indefinite article *a/an* as a marker for nonspecific count nouns and the definite article *the* for specific nouns. This is because such an approach fails to take into account the fact that, rather than being markers of some local feature of a noun, English articles constitute a system that dynamically adapts to an evolving awareness of both the context of communication and our interlocutor's state of knowledge. Consider the following fact: if indeed *a/an* were always for a nonspecific noun and *the* were always for a specific noun, sentences like *I have a dog* or *I saw a huge bulldog this morning* would be permanently incorrect, since the dogs being referred to are very specific dogs. In this particular case, the speaker uses *a* because s/he believes that the listener is not aware of the referents. There is a similar problem with the commonly employed article usage rule stipulating that when a count noun is mentioned for the first time, *a/an* should be used. The issue is that *the* is in fact always used with a first-mention count noun when the referent can be identified (e.g. can be seen/heard) by the listener in the context. Consider the utterance *Could you please pass me the pen?* where *pen* is mentioned for the first time. In this case, in preparing to ask for the pen, the speaker has dynamically constructed a model of what his or her interlocutor is likely aware of, given the shared, physical context. It is thus clear that we must teach articles in context and help students understand how the speaker's/listener's knowledge/perspective affects the use of articles.

The tense/aspect system of English is also closely integrated into broader cognitive and cultural systems. In this case, these systems concern our cognitive ability to maintain a dynamically evolving construal of a discourse and the situation within which it occurs, and our cultural system of indexing these construals through tense/aspect manipulation. Understanding the discourse/situational context and the speaker/writer's construal in communication is therefore imperative in teaching English tenses/aspects, especially the use of those tenses/aspects that are closely related, such as the simple past and the present perfect, as both may refer to an action/event that occurred in the past (e.g. *I watched the play 'Hamlet' last Saturday* vs. *I've watched the play 'Hamlet'*). Teachers generally do a good job explaining that the present perfect is used to refer to a past action/event when the focus is on the result or the consequence of the past action in the present. However, without using examples in meaningful discourse/situational contexts, it would still be difficult for students to appreciate the difference between the two tenses/aspects. Hence, many teachers provide the students with simple scenarios like the following, where they ask students to explain which of the two tenses/aspects should be used in each blank and why:

Tom: *John, would you like to go and watch 'Hamlet' tonight?*
John: *Thanks for asking me, but I (see) it already.*
Tom: *When did you see it.*
John: *I (see) it last Friday.*

Another pair of closely related tenses/aspects, the present perfect and the present perfect progressive, may be effectively taught through contextualised examples and through an analysis of the speaker/writer's construal/perspective regarding the communication task at hand. For instance, we can have students compare the following examples adapted from Davies's (2008–) Contemporary Corpus of American English:

1   Psychologists *have studied* for years the effects of disasters on children. They have produced many important findings on the issue.
2   Scientists at the institute *have been studying* complex laboratory tests to find out the patterns of the resistance of the disease to treatment.

A close comparison should help students understand which construal is intended by the present perfect in example 1, and how that differs from the construal intended by the use of the present perfect continuous in example 2. In example 1, even though psychologists are likely still studying the effects of disasters and will likely continue, the writer chose the present perfect instead of the present perfect progressive to emphasise what psychologists have accomplished, rather than what they will continue to do. In contrast, in example 2, the focus is the ongoing nature of the study, since the scientists have not found out the patterns in question.

Similarly, discourse/situational context plays a very important role in word order. Here is an example taken from Celce-Murcia and Olshtain (2000: 56–57), showing how such information can and should be included in teaching the object placement in separable phrasal verbs:

> Edward gave up *his reward*.
> Edward gave *his reward* up.
> Edward gave *it* [his reward] up.

In sentence level-based autonomous analysis, the sentences are semantically equivalent. However, they are not semantically equivalent from an analysis that encompasses context and function. As mentioned earlier, word order in English is determined largely by whether the information in question is new or old. Therefore, sentence 1 "would be preferred in contexts where the direct object (i.e. the reward) was truly new or specifically emphasized information" but sentence 2 "would be preferred where the direct object had already been mentioned but was not sufficiently recent or well-established as old information to justify the use of the pronoun [it]" as in sentence 3 (Celce-Murcia and Olshtain, 2000: 56–57). Specifically, in response to a question like *What did Edward give up?* sentence 1 would be the right choice. In responding to a question such as *What did Edward do with his reward?*, the right response would be sentence 3. As for sentence 2, it would be an appropriate response for situations where "'reward' has a somewhat less recent mention, e.g. 'The reward – the whole thing – it's very embarrassing, isn't it? What did poor Edward decide to do?'" (Celce-Murcia and Olshtain, 2000: 57).

It is important to emphasise that teaching techniques involving the kinds of in-context comparisons used above do more than just illustrate the conditions of alternation; they make the learner step into the cognitive shoes of the speaker of the target language, so to speak, and adopt his or her perspective on the events in question (Tomasello, 1999), for it is well-known that tense/aspect systems often vary from language to language (e.g. English having no 'imperfect', a tense/aspect found in Romance languages). These inter-perspectival functions of social learning have long been recognised as a crucial element of human cultural transmission and a powerful way of teaching. Through contextualised examples, students can better understand how discourse/situational contexts and a speaker's construal/focus determine our lexicogrammatical choices and how such choices are often culturally prescribed acts of perspective taking.

Teaching prepositions and parts of speech: attending to conceptualisation/construal

Prepositions are critically important to the cooperative construction of meaning in everyday contexts. Consider the difference between getting somewhere *at 12:00*, *on Tuesday* or *in 2008*. Indeed, these small words are so important to establishing meaning that corpus studies have shown that twelve prepositions are among the fifty most frequently used words in English (Liu, 2013). Just as they are critically important, prepositions are simultaneously very difficult to learn. Their difficulty lies in the well-known fact that most prepositions are polysemous and multifunctional. Functionally, many prepositions also often work as adverbs or particles, i.e. used without a noun as their object (as in *The deal is on/off* and *give up*/give *up* something). A key point to remember is that the various meanings and functions of a preposition are all extended, often metaphorically, from a core, literal spatial meaning. Therefore, it is ill-advised in the teaching of prepositions to treat the locatives as canonical and the other uses as idiosyncrasies to be learned use-by-use in a rote fashion. The systems approach would allow us to work within a consistent framework, employing the embodied, spatial meanings of prepositions to assist learners in grasping their respective extended metaphorical meanings. Thus, understanding the semantic networks of prepositions and the conceptual motivations behind them is crucial for understanding the use of prepositions.

In fact, recent research has shown that exploring embodied conceptual motivations and using visual aids/body actions can significantly enhance L2 learning of prepositions and phrases involving preposition particles (Boers, 2000; Tyler, 2012). For example, Boers's (2000) study shows that having learners explore the embodied conceptualisation that *up* means 'higher/more' and is hence generally positive while *down* means 'lower/less' and is hence generally negative helped students more effectively learn verbal phrases involving the two prepositions as particles, such as *brighten/cheer/fire/go/move up* and *beat/break/fall/go/let/down*. In two studies reported in Tyler (2012), CL-based instruction with the use of visual aids (e.g. diagrams and video clips) was found to be significantly more effective than traditional teaching in helping learners grasp the use of prepositions *to/for/at*.

Here we would like to illustrate how visuals like Figures 29.2 and 29.3 (adapted from Liu, 2013: 151–152) may be used to help students better understand the semantic differences among *at, on* and *in*, three frequently used but also difficult-to-distinguish prepositions for referencing spatial/temporal locations. The two figures schematise these three spatial concepts in terms of the specificity of the preposition. Figure 29.2 shows that *at* typically designates a very small and hence maximally specific spatial/temporal point. *On* usually covers a surface or two-dimensional area, signifying a space less specific than that referred to by *at*. *In* is used for a three-dimensional space that can be either very large or small. The more literal pictures in Figure 29.3 help illustrate the semantic differences among *at on,* and *in* even when they are used in the same noun phrase: *at/on/in the corner*. After learning the general semantic patterns of the prepositions, we can help students deal with the exceptions. This should be much more effective than teaching without enabling students to see the patterns.

Knowing the 'sharp point' sense of *at* can also help understand (and explain) its use to identify a target (e.g. *bark/kick/shoot at someone/something*) and help explain the difference between *throwing something at someone* (as a target) and *throwing something to someone* (as a goal/receiver) (Tyler, 2012: 151–153). Similarly, knowing the 'on two-dimensional surface' meaning of *on* can

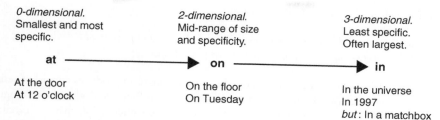

Figure 29.2 Semantic and usage differences among *at, on* and *in*

Source: Adapted from Liu, 2013: 151–152, by permission of Taylor & Francis, parent company of Routledge.

Figure 29.3 Illustration of the semantic differences among *at, on* and *in*

Source: Adapted from Liu, 2013: 151–152, by permission of Taylor & Francis, parent company of Routledge.

help one appreciate its extended meaning of being secure or being where it is supposed to be, e.g. *on target/topic/time/track*. Also, knowing the three-dimensional meaning of *in* can assist us in explaining the metaphorical use of *in* in phrases such as *in condition/control/shape/trouble,* where a state is conceptualised as a three-dimensional thing. It is also important to reiterate that, as shown in the aforementioned example of *went over* vs. *went through a report,* construal plays an extremely important role in the use of prepositions.

Similarly, conceptualisation/construal plays an equally important role in the classification of parts of speech, a critical point often overlooked in our teaching. While common definitions (e.g. a noun is a thing or person and a verb refers to an action) may work for beginning learners, such definitions are inadequate or problematic for many words, such as noun-turned-verbs (e.g. *baby* in *Don't baby me,* or *room* in *roomed with someone*) and nouns that actually express an action (e.g. *completion* and *fight*). A conceptualisation/construal-based definition can help explain these difficult cases. A noun in CL refers to anything that is conceptualised/construed as a 'reified thing' that is static and holistic, while a verb designates what is construed as a process, which is relational and sequential in nature, a definition system clearly illustrated by Langacker (1999) with the word *yellow*. Typically used as an adjective, *yellow* can also function as a noun referring to a particular thing in the realm of colour (e.g. *The yellows are winning*) and also as a verb expressing a process in which the colour of a given thing gradually changes into the colour of yellow (e.g. *The shirt yellowed with age*). This conceptualisation-based approach can be used to help learners better understand difficult parts of speech issues, including the common practice and value of 'nominalisation' in formal writing, where verb phrases are turned into noun phrases, as shown in the transformation of sentence A into B below:

A   *Tom completed the project in a timely manner and as a result he received a bonus.*
B   *Tom's timely completion of the project earned him a bonus.*

By construing the process of a verb as a static thing, nominalisation produces concise statements that contain equal amounts of information. Such a practice is difficult to deal with pedagogically, when noun-ness is assumed to be inherent to the things being named rather than the product of the way they are construed (Langacker, 1999; Taylor, 2002).

Teaching collocations and constructions: stressing meaning/function in lexicogrammar

Collocations in L2 pedagogy have been treated largely as arbitrary lexical units whose learning relies heavily on memorisation (Lewis, 2000). However, recent corpus-based cognitive analysis (e.g. Liu, 2010) has shown that collocations are generally motivated (i.e. not arbitrary but having a semantic or logical reasoning) if examined intra-lingually. When we focus our teaching on the motivations for collocations, we can help students grasp their use more effectively. Table 29.1 provides an example of how this can be done in learning the typical noun collocations of four common English verbs: *make/take/do/have*. These verbs have often been labelled 'delexicalised' or 'light' verbs (i.e. verbs that have little meaning when used in collocation with other words). The basic idea is that when students conduct a close analysis based on their encyclopedic knowledge (knowledge based on life experience and learning, see Taylor, 2002: 439–442), they will see that these collocations are actually motivated by the core meanings of the verbs.

Specifically, we can ask students to discuss which verb and its collocations involve more initiation, planning and effort. It should not be difficult for them to tell that *make* and its collocations do, for we know that it <u>generally</u> requires more initiation, planning and effort to *make* something than to *take* or *do* something and that *making a change/commitment/decision/effort* etc. <u>usually</u> entails more initiation and effort than *taking a break/bus/chance/nap* or *doing chores/ dishes/errands/homework* etc. Empirical studies have shown that understanding the motivations of lexical usages significantly enhances students' learning (e.g. Boers, 2000). Making students aware of this semantic dimension based on their encyclopedic knowledge of the world and then asking

Table 29.1 Typical noun collocations of *make/take/do/have*

Make	Take	Do	Have
Make a case	Take a bath	Do business	Have an affair
Make a change	Take a break	Do chores	Have an accident
Make a choice	Take a bus/taxi	Do dishes	Have an argument
Make a commitment	Take a chance	Do drugs	Have a conversation
Make a contribution	Take a look	Do errands	Have difficulty
Make a decision	Take a nap	Do exercises	Have a dream
Make a difference	Take an offer	Do harm	Have experience
Make an effort	Take a rest	Do homework	Have a feeling
Make a living	Take a phone call	Do laundry	Have fun/a good time
Make a mistake	Take a shower	Do research	Have a look
Make a phone call	Take a test	Do things	Have a problem
Make progress	Take a walk	Do work	Have trouble

Source: From Liu, 2013: 199, by permission of Taylor & Francis, parent company of Routledge.

them to explore how these collocations are different accordingly can guide students to uncover the typical meanings and motivations of the verbs for themselves. They may notice that the *do* collocations <u>frequently</u> refer to routine, often daily, activities. They should also find that that the verb *have* here is in the sense of 'experience' rather than 'possess', because the verb *have* can be replaced by the verb *experience* in most of the *have* collocations without any change of meaning, e.g. *experience* (instead of *have*) *a/an accident/break/difficulty/dream/ feeling/fun/problem* etc. In short, analysis like this should help learners better grasp the semantic patterns and then the use of the collocations. Again, after exploring the general semantic usage patterns of these common verbs, we can discuss the exceptions. In fact, there are reasons for many of the exceptions, some of which we know although some of which we do not know yet. For example, the reason we say *students take tests* (an activity that is clearly not easy), not *make tests,* is because the latter has been blocked by the fact that teachers make tests.

As explained earlier, of the three types of constructions mentioned earlier (i.e. filled/prefabricated, partially-filled/semi-prefabricated and unfilled/schematic), the schematic constructions (such as the aforementioned 'cause to receive' construction) are the most productive and are therefore very important in L2 learning. High token and type frequency is critical in learning this type of construction. Given the limited amount of input available in L2 learning (especially in a foreign language learning context), we should first provide students with adequate input of the prototypical form of the construction being taught before we move onto the less prototypical forms. This is because research has shown that skewed input and practice of the prototypical form of a construction facilitate its acquisition (Goldberg, 2006; Ellis, 2012). Let us look at the *V+N+Adj* construction, part of what Goldberg (1995: 180–198) calls the 'resultative construction', as shown in the following examples (2–4 from Goldberg):

1   *He made her happy.*
2   *She painted the house red.*
3   *Harry shot Sam dead.*
4   *He talked himself hoarse.*

This construction typically means the verb/action causes a change of state in the object/patient; the *make X adj* is the most prototypical form, whereas *talk oneself adj* is arguably the least prototypical in the group. First, therefore, expose students to many examples of the prototypical form and some other common forms of the construction by either having them do a corpus search or providing them with selected corpus examples, when no corpus is easily accessible. Then, have students identify, from the examples, the key components (*V+N+Adj*) and the change-of-state meaning of the construction. Afterwards, ask students to find more examples of the construction in a corpus and have them produce meaningful sentences of their own, based on the examples. That is, students should be encouraged to use the construction creatively (Holme, 2009).

While the last step (having students use the construction to generate their own sentences) is crucial in construction learning, it is also important to note that while encouraging students to use constructions creatively, teachers should simultaneously help students understand the constraints on each specific construction. This is because schematic constructions often have constraints (Goldberg, 1995, 2006; Taylor, 2002) that are not evident to L2 learners, who subsequently over-generalise their use. In the case of this resultative construction, learners may say:

★*She shot him wounded/killed.* (adapted from Goldberg, 1995; Taylor, 2002)

Teachers can use such errors to help students understand the constraints and restrictions about this resultative construction. Here, the ★*shot him wounded* example violated the 'end-of-state' constraint, which stipulates that the resulting state generally must be an end state, such as '*dead, open/shut, free . . .*' (Goldberg, 1995: 195). In contrast, the *★shot him killed* example violated the 'restriction against deverbal adjectives', i.e. "resultatives cannot be adjectives derived from either present or past participles" (Goldberg, 1995: 197). Awareness of such constraints can help L2 learners avoid overextending the use of the construction.

In every language, there are a large number of prefabricated multi-word constructions, including formulaic sequences and idioms, that are critical to fluent language production. These include sequences like *in spite of* and *in order to*, and it is important to teach these structures along with their functions and the contexts they are typically used in (Liu, 2013). This can be easily done today because studies (e.g. Biber et al., 1999) have so far identified not only many of the most common multi-word constructions in various registers (e.g. spoken, news, academic writing and medicine) but also their main functions (e.g. ideational/informational, interpersonal and/or textual/discoursal functions). For example, *I wonder if you + v* and *Could/would you please + v* are common formulae for making a request, while *data/results/surveys show/indicate/suggest that-clause* is a frequent construction in academic writing for reporting and/or interpreting research results. Also, we now know that, excluding phrasal verbs, most idioms (e.g. *chicken out/ drop the ball/hit a homerun*) are not highly frequent and are used typically to express evaluations, often negative ones, of an individual/event for a heightened effect (Moon, 1998). In teaching the highly frequent formulaic constructions, teachers often draw students' attention to these constructions by, among other things, highlighting them in the teaching material and also guide students in exploring the functions of the constructions in context. In ESP and EAP classes, teachers also often provide students with a list of the most common constructions and their main functions in the students' discipline/field of study. Such lists are readily available today. Of course, most importantly, teachers should engage students in speaking and writing activities that require them to use the constructions they are learning.

Given that multi-word constructions are often language-specific, it is important to help students pay special attention to the constructions that differ from those in their native language. This is especially the case with idioms, because many idioms are products of specific cultural practices, and they reflect their speakers' cultural perspectives and values (Kövecses, 2006; Liu, 2013). While culture-specific idioms may be unnecessary for learners of international English, they are important for ESL learners in an English-speaking country. From a CL perspective, most idioms are based on conceptual metaphors, e.g. *dropped the ball* (made a serious mistake) is based on the conceptual metaphor that 'life is competition/game' and *being down in the dumps/being on cloud nine* are based on the conceptual metaphor that 'being down is negative while being up is positive'. These idioms, therefore, are best taught not just as curious word combinations but also as windows into a culturally conditioned cognitive milieu. Thus, it is very helpful to provide learners with the cultural information and the conceptual motivations behind the idioms being learned.

Challenges and debates

As with any teaching approaches, there are challenges involved in teaching language as a comprehensive system. The greatest challenge is arguably the complexity of the issues covered, such as construal and discourse/situational context. These issues are especially difficult for beginning and low-level students. Given the fairly widely accepted view that simple and clear lexicogrammatical explanations that sacrifice some accuracy are more helpful for beginning/low-level students than elaborate accurate explanations (Liu, 2013), it is debatable whether and/or to what extent such complex systems issues should be addressed in teaching low-level students.

Another challenge is the amount of time required to cover all of these complex issues, considering especially the limited instruction time L2 teachers generally have and the large amount of input/output required for learning the various types of constructions, especially schematic constructions.

Another important challenge or issue of debate is whether lexis and grammar can always be taught together effectively. Perhaps, in some cases (e.g. for lower-level students struggling with basic grammatical issues like tense/aspect and word order), it may be helpful to have classes devoted exclusively to essential grammar skills. By the same token, there may be some words (e.g. technical vocabulary) that can be effectively learned simply as vocabulary items without any discussion of grammar. One more challenge is related to determining language teaching content and sequencing. As noted earlier, it is not easy to determine what is most meaningful and useful for the learner, especially when we also need to consider other important factors, such as the accessibility of the language according to the students' proficiency level and background. Furthermore, we also have to make sure that sequencing determined by usefulness does not result in knowledge gaps. An additional challenge is the aforementioned issue of how to promote creative use of the target language constructions being taught while simultaneously helping students understand the constraints on these constructions.

Future directions

It should be clear from the foregoing discussion that it is important to present language as it is embodied in ourselves and embedded in our social, cultural and cognitive systems. There are, of course, challenges involved in implementing this approach. However, these challenges should not stop us from trying to implement and enhance this meaningful, though complex, approach to language teaching, because it may help make language teaching more engaging and effective. Furthermore, as reported earlier, research has provided encouraging evidence for the use of this approach. With dedication and effort from all teachers, we are sure we can and will make teaching language as a comprehensive system a successful endeavour.

Discussion questions

- This chapter has mentioned some pedagogical implications and challenges the systems view of language brings to language teaching. What is your take on them, and what other implications and challenges do you see?
- How far do you agree that lexis and grammar are the two ends of one continuum? What advantages and disadvantages (or challenges) do you see in integrating lexis and grammar in language teaching?
- Consider these ways of describing the same event: *he went home* and *he made his way home*. How are they different in terms of the way they construe the action of *going*? How do you teach students the issue of construal in questions like this so they can use language to effectively communicate their meaning?

Related topics

Cognitive perspectives on classroom language learning; Complexity and language teaching; Corpora in the language classroom; Language and culture in ELT; Sociocultural theory and the language classroom; Teaching language skills.

Further reading

Coffin, C., Donohue, J. and North, S. (2009) *Exploring English grammar: From formal to functional.* London: Routledge. (This textbook offers teachers a clear functional account for context and motivation in the choice of structure.)

Fontaine, L., Bartlett, T. and O'Grady, F. (eds) (2013) *Systemic functional linguistics: Exploring choice.* Cambridge: Cambridge University Press. (This edited volume renders a broadly based and fresh approach to the role of choice and perspective in systemic functional linguistics.)

Littlemore, J. (2011) *Applying cognitive linguistics to second language learning and teaching.* New York: Palgrave McMillan. (This book is a deeply suggestive inquiry into the ways in which cognitive linguistics can transform language pedagogy.)

Pütz, M., Niemeier, S. and Dirven, R. (eds) (2001) *Applied cognitive linguistics II: Language pedagogy.* Berlin: de Gruyter. (A collection of useful articles exploring how cognitive linguistics may inform language pedagogy.)

Tomasello, M. (2009) *Constructing a language: A usage-based theory of language acquisition.* Cambridge, MA: Harvard University Press. (A comprehensive book on usage-based theory of language development, informed by linguistics, cognitive science, developmental psychology and culture.)

References

Biber, D., Johansson, S., Leech, G., Conrad, S. and Finegan, E. (1999) *Longman grammar of spoken and written English.* London: Longman.

Bloomfield, L. (1933) *Language.* New York: Henry Holt.

Boers, F. (2000) 'Metaphor awareness and vocabulary retention'. *Applied Linguistics,* 21/4. 553–571.

Celce-Murcia, M. and Olshtain, E. (2000) *Discourse and context in language teaching: A guide for language teachers.* Cambridge: Cambridge University Press.

Chomsky, N. (1957) *Syntactic structures.* The Hague/Paris: Mouton de Gruyter.

Davies, M. (2008–) *The Corpus of Contemporary American English: 520 million words, 1990–present.* Retrieved from http://corpus.byu.edu/coca/.

Ellis, N. (2012) 'Frequency-based accounts of SLA', in S. Gass and A. Mackey (eds) *Handbook of second language acquisition.* London: Routledge. 193–210.

Gallese, V. and Lakoff, G. (2005) 'The brain's concept: The role of the motor system in conceptual knowledge'. *Cognitive Neuropsychology,* 22/3. 455–479.

Goldberg, A. E. (1995) *Constructions: A construction grammar approach to argument structure.* Chicago: Chicago University.

Goldberg, A. E. (2006) *Constructions at work.* Oxford: Oxford University Press.

Halliday, M.A.K. (1994) *An introduction to functional grammar* (2nd ed.). London Arnold.

Holme, R. (2009) *Cognitive linguistics and language teaching.* New York: Palgrave McMillan.

Howarth, P. (1998) 'Phraseology and second language proficiency'. *Applied Linguistics,* 19/1. 22–44.

Hunston, S. and Francis, J. (2000) *Pattern grammar: A corpus-driven approach to the lexical grammar of English.* Amsterdam: Benjamins.

Kövecses, Z. (2006) *Language, mind, and culture.* Oxford: Oxford University Press.

Langacker, R. (1987) *Foundations of cognitive grammar: Theoretical prerequisites.* Stanford, CA: Stanford University.

Langacker, R. (1991) *Foundations of cognitive grammar: Descriptive application.* Stanford, CA: Stanford University.

Langacker, R. (1999) *Grammar and conceptualization.* Berlin: de Gruyter.

Langacker, R. (2008) 'Cognitive grammar as a basis for language instruction', in P. Roberson and N. Ellis (eds) *Handbook of cognitive linguistics and second language acquisition.* London: Routledge. 66–88.

Larsen-Freeman, D. and Cameron, L. (2008) *Complex system and applied linguistics.* Oxford: Oxford University Press.

Lewis, M. (2000) *Teaching collocation: Further developments in the lexical approach.* Boston: Heinle & Heinle.

Liu, D. (2010) 'Going beyond patterns: Involving cognitive analysis in the learning of collocations', *TESOL Quarterly,* 44/1. 4–30.

Liu, D. (2013) *Describing and explaining grammar and vocabulary: Key theories and effective practices.* London: Routledge.

Moon, R. (1998) *Fixed expressions and idioms in English.* Oxford: Clarendon Press.

Saussure, F. D. (1916) *Cours de linguistique générale*, eds. C. Bally and A. Sechehaye, with the collaboration of A. Riedlinger, Lausanne and Paris: Payot. (Translation by Baskin, W. (1977) *Course in general linguistics*. Glasgow: Fontana/Collins.)

Sinclair, J. (1991) *Corpus, concordance and collocation*. Oxford: Oxford University Press.

Talmy, L. (2000) *Toward a cognitive semantics, vol. 1: Concept structuring systems*. Cambridge, MA: MIT Press.

Taylor, J. R. (2002) *Cognitive grammar*. Oxford: Oxford University Press.

Tomasello, M. (1999) *The cultural origins of cognition*. Cambridge, MA: Harvard University Press.

Tyler, A. (2012) *Cognitive linguistics and second language learning: Theoretical basics and experimental evidence*. London: Routledge.

30

Teaching language skills

Jonathan Newton

Introduction

Over the past century, language teaching methods have tended to emphasise certain of the four skills of listening, speaking, reading and writing while downplaying the role of others. For instance, the grammar-translation method, popular in Western language education during the early twentieth century, placed great importance on reading and writing, with a focus on sentence level grammar and translation practice. In contrast, the direct method emphasised learning through oral communication, typically in the form of teacher-directed question-and-answer dialogues. The audiolingual method, which emerged in the mid-twentieth century, focused on carefully controlled speaking practice via drills and scripted dialogues; the role of listening was primarily to provide a model for speaking. In a dramatic contrast, comprehension-based approaches inspired largely by Krashen's influential monitor hypothesis (Krashen, 1982) insisted on the necessity and sufficiency of understanding input (i.e. listening and reading for meaning) for acquiring a second language. Consequently, speaking and writing were relegated to secondary roles. Summing up these pendulum swings, Celce-Murcia (2001: 3) comments that "language teaching is a field in which fads and heroes have come and gone in a manner fairly consistent with the kinds of changes that occur in youth culture". Adamson (2006: 615) argues, however, that language teaching fashions are not random but "mirrors of the contemporary sociocultural climate". (See Hall, this volume, ch. 15 for further discussion of language teaching methods and language teaching 'fashions'.)

How does all this inform the teaching of language skills at this point, early in the twenty-first century? More than ever, the English language teaching profession is able to draw on a large body of recent multi-disciplinary scholarship from fields such as linguistics, applied linguistics, psychology, cognitive science and education, and so, arguably, to distance itself from reactive methods trends. But while such scholarship has made a huge contribution to our understanding of the four skills and how to teach them, we are some way from consensus on many of the critical issues. Not surprisingly, then, addressing in a single chapter the wide-ranging, multifaceted topic of teaching language skills is not without its challenges, including how to do justice to the range of issues and debates on any one of the four skills, let alone all four. But along with this challenge comes the opportunity to explore synergies across the various skill areas. The chapter begins with a discussion of issues common across the four skills before looking at each skill in turn. It concludes with a discussion of future directions in teaching language skills.

Critical issues in teaching skills

The nature and role of practice

Skills are not innate; they are learned through practice (Proctor and Dutta, 1995), typically in the form of focused rehearsal of the sub-skills which make up skilled performance, e.g. learning to perfect a tennis stroke involves practising sub-skills such as adopting a particular grip, learning to position feet and body and automatising the mechanics of the stroke itself. In language learning, practice can be defined as "specific activities in the second language, engaged in systematically, deliberately, with the goal of developing knowledge of and skills in the second language" (DeKeyser, 2007: 1). We see this view of practice in the well-known 'presentation, practice and production' (PPP) approach to language teaching, in which the practice stage involves careful, controlled rehearsal of discrete language structures and/or functions. The aim is for the learner to proceduralise declarative knowledge of targeted forms and functions (e.g. that in English we use *verb stem +ed* to mark past action) prior to (supposedly) being able to use these forms with ease and accuracy in the third stage of production/communicative performance.

The value of this type of practice is hotly debated in ELT. It has suffered from association with behaviourist theories of learning and from its link to the largely discredited belief that language is best acquired through careful, sequentially staged practice of rule-based structures (Skehan, 1996; Doughty, 2003; Klapper, 2003). While advocates of PPP treat communicative use of language as a goal or outcome of practice, others, especially those who advocate task-based approaches, such as Willis and Willis (2007), see communicative use as essential to the whole learning process, and even as a preferred starting point (see Van den Branden, this volume, for further discussion of task-based language teaching).

But in rejecting practice by association, we run the risk of throwing the baby out with the bathwater. As Gatbonton and Segalowitz (2005) argue, ELT practitioners in the communicative language teaching (CLT) paradigm have largely failed to effectively integrate practice into communicative teaching. As a result, teachers too often fall back on the kind of repetitive pattern practice that scholars such as DeKeyser (1998) argue is of little value. Gatbonton and Segalowitz propose an alternative to the PPP approach under the acronym ACCESS – *automatization in communicative contexts of essential speech elements*. As the name suggests, in this approach, learners always practice useful utterances in the context of genuine communication. The approach consists of three phases, each involving communication activities: a creative automatisation phase in which essential speech segments are elicited; a language consolidation phase in which learners strengthen control of these utterances; and a free communication phase. A justification for this performance-oriented view of practice can be seen in the *transfer-appropriate processing* (TAP) model of memory (Goldstein, 2008) which, in simple terms, states that the way we process information determines the facets we will remember/get better at. For teaching language skills, the implication is that the kind of processing required in a target task should be mimicked in the classroom practice activities that are intended to prepare for that task; learners need opportunities to *practice the performance*. This is in many ways implicit in much of CLT in the use of role plays and other forms of group work. The TAP model provides one explanation for why form-focused drills are not adequate preparation for communicative performance, a point that DeKeyser (1998) argues persuasively.

So while it is clear that some form of practice is central to teaching language skills, just what kind of practice is appropriate and the extent to which practice should be separate or integrated into communicative use are issues of ongoing debate (see also Collins and Marsden, this volume, for further discussion of 'practice'). Similarly there are differing positions on how teaching should address bottom-up and top-down processing skills in relation to listening and reading, a topic we turn to next.

Bottom-up and top-down processes

A key issue in teaching the language skills concerns how much teachers should focus on top-down processing skills such as global comprehension of whole texts, on the assumption that, in the process, sub-skills will take care of themselves. In top-down processes, we draw meaning from around or outside a text (e.g. from topic-related background knowledge and experience) to help make sense of it. For example, a listener or reader draws on prior knowledge and on content and rhetorical schemata to construct meaning. These processes are largely inferential – the listener/reader draws on what they know of the context of communication to construct a representation of the message that is simultaneously emerging from the text. In the classroom, top-down processing is encouraged by getting learners to listen or read about a topic which is familiar to them, where the organisation and other genre conventions are familiar to them, where their attention is strongly focused on the message and where there is not a concern for linguistic detail.

Alternatively, we might approach skill learning in a different way – to what extent do learners benefit from practising bottom-up processing skills? Bottom-up processes are those by which we extract information from the linguistic elements in a written or spoken text to construct meaning. In listening, for example, bottom-up processes involve perceiving and parsing incoming speech and attending to auditory-phonetic, phonemic, syllabic, lexical, syntactic and semantic information to do so (Rost, 2011). Similarly, for reading, bottom-up processes include word recognition (and the sub-processes this implies), lexico-syntactic processing (e.g. processing affixes/stems, phrases and clauses) and semantic processing (e.g. assembling propositions) (Grabe and Stoller, 2011). For the proficient language user, these processes are fast and require little conscious awareness or effort. However, for the language learner, these processes are typically slower and require much more conscious effort. In the context of meaning-focused language use, this leads to an inevitable trade-off between the attention the learner has available for bottom-up processing on the one hand and for higher order sense-making processes on the other. Practice devoted to bottom-up processes would seem a natural response to this issue.

However, widely adopted communicative approaches to teaching the receptive skills have tended to place a much greater emphasis on top-down skills, with rather less attention paid to the skills and knowledge required for fast, accurate processing of the linguistic elements in the input. Such approaches emphasise global listening, skimming/scanning skills, making predictions and constructing meaning from context cues in and beyond the text, and drawing on personal experience of the topic to make sense of input. We see parallels to this approach in Krashen's (1982) input hypothesis, in which he argued that the most important process for acquiring a second language was comprehending meaningful input through listening and reading for meaning. Consequentially, he argued, teachers should deliberately avoid detailed explication of the formal properties of that input. However, Krashen's claims, and teaching approaches that followed from them, have been widely criticised on both theoretical and empirical grounds. A key weakness is that they fail to provide L2 learners with sufficient opportunities to develop the necessary sub-skills for L2 listening (Field, 2008; Vandergrift and Goh, 2012; Cauldwell, 2013) and reading (Bernhardt, 1991; Segalowitz and Hulstijn, 2005). For instance, Field (2011) argues that many of the comprehension activities used in classrooms to teach listening, such as answering questions about the meanings in a text, focus too much on the product of listening (i.e. comprehension) and so fail to help learners with the listening process. In short, as Field notes, such activities confuse *teaching* listening with *testing* listening.

As we shall see in the following sections, for both listening and reading, research evidence shows conclusively that bottom-up and top-down processes do not occur independently but are interactive and recursive. The implication for teaching is clear; learners need opportunities for guided practice of bottom-up and top-down processing strategies both separately and in concert.

Teaching the four skills

The following sections discuss each skill in turn, beginning with the two receptive skills of listening and reading before addressing the productive skills of speaking and writing.

Teaching listening skills

Cauldwell (2013: 6) describes the kind of comprehension approach advocated by Krashen (see above) and prevalent in many published textbooks as "an over-reliance on osmosis"; that is, it works on the maxim "listen a lot and your listening skills will improve automatically". Cauldwell contends that such an approach draws too heavily on research into the role of listening in first language acquisition and so overlooks the importance for L2 learners of instruction in speech perception processes. As Vandergrift and Goh (2012: 4) claim, "compared with writing and reading, or even speaking, . . . the development of listening has received the least systematic attention from teachers and instructional materials."

To what extent might learners benefit from being taught how to listen in a second language? Cauldwell (2013) argues that direct and deliberate teaching of perceptual processing skills is essential but that teachers need to better understand the phonology of fast speech in order to carry it out. Field (2003) also advocates more attention to bottom-up listening skills so as to assist learners with lexical segmentation – with parsing the speech stream so as to distinguish word boundaries. Field identifies three speech phenomena that make lexical segmentation particularly difficult for language learners and which therefore require attention through explicit instruction: (1) reduced forms (i.e. contractions such as *I'd,* weak forms such as unstressed articles, and chunks such as *Howyadoing? –* 'How are you doing?'); (2) assimilation and elision (i.e. changes to the beginnings and endings of words in connected speech, e.g. *this show – thi show*); and (3) resyllabification (i.e. *past her-> pastor*). Lynch and Mendelsohn (2002: 207) suggest a similar but expanded range of instructional targets: discriminating between similar sounds; coping with and processing fast speech; processing stress and intonation differences; processing the meaning of different discourse markers; and understanding communicative functions and the non-one-to-one equivalence between form and function (e.g. a declarative sentence such as *It's cold in here* performing a directive function *Please close the window*). These authors support teachers taking more time to raise awareness of such speech phenomena and to provide opportunities for learners to develop control over perceptual processes through activities such as dictations and repeated listening to authentic speech samples.

Skilled listening is, of course, more than successfully segmenting the speech stream. As Vandergrift (2007: 193) notes, skilled L2 listening also involves "a skilful orchestration of metacognitive and cognitive strategies". Raising learners' metacognitive awareness of how they listen and how to effectively manage the listening process are, therefore, important teaching goals (Vandergrift and Goh, 2012). To illustrate the point, a study by Vandergrift and Tafaghodtari (2010) showed that tertiary French as a second language students who were given metacognitive listening strategy training outperformed their peers in subsequent listening comprehension tests. The training led the learners through the metacognitive processes characteristic of successful L2 listening, including predicting, monitoring, evaluating and problem-solving. The authors conclude that listening performance improves when "listening practice includes opportunities to explain or reflect on the decisions required during the listening task" (p. 488).

By way of summary, and building on all these themes, Newton (2009) argues that to be effective, a listening programme should include five core components: extensive meaning-focused listening; guided diagnosis of miscomprehension problems; listening skills training and practice; listening strategy training; and making links to listening opportunities beyond the classroom.

Teaching reading skills

As with listening, teaching reading skills requires the teacher to be familiar with the range of lower and higher level processes that make up skilful reading and with how to sequence teaching to ensure learners have opportunities to develop skilful control over these processes. Drawing on an extensive review of L2 reading research, Grabe and Stoller (2011: 130) identify the following list of abilities L2 readers need to develop: efficient word recognition and automatic access to a large vocabulary; reading comprehension skills for extracting meaning from phrase, clause, paragraph and discourse text structures; applying reading strategies to difficult texts; setting and adjusting reading goals; inferencing and using prior knowledge; synthesising these processes for critical reading comprehension; and maintaining motivation to read extensively and for an extended period of time. Although this list seamlessly integrates bottom-up and top-down reading processes, the reading teacher is still faced with the question of how much emphasis to place on deliberate teaching and practice of reading sub-skills in comparison to other components such as extensive reading and comprehension-based reading activities. To help answer this question, we will now turn our attention to lower level (i.e. bottom-up) reading processes.

Skilled L2 readers activate highly automatised bottom-up text processing skills to make sense of text and to serve higher level comprehension and inferential goals (Hulstijn, 1991; 2001). This is a different picture of reading to that proposed by Goodman (1967), who claimed that effective readers draw on higher level processing skills to shortcut lower level text processing. In fact, a lack of automatic word recognition skills greatly hinders the reading process. Without these skills, the learner's attention to higher level text processing is compromised by fixations on problematic surface structures. Readers facing such challenges read more slowly (and by implication, less) and at lower levels of comprehension.

One priority for learners seeking to improve reading skills is therefore developing automaticity (i.e. fluency) in word recognition so as to free up cognitive resources for comprehending and interpreting text (Segalowitz and Hulstijn, 2005). In a study involving Japanese university students, Akamatsu (2008) showed that training in word-recognition through a word chains task in which the students drew lines to separate words written with no spaces led to improved word-recognition performance in both speed and accuracy. Furthermore, as Grabe and Stoller (2011: 13) note, "reading is fundamentally a linguistic process . . . though this aspect of reading is often downplayed." For teachers, this means helping learners to adopt efficient vocabulary learning strategies to rapidly expand their vocabulary knowledge. Research shows that an effective way to achieve this is through deliberate word learning using flash cards, combined with extensive reading of appropriately graded readers in which these words are met in meaningful contexts (Nation, 2013).

In fact, extensive reading is widely regarded by reading and vocabulary researchers as the cornerstone to developing reading ability and a wide vocabulary (Grabe and Stoller, 2011; Waring, 2012). Unfortunately, however, as Waring notes, extensive reading is too often treated as supplementary to a main programme, an option to be omitted if there is no time for it. Considering the strength of the evidence for its benefits, Waring argues that extensive reading should be at the core of every reading programme.

Opportunities for repeated reading have also been shown to improve reading fluency and to improve comprehension. For instance, a study by Gorsuch and Taguchi (2008) showed that Vietnamese university EFL students improved both their reading fluency and text comprehension though a repeated reading procedure which involved reading a short, simplified text five times. However, neither this or Akamatsu's (2008) study noted previously present a viable pedagogic proposal for automatising word recognition. They offer useful research techniques, but these are of limited practical use in a typical EFL situation. In this regard, extensive reading remains the strongest contender.

A key issue facing the reading teacher is the extent to which L2 learners can access their L1 reading skills when reading in the L2 (Carrell, 1991; Bernhardt and Kamil, 1995; Walter, 2007). Scholars agree that, although L1 and L2 reading draw on the same underlying cognitive processes, learners need to achieve a threshold level of L2 proficiency in order to access their L1 reading skills. Below that level, access is constrained by lack of automaticity of basic local text decoding skills such as letter and word recognition, which rob attention in working memory. However, just what that threshold level is has proved difficult to define. Related factors such as the linguistic difference between L1 and L2 and the social context of education in both languages (including differences in valued literacy practices in both languages) also impact strongly on L2 reading (Grabe and Stoller, 2011).

Finally, a challenge for teaching reading skills is that reading not only involves a complex array of sub-processes such as those listed above, but reading is done for many different purposes involving many different text types, all of which shape the process of reading. We read a newspaper story for a different purpose and thus in a different way from the way we read a poster, an Internet page, a technical manual, a cartoon, an email message and so on. With forms of digital text continuing to expand, this complexity is also increasing. And as digital literacy is incorporated into the goals of ELT reading instruction, it brings heightened levels of intertextuality and text-reader interactivity, which in turn offer new opportunities and challenges for the teaching of reading skills.

Teaching speaking skills

Since the heyday of CLT in the 1970s, most approaches to teaching speaking skills have sought to engage learners in meaning-focused, communicative tasks in one way or another (see Thornbury, this volume, for further discussion of CLT). A key issue of debate is where this communicative practice belongs in a teaching/learning cycle, an issue we met earlier in this chapter in the discussion of the role of practice in language teaching. A closely related issue concerns how teachers can ensure due attention is given to different aspects of speaking, namely to complexity (grammatical and lexical), accuracy and fluency (CAF). In what is known as the trade-off hypothesis, Skehan (1998) argues that these dimensions compete for the learner's limited cognitive resources and that the type of classroom activities teachers set for learners and how these activities are implemented will lead learners to give preferential attention to certain of the three CAF components, but not to all three. This has important implications for teaching speaking. For example, research has shown that when learners are provided with planning time prior to performing an oral production task, their language production tends to be more fluent and either more accurate or more complex, but not both (Skehan and Foster, 1999). Factors such as what type of planning is provided and how complex the task is also have a strong effect on how learners allocate their attention to these three aspects of speaking. We now turn to look more closely at teaching focused on one of these aspects – teaching to develop spoken fluency.

ELT curricula typically identify the language content and skills to be taught and learnt in a programme. What may be less clearly articulated are the opportunities available for learners to develop fluent control over this material in order to perform at a higher skill level. This is a problem for learners; if the items that have been learned are not readily available for fluent use, then the learning has been for little purpose. At its simplest level, to develop fluency requires extensive and often repetitive practice. This would not be seen as unusual for anyone learning a musical instrument or a sport. And yet, in ELT, it is an often overlooked component of teaching. Why? There are no doubt many reasons. Curricula may simply underestimate the amount of effort required to build fluency, or, given constrained classroom time, teachers may view fluency as the learners' responsibility. Also, in many parts of the world, high stakes assessment does not give due weight to speaking. And finally, the kind of communicative activities associated with fluency are often seen as impractical in the large classes typical of ELT in many parts of the world (see Shamim and Kuchah, this volume for further discussion of teaching large classes).

How can teachers help learners to develop communicative fluency without reverting to demotivating, repetitive form-practice? Research indicates that spoken fluency is likely to develop if three main conditions are met (Nation and Newton, 2009). First, the activity must be meaning focused so that the learners are communicating a message and experiencing the 'real time' pressures of normal communication. Second, the learners should take part in activities where all the language items are within their previous experience. This means that the learners work with largely familiar topics and types of discourse which make use of known vocabulary and structures. Third, there is support and encouragement for learners to perform at a higher level; for instance, they are encouraged to use larger planned chunks of language (i.e. formulaic sequences) (Wood, 2006), they are given planning time or they are encouraged to increase the speed at which they produce or comprehend text. Increased speed can be achieved through a timed or speed reading programme, or in the case of speaking, through the timed 4–3–2 speaking activity which we will discuss next.

The 4–3–2 activity meets all three conditions for fluency development outlined previously (meaningful, familiar topic/language, pressure to improve performance) and so is worth looking at in some detail. In this activity, learners give a short talk on a familiar topic three times consecutively, each time to a different partner, and with the time reducing from four to three to two minutes on each occasion. De Jong and Perfetti (2011: 31) carried out an empirical study into the effects of the 4–3–2 activity on spoken fluency. Using intermediate ESL students at a US university, they compared the performance of students who performed the activity (as described above) with students who spoke on a *new* topic each time. They found that while fluency increased for both groups, only the group who spoke on the same topic each time maintained their improved fluency on a post-test in which they gave a two-minute talk on a new topic. They conclude that "[s]peech repetition in the 4/3/2 task may cause changes in underlying cognitive mechanisms, resulting in long-term and transferable effect on performance fluency". This is an important outcome for teachers who are unsure of the value of task repetition.

But what happens to accuracy and errors under the pressure to speak in less and less time? This question was addressed in a study by Boers (2014) involving ten adult ESL learners performing 4–3–2 activities. As with De Jong and Perfetti (2011), Boers found fluency improvements across the iterations of the talk. However, he also found a high number of errors being repeated from the first to the third talk. He argues that this is an unintended by-product of the performance pressure created by reduced time for each talk. This pressure forces learners to fall back on verbatim duplication rather than attending to the accuracy or complexity of their utterances. To counter this risk of errors being reinforced, Boers suggests relatively simple pedagogic interventions such as providing guided planning time and/or corrective feedback after the first talk.

Only a relatively small amount of knowledge is needed for successful language use (Crabbe and Nation, 1991). But as in the 4–3–2 activity, where the goal is fluency, learners need substantial opportunities for communicative practice. Indeed, as early as 1985, Brumfit suggested that "[r]ight from the beginning of the course, about a third of the total time could be spent on this sort of fluency activity, and the proportion will inevitably increase as time goes on" (1985: 12). A critical issue for English language teachers and curriculum designers is to ensure fluency opportunities are given due attention in a programme.

No account of teaching speaking skills would be complete without addressing the role of corrective feedback (CF). However, since oral CF is the sole topic of Mackey, Park and Tagarelli's discussion in this volume, readers should refer to that chapter for a comprehensive discussion of this topic.

Teaching writing skills

The teaching of L2 writing skills has drawn extensively on trends in L1 writing pedagogy and the theories of writing on which they are based, theories drawn from fields such as composition studies, contrastive rhetoric and genre theory. However, basing L2 writing pedagogy on L1 practices fails to take sufficient account of the unique challenges of writing in a second language, a problem noted earlier in this chapter in relation to teaching listening skills. Not surprisingly, as L2 writing research emerged as a field in its own right in the 1980s, it identified differences in L1 and L2 writing processes and the challenges that learners face with regard to rhetorical preferences and command of English structure and vocabulary. As the field has developed, therefore, it has sought to critically re-evaluate the legitimacy of L2 writing instruction practices and values in reaction to the native writer bias in the source discipline of composition studies (Silva et al., 1997).

More recently, there have also been calls for L2 writing instruction to make better connections to the experience and knowledge of multilingual writers, and in so doing avoid the trap of seeing them as novice writers (Canagarajah, 2012). As Manchón (2012: 10) argues, the teaching of writing "needs to take a multilingual stance and do justice to the resources and strengths of multilingual writers". This involves questioning the assumption that learners should appropriate the values and expectations of writing in English, an issue addressed in the New Literacy Studies movement (Barton and Hamilton, 1998). Hyland (2012: 18) captures these various strands when he observes, "modern conceptions of learning to write see writing as a social practice, embedded in the cultural and institutional contexts in which it is produced and the particular uses that are made of it."

Among the various approaches to teaching L2 writing, process and genre approaches have been the most influential in recent years. Process approaches are probably the more influential of the two, particularly in higher education settings in North America. These approaches draw heavily on models of L1 writing, notably the cognitive process model proposed by Flower and Hayes (1981), which focus on the processes a writer goes through to produce text. Steps include planning, generating ideas, drafting, reviewing and revising, editing and publishing. Process-based writing instruction encourages learners to develop metacognitive awareness of their writing processes, reflecting on themselves as a writer and the text emerging at each writing stage. The teacher guides learners through the process and responds to emerging ideas and text with feedback, although peer response and self-reflection are also important sources of input (Hyland, 2003). A focus on language form tends to be discouraged until later in the process, reflecting misgivings over the effectiveness of corrective feedback in writing (e.g. Truscott, 1996). Recent research has, however, largely lent support to the positive role that feedback on grammar can play in L2 writing development (Bitchener and Ferris, 2012).

Process approaches have been criticised for being overly focused on the writer and the writer's internal world and giving insufficient attention to the social nature of writing (Hyland, 2003, 2012). Indeed, as Ortega (2012) notes, L1 scholarship has in recent years distanced itself from the expressive orientation of process approaches in search of a more socially and politically informed understanding of writing as social literacy.

The genre approach, another influential approach to teaching L2 writing skills, emphasises the nature of writing as purposeful activity, as a way of "getting something done" (Hyland, 2003: 18). A genre is a "goal oriented, staged social process" (Hyland, 2003: 19) within which linguistic patterns and choices reflect and construct socially conventional ways of achieving a given purpose. Learning to write from a genre perspective is a process of joining a discourse community. Genre-based L2 writing instruction emphasises awareness of how texts work and encourages learners to work with a metalanguage for describing genre features and structures, whether in academic contexts (Swales, 1990; see also Starfield, and Basturkmen and Wette, this volume) or primary school classrooms (Derewianka, 1991; Ahn, 2012). Grammar awareness is encouraged for the purpose of helping learners understand how language choices serve the socially defined purpose of a text. For example, in teaching a persuasive genre, a teacher might focus on how modal verbs are used to convey levels of certainty or logical necessity in support of the text's persuasive purpose.

A genre approach typically involves learners analysing the structure, content and language of model texts and drawing on this textual awareness to construct their own text, often jointly with the teacher (Hyland, 2003: 21). This reliance on models has drawn criticism for the way it can lead to an overly prescriptive approach to teaching writing focused on text reproduction rather than on creative, agentive writing processes (e.g. Badger and White, 2000: 157; Luke, 1996). Hyland (2003: 22) describes this as "a tension between expression and repression".

A more recent distinction emerging in L2 writing instruction is between learning-to-write (LW) and writing-to-learn (WL) (Manchón, 2012). LW focuses on helping learners to express themselves in writing in a second language and draws on theoretical frameworks from composition studies, applied linguistics, and English for academic purposes (see Basturkmen and Wette, this volume). In contrast, WL emphasises the value of writing as a tool for learning content knowledge (i.e. in a subject such as geography) and language. WL draws on both sociocultural and cognitive SLA theorising (see Negueruela-Azarola and García, and Collins and Marsden, respectively, this volume). This distinction has proved useful regarding the contentious issue of the relevance of L2 writing research to foreign language contexts, research which, traditionally, has taken place in English-dominant countries. In this regard, Leki (2009) argues that "contrary to dogma in SL [second language] writing, with its now traditional de-emphasis of language learning, using writing to develop language proficiency may be a central aim of L2 writing in FL settings" (Manchón, 2012: 5). We can only hope that these two orientations to L2 writing instruction avoid the trap of "feed[ing] into compartmentalized professional or scholarly cultures and creat[ing] misalignments between teacher and student understandings of the value and roles of L2 writing" (Ortega, 2012: 237).

Future directions and concluding thoughts

The role of technology

Looking to the future, one obvious factor responsible for opening up new directions in teaching language skills is technology (see Gruba, Hinkelman and Cárdenas-Claros, and Kern, Ware and Warschauer, this volume). Indeed, the potential of new technologies is such that it would be difficult to find an aspect of language skill development for which a recent technological innovation is not available to deliver enhanced opportunities for English language teachers and learners. For the receptive skills, perhaps the most valuable contribution that technology offers is simply in opening up access to vast amounts of richly meaningful language input in the form of written, visual and audio-visual resources. Furthermore, thanks to technology, teachers and learners have unprecedented control over these resources. In the case of listening texts, for example, even the simplest media player provides the teacher and learner with the ability to stop, start and loop chunks of text at will. More advanced speed shifter software also allows the learner to speed up or slow down an audio recording. For reading, text-to-speech software converts written text to spoken text, and hyperlinks and online dictionaries provide rich embedded language support.

For the productive skills, technology exponentially increases opportunities for learners to practice speaking and writing and to receive immediate feedback and guidance from the teacher. For speaking, technology allows learners to analyse recordings of their voices and compare their recording to a model. Comparison can be aided by the visual display of wave forms and pitch contours, animations of the movement of articulatory organs when producing phonemes and words, and automatic conversion of the recorded speech into IPA symbols. For writing, practice is supported by the spelling and grammar checking capabilities of word processing programmes and by the editing power of writing via computer. Freely available software such as Jing allows teachers to provide multimodal feedback on writing via video screen capture software linked to voice recording. This has distinct benefits for teachers and learners. For teachers, being able to provide their feedback in spoken form saves time and allows easy elaboration. For learners, not only is the feedback more informative, but it also exposes them to meaningful spoken input.

As the term indicates, computer-mediated communication (CMC) also offers learners opportunities to develop their productive language skills through communicating online in modalities unhindered by time or space. Older forms of CMC such as email initially opened up these opportunities for writing-based communication, but Web 2.0 opened up synchronous CMC options for 'live' interaction via, for example, Skype, text chat, Twitter and other interactive platforms and forms of social media. Virtual worlds such as those available through Open Sim or Second Life allow teachers and communities of learners to create their own immersive learning environment. All of these capabilities are fully portable via mobile technology such as smart phones, offering even more opportunities for innovative pedagogy. Perhaps the biggest challenge for the teacher is keeping up with technological developments while avoiding being swamped by the tsunami of technological teaching options available to them.

Reframing the four skills: learning strands

This chapter has reviewed key issues in the teaching of language skills. After examining perspectives on practice and top-down and bottom-up processing, it examined critical issues and future directions in teaching the four skills. Typically, the discussion has centred on binaries such as top-down and bottom-up processes, accuracy and fluency, and writing-to-learn and learning-to-write. But, of course, a great deal of complex interplay lies behind these simple distinctions. How is the language teacher to manage these complexities? One option is to shift the focus away from skills *per se* and onto learning opportunities more generally. Taking this approach, Nation and Newton (2009) argue that teachers are better served by reframing the four skills within a framework of four learning strands, each representing a core type of learning opportunity. The first strand is learning through message-focused input, where the learner's primary attention is on the ideas and messages conveyed by the language and met in listening and reading (i.e. the receptive skills). The second strand is learning through message-focused output, that is, learning through speaking and writing (i.e. productive skills), where the learners' attention is on conveying ideas and messages to another person. To complement these two meaning-focused strands, the third strand, learning through deliberate attention to language items and features, allows for a focus on declarative language knowledge and, for example, on the bottom-up processing skills so important in listening and reading. The fourth strand is developing fluent use of known language items. The opportunities for learning language are called strands because they can be seen as long continuous sets of learning conditions that run through a whole language programme. Balancing these four strands, according to Nation and Newton (2009), ensures learners achieve development in each skill area along with fluent control of the sounds, spelling, vocabulary, grammar and discourse features of the language that underpin these skills. It offers an approach which integrates, rather than separates, skills.

To conclude, therefore, even without deliberate attempts to integrate the four skills, they naturally co-occur in classroom practice, such as when a listening comprehension activity requires learners to read questions before listening, then answer them in writing, or when a speaking activity requires learners first to read off prompts and/or write speaking notes. Similarly, skills are not separate in learner cognition and frequently co-occur in communicative use. Thus, a learning strands approach – focusing on meaningful input and output, deliberate attention to language, and fluent language use – offers ELT professionals a deliberate and principled pathway for teaching language skills.

Discussion questions

- To what extent do the many component sub-skills of each of the four skills need to be explicitly taught? To what extent can they be left to develop intuitively through rich communicative learning experiences? How does the answer change for different groups of learners?
- How can a learner's L1 skills and knowledge be valued and drawn on to enhance the teaching and learning of L2 language skills?
- How can the plea by researchers such as Grabe and Stoller (2011) and Field (2003) to practitioners to explicitly teach componential reading and listening skills be married to communicative and integrated teaching approaches?

Related topics

Cognitive perspectives on classroom language learning; Communicative language teaching in theory and practice; Content and language integrated learning; English for academic purposes; English for specific purposes; Errors, corrective feedback and repair; Sociocultural theory and the language classroom; Task-based language teaching.

Further reading

Field, J. (2011) *Listening in the language classroom*. Cambridge: Cambridge University Press. (This prize-winning book provides guidance on how to teach listening sub-skills, especially those focused on perceptual processes.)

Goh, C. and Burns, A. (2012) *Teaching speaking: a holistic approach*. Cambridge: Cambridge University Press. (This book provides an in-depth discussion of the nature of speaking and spoken discourse, and the design and implementation of speaking programmes and activities.)

Grabe, W. and Stoller, F. (2011) *Teaching and researching reading* (2nd ed.). New York: Pearson Longman. (This is a comprehensive treatment of reading, addressing issues of what and how to teach and how to research reading processes.)

Hyland, K. (2013) *Teaching and researching writing.* New York: Routledge. (This text explores writing pedagogy as well as providing guidance on how to carry out research on writing.)

References

Adamson, B. (2006) 'Fashions in language teaching methodology', in A. Davies and C. Elder (eds) *The handbook of applied linguistics.* Malden, MA: Blackwell Publishing Ltd. 604–622.

Ahn, H. (2012) 'Teaching writing skills based on a genre approach to L2 primary school students: An action research'. *English Language Teaching,* 5/2. 2–16.

Akamatsu, N. (2008) 'The effects of training on automatization of word recognition in English as a foreign language'. *Applied Psycholinguistics,* 29. 175–193.

Badger, R. and White, G. (2000) 'A process genre approach to teaching writing'. *ELT Journal,* 54/2. 153–160.

Barton, D. and Hamilton, M. (1998) *Local literacies: Reading and writing in one community.* London: Routledge.

Bernhardt, E. B. (1991) *Reading development in a second language.* Norwood, NJ: Ablex.

Bernhardt, E. B. and Kamil, M. L. (1995) 'Interpreting relationships between L1 and L2 reading: Consolidating the linguistic threshold and the linguistic interdependence hypotheses'. *Applied Linguistics,* 16/1. 15–34.

Bitchener, J. and Ferris, D. (2012) *Written corrective feedback in second language acquisition and second language writing.* New York: Routledge.

Boers, F. (2014) 'A reappraisal of the 4/3/2 activity'. *RELC Journal,* 45/3. 221–235.

Brumfit, C. J. (1985) *Language and literature teaching: From practice to principle.* Oxford: Pergamon.

Canagarajah, S. (2012) 'Writing to learn and learning to write by shuttling between two languages', in R. M. Manchón (ed.) *Learning-to-write and writing-to-learn in an additional language.* Amsterdam: John Benjamins. 111–132.

Carrell, P. L. (1991) 'Second language reading: Reading ability or language proficiency?' *Applied Linguistics,* 12. 158–179.

Cauldwell, R. (2013) *Phonology for listening.* Birmingham, UK: Speech in Action.

Celce-Murcia, M. (2001) *Teaching English as a second or foreign language.* London: Heinle and Heinle.

Crabbe, D. and Nation, I.S.P. (1991) 'A survival language learning syllabus for foreign travel'. *System,* 19/3. 191–201.

De Jong, N. and Perfetti, C. A. (2011) 'Fluency training in the ESL classroom: An experimental study in fluency development and proceduralization'. *Language Learning,* 61/2. 533–568.

DeKeyser, R. (1998) 'Beyond focus on form: Cognitive perspectives on learning and practising second language grammar', in C. Doughty and J. Williams (eds) *Focus on form in classroom second language acquisition.* Cambridge: Cambridge University Press. 42–63.

DeKeyser, R. (2007) 'Introduction: Situating the concept of practice', in R. DeKeyser (ed.) *Practice in a second language.* Cambridge: Cambridge University Press. 1–18.

Derewianka, B. (1991) *Exploring how texts work.* London: Heinemann.

Doughty, C. (2003) 'Instructed SLA: Constraints, compensation and enhancement', in C. Doughty and M. H. Long (eds) *The handbook of second language acquisition.* Malden, MA: Blackwell. 256–310.

Field, J. (2003) 'Promoting perception: Lexical segmentation in L2 listening'. *ELT Journal,* 57/4. 325–334.

Field, J. (2008) *Listening in the language classroom.* Cambridge: Cambridge University Press.

Field, J. (2011) *Listening in the language classroom.* Cambridge: Cambridge University Press.

Flower, L. and Hayes, J. R. (1981) 'A cognitive process theory of writing'. *College Composition and Communication,* 32/4. 365–387.

Gatbonton, E. and Segalowitz, N. (2005) 'Rethinking communicative language teaching: A focus on access to fluency'. *Canadian Modern Language Review,* 61. 325–353.

Goldstein, E. B. (2008) *Cognitive psychology: Connecting mind, research, and everyday experience* (2nd ed.). Belmont: Thomson Wadsworth.

Goodman, K. (1967) 'Reading: A psycholinguistic guessing game'. *Journal of the Reading Specialist,* 6. 126–135.

Gorsuch, G. and Taguchi, E. (2008) 'Repeated reading for developing reading fluency and reading comprehension: The case of EFL learners in Vietnam'. *System,* 36. 253–278.

Grabe, W. and Stoller, F. (2011) *Teaching and researching reading* (2nd ed.). New York: Pearson Longman.

Hulstijn, J. H. (1991) 'How is reading in a second language related to reading in a first language?', in J. H. Hulstijn and J. F. Matter (eds) *Reading in two languages.* Amsterdam: AILA. 5–10.

Hulstijn, J. H. (2001) 'Intentional and incidental second-language vocabulary learning: A reappraisal of elaboration, rehearsal and automaticity', in P. Robinson (ed.) *Cognition and second language instruction.* Cambridge: Cambridge University Press. 258–286.

Hyland, K. (2003) *Second language writing.* Cambridge: Cambridge University Press.

Hyland, K. (2012) 'Learning to write: Issues in theory, research, and pedagogy', in R. M. Manchón (ed.) *Learning-to-write and writing-to-learn in an additional language.* Amsterdam: John Benjamins. 17–36.

Klapper, J. (2003) 'Taking communication to task? A critical review of recent trends in language teaching'. *Language Learning Journal,* 27/1. 33–42.

Krashen, S. D. (1982) *Principles and practice in second language acquisition.* Oxford: Pergamon.

Leki, I. (2009) 'Preface', in R. Manchón (ed.) *Writing in foreign language contexts: Learning, teaching and research.* Bristol: Multilingual Matters. xiii–xvi.

Luke, A. (1996) 'Genres of power? Literacy education and the production of capital', in R. Hasan and A. G. Williams (eds) *Literacy in society.* London: Longman. 308–338.

Lynch, T. and Mendelsohn, D. (2002) 'Listening', in N. Schmitt (ed.) *An introduction to applied linguistics.* London: Arnold. 193–210.

Manchón, R. M. (2012) *Learning-to-write and writing-to-learn in an additional language.* Amsterdam: John Benjamins.

Nation, I.S.P. (2013) *Learning vocabulary in another language* (2nd ed.). Cambridge: Cambridge University Press.

Nation, I.S.P. and Newton, J. (2009) *Teaching ESL/EFL listening and speaking.* New York: Routledge.

Newton, J. (2009) 'Listening in the language classroom: Opportunity standards for effective pedagogy'. *Modern English Teacher,* 18/3. 52–58.

Ortega, L. (2012) 'Reflections on the learning-to-write and writing-to-learn dimensions of second language writing', in R. M. Manchón (ed.) *Learning-to-write and writing-to-learn in an additional language.* Amsterdam: John Benjamins. 237–250.

Proctor, R. W. and Dutta, A. (1995) *Skill acquisition and human performance.* Thousand Oaks, CA: Sage Publications.

Rost, M. (2011) *Teaching and researching listening* (2nd ed.). Harlow: Longman.

Segalowitz, N. and Hulstijn, J. (2005) 'Automaticity in bilingual and second language learning', in J. F. Kroll and A.M.B. De Groot (eds) *Handbook of bilingualism: Psycholinguistic approaches.* Oxford: Oxford University Press. 371–388.

Silva, T., Leki, I. and Carson, J. (1997) 'Broadening the perspective of mainstream composition studies: Some thoughts from the disciplinary margins'. *Written Communication,* 14. 398–428.

Skehan, P. (1996) 'Second language acquisition research and task-based instruction', in J. Willis and D. Willis (eds) *Challenge and change in language teaching.* Oxford: Macmillan Heinemann. 7–30.

Skehan, P. (1998) *A cognitive approach to language learning.* Oxford: Oxford University Press.

Skehan, P. and Foster, P. (1999) 'The influence of task structure and processing conditions on narrative retellings'. *Language Learning,* 49/1. 93–120.

Swales, J. (1990) *Genre analysis: English in academic and research settings.* Cambridge: Cambridge University Press.

Truscott, J. (1996) 'The case against grammar correction in L2 writing classes'. *Language Learning,* 46. 327–369.

Vandergrift, L. (2007) 'Recent developments in second and foreign language listening comprehension research'. *Language Teaching,* 40/3. 191–210.

Vandergrift, L. and Goh, C. (2012) *Teaching and learning second language listening: Metacognition in action.* New York: Routledge.

Vandergrift, L. and Tafaghodtari, M. (2010) 'Teaching L2 learners how to listen does make a difference: An empirical study'. *Language Learning,* 60/2. 470–497.

Walter, C. (2007) 'First to second-language reading comprehension: Not transfer, but access'. *International Journal of Applied Linguistics,* 17/1. 14–37.

Waring, R. (2012) 'Extensive reading in English language teaching', in H. P. Widodo and C. A. Cirocki (eds) *Innovation and creativity in ELT methodology.* Munich: Lincom Europa. 69–80.

Willis, D. and Willis, J. (2007) *Doing task-based teaching.* Oxford: Oxford University Press.

Wood, D. (2006) 'Uses and functions of formulaic sequences in second language speech: An exploration of the foundations of fluency'. *Canadian Modern Language Review,* 13. 13–33.

31

Teaching literacy

Amos Paran and Catherine Wallace

Introduction: teaching literacy or teaching reading and writing?

In an era when we talk about digital literacy, emotional literacy and visual literacy as well as linguistic literacy (Ravid and Tolchinsky, 2002), we need to clarify ways in which we understand the term 'literacy' and how it might differ from its traditionally conceived constituent parts, 'reading' and 'writing'. This chapter will therefore attempt to tease out these connections, with particular reference to those who are learning to read and write in a second language. We begin by defining the field, moving on to consider general issues which are currently of concern to teachers and identifying key areas of debate. We conclude by outlining the main implications for practice of recent developments and set out some possible future directions in literacy studies with reference to second language learners.

Defining the field

While 'reading' and 'writing' are conceptualised as individual, cognitive skills, 'literacy' is indexed to particular societies at a particular time in history: literacy is seen in terms of what it allows you to do, that is, what social roles you are able to play in your community and the wider society. Thus Brice Heath (1991) talks of "the sense of being literate (which) derives from the ability to exhibit *literate behaviours*" (1991:3; italics in original). Brian Street and his associates (see Street, 1984; Baynham and Prinsloo, 2009) within the field known as New Literacy Studies have continued to emphasise this view of literacy as social practice rather than the learning of specific skills.

A view of literacy as embedded in social and cultural life is clearly relevant to those reading and writing in English as a second or additional language, as learners may have experienced different values and attitudes (tied to their L1 literacy) about what it means to be literate. These attitudes and experiences are likely to impact on their acquisition of L2 literacy. In addition, there are different contexts of literacy learning in a second language and different kinds of learners, representing a wide range of needs and resources. The assumption in most EFL contexts (in contrast to contexts where learners have settled in English-dominant countries) has normally been that the learners are literate in their L1. However, current global migration patterns have led to a situation where many migrants need to achieve some sort of L2 literacy without being literate in their L1 (see also Simpson, this volume). In addition, with the growing focus on EFL for young learners (see Enever, this volume), L1 literacy may not be firmly in place before pupils are introduced to L2 literacy. The range of L2 literacy learners is therefore wide and might include: a child or young learner who is already literate in L1; an adult literate in L1; children or young learners learning English literacy without being literate in their L1; or an adult learning English with no L1 literacy. Within these broad groups are many special cases, such as learners in post-colonial contexts who receive most of their education through a colonial language such as English; for example, learners in a Zambian school learning all their school subjects through the medium of English are in a very different position from young Italians learning English as a foreign language in school.

In the EFL world, the 'four skills' approach has tended to predominate (see Paran, 2012; Waters, 2012; Newton, this volume) – that is, we teach listening, speaking, reading and writing. The difference between teaching literacy – a view we argue for here – and teaching reading as a language skill is that, in teaching reading, we are taking a limited view of the process, often focusing on decoding and comprehension, but no more. In teaching literacy, we are assuming a purpose or reason for reading; we are looking at reading as communication and at what readers will *do* with what they read – or what writers do with writing.

Our approach is a broad-based view of literacy as both practice and process. To the work on literacy as practice we add an important missing dimension, namely, a discussion of the pedagogies which might support literacy more effectively. In short, while favouring the term 'literacy' and viewing literacy as sociocultural practice, we believe that it is still helpful to talk about reading and writing as specific processes which can be learned and developed to high levels of expertise (see Wallace, 2005).

Current critical issues

The internationalisation of English presents new challenges, purposes and practices in the teaching of literacy. We identify five key areas particularly relevant to literacy in English as a second/foreign language: digital forms of literacy, literacy as part of language learning and cognitive development, biliteracy, literacy as part critical literacy, and access to literacy through extensive reading.

Digital literacy: new literacy forms

Quite apart from the wide range of concepts with which the word 'literacy' is aligned (concepts referred to in our introduction), the way in which communication is now increasingly mediated by screens rather than the printed page has impacted on our engagement with the written language and on traditional literacy behaviours. Even 'the screen' has shown itself to be a shifting concept, as users move from computers to tablets and mobile devices. New technologies are opening up literacy opportunities not just in wealthy countries but also in the nations of the South, as, for example, through a scheme providing Kindles for Ghanaian children (Hirsch, 2013) or through Plan Ceibal, a scheme providing every Uruguayan child with a laptop (Woods, 2015).

However, even within an increasingly digital world, skill with print literacy remains an essential tool to take full advantage of new, cutting edge literacy resources. The world of paper and tools for writing such as pens is still with us and remains relevant for many L2 learners, especially if they aspire to education through the medium of English, where the need to process text in a linear manner (linear literacy) still prevails. In an educational world which takes a celebratory view of technological advances, it is important both to continue educating for linear literacy and to take a critical literacy approach to digital literacies (see later in this chapter for discussion of critical literacy).

Literacy as part of language learning and cognitive development

Discussion of the cognitive consequences of literacy has a long and contentious history. Olson (1994) concludes that literacy is best seen as linked to the cultural and economic needs and development of societies, and not as necessarily enhancing individual cognition through the mere fact of learning to read and write. Other researchers suggest that literacy does result in cognitive differences. These are the result of the differences between oral and written language in terms of syntax and vocabulary, as well as morphology in some inflected languages (Ravid and Tolchinsky, 2002); enhanced metalinguistic awareness of formal aspects of language as a result of acquisition of grapheme-phoneme correspondence (Tarone, 2010); and the large quantity of exposure to language which literacy enables (Cunningham and Stanovich, 1998). Indeed, many professionals working with learners new to literacy in any language have observed a washback effect by which access to print makes features of the language visible in ways that accessing oral English alone does not. Wallace (1987) shows how the spoken language of an illiterate adult became more fully structured as her reading developed and as she became aware how written English worked.

One development in the last two decades has been the focus on the learning of second languages by low-educated adults and adolescents, known as LESLLA (used as the acronym for both the process and for the organisation focusing on researching it). This has been sparked by a rise in immigration and changes in immigration patterns, resulting in large numbers of low-educated migrants arriving in Western Europe and the USA. Although many of these migrants are multilingual, integration into the new society requires not only learning an additional language but also becoming literate in that language, with little or no support from previous L1 literacy. Learning L2 literacy will be different for these learners, and LESLLA teachers may therefore need a different knowledge base from that of other ESL/EFL teachers (Vinogradov, 2013; see also Simpson, this volume).

Biliteracy

Cummins (1979, 2000), in a well-known conceptualisation of second language proficiency, describes how learners are advantaged by a high level of literacy in the first language. This allows what he calls the 'threshold level' to come into effect, by which L1 literacy can support L2 literacy even when the languages are linguistically dissimilar, and literacy skills established in the first language will transfer into the language being acquired (see also Carroll and Combs, and Newton, this volume). Other scholars have pointed out that where the first language is very different syntactically and graphically, as in the use of different writing systems such as the logographic system of Chinese, there may be greater difficulties than with transfer between alphabetic systems. Nonetheless, the process of making meaning, whether as readers or writers, involves similar strategies across languages. Yet learners are rarely invited to discuss and compare the use of strategies across the language repertoires which they operate. We would argue that learners should be encouraged to work between their respective languages in reading and writing, rather than keeping them distinct in the language classroom (see also Levine and Reves, 1985).

The role of critical literacy

One aspect of literacy which strongly differentiates it from 'reading' or 'writing' is 'critical literacy' (sometimes called 'critical thinking' or 'critical reading'). Table 31.1, based on Macknish (2011: 447), provides an overview of different approaches, putting them on a continuum from critical thinking to critical literacy.

Table 31.1 The continuum of critical reading processes

←——————————————   ——————————————→

Evaluating texts analytically (critical thinking)				Considering texts from a power perspective (critical literacy)		
Critiquing the logic of texts.	Questioning the source, author's purpose and stance.	Identifying pre-suppositions.	Considering alternative construc-tions of texts.	Focusing on wider socio-political influences.	Critiquing language and power relations.	Uncovering author's hidden agenda.
Assessing the credibility of claims and evidence.	Showing scepticism. Identifying bias.	Detecting propaganda devices.	Considering multiple perspec-tives.	Examining underlying values and ideology.	Challenging the posi-tioning of readers and others.	Taking action for social trans-formation.
Identifying fallacies.		Employing intertextuality.		Showing critical language awareness.		Pursuing social justice.
Distinguish-ing fact and opinion.		Showing language awareness.	Identifying missing and/or mar-ginalised voices.		Challenging naturalised assump-tions.	

Source: Adapted from Macknish, 2011: 447

Paran (2003) provides examples focusing on the left of the table, looking at ways of developing the constituent elements of critical thinking, such as in-depth knowledge, intellectual skills and dispositions of thoughtfulness (Onosko and Newmann, 1994). Increasingly, these skills (sometimes divided into 'lower order' and 'higher order' thinking skills) appear on curricula and syllabuses and sometimes are even tested in national exams. Wallace's (2003) approach, on the other hand, is located on the right hand side of the table and focuses on critical literacy, drawing on Halliday's (1994) systemic functional grammar. This involves asking students to consider how the choices of structure and lexis in texts work to privilege some sets of participants over others, often the more powerful (such as men, white people or the native speaker) over the less powerful (such as women, black people or the L2 learner). Practically, this involves students exploring textual features at the level of what Halliday (1994) calls field (the topic of the text), tenor (how the reader is addressed and positioned) and mode (how the text is put together as a cohesive and coherent artefact). Such analyses enable learners to reach conclusions about the ideological impact of texts in their contexts of use, alerting them to the ways in which texts may marginalise the 'Other'. As Cooke and Simpson (2008:110) note, "a critical take on literacy recognizes that literacy practices are far more than cognitive processes and relate to other social constructions such as class, gender, ethnicity and political status."

Fundamental to a critical literacy approach is the work of the Brazilian educational theorist Paulo Freire. In the UK, his approach has been taken up by a number of colleges, who have taken an overtly political approach to the teaching of literacy to adult migrants. An example of this work is the REFLECT project (www.reflect-action.org), which uses texts as 'codes' (Freire, 1972) to aid conceptualisation of social issues which might affect the daily lives of participants. Examples might be discussion of strikes, action to support local initiatives or organisation of protest movements. Freire's problem-posing approach has also informed work in the US (Auerbach and Wallerstein, 2004) and in EFL contexts (see Schleppegrell and Bowman, 1995, for an example from Guinea-Bissau).

Extensive reading

Extensive reading (ER) has assumed increasing importance in the last three decades. It is now commonly seen as a major source of L2 input, with benefits in all areas of language learning (Day and Bamford, 1998). There is widespread evidence for the effectiveness of ER, including the 'book flood' studies in Fiji (e.g. Elley and Mangubhai, 1983) and Lightbown et al.'s (2002) study of young ESL learners in Canada.

Although much of the earlier research was problematic (e.g. groups were not sufficiently differentiated, or the ER groups were exposed to additional input), Grabe (2009) suggests that the quantity of research from different contexts amounts to substantial evidence for the importance of ER activities. The picture is now more nuanced, and a clearer picture is being developed of the way ER interacts with other pedagogies, the way in which different types and levels of ER may be suited to different learners (Al-Homoud and Schmitt, 2009), and the amount of ER that needs to be done for benefits to be noticeable. One area where ER has clear benefits is in improving reading rate, thus making an important contribution to the development of reading fluency (Grabe, 2010). From a literacy point of view, it is important to note that ER is a prime example of learning literate behaviours through engaging in the literacy behaviour itself.

Key areas of debate in EFL/ESL literacy

The English writing system

The issues involved in learning to read and write English are crucially linked to the location of the English script on the continuum of orthographic depth. Orthographically shallow scripts present a consistent 1:1 relationship between the written and the spoken form, so that the mastery of a set of rules allows the reader to read any word in the language. Common examples of orthographically shallow languages are Spanish, Hungarian and Korean. In orthographically deep languages, on the other hand, the relationship between written and spoken forms is opaque, and the written form gives hardly any clues to the spoken one. Logographic scripts such as Chinese are the most extreme example: the characters provide nearly no clues to the sound. Many languages are situated between these extremes: Hebrew, for example, normally represents only the consonants in the written form, but not the vowels. English orthography, which is basically morpho-phonemic, is also midway on the continuum: the grapheme-phoneme correspondences are often complex.

However, English has more consistent patterning than is commonly acknowledged, as argued long ago by Albrow (1972) and by Stubbs (1980). Albrow claims that if one views the English writing system as consisting of different subsystems within the larger system, "many of the so-called irregularities of our writing system can be regarded as regular" (Albrow, 1972: 7). Pedagogically, we might propose making literacy learners aware of three related key principles, as flagged by Albrow and Stubbs:

- English retains the spelling of morphological units, e.g. 'electric' and 'electricity'; 'right' and 'rightly'; 'rite' and 'ritual'.
- English shows its grammar in its *writing*, and this aids the making of analogy, e.g. 'cats', 'dogs'; 'jumped', 'managed', 'wanted'. In each case, the inflectional ending is pronounced differently but is consistent in spelling.
- We relate words through connections to *meaning,* not to sound similarities, e.g. a likely new word for a learner reader such as 'scholar' can be related to 'school'; 'knowledge' to 'know'.

Of course, there is no doubt that English presents more difficulties for absolute beginners to the language than many other orthographies. However, it is helpful to draw learners' attention to some key principles about the writing system to facilitate literacy development. This meta-linguistic knowledge helps learners become aware of the patterns in the English writing system which become evident to them when they engage in a larger variety of literacy behaviours and read more widely.

Becoming a reader

The phonics debate

We have argued that understanding how English works as a system, grammatically, morpho-logically and lexically, is helpful to the emerging L2 reader. However, how this understanding operates in learning to read is disputed. Some scholars, notably Goodman in his classic paper 'Reading: a Psycholinguistic Guessing Game' (1967/1982), have argued that all the levels of language are in play right from the beginning of learning to read: there has to be an inter-action between syntactic, lexical and graphophonemic levels of language which readers draw on variably as they process text (see also Newton, this volume). A counter view is that the initial stage of learning to read should focus on developing the ability to decode the printed word and the ability to connect the written symbols with the meanings stored in the reader's mental lexicon. Many current early reading approaches favour this second view, which is based on what is known as 'the simple view of reading'. From this perspective, reading comprehension is conceptualised as the product of word recognition (decoding) and general comprehension (see Stuart et al., 2008; for an L2 view, see Verhoeven, 2011). This has sometimes been inter-preted as focusing only on decoding, taught through what is known as 'phonics'. Two points are important, however. Firstly, advocates of the simple view of reading agree that comprehension processes also need to be focused on in classrooms (see Stuart et al., 2008). Secondly, for L2 readers, who come with limited comprehension of the second language, merely focusing on decoding may result in learners who are skilled in sounding out words but unable to attach meaning to them (see Wallace, 1988, 1992; Gregory, 2008), resulting in what is sometimes known as 'barking at print'.

Regardless of the differing perspectives on the sequence of acquisition of the language ele-ments involved, ultimately, skilled reading can only develop in a context of use. This context of use must be linked to purpose, implying a literacy approach to teaching reading. This applies to both L1 and L2 readers. Reading needs to be linked to a purpose determined by context, which may be academic, personal or professional. This context-sensitive view of reading also means that we read different things for different purposes in different ways.

Teaching reading in the classroom: classroom literacy events

Classrooms worldwide vary widely in the manner in which literacy is taught, the way in which texts are used, and, indeed, in what counts as a classroom literacy event. In some classrooms, the main literacy event is reading aloud. For example, one class of young adults in a London ESOL class centred around a simple story about a child encountering a burglar at night (Wallace, 2013). The teacher read the text aloud a total of four times; students, nominated by the teacher in turn, read the text sentence by sentence a total of five times. The text was then used as a vehicle for grammar teaching and plundered for discrete grammatical items (in this case, the simple past tense): a clear case of the 'text as a linguistic object' (TALO; Johns and Davies, 1983). In some classes in Taiwan, reading lessons involve students listening to a recording of the text while following it in their book; later, the teacher plays the recording sentence by sentence, with students engaged in choral reading of the text (Chen JenYu, personal communication). Williams (1998, 2007), in research into the teaching of reading in Zambia and Malawi, also describes classes where the main activity was pupils reading aloud in turn along with a fair amount of choral reading. Though reading aloud in various forms appears in many literacy events (see Duncan, 2015) and may have a role to play in teaching reading, what is important to note in these examples is how reading aloud in these classrooms, with its focus on phonological form, becomes more dominant than reading for meaning.

In stark contrast to the ESOL classroom described by Wallace (2013, and in the paragraph above) is a strategy favoured by another teacher in the same institute. The teacher devoted a considerable amount of time to preparing the learner-readers for the text, through pre-reading activities which prompted background knowledge in advance of the presentation of the text. Here we see him introducing the topic of the text:

1   T: have you been reading newspapers this week?
2   S: no
3   T: news on television?
4   S: yes
(. . .)
8   T: all right. Does this ring any bells, anti-social behaviour, the news this week?

This brief exchange leads to an extended discourse which frames the presentation of an authentic topical text, taken from the Internet, which deals with anti-social behaviour. The teacher draws on his learners' everyday knowledge of cultural behaviour, as well as language use, to frame the text to be introduced. He taps into his learners' knowledge of what might constitute anti-social behaviour, thus 'bringing the outside in' (see Cooke and Wallace, 2004).

Differences between classroom literacy events persist at other levels of instruction as well. Paran (2002) describes how two teachers, using the same unit of an EAP textbook, emphasised phases of the lesson in different ways. He characterises one teacher's approach as product-oriented, in which the aim was to reach 'the right answer' about the meaning of the text. The other teacher organised activities so that the students re-read the text a number of times and then discussed it in different group combinations, attempting to understand not only the text but also what their peers had made of it. This teacher emphasised that students would not get definite answers to queries and questions, and connected class activities to the discussion of texts in academic life, thus highlighting the contexts within which texts are read and discussed. The two teachers thus produced very different literacy events.

Importantly, the differences between the lessons discussed in this section are not merely technical: they go to the heart of what teachers believe the purpose of the lesson is and the way in which the teachers conceptualise their lessons as *literacy events*, rather than *reading lessons*.

Beyond the comprehension view of reading

The lessons described above lead us to consider the question of whether it is useful to talk of comprehension or whether we should use the term *interpretation*, thus privileging the sense the reader wishes to make of text over any inherent meaning within the text. In EFL textbooks worldwide, the default position continues to be that of the text as 'container' of meaning and of the reader as a 'comprehender' who extracts meaning from texts. This view is evident in the comprehension questions (often multiple choice or true/false), which typically follow reading texts in EFL textbooks, in effect testing how far learners have understood what is 'contained' in the text. This contrasts with literacy views which focus on the reader as interpreter (Kress, 2014), and with reader response theory, which argues for different roles of the reader (Iser, 1978; see also Hall, this volume, ch. 32). The pedagogic implications of literacy views are represented in a variety of approaches, sometimes described as DARTS (directed activities related to texts). Here, rather than being invited to take meaning from texts, readers are encouraged to bring knowledge and experience to the text and to make sense of texts in different kinds of ways (see Barr et al., 1981; Paran, 1991. This also reflects the differences between the teachers discussed in the previous section).

Here we would like to reaffirm that effective reading always involves interpretation as much as comprehension, though clearly we acknowledge that learners need to understand what they read and to take meaning *from* text. Indeed, what is taken from or brought to texts, and the balance between interpretation and comprehension, will vary depending on the genre, which in turn is linked to reader purpose. In reading a train timetable or a recipe, for instance, most readers aim to get reliable factual information in ways that are different from the ways in which information is taken from an academic article.

Becoming a writer: first and second language learners

Product-, process- and genre-oriented teaching

A common way of looking at the teaching of writing is to conceptualise it as embodying one of three approaches: focusing on the *product*, often narrowly reproducing models and templates provided by a textbook; focusing on the *process* of writing and its stages, including brainstorming, drafting, editing etc.; and focusing on the *genre*, involving a consideration of the way in which "the features of a similar group of texts depend on the social context of their creation" and taking into account that "those features can be described in a way that relates a text to others like it and to the choices and constraints acting on text producers" (Hyland, 2003: 21; see also this volume: Starfield; Basturkman and Wette; and Newton). Thus a genre-focused pedagogy will focus on the way in which textual linguistic elements reflect writer choices made with the purpose of conveying the writer's intent and will involve an understanding of why texts are produced in the way that they are. Of the three, viewing the teaching of writing as genre is clearly the one best aligned with a view of literacy as socially situated.

In our experience, the most prevalent approach in EFL contexts is still the product approach, with teachers and textbooks providing linguistic models which students are encouraged to work from and base their own writing on. Neither the process approach nor the genre approach have made real inroads into mainstream teaching of writing (partly because the focus has often been on writing to learn rather than learning to write; see below). Although, in L2 contexts, process writing received a great deal of attention in the 1980s and the 1990s in academic circles (e.g. Zamel, 1983; Raimes, 1985), in teachers' handbooks (White and Arndt, 1991) and in some cases in coursebooks (White and McGovern, 1994), this move was not widespread and was probably mainly confined to EAP situations. Likewise, genre-based pedagogy has spread in very specific contexts – at university level, or in L1 (see for example, Hyland, 2009) and in some ESL contexts. In many EFL contexts, discussion of genre has mainly paid lip service to this notion. For example, in many coursebooks, the genres that learners are asked to produce are taught through modelling exemplars of the genre, which then in effect serve as frames, scripts or indeed models which learners learn to fill with their own content. There are, however, notable exceptions.

Tribble (2010) shows how a genre approach can be adapted to test-taking situations at Cambridge First Certificate in English (FCE) (i.e. an upper-intermediate) level; Firkins et al. (2007) adopt a genre approach for work with low-proficiency learners; and de Oliveira and Lan (2014) describe the way a teacher working with English language learners in the US incorporates a genre-based pedagogy into teaching science in elementary school.

There have, over time, been attempts to bring together the different approaches, acknowledging the strengths of each (e.g. Badger and White, 2000; Hyland, 2011). Within EFL, this balance is particularly important: genre-based approaches may be less successful in EFL contexts where the genres learners need to produce are poorly defined and where it is important to focus on the crucial enabling skills that are needed for the production of a written text by a learner (see Atkinson, 2003).

Learning to write and writing to learn

An important distinction that has recently come to the fore is the distinction between 'learning to write' and 'writing to learn'. This goes to the heart of the purpose of writing: what and who do we write for? In particular, who and what does the L2 writer write for? The act of writing presupposes a reader and a purpose for writing. Indeed, Hyland (2011) has suggested a different tripartite conceptualisation of the teaching of writing from that offered earlier: focusing on the *writer*; focusing on the *text* (subdivided into focusing on text as 'product' and on text as 'discourse'); and focusing on the *reader*. In many EFL classrooms, the only purpose of writing is to learn the language, and writing "often means little more than learning to demonstrate grammatical accuracy and clear exposition with little awareness of a reader beyond the teacher" (Hyland, 2011: 22). Little wonder, for often there is no other reader than the teacher, and in many cases there is no reader at all. Writing in this situation becomes a way of gaining overall proficiency in the language.

One liberating element which has enabled L2 writing to focus on genuine communication has been technology (see Gruba, Hinkelman and Cárdenas-Claros, and Kern, Ware and Warschauer, this volume). The near-ubiquity of the Internet and the development of mobile learning mean that it is possible to create situations where writing has a purpose and has a reader. This can be achieved through pairing between classrooms around the world (see an extended example in Kern, 2000), or by encouraging learners to contribute to blogs and online discussion forums. Learners are also much more likely to be motivated to use electronic media than to use pen and paper (though teachers point out that this has downsides when it comes to exams).

Implications for ELT practice

Shifting from 'reading' and 'writing' to literacy

We see a number of broad practical implications for taking a literacy approach, as opposed to a skills one, in L2 learning and teaching.

Firstly, teachers can promote activities which encourage learners not just to read widely in their personal time beyond the classroom but to be literacy researchers. They may carry out simple literacy ethnographies, noticing who reads what kinds of things in public and personal spaces, for instance on the street, in people's homes, on public transport and within the home cultural context. In ESOL contexts, learners could carry out literacy ethnographies in the target cultural setting. In many EFL contexts, too, such ethnographies can be carried out online. In school, teachers may institute whole-school and whole-class reading where pupils document and share their responses to their reading and discuss ways of reading, sometimes in study groups. Whole-class writing exchanges with classrooms in other countries can extend this approach to writing as well. In this way, reading and writing are configured as shared social practices which are jointly constructed. It also means that talk frames literacy activity. Talk around text is an inherent part of the reading experience, particularly in classrooms which centre around critical reading (see Wallace, 2003). In the same way, talk around text should be an integral part of teaching writing: in fully developed genre-oriented writing classrooms, understandings of genre are developed through analysis and discussion of the context, the purpose and so on. Descriptions of genre-oriented writing classrooms (e.g. Myskow and Gordon, 2010; Tribble, 2010) clearly indicate the way in which understanding and researching genre are discussed at length within the teaching sequence.

A second implication is the importance of providing rich opportunities to *practise* literacy – in the case of reading, to engage in extensive reading of many different genres, as argued earlier. In the case of writing, this means an active engagement with genre, an understanding of the way genres function in social contexts and the opportunity to produce a variety of genres. Literacy is thus viewed as sociocultural practice.

Finally, in moving away from a discrete skills teaching approach, we see reading as supporting writing, and writing as leading learners back to the reading of favoured texts in order to reshape and refine their own texts. Readers are potential writers and writers are necessarily readers – first and foremost readers of their own work. Experienced readers and writers read with a 'writerly' eye, imagining how they themselves might craft a similar passage; however, they also write with a readerly eye, imagining a reader in the course of writing. For second language learners, much of this understanding is derived from experience of literacy in a first or in other languages, which is why we argue here for a bilingual/biliterate approach, which we turn to next.

Working between languages

There has been an ideological tension between communicative language teaching (see Thornbury, this volume), which emphasises the target language exclusively, and bilingual approaches, which legitimise a role for the learners' home language/s and advocate the active use of learners' bi- or multilingual resources (see also Carroll and Combs, and Kerr, this volume). There are few examples of bilingual approaches in ELT classrooms, partly because the global textbook is an artefact which is marketed across contexts and continents (see Gray, this volume). However, interesting use can be made of dual language texts in multilingual settings. This is even more productive when these texts are created by the learners themselves, as is the case with the English/Albanian texts described by Sneddon (2009) in the UK and the 'identity texts' produced by young people working in both the heritage language and English in Canada (Cummins et al., 2005). Cummins et al. (2005) describe how pupils may share their linguistic resources; one case recounts how a recently arrived pupil from Pakistan advises on the Urdu version of a dual language text while her English dominant peers are responsible for the English language version.

With the growth of linguistically diverse teaching and learning contexts world-wide, it becomes increasingly important to draw on learners' linguistic repertoires. Learners with literacy in a language other than English can become literacy experts as they present and explain different writing systems to class members. Teachers can make use of the enhanced metalinguistic awareness of bilingual students to invite explicit discussion of the way in which language systems make different choices about, for example, tense and aspect, linked to ways of looking at the world. Working between languages brings cognitive advantages as well as motivational ones, linked to learner identity. It allows bi- and multi-lingual learners to observe differences between languages at the level of the sentence and the overall text, including different generic conventions, and contributes to the development of language awareness (see Svalberg, this volume).

Working analytically with English

Carefully selected and designed reading and writing tasks can support L2 learners to see patterns in English grammar at different stages of their literacy development. These include, for early learners, using versions of 'sentence maker' activities which allow learners to physically (and nowadays, electronically as well) manipulate sentence structure and are thus helpful in drawing attention to syntactic possibilities. Once learners are reading and writing, whole-text activities (referred to above as DARTS) draw learners' attention to the way in which texts are put together. Included in these are a range of predicting and cloze activities and the ordering of textual elements. Analytical reading can in this way be taught in conjunction with contextualised grammar and vocabulary teaching.

This kind of analysis might include discussion of the interface between written and spoken language; learners can be asked to redesign and reassemble texts accompanied by what we call 'literate talk', that is, literacy-influenced talk, which is one potential outcome of this kind of close work with text. One goal of a literacy-based programme of study is to help learners see the connections between written and spoken language and to make them aware of "the multiple relationships among all levels of text structure and how they interact" (Kern, 2000: 93).

Future directions: literacy in ELT

The changing map of literacy

We have argued in this chapter that, in a globalised world, assumptions about literacy instruction in a second language, many of which are entrenched in ELT practice, may need to be challenged. As a result of recent migration patterns, homogenous groups of learners are a phenomenon of the past in many countries. English language classes now often consist of new immigrants with rich language repertoires but little formal education learning alongside students with a low level of English but who are highly educated through the medium of their first language. This means that profiles of learners will vary and that learners' English language and literacy immediate and longer term needs will vary. This is true not only of ESOL classrooms, but also of urban classrooms in many countries in Europe and beyond, where EFL learners come from a large variety of language backgrounds.

There is also an ever wider number of literacy resources, many technological. The challenge for many learners may be to understand the culturally located ways in which these resources are used. How does one phrase an email message to one's professor? On what occasion is a written letter still a culturally appropriate form of communication? In short, a changing landscape relates to new technologies, a wider range of second language learners with different needs and resources and educational histories, and the role of English language literacy in international settings.

The importance of critical literacy in ELT

One overriding need in a globalised world where English, for the immediate future, serves as the global language, is for critical literacy. If L2 learners are to be active interpreters and creative designers of English language texts, they need an understanding of the manner in which texts, both academic and everyday, invite us to adopt certain views of the world. They need both to 'read back' and to 'write back'. The ESOL world in the UK has given strong attention to critical literacy, as discussed above; however, the EFL world has remained much more cautious about engaging with politically sensitive issues. This is partly because the use of the global textbook tends to favour a safe, sanitised set of discourses which minimises the risk of offence to particular cultural, religious or ethnic groups (see Gray, 2010; also, Gray, this volume). This caution may be misplaced. In many countries where English is taught to a high level in secondary education, the objectives of a critical approach align with those of the educational system. Many of our own international students, studying in the UK before returning to their own home contexts, are keen to adopt a more critical pedagogy for the twenty-first century, to take part in the debates of our age which are global debates and which, for the foreseeable future, will by and large be conducted through the medium of English. The intersection between literacy and criticality is likely to assume additional importance in years to come.

Discussion questions

- How do you react to the suggestion that literacy is more a 'cultural practice' than a 'cognitive skill'? If you agree, can you think of examples in your own context?
- Do you agree with the characterisation of 'mainstream' ELT as not recognising the changing context for learners' L2 literacy? If that is the case, what is the cause of this phenomenon?
- How do you teach L2 literacy in your context? In what ways does it resemble or differ from the examples provided in this chapter?
- How far do you agree with the authors' conclusion that critical literacy plays a particularly important role in an era when English functions as the major world language?

Related topics

Bilingual education in a multilingual world; Communicative language teaching in theory and practice; Computer-mediated communication and language learning; ELT materials; English for academic purposes; English for speakers of other languages; English for specific purposes; Teaching language skills.

Further reading

Kern, R. (2000) *Literacy and language teaching*. Oxford: Oxford University Press. (This book integrates reading, writing and speaking in a way which emphasises the cultural and critical characteristics of literacy acquisition and use. Importantly, it suggests that all language teaching should be informed by a literacy approach.)

Sneddon, R. (2009) *Bilingual books – biliterate children: Learning to read through dual language books*. Stoke on Trent: Trentham. (Sneddon describes how children from a range of home language backgrounds who are literate in English but not in their mother tongue are able to transfer the skills already developed in their reading of English into the mother tongue.)

Wallace, C. (2013) *Literacy and the bilingual learner: Texts and practices in London schools*. Houndmills, Basingstoke: Palgrave Macmillan. (This book looks at the literacy practices of English language learners in London schools. It discusses children and young adults learning literacy in English and explores the way in which literacy is linked to learner identities and aspiration.)

References

Albrow, K. H. (1972) 'The English Writing System: notes towards a description'. Schools Council Programme in Linguistics and English Teaching: Papers Series II, Vol 2. London: Longman for the Schools Council.

Al-Homoud, F. and Schmitt, N. (2009) 'Extensive reading in a challenging environment: A comparison of extensive and intensive reading approaches in Saudi Arabia'. *Language Teaching Research*, 13/4. 383–401.

Atkinson, D. (2003) 'L2 writing in the post-process era: Introduction'. *Journal of Second Language Writing*, 12. 3–15.

Auerbach, E. and Wallerstein, N. (2004) *Problem posing at work: English for action* (2nd ed.). Edmonton, Alberta: Grass Roots Press.

Badger, R. and White, G. (2000) 'A process genre approach to teaching writing'. *ELT Journal*, 54/2. 16–26.

Barr, P., Clegg, J. and Wallace, C. (1981) *Advanced reading skills*. London: Longman.

Baynham, M. and Prinsloo, M. (eds) (2009) *The future of literacy studies*. Basingstoke: Palgrave Macmillan.

Brice Heath, S. (1991) 'The sense of being literate: Historical and cross-cultural features', in R. Barr, M. L. Kamil, P. Mosenthal and P. D. Pearson (eds) *Handbook of reading research, vol. II*. New York and London: Longman. 3–25.

Cooke, M. and Simpson, J. (2008) *ESOL: A critical guide*. Oxford: Oxford University Press.

Cooke, M. and Wallace, C. (2004) 'Case study four. Inside out/outside in: A study of reading in ESOL classrooms', in C. Roberts, M. Baynham, P. Shrubshall, D. Barton, P. Chopra, M. Cooke, R. Hodge, K. Pitt, P. Schellekens, C. Wallace and S. Whitfield (eds) *English for Speakers of Other Languages (ESOL) Case studies of provision, learners' needs and resources*. London: National Research and Development Centre for Adult Literacy and Numeracy. 94–113.

Cummins, J. (1979) 'Linguistic interdependence and the education development of bilingual children'. *Review of Educational Research*, 49/2. 222–251.

Cummins, J. (2000) *Language, power and pedagogy: Bilingual children in the crossfire*. Clevedon: Multilingual Matters.

Cummins, J., Bismilla, V., Chow, P., Cohen, S., Giampapa, F., Leoni, L., Sandhu, P. and Sastri, P. (2005) 'Affirming identity in multilingual classrooms'. *Educational Leadership*, 63/1. 38–43.

Cunningham, A. E. and Stanovich, K. E. (1998) 'What reading does for the mind'. *American Educator*, 22/1&2. 1–8.

Day, R. and Bamford, J. (1998) *Extensive reading in the second language classroom*. Cambridge: Cambridge University Press.

De Oliveira, L. C. and Lan, S-W. (2014) 'Writing science in an upper elementary classroom: A genre-based approach to teaching English language learners'. *Journal of Second Language Writing*, 25/1. 23–39.

Duncan, S. (2015) 'Reading aloud in Lewisham: An exploration of reading-aloud practices'. *Literacy*, 49/2. 84–90.

Elley, W. and Mangubhai, F. (1983) 'The impact of reading on second language learning'. *Reading Research Quarterly*, 19/1. 53–67.

Firkins, A., Forey, G. and Sengupta, S. (2007) 'Teaching writing to low proficiency EFL students'. *ELT Journal*, 61/4. 341–351.

Freire, P. (1972) *The pedagogy of the oppressed*. Harmondsworth: Penguin.

Goodman, K. S. (1967/1982) 'Reading: A psycholinguistic guessing game', in K. Goodman *Language and literacy: The selected writings of Kenneth S. Goodman, vol. 1: Process, theory research*. Edited and introduced by F. V. Gollasch. London: Routledge & Kegan Paul. 33–43.

Grabe, W. (2009) *Reading in a second language: Moving from theory to practice*. Cambridge: Cambridge University Press.

Grabe, W. (2010) 'Fluency in reading – Thirty-five years later'. *Reading in a Foreign Language*, 22/1. 71–83.

Gray, J. (2010) *The construction of English: Culture, consumerism and promotion in the ELT coursebook*. Basingstoke: Palgrave Macmillan.

Gregory, E. (2008) *Learning to read in a second language: Making sense of words and worlds* (2nd ed.). London: Sage.

Halliday, M.A.K. (1994) *An introduction to functional grammar* (2nd ed.). London: Arnold.

Hirsch, A. (2013) 'Kindles makes up for lack of books in Ghana's reading revolution'. *The Guardian*, December 13, 2013. Retrieved from http://www.theguardian.com/world/2013/dec/13/kindle-ghana-reading-revolution-worldreader-guardian-christmas-appeal

Hyland, K. (2003) 'Genre-based pedagogies: A social response to process'. *Journal of Second Language Writing*, 12/1. 17–29. doi:10.1016/S1060-3743(02)00124-8

Hyland, K. (2009) *Teaching and researching writing* (2nd ed.). Harlow: Longman.

Hyland, K. (2011) 'Learning to write: Issues in theory, research and pedagogy', in R. M. Manchón (ed.) *Learning-to-write and writing to learn in an additional language*. Amsterdam/Philadelphia: John Benjamins. 17–35.

Iser, W. (1978) *The act of reading: A theory of aesthetic response*. London: Routledge & Kegan Paul.

Johns, T. and Davies, F. (1983) 'Text as a vehicle for information: The classroom use of written texts in teaching reading in a foreign language'. *Reading in a Foreign Language*, 1/1. 1–19.

Kern, R. (2000) *Literacy and language teaching*. Oxford: Oxford University Press.

Kress G. (2014) 'Reading, learning and "texts" in their interaction with the digital media'. Paper presented at the Neoliberalism, Applied Linguistics and Education Conference, Institute of Education, London, June 27–28, 2014.

Levine, A. and Reves, T. (1985) 'What can the FL teacher teach the mother tongue reader?' *Reading in a Foreign Language*, 3/1. 329–339.

Lightbown, P., Halter, R. H., White, J. L. and Horst, M. (2002) 'Comprehension-based learning: The limits of 'Do it yourself''. *Canadian Modern Language Review/La Revue canadienne des langues vivantes*, 58/3. 427–464.

Macknish, C. J. (2011) 'Understanding critical reading in an ESL class in Singapore'. *TESOL Journal*, 2/4. 444–472.

Myskow, G. and Gordon, K. (2010) 'A focus on purpose: Using a genre approach in an EFL writing class'. *ELT Journal*, 64/3. 283–292.

Olson, D. (1994) *The world on paper: The conceptual and cognitive implications of writing and reading*. Cambridge: Cambridge University Press.

Onosko, J. J. and Newmann, F. M. (1994) 'Creating more thoughtful learning environments', in J. N. Mangieri and C. Collins Block (eds) *Creating powerful thinking in teachers and students. Diverse perspectives*. Fort Worth: Harcourt Brace College Publishers. 27–49.

Paran, A. (1991) *Reading comprehension: Year I. Burlington proficiency series*. Limassol: Burlington Books.

Paran, A. (2002) 'Current practices in teaching EAP reading'. *Revista Canaria de Estudios Ingleses*, 44. 187–199.

Paran, A. (2003) 'Helping learners to become critical: How coursebooks can help', in W. A. Renandya (ed.) *Methodology and materials design in language teaching*. Singapore. SEAMEO RELC. 109–123.

Paran, A. (2012) 'Language skills: Questions for teaching and learning'. *ELT Journal*, 66/4. 450–458.

Raimes, A. (1985) 'What unskilled ESL students do as they write: A classroom study of composing'. *TESOL Quarterly*, 19/2. 229–258.

Ravid, D. and Tolchinsky, L. (2002) 'Developing linguistic literacy: A comprehensive model'. *Journal of Child Language*, 29/2. 417–447.

Schleppegrell, M. J. and Bowman, B. (1995) 'Problem-posing: A tool for curriculum renewal'. *ELT Journal*, 49/4. 297–306.

Sneddon, R. (2009) *Bilingual books – Biliterate children: Learning to read through dual language books*. Stoke on Trent: Trentham.

Street, B. (1984) *Literacy in theory and practice*. Cambridge: Cambridge University Press.

Stuart, M, Stainthorp, R. and Snowling, M. (2008) Literacy as a complex activity: deconstructing the simple view of reading. *Literacy* 42, 2. 59–66. doi: 10.1111/j.1741-4369.2008.00490.x

Stubbs, M. (1980) *Language and literacy. The sociolinguistics of reading and writing*. London: Routledge and Kegan Paul.

Tarone, E. (2010) 'Second language acquisition by low-literate learners: An under-studied population'. *Language Teaching*, 43/1. 75–83.

Tribble, C. (2010) 'A genre-based approach to developing materials for writing', in N. Harwood (ed.) *English language teaching materials: Theory and practice*. Cambridge and New York: Cambridge University Press. 157–178.

Verhoeven, L. (2011) 'Second language reading acquisition', in M. L. Kamil, P. D. Pearson, E. Birr Moje and P. P. Afflerbach (eds) *Handbook of reading research, vol IV*. New York: Routledge. 661–683.

Vinogradov, P. (2013) 'Defining the LESLLA teacher knowledge base', in T. Tammelin-Laine, L. Nieminen and M. M. Martin (eds) *Low-educated second language and literacy acquisition. Proceedings of the 8th Symposium. Jyväskylä Studies in Humanities 208*. Jyväskylä, Finland: University of Jyväskylä. 9–24. Retrieved from https://jyx.jyu.fi/dspace/bitstream/handle/123456789/41907/978–951–39–5310–2_LESLLA.pdf?sequence=1

Wallace, C. (1987) 'Variability and the reading behaviour of L2 readers', in R. Ellis (ed.) *Second language acquisition in context*. Oxford: Prentice Hall. 165–178.

Wallace, C. (1988) *Learning to read in a multicultural society: The social context of second language literacy*. Oxford: Prentice Hall.

Wallace, C. (1992) *Reading*. Oxford: Oxford University Press.

Wallace, C. (2003) *Critical reading in language education*. Basingstoke: Palgrave Macmillan.

Wallace, C. (2005) 'Reading and expertise', in K. Johnson (ed.) *Expertise in second language learning and teaching.* Basingstoke: Palgrave Macmillan. 85–103.

Wallace, C. (2013) *Literacy and the bilingual learner: Texts and practices in London schools.* Basingstoke: Palgrave Macmillan.

Waters, A. (2012) 'Trends and issues in ELT methods and methodologies'. *ELT Journal,* 66/4. 440–449.

White, R. and Arndt, V. (1991) *Process writing.* London: Longman.

White, R. and McGovern, D. (1994) *Writing.* Hemel Hempstead: Prentice Hall.

Williams, E. (1998) Investigating bilingual literacy: Evidence from Malawi and Zambia. Education Research Paper no. 24. London: DfiD. Retrieved from http://r4d.dfid.gov.uk/PDF/Outputs/Misc_Education/paper24.pdf

Williams, E. (2007) Extensive reading in Malawi: Inadequate implementation or inappropriate innovation? *Journal of Research in Reading,* 30/1. 59–79.

Woods, P. (2015) 'Telepresence teaching in Uruguayan primary schools – Is it delivering results?', in T. Pattison (ed.) *IATEFL 2014: Harrogate conference selections.* Faversham: IATEFL. 91–94.

Zamel, V. (1983) 'The composing processes of advanced ESL students: Six case studies'. *TESOL Quarterly,* 17/2. 165–187.

32

Using literature in ELT

Geoff Hall

Introduction

Literature can inspire, excite and intrigue, and engagement and inspiration are desirable in education of all kinds. In this chapter, I argue that using literature in ELT can be useful to expand language learners' vocabulary, awareness of register, genre and linguistic knowledge generally. But a stronger claim that I shall also make is that the ways in which language is used in literary texts are actually centrally relevant to the needs of students in a wide range of situations in everyday life.

Historically, as the communicative language teaching (CLT) movement grew in Western countries from the 1970s (see Thornbury, this volume), literature often came to be seen as less relevant to ELT. For advocates of CLT, grammar-translation was 'the enemy' (simplistically speaking), and grammar-translation had always relied on literature; indeed, for many advocates of grammar-translation, the reading of literature had been seen as the ultimate reason for studying a foreign language. Thus, literature fell out of favour in ELT, whilst CLT concentrated on speaking, understood as everyday information exchanges, and reading and writing were initially neglected in favour of more immediate 'high surrender' practical speaking activities (Wilkins, 1976).

More generally, with increasingly dominant instrumental and vocational views of education in many parts of the world, literature has often fallen under suspicion across both L1 and L2 curriculums. Yet literature is still often taught for its own sake, particularly in less well-resourced parts of the world, its value unquestioned as reading material or for vocabulary development. Even in these contexts, however, clearly defined pedagogical principles for teaching literature or teaching with literature are often not articulated, which in some ways is as undesirable as not using literature at all.

Yet a more recent position on literature use, with the rise of pedagogical concerns about identity and the feelings of learners, resonates with ideas of learner-centredness, reader response and suspicion of classic literary canons and, from this, to creative writing, drama workshops and altogether more active and interrogative approaches to literature study which will be discussed later in this chapter.

A representative hostile view to the use of literature comes from Horowitz (1990), who argues that, even if 'necessary' language could be located incidentally and with difficulty in some literary texts, there are surely easier ways to teach it. According to this view, literature is a specialist concern for some advanced and thus probably older students only, most likely those intending to be teachers. At the school level, on the other hand, communicative classes offer students basic vocabulary and grammar, with language taught for the purpose of information exchange in the 'real world', and ignore literature. This supposedly more practical language of service encounters and the like (restaurants, hotels and stations) enables only limited meaningful engagement with the values and informing ideas of cultural groups who use the L2, as documents like the Common European Framework (Council of Europe, 2001) acknowledge. Users of an L2 will often want meaningful relations (Hanauer, 2012) with other users of that language, as well as wanting to use the language to elaborate their own identities and desires (Kramsch, 2006, 2009). This is where literature can provide an invaluable resource.

'Literature', in current approaches to language teaching and ELT, is emphatically literature with a small 'l' (McRae, 1991), texts which use language imaginatively or creatively but are not necessarily 'classic' texts. Thus, literary texts use language in ways that are better related to other uses of language such as advertising or conversation than split off as somehow utterly different or even qualitatively superior (as a 'classics' or 'canonical' view might imply). From this viewpoint, stories, biography, travel literature, journalism, play scripts, diaries and blogs are all literature. If *Jane Eyre* by Charlotte Brontë, *Things Fall Apart* by Chinua Achebe or any other classic writing is to be valued more highly than other texts, this is something students should be encouraged to do for themselves rather than just accepting hand-me-down knowledge. From this perspective, therefore, literature can be used to engage and motivate students, to get them to notice and work with language forms expressively, to explore new personal and imaginative worlds and to communicate authentically, for, as Heath (1996: 776) notes: "Literature has no rival in its power to create natural repetition, reflection on language and how it works, and attention to audience response on the part of learners."

Two basic questions can be asked about the use of literature in ELT (Carter, 2007: 4):

1   What *is* literature, and what therefore should be *selected* as a basis for teaching literature, and why?
2   How should it be taught and what is its overall place, internationally, in language education?

I will address these two essential questions in turn. The chapter initially examines the language of literature before considering how using literature might support L2 learning. The chapter then examines approaches to literature reading before clarifying how literature is best selected and used in ELT. I conclude the chapter with some more recent developments and likely future directions for uses of literature in ELT.

The language of literature

Literature has sometimes been assumed to use language in distinct ways and with unique features – and not features most obviously required for English language learners. Yet research has revealed that it is not so much that the language of literary texts is not to be found in other texts (e.g. unusual vocabulary or grammar) but rather that language tends to be used in different ways, for different purposes, and with greater variety. This unusual range of otherwise representative language used in literary texts can be seen as an advantage to the learner, if admittedly sometimes also a challenge – but it is the right kind of challenge for those who need to pay attention to language and to expand their repertoires beyond a minimal 'survival' core.

Adamson (1998), for example, demonstrates increasing vernacularisation across all genres of literature in English; modern English literary texts, including poetry and drama as well as novels and short stories, are increasingly characterised by ordinary, everyday language, including more spoken forms. Dorst (2015) shows that literary texts do not use more metaphors and figurative language than other kinds of writing; rather, metaphors in literary texts are more innovative (and so draw attention to themselves) and tend to be signalled more self-consciously. Lakoff and Johnson (1980) demonstrated the pervasively metaphorical nature of all everyday language use, and Carter (2004) identified the inherent and routinely creative uses of language in everyday exchanges between users; literary texts reflect and develop this. Meanwhile, dialects, sociolects, professional and occupational registers, representations of accent, style and variation, and genre mixing are to be found deployed throughout modern literature, but not in isolation, and often in foregrounded and highly contextualised ways which lend themselves well to learning. The jargon of a lawyer may be used for memorably comic purposes, or a careful formal register may show uneasy relationships between characters that the reader cares about. A character is shown moving from job interview to chat with a friend or a stranger on a train, with relevant changes in dialect and sociolect. Literature artfully prompts the attentive reader to notice the particular nature of any specialised language it uses, and more generally how language varies according to contexts of use.

Language use in literature, then, is uniquely representative of the wider language, and authors are able to draw on all the resources of that language for creative or imaginative purposes. It is also a use of language which often prompts its readers to consider its form and use particularly carefully (for example, 'why did s/he use that word?, what exactly does that mean?, why is that term repeated?'). Literary language will often 'draw attention to itself' (Jakobson, 1960). No other use of language does this to the same degree, and literature therefore offers unique 'affordances' (van Lier, 2000) for language learners who need to cope with language as it is used and as it can be used and to begin to use it for themselves for their own purposes. The language of literature is 'authentic' in that sense, i.e. if it is engaged with by learners. And, in fact, literary language is designed to prompt engagement.

Using literature: perspectives from second language learning theory and research

Literature and 'noticing'

Second language learning has traditionally been studied from cognitive and psychological perspectives within SLA research. These approaches give some good theoretical grounds for using literature in ELT. Literary texts require or can prompt deep reader or listener cognitive engagement – interaction with meaning but also with, or through, close attention to the linguistic forms of the text (i.e. 'focus on form', see also Svalberg, this volume). 'Noticing' (Schmidt, 1990), or paying conscious attention to a form that is not known or not known well enough and seeing how it can be used to make meaning, seems to be a precondition for much successful language learning. Readers of literature often recall exactly the words of a favourite or meaningful literary text or extract (Nell, 1988); those words in that order are particularly effective for them. Reading studies have recorded the tendency of readers to slow their reading rate as they read passages they later report to be meaningful, pleasurable or in some way important (Miall, 2007). Precise words matter, and favourite or enjoyed passages are often read more than once. This type of literary reading favours memorability and thus L2 learning. Additionally, the teacher using literature can exploit the importance of using this word rather than that one in a literary work (e.g. the choice of one tense rather than another that could have been selected, or the use of an indefinite not a definite article, a lexical choice, a choice of word order etc.).

Learning requires attention, then, but also requires *repeated* acts of attention (Ellis, 2002, 2005). In SLA research, 'connectionism' argues for the importance of repetition and recycling, or near recycling, of language in the acquisition of, for example, grammatical patterns, formulaic 'chunks' of language, collocations and specific lexical items (ibid.). Attending to a word or form once is not enough; nor is uninterested noticing (Schmidt, 1990). Thus, 'foregrounding', a basic feature of many literary texts in which the text by design draws attention to its linguistic forms (words and structures, sounds, spelling and so forth) signposts language for learners, enabling them to give the necessary attention to relevant linguistic features. This foregrounding often works in practice as exact or near repetition or other patterning, or through innovative figurative uses of language.

For example, compare, at a more obviously literary level, advertising, or the refrains and choruses of poems, ballads and lyrics right through to the repetitive prose styles of Dickens or D. H. Lawrence. 'Beans Meanz Heinz' (an advertising slogan from the UK with obvious phonological patterning) is a linguistically similar phenomenon to "And miles to go before I sleep / And miles to go before I sleep", the conclusion of Frost's poem 'Stopping by Woods on a Snowy Evening', in which a reader is likely to be prompted to pause and to reflect upon the deliberate repetition. Teachers can draw attention to patterning in a text through prediction activities or extensions of the technique. Rhyme, alliteration and assonance are all instances of such repetition, which can be used to teach phonology but also to show the way sound is used in the service of meaning. Similarly, Boers and colleagues have shown how phonologically motivated many idioms are in English; we remember such sayings often at least partly because of the insistent sound patterning (e.g. shop till you drop, happy as Harry) (see, for example, Boers et al., 2014). As noted above, everyday language use is surprisingly poetic, and awareness of such poetics, in principle as well in specific examples, can help both teachers and students.

Tolerance of ambiguity

Within research into individual differences (see MacIntyre, Gregersen and Clément, this volume), 'tolerance of ambiguity' is seen as a positive trait for language learners (Chapelle and Roberts, 1986) and reflects the extent to which learners persist with meaning-making activity even when their comprehension is limited. Emmott (1997) and others have shown how 'tolerance of ambiguity' is needed for the successful reading of much literature, and indeed that, arguably, a reader can become more tolerant of ambiguity through repeated engagement with literary texts and with the encouragement of teachers and more confident peers. Writers of detective novels will plant clues which may or may not help the reader solve the crime – an apparently 'good' character turns out to be less trustworthy than we thought, or a first-person narrator, the reader gradually realises, does not fully understand her own situation or fully tell the truth about it. These are all instances of the kind of tolerance of ambiguity successful literary reading requires and develops, and which, it is argued, can also enhance second language learning. (Of course, cinema and many other art forms often require the same tolerance of ambiguity – throughout the chapter, my idea of the 'literary' needs to be understood very broadly.)

Beyond processing and close attention to surface linguistic forms, approaches to second language learning also emphasise the value of learning to infer, i.e. 'to read between the lines', and to understand the significance of words beyond any literal or apparent meaning they might seem to have; this might be termed 'active meaning-making' (Grabe, 2009). All help fix language in the mind of learners more securely (Grabe, ibid.; Alderson, 2000), and literature scores highly here again. Sustained attention to language helps retention in longer-term memory and a fuller understanding of how words and expressions can be used, and this can be enhanced by appropriately designed tasks. Thus, literature may be of help to learners if tasks can be designed to prompt active engagement with the texts chosen.

Emotional investment

The desire to 'turn the page', to finish the book as well as to re-read and to tell others about one's reading, including emotional involvement in it, are all signs of the kind of engagement that will facilitate language learning. Ideas of 'hot cognition', i.e. the relevance of emotions to thinking and understanding, also recognise this: reading, just as with other uses of language, can set the heart racing, make us physically uncomfortable or affect our feelings and bodies in multiple ways. It will hardly surprise educators to be told that feelings are very much linked to learning (Sanford and Emmott, 2012).

Participation in a new community

Emerging relatively recently within the research literature, social, sociocultural or sociocognitive perspectives (see, for example, Negueruela-Azarola and García, this volume) provide further insights into second language learning. Learners in such a view are 'individuals' rather than brains ('cognition'), and individuals in turn are social beings (see, for example, Atkinson, 2011). Learning takes place in and through particular contexts and situations, which are important for the forms and directions learning will take. Language learning is figured as *appropriation* or *participation* in a new community of practice (Lantolf, 2000: 20) or even imaginative identification (Kramsch, 2009; also Dörnyei, 2010, on motivation). From this perspective, the task of the language learner is to find a voice through the new language, and this will be done by interacting under given conditions with speakers of the new language. Thus, we learn a new language by using it meaningfully with others. Reading is just such an interaction, as is talking about the reading we have been doing.

Literature offers language that learners can engage with in various ways, whether it be immersion, resistance, pleasure or irritation, but all these responses engage the individual in significant ways, with ideas that matter to them (see Duff and Maley (1990/2007) and Maley (2001) on 'non-triviality' of literary texts). Literature can explore what it means to be human, including death, life and love; illness and health; what is right and wrong; social identity, including gender, race and ethnicity, and sexual orientation; and feelings and emotions. Such issues can matter to a learner at a deeper level than a typical communicative 'directions to the station'-type task. Literary texts can motivate language learners to want to understand, to express themselves and to define their own position and new identity by using what the L2 and its texts offer. Thus, a frequent learner comment in second language creative writing programmes (Hanauer, 2010; Iida, 2012) is 'I could never have said / would never have thought of that in my own language.' The work of Norton (2000) on gender and identity as factors in language learning or Pavlenko (2005), for example, on emotions in learner perspectives on language learning, or Dörnyei and Ushioda (2010) on the highly dynamic and contextual nature of motivation (see also Lamb, this volume) show how important feelings and specific learning situations and experiences are in determining the relation of a learner to a language and its texts. Wanting to engage with that language and to use it for one's own purposes are fundamental to success in language development, and imaginative and creative texts can be central in promoting and supporting such engagement (Kramsch, 2009).

Language play

One aspect of this engagement with a new language is the widely-observed phenomenon of 'language play' (Cook, 2000) – any teacher will have noticed instances of learner humour, repetitions or deliberate variations, language play as puns, (mis-)translations, mispronunciations, invented possible words or structures on a daily basis, both in classrooms and beyond. Language play can help learners ascertain the range of what is more or less acceptable or innovative in a language and learn how a language works by taking it apart and putting it back together again. The importance of language play in facilitating language development is noted by Lantolf (1997: 19), who writes, "I do not believe that language play, in and of itself, leads to successful SLA. . . . I do believe, however, that without language play learning is unlikely to occur." Similarly, Cook (2000: 204) notes that "There is good reason to regard [second] language play both as a means and an end of language learning" and that an "ability to play with language" could even be used as a "test of proficiency" (Lantolf and Cook both quoted in Belz, 2002: 204).

Research into 'language play' sees play as intrinsic to language learning. The ultimate examples of such ludic texts, once again, are broadly literary texts, whether jokes, stories and riddles, or puns or other 'bending' of the possibilities the language offers. This is the case in L2 learning as much as in first language development. Beard (1995) reports the links in L1 development between early language play and later success with literacy, vocabulary size and overall ultimate educational success. While less well researched, similar processes can be expected to apply to second language learner development.

Approaches to literature reading in ELT

Research into student attitudes (e.g. Martin and Laurie, 1993) reports that most language students are unconvinced when it comes to the use of literature in language education. They can be convinced by good teachers using literature imaginatively, but generally feel that it is not an efficient way to learn a second or foreign language. The teacher who intends to use literary texts in class will thus need to demonstrate how or why uses of literature are worthwhile. Similarly, there is real evidence of student resistance to non-standard English features in literary texts (Hoffstaedter-Kohn, 1991), rather as research shows teachers and students sceptical about the claims of ELF (English as a Lingua Franca) or doubting other 'World Englishes' variations (Jenkins, 2015). A challenging but important task for the English language teacher, today more than ever, is to teach the need to engage with English as a world language and to be at least aware of its full range of variation, as evidenced by literary texts of all kinds.

Reading literature in the classroom

Reader response, as developed by early theorists in literary studies such as Iser or Rosenblatt, generally informs uses of literature in ELT classrooms today, where more stylistic or 'close reading' approaches dominated in the past. Iser (1978) noted the need for successful readers of literature to actively fill in gaps in what the text tells us (i.e. to infer – see above), while Rosenblatt (1978/1994) emphasised that reading a literary text was an interactive aesthetic experience, not an exercise in fact finding. For Rosenblatt, what matters is the experience and what reading the text does for a reader, not reaching the meaning approved by one's teachers. As with approaches to first language reading, in methodological approaches to the reading of literature in a second language, educationists have generally moved toward such reader response approaches, particularly at school level, where the learner-reader is encouraged to express personal ideas and reactions to texts ('response') based on their knowledge and experiences up to that point.

Reader response approaches have been characterised by awareness of the importance of the reader to the construction of literary meaning. Not all readers read in the same way, and this can be an advantage rather than a problem in the classroom. Elliot (1990) and Ali (1994), for example, testify to the interest in and applications of reader response approaches in ELT. In the same tradition, Sell (1995) reports positively on reader response inspired uses of literary texts throughout ELT education in Finland, one of the most highly rated education systems in the world, from kindergarten to university. The relative lack of articles since the 1990s testifies to the acceptance of reader response since that time though the approach is not without problems. Some, for example, question the limitations of a personal approach to literature reading, and thus, reader response could still stand further investigation (Hall, 1999, 2015; Harding, 2014). The approach is seen as learner-centred and more likely to promote real and authentic communication in a language classroom, with similar advantages for second language learning to those claimed for communicative language teaching. 'Learning from literature' is promoted over 'teaching literature'. Lessons led by reader response approaches will feature much tentative exploration of individual readings, mediated by group work and further discussion and reflection as consensus emerges on the meaning of a text or until agreement to differ is reached, ideally all with continual reference back to the text itself: prompting reference to the text may be the role of the teacher in such discussions.

A key affordance of the literary text is for personally meaningful discussions. Kim (2004, concerning ELT) or Scott and Huntington (2007, concerning French language) show how more valuable text-based or text-originating discussions can proceed from this kind of open approach. Indeed, the Scott and Huntington article is particularly interesting not only because the classes described are low proficiency, but also for showing that a teacher can help facilitate, or in Vygotskian terms 'scaffold' (Vygotsky, 1978), more valuable discussions than took place in groups where a teacher was not present to facilitate. Where no teacher was present, the learners became fixated on linguistic detail and indeed on basic 'comprehension' with an apparent reluctance to enter into more significant discussions, though they could do this when led. There is often a tension between letting readers make sense for themselves, and 'teaching' the students what a text is about and why it is valued within the culture that originally produced it (typically in ELT, Britain or the USA).

Second language literature reading outside the classroom

When individuals attempt literature reading for themselves outside of classrooms, cognitive studies using 'think out loud' procedures (ToL), protocols or recalls (Gass and Mackey, 2000; Bowles, 2010) typically show (a) intensive processing of the language of literary texts, particularly of poetry or shorter texts, and (b) attempts to make connections both linguistically and to the world knowledge of the reader (see Hall, 2015, for further discussion). Where such solitary engagement with the text occurs, it would seem to be useful for language learning, at least in terms of the development of reading skills and incidental acquisition of vocabulary or structures. Elsewhere, emotions, pleasure, curiosity and engagement with characters (see, for example, the empathy research of Sklar, 2013) are all evidence of a text's potential suitability for language teaching and learning. Naturally, also reported are the difficulties of reading in a second language, including issues surrounding the additional demands on the working memory (see Collins and Marsden, this volume, for further discussion of working memory) and online cognition of the L2 user. These very real difficulties should never be underestimated. Readers of literature in a second language will usually need a lot of support and confidence-building activities before they will successfully and independently read extensively outside the classroom.

Extensive reading

Extensive reading is the general heading given to the reading of longer and complete texts, ideally for pleasure and for general understanding rather than to examine every detail (i.e. 'intensive reading'), which is more likely to happen in class (Day and Bamford, 1998). Literature use in ELT can clearly be pursued through extensive reading, as advocated by, for example, Elley and Manghubai (1983), Mason and Krashen (1997) and Day et al. (2011), and by Pigada and Schmitt (2006) researching incidental vocabulary acquisition through extensive reading. There is no doubt that many foreign language readers find increasingly well-written 'readers' specifically developed for the ELT market worthwhile, even if some educators hold serious reservations about the simplified texts often found, and there is still much to understand, for example concerning the contribution of glosses, marginal notes and other variations in presentation of these materials. Extensive reading of complete stories outside the classroom builds confidence, builds familiarity with the foreign language and facilitates the automatisation of processing of the foreign language so that readers can give less conscious attention to the linguistic surface in constructing meanings more quickly and efficiently. Research indicates that arguments for incidental vocabulary acquisition have probably been overstated, but some gains are measurable (e.g. Pigada and Schmitt, ibid.). A relevant and more recent development in this area is the formation of reading circles both face to face (Shelton-Strong, 2012) and through online communities of readers discussing their reading (Lima, 2013, 2014). I return to such developments in the chapter's section on recent developments and future directions for literature in ELT.

Literature in the ELT classroom

In this section, I turn more directly to practical issues in using literature in ELT. I have tried to indicate in previous sections some examples of what research findings might mean in practice for teachers and students, but there is never a direct and unarguable line from such applied linguistic research to the classroom. We need to learn from both second language learning research and educational research, including action research projects, which tell us what apparently works and does not work in actual classrooms. Paran (2008) makes a valuable critique of narrowly linguistic approaches to uses of literature in ELT which have neglected practical classroom and educational issues.

Generally, in terms of *how* and *what* to teach, which are the key questions for teacher-practitioners, the news is comforting. While training in the use of literature is unfortunately lacking in most ELT teacher education, the good news is that tasks (see Van den Branden, this volume) are a very effective way of engaging with literary texts. Precise principles for designing tasks for literary texts are provided by Duff and Maley (1990/2007), and include use of completion tasks, matching exercises, jigsaw activities and other classic CLT techniques. If literature is still itself found intimidating or unattractive by learners (and teachers!), this is a challenge for teacher trainers to tackle. But if literature, as has been argued, is language-in-use not unlike other uses of language, then, the same basic pedagogical techniques and methods can be used as for any other text, or as in established approaches to the teaching of reading. Stylistics, the linguistically informed systematic and principled study of texts, offers linguistic ways into interactive and exploratory study of a literary text. Related are the 'transformation' exercises of (perhaps the best example) Rob Pope (1995). A transformation can take the form of changing a source text into a different genre, for example a description of a landscape in a poem transformed into an estate agent's 'blurb'. A scene from a novel or short story can be dramatised, with students asked, for example, to add precise stage directions concerning movements, facial expressions or other details not present in the source text. Any discussion of existing differing translations of a text, or an attempt by students themselves to translate, will immediately raise questions of meaning and intention which can be very engaging.

Similarly, dramatisations (e.g. Elgar, 2002) or other performances, translations to the film medium as well as genre, style, narratology (e.g. Carter and Long, 1987, 1991) and indeed actual linguistic translations are now recognised to be of real learning value (Cook, 2010). The point to reiterate is that the literary text is a resource to learn from rather than an icon to be taught. Teachers and learners can and should play around with it to discover how it works and how perhaps it may be made to work better for them. The best tasks and activities will exploit to the full the specific features of the text. Literary texts do not only offer topics or themes. They offer valuable uses of language, and this is where its greatest affordances lie for language learners.

But selection of literature is not only a lesson-by-lesson or task-by-task issue; it is also a concern for wider syllabus design. Over 30 years ago, Brumfit (1981) highlighted a tension between increasingly impressive techniques for exploiting literary texts in classrooms and the relative absence of wider curriculum considerations and more longitudinal views beyond the single successful lesson: what texts to read, in what order and why. This observation often still applies today, though perhaps we are increasingly aware of it as ELT is more and more closely integrated into school level teaching. Enthusiasm for the use of literature in class needs to be tempered with wider thinking about the aims of the students and the outcomes looked for, including how learning on the programme will be assessed. Too often the approach to using literature in ELT has been opportunistic and short term rather than strategic, the 'fun' or undoubtedly valuable lesson in its own right taking precedence over longer term plans for L2 proficiency development. That said, some interesting literature-in-ELT syllabus documents are at last appearing (e.g. International Baccalaureate [IB] documents, Singapore Ministry of Education), and I note that these wider aims are not only to do with vocabulary building, genre and register learning, or better reading skills alone but part of wider educational aspirations for ethical citizenship and (inter-) cultural awareness. As Tate notes:

> I refuse to look at my students as primarily history majors, accounting majors, nursing majors. I much prefer to treat them as people whose most important conversations will take place outside the academy, as they struggle to figure out how to live their lives – that is, how to vote and love and survive, how to respond to change and diversity and death and oppression and freedom.
>
> *(1993: 320)*

The emergence of Modern Language Association (MLA) guidelines, American Council for Teaching of Foreign Languages (ACTFL) standards (from the USA), the Council of Europe's Common European Framework of Reference for languages (CEFR) (see chapter references) and other such documents informing language curriculums, teacher training and materials design demonstrate a growing interest in the role that literature and culture need to play in language education at the highest levels of planning and policy down to 'the next lesson'.

Further recent developments and future directions

Interest in culture and intercultural communication (see Kramsch and Zhu, this volume) is growing as more and more people come into contact more frequently, not always harmoniously, with those with different beliefs, ways of living, and ideas and aspirations than their own. New curriculum and syllabus statements in Europe and the US recognise the importance of raising cultural awareness and educating cultural intermediaries. This points to a renewed relevance for reading the literatures of other cultures. This is not only a question of, for example, coming to understand factual cultural features like the meaning of 'semi-detached house'. More importantly, through literature, we can get some idea of what it feels like to be 'like that', to do that, to believe that, or to belong to another cultural group. If imposed, such texts will do more harm than good; the challenge for educators is to foster tolerance rather than confirm prejudices – and this is much easier said than done. Bredella and Delanoy (1996), for example, report well-intentioned uses of cultural materials in Germany that seemed to reinforce rather than challenge negative learner stereotypes. It is also important to emphasise that literature can teach how like each other we often are, as well as sometimes how different. Literature alone cannot be sufficient for such learning but can contribute to it. One specific aspect of this interest in intercultural competence is the renewed interest in translation and own language use by those who will act as mediators in increasingly multicultural and multilingual worlds (Council of Europe, 2001; Cook, 2010; see Kerr, this volume) and a growing recognition of the mix of languages and varieties typical of literary text. Clearly, literary texts, and activities around literary texts, can be relevant to these important new educational imperatives. English, as we all know, is a world language, but by that same token, it is not quite the rather one-dimensional, native-speaker oriented standard language it was once believed to be (see Seargeant, this volume for further discussion).

Similarly, ELT is moving into schools and even early years education (see Enever, this volume), where once its predecessor, 'TEFL', was concerned almost exclusively with the teaching of adults. Younger learners are now the focus of a growing field of expertise as their numbers grow, and we see teenagers in secondary schools with ever higher levels of proficiency. Thus, Bland (2013) looks at the use of children's literature, young adult literature and cross-over literature aimed at both audiences, such as the *Harry Potter* books by J. K. Rowling or *The Curious Incident of the Dog in the Night-time* (Mark Haddon, 2003), which all originally had non-ELT audiences. Meanwhile, from nursery rhymes to stories and diaries (or blogs) to picture books and comics, literature seems to be ever more relevant for L2 learners.

A related phenomenon is that of multimodal literary texts and spin offs, also addressed by Bland (2013). Gaming, film and video all contribute to learners' visual literacy, literary literacy and critical cultural literacy. Adaptations of all kinds, including appropriations into other media and 'transformations', whereby a source text which originally inspired creativity is changed into a version no longer obviously or simply related (Sanders, 2015), are now the norm for literary work and are often subsumed into wider discussions of 'creativity'. As noted earlier in the chapter, reading groups and reading circles have never been more popular, in ELT as in the wider population (Shelton-Strong, 2012; Lima, 2013). Publishers, authors, retailers, newspapers and other media all encourage and support this burgeoning activity. Online reading groups have emerged (Lima, 2014), and the transnational possibilities of the Internet do seem to have some traction here as a complement to, surely, rather than ever replacing, the pleasure of the face-to-face meeting of those whose relations have developed partly or wholly through their reading group.

I close with creative writing and drama performance. One of the more welcome developments in literature study in L1 contexts, and now in ELT, is the rapid growth and popularity of literature as 'doing', something to try for yourself, as well as something to study in the work of expert published writers. Hanauer (2010, 2012) reported his development of ELT creative writing principles, and Spiro (2007), Iida (2012) and others (see, for instance, Disney, 2014) have provided many other examples of and justifications for such work. What was a rather marginal set of activities ten or twenty years ago is now unarguably a central use of literature in ELT.

Conclusion

What we call literature and how we teach it will undoubtedly go on changing, just as literature itself weaves in and out of fashion in ELT and elsewhere. Perhaps the fundamental guarantee of its continuing relevance and presence in whatever forms its study and reading may take in the future is that it is a most meaningful human activity and, as long as it is considered critically, one that can benefit all involved in learning, and L2 learning, as few other activities can.

Discussion questions

- Literatures in English are being produced and (re-)discovered from across the world with the ongoing globalisation of English. What opportunities and challenges does the use of literatures in English from Africa, Asia and others bring to ELT education?
- How can literary texts be used, adapted and developed best in the light of contemporary research in second language learning that points to the importance of play and creativity for learners?
- Few teacher training programmes have time for sessions on the use of literature, and many teachers are not themselves readers of literature. If claims for the value of literature in ELT made in this chapter are largely accepted, is this lack of specific training a problem? Or can the trained teacher simply be trusted to transfer techniques and principles learned elsewhere to the use of literature?

Related topics

Cognitive perspectives on classroom language learning; Communicative language teaching in theory and practice; Educational perspectives on ELT; Language and culture in ELT; Language curriculum design; Learner autonomy; Method, methods and methodology; Motivation; Questioning 'English-only' classrooms; Sociocultural theory and the language classroom; Teaching literacy; Task-based language teaching; World Englishes and English as a Lingua Franca.

Further reading

Carter, R. (2007) 'Literature and language teaching 1986–2006: A review'. *International Journal of Applied Linguistics*, 17/1. 3–13. (An overview of relevant research which argues for the study and development of long term aspects of literature teaching in ELT, such as its place in syllabus development and assessment.)

Hall, G. (2015) *Literature in language education*. Basingstoke: Palgrave Macmillan. (This thoroughly revised and updated second edition develops themes outlined in this chapter and also includes ideas and guidance for research projects in the area.)

Kramsch, C. (2006) 'Preview article: "The Multilingual Subject"'. *International Journal of Applied Linguistics*, 16/1. 97–110. (This paper previews Kramsch (2009), examining wider educational, intercultural and personal development considerations relevant to literature use in ELT.)

Maley, A. (2001) 'Literature in the language classroom', in R. Carter and D. Nunan (eds) *The Cambridge guide to TESOL*. Cambridge: Cambridge University Press. 180–185. (A very experienced practitioner's eye view of the field and related issues.)

Paran, A. (2008) 'The role of literature in instructed foreign language learning and teaching: An evidence-based survey'. *Language Teaching*, 41/4. 465–496. (A valuable and fully informed overview, which also argues for applied linguists to interact more fruitfully with language teachers around practical issues in literature, language development and education.)

References

ACTFL (American Council for Teaching of Foreign Languages) Standards. Retrieved from http://www.actfl.org/sites/default/files/pdfs/public/StandardsforFLLexecsumm_rev.pdf

Adamson, S. (1998) 'Literary language', in S. Romaine (ed.) *The Cambridge history of the English language, volume IV: 1776–1997*. Cambridge: Cambridge University Press. 589–692.

Alderson, C. (2000) *Assessing reading*. Cambridge: Cambridge University Press.

Ali, S. (1994) 'The reader response approach. An alternative for teaching literature in a second language'. *Journal of Reading*, 37/4. 288–296.

Atkinson, D. (ed.) (2011) *Alternative approaches to second language learning*. Abingdon: Routledge.

Beard, R. (ed.) (1995) *Rhyme, reading and writing*. London: Hodder & Stoughton.

Belz, J. A. (2002) 'Second language play as a representation of the multicompetent self in foreign language study'. *Journal of Language, Identity and Education*, 1/1. 13–39.

Bland, J. (2013) *Children's literature and learner empowerment*. London: Bloomsbury.

Boers, F., Lindstromberg, S. and Webb, S. (2014) 'Further evidence of the comparative memorability of alliterative expressions in second language learning'. *RELC Journal*, 45/1. 85–99.

Bowles, M. (2010) *The think aloud controversy*. New York: Routledge.

Bredella, L. and Delanoy, W. (eds) (1996) *Challenges of literary texts in the foreign language classroom*. Tubingen: Gunter Narr.

Brumfit, C. (1981) 'Reading skills and the study of literature in a foreign language'. *System*, 9/1. 243–248.

Carter, R. (2004) *Language and creativity. The art of common talk*. London: Routledge.

Carter, R. (2007) 'Literature and language teaching 1986–2006: A review'. *International Journal of Applied Linguistics*, 17/1. 3–13.

Carter, R. and Long, M. (1987) *The web of words*. Cambridge: Cambridge University Press.

Carter, R. and Long, M. N. (1991) *Teaching literature*. Harlow, Essex: Longman.

Chapelle, C. and Roberts, C. (1986) 'Ambiguity tolerance and field independence as predictors of proficiency in English as a second language'. *Language Learning*, 36/1. 27–45.

Cook, G. (2000) *Language play, language learning*. Oxford: Oxford University Press.

Cook, G. (2010) *Translation in language teaching*. Oxford: Oxford University Press.

Council of Europe (2001) *Common European framework of reference for languages: Learning, teaching, assessment*. Cambridge: Cambridge University Press.

Day, R. R. and Bamford, J. (1998) *Extensive reading in the second language classroom*. Cambridge: Cambridge University Press.

Day, R., Bassett, J., Bowler, B., Parminter, S., Bullard, N., Prentice, M., Mahmood, M., Stewart, D. and Robb, T. (2011) *Bringing extensive reading into the classroom*. Oxford: Oxford University Press.

Disney, D. (ed.) (2014) *Exploring second language creative writing*. Amsterdam: Benjamins.

Dörnyei, Z. (2010) The *psychology of the language learner. Individual differences in second language acquisition*. London: Routledge.

Dörnyei, Z. and Ushioda, E. (2010) *Teaching and researching motivation* (2nd ed.). London: Routledge.

Dorst, A. G. (2015) 'More or different metaphors in fiction? A quantitative cross-register comparison'. *Language and Literature*, 24/1. 3–22.

Duff, A. and Maley, A. (1990/2007) *Resource books for teachers: literature* (2nd ed.). Oxford: Oxford University Press.

Elgar, A. G. (2002) 'Student playwriting for language development'. *ELT Journal*, 50/1. 22–28.

Elley, W. B. and Manghubai, F. (1983) 'The impact of reading on second language learning'. *Reading Research Quarterly*, 19/1. 53–67.

Elliott, R. (1990) 'Encouraging reader-response to literature in ESL situations'. *ELT Journal*, 44/3. 191–198.

Ellis, N. (2002) 'Frequency effects in language acquisition'. *Studies in Second Language Acquisition*, 24/2. 143–188.

Ellis, N (2005) 'At the interface: Dynamic interactions of explicit and implicit language knowledge'. *Studies in Second Language Acquisition*, 27/2. 305–352.

Emmott, C. (1997) *Narrative comprehension: A discourse perspective*. Oxford: Clarendon Press.

Gass, S. and Mackey, A. (2000) *Stimulated recall methodology in second language research*. Mahwah, NJ: Erlbaum.

Grabe, W. (2009) *Reading in a second language*. Cambridge: Cambridge University Press.

Haddon, M. (2003) *The curious incident of the dog in the night-time*. London: Vintage.

Hall, G. (1999) 'Awareness, response and what might lie beyond'. *Language Awareness*, 8/1. 3–14.

Hall, G. (2015) *Literature in language education* (2nd ed.). Basingstoke: Palgrave Macmillan.

Hanauer, D. (2010) *Poetry as research. Exploring second language poetry writing*. Amsterdam: Benjamins.

Hanauer, D. (2012) 'Meaningful literacy: Writing poetry in the language classroom'. *Language Teaching*, 45/1. 105–115.

Harding, J. R. (2014) 'Reader response criticism and stylistics', in M. Burke (ed.) *The Routledge handbook of stylistics*. Abingdon: Routledge. 68–84.

Heath, S. B. (1996) 'Re-creating literature in the ESL classroom'. *TESOL Quarterly*, 30/4. 776–779.

Hoffstaedter-Kohn, P. (1991) 'Linguistic competence and poetic text processing', in E. Ibsch, D. Schram and G. Steen (eds) *Empirical studies in literature*. Amsterdam: Rodopi. 87–94.

Horowitz, D. (1990) 'Fiction and non-fiction in the ESL/EFL classroom: Does the difference make a difference? *English for Specific Purposes*, 9/2. 161–168.

Iida, A. (2012) The value of poetry writing. Cross-genre literacy development in a second language'. *Scientific Study of Literature*, 2/1. 60–82.

Iser, W. (1978) *The act of reading. A theory of aesthetic response*. London: Routledge & Kegan Paul.

Jakobson, R. (1960) 'Closing statement: Linguistics and poetics', reprinted in J. J. Weber (ed.) *The Stylistics Reader*. London: Arnold. 10–35.

Jenkins, J. (2015) *Global Englishes*. London: Routledge.

Kim, M. (2004) 'Literature discussions in adult SL learning'. *Language and Education*, 18/2. 145–166.

Kramsch, C. (2006) 'Preview article: "The multilingual subject"'. *International Journal of Applied Linguistics*, 16/1. 97–110.

Kramsch, C. (2009) *The multilingual subject*. Oxford: Oxford University Press.

Lakoff, G. and Johnson, M. (1980) *Metaphors we live by*. Chicago: University of Chicago Press.

Lantolf, J (1997) 'The function of language play in the acquisition of L2 Spanish', in W. R. Glass and A. T. Perez-Leroux (eds) *Contemporary perspectives on the acquisition of Spanish Vol 2*. Somerville, MA: Cascadilla Press. 3–24.

Lantolf, J. (ed.) (2000) *Sociocultural theory and second language learning*. Oxford: Oxford University Press.

Lima, C. (2013) 'Reading and discussing literature online', in T. Pattison (ed.) *IATEFL 2012 Glasgow conference selections*. Canterbury, UK: IATEFL. 88–89.

Lima, C. (2014) *Online reading groups*. Unpublished PhD thesis, Open University, Milton Keynes, UK.

Maley, A. (2001) 'Literature in the language classroom', in R. Carter and D. Nunan (eds) *The Cambridge guide to teaching English for speakers of other languages*. Cambridge: Cambridge University Press. 180–185.

Martin, A. L. and Laurie, I. (1993) 'Student views about the contribution of literary and cultural content to language teaching at the intermediate level'. *Foreign Language Annals*, 26/2. 188–207.

Mason, B. and Krashen, S. (1997) 'Extensive reading in English as a foreign language'. *System,* 25/1. 91–102.

McRae, J. (1991) *Literature with a small 'l'*. London: Macmillan.

Miall, D. S. (2007) *Literary reading: Empirical and theoretical studies*. New York: Peter Lang.

MLA (Modern Language Association). Retrieved from http://www.mla.org/

Nell, V. (1988) *Lost in a book: The psychology of reading for pleasure*. New Haven and London: Yale University Press.

Norton, B. (2000) *Identity and language learning: Social processes and educational practice*. Harlow, Essex: Longman.

Paran, A. (2008) 'The role of literature in instructed foreign language learning and teaching: An evidence-based survey'. *Language Teaching*, 41/4. 465–496.

Pavlenko, A. (2005) *Emotions and multilingualism*. Cambridge: Cambridge University Press.

Pigada, M. and Schmitt, N. (2006) 'Vocabulary acquisition from extensive reading'. *Reading in a Foreign Language*, 18/1. 1–18.

Pope, R. (1995) *Textual intervention. Critical and creative strategies for literary studies*. London: Routledge.

Rosenblatt, L. (1978/ 1994) *The reader, the text, the poem: The transactional theory of the literary work*. Carbondale, IL: Southern Illinois Press.

Sanders, J. (2015) *Adaptation and appropriation* (2nd ed.). Abingdon: Routledge.

Sanford, A. J. and Emmott, C. (2012) *Mind, brain and narrative*. Cambridge: Cambridge University Press.

Schmidt, R. (1990) 'The role of consciousness in second language learning'. *Applied Linguistics*, 11/1. 17–46.

Scott, V. M. and Huntington, J. A. (2007) 'Literature, the interpretive mode and novice learners'. *Modern Language* Journal, 91/1. 3–14.

Sell, R. D. (ed.) (1995) 'Literature throughout foreign language education'. *Review of ELT,* 5/1. London: Modern English Publications with The British Council.

Shelton-Strong, S. J. (2012) 'Literature circles in ELT'. *ELT Journal,* 66/2. 214–223.

Sklar, H. (2013) *The art of sympathy in fiction*. Amsterdam: Benjamins.

Spiro, J. (2007) *Storybuilding*. Oxford: Oxford University Press.

Tate, G. (1993) A place for literature in freshman composition. *College English*, 55/3. 317–321.

van Lier, L. (2000) 'From input to affordance: Social-interactive learning from an ecological perspective', in J. Lantolf (ed.) *Sociocultural theory and second language learning*. Oxford: Oxford University Press. 245–259.

Vygotsky, L. (1978) *Mind in society*. Cambridge, MA: Harvard University Press.

Wilkins, D. (1976) *Notional syllabuses*. Oxford: Oxford University Press.

Part VI

Focus on the language classroom

33

Complexity and language teaching

Sarah Mercer

Introduction

It has become customary to describe all kinds of different domains of language learning and teaching as 'complex'. However, the term complex has a very distinct meaning in complexity theories that does not mean the same as complicated. If something is complicated, it means that it may be composed of multiple components, but these can be separated into distinct parts. An example often given is of that an airplane engine, which is highly complicated, but which can be taken apart and reconstructed by experts. In contrast, something that is 'complex' makes sense as a whole and cannot be taken apart and put back together again. Instead, its character emerges from the unique interaction of its multiple components, rather like a holistic, organic view of a human being. In this chapter, we are concerned with aspects of language teaching that are complex, not just complicated.

Increasingly, academics and researchers are recognising and addressing complexity in learning and teaching a foreign language. Essentially, the field of ELT has been moving towards complexity perspectives for several years, making current developments perhaps less of a 'complexity turn' (Mercer, 2013) and rather more indicative of a growing sensitivity to complexity. What is new, however, is the more frequent explicit use of frameworks inspired by complexity theories to understand ELT learning and teaching contexts and processes.

In this chapter, I will refer to a range of complexity theories, first highlighting their diversity and then focusing on the key theoretical frame underlying this chapter, namely, dynamic systems theory. In the main part of the chapter, I will consider the ways in which 'systems thinking' might be employed in ELT and how this can be adapted in ways sensitive to the specific characteristics of the field. In particular, I will focus on possible implications of systemic frameworks for reflection and participant inquiry. I will also consider the potential implications of complexity thinking for the relationship between theory and practice and thus between practitioners and researchers. The chapter will conclude with a discussion of the challenges complexity theories pose for ELT and other cautionary warnings.

Complexity theories

Complexity theories are not covered by one single, unified theory. There are many interrelated branches across a vast range of disciplines, each of which has slightly differing foci and understanding of terms and processes. However, this diversity of theories is perhaps merely symptomatic of the inherent nature of complexity and the "inability of any single approach to capture what scientists mean by complex" (Page, 2010: 24). As Byrne and Callaghan (2014) suggest, complexity theories themselves are diverse and dynamic, and, whilst holding core characteristics, they can change according to their context of use. In this way, there may be a need for adaptations depending on contexts and domains in which the theories are employed. Various distinctions between the different theories have been classified as to whether they are seen as 'hard', 'restricted' and strongly mathematical, or 'softer' and more metaphorical, as has been the case in areas such as the social sciences and education (see, for example, Richardson and Cilliers, 2001; Morin, 2007; Byrne and Callaghan, 2014). From my own perspective as a teacher and researcher, I have found the most useful, readily accessible and intuitively appealing frames to be those concerned with 'complex dynamic systems' (CDS) and, indeed, this has perhaps been one of the most common approaches in ELT. For these reasons, I will concentrate on CDSs in this chapter.

'Dynamic systems theory' (DST) offers a theoretical framework for examining the nature and behaviour of complex dynamic systems (also known as complex adaptive systems, depending on the emphasis of the perspective taken (Larsen-Freeman and Cameron, 2008: 2); note that this is not a distinction of relevance in the context of this chapter, however). There is no single definition of a CDS, so instead they are often described in terms of their core characteristics. It is important to note that a system needs to exhibit these core characteristics to be defined as a CDS; otherwise, whatever is under consideration is simply perhaps complicated, as opposed to 'complex', as the term is understood in DST.

First, perhaps the most crucial characteristic is that the system is composed of *multiple interrelated elements* which, when viewed together, have collective *emergent* properties. As has been endlessly cited in relation to CDSs, 'the whole is more than the sum of the parts.' This means that the whole system cannot be understood by simply breaking it down into its component parts but has a quality which only 'emerges' and makes sense when the system is viewed as a whole. Another key characteristic, as the name suggests, is that a CDS is *dynamic* and constantly in a state of flux. This means it is continually adapting as a system and changing into a continually emergent state. This is reflected well in a core definition offered by Larsen-Freeman and Cameron (2008: 29), which explains that a dynamic system is "one that changes with time, and whose future state depends in some way on its present state". However, change may not be radically different in terms of the system state, but change can take the form of what is known as 'dynamic stability' (Larsen-Freeman and Cameron, 2008) or 'homeostasis', which means the system is continually changing but always retaining its overall composition and form. An example often used to explain this is that of a bath being filled with water. If the plug is taken out but water is going in at the same rate at which it is going out, the water will be moving in flux, but it will essentially maintain the same form. Another characteristic of a CDS is that change is *not easily predictable and is not linear* in nature. Given the highly interconnected nature of all the components of a system, this means that change in one part of a system is likely to lead to change elsewhere in the system, often in ways that are hard to predict. Furthermore, it is rarely one single cause that triggers change, but, rather, change can be due to a combination of factors or an accumulation of adjustments. Sometimes, however, dramatic changes can take place in a system emerging from small actions, depending on the system's state conditions at a certain point in time, in a process widely known as the 'butterfly effect'. Finally, a CDS typically tends to *self-organise*, meaning that the internal organisation of the system is not imposed on the system by an outside element or elements but that the system adjusts and organises itself into its typical functioning state.

It is important to note that not everything can be viewed as a CDS. If, for example, something contains multiple elements interacting but in a way in which they can be taken apart and re-connected together in a meaningful way, the elements may be classed as complicated but not complex, such as in the example of the airplane engine at the outset of the chapter. We must also remember that what is conceptualised as a CDS depends on the perspective taken. A CDS is not a 'real' thing, but we conceptualise a system as *representing* something real. We must not forget that the system remains a frame of perception in which the boundaries are imposed by our way of perceiving reality, and these may not necessarily reflect actual, real-world boundaries (Checkland and Poulter, 2006). We must also keep in mind that many examples of CDS are taken from the natural world and from mathematical processes. However, language education is special, as it involves humans, who have the unique capacity for conscious reflection and agency (e.g. Vallacher and Nowak, 2009; Easley and Kleinberg, 2010); thus, our understandings of CDSs in ELT must remain inherently social, accounting for our human capacity to reflect and deliberately and consciously act upon our understandings and experiences.

The history of complexity theories in SLA and ELT began in 1997, when Diane Larsen-Freeman introduced the idea of systems theory to the broader field of second language acquisition (SLA) with her paper entitled "Chaos/complexity science and second language acquisition". In it, she revisits conundrums in SLA and views them afresh through a complexity lens. Since then, there has been quite a large body of complexity-led research in the fields of SLA and first language acquisition (see, for example, special issues in *Developmental Review* (2005), *The Modern Language Journal* (2008) and *Language Learning* (2009), amongst others). However, the take-up across broader areas of the field of applied linguistics, including ELT, was perhaps triggered by the 2008 publication of the Larsen-Freeman and Cameron monograph *Complex systems and applied linguistics*. Following the publication of that book, work employing explicit complexity theory-based frameworks, in particular systems theory-based work, has emerged in diverse areas of SLA research beyond language acquisition studies, including language motivation, self, autonomy, classroom dynamics, teacher cognition, innovation etc. (see, for example, Feryok, 2010; Finch, 2010; Burns and Knox, 2011; Mercer, 2011a, b, c; Dörnyei et al., 2014; Kostoulas, 2014; Sade, 2014). A closely related, comparable body of work can be found in ecological perspectives on language learning and teaching typified by work in applied linguistics by van Lier (2004) and Kramsch (2008). These approaches also stress contextual diversity, the interaction of individuals and contextual factors, and the dynamism of those relationships and characteristics of factors across time and place. In particular, the foreign language classroom is seen as an ecological system nested within a hierarchy of other larger/broader systems such as the school, educational system and national and societal cultures (see, for example, Bronfenbrenner, 1979), and it is the interactions of all these layers of systems that generate unique conditions and settings.

Complexity theories and research in ELT

For researchers, working with DST empirically is challenging. In the past, often for empirical ease and in line with certain prevailing concepts of validity, research studies have often been designed to simplify and 'reduce' the complexity of language learning contexts and processes. To do this, fragments of the bigger picture of language classrooms and learning and teaching process have tended to be examined in relative isolation. The aim of such studies has typically been to generate more generalisable insights applicable to a wider range of settings. Whilst such studies have made valuable contributions to the knowledge base of ELT, there is increasing recognition of the value of additionally looking more closely at the complexity and inherent 'messiness' of real-world learners, teachers and classrooms (see, for example, Ushioda, 2009) by taking a more holistic view of processes and contexts. In order to 'embrace', rather than reduce or ignore complexity (Trueit and Doll, 2010), particular empirical approaches are required, for which more qualitatively oriented research designs are ideally suited.

Given the history of the field, ELT is already familiar with and open to qualitative, situated research, which tends to examine diversity, situatedness and uniqueness and which frequently takes a more holistic view of learners and settings. An important characteristic of qualitatively oriented studies is that their aim is not usually to generalise but rather to generate deeper, more nuanced understandings which meet the criteria of 'transferability'. This refers to the recognisability and applicability of insights to other contexts. In 'transferring' qualitative research findings, individuals who read a study interpret how and in what ways the findings are appropriate for their own setting, just as teachers can critically evaluate general principles of pedagogy for their specific contexts and purposes. As Larsen-Freeman (2013) notes, albeit in respect to learners, teachers do not simply 'transfer' or 'export' knowledge from one setting to another; rather, they 'transform' knowledge across contexts by interacting with it through the lens of their own interpretations of their situated experiences, reflections and co-constructed understandings.

The challenge for those researching within ELT has been how to research a CDS effectively, systematically, consistently and in a way that retains and reflects the system's core characteristics. One of the main challenges for any CDS study is therefore to define and set the boundaries of the system under investigation at the outset. The quest is to avoid reducing the system to distinct, separate variables (fragments of the whole) and also to retain a meaningful degree of holism and set of interrelationships as far as is empirically feasible. In this respect, Larsen-Freeman and Cameron (2008) suggest setting the boundaries of systems in terms of 'functional wholes', collective sets of variables which together function as a CDS in a meaningful and recognisable way. For example, a classroom, a language or a person's embodied psychology can all be seen as examples of systems that function as wholes and cannot easily be separated into component parts without losing some of the overall quality and meaning of the system.

Another important point to note here is that explicitly choosing to research from a DST perspective does not mean rejecting other types of research as invalid (Mercer, 2015). To do so would be extremely short-sighted and, as Block says (1996: 78), language learning is far too complex to be understood by one theory alone. Instead, complexity theories can serve as one more valuable tool and perspective to add to our existent research repertoire. To date, there have been some exciting developments and examples of innovative approaches to researching through this new lens requiring a fresh innovative set of empirical tools (see Dörnyei et al., 2014; see also MacIntyre, Gregersen and Clément, this volume). However, all research from a complexity perspective faces a major challenge. Whilst it can perhaps reflect reality more closely than more reductionist approaches, in an applied discipline such as ELT, we must ask what the added value of this perspective is for both the field as a whole and for practitioners, especially if practitioners already intuitively recognise many dimensions such as complexity, dynamism and systemic behaviours. Given the inherent underlying assumption that we cannot make predications and generalisations based on CDS research, what then is the useful output from such studies? How can researchers avoid their work being greeted by the ultimate 'so, what?' response (de Bot et al., 2005)?

Implications and relevance for ELT

In suggesting a role and aim for complexity-informed research, approaches such as appropriate methodology and postmethod pedagogy can perhaps give us some ideas of ways in which the theory can also be useful for practice (see also Mercer, 2013). For example, in Holliday's (1994) work on appropriate methodology and social contexts, he argues that each classroom is unique in its composition due to the interaction of multiple cultures, such as national, societal, institutional, subject and personal cultures. He suggests that whilst we may be able to make generalisations in terms of certain principles – for example, we know that classroom cultures are influenced by cultures outside the classroom – it is not possible for us to generalise about the precise nature and characteristics of a specific classroom (ibid.). This means that although it can be helpful for teachers to understand general principles, in practice, teachers have to work in ways that are 'appropriate' for their own settings and thus develop their own specific methodologies (see also Holliday, this volume).

In Kumaravadivelu's (2001, 2006) 'postmethod pedagogy', he questions the validity of pre-scribing fixed methods of how to teach, given the diversity, complexity and uniqueness of teach-ing and learning contexts. Instead, he suggests teachers should be empowered to critically reflect on and evaluate their own practice in sustainable ways, so that teaching can be sensitive to the local context and setting. He sees teachers not as being dictated to by theories and prescriptions from the academy but rather as constructing their own 'personal theories' based on their criti-cal reflection of both 'professional theories' and their own experiences in practice (O'Hanlon, 1993, cited in Kumaravadivelu, 2006: 172). This means that "the thinking teacher is no longer perceived as someone who applies theories, but someone who theorizes practice" (Edge, 2001: 6, as cited in Kumaravadivelu, 2006: 172; see also Hall, this volume, ch. 15 for further discussion of postmethod pedagogy).

Together, these approaches point to the inability to easily predict what will happen in class-rooms and thus also the difficulty of making pedagogical prescriptions applicable to all settings. Instead, collectively, they suggest the value of proposing a series of principles to guide pedagogic practice, thereby recognising some of the patterns in teaching encounters and yet the ultimate uniqueness of each experience and setting. They also all ascribe a central role to teachers, who are encouraged to critically engage with and evaluate 'global' or 'public' principles and theories in relation to their own specific practice (see also Mercer, 2013, 2015).

In other words, this perspective implies that the aim of research is not to provide prescriptive recipes for practice based on models of prediction but to offer principles to guide practice based on models of detailed understandings and possibly patterns. Indeed, whilst CDSs behave in unpredictable ways, this does not means that 'anything goes'. There is not an infinite number of possible outcomes of a system's development, as the past development of a system already lim-its the total range of possible outcomes (Byrne and Callaghan, 2014: 197); however, the exact and precise nature of the development of the system cannot be straightforwardly predicted. Instead, at most, we can search for patterns in systems and their behaviours, perhaps thinking, as expert teachers reportedly do, in terms of prototypicality (see, for example, Berliner, 2004). This means that one tangible and realistic practical output for research of a CDS could be to generate guidelines or principles based on deep, nuanced descriptions of systems and systemic behaviours in ways reminiscent of case study research based on qualities such as transferability.

Such an approach also assigns a critical role to teachers as autonomous, reflective agents mak-ing principled pragmatic decisions as appropriate for their unique needs and settings (see Adam-son, 2004). It implies that being an effective teacher is not just about having a broad body of knowledge but depends vitally on understanding how to apply that knowledge in ways sensitive to the specific context they work in. One key skill in developing such sensitive understandings is the ability to reflect effectively. As teachers, we can not only reflect on our own actual teaching practice but also on 'public' theories and other people's reported experiences (Williams, 2001: 26–27). This means teachers can be encouraged to critically reflect on insights and principles stemming from studies based on complexity theories, as well as on their own practice using the theories and related frameworks themselves.

Different degrees and types of reflection are suitable for different stages in a practitioner's career (Griffiths and Tann, 1992, cited in Williams, 2001). In respect to trainee teachers, I would agree with Tudor, who argues that we should be aiming to "empower trainee teachers with confidence to engage with and acknowledge complexity without fear of failing to meet ideal-ised, neat conceptions of supposed teaching practice" (Tudor, 2001: 209). To do this, a valuable component of teaching training programmes could be to include a complexity framework as a basis to reflect on and discuss classroom-based scenarios including trainees' own actual practical experiences in the language classroom. Clearly, there are challenges inherent in teacher training programmes which require a balance. Naturally, early stage teachers want and need clear defini-tive instructions of how to teach and concrete ideas for methods to work with. However, as with postmethod perspectives, I feel we would be somehow selling them short if we *only* provided them with such prescriptive recipes. Our current trainees will be teaching in a future filled with technological, linguistic, cultural and contextual developments, constraints and parameters we currently cannot as yet even imagine. Thus, whilst some degree of fixed support and specific ideas are necessary, teachers also need to develop the skills to reflect critically on their practice throughout their future careers. In this sense, it could be useful to work explicitly with complexity-informed reflective frameworks to promote trainees' critical reflective skills.

However, Hardman (2010) reports that experienced teachers can also find working with a complexity framework useful and comforting as they recognise the messiness from their daily practice reflected in and explained by these frameworks, potentially both when reading about others' experiences with them as well as reflecting on their own practice from within such a perspective. A particular form of complexity-informed reflection that all levels of teachers could work with is 'systemic thinking'. This is defined by Armson (2011: 288) as "a style of thinking that attends as much to the connections between things as to the things themselves, and to the connections between things and their wider context, and looks at things and their connections from more than one perspective". Systemic thinking tends to take a holistic view of a situation that can be conceptualised as a system, although it can also involve looking at a detailed aspect of the whole whilst being mindful of the bigger picture. It is a way of thinking that gives structure and boundaries to a 'messy' situation but retains the complexity without oversimplifying reality as it is perceived. Rather than being a particular study or intervention, systemic thinking should reflect more general 'habits of mind' (Booth Sweeney and Meadows, 1995: 1). It is not intended to find solutions to problems but is meant to be a way of being which seeks to continually improve a situation. Thus, embracing systemic thinking becomes a way of being in the classroom, not a short-termed intervention. (There are several excellent books on systemic thinking, which can provide inspiration for ELT-based approaches, for example, Booth Sweeney and Meadows, 1995; Meadows, 2009; Armson, 2011.)

Example of a complexity-informed reflective framework

Before working with any systemic reflective framework, we must firstly define what we mean by a CDS in the specific instance under consideration. Although we often highlight the fact that systems thinking closely reflects reality, we must remember, as noted above, that this is a lens that we bring to bear on a situation and serves as a frame through which we see it. A CDS is not reality *per se* but, as Checkland and Poulter (2006: 151), explain, systems are "social constructs", not "maps" of any kind of "real territory". In ELT, the system could be, for example, an inter-national ELT organisation, a school, a classroom, a learner, a teacher, a language and so forth. To illustrate systemic thinking in this chapter, I will consider the ELT classroom as a CDS, as others have already done (e.g. Finch, 2010; Bowsfield, 2004; Burns and Knox, 2011; Mercer, 2013).

Considering the ELT classroom in this way, we are aware of the multiple nested layers (such as the institution, culture, family etc.) and different facets and perspectives involved in language learning processes and classroom interactions (e.g. teacher, learner, curriculum etc.). In particular, it draws our attention to the centrality of group dynamics, the quality of relationships within the classroom, the nature of different temporal and contextual dynamics, and non-linear causality, as well as the strong interconnections between life inside and outside the language classroom (see Mercer, 2013, 2015).

Here, therefore, are a series of illustrative reflective questions inspired by systemic thinking, soft systems methodology and systemic research across a range of disciplines (in particular I have drawn upon Armson, 2011, but also Booth Sweeney and Meadows, 1995; Checkland and Poulter, 2006; Mason, 2008; Meadows, 2009). This basic framework can clearly be extended and adapted as appropriate to specific contexts, and it is by no means intended to be comprehensive; however, it is hoped these questions will help illustrate some of the types of thinking that could be prompted by reflecting on the ELT classroom as a CDS (see also Mercer, 2013, 2015):

1   If we think about the ELT classroom as a dynamic system, what other larger systems is it nested within? (e.g. the national culture or the school itself as a CDS). What smaller systems are nested within the classroom (e.g. an individual learner or a specific group work activity)? How do these multiple systems interact and define each other? How is life in the ELT classroom as a CDS connected to other systems beyond the classroom and school? How is life in the classroom as a whole defined by the behaviour of the various other systems nested within it?

2   What interconnections, relationships and interdependencies are there in relation to the ELT classroom as a CDS? This means focusing on all kinds of relationships, not only interpersonal ones (e.g. what relationships are there between learners, between learners and the teacher, between learners and the language, between learners and the coursebook, between teacher and the coursebook etc.). We can also consider relationships across domain boundaries reflecting on relationships between English and other school subjects and how these interconnect (e.g. the relationship of the learner or school or national culture towards English, or the relationship between English and other foreign languages or other subjects in the curriculum).

3   In particular, as teachers, we serve as a key point of influence within the classroom system. What relationships do we have in respect to and surrounding the classroom as a system? How might our relationships be affecting the system? Which of our relationships could we work on in order to improve the system as a whole (e.g. our relationships to our learners, to the school, to our colleagues, to the textbook, to the curriculum, to the classroom space etc.)?

4   Accepting the fundamentally dynamic nature of the ELT classroom as a system, what are the key drivers of change in the system? What things are likely to have a bigger effect on the system as a whole given their centrality in the system? How can we avoid thinking in terms of straightforward simplistic linear cause-and-effect such as 'if I do this, then that will happen'? What combined factors or what accumulated processes can lead to change? What things are especially dynamic or particularly stable? What changes in the system would we like to see, and what relationships could we focus on to potentially trigger these sorts of changes?

5   In evaluating our actions, we can reflect on both short-term and long-term as well as possible unanticipated outcomes of our actions. If we take a particular course of action, what would be the immediate as well as possible long-term effects of this (e.g. if we let a

moment of an individual's bad behaviour pass without comment, what are the short-term and possible long-term effects of this on the individual and class as a whole?)? What other relationships or aspects of the system might be affected by the action; in other words, what could be the knock-on ripple effect of the action?

6   We know within a CDS that sometimes small things can lead to big effects and changes through the 'butterfly effect'. We can ask ourselves what small changes could be made which may lead to bigger effects (e.g. reflecting on the use of teacher language, altering seating arrangements, redecorating the classroom, monitoring the mood, facial expression and body language of the teacher etc.)?

7   Complexity is also about multiple perspectives. How can we view life and experiences in the language learning classroom from multiple perspectives? What is our position from which we view the classroom? How is the way we are looking at our situation affecting how we act in the system? Is there a different way of interpreting a particular experience? Might other perspectives reveal different facets of classroom life and actions?

8   A final dimension to reflect on is the complexity and perpetual dynamism we engage with daily as English language teachers. This is what makes teaching both exciting and challenging. What about the diversity, uniqueness, complexity and dynamism of our setting can we not only appreciate but employ positively to further enhance the quality of the relationships in the classroom and the learning?

Systemic action research

Experienced practitioners may also wish to engage in more advanced professional development, and, here, ideas from systemic action research (e.g. Burns, 2007) may be useful. In general education, some scholars argue that an action research model is inherently a key methodological framework for embracing complexity (Phelps and Hase, 2002; Phelps and Graham, 2010), given that it allows for a practice-based approach to inquiry embedded in the real-world complexity and 'messiness' of actual classrooms. These authors assert that, in their conceptualisation, action research complements core understandings from complexity theories such as an acceptance of the unpredictability of open, nonlinear dynamics, the inseparability of contexts from the system and an interest in uniqueness and 'exceptions' as well as an embracing of reflective processes and feedback mechanisms.

A related approach is 'soft systems methodology' (SSM) (Checkland and Poulter, 2006), which is also in turn closely connected to systemic thinking. Whilst systemic thinking, systemic action research and SSM differ to various degrees in the specifics of the structured approach proposed, they all involve similar or comparable stages and stress their flexibility and responsiveness for individuals working with them. For the purposes of this chapter, I will offer an overview of the key stages typically involved in all three strands without any discussion of the particularities and differences between these specific approaches.

Often, such forms of reflective systemic inquiry begin with an exploratory phase to observe and find out about the nature of the situation, frequently involving a modelling stage in which a model of the system is created and, perhaps, a visual is drawn. Next follows a discussion stage in which multiple participants and perspectives discuss the model and its connection to reality, and then a particular action or an improvement to the system is proposed. This action is also debated in relation to the actual situation (rather than 'just' the situation conceived as a system), and then the action is taken. Then the cycle of feedback and reflection recommences (see Checkland and Poulter, 2006).

Whilst some teachers may find this form of reflective inquiry and systemic action research useful, we must exercise caution, as not all teachers may feel they have the time and resources to do so (Borg, 2007). Nevertheless, if systems thinking can become a way of being in and reflecting on our teaching contexts, working in this way need not necessarily add any additional time constraints if it were to be a habitual way of thinking about classroom life.

The relationship between theory and practice

Whilst teachers may wish to conduct their own research using systems thinking, approaches such as SSM also emphasise the benefits of multiple perspectives and dialogue, and thus perhaps some teachers may also wish to engage in collaborative projects with learners, colleagues or academics. As already noted, dynamic systems thinking reflects some of the features that many teachers already recognise intuitively from their practice, and now many researchers are starting to work with explicit frames and theories of CDSs. This could mean that teachers find and recognise their realities in the work of researchers and theorists more easily than was perhaps the case with more reductionist or abstracted frameworks, or statistical models. This offers the potential for practitioners and researchers to share conceptual understandings from complexity perspectives, which in turn could facilitate a shared discourse space for increased dialogue and cooperation for working together.

If dialogue and cooperation between practitioners and academic researchers is to function effectively, it needs to be based on a fundamental respect for each other, with neither party being perceived as having superior or more worthy forms of knowledge but rather as being genuine equal partners with a shared goal of seeking to improve classroom practice and language learners' learning. With such shared goals in mind and a common understanding of the nature of the classroom as a CDS, research could be done collaboratively with both parties sharing their insights, knowledge and expertise in a manner reminiscent of elements of 'deliberative dialogue' (see, for example, Schoem and Hurtado, 2001). The aim of deliberative dialogue is not to solve a problem but rather to give all participants a better sense of the situation and a deeper perspective on issues involved and possible solutions. The participants deliberate together, and discussion is aimed at finding the best course of action to continually improve practice. Thus, as London (n.d.) explains on his website (http://www.scottlondon.com/reports/dialogue.html):

> the objective is not so much to *talk* together as to *think* together, not so much to reach a conclusion as to discover where a conclusion might lie. Thinking together involves listening deeply to other points of view, exploring new ideas and perspectives, searching for points of agreement, and bringing unexamined assumptions into the open.

The implication is that both teachers and researchers could bring their resources, expertise and voices to the discussion of a jointly defined CDS in an attempt to better understand it with the ultimate aim of improving its functioning in practice. This means, for example, academics could bring the findings of systematic empirical research conducted from a complexity perspective to the table in the form of nuanced, detailed credible accounts of 'systems', drawing attention to systemic behaviour and any possible patterns. Practitioners could bring their experiential knowledge and practice-based expertise to the table, critically engaging with the research findings. The outcome of this process would thus hopefully come to reflect the combined knowledge that emerges from genuine dialogue between both parties. However, both must equally feel that they benefit from taking part in such collaboration, and both must come together with clear expectations about the nature of the partnership, the ensuing dialogue and any output from the process (such as classroom change, published papers or blogs, workshops with colleagues or conference presentations). However, the potential in collaborative work for enhancing our understandings of ELT would be considerable in uniting top-down and bottom-up perspectives. As Tsui (2003: 277) argues, "the theorization of practical knowledge and the 'practicalization' of theoretical knowledge are two sides of the same coin in the development of expert knowledge . . . and they are both crucial to the development of expertise."

Conclusions

At present, we are only just at the outset of working explicitly with complexity theories. Only with time will we be able to more thoroughly evaluate their potential for furthering our under-standings of ELT on theoretical, empirical and practical levels. However, as Hardman (2010: 6) explains, "perhaps the more immediately tangible insights come from applying complexity not to the descriptions of systems but to the limitations of our understanding." Indeed, thus far, complexity has already revolutionised various areas of research, challenging traditional linear cause-and-effect thinking, drawing attention to continual dynamism and highlighting intercon-nectedness, thereby opening the way for more holistic approaches to at least complement more reductionist or abstracted ways of thinking and researching.

However, we must also ensure that we engage critically with complexity theories to ensure we exploit and develop their full potential for the field of language learning and teaching. As Widdowson (2003: 3) points out, "the value of theory is not that it is persuasive but that it is provocative. You do not apply it, you appraise it. You use it as a catalyst for reflection." In this way, both educators and researchers should not feel dictated to by complexity theories, but they should be able to engage with them, make them their own and evaluate them in ways appropri-ate to their own unique experiences and settings (Mercer, 2015). Rather than seeing a theory as a 'law' to be adhered to and applied rigidly in a quest for generalisations and prediction, I share the view of Byrne and Callaghan (2014: 124), who see the status of a theory as 'a dialogical' frame for opening up conversations, reflections and discussions (see also Larsen-Freeman and Cam-eron, 2008). Indeed, any theory itself must also be understood as dynamic, with the potential for change and improvement. As Hardman (2010: 4) explains, "meanings shift when used in different fields" and transferring complexity theories to the field of ELT is most likely to involve change and adaptation as we become more familiar with and confident in exploring their potential for our field in ways that reflect the unique characteristics of our domain.

There remain challenges ahead to ensure that research can add to our understandings of ELT in ways that go beyond a mere description of what many practitioners, potentially at least, in part intuitively know. The way forward is likely to take inspiration from other complexity moves in the field, and these suggest some characteristics that are likely to be relevant to work from a CDS perspective. In sum, this means we must accept that top-down prescriptions are no longer appropriate and need not be the aim for research and theoretical thinking. Instead, we must find a balance between an understandable wish for simple solutions and ready-to-go recipes and, at the same time, a more realistic and honest stance which accepts the values of principles and pat-terns stemming from research but also the value of experiential knowledge and the importance of critical reflective skills as required for lifelong learning and practice. We need an approach which assigns a key role for autonomous, empowered, agentic, critically reflective teachers who have the skills to evaluate public theories and research findings in terms of their appropriacy for their own contexts. Both teachers and researchers can explore the rich potential offered by thinking systemically about the world of ELT in individual and collaborative ways and, whilst doing so, maintain a critical and reflective perspective on complexity theories and their future development and adaptation within our field.

Discussion questions

- To what extent do you agree that language classrooms are unpredictable and nonlinear? Can you think of examples from your own ELT practice of these characteristics?
- In your daily life as a teacher, what examples of systems' characteristics can you think of?
- In what ways do you feel that understanding classroom life, using a complexity lens, might lead to improvements in teaching and learning?
- To what extent do you think that it is reasonable and realistic to expect teachers to engage in systematic action research and/or deliberative dialogue as part of their professional, working lives?

Related topics

Appropriate methodology; Individual differences; Method, methods and methodology.

Further reading

Larsen-Freeman, D. and Cameron, L. (2008) *Complex systems and applied linguistics*. Oxford: Oxford University Press. (This is the key book about complex systems in applied linguistics and serves as an excellent introduction.)

Meadows, D. H. (2009) *Thinking in systems: A primer*. D. Wright (ed.) (1st ed.). London: Routledge. (A really useful, clearly written book to help develop systems thinking.)

A special issue of the journal *Revista Brasileira de Linguistica Aplicada*, 13/2, 2013, on complexity in language teaching. Open source. http://www.redalyc.org/toc.oa?id=3398&numero=29651 (This is an accessible and broad-ranging collection of papers applying complexity thinking to language teaching.)

References

Adamson, B. (2004) 'Fashions in language teaching methodology', in A. Davies and C. Elder (eds) *The handbook of applied linguistics*. Oxford: Blackwell. 614–622.

Armson, R. (2011) *Growing wings on the way: Systems thinking for messy situations*. Axminster: Triarchy Press.

Berliner, D. C. (2004) 'Expert teachers: Their characteristics, development and accomplishments', in I. Batllori, R. Obiols, A. E. Gomez Martinez, M. Oller, I. Freixa, J. Pages and I. Blanch (eds) *De la teoria. . . . a l'aula: Formacio del professorat ensenyament de las ciències sociais*. Barcelona, Spain: Departament de Didàctica de la Llengua de la Literatura I de les Ciències Socials, Universitat Autònoma de Barcelona. 13–28.

Block, D. (1996) 'Not so fast: Some thoughts on theory culling, relativism, accepted findings and the heart and soul of SLA'. *Applied Linguistics*, 17/1. 63–83.

Booth Sweeney, L. and Meadows, D. (1995) *The systems thinking playbook*. White River: Chelsea Green Publishing.

Borg, S. (2007) 'English language teachers' views of research: Some insights from Switzerland'. *ETAS Newsletter*, 24/2. 15–18.

Bowsfield, S. (2004) Complexity in the English language arts classroom: Prompting the collective. Proceedings of the 2004 complexity science and educational research conference. 147–154. Retrieved from http://www.complexityandeducation.ualberta.ca/conferences/2004/Documents/CSER2_Bowsfield.pdf

Bronfenbrenner, U. (1979) *The ecology of human development*. Cambridge: Harvard University Press.

Burns, A. and Knox, J. (2011) 'Classrooms as complex adaptive systems: A relational model'. *TESL-EJ*, 15/1. 1–25.

Burns, D. (2007) *Systemic action research: A strategy for whole system change*. Bristol: Policy Press.

Byrne, D. and Callaghan, G. (2014) *Complexity theory and the social sciences: The state of the art*. New York: Routledge.

Checkland, P. and Poulter, J. (2006) *Learning for action: A short definitive account of soft systems methodology and its use for practitioners, teachers and students*. Chichester: John Wiley & Sons.

De Bot, K., Verspoor, M. and Lowie, W. (2005) 'Dynamic systems theory and applied linguistics: The ultimate "so what?"' *International Journal of Applied Linguistics*, 15/1. 116–118.

Dörnyei, Z., Macintyre, P. and Henry, A. (eds) (2014) *Motivational dynamics in language learning*. Bristol: Multilingual Matters.

Easley, D. and Kleinberg, J. (2010) *Networks, crowds, and markets: Reasoning about a highly connected world*. New York: Cambridge University Press.

Edge, J. (2001) *Action research*. Washington, DC: TESOL.

Feryok, A. (2010) 'Language teacher cognitions: Complex dynamic systems?' *System*, 38/2. 271–279.

Finch, A. E. (2010) 'Critical incidents and language learning: Sensitivity to initial conditions'. *System*, 38/3. 422–431.

Griffiths, M. and Tann, S. (1992) 'Using reflective practice to link personal and public theories'. *Journal of Education for Teaching*, 18/1. 69–84.

Hardman, M. (2010) Learning to teach in urban complex schools. Paper presented at British Educational Research Association Conference, Warwick, September 4, 2010. Retrieved from https://www.academia.edu/890957/Learning_to_Teach_First_-_Participant_Perceptions

Holliday, A. (1994) *Appropriate methodology and social context*. Cambridge: Cambridge University Press.

Kostoulas, A. (2014) *A complex systems perspective on English Language teaching: A case study of a language school in Greece*. Unpublished PhD thesis, University of Manchester.

Kramsch, C. (2008) 'Ecological perspectives on foreign language education'. *Language Teaching*, 41/3. 389–408.

Kumaravadivelu, B. (2001) 'Toward a postmethod pedagogy'. *TESOL Quarterly*, 35. 537–560.

Kumaravadivelu, B. (2006) *Understanding language teaching: From method to postmethod*. Mahwah, NJ: Lawrence Erlbaum.

Larsen-Freeman, D. (1997) 'Chaos/complexity science and second language acquisition'. *Applied Linguistics*, 18/2. 141–165.

Larsen-Freeman, D. (2013) 'Transfer of learning transformed'. *Language Learning*, 63. 107–129.

Larsen-Freeman, D. and Cameron, L. (2008) *Complex systems and applied linguistics*. Oxford: Oxford University Press.

London, S. (n.d.) *Thinking together: The power of deliberative dialogue*. Retrieved from http://www.scottlondon.com/reports/dialogue.html

Mason, M. (2008) 'What is complexity theory and what are its implications for educational change?', in M. Mason (ed.) *Complexity theory and the philosophy of education*. Chichester: Wiley-Blackwell. 32–45.

Meadows, D. H. (2009) *Thinking in systems: A primer*. D. Wright (ed.) (1st ed.). London: Routledge.

Mercer, S. (2011a) 'Understanding learner agency as a complex dynamic system'. *System*, 39/4. 427–436.

Mercer, S. (2011b) 'The self as a complex dynamic system'. *Studies in Second Language Learning and Teaching*, 1/1. 57–82.

Mercer, S. (2011c). 'Language learner self-concept: Complexity, continuity and change'. *System*, 39/3. 335–346.

Mercer, S. (2013) 'Towards a complexity-informed pedagogy for language learning'. *Revista Brasileira de Linguística Aplicada*, 13/2. 375–398.

Mercer, S. (2015) 'Does foreign language teaching need complexity theory?', in A. Czejkowska, J. Hohensinner and C. Wieser (eds) *Forschende Vermittlung: Gegenstände, Methoden und Ziele fachdidaktischer Unterrichtsforschung*. Wien: Löcker. 109–123.

Morin, E. (2007) 'Restricted complexity, general complexity', in C. Gershenson, D. Aerts and B. Edmonds (eds) *Worldviews, sciences and us: Philosophy and complexity*. Singapore: World Scientific. 5–29.

O'Hanlon, C. (1993) 'The importance of an articulated personal theory of professional development', in J. Elliot (ed.) *Reconstructing teacher education: Teacher development*. London: The Falmer Press. 243–255.

Page, S. E. (2010) *Diversity and complexity*. Princeton, NJ: Princeton University Press.

Phelps, R. and Graham, A. (2010) Exploring the complementarities between complexity and action research: The story of Technology Together. *Cambridge Journal of Education*, 40/2. 183–197.

Phelps, R. and Hase, S. (2002) 'Complexity and action research: Exploring the theoretical and methodological connections'. *Educational Action Research*, 10/3. 507–524.

Richardson, K. A. and Cilliers, P. (2001) 'What is complexity science? A view from different directions'. *Emergence*, 3/1. 5–23.

Sade, L. A. (2014) 'Autonomy, complexity, and networks of learning', in G. Murray (ed.) *Social dimensions of autonomy in language learning*. Basingstoke: Palgrave Macmillan. 155–174.

Schoem, D. and Hurtado, S. (eds) (2001) *Intergroup dialogue: Deliberative democracy in school, college, community, and workplace*. Ann Arbor: The University of Michigan Press.

Trueit, D. and Doll, W. E. (2010) 'Thinking complexity: Being-in-relation', in D. Osberg and G. Biesta (eds) *Complexity theory and the politics of education*. Rotterdam: Sense Publishers. 135–151.

Tsui, A. (2003) *Understanding expertise in teaching: Case studies of second language teachers*. Cambridge: Cambridge University Press.

Tudor, I. (2001) *The dynamics of the language classroom*. Cambridge: Cambridge University Press.

Ushioda, E. (2009) 'A person-in-context relational view of emergent motivation, self and identity', in Z. Dörnyei and E. Ushioda (eds) *Motivation, language identity and the L2 self*. Bristol: Multilingual Matters. 215–228.

Vallacher, R. R. and Nowak, A. (2009) 'The dynamics of human experience: Fundamentals of dynamical social psychology', in S. J. Guastello, M. Koopmans and D. Pincus (eds) *Chaos and complexity in psychology: The theory of nonlinear dynamical systems*. Cambridge: Cambridge University Press. 370–401.

van Lier, L. (2004) *The ecology and semiotics of language learning: A sociocultural perspective*. Dordrecht: Springer.

Widdowson, H. (2003) *Defining issues in English language teaching*. Oxford: Oxford University Press.

Williams, M. (2001) 'Theory and practice in teacher education: Mind the gap', in V. Crew, C. Davison and B. Mak (eds) *Reflecting on language in education*. Hong Kong: The Hong Kong Institute of Education. 21–30.

34

Classroom talk, interaction and collaboration

Steve Walsh and Li Li

Introduction

This chapter looks at the important relationship between classroom talk, interaction and collaboration, a relationship which needs to be understood in order to maximise and enhance language learning. Learning, in this context, is viewed from a broadly sociocultural perspective, closely associated with learner participation, engagement and co-construction, where language acts as a mediating tool (see Negueruela-Azarola and García, this volume, for further discussion of sociocultural theory). Although participation in itself cannot always be equated with language learning, there is a strong and identifiable relationship between participation, collaboration and learning. For the purposes of this chapter, collaboration refers to the ways in which learning can be enhanced through interaction. It includes both the co-constructed learning which takes place in the second language classroom between teacher and students, and students and students, and also the ways in which teachers and teacher educators might collaborate in developing more detailed understandings of classroom interaction. This perspective, highlighting the importance of participation and collaboration, offers valuable insights into the learning and teaching process. Implications for teacher education and classroom practice are also discussed.

A key argument which we develop in the chapter is the need to place an understanding of classroom discourse at the centre of English and/or any second language teacher education or development programme. One way in which language teachers might improve their professional practice is to develop fine-grained, detailed understandings of their local context, something which they might achieve by examining the complex interplay between language, classroom interaction and learning.

A focus on classroom discourse

Why focus on classroom discourse?

As any teacher or learner knows, second language classrooms are highly complex, fast-paced, multi-party social contexts where talk and interaction are central to all activity. As Walsh puts it (2011: 168):

> In the rapid flow of classroom interaction, it is difficult to comprehend what is happening. Not only is the interaction very fast and involves many people, it has multiple foci; the

language being used may be performing several functions at the same time: seeking information, checking learning, offering advice and so on.

In a language classroom, it very quickly becomes apparent that learners access and acquire new knowledge and skills through the talk, interaction and collaboration which take place. Language is learned, problems are solved, new understandings accomplished and breakdowns repaired through the ensuing talk and according to the ways in which interaction is managed. Crucially, not only is language central to absolutely everything which takes place, it is also very often the goal of the interaction, the target of the talk; as Long (1983: 9) points out, language is "the vehicle and object of instruction".

So why should we, as teachers, teacher educators and researchers, focus on classroom discourse? First, there is a strong link between language and learning, with language playing a mediational role (Vygotsky, 1978); in other words, all learning requires language, the basic 'tool' which underpins or 'mediates' the learning process. To this end, interaction is central to learning, "the most important element in the curriculum" (van Lier, 1996: 5), a position echoed by Ellis (2000: 209) who tells us that "learning arises not *through* interaction, but *in* interaction" (original emphasis). As such, the relationship between talk, interaction and learning is central to classroom practice.

Second, 'good teaching' is concerned with more than good planning. As van Lier (1991) has commented, teaching has two essential ingredients: planning and improvising. The interactive decisions taken by teachers as they teach are at least as important as the planning which occurs before teaching (Bailey and Nunan, 1996). One way to access teachers' interactive, 'online' decision making (Walsh, 2006) is to look at their interactions with students. Good interactive decisions are ones which promote learning and learning opportunities and which reflect the pedagogic goals of the teacher, the goals of the learners, and the opportunities or constraints imposed by the context (see, for example, Seedhouse, 2004). Good decisions are those which are appropriate to the moment, not necessarily the ones which 'follow the plan'. Teachers may restrict or facilitate learning opportunities in their moment-by-moment decision making (Walsh, 2002). Their ability to make the 'right decision' entails an understanding of the complex relationship which prevails between talk, interaction and learning.

How might we focus on classroom discourse?

If it is accepted that teachers need to reflect on their practice as a way of developing more appropriate methodologies (Holliday, 1994; see also Holliday, this volume), there is a strong and compelling need for their reflections to be data led and evidence based (Mann and Walsh, 2013). Reflections are more likely to be meaningful and result in better teaching when they use some kind of evidence, such as a piece of material, a test score or a conversation with a student or colleague.

One way in which teachers might develop better understandings of their classroom practices is to study the interactions which take place in their own classrooms. By developing and extending their classroom interactional competence (CIC, Walsh, 2013) through reflection and dialogue, teachers will improve many aspects of their performance and promote engaged, dialogic learning environments. We return to this point in subsequent sections in this chapter.

However, there is as yet no widely available meta-language which can be used by teachers to describe classroom interaction. Understandings of interactional processes must begin with description (van Lier, 2000a), and understandings are co-constructed by teachers through dialogue with others about their professional world (Lantolf, 2000; Johnson, 2009). Description and dialogue, both of which are central to promoting CIC, require an appropriate meta-language, a language which can be used by teachers to talk about teaching and enhance understanding of their local context. We suggest that a more nuanced, qualitative approach to describing classroom discourse is needed to replace terms such as 'high' and 'low' teacher talk, or 'communicative' or 'uncommunicative' classrooms. Access to a more sophisticated, widely available meta-language and opportunities for dialogue are central to professional development (Edge, 2011). Expertise and understanding emerge through the insights and voices of L2 teachers (Bailey and Nunan, 1996); these voices need a language which allows concerns to be raised, questions to be asked and reflections to be discussed and shared.

Having outlined both the importance of classroom discourse and the need to understand the way in which it affects learning opportunities, the remainder of the chapter will first examine historical perspectives on classroom discourse before looking at its key features. We will then discuss appropriate methods of investigating classroom discourse before concluding with a consideration of future challenges in this area.

Historical perspectives

Classroom discourse has been researched extensively since the 1960s, when the advent of audio-recordings meant that classroom interactions could be recorded, transcribed and studied in some detail (Jenks and Seedhouse, 2015). Although the precise focus of these studies, the meaning of classroom discourse and what constitutes an appropriate approach for its study vary from one investigation to the next, a common theme is the need to explore the relationship between teacher and learner talk and learning.

Early work on classroom interaction focused on characterising patterns of discourse (e.g. Flanders, 1970), suggesting that classroom talk is structured and therefore can be categorised and quantified through description. The most influential work in this early period was arguably that of Sinclair and Coulthard (1975), who identified the three-part exchange structure, IRF – initiation-response-feedback – consisting of a teacher initiation in the form of a question, a student response and teacher feedback (see below for a fuller discussion). Subsequent studies in the 1980s made use of observation schedules to record what happened in classroom interactions and attempt to quantify specific features such as questions, responses, silence and so on.

Recognising the absence of a methodological framework for analysing classroom talk, Seedhouse (1996) argued for an 'emic' perspective, which adopts an institutional discourse conversation analysis approach (see below). Seedhouse (1996, 2004) demonstrates how a conversation analytic (CA) methodology is able to show the ways in which pedagogic goals and the language used to achieve them are inextricably linked. This line of research has generated a great deal of interest, resulting in a number of studies which provide detailed, emic perspectives on classroom discourse (e.g. Hall, 2009; Hellermann, 2011).

For example, based on the earlier work of Kramsch (1986), He and Young (1998) introduced a theory of interactional competence, which studied learners' discursive practices by focusing on turn-taking strategies, topic management and a range of interactional strategies used in various learning contexts. Young (2008) built on this work, proposing a number of linguistic and interactional resources used by learners such as turn taking, repair and so on. Developing learners' interactional competence requires their active participation in class (see also Hall et al., 2011; Young, 2013).

More recently, classroom discourse research has used interaction as a lens to investigate issues concerning learning and pedagogy. Areas of inquiry include what learning is and how learning can be promoted in class (Walsh and Li, 2013); teachers' decision making and pedagogical thinking (Li and Walsh, 2011; Fagan, 2012; Li, 2012, 2013; Morton, 2012); and how language teachers facilitate the development of learners' thinking skills in language learning by providing time, space and scaffolded help for students or hinder thinking skills by restricting student contributions and intervening too much (Li, 2011). All this work is clearly situated around notions of collaborative learning and highlights the participatory role of learners and how teachers can facilitate 'space for learning' (Walsh and Li, 2013).

Features of classroom discourse

In this section, we offer an overview of the most important features of second language classroom discourse, selected largely because they typify much of the interaction which takes place in classrooms and are prevalent in all parts of the world. They are control of patterns of communication, speech modification, elicitation and repair.

Control of the interaction

One of the most striking features of any classroom is that the roles of the participants (teacher and learners) are not equal; they are asymmetrical (as are many other institutional settings, for example doctor/patient, solicitor/client etc.). In language classrooms, teachers generally control patterns of communication by managing both the topic of conversation and turn taking, while students typically take their cues from the teacher, through whom they direct most of their responses. Even in the most decentralised and learner-centred classroom, teachers decide who speaks, when, to whom and for how long. Teachers are able to interrupt when they like, take the floor, hand over a turn, direct the discussion and switch topics. As Breen puts it, it is the teacher who "orchestrates the interaction" (1998: 119).

A teacher's ability to 'orchestrate the interaction' in this way not only determines who may participate and when, it also influences opportunities for learning (Walsh, 2002). By controlling participation structures, teachers also control the amount of 'space for learning' (Walsh and Li, 2013) students have; this is one of the key influences on learning and learning opportunities. Teachers may open up space by, for example, asking more open-ended questions, reducing 'teacher echo' and increasing their wait time (see below).

A key feature of classroom discourse, first proposed by Sinclair and Coulthard (1975), is a three-part exchange structure, also known as a triadic exchange structure. Typically in this exchange, for every contribution made by a student, the teacher makes two. This exchange structure is known as initiation-response-feedback (IRF; see above), or initiation-response-evaluation (IRE; Mehan, 1979), illustrated as follows:

Teacher	I:	what's the past tense of go?
Student	R:	went
Teacher	F:	went, excellent.

A consequence of this structure is that teachers clearly talk more than learners and occupy more of the interactional space of the classroom. Learners' opportunities to contribute are largely controlled by the teacher.

The IRF exchange structure has been influential in advancing understandings of classroom interaction (and spoken interactions more generally) in a number of ways. First, it helps us to appreciate that all classroom discourse is goal-oriented. The responsibility for establishing goals and 'setting the agenda' lies largely with the teacher. Pedagogic goals and the language used to achieve them are very closely related, even intertwined. Second, teachers have the main responsibility for what is said in the classroom and control the discourse not only through the special power and authority they have but also through their control of the discourse. They control who may speak and when, for how long and on what topic. They control turn taking through the use of IRF; not only do they initiate a response, they offer an evaluation – further evidence of control. Third, we see that learners take their cues from the teacher and rarely initiate a response. Their role, one which they are socialised into from a very early age, is to answer the teacher's questions, respond to prompts and so on. Fourth, an understanding of IRF – the 'building block' of classroom discourse – helps us to appreciate the special nature of classroom discourse and appreciate how teachers might vary interaction more and introduce alternative types of sequence.

A number of debates have emerged from studies on IRF. While some researchers believe that the exchange does not provide learners with opportunities to take initiatives (van Lier, 2000b) or is even negatively correlated with learning (Nystrand, 1997), others (e.g. Hall and Walsh, 2002: 196–197) argue that IRF users "have a more inquiry-based understanding of learning, which values the activities of exploration, hypothesis testing, and problem solving". In fact, the value of IRF in creating a learning opportunity to engage students lies in the task and pedagogical goal of the moment and how the teacher manages the F-move (e.g. Waring and Zhang, 2008). When a teacher is able to create a spiral IRF (Li, 2011), there is space for students to take the initiative, build on each other's contributions and therefore develop criticality through a sequence of teacher questions, learner answers and further teacher prompts.

Speech modification

A second feature of classroom discourse is teachers' speech modification, similar to the 'caretaker speech' employed by parents when speaking to very young children. The modification strategies used by teachers are conscious and deliberate and include: slower, louder, more deliberate speech; greater use of pausing and emphasis; and more exaggerated use of gestures and facial expressions to help convey meaning. Speech modification is used to help learners understand and to model new structures and vocabulary, for example. In many parts of the world, a teacher's articulation of the second language, for example English, may be the only exposure to the language that learners actually receive. It is important, therefore, that the L2 is modelled correctly and appropriately. Crucially, given the highly complex nature of classroom interaction, speech modification is necessary to ensure that everyone is following the *multilogue* (multi-party talk, Schwab, 2011) and taking part without getting lost.

There are a number of ways in which teachers use speech modification to create learning opportunities. At the simplest level, teachers employ a different range of linguistic resources to facilitate comprehension and assist the learning process. Through the use of simplified vocabulary, a more limited range of tenses and fewer modal verbs, clearer, slower pronunciation and a more extensive use of standard or non-idiomatic forms, teachers can greatly facilitate comprehension. On another level, teachers may modify their interactional resources to assist comprehension and help learners find their way. Key to this is the use of discourse markers (see, for example, Yang, 2014) to mark the beginnings and endings of various activities or stages in a lesson. Words such as *right, OK, now, so, all right* – which function typically as discourse markers – perform a very important function in signalling changes in the interaction or organisation of learning. The amount and type of organisational work performed by discourse markers is enormous since they signal both 'what is happening' in terms of teaching and learning and highlight particular linguistic features in the discourse.

In addition, teachers may use a range of strategies to both modify their speech and elicit speech modifications from learners. Strategies include: confirmation checks, where teachers confirm correct understanding; comprehension checks, used to ensure that learners understand the teacher; clarification requests, where students are invited to clarify a contribution; reformulation, rephrasing a learner's utterance; turn completion, finishing a learner's contribution; and backtracking, returning to an earlier part of a dialogue. These strategies operate at the level of interaction rather than solo performance; they are used to ensure that the discourse flows well and that the complex relationship between language use and learning is maintained. One interesting class of linguistic features used in classroom interaction is *backchannels* (words like *uh-huh, yeah, right, sure, OK*) – also known as acknowledgement tokens – which serve to 'oil the wheels' of the interaction and indicate 'listenership' (McCarthy, 2003) by acknowledging a turn and providing feedback.

Elicitation techniques

Elicitation techniques are the strategies teachers use to get learners to make a contribution during class. Typically, elicitation entails asking questions. Much of L2 classroom discourse is dominated by question-and-answer routines, with teachers asking most of the questions while learners ask correspondingly few questions. It is by asking questions that teachers are able to control the discourse (see the discussion of the IRF exchange, above), especially given that they know the answers to most of the questions they ask! Questions like these, where teachers already know the answer (for example, *what's the past tense of "go"?*) are called 'display' questions since they require learners to display what they know. Essentially, the defining characteristic of display questions is to check or evaluate understanding, concepts, learning, previous learning and so on.

More open-ended, genuine questions are called 'referential' questions. They are designed to promote discussion and debate, engage learners and produce longer, more complex responses which carry actual meaning (i.e. the teacher or listener does not know what the speaker/learner is going to say in advance). Such questions typically result in more 'natural' responses by learners, often longer and more complicated, and producing a more conversational type of interaction. Referential questions often begin with a *wh-* question such as *who, why, what*, etc. From a teaching and learning perspective, the distinction between display and referential is less important than the relationship between a teacher's pedagogic goal and choice of question – in other words, understanding what a question is actually *doing*. If the aim is to quickly check understanding or establish what learners already know, display questions are perfectly adequate. If, on the other hand, the aim is to promote discussion or help learners improve oral fluency, then referential questions are more appropriate. The extent to which a question produces a communicative response is less important than the extent to which a question serves its purpose at a particular point in a lesson.

Repair

Repair simply refers to the ways in which teachers deal with errors. It includes direct and indirect error correction. Error, repair and the possibilities surrounding corrective feedback are discussed in detail in the chapter by Mackey, Park and Tagarelli, this volume. However, it is worth summarising key points surrounding the relationship between repair and classroom discourse here.

Clearly, there is a range of forms of error correction available to a teacher at any point in time. As with all pedagogic strategies, some will be more or less appropriate than others at any given moment. Teachers may decide to ignore the error completely; signal that an error has been made and correct it; get learners to correct their own errors; or indicate that an error has been made and seek help from other learners to correct it. There is a close correlation between the choices teachers make when correcting errors and the four types of repair described by conversation analysts when studying naturally occurring conversation: self-initiated self-repair (i.e. I correct myself, unprompted), self-initiated other repair (i.e. I correct someone else, unprompted), other-initiated self-repair (i.e. someone prompts me to correct myself), and other initiated other repair (i.e. someone else prompts others to correct themselves) (see Sacks et al., 1974).

According to van Lier, "apart from questioning, the activity which most characterizes language classrooms is correction of errors" (1988: 276). He addresses one of the main debates confronting teachers when dealing with errors: should we avoid error correction at all costs since it affects the flow of classroom communication, or should we correct all errors so that learners acquire a 'proper' standard? Here, we suggest that the type of strategy used for error correction must relate to the pedagogic goals of the moment; for example, a highly controlled practice activity requires more error correction than one where the focus is oral fluency. The pedagogic goal and the language used to achieve it must be convergent – they should work together.

It is also probably fair to say that within the classroom, learners do expect to have their errors corrected. While it may not be appropriate in more naturalistic settings for speakers to correct each others' errors, in classrooms, this is both what learners want and expect. As Seedhouse (1997: 571) puts it, "making linguistic errors and having them corrected directly and overtly is not an embarrassing matter." Rather than deciding whether we should or should not correct errors, teachers would do well to consider the appropriacy of a particular strategy in relation to their intended goals. By adopting more conscious strategies and by understanding how a particular type of error correction impacts on the discourse, teachers can do much to tailor their error correction to the 'moment' and promote opportunities for learning.

Other issues

In addition to these features, others of note include 'feedback', which includes the strategies used by teachers to accept or modify a learner contribution, and 'confirmation checks' and 'clarification requests', actions which show acceptance or seek clarification of a learner contribution (see Mackey, Park and Tagarelli's chapter, this volume, for comprehensive discussion of these features). A further characteristic of classroom discourse, 'scaffolding', merits further brief discussion here, however.

Scaffolding in the L2 classroom refers to those supportive behaviours employed by a more advanced partner in collaboration with a less competent learner that aims to foster the latter's progress to a higher level of language proficiency (Memari-Hanjani and Li, 2014: 102). Scaffolding is "graduated", "contingent" and "dialogic" assistance/guidance (Aljaafreh and Lantolf, 1994: 495), which can be interpreted as the ways in which teachers (and learners) provide linguistic 'props' to assist learners in a language classroom. It is a typical feature of most language classroom discourse.

Appropriate methods of investigating classroom discourse

Previously in this chapter, we noted that the two main reasons for studying classroom interaction are that it promotes better understandings of learning and learning processes and that it facilitates teacher development. We turn now to the main approaches which have been used for such investigations.

Interaction analysis approaches

During the 1960s and 1970s, one of the most reliable, quantitative approaches to analysing interaction was thought to be through the use of observation instruments, or *coding systems*, to record what observers consider to be happening at any given moment. From these recordings and the ensuing statistical treatment, classroom profiles could be established, which, it was argued, provide an objective and 'scientific' analysis of the interaction. According to Brown and Rodgers (2002), over 200 different observation instruments exist. Essentially, these interactionist approaches to classroom discourse use some system of recording what observers see, often in the form of ticking boxes, making marks etc., usually at pre-specified time intervals throughout a lesson (e.g. every minute). Such instruments were regarded as being reliable since they offered a moment-by-moment record of 'what really happened' in the classroom (as we shall see shortly, however, these approaches have been critiqued).

According to Wallace (1998), observation schedules can be defined as either 'system-based' or '*ad hoc*'. System-based observation instruments normally have a number of fixed categories which have been pre-determined by extensive trialling in different classroom contexts. There are several advantages to using a fixed system: the system is ready-made – there is no need to design a completely new approach; because the system is well-known, there is no need for validation; any system may be used in real-time or following a recording; and comparisons between one system and another are possible. Examples include Bellack et al. (1966) and Flanders (1970).

The trend in later years was to include more and more categories designed to capture the complexities of classroom interaction. The COLT system (communicative orientation to language teaching), for example, was proposed by Allen et al. in 1984 (revised in 1995) and comprised 73 categories. Its principal goal was to enable the observer to make a connection between teaching methodology and language use, drawing heavily on the assumptions underpinning communicative language teaching (see Thornbury, this volume) and its goal of an interactive, 'communicative' classroom.

The main limitations of system-based interaction analysis approaches are the difficulty of matching interaction to pre-determined categories; they provide an etic (from the outside, by researchers or via pre-determined categories) rather than emic (from the inside, by participants or emerging from the classroom events themselves) perspective on the interaction; and a failure by observers to agree on 'what really happened' (i.e. amidst the complexity and rapid flow of a language class, different observers could interpret the same event in differing ways). In contrast, *ad hoc* approaches offer the construction of a more flexible instrument, which may, for example, be based on a specific classroom problem or area of interest. This approach allows specific details in the interaction to be studied and normally provides a more emic perspective.

Discourse analysis (DA) approaches

According to Seedhouse (2004: 56), "the overwhelming majority of previous approaches to L2 classroom interaction have implicitly or explicitly adopted what is fundamentally a discourse analysis approach." Perhaps the earliest and most well-known proponents of this approach are Sinclair and Coulthard (1975) who, in addition to identifying the IRF exchange system (see earlier in this chapter), used systemic functional linguistics (SFL; Halliday, 1985) analysis, and compiled a list of twenty-two speech acts representing the verbal behaviours of both teachers and students participating in primary classroom communication. The outcome for discourse analysis (DA) approaches is the development of a descriptive system incorporating a discourse hierarchy which moves from *lesson* at the highest level to *speech act* at the lowest. Speech acts offer a description of what is *done* with language by attributing functions to the interaction. While this is certainly useful and offers unique insights into the ways in which language and interaction are used to achieve particular goals, the main difficulty is that any utterance may perform a range of functions. The question 'what time does this lesson begin?' when asked by a teacher may, for example, perform the function of requesting information or admonishing a student who has turned up late to class. According to Stubbs (1983), it is almost impossible to say precisely what function is being performed by a teacher (or learner) act at any point in a lesson. As with any functional analysis, the precise meaning of an utterance is heavily dependent on local context.

Any attempt to analyse classroom data using a DA approach, therefore, involves some simplification and reduction. Matching utterances to categories may be problematic owing to the absence of a direct relationship between form and function. In general, DA approaches fail to take account of the more subtle forces at work such as role relations, context and sociolinguistic norms which have to be followed. In short, a DA treatment fails to adequately account for the dynamic nature of classroom interaction and the fact that it is socially constructed by its participants.

Conversation analytic (CA) approaches

Conversation analysis (CA) has its roots in sociology, stemming from an interest by its originators, Sacks et al. (1974), in 'ordinary conversation'. CA is based on the premise that social contexts are not static but are constantly being formed by participants through their use of language and the ways in which turn taking, openings and closures, sequencing of acts and so on are locally managed. Interaction is *context shaped* and *context renewing;* that is, one contribution is dependent on a previous one, and subsequent contributions create a new context for later actions. Under this microscopic view of context, one person's contribution is inextricably linked to that of another person. Order in spoken discourse is established through sequential organisation – the way in which one utterance is connected to another.

While CA has its origins in the study of ordinary conversation, its relevance to an institutional discourse setting, such as a classroom, cannot be ignored. In L2 classrooms, the goals and actions of participants are closely linked to, and to some extent constrained by, the institutional business of learning a language. A consequence is that the features of the interaction, such as turn and topic management, sequential organisation and choice of lexis, are all determined by that enterprise and by the roles of interactants. What CA can do is to uncover something of the detail of these interactions by looking at the ways in which contexts are co-created in relation to the goal-oriented activity in which they are engaged (Heritage, 2004: 224). Essentially, what takes place in an L2 classroom between teachers and learners, and learners and their peers, can be described as 'conversation'. It is, for the most part, two way; it entails turn taking, turn passing, turn ceding and turn seizing; and it makes use of topic switches and contains many of the features of 'ordinary' conversation such as false starts, hesitations, errors, silence, back channelling and so forth.

The main aim of CA is to view interaction through the eyes of the participants and account for the structural organisation of the interaction from this perspective. In this sense, the approach is strictly empirical. CA forces the researcher to focus on the interaction patterns emerging *from* the data rather than relying on any preconceived notions which they may bring *to* the data (Seedhouse, 2004). Central to this notion is that of context, which is dynamic and mutually constructed by the participants. Contexts are therefore constantly changing as a lesson progresses and according to local demands and constraints; talk is essentially goal oriented: participants are striving towards some overall objective related to the institution. Any analysis of the ensuing talk is *multi-layered;* because no one utterance is categorised in isolation and because contributions are examined in sequence, a CA methodology is much better equipped to interpret and account for the multi-layered structure of classroom interaction.

While we are not suggesting here that language teacher education or teacher development should make extensive use of CA, there is certainly an argument that fine-grained understandings of classroom interaction are central to promoting learning. The use of untranscribed recordings, for example, can be very useful and has much to offer in terms of fostering better understandings of the nature of interaction in the L2 classroom and enabling teachers to make changes to their practice.

Future directions

From the discussion in this chapter, and based on the research evidence from more than fifty years of research on classroom interaction, what challenges lie ahead for teachers and learners and how might some of those challenges be addressed?

Developing language teacher education

A very important observation is how little time is actually spent making language teachers aware of the importance of classroom interaction, in the ways suggested in this chapter. To our knowledge, very few ELT or TESOL teacher education programmes, either pre- or in-service, pay very much attention to classroom interaction. Typically, most teacher education programmes comprise a language awareness strand and a classroom methodology or pedagogy strand. Here, we would like to propose a 'third strand' on language teacher education programmes, focusing specifically on the relationship between interaction, participation, collaboration and learning. The aim of this component is to sensitise language teachers to the centrality of interaction to teaching and learning and to provide them with the means of acquiring close understandings of their local contexts. Rather than trying to make 'current' teaching methodologies work in contexts where they have little or no relevance, an understanding of local context is the first step in improving teaching efficacy and enhancing the learner experience – and an understanding of interaction and the ability of stakeholders to engage with the issues surrounding interaction, participation and learning lie at the heart of this challenge.

Related to the challenge of developing a detailed understanding of local context is the notion of classroom interactional competence (CIC, Walsh, 2013: 130), defined as "teachers' and learners' ability to use interaction as a tool for mediating and assisting learning". When studying transcripts of classroom discourse, it very quickly becomes apparent that levels of interactional competence vary hugely from one context and from one teacher to another. Some teachers, at some points in time, are very adept at managing interaction in such a way that learning and learning opportunities are maximised. Others use interactional strategies which 'get in the way' and which impede opportunities for learning (Walsh, 2002). By recording and analysing their own practice, teachers could develop and improve their interactions with students and establish more engaged, collaborative classes.

Developing classroom practice

In terms of addressing learner participation in the classroom, a number of challenges lie ahead. Perhaps the biggest and most difficult is the need to change the interactional structure of lessons so that learners might play a more equal role in classroom discourse. When we consider the ways in which learners are socialised into certain types of classroom behaviour, this is a huge challenge. In most content-based subjects, learners answer questions, respond to cues, follow the teacher's initiative, avoid interrupting and so forth. And yet, in a language classroom, a very different set of interactional traits is needed if learners are to play a more equal part in the discourse and to actively participate in learning. In language classrooms, we need learners to both ask and answer questions, to interrupt where appropriate, to take the initiative, seize the floor, hold a turn and so forth. In other words, there is a need for more equal roles in which learners and teachers collaborate in the process of co-constructing meanings. In such a learning environment, different interactional features prevail; turns are longer, for example, and there are more frequent topic changes. Overlaps and interruptions are more common, as are pauses. It is in this kind of environment that learners develop, since they are able to acquire the kinds of linguistic and interactional resources which will enhance the language learning process. Teachers, while still playing a more central role, would need a sophisticated understanding of classroom discourse in order to be able to manage the interaction.

And finally, it is impossible to consider future challenges without some mention of the place of technology in classroom discourse. Technology enhanced learning and the need to understand the ways in which technology, through interaction, mediates learning are key challenges in the future. There is a growing and pressing imperative to understand the ways in which technology might be embedded in classroom practices as a tool to assist and support learning (see, for example, Gruba, Hinkelman and Cárdenas-Claros, and Kern, Ware and Warschauer, this volume).

Conclusion

Such understandings of both face-to-face classroom discourse and the impacts of technology on classroom learning opportunities, and the development of good classroom practices, we suggest, can best be optimised through studies of classroom data and by looking at the ways in which interactions are created and managed. Appreciating the centrality of classroom discourse and the role of classroom talk, interaction and collaboration will help teachers and learners maximise opportunities for second language learning in class.

Discussion questions

- Which features of classroom interaction are important in your teaching, and how might you study them?
- Based on your own experience, what can teachers do to promote more engaged, collaborative classrooms?
- How would you like to improve or change the interactions which take place in your classes? How might you bring about those changes?
- How would you describe or define interactional competence in your context? How might you encourage it?

Related topics

Cognitive perspectives on classroom language learning; Communicative language teaching in theory and practice; Error, feedback and repair; Language teacher education; Sociocultural theory and the language classroom.

Further reading

Jenks, C. and Seedhouse, P. (eds) (2015) *International perspectives on ELT classroom interaction*. London: Palgrave Macmillan. (An international collection of papers on ELT classroom interaction which uses a range of methodologies for investigating classroom discourse and provides unique insights into a range of interactional phenomena.)

Walsh, S. (2013) *Classroom discourse and teacher development*. Edinburgh: Edinburgh University Press. (Develops many of the ideas put forward in this chapter and proposes ways of helping teachers to reflect on their interactional practices as a means of promoting professional development.)

References

Aljaafreh, A. and Lantolf, J. P. (1994) Negative feedback as regulation and second language learning in the zone of proximal development *Modern Language Journal*, 78/4. 465–483.

Allen, P., Fröhlich, M. and Spada, N. (1984) 'The communicative orientation of language teaching: An observation scheme', in J. Handscombe, R. A. Orem and B. P. Taylor (eds) *On TESOL '83: The question of control*. Washington, DC: TESOL. 231–252.

Bailey, K. M. and Nunan, D. (eds) (1996) *Voices from the language classroom*. Cambridge: Cambridge University Press.

Bellack, A., Kliebard, H., Hyman, R. and Smith, F. (1966) *The language of the classroom*. New York: Teachers College Press.

Breen, M. P. (1998) 'Navigating the discourse: On what is learned in the language classroom', in W. A. Renandya and G. M. Jacobs (eds) *Learners and language learning*. Anthology Series 39, Singapore: SEAMO Regional Language Centre. 115–143.

Brown, J. D. and Rodgers, T. (2002) *Doing applied linguistics research*. Oxford: Oxford University Press.

Edge, J. (2011) *The reflexive teacher educator in TESOL: Roots and wings*. London: Routledge.

Ellis, R. (2000) 'Task-based research and language pedagogy'. *Language Teaching Research*, 49/3. 193–220.

Fagan, D. S. (2012) 'Dealing with' unexpected learner contributions in whole-group activities: An examination of novice language teacher discursive practices'. *Classroom Discourse*, 3/2. 107–128.

Flanders, N. A. (1970) *Analysing teacher behaviour*. Reading, MA: Addison-Wesley.

Hall, J. K. (2009) 'Interaction as method and result of language learning'. *Language Teaching*, 43/2. 1–14.

Hall, J. K., Hellermann, J. and Doehler, S. P. (eds) (2011) *L2 Interactional competence and development*. Clevedon: Multilingual Matters.

Hall, J. K. and Walsh, M. (2002) 'Teacher–student interaction and language learning'. *Annual Review of Applied Linguistics*, 22. 186–203.

Halliday, M.A.K. (1985) *An introduction to functional grammar*. London: Edward Arnold.

He, A. W. and Young, R. (1998) 'Language proficiency interviews: A discourse approach', in R. Young and A. W. He (eds) *Talking and testing: Discourse approaches to the assessment of oral proficiency*. John Benjamins Amsterdam and Philadelphia. 1–24.

Hellermann, J. (2011) 'Members' methods, members' competencies: looking for evidence of language learning in longitudinal investigations of other-initiated repair', in J. K. Hall, J. Hellermann and S. P. Doehler (eds) *L2 interactional competence and development*. Bristol: Multilingual Matters Clevedon. 147–172.

Heritage, J. (2004) 'Conversational analysis and institutional talk: Analysing data', in D. Silverman (ed.) *Qualitative research: Theory, method and practice*. London: Sage Publications. 222–245.

Holliday, A. (1994) *Appropriate methodology and social context*. Cambridge: Cambridge University Press.

Jenks, C. and Seedhouse, P. (eds) (2015) *International perspectives on ELT classroom interaction*. London: Palgrave Macmillan.

Johnson, K. E. (2009) *Second language teacher education: A sociocultural perspective*. New York: Routledge.

Kramsch, C. (1986) 'From language proficiency to interactional competence'. *Modern Language Journal*, 70/4. 366–372.

Lantolf, J. P. (2000) *Sociocultural theory and second language learning*. Oxford: Oxford University Press.

Li, L. (2011) 'Obstacles and opportunities for developing thinking through interaction in language classrooms'. *Thinking Skills and Creativity*, 6/3. 146–158.

Li, L. (2012) 'Belief construction and development: Two tales of non-native English speaking student teachers in a TESOL programme'. *Novitas-ROYAL (Research on Youth and Language)*, 6/1. 33–58.

Li, L. (2013) 'The complexity of language teachers' beliefs and practice: One EFL teacher's theories'. *Language Learning Journal*, 41/2. 175–191.

Li, L. and Walsh, S. (2011) '"Seeing is believing": Looking at EFL teachers' beliefs through classroom interaction'. *Classroom Discourse*, 2/1. 39–57.

Long, M. (1983) 'Inside the "Black Box"', in H. Seliger and M. Long (eds) *Classroom oriented research in second language acquisition*. Rowley: Newbury House. 3–36.

Mann, S. and Walsh, S. (2013) 'RP or 'RIP': A critical perspective on reflective practice'. *Applied Linguistics Review*, 4/2. 291–315.

McCarthy, M. J. (2003) 'Talking back: "Small" interactional response tokens in everyday conversation'. *Research on Language in Social Interaction,* 36. 33–63.

Mehan, H. (1979) *Learning lessons: Social organization in the classroom.* Cambridge, MA: Harvard University Press.

Memari-Hanjani, A. and Li, L. (2014) 'Exploring L2 writers' collaborative revision interactions and their writing performance'. *System,* 44. 101–114.

Morton, T. (2012) 'Classroom talk, conceptual change and teacher reflection in bilingual science teaching'. *Teaching and Teacher Education,* 28/1. 101–110.

Nystrand, M. (1997) 'Dialogic instruction: When recitation becomes conversation', in M. Nystrand, A. Gamoran, R. Kachur and C. Prendergast (eds) *Opening dialogue: Understanding the dynamics of language and learning in the English classroom.* New York: Teachers College Press. 1–29.

Sacks, H., Schegloff, E. and Jefferson, G. (1974) 'A simplest systematics for the organisation of turn-taking in conversation'. *Language,* 50/4. 696–735.

Schwab, G. (2011) 'From dialogue to multilogue – A different view on participation in the English foreign language classroom'. *Classroom Discourse,* 2/1. 3–19.

Seedhouse, P. (1996) *Learning talk: A study of the interactional organization of the L2 classroom from a CA institutional discourse perspective.* Unpublished PhD thesis, University of York, UK.

Seedhouse, P. (1997) 'The case of the missing "no": The relationship between pedagogy and interaction'. *Language Learning,* 47/3. 547–583.

Seedhouse, P. (2004) *The interactional architecture of the second language classroom: A conversational analysis perspective.* Oxford: Blackwell.

Sinclair, J. McH. and Coulthard, M. (1975) *Towards an analysis of discourse: The English used by pupils and teachers.* Oxford: Oxford University Press.

Stubbs, M. (1983) *Discourse analysis: The sociolinguistic analysis of natural language.* Oxford: Blackwell; Chicago: University of Chicago Press.

van Lier, L. (1988) 'What's wrong with classroom talk?' *Prospect,* 3/3: 267–283.

van Lier, L. (1991) 'Inside the classroom: Learning processes and teaching procedures'. *Applied Language Learning,* 2/1. 48–64.

van Lier, L. (1996) *Interaction in the language curriculum: Awareness, autonomy and authenticity.* New York: Longman.

van Lier, L. (2000a) 'From input to affordance: Social-interactive learning from an ecological perspective', in J. P. Lantolf (ed.) *Sociocultural theory and second language learning.* Oxford: Oxford University Press. 245–259.

van Lier, L. (2000b) 'Constraints and resources in classroom talk: Issues in equality and symmetry', in C. N. Candlin and N. Mercer (eds) *English language teaching in its social context: A reader.* New York: Routledge. 90–107.

Vygotsky, L. S. (1978) *Mind in society: The development of higher psychological processes.* Cambridge: Harvard University Press.

Wallace, M. (1998) *Action research for language teachers.* Cambridge: Cambridge University Press.

Walsh, S. (2002) 'Construction or obstruction: Teacher talk and learner involvement in the EFL classroom'. *Language Teaching Research,* 6/1. 3–23.

Walsh, S. (2006) *Investigating classroom discourse.* London: Routledge.

Walsh, S. (2011) *Exploring classroom discourse: Language in action.* London: Routledge.

Walsh, S. (2013) *Classroom discourse and teacher development.* Edinburgh: Edinburgh University Press

Walsh, S. and Li, L. (2013) 'Conversations as space for learning'. *International Journal of Applied Linguistics,* 23/2. 247–266.

Waring, H. and Zhang, H. S. (2008) 'Using explicit positive assessment in the language classroom: IRF, feedback, and learning opportunities'. *Modern Language Journal,* 92/4. 577–594.

Yang, S. (2014) *Investigating discourse markers in Chinese college EFL teacher talk: A multi-layered analytical approach.* Unpublished PhD thesis, Newcastle University, Newcastle, UK.

Young, R. F. (2008) *Language and interaction: An advanced resource book.* London and New York: Routledge. London: Routledge.

Young, R. F. (2013) 'Learning to talk the talk and walk the walk: Interactional competence in academic spoken English'. *Ibérica,* 25. 15–38.

35

Errors, corrective feedback and repair

Variations and learning outcomes

Alison Mackey, Hae In Park and Kaitlyn M. Tagarelli

Introduction

Though it is obvious that most second language (L2) learners make errors in classroom settings, it is not always clear, from the teacher's perspective, how to deal with these errors. In a very early review of error correction in foreign language classrooms, Hendrickson (1978) posed five questions regarding error correction and ultimately called for more research to systematically answer these questions. They are:

1   Should learner errors be corrected?
2   If so, when should learner errors be corrected?
3   Which learner errors should be corrected?
4   How should learner errors be corrected?
5   Who should correct learner errors?

These questions, according to Lyster and Ranta (1997), turned out to be "deceptively simple", because answers are only now becoming clear after nearly four decades of research. There has been "a considerable amount of research on CF [corrective feedback]" (Lyster et al., 2013: 3), and in this chapter we try to examine how close the field of second language acquisition (SLA) has come to answering Hendrickson's fundamental questions as well as what else we have learned about error correction in foreign language settings (see Ellis and Shintani, 2014, for a recent review of how ELT manuals and guides have dealt with these issues over the years with respect to spoken and written corrective feedback).

This chapter examines the types of errors that L2 learners make when speaking, the feedback they receive from their interlocutors in classrooms (both their teachers and each other) and the ways in which learners can use that feedback to modify their original utterances and, hopefully, develop their interlanguage in the direction of the target language. We believe it will be helpful for English language teachers to consider what research has to say in relation to when, why and how feedback works. Using SLA research as one source of information (and reflecting upon their own experiences as another), teachers may garner a deeper understanding about how errors can be efficiently handled in instructional settings to promote L2 development.

Key definitions

In this chapter, we use the word *error* to refer to non-target-like utterances produced by learners. Although historically a distinction has been drawn between 'errors' and 'mistakes' (Corder, 1967) on the basis of whether incorrect utterances are systematic or slips of the tongue, this chapter makes no such distinction because this difference is most likely imperceptible in an authentic classroom setting.

Errors are, without a doubt, an inevitable part of language learning. There are many different kinds of errors that a learner can make, and these affect the kinds of feedback and repair that can follow. Errors vary according to linguistic form; for example, there are lexical errors, where the word used is incorrect; grammatical errors, where morphosyntax or word order is incorrect; and phonological errors, where pronunciation is incorrect. Pragmatic errors often violate some convention of meaning, even when the grammar is correct. The amount and type of errors that learners make depend on several factors, such as their level of L2 development and the amount and type of language they are producing at the time. Some errors may be due to some sort of transfer from the learner's L1 (e.g. Spada and Lightbown, 1999; Odlin, 2003), while others arise as part of the developmental stages that learners of all backgrounds progress through when learning a particular language (e.g. Dulay and Burt, 1974; Goldschneider and DeKeyser, 2001).

In this chapter we use the term *corrective feedback* to mean teacher (or peer/interlocutor) responses to learner utterances that contain errors, actual or perceived (see Ellis, 2006; Ellis and Shintani, 2014). According to Lyster et al. (2013), corrective feedback is "an inherent part of classroom practices in which teachers engage to achieve instructional objectives that include consolidation of students' L2 knowledge" (p. 2), and it "plays a pivotal role in the kind of scaffolding that teachers need to provide to individual learners to promote continuing L2 growth" (p. 1). In other words, corrective feedback is a tool that teachers use to turn errors into opportunities for L2 development. Corrective feedback provides negative evidence by signalling that a learner's utterance contained an error, but it can also provide positive evidence if the feedback contains the target form (e.g. in recasts, as we discuss later in the chapter). However, we should bear in mind that some researchers, for example, Ellis and Shintani (2014), argue that feedback is only effective if learners perceive it as corrective – that is, when learners see the feedback "as constituting negative evidence" (p. 261). Other researchers believe it is possible that learners may benefit from correction even if they do not seem to be aware of it at the time (Mackey, 2007). There are a number of different types of corrective feedback, which are described in detail later in this chapter.

Feedback can provide a connection between error and repair if it results in learners' responding in some way to the error, which has often been termed 'uptake' (Lyster and Ranta, 1997). For example, feedback may prompt learners to notice the gap or the distinction between their own non-target-like utterances and their teachers' correct utterances (Schmidt and Frota, 1986), and thus change their utterances to be more target-like. However, uptake does not necessarily lead to repair (e.g. a learner may simply acknowledge feedback without repair, or repair a different error), since the changes learners make to their utterances can take many forms (e.g. Mackey and Philp, 1998).

While the goal of this chapter is to help teachers understand when, why and how to use corrective feedback in the classroom, the research that informs this chapter comes from both classroom and laboratory studies. Corrective feedback has been shown to promote L2 learning in both settings (Mackey and Goo, 2007; Li, 2010). Although findings from classroom studies may translate more easily to real-world language classrooms, findings from controlled laboratory studies can provide more nuanced and deeper understandings of how error, feedback and repair work together in interactive settings.

In this chapter, we tackle the questions of how, when and why English language teachers should use corrective feedback in their classrooms, exploring learners' and teachers' perceptions about feedback as well looking at how effective feedback is in promoting learning. We explore different types of corrective feedback and present findings from research to help teachers make informed decisions about which types of feedback might be most effective in their own classrooms. Finally, we caution against using a one-size-fits-all approach to corrective feedback by providing an overview of the various factors, particularly linguistic targets and individual differences, that can influence how effective feedback can be.

Should teachers correct errors?

One of the questions some teachers wonder about is whether errors should be corrected at all in the language classroom. Teachers' opinions vary quite widely on this and often differ depending on their training and classroom experience. Teachers who subscribe to a non-interventionist approach to error correction (see, for example, the natural approach proposed by Krashen and Terrell, 1983), which gained some popularity in the 1980s, tend to believe that the primary intended focus of instruction is learning to communicate and that if communication of meaning is successful, correcting errors is not necessary. In other words, how one says something is less important than getting the intended message across. If meaning is successfully conveyed, errors are overlooked. From this perspective, positive evidence (sometimes termed 'input') alone is sufficient for language learning, and a learner error only receives attention if it hampers comprehensibility. Teachers who ascribe to these views often also believe that overt correction can harm learners' self-confidence as well as heighten their anxiety levels to an extent that is detrimental to language learning.

Turning to the other end of the continuum, in part because of worries that this approach to error led to learners who were 'fluently ungrammatical', research over the last few decades has looked into more form-oriented instruction, asking how effective it can be in L2 development. A convincing rationale for error correction can be found in this sort of research, seen in contemporary language teaching methods and theoretical approaches to learning, such as the interaction hypothesis (Mackey et al., 2012) and task-based language teaching (Ellis, 2005; Norris, 2010; Robinson, 2011; see Van den Branden, this volume), which view feedback as an integral part of making form-meaning connections in the course of communication.

Following these perspectives, most practitioners would agree that correcting all errors is not useful, realistic or possible, but that appropriate corrective feedback is likely to facilitate L2 developmental processes in two ways. First, corrective feedback can play a facilitative role in drawing learners' attention to discrepancies between their own interlanguage and the target language, a process that is central to restructuring of the interlanguage system (Schmidt, 1990, 1995, 2001; Ellis, 1991; Gass and Varonis, 1994). Corrective feedback in its more explicit forms (e.g. explicit correction, metalinguistic feedback) directly points to such disparity by supplying negative evidence that signals learners' incorrect use of target language. In the case of more implicit error correction such as recasts (i.e. reformulated versions of a learner's original incorrect utterance), it can present contrastive evidence in the form of models, without directly and overtly drawing learners' attention to errors. Long (2007: 4) points out that the provision of a recast after a learner error juxtaposes incorrect and correct utterances, thereby allowing "the learner to compare the two forms side by side, so to speak, and to observe the contrast". Once learners recognise the gap between their production and the information in corrections, they may be better able to modify their existing L2 knowledge towards the target norm.

Besides the fact that corrective feedback can serve as a catalyst for noticing-the-gap reference, it can also provide output opportunities for learners. Correction strategies that do not supply the target form (e.g. elicitation, clarification requests, confirmation checks) may prompt modified output (i.e. production by learners after instances of feedback, which may or may not be correct) and self-generated repair, allowing learners to reformulate their original incorrect utterances. The process of rephrasing one's original utterances in response to feedback is believed to facilitate L2 development in various ways (see Swain, 1985, 1995, 2005; Ellis and He, 1999; Izumi, 2003; McDonough and Mackey, 2006). For instance, corrective feedback enables learners to reflect on their original language and determine which part of their utterance was problematic. Through such self-monitoring processes, learners can gain more control over those target features and eventually enhance their fluency and automaticity of L2 processing. According to Swain's output hypothesis (1985, 1995, 2005), production also requires learners to engage in syntactic processing, which is not necessitated by comprehension of input. Swain notes that L2 learners "can fake it, so to speak, in comprehension, but they cannot do so in the same way in production" (1995: 127). In other words, self-correction in response to feedback can trigger deeper and more elaborate processing of L2 forms, helping learners establish memory traces that last longer.

In addition to theoretical support for the idea that learners benefit from correction, there is empirical support from recent research syntheses and meta-analyses (e.g. Keck et al., 2006; Russell and Spada, 2006; Mackey and Goo, 2007; Li, 2010; Lyster and Saito, 2010). These reviews synthesised the findings of primary research that examined the effectiveness of oral corrective feedback either in their entirety or in part, with the overall conclusion being that corrective feedback *is* beneficial to L2 development. Lyster and Saito (2010), who exclusively focused on the effects of oral corrective feedback in classroom settings, found that corrective feedback was moderately beneficial for learners' L2 development in comparison to the control group that received no corrective feedback, irrespective of instructional settings (second or foreign language classrooms). Mackey and Goo's findings also support the notion of developmental benefits for feedback. Interestingly, meta-analyses suggest that the effect of corrective feedback is maintained over time, without any significant differences between learners' scores on immediate and delayed posttests. These findings demonstrate the long-term pedagogical value of corrective feedback, suggesting that teachers' use of corrective feedback in the classroom should be encouraged.

As well as this empirical evidence that substantiates the utility of corrective feedback, research into learner and teacher preferences about corrective feedback is also positive. Research of this kind examines learners' and/or teachers' evaluations in relation to how corrective feedback should be treated in the classroom. Findings (e.g. Cathcart and Olsen, 1976; Oladejo, 1993; Schulz, 1996, 2001; Jean and Simard, 2011) demonstrate that there is a mismatch in learners' and teachers' beliefs regarding corrective feedback. Notwithstanding teachers' concerns that corrective feedback may provoke learner anxiety and impact their motivation and self-confidence in a negative manner, corrective feedback is typically appreciated and welcomed by learners. For instance, Cathcart and Olsen's (1976) study indicated that adult English as second language (ESL) learners not only expressed a strong preference for corrective feedback, but they also wanted to be corrected more frequently than their teachers deemed necessary. More recently, Brown (2009) revealed that correcting oral errors was considered one of the effective teacher behaviours by university students from various language courses, suggesting that learners regard error correction as an essential part of the foreign language classroom. Although learners' beliefs about corrective feedback do not necessarily predict or guarantee their reactions to it, this line of research in teachers' beliefs and perceptions about feedback nevertheless lends support to the idea that the provision of corrective feedback is helpful for another reason – it is important for teachers to meet the needs and expectations of learners in the classroom. As Nunan (1995:140) puts it, "teachers should find out what their students think and feel about what and how they want to learn" in order to yield successful learning outcomes.

Altogether, then, the research suggests clear evidence to support teachers using corrective feedback in L2 development. Corrective feedback not only aids the processes of language acquisition, but it also meets learners' needs and expectations of the teacher. Once teachers decide to correct errors in the classroom, though, it is important to determine how those errors should be corrected. That is, what types of feedback are available to language teachers, and when should they be used?

Different types of corrective feedback

Over the years, a number of taxonomies of oral feedback strategies have been proposed (Allwright, 1975; Chaudron, 1977; Lyster and Ranta, 1997; Seedhouse, 1997; Ranta and Lyster, 2007; Sheen and Ellis, 2011). For example, Sheen and Ellis (2011) suggest nine feedback types on the basis of six basic strategies originally identified by Lyster and Ranta (1997). These feedback techniques are separated along two dimensions: 1) input-providing vs. output-prompting and 2) implicit vs. explicit. The former distinguishes feedback types on the basis of whether feedback provides or elicits (i.e. input-providing and output-prompting, respectively) the correction, while the latter has to do with the explicitness of the corrective force.

There are four feedback moves that are input-providing: conversational recasts, didactic recasts, explicit correction and explicit correction with metalinguistic explanation. These strategies provide both positive and negative evidence and demonstrate to learners how their incorrect utterances can be correctly reformulated. Recognising that recasts are "elastic in nature" (Mackey and Goo, 2007), Sheen and Ellis (2011) distinguish between *conversational recasts* (i.e. implicit) and *didactic recasts* (i.e. explicit). Conversational recasts (i.e. when the error, or phrase containing an error, is repeated back to the learner in its corrected form) are implicit in nature in that they occur when a learner's incorrect utterance causes a communication problem and that they usually take the form of confirmation checks. In contrast, if recasts occur when there is no communication breakdown, and the primary focus is on form, they are seen as serving a didactic function. In addition to didactic recasts, corrections (e.g. *It's "she walks to school", not "walk"*) and corrections with metalinguistic explanations (e.g. *It's "she walks to school", not "walk". You need -s on the verb because "she" is third-person singular*) are also classified as explicit input-providing feedback strategies.

Output-prompting feedback strategies, on the other hand, provide negative evidence to learners by signaling that their utterances are problematic. Learners are given an opportunity to self-correct their errors and produce modified output. Five strategies fall into the category of this sort of feedback: repetitions, clarification requests, metalinguistic clues, elicitations and paralinguistic signals. *Repetitions* (e.g. *She walk to school?*) and *clarification requests* (e.g. *What?, Huh?*) prompt learners to respond without breaking the communication flow. These are considered to be negotiation for meaning. On the other hand, the corrective force of *metalinguistic clues* (e.g. *You need past tense*), *elicitations* (e.g. *Say that again?*) and *paralinguistic signals* (i.e. a gesture or facial expression to indicate that the learner has made an error) is overt in that learners clearly recognise that their utterances are being corrected.

A number of studies have compared different types of corrective feedback in an attempt to investigate which feedback works best in the classroom. While some studies claim that there were no significant difference across different feedback types (e.g. Ammar and Spada, 2006; Loewen and Nabei, 2007; McDonough, 2007), others found different types of feedback had differential effects on L2 development (e.g. Long et al., 1998; Iwashita, 2003; Leeman, 2003; Ellis et al., 2006). A meta-analysis of oral corrective feedback with 33 studies in both classroom and laboratory contexts revealed that explicit feedback (i.e. metalinguistic feedback, explicit correction) was generally more effective than implicit feedback (i.e. recasts, negotiation such as clarification requests, elicitation and repetition) in the short term, while implicit feedback had more impact on L2 learning in the long term (Li, 2010). Another meta-analysis by Lyster and Saito (2010) examined oral corrective feedback in the classroom, with slightly different findings for efficacy of different feedback types (they looked at recasts, explicit correction, and prompts). They found prompts were more helpful than recasts, while the effects of explicit correction were indistinguishable from the other two feedback types.

However, this does not mean that recasts are not effective in the classroom. Goo and Mackey (2013) point out various problems inherent in making comparisons of recasts to other types of feedback (e.g. prompts) and suggest that the findings of 'apples-to-oranges' comparison studies must be interpreted with caution. For instance, in some recast-versus-prompt studies (e.g. Lyster, 2004; Ammar and Spada, 2006; Ammar, 2008; Lyster and Izquierdo, 2009), form-focused instruction was included as a part of the experimental treatment, making it difficult to conclude from these studies that any differential effects between prompts and recasts are free from the moderating role of the form-focused instruction. Also, modified output opportunities were not controlled for in quite a few of the studies comparing recasts and prompts (e.g. Lyster, 2004; Ammar and Spada, 2006; Ellis et al., 2006; Loewen and Nabei, 2007; Ammar, 2008; Yang and Lyster, 2010). In other words, prompts naturally elicit more modified output opportunities, while recasts naturally do not. We know that modified output is helpful for L2 development (Swain, 1985, 1995, 2005); thus the recast-versus-other-types-of-feedback comparison when participatory demands of the two feedback types are different is again one that gives an output advantage to non-recast types of feedback. In practice, however, such comparisons may be missing the mark in terms of providing practical considerations for language teachers.

To that end, researchers (Goo and Mackey, 2013; Lyster et al., 2013) have begun to express skepticism about comparing the relative efficacy of different feedback strategies, suggesting instead a need for a change of direction in corrective feedback research. They point out that it may not be worthwhile to make attempts to identify the single most effective feedback type when all feedback techniques are likely to play some facilitative role in L2 learning, and no researchers have suggested teachers should exclusively focus on one feedback type to the exclusion of others. Far from it; most researchers recognise that teachers need to have a variety of feedback tools in their toolbox. So, it is helpful to try to understand what feedback type is best employed when and where; in other words, to investigate in which conditions one can maximise the effectiveness of different feedback types so that teachers can be better informed about *when* to use *what*. Since variety in instructional practices may increase learners' interest as well as "the depth and the transferability of learning" (Lightbown, 2008: 40), we interpret current research to suggest that teachers can be encouraged to implement various feedback strategies in their teaching instead of adhering to one type of feedback – even if they *think* one kind is the most effective.

Factors that impact the effectiveness of feedback

There are a number of factors that can influence the degree to which corrective feedback is effective for language learning, and teachers should be aware of these factors so that they can assess the roles that they play in their own classrooms. Here we focus mainly on linguistic targets and individual differences before noting other factors that affect the efficacy of corrective feedback.

Linguistic targets

As mentioned above, the types of errors that learners make are quite varied linguistically, and teachers often struggle to determine which errors to correct. One thing to consider with respect to feedback and linguistic targets is that although mastery of an L2 is often associated with advanced morphosyntactic and pragmatic abilities in that language (e.g. Hyltenstam and Abrahamsson, 2003), successful communication may depend more on lexical and phonological skills, which are crucial to an interlocutor's ability to be understood. Mackey et al. (2000: 493) suggest that "issues of pronunciation and accurate lexical usage" in their study "had more potential to seriously interfere with understanding", and thus feedback on lexical and phonological errors was more accurately perceived as such than morphosyntactic feedback "due to the lack of importance of morphosyntax in comprehension". Isaacs and Trofimovich (2012) found that the importance, or relative lack thereof, of morphosyntax in comprehension was related to learners' L2 lexical and pronunciation skills. Lexical and phonological errors always had a general negative effect on learner comprehensibility, but morphosyntactic errors only hindered communication in learners that had otherwise good lexical skills and pronunciation. Therefore, focusing feedback on these more salient features of high communicative value may be the way to go in language classrooms.

Interestingly, research suggests that teachers provide most of their feedback on morphosyntactic errors (Lyster, 1998; Mackey et al., 2000; Carpenter et al., 2006; Kim and Han, 2007), possibly because some of the most difficult aspects of a second language fall within this domain (see DeKeyser, 2005). However, learners are less likely to accurately perceive the corrective nature of such feedback or subsequently successfully repair morphosyntactic errors compared to feedback on other utterances, such as those containing lexical or phonological mistakes (Mackey et al., 2000; Lyster et al., 2013). This was also a finding in Mackey and Goo's (2007) meta-analysis, which demonstrated that feedback in interaction is more effective for lexical than grammatical development.

However, this does not mean that corrective feedback does not play a role in morphosyntactic development, though efficacy of feedback may be related to feedback type. For instance, the efficacy of recasts on morphosyntactic development seems to depend, at least in part, on the saliency of the grammatical form and therefore of the recast (Ellis, 2007; Yang and Lyster, 2010). For example, since the past tense *-ed* morpheme is a particularly non-salient form, a recast correcting *He watch a movie* to *He watched a movie* might go unnoticed by a learner. For such non-salient forms, a metalinguistic explanation that explicitly provides learners with information on why their utterance was incorrect (Ellis, 2007) or a prompt that encourages learners to work out the error on their own and self-repair (Yang and Lyster, 2010) might be more beneficial. On the other hand, recasts modeling correct vocabulary (Egi, 2010; Dilans, 2010) and pronunciation (Saito and Lyster, 2012a, b; Saito, 2013) might be more salient than those targeting grammar and therefore can contribute to L2 development, particularly when learners are given the opportunity to practice the correct form after hearing a target-like model. Even so, other types of corrective feedback, like prompts and clarification requests, may increase the breadth and depth of vocabulary knowledge beyond the effect of recasts, presumably because they force learners to self-repair (Ellis and He, 1999; Dilans, 2010). However, it is important to note that the apparently added benefit of these sorts of feedback might simply be due to their more explicit nature as compared to recasts. When level of explicitness is held constant, recasts have been shown to be more effective (Mifka-Profozic, 2012). For pragmatic targets (e.g. requests, refusals, apologies, invitations), studies suggest that explicit instruction is more conducive to L2 development than implicit instruction (Kasper and Rose, 2002; Jeon and Kaya, 2006), but while focused research on corrective feedback shows some benefit for explicit over implicit feedback (Koike and Pearson, 2005; Takimoto, 2006), implicit feedback also seems to have a role in promoting L2 pragmatic development (Koike and Pearson, 2005; Nipaspong and Chinokul, 2010). However, this area is relatively under-researched, so it is difficult to make clear recommendations in relation to feedback on pragmatic errors.

In general, therefore, when considering different linguistic targets and types of feedback, it is important to keep in mind that how effective feedback is may depend on many things, including the type of error. Teachers need to carefully assess the types of errors that their students make and plan their feedback accordingly. In addition to this, knowing their students and their unique abilities helps teachers to effectively implement appropriate feedback techniques in the classroom.

Individual differences

Besides linguistic targets, the effects of corrective feedback are modulated by individual differences amongst learners (see MacIntyre, Gregersen and Clément, this volume). Long (1996: 452) highlights the importance of "internal learner capacities, particularly selective attention" in negotiation for meaning and L2 acquisition. Similarly, Trofimovich et al. (2007: 192) suggest that the "cognitive constructs of attention, memory, and language aptitude 'shape' L2 interaction on a minute-by-minute basis". In language classrooms, learners need to balance multiple resources to effectively communicate and develop their interlanguage, including maintaining representations of input and output in short-term memory, accessing L2 knowledge from long-term memory, processing feedback and making comparisons between their own utterances and target-like utterances, and forming modified representations of L2 knowledge in long-term memory. Some researchers have suggested that during interaction, L2 learners are exposed to more information than they can process and therefore need a way to sort through all of the input and extract the most relevant information (Gass et al., 2003; Gass and Mackey, 2007).

Helpfully, research so far on how individual differences such as working memory (WM; see also Collins and Marsden, this volume, for further discussion) are related to the relationship between interaction and L2 development suggests some clear trends. First, of the studies that have looked at the relationship between WM and corrective feedback, most have found a positive relationship between WM or phonological short-term memory (a part of WM) and some aspect of language learning, whether it be noticing of feedback (Mackey et al., 2002; Sagarra, 2007), production of modified output (Sagarra, 2007), or L2 development (Goo, 2012; Mackey et al., 2002; Payne and Whitney, 2002; Sagarra, 2007). One study conducted by Trofimovich et al. (2007) did not find a relationship between WM and interaction, but this could be because effects of WM are often not seen until a delayed posttest that takes place around two weeks after treatment (Mackey et al., 2002; Payne and Whitney, 2002), and the delayed posttest in Trofimovich et al.'s (2007) study was two to twelve minutes after treatment. Second, the effects of WM interact with other factors, such as context of feedback (e.g. computer-assisted language learning appears to level out the effects of WM; Payne and Whitney, 2002; Sagarra, 2007) and the types of feedback that learners receive (Goo, 2012). Third, there is evidence that other individual differences relate to feedback, interaction more generally and L2 development, including anxiety (Sheen, 2008), creativity (McDonough et al., 2015), attentional control and analytic ability (Trofimovich et al., 2007), but these factors need more research. Finally, most of this research is done on college-aged students, and more research is needed on other populations, such as children (see

Ando et al., 1992 for a working memory study) and older adults (Mackey and Sachs, 2012, also for working memory).

So, this line of research suggests certain patterns exist in the relationship between individual differences, corrective feedback, and L2 development; we should note, though, that as yet it is not conclusive. Many of the studies have very small sample sizes, and the authors recommend caution in drawing conclusions from this experimental data. Additionally, many of these studies focus on one or two aspects of the relationship between individual differences, feedback and L2 development. It is also still not entirely clear exactly *how* individual differences like WM promote L2 development. Is it because having more working memory capacity can help learners to notice feedback? Or does good working memory lead to successful repair? Do certain individual differences give learners a general advantage in communicative tasks? How do other factors like motivation (see Lamb, this volume) – which is likely to be related to cognitive processes and strategies, reasoning, problem solving and decision making, and therefore is likely to be related to language learning outcomes (Dweck et al., 2004) – interact with how different learners approach and/or benefit from corrective feedback in classrooms? These are all highly interrelated questions that need to be teased apart. However, what these studies clearly show is that learners differ in multiple ways, and these may impact how learners respond to feedback in the classroom.

Additional considerations

A few other factors, in addition to linguistic targets and individual differences, that may influence the efficacy of corrective feedback have been studied. For example, children might be more sensitive to corrective feedback than older learners, particularly when it guides them to notice errors (Oliver, 2000; Mackey and Oliver, 2002; Lyster and Saito, 2010). This suggests that teachers should choose feedback moves particularly carefully based on the age of their learners. Additionally, while the teacher is often the only fully competent speaker in the room, this does not mean that teachers should be the only ones providing feedback. Peer feedback may be particularly important for language development, as it "benefits both providers and receivers" (Mackey, 2012), giving learners the opportunity to both receive feedback, as they do with teachers, and provide it, which draws on a different set of autonomous language skills.

Conclusion

In the years since Hendrickson (1978) first raised the questions of whether, when and how to provide feedback, research has proliferated, both experimental and classroom-oriented. There is now general consensus that a wide range of different types of feedback, including the most implicit kind (i.e. recasts), are developmentally effective. These effects are mediated by contexts and target forms. Overall, therefore, research suggests that there is no single most effective feedback type and that the best strategy for approaching learner errors should involve a mixed bag of feedback moves.

However, there are still a number of open questions for teachers in relation to feedback in the classroom. Most importantly, perhaps, the efficacy of feedback may depend on the characteristics of a particular classroom and the students in it. And while teacher feedback may have obvious value for learner L2 development, emerging research suggests that training learners to provide peer-feedback can be beneficial as well (Fujii et al., 2011; Sato and Lyster, 2012).

In conclusion, we have aimed to provide language teachers with a practical overview of corrective feedback informed by empirical findings from SLA research. However, it is important to keep in mind that each classroom is different, and what works for one group of students may not work as well for another. Only the teachers themselves understand the unique dynamics of their own classrooms.

Discussion questions

- How are errors treated in your classroom, and why are they treated in this way?
- To what extent do your learners expect explicit, teacher-led corrective feedback, and why?
- Are there any particular errors (e.g. morphosyntactic, phonological, lexical, semantic errors) that you believe are relatively easier for (a) teachers to correct, and (b) learners to notice?
- To what extent does task type affect the quality and quantity of corrective feedback in your classroom?

Related topics

Classroom talk, interaction and collaboration; Cognitive perspectives on classroom language learning; Individual differences; Language awareness; Task-based language teaching.

Further reading

Ellis, R. and Shintani, N. (2014) *Exploring pedagogy through second language acquisition research.* London, New York: Routledge. (Chapter 10 of this volume reviews corrective feedback from the perspective of teachers' manuals and SLA research.)

Lyster, R. and Saito, K. (2010) 'Oral feedback in classroom SLA'. *Studies in Second Language Acquisition, 32/2.* 265–302. (This meta-analysis examines the effectiveness of corrective feedback in classroom settings.)

Mackey, A. and Goo, J. (2007) 'Interaction research in SLA: A meta-analysis and research synthesis', in A. Mackey (ed.) *Conversational interaction in SLA: A collection of empirical studies.* New York: Oxford University Press. 408–452. (Drawing on empirical research studies, this chapter provides an overview and meta-analysis of the findings of research into interaction and its relationship to grammar and vocabulary acquisition.)

References

Allwright, R. (1975) 'Problems in the study of the language teacher's treatment of learner error', in M. K. Burt and H. C. Dulay (eds) *TESOL '75 new directions in second language learning, teaching and bilingual education.* Washington, DC: TESOL. 96–109.

Ammar, A. (2008) 'Prompts and recasts: Differential effects on second language morphosyntax'. *Language Teaching Research, 12/2.* 183–210.

Ammar, A. and Spada, N. (2006) 'One size fits all? Recasts, prompts, and L2 learning'. *Studies in Second Language Acquisition, 28.* 543–574.

Ando, J., Fukunaga, N., Kurahashi, J., Suto, T., Nakano, T. and Kage, M. (1992) 'A comparative study of the two EFL teaching methods: The communicative and grammatical approach'. *Japanese Journal of Educational Psychology, 40/3.* 247–256.

Brown, A.V. (2009) 'Students' and teachers' perceptions of effective foreign language teaching: A comparison of ideals'. *Modern Language Journal, 93/1.* 46–60.

Carpenter, H., Jeon, S., MacGregor, D. and Mackey, A. (2006) 'Recasts as repetitions: Learners' interpretations of native speaker responses'. *Studies in Second Language Acquisition, 28/2.* 209–236.

Cathcart, R. L. and Olsen, J.E.W.B. (1976) 'Teachers' and students' preferences for error correction of classroom conversation errors', in J. F. Fanselow and R. H. Crymes (eds) *On TESOL '76: Selections based on teaching done at the 10th annual TESOL convention.* Washington, DC: TESOL. 41–53.

Chaudron, C. (1977) 'A descriptive model of discourse in the corrective treatment of learners' errors'. *Language Learning, 27/1.* 29–46.

Corder, S. P. (1967) 'The significance of learner's errors'. *International Review of Applied Linguistics in Language Teaching,* 5/1–4. 161–170.

DeKeyser, R. M. (2005) 'What makes learning second-language grammar difficult? A review of issues'. *Language Learning,* 55/S1. 1–25.

Dilans, G. (2010) 'Corrective feedback and L2 vocabulary development: Prompts and recasts in the adult ESL classroom'. *Canadian Modern Language Review,* 66. 787–815.

Dulay, H. C. and Burt, M. K. (1974) 'Natural sequences in child second language acquisition'. *Language Learning,* 24/1. 37–53.

Dweck, C. S., Mangels, J. and Good, C. (2004) 'Motivational effects on attention, cognition, and performance', in D. Y. Dai and R. J. Sternberg (eds) *Motivation, emotion, and cognition: Integrated perspectives on intellectual functioning.* Mahwah, NJ: Erlbaum. 41–55.

Egi, T. (2010) 'Uptake, modified output, and learner perceptions of recasts: Learner responses as language awareness'. *Modern Language Journal,* 94/1. 1–21.

Ellis, R. (1991) 'Grammar teaching practice or consciousness-raising?' in R. Ellis (ed.) Second language acquisition and second language pedagogy. Clevedon, UK: Multilingual Matters. 232–241.

Ellis, R. (2005) 'Instructed language learning and task-based teaching', in E. Hinkel (ed.) *Handbook of research in second language teaching and learning.* Mahwah, NJ: Lawrence Erlbaum. 713–728.

Ellis, R. (2006) 'Researching the effects of form-focused instruction on L2 acquisition'. *AILA Review,* 19. 18–41.

Ellis, R. (2007) 'The differential effects of corrective feedback on two grammatical structures', in A. Mackey (ed.) *Conversational interaction in second language acquisition: A series of empirical studies.* Oxford: Oxford University Press. 339–360.

Ellis, R. and He, X. (1999) 'The roles of modified input and output in the incidental acquisition of word meanings'. *Studies in Second Language Acquisition,* 21/2. 285–301.

Ellis, R., Loewen, S. and Erlam, R. (2006) 'Implicit and explicit corrective feedback and the acquisition of L2 grammar'. *Studies in Second Language Acquisition,* 28/3. 339–368.

Ellis, R. and Shintani, N. (2014) *Exploring pedagogy through second language acquisition research.* London, New York: Routledge.

Fujii, A., Mackey, A. and Ziegler, N. (2011) *Metacognitive instruction and learning through task-based interaction.* Paper presented at the 4th Biennial International Conference on Task-Based Language Teaching. University of Auckland, New Zealand.

Gass, S. and Mackey, A. (2007) 'Input, interaction, and output in second language acquisition', in B. Van-Patten and J. Williams (eds) *Theories in second language acquisition: An introduction.* Mahwah, NJ: Lawrence Erlbaum. 175–200.

Gass, S., Svetics, I. and Lemelin, S. (2003) 'Differential effects of attention'. *Language Learning,* 53/3. 497–545.

Gass, S. and Varonis, E. (1994) 'Input, interaction and second language production'. *Studies in Second Language Acquisition,* 16/3. 283–302.

Goldschneider, J. M. and DeKeyser, R. M. (2001) 'Explaining the "natural order of l2 morpheme acquisition" in English: A meta-analysis of multiple determinants'. *Language Learning,* 51/1. 1–50.

Goo, J. (2012) 'Corrective feedback and working memory capacity in interaction driven L2 learning'. *Studies in Second Language Acquisition,* 34/3. 445–474.

Goo, J. and Mackey, A. (2013) 'The case against the case against recasts'. *Studies in Second Language Acquisition,* 35/1. 127–165.

Hendrickson, J. (1978) 'Error correction in foreign language teaching: Recent theory, research, and practice'. *Modern Language Journal,* 62/8. 387–398.

Hyltenstam, K. and Abrahamsson, N. (2003) 'Maturational constraints in SLA', in C. J. Doughty and M. H. Long (eds) *Handbook of second language acquisition.* Malden, MA: Blackwell. 539–588.

Isaacs, T. and Trofimovich, P. (2012) 'Deconstructing comprehensibility: Identifying the linguistic influences on listeners' L2 comprehensibility ratings'. *Studies in Second Language Acquisition,* 34/3. 475–505.

Iwashita, N. (2003) 'Negative feedback and positive evidence in task-based interaction: Differential effects on L2 development'. *Studies in Second Language Acquisition,* 25/1. 1–36.

Izumi, S. (2003) 'Comprehension and production processes in second language learning: In search of the psycholinguistic rationale of the output hypothesis'. *Applied Linguistics,* 24/2. 168–196.

Jean, G. and Simard, D. (2011) 'Grammar learning in English and French L2: Students' and teachers' beliefs and perceptions'. *Foreign Language Annals,* 44/4. 465–492.

Jeon, E. and Kaya, T. (2006) 'Effects of L2 instruction on interlanguage pragmatic development: A meta-analysis', in J. Norris and L. Ortega (eds) *Synthesizing research on language learning and teaching*. Philadelphia, PA: John Benjamins. 165–211.

Kasper, G. and Rose, K. (2002) *Pragmatic development in a second language*. Oxford: Blackwell.

Keck, C., Iberri-Shea, G., Tracy-Ventura, N. and Wa-Mbaleka, S. (2006) 'Investigating the empirical link between task-based interaction and acquisition', in J. Norris and L. Ortega (eds) *Synthesizing research on language learning and teaching*. Amsterdam: Benjamins. 91–131.

Kim, J. and Han, Z. (2007) 'Recasts in communicative EFL classes: Do teacher intent and learner interpretation overlap?', in A. Mackey (ed.) *Conversational interaction in second language acquisition: A series of empirical studies*. Oxford: Oxford University Press. 269–297.

Koike, D. and Pearson, L. (2005) 'The effect of instruction and feedback in the development of pragmatic competence'. *System*, 33/3. 481–501.

Krashen, S. D. and Terrell, T. (1983) *The natural approach: Language acquisition in the classroom*. New York: Prentice Hall.

Leeman, J. (2003) 'Recasts and second language development: Beyond negative evidence'. *Studies in Second Language Acquisition*, 25/1. 37–63.

Li, S. (2010) 'The effectiveness of corrective feedback in SLA: A meta-analysis'. *Language Learning*, 60/2. 309–365.

Lightbown, P. (2008) 'Transfer appropriate processing as a model for class second language acquisition', in Z. Han (ed.) *Understanding second language process*. Clevedon, UK: Multilingual Matters. 27–44.

Loewen, S. and Nabei, T. (2007) 'Measuring the effects of oral corrective feedback on L2 knowledge', in A. Mackey (ed.) *Conversational interaction in second language acquisition: A collection of empirical studies*. Oxford: Oxford University Press. 361–377.

Long, M. H. (1996) 'The role of the linguistic environment in second language acquisition', in W. C. Ritchie and T. K. Bahtia (eds) *Handbook of second language acquisition*. New York: Academic Press. 413–468.

Long, M. H. (2007) *Problems in SLA*. Mahwah, NJ: Lawrence Erlbaum.

Long, M. H., Inagaki, S. and Ortega, L. (1998) 'The role of implicit negative feedback in SLA: Models and recasts in Japanese and Spanish'. *Modern Language Journal*, 82/3. 357–371.

Lyster, R. (1998) 'Negotiation of form, recasts, and explicit correction in relation to error types and learner repair in immersion classrooms'. *Language Learning*, 48/2. 183–218.

Lyster, R. (2004) 'Differential effects of prompts and recasts in form-focused instruction'. *Studies in Second Language Acquisition*, 26/3. 399–432.

Lyster, R. and Izquierdo, J. (2009) 'Prompts versus recasts in dyadic interaction'. *Language Learning*, 59/2. 453–498.

Lyster, R. and Ranta, L. (1997) 'Corrective feedback and learner uptake: Negotiation of form in communicative classrooms'. *Studies in Second Language Acquisition*, 19/1. 37–66.

Lyster, R. and Saito, K. (2010) 'Oral feedback in classroom SLA'. *Studies in Second Language Acquisition*, 32/2. 265–302.

Lyster, R., Saito, K. and Sato, M. (2013) 'Oral corrective feedback in second language classrooms'. *Language Teaching*, 46/1. 1–40.

Mackey, A. (2007) 'Introduction: The role of conversational interaction in second language acquisition', in A. Mackey (ed.) *Conversational interaction in second language acquisition: A collection of empirical studies*. Oxford: Oxford University Press. 1–26.

Mackey, A. (2012) *Input, interaction and corrective feedback in L2 classrooms*. Oxford: Oxford University Press.

Mackey, A., Abbuhl, R. and Gass, S. M. (2012) 'Interactionist approaches', in S. Gass and A. Mackey (eds) *The Routledge handbook of second language acquisition*. New York, NY: Routledge. 7–23.

Mackey, A., Gass, S. and McDonough, K. (2000) 'How do learners perceive interactional feedback?' *Studies in Second Language Acquisition*, 22/4. 471–497.

Mackey, A. and Goo, J. (2007) 'Interaction research in SLA: A meta-analysis and research synthesis', in A. Mackey (ed.) *Conversational interaction in SLA: A collection of empirical studies*. New York: Oxford University Press. 408–452.

Mackey, A. and Oliver, R. (2002) 'Interactional feedback and children's L2 development'. *System*, 30/4. 459–477.

Mackey, A. and Philp, J. (1998) 'Conversational interaction and second language development: Recasts, responses and red herrings?' *Modern Language Journal*, 82/3. 338–356.

Mackey, A., Philp, J., Egi, T., Fujii, A. and Tatsumi, T. (2002) 'Individual differences in working memory, noticing of interactional feedback and L2 development', in P. Robinson (ed.) *Individual differences and instructed language learning*. Amsterdam: John Benjamins. 181–209.

Mackey, A. and Sachs, R. (2012) 'Older learners in SLA research: A first look at working memory, feedback, and L2 development'. *Language Learning*, 62/3. 704–740.

McDonough, K. (2007) 'Interactional feedback and the emergence of simple past activity verbs in L2 English', in A. Mackey (ed.) *Conversational interaction in second language acquisition: A collection of empirical studies.* Oxford: Oxford University Press. 323–338.

McDonough, K., Crawford, W. and Mackey, A. (2015) 'Creativity and EFL students' language use during a group problem-solving task'. *TESOL Quarterly*, 49/1. 188–199.

McDonough, K. and Mackey, A. (2006) 'Responses to recasts: Repetitions, primed production and linguistic development'. *Language Learning*, 56/4. 693–720.

Mifka-Profozic, N. (2012) *Oral corrective feedback, individual differences and L2 acquisition of French past tenses.* Unpublished doctoral dissertation, University of Auckland, New Zealand.

Nipaspong, P. and Chinokul, S. (2010) 'The role of prompts and explicit feedback in raising EFL learners' pragmatic awareness'. *University of Sydney Papers in TESOL*, 5. 101–146.

Norris, J. M. (2010) 'Task-based teaching and testing', in M. H. Long and C. J. Doughty (eds) *The handbook of language teaching.* Oxford: Wiley-Blackwell. 578–594.

Nunan, D. (1995) 'Closing the gap between learning and instruction'. *TESOL Quarterly*, 29/1. 133–158.

Odlin, T. (2003) 'Cross-linguistic influence', in C. J. Doughty and M. H. Long (eds) *Handbook of second language acquisition.* Malden, MA: Blackwell. 436–486.

Oladejo, J. (1993) 'Error correction in ESL: Learners' preferences'. *TESL Canada Journal*, 10/2. 71–89.

Oliver, R. (2000) 'Age differences in negotiation and feedback in classroom and pairwork'. *Language Learning*, 50/1. 119–151.

Payne, J. S. and Whitney, P. J. (2002) 'Developing L2 oral proficiency through synchronous CMC: Output, working memory, and interlanguage development'. *CALICO Journal*, 20/1. 7–32.

Ranta, L. and Lyster, R. (2007) 'A cognitive approach to improving immersion students' oral language abilities: The awareness–practice–feedback sequence', in R. DeKeyser (ed.) *Practice in a second language: Perspectives from applied linguistics and cognitive psychology.* Cambridge: Cambridge University Press. 141–160.

Robinson, P. (2011) 'Task-based language learning: A review of issues'. *Language Learning*, 61 [Supplement 1]. 1–36.

Russell, J. and Spada, N. (2006) 'The effectiveness of corrective feedback for the acquisition of L2 grammar. A meta-analysis of the research', in J. M. Norris and L. Ortega (eds) *Synthesizing research on language learning and teaching.* Philadelphia: John Benjamins. 133–164.

Sagarra, N. (2007) 'From CALL to face-to-face interaction: The effect of computer-delivered recasts and working memory on L2 development', in A. Mackey (ed.) *Conversational interaction in second language acquisition: A series of empirical studies.* Oxford: Oxford University Press. 229–248.

Saito, K. (2013) 'Re-examining effects of form-focused instruction on L2 pronunciation development: The role of explicit phonetic information'. *Studies in Second Language Acquisition*, 35/1. 1–29.

Saito, K. and Lyster, R. (2012a) 'Effects of form-focused instruction and corrective feedback on L2 pronunciation development of /ɹ/ by Japanese learners of English'. *Language Learning*, 62/2. 595–633.

Saito, K. and Lyster, R. (2012b) 'Investigating the pedagogical potential of recasts for L2 vowel acquisition'. *TESOL Quarterly*, 46/2. 385–396.

Sato, M. and Lyster, R. (2012) 'Peer interaction and corrective feedback for accuracy and fluency development: Monitoring, practice, and proceduralization'. *Studies in Second Language Acquisition*, 34/4. 591–626.

Schmidt, R. (1990) 'The role of consciousness in second language learning'. *Applied Linguistics*, 11/2. 129–158.

Schmidt, R. (1995) 'Consciousness and foreign language learning: A tutorial on the role of attention and awareness in learning', in R. Schmidt (ed.) *Attention and awareness in foreign language learning.* Honolulu: University of Hawaii Press. 1–63.

Schmidt, R. (2001) 'Attention', in P. Robinson (ed.) *Cognition and second language acquisition.* Cambridge: Cambridge University Press. 3–32.

Schmidt, R. and Frota, S. (1986) 'Developing basic conversational ability in a second language: A case study of an adult learner of Portuguese', in R. R. Day (ed.) *Talking to learn: Conversation in second language acquisition.* Rowley, MA: Newbury House. 237–326.

Schulz, R. (1996) 'Focus on form in the foreign language classroom: Students' and teachers' views on error correction and the role of grammar'. *Foreign Language Annals*, 29/3. 343–364.

Schulz, R. (2001) 'Cultural differences in student and teacher perceptions concerning the role of grammar instruction and corrective feedback: USA–Colombia'. *Modern Language Journal*, 85/2. 244–258.

Seedhouse, P. (1997) 'The case of missing "no": The relationship between pedagogy and interaction'. *Language Learning*, 47/3. 547–583.

Sheen, Y. (2008) 'Recasts, language anxiety, modified output, and L2 learning'. *Language Learning,* 58/4. 835–874.

Sheen, Y. and Ellis, R. (2011) 'Corrective feedback in language teaching', in E. Hinkel (ed.) *Handbook of research in second language teaching and learning, vol. 2.* New York: Routledge. 593–610.

Spada, N. and Lightbown, P. M. (1999) 'Instruction, first language influence, and developmental readiness in second language acquisition'. *Modern Language Journal,* 83/1. 1–22.

Swain, M. (1985) 'Communicative competence: Some roles of comprehensible output in its development', in S. M. Gass and C. G. Madden (eds) *Input in second language acquisition.* Rowley, MA: Newbury House. 235–253.

Swain, M. (1995) 'Three functions of output in second language learning', in G. Cook and B. Seidlhofer (eds) *Principle and practice in applied linguistics.* Oxford: Oxford University Press. 125–244.

Swain, M. (2005) 'The output hypothesis: Theory and research', in E. Hinkel (ed.) *Handbook of research in second language teaching and learning.* Mahwah, NJ: Lawrence Erlbaum Associates. 471–483.

Takimoto, M. (2006) 'The effects of explicit feedback on the development of pragmatic proficiency'. *Language Teaching Research,* 10/4. 393–417.

Trofimovich, P., Ammar, A. and Gatbonton, E. (2007) 'How effective are recasts? The role of attention, memory, and analytic ability', in A. Mackey (ed.) *Conversational interaction in second language acquisition: A series of empirical studies.* Oxford: Oxford University Press. 171–195.

Yang, Y. and Lyster, R. (2010) 'Effects of form-focused practice and feedback on Chinese EFL learners' acquisition of regular and irregular past tense forms'. *Studies in Second Language Acquisition,* 32/2. 235–263.

36

Questioning 'English-only' classrooms

Own-language use in ELT

Philip Kerr

Introduction and issues of terminology

Putting aside the thorny issue of which, or whose, English would be represented, an English-only policy in an English language classroom presents relatively few problems from a terminological perspective. It presumably means precisely what it says: a monolingual approach with no other languages permitted. Problems rapidly arise, however, when we wish to discuss the alternatives. How do we refer to the language(s), other than English, that might be used in a bilingual classroom that does not adhere to the English-only line?

'Mother tongue', 'native language' and 'first language' (or 'L1') are all problematic to varying degrees because of their emotive force or a lack of precision or accuracy (Rampton, 1990; Kecskes and Papp, 2000: 1–2; Cook, 2010: xxi–xxii; Hall and Cook, 2012: 273–274). Cook (2010), and subsequently Hall and Cook (2012, 2013) and Kerr (2014), use the term 'own language' to refer to "the language which the students already know, and through which (if allowed) they will approach the new language" (Cook, 2010: xxii). 'Own language' is not without its own shortcomings, not least as it does not differentiate clearly between monolingual and bilingual language learners. It will, however, be the preferred choice in this chapter.

An English-only policy necessarily precludes the use of translation as a classroom activity, and it is around the question of translation that the discussion of the relative merits of monolingual and bilingual language teaching has primarily centred. But translation is only one of many classroom activities that involve the learners' own language, and translation itself has many different guises. Own-language activities have come to be associated with translation, and translation has come to be associated with the particular kind of translation practised in grammar-translation approaches. In this chapter, 'own-language activities' will refer to all classroom activities that involve the use of the learners' own language, and 'translation' will refer to a subset of these.

Teacher practices and attitudes

The belief that English, as a new language, is best learnt in an English-only environment, through processes resembling in some ways first-language acquisition, is widespread and seductive.

To many people, it is self-evident that the more a learner is surrounded by English, the more English they will learn. From this perspective, the less use that is made of their own language, the more they will make progress in English. In an optimisation of this perspective, zero use of the learners' own language is the ideal to be aspired to.

In the twentieth century, a global industry of private English language schools grew up that catered to this belief. Employing, wherever possible, native-speaker teachers (NESTs in Medgyes' (1994) terminology; for discussion of the complexities surrounding the term 'native speaker', see Llurda, this volume), who often could not speak the language of their students, the English-only environment that these schools offered proved popular and commercially successful. Some of the larger and more influential chains of schools made, and still make, a point of their English-only policy in their marketing. One of the most well-known, Berlitz, describes its patented method as follows:

> Talk and think in your target language from the very beginning. . . . By continually using the new language and interacting with native speaker instructors and other students on the course, you will be immediately submerged in your new language. You learn faster and your learning progress is significantly greater than in bilingual teaching sessions.
>
> *(Berlitz, n.d.)*

Inlingua, with 320 schools in 36 countries, similarly employs native speakers, and the first of its ten pedagogical principles is "only the target language is used" (Inlingua, n.d.).

The connection between the private sector of English language teaching and the monolingual approach can be seen in the results of the only large-scale investigation into own-language use. Teachers in private institutions are approximately twice as likely as their counterparts in state institutions to adopt an English-only policy (Hall and Cook, 2013: 42).

State-sponsored English language teaching has, in many places, followed the lead of the private language schools. In some cases, there has been a blanket prohibition on own-language use. Mouhanna (2009: 3), for example, reports that many institutions in the UAE have banned "the use of L1 in the classroom which is commonly perceived to be an impediment to EFL learning". In Hong Kong, teachers are exhorted to "teach English through English" (Littlewood and Yu, 2011: 66). More frequently, there is a recognition that, although an English-only environment is the ideal, own-language use may be unavoidable at times. Macaro (2000: 171) cites the example of France, where the learner must be "led gradually towards distancing himself / herself from the mother tongue", and Lee (2012) discusses the case of Seoul, South Korea, where a proposed policy of 'teaching English in English' has been modified to allow teachers more flexibility in their use of Korean in English language classrooms.

In an attempt to uncover global practices, Hall and Cook (2013) carried out a survey of 2,785 primary, secondary and tertiary teachers of English in 111 countries. Nearly three quarters of the respondents felt that they could exercise their own judgement in deciding on an appropriate balance of English and own-language use, but 63 per cent suggested that their school or institution expected classes to be taught only in English and 46 per cent believed that English-only teaching was favoured by their educational ministries (Hall and Cook, 2013: 20). The institutional preference for English-only approaches was also reflected in the overwhelming number of respondents, who reported that "both the pre-service and in-service teacher-training programmes that they had experienced discouraged own-language use in the ELT classroom" (ibid.: 21).

The textbooks that currently form the basis of most instructional programmes may also shed some light on policies regarding own-language use, since these are often selected by institutions and ministries rather than by individual teachers. This is especially the case in the primary and secondary sectors, where lists of 'approved' books are commonly drawn up. Textbooks can be entirely in English, or they can contain own-language features. The latter typically include rubrics, translated word lists and grammar explanations, including contrastive analysis, in the students' own language. Sales figures are closely guarded commercial secrets, but it is clear that the use of textbooks with own-language features is widespread. In Poland, for example, books that are designed to prepare students for the Matura examination invariably include own-language features. Without these, ministerial approval will not be granted. This is despite the fact that English-only approaches are actively promoted in teacher training courses in the country. In Greece, textbooks are usually accompanied by supplementary books, known as 'Companions', which contain bilingual word lists and additional grammar explanations, usually in Greek. In China and Japan, textbooks produced by local publishers invariably have rubrics written in the local language (Ellis and Shintani, 2014: 227). The number of country-specific versions (i.e. with some information in the local language) of international English-only textbooks is also growing. Likewise, language learning apps with bilingual features are growing in popularity.

Insights into actual classroom practices are harder to gain. The observation or recording of classes in order to measure teachers' own-language use is likely to provide a distorted picture of everyday unobserved, unrecorded realities. The reasons for this will be explored later in this section. Self-reporting is sometimes used by researchers as an alternative, but this, too, is not very reliable. Two general pictures, however, emerge from the research. First, there is a wide variation in the amount of own-language use, ranging from 0 per cent to 90 per cent of classroom time (Levine, 2014: 335), but strict English-only approaches are "rarely encountered" (Macaro, 1997: 96). Second, the average overall amount of reported own-language use is somewhere between 20 per cent (Levine, 2014: 335) and something in excess of 40 per cent (Littlewood and Yu, 2011: 67). Outside of contexts where students come from multiple language backgrounds or where the teacher does not share the students' language, some degree of own-language use on the part of the teacher appears to be the norm. It is, as Hall and Cook (2012: 16) put it, "a part of many teachers' everyday classroom practice."

A wide range of variables are to be expected in attempts to calculate averages in English language teaching as a whole, given the very heterogeneous nature of the enterprise. A widely cited reason for increased own-language use is the learners' language level and age (which often correlate). Swain and Lapkin (2000: 267) have argued that greater own-language use is needed with "lower-achieving students". With fewer linguistic resources in English, they can "get more easily frustrated" (Macaro, 2000: 68), and it is no surprise to find that teachers use the students' own language approximately twice as often with lower levels as they do with the higher (Hall and Cook, 2013: 45). In addition to language level, larger class size, the early stages of a course, longer lessons and the previous learning experiences of the students may all entail proportionately greater own-language use. The particular activity at any given point of a lesson will also have an impact on the teacher's perception of the need to use the shared language. All of these variables will interact with each other, creating such a wide variety of classroom circumstances that one researcher has concluded that decisions about appropriate own-language use "cannot be predetermined nor easily generalized from one context to another" (Edstrom, 2009: 14)

The functions of teachers' own-language use

Easier to describe than the amount of teachers' own-language use is the range of functions that they use it for. A number of studies (e.g. Polio and Duff, 1994; Rolin-Ianziti and Varshney, 2008; Littlewood and Yu, 2011) have investigated these functions, and the results are similar.

'Medium-oriented' or 'core' functions
(i.e. concerned with the teaching of language)
- Teaching, explaining and checking understanding of grammar, vocabulary and texts

'Framework' and 'social' functions
(i.e. concerned with the management of the classroom)
- Managing personal relationships in the classroom (e.g. building rapport, maintaining discipline)
- Giving instructions for classroom and homework tasks
- Giving administrative information
- Lightening cognitive load
- Discussing methodological options

Figure 36.1 Functions of own-language use by the teacher

Combining two classificatory systems (Ellis, 1994; Kim and Elder, 2005), these functions are summarised in Figure 36.1.

Any given own-language intervention by the teacher can serve more than one function, so the categories are not always mutually exclusive. Interventions from either category can also be either planned / strategic or unplanned / compensatory (Pennington, 1995). The word "crutch" has been used by Cohen (2011) and Littlewood and Yu (2011) to refer to this compensatory function. In both cases, but particularly for the latter, the decision to use the learners' language may be motivated by a desire to "speed things up" (Macaro, 2005: 69). Time-saving is one of the most frequently cited reasons for own-language use by teachers: the "time saved by communicating in the mother tongue can be used for more productive activities" (Harbord, 1992: 352). Finally, in both categories, teachers may use the shared language because they are tired. Edstrom (2009: 14), in an evaluation of her own practice, "identified many instances in which [she] could have used the L2 and could identify no reason, other than laziness, for having done so". A lack of confidence in one's own English language proficiency, which has been reported in many studies (Littlewood and Yu, 2011: 69), may also be a contributing factor.

Hall and Cook (2013) found that own-language use by teachers was more common for the 'medium-oriented' or 'core' functions than it was for 'framework' and 'social' functions. As can be seen from Table 36.1, own-language use is most common in 'medium-oriented' functions, with a significant majority of teachers using this when 'explaining when meanings in English are unclear' and 'explaining grammar'.

For all of these functions, the greater use of the shared language in the state sector is noteworthy. Although the survey provides an insight into the relationship between function and own-language use, it does not give any information about the amount of time devoted to these functions. Teachers in the state sector use the shared language significantly more than their private sector counterparts for explanations, but are they in explanatory mode more often, too? Own-language maintenance of discipline shows a wide difference between state-sector and private sector teachers, and here it is not unreasonable to assume that the private sector, which typically has smaller class sizes and more motivated students, may require fewer disciplinary interventions.

It is probably advisable to treat the statistics for own-language use that emerge from self-reporting research and surveys as minima. There is, as Hall and Cook (2012: 285) observe, a

Table 36.1 A comparison of teacher own-language use by function and sector

	Functions*	Overall per cent of respondents using own language 'rarely' or 'never'	Per cent of respondents in the private sector using own language 'rarely' or 'never'	Per cent of respondents in the state sector using own language 'rarely' or 'never'
'medium-oriented' functions	explaining when meanings in English are unclear	28	39.9	19.5
	explaining vocabulary	38.5	47.4	32.3
	explaining grammar	41.9	57.1	30.7
'framework' or 'social' functions	developing rapport	46.8	55.0	41.0
	maintaining discipline	49.6	62.8	39.4
	giving instructions	56.9	67.9	49.0

* Three functions from the survey have been omitted from this table. These are the correction of spoken errors, feedback on written work and testing.

Source: Data extracted from Hall and Cook's survey (2013).

tendency for teachers to under-report their own-language use. Edstrom (2006), for example, estimated her own use of her own language at between 5 and 10 per cent of total teacher talking time. On investigation, she discovered it was more like 23 per cent. Other researchers (e.g. Polio and Duff, 1994; Árva and Medgyes, 2000) have found similar differences between teachers' stated and actual own-language use. In the light of this evidence, Levine (2014: 6) concludes that own-language use is the "unmarked language of communication in many arguably crucial moments of communication in the classroom".

The tension between attitudes and practice

In Hall and Cook's survey (2013: 17), 61.4 per cent of teachers believe or strongly believe that own language should be excluded from or limited in English language classrooms; a similar number believe that such an approach is institutionally approved of. Yet an even greater number report regular or systematic use of own language for a wide range of teacher-talk functions. Under-reporting of own-language use is hardly surprising, therefore. "The teachers' professed desires about L1 use," write Copland and Neokleous (2011: 271), "are clearly in conflict with their class-room realities, leaving them feeling damned if they speak L1 and damned if they do not."

A number of researchers (e.g. Mitchell, 1988; Macaro, 2000, 2005; Littlewood and Yu, 2011) have reported feelings of 'guilt' on the part of teachers when they 'resort' to using own language. The choice of the word 'resort' rather than the more neutral 'use' is itself revealing in the way that it suggests that teachers see their use of own language as a crutch. The number of teachers experiencing feelings of guilt may not form a majority: Hall and Cook's survey (2013: 41) found that 36 per cent felt guilty, compared to 37.9 per cent who did not. Nevertheless, feelings of guilt are clearly widespread, a situation which, as Macaro (2005: 69) observes, is not "a healthy outcome of a pedagogical debate".

Macaro (2000: 180–181) suggests that teachers' attitudes towards own-language use can be grouped into three categories. The first of these he calls 'the total exclusion position'. where no pedagogical value in own-language use is seen. The second, 'the maximalist position', is similar to the first, except that it acknowledges that, in the real world of the classroom, considerations of affect and discipline may override the desire for total exclusion. This position has "a more socio-cultural dependence" than the former. Third, 'the optimal use position' sees some pedagogical value in own-language use. How and why have the first two positions come to predominate in teachers' thinking?

The tradition of own-language exclusion

The influence of the private sector in English language teaching on attitudes towards own-language use has already been mentioned in the brief discussion of the genesis of 'the maximalist position'. As we will see, this influence has continued to the present day. Historical accounts of English-language teaching often begin with grammar-translation approaches of the nineteenth century, a method in which "much of the lesson is devoted to translating sentences into and out of the target language" (Richards and Rodgers, 2014: 6). Adopting a "procession of methods" approach (Howatt and Smith, 2014: 76; see also Hall, this volume, ch. 15), such histories then move on to the Reform movement of the late nineteenth century, where translation is relegated to a subordinate role, "although the native language could be used in order to explain new words or check comprehension" (Richards and Rodgers, 2014: 11). The decisive moment of change within this narrative comes with the advent of the direct method, whose most strident champion, Berlitz (1916: 3–4), described all own-language use in the learning of another language as "necessarily defective and incomplete".

The problem with such accounts is that, although the activity of language teaching in its succeeding historical phases appears to have some sort of continuity, the purposes of this activity were very different. Grammar-translation teaching was "devised and developed for use in secondary schools" (Howatt with Widdowson, 2004: 151), and the point of studying a language was to learn to read literature or "to benefit from the mental discipline and intellectual development that result from foreign language study" (Richards and Rodgers, 2014: 6). The Reform movement was, similarly, concerned with language teaching in secondary schools, but shifted emphasis away from literature to the oral production of language. The direct method, as exemplified by Berlitz, maintained the interest in oral production but had a very different orientation. The method was popularised, not in secondary schools, but in language schools, usually located in industrial towns with strong international trade links, where the adult students were learning English for strictly utilitarian purposes such as preparing for emigration to an English-speaking country or dealing with English-speaking clients (Howatt with Widdowson, 2004: 224–226).

The direct method failed to make significant inroads into secondary schools, partly because of an unrealisable requirement for NESTs and partly because the banning of own language was impracticable (Laviosa, 2014: 12). However, the assumption that the primary purpose of language learning was utilitarian, even when the learners were children rather than adults, took a firm and increasing hold. In schools, a combination of the ideas of the Reform movement and some of the practices of the direct method led to the oral method of Harold Palmer and the situational language teaching of A.S. Hornby (Richards and Rodgers, 2014: 44–57). In neither of these was own-language use banned, but its use was to be as limited as possible. Negative attitudes towards own-language use were reinforced with the emergence of audiolingualism. Here, interest shifted once more away from teenagers to young adults at colleges and universities, and this shift (as with Berlitz) was accompanied by a hardening of attitudes towards own-language use. With a psychological grounding in behaviourist habit formation, audiolingualism sought to avoid errors, and errors were considered to be "the result of L1 interference" (Ellis, 1990: 25). Ergo, the learner's own language was to be avoided, too. Nelson Brooks, who coined the term 'audiolingual', did, however, allow translation as "a literary exercise at an advanced level" (Brooks, 1964: 142). The concession to own-language use only for less utilitarian purposes is striking. (See Hall, this volume, ch. 15 for further discussion of the methods and approaches outlined in this section.)

In the above account, I have highlighted the connections between the purposes (utilitarian or otherwise) and subjects (adults or children, fee-paying or free) of language teaching, on the one hand, and the processes of teaching (exclusion or admission of own language) on the other (Laviosa, 2014: 4). Jumping to the present day, utilitarian (or vocational approaches) to English language learning have become so ubiquitous that it is "difficult to challenge [them] in the present climate where education has come to be seen in almost entirely instrumental terms" (Lawes, 2010). At the same time, the last 25 years have seen a huge rise in educational discourse (including the discourse of English language teaching) of what has been termed 'learnification' (Biesta, 2004, 2010), an overriding concern with how something is learnt as opposed to an interest in the purposes of that learning and the social relationships through which it takes place. The predominance of 'the maximalist position' on English-only can be better understood through a consideration of these broader educational trends.

Curricular objectives for the teaching of English in secondary schools usually underline a utilitarian purpose, but it is rare for this to be the only objective. Others include the awareness raising of aspects of the culture of English-speaking countries (including literature; see Hall, this volume, ch. 32), the development of intercultural competence (see Kramsch and Zhu, this volume) and the development of general language awareness (see Svalberg, this volume). When these other objectives are brought more to the fore, the more there are reasons for not adopting an English-only policy.

An issue ignored: 'The elephant in the room'

Yet in the literature for English language teachers in training, it is rare to find injunctions against own-language use. More often, the issue is simply ignored, or given only passing or historical reference. For example, two of the most well-known and best-selling handbooks for pre-service teachers, Harmer (1983) and Scrivener (1994), paid very little attention to own-language use in their early editions. These handbooks are widely used in teacher training colleges (i.e. for secondary school teachers) around the world, but were initially conceived for and sold to the market of predominantly NESTs, studying for qualifications such as the Cambridge English CELTA, a qualification for teaching adults, primarily in private language schools. In later editions (e.g. Scrivener, 2011; Harmer, 2015), more space has been given to own-language use. It is probably not a coincidence that this change has taken place at the same time as the market for books like these has grown rapidly in state-sponsored sectors.

At ELT conferences around the world, such as those organised by organisations such as the TESOL International Association and IATEFL (International Association of Teachers of English as a Foreign Language) and their affiliates, own-language use has been similarly ignored. Once again, it is noticeable that there is a disproportionate representation of NESTs, working in or with a background in the private sector, often with adults, among the organisers and plenary speakers of these conferences. Here, too, though, there are indications of change, with, for example, five sessions related to own-language use at the 2015 international IATEFL conference in the UK.

The arguments against own-language use

For such a widely shared belief, there are extremely few contemporary or near-contemporary published enumerations of the reasons why a policy of English-only is desirable in English language classrooms. Slightly more frequent are lists of the disadvantages of translation, and these (e.g. Newson, 1998) suffer from the 'straw man' fallacy where a particular and limited approach to translation is criticised. The arguments most frequently advanced against own-language use are the following:

1   Translation is less important than the four skills of reading, writing, listening and speaking and, in any case, is not a useful skill for most learners to acquire.
2   Time spent using own language is time lost using English.
3   Learners need to learn to think in English, and own-language use discourages them from doing so.
4   Own language use encourages the false belief that there is a word-for-word equivalence between languages and, therefore, leads to language interference problems.

Counter-arguments have been put forward by Malmkjær (1998), Vermes (2010), Cook (2010), Hall and Cook (2012), Laviosa (2014) and Ellis and Shintani (2014), among many others, and these counter-arguments have yet to be rebutted. Thus, the argument that translation is not a useful skill to acquire relies on a very narrow definition of translation. If translation is understood more broadly as mediation between speakers of two languages, it is hardly contentious to argue that it is a skill of paramount importance, "on a par at least with the traditional four skills" (Cook, 2008: 81). The reasons for the importance of this kind of mediation will be explored further in the next section.

The second argument, concerning time, falsely assumes that language use in the classroom is a zero-sum game. Some time spent on particular kinds of own-language activities may lead to more production of English than would otherwise be the case. As we saw earlier, own-language use by teachers is often motivated by a desire to save time, which can then be devoted to more productive activities.

Meanwhile, the relationship between thought and language is extremely complex, and the notion of 'thinking in a language' is therefore not as straightforward as it might appear (Cohen, 2011: 234–255). The idea that English language learners need to learn to think in English assumes that English and their own language are compartmentalised as separate systems in their minds. This, in turn, suggests that the task of English language learners is to leave their own language behind them and to attempt to become more like native speakers of English. However, it is unlikely that different languages are stored in different parts of the brain as completely separate systems (Grosjean, 1989). Research into word associations (e.g. Spivey and Hirsch, 2003) shows that the brain processes knowledge of two or more languages in parallel, at least to some extent. Learners will not, therefore, leave their own language behind them: learning English as a new language is a journey towards compound bilingual (or multilingual) competence (Kecskes and Papp, 2000; see also Carroll and Combs, this volume).

Learners cannot therefore be prevented from thinking in their own language. Except for the most advanced learners, the language of thought is inevitably their own language (Macaro, 2005: 68; Turnbull and Dailey-O'Cain, 2009: 5–6). In some respects, this may be no bad thing. Research has shown that own-language thinking may be beneficial to learners of another language when they are reading, as it more readily enables them, among other things, "to chunk material into semantic clusters, to keep their train of thought, to create a network of associations" (Cohen, 2011: 233).

The fourth argument against own-language use is more fully stated by Lado:

> (1) few words if any are fully equivalent in any two languages, (2) the student, thinking that the words are equivalent, erroneously assumes that his translation can be extended to the same situations as the original and as a result makes mistakes, and (3) word-for-word translations produce incorrect constructions.
>
> *(Lado, 1964: 53–54)*

Lado saw the influence of the learner's own language on the acquisition of the new one as entirely negative, and the term 'interference', still widely used by teachers, reflects this. More recently, however, it has been recognised that 'language transfer' (a term that is now preferred to 'interference') is a complex phenomenon which can operate two ways (i.e. the new language can also influence the own language) and is not necessarily negative (Ellis and Shintani, 2014: 235–240). Transfer is known to take place in all learning situations, and not just those where translation is used, so transfer cannot be the consequence of translation (Vermes, 2010: 89). Translation may, indeed, be a useful tool to deal with the phenomenon of transfer. Learners' awareness of false friends, for example, is most efficiently raised by direct comparison of the two languages. Word-for-word translation exercises (from English to the learners' own language) may, in fact, be one of the most effective ways of promoting the noticing of differences between languages (Laufer and Girsai, 2008).

There is no research which demonstrates that instructional approaches employing translation and other own-language activities result in more significant transfer effects than with monolingual approaches. There is, however, now ample research which demonstrates the positive effects of translation (e.g. bilingual dictionaries and bilingual wordlists) in the learning of vocabulary (Nation, 1997).

The arguments for own-language use (1): different purposes

Some of the most forceful arguments for own-language use come from those who are seeking to steer English language teaching away from a purely utilitarian approach in the framing of the goals of the enterprise. One of the clearest statements of this kind comes from the MLA Ad Hoc Committee on Foreign Languages (2007) document, 'Foreign Languages and Higher Education: New Structures for a Changed World'. It argues that the desired outcome of language teaching in higher education should be "educated speakers who have deep translingual and transcultural competence". It moves away from the goal of attempting to "replicate the competence of an educated native speaker", a goal which is "not necessarily useful, desirable or obtainable" (Hall and Cook, 2013: 8). Instead, the process of English language learning, during which functional language abilities are acquired, is seen as facilitating the development of "critical language awareness, interpretation and translation [skills], historical and political consciousness, social sensibility, and aesthetic perception" (MLA Ad Hoc Committee on Foreign Languages, 2007). From this perspective, own-language use plays a necessary and central role, and translation is a valuable skill in its own right (Laviosa, 2014: 1). Although this report is concerned with higher education, its recommendations may also be viewed as relevant to secondary schools.

A similar position is also clearly stated in the introductory chapter of the Common European Framework of Reference for Languages (Council of Europe, 2001: 1–8), which informs the English language education policies of many countries both in Europe and beyond. Here, the purpose of language learning and teaching is presented as the promotion of plurilingualism, an approach which recognises that language is used in cultural contexts and that languages and cultures are not kept 'in strictly separated mental compartments'. Rather, the lifelong task of language learning is to develop "a communicative competence to which all knowledge and experience of language contributes and in which languages interrelate and interact" (ibid.: 4).

In ecological approaches such as these, intercultural awareness is both an enabler of language proficiency and an outcome of reflection on language proficiency (Kramsch, 1993: 8). Teaching English, or any other language, is "teaching the very core of what it means to become multilingual . . . teaching language as a living form, experienced and remembered bodily, with a relation to an Other that is mediated by symbolic forms" (Kramsch, 2009: 191).

The decision to include or exclude own-language activities in English language teaching is not, therefore, just a process option in pursuing instrumental goals (although it is that, as well). Inclusion is a corollary of reframing the purposes of language teaching towards purposes that are more broadly educational, as opposed to training-oriented. As a result, it is not a surprise to find that such approaches find a more welcoming climate in state-sponsored higher education (e.g. Canagarajah, 2013; Laviosa, 2014) than they do in private language schools.

The arguments for own-language use (2): learner practices and attitudes

Contemporary constructivist theories of learning assume that the learning of anything new is always built upon previous knowledge and experiences. For low-level language learners, the most significant previous knowledge is their knowledge of their own language. It "lays the foundation for all other languages we might want to learn . . . it is the most valuable resource, indeed the critical one, that a talking child brings to the classroom" (Butzkamm and Caldwell, 2009:13). A comparison of English, the new language, with one's own language is to be expected, and it is what we find. In Hall and Cook's survey (2013), teachers reported that their students used their own languages to a significant degree in the classroom, and that, most frequently, they did this when studying vocabulary and grammar (Hall and Cook, 2013: 40). Also, as may now be expected, the students' own-language use was higher in state-sponsored institutions than in private schools.

Surveys of learners' attitudes towards own-language use (e.g. Chavez, 2003; Rolin-Ianziti and Varshney, 2008; Lee, 2012) have consistently shown that a majority have positive attitudes towards it, especially when they are at a low level. This preference is also shown by the huge commercial success of online language learning programmes such as Duolingo, which are organised around translation exercises. Many learners, it seems, are happy to use their own language as a cognitive tool in their language learning.

Building on constructivist theories of learning, sociocultural accounts of learning see language development as "a mediated, collaborative process driven by social interaction" (Levine, 2011: 24; see Negueruela-Azarola and García, this volume). Own-language use can play an important role in this collaborative process, besides the 'medium-oriented' function of coming to a better understanding of vocabulary items and grammar. Studies (e.g. Antón and DiCamilla, 1999; Swain and Lapkin, 2000) have found a range of 'framework' or 'social' functions in students' own-language use. These may be divided into two broad groups. First, there are those uses of own language in which students prepare for a classroom task by, for example, coming to a joint understanding of the requirements of the task and the best strategic approach to it. They may also use own language to "maintain each other's interest in the task throughout its performance" (Swain and Lapkin, 2000: 254). Own-language use may reduce the cognitive load and, in so doing, transform a task from something that is excessively challenging (and may not therefore be completed) to something that can be done and from which learning may result. Hall and Cook's survey (2013: 40) found this use of own language to be very common: only 30 per cent of teachers reported that their students never used own-language for this purpose. The second group of functions is concerned with interpersonal interactions and creating a positive learning environment. Own-language use may be more appropriate for the expression of, for example, concern and sympathy (Kim and Elder, 2005); it may limit the possibilities of embarrassment or negative peer evaluation; it may allow adolescents to express and explore their emerging identities by 'talking the right talk' (Tarone and Swain, 1995). Whilst some of these uses may be seen by teachers as 'off-task', or even disciplinary matters, effective classroom management invariably entails some tolerance of off-task behaviour.

Conclusion

For applied linguists, there are probably few aspects of English language teaching that are less contentious than the question of English-only classrooms. The claim that English is best learnt in an English-only environment is, at best, "not proven" (Macaro, 2000: 174), and, at worst, "detrimental" and "untenable" (Turnbull and Dailey-O'Cain, 2009: 182–186). There is a very clear consensus that some own-language use can support the learning of a new language. The historical arguments in favour of excluding own language are "based on a limited view of translation" (Vermes, 2010: 91) and do not take account of teaching and learning contexts (Ellis and Shintani, 2014: 233). On the whole, their roots were to be found in political and commercial considerations (Cook, 2010: xvi) rather than in any "considered pedagogic principle" (Widdowson, 2003: 160).

However, the popular received wisdom that new languages are best learnt in something approaching a 'naturalistic' setting, preferably with NEST teachers, is promoted and catered to by the private sector, which benefits from the contemporary dominant political narrative in which the private sector is more dynamic and efficient than the public. Huge private sector inroads into public education (Ball, 2012) are likely to strengthen the case for more vocational approaches to language education. The tests and the technologies that are sold by the private sector are largely incompatible with the ecological classroom approaches that underpin so many of the critiques of English-only. Discussions about changes to own-language policies will take place within this broader context.

Yet most teachers will need little persuading, since the emerging critical consensus on own-language use confirms their own practice-driven understanding of language classrooms. An 'English-mainly', as opposed to 'English-only', approach is already the norm. Of more concern to them will be the practical questions of how much own-language use, and of what kind, is appropriate (Sampson, 2012). The answers to both questions can be informed by research, but, ultimately, answers will be reached by teachers themselves as they explore their own local contexts (Hall and Cook, 2012: 296).

A move away from own-language use as a 'crutch' and towards more principled practices will be facilitated by two changes within English language teaching. The first is the incorporation of own-language issues in teacher training and development. There are already signs of this taking place in some contexts, and the greater prominence given to these issues in the recent literature for teachers in training (e.g. Harmer, 2012), as well as at conferences, is likely to accelerate acceptance. Secondly, the appearance of more practical suggestions in published form will provide teachers with more options to explore. Duff's *Translation* (1989) and Deller and Rinvolucri's *Using the Mother Tongue* (2002) were for a long time the only practical handbooks available.

Recent years have seen the publication of Butzkamm and Caldwell's *The Bilingual Reform* (2009) and Kerr's *Translation and Own-Language Activities* (2014), and both offer an extensive variety of own-language activities for general English contexts, including secondary schools. For university teachers, González Davies (2004) offers almost one hundred tasks, activities and projects, and, more recently, Levine (2011) and Laviosa (2014) have added substantially to the number of practical possibilities. At the same time, it is no longer rare to find textbooks (and their accompanying manuals for teachers) that include suggestions for own-language use. The elephant in the room is becoming increasingly visible.

Discussion questions

- As a learner of another language, what did you, your fellow students and your teachers use own language for? How did everyone feel about these uses?
- In your own institutional teaching context, how much variation is there in the attitudes that are expressed regarding own-language use?
- In your own teaching context, what are (or would be) the most important functions of own-language use by (a) students and (b) teachers?
- Why do you think that own-language use has been an 'elephant in the room' for so long?
- What potential dangers do you see in the legitimation of own-language activities? How significant are these dangers in your own context or other contexts that you know about?

Related topics

Bilingual education in a multilingual world; Method, methods and methodology; 'Native speakers', English and ELT.

Further reading

Cook, G. (2010) *Translation in language teaching*. Oxford: Oxford University Press. (This award-winning book is probably more responsible than any other for reigniting interest in own-language issues.)

Hall, G. and Cook, G. (2012) 'Own-language use in language teaching and learning'. *Language Teaching*, 45/3. 271–308. (A 'state-of-the-art' survey of this area which is the most comprehensive examination of the research literature.)

Kerr, P. (2014) *Translation and own-language activities*. Cambridge: Cambridge University Press. (Currently the most extensive handbook of practical classroom activities.)

References

Antón, M. and DiCamilla, F. (1999) 'Socio-cognitive functions of L1 collaborative interaction in the L2 classroom'. *Modern Language Journal, 83/2.* 233–247.

Árva, V. and Medgyes, P. (2000) 'Native and non-native teachers in the classroom'. *System, 28/3.* 355–372.

Ball, S. J. (2012) *Global Education Inc.* Abingdon: Routledge.

Berlitz, M. D. (n.d.) Company website. Retrieved May 3, 2015, from http://www.berlitz.co.uk/about_us/tradition/berlitz_method/

Berlitz, M. D. (1916) *Method for teaching modern languages* (Revised American ed.) New York: M. D. Berlitz.

Biesta, G.J.J. (2004) 'Against learning. Reclaiming a language for education in an age of learning'. *Nordisk Pedagogik*, 24/1. 70–82.

Biesta, G.J.J. (2010) *Good education in an age of measurement.* Boulder, CO: Paradigm Publishers.

Brooks, N. (1964) *Language and language learning: Theory and practice* (2nd ed.). New York: Harcourt Brace.

Butzkamm, W. and Caldwell, J.A.W. (2009) *The bilingual reform.* Tübingen: Narr Verlag.

Canagarajah, S. (2013) *Translingual practice.* Abingdon: Routledge.

Chavez, M. (2003) 'The diglossic foreign-language classroom: Learners' views on L1 and L2 functions', in C. Blyth (ed.) *The sociolinguistics of foreign-language classrooms: Contributions of the native, the near-native and the non-native speaker*. Boston: Thomson / Heinle. 163–208.

Cohen, A. D. (2011) *Strategies in learning and using a second language* (2nd ed.). Harlow: Pearson Education.

Cook, G. (2008) 'An unmarked improvement: Using translation in ELT', in B. Beavon (ed.) *IATEFL 2007 Aberdeen conference selections*. Canterbury: IATEFL. 76–86.

Cook, G. (2010) *Translation in language teaching*. Oxford: Oxford University Press.

Copland, F. and Neokleous, G. (2011) 'L1 to teach L2: Complexities and contradictions'. *ELT Journal*, 65/3. 270–280.

Council of Europe (2001) *Common European Framework of Reference for Languages: Learning, teaching, assessment*. Cambridge: Cambridge University Press.

Deller, S. and Rinvolucri, M. (2002) *Using the mother tongue*. Peaslake, Surrey: Delta Publishing.

Duff, A. (1989) *Translation*. Oxford: Oxford University Press.

Edstrom, A. (2006) 'L1 use in the L2 classroom: One teacher's self-evaluation'. *Canadian Modern Language Review*, 63. 275–292.

Edstrom, A. (2009) 'Teacher reflection as a strategy for evaluating L1/L2 use in the classroom'. *Babylonia*, 1. 12–15.

Ellis, R. (1990) *Instructed second language acquisition*. Oxford: Blackwell.

Ellis, R. (1994) *The study of second language acquisition*. Oxford: Oxford University Press.

Ellis, R. and Shintani, N. (2014) *Exploring language pedagogy through second language acquisition research*. Abingdon: Routledge.

González Davies, M. (2004) *Multiple voices in the translation classroom*. Amsterdam: John Benjamins.

Grosjean, F. (1989) 'Neurolinguists, beware! The bilingual is not two monolinguals in one person'. *Brain and Language*, 36/1. 3–15.

Hall, G. and Cook, G. (2012) 'Own-language use in language teaching and learning' *Language Teaching*, 45/3: 271–308.

Hall, G. and Cook, G. (2013) *Own-language use in ELT: Exploring global practices and attitudes in ELT*. London: British Council.

Harbord, J. (1992) 'The use of the mother tongue in the classroom'. *ELT Journal*, 46/4. 350–355.

Harmer, J. (1983) *The practice of English language teaching* (1st ed.). Harlow: Longman.

Harmer, J. (2012) *Essential teacher knowledge*. Harlow: Pearson Education.

Harmer, J. (2015) *The practice of English language teaching* (5th ed.). Harlow: Longman.

Howatt, A.P.R. and Smith, R. (2014) 'The history of teaching English as a foreign language, from a British and European perspective'. *Language and History*, 57/1. 75–95.

Howatt, A.P.R. with Widdowson, H. G. (2004) *A history of English language teaching* (2nd ed.). Oxford: Oxford University Press.

Inlingua (n.d.) Company website. Retrieved May 3, 2015, from http://inlingua-bern.ch/en/about-inlingua/method/

Kecskes, I. and Papp, P. (2000) *Foreign language and mother tongue*. Mahwah, NJ: Lawrence Erlbaum.

Kerr, P. (2014) *Translation and own-language activities*. Cambridge: Cambridge University Press.

Kim, S.-H. and Elder, C. (2005) 'Language choices and pedagogical functions in the foreign language classroom: A cross-linguistic functional analysis of teacher talk'. *Language Teaching Research*, 9/4. 355–380.

Kramsch, C. (1993) *Context and culture in language teaching*. Oxford: Oxford University Press.

Kramsch, C. (2009) *The multilingual subject*. Oxford: Oxford University Press.

Lado, R. (1964) *Language teaching: A scientific approach*. New York: McGraw-Hill.

Laufer, B. and Girsai, N. (2008) 'Form-focused instruction in second language vocabulary learning: A case for contrastive analysis and translation'. *Applied Linguistics*, 29. 694–716.

Laviosa, S. (2014) *Translation and language education*. Abingdon, OX: Routledge.

Lawes, S. (2010) 'Why learning languages matters'. *The Independent Blog*, November 17, 2010. Retrieved May 12, 2015, from http://blogs.independent.co.uk/2010/11/19/why-learning-languages-matters/

Lee, J. H. (2012) 'Reassessment of English-only approach in EFL context in view of young learners' attitudes, language proficiency, and vocabulary knowledge'. *Multilingual Education*, 2. 5. Retrieved March 31, 2015, from http://www.multilingual-education.com/content/pdf/2191–5059–2–5.pdf

Levine, G. S. (2011) *Code choice in the language classroom*. Bristol: Multilingual Matters.

Levine, G. S. (2014) 'Principles for code choice in the foreign language classroom: A focus on grammaring'. *Language Teaching*, 47/3. 332–348.

Littlewood, W. and Yu, B. (2011) 'First language and target language in the foreign language classroom'. *Language Teaching*, 44/1. 64–77.

Macaro, E. (1997) *Target language, collaborative learning and autonomy*. Clevedon: Multilingual Matters.

Macaro, E. (2000) 'Issues in target language teaching', in K. Field (ed.) *Issues in modern foreign languages teaching*. Abingdon, Oxon: Routledge. 171–189.

Macaro, E. (2005) 'Codeswitching in the L2 classroom: A communication and learning strategy', in E. Llurda (ed.) *Non-native language teachers: Perceptions, challenges and contributions to the profession*. New York: Springer. 63–84.

Malmkjær, K. (ed.) (1998) *Translation and language teaching*. Manchester: St Jerome.

Medgyes, P. (1994) *The non-native teacher*. Houndsmills: Macmillan.

Mitchell, R. (1988) *Communicative language teaching in practice*. London: CILT.

MLA Ad Hoc Committee on Foreign Languages (2007) *Foreign languages and higher education: New structures for a changed world*, 1–12. Retrieved May 15, 2015, from www.mla.org/flreport

Mouhanna, M. (2009) 'Re-examining the role of L1 in the EFL classroom'. *UGRU Journal*, 8. 1–19. Retrieved May 3, 2015, from http://www.academia.edu/7046855/Re-Examining_the_Role_of_L1_in_the_EFL_Classroom

Nation, P. (1997) 'L1 and L2 use in the classroom: a systematic approach'. *TESL Reporter*, 30/2. 19–27.

Newson, D. (1998) 'Translation and foreign language learning', in K. Malmkjær (ed.) *Translation and language teaching*. Manchester: St Jerome. 63–68.

Pennington, M. C. (1995) *Eight case studies of classroom discourse in the Hong Kong secondary English class*. Hong Kong: City University of Hong Kong Department of English.

Polio, C. and Duff, P. (1994) 'Teachers' language use in university foreign language classrooms: A qualitative analysis of English and target language alternation'. *Modern Language Journal*, 78/3. 313–326.

Rampton, B. (1990) 'Displacing the 'native-speaker': expertise, affiliation and inheritance'. *ELT Journal*, 44/2. 97–101.

Richards, J. C. and Rodgers, T. S. (2014) *Approaches and methods in language teaching* (3rd edition). Cambridge: Cambridge University Press.

Rolin-Ianziti, J. and Varshney, R. (2008) 'Students' views regarding the use of the first language: An exploratory study in a tertiary context maximising target language use'. *The Canadian Modern Language Review*, 65/2. 249–273.

Sampson, A. (2012) 'Learner code-switching versus English only'. *ELT Journal*, 66/3. 292–303.

Scrivener, J. (1994) *Learning teaching: A guidebook for English language teachers* (1st ed.). Oxford: Macmillan.

Scrivener, J. (2011) *Learning teaching: A guidebook for English language teachers* (3rd ed.). Oxford: Macmillan.

Spivey, M.V. and Hirsch, J. (2003) 'Shared and separate systems in bilingual language processing: Converging evidence from eyetracking and brain imaging'. *Brain and Language*, 86. 70–82.

Swain, M. and Lapkin, S. (2000) 'Task-based second language learning: The use of the first language'. *Language Teaching Research*, 4/3. 251–274.

Tarone, E. and Swain, M. (1995) 'A sociolinguistic perspective on second language use in immersion classrooms'. *Modern Language Journal*, 79. 24–46.

Turnbull, M. and Dailey-O'Cain, J. (eds) (2009) *First language use in second and foreign language learning*. Bristol: Multilingual Matters.

Vermes, A. (2010) 'Translation in foreign language teaching: A brief overview of pros and cons'. *Eger Journal of English Studies*, X. 83–93.

Widdowson, H. G. (2003) *Defining issues in English language teaching*. Oxford: Oxford University Press.

37

Teaching large classes in difficult circumstances

Fauzia Shamim and Kuchah Kuchah

Introduction

The phenomenon of large classes in mainstream primary, secondary and higher education has been discussed for more than a century now, particularly in well-resourced contexts. However, discussion of large classes is now becoming increasingly noticeable within the literature of ELT, mainly for the following reasons:

1   The phenomenal spread of English around the globe (Graddol, 2006; Copland et al., 2014).
2   The demand for quality teaching (Buckingham, 2003; UNESCO, 2005). Quality teaching is normally found to be a challenge in large classes.
3   The promotion of communicative language teaching (see Thornbury, this volume), with its focus on student-student interaction for increased language learning opportunities within the ESL/EFL classrooms, and the challenges in organising and managing 'interactive' teaching for a large number of students.
4   The 'education for all' movement, which has led to increased enrollments at the primary level without a concomitant increase in resources, particularly in developing countries (see O'Sullivan, 2006; Nakabugo, 2008; Sawamura and Sifuna, 2008; Kuchah, 2013; see also Enever, this volume, for discussion of primary ELT).

In addition to the phenomenon of large classes, there is also increasing evidence in the ELT literature, from a variety of educational contexts in the world, which indicates that a large proportion of teaching-learning of English takes place in 'difficult circumstances' (West, 1960; Maley, 2001; Benbow et al., 2007). This, unfortunately, has not been given sufficient attention in the discourse of language pedagogy. The focus in this chapter will therefore be on teaching English in large classes in difficult circumstances. We begin by defining the two key terms: 'large classes' and 'difficult circumstances'. In the next section, we outline the major issues surrounding teaching English in large classes within the kind of difficult circumstances we describe. This is followed by a brief discussion of ways of developing good practice in large classes, including the role of teacher education programmes and teacher research. Next, contemporary policy debates on class size are presented and their implications for decisions about class size discussed. Finally, recommendations are made for future directions in pedagogy for and research into large classes.

What is a 'large class'?

To date, there is no agreement on what constitutes a 'large class'. Large classes have been defined in various ways by teachers (and researchers) working in similar and different contexts. For example, large classes were defined as comprising 22–25 students in K-3 classes (8–9 years old) in an influential class size study in North America (Finn and Achilles, 1990). However, 25 students is considered a small class by teachers in developing countries. For example, in Pakistan, large classes may comprise 40–100 students in state secondary schools and 200 or more students at the tertiary level (Shamim, 1993; Sarwar, 2001; Bughio, 2012); in Cameroon, a large class could comprise 235 students in a secondary school (Kuchah and Smith, 2011); in Bangladesh, up to 150 students (Emery, 2013); and in Syria, large classes of 400+ students have been reported at the university level (Ajjan, 2012).

The varying perspectives of teachers regarding class size also makes it difficult to define large classes in terms of a single numerical value. Research evidence indicates that in order to fully understand the phenomenon of large classes, we need to look beyond mere numbers into other relevant contextual factors such as the teachers' previous experience of class size, the average class size in their context (Coleman, 1989), limited classroom space and/or inadequate provision of resources for the number of students present in a class and the teachers' teaching style (Shamim, 1993). Hence, the definition of large classes is more a matter of teachers' threshold levels (Shamim, op. cit.: 143–144) and other contextual factors than simply the number of students present in a class (Ajjan, 2012; Kuchah, 2013).

Yet while there is no universal definition of a large class, there seems to be a general agreement that 40 or more students in a class can pose a number of challenges for effective teaching and learning (see Watson-Todd, 2006), particularly in 'difficult circumstances'. This will be the working definition of a large class in this chapter.

What are difficult circumstances?

The issue of difficult circumstances in ELT was first brought to light by West (1960) in his book *Teaching English in difficult circumstances*. West drew attention to ELT challenges in classrooms consisting of "over 30 pupils (more usually 40 or even 50), congested on benches . . ., ill-graded, with a teacher who perhaps does not speak English well . . ., working in a hot climate" (p. 1). Difficult circumstances include, but may not be limited to, insufficient and/or outdated textbooks, crowded classrooms with limited space, and lack of adequate resources and facilities for teaching-learning, including ICT. These difficult circumstances are compounded, particularly in resource poor environments, if the teachers do not have adequate English language and/or pedagogical skills, as is evident in the following description of teaching English in large classes at a university in Pakistan:

> On the one hand, there is a lack of infrastructure; on the other hand, teachers are poorly trained in language teaching. There is a lack of resources, a lack of suitable furniture for language teaching, and an absence of visual aids. Although there is a change in the syllabus from being literature-oriented to language-oriented, the implementation of this syllabus is still a problem as teachers are less motivated to change their teaching methods due to a lack of required training. . . . Reluctance to introduce any change is also due to the sociocultural

influences on the teaching. Teachers transfer knowledge rather than sharing it. Therefore, teachers consider that changing teaching methods is difficult because of the learners' traditional orientation and behaviour for classroom learning.

(Bughio, 2012: 135)

Needless to say, the challenges of teaching large classes increase manifold in these difficult circumstances. (Some contextual variables that have been found to interact with class size will be discussed in detail later in the chapter.)

Main issues in teaching large classes

In this section, first, we outline a problem-oriented perspective on large class teaching and the solutions often proposed for these problems. Then, we problematise this problem-solution approach to developing an effective pedagogy for large classes, using the illustrative example of group work – a proposed solution found in the literature – to argue for the need to develop context-appropriate methodological principles and practices for large classes, i.e. pedagogies which take account of all the contextual variables *including the difficult circumstances*. Finally, we discuss how large class sizes might interact with other variables in language teaching and learning

A 'problems and solutions' approach to large class teaching

Recent surveys of the existing literature on large class teaching show that it mainly focuses on problems in large classes and suggested 'solutions' (Shamim, 2012; Anmpalagan et al., 2012). Anmpalagan et al. summarised ten major challenges identified by practitioners in teaching English in large classes and their suggested responses to address these difficulties (see Table 37.1).

A closer look at Table 37.1 indicates that teachers' reported problems in large classes pertain to classroom management, including managing pair and group work and students' on-task behaviour; interactional and affective factors such as getting to know the students; assessment and feedback; and limited resources. Some of these problems are related to other difficult circumstances such as the physical aspects of the classroom and mixed-ability classes; a few stem from the teachers' desire to promote active learning with the large class (for further discussion of these issues, see the section on 'Large classes and other variables' later in the chapter).

As Table 37.1 shows, the teachers' responses to problems in teaching English in large classes focus mainly on developing 'solutions' to discrete problems, such as the teacher raising her hand to get the students' attention when they are working in pairs or groups (also see Shamim et al., 2007).

Pedagogical solutions to deal with large classes have also been suggested by ELT methodologists. For example, Ur (2012: 276–279) provides a list of solutions to problems of discipline, assessment, suitable materials, participation and individual awareness posed by large heterogeneous classes. These include collaborative learning through peer teaching; individualisation of learning through student selected materials; and personalisation of tasks to allow for individual responses based on learners' own experience, opinions and imagination, as well as varying between compulsory and optional activities for each student and using open-ended cues to generate free discussion. She argues, for example, that varying topics, methods and texts, as well as making activities interesting, can solve problems of discipline in such classes. Hess' (2001) book dedicated entirely to teaching large multilevel classes suggests a series of activities for achieving key solutions to large class problems. These solutions include knowing students, motivating and activating students, maintaining interest and momentum, dealing with written work, effective

Table 37.1 Large class teaching: challenges and possible responses (based on Anmpalagan et al., 2012)

	Challenge	Possible response
1	'I have too much homework to mark. It is impossible to give effective feedback to everyone.'	Use peer feedback.
2	'Not all students participate due to being in a large class.'	Introduce or increase pair/group work.
3	'It is difficult to get students' attention to stop them working on a pair or group task.'	Raise your (i.e. the teacher's) hand and train students to do the same.
4	'The noise level in my class is too high.'	Establish a code of behavior.
5	'Students in a large class often have mixed abilities. It is difficult to cater for students with such different levels and needs.'	Get written feedback from students about lessons.
6	'It is difficult to achieve rapport with the students.'	Increase your availability.
7	'Students' individual responses are difficult to hear.'	Ask other students to repeat or paraphrase.
8	'It is difficult to promote active learning in large classes when resources such as textbooks, flash cards are limited.'	Enlist students' help in gathering material.
9	'It is difficult to know/use students' names in a large class.'	Have students make profile cards.
10	'I am sometimes in despair at my inability to manage a large class.'	Discuss difficulties more with other teachers.

group work, individualising and personalising student work, and making students responsible for their own learning as well as establishing classroom routines and procedures. More recently, Akoue et al. (2015) have also put together a list of activities for dealing with the challenges of classroom management, individual differences, student reticence, and assessment that large classes with minimal resources may pose. Amongst other things, these solutions include providing a variety of activities, appropriate pacing of content, developing collaborative learning, personalisation of content and the establishment of classroom routines.

Problematising the 'problems-solutions' approach

The suggestions and 'solutions' to large class teaching outlined above are mainly 'teaching tips', however, and although they may be relevant to teachers for teaching a large class on a Monday morning, there is hardly any critical discussion of their use, particularly in large classes that take place in difficult circumstances. Furthermore, most of these solutions represent 'best practices' in ELT more generally, i.e. desirable for teaching English effectively irrespective of class size. Moreover, as these 'solutions' have been developed mainly in small class contexts in BANA contexts (i.e. communicative language teaching-oriented, mainly Western private sector ELT (Holliday, 1994); see also Holliday, this volume), they pose problems when applied in large classes in difficult circumstances.

To illustrate this point, let us critically examine one suggestion for large class teaching that abounds in the literature, that is, group work (e.g. Sarwar, 2001; Smith, 2001, 2003; Shamim et al., 2007). It is believed that teachers who use group work appropriately in large classes are able to maintain an appropriate working agenda by empowering students to support each other in smaller groups, thus minimising the risk of student non-participation that is often associated with large class teaching. However, the practical challenges in some low income countries – such as physical space in the classroom, limited resources and time constraints – impose on teachers the further constraint of working in extremely crowded classrooms where group work might not be a contextually appropriate practice. This is evident in the following interview excerpt from a large class teacher in Pakistan:

> Teachers have lack of resource [sic], lack of space to arrange group activities as the number of students is high and classes are not big enough to arrange group activities. And shortage of timing is also another problem to complete the activity.
>
> *(Bughio, 2012: 126)*

Keeping this in mind, Harmer (2009) makes a case for teacher-fronted pedagogic practices that engage learners intellectually and verbally. He argues that teacher-fronted lessons do not necessarily imply student passiveness. In large class contexts, teachers and learners can actually benefit from teacher-controlled activities when such activities require students to be actively engaged in thinking about language and meaning. When teachers make use of activities that attract the interest and attention of learners, and demand both individual and pair responses to tasks, class size ceases to be an issue. This perspective chimes with research findings (e.g. Ajjan, 2012; Kuchah, 2013) which reveal that in very large class contexts where organising group work may be practically impossible, students tend to value activities that engage them intellectually. In other words, for these students, "being mentally engaged is as important a criterion of successful teaching as being kept verbally active" (Ajjan, 2012: 270). It seems therefore that for large classes, classroom interaction needs to be redefined to take into consideration cognitively engaging activities which may not necessarily involve extended verbal exchanges.

Large classes and other variables in teaching and learning

Large classes often interact with and upon other teaching-learning variables in a given context (Shamim, 1993). Accordingly, problems in teaching English in a large class can be exacerbated by a host of other variables in the context. In this section, we discuss three variables in particular. These are heterogeneous or mixed-ability classes, the culture of teaching-learning, and learner and teacher preferences.

Heterogeneous classes

Large classes are often heterogeneous. Thus, the problem of a large class is compounded due to a large number of learners of differing abilities in the class. This "[d]iversity among students confuses and puts too much pressure on their teachers leaving them mentally and physically exhausted" (Bahanshal, 2013). To address the problem of large heterogeneous classes, Naidu and her colleagues (1992) undertook classroom-centred research in a higher education setting in India and came up with what, according to them, were culturally acceptable 'solutions', such as involving learners in developing reading comprehension questions for their peers for the prescribed texts. As discussed in a later section of this chapter, the value of teachers' active engagement in research in the setting of their own classrooms is vital for effective teaching in their large classes.

The culture of teaching and learning

The culture of teaching and learning in an educational setting, such as established teacher-learner roles, as well as the cultural norms of interaction in the wider community, can impact on what happens in the classroom irrespective of class size (Shamim, 1993; Coleman, 1996). In most ELT literature, it is suggested that learner-centred teaching, often associated with smaller classrooms, may potentially be able to provide more learning opportunities and can be realised by employing various classroom management and interaction strategies such as pair and group work. However, this is often not the case in educational settings where the local culture, regardless of class size, may not be amenable to using a learner-centred approach in general and pair/group work in particular (see for example, Li, 1998; Bawazeer, 2013). This is often the case in low-resource contexts where the teacher is the only source of language input. In such classrooms, where the teacher is considered the 'fountain of all knowledge' and a 'guru', pair/group work may be seen as preventing time for necessary language input; large class sizes add to the difficulties of introducing a culture change and, more importantly, new roles and responsibilities for teachers and learners in the classroom (Bughio, 2012). As will be discussed shortly, this may necessitate using context appropriate strategies (Holliday, 1994), including teacher-centred pedagogy, to maximise learning in large classes.

Learner and teacher preferences

Learners and teachers may also have their own preferences for ways of teaching and learning. Khati's study (2010) of learner preferences in large multilevel secondary school classes in Nepal indicated that the students prefer to be called by their first names in the class. At the same time, they liked to engage in challenging activities and preferred their teachers to do additional activities outside the textbook. However, as mentioned earlier, teachers, particularly if they are teaching more than one large class at a time, find it difficult to learn the names of all their students. More importantly, on the one hand, not knowing their learners individually can be stressful for teachers; on the other, it is likely to demotivate the learners who want to be recognised as individuals in their large class.

A recent global survey of the challenges faced by primary ELT teachers (Copland et al., 2014) revealed that although large classes were a predominant issue, there were contextual variations in teachers' perceptions about the role of small classes in improving the quality of teaching and learning. The study revealed that:

> In the UAE, where most classes are relatively small (20+), it [small class size] was ranked first. In contrast, in Colombia, where classes are generally large (30+), and in Tanzania, where they are very large (40+), smaller classes are not judged as important as many other factors. This finding illustrates the complex interplay of local realities and educational norms where notions of acceptable classroom behaviour and classroom roles may vary.
>
> *(Copland et al., 2014:13)*

As noted above, this necessitates developing context appropriate strategies after a careful analysis of all local variables, thus recognising and addressing the potential threats and capitalising on the positive aspects of a context, to maximise opportunities for teaching and learning in large classes (Holliday, 1994; Kuchah and Smith, 2011).

Developing good practice in large class teaching

Developing context-appropriate methodology

In this section, we examine a proposal for developing context-appropriate methodology for teaching large classes. This proposal is different from the simplistic 'problem-solution' approach discussed above in three main ways: it is based on a careful analysis of all the variables in teaching large classes in difficult circumstances as well as available research in the field; it represents a contextually appropriate response to the challenges of large class teaching; and it attempts to establish some principles for the practice of teaching English in large classes.

As early as 1960, Michael West made a case for pedagogic practices which encouraged students in large classes in difficult circumstances to be more involved in developing their own learning. Central to his argument was the point that the larger and less well-resourced a class, the more important it is to help students to be able to learn for themselves. Recent developments in the field of learner autonomy, in the classroom as well as in out-of-class settings, are revealing insights about the value of autonomy-related practices for large class contexts where other difficult circumstances are present (see Benson, this volume, for further discussion of learner autonomy). Although the literature on learner autonomy in developing countries, where the majority of large classes are taught, is unfortunately very sparse, there are significant voices from these contexts (e.g. Sarwar, 2001; Fonseka, 2003; Kuchah and Smith, 2011) which point to learner autonomy as a way ahead for large and under-resourced classrooms.

For example, the following vignette from an overcrowded classroom in Cameroon offers a glimpse of a teacher's (Kuchah, this chapter's second author) initial dilemma in teaching large classes in difficult circumstances, which in this case included few textbooks and temperatures of up to 46 degrees Celsius and sets the basis for the autonomy-related practice he later developed with his students:

> It was clear to him [the teacher] from the very first day that all the group and pair work language activities he had envisaged were not going to work, and that he needed to think seriously about how to go about things. His wonderful ideas about communicative language teaching and his interactive activities certainly seemed to have their place elsewhere! Observing his other colleagues, teachers of history, science, and so on, Kuchah discovered that they basically dictated notes that students copied, and gave a few explanations in the process. He reflected that dictating notes would certainly not work for him, given that English was a foreign language to these students. A way out seemed to be to resort to a teacher-centred practice focusing more on grammar and vocabulary, providing rules and giving practice exercises from the textbook.
>
> *(Kuchah and Smith, 2011: 121)*

Kuchah's initial response to teaching a large class of 235 adolescents in a remote part of Cameroon was based on 'survival' instincts. Subsequently, he sought to re-negotiate learning goals and learning activities with his learners to experiment with a 'new' pedagogy – the pedagogy of autonomy – for increased learner engagement through the sharing of resources and responsibility for learning between the learners and the teacher. This included the teacher encouraging students to reflect and find answers to questions related to *what* they wanted to achieve from each lesson, *how* they intended to go about achieving mutually agreed objectives, and *where* they could find learning resources to meet their objectives (for details, see Kuchah and Smith, 2011).

The literature on learner autonomy (e.g. Holec, 1981; Little, 1991; Dam, 2008; Benson, this volume) encourages pedagogic practices that aim at enabling students to be responsible for their own learning. This includes helping them to take decisions about the goals, content, process and assessment of learning, both collectively and individually. As was argued by West (1960) and also demonstrated in the work of Fonseka (2003), Sarwar (2001) and Kuchah and Smith (2011), encouraging learners in large under-resourced classrooms to take control of various aspects of their learning may be a way of helping them develop a sense of ownership of the learning process and self-regulating their learning. There is ample evidence from these studies showing that when teachers share responsibility for teaching and learning with students, the latter are able to facilitate learning, thus dissipating many of the challenges of difficult circumstances.

While it must be said that problems of lack of space and infrastructure are largely dependent on stakeholders other than the teacher, it cannot be denied that the interactional and affective relationships within the classroom rest on teachers' shoulders and, by extension, on the nature of the training/education that prepares teachers for contexts in which large classes and other difficulties are the norm. In what follows, we look at ways in which teacher education can better prepare teachers to deal with the challenges of their working contexts in English language teaching and learning in difficult circumstances with large classes.

The role of teacher education programmes

Recent developments in ELT have seen a growing demand for research that recognises both teacher and student agency as an important part of the generation of good practice, especially in difficult circumstances where teachers and learners need to re-negotiate learning goals to meet the limited resources available to them (e.g. Smith, 2011). It is also incumbent on teacher educators to pay attention to social aspects of classroom learning (Wedell and Lamb, 2013) in terms of how teachers can develop positive rapport with language learners, especially in large class contexts where such personal connections between teacher and students may not be easy to establish on a one-to-one basis. In this regard, Kuchah's (2013) study specifically incorporated a teacher development component into the research design – based on what Kuchah himself terms an 'enhancement approach' – which consisted of workshop discussions with groups of teachers watching videos of lessons taught and selected as successful by their peers and identifying the positives (rather than the negatives) of these lessons. Discussions of each videoed lesson were further enriched and extended with insights from students' perspectives of good ELT practice in the context of their large classes. The findings of this study reinforce the claim that teachers are more likely to accept pedagogic innovation when it is seen to emanate from, or be endorsed by, their peers rather than when it is imposed on them by external 'experts' and/or policy makers (Kao et al., 2013).

Garet et al. (2001) have argued that sustained and intensive professional development which focuses on academic subject matter (content), gives teachers opportunities for 'hands-on' work (active learning) and is integrated into the daily life of the school (coherence) is more likely to have an impact on teachers' learning and practice than is shorter professional development in the form of one-off workshops (see also Johnson, this volume, for further discussion of language teacher education). Unfortunately, in most mainstream educational institutions in the developing world where large classes exist, teachers and even educational authorities can hardly afford time for sustained professional development opportunities, as these may keep the few available teachers away from their classrooms. This is even more the case in mainstream primary schools where teachers are general subject rather than (specifically) English teachers and where the absence of a teacher from class means that nothing is learned. In this regard, a pilot Teacher Association research project has been developed between the Cameroon ELT Association (CAMELTA) and the International Association of Teachers of English as a Foreign Language (IATEFL) Research Special Interest Group (ReSIG) to explore the potential contribution of teacher association research to teacher education (see Smith and Kuchah, 2014); the aim is to help teachers generate pedagogic knowledge, principles and practices which are appropriate to their specific contexts (Kuchah, 2013).

Supporting teacher research

The social construction of good practices involving teachers, as opposed to the handing down of recommended practices, is now being encouraged in some tertiary learning contexts. This has resulted in the mapping of research concepts like action research (Burns, 2010) and exploratory practice (Allwright, 2003, 2005; Allwright and Hanks, 2009), which legitimise teachers' knowledge and highlight the importance of reflective inquiry into the experiences of teachers as mechanisms for change in classroom practice (Lieberman, 1995; Johnson, 2006). Accordingly, there is a growing interest in identifying ways to facilitate teacher research in language teaching, both in teacher education programmes and in teachers' everyday life and work contexts (Borg, 2013; Borg and Sanchez, 2015; Smith et al., 2015).

As we have shown earlier, there are suggested solutions in the literature for dealing with large classes, mainly based on ideas promoted by expert handbooks and guides. Yet the dearth of research on the *effectiveness* of strategies for large class teaching is noticeable. However, recently, there have attempts by individual teachers and researchers to undertake and/or support action research in large classes. For example, Khurram (forthcoming) found, through action research in her large university classes in Pakistan, that learner motivation and involvement in large ESL classes could be improved by using techniques that engage the learners both affectively and cognitively. Meanwhile, Bughio (2012) worked as teacher-collaborator with a group of volunteer teachers at a university in Pakistan. The major aims were to increase meaningful classroom interaction by introducing group work and developing learner responsibility for self and peer learning. A learner-centred methodology was introduced for this purpose after a careful analysis of the variables that were found to affect teaching-learning of English in the large classes in that context, including factors outside the control of the teacher such as the physical structure of the classrooms. This indicates that action research and exploratory practice by teachers acting as researchers offer us the chance to investigate and support large class teaching in sustainable, localised and 'bottom-up' ways.

However, a major issue that needs further research and discussion is how to ensure continuity of teacher research once the support from the researcher/project is withdrawn, particularly in difficult circumstances.

From classroom practice to policy: does class size actually matter?

Having examined the practice of teachers in large classes and discussed ways in which teachers might develop successful classroom practices, we now return to two key contemporary debates in large class teaching, research and policy, both in difficult circumstances and well-resourced contexts. They are: whether small classes are better than large classes, particularly in terms of learner achievement, and, where resources are limited, what are the alternatives to reducing class size? These are questions that are arguably the domain of policy and policy makers rather than teachers (generally, teachers cannot affect class size; policy makers can). In this section, we will discuss these issues using the available research evidence.

Are small classes better than large classes?

The relative merits of small classes compared to large classes still forms an important part of teacher discourse. However, the majority of studies focusing on the relationship between class size and achievement and also class size and non-achievement variables, such as classroom processes, have been conducted in North America and Europe (see for example, Finn and Achilles, 1990;

Blatchford, 2012) – contexts that are vastly different from those that characterise the teaching-learning of large classes in difficult circumstances. Hence, the findings of these studies cannot be applied to developing country contexts, which are the focus of this chapter. This is because, among other things, what is considered a large class in well-resourced contexts is considered to be either a small or a 'normal' size class in the developing countries (Coleman, 1989, and also as we have seen in this discussion).

Interestingly, while large classes are a reality for many teachers in difficult circumstances, there is a dearth of research on class size effects in these contexts. One example is Michaelowa's (2001) study of pedagogic practices and learning outcomes in five francophone sub-Saharan African countries. The study findings revealed that even an increase in class size above 62 students in a classroom only modestly affected learning. Similarly, O'Sullivan (2006) found examples of good practice in large primary classes of more than 70 children in Uganda, thereby suggesting that effective teaching of large classes is possible even in difficult circumstances, as we have suggested in this chapter.

Alternatives to reducing class size: policy options

Asadullah (2005) studied the effects of class size on achievement in Bangladesh using national secondary school survey data. Based on the findings, which did not show any beneficial effects of smaller classes, he concluded that "reduction in class size is not efficacious in a developing country like Bangladesh" (p. 220). Interestingly, despite contextual differences, this resonates with the findings of meta-analyses of many influential studies conducted in other developing world contexts as well as in the USA, where Hanushek (1995, 1998) showed that there is no significant difference in learning outcomes between smaller and larger classes.

This has led to suggestions that discussions about the effects of class size on teaching and learning in general may be less relevant than discussions about teacher effectiveness or improving teachers' pedagogic practices in relation to their particular context. Buckingham (2003: 71) argues strongly that:

> class size has less effect when teachers are competent; and the single most important influence on student achievement is teacher quality. Research shows unequivocally that it is far more valuable, both in education and fiscal terms, to have good teachers than lots of teachers.

Buckingham's argument supports conclusions from previous studies by Staasz and Stecher (2000) and Stecher and Bohrnstedt (2000) that teacher quality is the most important variable for effective teaching-learning in a classroom.

This body of evidence brings to the fore the need for alternative ways of addressing the issue of large classes and other difficult circumstances. Based on these perspectives, this chapter has therefore argued for a bottom-up approach to teacher education which recognises the important role of both teacher and student agency in generating appropriate and effective language teaching practices in large class contexts.

Conclusion

Research into the affective and interactional potential and possibilities of English language teaching and learning in difficult circumstances is still very sparse despite the growing demand for English language education and the ever rising number of students in classrooms around the developing world. Future developments in this area will therefore need to build around a research agenda which not only looks at the constraints posed by such contexts but also at the potential for such contexts to enhance quality learning. Bottom-up research which considers class size as an important socio-cultural variable (Locastro, 2001), and promotes an enhancement approach (Kuchah, 2013) which takes on board the classroom experiences and practices of both students and teachers, may provide insights into the social dynamics of large classes.

Moreover, professional development opportunities have to take into account the critical importance of teachers' working contexts and promote teacher creativity and the building of craft knowledge (Lieberman, 1995). Additionally, teacher education for large class contexts needs to develop a curriculum which emphasises creativity and pedagogic inventiveness and encourages trainees to reflect on their day-to-day practices, aligning these with learner needs, abilities and expectations. This requires training teachers in ways of developing a 'pedagogy for autonomy' but also encouraging 'pedagogies of autonomy' that reflect teachers' pragmatic responses to their contextual challenges rather than practices imposed on teachers from powerful outsiders to their classroom realities. What is more, the discourse of learner-centredness needs to consider learner perspectives (Ajjan, 2012; Kuchah and Pinter, 2012; Kuchah, 2013). Finally, research into learner agency needs to become an important part of teacher development, if we must bridge the gap between teaching agendas and learning agendas.

Yet fundamentally, the question remains: is class size a problem? Allwright (1989) asked this more than 25 years ago. He pointed out, rightly in our view, that it is both a pedagogical and a political question. Large classes will continue to be the reality for teachers and learners in many countries in the world. Usually, however, large classes are not highlighted as a problem in official figures and reports due to differences often found between government statistics based on overall student-teacher ratios and the number of students actually present in different classes (O'Sullivan, 2006). As a result, large classes are often an 'invisible' difficult circumstance (Coleman, forthcoming). More importantly, policy makers, even in developed countries, "want to know the most cost-effective means to achieving the desired outcome" (White, 2013: 4). In this regard, reducing class sizes is an expensive educational reform, with less than convincing evidence for its effect on student learning outcomes. This necessitates a shift in focus from researching effects of class size *per se* to developing appropriate approaches to large class teaching. More specifically, practitioners need to move away from the problem-solution approach, instead developing context-appropriate methodologies for large class teaching. The major challenge for practitioners, both teachers and teacher educators, is to develop teacher and teaching quality for increased student engagement and learning in large classes.

Discussion questions

- How would you define a 'large class'? What is considered to be a 'large class' in your professional context?
- How might autonomy be introduced and developed in large classes? And how realistic is this in your professional context?
- To what extent do you think that teachers can undertake teacher research in their own, large class context? What support do they need in developing context-appropriate methodology?
- Should the focus of policy be on reducing class size or improving teaching quality? Which of these educational reforms might be most effective in improving learning outcomes in your professional context?

Related topics

Appropriate methodology; Classroom talk, interaction and collaboration; Communicative language teaching in theory and practice; Language teacher education; Learner autonomy.

Further reading

Coleman, H. (1990) 'The relationship between large class research and large class teaching'. *SPELT Newsletter,* 5/1. 2–9, reprinted (2015) in *SPELT Quarterly Journal*, 30/1. 2–10. (This paper provides a summary of teachers' self-reported challenges in large class teaching and suggests some principles for improving practice in large classes.)

Kuchah, K. and Smith, R. (2011) 'Pedagogy of autonomy for difficult circumstances: Principles from practice'. *International Journal of Innovation in Language Learning and Teaching,* 5/2. 119–139.

Kuchah, K. and Shamim, F (eds) (forthcoming) *International perspectives on teaching English in difficult circumstances.* Basingstoke: Palgrave Macmillan. (This edited collection comprises a section on the policy, research and practice in teaching English in large classes in difficult circumstances.)

Online: http://www.tandfonline.com/doi/abs/10.1080/17501229.2011.577529 (This article discusses a contextually appropriate 'pragmatic' response of a large-class teacher in an under-resourced secondary school in Cameroon, and principles are derived for developing learner autonomy.)

O'Sullivan, M. C. (2006) 'Teaching large classes: The international evidence and a discussion of some good practice in Ugandan primary schools'. *International Journal of Educational Development,* 26/1. 24–37. (O'Sullivan argues for the use of available resources in a context for the effective teaching of large classes, illustrating this with some examples from primary classrooms in Uganda.)

Shamim, F. (2012) 'Teaching English in large classes', in A. Burns and J. Richards (eds) *The Cambridge guide to pedagogy and practice in second language teaching.* Cambridge: Cambridge University Press. 95–102. (This chapter summarises the available literature on teaching English in large classes.)

References

Ajjan, M. (2012) *Teaching and learning in large tertiary Syrian classes: An investigation into students' and tutors' perspectives.* Unpublished PhD thesis, Centre for Applied Linguistics, University of Warwick, UK.

Akoue, B., Ndong, J. N., Allogo, J. and Tennant, A. (2015) *Starter teachers: A methodology course for the classroom (section 3).* London: The British Council.

Allwright, D. (1989) 'Is class size a problem'? *Lancaster-Leeds Language Learning in Large Classes Research Project.* Report no. 3. Retrieved from http://eric.ed.gov/?id=ED322754

Allwright, D. (2003) 'Exploratory practice: Rethinking practitioner research in language teaching'. *Language Teaching Research,* 7/2. 113–141.

Allwright, D. (2005) 'Developing principles for practitioner research: The case of exploratory practice'. *Modern Language Journal,* 89/3. 353–366.

Allwright, D. and Hanks, J. (2009) *The developing language learner: An introduction to exploratory practice.* London: Palgrave Macmillan.

Anmpalagan with Smith, R., Ajjan, M. and Kuchah, H. (2012) 'Large class teaching challenges and responses'. Retrieved from http://www.warwick.ac.uk/telc/strategies/

Asadullah, M. N. (2005) 'The effect of class size on student achievement: Evidence from Bangladesh'. *Applied Economics Letters,* 12/4. 217–221.

Bahanshal, D. A. (2013) 'The effects of large classes on English teaching and learning in Saudi schools'. *English Language Teaching,* 6/11. 49–59.

Bawazeer, K. (2013) 'Using group learning strategies to enhance the acquisition of English in Saudi Arabia'. *AWEJ,* 4/2. 48–63.

Benbow, J., Mizrachi, A., Oliver, D. and Said-Moshir, L. (2007) 'Large class sizes in the developing world: What do we know and what can we do?' *American Institute for Research Under the EQUIP1 LWA.* Retrieved from http://www.equip123.net/docs/E1-LargeClassrooms.pdf

Blatchford, P. (2012) 'Three generations of research on class size effects', in K. R. Harris, S. Graham and T. Urdan (eds) *APA educational psychology handbook: Volume 2: Individual differences and cultural and contextual factors.* Washington, DC: American Psychological Association. 529–554.

Borg, S. (2013) *Teacher research in language teaching: A critical analysis.* Cambridge: Cambridge University Press.

Borg, S. and Sanchez, H. S. (eds) (2015) *International perspectives on teacher research.* Basingstoke: Palgrave Macmillan.

Buckingham, J. (2003) 'Class size and teacher quality'. *Educational Research for Policy and Practice,* 2/1. 71–86.

Bughio, F. A. (2012) 'Improving English language teaching in large classes at university level in Pakistan'. Unpublished PhD thesis, University of Sussex, UK. Sussex Research Online. Retrieved from http://sro.sussex.ac.uk/

Burns, A. (2010) *Doing action research in English language teaching.* New York: Taylor and Francis.

Coleman, H. (1989) 'How large are large classes'? *Lancaster-Leeds Language Learning in Large Classes Research Project.* Report No. 4. Retrieved from http://files.eric.ed.gov/fulltext/ED322759.pdf

Coleman, H. (ed.) (1996) *Society and the classroom: Social explanations for behavior in the language class.* Cambridge: Cambridge University Press.

Coleman, H. (forthcoming) 'An almost invisible 'difficult circumstance': the large class', in K. Kuchah and F. Shamim (eds) *International perspectives in teaching English in difficult circumstances.* Basingstoke: Palgrave MacMillan.

Copland, F., Garton, S. and Burns, A. (2014) 'Challenges in teaching English to young learners: Global perspectives and local realities'. *TESOL Quarterly,* 48/4. 738–762.

Dam, L. (2008) 'How do we recognize an autonomous classroom? Revisited' in P. Benson, L. Dam, L. Legenhausen and R. Manchón (eds) *Learner autonomy: What does the future hold? [Proceedings of TESOL symposium, faculty of languages, University of Sevilla, Spain].* Alexandria, VA: TESOL. 13–27.

Emery, H. (2013) 'A global study of primary English teachers' qualifications, training and career development', in S. Sheehan (ed.) *British council ELT research papers 1.* London: British Council. 69–104. Retrieved from http://englishagenda.britishcouncil.org/research-papers/global-study-primary-english-teachers%E2%80%99-qualifications-training-and-career-developmen

Finn, J. D. and Achilles, C. M. (1990) 'Answers and questions about class size: A statewide experiment'. *American Educational Research Journal,* 27/3. 557–577.

Fonseka, E.A.G. (2003) 'Autonomy in a resource-poor setting: Enhancing the carnivalesque', in D. Palfreyman and R. Smith (eds) *Learner autonomy across cultures: Language education perspectives.* New York: Palgrave Macmillan. 147–163.

Garet, M. S., Porter, A. C., Desimone, L., Birman, B. F. and Yoon, K. S. (2001) 'What makes professional development effective? Results from a national sample of teachers'. *American Educational Research Journal,* 38/4. 915–945.

Graddol, D. (2006) *English next.* London: The British Council.

Hanushek, E. A. (1995) 'Interpreting recent research on schooling in developing countries'. *The World Bank Research Observer,* 10/2. 227–246.

Hanushek, E. A. (1998) 'The evidence on class size'. (Occasional Paper Number 98–1). Rochester, NY: W. Allen Wallis Institute of Political Economy University of Rochester. Retrieved from http://edpro.stanford.edu/hanushek/admin/pages/files/uploads/evidence.size.mayer-pererson.pdf

Harmer, J. (2009) 'Making large classes smaller'. *Talk,* May 29, 2009, Santiago – *Programa Inglés Abre Puertas, Ministry of Education, Chile.* Retrieved from http://www.youtube.com/watch?v=TSc-S_rbwYM&feature=related

Hess, N. (2001) *Teaching large multilevel classes.* Cambridge: Cambridge University Press.

Holec, H (1981) *Autonomy in foreign language learning.* Oxford: Pergamon.

Holliday, A. (1994) *Appropriate methodology and social context.* Cambridge: Cambridge University Press.

Johnson, K. E. (2006) 'The sociocultural turn and its challenges for second language teacher education'. *TESOL Quarterly,* 40/1. 235–257.

Kao, S. H., Grima, A. C. and Kuchah, K. (2013) 'Co-constructing learner autonomy for young learners: learner efforts, teacher reflections, policy development', in A. Barfield and N. Delgado (eds) *Autonomy in language learning: Stories of practices.* Canterbury, England: IATEFL Learner Autonomy SIG. 13–23.

Khati, A. R. (2010) 'Exploring common expectations from students in large multilevel secondary level English classes'. *Journal of NELTA,* 15/1–2. 98–105. Retrieved from www.nepjol.info/index.php/NELTA/article/download/6131/5028

Khurram, B. A. (forthcoming) 'Promoting learner involvement in a large university level ESL class in Pakistan', in K. Kuchah and F. Shamim (eds) *International perspectives in teaching English in difficult circumstances.* Basingstoke: Palgrave MacMillan.

Kuchah, K. (2013) *Context-appropriate ELT pedagogy: An investigation in Cameroonian primary schools.* Unpublished PhD thesis, Centre for Applied Linguistics, University of Warwick, UK.

Kuchah, H. and Pinter, A. (2012) 'Was this an interview?' Breaking the power barrier in adult-child interviews in an African context'. *Issues in Educational Research*, 22/2. 283–297.

Kuchah, K. and Smith, R. (2011) 'Pedagogy of autonomy for difficult circumstances: Principles from practice'. *International Journal of Innovation in Language Learning and Teaching*, 5/2. 119–139. Retrieved from http://www.tandfonline.com/doi/abs/10.1080/17501229.2011.577529

Li, D. (1998) '"It's always more difficult than you plan and imagine": Teachers' perceived difficulties in introducing the communicative approach in South Korea'. *TESOL Quarterly*, 32/4. 677–703.

Lieberman, A. (1995) 'Practices that support teacher development: Transforming conceptions of professional learning', in F. Stevens (ed.) *Innovating and Evaluating Science Education*. NSF Evaluation Forums 1992–1994. Retrieved from http://128.150.4.107/pubs/1995/nsf95162/nsf_ef.pdf#page=58.67–78

Little, D. (1991) *Learner autonomy 1: Definitions, issues and problems*. Dublin: Authentik.

Locastro, V. (2001) 'Teaching English to large classes'. *TESOL Quarterly*, 35/3. 493–506.

Maley, A. (2001) 'The teaching of English in difficult circumstances: Who needs a health farm when they're starving'? *Humanising Language Teaching*, 3/6 (November 2001). Retrieved from http://www.hltmag.co.uk/nov01/martnov014.rtf

Michaelowa, K. (2001) 'Primary education quality in francophone sub-Saharan Africa: Determinants of learning achievement and efficiency considerations'. *World Development*, 29/10. 1699–1716.

Nakabugo, M. G. (2008) 'Universal primary education for growth? The paradox of large classes in Uganda'. *Journal of International Cooperation in Education*, 11/1. 117–130.

Naidu, B., Neeraja, K., Shivakumar, J. and Viswanatha, V. (1992) 'Researching heterogeneity: An account of teacher-initiated research into large classes'. *ELT Journal*, 46/3. 252–263. doi: 10.1093/elt/46.3.252

O'Sullivan, M. C. (2006) 'Teaching large classes: The international evidence and a discussion of some good practice in Ugandan primary schools'. *International Journal of Educational Development*, 26/1. 24–37.

Sarwar, Z. (2001) 'Adapting individualization techniques for large classes', in D. Hall and A. Hewings (eds) *Innovation in English language teaching: A reader*. London: Routledge. 127–136.

Sawamura, N. and Sifuna, D. N. (2008) 'Universalizing primary education in Kenya: Is it beneficial and sustainable'? *Journal of International Cooperation in Education*, 11/3. 103–118.

Shamim, F. (1993) *Teacher-learner behaviour and classroom processes in large ESL classes in Pakistan*. Unpublished PhD thesis, School of Education, University of Leeds, UK. Retrieved from etheses.whiterose.ac.uk/495/1/uk_bl_ethos_397452_pdf.pdf

Shamim, F. (2012) 'Teaching English in large classes', in A. Burns and J. Richards (eds) *The Cambridge guide to pedagogy and practice in Second language teaching*. Cambridge: Cambridge University Press. 95–102.

Shamim, F., Negash, N., Chuku, C. and Demewoz, N. (2007) *Maximising learning in large classes: Issues and options*. Addis Ababa: The British Council. Retrieved from http://www.teachingenglish.org.uk/sites/teacheng/files/ELT-16-screen.pdf

Smith, R. (2001) 'Group work for autonomy in Asia: Insights from teacher-research'. *AILA Review*, 15. 70–81.

Smith, R. (2003) ' Pedagogy for autonomy as (becoming-) appropriate methodology', in D. Palfreyman and R. Smith (eds) *Learner autonomy across cultures: Language education perspectives*. New York: Palgrave Macmillan. 129–146.

Smith, R. (2011) 'Teaching English in difficult circumstances: A new research agenda', in T. Pattison (ed.) *IATEFL 2010 conference selections*. Canterbury: IATEFL. 78–80.

Smith, R. and Kuchah, H. K. (2014) '"Teacher association research" – an innovative form of teacher-research'. *Voices 236* (IATEFL Newsletter January–February). Canterbury, UK: IATEFL. 22–23.

Smith, R., Rebolledo, P., Shamim, F. and Wyatt, M. (2015) 'Teacher development around the world', in T. Pattison (ed.) *IATEFL 2014 Harrogate conference selections*. Kent: IATEFL. 197–201.

Staasz, C. and Stecher, B. M. (2000) 'Teaching mathematics and language arts in reduced size and non-reduced size classrooms'. *Educational Evaluation and Policy Analysis*, 22/4. 313–329.

Stecher, B. M. and Bohrnstedt, G. W. (eds) (2000) *Class size reduction in California: The 1998–99 evaluation findings*. Sacramento, CA: California Department of Education.

UNESCO (2005) *Education for all global monitoring report: The quality imperative*. Paris: UNESCO.

Ur, P. (2012) *A course in language teaching: Practice and theory* (2nd ed.). Cambridge: Cambridge University Press.

Watson-Todd, R. (2006) 'Why investigate large classes?' *KMUTT Journal of Language Education. Special Issue: Large Classes*, 9. 1–12. Retrieved from http://arts.kmutt.ac.th/sola/rEFL/Vol9_Reflections_Large_Classes.pdf

Wedell, M. and Lamb, M. (2013) 'Inspiring English teachers: A comparative study of learner perceptions of inspirational teaching'. ELT *Research Papers 13–03*. London: British Council. Retrieved from https://www.teachingenglish.org.uk

West, M. (1960) *Teaching English in difficult circumstances*. London: Longmans, Green. Reissued in Smith, R. C. (ed.) (2005) *Teaching English as a foreign language, 1936–1961, vol. VI*. Abingdon: Routledge.

White, H. (2013) 'What works, what doesn't work and why: A briefing for decision makers'. *Evidence Matters*, 3. 1–4. Retrieved from http://www.3ieimpact.org/media/filer_public/2013/09/10/evidence_matters_edu.pdf

38

Computer-mediated communication and language learning

Richard Kern, Paige Ware and Mark Warschauer

Introduction

The use of computers for communication between individuals goes back to the 1960s, but it was not until the spread of email and the arrival of the World Wide Web in the 1990s that language educators began to make significant use of computer-mediated communication (CMC) as one dimension of the larger effort to explore computer-assisted language learning (CALL). Initially, most CMC projects took place within a single class and used text-based synchronous (i.e. real-time) platforms such as chat and instant messaging. Early research focused on learners' attitudes and motivation (Beauvois, 1997), comparisons of interactional dynamics in online versus face-to-face environments (Kern, 1995; Warschauer, 1996) and linguistic descriptions of online discourse (Chun, 1994; Kern, 1995; Warschauer, 1996).

These early studies suggested that use of synchronous CMC environments offered language learners more opportunities to express themselves (in writing) during class sessions – fostering greater overall amounts of language production (Kern, 1995) as well as a wider variety of language forms and functions (Chun, 1994). CMC also promoted more balanced participation than face-to-face discussion (Warschauer, 1996) and reduced anxiety (Satar and Özdener, 2008); however, see Jebali (2014), who found no anxiety effects and better performance in face-to-face discussion than via CMC. Use of synchronous CMC appeared to stimulate motivation, free expression of ideas, the articulation of differences of opinion, the multiplication of perspectives on discussion topics and the levelling of power and status differences between teachers and students (Kern, 1995).

On the other hand, the use of text-based CMC also had some problematic aspects. Teachers were found to have less control over classroom discourse, and the rapid pace of discussions sometimes exceeded students' ability to keep up. Moreover, since learners' language contained many non-normative forms, their texts did not model the kind of language most teachers wanted them to read. Even if online participation was more democratic in the sense that shyer students often participated as much as their more outgoing peers, interactions were sometimes anarchic and discussions often lacked coherence (Kern, 1995). Thus, the considerable differences between electronic and face-to-face discussion led to recommendations that they be used for distinct purposes. Warschauer (1996), for example, recommended that written electronic discussion be used as a prelude to oral discussion to generate ideas that could later be examined and debated orally or incorporated into formal essays. In this way, face-to-face and electronic discussions could be combined in various ways to highlight the advantages of each medium.

In the sections below, we review recent CMC research as it relates to second language acquisition (SLA), with particular focus on two important areas of particular pedagogical interest: feedback on learners' writing and speaking and telecollaboration in language and intercultural learning. We then discuss three aspects of CMC that merit greater debate: 'missed' communication, the neutrality of technological interfaces, and the vexed question of determining the 'effectiveness' of CMC for learning. We conclude with a discussion of future directions in the field.

Critical discussion of main current issues

SLA-grounded research

Research in CALL is informed by a number of perspectives within SLA theory, which is traditionally anchored in a psycholinguistic focus on individual learner use and acquisition of linguistic forms. According to Chapelle (2005), interactionist SLA theory has been the most widely used in CALL research and has underlain a number of studies focused on negotiation of meaning, modified input and learner attention to language form. CMC studies taking an interactionist SLA perspective often rely on quasi-experimental designs and discourse analysis inventories to document learner use and acquisition of particular language forms and, to some extent, learners' meta-linguistic understandings of the target language. For example, researchers have examined how particular tasks can be purposefully designed to encourage episodes of negotiation of meaning (Blake, 2000; Pellettieri, 2000), how task type affects focus on form (Yilmaz, 2011) and how CMC environments can foster a wider range of learner interactions beyond these anticipated negotiations (Kötter, 2003). A number of researchers have also examined how learners paired with local peers or distant partners can provide the necessary conditions for noticing and uptake of targeted morphological, syntactic and semantic forms. These studies include, for example, examinations of chat-based feedback, which found gains in learners' metalinguistic awareness of grammatical forms (O'Rourke, 2005); documentation of instant messaging interactions that illustrated how learners took up suggestions within the context of the chat room (Sotillo, 2005); and research that structured chatting around a series of tasks, which confirmed learner uptake on particular lexical items (Smith, 2005).

Another perspective on CMC, involving qualitative rather than experimental methods, is conversation analysis (González-Lloret, 2011). Conversation analysis can be applied not only to teacher-controlled CMC projects but also to learners' use of CMC outside of school settings to study how language is acquired through interaction. Tudini (2010) studied learners of Italian interacting with Italian peers as well as adults of diverse professional backgrounds, focusing largely on repair sequences. She recommended that learners become reflective analysts of their own acquisition by being introduced to conversational repair broadly, so as to become aware of forms of repair other than correction. Jenks (2014) studied multiparty voice-chat by speakers of English as an additional language, using conversation analysis as his primary method of analysis. He showed how vocal cues, such as intonation, are used during voice chat and explored differences in turn-taking practices between text and voice chat, showing that interactional competencies vary according to the particular medium used. Jepson (2005) also compared chat mediums and found that repair moves were significantly higher in voice chat than in text chat (and were frequently motivated by pronunciation difficulties).

In experimental studies, researchers have begun to target specific practices within the context of asynchronous text-based chat. For example, Sauro (2009) assessed the benefits of two different types of corrective feedback for learners of English: feedback that recast learners' errors or metalinguistic feedback that informed learners of the nature of their errors. With respect to the language feature of interest (article omission with abstract nouns such as 'work', 'love', 'culture'), Sauro found no differences between the two treatment groups, though the metalinguistic group out-performed the control group. Sauro and Smith (2010) adopted a different approach and assigned students to one of two groups: those who were given additional time to self-correct their writing prior to sending it and those who were not. They found that learners who self-corrected showed greater lexical variety and linguistic complexity.

The focus on corrective feedback in the above studies reflects interests common to interactionist SLA research. However, in recent years, researchers have begun to explore two other domains for peer feedback: idea development, which emphasises meaning generation across the multiple phases of writing, and genre awareness, which emphasises an awareness of register, rhetoric, audience and context. We will treat these areas in the following section.

Feedback on writing and speaking

Feedback provided by classroom peers, teachers or distant partners can be delivered through a number of technological means, including word processing software, commercially developed programmes and instructors' creative uses of Moodle, Google Docs, blogging and wiki interfaces (i.e. platforms that allow learners to create and share content online). Ware and Kessler (2013) categorised feedback studies according to the *focus* of the feedback (form, idea development or genre awareness) as well as the *strategies* used to deliver feedback. Strategies for delivering feedback include using transcripts of interactions for guiding learners' meta-reflection; analyzing models for effective strategies; and offering guidance in expanding writing range across different genres.

Several recent studies add insights about peer feedback. In analyzing synchronous chat logs of learners in Japan and Australia, Bower and Kawaguchi (2011) found that learners typically focused on communicating ideas unless they were instructed to offer explicit corrective feedback. Darhower (2008) came to a similar conclusion in his study of learners in the US and Puerto Rico. Ware and O'Dowd (2008) conducted a quasi-experimental study in which US and Chilean students were not given instructions to offer error corrections or comments on language form. Students in a US-Spain partnership, however, were given explicit instructions to provide feedback on form. Ware and O'Dowd found that both groups rarely provided corrections. They concluded that learners' tentative engagement with error correction reflected their desire not to be overly didactic and their insecurity about their own language expertise.

More CMC feedback research has been done on student writing than on speech, though with technological advances that enable video and audio to be better exchanged, this situation is changing rapidly. Most studies on feedback on speech have focused on a number of automated feedback programmes (for a review, see Ware and Kessler, 2013). The primary drawback to these automated systems is their still-limited ability to provide learners with individually tailored feedback, which therefore underlines the need for better systems to enable teachers to give feedback electronically. Delivery mechanisms for providing feedback include a range of web-based tools, many of which use a version of automated speech recognition (ASR). Several popular tools which allow instructors to provide voice- and text-based responses (and students to leave messages and comments) include Wimba voice boards, Voxopop, Moodle Nanogong,

Google Voice and Portable PoodLL. Recommended areas of research include developing a better understanding of the advantages and disadvantages of human feedback in relation to automated programmes, examining student use of feedback and documenting pedagogical pitfalls (e.g. schools' inadequate investment in professional development opportunities, students' inability to use software autonomously, institutional constraints that limit teachers' use of software and over-reliance on automated software).

While SLA research tends to focus strictly on language acquisition, much pedagogical use of CMC is not targeted on language *per se* but rather on communicative exchange and intercultural learning. We now turn to that side of CMC.

Telecollaboration and intercultural learning

Telecollaboration involves establishing online educational exchanges between language learners and speakers of the target language. Traditionally, telecollaboration projects have been established between partner classes in schools and universities, but in recent years they have come to transcend institutional boundaries, as in the case of MMOGs, or massively multiplayer online games (Thorne et al., 2009; Thorne, 2010; Rama et al., 2012; Thorne and Fischer, 2012).

A number of books and review articles have surveyed research on telecollaboration (e.g. Kern et al., 2008; Guth and Helm, 2010; Dooly and O'Dowd, 2012; Blake, 2013). Rather than provide a comprehensive review here, we will focus on the intercultural learning dimension of telecollaboration, which is most relevant to many English teachers' practice.

One of the best known and the most longstanding telecollaborative projects is *Cultura,* which exemplifies the cultural turn in online pedagogy (Furstenberg and Levet, 2014). Developed at MIT in the late 1990s, *Cultura* aims to facilitate language learners' collaborative exploration of the concepts, values, beliefs and attitudes that underlay their respective cultures. Culture is approached dialogically and critically through a series of activities that involve juxtaposing materials from both cultures, analyzing and interpreting those materials, and responding to others' interpretations. In addition to working with a variety of texts, questionnaires, images and films, students 'meet' in an online forum that gives them time to read, think and formulate answers to partners' questions. Their discussion of these questions (in writing) leads to new questions, feeding an ongoing process of reflection, discussion and further reflection. The idea is not to arrive at definitive conclusions about the other culture but to glimpse aspects of the culture through the very process of discussion.

While a number of studies have found promising results regarding the viability of telecollaboration for providing motivating language practice and developing intercultural awareness (e.g. von der Emde and Schneider, 2003), other studies show that intercultural contact does not necessarily lead to cultural understanding (Belz, 2002, 2003; Thorne, 2003; Ware, 2005; O'Dowd, 2006). Language ability, linguistic style, academic context and institutional culture are all factors that can affect learners' negotiation of meaning and cultural understanding. Two of the most significant, yet subtle, factors are the medium and genre of interaction.

In her study of telecollaboration between German students of English and American students of German, Ware (2005) found that the nature of the CMC medium, which often favours speed and brevity over sustained attention, can have a negative influence on students' communicative choices, leading to disengagement and missed opportunities for intercultural learning (see the section later in the chapter on 'missed communication'). Thorne (2003) added that while a particular medium may influence communicative practices, it does not *determine* them. Rather, communicative patterns are negotiated dynamically through 'cultures of use' (i.e. the norms and attributions that evolve out of everyday use of a medium). The cultures of use relevant to a given

CMC medium (e.g. email, chat room, instant messaging) can differ across social, generational, institutional and national groups and can affect discourse in various ways, from the choice of an appropriate topic to the level of formality (including non-normative spelling and capitalisation, the use of emoticons and emoji, and so on).

Kramsch and Thorne (2002) proposed that intercultural CMC exchanges sometimes go awry not just because of linguistic misunderstandings but also because of clashes in cultural frames and the stylistic conventions of particular genres. Hanna and de Nooy (2009) underscored the importance of communicative genres in their case study of two British and two American learners of French who participated in an online forum sponsored by the newspaper *Le Monde*. They showed that the ease with which the learners entered the online discussion with native speakers of French was deceptive because the genre called 'discussion' is not universal but varies across cultures. In the context of this French online forum discussion, politeness and linguistic accuracy were much less important than a willingness to be socialised into and to follow the online community's discourse rules. In other contexts, however, attention to politeness and linguistic accuracy might be far more important. Therefore, genre and culture interact to shape the conditions and constraints of communicative contexts and, by extension, communicative competence. Taken as a whole, then, intercultural CMC studies underline the fact that online contact does not automatically produce intercultural understanding, which requires sustained negotiations of differences in genres, interaction styles, local institutional cultures and culture more broadly.

As mentioned earlier, online collaboration is not always academic in nature, and, as digital devices are routinely used for everyday communication, the boundaries between in-school and out-of-school language learning contexts are becoming increasingly blurred – a point we take up in the next section.

In and out of school

The growing prevalence of social media has meant that students often communicate online outside of school. In some cases, their CMC use directly overlaps with school-based activities. In many more cases, it does not, but may contribute to students' language learning nonetheless.

Black (2008) carried out a study of adolescent English learners using fan fiction websites. These sites involve tens of thousands of people posting their own stories related to the characters or settings of novels, movies, television shows, manga or other fictional media. Readers offer praise, suggestions and feedback on writing, and authors follow up with discussion and dialogue. Black presents case studies of English learners who honed their writing, communication and media skills, while developing their identity and self-confidence, through fan fiction communities. Other new media genres, such as video games and virtual worlds, also provide opportunities for language and literacy development through computer-mediated interaction. Zheng et al. (2009), for example, document the English language communication that takes place when middle-school students in China and the U.S. interact in the Quest Atlantis virtual world. Similarly, Rama et al. (2012) study the affordances for language learning offered when college students play World of Warcraft in a language they are learning. Both studies conclude that the intermingling of native and non-native speakers and non-threatening communication tasks facilitate the kinds of risk-taking (by learners) and feedback (by native speakers) that can accelerate learners' language development.

Key areas of debate

Pedagogical uses of CMC are not without some controversy, and we will deal with three debates tied to the following assumptions: that affording learners the opportunity to engage online with native speakers will be productive, that technologies are neutral and that assessing effectiveness is unproblematic.

Missed communication

When social interaction is theorised as being jointly constructed among participants, online communication requires a mutual commitment for individuals to converse through multiple layers of context: linguistic, situational, cultural and virtual. Successful communication online might therefore be viewed as a joint commitment among participants to develop and sustain interaction even in the face of potential contextual ambiguity. For example, in Ware (2005: 66), students construed the context in a variety of ways: as a chance to develop an informal online friendship, as a formal task to be completed for their course grade and as an opportunity to receive feedback on their linguistic output. When linguistic, situational or cultural misunderstandings developed, in part because of these differences in perceived context, participants would often retreat by ignoring the problem, redirecting the conversation or withdrawing from the conversation entirely. Such avoidance of engagement is what Ware described as "missed" communication, or "missed opportunities for approximating the kind of rich, meaningful intercultural learning that instructors often intend with telecollaborative projects". Communication in telecollaboration "fails", as O'Dowd and Ritter (2006: 624) have argued, when projects end in "low levels of participation, indifference, tension between participants, or negative evaluation of the partner group or their culture".

O'Dowd and Ritter (2006) propose four types of causes of missed communication: individual, classroom, socio-institutional and interactional. Individual differences in motivation, expectations, background knowledge and time investment can lead to tensions in how involved and aware participants are likely to be during the exchange (Ware, 2005). At the classroom level, the quality of learner interaction can be affected by the relationship between the organising teachers (Belz and Müller-Hartmann, 2003), the strategic task design and sequencing (O'Dowd and Ware, 2009) and the instructional time available for learners to process and reflect on their online interactions (O'Dowd and Ritter, 2006). Additionally, socio-institutional factors can impose formidable logistic and pedagogical challenges. Differences in semester schedules and time zones make it difficult to align calendars and develop a smooth rhythm for steady interaction (Belz, 2002). Course expectations and assessment norms at different institutions might differ considerably, with more or less emphasis placed on basic participation, formal linguistic accuracy or critical analysis (O'Dowd, 2010). Finally, at the interactional level, language norms can differ considerably, not only across classrooms but also within individual participant groups. Turn-by-turn analyses along sociolinguistic, pragmatic and discursive lines have illustrated the many points at which communication can break down (Belz, 2003; Ware and Kramsch, 2005).

Many pedagogical recommendations have emerged from this body of work focused on missed communication. O'Dowd and Ritter (2006), for example, argue for a three-pronged approach that emphasises engaging students in discussions of examples of failed exchanges, ensuring that instructors are communicating consistently and encouraging participants to adopt an action research perspective. Ware and Kramsch (2005) suggest that instructors cultivate an intercultural stance in which learners seek a "decentered perspective" (p. 202) from which they can learn to make sense of their partners' words by interpreting them, not only by using their own individual interpretive lens but also by taking on perspectives that are informed by other possible interactional styles, situational contexts or historical understandings beyond those that are most familiar to them. For example, if one international partner in telecollaboration uses a formal form of personal pronoun to address the other partner, such word choice could be interpreted in a variety of ways, including as an attempt to create interactional distance, to signal respect or to invite formality. Such a dialogic approach is growing among researchers interested in CMC for intercultural understanding. Belz (2002), for example, advocates exploring the linguacultural faultlines that emerge in online interaction, and Guth and Helm (2010) suggest that working through conflicts is an important skill for any intercultural encounter.

Dialogic approaches to intercultural understanding map well onto other types of international partnerships that promote similar goals of global dialogue and intercultural understanding. Helm et al. (2012) documented a new type of pedagogical structuring in which language instructors offered students the opportunity to satisfy part of their course requirements by participating in a non-governmental organisation (NGO) project focused on intercultural interactions. In this case study, Italian and Palestinian students learning English participated in the Soliya Connect Programme, an NGO project whose goal is to increase dialogue among individuals from different cultures. This novel approach positions the language instructor as a co-facilitator within a larger infrastructure built around developing intercultural understanding. These pedagogical recommendations share a rigorous and creative rethinking of the goals of telecollaboration and its role in the language curriculum. (See also Kramsch and Zhu, this volume, for discussion of language, culture and online cultures in ELT.)

Technology as 'neutral conduit' versus 'social actor'

When people communicate via technology, their language is mediated materially by some kind of device and its interface. Some consider these devices and interfaces to be neutral conduits (Rheingold, 1993; Negroponte, 1995). Others, however, point out that both hardware and software influence how we use language and, in the case of videoconferencing, how we express ourselves visually (Kappas and Krämer, 2011). For example, Parkinson and Lea (2011) found that when people videoconference with people they do not know well, they tend to compensate for relatively intimate visual contact by talking about less personal topics in order to increase social distance. "Paradoxically," they write, "one consequence may be that [videoconferencing] produces less intimacy than text-based or audio-only communication, because, in the latter cases, interactants may seek to increase rather than decrease the emotional relevance of the conversation itself when fewer alternative cues are available" (p. 103). Each medium has its own particular human–material interface and corresponding conventions that must be mastered. How well one knows the workings of these interfaces makes a difference in how communication unfolds (with inexperienced users being at a disadvantage), and the technologies themselves impose their own constraints that can produce misunderstandings (for example, when a transmission delay occurs, interlocutors sometimes wonder whether the desynchronised smiles, gestures or facial expressions they see onscreen are responses to what they are saying *right now* or whether they correspond to what they said a moment earlier).

Related to the issue of technology neutrality is the question of cultural bias of computer technology. For example, even though computers allow writing in all Unicode-encoded scripts via software workarounds, they come standard with ASCII keyboards that lend themselves most easily to Roman alphabetic writing. Computers also come standard with one keyboard and one monitor, implying that they are intended to be used by single individuals. But in some non-Western contexts, the 'computer user' is often a collective, involving the household and extended family (Bell et al., 2005). In one study, Japanese engineers reported that they rarely if ever wrote texts in isolation and avoided using computers set up for just one user (Haas, 1996: 228).

While such issues may not seem directly relevant to pedagogical uses of CMC, a similar, perhaps subtler form of culture bias is evoked in Thorne's (2003) work on *cultures of use* (mentioned previously in the telecollaboration section). Popular email clients like Gmail or Yahoo, social networking sites like Facebook or Orkut, text and video-chat clients like Skype or Google Hangouts can be used in different ways, for different purposes, and with different expectations by different people in different settings. Consequently, decisions made by teachers (for example, choosing email as a platform to encourage friendly, personal communication among students) may backfire if students do not associate email with that kind of activity in their day-to-day lives.

People may not ordinarily think of technology as being a social actor, yet psychological studies have shown that people tend to relate to computers and television like they do to people and places in the real world (Reeves and Nass, 1996). This body of research, which Reeves and Nass refer to variously as "media equation", "social responses to communication technologies" or "computers as social actors", shows, for example, that people treat computers with female voices differently than those with male ones; they feel encroached upon by large faces on a screen; and they can have the same physical responses to on-screen motions as to real-life motions. Bolter and Grusin (2000) also argue that media and reality are inseparable, though less from a psychological and sociological perspective and more from a cultural and historical perspective.

In today's media saturated world, it is difficult to factor out the technological from the social and the social from the technological. To date, CMC research in the context of language education has not paid much attention to techno-social relationships, but it seems that the focus of future research should be not unidirectional, as in 'how technology affects language', but rather interactive, as in how people deal creatively with the resources that new technologies offer them to do traditional activities in new ways, or to invent whole new social practices.

Measuring effectiveness

The seemingly simple question, 'Does CMC improve language learning?' turns out to be not so simple to answer, because many intervening variables come into play. We have seen that CMC can be used in myriad ways in myriad contexts. Consequently, the judgment of effectiveness cannot be separated from the specificities of the learners, the setting, the task(s), the form of assessment and so on. Furthermore, the researcher's theoretical stance on what 'counts' as acquisition makes a difference. For example, Blake (2000) found that CMC provided a good environment for negotiating meaning. However, his data showed a predominance of *lexical* negotiations and relatively few *syntactic* negotiations, leaving open questions about the extent to which CMC fosters grammatical development. On the other hand, if we view language learning from a broad semiotic perspective, we will be less interested in whether learners successfully acquire a particular linguistic structure and more interested in how they use their available linguistic, cognitive, social and material resources to deal with specific communicative situations. The variability in contexts and uses of CMC is such that teachers and researchers need to understand effectiveness in terms of the specifics of *what* particular learners do with computers, *how* they do it and what it *means* to them. As a consequence, the effectiveness question cannot be answered in any generic or absolute sense but only in a highly context-specific sense.

Future developments

Future CMC projects will inevitably incorporate an increasing variety of platforms, will involve both in-school and out-of-school contexts, and will be designed for varied purposes. Two current areas that will most likely grow in sophistication and significance are multimodal CMC and automated conversation.

Multimodality and videoconferencing

As sound and video technologies become increasingly integrated into websites and documents, writing will increasingly share the stage with other modes of expression, and people will be faced with more choices than ever about how to communicate. Should a given idea be expressed through speech? In writing? With a photograph? A video? A combination thereof? Should colour or sound be incorporated? How will it be organised spatially? Each choice entails subsequent decisions about the particular mediational tools and techniques to be used and the most appropriate styles and forms of language to employ. These decisions matter, because just as technologies are not neutral conduits, neither are modes of expression or language itself.

Multimodal communication is of course not new, but what is new in digital environments is that verbal, visual and sonic modes are all represented numerically and thus share a common architecture. This means that tools for 'writing' may be used to compose in other modes (for example, voice tracks for video animations can be produced by typing on a keyboard). 'Authoring', 'composing' or 'designing' are therefore more apt terms than 'writing', even though the biomechanical processes look identical to those involved in writing text. Digital representation also means that anyone who has access to the requisite computer software has the means to create, transform or re-mediate content and to disseminate it widely on the Internet, potentially attracting massive audiences. Whereas the rhetorical decisions involved in technology-mediated communication used to be reserved for specialists, they are now often in the hands of 'ordinary people'. This creates an important challenge for language educators.

Kress (2010), Kress and van Leeuwen (1996, 2001) and van Leeuwen (2005) have written extensively on multimodality, emphasising the different affordances of different media and how important it is for educators to understand what those affordances are, to help learners develop a conscious understanding of the 'invisible' processes that go into their multimodal creations. Multimodality is directly relevant to pedagogical CMC in many ways, but we will focus on just one here: the increasing use of videoconferencing in telecollaborative exchanges.

Videoconferencing has become a widely used platform for pedagogical CMC projects (e.g. Wang, 2006, 2007; Develotte et al., 2008; Jauregi et al., 2011). This immediately raises the question of how the audiovisual medium affects learner interactions. One researcher who explored this is Yanguas (2010), who investigated how learners in video and audio CMC groups negotiated for meaning during task-based interaction, compared to face-to-face communication and traditional text-based CMC interactions. He found differences in the way the audio and video groups negotiated for meaning, and similarities between oral CMC and face-to-face turn-taking patterns (though these were quite different from those found in written synchronous CMC). Develotte et al. (2008) analysed how American learners of French and their French tutors made use of specific video and textual affordances in MSN videoconferences and found that video augmented the tutors' palette of resources and facilitated their lesson planning, helped them to gauge the comprehension of their students and to give encouraging feedback, and allowed them to introduce a ludic dimension that would have been difficult to replicate in writing alone. Students reported that video supported their learning by providing nonlinguistic cues and it allowed them to see their French partners interact between themselves, which they found particularly enjoyable and helpful. Written chat was used in a variety of ways to complement the voice and video features. Significantly, writing was almost always done simultaneously with listening or speaking, and it served multiple functions. A frequent use of writing by the tutors was to correct students' errors or interject encouragements in such a way as not to interrupt the flow of conversation, with the added benefit of providing a written record of spoken errors that students could save for review.

Research on multimodal CMC is in its early stages, but is starting to take account of students' awareness of the complexities of learning and expression in hypermediated environments (Malinowski, 2014) and the specific ways the screen interface refracts participants' interactions and understandings (Malinowski and Kramsch, 2014). A question for future research is whether videoconferencing ameliorates that problem (e.g. enhancing communication by virtue of its visual immediacy, voice transmission and potential to create a greater sense of personal contact) or whether it merely creates other problems. O'Dowd (2006) took a first step in this direction by studying the use of videoconferencing in tandem with e-mail to compare their respective contributions in intercultural exchanges. He found that although e-mail was a more effective platform for providing in-depth background on issues, participants' differences of opinion tended to be left unexplored in this medium, whereas in face-to-face videoconferencing students were, "in a way, *obliged by the nature of the medium* to delve further into the topics in question to find out why the other group felt the way it did. It was when they did this that the link between their partners' behavior and beliefs and the personal, social, and historical factors began to emerge" (p. 104, our emphasis).

Finally, an important question raised by multimodality is whether communicative abilities learned via CMC can transfer to other, non-CMC contexts or modalities, such as face-to-face speech. Abrams (2003) found that students who engaged in synchronous CMC the day before an in-class oral discussion produced more discourse during that discussion than students who had not used CMC or had used asynchronous CMC. Mendelson (2014) presented case studies of individual students who displayed transfer between chatting and speaking, but in very different ways.

Automated conversation

Automated conversation involving chatbots or agents is another promising area for CMC in language learning. Chatbots have existed since at least the mid-1960s, when an MIT professor introduced ELIZA (Weizebaum, 1966). Today, automated 'bots' are widely used in the commercial world to solicit information from customers. In a review of bots for language learning, Fryer and Carpenter (2006) suggested a number of possible advantages they might offer: for example, students feel more relaxed when communicating with bots than with human beings; bots can repeat material endlessly without getting tired or impatient; bots can communicate in both text and synthesised speech; and bots can be designed to provide a variety of specific feedback on either grammar or spelling. In the future, bots could be designed for very specific purposes; for example, they could be combined with automated writing evaluation programmes to converse with students about how they plan to revise their papers.

Newer and more complex than bots, but also of great potential interest for language learning, are automated conversation agents. Such agents do not communicate one-to-one with students. Rather, they 'listen in' to small group online discussions, monitor the conversations and intercede according to what has already been said to stimulate more advanced conversation. For example, a team of researchers at Carnegie Mellon University has developed automated agents that ask students to revoice (e.g. 'So are you saying that the two people are equally at fault?'), to agree or disagree ('Do you agree or disagree with what she said, and why?') and to explain others' perspectives ('Why do you think he thinks that way?' e.g. Adamson et al., 2014). To date, these bots have been used to support more critical thinking in general classrooms rather than being targeted at language learners specifically. However, it is easy to imagine the special benefit for language learning if such bots were incorporated into small group online discussions.

Conclusion

For many students, online environments represent far more than a place to learn or practice language. Rather, they are sites where much of learners' real-world language use takes place. CMC is thus becoming not only more varied and complex, but also increasingly important in language education. The global growth of the Internet, the proliferation of mobile devices, and the development of new capabilities for automated and multimodal interaction make it likely that the role of CMC in second language teaching and research will continue to expand in the future.

Discussion questions

- In what ways might CMC differ from face-to-face interaction? Consider interactional differences as well as how language is used in different forms of CMC. Given that interaction has a central place in the creation of learning opportunities, what might these differences mean for the language that might be learned?
- To what extent do learners in your professional context engage in CMC in English in the classroom and beyond the classroom? What kinds of interactions do they engage in, and what might they learn as a result?
- To what extent do you think that developments in CMC might help autonomous language learning?
- To what extent do you think that the lack of control over language forms in CMC might lead learners to use non-standard English? To what extent is this a problem?
- What opportunities are there for the development of CMC for language learning in your context, both for learners within school settings and also for learners beyond the classroom (e.g. through online game-playing)? What are the barriers to such developments?

Related topics

Cognitive perspectives on classroom language learning; Error, corrective feedback and repair; Language and culture in ELT; New technologies, blended learning and the 'flipped classroom'; Sociocultural theory and the language classroom.

Further reading

Barton, D. and Lee, C. (2013) *Language online: Investigating digital texts and practices.* London: Routledge. (An examination of a variety of areas of current interest in online communication, including identity, multilingualism, language education and methodologies.)

Goodfellow, R. and Lamy, M.-N. (eds) (2009) *Learning cultures in online education.* London: Continuum International Publishing. (This book discusses cross-cultural education, computer-mediated interaction by marginalised groups, the growth of new forms of knowledge production and the spread of social network phenomena and their use in education.)

Jones, R. H., Chik, A. and Hafner, C. A. (eds) (2015) *Discourse and digital practices: Doing discourse analysis in the digital age.* London: Routledge. (This draws on contributions from leading scholars to explore ways that digital literacy practices such as text-based online communication, video gaming and social networking can be analysed using discourse analytic approaches and tools.)

Liddicoat, A. J. and Scarino, A. (2013) *Intercultural language teaching and learning.* Oxford: Wiley-Blackwell. (This book provides an overview of key areas of intercultural education, including programme evaluation, teacher collaboration and conceptual models of language and culture teaching.)

Thomas, M., Reinders, H. and Warschauer, M. (eds) (2013) *Contemporary computer-assisted language learning.* Huntingdon, UK: Bloomsbury Publishing. (An edited collection that covers broad areas of computer-assisted language learning for diverse contexts and environments.)

References

Abrams, Z. I. (2003) 'The effect of synchronous and asynchronous CMC on oral performance in German'. *Modern Language Journal*, 87/2. 157–167.

Adamson, D., Dyke, G., Jang, H. and Rosé, C. P. (2014) 'Towards an agile approach to adapting dynamic collaboration support to student needs'. *International Journal of Artificial Intelligence in Education*, 24. 92–124.

Beauvois, M. H. (1997) 'Computer-mediated communication: Technology for improving speaking and writing', in M. D. Bush (ed.) *Technology enhanced language learning*. Lincolnwood, IL: National Textbook Company. 165–184.

Bell, G., Blythe, M. and Sengers, P. (2005) 'Making by making strange: Defamiliarization and the design of domestic technologies'. *ACM Transactions on Computer-Human Interaction*, 12/2. 149–173.

Belz, J. A. (2002) 'Social dimensions of telecollaborative foreign language study'. *Language Learning & Technology*, 6/1. 60–81.

Belz, J. A. (2003) 'Linguistic perspectives on the development of intercultural competence in telecollaboration'. *Language Learning & Technology*, 7/2. 68–99.

Belz, J. A. and Müller-Hartmann, A. (2003) 'Teachers as intercultural learners: Negotiating German-American telecollaboration along the institutional fault line'. *Modern Language Journal*, 87/1. 71–89.

Black, R. W. (2008) *Adolescents and online fan fiction*. New York: Peter Lang.

Blake, R. J. (2000) 'Computer mediated communication: A window on L2 Spanish interlanguage'. *Language Learning & Technology*, 4/1. 120–136.

Blake, R. J. (2013) *Brave new digital classrooms: Technology and foreign-language learning* (2nd ed.). Georgetown, Washington, DC: Georgetown University Press.

Bolter, J. D. and Grusin, R. (2000) *Remediation: Understanding new media*. Cambridge, MA: MIT Press.

Bower, J. and Kawaguchi, S. (2011) 'Negotiation of meaning and corrective feedback in Japanese/English eTandem'. *Language Learning & Technology*, 15/1. 41–71.

Chapelle, C. A. (2005) 'Interactionist SLA theory in CALL research', in J. L. Egbert and G. M. Petrie (eds) *CALL research perspectives*. Mahwah, NJ: Erlbaum. 53–64.

Chun, D. M. (1994) 'Using computer networking to facilitate the acquisition of interactive competence'. *System*, 22/1. 17–31.

Darhower, M. A. (2008) 'The role of linguistic affordances in telecollaborative chat'. *CALICO Journal*, 26/1. 48–69.

Develotte, C., Guichon, N. and Kern, R. (2008) '"Allo Berkeley? Ici Lyon . . . Vous nous voyez bien?" Etude d'un dispositif de formation en ligne synchrone francoaméricain à travers les discours de ses usagers'. *Alsic (Apprentissage des Langues et Systèmes d'Information et de Communication)*, 11/2. 129–156.

Dooly, M. and O'Dowd, R. (eds) (2012) *Researching online foreign language interaction and exchange*. New York: Peter Lang.

Fryer, L. and Carpenter, R. (2006) 'Emerging technologies: Bots as language learning tools'. *Language Learning & Technology*, 10/3. 8–14.

Furstenberg, G. and Levet, S. (2014) '*Cultura*: From then to now: Its origins, key features, and how it has evolved. Reflections on the past and musings on the future', in D. Chun (ed.) *Cultura-inspired intercultural exchanges: Focus on Asian and Pacific languages*. Honolulu: University of Hawai'i, National Foreign Language Resource Center. 1–31.

González-Lloret, M. (2011) 'Conversation analysis of computer-mediated communication'. *CALICO Journal*, 28. 308–325.

Guth, S. and Helm, F. (eds) (2010) *Telecollaboration 2.0: Language, literacies and intercultural learning in the 21st century*. Bern: Peter Lang.

Haas, C. (1996) *Writing technology: Studies on the materiality of literacy*. Mahwah, NJ: Erlbaum.

Hanna, B. E. and de Nooy, J. (2009) *Learning language and culture via public Internet discussion forums*. Basingstoke: Palgrave Macmillan.

Helm, F., Guth, S. and Farrah, M. (2012) 'Promoting dialogue or hegemonic practice? Power issues in telecollaboration'. *Language Learning & Technology*, 16/2. 103–127.

Jauregi, K., de Graaff, R., van den Bergh, H. and Kriz, M. (2011) 'Native/non-native speaker interactions through video-web communication: A clue for enhancing motivation?' *Computer Assisted Language Learning*, 25/1. 1–19.

Jebali, A. (2014) 'Does CMC reduce foreign language classroom anxiety?', in P. Zaphiris and A. Ioannou (eds) *Learning and collaboration technologies. Technology-rich environments for learning and collaboration*. Heraklion, Crete, Greece: HCI International. 277–287.

Jenks, C. (2014) *Social interaction in second language chat rooms*. Edinburgh: Edinburgh University Press.

Jepson, K. (2005) 'Conversations – and negotiated interaction – in text and voice chat rooms'. *Language Learning & Technology*, 9/3. 79–98.

Kappas, A. and Krämer, N. C. (eds) (2011) *Face-to-face communication over the Internet: Emotions in a web of culture, language and technology*. Cambridge: Cambridge University Press.

Kern, R. (1995) 'Restructuring classroom interaction with networked computers: Effects on quality and characteristics of language production'. *Modern Language Journal*, 79/4. 457–476.

Kern, R., Ware, P. D. and Warschauer, M. (2008) 'Network-based language learning and teaching', in N. Van Deusen-Scholl and N. Hornberger (eds) *Encyclopedia of language and education, second revised edition, vol. 4*. Heidelberg: Springer. 281–292.

Kötter, M. (2003) 'Negotiation of meaning and codeswitching in online tandems'. *Language Learning & Technology*, 7/2. 145–172.

Kramsch, C. and Thorne, S. L. (2002) 'Foreign language learning as global communicative practice', in D. Block and D. Cameron (eds) *Globalization and language teaching*. London: Routledge. 83–100.

Kress, G. (2010) *Multimodality: A social semiotic approach to contemporary communication*. London: Routledge.

Kress, G. and van Leeuwen, T. (1996) *Reading images: The grammar of visual design*. London: Routledge.

Kress, G. and van Leeuwen, T. (2001) *Multimodal discourse: The modes and media of contemporary communication*. London: Arnold.

Malinowski, D. (2014) 'Drawing bodies and spaces in telecollaboration: A view of research potential in synaesthesia and multimodality, from the outside'. *Pedagogies*, 9/1. 63–85.

Malinowski, D. and Kramsch, C. (2014) 'The ambiguous world of heteroglossic computer-mediated language learning', in A. Blackledge and A. Creese (eds) *Heteroglossia as Practice and Pedagogy*. Heidelberg: Springer. 155–178.

Mendelson, A. (2014) 'Write to speak revisited: An ecological investigation of transfer between chatting and speaking in foreign languages'. Unpublished PhD Dissertation, University of California, Berkeley.

Negroponte, N. (1995) *Being digital*. New York: Alfred A. Knopf.

O'Dowd, R. (2006) 'The use of videoconferencing and e-mail as mediators of intercultural student ethnography', in J. A. Belz and S. L. Thorne (eds) *Computer-mediated intercultural foreign language education*. Boston: Heinle & Heinle. 86–120.

O'Dowd, R. (2010) 'Issues in the assessment of online interaction and exchange', in S. Guth and F. Helm (eds) *Telecollaboration 2.0: Language, literacies and intercultural learning in the 21st century*. Bern: Peter Lang. 337–360.

O'Dowd, R. and Ritter, M. (2006) 'Understanding and working with "failed communication" in telecollaborative exchanges'. *CALICO Journal*, 23/3. 623–642.

O'Dowd, R. and Ware, P. (2009) 'Critical issues in telecollaborative task design'. *Computer Assisted Language Learning*, 22/2. 173–188.

O'Rourke, B. (2005) 'Form-focused interaction in online tandem learning'. *CALICO Journal*, 22/3. 433–466.

Parkinson, B. and Lea, M. (2011) 'Video-linking emotions', in A. Kappas and N. C. Krämer (eds) *Face-to-face communication over the Internet: Emotions in a web of culture, language and technology*. Cambridge: Cambridge University Press. 100–126.

Pellettieri, J. (2000) 'Negotiation in cyberspace: The role of *chatting* in the development of grammatical competence', in M. Warschauer and R. Kern (eds) *Network-based language teaching: Concepts and practice*. Cambridge: Cambridge University Press. 59–86.

Rama, P. S., Black, R. W., Van Es, E. and Warschauer, M. (2012) 'Affordances for second language learning in World of Warcraft'. *ReCALL*, 24/3. 322–338.

Reeves, B. and Nass, C. (1996) *The media equation: How people treat computers, television, and new media like real people and places*. Stanford, CA: CSLI Publications/Cambridge University Press.

Rheingold, H. (1993) *The virtual community: Homesteading on the electronic frontier*. Reading, MA: Addison-Wesley.

Satar, H. M. and Özdener, N. (2008) 'The effects of synchronous CMC on speaking proficiency and anxiety: Text versus voice chat'. *Modern Language Journal*, 92/4. 595–613.

Sauro, S. (2009) 'Computer-mediated corrective feedback and the development of L2 grammar'. *Language Learning & Technology*, 13/1. 96–120.

Sauro, S. and Smith, B. (2010) 'Investigating L2 performance in text chat'. *Applied Linguistics*, 31/4. 554–577.

Smith, B. (2005) 'The relationship between negotiated interaction, learner uptake, and lexical acquisition in task-based computer-mediated communication'. *TESOL Quarterly*, 39/1. 33–58.

Sotillo, S. (2005) 'Corrective feedback via instant messenger learning activities in NS-NNS and NNS-NNS dyads'. *CALICO Journal,* 22/3. 467–496.

Thorne, S. L. (2003) 'Artifacts and cultures-of-use in intercultural communication'. *Language Learning & Technology,* 7/2. 38–67.

Thorne, S. L. (2010) 'The "intercultural turn" and language learning in the crucible of new media', in S. Guth and F. Helm (eds) *Telecollaboration 2.0: Languages, literacies and intercultural learning in the 21st century, vol. 1.* Bern: Peter Lang. 139–164.

Thorne, S. L., Black, R. W. and Sykes, J. M. (2009) 'Second language use, socialization, and learning in Internet interest communities and online gaming'. *Modern Language Journal,* 93. 802–821.

Thorne, S. L. and Fischer, I. (2012) 'Online gaming as sociable media'. *ALSIC: Apprentissage des Langues et Systèmes d'Information et de Communication,* 15/1. doi: 10.4000/alsic.2450. Retrieved from https://alsic.revues.org/2450.

Tudini, V. (2010) *Online second language acquisition: Conversation analysis of online chat.* London: Continuum.

van Leeuwen, T. (2005) *Introducing social semiotics.* London: Routledge.

von der Emde, S. and Schneider, J. (2003) 'Experiential learning and collaborative reading: Literacy in the space of virtual encounters', in P. Patrikis (ed.) *Reading between the lines: Perspectives on foreign language literacy.* New Haven: Yale University Press. 118–143.

Wang, Y. (2006) 'Negotiation of meaning in desktop videoconferencing-supported distance language learning'. *ReCALL,* 18/1. 122–145.

Wang, Y. (2007) 'Task design in videoconferencing-supported distance language learning'. *CALICO Journal,* 24/3. 591–630.

Ware, P. (2005) '"Missed" communication in online communication: Tensions in a German- American telecollaboration'. *Language Learning & Technology,* 9. 64–89.

Ware, P. and Kessler, G. (2013) 'CALL and digital feedback', in M. Thomas, H. Reinders and M. Warschauer (eds) *Contemporary computer-assisted language learning.* Huntingdon, UK, Bloomsbury. 323–340.

Ware, P. D. and Kramsch, C. (2005) 'Toward an intercultural stance: Teaching German and English through telecollaboration'. *Modern Language Journal,* 89/2. 190–205.

Ware, P. D. and O'Dowd, R. (2008) 'Peer feedback on language form in telecollaboration'. *Language Learning & Technology,* 12/1. 43–63.

Warschauer, M. (1996) 'Comparing face-to-face and electronic discussion in the second language classroom'. *CALICO Journal,* 13/2. 7–26.

Weizebaum, J. (1966) 'ELIZA—A computer program for the study of natural language communication between man and machine'. *Communications of the ACM,* 9/1. 36–45.

Yanguas, I. (2010) 'Oral computer-mediated interaction between L2 learners: It's about time!' *Language Learning & Technology,* 14/3. 72–93.

Yilmaz, Y. (2011) 'Task effects on focus on form in synchronous computer-mediated communication'. *Modern Language Journal,* 95. 115–132.

Zheng, D., Young, M. F., Wanger, M. M. and Brewer, R. E. (2009) 'Negotiation for action: English language learning in game-based virtual worlds'. *Modern Language Journal,* 93/4. 498–511.

39

Values in the ELT classroom

Julia Menard-Warwick, Miki Mori, Anna Reznik
and Daniel Moglen

Introduction

In this chapter, four authors based in a California university explore the ways in which teachers engage with questions of 'values' in English language classrooms across social contexts. First, we address the topic as it appears in previous literature, followed by an exploration of two data examples in which specific values are discussed in particular classrooms. We end with implications for understanding values in ELT.

We examine this topic first because teaching English always involves values. Teachers make decisions based on values, and, during lessons, students and teachers express particular values. Second, we discuss values because we recognise that talking about values often *is* a value within the popular methodological paradigm of communicative language teaching (CLT, further discussed in the following section). Since CLT values communication, *talking about values* is valuable insofar as this practice encourages students to communicate more extensively and passionately than they might otherwise. From this perspective, it may not matter *which* values an individual student articulates. At the same time, of course, many teachers hope that students will develop more 'enlightened' attitudes through discussing controversial topics (for examples, see below).

Framework and definitions

In recent decades, CLT has been the pedagogical approach most widely advocated in ELT training programmes around the world (see Thornbury, this volume). This approach considers communication, often via speaking, as the central way students learn a language (as opposed to grammar-based instruction, which focuses on acquiring rules). Thus, classroom activities encourage students to give their opinions on a topic. In order to address why sharing opinions is valued, we consider the larger framework, or belief system, in which CLT is situated. For that, we identify neoliberalism (Holborow, 2012a), the predominant ideology in globalised contexts, as one framework through which to understand ELT and the expression of values.

Defining 'values'

Before elaborating on this framework, we will discuss our definition of 'values' and related terms, as well as how these differ from the understandings of others in the field. We use *values* to refer to appraisals of rightness/wrongness (similar to Johnston, 2003), but we reserve *morality* for values within sustained, coherent systems of belief (e.g. religious prohibitions against engaging in sexual behaviour outside of heterosexual marriage). With Johnston, we define *ethics* as "codified standards and rules governing professional practice" (ibid.: 11), i.e. values within institutional contexts. An example is the common prohibition against plagiarism. However, whereas Johnston defines *ideology* as values within political contexts, we favour a linguistic anthropological definition of ideology as beliefs "constructed in the interest of a specific social or cultural group" (Kroskrity, 2000: 8). Moreover, we argue that ideologies are often instantiated in language as *discourses*, characteristic ways of referring to and evaluating particular topics (e.g. feminist discourse). Thus, values often enter classrooms in the form of competing discourses, which may clash with each other in classroom interactions (Menard-Warwick, 2013).

To better frame our discussion, we will distinguish *values about* and *values within*, where 'values about' refers to the evaluation of particular topics in classroom discussions and 'values within' refers to perspectives enacted through classroom interaction and pedagogical policies. For example, if students agree in a classroom discussion that women should pursue careers on the same basis as men, this is a value *about* gender; if participation structures in an English class encourage female students to speak out, this can be seen as a value *within* the pedagogy of this particular classroom.

Considering values in communicative language teaching

The debate on teaching values in the classroom (i.e. 'values about') can be traced back to Kelly (1986), who argued in favour of the *committed impartiality* approach, in which the teacher freely states her views on controversial issues and then allows "competing perspectives [to] receive a fair hearing through critical discourse" (p. 130). However, the inherent problem with this approach is the teacher's role as an authority figure in the classroom with whom students may fear to disagree (Miller-Lane et al., 2006). Thus, teachers may aim for neutrality (not stating their own opinions) in order to avoid intimidating and silencing more sensitive students.

The teacher's dilemma becomes even more pronounced in an ESL classroom, where learners may come from a wide variety of cultures. Oster (1989), while arguing in favour of teaching critical reading of literature, pointed out how self-disclosure may feel threatening to an ESL student, since the amount of information that is proper to disclose about oneself differs from culture to culture. Oster also noticed that the students' cultural norms dictated their understanding of the texts: thus, a Chinese student's family values resulted in her condemnation of a protagonist who did not behave with the respect understood to be due to one's father, labelling him as someone who needs "a mental doctor" (ibid.: 92). Another dilemma that teachers face is their responsibility to students vis-a-vis their role as outlined by the institution. In Ajayi's (2008) study, several teachers complained of the narrow scope of the ESL syllabus and stated that they avoided controversial topics, such as abortion, sex education etc., for fear of losing their jobs.

Indeed, when political considerations enter the classroom, the situation becomes increasingly complicated. Canagarajah (1993, 1999) conducted one of the first in-depth explorations of clashing values in ELT, specifically examining dilemmas inherent in the use of Western textbooks and CLT methodology in rural Sri Lanka. Describing students' conflict as "how to learn English . . . without being inducted into the values embodied by the language and (Western-influenced) curriculum" (1999: 96), he found that his students refused to participate in classroom 'communicative' activities which were based on discursive values that they did not share, such as the importance of budgeting money for future needs.

While Canagarajah's work is situated in a local context and deals mostly with cultural politics, Johnston (2003) expanded the discussion of values in ELT classrooms to a wider variety of issues, including assessment, L1 use in the classroom, and the teacher's personal beliefs. As an example of a value-laden (both 'values within' and 'values about') dilemma at the heart of CLT, Johnston offered the example of a teacher who asked students for their opinion about the rules of driving ('values about'); however, when no one volunteered, he said "say something, it does not matter, it is not important" (ibid.: 29). While there is no overt conflict here of the kind illustrated by Canagarajah, there nevertheless seems to be opposing messages about what should be communicated in a classroom and how. This leads to a missed opportunity: unable to inspire an exchange of ideas, the teacher creates the impression that language is learned only for its own sake ('values within'). Central to Johnston's work is the teacher's inner conflict as s/he faces these issues, and he argues that this conflict does not have a simple, one-fits-all solution; rather, the solution depends heavily on the situation and on the values held by a particular teacher.

Although we agree with Johnston that solutions to pedagogical dilemmas will vary depending on context, we additionally argue that these kinds of conflicts and missed opportunities in ELT classrooms arise most frequently when English instruction transmits practices and values associated with globalisation (Menard-Warwick, 2013). Tending to originate in Western society, these lifeways have spread around the planet in recent years as English becomes the *de facto* lingua franca of the world (see Seargeant, this volume). Products from corporations such as Coca Cola, Starbucks and McDonald's, along with widely accessible American TV and movies, allow people around the world to glimpse (and in some cases adopt) Western language and culture (see also Pennycook, this volume).

Considering the scope of neoliberalism in ELT

While this globalised culture is hardly uniform, many of its values can be seen as manifestations of neoliberal ideology. Bell Lara and Lopez define neoliberalism as "the premise that freedom of choice and the rational calculation of economic actors . . . is the principle underlying human behaviour" (2007: 18). From this perspective, individuals are responsible for their own futures and should expect nothing from the larger global society – other than the protection of rights, especially property rights (Hershberg and Rosen, 2006). While neoliberalism has primarily been linked to the free market principles on which the global *economy* is based, the definition given by Bell Lara and Lopez suggests the broader implications for *lifestyles* based on freedom of choice. As Holborow points out, in this discursive context, the economic metaphor of entrepreneurship is now being applied to a wide range of fields, "from social work to personal development" (2012b: 53). She additionally notes that "within applied linguistics. . . neoliberalism has been seen to intersect with English as a dominant language" (2012a: 26).

Thus, because English is the dominant language of financial transactions within the globalised economy, it also necessarily dominates the 'linguistic market', in which language has a monetary exchange value, both metaphorically and practically. In this way, English and English language teaching themselves have become commodities. Similarly, it has long been argued within cognitive linguistics that the *conduit metaphor* for communication is embedded in the structures of the English language, as seen in expressions like 'I *gave* you that idea', or 'your concept *came across* beautifully' (Reddy, 1970: 311–312). In this view, language serves as a conduit for ideas and texts that become commodified packages that are passed (or potentially sold) from one interlocutor to another. The terms *input* and *output*, widely associated with ELT around the globe, have been critiqued from a sociocultural perspective as based in the conduit metaphor (Platt and Brooks, 1994; see also Negueruela-Azarola and García, this volume). In this version of CLT, it doesn't matter what's *in* the package, as implied by the teacher that Johnston observed (2003). Moreover, with language commodified, the need arises for regulation and surveillance to protect intellectual property in the linguistic marketplace (Bloch, 2012); we shall return to this issue shortly, when discussing value dilemmas surrounding plagiarism in student writing.

As English reigns as the language of science, business and travel within the global linguistic 'free market', the number of L2 learners is rapidly increasing. Certainly, English learners come from a multitude of backgrounds and study English for various purposes, but the hegemony of English (Edge, 2006) as cultural capital in the global marketplace creates the general context for student learning. Moreover, the international dominance of the language reveals itself in the classroom through the curriculum, such as in the widespread focus on gatekeeping assessments such as TOEFL/TOEIC. While English-only classroom policies (see Carroll and Combs, and Kerr, this volume) enact the ideology that standard English is *the* sole essential form of cultural capital in the global marketplace (Menard-Warwick, 2013), the predominance of English increases resistance to what is widely considered to be the language of colonialism or imperialism (Canagarajah, 1999; Kumaravadivelu, 2006; Menard-Warwick, 2013; see Pennycook, this volume, for further discussion).

Indeed, the privileging of Western cultural practices in the context of contemporary global neoliberalism has a profound effect on conflicts over values in English classrooms. Perspectives on gender and sexuality that are discursively connected to ELT tend to promote individual free choice within commodified lifestyle options, with some lingering bias towards 'mainstream' Western-style heterosexual relationships. This has been especially well-researched in Japan, where commercial language schools market conversation classes taught by attractive Anglo males to women who dream of Hollywood-style romance (Takahashi, 2013; see also Kramsch and Zhu, this volume, for further discussion of the links between language, culture and ELT in the contemporary world).

However, especially (but not only) in Islamic contexts, researchers have noted alarm at the prospect of ELT promoting the global free market in gender and sexuality. In an analysis of essays by Moroccan English majors, Sellami (2006) found negative representations of English-speaking societies. Students portrayed Westerners as "slaves of sex, money, and alcohol" (ibid.: 179), individualistically seeking pleasure. In response to this cultural threat, ELT professionals in the Middle East have organised *TESOL Islamia*, an organisation with stated goals "to promote ELT in ways that best serve the . . . interests of the Islamic world" (Kumaravadivelu, 2006: 14). In this way, although English is recognised as linguistic capital, it is separated from Western culture. To further explore conflicts relating to values in ELT, in the next section we examine data collected in classroom settings.

Classroom data on conflicting values

In this section, we use classroom observation data to explore value-laden issues that impact ELT. First, we examine comments by California teachers that construct plagiarism as 'danger', in juxtaposition with interview and essay data where a student expresses uncertainty about academic citation standards and is found to be quoting without attribution. Then, we analyse discussions in Californian and Chilean classrooms, where competing ideologies of the family affect attitudes toward divorce. All names in this section are pseudonyms, except for researchers Miki and Julia.

Values within the classroom: plagiarism and writing practices

Within contemporary global society, the commodification of language has led to increased attention toward plagiarism in student writing, as an ethical issue based on the social constructs of privatisation and ownership (Thompson and Pennycook, 2008; Bloch, 2012). From this perspective, inappropriate use of quoted material becomes metaphorically 'theft' or 'crime'. In classrooms, talking about the 'dangers' of plagiarism (see data section below) shows teachers' participation in the discourse of intellectual property (Bloch, 2012). In reviewing citation practices for writing assignments in Western academic contexts, teachers and students frequently discuss plagiarism in terms of ownership and stealing. Students are always 'in danger' of plagiarising, and teachers are positioned 'to police' student writing (Anson, 2008). At times the very choice of vocabulary suggests a potential breach of trust between teacher and student (Buzzelli and Johnston, 2002). In observations of two California university writing classrooms conducted in 2012, Miki examined how the issue of plagiarism was presented by teachers to students from a wide variety of linguistic and cultural backgrounds.

Teacher perspectives

For example, Teacher Karla cautioned her students about the slippery slope between paraphrasing and plagiarism:

> You have to be really careful when you paraphrase, it's sort of the most dangerous area for plagiarism. You have to compose your own sentences completely and you have to be careful not to just use the author's sentence . . . and replace every 4 words or something. That's called patchwriting and that's technically plagiarism.

In another classroom, while similarly noting the danger of plagiarism, Teacher Ann emphasised the importance of correct citation:

> You also want to say 'I've done my homework. I know what's out there' and you want to make sure the bibliographic information is correct so you're not being accused of plagiarism, which means you're not giving credit correctly to somebody.

She emphasises the social value of recognising another person's ideas by explicitly acknowledging them in a text. Such values influence ethical considerations for how to 'handle' transgressive acts, with many educational institutions mandating disciplinary sanctions that range from failing grades for essays to expulsion from the academy. However, Karla's use of 'technically' in 'technically plagiarism' and Ann's employment of an agentless passive, 'being accused of', suggest distancing from university policies and a lack of commitment to the underlying values that drive them.

To illustrate, during a subsequent interview, Ann explained her recent enforcement of the university plagiarism policy:

> And actually I turned someone in for plagiarism in our class. Even after I went over citation two or three times . . . it was more like sloppy citation like, you could tell there was a source but the writer never . . . referenced it at all.

She mentioned this during a discussion about student abilities, where she explained that many students have insufficient knowledge of citation rules. Nevertheless, Ann did report the student, and she explained her decision by saying that she 'went over citation two or three times'. However, she seemed to be giving something of a 'confession': she did not want to turn in the student for plagiarism but found it her duty to enact the ethics of the academy. Teachers in such cases are involved in a conflict of values, the solution to which is not always clear-cut, especially when dealing with English learners.

Student perspectives

With regard to student perspectives, an interview with Alejandro, an L1 Spanish bilingual student from Ann's class, showed that students may share similar values and ethics as the academy but lack the skills to demonstrate these values. In this interview, he discussed the second draft of his essay, in which two sentences were taken directly from a book. Not realising the source of the sentences, Miki, the interviewer, asked why he had put a quotation mark at the end though not at the beginning. Alejandro replied, 'I don't know why I put a quote; it's more kind of like paraphrase' then added, 'I haven't looked up how to cite yet.' The sentences remained citationless in the final draft, and Miki later discovered that Alejandro had copied them directly (thus committing plagiarism). However, this transgression of the rules was only noted as part of her research (Mori, 2014), and she declined to report him.

In a follow-up email, Alejandro said that he preferred to paraphrase rather than quote so as not to 'have to worry about plagiarising'. In Miki's analysis, Alejandro understood the importance of citation, but his drafting practices prevented him from quoting and citing correctly. Like one student chronicled by Thompson and Pennycook, he perhaps "struggled to come to terms with the version of language and knowledge that looked to (him) like the privatization of natural resources rather than the use of shared commodities" (2008: 134).

In the context of plagiarism and writing, neoliberal discourses of language as an individual commodity (Bloch, 2012) or a "privatiz(ed) natural resource" (Thompson and Pennycook, 2008: 134) compete with broader ideas of language as social, learned from others and belonging to no one (Thompson and Pennycook, 2008). In addressing plagiarism, ELT practitioners may want to consider if there is "more value in educating the student than in punishing (him)" (Johnston, 2003: 8), and in doing so, they have to rely on their personal values as well as their knowledge of the particular students' situation. Such cases perhaps call for balancing the ethical perspectives of the institution, the instructor and the students.

Values about a topic: discussing divorce in the classroom

While plagiarism can be seen as primarily an *ethical* issue, with plagiarism prevention policies enacted as a value *within* classrooms at the behest of educational institutions, the next two examples illustrate *moral* conflicts in which values *about* family life are explored in the classroom. The data excerpts highlight the power inequality between teacher and students and, therefore, students' right to remain silent or to make their voice heard (Buzzelli and Johnston, 2002). Julia conducted both of these classroom observations in 2005, the first in California and the second in Chile.

The classroom in California

In the first of these classroom interactions, Melinda, an Anglo teacher of a linguistically and culturally diverse class of adult immigrants in California, led an ESL activity on greeting cards ('Anglo' is a Californian term for a person with European ancestry and an L1 English-speaking background). She started by asking her students when they usually sent greeting cards; as the students listed festive occasions, she added 'divorce' to the list. When several students protested that they had never seen such a card, she erased her suggestion, but then wrote it again, on the top of the list, making it a topic for discussion:

> **Melinda**: What would a card say if it was all about congratulations and divorce?
> **Students**: ((laughing))

Tina:	I never see that.
Melinda:	A lot of people are happy when they get a divorce.
Student:	Not all people.
Melinda:	Not all people, but some people. What would it say?
Tina:	Hurray ((laughing)).
Melinda:	Okay.
Tina:	I never see that card before. I am still married.
Andre:	I saw it.
Melinda:	You saw it, Andre? You've seen them?
Andre:	Yes.
Melinda:	Uh-huh.
Lena:	Enjoy, enjoy your single life again.
Melinda:	Okay, 'Hurray, enjoy your single life again.' That was pretty good.

Melinda pursued this controversial topic, despite her students' puzzlement at the framing of divorce as a happy occasion. She established her position by stating that 'A lot of people are happy when they get a divorce' (as a teacher, her authority to express an opinion was unquestionable). When a student protested, 'Not all people', she persisted until a student proposed a satisfactory line, after which she changed the topic.

In an interview after the lesson, Melinda stated that she had no plans to talk about divorce and that her motivation for doing so was to 'be goofy', to relieve the boredom of a conventional activity, since students pay better attention to something that is 'a little shocking'. However, she added that she wanted her students to think critically about an issue that 'has a lot of acceptability here, . . . and not necessarily where they're from'. At the same time, we should note that Melinda herself is divorced; in the interview, she stated that she routinely answers students' inquiries of her marital status as being a 'happily divorced woman' (Menard-Warwick, 2013: 112). In light of this information, the class discussion can be seen not only as a conflict of ideologies between contemporary California and 'where the students are from' but also between the teacher's personal values and those of at least some of her students. Melinda's insistence on the fact that 'not all people, but some people' can be happy after a divorce may reflect more than a desire to make students think critically about a value-laden issue; it could also stem from a desire to validate her personal choices. At the same time, Melinda's position of power in the classroom could explain the students' reticence. In any case, her emphasis on the potential benefits of marital dissolution seems to originate from the ideology, widespread in globalised contexts, that individuals are primarily responsible for their own happiness (Hershberg and Rosen, 2006).

The classroom in Chile

In another 2005 observation, Julia saw how the issue of divorce was handled in an EFL class in Chile, where, unlike in Melinda's classroom, the students and teacher all came from similar national, linguistic and cultural backgrounds. The term *moral* in this case is appropriate since the issue of divorce, for some students, is linked to their religious beliefs. A traditionally Catholic society, Chile was the last country in the Western Hemisphere to legalise divorce (Ross, 2004), approximately a year before this observation. Such cultural changes in Chile are widely seen as resulting from globalisation, while English learning has been promoted by the Chilean government as an important means of participation in the globalised world (Menard-Warwick, 2013).

The students in this class were practising English teachers themselves, but *also* English learners, since they were enrolled in a professional development course designed to improve their speaking skills in the language. Their professor, Genaro, had spent most of his life teaching English in Chile but had earned a doctorate from a US university and was thus familiar with both traditional Chilean and contemporary 'globalised' perspectives on gendered issues. The lesson topic was job interviews for schoolteachers, and the students were to engage in role-play. Genaro divided the class in groups and asked them to come up with questions for prospective candidates 'regarding controversial topics nowadays'. The following dialogues then took place:

1. **Maricela**: Are you married? Do you live with your family?
   Paola: I live with my husband and my daughter, and I consider family a very important factor because students need the support of their families.
2. **Sofía**: Are you married, do you have a family?
   Carmen: Yes, I am married and I have two boys. I live near the beach.
   Sofía: Are you happy?
   Carmen: Yes.
3. **Marco**: I am the headmaster here, I am interested in a person to teach our children. What do you think about divorce?
   Renate: I believe in the family living together, both mother and father living together. But nowadays life has changed a lot, and everyday we see more and more people divorced and that affect our children very much, and I think there is nothing we can do to avoid it, we have to work and do our best with those children.

(Menard-Warwick, 2013: 213. Reproduced with permission)

It is interesting to note that of the three women roleplaying interviewees, Paola and Renate were separated from their husbands. Therefore, one may wonder about the motives that made them profess belief in traditional family values.

One clear reason was mentioned by Genaro in an after-class interview: the conflict between the women's lifestyles and what is perceived to be moral by the larger society, where the Catholic Church remains influential.

Julia: People have to hide it [being divorced] in an interview like that?
Genaro: No, not necessarily, [...] but perhaps if you are going to, if you are applying for a post in a religious school, probably they are going to consider it more carefully, [...] for example I remember the first, well it was more than 30 years ago, but anyway, things have changed a lot, [...] I began working at the Catholic school run by nuns, and the first question she asked me, even before asking me where I had gotten my degree, was 'are you married?'

Genaro defended his choice of topic; even though he stated that 'things have changed a lot'; this emphasis on cultural changes, often connected to gender, emerged as a common theme in Julia's research (Menard-Warwick, 2013). It is interesting to hear Marco, roleplaying the headmaster, confirm his position by implying a direct relation between the candidate's family values and the possibility of employment. The three women who played candidates agreed in this mock interview that traditional marriage was an important value for them. While Carmen simply stated that she was happily married, Paola stressed the importance of family support for her students, and Renate brought up the negative effects of divorce on students' lives (although she avoided mentioning her own marital status).

In a research interview, Renate articulated her understanding of the effects of family break-down on her students:

> They are not interested in studying [. . .] most of them come from really poor families [. . .] single parent, mono-parental in Spanish [. . .] they spend the whole day alone because the mother or the father is working, [. . .] I feel they are not interested in learning anything, they just (get) home and turn the television on and watching those stupid programmes they have here.

Therefore, Paola's pretending to be married, as well as Renate's avoidance of the issue during her mock interview, may result from a real moral dilemma: the fact that they do espouse traditional values and that divorce remains a painful topic for them.

Comparing the two classrooms

While Melinda's class discussion illustrates how some teachers try to encourage students to adopt 'liberalised' global values on gender and sexuality, Genaro's roleplay activity reminds us that many English learners are embedded in traditional structures of authority, where open adoption of globalised perspectives remains risky. In any case, like Melinda, Genaro exercises his authority by making his students engage in a value-laden discussion. One may argue that he is motivated by the students' needs, trying to prepare them for real-life job interviews, just as Melinda's students may benefit (she argues) from a clearer understanding of California culture.

However, taken together, the two examples demonstrate that ELT practitioners need to approach topics of moral complexity with utmost care, being aware of the goals that they are trying to achieve while remembering that students may have had painful experiences with issues like divorce. Teachers may be unable to avoid having plagiarism policies, as this represents a value *within* their classrooms; however, it is far rarer for teachers to need classroom policies on issues like divorce (values *about*). Nevertheless, they should consider how best to address controversy in the classroom, as we discuss in the final section of this paper.

Implications, challenges, future directions

In this section, we make recommendations for how educators can best approach value conflicts in their classrooms, while also suggesting directions for future research. Our central argument is that conflicting values in the ELT classroom should be examined and made explicit: we are not arguing for or against neoliberal ideologies; we take no specific position on the Islamic concerns, plagiarism policies or divorce controversies cited above (Kumaravadivelu, 2006; Sellami, 2006; Menard-Warwick, 2013; Mori, 2014). However, we do recommend that teachers critically address their own ideologies and those of the curriculum while integrating sociohistorical considerations into pedagogy.

The self-reflecting teacher

Critical self-reflection while teaching can create a starting place for effectively addressing values in the classroom. Practitioners can begin by considering their upbringing and education, including their training for English language teaching. In our experience, when instructors' deconstruct their personal and educational histories, this creates leverage for teasing apart values in the classroom. We recommend that teachers focus on specific experiences and try to be explicit in interpreting how these experiences inform their pedagogy. That is, teachers might first ask themselves how they learned academic citation practices or became socialised into particular views on gender and sexuality – and next reflect on the extent to which they can or should promote these perspectives in their current ELT context. In this way, teachers can develop awareness of their own social and cultural identities and the constraints and resources these provide for their teaching (Menard-Warwick, 2013).

In reflecting on their educational practice, teachers also need to consider how values impact the classroom through policies and structures of the educational system – for example, tests and grades. While teachers may have little latitude to change such practices, they nevertheless should ponder the extent to which examinations index a lack of trust or grading reflects the value of individual competition (Buzzelli and Johnston, 2002). Individually or collectively, teachers might consider how policies likewise determine how ideologies and values affect student agency. As Buzzelli and Johnston write, the teacher, as the authority in the classroom, has the power to "make B do something that B would not ordinarily do" (2002: 70). However, these authors emphasise that with authority comes responsibility: teachers need to be sure that they indeed have students' best interests at heart. In this regard, it is essential that practitioners factor into their reflections the socio-historical characteristics of their particular classroom, such as geographical location, learner goals, local traditions and institutional setting.

Addressing conflicts for values *about* and values *within* a classroom

To give an example of a value *within* classroom pedagogies, CLT emphasises the right for students to speak in class, and such a *voice* can create opportunity for *choice* (Buzzelli and Johnston, 2002), discussed earlier as being central to neoliberal intersections with ELT. However, simply advocating free choice does not necessarily lead to voice, as many students have little desire to speak up in classrooms. However, if choice is taken seriously, students must retain the right to be silent. Moreover, if students are seen as having a right to *voice/choice* in the language classroom, the question arises as to whether this voice is (allowed to be) multilingual. An important area to explore with students is the language ideologies in the institution or societal context that shape policies around classroom language use (see also Carroll and Combs, this volume). However, this will only be possible when teachers have first examined their own language ideologies and are able to articulate them (Menard-Warwick, 2013).

To give another example, values *about* gender roles and sexual orientation create controversy in many global contexts, as seen in the divorce discussions above. While explorations of these issues will be most compelling when connected to the social histories of the students, they are often too personal and controversial to simply ask students for their own experiences. Furthermore, teachers need to consider how content and activities in a text are often rife with value-laden and ideological messages regarding what is normal and expected in an English language classroom and/or English medium setting. Aside from divorce, another set of potentially divisive issues revolve around gender identities and the assumed importance of heterosexual coupling (Takahashi, 2013; see also Gray, this volume). To avoid imposing globalised values on their students, we recommend that teachers raise gender issues in ways that connect with students' own backgrounds but that do not require self-disclosure. A good example is Ó'Móchain's (2006) use of local 'queer narratives' to frame discussions of sexualities in an English class at a Japanese college. This would be a fruitful area for future research.

The complex relationship between language, nationality, race and culture is another site of classroom conflict in need of increased attention by researchers and teachers. Discussions in this area often assume that such categories are valid, fixed and mutually exclusive, so that each student necessarily represents a particular nationality, race and culture. However, nations can contain multiple races and ethnic groups, such as in China (Han, Tibetan, Uyghur etc.), while any conclusions on 'Asian culture' assumes the similarity of three billion people (Chinese, Indian, Japanese etc.) (Kumaravadivelu, 2003). Ideologies around these topics often interact with power dynamics regarding multilingualism, legitimacy and prestige, as well as with the language learning process, such as what gets taught and who participates. Whenever multiple languages and cultures come in contact, teachers are faced with determining the boundaries of acceptable language – especially given many students' goal to acquire 'standard' English as cultural capital in the global marketplace (Menard-Warwick, 2013) or simply to pass high stakes examinations (Canagarajah, 1993).

Considering conflicts and adjusting curriculum

Finally, we recommend that ELT practitioners address the potential conflicts between their own identities as reflective teachers and their students' socio-historically situated goals for learning. Although teachers vary widely in the amount of control they have over the course curriculum and approach to teaching, they need to feel that they have (some) agency in their classrooms – while at the same time ensuring that their students do as well. To this end, Auerbach (1992) describes a family literacy programme for immigrants in which language development was situated within the larger process of social change in immigrant communities. In these classes, English learners were included in curricular decision-making, while discussion activities aimed to bring oppressive social structures into conscious awareness so that learners could collectively take action for social improvement. This pedagogical method, referred to as the *participatory approach*, stems from the groundbreaking work by Paulo Freire (1999), which emphasises dialogue between teachers, students and texts (see also Simpson, this volume).

While participatory curriculum development is only possible in a few teaching contexts, the emphasis on dialogue, which is its most important feature, is more widely applicable (Kramsch, 1993). To resist tendencies that silence students, we recommend that teachers promote dialogue aimed at problematising values (Kubota, 1999) with the goal of facilitating students' ability to comprehend value-laden issues from multiple perspectives (Byram et al., 2002). Teachers may worry that such discussions will only reinforce students' original prejudices, but, in our experience, teacher facilitation can help students broaden their views without necessarily changing them (Menard-Warwick, 2013).

In some classrooms, curricular demands or political situations may make it impossible to problematise controversial issues. Nevertheless, teachers should recognise the value for learners of exploring controversial topics in order to communicate better with individuals from different backgrounds. To draw upon an example from the research literature which we have previously noted, if Moroccan students see English speakers as prototypically "slaves of sex, money, and alcohol" (Sellami, 2006), it is going to be difficult for them to work with the Canadian visiting professor at their university or the Australian tourist who checks into their hotel or hospital. While teachers in such contexts should feel under no obligation to promote 'mainstream Western values' on sex, alcohol or financial planning (Canagarajah, 1993), it would be helpful for students who are offended by trends in the global media to understand the diversity of perspectives that exist in English-speaking countries and to realise that it is possible to find points of agreement as well as disagreement with English-speaking individuals.

The utility of this approach to classroom learning and values comes from its recognition of values (and ideologies) and its promotion of possibilities for engaging, challenging and articulating such perspectives. In addressing these issues, teachers might ask opinionated students to provide evidence for their views, while at the same time providing space for less proficient or outspoken individuals to join in on the reflection (e.g. by the use of their L1 or through journaling). It is not enough to value heated discussions in order to promote speaking practice. Rather, it is essential that discussions of ideologies, morals and ethics promote listening and comprehending and not merely the articulation of strongly held opinions (Kramsch, 1993). Teachers facilitating discussions may want to ask students to respond directly to the comments of other students or to assertions in texts, keeping in mind that the goal is not agreement but rather *understanding* (Byram et al., 2002; Menard-Warwick, 2013). Moreover, given classroom power dynamics, teachers need to recognise that student discomfort or resistance may appear in the form of silence and disengagement. For this reason, the promotion of reflective learning should go beyond addressing controversial issues (values *about*) but more importantly initiate conversations about values *within* teaching and the curriculum.

Conclusion

In sum, the consideration of values, ethics and ideologies in English language teaching is important, and it can be explored along a variety of lines. Given that these topics are challenging and difficult to embark on alone, engaging with other ELT practitioners may help instructors to understand the roles of values and ideologies in their work. Though some groundbreaking research has been done, more practitioners and researchers need to turn their attention to these often taboo and seemingly invisible aspects of English language classrooms. While the term 'reflective teaching' has perhaps been overused and used too imprecisely (Fat'hi and Behzadpour, 2011), we argue for increased research on how reflective teaching can inform pedagogical approaches to values in ELT. Therefore, practitioners need to focus not only on particular values in the classroom but also on how research and praxis can lead to a better understanding of values.

Transcription conventions

[. . .]	Text omitted
[text]	Author's paraphrase or background information
()	Transcriptionist doubt
(())	Comment on paralinguistic features (e.g. laughter)

Discussion questions

- Consider a memorable classroom interaction that involved conflict. What values were demonstrated via the interaction? If values were discussed, what were they? Was there continuity between values enacted (i.e. observed) in classroom practice and those that were discussed by the students?
- In TESOL Islamia, the stated goal is "to promote ELT in ways that best serve the sociopolitical, sociocultural, and socioeconomic interests of the Islamic world" (Kumaravadivelu, 2006: 14). To what extent is it possible to separate the English language from the Western values associated with it? What are the advantages and disadvantages of doing so?
- What are some (implicit or explicit) language ideologies that you have encountered in language classes that you have taken or in your teacher training? How have these ideologies affected your own teaching?

- Buzzelli and Johnston discuss a teacher's power to "make B do something that B would not ordinarily do" (2002: 70) with B's best interest in mind. What are some ways for a teacher to persuade students that, in introducing conflicting values, s/he is guided by their best interests?
- How should teachers react when they find their personal values under attack during a class-room interaction? Should their position of power prevent them from voicing their opinion?

Related topics

Bilingual education in a multilingual world; Communicative language teaching in theory and practice; ELT materials; Language and culture in ELT; Politics, power relationships and ELT; Questioning 'English-only' classrooms.

Further reading

Edge, J. (ed.) (2006) *(Re)locating TESOL in an age of empire.* Houndmills, UK: Palgrave Macmillan. (A provocative collection of papers geared towards ELT practitioners and researchers interested in the impact of English in a globalised and conflicted world.)

Howard, R. M. and Robillard, A. E. (eds) (2008) *Pluralizing plagiarism: Identities, contexts, pedagogies.* Portsmouth, NH: Boynton/Cook/Heinemann. (A variety of research studies on plagiarism and writing, including proposed pedagogical practices.)

Johnston, B. (2003) *Values in English language teaching.* New York: Routledge. (The most comprehensive and focused treatment of the topic of this article.)

Kumaravadivelu, B. (2007) *Cultural globalization and language education.* New Haven, CT: Yale University Press. (Thoughtful discussion of the limitations of Western cultural norms for ELT in the age of globalisation.)

Menard-Warwick, J. (2013) *English language teachers on the discursive faultlines: Identities, ideologies, pedagogies.* Bristol, UK: Multilingual Matters. (Contrasting case studies that examine how English teachers in Chile and California deal with value-laden issues.)

References

Ajayi, L. (2008) 'ESL theory practice dynamics: The difficulty of integrating sociocultural perspectives into pedagogical practice'. *Foreign Language Annals,* 41/4. 639–659.

Anson, C. M. (2008) 'We never wanted to be cops: Plagiarism, institutional paranoia, and shared responsibility', in R. M. Howard and A. E. Robillard (eds) *Pluralizing plagiarism: Identities, contexts, pedagogies.* Portsmouth, NH: Boynton/Cook/Heinemann. 140–157.

Auerbach, E. (1992) *Making meaning, making change: Participatory curriculum development for adult ESL literacy.* Washington, DC: Center for Applied Linguistics.

Bell Lara, J. and López, D. L. (2007) 'The harvest of neoliberalism in Latin America', in R. A. Dello Buono and J. Bell Lara (eds) *Imperialism, neoliberalism, and social struggles in Latin America.* Leiden & Boston: Brill. 17–35.

Bloch, J. (2012) *Plagiarism, intellectual property and the teaching of L2 writing.* Tonawanda, NY: Multilingual Matters.

Buzzelli, C. A. and Johnston, B. (2002) *The moral dimensions of teaching: Language, power, and culture in classroom interaction.* New York: RoutledgeFalmer.

Byram, M., Gribkova, B. and Starkey, H. (2002) *Developing the intercultural dimension in language teaching.* Retrieved October 5, 2012, from http://www.coe.int/t/dg4/linguistic/source/guide_dimintercult_en.pdf

Canagarajah, A. S. (1993) 'Critical ethnography of a Sri Lankan classroom: Ambiguities in student opposition to reproduction through ESOL'. *TESOL Quarterly,* 27/4. 601–626.

Canagarajah, A. S. (1999) *Resisting linguistic imperialism in English teaching.* Oxford: Oxford University Press.

Edge, J. (2006) 'Background and overview', in J. Edge (ed.) *(Re-)locating TESOL in an age of empire.* Houndmills, UK: Palgrave Macmillan. xii–xix.

Fat'hi, J. and Behzadpour, F. (2011) 'Beyond method: The rise of reflective teaching'. *International Journal of English Linguistics,* 1/2. 241–251.

Freire, P. (1999) *Pedagogy of the oppressed* Myra Bergman Ramos (trans.) (20th anniversary ed.). New York: Continuum Publishing.

Gray, J. (2013) 'LGBT invisibility and heteronormativity in ELT materials', in J. Gray (ed.) *Critical perspectives on language teaching materials*. Basingstoke, UK: Palgrave Macmillan. 40–63.

Hershberg, E. and Rosen, F. (2006) 'Turning the tide?', in E. Hershberg and F. Rosen (eds) *Latin America after neoliberalism: Turning the tide in the 21st century?* New York: New Press. 1–25.

Holborow, M. (2012a) 'What is neoliberalism? Discourse, ideology, and the real world', in D. Block, J. Gray and M. Holborow (eds) *Neoliberalism and applied linguistics*. New York: Routledge. 14–32.

Holborow, M. (2012b) 'Neoliberal keywords and the contradictions of an ideology', in D. Block, J. Gray and M. Holborow (eds) *Neoliberalism and applied linguistics*. New York: Routledge. 33–55.

Johnston, B. (2003) *Values in English language teaching*. New York: Routledge.

Kelly, T. E. (1986) 'Discussing controversial issues: Four perspectives on the teacher's role'. *Theory and Research in Social Education*, 25. 113–136.

Kramsch, C. (1993) *Context and culture in language teaching*. Oxford: Oxford University Press.

Kroskrity, P. V. (2000) 'Regimenting languages: Language ideological perspectives', in P. Kroskrity (ed.) *Regimes of language: Ideologies, polities, and identities*. Santa Fe, NM: School of American Research Press. 1–34.

Kubota, R. (1999) 'Japanese culture constructed by discourses: Implications for applied linguistic research and English language teaching'. *TESOL Quarterly*, 33/1. 9–35.

Kumaravadivelu, B. (2003) Problematizing cultural stereotypes in TESOL. *TESOL Quarterly*, 37/4. 709–719.

Kumaravadivelu, B. (2006) 'Dangerous liaison: Globalization, empire, and TESOL', in J. Edge (ed.) *(Re-)locating TESOL in an age of empire*. Houndmills, UK: Palgrave Macmillan. 1–26.

Menard-Warwick, J. (2013) *English language teachers on the discursive faultlines: Identities, ideologies, pedagogies*. Bristol, UK: Multilingual Matters.

Miller-Lane, J., Denton, E. and May, A. (2006) 'Social studies teachers' views on committed impartiality and discussion'. *Social Studies Research and Practice*, 1. 30–44.

Mori, M. (2014) *Negotiating Ownership when incorporating outside sources: A qualitative study with multilingual undergraduate students* (Doctoral dissertation). Retrieved March 8, 2015, from Proquest Dissertations and Theses http://search.proquest.com/docview/1665571794.

Ó'Móchain, R. (2006) 'Discussing gender and sexuality in a context-appropriate way: Queer narratives in an EFL college classroom in Japan'. *Journal of Language, Identity, and Education*, 5. 51–66.

Oster, J. (1989) 'Seeing with different eyes: Another view of literature in the ESL class'. *TESOL Quarterly*, 23. 85–103.

Platt, E. and Brooks, F. B. (1994) 'The "acquisition-rich environment" revisited'. *Modern Language Journal*, 78/4. 497–511.

Reddy, M. R. (1970) 'The conduit metaphor – a case of frame conflict in our language about language', in A. Ortony (ed.) *Metaphor and thought*. Cambridge: Cambridge University Press. 284–324.

Ross, J. (2004) Chile defies church and legalizes divorce. *The Guardian,* March 11, 2004. Retrieved March 13, 2014, from http://www.theguardian.com/world/2004/mar/12/chile

Sellami, A. (2006) 'Slaves of sex, money, and alcohol: (Re-)locating the target culture of TESOL,' in J. Edge (ed.) *(Re-)locating TESOL in an age of empire*. Houndmills, UK: Palgrave Macmillan. 171–194.

Takahashi, K. (2013) *Language learning, gender and desire: Japanese women on the move*. Bristol, UK: Multilingual Matters.

Thompson, C. and Pennycook, A. (2008) 'Intertextuality in the global contact zone', in R. M. Robillard and A. E. Howard (eds) *Pluralizing plagiarism: Identities, contexts, pedagogies*. Portsmouth, NH: Boynton/Cook/Heinemann. 124–139.

Index